BF
321
.A82
1993

Attention and
performance XIV.

$75.00

DATE			

BAKER & TAYLOR

Attention and Performance XIV

Attention and Performance

Attention and Performance XIV: Synergies in Experimental Psychology, Artificial Intelligence, and Cognitive Neuroscience, edited by David E. Meyer and Sylvan Kornblum, 1992

Attention and Performance XIV

Synergies in Experimental Psychology, Artificial Intelligence, and Cognitive Neuroscience

edited by David E. Meyer and Sylvan Kornblum

This book is based on the papers that were presented at the Fourteenth International Symposium on Attention and Performance held at the University of Michigan, Ann Arbor, Michigan, July 9–13, 1990.

A Bradford Book
The MIT Press
Cambridge, Massachusetts
London, England

This book was set in Palatino by Asco Trade Typesetting Ltd., Hong Kong and was printed and bound in the United States of America.

ISSN: 1047-0387
ISBN: 0-262-13284-2

Contents

Preface

HISTORICAL BACKGROUND

This book commemorates the twenty-fifth anniversary of the international series of Attention and Performance symposia. The advent of the series dates back to the summer of 1966 when in Driebergen, The Netherlands, Andries F. Sanders, a Dutch experimental psychologist and ergonomicist, convened a group of colleagues from Europe, Britain, and North America to discuss their burgeoning research on "performance theory" and "human information processing." During these discussions, several topics that formed the then-prevailing core of performance theory were explored, including eye movements and visual search, attention and the single-channel hypothesis, short-term memory and information processing, reaction processes and mental chronometry, vigilance and sustained performance of continuous tasks, and physiological correlates of attention. The outcome of this exploration became embodied in a volume of proceedings (Sanders 1967) that, along with the symposium itself, was deemed to be an overall success (for a review, see Laming 1968).

Inspired by the success of Sanders's first venture and by a desire to continue pursuing various aspects of performance theory on a regular intimate basis thirteen further international Attention and Performance symposia have been organized since 1966 (table 1). Except for one symposium organized by Koster (1969) on reaction time, the early symposia of the series typically had eclectic themes, spanning many general areas related to human information processing (e.g., Sanders 1970; Kornblum 1973; Rabbitt and Dornic 1975; Dornic 1977; Requin 1978; Nickerson 1980; Long and Baddeley 1981). More recently, however, the symposia have focused on specific topics such as the control of language processes (Bouma and Bouwhuis 1984), the neuropsychology of attention and cognition (Posner and Marin 1985), reading (Coltheart 1987), and motor control (Jeannerod 1990). Similarly, there has been a diversity of symposium organizers, participants, and meeting sites.

Accompanying the evolution of the Attention and Performance symposium series, a formal administrative organization, the International Association for the Study of Attention and Performance (IASAP), was created to facilitate the planning of future symposia and the preparation of published proceedings. The IASAP has a constitution and a set of bylaws (see Dornic 1977, appendix;

Table 1 List of Attention and Performance Symposia to Date

Symposium Number	Location	Year	Organizers	Topic
I	The Netherlands	1966	A. F. Sanders	Attention and Performance
II	The Netherlands	1968	W. Koster	Reaction Time
III	The Netherlands	1969	A. F. Sanders	Information Processing
IV	United States	1971	S. Kornblum	Information Processing
V	Sweden	1973	P. Rabbit and S. Dornic	Information Processing
VI	Sweden	1975	S. Dornic	Information Processing
VII	France	1976	J. Requin	Information Processing
VIII	United States	1978	R. Nickerson	Information Processing
IX	Great Britain	1980	J. Long and A. Baddeley	Information Processing
X	The Netherlands	1982	H. Bouma and D. Bouwhuis	Language Processes
XI	United States	1984	M. I. Posner and O. Marin	Attention and Neuropsychology
XII	Great Britain	1986	M. Coltheart	Reading
XIII	France	1988	M. E. Jeannerod	Motor Control
XIV	United States	1990	D. E. Meyer and S. Kornblum	Silver Jubilee

Kornblum 1987), administered jointly by a chairperson, an executive committee, and an advisory council whose memberships change periodically according to procedures specified in the constitution and bylaws. A major function of these procedures is to maintain the symposium series, to bring new blood and ideas into the organization, and to ensure that it continues to achieve its original objectives which, as the IASAP constitution states, are "to increase and disseminate knowledge in the area of human attention, performance, and information processing, and to foster international communication in this area."

Of course, despite the best intentions and efforts of the IASAP, not all symposia in the Attention and Performance series have enjoyed equally high success. Reactions to some of them have been mixed (Broadbent 1986; Henderson 1974; Hinrichs 1982; Kantowitz 1977, 1981; Mostofsky 1971; Sanders 1984; Seidenberg 1985; Shaffer 1984). Among criticisms expressed by reviewers over the years has been the concern that some past symposia dealt with too broad a mix of topics, which resulted in books that seemed very much like volumes of an ordinary journal on general information processing. In contrast, other symposia were sometimes viewed as having too narrow a focus and being too idiosyncratic in their choice of topics. Reviewers have also bemoaned the price of the volumes, which they usually thought was too high. Intellectually more telling critiques have suggested that the series placed undue emphasis on simple experimental paradigms and chronometric measurements (e.g., reaction time) whose relevance was mostly restricted to simple input-output processes. This, they argued, diminished the symposia's relevance to the emerging and changing needs in the fields of applied cognitive science and human-factors engineering.

Overall, however, the Attention and Performance symposium series has received strongly positive reviews (e.g., see Broadbent 1986; Carr 1989; Pashler and Johnston 1986; Zelaznik 1991). As Broadbent (1986, 158) emphasized, the movement represented by these symposia "has ... brought us from almost total ignorance to a fair knowledge of a lot of empirical relationships, it has excluded certain simpleminded theories, and it has reached reasonable certainty about some of the principles necessary for the ultimate correct theory.... Above all, [it] has produced a variety of techniques that are of applied value, that are already of use in neuropsychology and increasingly in psychopharmacology, and which can thus be used to link psychological function to the brain. This seems a fair haul for twenty years of work by a rather small community...." So, on balance, it is fair to conclude that the symposium series has continued to fulfill its originally intended function.

OBJECTIVES OF ATTENTION AND PERFORMANCE XIV

The twenty-fifth anniversary of the first Attention and Performance symposium fell during August 1991. In anticipation and in celebration of this special occasion, a silver jubilee symposium was held the week of July 9–13, 1990, in Ann Arbor, Michigan, at the North Campus Commons of the University of Michigan. It was also the fourteenth symposium of the series, which—with a couple of exceptions—has occurred regularly on a biannual basis. In addition to local participants, a total of fifty-seven investigators from eleven countries took part in Attention and Performance XIV (see the List of Participants and Contributors). Their presentations and discussions, subsequently revised and edited, provide the content of this book.

Our goals for Attention and Performance XIV were threefold. First, following a request from the IASAP executive committee, we wanted the symposium to include a retrospective and prospective as well as contemporary outlook. It was therefore devoted in roughly equal measure to assessing past accomplishments, surveying important current projects, and identifying attractive directions for future research on various aspects of human attention and performance. Our second goal was to make the symposium stimulating, lively, and freewheeling, but without unduly compromising thoughtful rigorous discourse. Hence, its format contained liberal portions of several intellectual ingredients, including evaluative tutorial reviews, integrative reports of recent programmatic research projects, and speculative prognostications. Our third goal was to highlight and promote growing interdisciplinary syntheses that have emerged not only in psychology and cognitive science broadly defined, but also in the specific fields of attention and performance research. As a result, the presentations at Attention and Performance XIV reflected several complementary scientific approaches, ranging from experimental psychology, artificial intelligence, neurophysiology, and cognitive neuroscience to applied cognitive psychology. The inclusion of such varied approaches is intended to acknowledge how research relevant for understanding attention, information processing, and performance has both progressed and become much more diversified over the past twenty-five years.

Of course, it was not possible to include all potentially relevant topics as part of Attention and Performance XIV. With the limited time, space, and financial resources available to us, some selectivity was required. So, after again seeking suggestions from the IASAP executive committee and advisory council, we chose to focus on five core topics: (1) visual information processing; (2) attention; (3) learning and memory; (4) mental chronometry and processing dynamics; and (5) motor control and action. Our choices stemmed from several considerations. Most of the selected topics were major ones at the time of the first Attention and Performance symposium (Sanders 1967). Furthermore, sustained pursuit of them has, in each case, yielded substantial progress over the past twenty-five years, and it seems likely that this progress will continue for the foreseeable future. Equally noteworthy is that these topics have attracted researchers from a variety of scientific disciplines and perspectives, whose joint contributions illustrate how interdisciplinary endeavors can produce significant advances toward understanding the substrates of attention and performance.

The selection of the participants for Attention and Performance XIV was likewise intended to achieve certain other complementary objectives. Obviously, the participants had to be experts on the topics at hand, and they had to accept our invitation to attend the symposium. Also, in accord with the IASAP bylaws (Kornblum 1987), they had to represent a variety of countries and levels of seniority. However, they could not number more than sixty-five, thus maintaining an overall air of intimacy and leisure in the proceedings.

CONTENTS OF THE PRESENT BOOK

The main body of this book contains seven parts.

Part I consists of a single chapter: the Association Lecture. It appears here because such lectures have been a traditional part of the last six Attention and Performance symposia. Their purpose is to offer an inspirational forum for prominent attention and performance researchers who, as described in the bylaws of the IASAP, will "have done honor to the Association by accepting to present these lectures."

Consistent with this description, Professor David Rumelhart presented the Association Lecture at Attention and Performance XIV. His participation and presentation seem especially apt in light of our stated objectives for the symposium. Most notably, through the development and application of the connectionist theoretical framework (Rumelhart 1989), he has demonstrated how a combination of experimental psychology, computational modeling, and cognitive neuroscience perspectives can advance research on attention and performance. Extending these demonstrations, the Association Lecture by Professor Rumelhart (coauthored with Peter Todd) takes us further toward a systematic treatment of memory structure and semantic knowledge representation, both of which have become integral parts of performance theory over the past twenty-five years (see part IV, this volume).

Following the Association Lecture, parts II through VI cover the five core topics of Attention and Performance XIV. Each part starts with a brief introduction followed by a keynote tutorial chapter. Next come several chapters that summarize results from integrative programs of research by various investigators who have been actively pursuing the topic at hand. A discussant's commentary then integrates these topical contributions.

The authors of the keynote tutorial chapters have produced their contributions with a particular charge in mind. To be specific, they were asked to include three basic components: (1) a concise general evaluative review of research progress made during the past twenty-five years; (2) a clear thoughtful sketch of the most important and promising issues, objectives, approaches, and perspectives for research in the next twenty-five years; and (3) discretionary summaries from their own personal research that would help support the main points being made. Our intent was to encourage eclectic and imaginative contributions.

In contrast, the authors who contributed chapters more heavily based on their own integrative programs of research began with a somewhat different charge. They were asked to present an overview of their recent research as it relates to the part of the symposium in which they were participating. We especially encouraged them to emphasize what seemed most distinctive and offered the most promising directions for further advances.

The discussants' commentary chapters for each part of the symposium had yet another purpose. Discussants were asked to make constructive, evaluative, integrative comments. They were also encouraged to express their own personal views about where research should be going.

Finally, part VII is a general discussion that integrates and evaluates the different parts of the symposium. Another equally important purpose of this part is to take stock of the attention and performance research enterprise at large. We asked the general discussant to assess the enterprise's most important products during the past twenty-five years and to prescribe what its major aims during the next twenty-five years should be. The general discussant thus had the challenging role of bringing Attention and Performance XIV to a satisfying close.

To fill the general discussant's role, we invited Professor Donald Broadbent. This invitation again seemed highly natural and appropriate. For many years, Broadbent has been among the preeminent leaders of attention and performance research, and he now stands as the field's widely acknowledged godfather. Who else could better comment on its past progress, current status, and future prospects? Also, having Professor Broadbent be the general discussant of Attention and Performance XIV was most fitting because the occasion happened to coincide with his official retirement from the academic position that he has long held at the University of Oxford. We are honored that Professor Broadbent agreed to look backward and forward with us during the symposium, and we wish to take this occasion to recognize the many significant scientific contributions that he has made throughout his professional career.

It should be noted that this book has also benefited from a careful review process after the Attention and Performance XIV symposium ended. For most chapters, at least two referees made comments about suggested additions and revisions. Although the incorporation of these comments necessarily delayed the book's publication, we hope that both the symposium's contributors and future readers will find the wait to have been well worthwhile.

STATE-OF-THE-ART AND FUTURE PROSPECTS

Fortunately, in our opinion, the contents of the present volume make it clear that the enterprise of attention and performance research has been reasonably fruitful to date, is alive and well, and on course toward exciting new developments. Despite difficult hurdles encountered along the way, research efforts during the past twenty-five years have yielded substantial progress. What lies ahead promises even greater progress. For example, we are optimistic about the prospects offered by combining sophisticated experimental psychology procedures with neuropsychological assessments, brain-imaging techniques (MRI, PET, etc.), and quantitative analyses of event-related brain potentials. Perhaps future results from these, when interpreted through precise computational models, including connectionism, will yield an integration and elaboration of the already-identified theoretical principles that Broadbent (1986) mentioned earlier. Certainly it is the sort of interdisciplinary synthesis embodied in Attention and Performance XIV that can lead to such advances.

At the same time, however, many challenges lie ahead. Attention and performance research needs to continue expanding its horizons beyond studies based primarily on "small simple" paradigms and the twin behavioral measures of reaction time and response accuracy. As some contributors to the present book have forcefully stressed, much more intense effort should be expended on quantifying and computationally modeling complex high-level control processes in naturalistic situations (e.g., see chapters by Allport, Broadbent, Duncan, and Gopher). More effort should also be expended on pursuing topics such as individual differences, psychophysiological energetics, and so forth. Perhaps the present volume of proceedings will help pave the way toward these types of objective. If it does, then Attention and Performance XIV will have been an ultimate success.

ACKNOWLEDGMENTS

The organization of Attention and Performance XIV and the production of this book have been facilitated enormously by many institutions and people who contributed their intellectual ideas, financial resources, personal time, and moral support. We wish to acknowledge all of these contributions at least implicitly, and to mention some of them explicitly herewith. First, special thanks should go to the participants who traveled from near and far to attend the symposium. Without their enthusiastic involvement, no scientific exchange or book like this would have emerged. Secondly, the detailed comments by our referees about initial drafts of the book's chapters are greatly appreciated. As the chapter authors already know, these comments often led to substantial improvements. We are likewise grateful to the executive committee and advisory council of the IASAP for their inputs to the planning of the symposium and to the selection of the topics that were finally included.

In addition, the organization of the symposium and the production of this book have been much enhanced by contributions from several other sources. Most notably, the North Campus Commons at the University of Michigan provided ample space and guidance to deal with the physical needs of the symposium. The production staff of our publisher, The MIT Press, greatly aided our editorial efforts while adhering to their high standards of manufacturing a handsome volume and marketing it at a reasonable price. And last, but not least, diligent help was given by our graduate students and administrative and technical staff at Michigan. In particular, we thank Matt Kurbat, Mary Lassaline, April Main, Donna Pineau, Paul Price, Cindy Vance, and Tony Whipple for their assistance before, during, and after the symposium.

Funding for Attention and Performance XIV was obtained through the United States Office of Naval Research and Air Force Office of Scientific Research. We owe a debt of gratitude to both Al Fregley at the AFOSR and Harold Hawkins at the ONR for their continued financial support.

David E. Meyer
Sylvan Kornblum

Ann Arbor, Michigan

REFERENCES

Bouma, H., and Bouwhuis, D. (Eds.) (1984). *Attention and performance X: Control of language processes*. Hillsdale, NJ: Lawrence Erlbaum.

Broadbent, D. E. (1986). The enterprise of performance. *Quarterly Journal of Experimental Psychology, 38A*, 151–162.

Carr, T. H. (1989). At the cutting edge of research on reading. Review of *Attention and performance XII*, by M. Coltheart (Ed.). *Contemporary Psychology, 34*, 935–937.

Coltheart, M. (Ed.). (1987). *Attention and performance XII: The psychology of reading*. London: Lawrence Erlbaum.

Dornic, S. (Ed.). (1977). *Attention and performance VI*. Hillsdale, NJ: Lawrence Erlbaum.

Henderson, L. (1974). Review of *Attention and performance IV*, by S. Kornblum (Ed.). *British Journal of Psychology, 65*, 571–572.

Hinrichs, J. V. (1982). The International Journal of Information Processing? Review of *Attention and performance IX*, by J. Long and A. Baddeley (Eds.). *Contemporary Psychology, 27*, 971–972.

Jeannerod, M. (Ed.). (1990). *Attention and performance XIII. Motor representation and control*. Hillsdale, NJ: Lawrence Erlbaum.

Kantowitz, B. H. (1977). Zeitgeist at $25 per Kilogram. Review of *Attention and performance V*, by P. Rabbitt and S. Dornic (Eds.). *Contemporary Psychology, 22,* 452–454.

Kantowitz, B. H. (1981). More Zeitgeist at a better price. Review of *Attention and performance VIII*, by R. Nickerson (Ed.). *Contemporary Psychology, 26,* 879–880.

Kornblum, S. (Ed.). (1973). *Attention and performance IV*. New York: Academic Press.

Kornblum, S. (1987). Attention and Performance Symposia: Modus Operandi. In M. Coltheart (Ed.), *Attention and performance XII: The psychology of reading*, 689–691. London: Lawrence Erlbaum.

Koster, W. (Ed.). (1969). *Attention and performance II*. Amsterdam: North-Holland.

Laming, D. R. J. (1968). Review of *Attention and performance*, by A. F. Sanders (Ed.). *Quarterly Journal of Experimental Psychology, 20,* 314–315.

Long, J., and Baddeley, A. D. (Eds.). (1981). *Attention and performance IX*. Hillsdale, NJ: Lawrence Erlbaum.

Mostofsky, David, J. (1971). Review of *Attention and performance III*, by A. F. Sanders (Ed.). *American Journal of Psychology, 84,* 453–454.

Nickerson, R. S. (Ed.). (1980). *Attention and performance VIII*. Hillsdale, NJ: Lawrence Erlbaum.

Pashler, H., and Johnston, J. C. (1986). Multiple approaches to attention mechanisms. Review of *Attention and performance XI*, by M. I. Posner and O. Marin (Eds.). *Contemporary Psychology, 31,* 856–857.

Posner, M. I., and Marin, O. S. M. (Eds.). (1985). *Attention and performance XI*. Hillsdale, NJ: Lawrence Erlbaum.

Rabbitt, P. M. A., and Dornic, S. (Eds.). (1975). *Attention and performance V*. London: Academic Press.

Requin, J. (Ed.). (1978). *Attention and performance VII*. Hillsdale, NJ: Lawrence Erlbaum.

Rumelhart, D. E. (1989). The architecture of mind: A connectionist approach. In M. I. Posner (Ed.), *Foundations of cognitive science*, 133–159. Cambridge, MA: MIT Press.

Sanders, A. F. (Ed.). (1967). *Attention and performance*. Amsterdam: North-Holland.

Sanders, A. F. (Ed.). (1970). *Attention and performance III*. Amsterdam: North-Holland.

Sanders, A. F. (1984). Ten symposia on attention and performance: Some issues and trends. In H. Bouma and D. Bouwhuis (Eds.), *Attention and performance X: Control of language processes*, 3–13. Hillsdale, NJ: Lawrence Erlbaum.

Seidenberg, M. S. (1985). Low-level language processes. Review of *Attention and performance X*, by H. Bouma and D. Bouwhuis (Eds.). *Contemporary Psychology, 30,* 946–947.

Shaffer, H. (1984). Review of *Attention and performance IX*, by J. Long and A. Baddeley (Eds.). *Quarterly Journal of Experimental Psychology, 36A,* 683–684.

Zelaznik, H. (1991). Advances in motor representation and control. Review of *Attention and performance XIII*, by M. Jeannerod (Ed.). *Contemporary Psychology, 36,* 967–968.

Participants and Contributors

Alan Allport
Department of Experimental
Psychology, University of Oxford,
South Parks Road, Oxford OXI
3UD, ENGLAND

Donald E. Broadbent
Department of Experimental
Psychology, University of Oxford,
South Parks Road, Oxford OXI
3UD, ENGLAND

Claus Bundesen
Psychology Laboratory,
Copenhagen University, Njalsgade
90, DK-2300, Copenhagen S,
DENMARK

Susan Chipman
Cognitive Science, 1142 CS, Office
of Naval Research, Arlington,
VA 22217-5000, USA

Michael Coles
Department of Psychology,
University of Illinois, 603 E. Daniel,
Champaign, IL 61820, USA

Max Coltheart
Department of Psychology, School
of Behavioral Sciences, MacQuarie
University, Sydney, NSW,
AUSTRALIA

John Duncan
MRC Applied Psychology Unit, 15
Chaucer Road, Cambridge CB2 2EF,
ENGLAND

Martha J. Farah
Department of Psychology,
University of Pennsylvania,
Philadelphia, PA 19104, USA

Jennifer Freyd
Department of Psychology,
University of Oregon, Eugene, OR
97403, USA

Daniel Gopher
Industrial Engineering and
Management, Technion, Haifa,
32000 ISRAEL

Peter C. Gordon
Department of Psychology, Harvard
University, Cambridge, MA 02138,
USA

Harold Hawkins
Personnel & Training Research
Program, Office of Naval Research,
Code 1142 PT, Arlington, VA
22217-5000, USA

Steven Hillyard
Department of Neuroscience, M008,
University of California, San Diego.
La Jolla, CA 92093, USA

Douglas L. Hintzman
Department of Psychology,
University of Oregon, Eugene, OR
97403, USA

David Howard
Department of Psychology, Birkbeck
College, Malet Street, London
WC1E 7BT, ENGLAND

Glyn W. Humphreys
Department of Psychology, The
University of Birmingham, P.O. Box
363, Birmingham B15 2TT,
ENGLAND

Michael S. Humphreys
Department of Psychology,
University of Queensland, St. Lucia,
4067, AUSTRALIA

David E. Irwin
Department of Psychology,
University of Illinois,
Champaign, IL 61820 USA

Richard Ivry
Department of Psychology,
University of California-Berkeley,
Berkeley, CA 94720, USA

John Jonides
Department of Psychology,
University of Michigan, Ann Arbor,
MI 48109, USA

Mitsuo Kawato
Human Information Processing,
Research Laboratories,
2-2 Hikaridai,
Seika-Cho, Soraku-gun,
Kyoto 619-02, JAPAN

Steven Keele
Department of Psychology, Colleges
of Arts and Sciences, University of
Oregon, Eugene, OR 97403, USA

Sylvan Kornblum
Mental Health Research Institute,
University of Michigan, 205 Zina
Pitcher Place, Ann Arbor, MI
48109-0720, USA

Stephen M. Kosslyn
Department of Psychology, William
James Hall, Harvard University,
Cambridge, MA 02138, USA

Gordon D. Logan
Department of Psychology,
University of Illinois, 603 E. Daniel,
Champaign, IL 61820, USA

Laurence T. Maloney
Psychology Department, New York
University, 6 Washington Place,
New York, NY 10003, USA

James L. McClelland
Department of Psychology,
Carnegie-Mellon University,
Pittsburgh, PA 15213-3890, USA

Janet Metcalfe
Department of Psychology,
Dartmouth College, Hanover,
NH 03755 USA

David E. Meyer
Department of Psychology,
University of Michigan, 330 Packard
Road, Ann Arbor, MI 48109,
USA

Stephen Monsell
Department of Experimental
Psychology, University of
Cambridge, Downing Street,
Cambridge CB2 3EF, ENGLAND

Gijsbertus Mulder
Institute of Experimental
Psychology, University of
Groningen, Grote Kruisstyaat 2/1,
9712 TS Groningen,
THE NETHERLANDS

Allen Osman
Department of Psychology C-OO9,
University of California-San Diego,
La Jolla, California 92093, USA

John Palmer
Department of Psychology,
University of Washington, Seattle,
WA, 98195, USA

Harold Pashler
Department of Psychology C-009,
University of California-San Diego,
La Jolla, CA 92093, USA

Karalyn E. Patterson
MRC Applied Psychology Unit,
15 Chaucer Road, Cambridge CB2
2EF, ENGLAND

Michael I. Posner
Department of Psychology, Colleges
of Arts and Sciences, University of
Oregon, Eugene, OR 97403, USA

Wolfgang Prinz
Max-Planck-Institute for
Psychology, Post Fach 44 01 09,
D-8000 Munich 44, GERMANY

Jeroen G. W. Raaijmakers
TNO Institute for Perception, P.O.
Box 23, 3769 ZG,
Soesterberg, THE NETHERLANDS

Jean Requin
Cognitive Neuroscience Laboratory,
CNRS-LNF1, 31 Chemin
Joseph-Aiguier,
13402 Marseille, Cedex 9, FRANCE

Seth Roberts
Department of Psychology,
University of California-Berkeley,
Berkeley, CA 94720, USA

Henry L. Roediger III
Department of Psychology, Rice
University, Houston,
TX 77251-1892, USA

David A. Rosenbaum
Department of Psychology,
University of Massachusetts,
Amherst, MA, USA

David E. Rumelhart
Department of Psychology, Stanford
University, Stanford, CA
94305-2130, USA

Andries F. Sanders
Vrije Universiteit, Vakgroep
Psychonomie, DeBoelelaan 111,
B-106, 1081 HW Amsterdam,
THE NETHERLANDS

Giuseppe Sartori
Department of Physiological
Psychology, University of Padova,
Padova, ITALY

Roger Schvaneveldt
Department of Psychology, New
Mexico State University, Las Cruces,
NM 88003, USA

Richard Schweickert
Psychological Sciences, Purdue
University, West Lafayette, IN
47907, USA

George Sperling
Department of Cognitive Science,
SST, University of California at
Irvine, Irvine, CA 92717, USA

Larry R. Squire
Department of Psychiatry (116),
V.A. Medical Center, 3350 La Jolla
Village Drive, San Diego, CA
92161, USA

Saul Sternberg
Psychology Department, University
of Pennsylvania, Walnut Street 3815,
Philadelphia, PA 19104-6196, USA

Anne Treisman
Department of Psychology,
University of California-Berkeley,
Berkeley, CA 94720, USA

Shimon Ullman
Artifical Intelligence Laboratory,
Massachusetts Institute of
Technology, 545 Technology
Square, Cambridge, MA 02139,
USA

Carlo Umilta
Dipartimento di Psicologia Generale,
University di Padova, Piazza
Capitaniato 3, 35139 Padova,
ITALY

Paolo Viviani
Psychology and Education Sciences,
University of Geneva, 24 rue
General Dufour, Ch-1211, Geneva 4,
SWITZERLAND

Dirk Vorberg
Philipps-Universität Marburg,
Fachbereich Psychologie, Gutenberg
strasse 18, Marburg, D-3500, WEST
GERMANY

Alan M. Wing
MRC Applied Psychology Unit, 15
Chaucer Road, Cambridge CB2 2EF,
ENGLAND

Howard Zelaznick
Department of Physical Education,
Purdue University, West Lafayette,
IN 47907, USA

1. George Sperling	18. Glyn W. Humphreys	35. David Howard
2. Anne Triesman	19. Michael S. Humphreys	36. Alan M. Wing
3. Martha J. Farah	20. Gijsbertus Mulder	37. Henry L. Roediger III
4. Harold Pashler	21. Richard Schweickert	38. Wolfgang Prinz
5. Saul Sternberg	22. Andries F. Sanders	39. Seth Roberts
6. Susan Chipman	23. Allen Osman	40. Howard Zelaznick
7. Max Coltheart	24. Mitsuo Kawato	41. Jean Requin
8. Donald E. Broadbent	25. Claus Bundesen	42. Michael Coles
9. Gordon D. Logan	26. David E. Irwin	43. Harold Hawkins
10. Janet Metcalfe	27. Stephen Monsell	44. David E. Meyer
11. Dirk Vorberg	28. Paolo Viviani	45. Steven Hillyard
12. Jennifer Freyd	29. Carlo Umilta	46. Douglas L. Hintzman
13. Shimon Ullman	30. Giuseppe Sartori	47. David E. Rumelhart
14. Sylvan Kornblum	31. Steven Keele	48. Alan Allport
15. John Palmer	32. Jeroen G. W. Raaijmakers	49. Roger Schvaneveldt
16. Peter C. Gordon	33. Michael I. Posner	50. Charles Woringham
17. John Duncan	34. Daniel Gopher	

I   Association Lecture

1 Learning and Connectionist Representations

David E. Rumelhart and Peter M. Todd

1.1 INTRODUCTION: REPRESENTATIONAL TOOLS IN CONNECTIONIST NETWORKS

Connectionist modeling is undergoing a renaissance. As the merits of brain-style computation (Rumelhart 1990) have become apparent, a bewildering variety of connectionist applications has cropped up throughout the cognitive sciences and engineering (for instance, see Lippmann, Moody, and Touretzky 1991). One of the central issues in all of these models is the representation of knowledge in the connectionist network. Getting a coherent picture of "what goes on" inside a network as it develops, manipulates, and alters the representation of the knowledge it processes is vital for our understanding of connectionist information processing, and likely for our understanding of the minds these systems model. In this chapter we explore the sorts of representations that connectionist systems employ and the crucial role learning plays in constructing them.

The representational materials that connectionist systems have to work with are remarkably simple. A connectionist network can basically be described as a collection of simple processing units, each of which has a current *state of activation*, linked together by a set of connections, each of which has a current *strength* or *weight* (see fig. 1.1). The weighted connections modify the activation values that they pass among the processing units. One set of units is typically assigned the special role of receiving inputs from the "external world"; these input units have their activation values set (at least in part) by an external stimulus. Another set of units is usually designated as the outputs of the system; the activation values of these output units is monitored as the final result of processing by the network. Units that fall into neither of these classes are often called hidden units, and they play a key role in the representation of knowledge in the network. We can further abstract the system's description to a simple vector $A[i]$ of activation values of all the units in the network, and a matrix $W[i, j]$ of the weights on the connections between units in the network. From this standpoint, there are now basically just two representational formats in which information is held in a connectionist network.

The first is the overall pattern of activation, $A[i]$, across all the units of the network. This pattern of activation corresponds to the *state of processing* of

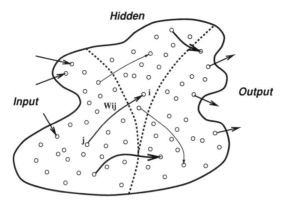

Figure 1.1 Generalized structure of a connectionist network, showing the input, hidden, and output processing units (e.g., i and j) and weighted interconnections (e.g., Wij).

the system at any point in time and determines what information is currently being represented and acted on by the network. It is important to note that this representational format achieves its meaning not through its internal structure, but through its relationship to the structure and meaning of the inputs and outputs of the system. While we usually impose a semantic interpretation on the network's inputs and outputs, the network is typically under no constraints to develop internal representations that we can comprehend and instead will come up with whatever best fits the task (i.e., the input-output mapping) at hand. Thus there may be no simple interpretation of the network's overall pattern of activation in terms easily understood by a human observer. The meaning of the pattern is rather determined by what causes it and what it causes (i.e., the network's inputs and outputs, respectively).

The second representational format in a connectionist system is the pattern of connectivity in the network, that is, the matrix $W[i, j]$ of connection strengths among the units of the network. This pattern is even more difficult to interpret than the pattern of activation in the network. Yet the pattern of connectivity is, in a sense, the more critical representational tool in connectionist networks, since it corresponds to the current *state of knowledge* of the system. The knowledge stored in the network's connectivity determines the effects of the inputs on the system's overall pattern of activation, and the effects of that activation on the behavior and outputs of the system as a whole. Thus, the network's pattern of activation can be thought of as simply a consequence of the pattern of connectivity of the system. As we will see, learning serves to modify the connection strengths in the network—its knowledge—so that it will produce the proper activations (particularly at the outputs) in response to various inputs—its processing.

These connectionist representational tools may seem at first unduly weak when compared to the formal logic predicates, semantic networks, frames and scripts, and other relatively sophisticated schemes for representing knowledge developed over the years in artificial intelligence (AI) and cognitive science (cf. Rumelhart and Norman 1988, Brachman and Levesque 1985). But there are in fact great advantages inherent in these simpler representational devices. Before turning to a detailed discussion of connectionist representation methods, it is useful to gain a historical perspective on this issue, by looking briefly at the history of representational systems and the (negative) correlation between interest in learning systems and interest in complex representation schemes. Many early AI systems, such as Oliver Selfridge's Pandemonium model of pattern recognition (Selfridge 1959), Frank Rosenblatt's perceptron model (Rosenblatt 1962), and the checkers-playing system of Arthur Samuel (Samuel 1959), had a strong focus on learning but a relatively weak and simple representational format. As interest in more sophisticated representation schemes grew, interest in learning per se correspondingly diminished. The idea was roughly that if we didn't know how the information was ultimately to be represented, we couldn't know what exactly should be learned in the first place. This view appears to have dominated most AI research during the 1970s.

With the 1980s, however, came some change of heart. Many researchers have recently developed increasingly simplified representational systems for which relatively simple learning procedures can be defined. One example of such work is the Soar system developed by Allen Newell and his colleagues (Newell 1990). They dropped many of the most complicated aspects of 1970s-era representation schemes and retained only a rather streamlined representational system, further enabling them to develop appropriate learning rules for the system. The connectionist paradigm goes one step further in simplifying its representational system and focusing even more on learning as a mechanism for developing representations. Given the large numbers of units and connections in a typical network, it is virtually impossible to "hand-wire" a connectionist system capable of very sophisticated behavior. This results in an increasing dependence on learning rules and mechanisms to "wire up" networks, and thereby to determine the details of connectionist representational formats. In the remainder of this chapter, we will focus on the distinctions made among the classes of such representations, the reasons and mechanisms for learning them, and some of the examples of their usefulness in connectionist systems.

1.2 DISTRIBUTED VERSUS LOCALIST REPRESENTATIONS

Perhaps the simplest representational scheme within the connectionist framework is the *localist* representation system (cf. Feldman and Ballard 1982). In this case, each unit in a network corresponds to a single concept. This one-concept—one-unit representational system has the advantage of simplicity and clarity. First of all, it is easy to see how the units should connect to one another—"hand-wiring" of localist networks is little problem. Furthermore, when a set of concepts is to be represented, we simply turn on each of the units corresponding to those individual concepts. McClelland and Rumelhart employed such a localist scheme in a word perception model designed to account for the word-superiority effect, the phenomenon in which letters are

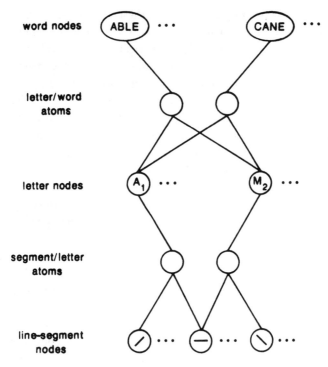

Figure 1.2 Example of a connectionist network using localist representations for word perception from letters and their subfeatures.

more easily recognized when presented in the context of normal words than in random letter strings (McClelland and Rumelhart 1981; Rumelhart and McClelland 1982). As seen in figure 1.2, this network had three sets of interconnected localist units: features, letters, and words. Connecting the units in this network was quite straightforward. Visual feature units were connected to the letters that contained them (e.g., vertical and horizontal bar detecting units were connected to the "T" letter unit), and letter units were similarly connected to the words in which they were found (e.g., "T" and "R" were connected to the word unit representing "CART"). Very useful results were obtained from this relatively simple model; but, as is typical of localist systems, the representations it used were all predetermined and of little interest compared to its processing behavior.

An alternative and rather more powerful representational system is the *distributed* representation format (described in detail in Hinton, McClelland, and Rumelhart 1986). In this case, a concept is represented not by the activation of a single unit, but rather by a pattern of activation over several units at once. Thus, each concept incoporates many units, and each unit participates in the representation of many concepts. It is useful to think of the individual units as representing what Hinton calls *microfeatures* (Hinton, McClelland, and Rumelhart 1986). A particular concept, then, is represented by a particular pattern of microfeatures. This leads to a natural measure of similarity between

Rumelhart and Todd

concepts: two concepts are similar to the extent that they share the same set of microfeatures. The key role of similarity as a fundamental processing strategy makes distributed connectionist systems unique, as we will see in the next section.

Because learning in a distributed-representation network occurs as modification of connections among microfeatures rather than among concepts directly, generalization and transfer of learning between concepts is inescapable. Increasing or decreasing connection strengths among the microfeatures of one concept inevitably affects the representation—and thus the meaning and consequences—of other concepts. This transfer of learning or generalization process can be both good and bad: good in that similar concepts should generally be responded to similarly, but bad, however, when important distinctions must be made between concepts that are very similar. In the former case, the system must learn which common microfeatures similar concepts share, while in the latter case, it must learn distinctive microfeatures that differentiate otherwise similar concepts. Learning is thus a key means of discovering relevant representations in both cases.

Another important aspect of distributed representations is their ability to represent a very large number of potential concepts in terms of a finite number of representational elements. If we use localist representations, with one unit corresponding to one concept, then with n units we have a vocabulary of n possible concepts. This finiteness of concept vocabulary is somewhat worrying—the combinatorics of the situation are definitely not in our favor. However, in a distributed representation we can have an enormous vocabulary of possible concepts with a relatively small number of representational elements. For example, if we have n binary units (which can take on activations of 0 or 1 only) available, we have a vocabulary of 2^n concepts we can possibly represent. For even small values of n, such as 100 or 1000, the vocabulary of possible concepts is 2^{100} or 2^{1000}—enormous numbers by any measure.

Of course, we pay a price for this large vocabulary. In a distributed representation we can represent any one of a very large number of concepts at one time, but we cannot represent many concepts at the same time. In a localist representation, as we mentioned earlier, we can simultaneously represent any desired combination of the possible individual concepts. Generally, in the parallel distributed processing (PDP) connectionist framework, we believe that the advantage of a large vocabulary of possible distributed concepts outweighs the advantage of being able to simultaneously represent arbitrary combinations of localist concepts. And it is still possible to represent a number of distributed concepts simultaneously, provided that number is reasonably small.

Perhaps the most serious disadvantage of distributed representations is our inability to easily interpret the complex patterns developed over the course of learning. It is this difficulty of interpretation and understanding that makes distributed representations seem so mysterious. But as we will demonstrate in the following sections, the patterns need not always be so enigmatic.

1.3 LEARNING REPRESENTATIONS IN CONNECTIONIST NETWORKS

Figure 1.3 illustrates a very simple connectionist network. It consists of two layers of units, the input units and output units, connected by a set of weights. As a result of the particular connectivity and weights of this network, each pattern of activation presented at the input units will induce another specific pattern of activation at the output units. This simple architecture is useful in a number of ways. If the input and output patterns all use distributed representations—namely, if they can all be described as sets of microfeatures—then this network will exhibit the important property mentioned in the previous section that "similar inputs yield similar outputs," along with the accompanying generalization and transfer of learning. Such two-layer networks behave this way because the activation of a particular output unit is given by a relatively smooth function of the weighted sum of its inputs. Thus, a slight change in the value of a particular input unit will yield a similarly slight change in the values of the output units.

Although this similarity-based processing is mostly useful, it does not always yield the correct generalizations. In particular, in a simple network of the kind shown in figure 1.3, the similarity metric employed is determined by the nature of the inputs themselves. And the "physical similarity" we are likely to have at the inputs (based on the structure of stimuli from the physical world) may not be the best measure of the "functional" or "psychological" similarity we would like to employ at the output (to group together appropriate similar responses). For example, it is probably true that a lowercase *a* is physically less similar to an uppercase *A* than to a lowercase *o*, but functionally and psychologically, a lowercase *a* and an uppercase *A* are more similar to one another than are the two lowercase letters. Thus, physical relatedness is an inadequate similarity metric for modeling human responses to letter-shaped visual inputs. It is therefore necessary to transform these input patterns somehow from their initial physically derived format into another representational form in which patterns requiring similar (output) responses are indeed similar to one another. This involves learning new representations.

Output

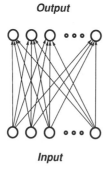

Input

Figure 1.3 A simple two-layer connectionist network consisting solely of input units connected to output units.

Figure 1.4 illustrates a simple layered feedforward network, in which information (activation) flows up from the input units at the bottom, through successive layers of internal ("hidden") units, to create the final response at the layer of output units on top. Such a network is useful for illustrating how an appropriate psychological or functional representation can be created. If we think of each input vector as a point in some multidimensional space, we can think of the similarity between two such vectors as the distance between their two corresponding points. Furthermore, we can think of the weighted connections from one layer of units to the next as implementing a transformation that maps each original input vector into some new vector. This transformation can create a new vector space in which the relative distances among the points corresponding to the input vectors are different from those in the original vector space, essentially rearranging the points. And if we use a sequence of such transformations, each involving certain nonlinearities, by "stacking" them between successive layers in the network, we can entirely rearrange the similarity relations among the original input vectors.

Thus, a layered network can be viewed simply as a mechanism for transforming the original set of input stimuli into a new similarity space with a new set of distances among the input points. For example, it is possible to move the initially distant "physical" input representations of a lowercase a and an uppercase A so that they are very close to one another in a transformed "psychological" output representation space, and simultaneously to transform the distance between the lowercase a and a lowercase o output representations so that they are rather distant from one another. (Generally, we seek to attain a representation in the second-to-last layer that is sufficiently transformed for us to rely on the principle that similar patterns yield similar

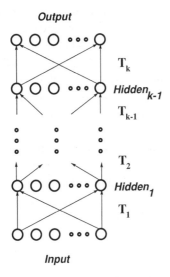

Figure 1.4 A multilayer connectionist network with several hidden layers interposed between the input and output layers; each hidden layer computes a transformation **T** of the representation structure.

Learning and Connectionist Representations

outputs at the final layer.) The problem is to find an appropriate sequence of transformations that accomplish the desired input-to-output change in similarity structures.

The *backpropagation* learning algorithm is a simple procedure for discovering such a sequence of transformations. In fact, we can see the role of learning in general as a mechanism for constructing the transformations that will convert the original physically based configuration of the input vectors into an appropriate functional or psychological space, with the proper similarity relationships between concepts for making generalization and transfer of learning occur automatically and correctly. The details of the backpropagation learning procedure are described in Rumelhart, Hinton, and Williams (1986) and will not be repeated here. However, the basic idea is the following: A performance measure is defined for how well a network satisfies some set of predefined criteria, such as producing a desired output for a given input. Backpropagation works by simply computing the gradient of this performance measure with respect to each of the weights in the network and then modifying those weights to improve the performance measure on a subsequent learning trial (e.g., the next input–desired output pair). This simple gradient search method has turned out to be quite effective in developing new and appropriate representations for many rather complex problems, by constructing similarly complex sequences of transformations.

In the remainder of the chapter, we will describe three different examples of the application of such a simple learning procedure and illustrate the interesting and useful representations it can create.

1.4 AUTOENCODERS

Perhaps the simplest mechanism for creating new and useful representations is the autoencoder.[1] The basic architecture of the autoencoder is illustrated in figure 1.5. The network has what may be called an hourglass architecture. The input and output vectors are of high and equal dimensionality—that is, there are n input units and n output units, where n is relatively large. The middle layer of hidden units has much lower dimensionality, containing m units, with $m \ll n$. The target for the output units is simply the input vector. Thus, the goal of an autoencoder is to take a high-dimensional input vector, recode it in a lower-dimensional space, and then use this low-dimensional representation to reproduce the original input vector again. This process of recoding is similar in many respects to ordinary principle components analysis (PCA). However, since the hidden units and output units are usually nonlinear, the network performs a nonlinear variant of PCA.

To illustrate how an autoencoder network can find a useful re-representation of its input, consider the set of visual patterns illustrated in figure 1.6. Imagine the set of characters that can be created out of the four line segments shown in the figure. We can create the letter O by having all four line segments on. We can create the letter L by turning on left and bottom line segments. The letter C consists of the top, bottom, and left line segment, and so forth.

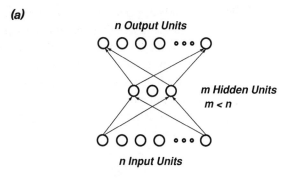

n Output Units

m Hidden Units
m < n

n Input Units

(b)

Internal Representation

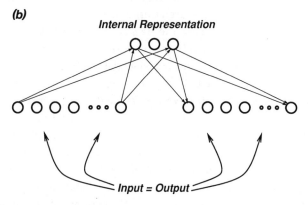

Input = Output

Figure 1.5 Basic structure of an autoencoder network (a) showing its hourglass architecture, and (b) emphasizing the identity of inputs and outputs.

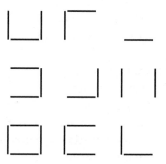

Figure 1.6 Examples of characters created from a set of four line segments, for use in an autoencoding experiment.

There are a total of sixteen possible images that can be constructed out of the four line segments. This includes the image in which no line segments are on. Now imagine that we use a 10 × 10 square array of pixels as our input and simply turn on just those pixels along each edge of the square corresponding to the line segments in the desired character. In this experiment, we know a priori that all sixteen possible input characters can be created out of four underlying features (line segments). It doesn't matter that the inputs are one hundred-dimensional vectors—there is a simple and much more compact representation of the set of input vectors that can actually occur. We want to see if a network can actually learn this simpler representation.

In a series of experiments involving a network with one hundred input units, four hidden units, and one hundred output units, trained on all sixteen characters as input and output using the backpropagation learning algorithm, we found that the four hidden units always turned out to correspond to the four underlying line segments. The autoencoder had effectively extracted the underlying structure of the population of input (and output) vectors and had learned the proper connection weights needed to implement the transformations back and forth between the full 100-dimensional vector representation and the reduced four-dimensional representation. In a variation on this experiment we used noisy input character vectors. In this case, the input essentially consisted of the desired line segments superimposed on a field of noise, so that each element of the input vector had a .25 probability of having the wrong value. (That is, units that were supposed to be on would be off 25 percent of the time, and vice versa.) This generated a very messy set of input vectors for the network to try to learn. But since the noise was random and unpredictable, it could not be extracted in the form of stable features of the input to be used in the reduced representation. Rather, we found that the four hidden units again picked up the four reliable underlying features—the line segments—of the character set.

This robust behavior under noisy data conditions is a further demonstration of the ability of PDP connectionist systems to learn useful distributed representations and to generalize and transfer that learning appropriately between inputs. In particular, with the autoencoder we have a system capable of extracting those features from the input vectors that are best able to predict the structure of the entire vector. Since the noise in the previous example was unpredictable it was ignored, and only the useful features were learned. In this way, the network builds representations that have as much information as possible about the input patterns, but that are also as concise as possible.

With slight modifications in the hourglass network architecture, we can build what are basically autoencoders that ignore other irrelevant aspects of the input. Imagine, for instance, that we have a large visual field that somewhere contains a single much smaller character of the type described earlier in this section. We may be interested in the character itself, without caring where it occurs—in essence, we want a sort of position-invariant attentional mechanism that represents the *type* of character and ignores its spatial location. A network that will do precisely this is shown in figure 1.7. The input visual field

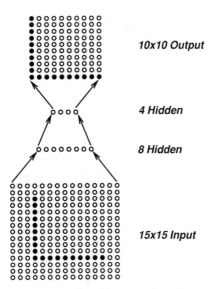

10x10 Output

4 Hidden

8 Hidden

15x15 Input

Figure 1.7 Modified autoencoder architecture for abstracting location-invariant features from a character in a larger visual field.

is a 15 × 15 array, in which our 10 × 10 character can appear at any of 36 (6 × 6) positions. The output is the same 10 × 10 character in canonical position. Feeding into the output is our layer of four hidden units, as before. But we also add one more layer to this network, consisting of eight hidden units, interposed between the input array and the four-unit hidden layer. The task of this second hidden layer is to create an intermediate representation of the input visual stimuli in which the position information has been discarded. The four-unit hidden layer can then transform that representation into one that is more useful at the output layer. This network was trained using only eleven of the sixteen possible characters, those that have two or more segments so that their position in the input array can be unambiguously determined. Each of these characters was presented at each of the thirty-six positions in the input, for a total of 396 training patterns. Once the network had learned to perform this task suitably well, we found that as before the four-unit hidden layer had adopted a one-unit-per-line-segment representation. Thus, again only the information needed for the task at hand—reconstructing the character and ignoring its position—was abstracted by the network for its auto-encoded representation.

1.5   REPRESENTING SEMANTIC NETWORKS IN CONNECTIONIST SYSTEMS

One of the classic representational systems much studied in the 1970s was the *semantic network* (Quillian 1968; Collins and Quillian 1970). Figure 1.8 shows a fairly standard example of a semantic network, represented as a tree structure that can be interpreted as a concise summary of a large number of individual

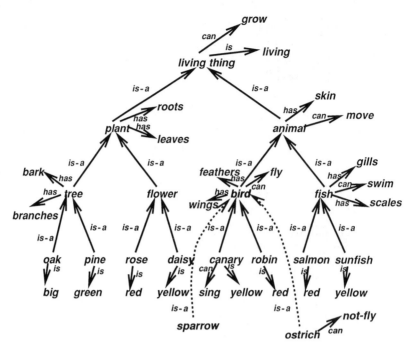

Figure 1.8 A semantic network encoding explicit and implicit ("inherited") facts about plants and animals.

facts. For example, the semantic network in figure 1.8 directly encodes the fact that a canary is a bird, a bird can fly, a bird is an animal, an animal has skin, an animal is a living thing, and a living thing can grow. It also contains the fact that a canary can fly, a canary has skin, and so forth. These secondary facts are implicit in the network through the principle of *inheritance*: if an *x* is a *y* and a *y* has a certain property, then generally speaking *x* can be said to have inherited that property. Inheritance allows a great number of implicit facts to be captured in a semantic network. How can we represent this collection of facts and inferences in a connectionist network?

In answering this question, one might first be tempted to design a localist representation in which each term or node of the semantic network such as *canary* or *bird* or *sing* is represented by a single unit in a connectionist network; then when the *canary* unit is activated, perhaps it would activate the units for *sing* and *yellow* and *bird* and *animal* and so on. This way of modeling semantic networks may be straightforward and easily followed, but it adds little to the representational characteristics of the traditional semantic network. (But see Shastri 1988a, b for an essentially localist connectionist instantiation of a semantic network that shows useful processing abilities.)

A more interesting approach is to represent the semantic network's information in a distributed fashion. With this approach, the problem becomes how to represent terms such as *canary* and *robin* and relations such as *is-a*, *has*, and *can* as distributed patterns in our connectionist network. One possible solution is shown in figure 1.9—a simple connectionist network architecture designed to

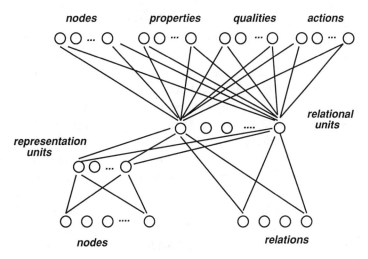

Figure 1.9 A connectionist network designed to learn distributed representations for the facts contained in a semantic network.

learn the appropriate distributed representations for the concepts in a semantic network. The idea is to train the network to map from concept-relation pairs as inputs to a listing of all terms that stand in that relation to that concept as outputs. For example, given *canary* and *can* as inputs, we want to produce *sing*, *fly*, *move*, and *grow* as outputs. Similarly, given *daisy* and *is* as inputs we want *yellow* and *living* as outputs, and *tree* and *has* as inputs should produce *bark*, *leaves*, and *roots*. If we represent these inputs and outputs in a localist fashion, then in order to perform this mapping the network will have to learn to reencode the localist representations of the inputs into appropriate distributed representations at the hidden layers from which the outputs can be produced. Hinton (1986) has employed a similar method to learn about family relationships.

To get the network to perform this mapping, we trained it in the following way. First, all the facts contained in the semantic network (both explicitly, and implicitly via inheritance) were converted into input/output training pairs. Each fact in the semantic network has the form *term1-relation-term2*; to convert these into training pairs for the network, we essentially collected all the facts that related to a specific *term1* and *relation* and compressed them into a single statement of the form *term1-relation-⟨set of terms⟩*. Thus the facts *bird has feathers* and *bird has wings* were compressed into the single statement *bird has ⟨feathers and wings⟩*. These compressed facts were turned into the training pairs by using the first two parts, *term1* and *relation*, as inputs, and the last part, *⟨set of terms⟩*, as the outputs.

After constructing these input/output pairs, training the network then consisted of turning on the "node" input unit corresponding to *term1* (e.g., *bird*, *fish*, *daisy*, etc.) and the "relation" input unit corresponding to *relation* (i.e., *is-a*, *has*, *is*, or *can*) (see fig. 1.9). The output units corresponding to each of the terms in *⟨set of terms⟩* were also turned on. Depending on the relation type turned on in the input, the outputs turned on would all be in one of the four clusters of output units corresponding to nodes, properties, qualities, or actions in the semantic network. For example, if the relation type was *is-a* in the input, then only node output units would be turned on (e.g., *living-thing*); if the relation type *has* was turned on, then some set of the property units would be turned on (e.g., *feathers*); the relation *is* would turn on qualities (e.g., *red*); and the relation *can* would turn on actions (e.g., *swim*). The network was trained on input-output pairs of this type by backpropagation until it was able to produce correctly the appropriate pattern over the output units for each input pattern. This required several hundred pairings of each input-output pair.

The network architecture used here is slightly more complicated than a standard three-layer form. The node input units project first onto a layer of hidden units called representation units, before being combined with the relation inputs at the second hidden layer, made up of what we call relational units. This structure is used because we want the first layer of weights to transform the localist input representations of the node terms into distributed representations of the concepts involved, at the representation units. These distributed representations interact with the relational inputs through the layer of relational hidden units and then finally project onto the output units.

The distributed representations of the node input concepts developed at the representation unit hidden layer are our main concern in this experiment. We expect that similar concepts will have similar representations at this transformed level, in spite of the fact that at the input level all concepts are equally similar to one another (since they are represented in a localist manner and thus have no inherent differential similarity). This representational structure will develop because similar responses at the output level are to be given to similar concepts at the input level, but since this similarity is not captured in the input representation, it must be introduced in the distributed hidden-layer representation. Thus, for example, on the whole *oak* and *pine* are to be responded to similarly. As a result, the distributed representation of *oak* and of *pine* should be very similar.

Figure 1.10 shows the representations developed from one experiment, in which we used eight representation hidden units. The figure is essentially the semantic network "tree" of concepts laid on its side. Thus, to the left we see the leaves of the tree—*oak, pine, rose, daisy,* and so forth; to their right we find the representations for the next higher order terms—*tree, flower, bird,* and *fish;* then further right are the still higher order terms—*plant* and *animal,* and finally at the far right we have the representation for *living-things.* The representations are shown in terms of the weights from the node input units to the representation hidden units. Positive weights are indicated by pluses, negative weights by minuses, and weights near zero by "?"s. What we find is that the major conceptual dimensions of the semantic network are represented by particular features in the connectionist network. For example, the first feature is positive for all plants, and negative (or at least *not* positive, in the case of *fish*) for all animals. Thus, feature 1 seems to represent the plant/animal distinction (though it is purely chance that the *first* unit out of all eight picked up this

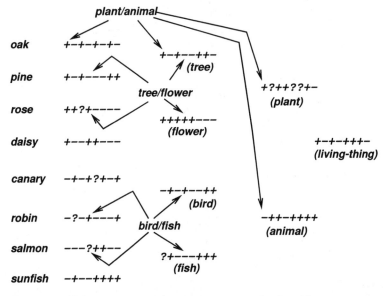

Figure 1.10 The representations for various concepts developed by a connectionist network with eight hidden units, showing interpretations of some of the microfeatures.

feature, as we will see in the next example). Similarly, if we are representing a plant, then feature 4 captures the tree/flower distinction; and interestingly this very same feature (hidden unit 4) encodes the bird/fish distinction in the case of animals. This ability for the same unit to represent different things conditional on the value of some other unit is a useful way in which connectionist representations differ from simple feature lists. By using hidden units for "double-duty" (or triple or more) conditional encoding of microfeatures, distributed representations can be much more compact than feature-list representations that have different slots allocated in the case of different concept types.

Figure 1.11 shows the results of another experiment, this time with six rather than eight representation hidden units. Here again we see that one feature, in this case the fifth, represents the plant/animal distinction, while feature 1 represents the bird/fish distinction (for animals) and feature 4 the tree/flower distinction (for plants). (The doubling up onto the same hidden unit we saw for these features in the previous example is absent here; there are enough hidden units for the representations that doubling up is not required but may happen in some cases nonetheless.) The other three features are rather more difficult to interpret and appear to represent the remaining idiosyncratic characteristics of the various node concepts.

One of the primary features of the semantic network is its inheritance property, as we mentioned earlier. New information can be added to the network and it will "inherit" many additional facts. For example, we could add the fact that a *sparrow is-a bird* to the semantic network, as indicated in figure 1.8 by the dotted line (an *is-a* link) from *sparrow* to *bird*. If we know that a *sparrow is-a bird*, we also immediately know by inheritance from *bird*, *animal*, and *living-thing* that a *sparrow can fly*, a *sparrow has feathers*, a *sparrow has skin*,

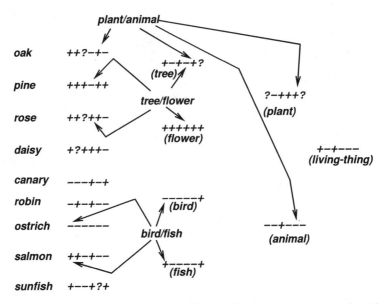

Figure 1.11 Representations developed by another connectionist network, with six hidden units.

a *sparrow can grow*, and so on—all of which is captured naturally and directly by the semantic network representation. Now switching back to our connectionist model we can ask, if we train the PDP network on the fact that a *sparrow is-a bird*, will it correctly generalize to these additional characteristics?

To answer this question, we first trained the six-representation-unit network without any initial concept of *sparrow* (but with an unused node input unit for later use) and achieved the representations illustrated in figure 1.11. After this, we further trained the network on just the proposition that a *sparrow is-a bird*. This was achieved by presenting *sparrow* and *is-a* as the two inputs (turning on the previously unused node input unit to stand for *sparrow*) and *bird* as the desired output. The difference between the actual activation on the *bird* output unit and the desired output (1.0) was backpropagated as the error signal to use in modifying the weights in the network. The error from the *bird* output unit was the only error signal used in training on this additional fact. Furthermore, only the weights from the new *sparrow* input unit to the representation hidden units were changed during learning—all other weights in the network were kept fixed, so that the other representations would not be adversely affected by this further training.

Now in order for *sparrow* to turn on *bird*, the pattern over the representation units for *sparrow* must be similar to the patterns for other node input concepts that turn on *bird*. This is in fact what happens, as we find in the representation developed for *sparrow* illustrated in figure 1.12. We see that *sparrow* has developed a pattern roughly halfway between *canary* and *robin*, perhaps a bit closer to the latter. The figure also shows the generalization results. Although the network had not been taught anything explicitly about what a *sparrow* has or can do (nothing in fact other than that it *is-a bird*), it correctly inferred that a

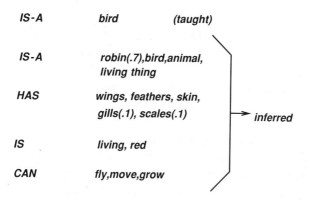

Figure 1.12 Representation developed for a new *sparrow* concept, showing its resulting inferred attributes.

sparrow can fly, can move, can grow, has wings, has feathers, has skin, is-an animal, is-a living-thing, is living, and *is red* (a good guess as to its color). The network's representation of *sparrow* also gives a strength of 0.1 for having *gills* and *scales* (erroneously, but ignorably) and a value of essentially 0.0 for every other inappropriate quality, property, and action. Thus, we see that the connectionist network provides a rather good generalization mechanism that emulates the inheritance mechanism of the semantic network, turning on the expected implications of a new concept and ignoring the low-likelihood ones. But, importantly, the connectionist network achieves all this using a very different similarity-based learning and processing mechanism.

Another feature of semantic networks is the so-called cancellation principle. This is illustrated by the example of the ostrich. Although the ostrich is a bird, the ostrich cannot fly; therefore, the normal inheritance mechanism must somehow be thwarted in this case. This can be done in traditional semantic networks by adding the direct characteristic to *ostrich* that it *can not-fly* (as shown in fig. 1.8), and by adding the general principle that no inherited property can override an explicitly stated property of a concept. (We add the *not-fly* action here rather than adding a new type of *cannot* link.) How does the connectionist network emulate this principle? Quite simply—we just train the network with the fact that an *ostrich is-a bird* and has all the usual *bird* attributes, except that we explicitly teach the network that an *ostrich can not-fly.* We do this by turning off the *fly* output unit (giving it a desired activation value of 0.0) when *ostrich* and *can* are given as inputs. Figure 1.11 illustrates the representation thereby attained for *ostrich*—in this case all minuses. This representation captures all the desired facts (and the new exception) about ostriches.

Having trained the network on *ostrich*, we then wanted to see how it generalized to other flightless birds. We further taught the network about a new thing we called an *emu*: an *emu is-a bird*, but an *emu can not-fly*. We trained the network on these two facts about this new creature as we did for the *sparrow*, by sending error signals back only from the *bird* and *fly* output units and changing only the weights on the connections from the new *emu* input unit to the representation hidden units. We found that the network discovered a representation for *emu* that was exactly the same as that for *ostrich*. Therefore its responses to all queries were also the same as those for *ostrich*: it said that an *emu is large, has feathers, has wings, is-an animal, is-a living-thing*, and so on. Since the *ostrich* was the only example of a flightless bird that the network knew about, it simply assimilated *emu* to *ostrich* and thereby gave the right answers to essentially every query about emus.

We ran one final experiment in which we presented the network with still another flightless bird—this time the penguin. We taught the network that a *penguin is-a bird*, that a *penguin can not-fly*, but that it *can swim*. In this case we found that the network mistakenly generalized by asserting that, in addition to being a *bird*, the *penguin is-a fish*, and that it *has gills* and *has scales* as well as *has feathers* and other *bird* attributes. Not happy with this result, we tried again. This time we taught the network explicitly that the *penguin is-a bird*, the *penguin is-a not-fish*, the *penguin can not-fly*, but the *penguin can swim*. We found that the network could not both turn on the output unit for *swim* and turn off the unit for *fish*. That is, by modifying weights only from the penguin input unit to the representation hidden units, we were unable to make the system differentiate between being able to *swim* and being a *fish*. Presumably this is because the network had learned that whenever anything *is-a fish*, it *can swim*, and vice versa, and it made use of this redundancy to form appropriate generalizations. The only way the network could assimilate this new swimming penguin fact was to allow it to modify other connections—then it could eventually learn this peculiar proposition.

The case of the penguin illustrates another important feature of connectionist networks: they work by representing certain classes of concepts as similar to one another, and by exploiting the redundancies among the characteristics of the concepts within a class to make generalizations. Usually these generalizations are appropriate, as when the network responded the same way for *emu* and *ostrich*, but sometimes they are not, as when the network had a hard time learning that penguins can swim but aren't fish. The network essentially ends up reflecting the structure of the world (as we humans parse it, since we make the training sets). To the extent that there are correlations or commonalities among the (micro)features we perceive for various fishes or various birds, the network will be able to correctly generalize between members of these categories.

Finally, before leaving this semantic network example, it will be useful to look at another way of viewing the representations developed in these experiments. Figure 1.13 shows a hierarchical clustering view of the hidden unit representations for still another experiment in this series. Here we see that on the whole, animals are clustered separately from plants, trees are clustered separately from flowers, and fish are clustered separately from birds. In addi-

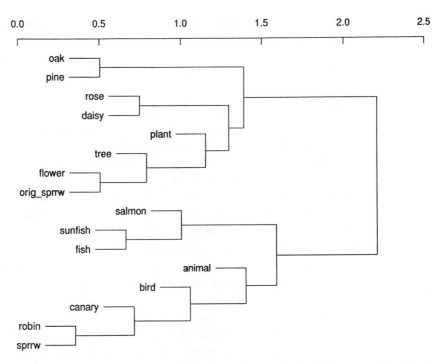

Figure 1.13 Hierarchical clustering of the representations developed by a connectionist network, showing similarity and hierarchy relations among the concepts.

tion, the most similar pairs in the figure are those of the same type at the same (low) level in the semantic network hierarchy (e.g., *oak* and *pine*). Finally, we can see how the representation of one concept, the *sparrow* described earlier, changed during the course of learning. In the already fully trained network, the original representation of *sparrow* was determined simply by the random initial setting of the weights from its corresponding input node unit. This ended up by chance to be very close to the learned representation of *flower*, as shown. However, after the previously trained network was further taught that a *sparrow is-a bird*, we see that the *sparrow* representation moved to be very close to that for *robin*, as we illustrated in figure 1.12.

We've seen in this example that connectionist learning algorithms can create new representations that abstract the important features from a set of input-output relations. A trained network can use the features in this transformed representation to provide appropriately generalized responses when it learns about new concepts. Knowing only one characteristic of a new concept—for example, that it *is-a bird*—the connectionist network can correctly infer its other major attributes. Although this behavior is compelling and suggestive, it is of course unrealistic to imagine that humans learn and develop concepts based on just this sort of mechanism. Our own concept formation processes are no doubt much more complex. In the next section we will show how connectionist networks can build representations that may come closer to the kind that people apparently employ.

1.6 CONNECTIONIST REPRESENTATIONS AND HUMAN JUDGMENTS OF SIMILARITY

In the previous sections we showed how connectionist systems can develop representations that work for performing particular tasks. For a psychological model, however, in addition to seeking representations that just *work*, we would like to constrain the network somehow to develop internal representations that resemble those employed by humans. One way to do this is to impose human similarity structures onto the network's representations, rather than giving it free rein to modify the similarity structures as needed. In particular, if we are interested in reconstructing internal human representations of input stimuli based on human judgments of similarity between those stimuli, then if we construct a network that is constrained to produce the same similarity structure between *its* internal representations of the inputs, the two representational systems—human and network model—should match. Several years ago we carried out a series of experiments designed to test this hypothesis (Todd 1987, 1988; see Todd and Rumelhart 1993 for more details.)

The basic idea is illustrated in figure 1.14. Essentially, we want a network to learn a mapping from its inputs to an internal representation, as usual, but this time we want a natural similarity measure over these representations to mimic human judgments of similarity between the inputs. The network's internal representations will then be a model of those the humans employed to make their similarity judgments. In our previous examples, the networks developed a similarity structure over their internal representations that would work to produce the desired outputs; here, since we want to constrain the network's representations to match the ones humans use in making similarity judgments, we use a little trick: we make the network's desired outputs *be* the human similarity judgments. To do this, we have to construct a network that compares two input stimuli at a time and produces an output corresponding to their similarity.

The network architecture for this purpose is shown in figure 1.15. Here we have used two instances of the encoder network from figure 1.14, whose outputs (the internal representations) are compared by a comparison subnetwork that produces the final similarity judgment as output. Humans probably

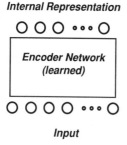

Figure 1.14 A simple encoder network that maps inputs into internal representations, for use in a psychological model of human representations.

have just one copy of something analogous to the encoder subnetwork and use it twice in succession to compare two sequentially presented stimuli; in the network we have converted this use of the encoder twice in time into using two copies of it in parallel simultaneously. The weights in both copies of the encoder network are kept equal throughout training (that is, the two encoders are always constrained to be identical and hence use the same encoding strategy on both input stimuli).

To train this network, we first collect human similarity judgments on pairs of stimuli and encode these stimuli into an appropriate form for use as network inputs with the corresponding similarity value as desired output. Then, for each judgment, one stimulus, S_1, is inserted into the left set of input units, and the other, S_2, is inserted into the right set. Each input stimulus is then mapped through its own copy of the same encoder subnetwork, to produce two corresponding internal representations, X_1 and X_2, at the two-part hidden-unit representation layer. These two representations are then compared using the fixed comparison subnetwork, which embodies some theory of how similarity judgments are made. The final output of this comparison network is the predicted similarity of stimuli S_1 and S_2. This predicted similarity is compared to the actual human similarity judgment, and the difference between them is used as an error signal to modify the weights in (both copies of) the encoder subnetwork. The weights in the comparison subnetwork are held fixed throughout training. In this way, only the mapping from input stimuli to internal representation can change during training; the similarity comparison method itself is assumed to remain constant for humans (at this time scale), and so it is kept constant in the network model as well. We train the encoder networks in this way until the similarity judgments are predicted as accurately as possible. The final results we are interested in are the internal representa-

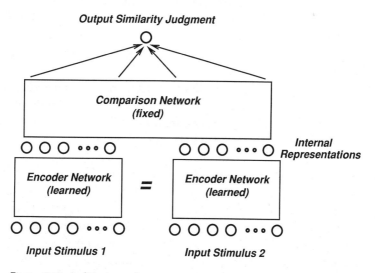

Figure 1.15 Architecture of a connectionist network for mapping from pairs of stimuli to their human-judged similarity, via a learned psychological encoding and a fixed comparison subnetwork.

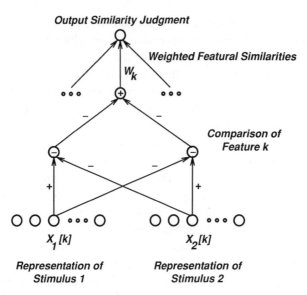

Figure 1.16 The subnetwork structure for comparing two featural dimensions using a Hamming-like similarity metric, showing the signs of the weights and biases (within unit circles) used.

tions developed by the network, which we expect will mimic those used by humans to represent these stimuli.

This procedure for modeling human representations can be carried out under a wide variety of assumptions about the nature of the similarity comparison subnetwork. For example, we can easily implement a simple Euclidian-distance measure of similarity between the representation vectors. In this case our procedure acts very much like standard multidimemional scaling (MDS; see Shepard 1980), finding representations in which individual hidden units capture real-valued featural dimensions of the stimuli. In most of our experiments we have employed something close to Hamming distance as our similarity metric, because it is a rough measure of pattern overlap, particularly suited to the sort of microfeature-vector pattern representations developed in PDP systems.

Figure 1.16 illustrates the basic structure of our comparison subnetwork for computing the Hamming-style similarity measure. The featural dimensions are compared individually; here we see the comparison of feature k alone. If feature k is about equally present in both input S_1 and input S_2, that is, if hidden units $X_1[k]$ and $X_2[k]$ have roughly equal activation values, then the comparison unit at the top of the subnetwork will also have a high activation value and will contribute strongly to the overall similarity judgment based on this feature match. If, however, feature k is present in greatly different amounts in the two input stimuli, then the output for this feature comparison will be small, indicating dissimilarity. The comparison results for each featural dimension are independently weighted and summed to form the final predicted similarity value. The entire similarity-judging feature abstraction network with this comparison subnetwork structure inserted is illustrated in figure 1.17.

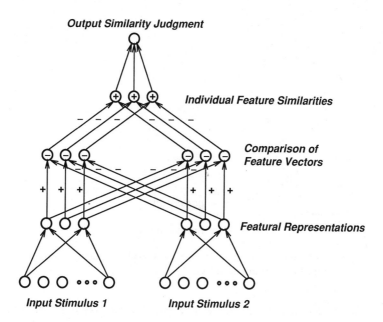

Output Similarity Judgment

Individual Feature Similarities

Comparison of Feature Vectors

Featural Representations

Input Stimulus 1   **Input Stimulus 2**

Figure 1.17 The structure of the similarity-judging network, with the Hamming-like comparison subnetwork inserted for three features.

Table 1.1 Similarity Measures between Kinship Terms

	F	B	S	GS	U	N	C
GF	.7	.1	.2	.8	.2	.1	.1
F		.4	.7	.2	.3	.1	.1
B			.7	.2	.2	.2	.2
S				.5	.1	.1	.1
GS					.1	.1	.2
U						.6	.7
N							.8

We have carried out a number of experiments with this paradigm, and in this section we provide the results of two of them to illustrate the basic characteristics of the methodology. In the first experiment we employed data provided by Roy D'Andrade (personal communication, conversation, 1986) on judgments of similarities among kinship terms. The terms employed were *grandfather, father, brother, son, grandson, uncle, cousin,* and *nephew*. The matrix of similarities between these terms is given in table 1.1. We used this data to train our network by constructing pairs of localist representations of the terms as inputs (i.e., eight input units for each stimulus, with one turned on at a time), with their corresponding similarity value as the desired output. So, for example, to train the network on the pair $\langle$ *grandfather, brother* $\rangle$, we turn on the unit in S_1 corresponding to *grandfather* and the unit in S_2 corresponding to

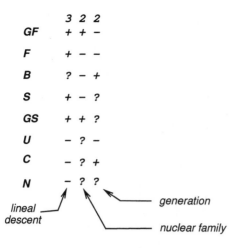

	3	2	2
GF	+	+	−
F	+	−	−
B	?	−	+
S	+	−	?
GS	+	+	?
U	−	?	−
C	−	?	+
N	−	?	?

lineal descent / generation / nuclear family

Figure 1.18 Representations developed by a similarity-judging network for kinship terms, showing the three features discovered.

brother and use 0.1 as the desired output value. We used three representation hidden units in this example.

The representations developed by the network are illustrated in figure 1.18. The three features extracted correspond to rather plausible categories and are weighted in ratios of approximately 3 to 2 to 2; that is, the first feature was the most important in terms of determining the similarity, and the second two features were about equally important. The first feature appears to correspond roughly to the dimension of lineal descent: *grandfather, father, son,* and *grandson* are all given the same featural value (+) and all belong to the same line of descent. *Uncle, cousin,* and *nephew* are given a very different value (−), and *brother* is classified somewhere between. The second dimension appears to correspond to distance from the nuclear family. Thus, *father, brother,* and *son* are all classified together and all belong to the same nuclear family. Likewise, *grandfather* and *grandson* are both equally distant from the nuclear family and so are classified together with the same feature value, as are *uncle, cousin,* and *nephew.* The third dimension appears to correspond to generation. In this case all of those older than ego (self) are classified together, namely, *grandfather, father,* and *uncle.* Similarly, those younger—*son, grandson,* and *nephew*—are classified together, as are those of the same generation—*brother* and *cousin.* These featural dimensions discovered by the network are all readily interpretable by a human observer, supporting our hypothesis that the network is picking up the same types of features that people use to represent these concepts. (See Hinton 1986 for an alternative and less psychologically motivated network representation of family relation concepts.) Finally, it is interesting that all three dimensions appear to employ trinary values. Since our comparison subnetwork simply checks to see whether the feature values are significantly different from one another, a trinary system is easily attained.

One of the particularly nice features of the architecture we have employed here is that we need not use localist representations for our input stimuli. For instance, consider the case in which the input stimuli are geometric forms, like those shown in figure 1.6, presented in pairs with their corresponding similarity value. Now when the network learns how to encode the input stimuli, it is picking up something about the relationship between the input's geometric structure and its internal representation—in this case, that four units alone can capture the structure inherent in the collection of "line segments" presented over the input units. This suggests that if we train the network on a *subset* of the geometric forms in the pair comparisons, we could then present it with new examples and it could "predict" their featural representations and their proper similarity value—even though it has never seen these stimulus patterns before. Furthermore, this generalization to new stimuli should match how humans would generalize. In a final experiment we illustrate these properties.

For this experiment we chose a set of data from a study by Rothkopf (1957; also reported in Shepard 1963), in which subjects indicated the similarity among pairs of Morse codes for individual letters and numerals (through intercode confusions). Since the maximum length of a single Morse code for a letter or numeral is a collection of five dots and dashes, we represented each code with ten input units, one for a dot and one for a dash for each of the five possible positions. A dot in a particular position would turn on the first of the pair of input units, a dash the second, and the absence of both (indicating that we were beyond the end of the code) would mean that neither unit at that position was turned on. Thus the letter E (Morse code ".") was converted into the input vector $\langle 1, 0, 0, 0, 0, 0, 0, 0, 0, 0 \rangle$, and the numeral 0 (Morse code "$-----$") was converted into $\langle 0, 1, 0, 1, 0, 1, 0, 1, 0, 1 \rangle$. In this way all the letters and numerals could be easily represented.

We ran several simulations in which we trained a network with two featural representation hidden units on a subset of these Morse codes and then tested its generalization ability on the untrained patterns. In one case, we trained the network on pairs using thirty-one out of the thirty-six total letters and numbers, leaving out I, D, H, V, and 1 completely from the training set. The resulting representations of all thirty-six codes are illustrated in figure 1.19, where we've graphed the activation values of the two feature units on the x and y axes. The interpretation of the two featural dimensions is readily seen. The x-axis dimension corresponds to the length of the code for the letter or number involved. On the far left of the figure we see the short codes, and on the far right the long codes. The y-axis feature roughly corresponds to the proportion of dots or dashes in the code. Near the top we see the codes for E, S, H, and 5, which consist entirely of dots, and at the bottom we see 0, O, and M, which consist entirely of dashes. Intermediate values along both dimensions correspond to the medium-length, mixed dot-and-dash codes.

These are the same features that Shepard found with his MDS analysis (Shepard 1963), but in this case they were more easily interpreted, as follows. Often, the spatial configurations of the stimuli that MDS discovers must be rotated before the dimensions can be interpreted properly. But because of anisotropies in our network's stimulus-to-representation mapping (from the

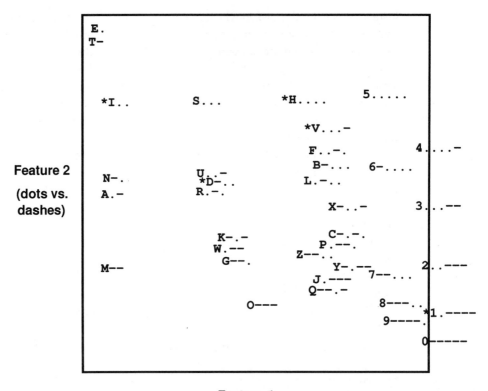

Figure 1.19 Representations developed by a similarity-judging network for Morse code signals, with the two features plotted on the two axes and showing the locations generalized to for five previously unseen codes (starred).

logistic activation functions used), the features came out directly from the two hidden units without the need for rotation. As in the previous example, the features have psychological meanings that we can ascribe to the human representations of these stimuli. Furthermore, the network in this case can generalize to new stimuli; the codes that the network never saw during training are indicated by stars in the positions they are encoded to by the learned representational mapping. Obviously these codes have taken their appropriate place in the representational format. The network has been able to abstract the basic features underlying the human similarity judgments of Morse code signals, and can generalize from those features to predict the similarities among stimuli it has never before seen—something that is quite impossible with standard MDS.

1.7 CONCLUSION

In this chapter we have shown the important role that learning and similarity play in the construction of representations in connectionist networks. Simple learning procedures such as the backpropagation algorithm can discover sequences of transformations that create the different internal distributed representations needed to perform a given input-output mapping task. Along the way, these transformations must alter the physically based similarity relations among the input vectors into the psychological and functional similarities required at the output. The representations learned as a result at the hidden layers will embody similarity relations that allow proper generalization to and transfer of learning between new stimuli. This similarity-based ability to learn and modify internal representations is an essential feature of any complex information processing system. The examples we described of autoencoders, connectionist semantic networks, and psychological similarity judgment models serve to illustrate the power and variety of representation learning approaches all captured under the unified paradigm of brain-style computation.

NOTE

1. The idea of using the autoencoder to re-represent input patterns was first suggested to me in 1985 by Geoffrey Hinton. It has since become a popular method.

REFERENCES

Brachman, R. J., and Levesque, H. J. (Eds.). (1985). *Readings in knowledge representation*. Los Altos, CA: Morgan Kaufmann.

Collins, A. M., and Quillian, M. R. (1970). Facilitating retrieval from semantic memory: The effect of repeating part of an inference. In A. F. Sanders (Ed.), *Attention and performance III*. Amsterdam: North Holland.

Feldman, J. A., and Ballard, D. H. (1982). Connectionist models and their properties. *Cognitive Science, 6*, 205–254.

Hinton, G. E. (1986). Learning distributed representations of concepts. In *Proceedings of the Eleventh Annual Conference of the Cognitive Science Society*, 1–12. Hillsdale, NJ: Lawrence Erlbaum Associates.

Hinton, G. E., McClelland, J. L., and Rumelhart, D. E. (1986). Distributed representations. In D. E. Rumelhart and J. L. McClelland (Eds.), *Parallel distributed processing: Explorations in the microstructure of cognition. Vol. 1: Foundations*. Cambridge, MA: MIT Press/Bradford Books.

Lippmann, R. P., Moody, J. E., and Touretzky, D. S. (Eds.). (1991). *Advances in neural information processing 3*. San Mateo, CA: Morgan Kaufmann.

McClelland, J. L., and Rumelhart, D. E. (1981). An interactive activation model of context effects in letter perception: Part 1. An account of basic findings. *Psychological Review, 88*, 375–407.

Newell, A. (1990). *Unified theories of cognition*. Cambridge, MA: Harvard University Press.

Quillian, M. R. (1968). Semantic memory. In M. Minsky (Ed.), *Semantic information processing*. Cambridge, MA: MIT Press.

Rosenblatt, F. (1962). *Principles of neurodynamics*. New York: Spartan.

Rothkopf, E. Z. (1957). A measure of stimulus similarity and errors in some paired-associate learning tasks. *Journal of Experimental Psychology, 53*, 94–101.

Rumelhart, D. E. (1990). Brain style computation: Learning and generalization. In S. F. Zornetzer, J. L. Davis, and C. Lau (Eds.), *An introduction to neural and electronic networks*. San Diego: Academic Press.

Rumelhart, D. E., Hinton, G. E., and Williams, R. J. (1986). Learning internal representations by error propagation. In D. E. Rumelhart and J. L. McClelland (Eds.), *Parallel distributed processing: Explorations in the microstructure of cognition. Vol. 1: Foundations*. Cambridge, MA: MIT Press/ Bradford Books.

Rumelhart, D. E., and McClelland, J. L. (1982). An interactive activation model of context effects in letter perception: Part 2. The contextual enhancement effect and some tests and extentions of the model. *Psychological Review, 89*, 60–94.

Rumelhart, D. E., and Norman, D. A. (1988). Representation in memory. In R. C. Atkinson, R. J. Herrnstein, G. Lindzey, and R. D. Luce (Eds.), *Stevens' handbook of experimental psychology*. New York: Wiley. Extracts of chapter reprinted as "Representation of Knowledge" in A. M. Aitkenhead and J. M. Slack (Eds.), (1985), *Issues in cognitive modeling*. London: Lawrence Erlbaum Associates.

Samuel, A. (1959). Some studies in machine learning using the game of checkers. *IBM Journal of Research and Development, 3*, 210–229.

Selfridge, O. (1959). Pandemonium: A paradigm for learning. In *Symposium on the mechanization of thought processes*. London: HM Stationery Office.

Shastri, L. (1988a). *Semantic networks: An evidential formalization and its connectionist realization*. Los Altos, CA: Morgan Kaufmann/London: Pitman.

Shastri, L. (1988b). A connectionist approach to knowledge representation and limited inference. *Cognitive Science, 12*, 331–392.

Shepard, R. N. (1963). Analysis of proximities as a technique for the study of information processing in man. *Human Factors, 5*, 33–48.

Shepard, R. N. (1980). Multidimensional scaling, tree-fitting, and clustering. *Science, 210*, 390–398.

Todd, P. M. (1987). *Abstracting musical features using a parallel distributed processing approach*. Master's thesis, UC San Diego Institute for Cognitive Science, La Jolla, CA.

Todd, P. M. (1988). *A connectionist multidimensional scaling method allowing semantic generalization*. Unpublished manuscript, Stanford University Psychology Department, Stanford, CA.

Todd, P. M., and Rumelhart, D. E. (1993). Feature abstraction from similarity ratings: A connectionist approach. In Y. Chauvin and D. E. Rumelhart (Eds.), *Backpropagation: Theory, architectures, and applications*. Hillsdale, NJ: Lawrence Erlbaum Associates.

II   Visual Information Processing

Introduction

In 1966, at the time of the first Attention and Performance symposium, visual information processing already constituted a basic topic of performance theory, and many exciting developments were taking place with respect to it. Hubel and Wiesel (1962) had recently published their seminal discoveries about elementary feature detectors in the cat's visual cortex. Research on human iconic memory was blossoming because of Sperling's (1960) introduction of the partial-report procedure and demonstration of intriguing iconic-memory phenomena. And studies of visual search were underway in response to theoretical proposals by Neisser (1963) and others about serial versus parallel processing.

The pursuit of such investigations has continued and expanded greatly over the past twenty-five years. We now know much more about the nature of iconic memory (e.g., Coltheart 1984) and the role of eye movements in visual perception and cognition (e.g., Rayner 1984). Investigators have also made substantial progress toward understanding the neurophysiological substrates of visual information processing, as evidenced, for example, in the identification of separate visual pathways that process object and location information (Ungerleider and Mishkin 1982). Meanwhile, at higher cognitive levels, more has been learned as well about visual imagery (e.g., Kosslyn 1980) and mental transformations of objects in the mind's eye (e.g., Shepard and Cooper 1983). Perhaps most notably, rigorous computational analyses have shed considerable light on what sorts of information are logically required for constructing formal knowledge representations of visual scenes (Marr 1982). Given this sort of progress, part II of *Attention and Performance XIV* is devoted to surveying our present understanding of visual information processing, assessing how we got here, and making our best guesses about where we may go next to obtain even deeper insights into various perceptual and cognitive aspects of vision. Consistent with the goals of the symposium, the present chapters on this topic take various complementary approaches in the exploration of the visual system and analysis of its characteristics at different levels.

Here Van Kleeck and Kosslyn provide a keynote tutorial review in which they outline a taxonomic perspective on the evolution of visual information processing research. A major theme of their chapter is that since *Attention and Performance I*, the field of visual information processing has gone through three research phases that include an "era of cognitive psychology," an "era of cognitive science," and an "era of cognitive neuroscience." Illustrating the different research styles associated with these phases, which are all of course still in vogue, other contributors to part II take us on tours of their own recent research projects. In particular, Maloney formulates an elegant mathematical framework to account for mechanisms of color constancy and color perception that, with certain assumptions, allow surface colors to be identified despite variations of spectral information across adjacent spatial regions. Pursuing other important visual features, a powerful computational treatment of three-dimensional object recognition is developed by Ullman, who shows how cues from combinations of two-dimensional views can be cleverly integrated to recognize objects in three dimensions without having "three-dimensional object models." Moving on from visual information processing about static objects, Freyd takes steps to describe dynamic mental representations of objects in motion. Her contribution offers five "hunches" about what these representations may be like. Next, Irwin treats the occurrence of motion in visual information processing from a related slant. His question is: How do people combine information obtained from successive glimpses of a visual scene in order to arrive at an integrated representation of the visual world? To answer this question, he reviews the literature on information integration across saccadic eye movements and reports further experiments to augment this literature. On the assumption that visual attention is highly correlated with the direction of a person's gaze, the chapter by Humphreys and Riddoch is also, at least indirectly, related to issues treated by Irwin. To be specific, they report interesting new neuropsychological data about dissociations between space-based and object-based attention systems, which help extend our characterization of processing deficits such as "visual neglect."

Finally, as the discussant for this section, Treisman explains more fully how all of these chapters fit neatly together in reaching general theoretical statements about the nature of the visual system's intermediate representations for objects and events.

REFERENCES

Coltheart, M. (1984). Sensory memory. In H. Bouma and D. G. Bouwhuis (Eds.), *Attention and performance X*, 259–285. Hillsdale, NJ: Lawrence Erlbaum Associates.

Hubel, D. H., and Wiesel, T. N. (1962). Receptive fields, binocular interaction, and functional architecture in the cat's visual cortex. *Journal of Physiology, 160*, 106–154.

Kosslyn, S. M. (1980). *Image and mind.* Cambridge, MA: Harvard University Press.

Marr, D. (1982). *Vision.* San Francisco: W. H. Freeman.

Neisser, U. (1963). Decision time without reaction time: Experiments in visual scanning. *American Journal of Psychology, 76*, 376–385.

Rayner, K (1984). Visual selection in reading, picture perception, and visual search—A tutorial review. In H. Bouma and D. G. Bouwhuis (Eds.), *Attention and performance X*, 67–96. Hillsdale, NJ: Lawrence Erlbaum Associates.

Shepard, R. N., and Cooper, L. N. (1983). *Mental images and their transformations*. Cambridge, MA: MIT Press.

Sperling, G. (1960). The information available in brief visual presentations. *Psychological Monographs, 74*, Whole No. 498.

Ungerleider, L. G., and Mishkin, M. (1982). Two cortical visual systems. In D. J. Ingle, M. A. Goodale, and R. J. W. Mansfield (Eds.), *Analysis of visual behavior*, 549–586. Cambridge, MA: MIT Press.

2

Visual Information Processing: A Perspective

Michael H. Van Kleeck and Stephen M. Kosslyn

The study of visual information processing has produced remarkable insights over the past twenty-five years. Researchers have discovered a host of phenomena that seem to reflect basic principles of vision and the use of visual information in cognition. We believe that this work has led to the verge of a new era, and in this chapter we develop the grounds for our optimism. In brief, it is our view that the next twenty-five years will see many computationally sophisticated theories that incorporate behavioral and neurobiological data. Such theories will flourish in part because researchers will skillfully exploit the power of new neuroimaging and computer simulation technologies, which will allow them to answer subtle questions about the component subsystems of vision.

In this chapter we will explicate research goals that are based on past progress and future opportunities. In the first part, we provide a brief, general review of important trends in the study of visual information processing over the past twenty-five years. For present purposes, *visual information processing* is defined to include only the manipulations and transformations of visual information that take place after the transduction of light energy into nerve signals in the cerebral cortex. Thus, for example, the vast body of research on the retina is excluded (for a review, see Dowling 1987). In addition, because our focus is on human vision, we will mention work on nonhuman animals only to the extent that it has been incorporated into theories of human visual processing. Of necessity, even within this reduced domain, the review will not attempt exhaustive coverage but rather will use selected examples to highlight important issues and approaches. Our primary concern is not to summarize results in particular content areas but rather to chart the evolution of research strategies and methods. This historical sketch will set the stage for a discussion of the most promising issues, approaches, and objectives for the next twenty-five years of research on visual information processing.

2.1 THE PAST TWENTY-FIVE YEARS: THREE MOVEMENTS

Research on visual information processing over the past twenty-five years can be very roughly divided into three phases. We characterize each in terms of the goals of theorizing and the form of the theories themselves.

The first phase, extending from the early 1960s to about 1975, can be called the era of psychophysics and cognitive psychology. In this era, the primary goal of theories was to account for behavioral data obtained in laboratory experiments; from these data, theorists induced types of internal "codes" and general principles of information processing.

The second phase, extending from about 1975 to 1985, was the era of cognitive science. In this phase, the goal was to provide behavioral theories sufficiently precise to allow building a machine that mimicked human behavior; theorists posited data structures and processes that operated on them.

Finally, the third phase, extending from about 1985 to the present, is the era of cognitive neuroscience. In this era, the goal is to specify how individual neural structures process information, and theorists specify data structures and processes that are implemented directly in the brain.

It is important to realize that each era did not replace the previous ones; rather, it supplemented the goals of the previous ones. All of the goals and methods of the first era were incorporated into the second, and all of the goals and methods of the first two eras are still respected in the third. The development has been the addition of further requirements, not the replacement of earlier ones with new ones. In addition, by speaking of phases and eras we do not intend to imply strict disjunctions between periods; the labels are applied primarily for expository convenience, to highlight changes that developed gradually from one period to the next. Indeed, there is considerable overlap between the eras, and relatively "pure" forms of all three approaches are still represented in the journals today. But we argue that our characterization captures significant trends, as reflected by the number of researchers in each era who began to consider certain types of goals and theoretical perspectives. With these caveats in mind, we will consider each of the three eras in turn.

Psychophysics and Cognitive Psychology (1965–1975)

During this period, psychophysicists and cognitive psychologists charted the nature of visual information processing with a wide variety of techniques, and theories were designed to explain the results of such experiments. Psychophysicists, for example, investigated the structure and dynamics of early visual processing via studies of selective adaptation, visual masking, magnitude estimation, and subthreshold summation (e.g., Blakemore and Campbell 1969; Gilinsky 1967; Kulikowski, Abadi, and King-Smith 1973; Schiller and Smith 1965; Sekuler 1966; for a brief review, see Spoehr and Lehmkuhle 1982). Cognitive psychologists used chronometric and error data to delineate principles of visual information processing in a wide variety of higher-level domains, such as visual attention (e.g., Posner and Boies 1971; Treisman 1969; see also Navon 1977), letter and word processing (e.g., Estes 1975; Reicher 1969), picture and scene processing (e.g., Biederman 1972; Potter and Faulconer 1975), and visual mental imagery (Paivio 1971; Shepard and Metzler 1971).

Despite the wide variety of techniques used during this period, most studies had several features in common. These features can be divided into two classes: those concerning the nature of the data, and those concerning the nature of the theories constructed from the data.

Restrictions on Data   The data collected during these years were almost entirely behavioral; psychologists noted the stimulus-response relations established by the visual system. Although electrophysiological investigations were not unknown during this period (e.g., Donchin and Lindsley 1969; Harter and White 1967), mainstream work in visual information processing at this time relied primarily upon three simple behavioral measures: response times, error rates, and detection thresholds. The limitations imposed by these measures were compounded by the restricted setting in which the measures were collected, namely the psychological laboratory, where the stimulus situation had been reduced to bare essentials. Ecologically valid studies were rare during this period.

Subject populations typically were also very restricted, consisting primarily of college students who were majoring in psychology. Not all researchers studying vision at this time used such limited populations; neuropsychological research, for example, frequently examined brain-damaged patients across a wide age range and compared them to normal control subjects (e.g., De Renzi, Faglioni, and Scotti 1971; Newcombe and Russell 1969). In addition, some developmental psychologists studied visual information processing (e.g., see Gibson 1969). Nonetheless, the majority of psychologists working on visual information processing did not test a broad range of subject populations.

The Nature of Theories   Theories were formulated expressly to account for the restricted behavioral data just described. These theories typically specified the nature of mental codes or general principles of visual information processing. For example, Paivio (1971) distinguished between verbal and imaginal memory codes, and Posner (1978) distinguished between name and physical codes used in visual matching. These codes were not specified formally; their characteristics were simply described verbally. Similarly, Shepard and Metzler (1971) discovered an important principle about visual-mental imagery, namely that people transform visual shapes incrementally from one orientation to another, but the mechanisms underlying that principle were not explained. And Egeth (1966) argued that parallel processing was used to encode certain kinds of displays, but did not specify how such processing could occur.

Because the experimental tasks were often highly simplified or artificial, the theories tended to account for relatively circumscribed domains of behavior. Indeed, "theories" were relatively rare in this era, if we take a theory to be a set of principles that account for the observed regularities in a domain; instead, most researchers posited models of specific tasks (cf. Kosslyn 1980, chap. 5). Most of these models, especially in cognitive psychology but also to some extent in psychophysics, were not stated explicitly (either mathematically or in computer simulations); in some cases, mathematical descriptions were used to capture the regularities in the data (e.g., see Estes 1975), but these descriptions did not specify mechanisms.

Growing Dissatisfaction   The limitations of work on visual information processing during this period did not go unnoticed. Alan Newell (1973), for example, eloquently pointed out that the limited scope and vague specification of these models made it difficult to see how they could ever add up to a comprehensive theory of visual information processing. Newell criticized experimentalists for "playing 20 questions with nature"—for endlessly seeking poorly related fragments of information by investigating binary oppositions, such as serial versus parallel, preattentive versus attentive, and the like. Newell was not the only critic. Ulric Neisser had helped define the new field of cognitive psychology with his optimistic book, *Cognitive Psychology* (1967), but he took a more cautious stance nine years later in *Cognition and Reality* (1976). Lamenting the fact that most studies were ignoring important aspects of information processing used in everyday life, he called for a more ecologically valid approach to the study of cognition, and for more attention to the complexity and sophistication of human cognitive processes.

The emergence of the next phase of work in visual information processing—the era we have called cognitive science—was in part a response to the problems identified by commentators such as Newell and Neisser.

Cognitive Science (1975–1985)

By 1975, research in psychophysics and cognitive psychology had produced an extensive database and a refined set of techniques for studying visual information processing (e.g., Puff 1982). The database was like a collection of pieces of a puzzle, and computational theorizing offered a way to start putting them together. The goal of this theorizing was to analyze what would be required to build a machine that could mimic aspects of human performance in the natural world, solving the problems posed by the environment—not simply those examined in psychologists' laboratories. To this end, the cognitive science approach attempted to specify the data structures and processes that are used when one performs a task.

The towering figure of this era was David Marr (1982). Marr made two major contributions to theories of visual information processing. First, he emphasized the importance of dividing processing into modules. Researchers in computer vision before him had typically attempted to proceed from a digitized picture to object identification in a single step (e.g., see Winston 1975). Marr broke processing into a set of phases, which he called the "primal sketch," the "$2\frac{1}{2}$-D sketch," and the "3-D model." Roughly speaking, the primal sketch specifies the edges of objects, the $2\frac{1}{2}$-D sketch specifies visible surfaces (the "$\frac{1}{2}$-D indicates that one does not see the occluded portion of the third dimension), and the 3-D model specifies the volumetric structure of an object.

Although the terminology sometimes differed, the concept of modularity was familiar to cognitive psychologists, who often inferred "stages" in which particular codes were used or principles were evident (e.g., Atkinson and Shiffrin 1968; Sternberg 1969). These inferences, however, were based partly on intuition, but primarily on data from laboratory experiments; the stages were posited to account for empirical findings. Marr had a different idea of how to formulate a theory; he did not begin by trying to account for specific results from laboratory experiments (although he did, of course, ultimately want to provide such accounts). Rather, he considered the problems that must be solved by any system that can see the natural world as we do (e.g., any system must be able to segregate figure from ground, which requires locating edges under a variety of circumstances). His analyses of those problems led to specific hypotheses about the modules that might underlie the behavior.

Whether or not Marr's theory survives the test of time, some aspects of it probably will. The reason we feel confident in making this assertion is that his theory rested on a careful, ecologically valid analysis of what the visual system can do. It is this kind of analysis that lies at the heart of Marr's other major contribution, which was to highlight the importance of understanding information-processing systems at multiple levels of analysis. He distinguished three such levels (Marr 1982).

The first level was the "theory of the computation." A theory of a computation is an argument for specifying a particular component of information processing. This argument consists of an analysis of an aspect of what the visual system can do (e.g., detect edges under a variety of circumstances) on the basis of particular input. Viewed purely as isolated instances of formal data, the input may not be sufficient to determine a unique solution. Accordingly, a large part of the analysis consists in specifying the real-world regularities and constraints that the visual system can exploit to derive unique solutions to otherwise underdetermined problems. A theory of a computation specifies *what* is done by an information-processing component; Marr typically formulated such theories mathematically (e.g., for edge detection, in terms of zero-crossings in the second derivative of the function relating intensity and position).

The second level distinguished by Marr was the theory of the representation and algorithm. This level specifies representations for the input and output of a computation and describes *how* a computation is carried out. The same information can be represented in numerous different ways, each of which makes different information explicit. For example, as children just learning to add often discover, representing small numbers on one's fingers makes it easy to add the numbers, because a quick counting process can be used. In contrast, the finger representation is ill suited for multiplication; arabic numerals work better (especially as the numbers increase in size), because arabic numerals make powers of ten explicit. An effective algorithm thus must rely on a representation suited to the computation, which is operated on to produce the requisite output.[1]

Much of the work in the cognitive science of vision by psychologists focused on this second level of analysis. For example, Palmer (1977) developed a theory of how parts of objects are organized and represented, and Stevens and Coupe (1978) provided evidence that descriptions of spatial relations are used to represent complex objects. In addition, Treisman and Gelade's (1980) work on attention specified how different kinds of stimuli are represented, either as conjunctions of features or individual features. (Recall that each era incorporated the goals and methods of the previous ones; hence, at the same time that the cognitive science focus emerged, research in the tradition of psychophysics and cognitive psychology was still making important contributions; e.g., Garner 1974.)

Finally, the third level identified by Marr was the theory of the implementation. This level specifies how representations and algorithms are instantiated in a particular machine, such as a human brain or digital computer. Marr drew a relatively sharp line between the first two levels, on the one hand, and the physical realization of representation and algorithm, on the other. He acknowledged that one can gain hints about information processing from studying the brain, but he emphasized the relative independence of the first two levels from the implementation. This emphasis fit well with his interest in artificial intelligence and in using facts about biological information processing to guide the construction of seeing machines.

Marr's case for multiple levels of analysis had at least two important effects. First, his separation of the implementational level from the computational and representational/algorithmic levels encouraged careful formal analyses of the abstract properties of visual computations. The general nature of these investigations can be characterized as follows. Many of the problems of early vision belong to the science of "inverse optics" (Poggio, Torre, and Koch 1985). Whereas classical optics specifies how 2-D images result from 3-D objects, inverse optics concerns the recovery of 3-D information from the 2-D image. What makes inverse optics difficult is the fact that there is always more than one possible solution: any given 2-D image could in principle have resulted from any one of an infinite number of 3-D objects under an appropriate projection.

The key to computational analyses of the problems of inverse optics is the discovery of natural constraints or regularities that will allow a unique solution to be found (e.g., Marr and Poggio 1976; Marr 1982). For example, most adjacent points of light on the retina typically are reflected from surfaces that are at roughly the same distance from the viewer. This constraint turns out to be useful in computing distance information from the disparities in the images striking the two eyes (stereo). Marr and his colleagues at MIT used this approach to investigate many central problems in visual information processing, including stereo vision (Marr and Poggio 1976), the inference of structure from motion (Ullman 1979), the measurement of visual motion (Hildreth 1984), and visual parsing (Hoffman and Richards 1984).

The second important effect of Marr's separation of the implementational level from the computational and representational/algorithmic levels was to encourage the use of computer simulation models. The topics investigated via computer simulations in this period ranged from relatively circumscribed areas such as letter and word perception (e.g., Wolford 1975; McClelland and Rumelhart 1981; Rumelhart and McClelland 1982) to broader domains such as visual mental imagery (Kosslyn and Shwartz 1977) and the visual analysis and segmentation of real-world scenes (e.g., Marr 1976).

Growing Dissatisfaction   Much of Marr's work focused on relatively "early" visual information processing, such as edge detection and stereo. These are good problems to study in part because geometry itself places constraints on their solutions. The farther into the system one goes, however, the less important are properties of surfaces and objects as constraints on information processing. Marr at one point seemed to believe that theories of the computation are like theorems in mathematics; given a precise enough statement of the problem and the constraints imposed by the available input, one could almost prove that a certain type of processing was required (see Marr and Nishihara 1978, 16; for a discussion, see Kosslyn and Maljkovic 1990). Unfortunately, this approach will not implicate a unique theory; alternative explanations are always possible.

This problem of multiple alternative theories had become evident to many researchers by 1978, with the publication of John Anderson's article on the structure process trade-off problem. The problem hinges on the fact that properties of representations are only expressed via properties of the processes that operate on them; a given behavioral result always reflects the joint properties of the structure and process. Hence, a very large range of representations could be used when one performs any given task, with differences in the processes compensating for differences in the representations.

For example, the problem of structure/process trade-offs stymied research on visual mental imagery, making it very difficult to delineate the nature of the data structures that underlie the experience of visualizing. Consider two much-debated theories: Whereas one theory posited that images are spatial, depictive displays that can be scanned incrementally (and thus more time is required to scan farther distances), another posited that image representations are serially ordered lists of properties, which are searched sequentially (see Kosslyn 1980 for a discussion of the two classes of theories). Although these representations are very different, the differences are obscured by the corresponding differences in the processes that operate upon them. This problem is unavoidable as long as one can arbitrarily choose properties of data structures and processes.

One source of additional constraints on theories comes from studies of the brain itself. Despite the focus on visual computations per se during the cognitive science era, the implementational level of analysis was not ignored. Indeed, Marr himself always looked to the biological substrate for inspiration (e.g., Marr 1974, 1976). In the 1980s, however, the neural basis of visual information processing began to receive increased attention within the mainstream of experimental psychology. Thus began the third period that we have identified, the era of cognitive neuroscience.

Cognitive Neuroscience (1985–Present)

Cognitive neuroscience emphasizes the idea that "the mind is what the brain does." Visual information processing is to be understood as a set of computations carried out by specific parts of the brain. Thus, research in this era not only promotes theories that can account for the behavioral properties of the system and that are specified in terms of computations, but also requires that the inferred computations be consistent with facts about the brain. Much of the theorizing in this era involves *neural network models* (also known as *connectionist* or *parallel distributed processing* models) of varying degrees of biological realism; these models specify relationships between the individual elements that make up networks (e.g., McClelland and Rumelhart 1986; Rumelhart and McClelland 1986a, in particular, 110–146). Some theories, however, operate at a higher level of analysis and simply specify the input-output relations that individual networks must produce (e.g., Kosslyn et al. 1990; Posner 1988; Posner and Petersen 1990).

It is not surprising that visual information processing is, along with memory, one of the first areas of experimental psychology to profit from the cognitive neuroscience approach. In both cases, we are fortunate in having animal models of human processing. Since the pioneering work in the 1950s and 1960s by Kuffler (1953), Hubel and Wiesel (1962, 1968), and Mountcastle (1957), neuroscientists have been steadily extending our understanding of visual areas and pathways in nonhuman animals. In addition, studies of visual dysfunctions following brain damage in humans have an even longer history (e.g., Holmes 1918, 1919; Riddoch 1917). Thus, many neural constraints on theorizing have been available for the asking.

These neural constraints are both powerful and straightforward. For example, one major finding in research with nonhuman primates is that different sorts of visual information are processed in separate *streams*. Information about object properties (such as shape, texture, and color) is processed along one pathway, whereas information about spatial properties (such as location and size) is processed along another pathway (Ungerleider and Mishkin 1982). This separation has obvious implications for theories of visual information processing (e.g., Kosslyn et al. 1990; Treisman and Gormican 1988). Furthermore, various distinct areas with different physiological properties have been identified along these pathways. For example, areas involved in the early phases of processing turn out to be organized topographically, preserving the physical layout of a stimulus (with some magnification and distortion). This sort of organization makes certain kinds of local computations very easy (e.g., see Johnston 1986).

To be sure, neurobiological constraints had not been completely ignored by investigators of visual processing in normal human subjects. In psychophysics, for example, the fact that only cortical cells are sensitive to orientation was used to provide a rough determination of the anatomical locus of sine-wave grating adaptation effects: The reduction of such effects by changes in grating orientation was taken to imply a central rather than peripheral locus for the effects (Blakemore and Campbell 1969). Similarly, European cognitive psychologists have long considered the behavioral deficits following damage when formulating theories of intact systems (e.g., for reviews, see Humphrey and Riddoch 1987). What is new in cognitive neuroscience is the use of detailed neuroscientific knowledge in conjunction with computational analyses and behavioral data to motivate systems-level theories of visual information processing (see Kosslyn and Koenig, 1992). These data are being used to specify subsystems and the representations and processes within them. This cognitive neuroscience approach has recently been used to construct integrative theories in areas such as visual attention (Posner 1988; Posner and Petersen 1990), visual mental imagery (Kosslyn 1987, 1988), and visual object recognition (Biederman 1987; Biederman et al. 1988; Feldman 1985; Kosslyn et al. 1990).

In our opinion, cognitive neuroscience represents the most promising approach for studies of visual information processing in the years to come. Accordingly, rather than dwelling further here on this approach, we will consider it further in the course of our survey of issues and objectives for the study of visual information processing over the next twenty-five years.

2.2   THE NEXT TWENTY-FIVE YEARS: ISSUES AND APPROACHES

In this section we set forth what we take to be the most important issues and approaches for the next quarter century of research on visual information processing.

Developing Interactions

Cognitive neuroscience depends on interactions among computational, neuro-scientific, and behavioral approaches. We expect developments in each field to bring them closer together, making the confluence of approaches even more powerful.

Computational Theorizing   We expect to see three kinds of developments in computational theorizing (which specifies how one could build a device to behave in certain ways). First, we expect theories typically to be motivated by more careful analyses of what is computed, exploiting the virtues of Marr's method of developing theories of the computation. Much current neural network modeling suffers from too little analysis of the problem to be solved. For example, Rumelhart and McClelland (1986b) assumed that a distinct subsystem produces the past-tense form of verbs, but Pinker and Prince (1988) showed that this is not likely to be correct; common sense is not always a good guide to which aspects of behavior are accomplished by distinct subsystems (each of which corresponds to a separate network). We expect to see many more neural network models motivated by Marr-like theories of what is computed, which will be supplemented by information about the neurophysiology and neuroanatomy of the visual system.

Work along these lines is already beginning to appear and has addressed how the visual system derives shape from shading (Lehky and Sejnowski 1988), recovers craniotopic location from retinotopic location and eye position (Zipser and Andersen 1988), and encodes shape versus location (Rueckl, Cave, and Kosslyn 1989). For example, Lehky and Sejnowski (1988) found that in learning to compute shape from shading, their network developed units whose response properties resembled those of cortical "edge" and "bar" detectors, which had not previously been linked to shading. Such simulations can elucidate how particular visual problems are solved and can suggest hypotheses for subsequent neurobiological investigations.

We also expect computational theories to make increased use of sophisticated formal analyses, often to justify specific componential decompositions. These analyses will be promoted in part by the widespread availability of computer programs with mathematically oriented symbol manipulation capabilities, such as *Mathematica* (Wolfram 1988). Such programs will bring rigorous abstract analyses of visual problems within the reach of researchers whose technical ability with the mechanics of mathematics lags behind the sophistication of their conceptual insights. Furthermore, when formal analyses yield equations that have no analytic solutions, the powerful desktop workstations of the 1990s and beyond will permit numerical approximations to be computed quickly and easily.

A second direction in which we foresee major developments is in the "neural plausibility" of computational theories. The fast chips and large memories of the new workstations will enable simulations of visual processes to incorporate increasing amounts of detail about the neuroanatomy and neurophysiology of specific neural networks. We expect to see this trend first in theories of relatively low-level vision, such as motion and edge detection. However, we also expect a "trickle up" phenomenon: The relatively high-level input-output mappings computed by recent neural network models in psychology (e.g., McClelland and Rumelhart 1986; Rumelhart and McClelland 1986a) will be grounded in the more biologically realistic architectures of current models of lower-level neural functions (e.g., Koch and Segev 1989; MacGregor 1987). A promising development in this regard is the recent development of VLSI chips that mimic neural circuitry (Mead 1988).

Third, we expect to see theories and models that focus less on laboratory phenomena, such as the "word-superiority effect" (e.g., McClelland and Rumelhart 1981), and more on real-world phenomena—including the effects of brain damage on behavior (e.g., Patterson, Seidenberg, and McClelland 1989). In some cases, these phenomena may even be placed in an evolutionary context (e.g., see Cosmides 1989). Many a psychological theory reared in the hothouse of the laboratory has withered when exposed to the messy realities of real-world situations (cf. Neisser 1976). No theory can be expected to account for all the complexities of such situations, but the attempt to describe and predict at least some real-world phenomena serves as an important check on the viability of a theory. Accordingly, research on visual information processing could benefit from increased attention to such applied areas as education, human factors in instrument and computer design, rehabilitation following brain damage, and of course, machine vision.

Neural Considerations   We expect discoveries in neuroscience to have an increasingly large influence on work in human visual information processing. Such cross-fertilization will occur in several ways. First, research with awake behaving monkeys, such as that by Moran and Desimone (1985), Shiller and Logothetis (1990), and others, will gradually merge with research on humans as the issues converge. Indeed, we expect close collaborations between researchers examining primates and those studying humans. These interactions will cut both ways; not only will experimental psychologists incorporate neuroscientific knowledge into their explanations of behavioral results, but also visual neuroscientists will increasingly test their neuron- and pathway-level findings against data from experiments on higher-level perceptual phenomena. For example, Livingstone and Hubel (1988) noted remarkable consistencies between human perceptual experiments and their own anatomical and physiological findings on selectivity for form, color, movement, and depth in the visual system of monkeys. Indeed, Livingstone and Hubel (1987) even devised perceptual experiments of their own to test in humans the implications of the data that they obtained from monkeys. Such cross-fertilization between disciplines, via the exchange of data, experimental techniques, and theory, holds great promise for the progress of research in visual information processing over the next twenty-five years.

Second, we expect to see increased attention to the vast literature on visual dysfunctions following brain damage or neurological disease (for reviews, see Benton 1985; Damasio 1985; Ellis and Young 1988; Farah 1990; Kosslyn and Koenig 1992; Warrington 1985). This literature serves as a bridge between animal models and theories of human information processing. As our understanding of visual information processing grows in sophistication, new and more refined studies of visual dysfunctions can also be carried out to distinguish among theoretical alternatives. Posner and his colleagues, for example, have developed a theory of the components of visual attention based in part on their investigations of changes in attentional abilities in patients with parietal, thalamic, or midbrain lesions (for a summary, see Posner 1988; Posner and Petersen 1990). We expect to see more such work, especially in conjunction with new techniques for using magnetic resonance imaging to localize lesions in the human brain (e.g., Jouandet et al. 1989).

Drawing inferences from human lesion data to the functional architecture of normal visual cognition is not entirely straightforward. For example, one cannot assume that brain damage only causes a local modification to the cognitive system, so that apart from this local modification the cognitive systems of brain-damaged patients remain essentially equivalent to those of normal subjects (cf. Caramazza 1986). Rather, intact functions might be reorganized or modified, new functions might be created, or existing strategies might be used in new contexts (for a discussion, see Kosslyn and Van Kleeck 1990, the reply by Caramazza 1992, and the counter by Kosslyn and Intriligator 1992). Such complexities cry out for computer simulation modeling, and we expect to see such a confluence of approaches in the near future (Kosslyn et al. 1990 offer an initial effort in this direction).

Third, we also expect to see an increasing number of studies that use sophisticated behavioral tasks in conjunction with computational analyses and neuroactivation measurement techniques. A wide variety of such techniques are now available, including positron emission tomography (PET; see Pawlik and Heiss 1989; Raichle 1987), electroencephalography (EEG; see Donchin et al. 1986), magnetoencephalography (MEG; see Beatty et al. 1986), and measurement of regional cerebral blood flow (rCBF; see Knezevic et al. 1988). For example, the Washington University group has used PET measures in conjunction with a series of behavioral tasks that were designed using informal "theories of the computation." Each task was posited to recruit a specific set of computations, and the researchers isolated the brain areas involved in specific computations by subtracting the pattern of cerebral blood flow induced by one task from that induced by another (e.g., Petersen et al. 1988). Kosslyn et al. (1992) have recently used PET in conjunction with behavioral tasks that originally were developed to study the functional equivalence of imagery and perception (Podgorny and Shepard 1978). This approach has produced evidence that topographically organized parts of human visual cortex are recruited during visual mental imagery. We foresee much more work along these lines, especially if the cost of such research decreases.

In all of the above cases, we expect to see a large influence of computational theorizing. Not only will such theories define the issues that guide empirical work, but discoveries about the neural implementation of processing will also immediately reshape computational theories—which in turn will promote additional studies of the brain. The dynamic interplay between computational theorizing and studies of neural systems will typically be done by teams of researchers. Such teams are already developing, for example in Robert Wurtz's laboratory at the National Eye Institute.

Behavioral Tasks and Measurements   Behavioral data are the backbone of research in psychophysics and cognitive psychology, and such data are essential if we are to understand the function of neural tissue. Indeed, the recent work on PET scanning would have been impossible without the behavioral techniques developed in experimental psychology. Such techniques will probably be further enriched in several ways. First, the repertoire of behavioral measures will be expanded. For example, we could measure not only the time to press a key, but also the force with which the key is pressed and the speed with which the key travels from its completely open to completely closed positions. Such measures might allow us to assess the confidence with which a response is made. In addition, although some interesting results have been reported using patterns of eye movements as the dependent measure (e.g., see

Carpenter, Just, and Shell 1990; Senders, Fisher, and Monty 1978), these results simply scratch the surface of what can be done with eye-tracking techniques.

Second, behavioral data will also be enriched as researchers test more varied populations of subjects. For example, the population of normal subjects should be sampled across a wide variety of ages, not just the 18–21-year-old range that is common in university research. Studies of cognitive development in younger subjects can provide important clues to the cognitive architecture of adults (e.g., for a relatively early example of this promise bearing fruit, see Siegler 1978). The testing of elderly subjects also holds significant theoretical and practical interest; not only can selective impairments in visual abilities with increasing age shed light on the functional architecture of the visual system, but they also bear on the medical needs of an increasingly large segment of the American population. Finally, the broadening of the experimental subject base should not be limited to normal subjects but should also include neurological patients, as discussed in more detail below.

Collaboration and Communication

The multidisciplinary nature of cognitive neuroscience is both its strength and its weakness. Under ideal conditions, the diversity of viewpoints within cognitive neuroscience strengthens theories by placing multiple constraints on them. In practice, however, it is far from easy to weld many diverse and sometimes unfamiliar viewpoints into an integrated whole; it is much easier to pursue more limited investigations in one's own specialty area. Of course, this problem of integration versus fragmentation is not confined to cognitive neuroscience. Indeed, in reviewing the state of cognitive psychology in 1975, at the end of the first period identified in our historical review, Alan Allport wrote that the field was marked by "a curious parochialism in acknowledging even the existence of other workers, and other approaches ... and underlying all else the near vacuum of theoretical structure within which to interrelate different sets of experimental results, or to direct the search for significant new phenomena" (1975, 152).

To avoid the danger of fragmentation, it is incumbent on researchers in visual cognitive neuroscience to adopt theoretical frameworks that draw on behavioral data, computational analyses, and neurobiological facts. To submit such theories to experimental test, it will be necessary to reduce the traditional reliance on narrowly focused series of experiments and instead to consider converging evidence from multiple approaches. Such an approach will necessarily involve widespread collaborations.

Collaboration   No single researcher can hope to master completely the multiple areas of expertise that will serve as building blocks for theories of visual information processing. Furthermore, as theories increase in complexity and subtlety, experimental tests of them may require specific populations (e.g., brain-damaged patients with focal lesions in specific loci) that are not widely accessible to individual researchers. Furthermore, tests of theories may require resources, such as PET scanning equipment, that are beyond the reach of many institutions.

Collaboration across disciplines seems likely to be the norm. Indeed, funding agencies, such as the National Institutes of Health and the Office of Naval Research, have begun to earmark support for collaborative cross-disciplinary research. The James S. McDonnell Foundation has recently taken an active role in promoting cognitive neuroscience, first by sponsoring summer institutes in cognitive neuroscience at Harvard University and Dartmouth University, and more recently by establishing (in conjunction with the Pew Charitable Trusts) a multimillion-dollar program to establish centers for cognitive neuroscience.

In response to these changes, graduate education should prepare experimental psychologists to understand the viewpoints and vocabularies of future co-workers. Students need to understand not only the basic empirical and conceptual foundations of the different fields, but also the general issues that have shaped those fields. Without such a grounding, it will be difficult to work well with researchers in other disciplines. One measure of having acquired the necessary knowledge is the ability to comprehend journal articles in the various disciplines that contribute to cognitive neuroscience.

Communication   Finally, the interdisciplinary nature of cognitive neuroscience requires a smooth flow of information among researchers. Two major impediments to communication can be identified immediately. First, there is too much information to absorb within even one discipline, let alone several. Second, it often is difficult to know how to evaluate material in another area. Both problems could be addressed by creating a new kind of journal that published page-length summaries and evaluations of research that bears on specific issues. The summaries should be written in the accessible style of those that presently grace the beginning of each issue of *Science*, and the evaluations should be made by experts who have no particular axe to grind. Because the standard journal review process already depends on such evaluations (although at a more detailed level than that envisioned here), it should not be difficult to recruit suitable contributors.

Even if such summary journals become widely available, however, advances in information technology will also play an important role. For example, the increasing availability of computerized bibliographies and databases, such as the American Psychological Association's PSYCINFO, will allow researchers to extract information quickly and efficiently from a wide variety of sources. Electronic publication of abstracts on international computer networks has already begun to speed the availability of new research results. The same networks also host exchanges of letters on current research topics. In this way, computer networks can draw the entire worldwide community of vision scientists into discussions that formerly took months or years to penetrate beyond the major research centers.

Computer networks and increasingly affordable mass storage devices may also promote more widespread sharing of raw data. Such sharing would allow more researchers to contribute their insights about particular findings and would provide more extensive foundations for related studies. In this way, the sharing of raw data would maximize the benefits from each individual study. This efficiency and cost-effectiveness will be especially important because of the expensive equipment, complex techniques, and special subject populations required for many types of research in cognitive neuroscience.

Given the importance of computer simulation work in research on visual information processing, it is also necessary to provide channels for the distribution of the simulation programs. To allow simulation researchers to build on each other's work, not only executable versions of programs but also source code should be made available. Neural net modelers have set an admirable example in this regard, as evidenced by the availability of the Rochester Connectionist Simulator (Goddard, Lynne, and Mintz 1986), the MIRRORS/II connectionist simulation environment (D'Autrechy et al. 1988), the GENESIS neural network system (Wilson et al. 1988), the DESCARTES simulation environment for hybrid connectionist architectures (Lange et al. 1989), and programs that accompany McClelland and Rumelhart's widely read *Explorations in Parallel Distributed Processing* (1988).

2.3   CONCLUSIONS

These are exciting times in which to be a researcher interested in visual information processing. We suggested at the outset that this area is poised to make a major leap forward. The reasons for our optimism are straightforward.

During the first era of research in this field, researchers developed sophisticated methodologies and discovered a host of phenomena that had to be accounted for by all subsequent theories. The phenomena characterize the behavior of the visual information-processing system, and provide insight into general principles of its operation and the kinds of information it represents.

During the second era, researchers grappled with the form of explicit theories of visual information processing, and a widespread consensus emerged that human information processing would be best understood using the vocabulary of computation. In the course of trying to develop such theories, many issues came into sharp focus. We began to understand alternative possible ways of representing and processing information, even if the means were not always available for deciding among them.

In the most recent era, new means for distinguishing among theories have become available. In particular, the new brain-scanning techniques allow us to localize activation in the brain during information processing and to localize lesions that disrupt information processing in specific ways. Furthermore, the widespread availability of powerful computers and the development of formalisms for modeling brainlike computation allow us to formulate rigorous theories of complex neural information processing. By rooting our theories in the brain, we gain powerful constraints and keep ourselves from adjusting our theories facilely, as was possible during the era of cognitive science. We now must describe what is accomplished by specific brain structures, and we can no longer arbitrarily alter these characterizations to account for data.

One of the most exciting aspects of the trajectory we have charted is that it lands us squarely in the realm of natural science. As soon as we begin to consider the brain, we begin to relate our concerns to those of biologists, geneticists, chemists, and physicists. Not only are we in a position to take advantage of discoveries and techniques in these fields, but we in turn can produce research results relevant to some of their concerns.

In short, research in visual information processing has matured dramatically in the past twenty-five years. The cognitive neuroscience approach that has emerged provides a solid scientific foundation for the next twenty-five years, which will surely bring us many steps closer to understanding the daunting complexities of our seemingly effortless visual abilities.

NOTES

Preparation of this chapter was supported in part by a National Science Foundation Graduate Fellowship and an MIT/Fairchild Postdoctoral Fellowship (M. H. Van Kleeck) and Air Force Office of Scientific Research Grant 88-0012, supplemented by funds from the ONR, and NSF Grant BNS 90 09619 (S. M. Kosslyn). We thank Lynn Hillger for valuable comments on a draft of the chapter.

1. The distinctions among the various levels are not as clear as they might seem at first glance. For example, the operation of addition can be a computation in its own right or part of an algorithm for computing the mean. Kosslyn and Maljkovic (1990) examine the force of these distinctions in detail.

REFERENCES

Allport, D. A. (1975). 'The state of cognitive psychology': A critical notice of W. G. Chase (ed.), *Visual information processing*. In *Quarterly Journal of Experimental Psychology, 27,* 141–152.

Anderson, J. R. (1978). Arguments concerning representations for mental imagery. *Psychological Review, 85,* 249–277.

Atkinson, R. C., and Shiffrin, R. M. (1968). Human memory: A proposed system and its control processes. In K. W. Spence and J. T. Spence (Eds.), *The psychology of learning and motivation: Advances in research and theory*, Vol 2. New York: Academic Press.

Beatty, J., Barth, D. S., Richer, F., and Johnson, R. A. (1986). Neuromagnetometry. In M. G. H. Coles, E. Donchin, and S. Porges (Eds.), *Psychophysiology: Systems, processes, and applications,* 26–42. New York: Guilford Press.

Benton, A. (1985). Visuoperceptual, visuospatial, and visuoconstructive disorders. In K. M. Heilman and E. Valenstein (Eds.), *Clinical neuropsychology,* 2d ed., 151–185. New York: Oxford University Press.

Biederman, I. (1972). Perceiving real-world scenes. *Science, 177,* 77–80.

Biederman, I. (1987). Recognition-by-components: A theory of human image understanding. *Psychological Review, 94,* 115–147.

Biederman, I., Blickle, T. W., Ju, G., Hilton, J. H., and Hummel, J. E. (1988). Empirical analyses and connectionist modeling of real-time human image understanding. In *Program of the Tenth Annual Conference of the Cognitive Science Society,* 251–256. Hillsdale, NJ: Lawrence Erlbaum.

Blakemore, C., and Campbell, F. W. (1969). On the existence of neurons in the human visual system selectively sensitive to the orientation and size of retinal images. *Journal of Physiology, 203,* 237–260.

Caramazza, A. (1986). On drawing inferences about the structure of normal cognitive systems from the analysis of patterns of impaired performance: The case for single-patient studies. *Brain and Cognition, 5,* 41–66.

Caramazza, A. (1992). Is cognitive neuropsychology possible? *Journal of Cognitive Neuroscience, 4,* 80–95.

Carpenter, P. A., Just, M. A., and Shell, P. (1990). What one intelligence test measures: A theoretical account of the processing in the Raven Progressive Matrices test. *Psychological Review, 97,* 404–431.

Cosmides, L. (1989). The logic of social exchange: Has natural selection shaped how humans reason? Studies with the Wason selection task. *Cognition, 31,* 187–276.

Damasio, A. R. (1985). Disorders of complex visual processing: Agnosias, achromatopsia, Balint's syndrome, and related difficulties of orientation and construction. In M-M. Mesulam (Ed.), *Principles of behavioral neurology,* pp. 259–288. Philadelphia, PA: F. A. Davis.

D'Autrechy, C. L., Reggia, J. A., Sutton, C. G., and Goodall, S. M. (1988). A general-purpose simulation environment for developing connectionist models. *Simulation, 51,* 5–19.

De Renzi, E., Faglioni, P., and Scotti, G. (1971). Judgment of spatial orientation in patients with focal brain damage. *Journal of Neurology, Neurosurgery, and Psychiatry, 34,* 489–495.

Donchin, E., Karis, D., Bashore, T., Coles, M., and Gratton, G. (1986). Cognitive psychophysiology and human information processing. In M. G. H. Coles, E. Donchin, and S. Porges (Eds.), *Psychophysiology: Systems, processes, and applications.* New York: Guilford Press.

Donchin, E., and Lindsley, D. B. (1969). *Average evoked potentials: Methods, results, and evaluations.* Washington, D.C.: Scientific and Technical Information Division, National Aeronautics and Space Administration.

Dowling, J. (1987). *The retina: An approachable part of the brain.* Cambridge, MA: Harvard University Press.

Egeth, H. (1966). Parallel versus serial processes in multidimensional stimulus discrimination. *Perception and Psychophysics, 1,* 245–252.

Ellis, A. W., and Young, A. W. (1988). *Human cognitive neuropsychology.* Hillsdale, NJ: Erlbaum.

Estes, W. K. (1975). Some targets for mathematical psychology. *Journal of Mathematical Psychology, 12,* 263–282.

Farah, M. J. (1990). *The agnosias.* Cambridge, MA: MIT Press.

Feldman, J. A. (1985). Four frames suffice: A provisional model of vision and space. *Behavioral and Brain Sciences, 8,* 265–289.

Garner, W. R. (1974). *The processing of information and structure.* Hillsdale, NJ: Erlbaum.

Gibson, E. J. (1969). *Principles of perceptual learning and development.* New York: Appleton-Century-Crofts.

Gilinsky, A. S. (1967). Orientation-specific effects of patterns of adapting light on visual acuity. *Journal of the Optical Society of America, 58,* 13–18.

Goddard, N., Lynne, K. J., and Mintz, T. (1986). Rochester connectionist simulator. Technical report TR-233, Department of Computer Science, University of Rochester.

Harter, M. R., and White, C. T. (1967). Perceived number and evoked cortical potentials. *Science, 156,* 406–408.

Hildreth, E. C. (1984). *The measurement of visual motion.* Cambridge, MA: MIT Press.

Hoffman, D. D., and Richards, W. A. (1984). Parts of recognition. *Cognition, 18,* 65–96.

Holmes, G. (1918). Disturbances of visual orientation. *British Journal of Ophthalmology, 2,* 449–468, 506–615.

Holmes, G. (1919). Disturbances of visual space perception. *British Medical Journal, 2,* 230–233.

Hubel, D. H., and Wiesel, T. N. (1962). Receptive fields, binocular interaction and functional architecture in the cat's visual cortex. *Journal of Physiology (London), 166,* 106–154.

Hubel, D. H., and Wiesel, T. N. (1968). Receptive fields and functional architecture of monkey striate cortex. *Journal of Physiology (London), 195,* 215–243.

Humphreys, G. W., and Riddoch, M. J. (Eds.). (1987). *Visual object processing: A cognitive neuropsychological approach.* London: Erlbaum.

Johnston, A. (1986). A spatial property of the retino-cortical mapping. *Spatial Vision, 1,* 319–331.

Jouandet, M. L., Tramo, M. J., Herron, D. M., Hermann, A., Loftus, W. C., Bazell, J., and Gazzaniga, M. S. (1989). Brainprints: Computer-generated two-dimensional maps of the human cerebral cortex in vivo. *Journal of Cognitive Neuroscience, 1,* 88–117.

Knezevic, S., Maximilian, V. A., Mubrin, Z., Prohovnik, I., and Wade, J. (Eds.). (1988). *Handbook of regional cerebral blood flow.* Hillsdale, NJ: Erlbaum.

Koch, C., and Segev, I. (Eds.). (1989). *Methods in neuronal modeling: From synapses to networks.* Cambridge, MA: MIT Press.

Kosslyn, S. M. (1980). *Image and mind.* Cambridge, MA: Harvard University Press.

Kosslyn, S. M. (1987). Seeing and imagining in the cerebral hemispheres: A computational approach. *Psychological Review, 94,* 148–175.

Kosslyn, S. M. (1988). Aspects of a cognitive neuroscience of mental imagery. *Science, 240,* 1621–1626.

Kosslyn, S. M., Alpert, N. M., Maljkovic, V., Weiss, S. B., Thompson, W. L., Hamilton, S. E., Chabris, C. F., and Buonanno, F. S. (1992). Visual mental imagery activates primary visual cortex: A PET study. Unpublished manuscript, Harvard University, Cambridge, MA.

Kosslyn, S. M., Flynn, R. A., Amsterdam, J. B., and Wang, G. (1990). Components of high-level vision: A cognitive neuroscience analysis and accounts of neurological syndromes. *Cognition, 34,* 203–277.

Kosslyn, S. M., and Intriligator, J. M. (1992). Is cognitive neuropsychology plausible? The perils of sitting on a one-legged stool. *Journal of Cognitive Neuroscience, 4,* 96–106.

Kosslyn, S. M., and Koenig, O. (1992). *Wet mind: The new cognitive neuroscience.* New York: Free Press.

Kosslyn, S. M., and Maljkovic, V. (1990). Marr's metatheory revisited. *Concepts in Neuroscience, 1,* 239–251.

Kosslyn, S. M., and Shwartz, S. P. (1977). A simulation of visual imagery. *Cognitive Science, 1,* 265–295.

Kosslyn, S. M., and Van Kleeck, M. H. (1990). Broken brains and normal minds: Why Humpty-Dumpty needs a skeleton. In E. L. Schwartz (Ed.), *Computational neuroscience.* Cambridge, MA: MIT Press.

Kuffler, S. W. (1953). Discharge patterns and functional organization of mammalian retina. *Journal of Neurophysiology, 16,* 37–68.

Kulikowski, J. J., Abadi, R., and King-Smith, P. E. (1973). Orientational selectivity of grating and line detectors in human vision. *Vision Research, 13,* 1479–1486.

Lange, T. E., Hodges, J. B., Fuenmayor, M. E., and Belyaev, L. V. (1989). DESCARTES: Development environment for simulating hybrid connectionist architectures. In *Program of the eleventh annual conference of the Cognitive Science Society*, 698–705. Hillsdale, NJ: Erlbaum.

Lehky, S. R., and Sejnowski, T. J. (1988). Network model of shape-from-shading: Neural function arises from both receptive and projective fields. *Nature, 333*, 452–454.

Livingstone, M. S., and Hubel, D. H. (1987). Psychophysical evidence for separate channels for the perception of form, color, movement and depth. *Journal of Neuroscience, 7*, 3416–3468.

Livingstone, M., and Hubel, D. (1988). Segregation of form, color, movement, and depth: Anatomy, physiology, and perception. *Science, 240*, 740–749.

McClelland, J. L., and Rumelhart, D. E. (1981). An interactive activation model of context effects in letter perception: Part 1. An account of basic findings. *Psychological Review, 88*, 375–407.

McClelland, J. L., and Rumelhart, D. E. (1986). *Parallel distributed processing: Explorations in the microstructure of cognition. Vol. 2: Psychological and biological models.* Cambridge, MA: MIT Press.

McClelland, J. L., and Rumelhart, D. E. (1988). *Explorations in parallel distributed processing: A handbook of models, programs, and exercises.* Cambridge, MA: MIT Press.

MacGregor, R. J. (1987). *Neural and brain modeling.* San Diego, CA: Academic Press.

Marr, D. (1974). The computation of lightness by the primate retina. *Vision Research, 14*, 1377–1388.

Marr, D. (1976). Early processing of visual information. *Philosophical Transactions of the Royal Society of London, 275*, 483–524.

Marr, D. (1982). *Vision: A computational investigation into the human representation and processing of visual information.* New York: W. H. Freeman.

Marr, D., and Nishihara, H. K. (1978). Visual information processing: Artificial intelligence and the sensorium of sight. *Technology Review, 81*, 2–23.

Marr, D., and Poggio, T. (1976). Cooperative computation of stereo disparity. *Science, 194*, 283–287.

Mead, C. (1988). *Analog VLSI and neural systems.* Reading, MA: Addison-Wesley.

Moran, J., and Desimone, R. (1985). Selective attention gates visual processing in the extrastriate cortex. *Science, 229*, 782–784.

Mountcastle, V. B. (1957). Modality and topographic properties of single neurons of cat's somatic sensory cortex. *Journal of Neurophysiology, 20*, 408–434.

Navon, D. (1977). Forest before trees: the precedence of global features in visual perception. *Cognitive Psychology, 9*, 353–383.

Neisser, U. (1967). Cognitive psychology. New York: Appleton-Century-Crofts.

Neisser, U. (1976). *Cognition and reality: Principles and implications of cognitive psychology.* New York: W. H. Freeman.

Newcombe, F., and Russell, W. R. (1969). Dissociated visual perceptual and spatial deficits in focal lesions of the right hemisphere. *Journal of Neurology, Neurosurgery, and Psychiatry, 32*, 73–81.

Newell, A. (1973). You can't play 20 questions with nature and win. In W. G. Chase (Ed.), *Visual information processing*, 283–308. New York: Academic Press.

Paivio, A. (1971). *Imagery and verbal processes.* New York: Holt, Rinehart and Winston.

Palmer, S. E. (1977). Hierarchical structure in perceptual representation. *Cognitive Psychology, 9*, 441–474.

Patterson, K. E., Seidenberg, M. S., and McClelland, J. L. (1989). Connections and disconnections: Acquired dyslexia in a computational model of reading processes. In R. G. M. Morris (Ed.), *Parallel distributed processing: Implications for psychology and neurobiology*. New York: Oxford University Press.

Pawlik, G., and Heiss, W. D. (1989). Positron emission tomography and neuropsychological function. In E. D. Bigler, R. A. Yeo, and E. Turkheimer (Eds.), *Neuropsychological function and brain imaging*, 65−138. New York: Plenum Press.

Petersen, S. E., Fox, P. T., Posner, M. I., Mintun, M., and Raichle, M. E. (1988). Positron emission tomographic studies of the cortical anatomy of single-word processing. *Nature, 331*, 585−589.

Pinker, S., and Prince, A. (1988). On language and connectionism: Analysis of a parallel distributed processing model of language acquisition. In S. Pinker and J. Mehler (Eds.), *Connections and symbols*, 73−193.

Podgorny, P., and Shepard, R. N. (1978). Functional representations common to visual perception and imagination. *Journal of Experimental Psychology: Human Perception and Performance, 4*, 21−35.

Poggio, T., Torre, V., and Koch, C. (1985). Computational vision and regularization theory. *Nature, 317*, 314−319.

Posner, M. I. (1978). *Chronometric explorations of mind*. Hillsdale, NJ: Erlbaum Associates.

Posner, M. I. (1988). Structures and functions of selective attention. In T. Boll and B. K. Bryant (Eds.), *Clinical neuropsychology and brain function: Research, measurement, and practice*, 169−202. Washington, DC: American Psychological Association.

Posner, M. I., and Boies, S. J. (1971). Components of attention. *Psychological Review, 78*, 391−408.

Posner, M. I., and Petersen, S. E. (1990). The attention system of the human brain. In W. M. Cowan, E. M. Shooter, C. F. Stevens, and R. F. Thompson (Eds.), *Annual Review of Neuroscience*, 25−42. Palo Alto, CA: Annual Reviews, Inc.

Potter, M. C., and Faulconer, B. A. (1975). Time to understand pictures and words. *Nature, 253*, 437−438.

Puff, C. R. (Ed.) (1982). *Handbook of research methods in human memory and cognition*. New York: Academic Press.

Raichle, M. E. (1987). Circulatory and metabolic correlates of brain function in normal humans. in F. Plum (Ed.), *Handbook of physiology: Section 1, the nervous system. Vol. 5, Pts. 1 & 2: Higher functions of the brain*. Oxford: Oxford University Press.

Reicher, G. M. (1969). Perceptual recognition as a function of meaningfulness of stimulus material. *Journal of Experimental Psychology, 81*, 275−280.

Riddoch, G. (1917). Dissociation of visual perceptions due to occipital injuries, with especial reference to appreciation of movement. *Brain, 40*, 15−57.

Rueckl, J. G., Cave, K. R., and Kosslyn, S. M. (1989). Why are "what" and "where" processed by separate cortical visual systems? A computational investigation. *Journal of Cognitive Neuroscience, 1*, 171−186.

Rumelhart, D. E., and McClelland, J. L. (1982). An interactive activation model of context effects in letter perception: Part 2. The contextual enhancement effect and some tests and extensions of the model. *Psychological Review, 89*, 60−94.

Rumelhart, D. E., and McClelland, J. L. (1986a). *Parallel distributed processing: Explorations in the microstructure of cognition. Vol. 1: Foundations*. Cambridge, MA: MIT Press.

Rumelhart, D. E., and McClelland, J. L. (1986b). On learning the past tenses of English verbs. In J. L. McClelland and D. E. Rumelhart (Eds.), *Parallel distributed processing: Explorations in the microstructure of cognition. Vol. 2: Psychological and biological models,* 216–271. Cambridge, MA: MIT Press.

Schiller, P. H., and Logothetis, N. K. (1990). The color-opponent and broad-band channels of the primate visual system. *Trends in Neuroscience, 13,* 392–398.

Schiller, P. H., and Smith, M. C. (1965). A comparison of forward and backward masking. *Psychonomic Science, 3,* 77–78.

Sekuler, R. W. (1966). Choice times and detection with visual backward masking. *Canadian Journal of Psychology, 20,* 34–42.

Senders, J. W., Fisher, D. F., and Monty, R. A. (1978). *Eye movements and the higher psychological functions.* Hillsdale, NJ: Erlbaum.

Shepard. R. N., and Metzler. J. (1971). Mental rotation of three-dimensional objects. *Science, 171,* 701–703.

Siegler, R. S. (1978). *Children's thinking: What develops?* Hillsdale, NJ: Erlbaum.

Spoehr, K. T., and Lehmkuhle, S. W. (1982). *Visual information processing.* San Francisco: W. H. Freeman.

Sternberg, S. (1969). The discovery of processing stages: Extensions of Donders' method. In W. G. Koster (Ed.), *Attention and Performance II,* 276–315. Amsterdam: North-Holland.

Stevens, A., and Coupe, P. (1978). Distortions in judged spatial relations. *Cognitive Psychology, 10,* 422–437.

Treisman, A. (1969). Strategies and models of selective attention. *Psychological Review, 76,* 282–299.

Treisman, A., and Gormican, S. (1988). Feature analysis in early vision: Evidence from search asymmetries. *Psychological Review, 95,* 15–48.

Treisman, A. M., and Gelade, G. (1980). A feature-integration theory of attention. *Cognitive Psychology, 12,* 97–136.

Ullman, S. (1979). *The interpretation of visual motion.* Cambridge, MA: MIT Press.

Ungerleider, L. G., and Mishkin, M. (1982). Two cortical visual systems. In D. J. Ingle, M. A. Goodale, and R. J. W. Mansfield (Eds.), *Analysis of visual behavior,* 549–586. Cambridge, MA: MIT Press.

Warrington, E. K. (1985). Agnosia: The impairment of object recognition. In J. A. M. Frederiks (Ed.), *Handbook of clinical neurology, Vol. 45. Clinical neuropsychology,* 333–349. Amsterdam: Elsevier Science.

Wilson, M. A., Upinder, S. B., Uhley, J. D., and Bower, J. M. (1988). GENESIS: A system for simulating neural networks. In D. S. Touretzky (Ed.), *Advances in neural information processing systems I,* 485–492. San Mateo, CA: Morgan Kaufmann.

Winston, P. H. (Ed.). (1975). *The psychology of computer vision.* New York: McGraw-Hill.

Wolford, G. (1975). Perturbation model for letter identification. *Psychological Review, 82,* 184–199.

Wolfram, S. (1988). *Mathematica: A system for doing mathematics by computer.* Reading, MA: Addison-Wesley.

Zipser, D., and Andersen, R A. (1988). A back-propagation programmed network that simulates response properties of a subset of posterior parietal neurons. *Nature, 331,* 679–684.

3 Color Constancy and Color Perception: The Linear-Models Framework

Laurence T. Maloney

Computational color vision has two distinct but complementary goals. The first is to predict the color judgments of human observers given a physical description of the environment; the second goal is to derive, by algorithm, useful information concerning the spectral reflectance properties of objects in a scene.

The color experience of the human observer is affected by many factors: by contrast between nearby surfaces, by afterimages, and by the spectral composition of the illuminant of the scene being viewed. It is difficult, for example, to anticipate what a human observer would experience in viewing, under various illuminants, the chromatically and spatially complex displays found in modern military and commercial planes. Success at the first goal cited above would ease the design of such chromatic displays and other human-computer interfaces using color. Helson (1938) and Judd (1940) developed the first comprehensive program of measurement and modeling directed toward the solution of this as yet unsolved problem.

A solution to the second goal is immediately relevant to robotics applications that need information (analogous to color) concerning the surface properties of objects. For the purposes of these applications, "color" is viewed as an intrinsic property of a surface, and the goal of color vision is taken to be the recovery of the *intrinsic color* of objects, just as the goal of computational spatial vision is to recover shape and location information: "Colours have their greatest significance for us in so far as they are properties of bodies and can be used as marks of identification of bodies" (Helmholtz [1896] 1962, 286).

A successful computer vision algorithm (in this sense) would return estimates of color, specific to each object, that were influenced by neither the colors of other objects present in the scene nor the nature of the illuminant: "Hence in our observations with the sense of vision we always start out by forming a judgment about the colours of bodies, eliminating the difference of illumination by which a body is revealed to us" (Helmholtz [1986] 1962, 287). An algorithm that achieves this criterion is perfectly *color constant*. At a minimum, a color vision system that exhibits perfect color constancy must eliminate the influence of the illuminant and the influence of other objects present in a scene from color estimates associated with a given object.

As the above comment by Helmholtz indicates, human color vision does achieve some degree of color constancy: "With moderate departures from daylight in the spectral distribution of energy in the illuminant, external objects are seen ... nearly in their natural daylight colors" (Judd 1940). This chapter summarizes recent work in computational color vision that aims to explain how approximate color constancy is possible for a biological vision system. The algorithms that are examined represent simple and accurate ways to deduce the surface properties of objects from the spectral information available in an image of a scene. As such, they primarily address the second goal above. Yet, to the extent that human color vision is approximately color constant, work toward the second goal of computation color vision may also address the first. In asking how color constancy is possible in human vision, those of us involved in developing the algorithms hope to illuminate how color vision operates.

The algorithms share a common framework of assumptions about the environment, notably that the possible lights and surfaces in a scene are sharply constrained to fit *linear models* with small numbers of parameters. The chapter also summarizes recent attempts to evaluate these assumptions about the environment. This common Linear-Models Framework is relevant to devising and evaluating tests of human color vision and its potential constancy. I discuss some of the consequences entailed by accepting these algorithms and their assumptions as models of human color vision.

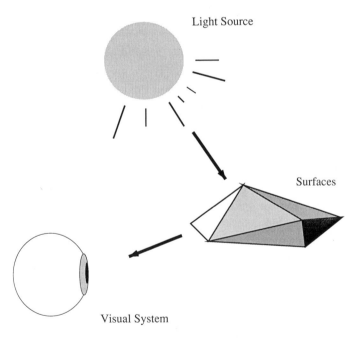

Figure 3.1 The surfaces of objects in a scene are illuminated by the light source. Information about both surfaces and light source arrives at the visual system.

This chapter does not review previous work evaluating the constancy (inconstancy) of human color vision. The reader is referred to Boynton (1979) for an introduction to issues in the study of human color vision and to Brainard and Wandell (1991) and Brainard (1989) for an excellent review of the implications of the Linear-Models Framework for such work. Nor does this chapter attempt to summarize the literature on alternative approaches to color constancy using "lightness" algorithms. These algorithms, of which Kries's model of adaptation (Kries [1902] 1970) and Land's retinex theory (Land and McCann 1971; Land 1983) are the most notable examples, are reviewed in Hurlbert (1986) and critiqued in Brill and West (1981), West and Brill (1982), and Brainard and Wandell (1986). Linear models are potentially useful in processing color information in a variety of industrial applications including photography, color reproduction, and computer vision (see Wandell 1987). The Linear-Models Framework has unexpected implications for philosophical analyses of the status of color. The reader is referred to Hilbert (1987) for a highly readable summary and analysis of the main issues.

3.1 NOTATION AND FRAMEWORK

The following notation is needed to link perceptual processing and the physical structure of a scene illuminated by a single light source. In this chapter, I will only consider scenes (or regions of scenes) in which the illuminant may be assumed to be uniform. This structure is summarized in figure 3.1. In brief, light from the light source (E) impinges on surfaces. The surfaces, in turn, emit light. The light emitted ("reflected") by each surface excited by the illuminant is termed the color signal (L). This color signal is absorbed by photoreceptors (R) in a visual system.

- Let $E(\lambda)$ denote the spectral power distribution of the ambient illuminant at each wavelength λ in a fixed interval of the electromagnetic spectrum.
- Let $S^x(\lambda)$ denote the reflectance of a patch of surface at wavelength λ (the superscript x indexes the location of the surface patch in the scene or, equivalently, on the retina).
- Let $L^x(\lambda) = E(\lambda)S^x(\lambda)$ denote the spectral power distribution of the illuminant reflected by the surface, termed the *color signal*.
- Let $R_k(\lambda)$, $k = 1, 2, \ldots, P$ denote the spectral sensitivity of P distinct types of photoreceptors. In human color vision, for example, P is typically taken to be 3.

The initial information available to a color vision system at a single retinal location is the quantum catch of each of the P classes of receptor:

$$\rho_1^x = \int L^x(\lambda) R_1(\lambda) d\lambda = \int E(\lambda) S^x(\lambda) R_1(\lambda) d\lambda.$$

$$\rho_2^x = \int L^x(\lambda) R_2(\lambda) d\lambda = \int E(\lambda) S^x(\lambda) R_2(\lambda) d\lambda.$$

$$\vdots \qquad\qquad\qquad\qquad\qquad\qquad\qquad\qquad (1)$$

$$\rho_P^x = \int L^x(\lambda) R_P(\lambda) d\lambda = \int E(\lambda) S^x(\lambda) R_P(\lambda) d\lambda.$$

The preceding equations hold precisely when all the physical processes shown in figure 3.1 can be treated as linear systems. The P numbers at each location form a vector $\rho^x = [\rho_1^x, \ldots, \rho_P^x]$. Inspection of equation (1) discloses that the entries of the vector ρ^x at each location x depend as much on the light $E(\lambda)$ as on the surface reflectance $S^x(\lambda)$. Any color constancy algorithm must derive, from these values, estimates of color that depend on $S^x(\lambda)$ at each location x but do not vary (or vary only slightly) with changes in the illuminant $E(\lambda)$. Estimates of color that depend on the surface but not on the illuminant are termed *intrinsic colors*.

Intrinsic colors preserve partial information about surfaces and how they interact with light. An example may help to illustrate the relation between intrinsic colors and color constancy. Suppose that a visual system views a scene illuminated by an unknown light source, $E(\lambda)$. Assume that the only information it has about the scene are the quantum catches of its photo-receptors ρ^x under the unknown illuminant. Suppose further that, based on these quantum catches, it is able to compute what the quantum catches of each receptor would be for the same scene under a fixed reference illuminant $E_0(\lambda)$ and that it can succeed in this computation no matter what unknown light source $E(\lambda)$ is present in the scene. Then the computed quantum catches satisfy the definition of intrinsic colors for they do not vary with changes in the (unknown) illuminant. Such a hypothetical visual system would be color constant if it bases its color perception on the predicted quantum catches corresponding to the reference illuminant.

Such a visual system, color constant under all possible light sources, $E(\lambda)$, is impossible. Sallstrom (1973) showed that, without further restrictions on possible lights and surfaces that may be present in a scene (or equivalent side information about the scene), it is not possible to derive color estimates that depend primarily on surface reflectance. He proposed restricting consideration to lights and surface reflectances that lie in low-dimensional function subspaces, as described next. Maloney and Wandell (1986) term these constraints on light and surface *linear models*.

3.2   LINEAR MODELS OF LIGHT AND SURFACE REFLECTANCE

The functions $E(\lambda)$, $S^x(\lambda)$, and $R^k(\lambda)$ are assumed to be drawn from $\mathbf{C}_v$, the *linear function space* of continuous functions of λ that are zero outside the visible spectrum ("piecewise-continuous" may be substituted for "continuous" here and throughout the remainder of the chapter). C_v is a linear function space, a vector space whose elements are functions. (Apostol 1969, chaps. 1 and 2, is an excellent introduction to linear function subspaces. See also Maddox 1970; Young 1988. Strang 1988 is a standard introduction to finite-dimensional linear algebra.) C_v is assumed to have a *Schauder basis* $E_i = 1, 2, 3, \ldots$ such that for any light $E(\lambda)$, there are unique real numbers ε_i such that

$$E(\lambda) = \sum_{i=1}^{\infty} \varepsilon_i E_i(\lambda). \tag{2}$$

The real numbers ε_i are the *coordinates* corresponding to the light $E(\lambda)$ in the space C_v. The infinite vector $\varepsilon = [\varepsilon_1, \ldots, \varepsilon_i, \ldots]$ determines $E(\lambda)$. Just as in the finite-dimensional case, there are many possible bases from which to choose. Any illuminant with continuous spectral power density can be perfectly captured by an expansion with respect to an infinite-dimensional basis of C_v. The representation in equation (2) in no way constrains the possible illuminants present in the scene. The monomials in λ, $(1, \lambda, \lambda^2, \lambda^3, \ldots)$ restricted to the visible spectrum could serve as a basis. The *Fourier basis* formed of sinusoids and cosinusoids whose periods exactly divide the length of the visible spectrum serves as a second possible choice of basis, a basis first used in modeling color vision by Yilmaz (1962). Our choice of basis for the lights $E(\lambda)$ will be guided by empirical considerations detailed below.

Not every set of coordinates $\varepsilon = [\varepsilon_1, \ldots, \varepsilon_i, \ldots]$ corresponds to a physically possible light $E(\lambda)$; some coordinates correspond to spectral power densities with negative power at some point of the visible spectrum. The "physically realizable" lights form a convex set in C_v analogous to the region within the spectral locus in CIE coordinates (Wyszecki and Stiles 1982).

The basis $E_i(\lambda)$, $i = 1, 2, 3 \ldots$ could also serve to express the coordinates of the surface reflectances. I will instead choose a second basis $S_j(\lambda)$, $i = 1, 2, 3 \ldots$ specifically to express the coordinates of the surface reflectances $S^x(\lambda)$:

$$S^x(\lambda) = \sum_{j=1}^{\infty} \sigma_j^x S_j(\lambda). \tag{3}$$

The infinite vector $\sigma = [\sigma_1^x, \ldots, \sigma_j^x, \ldots]$ determines $S^x(\lambda)$. The choice of this second basis will also be guided by empirical considerations. Mathematically speaking, *any* continuous light or surface reflectance can be expanded as in equations (2) or (3) with respect to either basis. Note that while the coordinates σ_j^x of $S^x(\lambda)$ vary with location, the fixed basis elements do not. A single basis is used to model surface reflectance at each location in the scene.

We substitute equations (2) and (3) into equation (1) to get

$$\rho_k^x = \sum_{i=1}^{\infty} \sum_{j=1}^{\infty} \varepsilon_i \sigma_j^x E_i(\lambda) S_j(\lambda) R_k(\lambda). \tag{4}$$

The product $E_i(\lambda) S_j(\lambda) R_k(\lambda)$ contains only fixed elements independent of the particular scene viewed. The specific illuminant enters into the visual process only through its coordinates ε_i, $i = 1, 2, \ldots$, and the spectral reflectance functions only through the coordinates at each location, σ_j^x, $j = 1, 2, \ldots$. The equation above is exact within the framework of assumptions adopted so far. Equation (4) merely restates equation (2) with respect to two infinite-dimensional coordinate systems; it can no more be solved for information about the surface reflectance (about the σ^x) independent of the light than could equation (2). Any of the coordinates σ_j^x could serve as an intrinsic color—if we could reliably estimate it despite changes in the illuminant. But, in the equation above, information about light and surface is irreversibly tangled.

Following Sallstrom (1973), we next replace the infinite summations above (that perfectly capture light and surface reflectance) by *finite* summations:

$$E_\varepsilon^x(\lambda) = \sum_{i=1}^{M} \varepsilon_i E_i(\lambda) \tag{5}$$

$$S_\sigma^x(\lambda) = \sum_{j=1}^{N} \sigma_j^x S_j(\lambda).$$

The class of lights that can be represented in this way for a fixed value of M, and fixed basis elements $E_1(\lambda)$, $E_2(\lambda)$, ... $E_M(\lambda)$ is termed a *linear model of light* with dimension M. A linear model of surface reflectances with dimension N is defined analogously. The values of M and N chosen are arbitrary; in practice, most attention has gone to the cases $M = 2$, 3 and $N = 2$, 3, or 4. The finite-dimensional vectors $\varepsilon = [\varepsilon_1, \ldots, \varepsilon_M]$ and $\sigma^x = [\sigma_1^x, \ldots, \sigma_N^x]$ still denote the coordinates of light and surface within their respective linear models. The subscripted variables E_ε and S_σ^x will denote lights and surfaces constrained to lie in finite-dimensional linear models. Figure 3.2 shows measurements (circles) of the spectral reflectance of four natural surfaces taken from Krinov (1947). Each of 337 Krinov spectral reflectance curves was fit to a linear model with $N = 3$ chosen as described in Maloney (1986). The values of R^2 (least-squares goodness-of-fit between data and model) obtained ranged from 0.921 to 0.999 with median 0.993. The two best and two worst fits are shown in figure 3.2.

Algorithms for the processing of the initial spectral information proposed by Brill (1978, 1979), Buchsbaum (1980), and Maloney and Wandell (1986) are most effectively presented if we assume that finite-dimensional models of light and surface reflectances with low values of M and N accurately model lights and surfaces present in the environment. In the next section, we assume that the truncated summations (linear models) are, in fact, exact models of the environment and direct our attention to the operation of the algorithms. In section 3.4, we summarize evidence related to the accuracy of fit of linear models (with small numbers of parameters) to measurements of the spectral power distribution of daylight, to other classes of illuminants, and to measurements of surface spectral reflectance for a variety of materials.

3.3 THE LINEAR-MODELS APPROACH

Substituting equation (5) into equation (1) permits us to express the relationship between the light, surface reflectances, and receptor responses by the

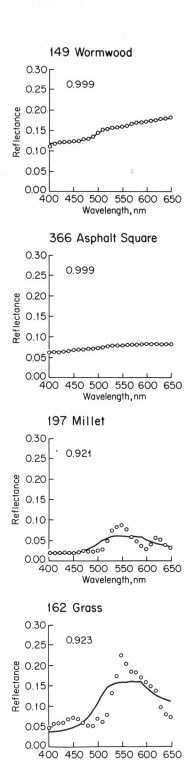

Figure 3.2 The circles are measurements of spectral reflectance taken from Krinov (1947). The curves are linear model approximations for a linear model with three basis elements ($N = 3$) chosen as described in Maloney (1986).

Linear-Models Framework

matrix equation

$$\rho^x = \Lambda_\varepsilon \sigma^x, \tag{6}$$

where ρ^x is, as above, the vector formed from the quantum catches of the P receptors at location x. The matrix Λ_ε is P by N, and its kjth entry is of the form $\int E_\varepsilon(\lambda) S_j(\lambda) R_k(\lambda) d\lambda$. The matrix Λ_ε depends only on the light (as the basis elements S_j and receptor spectral sensitivities R_k are fixed independent of any particular scene). This matrix captures the role of the light in transforming surface reflectances at each location x into receptor quantum catches.

The coordinates $\sigma = [\sigma_1^x, \ldots, \sigma_N^x]$ (or any convenient transform of them) serve as intrinsic colors, namely, the quantities we seek to estimate given the ρ^x at each location. Various limits on recovery of the σ^x are dictated by equation (6). We consider the limits on recovery when (1) the light on the scene is assumed to be known, and (2) the light on the scene is unknown.

Known Light

In the simple case in which the ambient light, and (therefore) the lighting matrix Λ_ε, is known, we see that to recover the N weights that determine the surface reflectance we need merely solve a set of simultaneous linear equations. The recovery procedure reduces to matrix inversion when $P = N$. That is,

$$\Lambda_\varepsilon^{-1} \rho^x = \sigma^x, \tag{7}$$

where the quantities on the left-hand side are all known or computable from known quantities. Recovery is also possible when $P > N$ whenever Λ_ε corresponds to an injective (1-1) linear transformation. If P is less than N equation (6) is underdetermined and there is no unique solution. (See Maloney 1984 for a discussion of the invertibility of the various matrices referenced above and below.)

Unknown Light

If the ambient light is unknown then it is easy to show that we cannot do as well: we cannot, in general, recover the ambient light vector ε or the spectral reflectances even when $P = N$. The matrix Λ_ε is square. For any ε such that Λ_ε is nonsingular there is a set of surface reflectances that satisfy equation (6). *Any* such choice of a light vector ε and corresponding surface reflectances σ^x could have produced the observed quantum catches. Even if we restrict attention to the convex subset of physically realizable lights, such confusions are possible for many choices of lights and surfaces. It is, however, possible to invert equation (6) to obtain estimates of σ^x with additional assumptions, or side information about the scene. Each of the linear-models algorithms, described next, takes a distinct approach to the determination of Λ_ε. Once Λ_ε is known, the intrinsic colors of surfaces (here the σ^x) may be computed by means of equation (7) as in the known light case.

The Algorithms of Brill and of Buchsbaum

Brill (1978, 1979) considers the case where $P = N = 3$ and there are three reference surfaces available in the scene at known locations x_1, x_2, and x_3. (Brill's algorithm requires no restriction on the illuminant $M = \infty$). Then the quantum catches ρ^x at these locations (among others) are known and we have the simultaneous matrix equations:

$$\rho^{x_1} = \Lambda_\varepsilon \sigma^{x_1}$$
$$\rho^{x_2} = \Lambda_\varepsilon \sigma^{x_2} \qquad (8)$$
$$\rho^{x_3} = \Lambda_\varepsilon \sigma^{x_3}.$$

Both sides of each equation are known. If the reference surfaces σ^{x_l}, $l = 1, 2, 3$ are linearly independent, then it is possible to solve for Λ_ε (if the σ^{x_i} are taken as the basis of the space of surfaces, then the matrix RHO whose columns are ρ^{x_i}, $i = 1, 2, 3$ is the inverse of the desired Λ_ε. If another basis is desired, then Λ_ε is simply the inverse of the matrix RHO premultiplied by the matrix that changes from the σ^{x_i} basis to the desired basis (see Strang 1988). Once Λ_ε is known, we invert equation (6) and solve for the coordinates (intrinsic colors) of all sources in the scene.

Buchsbaum (1980) assumes that $M = N = 3$, and requires that the location of one reference surface σ^{x_0} be known. To understand how his algorithm works, we must define

$$\Lambda_1 = \Lambda_{[1,0,0]}$$
$$\Lambda_2 = \Lambda_{[0,1,0]}$$
$$\Lambda_3 = \Lambda_{[0,0,1]},$$

the light matrix Λ_ε for each of the known basis lights. Then, the quantities

$$\rho^{x_1} = \Lambda_1 \sigma^{x_0}$$
$$\rho^{x_2} = \Lambda_2 \sigma^{x_0} \qquad (9)$$
$$\rho^{x_3} = \Lambda_3 \sigma^{x_0}$$

are all known once the reference surface σ^{x_0} is given. These are the quantum catches corresponding to the reference surface under each of the basis lights in turn. It can be shown that (see Maloney 1984, ch. 3)

$$\Lambda_\varepsilon = \varepsilon_1 \Lambda_1 + \varepsilon_2 \Lambda_2 + \varepsilon_3 \Lambda_3, \qquad (10)$$

giving the following expression for the quantum catch of the reference surface under an unknown light ε:

$$\rho^{x_0} = \Lambda_\varepsilon \sigma^{x_0} = \varepsilon_1 \rho^{x_1} + \varepsilon_2 \rho^{x_2} + \varepsilon_3 \rho^{x_3}. \qquad (11)$$

If the fixed vectors ρ^{x_l}, $l = 1, 2, 3$ are linearly independent, then the above equation can be solved for ε given ρ^{x_0}. (The coordinates of the light ε are precisely the coordinates of the reference surfaces' quantum catches ρ^{x_0} with respect to the basis $\{\rho^{x_1}, \rho^{x_2}, \rho^{x_3}\}$.) In summary, a single reference surface permits estimating the light when $P = N = M = 3$. Once ε is known, equation (6) may be solved for the intrinsic colors of surfaces.

The algorithm of Brill generalizes to the case where $P = N$ takes on any value; it then requires N linearly independent reference surfaces. Buchsbaum's algorithm generalizes to arbitrary $M = N = P$ requiring still only a single reference surface. Both algorithms can be applied to a visual system with any number of types of receptors P.

Brill's algorithm, however, makes no asumptions about the illuminant (M) and can potentially function in environments where the physical assumptions of Buchsbaum's algorithm are not met. Note that the three fixed quantum catches ρ^{x_l}, $l = 1$, 2, 3 generated by the single reference surface under the known basis lights serve much the same role as Brill's three reference surfaces: they "pin down" the light matrix.

In either algorithm, the quantum catch corresponding to one reference surface may be replaced by the average quantum catch in the scene *if* we assume that the average of the intrinsic colors of the scene is known. If, for example, we assume that the average intrinsic color of a scene is "gray," then this "gray" σ^{x_0}, paired with ρ^{x_0}, the average of the observed quantum catches in the scene, permit estimation of the illuminant using Buchsbaum's algorithm. The assumption concerning the average of the intrinsic colors in a scene is sometimes termed the *Grayworld* assumption.

The remaining algorithms each devise a method of estimating the coordinates of the light ε and then use equation (7) to solve for intrinsic colors exactly as in the Known Light case. They differ only in how they go about determining the light. The use of reference surfaces in these first two algorithms makes them implausible candidates for a model of human color vision. The remaining algorithms illustrate several ways of dispensing with reference surfaces.

The Algorithm of Maloney and Wandell

Maloney and Wandell (1986) assume that there are more classes of receptors than degrees of freedom in surface reflectances $P > N$. Assume that there are $P = N + 1$ linearly independent receptors to spectrally sample the image at each location. Then Maloney and Wandell compute the light coordinates ε and the N-dimensional surface reflectance vectors σ^x given the $N + 1$ dimensional receptor response vector ρ^x at each location. Then, the matrix Λ_ε is a linear transformation from the N-dimensional space of surface reflectances σ^x into the $N + 1$-dimensional space of receptor quantum catches ρ^x. As Λ_ε is a linear transformation, the receptor responses must fall in a proper subspace of the receptor space. In the case $P = 3$, $N = 2$, the vectors ρ^x must lie on a plane in the three-dimensional receptor space (see fig. 3.3). The particular subspace is determined by Λ_ε and therefore by the lighting parameter ε.

Under circumstances detailed in Maloney (1984), knowledge of the plane determines the light ε up to an unknown constant. The outcome of the algorithm consists of estimates of the intrinsic colors of surfaces known up to a single common "lightness" scaling factor C. That is, if ε is the true light and

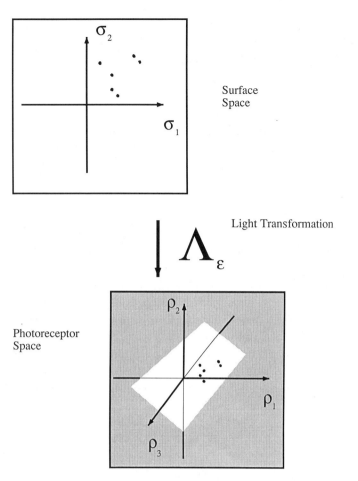

Figure 3.3 Illustration of the solution method of Maloney and Wandell (1986) in the case where there are three classes of receptors ($P = 3$) and two degrees of freedom in the model of surface reflectances ($N = 2$). The receptor quantum catches lie on a plane through the origin in the three-dimensional space of receptor quantum catches ρ^x.

σ^{x_1}, σ^{x_2}, ..., ρ^{x_z} are the true intrinsic colors at Z locations, the algorithm returns a normalized estimate of the light $\bar{\varepsilon} = (1/C)\varepsilon$ and corresponding estimates of the surface properties $\bar{\sigma}^{x_1} = C\sigma^{x_1}, \ldots, \bar{\varepsilon}^{x_z} = C\sigma^{x_z}$ where C is a unknown scaling factor common to all the estimates. (In contrast, the "reference surface" algorithms above can use the reference surface to estimate the absolute power output of the illuminant.) Once the normalized value $\bar{\varepsilon}$ is known, the matrix $\Lambda_{\bar{\varepsilon}}$ can be inverted to recover the normalized intrinsic colors, $\bar{\sigma}^x$ above. Maloney and Wandell (1986) propose a two-step procedure to estimate normalized light and surface reflectance properties. First, they determine the plane spanning the receptor quantum catches. Second, knowledge of the plane in figure 3.3 permits recovery of the normalized ambient light vector $\hat{\varepsilon}$ by computations detailed in Maloney (1984). These computations use the vector at the origin normal to the plane in figure 3.3. This vector serves a role analogous to the reference surface in Buchsbaum's algorithm: it is a recoverable landmark that moves as a function of the illuminant. By requiring $P > N$, Maloney and Wandell are able to replace Buchsbaum's reference surface with a geometrical landmark that serves the same purpose.

Other Work in the Linear-Models Framework

D'Zmura and Lennie (1986) and Lee (1986) additively decompose surface reflectance into a matte and a specular component as suggested by Shafer (1985) and Klinker, Shafer, and Kanade (1988). They then use the specular component of the scene to effectively view the illuminant "in a mirror," thereby determining ε. (Indeed, a mirror would serve quite well as a reference surface in Buchsbaum's algorithm.)

Each of the algorithms described so far recovers light and surface properties exactly when its assumptions are satisfied and its input is noiseless. Errors in estimated surface properties, then, are due solely to failures of the Linear-Models Framework or random errors in the initial photoreceptor measurements. In contrast, Rubner and Schultern (1989) use linear models in combination with a regularization approach to constrain and estimate the illuminant heuristically, and Funt and Drew (1988) apply the Linear-Models Framework to scenes in which the illuminant is not assumed constant across the region of application of the algorithm. These algorithms are heuristic in nature; they need not produce exact estimates of light and surface properties even when their explicit assumptions are fulfilled.

3.4 APPLICABILITY OF THE LINEAR-MODELS APPROACH

The linear-models algorithms function in environments where light, surface reflectance, and the number of photoreceptor classes available satisfy the assumptions made in the preceding section. Each of the algorithms can tolerate some degree of discrepancy between the idealizations implicit in the use of linear models of surface and light, and the actual complexity of surfaces and lights available in the environment. Perturbation analyses of some of the algorithms are found in Brill (1978, 1979), Buchsbaum (1980), Maloney (1984), and Wandell (1987).

Fundamentally, the Linear-Models Framework requires that lights and surfaces in environments of interest be simple. Several authors (Lythgoe 1979; MacAdam 1981; Stiles, Wyszecki, and Ohta 1977) have expressed the opinion that empirical surface reflectances are smooth, constrained curves. Nassau (1983) and Weisskopf (1968) describe some of the physical processes that constrain certain classes of surface reflectances (see Maloney 1986 for discussion).

In this section I review evidence concerning the fit of linear models to empirical surface reflectances and to daylight. The following notational conventions are used for finite and infinite sums and their products. Subscripted terms like E_i or R_k will always denote individual functions. Superscripted terms like E^M denote an implicit summation. If the superscript is capitalized, the summation is taken from 1 to the superscript. For example,

$$E^M(\lambda) = \sum_{i=1}^{M} \varepsilon_i E_i(\lambda). \tag{12}$$

If it is lowercase, the summation is taken from the corresponding uppercase character plus 1 to infinity. For example,

$$E^m(\lambda) = \sum_{i=M+1}^{\infty} \varepsilon_i E_i(\lambda). \tag{13}$$

If we let

$$E(\lambda) = E^0(\lambda) = \sum_{i=1}^{\infty} \varepsilon_i E_i(\lambda), \tag{14}$$

we have the identity, $E^0 = E^M + E^m$ for any $M > 0$.

Similar conventions are adopted for the surface reflectance terms

$$S(\lambda) = S^0(\lambda) = S^N + S^n. \tag{15}$$

In this notation we may summarize the Linear-Models Framework as the claim that S^N is a satisfactory approximation to S and that E^M is a satisfactory approximation to E, even for small values of M and N. When a surface reflectance is superscripted by location, the variable x will always be used. The double meaning of superscripts for surface reflectance can therefore be disambiguated.

The expression $E^M S^N$ or $E^M S^n$ denotes the product of two summations. We also denote such a product by, for example,

$$L^{Mn} = E^M S^n = \sum_{i=1}^{M} \sum_{j=N+1}^{\infty} E_i(\lambda) S_j(\lambda) \tag{16}$$

Formal multiplication gives

$$L = L^{MN} + L^{Mn} + L^{mN} + L^{mn}. \tag{17}$$

The discrepancy between L and L^{MN} is

$$L^{Mn} + L^{mN} + L^{mn}. \tag{18}$$

This overall error term is the sum of three terms corresponding to (1) the model light E^M shining on the nonmodel surface S^n, (2) the nonmodel light E^m shining on the model surface S^N, and (3) the nonmodel light E^m shining on the nonmodel surface S^n. We can view the scene, then, as the superposition of two scenes: the model scene L^{MN}, whose properties we wish to estimate, and the error scene, $L^{Mn} + L^{mN} + L^{mn}$, whose presence perturbs our estimates. Intuitively speaking, we would like to make the model scene as bright as possible compared to the error scene. It is interesting to note that we no longer seek to estimate the true surface reflectance of objects but rather the simplified, or idealized representation S^N. It is the parameters of this somewhat abstract but objective representation that now correspond to *intrinsic colors* (see Hilbert 1987).

The error term in equation (18) depends, first of all, on the bases E_i and S_j. For example, the use of different bases for illuminants and surfaces can reduce the magnitude of equation (18). Maloney (1986) analyzed 462 surface spectral reflectance functions of Munsell color samples (Nickerson 1957; described in Kelley, Gibson, and Nickerson 1943) measured at 10 nm intervals from 400 nm to 700 nm inclusive and a set of surface reflectances of "natural formations" (due to Krinov 1947) measured at 10-nm intervals from 400 to 650 nm. He used characteristic vector analysis (see, e.g., Mardia, Kent, and Bibby 1979) to compute the first few functions of an empirical basis designed to model an available set of surface reflectances. The results of the analysis suggest that all of the surface spectral reflectance functions could be approximated essentially perfectly by linear models S^N with $N = 7$. The values of σ_j in a particular approximation typically decreased rapidly with increasing j. Parkkinen, Hallikainen, and Jaaskelainen (1989) measured a larger set of Munsell color samples at 5-nm intervals across the visible spectrum and report a limit of $N = 8$.

Judd, MacAdam, and Wyszecki (1964) report summary results for a large set of measured spectral power distributions of daylight. Their results and later, more extensive work by other researchers (Das and Sastri 1965; Sastri and Das 1966, 1968; Dixon 1978) indicate that sampled daylight may also be described by a small number of basis elements (possibly as small as $M = 3$). These computations have not been confirmed or extended using the original data samples that are apparently not available. Maloney (1984) analyzes a class of illuminants often used to approximate phases of daylight, *blackbody radiators* with temperatures between $1900°K$ and $10300°K$. He found that when M was as small as 3 the truncated linear model provided essentially perfect fits.

These results suggest that although low-dimensional linear models provide good approximations to daylight spectral power distributions and surface reflectances, further measurement and analyses are needed to establish any such claim.

3.5   THE CHOICE OF PHOTORECEPTORS

The error term in equation (18) depends on the choice of basis elements, but its impact on the visual system depends also on the choice of spectral sensitivity functions R_k for the different classes of receptors. Returning to equation (18), we note that the perturbation in the quantum catch of the kth photoreceptor class due to these terms is

$$\Delta\rho_k = \int L^{Mn}R_k + \int L^{mN}R_k + \int L^{mn}R_k. \tag{19}$$

(The variable of integration λ is omitted for clarity.) Can the spectral sensitivity $R_k(\lambda)$ be chosen so that the error term in equation (19) is sharply reduced while preserving the quantum catch due to the term L^{MN}? Can we use R_k to enhance the effective fit between linear models and world? Barlow (1982) argued that the broad, smooth shapes of the spectral sensitivities of human photoreceptors serve, in effect, to low-pass filter and simplify the spectral power distribution of the light incident on the receptors. Maloney (1986) reanalyzed the sets of empirical surface reflectances described above, taking into account the smoothing induced by human photoreceptors, and determined that this smoothing led to effectively perfect fits with four basis elements—an improvement over the unweighted fits. The shapes of the spectral sensitivity functions do serve to enhance the fit between linear model and the data sets considered. Maloney (1984, 1986), Brainard, Wandell, and Cowan (1989), and Maloney (1990) propose methods for choosing optimal receptors according to various criteria.

3.6 CHROMATIC ADAPTATION

The Linear-Models Framework and the algorithms summarized above are directed toward the second goal of computation color vision: the estimation of stable intrinsic colors of surfaces. Yet, several of the results have implications for the first goal, the prediction of human color judgments. Brill and West (1981), West and Brill (1982), Maloney and Wandell (1986), and Brainard and Wandell (1991) discuss possible links between the Linear-Models Framework and the study of human color vision. I conclude by discussing two such links.

First, if any of the algorithms of Brill or Buchsbaum or Maloney and Wandell are used across a range where their assumptions are satisfied, then they provide perfectly stable estimates of surface properties despite changes in the illuminant. The lights and surfaces across such a range, described by linear models, may be markedly different in their physical properties and still permit perfect color constancy. *Large* changes in the physical light are consistent with perfect color constancy for these models. Yet, once lights or surfaces are drawn from outside the linear models to which the algorithms are attuned, the estimates of surface properties will fail to be constant for almost all changes in the light. If the linear models of lights and surfaces are only approximations to physical lights and surfaces, then the models will be approximately color constant. Consequently, if one were to select lights and surfaces haphazardly, one would almost certainly conclude that a visual system embodying one of the algorithms above was at best approximately color constant, failing less on some occasions than on others. It would be easy to overlook the class of lights and surfaces where the algorithms operate flawlessly. The existence of such *privileged spaces* of lights and surfaces is perhaps the most significant prediction of the Linear-Models Framework for the study of human color vision.

Brainard and Wandell (1991) and Brainard (1989) measured chromatic adaptation in reponse to illuminant changes simulated on a CRT display. The simulated illuminants and surface reflectances were drawn from Judd, Mac-Adam, and Wyszecki's linear model of daylight and a linear model derived from Nickerson's Munsell sample measurements. Their results were consistent with hypotheses concerning chromatic adaptation and privileged spaces predicted by the Linear-Models Framework.

Second, W. S. Stiles suggested that the study of color vision be considered as the study of two processes, *local retinal adaptational state* and the process that selects the local state, *the control of adaptation*: "we anticipate that a small number of variables—adaptation variables—will define the condition of a particular visual area at a given time, instead of the indefinitely many that would be required to specify the conditioning stimuli. The adaptation concept—if it works—divides the original problem into two: what are the values of the adaptation variables corresponding to different sets of conditioning stimuli, and how does adaptation, so defined, modify the visual response to given test stimuli" (1961). Figure 4 schematizes Stiles's proposal.

The Linear-Models Framework naturally identifies the possible *local retinal adaptational states* with the matrices Λ_ε^{-1}, the matrices that compensate for each of the possible illuminants ε. The notion of identifying retinal adaptational states with a class of matrices is at least as old as Kries ([1902] 1970). See Hurvich (1981) and Wyszecki and Stiles (1982) for illustrations. If A denotes the retinal state matrix, ρ^x the excitation of the photoreceptors classes at

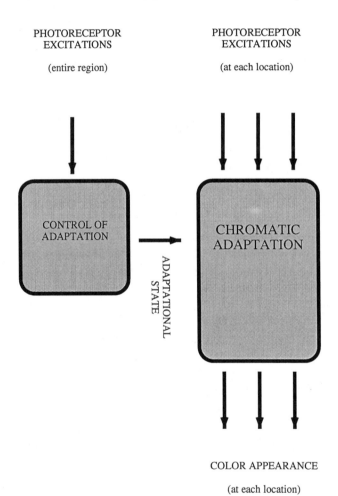

Figure 3.4 Schematic diagram of Stiles's model of adaptation. *Local adaptational state* is characterized as a small number of variables that control the relation between photoreceptor excitations at a retinal location and the excitations of internal "mechanisms" that determine color appearance at that location (on the right). Information drawn from large regions of the retina (on the left) is used to set or *control* the *adaptational state*.

location x, then the action of local retinal adaptation is described by

$$A\rho^x = \mu^x \tag{20}$$

where μ is a vector $[\mu_1, \ldots, \mu_R]$ of excitations of hypothetical "mechanisms" that determine color appearance. Over a privileged range of lights and surfaces where the biological vision system is color constant, the above becomes

$$A_\varepsilon \rho^x = \mu^x = F(\sigma^x). \tag{21}$$

On the left-hand side, the adaptational state matrix is now a function of the illuminant ε as it compensates for the effects of the illuminant. On the right-hand side, the excitations of the mechanisms are now a function F of the intrinsic colors of the surfaces at each location. A comparison of equation (21) with the inversion equation common to the linear-models algorithms,

$$\Lambda_\varepsilon^{-1} \rho^x = \sigma^x, \tag{22}$$

brings out the analogy between the linear models approach and current theories of local retinal adaptational state: *under conditions where the biological visual system is color constant,* local retinal state satisfies $A = F\Lambda_\varepsilon$ where Λ_ε is determined by the Linear-Models Framework and F is a fixed unknown function determined by the internal representation of surface properties in the visual system. The linear-models approach is potentially a tool to predict and model local adaptational state in color vision.

Taken as models of chromatic adaptation the linear-models algorithms highlight the control mechanisms of adaptation, the second of Stiles's processes. Each of the linear-models algorithms described above can be taken as a theory of the sources of information in a scene that affects local adaptational state (Maloney and Varner 1986). The Linear-Models Framework is potentially useful in not only the study of local adaptational state but also the complex mapping between the properties of realistic scenes and local adaptational state envisioned by Stiles.

NOTE

I thank David H. Brainard, Sylvan Kornblum, and John Palmer for helpful suggestions. This work was supported by a grant from the National Eye Institute EY08266.

REFERENCES

Apostol, T. M. (1969). *Calculus.* Vol. 2, 2d ed. Waltham, MA: Xerox.

Barlow, H. B. (1982). What causes trichromacy? A theoretical analysis using comb-filtered spectra, *Vision Research, 22,* 635.

Boynton, R. M. (1979). *Human Color Vision.* New York: Holt, Rinehart, & Winston.

Brainard, D. H. (1989). *Understanding the illuminant's effect on color appearance.* Ph.D. dissertation, Stanford University, Stanford, CA.

Brainard, D. H., and Wandell, B. A. (1986). An analysis of the retinex theory of color vision. *Journal of the Optical Society of America A, 3,* 1651–1661.

Brainard, D. H., and Wandell, B. A. (1991). A bilinear model of the illuminant's effect on color appearance. In M. S. Landy and J. A. Movshon, (Eds.), *Computational Models of Visual Processing.* Cambridge, MA: MIT Press.

Brainard, D. H., Wandell, B. A., and Cowan, W. B. (1989). Black light: How sensors filter spectral variation of the illuminant. *IEEE Transactions on Biomedical Engineering,* T-BME 36, 140–149.

Brill, M. H. (1978). A device performing illuminant-invariant assessment of chromatic relations. *Journal of Theoretical Biology, 71,* 473.

Brill, M. H. (1979). Further features of the illuminant-invariant trichromatic photosensor. *Journal of Theoretical Biology, 78,* 305.

Brill, M. H., and West, G. (1981). Contributions to the theory of invariance of color under the condition of varying illumination. *Journal of Mathematical Biology, 11,* 337–350.

Buchsbaum, G. (1980). A spatial processor model for object colour perception. *Journal of the Franklin Institute, 310,* 1.

Buchsbaum, G., and Gottschalk, A. (1984). Chromaticity coordinates of frequency-limited functions. *Journal of the Optical Society of America, 1,* 885–887.

Cohen, J. (1964). Dependency of the spectral reflectance curves of the Munsell color chips. *Psychonomic Science, 1,* 369.

Das, S. R., and Sastri, V. D. P. (1965). Spectral distribution and color of tropical daylight. *Journal of the Optical Society of America, 55,* 319.

Dixon, E. R. (1978). Spectral distribution of Autralian daylight. *Journal of the Optical Society of America, 68,* 437.

D'Zmura, M., and Lennie, P. (1986). Mechanisms of color constancy. *Journal of the Optical Society America A, 3,* 1662–1672.

Funt, B. V., and Drew, M. S. (1988). Color constancy computation in near-Mondrian scenes using a finite dimensional linear model. In *Proceedings of the Computer Society Conference on Computer Vision and Pattern Recognition, 862,* 544–549. Ann Arbor, Michigan: Computer Society Press.

Helmholtz, H. von ([1896] 1962). *Helmholtz's Treatise on Physiological Optics.* Ed. J. P. C. Southall. Vol. 2. New York: Dover.

Helson, H. (1938). Fundamental problems in color vision. I. The principle governing changes in hue saturation and lightness of non-selective samples in chromatic illumination. *Journal of Experimental Psychology, 23,* 439.

Hilbert, D. R. (1987). *Color and Color Perception; A Study in Anthropocentric Realism.* Stanford. California: CSLI.

Hurlbert, A. (1986). Formal connections between lighness algorithms. *Journal of the Optical Society of America A, 3,* 1684–1693.

Hurvich, L. M. (1981). *Color Vision.* Sunderland, MA: Sinauer.

Judd, D. B. (1940). Hue saturation and lightness of surface colors with chromatic illumination. *Journal of the Optical Society of America, 30,* 2.

Judd, D. B., MacAdam, D. L., and Wyszecki, G. (1964). Spectral distribution of typical daylight as a function of correlated color temperature. *Journal of the Optical Society of America, 54,* 1031.

Kelley, K. L., Gibson, K. S., and Nickerson, D. (1943). Tristimulus specification of the *Munsell Book of Color* from spectrophotometric measurements. *Journal of the Optical Society of America, 33,* 355.

Klinker, G. J., Shafer, S. A., and Kanade, T. (1988). The measurement of highlight in color images. *International Journal of Computer Vision, 2,* 7–32.

Kries, J. von ([1902] 1970). Chromatic adaptation. In D. L. MacAdam (Ed.), *Sources of Color Science.* Cambridge, MA: MIT Press.

Krinov, E. L. (1947). *Spectral reflectance properties of natural formations.* Technical translation, TT-439, National Research Council of Canada.

Land, E. H. (1983). Recent advances in retinex theory and some implications for cortical computations: Color vision and the natural image. *Proceedings of the National Academy of Sciences, 80,* 5163–5169.

Land, E. H., and McCann, J. J. (1971). Lightness and retinex theory. *Journal of the Optical Society of America, 61,* 1–11.

Lee, H. (1986). Method for computing the scene-illuminant chromaticity from specular highlights. *Journal of the Optical Society of America A, 3,* 1694–1699.

Lythgoe, J. N. (1979). *The Ecology of Vision.* Oxford: Clarendon.

MacAdam, D. L. (1981). *Color Measurement. Theme and Variations.* Berlin: Springer-Verlag.

Maddox, I. J. (1970). *Elements of Functional Analysis.* Cambridge: Cambridge University Press.

Maloney, L. T. (1984). *Computational approaches to color constancy.* Ph.D. Dissertation, Stanford University. Reprinted as Stanford Applied Psychology Laboratory Report 1985–01 (1985).

Maloney, L. T. (1986). Evaluation of linear models of surface spectral reflectance with small numbers of parameters. *Journal of the Optical Society of America A, 3,* 1673–1683.

Maloney, L. T. (1990). Photoreceptor spectral sensitivities and color correction. In M. H. Brill (Ed.), *Perceiving, Measuring, and Using Color,* Proceedings of the SPIE 1250, 103–110. Washington, D.C.: SPIE.

Maloney, L. T., and Varner, D. C. (1986). Chromatic adaptation, the control of chromatic adaptation, and color constancy (abstract). *Optics News, 12,* 134.

Maloney, L. T., and Wandell, B. A. (1986). Color constancy: A method for recovering surface spectral reflectance. *Journal of the Optical Society of America A, 3,* 29.

Mardia, K. V., Kent, J. T., and Bibby, J. M. (1979). *Multivariate Analysis.* London: Academic Press.

Nassau, K. (1983). *The Physics and Chemistry of Color: The Fifteen Causes of Color.* New York: Wiley.

Nickerson, D. (1957). Spectrophotometric data for a collection of Munsell samples. Washington, D.C.: U.S. Department of Agriculture.

Parkkinen, J. P. S., Hallikainen, J., and Jaaskelainen, T. (1989). Characteristic spectra of Munsell colors. *Journal of the Optical Society of America A, 6,* 318–322.

Rubner, J., and Schultern, K. (1989). A regularized approach to color constancy. *Biological Cybernetics, 61,* 29–36.

Sallstrom, P. (1973). *Colour and physics: Some remarks concerning the physical aspects of human colour vision.* Institute of Physics Report, 73–09, University of Stockholm.

Sastri, V. D. P., and Das, S. R. (1966). Spectral distribution and color of north sky at Delhi. *Journal of the Optical Society of America, 56,* 829.

Sastri, V. D. P., and Das, S. R. (1968). Typical. spectra distributions and color for tropical daylight. *Journal of the Optical Society of America, 58,* 391.

Shafer, S. A. (1985). Using color to separate reflectance components. *Color Research and Applications, 10,* 210–218.

Stiles, W. S. (1961). Adaptation, chromatic adaptation, colour transformation. *Anales Real Soc. Espan. Fis. Quim., Series A, 57,* 149–175.

Stiles, W. S., Wyszecki, G., and Ohta, N. (1977). Counting metameric object-color stimuli using frequency-limited spectral reflectance functions. *Journal of the Optical Society of America, 67,* 779.

Strang, G. (1988). *Linear Algebra and Its Applications.* New York: Harcourt, Brace, Jovanovich.

Wandell, B. A. (1987). The synthesis and analysis of color images. *IEEE Transactions on Pattern Analysis and Machine Intelligence,* PAMI-9, 2–13.

Weisskopf, V. F. (1968). How light interacts with matter. *Scientific American, 219,* 59–71.

West, G., and Brill, M. H. (1982). Necessary and sufficient conditions for von Kries chromatic adaptation to give color constancy. *Journal of Mathematical Biology, 15,* 249–258.

Wyszecki, G., and Stiles, W. S. (1982). *Color Science; Concepts and Methods, Quantitative Data and Formulas.* 2d ed. New York: Wiley.

Yilmaz, H. (1962). Color vision and a new approach to color perception. In *Biological Prototypes and Synthetic Systems, Vol. 1.* New York: Plenum.

Young, N. (1988). *An Introduction to Hilbert Space.* Cambridge, England: Cambridge University Press.

4 The Visual Recognition of Three-dimensional Objects

Shimon Ullman

The task of visual object recognition is performed efficiently and effortlessly by humans, including young children. Simpler animals, such as the pigeon, also exhibit a remarkable capacity to classify and recognize objects. In contrast, the task has proved to be exceedingly difficult in artificial systems. This is an intriguing contrast: it suggests that a better understanding of the recognition problem, and, in particular, why the task is so natural for biological systems and so difficult to mimic in artificial systems, may give us insights regarding some fundamental principles of brain organization.

In approaching the recognition problem, it may appear initially that the problem could perhaps be overcome by using a sufficiently large and efficient associative memory system. In performing recognition, we are trying to determine whether an image we currently see corresponds to an object we have seen in the past. It might be possible, therefore, to approach object recognition by storing a sufficient number of different views associated with each object, and then compare the image of the currently viewed object with all the views stored in memory (Abu-Mostafa and Psaltis 1987). Several mechanisms, known as associative memories, have been proposed for implementing this "direct" approach to recognition. These mechanisms, usually embodied in neuronlike networks, can store a large number of patterns (P_1, $P_2, \ldots, P_n$), and then, given an input pattern Q, they can retrieve the pattern P_i that is most similar to Q (Willshaw, Buneman, and Longuet-Higgins 1969; Kohonen 1978; Hopfield 1982).

Have associative memories of this type solved the problem of object recognition? Discussions of associative memories sometimes suggest that they have. When the system has stored a representative view, or a few views, of each object, a new view would automatically retrieve the stored representation that most closely resembles it.

The problem with using an associative memory directly to recognize objects from their images is that the notion of similarity used in associative memories is a restricted one. The typical similarity measure used is the so-called "Hamming distance." (This measure is defined for two binary vectors. Suppose that **u** and **v** are two binary vectors, namely, strings of 1's and 0's. The Hamming distance between **u** and **v** is simply the number of coordinates in which they differ.)

Such a simple similarity measure may be appropriate for some special applications and for certain nonvisual domains, such as olfaction (Freeman 1979). For the general problem of visual object recognition this direct approach is implausible for two reasons. First, the space of all possible views of all the objects to be recognized is likely to be prohibitively large. The second, and more fundamental reason, is that the image to be recognized will often not be sufficiently similar to any image seen in the past. There are four main sources for this variability, and it seems to me that the success of any recognition scheme will depend on its ability to cope with these four problems.

The first source of variability comes from photometric effects, namely, the positions and distribution of light sources in the scene (including effects of mutual illumination by other objects, the relative orientation of the object with respect to the light sources, etc.). Illumination effects of this type can drastically change the light intensity distribution in the image, but they usually do not affect our ability to recognize the objects in the image.

The second source is the effect of context. By "context" I mean here the setting of the object in the scene. Objects are rarely seen in isolation: they are usually seen against some background, next to, or partially occluded by, other objects. Even when the image contains a familiar object, if we compare the image as a whole with images we have seen in the past, it is unlikely to match closely any image of the same object seen in the past.

The third reason for the variability between new and old images has to do with the effect of viewing position. Three-dimensional objects can be viewed from a variety of vantage points (directions and distances) that can give rise to widely different projections. It is sometimes difficult to appreciate this effect of viewing direction. Two views of the same object separated by, say, 20–30 degrees usually appear perceptually quite similar. When the two two-dimensional projections are superimposed, however, it becomes apparent how different they can become with even a modest change in viewing direction.

The fourth and final reason is the effect of changing shape. Many objects, such as the human body, can maintain their identities while changing their three-dimensional shapes. To identify such objects correctly, the recognition scheme must therefore be able to deal with the effects induced by changes in shape.

In this chapter I will deal with aspects of the second and third of these sources of variability, the effects of context and of viewing position. Before doing this, however, I will comment briefly on the first source, the photometric effects. How can a recognition system deal with such changes in illumination conditions? The answer is not entirely known, but there has been one dominant approach to the problem that is based on the notion of edge detection. The idea is to find features in the light intensity distribution forming the image that are affected as little as possible by changes in the illumination conditions. The best-known example of such features are intensity edges, namely, contours where the light intensity changes relatively abruptly from one level to another. Such edges are often associated with object boundaries and with material changes on an object's surface. When the illumination changes, the absolute light intensities change as well, but the locations of edges that are caused by physical surface discontinuities on the whole remain stable.

This process of edge detection is illustrated in figure 4.1. Figure 4.1a is a grey-level image, and 4.1b is its edge-contour image. The edge image contains most of the relevant information in the original image. The advantage of this edge image is that, unlike the original image, it will change only little when the illumination conditions change. This invariance is not complete, however: some object edges might appear or disappear, some spurious edges will result from shadows and specularities, and so forth. It is also unclear as yet to what extent contour information of this kind is sufficient for the purpose of recognition.

4.1   CONTEXT EFFECTS: SEGMENTATION AND SELECTION

The second source of variation listed above is the effect of varying context. The main approach that has been proposed to deal with this context problem is to precede the actual recognition and matching process by a stage called "segmentation" or "selection." The general idea is to select a region that contains an object to be recognized out of the image and "hand it over" to the recognition process, which can then selectively process this region, and ignore the rest of the image. Such a process is desirable from a computational standpoint. In a recent formal analysis, Grimson (1990) has shown that even a moderately efficient segmentation stage would be highly beneficial for subsequent matching processes. His analysis has shown that, under fairly general assumptions, the problem of matching the image of an isolated object with an internal model requires a polynomial number of steps (on the order of $(m^2 + ams)$, where m is the number of model features, s the number of image features, and a a small constant). If, however, the object is not separated from the background, the problem becomes exponential. If one assumes a selection process that identifies a subset of the image features as belonging to a single object, then, even if the process is imperfect (i.e., it identifies only a part of the object features and also introduces some spurious ones), the complexity of the problem is reduced again to a low-order polynomial.

There are several lines of evidence supporting the notion that in human vision the recognition process is indeed preceded by a somewhat independent segmentation and selection stage. One type of evidence comes from patients with different types of visual agnosia. For example, it seems that some patients have difficulty recognizing objects when the task requires separation of the object from nearby or occluding stimuli but can recognize the same objects well when each object is shown in isolation, well separated from other objects in the scene. Observers with intact visual systems may also have difficulties recognizing an object when the task of separating the object from the background becomes perceptually difficult (Kundel and Nodine 1983). Another type of evidence comes from images containing occlusion. Bregman (1984) has shown that occluded objects that are recognizable when the occluding surface is made explicit become unrecognizable when the occluder is not shown,

a

b

Figure 4.1 Edge images may be used to minimize variations due to illumination effects. (a) Original grey-level image. (b) An edge image of the original image.

despite the fact that the two images (with and without the occluder) contain the same information regarding the occluded object that is to be recognized. The reason seems to be that, in the presence of the visible occluder, the perceptual system "automatically" groups together different parts that belong to the same object. When the occluder is not shown explicitly, the perceptual system fails to make this initial grouping. It is interesting to note that the grouping process appears to be low-level and automatic. Even when one knows which object to look for in the image, when the occluder is not visible it is not easy to replace the automatic grouping process by a conscious attempt to group together the relevant parts of a given object. It is as if some autonomous processes make certain decisions regarding which regions and contours in the image should be considered together as a single entity.

A related phenomenon has recently been studied by Nakayama, Shimojo, and Silverman (1989). They constructed partially visible human faces by interposing horizontal stripes that had no information about the face. The stripes could appear either in front of or behind the face. The two versions contain identical visible portions of the face: In one case the face appears to be visible behind an occluding fence; in the other case, unrelated parts of the face appear to float in front of the background. This study has shown that the faces are much more recognizable when they appeared to be in the back, compared to being in front. Again, the problem seems to be that segmentation is successful in one case, but not in the other.

Some examples of segmentation processes can be observed in figure 4.2a–d. When we look at an image such as figure 4.2a, it appears to us that our attention is somehow immediately drawn to the main object, which we then recognize as a car. For most observers, the car is found immediately, without the need to scan the image systematically and without first attempting to recognize some structures in other parts of the image.

Structures that attract our attention need not be recognizable objects. In figure 4.2b–d, for example, a number of round blobs are relatively easy to detect as the most salient, figurelike structures in these images.

In examining the processes that make such structures salient in our perception, it is useful to draw a distinction between local and global (or structural) saliency. Our attention is sometimes drawn to an item in the image because this item differs in some local property from neighboring elements; for example, a green dot in an image of red dots, or a vertical line segment surrounded by horizontal ones. This phenomenon of local saliency has been investigated in a number of psychological studies (e.g., Treisman and Gelade 1980; Julesz 1981). In other cases (such as fig. 4.2c–d) the salient structure has no conspicuous local part, with a distinguishing local property such as color, orientation, contrast, or curvature. Although the elements comprising the structure are not individually salient, their arrangement makes the figure as a whole somehow globally conspicuous. In the more general case, the saliency of an image structure may be determined by the combination of both local and global aspects.

The section below describes a model that has been developed to extract certain classes of globally salient structures from images. This process is not

a

Figure 4.2 The perception of salient structures. The car in (a) attracts our attention; we can find it without scanning the image exhaustively. (b)–(d) do not contain recognizable objects, but certain structures in the image are more salient and figurelike than others. The saliency in (c) and (d) is global rather than local.

intended to provide a full solution to the selection problem on its own, but, as discussed at the end of this section, it offers a useful stage in solving the problem.

Detecting Globally Salient Image Structures

The model for extracting salient image structures proceeds by computing a measure of saliency at each point in the image. A successful model of this type will assign high saliency measure to image structures that are also salient in human perception and should provide an efficient method for extracting from the image the conspicuous structures such as the car or the blobs in figures 4.2b–d.

For simplicity, the input image is assumed to be composed of contours. Such contours may be, for example, the lines and edges extracted from the image by line and edge detection processes. The saliency measure in the model increases with the contour's length and decreases with its curvature or curvature variation; that is, the measure is designed to favor image contours that are long and smooth. In this account I will concentrate on a somewhat simpler version that does not take curvature variation into account: the saliency measure increases with overall length and decreases with total curvature. The

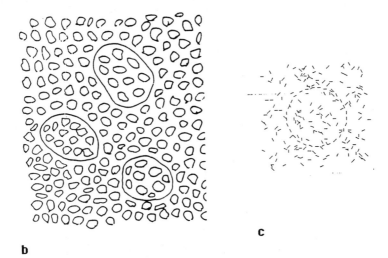

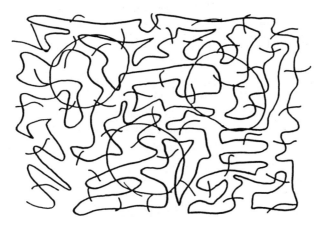

c

b

d

Figure 4.2 (continued)

use of length and curvature parameters was motivated by psychophysical observations, and the exact form of the saliency measure was determined by computational considerations that are discussed in more detail below.

In defining the mathematical form of the saliency measure, it is convenient to consider first a single contour Γ in the image and ignore all others. Let p be a point on Γ and $S_\Gamma(p)$ be the saliency measure at point p assuming that Γ is the only relevant curve. The saliency at p is then given by

$$S_\Gamma(p) = \sum_i w_i \sigma_i.$$

In this expression σ_i is the local saliency of the ith edge element along the curve (fig. 4.3a). For now, σ_i can be thought of simply as having the value "1" for every edge element i, and "0" if the edge element is missing (i.e., there is a gap in the curve). More generally, the values of σ_i provide the link between

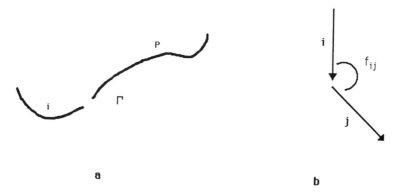

a
b

Figure 4.3 The saliency computation. (a) The contribution of element i to the saliency at p depends on the total curvature between the two locations. For details see text. (b) Two neighboring line elements in the network for computing global saliency. The "coupling constant" $f_{i,j}$ between them decreases with the angle between the two elements.

local and global saliency. The idea is that the σ_i's are determined by a local saliency measure; they increase, for example, for higher contrast, or when the ith edge element differs significantly from its neighbors in color or orientation, and so forth. In this manner the scheme can provide measure of the global saliency based on length and curvature, while at the same time taking into account the local saliency of the individual components.

In the expression above the overall saliency is obtained by a weighted sum of the local contributions σ_i along Γ. The weight w_i of the ith element is

$$e^{-c_i},$$

where c_i is the total curvature of the contour from p up to the ith element (a slight extension of this definition is introduced below).

The saliency measure defined so far depends on a particular curve Γ. The final saliency at p is given by

$$S(p) = max_{\Gamma} S_{\Gamma}(p).$$

The maximum is taken over all possible curves terminating at p. (This computes the contribution to p from one side of the curve; the contribution from the other side is determined in a similar way.) In practice, it is also convenient to use this definition limited to curves of length N:

$$S_N(p) = max_{\Gamma_N} S_{\Gamma_N}(p),$$

where Γ_N stands for Γ restricted to length N. It is important to realize that the optimum is sought over all possible curves, including fragmented ones. In the case of the fragmented circle in figure 4.2c, for example, the scheme will in effect consider all the possible curves running through any number of the individual line segments in the figure. This task may appear prohibitive: to determine the salient figure, one must consider all possible curves through all the elements in the image, and along each one integrate the curvature-based saliency measure defined above. As it turns out, this saliency measure can in fact be computed by a surprisingly simple, locally connected, network described below.

Computing Global Saliency by a Simple Local Network

To detect the globally salient structures in the image, the saliency measure $S(p)$ is computed at each image point p by a locally connected network of processing units. The processing elements can be thought of as local "line detectors" that respond to the presence of lines or edges in the image. The entire image is covered by a grid of $n \times n$ points, where each point corresponds to a specific x, y location in the image. At each point p there are k "orientation elements" coming into p from neighboring points, and the same number of orientation elements leaving p to nearby points. Each orientation element p_i (the ith orientation element at point p) responds to an input image by signaling the presence of the corresponding line segment in the image. A lack of activity at p_i means that the corresponding line segment is not present in the image. The activity level of the element p_i, denoted by E_{p_i}, will eventually correspond to the saliency of this line element. The initial activity is determined by the local saliency of the element, denoted by σ_i. This local saliency is determined by comparing the element in question with surrounding elements along a number of dimensions. For example, if the ith element has high contrast, or if it is very different from the surrounding elements in color, orientation, or direction of motion, then its local saliency will be high. To account for global rather than local saliency, the activity $E(p_i)$ is then modified by interactions with the neighboring elements, so that eventually it also measures the length and the curvature of the contour passing through p_i.

The activity $E(p_i)$ is updated by the following simple local computation:

$$E_{p_i}^{(0)} = \sigma_i$$

$$E_{p_i}^{(n+1)} = \sigma_i + \rho_i \max_{p_j} E_{p_i}^{(n)} f_{i,j},$$

where p_j is one of k possible neighbors of p_i. In this formula, $f_{i,j}$ are "coupling constants" between neighboring line elements. Their values in the model are given by

$$f_{i,j} = e^{-(2\alpha_{ij}\tan(\alpha_{ij}/2))/\Delta s},$$

where α_{ij} is the angle between the successive elements i and j (see fig. 4.3b). The main property of these coupling constants is that they decrease with the angle between successive elements. The particular choice of the coupling constants above ensures that the computed saliency will depend directly on the total curvature along the contour. In terms of these constants, the discrete approximation to the total curvature measured along $p_i, \ldots, p_j$ is obtained by

$$e^{C_{i,j}} = \prod_{k=i}^{j-1} f_{k,k+1}$$

where $C_{i,j}$ is the total curvature (squared) between elements i and j. This quantity is equal to unity for a straight line and decays to zero as the curvature increases. The factors ρ_i are of secondary importance; they make the contributions of faraway locations smaller than those of nearby elements along the curve (for more detail, see Ullman and Shashua 1988).

The updating formula is in fact a very simple one, and the saliency computation as defined above is simple and local. At each step in the iteration at a given element, the element simply adds the maximal contribution of its k neighbors to its original local saliency σ_i.

The interesting point about this computation is that by using this simple updating formula the quantity E_{p_i} computes the desired measure $S(p)$, defined above, at every point p. It is remarkable that such a simple local computation is sufficient for this task. The saliency measure S at a point p in the image is in fact a rather elaborate measure. For each possible curve Γ passing through p, it must compute a measure S_Γ and select the best one (with highest S_Γ). The computation achieves all of this without explicitly tracing and then examining different curves. Although the number of possible curves of length N increases exponentially as the number N grows, the computation is only linear in the length N.

Figure 4.4 shows examples of the computation applied to three figures. The first is the car image in figure 4.2a (only a portion of the image is shown). The figure on the left is a "saliency map" after thirty iterations of the computation. In this representation, the wider, lighter contours are those with higher saliency $E(p)$. It can be seen that the activity in the background is reduced compared with the activity in the figure. The figure on the right shows the five most salient contours by the end of the thirty iterations.

Although the process successfully selects the main object in this image, it should be noted that, in general, the saliency computation described above is not intended to model the entire process of selecting a candidate object from the image. A more plausible view is that such a selection process is obtained in two stages. The first stage, which is applied uniformly and parallel across the entire image, selects and "highlights" a small number of contours. A candidate object can then be selected by processing these preferred contours further. This second stage can be more attentive and applied preferentially to the contours selected in the first stage, rather than to all the contours in the image.

Figure 4.4b shows a fragmented circle embedded in increasing amounts of noise. The left column illustrates the input figures. It can be noted that in the first two images the circle is immediately discernible by our perceptual system despite the gaps and the high noise level. The second column shows the saliency map after ten iterations, and the right column shows the most active (salient) contour by the end of the ten iterations. The performance of the scheme appears to be comparable to human perception. It is also worth noting that the gaps in the original figure are filled in the course of the computation.

Figure 4.4c was supplied to us by Professor J. Beck from the University of Oregon. Beck has noted that the figure is a challenging one, but still perceivable by human observers. It is also interesting because it is not a simple closed

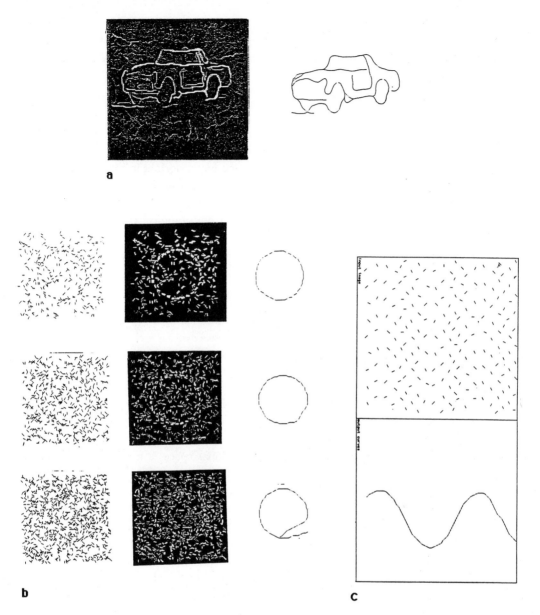

Figure 4.4 Results of the saliency computation. (a) A portion of the car image in 4.2a. Left: the saliency map after 30 iterations. Right: the five most active (salient) contours after thirty iterations. (b) A fragmented circle embedded in an increasing amounts of noise. Left: original images. Center: the saliency map after ten iterations. Right: the most salient contour following ten iterations. (c) A sinusoidal curve in background noise. Top: the input figure. Bottom: the most salient contour in the Input image.

compact figure. Schemes that are sensitive specifically to bloblike structures will not be able to extract such long curved structures. The scheme described above has some preference for closed figures, but, like human vision, can detect any smooth extended structure.

In summary of this discussion on the selection of salient image structures, a number of points are worth noting.

1. There are good reasons to believe, based on psychophysical and computational considerations, that processes involved in segmenting the image and selecting structures for further processing are important in the early stages of visual information processing. The lower-level visual areas in the hierarchy of visual areas, such as V1 and V2, may be involved in this type of processing. The saliency map itself may also have a physiological counterpart, but not necessarily in V1 or V2.

2. Segmentation and selection probably involve a number of different processes that depend on both local (e.g., contrast, color, and motion) and global (e.g., length and overall curvature) properties.

3. The (global) saliency of a contour in the image increases when the contour is long and smooth.

4. The extraction of smooth long contours can be obtained by a simple network of locally interacting line elements.

4.2   COMPENSATING FOR VIEWING DIRECTION

The problem of compensating for changes in the image induced by different orientations of objects in three-dimensional space is a difficult one, and a number of schemes have been proposed over the years as possible models for how the visual system may overcome this problem. The large number of shape-based object recognition schemes that have been proposed in the past can be divided into three broad classes (Ullman 1989): invariant properties methods (e.g., Tou and Gonzales 1974), object decomposition methods (e.g., Biederman 1985), and alignment methods (Ullman 1989). In this section I will briefly discuss the alignment approach in general and present the outline of a new scheme that differs from previous ones in that it uses collections of two-dimensional images instead of storing three-dimensional object models. This scheme appears to be simpler and more direct than alternative ones and might correspond more closely to some of the processes used by biological visual systems in recognizing three-dimensional objects.

The Alignment Approach to Recognition

To introduce the alignment approach, it is convenient to view visual recognition as a problem involving search in a large space: given a viewed object, a best match is sought in the space of all stored object models and all of their possible views. If V denotes the viewed object, (M_i) is the set of different object models stored in memory, and (T_{ij}) is the set of allowable transformations that can be applied to object model M_i, then the goal of the search is to find a particular model and a particular transformation that will maximize some measure of fit F between the object and the model. That is, the search for a maximum in $F(V, (M_i T_{ij}))$ over all possible object models M_i and their transformations T_{ij}.

The basic idea of the alignment approach is to decompose this search into two stages. First, determine the transformation between the viewed object and the object model, for all candidate models. This is the *alignment* stage. Second, determine the object model that best matches the viewed object. At this stage, the search is over all possible models but not over their possible views, since the transformation has already been determined uniquely in the alignment stage. In terms of the maximization problem stated above, the idea is to determine for each potential object model a unique transformation T_{ij} that aligns M_i and V optimally. The search for the best match is now reduced to finding the maximum in $F(V, M_i)$ only, that is, a search over the set of objects but not over their different views.

This decomposition of the problem may seem at first somewhat unexpected: how can the viewing position be determined prior to the identification of the correct object? Before discussing methods for performing such alignment, let me comment on the motivation underlying this decomposition. The basic idea is that the space of possible transformations is considerably more constrained than the set of possible objects. The set of all possible objects is large and unconstrained. In contrast, the set of possible transformations is often captured by a small number of parameters. For example, the transformations in viewing direction are described by the six parameters of rigid motion, namely, translation and rotation in three-dimensional space. This simpler structure makes it easier to first determine the transformation in viewing direction. As discussed below, the transformation can be recovered, for example, on the basis of very limited and partial information. Once the effect of viewing direction has been factored out, the determination of the best-fitting model is considerably facilitated.

Alignment by Transforming a Three-Dimensional Model

An example of using the alignment approach to three-dimensional object recognition was described in Ullman (1989). This scheme uses a small number of corresponding image and model features to recover the required transformation. In particular, the alignment can be performed on the basis of three corresponding feature points in the viewed object and the stored internal model. These features can be, for example, corner points, concavities on the object's silhouette, or the centers of salient blobs. These feature points that are used for alignment are called "anchor points."

The alignment process then proceeds in the following manner. For each object to be recognized, the recognition system stores an internal model M_i. This internal model consists of a contour image of the object. It contains the orthographic projection of the object's contour, together with the depth values associated with each contour point. (Different contours in the model may carry different weights, but we will not consider here such possible elaborations.)

The system is now given a view V of an unknown object, and the problem is to decide, for a given model M_i, whether or not V is a possible view of M_i. To reach a decision, we can first ignore the entire image of the object and examine only the three anchor points. Let (P_1, P_2, P_3) be the three-dimensional coordinates of the three anchor points in the model, and (p_1, p_2, p_3) the two-dimensional coordinates of the corresponding points in the image. The crucial point is that the model M_i and the view V can be aligned in a unique manner given only the coordinates P_1, P_2, P_3, (known in the model) and p_1, p_2, p_3, (recovered from the image). In other words, the rotation in space, translation, and scaling, possibly relating M_i to V, is determined on the basis of the three corresponding points. The recovered transformation is now applied to the internal model M_i. This operation is similar to a "mental rotation": the internal model is rotated, translated, and scaled by the amount prescribed by the alignment stage. Following the transformation, if M_i is indeed the correct model, V and M_i should agree closely, since the source of incongruence (the difference in viewing direction) has already been removed.

The fact that three anchor points are sufficient for alignment is shown in Ullman (1989). Two comments are noteworthy in this regard. First, the alignment stage does not require the extraction of three-dimensional information from the image; the two-dimensional coordinates of the features suffice. Three-dimensional information could be used, when available, to simplify the alignment stage somewhat, but the plocess can proceed in the absence of precise three-dimensional information. Second, the use of feature points is only one possible option; lines or dominant directions associated with the object can also be used for alignment.

Many extensions of this basic scheme are possible. One extension worth mentioning is that the internal object model is not necessarily limited to contour information. More abstract descriptions, "pictorial labels," could be used in addition to the raw contour information. Such a label may describe, for example, local textural properties (e.g., the "bushy" tail of a squirrel). When the image and model are brought into alignment, they can then be compared not only at the precise contour level, but also at a more abstract level. For more details on the use of pictorial descriptions see Ullman (1989).

The Combination of Two-Dimensional Views

In the alignment scheme described above, as well as in most other recognition theories, it has been assumed that the visual system somehow stores and manipulates three-dimensional object models. When confronted with a novel two-dimensional image of the object, the system deduces whether it is a possible view of one of the already stored three-dimensional objects.

In this section I describe an alignment method that does not use explicit three-dimensional models. Instead, it uses directly small collections of two-dimensional images. The new approach has several advantages. First, there is no need in this scheme to explicitly recover and represent the three-dimensional structure of objects. Second, it handles all the rigid three-dimensional transformations, but it is not restricted to such transformations. Third, the processes involved are often simpler than in previous schemes. Fourth, it becomes easier to acquire new object models.

In this approach, a three-dimensional object is represented by the linear combination of two-dimensional images of the object. If $M = M_1, \ldots, M_k$ is the set of pictures representing a given object, and P is the two-dimensional image of an object to be recognized, then P is considered an instance of M if $P = \sum_{i=1}^{k} \alpha_i M_i$ for some constants α_i.

What I mean by a linear combination of views is the following. Suppose that (x_i, y_i), (x_i', y_i'), (x_i'', y_i'') are the coordinates of corresponding points (i.e., points in the image that arise from the same point on the object) in three different views. Let X_1, X_2, X_3, be the vectors of x-coordinates of the points in the three views. Suppose that we are now confronted with a new image, and X' is the vector of the x-coordinates of the points in this new view. If X' arises from the same object represented by the original three views, then it will be possible to express X' as the linear combination of X_1, X_2, X_3. That is, $X' = a_1 X_1 + a_2 X_2 + a_3 X_3$ for some constants a_1, a_2, a_3. Similarly, for the y-coordinates, $Y' = b_1 Y_1 + b_2 Y_2 + b_3 Y_3$ for some constants b_1, b_2, b_3. Note that in general, different coefficients are required for the x and y components. In more pictorial terms, we can imagine that each of the three points x_i, x_i', x_i'' has a mass associated with it. The mass at x_i, x_i', x_i'' is a_1, a_2, a_3, respectively (the same weights are used for all triplets). The linear combination of the points is now their center of mass. The linear combination property is expressed by the following theorem:

Theorem. *All possible views of a rigid object that can undergo rotation in space, translation, and scaling are spanned by the linear combinations of three views of the object.*

The theorem assumes orthographic projection and objects with sharp bounding contours. For objects with smooth bounding contours, the number of views required is five rather than three. (Objects with smooth bounding contours, such as an egg or a football, are more complex because the object's silhouette is not generated by fixed contours on the object. The bounding contours generating the silhouette move continuously on the object as the viewing position changes.) If the object is close to the camera and the perspective effects become large, the space spanned by all the object's views will no longer be linear but will become slightly curved. Algorithms have been developed (e.g., the RBF method mentioned below) to handle these cases, without requiring a strict linear combination. Finally, it should be noted that, due to self-occlusion, three views are insufficient for representing an object from all orientations. That is, a different set of views will be required to represent, for example, the "front" and the "back" of the same object.

Figure 4.5 shows an example of using linear combinations of views to compensate for changes in viewing direction. Figure 4.5a shows three different views of a car (a VW). The figure shows only those edges that were extracted in all three views; as a result, some of the edges are missing. Figure 4.5b shows two new views of the VW car. These new images were not obtained from novel views of the car. They were generated instead by using linear combinations of the first three views. Figure 4.5c shows two new views of the VW, obtained from new viewing positions. Figure 4.5d superimposes these new views and the linear combinations obtained 4.5c. It can be seen that the novel views are matched well by linear combinations of the three original views. For comparison, Figure 4.5e shows the superposition of a different but

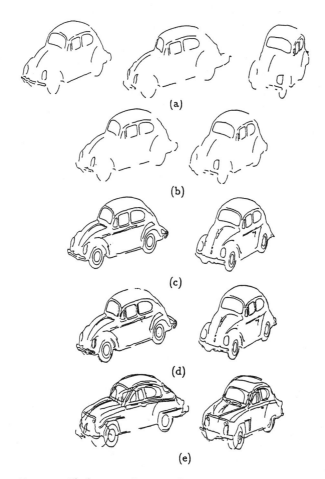

(a)

(b)

(c)

(d)

(e)

Figure 4.5 The linear combination of 2-D views. (a) Three views of a car (VW). Due to technical reasons, only some of the edges are illustrated. (b) Two new views of the VW. These new views were obtained by linear combinations of the views in (a). (c) Two novel views of the VW. (d) Superposition of the images in (c) and the linear combinations in (b). The new views are matched well by linear combinations of the original views. (e) The best matching linear combination to a similar, but different, car (a Saab). The match is less precise, illustrating that the linear combination method can make fine distinctions between similar objects seen from novel viewing positions.

similar car (a Saab), with the best matching linear combinations of the VW images. As expected, the match is not as good. This illustrates that the linear combination method can be used to make fine distinctions between similar three-dimensional objects in novel viewing directions.

Using Combinations of Views for Recognition The preceding section has stated and illustrated the fact that a novel view of a three-dimensional object can be matched by combinations of a small number of two-dimensional images. In this section I consider briefly how this property may be used in a process for three-dimensional object recognition. There are several possible ways in which this can be accomplished. I briefly mention two possible methods. For a more complete discussion see (Ullman and Basri 1989).

The Use of a Linear Mapping The linear combination property can be used to construct a linear operator that maps each view of a given object to a predefined vector, which identifies the object. We assume in this section that a correspondence has been established between the viewed object and the stored model. We then use a linear mapping to test whether the viewed object is a linear combination of the model views.

Suppose that a pattern P is represented by a vector $\mathbf{p}$ of its coordinates (e.g., $(x_1, y_1, x_2, y_2, \ldots, x_n, y_n)$). Let P_1 and P_2 be two different patterns representing the same object. We can now construct a matrix L that maps both $\mathbf{p}_1$ and $\mathbf{p}_2$ to the same output vector $\mathbf{q}$. That is, $L\mathbf{p}_1 = L\mathbf{p}_2 = \mathbf{q}$. Any linear combination $a\mathbf{p}_1 + b\mathbf{p}_2$ will then be mapped to the same output vector $\mathbf{q}$, multiplied by the scalar $a + b$. We can choose, for example, $\mathbf{q} = \mathbf{p}_1$, in which case any view of the object will be mapped by L to a selected "canonical view" of it.

We have seen above that different views of the same object can be expressed as linear combinations $\sum a_i \mathbf{p}_i$ of a small number of representative views, P_i. If the mapping matrix L is constructed in such a manner that $L\mathbf{p}_i = \mathbf{q}$ for all the views P_i in the same model, then any combined view $\hat{\mathbf{p}} = \sum a_i \mathbf{p}_i$, will be mapped by L to the same $\mathbf{q}$ (up to a scale), since $L\hat{\mathbf{p}} = (\sum a_i)\mathbf{q}$.

L can be constructed as follows. Let $\{\mathbf{p}_1, \ldots, \mathbf{p}_k\}$ be k linearly independent vectors representing the model pictures (we can assume that they are all linearly independent since a picture that is not is obviously redundant). Let $\{\mathbf{p}_{k+1}, \ldots, \mathbf{p}_n\}$ be a set of vectors such that $\{\mathbf{p}_1, \ldots, \mathbf{p}_n\}$ are all linearly independent. We define the following matrices:

$P = (\mathbf{p}_1, \ldots, \mathbf{p}_k, \mathbf{p}_{k+1}, \ldots, \mathbf{p}_n)$

$Q = (\mathbf{q}, \ldots, \mathbf{q}, \mathbf{p}_{k+1}, \ldots, \mathbf{p}_n)$.

We require that

$LP = Q$.

Therefore:

$L = QP^{-1}$.

Note that since P is composed of n linearly independent vectors, the inverse matrix P^{-1} exists, therefore L can always be constructed.

By this definition we obtain a matrix L that maps any linear combination of the set of vectors $\{\mathbf{p}_1, \ldots, \mathbf{p}_k\}$ to a scaled pattern $\alpha\mathbf{q}$. Furthermore, it maps any vector orthogonal to $\{\mathbf{p}_1, \ldots, \mathbf{p}_k\}$ to itself. Therefore, if $\hat{\mathbf{p}}$ is a linear combination of $\{\mathbf{p}_1, \ldots, \mathbf{p}_k\}$ with an additional orthogonal noise component, it would be mapped by L to $\mathbf{q}$ combined with the same amount of noise.

In our implementation we have used $L\mathbf{p}_i = 0$ for all the view vectors $\mathbf{p}_i$ of a given object. The reason is that if a new view of the object $\hat{\mathbf{p}}$ is given by $\sum a_i\mathbf{p}_i$ with $\sum a_i = 0$, then $L\hat{\mathbf{p}} = 0$. This means that the linear mapping L may send a legal view to the zero vector, and it is therefore convenient to choose the zero vector as the common output for all the object's views. If it is desirable to obtain at the output level a canonical view of the object such as $\mathbf{p}_1$ rather than the zero vector, then one can use as the final output the vector $\mathbf{p}_1 - L\hat{\mathbf{p}}$.

The decision regarding whether or not $\hat{\mathbf{p}}$ is a view of the object represented by L can be based on comparing $\|L\hat{\mathbf{p}}\|$ with $\|\hat{\mathbf{p}}\|$. If $\hat{\mathbf{p}}$ is indeed a view of the object, then this ratio will be small (exactly 0 in the noise-free condition). If the view is "pure noise" (in the space orthogonal to the span of $(\mathbf{p}_1, \ldots, \mathbf{p}_k)$) than this ratio will be equal to 1.

The description of the linear mapping scheme above outlines the method in its simplest form. A practical implementation will require a number of modifications and extensions (as discussed in Ullman and Basri 1989). The simple scheme demonstrates, however, how compensation for the viewing direction (as well as other transformations) may he achieved by processes that are low-level in nature, operating directly on collections of two-dimensional views.

The Use of Radial Basis Functions (RBF)   An alternative scheme for combining two-dimensional views is the Radial Basis Functions (RBF) method and its extensions described by Poggio and Girosi (1989). The basic idea of the scheme, which will not be reviewed here, is to use again two-dimensional views, and then treat recognition as an approximation problem in the space of possible views. Given a number of two-dimensional views representing a single three-dimensional object, an approximation method is used to interpolate smoothly between the known views. The method used for interpolation is the so-called RBF method. This method interpolates a function between known data points by using a linear superposition of basis functions, centered on the known data points.

This method has the advantage that it is not limited to linear combinations of images; nonlinear combinations are also possible. To take full advantage of the results mentioned above (that the set of views of a given object spans a very low-dimensional subspace in the space of possible views) the basic RBF method should be modified to allow the basis functions to be long and narrow rather than radial (and pointing in different directions in different parts of the space). Such an extended scheme may combine in an optimal manner the desired properties of the two methods, but it will not be considered here further.

The schemes described above leave many problems unanswered. For example: how correspondence between image and model features may be established, the treatment of nonrigid transformations, general object classification as opposed to precise identification, and extending the scheme to deal with a large "library" of internal model.

These problems require considerable more research, both empirical and computational. In considering these problems, it should be emphasized that recognition is probably more than a single process; there may be many and quite different processes used by the visual system to classify and identify visual stimuli. Object recognition may be analogous in this respect to the perception of three-dimensional space: the perception of depth and three-dimensional shape is not a single module but is mediated by a number of interacting processes that utilize various sources of information, such as binocular disparity, motion parallax, surface shading, contour shape, and texture gradients. Similarly, visual object recognition is probably better viewed not as a single module but as a collection of interacting processes.

There is suggestive evidence —for instance, from the impressive ability of simpler animal to perform efficiently visual recognition—that these processes include a powerful component that is low-level and pictorial rather than abstract and symbolic in nature, and the combination of two-dimensional views is a candidate for such a component.

The following points summarize the main conclusions regarding the compensation for viewing direction.

1. In contrast with methods that use three-dimensional object models, the method outlined above use directly small collections of two-dimensional images.

2. The scheme suggests that a particular view of a given two-dimensional object will be represented in the visual system by the combined activity of units, where each unit is tuned in a broad manner to a particular two-dimensional view. This seems to be in general agreement with physiological findings regarding face-selective cells in the primate visual cortex (Perret et al. 1985). These cells usually respond best to a particular two-dimensional view of a face, but the response is broadly tuned and usually covers similar faces as well as the same face from a range of viewing directions.

3. The use of combinations of two-dimensional views in recognition appears more direct and straightforward than do schemes that store and manipulate three-dimensional models, and may be more biologically plausible. The scheme is similar in certain respects to the direct use of an associative memory for two-dimensional patterns, but with a crucial difference. Given an input pattern, the system is not required to have an exact replica of the pattern already stored in memory. Instead, it is trying to establish whether the input pattern can be matched by combinations of small sets of stored patterns. As it turns out, such combinations are sufficient to compensate for the variations induced by changes in viewing direction.

NOTE

I thank my students and collaborators in this work Amnon Shashua and Ronen Basri. S. U. and A. S. were supported in part by NSF grant IRI-8900207.

REFERENCES

Abu-Mostafa, Y. S., and Psaltis, D. (1987). Optical neural computing. *Scientific American, 256,* 66–73.

Biederman, I. (1985). Human image understanding: Recent research and a theory. *Computer Vision, Graphics, and Image Processing, 32,* 29–73.

Bregman, A. S. (1984). Auditory scene analysis. In *Proceedings of the Seventh International Conference on Pattern Recognition,* 168–175. Montreal:

Freeman, W. J. (1979). EEG analysis gives model of neuronal template matching mechanism for sensory search with olfactory bulb. *Biological Cybernetics, 35,* 221–234.

Grimson, W. E. L. (1990). The effect of indexing on the complexity of object recognition. M.I.T. A.I. Memo No. 1226.

Hopfield, J. J. (1982). Neural networks and physical systems with emergent collective computational abilities. *Proc. Nat. Acad. Sci. USA, 79,* 2554–2558.

Julesz, B. (1981). Textons, the elements of texture perception, and their interactions. *Nature, 290,* 91–97.

Kohonen, T. (1978). *Associative Memories. A System Theoretic Approach.* Berlin: Springer-Verlag.

Kundel, H. L., and Nodine, C. F. (1983). A visual concept shapes image perception. *Radiology, 146(2),* 363–368.

Nakayama, K., Shimojo, S., and Silverman, G. H. (1989). Stereoscopic depth: Its relation to image segmentation, grouping, and the recognition of occluded objects. *Perception, 18,* 55–68.

Perret, D. I., Smith, P. A. J., Potter, D. D., Mistlin, A. J., Head, A. S., Milner, A. D., and Reeves, M. A. (1985). Visual cells in the temporal cortex sensitive to face view and gaze direction. *Proc. Roy. Soc., B, 223,* 293–317.

Poggio, T., and Girosi, F. (1989). A theory of networks for approximation and learning. M.I.T. A.I. Memo No. 1140.

Tou, J. T., and Gonzales, R.C. (1974). *Pattern Recognition Principles.* Reading, MA: Addison-Wesley.

Treisman, A., and Gelade, G. (1980). A feature integration theory of attention. *Cog. Psychol., 12,* 97–136.

Ullman, S. (1989). Aligning pictorial descriptions: An approach to object recognition. *Cognition, 32(3),* 193–254.

Ullman, S., and Basri, R. (1989). Recognition by linear combination of models. M.I.T. A.I. Memo No. 1152.

Ullman, S., and Shashua, A. (1988). Structural saliency: The detection of globally salient structures using a locally connected network. M.I.T. A.I. Memo No. 1061.

Willshaw, D. J., Buneman, O. P., and Longuet-Higgins, H. C. (1969). Non-holograhic associative memory. *Nature, 222,* 960–962.

5 Five Hunches about Perceptual Processes and Dynamic Representations

Jennifer J. Freyd

5.1 INTRODUCTION

In everyday encounters with the world we interact with a dynamic environment. Whether hunting game in the Serengeti, fleeing tigers in the Himalayas, traversing the streets of New York, driving on a Los Angeles freeway, dancing the tango, feeding an infant, or cooking dinner with a spouse, a human must coordinate his or her movements with the movements of another moving being.

Most events of consequence, and many more mundane events, involve motor action from the perceiver that is related to action by others. This is true even if the current environment contains no active objects besides the perceiver, for the perceiver may well be planning to act on the environment (by walking through it or by manipulating an object within it). Although it is certainly true that we can sit back passively and perceive events with little direct influence on them, this capacity may well be a by-product of a perception/action system that has evolved to guide adaptive motor actions in the world.

This perspective on perception, that perception is really a perception/action system, has been pushed by others (for instance, Gibson and his followers). I take this perspective too, but I take it in a direction different from Gibson's ecological approach, which postulates direct perception of the affordances of the environment (see Gibson 1979). Along with Shepard (1984), my direction is toward the investigation of perceptual representation. In particular, I theorize that perceptual representations are *dynamic* (Freyd 1987) and that static stimuli invoke dynamic mental representations.

But what is a mental representation? One of my ambitions in this chapter is to suggest an understanding of mental representation that follows from the perspective that human perceivers are especially well suited for interacting with a dynamic environment. In this context I will attempt to break down the structure/process distinction that has dominated cognitive psychology. A second idea I will suggest in this chapter relates to a possible temporal isomorphism between the internal and external worlds. A third goal is to sketch a theory of art perception that follows from my claim that static stimuli point the way to dynamic representations. A fourth aim is to share some ideas about the implications my perspective might have for network models of perceptual processes and representations. My fifth ambition for this chapter is to suggest that although perceptual representations are dynamic, shareable representations (that is, representations that can be readily shared between people) may be more static than dynamic.

Before elaborating on these new hunches, I review briefly some of my empirical and theoretical work on picture perception, representational momentum, and the theory of dynamic mental representations. I then turn to the new ideas. These developments are not yet definitive findings; instead, they are offered as new directions for research.

5.2 REVIEW OF EMPIRICAL AND THEORETICAL RESULTS ON DYNAMIC MENTAL REPRESENTATIONS

I began thinking about dynamic mental representations in the context of two perceptual puzzles: (1) How can readers make sense of handwritten letters and words when there is such variety in the stimulus? (2) How can some static pictures and photographs lead to the phenomenal experience of implied movement?

My answer to question 1 invoked the past: Readers may use handwritten material as a static trace of a dynamic process (Freyd 1983a, 1987; see also Watt 1980). If so, our ability to decode handwritten material may partly depend on our knowledge of how the material was created. Freyd (1983a) demonstrated that knowledge of drawing method influences the recognizability of distorted artificial characters. Babcock and Freyd (1988) found that perceivers are sensitive to information in the static trace that specifies the manner in which a character was drawn. Using actual hand-drawn characters, DeKay and Freyd (in press) showed that drawing method influenced the subsequent discriminability of characters. Zimmer's (1982) results suggest that the relative weight of dynamic versus static information in handwriting recognition varies as a function of legibility and communicative demands. Taken together these findings point to the importance of dynamic information in a perceptual domain that is on the surface static.

My answer to question 2 invoked the future. Consider one sort of static picture that can imply motion—snapshots of objects and creatures captured in the middle of an event. I hypothesized that people might perceive implicit motion when presented with such pictures of "frozen" motion (as in fig. 5.1), where perceiving implicit motion could mean the movement an object would undergo were it to be thawed. These two answers—invoking the past and the future—were united by the idea that some, and perhaps all, perceptual representations include a temporal dimension.

My experimental investigation of question 2 began with a test of the hypothesis that frozen-action photographs might involve the representation of dynamic information (Freyd 1983b). Using pairs of before-and-after pictures taken from action scenes, individual stills were presented to subjects tachistoscopically. The subjects were instructed to look at one picture and hold it in

Figure 5.1 A "frozen-action" photograph that conveys the future of the captured event.

memory, and then to view a second picture and decide as rapidly as possible whether the second frame was "the same as" or "different from" the first. They were shown the pairs in either real order or backward order. Subjects took longer to correctly indicate that the second frame was different when the pair was in real-world temporal order. (The mean response times were 847 ms for real-world and 788 ms for backward correct responses; error rates were higher, but not significantly so, for real-world than for backward test orders.)

Development of the theory of dynamic representations has been heavily influenced by results from studies of *representational momentum*. In our first study on this topic, Finke and I (Freyd and Finke 1984) demonstrated that when a rotation of a visual pattern is implied, an observer's memory for the pattern orientation tends to be displaced forward in the direction of the implied rotation. In a similar, subsequent study (Freyd and Finke 1985), subjects were presented with a static figure in a sequence of orientations sampled from a possible path of rotation (see fig. 5.2). Subjects were instructed to remember the third orientation they saw and were presented with a fourth orientation that was either the same as, or different from, the third. Test orientations were varied parametrically around true-same. We found a generally symmetric unimodal distribution of "same" responses centered not on true-same but on a forward rotation from true-same. That is, subjects showed a shift in memory for position. Effects similar to those found for implied rotational motion (e.g., Cooper et al. 1987; Freyd and Finke 1984, 1985; Freyd and Johnson 1987; Kelly and Freyd 1987; Verfaillie and d'Ydewalle 1991) have

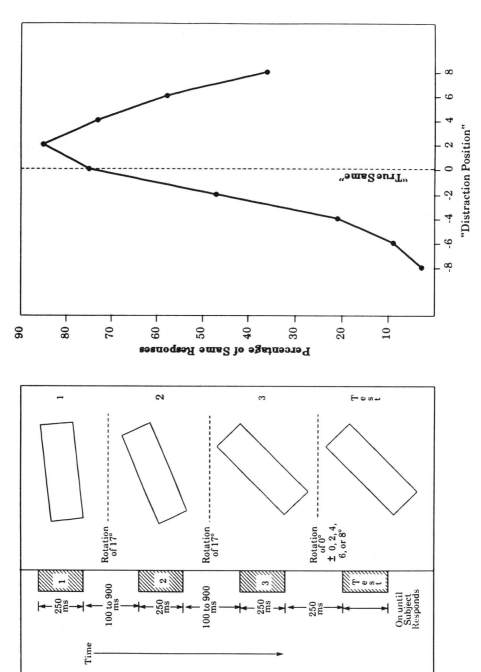

Figure 5.2 Schematic depiction of stimuli and results from a representational momentum experiment (Freyd and Finke 1985).

been discovered for implied translational motion (e.g., Finke and Freyd 1985; Finke, Freyd, and Shyi 1986) and for an implied spiral path (Freyd and Taylor 1990). When the transformation is subjectively continuous (as in animation), the memory displacements may be even bigger (e.g., Faust 1990; Hubbard and Bharucha 1988; Hubbard 1990), although it is difficult to directly evaluate the role of subjective continuity independent from other parameters known to influence the memory shifts such as implied velocity and final stimulus duration (Faust 1990).

Finke and I termed this phenomenon "representational momentum" (Freyd and Finke 1984) because of its similarity to physical momentum, in which a physical object continues along its path of motion through inertia. As with physical momentum, representational momentum is proportional to the implied velocity of motion (e.g., Freyd and Finke 1985; Finke, Freyd, and Shyi 1986), and it also varies with the implied acceleration (and thus implied final velocity) of the pattern (Finke, Freyd, and Shyi 1986). In addition, the amount of memory distortion follows a continuous stopping function for the first 250 ms or so of the retention interval (Freyd and Johnson 1987). Furthermore, these parametric effects have been demonstrated in a nonvisual domain. Using sequences of pitches, Kelly, DeKay, and I (Freyd, Kelly, and DeKay 1990; Kelly and Freyd 1987) replicated the basic phenomenon and showed that it behaved similarly to the visual case with changes in implied velocity, implied acceleration, and retention interval.

Appropriately, representational momentum effects do not obtain under various boundary conditions. When the order of the first two items in the inducing display is reversed, thus disrupting the coherence of the implied transformation, the memory asymmetry disappears (Freyd and Finke 1984; see also Freyd and Johnson 1987; Freyd, Kelly, and DeKay 1990). When the shapes of objects are radically altered from item to item in an implied rotation, momentum effects do not emerge (Kelly and Freyd 1987). And when the inducing display ends with an implied final velocity of zero, the momentum disappears (Finke, Freyd, and Shyi 1986). Similarly, an implied deformation of a rectangle into a perfect square produced no memory asymmetry, suggesting that when the inducing display ends with an item that is prototypical of a category, internal transformations may be halted (Kelly and Freyd 1987).

Although the similarities between physical and representational momentum might be taken as evidence that through natural selection, or the child's interaction with the environment, the human visual system has adaptively acquired rules that mimic physical momentum, I prefer an alternative view (Freyd 1987; see also Finke and Freyd 1989). I understand representational momentum as a necessary characteristic of a representational system with spatiotemporal coherence, just as physical momentum is a property of objects embedded in a spatiotemporal world. I therefore predict representational momentum effects for any dimension affording continuous transformation. From this perspective, representational momentum, rather than being directly adaptive (as in fig. 5.3A), may be a necessary product of the adaptive advan-

(A)

| Physical Momentum | ⟶ | Representational Momentum |

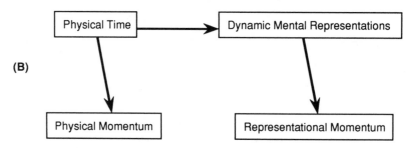

(B)

Figure 5.3 Representational momentum, rather than (A) being directly adaptive, may be (B) a necessary product of the adaptive advantage of anticipatory computations and a more general internalization of time (as suggested in Freyd 1987; Freyd, Kelly, and DeKay 1990).

tage of anticipatory computations and a more general internalization of time (as in fig. 5.3B).

Of relevance to this interpretation of representational momentum is evidence that the phenomenon is apparently not particularly cognitively penetrable. The memory task offers subjects an objective correct answer, and obtaining that correct answer requires that the subjects refrain from transforming the stimuli to be remembered; subjects reliably show the effect despite the demand characteristics. Moreover, despite practice and feedback the effect persists (Freyd and Finke 1985). Recently, Hubbard and Bharucha (1988), Ranney (1989), and Finke and Freyd (1989) debated the extent to which representational momentum is penetrable. Finke and Freyd (1989) propose that while the path of extrapolation may be influenced by contextual factors, the forward memory shifts cannot be eradicated by manipulations of conscious beliefs. We thus argue that representational momentum is relatively impenetrable—that is, subjects cannot instantaneously halt the represented motion no matter what they think or attempt. This points to the inextricability of time in representation.

In a line of investigation related to representational momentum studies I have continued to explore the perception of dynamic information in static pictures (Freyd 1983b; Freyd, Pantzer, and Cheng 1988; Freyd and Pantzer 1989). Freyd, Pantzer, and Cheng (1988) hypothesized that implicit physical forces might be one way pictures depicting stable scenes lead to dynamic representations. We presented subjects with drawings of scenes in equilibrium (e.g., a plant hanging from a hook; a box resting on a spring) followed by a depiction of the same scene suddenly in disequilibrium (the plant minus the hook; the spring minus the box) but without any change in position of the to-be-remembered object (the plant, the spring). Subjects made more memory errors in the direction predicted by the disequilibrium than in the opposite

Figure 5.4 An example of a stable still life conveying physical forces in equilibrium: Photograph of a figurehead from the ship *Centennial*, ca. 1875, wood, painted white (courtesy of The Fine Arts Museums of San Francisco, Museum Collection).

direction (thus the plant was misremembered farther down, the spring farther up). This result suggests that lurking behind the phenomenal sense of concreteness one has when viewing some pictures or scenes (as in figure 5.4) may be an underlying representation of physical forces.

Freyd and Pantzer (1990) recently investigated the dynamics of simple static patterns. Some simple static patterns like arrows can produce a compelling sense of directionality (see fig. 5.5). Even equilateral triangles, which lack a conventional interpretation, appear to point in one particular direction at any one time (Attneave 1968; Palmer 1980). We found memory distortions for arrows and triangles in the direction in which they appeared to point, suggesting that the phenomenal sensation of directionality is based on a dynamic mental representation.

These experiments, investigating the perception of dynamic information in static patterns, plus the studies exploring representational momentum, are the empirical basis for my claim that just as time is a dimension in the external world, inseparable from other physical dimensions, so might time be a dimension in the represented world. I have proposed two criteria for dynamic mental representations (these criteria were suggested in Freyd 1987, but they have

Figure 5.5 Simple static patterns like arrows and triangles may point.

been further developed since then):

1. A dynamic mental representation is one in which the temporal dimension is inextricably embedded in the representation. The representing dimension for time could not be removed from the representation while still preserving a coherent representation. It is mandatory, necessary, and unavoidable.

2. The internal temporal dimension is inherently like external time (at least to a first approximation). For a representation to be dynamic, at least two particular aspects of the temporal dimension in our external world must also be consequences of the inherent structure of the representing dimension.

a. The temporal dimension must be directional; the external time humans confront goes forward.

b. The temporal dimension must be continuous (or as continuous as the mechanics of neural networks permit, which presumably operate at less fine temporal resolution than do potential quantum effects in physical time). Operationally, continuity will mean that between any two points of time, another point of time exists.

Because the continuity criterion is of special relevance to many of the ideas that are discussed in the remainder of this chapter, I will briefly describe the experiment on representational momentum that I think supports this criterion most compellingly. Experiment 1 of Freyd and Johnson (1987) used a standard inducing sequence of three rectangles, each presented ahead of the last by 17 degrees of rotation. As usual, we asked subjects to remember the third position. The test positions were varied parametrically around that third position. Nine retention intervals were used, ranging from 10 to 90 ms in steps of 10 ms. Based on the analogy to an inertial object being stopped, a monotonic relationship was predicted for the relationship between estimated memory shift and retention interval. In fact we found an approximately linear relationship ($r = .98$) between these variables (see fig. 5.6). Other experiments indicate that the memory shift grows for at least the first 200 ms for the standard inducing display using three rectangles.

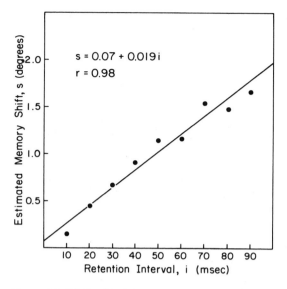

Figure 5.6 Relationship between retention interval (10–90 ms) and memory shift found by Freyd and Johnson (1987).

The strong relationship between memory shift and retention interval may be considered evidence in support of the continuity criterion of dynamic representations. According to this interpretation, our test items constituted probes at 10-ms intervals of the current state of the mental representation. The results indicate that the memory shift increased by minute (fractions of a degree of rotation), but highly predictable, amounts in those small time periods. This finding suggests that Cooper's (1976) probing of mental rotation can be considered in terms of the temporal continuity that it implies (as opposed to the spatial continuity that has been discussed most often). Our results, however, use a much finer gradation of probe times and also are less likely to be influenced by expectations, beliefs, tacit knowledge, or demand characteristics (see Finke and Freyd 1989).

5.3 FIVE HUNCHES

My recent thinking about dynamic representations has suggested to me some new avenues for exploration. For the remainder of this chapter I will turn to five of those new directions.

Hunch 1: Mental representations are a level of analysis.

According to the standard view in cognitive psychology a mental representation is a mental thing—a data structure, as opposed to a mental process (e.g., Anderson 1990, Palmer 1978). Perhaps this definition of representation falls out of the computer metaphor. Whatever its genesis, it has tended to force a notion of representation that is implicitly static. That structure and process models may be formally equivalent is not a new idea (e.g., Anderson 1978);

what is not generally recognized is the extent to which we continue to assume structure/process dualism in theories of mental representation.

One reason to question the structure definition of mental representation is that it seems implausible to suppose that on-line, ongoing computation involves structures that are physically distinct from processes. Indeed, I think the only reason this idea has persisted is that structures have been considered to have some permanence, whereas processes occur in time. Static data structures have some appeal as a description of long-term memory. My struggle with the notion of mental representation, however, is not for the permanent storage of information, but for the active, on-line representation of the external world. The mental representations I want to understand are in the domain of "working" memory, not long-term memory. I do not reject the notion of structure when it refers to the physical architecture of the brain. Instead I reject the idea that active mental representations are separate, static things in the mind.

If mental representations are not static structures, what are they? My proposal is that mental representations are a level of analysis through which we can understand mental mechanisms. But this level of analysis is not trivial; it is crucial, for it allows us to examine the relationship between information in the world and information in the mind. Examining this relationship is the focus of much work in cognitive psychology, whether the phrase "mental representation" gets used or not. In questioning the correspondence between internal and external worlds, investigators have generally focused on two questions: (1) What information is represented?, and (2) How is that information represented (e.g., is continuous information in the world represented discretely in the mind)?

Along with "what" information and "how" we represent it, I propose that we also consider what might be called the "why" questions: why do we represent certain information? What functions of the mind get aided by representing particular sorts of information? My perspective suggests that it is especially important to represent information about the future. Earlier I pointed out that when people interact with the world, they need to be sensitive to real-time change or movement. More than simply to perceive movement, it is highly advantageous to anticipate movement. Even if we are interacting with a static object, for instance when we walk about or start to lift an object, we need to anticipate the effect of our motor movements on the environment. The advantages to anticipating movement suggest that representations of the world might emphasize future time. Yet, classically, time has been a symptom of mental processes, as in chronometric analyses of processes (e.g., Posner 1978; Shepard and Cooper 1982). Thinking of mental representations as a level of analysis of processes allows time to be inextricably part of the structure. With time inside, not outside, the mental representation, the dynamic present and the anticipated future can both be easily represented.

This monist reconceptualization of mental representation, based on a central role for time in the mind, has potential application in a number of areas of cognitive psychology. At a general level, it could facilitate a new sort of interaction between investigators focusing on so-called mental "processes" and those focusing on so-called mental "structures." For instance, we might be able to reconsider theories of attention allocation in terms of the dynamics of mental representation and integrate what is known about aspects of object recognition.

Similarly, seeing mental representations as a level of analysis through which we can understand mental mechanisms may cast new light on a classic debate. Is perception direct and unmediated (e.g., Gibson 1979) or does it instead depend on inferences or mental representations (e.g., Helmholtz [1894] 1971; Shepard 1984)? Whereas we may well still want to debate the extent to which inference is used in perception, a perceiving organism with information about the world has a representation since "representation" refers to the correspondence between information in the world and information in the mind. I would pose the "unconscious inference" question in terms of the knowledge embedded in the representational structure that constrains and shapes the incoming information such that "inferences" are automatically computed given the match between the information coming in and the built-in knowledge. For instance, Shiffrar and Freyd (1990) demonstrated that interpolated paths of apparent motion for views of the human body follow anatomical constraints. I interpret this finding in terms of knowledge built into the visual system that automatically "infers" the plausible path of motion.

The level-of-analysis view of representation, in which time is thus inside of representation, also leads to a reconceptualization of our immediate experience with the world. If anticipatory computations are part of the reality we represent, one might say that the mentally represented world is constantly falling forward in time.

Hunch 2: Time allows an easy isomorphism between the internal and external worlds.

I have suggested that dynamic representations make good sense. It seems highly advantageous to be able to perceive certain events and make anticipatory computations concerning them. Any creature interacting with the physical world would be aided by a dynamic analysis in which the future was represented mentally.

There may be additional advantages to dynamic representations. In particular, time is unlike all other physical dimensions, in that it may be especially well suited for a simple isomorphism between the internal and external worlds—time may represent time. Shepard (1981) distinguished between simple, first-order isomorphisms and second-order isomorphisms in representation. He argued that in certain domains first-order isomorphisms are unlikely: When we represent the color green in the world, our neurons don't turn green. Shepard prefers second-order isomorphisms for domains like color. These isomorphisms are characterized by a correspondence between perceiving the world and representing the world. In the perception of a real-world rotation, for instance, the mind represents the spatial continuity of the rotation. When we imagine a rotation, the mental representation similarly reflects the spatial continuity of physical rotations.

Although early visual processing (in which retinotopic maps are used) may be characterized by a simple isomorphism of spatial dimensions, at least, it is unlikely that later cognitive processing of the world includes many first-order isomorphisms for most real-world dimensions. The dimension of time, however, seems inherently well suited for a simple isomorphism between the internal and external worlds. This is not to say that there may not be scaling factors between event time and represented time, but instead to suggest that a one-to-one correspondence may sometimes exist.

The proposition that mental time is simply isomorphic with external time is consistent with the "continuity" criterion proposed for dynamic representations (Freyd 1987). But whereas in the past I have been careful to leave open the possibility that the mental temporal dimension might be something other than time (yet that shares inherent constraints with time), I now lean toward the proposition that time represents time. Even more than that, I now speculate that time may represent aspects of other dimensions. For instance, the continuity of time may allow us to represent continuity along a variety of continuous dimensions in the world, by avoiding the problem of simultaneously representing an infinite number of values with a finite brain (see Johnson-Laird 1983). Time may also do extra mental work for us by implementing the perceptual phenomenon of directionality, even when the directionality relates to a dimension that is not temporal in the world (Freyd and Pantzer 1989).

Hunch 3: Static art points to dynamic representations.

Arnheim (1974, 1988) and others have argued convincingly that a key component of art appreciation is the excitement generated by configural tension and other sorts of implicit dynamics. Surely many would agree that painters, sculptors, architects, and now photographers have long exploited the power of implied dynamics. Sometimes the implied dynamics is explicit, as in Michelangelo's David or the dancers in figure 5.7.

In other cases the dynamic tension is more abstract, as in Matisse's paintings, the Sydney opera house (see Arnheim 1988), or figure 5.8. Arnheim argues that dynamic tension in abstract works comes from various configural sources of unbalance. Yet another possibility for the source of dynamic tension in abstract forms (such as the patterns in fig. 5.5) is suggested by a new collaboration I have begun with Geoffrey Miller, in which we are investigating cues of animacy in the dynamics of simple displays. Perhaps arrows and triangles can invoke forward memory distortions (as found by Freyd and Pantzer 1990) and the sensation of pointing, by virtue of activating perceptual representations of animate creatures that have a directionality to them. This may relate to adaptive anticipatory computations if it is the case that animals appear to point in a direction in which they are more likely to move.

In addition to abstract and explicit implications of dynamics in static art, I believe that dynamic tension may come from the medium, too, as in Japanese

Figure 5.7 An example of explicit implied dynamics in static art: Photograph of Pavlova and Mordkin in *"Bacchanale Russe,"* 1912, bronze, by Malvina Hoffman (courtesy of The Fine Arts Museums of San Francisco, gift of Alma de Bretteville Spreckels).

calligraphy, or the paintings of Jackson Pollock, both of which may be perceived partly in terms of the creation process (see Freyd 1983a), or in the figure 5.9 where the contrast of light and dark seems to shimmer almost, or the paintings of Mondrian, where there may be a dynamic tension between the surface of the painting with visible brush marks and the cool geometry of the design (see Freyd 1987).

But given this power of implied dynamics in static art, what is the perceptual basis for the aesthetic experience? The experiments using static pictures (Freyd 1983b; Freyd, Pantzer, and Cheng 1988; Freyd and Pantzer 1989) suggest to me an explicit model for aspects of the perception of art. In those experiments, the retention interval used between the static picture to remember and the test item was in the range of 250–500 ms. That fraction of a second was sufficient to produce a memory distortion.

When viewing a static photograph, observers make a sequence of discrete eye movements (saccades). These eye movements are typically also in the range of 250–500 ms. This suggests to me that when the eye lands on a "dynamic" part of the static art (for instance, the top of a Roman column, or a

Figure 5.8 An example of abstractly implied dynamics in static art: *Orange* (Composition with Chessboard) by Vassily Kandinsky, 1923, color lithograph (courtesy of The Fine Arts Museums of San Francisco, gift of Mrs. J. Wolf in memory of Miss Rachael Abel).

tensed muscle in a statue, or a thick brush mark on a painting surface) and then moves again to another location, in between those saccades the memory for the first part of the art might be slightly shifted in the direction of the implied dynamics. When the eye then later returns to the spot of dynamic tension, there would likely be a small discrepancy between the memory for that spot and the immediate perception of the information—and this discrepancy may be a source of aesthetic excitement.

Hunch 4: Temporal continuity in representation depends on asynchrony in neural networks.

The continuity criterion for dynamic mental representations might appear incompatible with the fact that in many cases individual neurons fire discretely (Kandel and Schwartz 1985; cf. Requin, Riehle, and Seal, chap. 30). Although cognitive theories are often held immune to consideration of the details of neural implementation, it seems desirable to attempt to reconcile one's cognitive models with what is known about the brain. My hunch is that temporal continuity is achieved, despite the nature of individual neural firings, through the asynchrony that may exist between neural connections working together in a network.

Figure 5.9 An example of dynamics implied by the medium used in static art: *New York Rooftops*, by Georgia O'Keefe, 1925–1930, charcoal on laid paper (courtesy of The Fine Arts Museums of San Francisco, Achenbach Foundation for Graphic Arts, gift of Mrs. Charlotte Mack).

An underlying continuous system is supported by empirical results in cognition, perception, and motor behavior (Freyd 1987; Shepard and Cooper 1982), and neuroscience (e.g., Georgopoulos et al. 1989; Poggio 1984). At the neural level, a number of interesting phenomena seem to depend on phase differences between the firings of groups of neurons (Freeman 1981; Gerstein 1970; Toyama, Kimura, and Tanaka 1981). At least one neural computational device is known to depend on a kind of orchestrated synaptic asynchrony. Sound localization in the barn owl involves a brain nucleus to which neurons from each ear enter at opposite sides and interdigitate through dendritic connections. The cells in this region then discharge maximally when inputs from the two sides arrive simultaneously (Takahashi 1989). Thus, predictable temporal asynchrony in dendritic transmissions underlies this computational device.

Some current connectionist networks approximate continuity not through asynchrony but through a range of values associated with neural activations that are synchronously and uniformly updated (see Jordan 1986; Smolensky 1988). Discrete time slices and a global clock are computationally convenient. Analysis of distributed processing systems without global clocks is much more difficult than reasoning about synchronous systems (Lamport 1978). Since any continuous process can be modeled discretely without detection depending on the resolution of the measurement instrument, current PDP models might be highly compatible with my continuity criterion if the cycle time of the model is not constrained by biological data. Further, a description of networks that approximates continuous activation updates in discrete time slices may be a good approximation to a formal description of neural networks that assumes discrete firings distributed continuously and stochastically over time. If the activation level of a processing element is reconceptualized as its expected value, for instance, the two models may prove identical under some conditions.

It is likely, nonetheless, that there are subtle differences between these synchronous and asynchronous models; for instance, the probability distribution around the expected value of a processing element may depend on whether we assume discrete but asynchronous firings or continuous activation values. A synchronous firing model makes modeling of phase relationships between neuronal responses awkward. More important, allowing for asynchrony in the firing of individual processing elements permits parsimonious models where information is carried not directly by patterns of activation but by their emergent rhythmic patterns of activity (Shastri and Ajjanagadde 1990). Shastri and Ajjanagadde, in fact, present a model in which asynchrony coupled with phase drift predict bounds on the number of items in short-term memory.

While awaiting more formal investigation of asynchronous PDP systems, connectionist modelers should at least be alert for artifacts caused by the temporal resolution they happen to choose.

Hunch 5: Shareability may constrain dynamic mental representations.

How can humans mentally represent the vast complexity and continuity of the world when necessary for perception and action, and at the same time represent a world simple enough to allow conscious thought and communication? I've already pushed the notion of dynamic mental representations as a way to handle the vast complexity and continuity of the world when necessary for perception and action. But are dynamic representations conducive to information sharing? Are they even available to conscious thought?

Shareability (Freyd 1983c, 1990) is a theory about knowledge structure and mental representation that considers the consequences of the fact that humans depend heavily on the sharing of information. Shareability claims that at least some of the properties we observe in knowledge structures emerge during the sharing process and specifically do not directly reflect inherent constraints on individual minds. This theoretical position is at odds with the viewpoint, dominating most of linguistics and cognitive psychology, that observed structure directly reveals innate or learned constraints of the human mind. Shareability does not deny that ultimately the constraints have their roots in the individual mind, but it claims that there are emergent properties that are qualitatively unique to the process of information sharing.

The shareability constraint that I have been most interested in pursuing further is that shared information becomes more categorical than it is when originally represented in the individual mind. I believe this claim touches on a basic and fundamental problem in psychology: What is the basis of categorization? The accepted position in the field is that the need and the ability to categorize information stem from the individual (e.g., see Pinker and Bloom 1990). Shareability is an alternative position, which claims that in some situations at least, categorization takes place only because information is shared. It occurs because of the greatly reduced channels of information flow between two or more separate minds, in comparison to the representational capacities of the individual mind, combined with the strong pressure to minimize information loss.

Suppose, for instance, that a group of rafters attempt to share information about the properties of currents in a river, for which only some rafters have direct perceptual experience. If each individual's representation of the information includes fine-grained or continuous information about the river currents, there will initially be enormous potential for information distortion when sharing this information over a group of people. However, across time and an increasing number of individuals sharing the information, certain modal values will emerge as anchors within the shared structure (perhaps partly based on mutual knowledge accessed through analogy or metaphor; see Freyd 1983c). The sharing process will thus behave like a discrete filter that is relatively stable across time and space. Similarly, a tacit agreement on a small number of categories along potentially continuous dimensions will minimize increasing information loss. Even without such agreement, shareability predicts that there will be convergence on modal values (Freyd 1990). In other words, the fine-grained or continuous information is traded for stability over time and space.

Shareability predicts that private knowledge is often represented with dimensions that capture the continuous structure of real-world dimensions, but that shared knowledge is constrained by properties that emerge in communication (such as limitations of the communication medium and the pressure to minimize information loss), so that shared knowledge is represented with dimensions in which underlying continua are partitioned into discrete categories. The theory of dynamic mental representations proposes that for perception and related processes, the temporal dimension in the representations does reflect the continuous structure of time in the real world. This proposal, taken together with shareability, predicts that dynamic mental representations are not directly shareable and that, in particular, the continuity of the temporal dimension may be lost in shared knowledge. If we further suppose that our most consciously accessible representations are already in a format appropriate for sharing, this might explain why the hypothesis that representations are dynamic seems at odds with conscious experience.

Although I have argued that the continuity of a temporal dimension is basic to representations serving much of cognitive processing, such as perceptual processing, the continuity property may be limited to only some cognitive modules. It might make sense, for instance, to quantize the temporal dimension in conscious representations, assuming that the representations serving consciousness have evolved to be most shareable (given that we are a social species). It may even be that continuity is limited to the module in which the representation resides; that is, it may be that continuous information is not shareable from module to module within the individual mind. In other words, module-to-module communication might lead to a kind of shareability within the mind (Freyd 1983c).

The possibility that continuity and discrete categories both exist due to the contrast between nonshared and shared mental processing units (whether we consider the units to be individual brains or individual modules within a brain) may shed some light on the mixed empirical evidence on how discrete versus continuous are mental representations. The mixed empirical evidence has fueled many debates, including some current controversy surrounding connectionist versus symbolic models of cognition (e.g., see Pinker and Prince 1988). Perhaps mental representations are continuous within an individual brain or individual brain module, but at larger levels of interaction and analysis, shareability has the effect of partitioning that continuity into discrete categories.

Shareability predicts that analyzable constraints will emerge when knowledge is being shared. It is likely that such constraints would have an effect on dynamic information, for such information is considered continuous, and shareability predicts that underlying continua will be represented as categories. The existence of qualitatively different sorts of mental representations may account for our ability to represent, when necessary for perception and action, a great deal of the complexity and continuity of the real world, and also for our ability to represent the world with sufficient economy and simplicity so that when necessary we can communicate our knowledge about the world.

5.4 CONCLUDING REMARKS

Five new hunches have been proposed based on earlier empirical and theoretical work on dynamic representations. Hunch 1 takes the importance of time in human cognition toward a monistic view of the structure/process dichotomy such that the study of mental representations refers to a level of analysis of mental mechanisms. This level addresses the relationship between information in the mind and information in the world. Hunch 2 proposes that mental time represents time in the world (and the anticipated world).

Hunches 1 and 2 thus pursue the implications dynamic information has for theories of representation at the cognitive level. Hunch 3 is a proposal for a new empirical application of dynamic representations—the perception of motion in art—and a proposal for a cognitive computational model that might underly aspects of aesthetic excitement. Hunch 4 moves "down a level" and considers issues related to the neural basis of dynamic representations. Hunch 5 moves "up a level" by addressing the discrepancy between internal dynamic representations and representations that people share with one another.

Each of these hunches is speculative by nature; it is hoped that at least one hunch is pointing in the right direction.

NOTE

The research reviewed here was supported by NSF Presidential Young Investigator Award BNS-8451356 and NIMH Grant R01-MH39784. The manuscript was prepared while I was supported by a Guggenheim Fellowship and a Research Scientist Development Award from NIMH (K02-MH00780), and while I was a Fellow at the Center for Advanced Study in the Behavioral Sciences (NSF BNS87-00864).

I am indebted to many colleagues for their comments on the work and ideas described here, including Mark Faust, Mike Kelly, Geoffrey Miller, Kathleen Much, Teresa Pantzer, Mike Posner, Jim Stigler, Roger Shepard, and most especially J. Q. Johnson.

REFERENCES

Anderson, J. R. (1978). Arguments concerning representations for mental imagery. *Psychological Review, 85*, 249–277.

Anderson, J. R. (1990). *Cognitive Psychology and Its Implications*. 3d ed. New York: W. H. Freeman and Company.

Arnheim, R. (1974). *Art and Visual Perception*. Rev. ed. Berkeley: University of California Press.

Arnheim, R. (1988). Visual dynamics. *American Scientist, 76*, 585–591.

Attneave, F. (1968). Triangles as ambiguous figures. *American Journal of Psychology, 81*, 447–453.

Babcock, M. K., and Freyd, J. J. (1988). The perception of dynamic information in static handwritten forms. *American Journal of Psychology, 101*, 111–130.

Cooper, L. A. (1976). Demonstration of a mental analog of an external rotation. *Perception & Psychophysics, 19*, 296–302.

Cooper, L. A., Gibson, B. S., Mawafy, L., and Tataryn, D. J. (1987). Mental extrapolation of perceptually-driven spatial transformations. Paper presented at the Twenty-eighth Annual Meeting of the Psychonomic Society, Seattle, WA, November.

DeKay, M. L., and Freyd, J. J. (N.d.). The effects of drawing method on the discriminability of characters. *Visible Language*. In press.

Faust, M. (1990). Representational momentum: A dual process perspective. Ph.D. dissertation, University of Oregon, Eugene, OR.

Finke, R. A., Freyd, J. J. (1985). Transformation of visual memory induced by implied motions of pattern elements. *Journal of Experimental Psychology: Learning, Memory, and Cognition, 11*, 780–794.

Finke, R. A., and Freyd, J. J. (1989). Mental extrapolation and cognitive penetrability: Reply to Ranney, and some other matters. *Journal of Experimental Psychology: General, 118*, 403–408.

Finke, R. A., and Freyd, J. J., Shyi, G. C.-W. (1986). Implied velocity and acceleration induce transformations of visual memory. *Journal of Experimental Psychology: General, 115*, 175–188.

Freeman, W. J. (1981). A physiological basis of perception. In *Perspectives in Biology and Medicine*. Chicago, IL: University of Chicago Press.

Freyd, J. J. (1983a). Representing the dynamics of a static form. *Memory & Cognition, 11*, 342–346.

Freyd, J. J. (1983b). The mental representation of movement when static stimuli are viewed. *Perception & Psychophysics, 33*, 575–581.

Freyd, J. J. (1983c). Shareability: The social psychology of epistemology. *Cognitive Science, 7*, 191–210.

Freyd, J. J. (1987). Dynamic mental representations. *Psychological Review, 94*, 427–438.

Freyd, J. J. (1990). Natural selection or shareability? [A commentary]. *Behavioral and Brain Sciences, 13*, 732–734.

Freyd, J. J., and Finke, R. A. (1984). Representational momentum. *Journal of Experimental Psychology: Learning, Memory, and Cognition, 10*, 126–132.

Freyd, J. J., and Finke, R. A. (1985). A velocity effect for representational momentum. *Bulletin of the Psychonomic Society, 23*, 443–446.

Freyd, J. J., and Johnson, J. Q. (1987). Probing the time course of representational momentum. *Journal of Experimental Psychology: Learning, Memory, and Cognition, 13*, 259–268.

Freyd, J. J., Kelly, M. H., and DeKay, M. (1990). Representational momentum in memory for pitch. *Journal of Experimental Psychology: Learning, Memory, and Cognition, 16*, 1107–1117.

Freyd, J. J., and Pantzer, T. M. (1989). Static patterns moving in the mind. Paper presented at the Inaugural Fred Attneave Lecture, Eugene, OR, May.

Freyd, J. J., Pantzer, T. M., and Cheng, J. L. (1988). Representing statics as forces in equilibrium. *Journal of Experimental Psychology: General, 117*, 395–407.

Freyd, J. J., and Taylor, K. (1990). *Naive physics, representational momentum, and a spiral tube*. Paper delivered at the Thirty-first Annual Meeting of the Psychonomic Society, New Orleans, LA, November.

Georgopoulos, A. P., Lurito, J. T., Petrides, M., Schwartz, A. B., and Massey, J. T. (1989). Mental rotation of the neuronal population vector. *Science, 243*, 234–236.

Gerstein, G. L. (1970). Functional association of neurons: Detection and interpretation. In F. O. Schmitt (Ed.), *The Neurosciences: Second Study Program*. New York: Rockefeller University Press.

Gibson, J. J. (1979). *The Ecological Approach to Visual Perception*. Boston: Houghton Mifflin.

Helmholtz, H. von. ([1894] 1971). The origin and correct interpretation of our sense impressions. In R. Kahl (Ed.), *Selected Writings of Hermann von Helmholtz*, 501–512. Middletown, CT: Wesleyan University Press.

Hubbard, T. L. (1990). Cognitive representations of linear motion: Possible direction and gravity effects in judged displacements. *Memory & Cognition, 18*, 299–309.

Hubbard, T. L., and Bharucha, J. J. (1988). Judged displacement in apparent vertical and horizontal motion. *Perception & Psychophysics, 44*, 211–221.

Johnson-Laird, P. N. (1983). *Mental Models*. Cambridge, MA: Harvard University Press.

Jordan, M. I. (1986). Serial order: A parallel distributed processing approach. ICS technical report 8604, Institute for Cognitive Science, UCSD, San Diego.

Kandel, E. R., and Schwartz, J. H., Eds. (1985). *Principles of Neural Science*. 2d ed. New York: Elsevier.

Kelly, M. H., and Freyd, J. J. (1987). Explorations of representational momentum. *Cognitive Psychology, 19*, 369–401.

Lamport, L. (1978). Time, clocks and the ordering of events in a distributed system. *Communications of the ACM, 21,* 558–565.

Palmer, S. E. (1978). Fundamental aspects of cognitive representation. In E. Rosch and B. B. Lloyd (Eds.), *Cognition and Categorization,* 259–303. Hillsdale, NJ: Erlbaum.

Palmer, S. E. (1980). What makes triangles point: Local and global effects in configurations of ambiguous triangles. *Cognitive Psychology, 12,* 285–305.

Pinker, S., and Bloom, P. (1990). Natural language and natural selection. *Behavioral and Brain Sciences, 13,* 707–784.

Pinker, S., and Prince, A. (1988). On language and connectionism: Analysis of a Parallel Distributed Processing model of language acquisition. *Cognition, 28,* 73–193.

Poggio, T. (1984). Vision by man and machine. *Scientific American, 250 (4),* 106–115.

Posner, M. (1978). *Chronometric Explorations of Mind.* Hillsdale, NJ: Erlbaum.

Ranney, M. (1989). Internally represented forces may be cognitively penetrable: Comment on Freyd, Pantzer, and Cheng. *Journal of Experimental Psychology: General, 118,* 399–402.

Shastri, L., and Ajjanagadde, V. (1990). From simple associations to systematic reasoning: A connectionist representation of rules, variables and dynamic bindings. Technical report MC-CIS-90-05, LINC Lab 162, Computer and Information Science Department, University of Pennsylvania.

Shepard, R. N. (1981). Psychophysical complementarity. In M. Kubovy and J. R. Pomerantz (Eds.), *Perceptual Organization,* 279–341. Hillsdale, NJ: Erlbaum.

Shepard, R. N. (1984). Ecological constraints on internal representation: Resonant kinematics of perceiving, imagining, thinking, and dreaming. *Psychological Review, 91,* 417–447.

Shepard, R. N., and Cooper, L. A. (1982). *Mental Images and Their Transformations.* Cambridge, MA: MIT Press/Bradford Books.

Shiffrar, M., and Freyd, J. J. (1990). Apparent motion of the human body. *Psychological Science, 1,* 257–264.

Smolensky, P. (1988). On the proper treatment of connectionism. *Behavioral and Brain Sciences, 11,* 1–74.

Takahashi, T. T. (1989). The neural coding of auditory space. *Journal of Experimental Biology, 146,* 307–322.

Toyama, K., Kimura, M., and Tanaka, T. (1981). Cross correlation analysis of interneuronal connectivity in cat visual cortex. *Journal of Neurophysiology, 46,* 191–201.

Verfaillie, K., and d'Ydewalle, G. (1991). Representational momentum and event course anticipation in the perception of implied periodical motions. *Journal of Experimental Psychology: Learning, Memory, and Cognition, 17,* 302–313.

Watt, W. C. (1980). What is the proper characterization of the alphabet? II: Composition. *Ars Semeiotica, 3,* 3–46.

Zimmer, A. (1982). Do we see what makes our script characteristic or do we only feel it? Modes of sensory control in handwriting. *Psychological Research, 44,* 165–174.

6 Perceiving an Integrated Visual World

David E. Irwin

6.1 INTRODUCTION

When we scan the environment, view pictures, or read, our eyes move rapidly from point to point in space several times each second. These rapid eye movements, or *saccades*, are separated by brief time periods called *fixations* during which the eyes are relatively still. Eye movements occur because the visual world contains more information than can be perceived in a single fixation; they allow us to orient our high-resolution foveal vision on objects of interest in the environment so that we can make out their fine detail. Saccades and fixations occur very frequently; based on the conservative assumption that saccadic movements are executed on average twice each second, the typical viewer makes well over 100,000 saccades each day.

This method of information acquisition from the environment produces several problems for human perception. One problem is that during a saccade visual stimulation sweeps across the retinas at velocities of several hundred degrees per second, producing a blur or smear. Ordinarily we don't perceive this blur, nor do we perceive the world whizzing by when the eye is in motion. This blanking of vision during saccades is called *saccadic suppression*, and it appears to be due primarily to visual masking—the clear, bright fixations that precede and follow the saccade mask the perception of the low-contrast retinal blur that is present during the eyes' movement (Campbell and Wurtz 1978). Because of saccadic suppression, we acquire visual information from the world only during fixations, when the eyes are still. Consequently, our visual information about the world is registered in isolated glimpses that are separated in time. Furthermore, the contents of these isolated glimpses are not identical; the retinal positions of objects in the world change from one fixation to the next, so that an object in the periphery during one fixation may suddenly appear at the fovea during the next. Despite this rapidly changing and temporally discontinuous visual input, we ordinarily perceive the world as unified, stable, and continuous, with objects maintaining their positions in space. For over a century psychologists have wondered about the processes that underlie this quality of perception. The most common hypothesis is that somehow the contents of successive fixations are combined, or integrated, across eye movements in such a way as to produce a coherent representation of the visual environment. This chapter summarizes what is known about information integration across eye movements and how this integration relates to the perception of a stable and continuous visual environment across changes in eye position.

The plan of the chapter is as follows. First, the hypothesis that perceptual stability results from the integration of successive "snapshots" of individual fixations is considered. Experimental evidence indicates that this hypothesis is incorrect. The later sections of the chapter summarize what is known about the kinds of information that are integrated across saccades, what these findings reveal about the mechanisms underlying integration, and what the implications of this evidence are for understanding the perception of a stable and continuous visual environment.

The Spatiotopic Fusion Hypothesis

Helmholtz ([1867] 1925) was among the first to note that objects in the world appear to maintain a constant direction with respect to the viewer even though their positions on the retina change when the eyes move. This phenomenon, usually called *visual direction constancy*, suggests that humans are somehow able to attend to, or to compute, the environmental or spatial (as opposed to retinal) coordinates of objects in the world. For example, the egocentric direction of an object with respect to the head could be determined on the basis of the position of the object on the retina and the position of the eyes in the head. The classic idea of how retinal information is transformed into spatial coordinates is that of cancellation theory, which claims that changes in the retinal position of an image are canceled by the corresponding change in eye position (e.g., Holst and Mittelstaedt [1950] 1971). According to this theory, whenever the eyes move a copy of the motor signals sent to the eyes is also sent to a comparator that matches the motor information against the retinal image motion generated by the eyes' movement; because these two sources of information match, the spatial locations of objects in the world appear constant. Although the details of the matching process used in cancellation are rather vague (e.g., what is the format of the two sources of information that permits them to be compared?), one possibility is that the contents of the previous fixation are mentally "shifted" to compensate for the eye movement, then superimposed with the contents of the new fixation to yield a stable, integrated, composite representation of the visual environment. This hypothesis, which I'll call the *spatiotopic fusion hypothesis*, holds that the visible contents of successive fixations are spatially reconciled across changes in eye position and superimposed according to environmental coordinates at an early stage of perceptual processing. Several investigators have proposed that spatiotopic fusion may be the mechanism by which visual information is integrated across saccades (e.g., Banks 1983; Breitmeyer, Kropfl, and Julesz 1982; Breitmeyer 1984; Jonides, Irwin, and Yantis 1982; McConkie and Rayner 1976; Trehub 1977). The first clear statement of this hypothesis was formulated by McConkie and Rayner (1976), who suggested that while a new fixation overrides, or masks, the retinal activity pattern of the prior fixation, at another level in the perceptual system (in what they called the *integrative visual buffer*) the contents of the two fixations are spatially integrated into a single representation of the stimulus. Note that the spatiotopic fusion hypothesis implicitly assumes that integration across eye movements and perceptual stability are intimately linked: Successive visual snapshots comprise the information combined across saccades, and the outcome of this combination is a unified and stable percept of the visual environment.

The view that the contents of successive fixations are integrated in memory according to their environmental coordinates to yield a unified representation of the visual environment is intuitively appealing; it explains in a simple and satisfying way why the world looks stable and continuous across eye movements. The empirical evidence regarding this hypothesis is less than compelling, however; this evidence is reviewed next.

6.2   DOES SPATIOTOPIC FUSION OCCUR ACROSS SACCADES?

In order to determine whether the contents of successive fixations are spatially superimposed to form a composite representation of the visual environment, an experimental task must satisfy at least two criteria. First, successful performance of the task must require the combination or interaction of information viewed in separate fixations; if the task can be performed solely on the basis of information obtained in a single fixation, it has little relevance for transsaccadic integration. I will refer to this as the *fixation interaction* criterion. Second, accurate performance of the task must depend upon spatial overlap across successive fixations; that is, performance should be disrupted if the target changes its position during the saccade, or at the very least such changes should be detectable. If the contents of successive fixations are aligned according to their spatial coordinates and integrated across eye movements, then displacing one of the stimuli during the saccade should cause misalignment and disrupt the integration process. This criterion will be referred to as the *spatial overlap* criterion. Although several investigations conducted over the last twenty years appeared at one time to provide support for the spatiotopic fusion hypothesis, subsequent research or analysis has shown that they failed to satisfy at least one of these two criteria. In addition, there exists substantial evidence against the hypothesis that spatiotopic fusion occurs across saccades. These results point to the conclusion that the contents of successive fixations are not spatially superimposed across eye movements to form a composite representation of the visual environment. The evidence leading to this conclusion is summarized below.

Davidson, Fox, and Dick (1973). One of the earliest demonstrations that seemed to support the existence of spatiotopic integration across saccades was provided by Davidson, Fox, and Dick (1973). In their experiment, subjects made saccades back and forth between two fixation points. Shortly before the onset of a given saccade, a horizontal string of five letters was briefly presented; these letters were so arranged that the second letter of the string

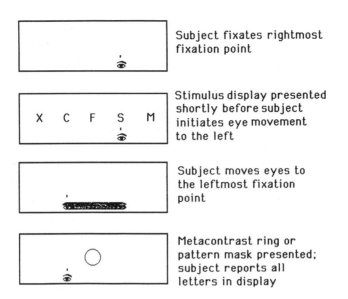

Figure 6.1 Schematic illustration of the procedure in the Davidson, Fox, and Dick (1973) experiment.

was directly above one fixation point and the fourth letter of the string was directly above the other (see fig. 6.1). Following the completion of the saccade, a mask or metacontrast ring was presented at one of the five letter locations and the subject attempted to report all five letters in the display. The question of interest was whether the mask would interfere with the perception of the letter that had been presented at the same spatial position as the mask, or with the perception of the letter whose retinal coordinates were stimulated by the mask. For example, if the subject made an eye movement to the left (from the point under the fourth letter to the point under the second letter) and the mask was presented where the third letter had been, would report of the third letter be inhibited (same spatial coordinates) or would report of the fifth letter be inhibited (same retinal coordinates)? Davidson, Fox, and Dick found that the mask interfered with report of the letter that had the same retinal coordinates as the mask, but subjects reported that they "saw" the mask in its correct spatial position. For the situation described above (and depicted in fig. 6.1), for example, report of the fifth letter was inhibited, but subjects reported that the mask appeared to occupy the same location as the third letter. This experiment thus appears to be consistent with the spatiotopic fusion hypothesis as described by McConkie and Rayner (1976): Masking occurred at a retinotopic level, but integration of the pre- and postsaccadic displays occurred at a spatiotopic level.

Van der Heijden, Bridgeman, and Mewhort (1986) criticized the Davidson, Fox, and Dick experiments on several methodological grounds, chief among which was that subjects' accurate report of the spatial location of the mask could have been based on information present in the second fixation only, such as the fixation point; in other words, spatiotopic fusion is not required to explain the apparent dissociation between the effective locus of the mask and its apparent spatial position, in violation of the fixation interaction criterion.

Irwin, Brown, and Sun (1988) reexamined the Davidson, Fox, and Dick (1973) experiments in an attempt to provide a more objective test of the spatiotopic fusion hypothesis. Using a procedure very similar to that of Davidson, Fox, and Dick, Irwin and colleagues also found that a mask presented after a saccade interfered with the report of a letter that shared the same retinal coordinates as the mask. The mask appeared to be superimposed over the letter whose report was inhibited, however; there was no dissociation between the effective locus of the mask and its apparent spatial position. In order to investigate integration more directly, Irwin, Brown, and Sun conducted a second experiment in which a bar marker, instead of a mask, was presented after the saccade and subjects were instructed to report the identity of the letter that appeared underneath the bar. If integration across saccades occurs on the basis of shared spatial coordinates, subjects should have reported the letter that occupied the same *spatial position* as the bar marker. Using timing conditions similar to those used by Davidson, Fox, and Dick, however, Irwin and colleagues found that subjects reported the letter that had the same *retinal coordinates* as the bar marker, providing evidence for retinotopic integration across saccades. In an effort to determine why results different from those of Davidson, Fox, and Dick were obtained, Irwin, Brown, and Sun conducted a third experiment in which a postsaccadic bar marker was presented over one of the presaccadic letter positions, but in addition a visual landmark was presented after the saccade so that subjects could localize the bar's spatial position. Under these conditions, subjects still reported that the letter that shared the same retinal coordinates as the bar marker appeared to be underneath it, but they were also able to accurately specify the bar's spatial position. Thus, this experiment demonstrated that subjects could apparently "dissociate" retinotopic and spatiotopic information across an eye movement, but, consistent with the conjecture of Van der Heijden, Bridgeman, and Mewhort (1986) subjects' ability to report the spatial location of the bar marker was in fact based on retinal information (the visual landmark) present in the second fixation only, rather than on spatiotopic fusion. Because visual landmarks were present in the Davidson, Fox, and Dick experiment, their results can be explained solely in retinotopic terms; based on the criterion that integration performance must involve the interaction of successive fixations, the Davidson, Fox, and Dick experiment provides no convincing support for the spatiotopic fusion hypothesis.

Ritter (1976). Another study often cited as favoring the spatiotopic fusion hypothesis was conducted by Ritter (1976). In Ritter's experiment a patch of light was briefly presented in the visual periphery just before the onset of a saccade, and then it was presented again sometime after the saccade had ended. The two light flashes were presented at the same spatial location, but they stimulated different retinal locations because of the eye movement. The subjects' task was to report whether they saw one light flash or two. The two light flashes were seen as a single flash when the interval separating them was less than about 75 ms; at longer intervals, two separate flashes were seen. This result suggests the existence of a briefly lasting memory that summates visual information from successive fixations according to its spatial, rather than retinal, coordinates, consistent with the spatiotopic fusion hypothesis. An alternative explanation, however, is that the offset of the light was simply not detected during the critical 75-ms interval because of saccadic suppression, which occurs not only during a saccade but for some time before and after it as well (Latour 1962; Volkmann, Schick, and Riggs 1968). Thus, Ritter's research does not satisfy the fixation interaction criterion. Ritter attempted to rule out saccadic suppression as an explanation by conducting a control experiment in which subjects had to detect whether a light changed its position during a saccade. However, the detection of light displacement during a saccade is different from the detection of light offset. The control is therefore irrelevant. To elaborate, several investigators have demonstrated that stimulus displacements during a saccade can be detected only if the magnitude of the displacement is large—approximately 10–30 percent of the saccade's extent (e.g., Bridgeman, Hendry, and Stark 1975; Mack 1970; Whipple and Wallach 1978). In Ritter's control experiment, the stimulus was displaced by 50 percent of the saccade's extent. These displacements were easily detected, but smaller displacements would not have been; had Ritter used smaller displacements in his control condition, he would have concluded correctly that his "integration" results could be explained in terms of saccadic suppression. Of course, the fact that stimulus displacements during a saccade are frequently undetectable is itself inconsistent with the spatiotopic fusion hypothesis, because it violates the spatial overlap criterion.

Wolf, Hauske, and Lupp (1978, 1980). Wolf, Hauske, and Lupp (1978, 1980) reported results quite similar to those of Ritter (1976). Wolf, Hauske, and Lupp (1978) had subjects discriminate between gratings that varied in spatial frequency following a saccade to a target location. They found that the threshold for a 3.2 cycle/degree (cpd) grating decreased if a suprathreshold "priming" grating of the same spatial frequency was presented at the same spatial location before the saccade. This finding suggests a position-specific summation of visual information across saccades, consistent with the spatiotopic fusion hypothesis. Wolf, Hauske, and Lupp (1980) replicated this result and showed further that misaligning the prime and the target in the range of 0–180 degrees of phase led to a decrease in performance that was monotonic with the phase shift; this finding is consistent with the spatial overlap criterion. These two studies thus seemed to provide support for a visual memory capable of summating information from successive fixations based on their spatial coordinates.

However, the results of Wolf, Hauske, and Lupp (1978, 1980) were recently reexamined by Irwin, Zacks, and Brown (1990), who identified three potential problems with Wolf, Hauske, and Lupp's experimental procedure that called their results into question. First, the phosphor used by Wolf and his colleagues (P31) decays relatively slowly, so that it is possible that their results were due to phosphor persistence on their display rather than to visual persistence in memory; this would violate the fixation interaction criterion. Second, not all of the Wolf, Hauske, and Lupp experiments used forced-choice methods for establishing threshold values, so that their finding of threshold decreases under spatial priming conditions may have been due to criterion shifts, rather than to changes in sensitivity. Finally, there was substantial retinal overlap between the pre- and postsaccadic displays in some of the Wolf, Hauske, and Lupp experiments; for example, in Wolf, Hauske, and Lupp (1978) the presaccadic fixation point was 2 degree to the left of the prime/target area that subtended 8 degree of visual angle. If subjects saccaded to the center of this area, the leftmost 2 degree of the prime would overlap on the retina with the rightmost 2 degree of the target; consequently, the integration found in these experiments may have been retinotopic, rather than spatiotopic, in origin.

Given these possible problems, Irwin, Zacks, and Brown (1990) attempted to replicate the Wolf, Hauske, and Lupp (1978, 1980) findings using a similar, but improved, procedure. In order to eliminate concerns about criterion shifts, Irwin, Zacks, and Brown employed a forced-choice procedure for estimating thresholds. In order to to ensure that any integration that they found was spatiotopic rather than retinotopic in origin, Irwin and his colleagues used a relatively small prime/target area far enough away from the presaccadic fixation point to eliminate any retinal overlap between the presaccadic prime and the postsaccadic target. In order to eliminate the artifactual effects of phosphor persistence, Irwin, Zacks, and Brown presented the prime and the target on separate parts of a display that subjects viewed through an optical system consisting of electromechanical shutters, prisms, and a beam-splitter. The prime was visible only when one shutter was open, and the target was visible only when a different shutter was open. When the shutters were closed, the prime and the target (and any phosphor persistence) were blocked from view. The prisms and the beam-splitter were used to optically combine the prime and target images so that they appeared to occupy the same spatial position. Under these experimental conditions, Irwin, Zacks, and Brown found no evidence for spatiotopic interaction across saccades: The threshold for detecting a target grating presented after a saccade was unaffected by presenting a grating with the same spatial frequency in the same spatial location before the saccade. These results suggest that the findings of Wolf, Hauske, and Lupp were due to some factors other than spatiotopic integration across eye movements.

Jonides, Irwin, and Yantis (1982) and Breitmeyer, Kropfl, and Julesz (1982). Two additional studies once thought to be supportive of the spatiotopic fusion hypothesis were reported by Jonides, Irwin, and Yantis (1982) and by Breitmeyer, Kropfl, and Julesz (1982). These two studies used very similar experimental procedures and yielded similar results. In the Jonides, Irwin, and Yantis study, subjects were presented with twenty-four of the twenty-five dots in a 5 × 5 dot matrix in two separate visual time frames; there were twelve dots per frame (see fig. 6.2). The two frames were presented in the same spatial region of the display, but the subject saw one frame during one fixation (peripherally) and the second frame only after a saccade had been made to the

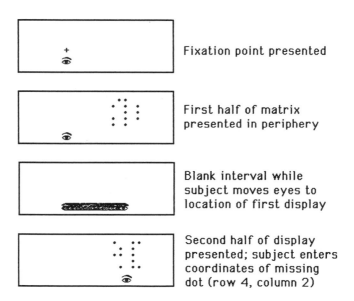

Fixation point presented

First half of matrix presented in periphery

Blank interval while subject moves eyes to location of first display

Second half of display presented; subject enters coordinates of missing dot (row 4, column 2)

Figure 6.2 Schematic illustration of the procedure in the Jonides, Irwin, and Yantis (1982) experiment.

second display location. The subjects' task was to identify the location, in the 5×5 matrix, of the missing dot (i.e., the location in which no dot had been presented). Thus, this task required subjects to integrate the two frames of dots according to their spatial coordinates. In order to assess subjects' performance during the integration task, a no-saccade control condition, which mimicked the retinal layout of the saccade condition but in which the two frames did not overlap spatially, was also conducted. In this control, the first frame was presented in the periphery and the second frame was presented at the fovea while the subject maintained fixation at the original fixation point. Jonides, Irwin, and Yantis found that accuracy in the saccade condition was nearly ten times higher than accuracy in the control condition, even though the information at the retina in the two conditions was roughly identical. Breitmeyer, Kropfl, and Julesz used a 6×6 matrix, and presented twenty-eight elements in the first frame and seven or eight elements in the second frame. The subject's task was to report whether the 6×6 matrix had been completely filled or not by the combination of dots in the two frames. The only condition in which accuracy was above chance was one in which the first frame appeared in the periphery and the second frame appeared at the same spatial location following a saccade, as in the Jonides, Irwin, and Yantis study. Thus, both of these studies suggest that information in two displays having the same spatial coordinates can be integrated into a spatially reconciled form across eye movements. This would be consistent with the spatiotopic fusion hypothesis.

Unfortunately, the highly accurate performance reported by Jonides, Irwin, and Yantis (1982) in their saccade condition appears to have been due to the persistence of the phosphor on the display scope that they used, rather than to persistence in memory. These investigators found that when filters were placed over the display in order to reduce the visibility of the decaying phosphor trace, or when fast-decaying, light-emitting diodes were used for stimulus presentation, integration accuracy in the saccade condition fell to the level of performance found in the no-saccade control condition (Irwin, Yantis, and Jonides 1983; Jonides, Irwin, and Yantis 1983). In other words, when phosphor persistence was eliminated, all evidence in favor of spatiotopic fusion vanished. Breitmeyer, Kropfl, and Julesz (1982) used the same phosphor as Jonides, Irwin, and Yantis did, so that it is possible that the former's results were also caused by phosphor persistence. An additional weakness of the Breitmeyer, Kropfl, and Julesz experiment is that eye position was not monitored. The duration of the first frame in the Breitmeyer, Kropfl, and Julesz study was set at 200 ms, and the interstimulus interval was set at 40 ms. Given these values, it is entirely possible (and quite likely) that a subject would have initiated and completed a saccade before frame 1 had ended. If this in fact happened, then the subject would have viewed both frames within the same fixation, thus violating the fixation interaction criterion. Furthermore, Di Lollo (1977, 1980) has shown that integration accuracy can be very high under these conditions. The original Jonides, Irwin, and Yantis (1982) findings have been the subject of a number of unsuccessful replication attempts, in which a range of stimuli, exposure durations, and interstimulus intervals have been used (Bridgeman and Mayer 1983; Irwin, Brown, and Sun 1988; O'Regan and Levy-Schoen 1983; Rayner and Pollatsek 1983). Although an exhaustive parametric variation of duration and interstimulus interval has not been conducted, it would appear, based on the existing studies, that people simply cannot mentally superimpose different visual patterns viewed in successive fixations and produce a percept of an integrated composite pattern.

Failures to find evidence for spatiotopic fusion across saccades. Additional negative evidence regarding the spatiotopic fusion hypothesis has been provided by experiments examining transsaccadic integration during reading and picture viewing. Several investigations have demonstrated that changing the visual characteristics of words and pictures (such as letter case and object size), or their spatial positions, during an eye movement has little or no disruptive effect on reading, word naming, or picture naming (e.g., McConkie and Zola 1979; McConkie et al. 1982; O'Regan 1981; Pollatsek, Rayner, and Collins 1984; Pollatsek, Rayner, and Henderson 1990; Rayner, McConkie, and Zola 1980). For example, McConkie and Zola (1979) monitored the subjects' eye position while they were reading text composed of alternating-case letters (e.g., "ThE dOg BaRkEd"). Changing the case of the letters during a saccade (e.g., to "tHe DoG bArKeD") had no perceptible effect on the subjects' eye movements, and subjects also failed to notice that any changes had occurred. If information integration across saccades relies on precise spatial reconciliation and superposition of visual information in memory, then, based on the spatial overlap criterion, one would expect such stimulus changes to be extremely disruptive.

6.3 INTERIM SUMMARY

There does not appear to be any convincing experimental evidence that satisfies the two criteria that have been proposed for demonstrating the existence of spatiotopic fusion across saccades. This, plus the substantial negative evidence that has been cited, leads to the conclusion that the perception of a stable and continuous visual environment across eye movements does not depend upon a low-level, spatial superposition of the visible contents of successive fixations in a specialized transsaccadic memory buffer. Despite the intuitive appeal of the spatiotopic fusion hypothesis, it appears to be wrong.

What Is Integrated across Saccades?

Given the demise of the spatiotopic fusion hypothesis, the two fundamental questions remain: Why does the world look stable and continuous across changes in eye position, and what kinds of information are integrated across eye movements and stored in one's mental representation of a scene? It should be noted that these are logically separate questions—that is, the mechanisms underlying our perception of a stable world need not be the same as those underlying the integration of information across eye movements. As noted earlier, the spatiotopic fusion hypothesis assumes, implicitly, that perceptual stability results from the combination of visual snapshots of successive fixations. However, as we have just seen, spatiotopic fusion appears to be nonexistent. It may, therefore, be useful to address the questions of information integration and perceptual stability across saccades separately. This section considers the first issue: What kinds of information are integrated across eye movements?

6.4 EVIDENCE FROM READING

The considerable research on integration across saccades during reading has recently been reviewed by Pollatsek and Rayner (in press) and will only be summarized briefly here. The main paradigm used in this research is called the *parafoveal preview* technique. In this paradigm, subjects are presented with a string of letters (the preview) in the parafovea (i.e., just outside the fovea, approximately 1–5 degrees from the fixation point). When a saccade is initiated to the preview's spatial location, the letter string is removed and replaced by another letter string that the subject names (or, in some experiments, categorizes as a word/nonword or as a member of some semantic category). The question of interest is: What are the characteristics of the parafoveal presaccadic preview that facilitate the recognition of the postsaccadic target string? These characteristics are assumed to have been extracted from the presaccadic stimulus and integrated with the postsaccadic stimulus during its processing.

One of the first and most important studies of this type was conducted by Rayner, McConkie, and Zola (1980), who found that a parafoveal preview produced significant facilitation for the naming of a postsaccadic target when the preview and the target were the same word. The benefit of the preview did not depend on the existence of physical identity between the preview and the target; the same amount of facilitation was found whether the preview and the target were presented in the same case or not (e.g., truck vs. TRUCK). Furthermore, almost as much facilitation was found when only the first two or three letters of the preview matched the target (e.g., TRAIN-TRASH) as when the whole words matched. However, when the preview and the target shared the first phoneme but had different first letters (e.g., ROUGH as the preview and WRITE as the target), no facilitation was obtained, which implies that the benefit of the preview was based on something other than a phonemic code. Based on these results, Rayner, McConkie, and Zola concluded that some abstract identity code for the first two or three letters in the parafoveal preview was extracted during the first fixation, and then integrated with information about the postsaccadic target when the latter was presented.

Subsequent research by these and other investigators has, for the most part, supported this conclusion (Pollatsek and Rayner, in press), except for a recent report by Pollatsek et al. (1992) which suggests that, under some circumstances, a phonemic code may provide a preview benefit. These investigators found that a parafoveal preview that was a homophone of the postsaccadic target (e.g., CITE-SITE) produced more facilitation than did a parafoveal preview that was visually similar to the target but was not homophonous with it (e.g., CAKE-SAKE). There appears to be no conclusive evidence supporting the idea that semantic or morphemic information is extracted from a parafoveal preview (Balota and Rayner 1990; Pollatsek and Rayner, in press).

A possible source of controversy is the question of whether preview benefits only occur when words are presented in isolation, as in the studies reported above, or whether they also occur during reading of continuous text. For example, McConkie et al. (1982) found that when the initial letter of a word in a text was changed (e.g., changing *w*eedy, to *s*eedy) across successive fixations, the durations of fixations on that word were not significantly different from those found when the inititial letter of the word was not changed. Balota, Pollatsek, and Rayner (1985) argued that this null effect was due to a lack of statistical power, and to the use of low-frequency target stimuli that were relatively unconstrained by the preceding sentence context. When these problems were remedied, Balota, Pollatsek, and Rayner (1985) found a significant effect of parafoveal orthographic priming in the reading of continuous text.

6.5   EVIDENCE FROM PICTURE PERCEPTION

In addition to studies of transsaccadic integration during reading, several experiments have examined the integration of pictorial information across fixations. Pollatsek, Rayner, and Collins (1984) investigated this issue using a paradigm very similar to that used in the reading studies described above. A simple line drawing of an object was presented in the visual periphery (i.e.,

5–10 degrees from the fixation point); when the subject initiated a saccade toward this stimulus, it was removed and replaced with a stimulus that the subject named as quickly as possible. A large benefit in naming time was found when the presaccadic and postsaccadic stimuli were the same drawing. This was true even when the two stimuli were not physically identical—making one of the stimuli 10 percent larger than the other did not influence the preview benefit. This result rules out a spatiotopic fusion explanation for these findings. Two other results indicate that some visual aspects of the presaccadic stimulus were important for integration, however. First, when different pictures of the same concept (e.g., two different pictures of a dog) were used as preview and target, less facilitation was found than when the preview and target were identical. Second, visual (i.e., physical) similarity between the preview and the target was found to shorten the naming time for the target even when the preview and the target represented different concepts; for example, the peripheral presentation of a drawing of a carrot facilitated naming time for a postsaccadic drawing of a baseball bat. Pollatsek, Rayner, and Collins (1984) concluded that some visual features and some abstract identity information about the presaccadic stimulus were extracted during the first fixation and subsequently combined with the information extracted from the postsaccadic stimulus to facilitate the latter's identification and naming. Similar results were reported by Pollatsek, Rayner, and Henderson (1990).

6.6   EVIDENCE FROM OTHER VISUAL TASKS

Other studies report additional evidence that visual information can persist and be used across saccades. Using a letter-matching task, Posner and Keele (1967) and Hansen and Sanders (1988) found that physical matches were made more quickly than name matches even when the two letters were viewed in separate fixations. Furthermore, Hansen and Sanders (1988) found that when both the first and second stimulus were visually degraded, processing of the second stimulus was faster than when only the second stimulus was degraded; these results suggest that visual features of the two stimuli were compared across eye movements, rather than abstract name codes (see also Sanders and Houtmans 1985).

Palmer and Ames (1989) have also found evidence for memory for visual features across eye movements. In their experiments, subjects were presented with study displays that contained two objects, such as vertical lines of slightly different lengths. In one condition (the movement condition), subjects fixated each of the two lines in turn, and then returned their eyes to a central fixation point midway between the two objects. In another condition (the fixation condition), subjects maintained fixation at the central fixation mark throughout the trial. In both conditions the initial display was erased after a second or so; then, a comparison stimulus and an arrow pointing to one of the two previously studied locations were presented at the central fixation location. Subjects were required to judge whether the comparison stimulus was longer or shorter than the previously presented study stimulus. The data consisted of the thresholds for making this line-length judgment. Palmer and Ames found that the threshold in the movement condition was much lower than that obtained in a version of the fixation condition in which widely separated stimuli were used, and was almost as low as that obtained in a version of the fixation control condition in which the study stimuli were presented near the fovea. These results indicate almost perfect memory for line-length information across successive fixations. Other experiments generalized these results to other visual aspects of objects, such as size and shape.

Hayhoe, Lachter, and Feldman (1991) reported evidence for integration of precise spatial information for single dots presented in successive fixations. In their experiment, three dots were presented in a region subtending approximately 15 degree of visual angle; subjects judged whether the dots formed a right triangle. The precision with which subjects could make this judgment was determined under conditions in which the eyes were stationary, and also under conditions in which the eyes moved between successive dot presentations. When the eyes were stationary and the dots were presented simultaneously, precision was very high; thresholds of 2–4 degree deviation from right triangularity were found. Precision declined only slightly as the interval between successive dot presentations increased to 800 ms when the eyes were stationary. Very similar threshold estimates were found when the eyes moved between successive dot presentations, at least when a stable visual landmark (a central fixation point) was continuously present. When the visual reference point was removed, and the three dots were presented in total darkness with intervening eye movements, thresholds increased by a factor of 1.5–2 for three of the four subjects, while one subject was no longer able to perform the task. These results indicate that precise spatial information about several points can be held in a slowly decaying, maplike representation across several eye movements, especially when a fixed visual reference point is available.

Additional evidence that visual information from successive fixations can be compared across eye movements has been found by Irwin, Zacks, and Brown (1990). Their experimental procedure was based on one that Phillips (1974) used to study memory within individual fixations. Phillips presented two random-dot patterns separated in time; subjects had to judge whether these two patterns were identical or different. Phillips found that with short interpattern intervals (20 ms), subjects were nearly perfect at making this judgment; however, as interpattern interval increased, accuracy decreased. Irwin, Zacks, and Brown modified Phillips's procedure so that one pattern was presented while the subject was fixating one part of a display and the second pattern was presented following a saccade to a new location. In this way, memory across eye movements could be studied. Irwin and colleagues used patterns that contained seven randomly arranged dots, and they used only one interpattern interval (250 ms); under these conditions, they found that the accuracy of the same-different judgment across eye movements was about 70 percent. Physically displacing the second pattern with respect to the first, so that the two patterns appeared in different spatial locations in successive fixations, had no effect on accuracy. This result indicates that visual information is retained across saccades in a location-independent representation.

In an attempt to further define the characteristics of this location-independent memory, Irwin (1991) varied interpattern interval, pattern displacement, and pattern complexity in the transsaccadic Phillips task. Recognition accuracy declined only slightly as interpattern interval increased from 1 to 5000 ms. As in Irwin, Zacks, and Brown (1990), there was also little effect on recognition accuracy of spatially displacing the postsaccadic pattern with respect to the presaccadic pattern. Pattern complexity, on the other hand, had a large effect on performance: Simple patterns were recognized much more accurately than complex patterns, regardless of interpattern interval. In sum, these results indicate that transsaccadic integration relies on a limited-capacity, long-lasting, location-independent memory.

6.7 SUMMARY

The research reviewed above suggests that, during reading, visual features of the stimulus environment are not integrated across saccades. Rather, abstract letter-identity codes are extracted from the parafovea of one fixation and integrated with the foveal contents of the subsequent fixation to speed its processing. Outside the reading domain, however, there is evidence that visual features of successive fixations can be compared and combined across eye movements. When pictures are used as stimuli, abstract object codes can also be combined from one fixation to the next. What these findings suggest about the potential mechanisms underlying integration across eye movements is discussed next.

Mechanisms of Transsaccadic Integration

The research summarized above suggests the operation of at least two different processing systems in transsaccadic integration. One system, whose existence is demonstrated by the experiments of Palmer and Ames (1989), Hayhoe, Lachter, and Feldman (1991), Irwin, Zacks, and Brown (1990), and Irwin (1991), appears to retain visual information from a fixation so that it can be compared or combined with visual information contained in a subsequent fixation. Although the results of Palmer and Ames, Hayhoe, Lachter, and Feldman, and Irwin, Zacks, and Brown provide little information about the capacity or time course of this system, the results of Irwin (1991) suggest that it has a limited capacity and a long duration. In addition, the representations contained in this system do not appear to be strictly tied to absolute spatial positions. This system is similar to visual short-term memory, which is capable of maintaining information about visual form for long temporal intervals (e.g., Cermak 1971; Phillips 1974) in a location-independent format (e.g., Phillips 1974). Visual short-term memory can, however, maintain precise spatial information under some circumstances; the data on performance of mental rotation of complicated visual forms (e.g., Shepard and Metzler 1971; Tarr and Pinker 1989) attests to this fact, as do demonstrations that visual images preserve metric spatial information (e.g., Kosslyn, Ball, and Reiser 1978; Pinker 1980; Pinker and Finke 1980). In sum, visual short-term memory appears to be perfectly capable of explaining the maintenance of visual information across eye movements, as found in the experiments summarized above.

It is not immediately obvious how visual short-term memory could explain the parafoveal preview benefits found in reading and picture-viewing experiments, however. To explain these findings, a second transsaccadic integration system is required. The processing facilitation found in reading and picture viewing would seem to require priming of already existing representations of words and objects in long-term memory, rather than the mere maintenance of letter codes and object codes in short-term memory. In fact, an explanation of transsaccadic integration based on priming of long-term memory representations has been offered by Pollatsek and Rayner (in press). They proposed that a parallel processing model of word recognition, of the type developed by McClelland and Rumelhart (1981) and by Paap et al. (1982), might explain how transsaccadic integration during reading is carried out. According to this proposal, abstract letter-identity codes extracted from the parafoveal preview might excite a neighborhood of lexical entries in memory that begin with these letter codes. The processing of a target word that shared these letter codes would be facilitated as a result of this excitation when it was encountered during the next fixation. A similar mechanism might account for the benefits of parafoveal preview in picture viewing (Pollatsek, Rayner, and Henderson 1990). In this case, it is possible that the parafoveal visual form activates a neighborhood of visually similar entries in a lexicon of stored visual representations, while at the same time information about the identity of the parafoveal object primes retrieval pathways in semantic memory. The outcome of these sources of activation would be a facilitation in identifying and naming the target stimulus viewed during the next fixation.

Although different mechanisms are being proposed to account for parafoveal priming effects and for transsaccadic comparison and combination effects, both accounts share the notion that general-purpose memory stores (i.e., visual short-term memory and long-term memory) underlie the integration of information across eye movements. In other words, transsaccadic integration appears not to rely on a specialized memory buffer whose only function is to combine information across eye movements, but rather it occurs as a consequence of ordinary memory processes that operate both within and across fixations. This conclusion is supported by the fact that no-saccade control conditions that were included in many of the experiments reported above invariably yielded patterns of performance that were very similar to those found in the saccade conditions (e.g., Irwin, 1991; Palmer and Ames 1989; Pollatsek, Rayner, and Henderson 1990; Rayner, McConkie, and Zola 1980). In sum, despite intuitions to the contrary, there appears to be no specialized memory buffer for combining information across eye movements.

Implications for Perceptual Stability

Although our conscious experience of a stable and continuous visual world across eye movements seems intuitively to demand the existence of a very detailed, high-capacity buffer, capable of spatially summating the visual contents of successive fixations, the experimental evidence indicates that no such memory exists. Instead, information integration seems to involve the accumulation and the combination of limited amounts of visual information in short-term memory, and the priming of long-term memory representations. How could such operations produce the perception of a stable and continuous visual world, as is ordinarily experienced across changes in eye position? In order to achieve perceptual stability, the human perceptual system must solve two problems: smearing of visual information across the retina while the eye is moving, and changes in the retinal positions of objects from one fixation to the next. During individual fixations the retinal image *is* relatively stable and continuous. Therefore, if retinal smear during saccades can be eliminated, and if changes in retinal positions across fixations can somehow be accounted for, then perceptual stability will have been achieved. As noted earlier, saccadic suppression eliminates the perception of retinal blur during saccades. The only remaining question, therefore, is that of the change in the retinal images of objects across successive fixations: Why don't changes in the retinal positions of objects from one fixation to the next cause perceived motion or perceived instability?

A possible answer to this question was offered by Irwin, Zacks, and Brown (1990), who found that subjects could accurately determine whether two random-dot patterns viewed in successive fixations were identical or different, even when the two patterns were presented at different spatial locations in the two fixations. These results suggest that what subjects remembered from one fixation to the next were the spatial relationships between the elements in the pattern (i.e., the relative positions of the dots with respect to each other), rather than the absolute position of the pattern, or the absolute positions of the individual elements in the patterns. In other words, subjects appeared to rely on object-relative, or exocentric, coordinates (Mack 1986) rather than on egocentric coordinates. Irwin, Zacks, and Brown hypothesized that the perception of a stable visual environment across eye movements might also arise from the use of an exocentric coding strategy. Subjects might code the relative positions of objects with respect to each other during individual fixations. Because these relative positions don't change from one fixation to the next, they lead to a stable percept of the environment even though the retinal positions of the objects themselves do change. This view of perceptual stability across saccades is consistent with the ecological theories of perception proposed by Gibson (1966, 1979) and by Haber (1985), which claim that stimulus invariants in the environment (in this case, relative position) allow the viewer to apprehend the world as stable and continuous.

The perception of a stable visual world cannot be explained solely in terms of relative position information, however. It has been known for over a century that sensorimotor information can also influence perceptual stability in some situations. Helmholtz ([1867] 1925), for example, noted that when the eye is passively displaced (e.g., by pressing on the canthus), the world appears to move in the direction opposite to the displacement. Other studies have shown that when the eye is prevented from moving (e.g., by paralysis of the oculomotor muscles) and a saccade is attempted, the world appears to move in the direction of the intended eye movement (e.g., Stevens et al. 1976). These phenomena suggest that perceptual stability depends, at least in part, on nonvisual eye position information provided by the oculomotor system. Further evidence for this point is provided by the fact that subjects can, at least to some degree, localize isolated visual stimuli across changes in eye position even when these stimuli are presented briefly and in total darkness (e.g., Matin 1972; Hayhoe, Lachter, and Feldman 1991). This indicates that spatial position can be represented in memory even when relational visual cues are absent.

Despite the fact that sensorimotor information appears to play a role in visual localization and perceptual stability across eye movements, it is interesting to note that the influence of sensorimotor variables can be modified or overcome by visual context. For example, Matin (1976) has shown that localization judgments are greatly improved in the presence of a visual landmark in the experimental environment. Hayhoe, Lachter, and Feldman (1991) also found that subjects' ability to integrate successively presented dots across eye movements was improved when a stable visual reference point was provided. Additional evidence for the claim that relative position information can overcome sensorimotor information is provided by the fact that the spatial localization errors that occur when the eyes are paralyzed occur only in the dark, but not in normally illuminated, structured visual environments (Matin et al. 1982). Similarly, the illusory displacements of the world that are generated by passively displacing the eye are greatly reduced when subjects view a normal visual environment (Stark and Bridgeman 1983). These results suggest that perceptual stability across eye movements relies on some combination of sensorimotor information and relative visual position information (cf. Bridgeman and Graziano 1989; Hayhoe, Lachter, and Feldman 1991; Matin 1986; Shebilske 1986), with the visual information having a dominant effect.

One final factor that needs to be considered is the apparent limited-capacity nature of "transsaccadic" memory. If visual short-term memory actually is the mechanism by which visual information is retained across eye movements, its limited capacity would severely restrict a viewer's ability to detect changes across successive fixations. It is possible, in fact, for the world to change in many ways between one fixation and the next without a viewer noticing the change. This situation is simulated in figure 6.3. The top drawing in this figure differs from the bottom drawing in several respects, but these differences do not automatically emerge as one alternates fixation between the two drawings. In order to accurately compare the two drawings, one needs to attend to and encode a particular piece of a drawing. Similarly, unless an object in the world has been attended to and encoded into memory, any change it undergoes from

Figure 6.3 Demonstration that changes in the contents of successive fixations may not be easily detected. The top drawing is different from the bottom drawing in 8 details, but these are not detectable unless specific objects are attended to and encoded into memory. *Note:* From "Information Integration across Saccadic Eye Movements" by D. E. Irwin, 1991, *Cognitive Psychology, 23,* 452. Copyright 1991 by Academic Press. Reprinted by permission.

one fixation to the next might not be detected. Perceptual stability may be the result of our relative insensitivity to change across eye movements, rather than to sensorimotor information or to the constancy of the relative spatial positions of objects. It may be the case, for example, that the perceptual system merely assumes that the world remains stable across saccades, unless it is given obvious information to the contrary (MacKay 1973). This intriguing possibility requires further investigation.

Conclusions and Future Research Directions

It appears that the perception of a stable and continuous visual environment across eye movements is based more on the contents of the current fixation than on one's memory for the contents of previous fixations (cf. O'Regan and Levy-Schoen 1983). Perhaps this is not surprising when one considers that the duration of individual fixations is approximately ten times longer than the duration of individual saccades: Ninety percent of our viewing time is composed of stable and continuous vision. Future research should provide more information about what characteristics of individual fixations are remembered and combined across eye movements and should further define the properties of the memory systems involved in transsaccadic integration.

NOTE

Preparation of this chapter was supported by Grant BNS 89-08699 from the National Science Foundation to the author. I thank Mary Hayhoe, Sandy Pollatsek, and John Palmer for many helpful discussions regarding these issues, and Claus Bundeson, Sylvan Kornblum, and Keith Rayner for helpful comments on an earlier version of the chapter.

REFERENCES

Balota, D. A., and Rayner, K. (1990). Word recognition processes in foveal and parafoveal vision: The range of influence of lexical variables. In D. Besner and G. Humphreys (Eds.), *Basic processes in reading: Visual word recognition*. Hillsdale, NJ: Erlbaum.

Balota, D. A., Pollatsek, A., and Rayner, K. (1985). The interaction of contextual constraints and parafoveal visual information in reading. *Cognitive Psychology, 17*, 364–390.

Banks, W. P. (1983). On the decay of the icon. *Behavioral and Brain Sciences, 6*, 14.

Breitmeyer, B. G. (1984). *Visual masking: An integrative approach*. New York: Oxford University Press.

Breitmeyer, B. G., Kropfl, W., and Julesz, B. (1982). The existence and role of retinotopic and spatiotopic forms of visual persistence. *Acta Psychologica, 52*, 175–196.

Bridgeman, B., and Graziano, J. A. (1989). Effect of context and efference copy on visual straight ahead. *Vision Research. 29*, 1729–1736.

Bridgeman, B., Hendry, D., and Stark, L. (1975). Failure to detect displacement of the visual world during saccadic eye movements. *Vision Research, 15*, 719–722.

Bridgeman, B., and Mayer, M. (1983). Failure to integrate visual information from successive fixations. *Bulletin of the Psychonomic Society, 21*, 285–286.

Campbell, F. W., and Wurtz, R. H. (1978). Saccadic omission: Why we do not see a gray-out during a saccadic eye movement. *Vision Research, 18,* 1297−1303.

Cermak, G. W. (1971). Short-term recognition memory for complex free-form figures. *Psychonomic Science, 25,* 209−211.

Davidson, M. L., Fox, M. J., and Dick, A. O. (1973). Effect of eye movements on backward masking and perceived location. *Perception & Psychophysics, 14,* 110−116.

Di Lollo, V. (1977). Temporal characteristics of iconic memory. *Nature, 267,* 241−243.

Di Lollo, V. (1980). Temporal integration in visual memory. *Journal of Experimental Psychology: General, 109,* 75−97.

Gibson, J. J. (1966). *The senses considered as perceptual systems.* Boston: Houghton Mifflin.

Gibson, J. J. (1979). *The ecological approach to visual perception.* Boston: Houghton Mifflin.

Haber, R. N. (1985). Three frames suffice: Drop the retinotopic frame. *Behavioral & Brain Sciences, 8,* 295−296.

Hansen, W., and Sanders, A. F. (1988). On the output of encoding during stimulus fixation. *Acta Psychologica, 69,* 95−107.

Hayhoe, M., Lachter, J., and Feldman, J. (1991). Integration of form across saccadic eye movements. *Perception, 20,* 393−402.

Helmholtz, H. v. ([1867] 1925). *Treatise on physiological optics.* Ed. and trans. J. P. C. Southall. New York: Optical Society of America.

Holst, E. von, and Mittelstaedt, H. ([1950] 1971). The principle of reafference: Interactions between the central nervous system and the peripheral organs. In P. C. Dodwell (Ed. and Trans.), *Perceptual processing: Stimulus equivalence and pattern recognition,* 41−71. New York: Appleton.

Irwin, D. E. (1991). Information integration across saccadic eye movements. *Cognitive Psychology, 23,* 420−456.

Irwin, D. E., Brown, J. S., and Sun, J.-S. (1988). Visual masking and visual integration across saccadic eye movements. *Journal of Experimental Psychology: General, 117,* 276−287.

Irwin, D. E., Yantis, S., and Jonides, J. (1983). Evidence against visual integration across saccadic eye movements. *Perception & Psychophysics, 34,* 49−57.

Irwin, D. E., Zacks, J. L., Brown, J. S. (1990). Visual memory and the perception of a stable visual environment. *Perception & Psychophysics, 47,* 35−46.

Jonides, J., Irwin, D. E., and Yantis, S. (1982). Integrating visual information from successive fixations. *Science, 215,* 192−194.

Jonides, J., Irwin, D. E., and Yantis, S. (1983). Failure to integrate information from successive fixations. *Science, 222,* 188.

Kosslyn, S. M., Ball, T. M., and Reiser, B. J. (1978). Visual images preserve metric spatial information: Evidence from studies of image scanning. *Journal of Experimental Psychology: Human Perception and Performance, 4,* 47−60.

Latour, P. (1962). Visual threshold during eye movements. *Vision Research, 2,* 261−262.

McClelland, J. L., and Rumelhart, D. E. (1981). An interactive activation model of context effects in letter perception: Part 1. An account of basic findings. *Psychological Review, 88,* 375−407.

McConkie, G. W., and Rayner, K. (1976). Identifying the span of the effective stimulus in reading: Literature review and theories of reading. In H. Singer and R. B. Ruddell (Eds.), *Theoretical models and processes of reading,* 137−162. Newark, NJ: International Reading Association.

McConkie, G. W., and Zola, D. (1979). Is visual information integrated across successive fixations in reading? *Perception & Psychophysics, 25,* 221–224.

McConkie, G. W., Zola, D., Blanchard, H. E., and Wolverton, G. S. (1982). Perceiving words during reading: Lack of facilitation from prior peripheral exposure. *Perception & Psychophysics, 32,* 271–281.

Mack, A. (1970). An investigation of the relationship between eye and retinal image movement in the perception of movement. *Perception & Psychophysics, 8,* 291–298.

Mack, A. (1986). Perceptual aspects of motion in the frontal plane. In K. R. Boff, L. Kaufman, and J. P. Thomas (Eds.), *Handbook of perception and human performance,* Vol. 1, 17.1–17.38. New York: Wiley.

MacKay, D. M. (1973). Visual stability and voluntary eye movements. In R. Jung (Ed.), *Handbook of Sensory Physiology,* Vol. 8/3, 307–331. Berlin: Springer-Verlag.

Matin, L. (1972). Eye movements and perceived visual direction. In D. Jameson and L. M. Hurvich (Eds.), *Handbook of sensory physiology,* Vol 7/4, 331–379. Berlin: Springer-Verlag.

Matin, L. (1976). Saccades and extraretinal signal for visual direction. In R. A. Monty and J. W. Senders (Eds.), *Eye movements and psychological processes,* 205–219. Hillsdale, NJ: Erlbaum.

Matin, L. (1986). Visual localization and eye movements. In K. R. Boff, L. Kaufman, and J. P. Thomas (Eds.), *Handbook of perception and human performance,* Vol. 1, 20.1–20.45. New York: Wiley.

Matin, L., Picoult, E., Stevens, J. K., Edwards Jr., M. W., Young, D., and MacArthur, R. (1982). Oculoparalytic illusion: Visual-field dependent spatial mislocations by humans partially paralyzed with curare. *Science, 216,* 198–201.

O'Regan, J. K. (1981). The convenient viewing position hypothesis. In D. F. Fisher, R. A. Monty, and J. W. Senders (Eds.), *Eye movements: Cognition and visual perception.* Hillsdale, NJ: Erlbaum.

O'Regan, J. K., and Levy-Schoen, A. (1983). Integrating visual information from successive fixations: Does trans-saccadic fusion exist? *Vision Research, 23,* 765–768.

Paap, K. R., Newsome, S. L., McDonald, J. E., and Schvaneveldt, R. W. (1982). An activation-verification model for letter and word recognition: The word superiority effect. *Psychological Review, 89,* 573–594.

Palmer, J., and Ames, C. T. (1989). Measuring the effect of multiple eye fixations on size and shape discrimination. *Investigative Ophthalmology and Visual Science (Supplement), 30,* 159.

Phillips, W. A. (1974). On the distinction between sensory storage and short-term visual memory. *Perception & Psychophysics. 16,* 283–290.

Pinker, S. (1980). Mental imagery and the third dimension. *Journal of Experimental Psychology: General, 109,* 354–371.

Pinker, S., and Finke, R. A. (1980). Emergent two-dimensional patterns in images rotated in depth. *Journal of Experimental Psychology: Human Perception and Performance, 6,* 244–264.

Pollatsek, A., Lesch, M., Morris, R., and Rayner, K. (1992). Phonological codes are used in integrating information across saccades in word identification and reading. *Journal of Experimental Psychology: Human Perception and Performance, 18,* 148–162.

Pollatsek, A., Rayner, K., and Collins, W. E. (1984). Integrating pictorial information across eye movements. *Journal of Experimental Psychology: General, 113,* 426–442.

Pollatsek, A., and Rayner, K. (1992). What is integrated across fixations? In K. Rayner (Ed.), *Eye movements and visual cognition: Scene perception and reading.* New York: Springer-Verlag.

Pollatsek, A., Rayner, K., and Henderson, J. M. (1990). Role of spatial location in integration of pictorial information across saccades. *Journal of Experimental Psychology: Human Perception and Performance, 16,* 199–210.

Posner, M. I., and Keele, S. W. (1967). Decay of visual information from a single letter. *Science, 158,* 137–139.

Rayner, K., McConkie, G. W., and Zola, D. (1980). Integrating information across eye movements. *Cognitive Psychology, 12,* 206–226.

Rayner, K., and Pollatsek, A. (1983). Is visual information integrated across saccades? *Perception & Psychophysics, 34,* 39–48.

Ritter, M. (1976). Evidence for visual persistence during saccadic eye movements. *Psychological Research, 39,* 67–85.

Sanders, A. F., and Houtmans, M. (1985). There is no central stimulus encoding during saccadic eye shifts: A case against general parallel processing models. *Acta Psychologica, 60,* 323–338.

Shebilske, W. L. (1986). Baseball batters support an ecological efference mediation theory of natural event perception. *Acta Psychologica, 63,* 117–131.

Shepard, R. N., and Metzler, J. (1971). Mental rotation of three-dimensional objects. *Science, 171,* 701–703.

Stark, L., and Bridgeman, B. (1983). Role of corollary discharge in space constancy. *Perception & Psychophysics, 34,* 371–380.

Stevens, J. K., Emerson, R. C., Gerstein, G. L., Kallos, T., Neufeld, G. R., Nichols, C. W., and Rosenquist, A. C. (1976). Paralysis of the awake human: Visual perceptions. *Vision Research, 16,* 93–98.

Tarr, M. J., and Pinker, S. (1989). Mental rotation and orientation-dependence in shape recognition. *Cognitive Psychology, 21,* 233–282.

Trehub, A. (1977). Neuronal models for cognitive processes: Networks for learning, perception, and imagination. *Journal of Theoretical Biology, 65,* 141–169.

Van der Heijden, A. H. C., Bridgeman, B., and Mewhort, D. J. K. (1986). Is stimulus persistence affected by eye movements? A critique of Davidson, Fox, and Dick (1973). *Psychological Research, 48,* 179–181.

Volkmann, F. C., Schick, A., and Riggs, L. A. (1968). Time course of visual inhibition during voluntary saccades. *Journal of the Optical Society of America, 58,* 562–569.

Whipple, W. R., and Wallach, H. (1978). Direction-specific motion thresholds for abnormal image shifts during saccadic eye movements. *Perception & Psychophys, 24,* 349–355.

Wolf, W., Hauske, G., and Lupp, U. (1978). How pre-saccadic gratings modify post-saccadic modulation transfer functions. *Vision Research, 18,* 1173–1179.

Wolf, W., Hauske, G., and Lupp, U. (1980). Interactions of pre- and post-saccadic patterns having the same coordinates in space. *Vision Research, 20,* 117–125.

7 Interactions between Object and Space Systems Revealed through Neuropsychology

Glyn W. Humphreys and M. Jane Riddoch

7.1 INTRODUCTION

Early visual processing is undoubtedly massively parallel, occurring simultaneously across the visual field and involving the independent coding of image features along a number of dimensions (e.g., see Desimone and Ungerleider 1989 for a review of physiological evidence). Nevertheless, our ability to select and direct actions to multiple objects is severely limited. For instance, there are clear costs involved when there must be selection between two simultaneous relative to two successively presented target objects (e.g., Duncan 1984). Understanding how visual selection operates is critical for understanding visual information processing.

Normally, visual selection seems to involve interactions within a complex attentional network, whose components orient us to potentially significant locations in space and maintain attention on objects of current interest (e.g., Mesulam 1981; Posner and Peterson 1990). To understand how selection operates, we must specify the nature of the component attentional mechanisms and the ways in which they interact. In this chapter we attempt to delineate several important aspects of the attentional network determining visual selection, and we provide a new account of the relations between the visual attentional and object recognition systems. Our arguments are based on a consideration of both normal visual selection and the impairments that can disrupt selection after brain damage.

7.2 EVIDENCE FROM NORMAL SUBJECTS

Components of the Attentional Network

Evidence from work with normal subjects allows us to distinguish between components of the attentional network that respond in a data-driven way to appropriate external signals (such as abrupt light onsets) and components that seem to be under voluntary control.

Consider a study reported by Posner, Cohen, and Rafal (1982). They presented subjects with a peripheral cue before a target stimulus (to which a simple reaction-time response was made). In one condition the cue appeared on the opposite side of fixation from the target on 80 percent of trials, and on the same side of fixation as the target on only 20 percent of the trials. Despite the low likelihood of the cue and target appearing at the same location, reaction times (RTs) were faster if the target appeared at the cued location when the interval between the cue and the target was brief (100 msec or less). Only if there was a longer interval between cue and target were RTs faster when the target appeared on the side opposite the cue—as would be expected were subjects voluntarily attending to the most likely target location indicated by the cue. Results such as this suggest that "capture" of attention by appropriate external signals can take place even when subjects attempt voluntarily to attend to another location.

In a similar vein, Müller and Rabbitt (1989) presented subjects with a central (arrow) cue, informing them of the most likely location for a target (the target was three times more likely to appear at the centrally cued location than at each of three other potential target locations). This central cue was followed by an irrelevant peripheral light flash at a nontarget location. The task was to detect the target. Without the peripheral flash, performance was better when the cue correctly indicated the target's location relative to when the cue was incorrect; the detection of correctly cued targets was also better than that of targets in a neutral condition, in which the subjects were not given information about the likely target location. Thus, correctly cueing the target's location had a facilitatory effect on performance. The peripheral light flash, producing data-driven orienting, disrupted the facilitatory effect of valid central cues, produced by voluntary orienting. In this instance, the existence of distinct data-driven and voluntary attentional components is indicated by the disruptive effects of one on the other when the two are pitted against one another. Müller and Rabbitt's (1989) results suggest that at least some of the components within the attentional network interact in a mutually inhibitory way. In particular, they show that the data-driven orienting mechanism can inhibit operation of the voluntary orienting mechanism.

Other work suggests that the data-driven mechanism can itself be modulated. For instance, Yantis and Jonides (1990) presented subjects with two peripheral letters on each trial. One of the letters (the target) was either an *E* or an *H*; the other was an irrelevant distractor. Letters were presented at a location that had previously contained either no letter segments (*onset stimulus*) or a set of eight segments, some of which were removed to reveal the letter (*offset stimulus*). Of most relevance here is the condition where there was an onset target and an offset distractor, and the opposite condition in which there was an offset target and an onset distractor. Prior to targets and distractors appearing, subjects were given a central cue indicating the likely location of the target letter (the central cue was valid on 80 percent of the trials).

Reasoning from previous work (Yantis and Jonides 1984), Yantis and Jonides proposed that only the onset stimuli should engage the data-driven orienting mechanism. Some of their results supported this proposal. When the central cue was invalid (i.e., subjects were cued to the distractor's location), there was an RT advantage in responding to onset relative to offset targets; subjects found it easier to reorient attention from an invalid location when a stimulus onset provided the orienting cue. This is consistent with the onset target activating the data-driven orienting mechanism, orienting attention to the location so cued and inhibiting voluntarily attention to the centrally cued location.

However, Yantis and Jonides found little difference between onset and offset targets when the central cue was correct. When there was an offset target and an onset distractor, the distractor did not capture attention automatically, providing that subjects voluntarily directed attention to the centrally cued location (otherwise RTs should have again been slowed relative to the onset target condition). Apparently, data-driven orienting is modulated by voluntary attention (see also Müller and Humphreys 1991 for further supportive evidence on this point). For instance, voluntary attention to a centrally cued location may produce inhibition of data-driven orienting. In Yantis and Jonides's (1990) experiment, the data-driven mechanism may only have become effective again when subjects identified a distractor at the centrally cued location (on invalid trials), leading to a release from inhibition.

Further evidence on the modulation of orienting to targets comes from eye movement research, which suggests that orienting is affected when subjects maintain attention on a stimulus. Fischer and his colleagues (e.g., Fischer 1986; Fischer and Breitmeyer 1987) have reported that the time to initiate a saccade to a peripheral target is increased when subjects fixate and attend to a central stimulus before the target's onset, relative to when there is no central stimulus present. This delay in saccade initiation seems to stem from subjects maintaining their attention on the central stimulus. A similar delay is not incurred when subjects are instructed to fixate the central stimulus but not to attend to it. Maintaining attention on the central stimulus inhibits orienting to the peripheral target, slowing saccade initiation time.

A framework illustrating potential relations between mechanisms that maintain attention and mechanisms that orient attention to new locations, either in a data-driven or voluntary manner, is shown in figure 7.1. It is proposed that the attentional network contains at least three separate components, one concerned with maintaining attention at its current locus, one concerned with orienting attention in response to appropriate data-driven signals, and one concerned with voluntarily orienting attention to new locations. These components interact in a mutually antagonistic way, so that activation of one component leads to inhibition of the others.

Given that there are separate components within the attentional network, it should be possible for one component to be selectively affected by brain damage; for instance, particular brain lesions may affect data-driven or voluntary orienting. However, within the framework presented, we may also expect that a disorder within one component could also affect the operation of other components. For example, impairment of data-driven orienting should lead to

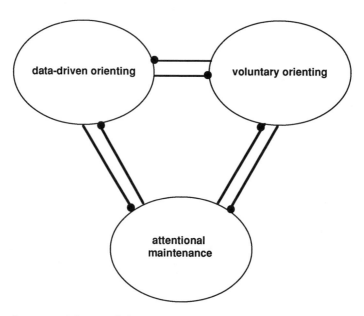

Figure 7.1 A framework for interactions between components of the normal attentional network. The framework contains separate mechanisms for data-driven and voluntary orienting, and for attentional maintenance. These mechanisms are presumed to act in a mutually inhibitory fashion.

the overmaintenance of attention, since the data-driven orienting mechanism will fail to inhibit the maintenance component in the normal way.

Space-based Orienting and Object-based Selection

The role of the orienting components of the attentional network seems to be to direct attention to locations of potential significance—for instance, to the location in the visual field where a sudden movement has been signaled. However, let us suppose that the signal is caused by a partially occluded animal moving behind some trees. In such a case, simply attending to the region of field where movement is signaled would not be efficient for action, since that region of field contains at least two objects, to which different actions might be required (e.g., reach to the animal, avoid the trees). There needs to be selection between the potential objects towards which action may be directed (cf. Allport 1987). Furthermore, selection needs to be based on objects rather than on regions of space—for instance, the animal may be selected and the trees rejected, even though they occupy overlapping positions in the visual field (see Duncan 1984; Humphreys and Bruce 1989 for discussion of the distinction between space- and object-based attention). Thus spatial orienting needs to be distinguished from the object-based process involved in selection for action.

Humphreys et al. (1991) have recently suggested how these two aspects of visual attention might be realized, if the operation of the attentional network is "yoked" to that of a separate system concerned with the recognition of known

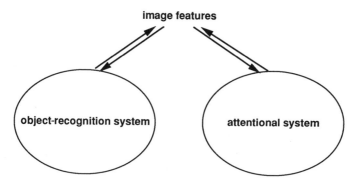

image features

object-recognition system

attentional system

Figure 7.2 Relations between the attentional system and the object-recognition system. Here image features activate both the attentional and the object-recognition systems. Visual selection occurs when a stable pattern of activation is established across the systems. Feedback from the object-recognition system leads to selection being object based.

objects. They proposed that attentional processes enhance the activation of image features at attended locations and inhibit those at unattended locations (e.g., see Downing 1988; Hawkins et al. 1990; Müller and Humphreys 1991 for evidence of attentional enhancement; see Moran and Desimone 1985 for evidence of attentional inhibition). This enhancement may be produced independently by each component in the attentional network. Also, the features activated can be coded in three-dimensional space, and not just in terms of their retinal locations (e.g., Downing and Pinker 985).

In parallel with this attentional activation, there can be activation of stored representations for known objects within a separate "object-recognition" system. Once activated, these stored representations feed back to support consistent image features. Because of this top-down support, image features for whole objects can sometimes be activated even when attention is directed only to a local part of the whole. The image features activated via the object-recognition system then activate the attentional system, leading to attention being engaged on the whole. Once a stable pattern of activation is achieved, the whole object can be selected for action.

Within this "yoked" system, selection is object based, even though attentional enhancement is to image features at particular locations in three-dimensional space. The coding and attentional enhancement of image features in three- rather than two-dimensional space fits with evidence indicating the importance of depth coding for image segmentation (e.g., Nakayama and Silverman 1986).

7.3 NEUROPSYCHOLOGICAL EVIDENCE

The argument for the existence of separate components within an attentional network is supported by neuropsychological evidence. We first cover this evidence and then discuss how neuropsychological data illustrate that orienting and selection are respectively space- and object-based selection.

Unilateral Visual Neglect

The main neuropsychological evidence for different components within the visual-attentional system comes from patients with unilateral visual neglect (cf. Heilman 1979). Patients with neglect typically fail to respond to stimuli on the side of space contralateral to their lesion. This is not simply due to the patients having a field cut. There is no clinical relationship between field defects and the severity of neglect (Halligan, Marshall, and Wade 1990), and many patients with neglect do not have field defects (e.g., see below). Also, neglect is intimately tied to attentional processes because it can be reduced when patients are cued to attend to the affected side (e.g., Posner, Cohen, and Rafal 1982; Riddoch and Humphreys 1983), and it can be increased under conditions of double simultaneous stimulation (producing the phenomenon of "extinction"; e.g., Volpe, LeDoux, and Gazzaniga 1979). That is, neglect is influenced by manipulations of attention to and from the affected side.

As with many neuropsychological syndromes, patients with neglect can exhibit a variety of different symptoms, some of which may occur independently in different patients (e.g., Riddoch 1990). Thus, the neglect syndrome probably consists of several functionally distinct impairments, and not all neglect patients need have the same underlying disturbance. This is consistent with the range of different lesions that neglect patients may have (Mesulam 1981). These different disturbances can be related to impairments of different components of the attentional network.

Posner and his colleagues have proposed that neglect can be related to selective impairments to one of three attentional processes concerned, respectively, with disengaging attention from previously attended objects, moving attention to new locations, and engaging attention on objects there. Their arguments are based on work examining whether spatial cues facilitate simple RT in groups of patients suffering different brain lesions. For instance, Rafal and Posner (1987) reported that, after unilateral lesions of the thalamus, patients may produce slowed responses to all contralateral stimuli, along with a relatively normal *pattern* of performance (RTs being faster when a target is in a cued relative to an uncued location). They attribute this slowed responding to unilateral impairment of the attentional engagement mechanism.

Furthermore, Posner, Rafal, Choate, and Vaughan (1985) examined the performance of patients with progressive supranuclear palsy (PSP) caused by degeneration of several midbrain structures including the superior colliculus. In these patients, responses to the affected side of space were relatively fast. However, the patients needed a long interval between the cue and the target in order to show a positive effect of cueing on the affected side. Posner et al. attribute this to a selective problem in moving attention.

Posner et al. (1984) also tested parietally lesioned patients. Such patients can show a relatively normal effect of cueing on the side contralateral to their lesion (though even in the case of valid cueing, RTs typically remain somewhat longer than when attention is cued to the ipsilateral side). More strikingly, the patients can be very impaired at responding to contralateral targets when their attention is cued to the unaffected (ipsilateral) side. This marked effect of invalid cueing suggests that the patients have problems disengaging attention from ipsilateral stimuli in order to detect contralateral targets.

Within a framework such as the one we have proposed (fig. 7.1), the attentional network will enter states that can be described by means of the terms *engage*, *disengage*, and *move*, according to the current balance of activation between the component mechanisms. When the maintenance mechanism is inhibited by one of the orienting mechanisms, attention will be "disengaged" from its current locus and "moved" to a location signaled by the orienting mechanism. Strong activation by the maintenance mechanism, and inhibition of the orienting mechanisms, will lead to attention being "engaged." Thus terms such as engage, disengage, and move may describe states of the system rather than the basic processing mechanisms.

Our attentional framework also allows finer-grained distinctions to be made. In particular, a problem with disengaging attention from ipsilateral stimuli, as occurs following parietal lesions, could stem from either of two causes: (1) a unilateral deficit in an orienting mechanism, such that contralateral stimuli no longer *attract* attention normally, or (2) abnormal inhibition of the orienting system(s) by the maintenance mechanism. That is, disengagement problems could reflect deficient contralateral *attraction* or abnormal ipsilateral *hold*. We believe that such finer-grained distinctions are supported by the neuropsychological literature. Relevant evidence is discussed in the next section.

Impaired Attentional Orienting

In at least some cases, visual neglect can be linked to impaired orienting to targets presented contralateral to the side of lesion, rather than to poor engagement, disengagement, or movement of attention. Riddoch and Humphreys (1987) had neglect patients carry out visual search tasks, in which they had to detect a predesignated target among varying numbers of irrelevant nontargets. Targets were defined either by a single disjunctive feature (e.g., search for a red circle among green circles) or by a conjunction of features (search for an inverted *T* among upright *T* nontargets, where all the stimuli share horizontal and vertical line elements). For disjunctive feature search, there were few differences in RTs to detect targets in the neglected and non-neglected fields, and RTs were relatively flat in each field. For conjunction search, RTs increased as a function of the number of nontargets present, and both the slope and the intercept of the search functions increased for targets in the neglected relative to the non-neglected field. For both disjunctive and conjunction searches, there was an increased probability of missing a target in the neglected field, though the number of nontargets did not affect the miss rate.

If we consider only the RT measure, it could be argued that neglect occurred for conjunction but not for disjunctive search. This argument would fit with the proposal that only conjunction search involves movements of attention (cf. Treisman and Gelade 1980). Neglect may be manifest only when patients have to move attention into the neglected field.

However, as we go on to show in the next section, RT costs to detect targets on the neglected side can be incurred in disjunctive search as the feature discrimination becomes more difficult. Rather than interpreting these data in terms of a possible qualitative difference between disjunctive and conjunction search, we suggest that neglect patients show a continuum of difficulty across different target-nontarget relationships, reflecting the relative discriminability of the target in the neglected field. Duncan and Humphreys (1989) have argued that visual search depends on the relationship between two continuous variables: (1) the similarity of the target to the nontargets, and (2) the similarity between the nontargets. These two variables scale one another, so that the effects of target-nontarget similarity become more severe as nontargets become less similar. This relationship can be represented as a "search surface" that becomes steeper as target-nontarget similarity increases and nontarget-nontarget similarity decreases. The search surface may also reflect how much an orienting mechanism, responding to the most salient differences between stimuli in the visual field, is activated by a target placed among different nontargets (in fact, this would be an inverse relation; the steeper the search surface, the lower the activation of the orienting mechanism).

In visual neglect a rescaling of this search surface may occur, with the activation function for neglect-side targets being abnormally decreased, producing exaggerated effects of target discriminability on search. According to this view, neglect becomes manifest in RTs as a function of target discriminability (itself determined by both target-nontarget and nontarget-nontarget similarity), not as a function of the contrast between conjunction and disjunctive feature targets. For instance, as the discriminability of targets relative to nontargets decreases, there may be an increased likelihood that the orienting mechanism is most strongly attracted by a nontarget, since differences between nontargets may become as salient as differences between targets and nontargets. Further, the probability of this should increase as display size increases (simply because there are then relatively more nontargets to targets). The net result is that subjects should orient to nontargets before targets, producing RT costs in detecting targets on the neglected side. Also, the orienting mechanism may sometimes fail to reach threshold. On such occasions, targets will be missed, but this may be unrelated to the number of nontargets present.

7.4   STUDY 1

To examine orienting impairments further, separated from possible impairments in disengaging attention, we have studied disjunctive search when the nature of nontargets in the non-neglected field was kept constant while target-nontarget discriminability varied. This manipulation is important: variation in the amount of neglect manifested by a given patient cannot be attributed to problems in disengaging attention from stimuli in the non-neglected field, when the stimuli in that field do not change in the conditions of interest.

Here targets were defined by their color, so that (in two tasks) nontargets were always green and targets were either red or yellow. Since the information in the non-neglected field is constant in these conditions, any variation in neglect reflects altered discriminability (and orienting) to neglect-side targets. We also examined the effects of nontarget-nontarget similarity, by including two conditions in which half the nontargets were green and half blue. This allowed us to examine how both target-nontarget and nontarget-nontarget similarity influence the degree of neglect, and thus to relate any data to the notion that the "search surface" (Duncan and Humphreys 1989) might be altered in the neglected and the non-neglected fields. All the target-nontarget discriminations were very easy for normal subjects, and in pilot studies there were typically slopes of under 5 msec per item for all the search conditions. This is consistent with the target in each case being defined by a salient disjunctive feature relative to the nontargets.

The Patient

The subject of our present study, H.C., was one of the patients reported in Riddoch and Humphreys (1987). H.C. suffered a right parietal lesion from a stroke at age seventy-five. He had a dense left hemiplegia but no visual field defect on perimetric testing. He was classified as manifesting unilateral neglect on standard clinical tests of copying and line cancellation, in which he omitted detail and missed target lines on the left side of the page.

Method

The data were collected in two test sessions. During each session, H.C. undertook four visual-search tasks where target-nontarget and nontarget-nontarget relations were varied orthogonally. Targets were either red (low target-nontarget similarity) or yellow (high target-nontarget similarity); nontargets were either green (high nontarget-nontarget similarity) or half green and half blue (low nontarget-nontarget similarity). These four tasks were administered in an ABCD and DCBA order in the two test sessions.

The stimuli were presented on cards (12.6 cm wide × 10 cm high) and viewed from about 30 cm. Each card contained thirty-two circles, eight per quadrant. Half the cards had a target present; on half of these, the target was to the left of center, on the other half it was to the right of center. On the remaining cards there was no target present. Target and nontarget circles were colored according to the particular task. Each card also contained a central digit, which H.C. was required to name at the start of each trial.

H.C. was told the target before each condition. He was also told that half the cards would contain the target while the other half would not. He responded yes or no, and responses were recorded via a stopwatch by an experimenter blind to the hypotheses. There were one hundred and twenty trials in each condition (60 per session), so that in each case the target was present thirty times in the left field and thirty in the right.

In pilot work we also examined the effects of the number of nontargets on H.C.'s ability to detect right-side targets in the condition where there was high target-nontarget similarity and low nontarget-nontarget similarity (with yellow targets and green-blue nontargets; this was when the search was most difficult). There were no effects of the number of nontargets present (his RTs were 2.4, 2.25, 2.5, and 2.45 sec respectively with 4, 6, 8, and 10 items per quadrant). This indicates that even in the most difficult task, H.C. did not show a pattern of RTs consistent with serial search to right-side targets. Thus, in each case it can be argued that the target comprised a disjunctive feature that can be detected via a spatially parallel search.

Rationale

The idea behind this study was as follows. If H.C. shows impaired orienting to stimuli presented contralateral to his lesion, then he should show marked effects of both target-nontarget and nontarget-nontarget similarity when targets are presented in his impaired (left) visual field. Such a result cannot be attributed to a disengagement problem, since the nontargets in H.C.'s right field stay the same under the different target-nontarget conditions; hence nontargets should *hold* H.C.'s attention to the same extent as target-nontarget similarity is varied. Also, since right-side targets in even the most difficult task can be detected via a parallel search process, the effects can be attributed to problems orienting to disjunctive features rather than to feature conjunctions.

Results

The RTs and error rates for left- and right-side targets in each task are given in table 7.1.

The RT data were analyzed by treating each correct response time as a separate observation. On target-present trials there were main effects of field, target-nontarget similarity, and nontarget-nontarget similarity ($F(1, 187) = 1008$, 922, and 525, respectively, all $p < 0.001$). All the interactions were significant, including the crucial three-way field × target-nontarget similarity × nontarget-nontarget similarity interaction ($F(1, 187) = 43.68$, $p < 0.001$). This interaction arose because the combined effects of target-nontarget similarity and nontarget-nontarget similarity were more pronounced in the left than in the right visual field.

For the target-absent RT data, there were also main effects of target-nontarget and of nontarget-nontarget similarity ($F(1, 156) = 512$ and 786, respectively, $p < 0.001$). The target-nontarget × nontarget-nontarget similarity interaction was also significant ($F(1, 156) = 13.44$, $p < 0.001$).

H.C. missed 30.8 percent (37/120) of the targets presented in the left visual field, relative to 7 percent (8/120) of the targets in the right visual field. The

Table 7.1 The Mean Correct RTs (in sec) and Percent Errors (%E) Made by H. C. in Study 1

Target-Nontarget Similarity	High (yellow)		Low (red)	
Nontarget-Nontarget Similarity	High (green)	Low (green-blue)	High (green)	Low (green-blue)
Left field present				
RT	2.34	4.13	1.92	2.88
(%E)	(26.7)	(30.0)	(40.0)	(26.7)
Right field present				
RT	1.95	2.35	1.86	2.10
(%E)	(7.0)	(10.0)	(3.3)	(7.0)
Absent				
RT	2.96	4.37	2.11	3.20
(%E)	(0.0)	(0.0)	(0.0)	(0.0)

effects of presentation field on miss rate was highly significant ($X^2 = 21.44$, $p < 0.001$). In the left field, there were no significant effects of either target-nontarget similarity (i.e., red vs. yellow targets, 20/60 vs. 17/60 misses, $X^2 < 1.0$), or of nontarget-nontarget similarity (i.e., green vs. green-blue non-targets, 20/60 vs. 17/60 misses; $X^2 < 1.0$). There were too few right field errors for analysis. On absent trials H.C. made no errors.

Discussion

The data show clear effects of both target-nontarget and nontarget-nontarget similarity in this neglect patient, with the combined effects of these two factors slowing his RTs dramatically for targets in the left field relative to those in the right field. In Duncan and Humphreys's (1989) terms, this suggests a complex and nonlinear shift in the scaling of the "search surface" in the neglected and non-neglected fields. This shift cannot be attributed to an attentional disengagement problem alone, since target discriminability was manipulated such that information in the non-neglected field remained constant.

We propose that the shift in the search surface reflects the unilateral impairment of an orienting mechanism normally activated by salient differences between stimuli in the visual field. Apparently the orienting mechanism takes disproportionally longer to be activated by targets on the neglected side relative to the non-neglected side of space as (1) target-nontarget similarity increases, and (2) nontarget-nontarget similarity decreases. Also, with H.C., there seems to be a high probability that the orienting mechanism never reaches threshold under any circumstance, producing target misses unrelated to both types of stimulus similarity. This may stem from inhibition of an already impaired orienting system by the attentional maintenance system. We will discuss such a possibility more fully in the next section.

7.5 STUDY 2

Object- and Space-Vision

According to the framework we have outlined, attentional orienting mechanisms respond to salient stimulus differences and move attention to the locations where these differences occur. That is, orienting mechanisms are inherently spatial. The behavior of patients with orienting problems should be spatially determined (e.g., they should involve neglect of one half of visual space). On the other hand, patients whose problems occur because the attentional maintenance mechanism exerts an abnormal *hold* may show object-based attentional abnormalities. Proper evaluation of these ideas requires patients with orienting problems to be separated from those with problems in attentional maintenance.

To assess the relations between space and object coding, we have recently examined patients with Balint's syndrome. Balint's syndrome typically has two fundamental characteristics: visual disorientation (such that only the object at the center of attention is "seen" at any one time) and optic ataxia (misreaching to stimuli using visual guidance) (e.g., Damasio 1985). In at least some Balint's syndrome patients, visual disorientation can be linked to an abnormal hold exerted by the attentional maintenance mechanism on orienting.

Subjects

The subjects were two patients with Balint's syndrome who had differing etiologies. One, S.P., suffered carbon monoxide poisoning that produced diffuse pronounced lesions of both occipital lobes and the right frontal lobe. He had a lower left quadrantinopia on perimetric testing. The other patient, S.A., had cerebral degeneration, initially most pronounced over the left parietal region but bilaterally sited over the parietal lobes at the time of testing. Several tests of her visual fields using Goldman perimetry produced rather inconclusive results, with either shallow fields or a lower-right quadrantinopia emerging. Both patients were diagnosed as having Balint's syndrome because (1) they seemed able to identify only the object at the center of their attention in interpreting pictures of complex scenes (ignoring surrounding stimuli), (2) they showed marked problems in responding to multiple simultaneously presented visual stimuli (Humphreys 1991), and (3) they had optic ataxia. Our investigations concerned their visual disorientation (points 1 and 2 above). S.P. was twenty-eight years old at the time of testing, and S.A. was seventy years old.

Tests of Visual Orienting

As noted above, to make conclusions about the distinction between object and space vision, it may be necessary to distinguish patients with orienting problems from those with problems due to abnormal maintenance of attention.

We did this by examining the patients' ability to use spatial cues for responses to stimuli presented at central and peripheral spatial locations. On each trial, the patients were presented with either a letter S or H, which they named as quickly as possible. The target letter appeared either in the center of the visual field or 4 degree left or right of center. Preceding the target was a cue, to the center, left, or right field. The cue was a single fixation cross, which fell at a location just above that of the target when the cue and target were in the same area of field (left, center, or right). There was no predictive relationship between the location of the cue and that of the target. The cue was presented for durations of 150 and 300 msec and followed immediately by the target (for 200 msec.).

Rationale

If patients are able to orient normally to briefly presented visual stimuli, responses to targets should be facilitated when targets fall in the same area of field as the cue (since attention will be oriented to the target's location by the cue). By examining performance at two SOAs, we also test the efficiency of the orienting mechanism as the duration of the cueing signal varies.

Results

Figure 7.3 illustrates the correct RTs for each patient as a function of the location of the target in the visual field relative to that of the cue, for cue-target SOAs of 150 and 300 msec.

Clear differences emerged between the performance of the two patients. S.A. showed a positive effect of cueing only at the longer SOA, and there was no cueing effect with a 150-msec SOA. This lack of a cueing effect at the short SOA is unlikely to reflect problems in moving attention (cf. Posner et al. 1985). For instance, there was no effect of cueing even at the central location, where attentional movements are not required. Also, in other experiments S.A. failed to show a cueing effect with a brief (50-msec) cue even after a 300-msec. SOA. Instead, we suggest that S.A. has an orienting problem, such that she fails to orient unless visual stimuli have sufficient energy (note though that she can detect the presence of briefly presented stimuli, as evidenced by her performance in perimetry tests).

S.P., however, appeared to have no problems in orienting. He showed a positive effect of cueing at each SOA: performance was facilitated when the target appeared at the cued location relative to when it appeared at an uncued location. This contrasts with what happens when S.P. is asked to detect multiple targets, where he is markedly impaired (see below). We suggest that the contrast occurs because, for S.P., there is abnormal inhibition of the orienting system(s) after attention is engaged on an object. Interestingly, some evidence of "abnormal hold" also occurred in the cueing data, since S.P.'s RTs were generally slower at the longer SOA, when attention might be engaged

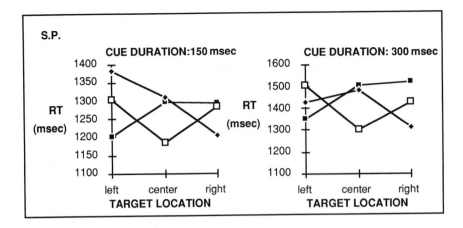

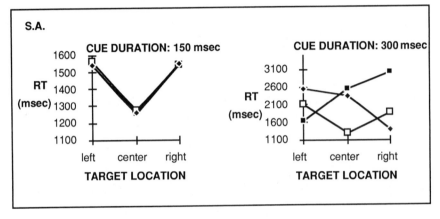

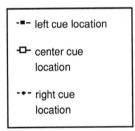

-■- left cue location

-□- center cue
location

-◆- right cue
location

Figure 7.3 Mean correct RTs (msec) of S.P. and S.A. to make choice responses for letter targets as a function of the position of a spatial cue relative to the target letter, at two SOAs.

Humphreys and Riddoch

by the cue (see fig. 7.3). It seems that, having attended to the cue, S.P. had some difficulty reorienting to the target.

This problem was also apparent in S.A.'s data. She too was slower overall at the longer cue duration. Difficulty in disengaging attention from the cue might be expected with S.A., due to (normal) inhibition from the attentional maintenance mechanism on an impaired orienting system.

7.6 STUDY 3

Tests of Object Vision and Space Vision

Given that our two patients, S.A. and S.P., had different functional impairments, we were interested in further examining whether they were sensitive to object or spatial information in visual-selection tasks. The patients were presented with displays of thirty-two colored circles. All the circles were either the same color (all red or all green) or half were red and half green. Over separate blocks of trials, displays were tachistoscopically presented for 500, 750, 1000, or 2000 msec (followed by a pattern mask). The patients simply had to decide whether all the circles were the same color or whether there were two different colors present. The circles were either *close* (the average center-to-center spacing was 0.3° visual angle) or *spaced* (the average center-to-center spacing was 1.2°).

This task might logically be performed by responding to each display as a whole, so that individual circles need not be selected as separate perceptual objects. However, pilot work using single circles of either the same or differing colors indicated that this was not how either patient performed the task; rather, the patients responded to individual circles, finding it particularly hard to judge when there were two circles of different colors present.

There were three conditions of interest (see fig. 7.4). In the *random* condition, the spaces between the colored circles contained sets of black lines. In the *single-object* condition the lines joined together circles of the same color. In the *mixed-object* condition, the lines joined together circles of opposite color. Circles of different colors were joined together only in the mixed-object condition. The average distance between the circles, and the average lengths of the lines, were the same in the mixed-object, the single-object and the random conditions.

Rationale

If patients are poor at selecting two circles of different colors from these displays, and if this problem is spatially determined, then they should perform better when the circles are closer together, but there should be no effects of the different "object" conditions (i.e., random vs. single vs. mixed). However, if their problems are object based, in that they have difficulty disengaging attention once it is directed to an object, then performance should be better in

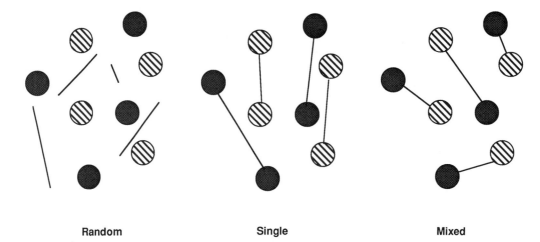

| Random | Single | Mixed |

Figure 7.4 Illustration of stimuli used to assess object-based versus spatially based selection in Balint's syndrome patients. Filled (blackened) circles in the figure represent green circles of the original display, and striped circles represent red circles of the original display.

the mixed-object than in the random and single-object conditions, since only in the mixed-object condition are the two colors present within a single object.

Results

For both patients, performance was best in the mixed-object condition. With *spaced* displays there was relatively little difference between performance in the single-object and random conditions. Averaging over exposure durations, S.P. scored about 64 percent correct in the mixed condition, relative to 57 and 55 percent in the single and random conditions; S.A. scored about 71 percent versus 58 and 57 percent in the mixed, single, and random conditions, respectively. Thus, for both patients, performance was better if they could select both colors from the same perceptual object.

With *close* displays, S.P scored 75 percent correct with mixed displays and 55 percent with single and random displays at each spacing. He was quite unaffected by spacing. S.A., however, performed better when the circles were closer together. With *close* displays she scored 90 percent, 75 percent, and 73 percent in the mixed, single, and random conditions.

Discussion

These results support our general distinction between different attentional disorders in neuropsychological patients. In particular, they link problems in visual orienting to a spatial property of displays—namely, the distances separate disparate elements in the field. In contrast, problems due to abnormal maintenance of attention are not affected by this spatial property, but by whether elements conjoin to form single objects.

S.A. has a major problem in orienting to salient signals in the visual field (study 2). For her, bringing disparate stimuli into closer proximity markedly enhances orienting and improves performance. She performs better with mixed rather than single-object or random displays because, once her attention is engaged on an object, there is inhibition of the impaired orienting system, leading to disengagement problems. She can then detect the presence of circles of different colors if they are part of the same object but is less likely to do so otherwise.

In contrast, S.P. does not have an orienting problem per se (study 2), but he has difficulty disengaging due to abnormal attentional "hold." Thus, S.P. can select single objects in the displays, be they single or joined circles, but has difficulty selecting multiple objects. However, S.P.'s performance is far from perfect even in the mixed-object condition, where one might expect good performance because different colored circles, when present, are joined into a single object. This suggests a residual deficit, which stems from the competition over what is first selected in each display. In particular, the different colors of the mixed objects can act as cues to segment the objects, so that paired circles are not always selected as unitary perceptual wholes.

7.7 GENERAL DISCUSSION

We have proposed a general framework for visual attention that assumes that behavior emerges from the interactions between components of an attentional network. The components of this network perform different computational roles. Some respond to salient stimulus differences and orient attention to their location in the visual field. Some allow attention to be oriented under voluntary control to new locations. Some produce the maintenance of attention on objects. Orienting mechanisms are space based, while visual selection is object based. We have attempted to account for certain neuropsychological disorders of visual attention in terms of selective impairment to parts of this attentional network.

Our proposal that patients have problems disengaging from selected *objects* fits with several previous findings in the literature. For instance, Luria (1959) described the case of a Balint's syndrome patient who "saw" a single triangle when two triangles of different colors were superimposed, but a Star of David when the triangles were the same colors. Kinsbourne and Warrington (1962) failed to find any effect of the distance between letters on letter report in patients impaired at identifying multiple briefly presented letters. Kartsounis and Warrington (1989) report a patient with visual neglect who correctly copied sets of overlapping shapes (such as the Olympic rings), but not sets of separate shapes occupying the same spatial area. In cases such as these, we suggest that patients have problems disengaging attention from previously attended objects; because the problem is object based, there are no effects of spatial separation between to-be-attended objects, along with some benefits when multiple stimuli can be coded and selected as single objects.

What about patients with orienting problems? Note here that the orienting mechanism may not be simply impaired; it may be *nonlinearly transformed*. In common clinical tasks used to assess visual neglect, such as line bisection, attention may not be oriented into the neglected field as a linear function of line length; rather, proportionately more neglect may occur with longer lines (cf. Bisiach et al. 1983; Riddoch and Humphreys 1983). The notion that a simple cut-off exists between neglected and non-neglected space may grossly oversimplify the situation.

A final and more general point concerns the implications of our argument for understanding the relations between object and space vision. Considerable neurophysiological evidence suggests the separation of object and space vision into two different cortical processing streams: a dorsal (occipital-parietal) stream concerned with spatial processing and a ventral (occipital-temporal) stream concerned with object recognition (e.g., Ungerleider and Mishkin 1982). We have suggested that a spatially based attentional system is yoked to the object recognition system by their effects on a common set of image features. In this way, visual selection comes to be object based rather than space based. This proposal illustrates how the dorsal and ventral processing streams may interact.

The distinction between components of the attentional system itself, and in particular between the attentional maintenance and orienting processes, is supported by work with both normal subjects and brain-damaged patients, while the neuropsychological evidence further links the orienting system(s) to spatially bound processes and selection to perceptual objects. We believe that more detailed neuropsychological work, which explores interactions between the components of the attentional network, will provide future important constraints on our understanding of attention and its influence on vision.

NOTE

This research was supported by grants from the Wolfson Foundation, and the Medical Research Council and the Science and Engineering Research Council of Great Britain. The proposals here have benefited from discussions with John Duncan and Hermann Müller, and the paper has gained from comments by Dave Meyer, Sylvan Kornblum, Anne Treisman, and an anonymous reviewer. Our thanks to Cathy Price and Philip Quinlan for their help with the experiments, and to the patients, H.C., S.A., and S.P., for their participation. Presentation of the research at Attention and Performance XIV was facilitated by a grant from the journal *Brain*.

REFERENCES

Allport, D. A. (1987). Selection for action: Some behavioural and neurophysiological considerations of attention and action. In H. Heuer and A. F. Sanders (Eds.), *Perspectives on Perception and Action*, 395–420. Hillsdale, NJ: Lawrence Erlbaum Associates.

Bisiach, E., Bulgarelli, C., Sterzi, R., and Vallar, G. (1983). Line bisection and cognitive plasticity of unilateral neglect of space. *Journal of Neurology, Neurosurgery, and Psychiatry, 48,* 141–144.

Damasio, A. R. (1985). Disorders of complex visual processing. In M. M. Mesulam (Ed.), *Principles of Behavioral Neurology, Contemporary Neurology Series*, 259–288. Philadelphia: Davis.

Desimone, R., and Ungerleider, L. G. (1989). Neural mechanisms of visual processing in monkeys. In F. Boller and J. Grafman (Eds.), *Handbook of Neuropsychology*, Vol. 2, 267–299. Amsterdam: Elsevier Science.

Downing, C. J. (1988). Expectancy and visual-spatial attention: Effects on perceptual quality. *Journal of Experimental Psychology: Human Perception and Performance.* 14, 188–202.

Downing, C. J., and Pinker, S. (1985). The spatial structure of visual attention. In M. I. Posner & O. S. M. Marin (Eds.), *Attention and Performance XI*, 171–188. Hillsdale, NJ: Lawrence Erlbaum Associates.

Duncan, J. (1984). Selective attention and the organization of visual information. *Journal of Experimental Psychology: General, 113*, 501–517.

Duncan, J., and Humphreys, G. W. (1989). Stimulus similarity and visual search. *Psychological Review, 96*, 433–458.

Fischer, B. (1986). The role of attention in the preparation of visually guided eye movements in monkey and man. *Psychological Research, 48*, 251–258.

Fischer, B., and Breitmeyer, B. (1987). Mechanisms of visual attention revealed by saccadic eye movements. *Neuropsychologia, 25*, 73–83.

Halligan, P. W., Marshall, J. C., and Wade, D. T. (1990). Do visual field deficits exacerbate visuo-spatial neglect? *Journal of Neurology, Neurosurgery, and Psychiatry, 53*, 487–491.

Hawkins, H. L., Hillyard, S. A., Luck, S. J., Mouloua, M., Downing, C. J., and Woodward, D. P. (1990). Visual attention modulates signal detection. *Journal of Experimental Psychology: Human Perception and Performance, 16*, 802–811.

Heilman, K. M. (1979). Neglect and related disorders. In K. M. Heilman and E. Valenstein (Eds.), *Clinical Neuropsychology*, 268–307. New York: Oxford University Press.

Humphreys, G. W. (1991). Neuropsychological studies of vision and attention: Balint's syndrome. In R. Gregory, J. Harris, P. Heard, D. Rose, and J. Cronly-Dillon (Eds.), *The Artful Brain*. Oxford: Oxford University Press.

Humphreys, G. W., and Bruce, V. (1989). *Visual Cognition: Computational, Experimental and Neuropsychological Perspectives*. London: Lawrence Erlbaum Associates.

Humphreys, G. W., Riddoch, M. J., Müller, H. M., and Donnelly, N. (1991). Where, what and why: On the interaction between ventral object vision and dorsal space vision in humans. Unpublished manuscript.

Kartsounis, L. D., and Warrington, E. K. (1989). Unilateral visual neglect overcome by cues implicit in stimulus arrays. *Journal of Neurology, Neurosurgery, and Psychiatry, 52*, 1253–1259.

Kinsbourne, M., and Warrington, E. K. (1962). A disorder of simultaneous form perception. *Brain, 85*, 461–486.

Luria, A. R. (1959). Disorders of "simultaneous perception" in a case of bilateral occipitoparietal brain injury. *Brain, 83*, 437–449.

Mesulam, M. M. (1981). A cortical network for directed attention and unilateral neglect. *Annals of Neurology, 10*, 309–325.

Moran, J., and Desimone, R. (1985). Selective attention gates visual processing in the extrastriate cortex. *Science, 229*, 782–784.

Müller, H. M., and Humphreys, G. W. (1991). Luminance increment detection: Capacity limited or not? *Journal of Experimental Psychology: Human Perception and Performance, 17*, 107–124.

Müller, H. M., and Rabbitt, P. M. A. (1989). Reflexive and voluntary orienting of visual attention: Time course of activation and resistance to interruption. *Journal of Experimental Psychology: Human Perception and Performance, 15*, 315–330.

Nakayama, K., and Silverman, G. H. (1986). Serial and parallel processing of visual feature conjunctions. *Nature, 320*, 264–265.

Posner, M. I., Cohen, Y., and Rafal, R. D. (1982). Neural systems of spatial orienting. *Proceedings of the Royal Society of London, B298*, 187–198.

Posner, M. I., and Peterson, S. E. (1990). The attention system of the human brain. *Annual Review of Neuroscience, 13*, 25–42.

Posner, M. I., Rafal, R. D., Choate, L. S., and Vaughan, J. (1985). Inhibition of return: Neural basis and function. *Cognitive Neuropsychology, 2*, 211–228.

Posner, M. I., Walker, J. A., Friedrich, F. J., and Rafal, R. D. (1984). Effects of parietal injury on covert orienting of attention. *The Journal of Neuroscience, 4*, 1863–1974.

Rafal, R. D., and Posner, M. I. (1987). Deficits in human visual spatial atention following thalamic lesions. *Proceedings of the National Academy of Science, 84*, 7349–7353.

Riddoch, M. J. (1990). Neglect and the peripheral dyslexias. *Cognitive Neuropsychology, 7*, 369–390.

Riddoch, M. J., and Humphreys, G. W. (1983). The effect of cueing on unilateral neglect. *Neurpsychologia, 21*, 589–599.

Riddoch, M. J., and Humphreys, G. W. (1987). Perceptual and action systems in unilateral visual neglect. In M. Jeannerod (Ed.), *Neurophysiological and Neuropsychological Aspects of Spatial Neglect*, 151–182. Amsterdam: Elsevier Science.

Treisman, A., and Gelade, S. (1980). A feature-integration theory of attention. *Cognitive Psychology, 12*, 97–136.

Ungerleider, L. G., and Mishkin, M. (1982). Two cortical visual systems. In D. J. Ingle, M. A. Goodale, and R. J. W. Mansfield (Eds.), *Analysis of Visual Behavior*, 549–586. Cambridge, MA: MIT Press.

Volpe, B. T., LeDoux, J. E., and Gazzaniga, M. S. (1979). Information processing in an "extinguished" visual field. *Nature, 282*, 722–724.

Yantis, S., and Jonides, J. (1984). Abrupt visual onsets and selective attention: Evidence from visual search. *Journal of Experimental Psychology: Human perception and Performance, 10*, 601–621.

Yantis, S., and Jonides, J. (1990). Abrupt visual onsets and selective attention: Voluntary versus automatic allocation. *Journal of Experimental Psychology: Human Perception and Performance, 16*, 121–134.

8 Representing Visual Objects

Anne Treisman

In discussing a group of papers one is expected to find some shared themes, to pull threads together. The task was difficult with this set of papers, all of which offer interesting and innovative treatments, but of apparently very diverse topics. Finding a highest common denominator is inevitably also something of a Rorschach test: the choice is likely to reflect not only the content of the papers but also the preoccupations of the discussant. The only general theme that seemed to me to appear in different guises in most if not all the papers was an attempt to define and characterize the nature of the intermediate representations formed by the visual system on the way to identifying objects and events.

I was primed to see this shared thread by the fact that Daniel Kahneman and I have also been exploring the possible role of temporary "episodic" structures that might act as collecting boxes for sensory data (Kahneman and Treisman 1984; Treisman 1986, 1988). We called them "object files." In our account, these object files act as an interface between simple feature maps and the stored descriptions or models that mediate object identification in a long-term recognition network. They are addressed by their spatiotemporal coordinates rather than by their content. They assemble all the incoming information relating to the currently attended stimulus, allowing the structured relations between the features to emerge. These temporary object files or tokens can then be matched to the stored types or canonical descriptions of known objects. They can also be updated as the sensory information changes when the object moves or transforms its shape or other properties, so preserving the identity and continuity of the perceived object.

We believe that some such temporary token representations are needed to explain the following perceptual phenomena: (1) the perception of arbitrary new conjunctions of features, even when two or more such conjunctions are simultaneously present, (2) the ability to see multiple identical instances of the same object at the same time, (3) the fact that the perceptual units selected by attention seem to be objects as wholes rather than their attributes (Kahneman 1973; Treisman, Kahneman, and Burkell 1983; Duncan 1984), (4) the dissociations found in some neuropsychological patients between their ability to match different views of the same object or to copy pictures of objects and their inability to identify the same objects (Farah 1990; Humphreys and

Riddoch 1987; Warrington and Taylor 1978), and (5) the perceptual unity we attribute to moving or changing objects. Kahneman, Treisman, and Gibbs (1992) have found supporting evidence for this last function in experiments testing object-specific priming and object-specific accumulation of feature information across intervals of time and space.

Starting from these general ideas, what can I learn from the other chapters in this volume to flesh out and make more precise an account of these intermediate object representations? To what extent do the chapters agree?

8.1 OBJECT IDENTIFICATION

Ullman's chapter deals directly with the problem of object recognition. He therefore has specific and explicit proposals concerning the nature of the representations that are matched to a mental dictionary of object models. He takes an unusually low-level approach, working with a two-dimensional pictorial image rather than requiring any prior analysis of the image into possible three-dimensional parts (e.g., the geons proposed by Biederman 1987), or forming a more abstract propositional description of its structure. In the first part of his chapter, he deals with the initial segmentation of the scene, defining some of the characteristics that make an image likely to attract attention and (in our terms) to be assigned to a separate object file. The retinal image is first transformed into an edge map resembling a complex, noisy, superimposed line drawing, within which real objects are usually characterized by longer, smoother contours than those that result from the background noise. Ullman develops economical algorithms for determining the Gestalt properties of good continuation, smoothness or minimum curvature, and extended length, allowing the extraction of contours that maximize those properties. So in noisy contexts the images likely to be selected as potential objects would be those with the least curvature and the best continuity of outline. These properties would not be the only ones giving high-priority access to object files; Ullman mentions the "pop-out" effect with locally salient features like a unique color, direction of motion, or stereoscopic depth. But even with more global properties, I would suggest the possibility of a reversed effect in which a single, very angular or wiggly line on a background of smooth curves would become the most salient unique element. We have already shown that a broken line or circle is easily detected in a background of continuous lines or closed circles (Treisman 1988; Treisman and Gomican 1988).

Once the selected contours have been extracted from the background, Ullman proposes that the identity of the object is retrieved by directly matching the spatial coordinates of the contours to those of the linear combination of a few prestored two-dimensional views for each possible model. The match may be made on points, or on oriented sets of points (picked up by linear receptive fields), or on local features such as closed blobs, cusps, deep concavities, or inflection points. Ullman (1989) even extended the set of possible features to include symbolic descriptions of spatially localized contours, for example "wiggly edge" for a cockscomb. This combination of spatial indexing with local propositional abstractions within a single representation is an interesting suggestion. We do seem to code many perceptual properties with global descriptions, the mental equivalents of words like *many*, *heterogeneous*, *furry*, and *jagged*, without storing the detail, yet without losing the analog properties of the more general spatial layout or of the global texture, color, size, and orientation.

Whatever format is used for the stored models, this format must also be explicit in the images to which they are matched. The amount of spatial detail available seems to be considerable (sufficient to distinguish a Saab from a Volkswagon). Perhaps there could be some prior selection of which points or contours are critical for any given vocabulary of objects, rather than an equally precise transmission of all contours for all images; Ullman does not discuss this possibility in chapter 4 (see, however, Ullman 1989). Another form of abstraction should also be noted: since the match between the current image and the stored models is made on spatial coordinates rather than on intensity values, the particular discontinuities that define the boundaries of the image are irrelevant—they could be defined by positive or negative contrast, by color, by motion, by texture or stereo depth, or they could be some composite best-fit boundaries emerging from a pooled representation (Cavanagh, Arguin, and Treisman 1990).

Ullman offers an elegant and economical way of identifying objects from relatively literal two-dimensional images, without much intervening recoding or analysis. An important new contribution is to show that the alignment problem, of compensating for differences of orientation in three-dimensional space before matching the image to possible models, can potentially be solved by prestoring just three two-dimensional views for the front of objects with sharp edges (five for objects with smoothly curved surfaces). This theory opens up exciting new possibilities, including a possible convergence of the underlying mechanisms used in object identification with those that mediate apparent motion. So far as my selected theme for discussion is concerned, it offers a low-level, two-dimensional analog view of the contents of possible object files and shows that this may be sufficient to access top-down information about the identity of the object currently in view.

Ullman does not intend his model to be taken as a full account of human object identification. Some extensions or modifications might be needed to deal with objects that allow a range of different relative sizes of their parts, or a range of different relative positions of parts within the whole (for example, the movable limbs of human and animal bodies, the varied shapes of oak trees and teapots). There are advantages in representing some classes of objects at two articulated levels, by the presence of a particular set of parts plus a particular range of relations between the parts, rather than as more global, unarticulated wholes. The occurrence of illusory recombinations of features also suggests that the articulation may have some psychological reality in human vision (Treisman and Paterson 1984). Another potential difficulty in applying the model to human object perception is that it identifies objects first at the most specific level—Saabs or VWs rather than cars—whereas there is some evidence that humans access first the "basic level" category before they identify the subcategory (Rosch et al. 1976). Perhaps Ullman's suggestion concerning prealignment to a prototype model could help on this point, as well as reducing the computational load when multiple models must be considered. Moreover, Ullman (1989) stated explicitly that the align-and-match method may be only one of several routes used by the human visual system to identify objects. Different classes of objects may require different specialized forms of analysis.

8.2 OBJECT MATCHING ACROSS SACCADES

Irwin's goal is also to determine the nature of the representations that are matched in perceptual processing. The match here is not to stored models but to a prior image of the same object resulting from the previous fixation. The aim is to determine the correspondence across eye movements that change the retinal location of all the features. Irwin offers compelling evidence that this correspondence is established not by point-to-point superimposition, but at a less detailed, more schematic level. Absolute location is lost, as is the detail of images any more complex than eight random dots. By varying the delay and the location of the postsaccadic presentation, Irwin shows a clear transition between a very transitory, detailed, retinotopic image and the more schematic visual memory that lasts up to five seconds and that seems to be independent of location. In fact he concludes that there *is* no specialized saccadic buffer memory separate from the general visual short-term store. This encourages the speculation that he could in fact be studying the same intermediate representation as Ullman.

Could the representations and the matching process be the same for, on the one hand, successive images of the same object in different retinal locations across successive intervals of time and, on the other hand, an input image and the long-term stored models in the object thesaurus? The critical information in both Ullman's images and Irwin's visual representations concerns the relative positions of parts or features. These typically remain stable across saccades that change their retinal locations. I am not sure how to compare the limited complexity of the stored images of Irwin's random dot patterns with the detail needed to distinguish Ullman's pictures of Saabs and VWs. It might be interesting to see if subjects would detect a difference between Ullman's two cars across saccades in Irwin's paradigm. Part of the apparent difference in capacity may be due to different demands on memory. In identifying an object, the sensory information typically remains present and the memory demands are on the long-term thesaurus of stored objects. On the other hand, in matching across saccades, information from the first fixation must be held in short-term visual memory to be compared with the second. The capacity of this temporary visual memory may well be more limited than that of the object representations in the permanent thesaurus.

An apparently inconsistent finding, throwing some doubt on the visuo-spatial quality of transsaccadic information, comes from the finding (Rayner,

McConkie, and Zola 1980) that transsaccadic priming is unaffected by a change in the case of letters, despite the change in spatial relations inherent in many same-letter pairs (e.g., *a* and *A*). Irwin, however, attributes this nonvisual letter priming and the visual spatial feature priming to separate memory systems. An alternative would be to allow different forms of information to combine in a single memory representation. Both Ullman's hybrid representations and our concept of object files allow the possibility of combining physical features with identity information. The object file is assumed to collate the feature information (initially available) with identity information once this has been retrieved by matching to long-term recognition memory.

Some results that we obtained while exploring the notion of object files contrast with those reported by Irwin (Kahneman, Treisman and Gibbs 1992). Instead of studying the integration of information across eye movements, we studied integration across movements of the object itself. We found evidence that new information associated with a previously presented object was selectively affected by prior information about the same object. For example, we presented two letters briefly inside two outline shapes (frames), then moved the empty frames to two new locations and presented a single letter in one of the two. Subjects were faster in naming this target letter if it matched the letter previously presented in the same frame at its prior location, but they were not affected at all by a match with a letter previously presented in the other (equidistant) frame. Thus information in our experimental paradigm was often integrated in a completely object-specific fashion, contrasting with the indifference to spatial location (and therefore to object continuity) observed by Irwin et al. A relevant difference may be that we presented two letters in the priming field; in pilot experiments with a single priming letter presented in one of two or three frames, the object specificity was much reduced. Perhaps a new stimulus is integrated with whatever past stimulus fits best; if two competing past histories are available, the one consistent with object continuity is chosen, but if only one possible candidate is available, the present and past letters will be integrated regardless of whatever object constraints are violated. Indeed, the single priming letter in our experiments did sometimes appear to jump in apparent motion to a new frame. It would be interesting to introduce competing objects in Irwin's transsaccadic tests to see if location (or object) specificity would then be observed.

8.3 A TEMPORAL DIMENSION IN OBJECT REPRESENTATIONS

Irwin and Freyd share an interest in the temporal dimension of visual processing. They are part of a new trend to explore change and movement in the context of object perception and to study events as well as static states. In Irwin's research, the changes result from the observer's active, exploratory role. The problem is to separate the effects of these extrinsically produced changes in the retinal image from those produced by movement of the objects themselves. Freyd's research, on the other hand, explores the dynamic interpretations that subjects spontaneously impose on many objectively static views. She too makes important new claims about the nature of visual object representations. Like Irwin's, her evidence comes from probing memory at short intervals after presentation. However, her experiments test a specific hypothesis: that mental representations are dynamic rather than static. Freyd claims that they have an intrinsic temporal dimension even when the stimuli themselves consist of one or more static views. Observers link an orderly sequence of pictures to infer continuous motion and then spontaneously continue the "momentum" in the implied direction. Even a single picture of an apparently moving object evokes this inference of changed location.

Like Irwin and Ullman, Freyd suggests an analog spatial representation that preserves the relative locations of elements over time and integrates them into a single perceptual object. The transformations occur progressively and continuously rather than in discrete time steps. However, this representation is clearly not just a sensory photograph; in several of Freyd's experiments, it must already have been interpreted. The movement inferred from a single picture can be affected by knowledge of the physical properties of the represented object—for example, the difference between a released spring (implying upward movement) and a falling weight (implying downward movement). The lines of the picture must be matched to the outlines of the physical objects they represent before this kind of knowledge can come into play to determine their inferred positions a moment later. Thus, Ullman's two-dimensional matching and model identification must already be completed at the time that Freyd's probes are presented. It is interesting that even *after* the objects have been identified, their representations appear to retain a dynamic, spatial, and temporal analog quality. The visual tokens of present stimuli (their object files, in our terms) seem to be retained, as well as a record of the types to which they are matched.

We see object files as containing the information that is reflected in subjective perceptual experience. Freyd, however, believes that conscious experience is more discrete and symbolic than these dynamic images, which she claims are not accessible to introspection. She attributes the categorical quality of awareness to the limited capacity constraints of shareability, whether with other people through language or between modular brain systems through neural connections within a single individual. The process of encoding ideas and experiences into speakable sentences (or into neural codes that can be compressed into limited communication channels) may feed back onto the perceptual experiences themselves, preventing conscious awareness of the more continuous, dynamic and analog images that she infers from her experiments. This is an interesting idea. However, I am not sure that the categorical and discrete quality Freyd attributes to mental experience reflects a generally shared impression. It seems fairly easy to fly a mental bird across a mental sky. On the other hand, Freyd is in good company with Milan Kundera, who remarked, "Memory doesn't film, memory takes photographs." Introspections often differ and may be difficult to use as evidence about the underlying mechanisms.[1]

What other findings might be relevant? If Freyd is right that shareability affects the perceptual precursors of what is to be communicated, we might expect it to affect other dimensions of experience besides the dynamic ones. Space, color, texture should all be perceived categorically. But when psychologists have looked for effects of language (e.g., nameability) on perceptual continua (as opposed to memory), they have had little success (Bornstein 1975; Carroll and Casagrande 1958; Heider and Olivier 1972). We do seem to perceive some distinctions categorically, particularly phonemic and musical contrasts (Cutting and Rosner 1974; Studdert-Kennedy 1975). Perhaps the critical factor is not so much whether we communicate the experiences, but (1) whether the stimuli arise from discrete sources or categories in the world (e.g., plucked vs. bowed instruments, cats vs. Pekingese dogs), and (2) whether our behavioral response must be categorical (e.g., fight or flight). It is important for us to distinguish whether someone is chasing us or merely following, whether a mushroom is edible or poisonous, because the implications for adaptive behavior are mutually exclusive. My guess is that animals would also show categorical perception in cases where evolution has faced them with critical choices between alternative interpretations of stimuli that are associated with mutually exclusive responses. We certainly sharpen our perception of distinctive features as we become expert in reading X rays for signs of malignancy, or in sexing chickens (Gibson 1969). Language may sometimes sharpen perception in the same way, but its effects may be less important than the constraints imposed by understanding the world and interacting successfully with it.

The issue of categorical versus continuous perception is also raised in Van Kleeck and Kosslyn (chap. 2; see also Kosslyn 1987; Kosslyn et al. 1990). He proposed an interesting possibility, together with some evidence supporting it: the suggestion was that we may compute both categorical relations (e.g., 'between', 'connected to') and metric or coordinate properties (e.g., 'two inches apart'), and that the left and right hemispheres may have become specialized to handle the two types of processing separately. The left hemisphere (with its language centers) would deal primarily with categorical relations, and the right hemisphere with the more continuous metric relations. Different tasks require different information: motor behavior, such as grasping, throwing, or reaching, requires fairly exact spatial coordinates, whereas object identification, which needs to be invariant across variation of size and absolute position, may depend more on categorical descriptions. Perhaps we set up parallel but connected object files in the two hemispheres, to represent these different properties of the same object.

8.4 OBJECT-BASED ATTENTION: EVIDENCE FROM NEUROPSYCHOLOGY

In general, Kosslyn emphasized the importance of combining behavioral, computational, and neural approaches to the same problems, and showed how the three interact and complement our understanding. Humphreys and

Riddoch (chap. 7) offer a good example of how neuropsychological evidence from patients with localized brain damage can throw light on visual processing. Their main interest is in distinguishing two forms of visual attention: a spatially based orienting to salient stimuli, and an object-based selection in which attention is engaged and held by one particular object at a time. They separate the two by contrasting patients with unilateral spatial neglect who fail to orient to stimuli on the neglected side, and patients with Balint's syndrome who appear to have trouble disengaging attention from a first object in order to process a second. The facilitating effect of linking lines, on the ability of two such patients to compare the colors of two objects, is a particularly intriguing example of object-bound attention. The lines apparently make a single perceptual unit of two otherwise separate shapes, allowing them to share the same object file and thus be compared without any need to disengage and switch attention.

Is the empirical evidence requiring a separation of spatial from object-based attention compelling? There is certainly evidence suggesting purely spatial effects of orienting. An example is the spatial gradient around a cued location that facilitates detection of a secondary target in the neighborhood of an attended stimulus (Hoffman, Nelson, and Houck 1983; Laberge 1983). There is also evidence for object-based attention when spatial distance is equated (Duncan 1984; Treisman, Kahneman, and Burkell 1983). What may be more arguable is the equation of space-based attention with orienting and of object-based attention with holding. Orienting may sometimes also be object based, but is initially more global and less finely tuned to details of the structure; as time passes attention would become more narrowly focused on the relevant contours (Murphy and Eriksen 1987). The neuropsychological deficits may correspond more closely to the distinction between the operations of engaging and disengaging attention (Posner et al. 1987), and only indirectly to the distinction between spatial and object-based attention.

It might be possible to dissociate these two types of attention, in normal subjects as well as in patients, by adapting our moving object paradigm. One could cue an object like an empty frame in one location (either by a local pointer or by flashing the frame itself), then move the frame immediately to another location while a second frame moves to the original location. One could then probe attention to a letter, either in the frame currently at the cued location (spatially based attention) or in the cued frame at its new location (object-based attention). Patients with Balint's syndrome should be impaired when the cue signals the old location but the new frame, because they have trouble disengaging from an object. In contrast, patients with neglect might have trouble orienting to the new location, even though the cued frame had moved to it. Tipper, Brehaut, and Driver (1990), using a similar method, have recently shown object-based rather than spatially based inhibition of return. Inhibition of return (Posner and Cohen 1984) is thought to reflect a decreased ability to attract an orienting response. Tipper, Brehaut, and Driver's result therefore confirms that orienting (as well as engagement) can sometimes be object-specific.

Some recent results in visual search have led me to propose a related distinction between two ways of controlling attention (Treisman 1988; Treisman and Sato 1990). Both are spatially mediated, but with one form of control the relevant locations can be selected independently of the objects they contain, while with the other the locations are defined solely by the relevant objects. The first form of attention is controlled by moving an attention "window" to selected areas within a master map of locations. Different feature maps are linked to the master map, so that all the features currently present in the attended window are thereby selected for further processing and can be integrated to specify a unitary object. The second form of attentional selection is controlled by inhibition from one or more of these feature maps acting on all master map locations that currently contain those irrelevant features. The effect is the same as that of the attention window: irrelevant items are gated and the features in the remaining locations are selectively passed on for further processing. (Equivalent effects could be achieved by selective activation from features of the attended objects; see also Wolfe, Cave, and Franzel 1989.) This feature-based selection allows attention to be restricted to relevant objects, even when they are spatially interspersed with irrelevant objects, provided that the relevant ones differ from the irrelevant ones in one or more salient and highly discriminable features, for example, one of two overlapping shapes defined by their color (Rock and Gutman 1981; Tipper 1985).

Humphreys and Riddoch's (chap. 7) spatial orienting would correspond to movement of the attention window to the particular location in the master map of locations that contains a spatial cue, or that corresponds to a more centrally interpreted instruction (e.g., high tone means top row). This type of spatial orienting aligns the attention window with the general area of the cue. Neighboring stimuli, that happen to fall close to the cued area, will therefore also receive some preferential processing, resulting in a spatial gradient around the center of the cued area (Laberge 1983). Humphreys and Riddoch's object selection would simply reflect the finer control from one or more feature maps, selectively sparing the master map locations that contain the relevant features of an attended object. This account predicts that attention should more easily select spatially integrated conjunctions (e.g., red vertical lines among red horizontal and green vertical lines) than spatially separated conjunction stimuli (e.g., a red patch adjacent to a black vertical line among red patches adjacent to black horizontal lines and green patches adjacent to black vertical lines). Grabowecky and Khurana (1990), working in my laboratory, have found large differences in search rates between these two conjunction search conditions, even when the complexity and heterogeneity of the displays were closely matched.

More challenging results for any account of either spatial or object-based visual attention are those described by Pylyshyn and Storm (1988). Their subjects were able to keep track of up to four of eight identical white dots moving randomly and independently of each other. Since the selected dots had no unique features not shared by the distractors, other than their individual spatiotemporal histories, selective activation from a feature map cannot mediate this selective tracking. Margaret Wilson and I (in preparation) have shown that attention is required to perform this task: our subjects' performance deteriorated when a competing visual task was imposed. Yantis (1989) reports evidence consistent with the idea that subjects represent the selected dots as the corners of a global shape, deforming over time, and that they maintain attention to this shape as a whole rather than to its component dots. Thus, selection in this task must be explained by downward control from an object representation at the level at which the four dots are assembled into a shared token or object file. However, attention also determines what gets entered into the single-object file; the process seems to depend on an interactive cycle which is easily broken, either when attention wanders or when the object distorts too drastically. The selected dots are defined only by their history and continuity of motion across space.

Maloney's chapter has the least direct relevance to the theme of object perception. Color constancy does, however, reflect the goal of perception as a means of discovering the real world of objects and events. Maloney proposes an elegant theory to account for how we might achieve a representation of real object colors despite changes in illumination, rather than simply responding to the wavelengths of the reflected light. Recent evidence suggests that the features that become salient in preattentive processing may include features of three-dimensional objects after the direction of illumination has been established (Ramachandran 1988; Enns and Rensink 1990). Further research may explore whether preattentive saliency (and therefore the features to be assembled in object files) reflects real-world colors or retinal colors.

How much convergence have we actually found between these different views of the role and content of object files (or their equivalents) in the chapters reviewed here? Several of the chapters pose some form of correspondence problem. It appears explicitly in Ullman's discussion (chap. 4) of how an image could be aligned with possible models, in Irwin's discussion (chap. 6) of transsaccadic integration, and in our updating of information in object files for moving objects; it is present more implicitly in Freyd's creation (chap. 5) of a single dynamic representation from a succession of static images. Ullman raised the possibility that alignment for object identification could use operations similar to those involved in apparent motion. The correspondence problem must also be solved for dichoptic images that result in fusion, stereopsis, or binocular rivalry. An obvious question is whether the correspondence is established at the same level—on the same tokens—in all these different visual processes, or whether a more general matching process is implemented at many different levels in parallel. In the case of stereopsis, the evidence points to multiple levels: Julesz's random dot stereograms are matched on local points or oriented blobs (Julesz 1971), but Ramachandran, Rao, and Vidyasagar (1973) have shown that abstracted boundaries can also be matched either stereoscopically or for apparent motion, even when they are defined by different features in the two images (e.g., differently oriented texture lines). Irwin's matching across saccades is clearly not a point-for-point correspondence and may also take place at two different higher levels: schematic visual features and letter or word identities. Some convergence of neural mechanisms to achieve this matching on inputs at several different levels of abstraction might represent a desirable economy for the visual system. We certainly need to maintain a single continued representation for what physically remains a single object across changing views and also to identify the same physical entities as the same meaningful types, with possible exceptions for the fairy-tale transformations of pumpkins into coaches and glass slippers back to clogs.

NOTES

Preparation of this article was supported by the Air Force Office of Scientific Research, Air Force Systems Command, USAF, under grant number AFOSR 87-0125 to Anne Treisman. The manuscript is submitted for publication with the understanding that the U.S. Government is authorized to reproduce and distribute reprints for governmental purposes, notwithstanding any copyright notation thereon.

1. "Rubens decouvrait une chose assez curieuse: la memoire ne filme pas, la memoire photographie.... Sa memoire erotique lui offrait un petit album de photos porno, mais aucun film porno" (M. Kundera, *Immortalité*, Gallimard, 1990, 375).

REFERENCES

Biederman, I. (1987). Recognition-by-components: A theory of human image understanding. *Psychological Review, 94,* 115–167.

Bornstein, M. H. (1975). Qualities of color vision in infancy. *Journal of Experimental Child Psychology, 19,* 401–419.

Carroll, J. B., and Casagrande, J. B. (1958). The function of language classification in behavior. In E. E. Maccoby, T. Newcomb, and E. L. Hartley (Eds.), *Readings in social psychology,* 3d ed., 18–31. New York: Holt, Rinehart and Winston.

Cavanagh, P., Arguin, M., and Treisman, A. (1990). Effect of surface medium on visual search for orientation and size features. *Journal of Experimental Psychology: Human Perception and Performance, 16,* 479–491.

Cutting, J. E., and Rosner, B. S. (1974). Categories and boundaries in speech and music. *Perception and Psychophysics, 16,* 564–570.

Duncan, J. (1984). Selective attention and the organization of visual information. *Journal of Experimental Psychology: General, 113,* 501–517.

Enns, J., and Rensink, R. A. (1990). Influence of scene-based properties on visual search. *Science, 247,* 721–723.

Farah, M. J. (1990). *Visual agnosia.* Cambridge, MA: MIT Press.

Farah, M. J. and Hammond, K. M. (1988). Mental rotation and orientation-invariant object recognition: Dissociable processes. *Cognition, 29,* 29–46.

Gibson, E. J. (1969). *Principles of perceptual learning and development.* New York: Appleton-Century-Crofts.

Grabowecky, M., and Khurana, B. (1990). Features were meant to be integrated. *Investigative Ophthalmology & Visual Science, 31*(4),105.

Heider, E. R., and Olivier, D. C. (1972). The structure of color space in naming and memory for two languages. *Cognitive Psychology, 3,* 337–354.

Hoffman, J. E., Nelson, B., and Houck, M. R. (1983). The role of attentional resources in automatic detection. *Cognitive Psychology, 51,* 379–410.

Humphreys, G. W., and Riddoch, M. J. (1987). The fractionation of visual agnosia. In G. W. Humphreys and M. J. Riddoch (Eds.), *Visual object processing: A cognitive neuropsychological approach.* London: Erlbaum.

Julesz, B. (1971). *Foundations of cyclopean perception.* Chicago: University of Chicago Press.

Kahneman, D. (1973) *Attention and effort.* Englewood Cliffs, NJ: Prentice-Hall.

Kahneman, D., and Treisman, A. (1984). Changing views of attention and automaticity. In R. Parasuraman and D. R. Davies (Eds.), *Varieties of attention.* New York: Academic Press.

Kahneman, D., Treisman, A., and Gibbs, B. (1992). The reviewing of object files: Object-specific integration of information. *Cognitive Psychology, 24,* 175–219.

Kosslyn, S. M. (1987). Seeing and imagining in the cerebral hemispheres. *Psychological Review, 94,* 148–175.

Kosslyn, S., Flynn, R., Amsterdam, J., and Wang, G. (1990). Components of high-level vision: A cognitive neuroscience analysis and accounts of neurological syndromes. *Cognition, 34,* 203–277.

Laberge, D. (1983). Spatial extent of attention to letters and words. *Journal of Experimental Psychology: Human Perception and Performance, 9,* 371–379.

Murphy, T. D., and Eriksen, C. W. (1987). Temporal changes in the distribution of attention in the visual field in response to precues. *Perception and Psychophysics, 42,* 576–586.

Posner, M. I., and Cohen, Y. A. (1984). Components of visual orienting. In H. Bouma and D. G. Bouhuis (Eds.), *Attention and Performance X,* 531–556. Hillsdale, NJ: Erlbaum.

Posner, M. I., Inhoff, A., Friedrich, F. J., and Rafal, R. D. (1987). Isolating attentional systems: A cognitive anatomical analysis. *Psychobiology, 15,* 107–121.

Pylyshyn, Z. W., and Storm, R. W. (1988). Tracking of multiple independent targets: Evidence for a parallel tracking mechanism. *Spatial Vision, 3,* 1–19.

Ramachandran, V. (1988). Perceiving shape from shading. *Scientific American, 259,* 76–83.

Ramachandran, V. S., Rao, V. M., and Vidyasagar, T. R. (1973). The role of contours in stereopsis, *Nature, 242,* 412–414.

Rayner, K., McConkie, G. W., and Zola, D. (1980). Integrating information across eye movements, *Cognitive Psychology, 12,* 206–226.

Rock, I., and Gutman, D. (1981). Effect of inattention on form perception. *Journal of Experimental Psychology: Human Perception and Performance, 7,* 272–285.

Rosch, E., Mervis, C. B., Gray, W. D., Johnson, D. M., and Boyes-Braem, P. (1976). Basic objects in natural categories. *Cognitive Psychology, 8,* 382–439.

Studdert-Kennedy, M. (1975). From continuous signal to discrete message. In J. F. Kavanagh and J. E. Cutting (Eds.), *The role of speech in language.* Cambridge, MA: MIT Press.

Tipper, S. P. (1985). The negative priming effect: Inhibitory effects of ignored primes. *Quarterly Journal of Experimental Psychology, 37A,* 571–590.

Tipper, S. P., Brehaut, J. C., and Driver, J. (1990). Selection of moving and static objects for the control of spatially directed attention. *Journal of Experimental Psychology: Human Perception and Performance, 16,* 492–504.

Treisman, A. (1986). Features and objects in visual processing. *Scientific American, 254,* 114–126.

Treisman, A. (1988). Features and objects: The fourteenth Bartlett memorial lecture. *Quarterly Journal of Experimental Psychology, 40A,* 201–237.

Treisman, A., and Gormican, S. (1988). Feature analysis in early vision: Evidence from search asymmetries. *Psychological Review, 95,* 15–48.

Treisman, A., Kahneman, D., and Burkell, J. (1983). Perceptual objects and the cost of filtering. *Perception and Psychophysics, 33,* 527–532.

Treisman, A., and Paterson, R. (1984). Emergent features, attention and object perception. *Journal of Experimental Psychology: Human Perception and Performance, 10,* 12–31.

Treisman, A., and Sato, S. (1990). Conjunction search revisited. *Journal of Experimental Psychology: Human Perception and Performance, 16,* 459–478.

Ullman, S. (1989). Aligning pictorial descriptions: An approach to object recognition. *Cognition, 32,* 193–254.

Warrington, E. K., and Taylor, A. M. (1978). Two categorical stages of object recognition. *Perception, 33,* 527–532.

Wolfe, J. M., Cave, K. R., and Franzel, S. L. (1989). Guided search: An alternative to the feature integration model for visual search. *Journal of Experimental Psychology: Human Perception and Performance, 15,* 419–433.

Yantis, S. (1989). Dynamic multielement attentional tracking. Paper presented at the Annual Meeting of the Psychonomic Society, Atlanta, GA.

III Attention

Introduction

The fact that attention can modulate the processing of simultaneous stimulus inputs has been known for many centuries (Boring 1950; James 1890). It was during the 1950s and early 1960s, however, that scientific research on attention reached full maturity, coincident with the information-processing revolution in cognitive psychology (Norman 1969). Indeed, this research became sufficiently prominent during the 1960s that the Attention and Performance symposia were established in order to pursue it specifically along with other related aspects of performance theory.

What especially excited investigators at that time were questions about the nature of selective attention and its effects on the speed and accuracy of information processing. Are individual stimuli selected for further processing on the basis of their elementary physical features or on the basis of their meanings? Does the selection process occur relatively early or late in a sequence of processing stages? To what extent can two or more stimuli be processed accurately at the same time? What does it take for stimulus processing to become highly rapid, automatic, and effortless? Initial tentative answers to these and other basic questions appeared in Broadbent's (1958) trend-setting book, *Perception and Communication*, where he proposed a filter theory of selective attention and extended previous work on the so-called single-channel hypothesis (cf. Welford 1952). Yet the answers provided by the filter theory did not seem entirely definitive, and other investigators had their own alternative theoretical ideas (e.g., Deutsch and Deutsch 1963; Moray 1959; Treisman 1960), which served to drive attention and performance research forward.

This drive has yielded numerous further advances in our empirical and theoretical understanding of attention over the past twenty-five years. For example, more data have been collected about whether selective attention occurs at an early or late stage of information processing, with some results supporting the early-selection hypothesis and others supporting late selection. Given the obtained mixture of evidence, some investigators have introduced new "single and multiple resource" theories to characterize attention and processing capacity more realistically (e.g., Kahneman 1973; Moray 1967; Navon and Gopher 1979; Wickens 1980). Much has been learned as well about the various functions of attention in visual and auditory information processing (e.g., Treisman and Gelade 1980), and about the automatization of processing through practice on tasks like visual search (e.g., Shiffrin and Schneider 1977). Contributing to these discoveries are innovative methodological techniques, including records of event-related brain potentials (e.g., Hillyard and Kutas 1983) and brain images (e.g., Laberge and Buchsbaum 1990; Posner and Petersen 1990) that supplement traditional behavioral measures of reaction time and response accuracy. In fact, sufficient progress has occurred that the fruits of attention and performance research are now yielding valuable benefits for practioners in applied domains such as human-factors engineering, where problems of mental-workload measurement and person-machine interface design must be solved (O'Donnell and Eggemeier 1986). Nevertheless, as the chapters in part III attest, some of the "progress" made to date may have been misguided, important challenges remain ahead, and the field must continue seeking additional ways of reconciling classic empirical and theoretical approaches with new methodologies and concepts.

In the latter vein, part III starts with a provocative keynote tutorial review by Allport. An important theme of this chapter is that recent neurophysiological and neuropsychological research reveals a multiplicity of brain loci where attention has modulatory effects on various aspects of information processing. Consequently, the classic questions about early versus late attentional selection, and the hypothesis of a single selective locus, may no longer be apropos. Some of Allport's points are reinforced in the chapter by Mangun, Hillyard, and Luck, who use a combination of event-related brain potentials, magnetic-resonance brain images, and behavioral data to explore the substrates of visual selective attention. As they show, selective attentional effects occur, among other places, at the levels of both the prestriate visual cortex and the dorsal occipito-parietal cortex. Also of considerable interest is that these effects occur relatively quickly (within 150 msec or less) after stimulus onset, consistent with an early-selection hypothesis. Further sustaining some classical notions about selective attention and processing capacity, Pashler argues that the human information-processing system may contain a "bottleneck" at the point where responses are selected for output, thereby explaining the persistent "psychological refractory period" effect, which constituted a principal basis for the original single-channel hypothesis (Welford 1952). Still, as the chapter by Sperling and Wurst illustrates, concepts congruent with late-selection effects of attention are alive and well too. In particular, Sperling and Wurst introduce a new theoretical construct, attentional "tags," through which traces of visual items may be selected for further processing after they have entered a short-term visual memory store. The explanatory utility of such a construct is exactly what Allport would anticipate in light of his ideas about the multiplicity of selective attentional loci.

Moreover, Gopher's chapter seems highly compatible in the present context. To be specific, he shows how the performance of multiple perceptual-motor tasks involves metalevel attentional control mechanisms acquired through extensive varied practice. Apparently, these mechanisms provide a flexible set of skills and strategies for optimizing multiple-task performance in the face of changing task demands. Such flexibility is, indeed, what one might expect, if selective attention can operate at multiple loci, spanning both perceptual and motor sites, as Allport suggests. Similar themes likewise carry through to Duncan et al.'s chapter on multiple-task performance in the operation of automobiles. As Duncan et al. argue, future research on attention and control must take better account of individual differences underlying performance strategies, and more vigorous efforts should be made to apply our current knowledge in real-world settings.

Fortunately, all of these preceding dictates are what Posner, the discussant of part III, would likewise have us heed. As his abstract eloquently concludes: "... isolating and relating different levels at which attention can (and should) be studied (is) important if cognitive-neuroscience links are to be instrumental to developments related to the 'decade of the brain' during the 1990's."

REFERENCES

Boring, E. G. (1950). *A history of experimental psychology*. New York: Appleton-Century-Crofts.

Broadbent, D. E. (1958). *Perception and communication*. London: Pergamon Press.

Deutsch, J. A., and Deutsch, D. (1963). Attention: Some theoretical considerations. *Psychological Review, 70*, 80–90.

Hillyard, S. A., and Kutas, M. (1983). Electrophysiology of cognitive processing. *Annual Review of Psychology, 34*, 33–61.

James, W. (1890). *The principles of psychology*. New York: Henry Holt.

Kahneman, D. (1973). *Attention and effort*. Englewood Cliffs, NJ: Prentice-Hall.

Laberge, D., and Buchsbaum, M. S. (1990). Positron emission tomographic measurements of pulvinar activity during an attention task. *Journal of Neuroscience, 10*, 613–619.

Moray, N. (1959). Attention in dichotic listening: Affective cues and the influence of instructions. *Quarterly Journal of Experimental Psychology, 9*, 56–60.

Moray, N. (1967). Where is capacity limited? A survey and a model. In A. F. Sanders (Ed.), *Attention and performance*. Amsterdam: North-Holland.

Navon, D., and Gopher, D. (1979). On the economy of the human processing system. *Psychological Review, 86*, 214–255.

Norman, D. A. (1969). *Memory and attention*. New York: John Wiley.

O'Donnell, R. D., & Eggemeier, F. T. (1986). Workload assessment methodology. In K. R. Boff, L. Kaufman, and J. P. Thomas (Eds.), *Handbook of perception and human performance*. New York: John Wiley.

Posner, M. I., and Petersen, S. E. (1990). The attention system of the human brain. *Annual Review of Neuroscience, 13*, 25–40.

Shiffrin, R. M., and Schneider, W. (1977). Controlled and automatic human information processing. II: Perceptual learning, automatic attending and a general theory. *Psychological Review, 84*, 127–190.

Treisman, A. M. (1960). Contextual cues in selective listening. *Quarterly Journal of Experimental Psychology, 12*, 242–248.

Treisman, A. M., and Gelade, G. (1980). A feature-integration theory of attention. *Cognitive Psychology, 12,* 97–136.

Welford, A. T. (1952). The "psychological refractory period" and the timing of high-speed performance—A review and a theory. *British Journal of Psychology, 43,* 2–19.

Wickens, C. D. (1980). The structure of attentional resources. In R. Nickerson (Ed.), *Attention and performance VIII,* 239–258. Hillsdale, NJ: Lawrence Erlbaum Associates.

9   Attention and Control: Have We Been Asking the Wrong Questions? A Critical Review of Twenty-Five Years

Alan Allport

9.1   A CRITICAL LOOK BACK

The twenty-five years since the first Attention and Performance symposium (Sanders 1967) have been a period of extraordinarily rapid growth and transformation within the cognitive sciences. Indeed, if some Rip van Winkle of experimental psychology were to return to the land of A&P after a quarter century of deep sleep, he could scarcely fail to be astonished at the extent to which the scientific horizons had expanded, compared to what he had known in the early 1960s. Transformation has occurred on almost all fronts in cognitive psychology[1] and neuropsychology, in the neurosciences, in robotics and artificial intelligence, and in connectionist modeling. He would be struck, too, by the growing recognition of conceptual as well as empirical interdependence among these very diverse disciplines in the movement toward an integrated cognitive neuroscience. In short, over this twenty-five-year period, the surrounding scientific landscape, the objectives, the questions being addressed, and the conceptual and empirical framework underlying them would appear changed almost beyond recognition.

Nonetheless, in contrast to so much change, if our reawakened Rip van Winkle were to turn to the psychology of attention, he might be surprised to find certain features of the contemporary landscape reassuringly familiar. To a remarkable extent, the same issues and controversies that dominated the psychology of attention twenty-five years ago have continued to preoccupy students of attention throughout this period. And, underlying these issues and controversies, certain enduring assumptions about the nature of attention and about the functional architecture of cognitive and perceptual-motor processes continue to exert their hold, even a quarter century later. Two (intertwined) controversies in particular are still widely perceived as the central, and the most fundamental, issues to be resolved. These are (1) the controversy over "early" versus "late" perceptual selection, where the question at issue is whether attentional selection occurs before or after the encoding of categorical stimulus identity; and (2) the question of which cognitive processes "require attention" (and are therefore "limited"), and which processes can be performed "without attention" (or "automatically"). Both issues have fueled extremely vigorous controversy over this long period.[2] After twenty-five years, both remain essentially unresolved.[3]

Why has so much effort been devoted to these two issues in particular, and why has it resulted in such a conspicuous lack of successful resolution?

Attentional "Limitations"?

The perceived centrality of these two issues, I believe, derives from a set of very widely shared assumptions about cognitive architecture and about the nature of attention. Fundamental to the latter is the idea that the *need for* selective attention arises from (even, is uniquely caused by) certain basic *limitations* of cognitive function or "limited processing capacity" in the brain. According to this view, the selective character of attentional processes is interpreted as a direct consequence of the postulated processing limitations, whatever these might be. For example, "If the brain had infinite capacity for information processing, there would be little need for attentional mechanisms" (Mesulam 1985). This conception of selective attention was articulated in its most influential form by Broadbent (1958, 1971, 1982). Thus, "selection takes place *in order to protect a mechanism of limited capacity,* the P system." "The obvious utility of a selection system is to produce an economy in mechanism. If a complete analysis were performed even on neglected messages, there seems *no reason for selection at all*" (Broadbent 1971, 178 and 147, italics added). Closely related assumptions are (1) that "attention" itself denotes a computational *resource* of some kind, severely limited in quantity, (2) which must thus be allocated selectively as a zero-sum process. (3) Attention is held to be essential for certain sorts of processing ("controlled" or "attentional" processing), while other sorts of processes ("automatic" processes) do not need attention (e.g., Kahneman 1973; Posner 1978, 1982; Shiffrin and Schneider 1977). Further, (4) attention, in this sense of limited computational resource, is fundamentally unitary. If we do not admit this latter assumption, the attempt to characterize cognitive processes in terms of those that do, or do not, require attention (or those that require *more,* or *less,* attention) appears at best an ambiguous enterprise, and at worst risks simple incoherence. There is a corollary assumption (5) that attention represents a resource that can, in some circumstances, be "divided," albeit with great difficulty (Shiffrin 1988).

Given these very basic intuitions about the nature of attention and about the causal origins of attentional selectivity, it is easy to see why these two issues (or groups of issues: the locus of selection and the characterization of processes that "require attention") should have been held to be of central importance. That is, (1) if we could experimentally determine the functional locus of the architectural constraints (early or late), that—supposedly— imposed the need for selectivity of processing, and (2) if we could characterize, in information-processing terms, those processes that fail or break down in the absence of attention, so the underlying argument runs, then we might at last begin to understand the nature of these mysterious limitations that—*ex hypothesi*—made such selectivity of processing necessary in the first place.

Of course, the debate over both of these issues—which sorts of processes require attention, and early and late selection—has taken a good many twists and turns over this long period. In particular, over the past decade, the theoretical opposition between early and late selection has been the subject of numerous sophisticated reformulations, including versions that explicitly combine aspects of *both* the traditional positions (e.g., Bundesen 1990; Duncan 1987; Johnston and Dark 1986; Kahneman and Treisman 1984; Mozer 1987; Pashler 1984, in press; Pashler and Badgio 1985, 1987; Treisman 1969; van der Heijden 1981, 1987; van der Heijden, Hagenaar, and Bloem 1984; Yantis and Johnston 1990). Some recent discussions of "automaticity" (Cohen, Dunbar, and McClelland 1990; Logan 1988, 1990) similarly make little or no reference to the construct of limited capacity. (See also Cheng 1985; Hirst et al. 1980; Neisser, Hirst, and Spelke 1981; Neumann 1987; Ryan 1983, for earlier critiques.) Nevertheless, the idea of a direct causal link between various postulated processing limitations (bottlenecks, limited capacity) and "the locus of selective attention" appears still to exert a powerful attraction as the obvious, or "default," starting point for discussions of selective attention.[4] According to this traditional viewpoint, "selection" (whether early or late) means selectivity of *processing*, that is, selective admission to, or processing by, the hypothetical, limited-capacity system(s); and the "locus of selection" is treated as equivalent to the stage in the system beyond which the postulated capacity limitation, or attentional bottleneck, occurs.

Perhaps the best-known current attentional theory that links attentional selectivity to intrinsic processing limitations, as the causal determinant, is Treisman's feature-integration theory (FIT) (Treisman and Gelade 1980; Treisman 1988). In FIT, the critical architectural constraint that imposes the need for selective attention derives from a potential ambiguity of coding, which can occur in parallel networks when confronted with more than one stimulus, the so-called binding problem (Hinton, McClelland, and Rumelhart 1986; Crick and Koch 1990). According to FIT, in order to separate correct from *illusory* conjunctions of separately coded visual features, attention must select one "object" (or, in some versions, one spatial "area") at a time, within a retinotopic master map of visual locations, so that correct feature conjunctions for that object (or for all objects within that area?) can be uniquely coded. As regards the perception of complex visual stimuli, FIT thus resembles a strong, "early selection" theory. It is distinguished, admirably, from traditional versions of early selection, however, in providing an explicit characterization of, and theoretical motivation for, the hypothesized capacity limitations that, according to FIT, necessitate the serial focusing of attention on each item in turn, if objects characterized by conjunctions of separable features are to be correctly perceived.[5]

Few Words, Many Meanings?

Clearly, the debates over early and late selection, and over the nature of attentional limitations, have shifted ground during this twenty-five-year period. Indeed, the continued failure to achieve consensus on the locus of selection may be attributable, in part at least, to differing interpretations of what is supposed to be at issue. For example, is early selection meant to refer to an *obligatory* process, or merely to an available strategy? If we are concerned with attentional limitations, the distinction is fundamental. For example, suppose that some parallel stimulus identification is possible—though not necessarily mandatory—as evidence from both alphanumeric stimuli (Duncan 1987; Pashler and Badgio 1987) and pictorial arrays (Hoffmann 1987) appears to show. Suppose also that (under different task instructions) we could convincingly show selective identification of just one item at a time from the same stimulus arrays. Then the latter selectivity of processing could not, in this case, be caused by (or diagnostic of) an intrinsic processing limitation. Identifying the locus of selection, in this case, would carry no implications for the locus of a hypothetical attentional bottleneck. Yet, in the debate over early versus late selection, this distinction between obligatory and optional selection is commonly ignored.

More fundamentally, what is meant by *selection*? Any kind of task-dependent modulation of sensory (or sensory-motor) neuronal responses? Spatial orienting? Selective facilitation? The gating out of unwanted information? Attentional tagging? Selective feature integration? Selective delay of processing? Making information "available to control responses and conscious experience"? "Entry to a limited-capacity short-term memory store"? All of these concepts, and many more, have been used as referents of the term *selection*. Unless all of these, astonishingly, denote one and the same underlying operation, there can be no a priori grounds to expect just one "locus of selection."

There is a further ambiguity, in that *selection* appears to be used sometimes to refer to a hypothetical *causal mechanism*, sometimes to the postulated *result*. Moreover, this postulated result is sometimes internal (selective *processing*), and sometimes behavioral (selective *response*). It is dreadfully confusing. For many reasons, the question that once appeared fundamental and clear-cut, about the locus of attentional selection, now looks confusingly ill-defined or (at best) fragmented into a variety of subquestions.

Similar, if not more confusing ambiguities surround the usage of the term *attention*. Johnston and Dark (1986) pointed to a crucial distinction between attention conceptualized as some hypothetical *causal agency*, which can be directed or focused on an entity (with the result that this entity may be "selected"), and attention as an *outcome* or resultant, characterizing the behavioral state of the organism as a whole. Practically all current theories of attention are *cause* theories in this sense. There is, nevertheless, frequent slippage between these very different senses of attention. Even as causal mechanism, a more subtle equivocation exists between attention conceptualized as some limited processing resource (which can be "directed") and an "attention system" conceptualized as controller, that directs or allocates the limited resource. Johnston and Dark (1986) also pointed out, very gently, that in most contemporary theories of attention, this postulated causal agency "has all the characteristics of a processing homunculus." In general, despite the ingenuity and subtlety of much of the experimental literature that has been devoted to these two enduring controversies, the key concepts (*selection, automaticity, attention, capacity,* etc.) have remained hopelessly ill-defined and/or subject to divergent interpretations. Little wonder that these controversies have remained unresolved.

Assumptions about Cognitive and Perceptual-Motor Architecture

The controversy over early and late selection was predicated on a number of rather strong assumptions about cognitive architecture and the organization of processing stages. In the light of current neuropsychological and neurophysiological evidence, many of these assumptions now appear questionable, or simply mistaken. Among such assumptions, on which nevertheless the intelligibility of this controversy evidently depends, can be listed the following:

1. Information processing follows a linearly ordered, unidirectional sequence of processing stages from sensory input to overt response, rather than (for example) operating in multiple, parallel, and perhaps reciprocal pathways. Only in a single, linearly ordered series of processing operations could we readily determine which operations logically precede which other ones; that is, which operations occur earlier or later.

2. Such a sequence of processing stages is, indeed, already known (or can be simply assumed a priori).

3. More specifically, the processing of nonsemantic attributes (i.e., the processing of attributes other than symbolic or categorical identity) occurs earlier in a logical/causal sequence of operations than does any semantic or categorical processing.

4. The processing of *spatial* attributes and relations, in particular, logically precedes the processing of categorical or semantic attributes.

5. For some variants of the early/late selection hypothesis, "intraperceptual processes" can be distinguished in a principled way from, and logically precede, so-called "postperceptual" processes.

The traditional dispute over early versus late selection appears to depend on this set of assumptions, or their equivalent, for its theoretical alternatives even to be formulated coherently. If these assumptions are wrong, then the question at issue lapses into incoherence.

Moreover, the continued search for *the* locus of selection must assume that

6. There is just *one*, or one principal, locus of attentional selection—certainly insofar as early and late selection are represented as mutually exclusive alternatives.

7. Attentional selection thus denotes one unique or uniform computational process—represented, very often, as the selective admission of privileged

information to a stage of "further processing" and/or the selective exclusion from this critical stage of all other, unattended information.

Perhaps most deep-seated of all is an assumption, explicit in a number of theories and implicit in others, that

8. There exists, in the brain, a unique and unitary "central system" (or "attentional system" or "central executive") of limited capacity, that can be bypassed only by "automatic" processes. Ex hypothesi, the central system or attentional system is responsible for all "controlled" processes, that is, for all cognitive processes that "require attention." (This hypothetical central system is therefore, necessarily, a general-purpose—or all-purpose—system of attention and control.)

These assumptions of the *unitary* character of attentional control (and/or of attentional limitations) logically underpin any attempt to partition cognitive processes into two sets: those that do and those that do not require attention. If, on the contrary, attention is *not* a unitary computational process, and does not depend on a single central system or on some unitary, limited processing resource, the question of which cognitive operations require attention remains ill-specified. What kind of attention? What is it that cognitive processes are supposed to require, when they require attention? Without an explicit computational theory of the functions of attention, the empirical question of which processes require attention is liable just to chase its own tail.

Questioning the Assumptions: A Look Ahead

The purpose of this tutorial chapter is to look again at these long-standing, underlying assumptions, in the light of available neurophysiological and neuropsychological evidence. With rare exceptions, the controversies over early and late selection, and over controlled versus automatic processing have relied on behavioral human-performance data based on normal, adult, human subjects. Consideration of a wider range of evidence, including neuropsychological studies of disorders of attention, as well as data on the neurophysiology and neuroanatomy of visual-motor control, calls in question many of the traditional assumptions on which these controversies were predicated. Such a review may also bring into better focus something of the *heterogeneity* of attentional functions, which preoccupation with these old controversies has tended to obscure.

Section 9.2 of this chapter summarizes evidence on visual-motor architecture in primates, including (1) major, parallel pathways serving *categorical* and *spatial* processing; (2) multiple, parallel, and *reciprocal* paths between sensory input and motor control; and (3) visual and spatial representation (attributes traditionally associated with supposedly early processing) in anterior, *action*-related systems (traditionally late stages of processing). Section 9.3 recapitulates conceptions of early selection as dependent, in particular, on spatial representation. In the brain, however, spatial encoding occurs at many different levels and with reference to different spatial coordinate systems. Evidence is reviewed on neurophysiological processes of spatial and nonspatial attention, orienting, and the attentional modulation of neuronal responsiveness, which operate at many different functional loci and implement several different principles of selectivity. In Section 9.4, implications of these findings for traditional conceptions of attention are assessed further, and considerably extended, in the light of neuropsychological disorders of spatial attention. Section 9.5 then turns to nonspatial, attentional, or executive control. Evidence is briefly surveyed, indicating a range of functionally separable, autonomous subsystems, responsible for different aspects of voluntary, executive control. Section 9.6 summarizes (some of) the *heterogeneity* of attentional functions and points to the empirical inadequacy of traditional conceptions of attention, seen as some functionally undifferentiated (and unspecified) causal mechanism. Recent data on the "psychological refractory period" are briefly reconsidered. The chapter ends (Section 9.7) with some concluding remarks on the task ahead.

9.2   ASPECTS OF VISUAL-MOTOR ARCHITECTURE

Parallel Processing of "What" and "Where"

As is well known, the extrastriate primate cortex contains over twenty different areas with a complex distribution of visual functions (Desimone and Ungerleider 1989; Maunsell and Newsome 1987). This branching network of visual areas appears to be grouped rather broadly into two or three major *parallel* systems: (1) a ventral system, including much of the inferior temporal lobe, that is crucial for form-based *object* recognition; and (2) a dorsal system that projects into the posterior parietal cortex and that is essential for (between object) *spatial* vision and visual-motor coordination (DeYoe and Van Essen 1988; Ungerleider and Mishkin 1982; Maunsell and Newsome 1987). Neuropsychological evidence points to a similar, modular separation into parallel, computationally autonomous systems in humans: that is, parallel systems responsible for object identification and for visual-spatial functions—"what" and "where" (e.g., Farah 1990; Levine, Warach, and Farah 1985; Newcombe, Ratliff, and Damasio 1987). (3) A third major visual pathway has been suggested that involves the superior temporal sulcus (STS) in the macaque and is responsible, among other things, for the coding of complex visual motion (Boussaoud, Ungerleider, and Desimone 1990).

Multiple, Reciprocal Pathways between Vision and Action

"Forward" connections throughout this network of visual areas are paralleled, in almost every case, by equally rich, reciprocal, "backward" connections—unlike what one might expect if cortical visual information processing were indeed a simple, unidirectional (forward) process. Schematic diagrams of the cortical visual system often represent these multiple visual areas without explicit, efferent connections beyond the so-called visual system itself. It is important to emphasize, however, that every one of these twenty-odd visual areas, including the primary visual cortex, has its own output pathways directly to different motor or action systems, including to subcortical structures in the tectum, brainstem, spinal cord, and caudate-putamen system, so that each visual area forms, in effect, a different parallel link between the sense organ (the retina) and the motor output (Creutzfeldt 1985). A stimulus that activates any cortical visual area thus also induces some behavioral disposition to *action* (Creutzfeldt 1988; see Levy 1990, for some recent reflections on this theme). Requin, Riehle and Seal (1988; chap. 30, this volume) have similarly emphasised the quantitative distribution of "sensory" and "motor" (and sensory-motor) function, at the single-unit level, throughout different cortical areas, at all levels in the system.

Different, extrastriate visual areas also project forward, individually and directly, to a different combination of regions in frontal cortex. For example, area 8a (the frontal eye field) receives projections directly from at least nine different, extrastriate visual areas. A different, but partially overlapping subset of (occipito-temporal) visual areas has reciprocal connections, respectively, with frontal areas 12 and 46 (Barbas 1988; Barbas and Pandya 1989). Similarly, there are rich and reciprocal connections between the parietal, visual-spatial systems (e.g., area 7a) and many other regions of frontal cortex, including again area 46 in the lateral frontal cortex (Goldman-Rakic 1987). Furthermore, these latter two regions (areas 7a and 46) project to over a dozen other regions in common, including both anterior and posterior cingulate cortex, as part of a reciprocal, parallel distributed network of cortical areas (Goldman-Rakic 1988a, 1988b). Likewise, different frontal regions maintain separate, parallel *efferent* pathways (Alexander, DeLong, and Strick 1986).

Visual-Spatial Functions in Anterior (Action-oriented) Systems

Correspondingly, many different anterior (frontal) areas exhibit specialized *visual* and *visual-spatial* functions. To illustrate in terms of areas already mentioned, Area 46 in the principal sulcus of the macaque frontal cortex appears to be responsible for certain visual-spatial "working memory" functions, mediating performance of a delayed manual response to a previously visually specified target location; microlesions within area 46 result in (nonretinotopic) spatially circumscribed deficits in such delayed visual response tasks, where *manual* responses are involved (Goldman-Rakic 1987, 1988a). A similar type of spatial working memory for visually specified locations, but where the task requires a delayed *oculomotor* response, appears to depend, instead, on cell populations in area 8a (frontal eye field) and in posterior parietal cortex (area LIP) (Gnadt and Andersen 1988; Goldberg and Bruce 1985; Goldberg and Colby 1989).

Rizzolatti and his colleagues have studied cell populations in frontal premotor cortex (inferior area 6), which selectively control different types of purposeful reaching and grasping actions of the hand, and which are also selective for the spatial direction of the object of reach, in terms of its body-centered (i.e., nonretinotopic) location (Rizzolatti and Gentilucci 1988; Rizzolatti et al. 1988). From this work, it appears that different "grasping" cells fire in advance of (and during) different types of hand movement: for example, pushing away, bringing to the mouth, full hand grasp, four-finger grip, and precision grip (between forefinger and thumb). Many of these premotor cells also have sensory (visual and tactile) receptive fields, with corresponding spatiotopic selectivity. Very interestingly, their sensory response appears also to be tuned to action-relevant stimulus characteristics. For example, some precision grip neurons are visually responsive, but only to small, convex visual objects that are within manual reach.

9.3   SELECTION BY LOCATION

What have these considerations of visual-motor architecture to do with early and late selection? Early selection was postulated originally to operate in terms of *simple physical characteristics* of the sensory input and, particularly, in terms of stimulus *location*. Protagonists of early selection have been attracted to the metaphor of a spatially defined spotlight of attention, as a characterization of the early selection mechanism (e.g., Broadbent 1982; Treisman 1988). Indeed, it has been argued, on the basis of a variety of experimental evidence, that visual selective-response tasks—more specifically, tasks conforming to what Kahneman and Treisman (1984) defined as the "filtering paradigm"—in which the to-be-selected visual items are cued by *non*spatial visual attributes such as color or size—may depend on (i.e., be mediated via) selective cueing of *location* (e.g., Butler and Currie 1986; Johnston and Pashler 1990; Kahneman and Treisman 1984; Nissen 1985; Styles and Allport 1986; van der Heijden 1991). Where there is no spatial separation of wanted and unwanted information, selective performance drops (Johnston and Dark 1986). Sperling and Wurst (see chap. 12), for example, describe a selection task in which to-be-attended and to-be-ignored stimuli appeared one after another in the same location, in rapid serial presentation. Under these conditions, "early perceptual filtering" cued by *non*spatial visual attributes was completely ineffective.

Thus, many of the visual phenomena proposed as indicators of so-called early selection could be redefined, more precisely and more appropriately, simply as indicators of *spatial* selectivity. Indeed, experimental demonstrations that the efficiency of visual selection (i.e., the efficiency of selective *response*) is affected by spatial separation of to-be-attended and to-be-ignored information are often taken, ipso facto, as confirmation of the early selection hypothesis.

How far do the mechanisms of selection by location in fact conform to the traditional characterization of the early selection hypothesis? This is the question to which we must now turn.

First, contrary to traditional assumptions, spatial location is far from being a "simple physical characteristic" so far as its coding in the brain is concerned. Behavioral and neurophysiological data, as well as computational considerations, reveal a complex system of coordinate transformations between different retina-based and nonretinotopic visual representations. These include visual representations that take account of eye and head position, others that code location in terms of arm- or body-centered coordinates, as well as visual representations based on environment-, and possibly object-centered, coordinate systems (e.g., Andersen 1987, 1989; Ellis et al. 1989; Feldman 1985; Hinton and Parsons 1988; Marr 1982; Nicoletti and Umiltà 1989; Presson, DeLange, and Hazelrigg 1989; Rizzolatti and Gentilucci 1988; Soechting, Tillery, and Flanders 1990; Zipser and Andersen 1988). Neuropsychological disorders of spatial attention (spatially selective "extinction" and "neglect"; see below) similarly reveal selective processes operating in a variety of *non*retinotopic spatial coordinates (e.g., Bisiach, Capitani, and Porter 1985; Calvanio, Petrone, and Levine, 1987; Driver and Halligan 1991; Farah et al. 1990; Làdavas 1987; Rizolatti and Gallese 1988). Disorders of spatial attention can also affect *nonsensory*, imaginal space (Bisiach and Luzzatti 1978; Bisiach et al. 1981).

Moreover, as already noted, visual representation of spatial relations ("where") evidently depends on processing pathways that are organized broadly *in parallel* with the processing of visual-form-based object identity ("what"). There seems to be no empirical basis for the assumption that spatial encoding, and spatial selectivity, are functionally *prior* to nonspatial, categorical encoding. The controversy over early versus late selection simply took it for granted that selective processes were (necessarily) *either* "precategorical" or "postcategorical." No other logical possibilities were entertained. In particular, the possibility of spatial processing pathways, subject to attentional modulation, that were neither functionally prior nor subsequent to "categorical" encoding but were organized in parallel was simply outside the terms of this traditional debate.

Indeed, the coding of visual-spatial relations and the attentional modulation of such spatial encoding (see below) occur at many different levels of visual processing and visual-motor control. That is, they are found both at levels which might be deemed relatively early in visual processing as well as at levels that are markedly late in relation to the control of action. (In the cortical visual system, the most notable exceptions are primary visual cortex, V1, and in V2, which mediate, arguably, the "earliest" cortical visual representations, where spatial-attentional modulation generally has *not* been found.) Very few experiments on visual attention with normal subjects have included manipulations that could differentiate among these different possible levels or domains of spatial representation. The fact that visual selective attention can show major effects of spatial variables (Johnston and Dark 1986; Kahneman and Treisman 1984), in general, tells us little about the level in the system at which these effects occur.

Spatially Selective Attentional Modulation and Spatial Orienting of Attention

Posner and his colleagues (Posner 1988; Posner et al. 1987; Posner and Peterson 1990; see also Fischer 1986) have identified at least three functionally separable components in a simple shift of visual-spatial attention, or spatial "orienting": disengagement from the present focus of attention, the movement of attention, and reengagement on the new target location. Further, they have presented evidence that each of these component processes depends, in part at least, on the integrity of *different* (and widely separated) brain structures. Thus, it appears that a number of separable component processes each play an essential part in the overall process of "selecting" a new focus of spatial attention. It follows that spatial selection (let alone *other* types of attentional selectivity) has not just one functional locus, but many.

Spatial orienting of visual attention is accompanied by *enhanced* neuronal responsiveness to visual stimuli appearing in the attended location (Goldberg and Bruce 1985; Goldberg and Segraves 1987; Petersen, Robinson, and Morris 1987; Robinson and Petersen 1986; Rugg et al. 1987). These spatially selective enhancement (SSE) effects have been found in many different spatiotopic ("where") coding systems, both cortical and subcortical, including posterior parietal cortex, frontal eye fields, superior colliculus, and the lateral pulvinar nucleus of the thalamus. Focal brain lesions in any one of these areas can result in spatially selective disturbances of both overt and covert attention, both in humans and in other primates (e.g., Milner 1987; Posner 1988; Vallar and Perani 1987; see also below). In contrast, SSE effects have not been found in primary visual cortex, V1, nor in V2, and focal lesions in V1 or V2 do not result in disorders of spatial attention. Further, the time course and other characteristics of the SSE effects recorded in these different brain sites appear to correspond well with the observed *behavioral* (RT) benefits of spatial-attentional cueing, resulting from peripheral versus central (i.e., symbolic) spatial cues, respectively (Fischer and Breitmeyer 1987; Posner 1988; Posner and Petersen, 1990; Wurtz, Goldberg, and Robinson 1980).

The attentional modulation of neuronal response within the spatiotopic ("where") visual system that has been identified so far involves spatially selective *enhancement* of neuronal responsiveness to visual stimuli. No evidence has been found, in the "where" system, of spatially selective inhibition or attenuation of responsiveness to the unattended or to-be-ignored visual fields. These spatiotopic attentional enhancement effects thus appear to be very different from the hypothetical selective gating or exclusion of sensory input, oriented towards economizing on mechanism, postulated by versions of *both* early and late selection theories.

In contrast, when visual attention is focused or "engaged" on a given location, the responsiveness of lower-level *oculomotor* mechanisms in the brainstem, which control saccadic movements of the eyes toward visual or other potentially distracting stimuli, is sharply reduced (Goldberg and Segraves 1987). As a result, "express saccades" are eliminated (Fischer 1986; Fischer and Breitmeyer 1987), and overt behavioral responses to stimuli in other, nonattended locations are markedly slowed (Posner 1988). Spatial-attentional engagement acts apparently as a sort of "hold" mechanism that inhibits overt (i.e., oculomotor) shifts of visual attention as well as inhibiting covert attentional orienting (cf. Humphreys and Riddoch, chap. 7); its effect appears to be, in part at least, to suppress extraneous *actions* (implicit and explicit), rather than to attenuate the *perceptual* quality of unattended visual-spatial input.

An interesting possibility is that these "behavioral inhibition" effects,[6] which appear temporarily to decouple the control of overt *response* from other, potentially competing but to-be-ignored sources of motor command—but operating in *spatially* selective terms—have an equivalent in the *non*spatial domain in the phenomena of "negative priming" (Allport, Tipper, and Chmiel 1985; Tipper 1985; Tipper and Driver 1988; Tipper, MacQueen, and Brehaut 1988). In the latter, actively ignored *categorical* codes appear, likewise, to be temporarily isolated from the control of actions, but in nonspatial terms.

Posner and his colleagues have argued that, before spatially focused visual attention can be shifted to a different location, it must first be "disengaged" from its current focus (Posner 1988; Posner et al. 1987). They have presented RT data consistent with the view that a major component of the unilateral "neglect" syndrome, resulting from posterior parietal injury, represents selective impairment of a mechanism of spatial-attentional disengagement. Recent research by other groups provides further support for this view (Baynes, Holtzman, and Volpe 1986; Brunn and Farah 1991; Morrow and Ratcliff 1988; see also section 9.4 below).

Implications for Early and Late Selection

It may be useful to summarize some implications of the data reviewed so far concerning traditional conceptions of early and late selection.

As we have seen, many authors have taken any evidence of *spatial* selectivity, in selective-response tasks, as ipso facto providing support for the early selection hypothesis. Similarly, observations of spatial-attentional modulation, occurring at short latencies following stimulus onset, have likewise been interpreted as evidence for early selection, meaning that "information is being gated or filtered at a fairly early stage of visual processing" (Hillyard, Munte, and Neville 1985, 67).

Now, if early selection means no more than spatially selective modulation of visual responsiveness in noncategorical, spatial domains of processing, there can be little argument that early selection is a reality. However, the hypothesis of early selection, about which so much controversy has centered, is by no means synonymous merely with spatial selectivity. Granted that spatially selective processes occur, including some with short onset latencies, *none* of the inferences that are associated with the traditional early versus late selection framework appear to follow as valid consequences.

• The systems showing spatially selective, attentional modulation of visual response (i.e., SSE effects) operate in parallel with, not functionally prior to, categorical ("what") systems. Coordination between attentional processes in spatial and categorical visual systems, and the causal consequences (if any) of modulation in one of these parallel systems on processing in another, are practically unknown. It is an area that urgently needs further research. However, no effects of this kind can be assumed a priori.

• Spatially selective attentional modulation has been found at many different, functional-anatomical loci. These include cortical and subcortical systems implicated in efferent, or *action-related* control functions. In terms of the traditional framework, these are relatively *late* stages of processing.

• Further, identifying the locus (or loci) of selection, in the sense defined above, offers no basis whatever for making inferences regarding the site of an attentional "bottleneck," or of "processing capacity limitations." Similarly, no inferences about obligatory categorical encoding can be derived from evidence of late (action-related) levels of spatial selection.

• Available evidence suggests that attentional modulation in noncategorical, spatial-vision systems takes the form of *enhancement* of neuronal responsiveness in attended locations, not attenuation of unattended locations. In addition to the selective enhancement of visual response, however, spatial-attentional engagement apparently entails the temporary decoupling of unattended visual locations from potential *motor* command. The behavioral costs (RT delays) for overt responses to stimuli in one location, following an "invalid" cue to a different location, appear to reflect the time cost of disengagement from the cued location, rather than withdrawal of "processing resources" from the uncued locations.

• Finally, selection, as defined operationally in terms of selective mapping of stimulus parameters to overt *response*, namely, "selection-for-action" (Allport 1987, 1989), is by no means logically equivalent to selectivity of implicit, knowledge-based *processing*. Efficient spatial selection-for-action, including selective response showing *no* interference from perceptual distractors, is compatible, in principle, with any level of categorical encoding of those distractors. The empirical issue, which still remains wide open, is an interesting one, but it perhaps does not have the central theoretical importance that was once supposed. (As an illustration of the empirical pitfalls in inferring "no processing" from "no interference," see, e.g., Driver and Tipper 1989.)

Attentional Modulation in the Processing of Visual Color and Form

Different principles of attentional modulation have been described in visual area V4 and in infero-temporal (IT) cortex, namely, within the ventral, object-identity ("what") pathway (cf. Rugg et al. 1987). Spitzer, Desimone, and Moran (1988) reported that increased attention, behaviorally evident when an animal had to carry out a relatively difficult visual discrimination, was accompanied by marked changes in the selectivity of tuning of visual responses in V4 units. That is, during the difficult discrimination task, the tuning bandwidth in the majority of cells that they sampled in V4 became narrower with respect to both wavelength and orientation, thus giving a stronger and more sharply peaked response to the "preferred" value for that cell.

Moran and Desimone (1985) had reported earlier a complex effect of spatially selective attention on color-selective units in V4 and in IT. They trained monkeys, in visual matching tasks, to respond selectively to a visual stimulus that was presented in a given, precued location (while maintaining fixation on one spot) and to ignore another, simultaneously presented, adjacent stimulus. When the attentional target and the distractor stimulus both fell within the receptive field of the *same* unit, and the target stimulus had a wavelength to which that unit was normally *not* responsive, V4 and IT unit responses to the (normally effective) distractor stimulus were attenuated. (This effect occurred in a majority of cells; in some units there were no attentional effects, while others even showed enhanced response to the to-be-ignored stimulus.) However, if the target stimulus fell outside the spatial receptive field of a given unit, there were no attentional effects, either facilitatory or inhibitory, on responses to the to-be-ignored stimuli. (IT cells generally lack the spatial selectivity necessary to show this effect.) Moreover, when both "attended" and "ignored" stimuli fell within the same receptive field, response to the to-be-ignored stimulus appeared to begin normally but was then modulated abruptly, around 100 ms after stimulus onset (Desimone and Moran 1987).

Crick and Koch (1990) have attributed these effects to a process of enhanced local competition between neurons in the same macrocolumn of cortical units, but not between neurons in different macrocolumns. (In IT, the enhanced local competition would presumably be among units coding *similar* visual attributes, rather than in terms of spatial overlap.) It is not clear to what extent the *same* mechanism might in fact be responsible both for the effects of increased sharpness of tuning and for the spatially selective modulation of response (attenuation, enhancement) in V4 units.[7] It is an interesting possibility. As Crick and Koch suggest, the idea that *attention facilitates local competition* may throw an interestingly new light on mechanisms of attention and deserves further study. Thus, according to their hypothesis, when a local stack of units (a macrocolumn) is not attended to, it can have multiple outputs. When it *is* attended to, its outputs will tend to be narrowed down, or disambiguated, to just "one." This idea is similar in some respects to suggestions put forward by Marcel (1980, 1983) about focal awareness. It offers a very different conception from the idea that attentional selection exists in order to protect a central mechanism of limited capacity (at some level) from overload.

9.4 NEUROPSYCHOLOGY OF SPATIAL ATTENTION

Unilateral Neglect

The phenomena associated with acquired disorders of spatial attention (DeRenzi 1982; Jeannerod 1987; Rizzolatti and Gallese 1988) provide a number of challenging constraints for theories of attentional function. In the most commonly described behavioral syndrome of "unilateral neglect," associated with posterior parietal injury, the resulting, gross lateral inattention is not restricted to a fixed region of egocentric space (e.g., the contralesional visual hemifield), but shows a left-to-right, continuous *gradient* or bias of attentional priority, among potentially competing objects of attention (Baynes, Holtzman, and Volpe 1986; Jeannerod and Biguer 1987; Kinsbourne 1977, 1987; Làdavas 1990). In other words the disturbance appears to reflect an enhanced attentional priority, and stronger attentional engagement, in one direction, as much as a diminished priority towards the other. The attentional gradient can be influenced by appropriate spatial cueing and by vestibular stimulation (Cappa et al. 1987; Riddoch and Humphreys 1987; Rubens 1985; Sieroff, Pollatsek, and Posner 1988).

The severity of this "perceptual" neglect, manifest in the visual-spatial domain, can depend also on a variety of *response* variables, such as which hand is used to indicate perceptual detection and (in some cases) on whether the responding hand is held to the right or left of the body (e.g., Coslett et al. 1986; Duhamel and Brouchon 1990; Joannette et al. 1986). Rizzolatti and his colleagues have shown that, in monkeys, microlesions in various frontal, premotor systems, controlling different categories of motor action, can produce highly selective forms of perceptual (i.e., visual) inattention, as well as high-level motor impairments. Lesions in different premotor areas provoked spatially selective visual inattention restricted to different egocentric regions of visual space. Thus, for example, they reported different types of spatial neglect confined to unilateral sensory space just around the mouth, or confined to "reaching" space, or restricted to distant, oculomotor space. The particular region of affected visual space depended on, and was congruent with, the particular categories of purposive motor acts disturbed by these different, prefrontal lesions (Rizzolatti and Camarda 1987; Rizzolatti, Gentilucci, and Matelli 1985; Rizzolatti and Gallese 1988). In the same way, sagittal interruption of the midbrain commissures, which abolishes *overt* orienting of head and eyes in the vertical direction, is accompanied by a corresponding perceptual neglect in the same vertical plane (Matelli et al. 1983).

Results of this kind illustrate dramatically the functional interdependence of attentional effects in the *perceptual* domain (defined in visual-spatial coordinates) and the organization of categories of motor *action*. They challenge traditional ideas of a neat, unidirectional sequence of processing stages, and they call into question any possibility of a simple distinction between perceptual and *post*perceptual (including, typically, motor- or action-related) processes. By the same token, the controversy over the locus of attentional selection, conceptualized as *either* "intraperceptual" or "postperceptual," is similarly called into question. (To my knowledge, a definition of perception, construed as occupying some determinate set of processing stages but *no further* in an ordered sequence of hypothetical stages, has never been seriously attempted. This is a prudent reticence perhaps. Nevertheless, ill-defined theoretical distinctions do not make good science.)

Spatially selective perceptual inattention, occurring as a result of focal brain injury, can reflect a variety of different spatial frames of reference. To illustrate with just two examples: a patient with left-sided neglect may selectively ignore stimuli to his or her left with reference to the *gravitational axis*, even though the head is tilted horizontally (Làdavas 1987); in contrast, lateralized neglect can also be evident with reference to an object's *principal axis*, despite marked rotation of that axis out of the vertical, and with head upright (Driver and Halligan 1991). Also, as noted earlier, lateralized neglect can include neglect of the contralesional side of remembered or imagined visual scenes (e.g., Bisiach and Luzzati 1978; Ogden 1985). These dramatic, varied disturbances of spatial attention clearly affect levels of spatial representation beyond the retinotopic encoding of elementary visual features, the level implicated, for example, in Treisman's attentional theory of visual feature integration (Treisman 1988). That is to say, visual spatial attention cannot operate uniquely in retinotopic coordinates, nor, uniquely, in terms of early visual processing levels. The occurrence of these diverse patterns of spatial neglect indicate, compellingly, that there are visual-spatial attentional functions, subject to selective disturbance, in a variety of different visual-spatial coding systems.

Furthermore, disorders of spatial attention can affect *just one* (or more) spatial representational domain and leave others intact. Thus, for example, spatial neglect can selectively affect subjects' reading of either the left or the right side of written words; further, this disorder, known as *neglect dyslexia*, can occur independently of—or even lateralized in the opposite direction to—neglect of nonlinguistic visual space (e.g., Caramazza and Hillis 1990a,b; Costello and Warrington 1987; Ellis, Flude, and Young 1987). The patient studied in detail by Caramazza and Hillis failed to read the *terminal* (i.e., in canonical, alphabetic representation, the "right") half of words, regardless of whether the word was presented visually in normal left-to-right orientation, or was mirror-reversed, or even if the words were orally spelled to the patient. Thus, the hemineglect was manifested within what appears to be a word-centered, orthographic space, which is evidently *not* retinotopic. Somewhat similar results have been reported regarding the neglect of left or right space in deaf signed language, where *syntactic* use of (body-centered) hemispace appears to be doubly dissociable from spatial attention in *nonlinguistic* activities (Bellugi, Poizner, and Klima 1989; Poizner, Bellugi, and Klima 1990). There is evidence also that hemineglect with respect to external visual space, and to the patient's own body, can occur as independent, dissociable disorders (Bisiach et al. 1986).

Since the spatial direction of attention can show gross disturbances in one or another of these different, spatial representational domains, without dislocation of spatial attention in other coding domains, it follows that there can be no single locus of spatial selection. On the contrary, it seems likely that functionally separable mechanisms of spatial selectivity, and of spatial attentional "engagement," exist in every one of these different spatial domains of representation, except possibly in the earliest cortical representations in V1 and V2.

Simultanagnosia

Even in the absence of gross contralateral neglect, patients with unilateral, posterior parietal injury often show contralateral perceptual "extinction": that is, when two (or more) visual objects are briefly presented simultaneously, side by side, the patient fails to identify, and even denies the occurrence of, more than one object, acknowledging only the one nearest to the ipsilesional side. In some cases of *bilateral* posterior parietal or parieto-occipital injury, the phenomenon of perceptual extinction can be seen in an extreme, and profoundly disabling, bilateral—or strictly, concentric—form, known as (dorsal) simultanagnosia (e.g., Coslett and Saffran 1991; Farah 1990; Holmes and Horrax 1919; Luria 1959; Luria, Pravdina-Vinarskaya, and Yarbuss 1963; Rizzo and Hurtig 1987).[8]

In dorsal simultanagnosia, only one object or part of an object can be seen at any one time, even though the patients often have full visual fields. For example, Hecaen and de Ajuriaguerra (1956) noted of their patient (Case 1) that, in lighting a cigarette, the patient failed to see the flame offered to him an inch or two away from the cigarette held between his lips, as "his eyes were fixed on the cigarette." As noted earlier, in cases of *unilateral* perceptual extinction the patients appear to have abnormal difficulty in disengaging spatial attention from one visual object in order to shift attention to another object in the contralesional direction (Posner et al. 1987; Morrow and Ratcliff 1988). In simultanagnosia, a similar impairment in the disengagement of spatial attention apparently affects shifts of attention in *any* direction. The patient's attention and phenomenal awareness appear locked on just one perceptually coherent object at a time, regardless of the object's size[9] or spatial separation. The patient studied by Luria, Pravdina-Vinarskaya, and Yarbuss (1963) was shown drawings of familiar objects tachistoscopically; the drawings varied in size, ranging from 6° to 20° of visual angle. When presented with the objects one at a time, the patient could name them, regardless of size; however, when two objects were presented simultaneously, even at the smallest size, he was able to identify only one.

Likewise, when shown outline drawings of multiple familiar objects spatially superimposed, the simultanagnosic patient typically succeeds in identifying only one object and denies that he can see any others (Farah 1990). Even long words may be read as a whole, whereas several words (or a sentence) covering the same visual extent cannot (Coslett and Saffran 1991; Williams 1970). The lexical status of a letter string (word or pseudoword) also determines whether the whole or only a part of the letter string can be overtly identified in simultanagnosia (Coslett and Saffran 1991), as in unilateral neglect (Sieroff, Pollatsek, and Posner 1988; see also Brunn and Farah 1991).

From observations of this kind, it appears that perceptual selectivity (or attentional engagement) in these patients is strongly influenced by higher-order encoding of lexical and visual-object identity. With real-world scenes, as with pictures, the patients report seeing either a single composite object as a whole, or else just one coherent part of the object at a time: for instance, the handlebars of a bicycle, a jug handle, a rider, but not the animal on which he is riding, and so forth. The level of analysis, in a hierarchy of part-whole relations, appears to be subject to limited voluntary control; the resulting selectivity, however, is describable *only* in terms of hierarchical, knowledge-based encoding, which must therefore be logically prior to (or exist independently of) the selection process. Parietal unilateral neglect, similarly, appears to operate at the level of whole (perceptually integrated) visual objects, and/or coherent parts of already hierarchically parsed, structural descriptions of those objects (e.g., Kartsounis and Warrington 1989; Kinsbourne 1987).

A related issue, on which the available evidence is regrettably only fragmentary, concerns the level of categorical or semantic encoding of visual information that has been phenomenally, and behaviorally, "extinguished." In a recent study of a simultanagnosic patient, Coslett and Saffran (1991) found very powerful facilitation effects of semantic relatedness between two briefly presented words, affecting whether the patient was able to report (and, indeed, claimed to "see") either just one or both of the words. Similarly, Marshall and Halligan (1988) reported an ingenious demonstration in a patient with profound unilateral neglect, showing that the evaluative significance of pictorial information in the neglected field (a house on fire), whose presence was explicitly denied by the patient, could bias her indirect (forced-choice) preference judgments. Further investigation of these and related issues, and replication of these findings in other patients, is clearly needed.

9.5 NONSPATIAL SELECTION AND CONTROL

The discussion so far has focused on *spatial* selectivity in visual selective-response tasks, since this is the area to which theories of early and late selection, and of automatic and controlled processing, have been most frequently addressed in recent years.[10] Nevertheless, there are *other* aspects of dynamic attentional (or "executive") control, many of which are *nonspatial* in operation: they include processes concerned with the moment-by-moment adjustment of behavioral goal priorities (see, for example, Helfman 1990), with the planning and sequencing of behavior, and with the maintenance and/or shifting of selective task "set." Theories of early and late selection have little (or nothing) to say about these processes of executive control, which—perhaps for this reason—have attracted relatively little research in psychological laboratories over the past twenty-five years. This very large, but neglected, area of research can only be dealt with briefly here.

One popular view attributes all such control processes to a unitary central executive or supervisory attentional system (SAS) (e.g., Baddeley 1986; Norman and Shallice 1986). Posner's conception of the "anterior attention system" appears somewhat similar (Posner and Petersen 1990; Posner and Rothbart 1991). Unfortunately, the concept of a central executive has yet to be elaborated in a way that avoids the homunculus problem, namely, the problem of practically unconstrained explanatory powers. As a consequence, the idea has yet—to my knowledge—to generate specific, hypothesis-testing research.

Shallice (1988) has proposed that the hypothetical central executive (or SAS) be identified broadly with frontal lobe function, and he briefly discussed neuropsychological evidence indicative of "modularity," or nonequipotentiality, between different frontal regions. Injury to dorsolateral frontal areas, for example, is generally associated with impaired performance in delayed response tasks, increased distractibility, and difficulty in shifting hypotheses (e.g., in the Wisconsin sorting task). Injury to inferior and orbital frontal cortex, on the other hand, is accompanied (among other symptoms) by inability to suppress well-learned or otherwise dominant response tendencies (cf. Fuster 1989; Shallice and Burgess, in press).

A different, and very striking dissociation between different types of executive functions can be illustrated in the case study of a patient, EVR, reported by Eslinger and Damasio (1985). A former accountant, EVR had undergone bilateral surgical ablation of orbital and lower mesial frontal cortex for removal of a large cerebral tumour. He showed a complex and disabling impairment in making practical decisions and in assigning social and professional priorities. This was attributed by Eslinger and Damasio to "a defect of analysis and integration of stimuli pertaining to real-life situations" (1739). For example, "deciding where to dine might take hours, as he discussed each restaurant's seating plan, particulars of menu, atmosphere, and management. He would drive to each restaurant to see how busy it was, but even then he could not finally decide which to choose. Purchasing small items required in-depth consideration of brands, prices, and the best method of purchase ..." (1732). Major financial and other decisions by EVR turned out disastrously, and he was dismissed from a succession of different jobs. In contrast to EVR's devastating, but selective, impairment of executive decision making and judgment, EVR performed normally on a range of laboratory tests of reasoning, flexible hypothesis testing, cognitive estimation, and resistance to distraction and memory interference (all of which have been proposed as functions of the general-purpose central executive or SAS). His measured IQ was superior (ninety-seventh to ninety-ninth percentile).

Besides neuropsychological case studies of human patients that show contrasting impairments of executive function, there is extensive evidence from monkeys showing local specialization and heterogeneity of function in frontal lobes for different aspects of executive and attentional control (e.g., Fuster 1989; Goldman-Rakic 1988a). PET-scan data in humans, recorded during performance of cognitive tasks in which different types of "executive" function are involved (Smith and Fetz 1987), reveal, likewise, very striking nonequipotentiality among different frontal areas for different components of attentional control. Roland (1985) identified three separable foci of increased metabolic activity in superior prefrontal cortex, associated with three different components of attentional control. One superior prefrontal area was apparently activated by specific task preparation, following instructions; a different, adjacent area of superior prefrontal cortex was highly activated during tasks that called for selective attention to a given stimulus dimension while ignoring other dimensions, as in many Stroop-like tasks; a third area was found to be active during conditional (if-then) or temporal sequencing of cognitive operations. A lateral midfrontal region of activation has also been reported during sustained auditory vigilance tasks, predominantly in the right hemisphere (Cohen et al. 1988). Using similar techniques, Posner and his associates (Petersen et al. 1989; Posner et al. 1988) have identified a very different frontal region of activation in anterior cingulate cortex, whose activation is correlated with implicit acts of attentional *target detection* in (nonspatial) monitoring tasks. Pardo et al. (1990) reported enhanced activation of anterior cingulate cortex during a Stroop color-word interference task. Recently, Passingham and others (Deiber et al. 1991) implicated the same or closely adjacent areas of anterior cingulate cortex and supplementary motor area (SMA) in the generation of self-selected, voluntary acts. Patients with Parkinson's disease show dramatically reduced activation in the region of the anterior cingulate (Playford, Passingham, and Nutt 1991).

Clearly, our current understanding of human, executive control processes is fragmentary in the extreme. Nevertheless, the results offered by these new techniques, together with neuropsychological analyses of the effects of localized injury or disease on diverse executive functions, and neurophysiological data in nonhuman primates, make the idea of a general-purpose, functionally undifferentiated central executive (or attentional control system)—responsible for all aspects of nonspatial, voluntary, attentional control—highly implausible. Earlier I emphasized the heterogeneity of attentional processes in spatially selective tasks. The much larger domain of nonspatial attentional control appears, correspondingly, even more heterogeneous. In exploring this latter area, however, we plainly have very much further to go.

9.6 PROCESSES THAT "REQUIRE ATTENTION"?

Multiple Attentional Functions

In this review, I have tried to indicate some of the multiplicity of different attentional functions involved in selective perceptual-motor control. The catalogue is, no doubt, seriously incomplete. Nevertheless, granted the limited nature of this review, the multiplicity and diversity of attentional control processes appear incontrovertible.

In the visual-spatial domain, there is evidence of attentional modulation at many different levels, and in different, parallel pathways from visual input to motor control. The continued search for *one* critical locus of selection is fruitless; there is no such locus. Moreover, the evidence reviewed here indicates that, in implementing visual-attentional selectivity, a number of qualitatively *different* mechanisms are involved. These include

• spatially selective *enhancement* of neuronal response, in predominantly spatiotopic ("where") systems, without corresponding inhibition or attenuation of responsiveness to visual stimuli in nonattended locations;

• raised thresholds of *motor* responsiveness with respect to stimuli outside the spatial focus of attention, as a consequence of (or as a component in) the spatial engagement of attention;

• in the figural or object-vision system, enhanced selectivity of tuning (i.e., narrower tuning bandwidth) and increased *local competition*, again, however, without entailing the suppression of functionally distant, unattended information.

Further, in *nonspatial* attentional control there is evidence to suggest that separable control mechanisms may be responsible for each of the following component processes:

• task-related suppression of prepotent response tendencies;

• maintenance of executive working memory in a variety of delayed-response tasks;

• selection-for-action among competing stimulus dimensions;

• temporal and conditional sequencing of cognitive operations;

• generation of implicit or endogeneous action choices, including implicit acts of "target detection" in continuous monitoring task;

• evaluation of consequences, and of relative priorities, in social (real-life) decision making.

The list is descriptive only, and certainly incomplete. There is no suggestion here that the executive control processes, thus labeled, cannot be functionally subdivided further. Experimental studies of the voluntary shifting of task "set," to control different, successive cognitive operations, provide additional, converging evidence of functionally separable components of executive or attentional control (Allport and Styles 1990, n. 1).

As noted by Johnston and Dark (1986), most contemporary theories of information processing in general, and selective attention in particular, view attention as some sort of causal mechanism. However, even a brief survey of the heterogeneity and functional separability of different components of spatial and nonspatial attentional control prompts the conclusion that, qua causal mechanism, *there can be no such thing as attention.* There is no *one* uniform computational function, or mental operation (in general, no *one* causal mechanism), to which all so-called attentional phenomena can be attributed. On the contrary, there is a rich diversity of neuropsychological control mechanisms of many different kinds (and no doubt many yet to be discovered), from whose cooperative and competitive interactions emerge the behavioral manifestations of attention. It follows that to ask, *Which cognitive processes require attention?* and to search for common characteristics of all such processes, in contradistinction to all "automatic" processes (which supposedly do *not* require attention), is an enterprise that, like the search for one unique locus of selection, is incapable of resolution.

It seems no more plausible that there should be one unique mechanism, or computational resource, as the causal basis of all attentional phenomena than that there should be a unitary causal basis of thought, or perception, or of any other traditional category of folk psychology. A vast range of behavioral effects has been attributed to attention. Which of these heterogeneous phenomena should in fact be causally grouped together, and which depend on *different* attentional mechanisms? Consider just a few such phenomena: negative priming; induced saliency; visual pattern masking and "demasking"; temporal grouping and phenomenal simultaneity; perceptual "retouch"; illusory conjunctions; illusory conjunctions in immediate postcategorical memory; semantic priming versus expectancy; voluntary, involuntary, and countervoluntary covert spatial orienting; express saccades; perceptual "prior entry"; Stroop-like interference effects; probe RT delays; load-dependency effects; shifting and engagement of selective set—between stimulus dimensions, between cognitive operations; language switching; attentional dyslexia; center-of-gravity effects in saccadic control; "dilution" of the Stroop affect; vigilance decrements; spatial route planning; exogenous and endogenous control of visual search trajectories; inhibition of return; keeping track of current, and completed, goals and subgoals; evaluation of action consequences; covert target detection; endogenous action choice; suppression of prepotent response tendencies; "planning and problem solving"; and so on. Most or all of these, and many other effects and abilities have been described as determined by, or the result of, a causal mechanism of attention (and/or of limitations or lapses of such a mechanism). Often such theories are quite local in scope and admit a multiplicity of other causal, attentional mechanisms. Certainly no comprehensive causal mechanism of attention has ever been specified, even in barest outline. Reference to attention (or to the central executive, or even to the anterior attention system) as an unspecified causal mechanism explains nothing.

Limited Capacity and the Psychological Refractory Period

It may be objected that many theories that represent attention as an undifferentiated, general-purpose causal mechanism or processing resource have in fact specified at least *one* causal property of the postulated central system, namely, its *limited capacity* (e.g., Baddeley 1986; Broadbent 1958; Kahneman 1973; Posner 1982; Shiffrin 1988). In support of this conception of a central, limited-capacity system as a causal determinant of performance limitations of many kinds, theorists have appealed to data from concurrent tasks (for commentary, see Allport 1980, 1989; Hirst 1986; Neumann 1987) and, in particular, to data from the psychological refractory period (PRP) paradigm (e.g., Baddeley 1990; Broadbent 1971, 1982; Kahneman 1973; McLeod 1978; McLeod and Posner 1984).[11] Recently, however, Pashler (1984) and Pashler and Johnston (1989) have shown very convincingly that the underadditive effects of stimulus manipulations on PRP delays are inconsistent with the predictions of graded, *capacity-sharing* models; instead, the data support a strict *response-postponement process* (Welford 1952; Smith 1967).

Pashler (1991; see also chap. 11) has also shown, moreover, that this postponement effect (attentional bottleneck?) does *not* apply to concurrent, voluntary (or nonautomatic) shifts of *visual attention*. Thus, he demonstrated that supposedly "attention-demanding" visual tasks, such as Treisman and Gelade's (1980) conjunction search, and spatially cued as well as postcategorically cued selective report tasks (report the highest digit, for example) are *not* affected by the same PRP delays. There were no PRP effects, provided that the latter tasks did not include a requirement for *overt* speeded (vocal or manual) response, even though these tasks were severely time-limited by pattern masking. In other words, the causal mechanisms responsible for directing voluntary, spatial shifts of attention, as well as the limited processing resource(s) postulated to underlie characteristic performance in these attention-demanding visual tasks, are functionally separable from the causal mechanisms responsible for response postponement in the PRP or "overlapping-tasks" paradigm.

Pashler (1991; chap. 11, this volume; Pashler and Johnston 1989) has interpreted the PRP response-postponement effects in terms of a central processing bottleneck, a stage of processing required for a wide range of decision- and response-related functions—though not for perceptual categorization or visual-spatial orienting—much as in the earlier tradition of late selection theories.[12] The idea of a processing bottleneck accords with the traditional view of attentional selectivity as fundamentally the *result* of (or determined by) intrinsic system limitations. In this particular case, however, the apparent system limitation is such that complex response decisions can be executed *simultaneously* (provided that they can be temporally "grouped" or coordinated), but cannot begin *asynchronously*.

What could be the origin of a behavioral constraint of this kind, since it is clearly not an example of informational "limited capacity"? (See Neumann 1987.) Is the bottleneck to be thought of as a *cause* of attentional selectivity (as traditionally supposed) or, on the contrary, can PRP response-postponement effects be understood as the *consequence* of other, coordinative processes involved in maintaining the coherence of purposeful action? Control processes are of course needed to implement the organism's temporary commitment to, or "engagement" in, a particular cognitive task and to protect ongoing action choices (also, ongoing, endogenous memory search) from interruption or capture by potentially related, but task-irrelevant, sources of information.

Practically nothing is known about such processes. Indeed, laboratory-based exploration of the mechanisms responsible for task set and related aspects of executive control has scarcely begun. Over the past twenty-five years, research on attention has been dominated by the idea of intrinsic processing *limitations*, and their functional locus, and has largely neglected to inquire what attentional processes might otherwise be *for*. What is urgently needed is the development of a *computational theory*, in the sense outlined by Marr (1982),[13] of the many different functions of attentional selectivity and control, in place of the altogether inadequate conception of the cognitive agent as a selective, but otherwise passive, information channel, which has been the guiding metaphor over the preceding twenty-five years.

There is a long way to go.

9.7 CONCLUDING REMARKS

As we inch our way toward a better understanding of mental functions, in terms of cognitive neurobiology, we should no doubt expect that many of our once-cherished ideas will need to be set aside, to be replaced by a different, and increasingly intricately articulated conceptual framework, linking cognitive and neurobiological processes at many different levels of description. Questions that made sense in terms of an earlier and simpler set of ideas come to be reformulated, or superseded, as the assumptions on which they were based are revised or discarded.

Two such questions, as I have tried to show, are (1) the issue of the so-called locus of selection, and (2) the attempt to characterize those processes that do, or do not, require attention. As traditionally posed, these questions rested on a variety of simplifying assumptions: in particular, assumptions about cognitive architecture, and about the computational status and unique causal origin of attentional selection—assumptions that, I have argued, were seriously mistaken. The preeminence accorded to these two questions over the past twenty-five years rested, furthermore, on belief in the possibility of a unitary (and simple) "theory of attention." Indeed, answers to these questions were frequently put forward as just that—as a putative theory of attention. This belief rested, in turn, on the assumption (implicit or explicit) that attentional functions were *all of one type* (possibly, in some recent formulations of just two types). The penalty for such wishful thinking is to be condemned forever to appeal, in one's theory, to ill-defined (or even completely undefined) causal mechanisms and constraints—attention, attentional resources, central processing system, (anterior) attentional system, central executive, further processing, and the like—whose explanatory horsepower is nil.

There is one way to escape from this dreadful penalty. It is by taking seriously the idea that attentional functions are of very many different kinds, serving a great range of different computational purposes. There can be no simple theory of attention, any more than there can be a simple theory of thought. A humbler but also a more ambitious task for the next twenty-five years will be to characterize, in cognitive neurobiological terms, as much as possible of this great diversity of attentional functions.

NOTES

1. In the early 1960s, cognitive psychology did not yet have a name; the term apparently gained general currency around 1967, following the publication of Neisser's (1967) book of that title.

2. For example, consider the following quotes: "The principal theoretical issue confronting attention research today concerns whether selection is 'early' or 'late'" (Hoffman 1986). "Among the most fundamental questions about the functional architecture of the human visual informa-

tion-processing system is the *locus* of selective attention. Of particular importance is whether *attentional limitations* occur before stimulus identification ... or after" (Yantis and Johnston 1990, italics added). A recent mathematical model of visual attention, by Bundesen (1990), similarly links limited-capacity processing and limited-capacity storage directly to the selectivity of attention, where "selection and recognition are viewed as two aspects of the same process."

A full bibliography of research related to, or discussed in terms of, one or both of these issues would be immense, amounting to a very large part of all psychological research on human information processing over this period. Both controversies were shaped initially, and most decisively, by the work of Broadbent (1958), Cherry (1957), Deutsch and Deutsch (1963), and Welford (1952). Some of the more salient, subsequent landmarks in the course of these two controversies include (among many others): Broadbent (1971, 1982), Duncan (1980, 1985), Hoffman (1979), Kahneman (1973), Kahneman and Treisman (1984), Keele and Neill (1979), Logan (1978, 1988), Norman (1968), Norman and Bobrow (1975), Pashler (1984, 1991), Pashler and Johnston (1989), Posner (1978, 1982), Shiffrin and Schneider (1977), Treisman (1960, 1969, 1988; Treisman and Gelade 1980). Recent reviews, offering some critical perspectives on and entry points into this very large literature include Allport (1989), Hirst (1986), Johnston and Dark (1986), Navon (1984), Neumann (1987), and van der Heijden (1991).

3. See, for example, Navon (1990), Shiffrin (1988), Yantis and Johnston (1990). As Shiffrin (1988), a leading exponent of the distinction, has noted, "Attempts to define necessary and sufficient criteria to distinguish automatic and attentive processes ... have not yet proven successful."

4. See n. 2 for some representative examples.

5. The conjunction-search phenomena, as well as the character of "illusory conjunctions" on which FIT was originally founded (Treisman and Gelade 1980; Treisman and Schmidt 1982), have since been qualified by a number of important exceptions, boundary conditions, and reinterpretations (e.g., Chmiel 1989; Duncan 1987; Houck and Hoffman 1986; Johnston and Pashler 1990; McClelland and Mozer 1986; McLeod, Driver, and Crisp 1988; Nakayama and Silverman 1986; Pashler 1987; Pashler and Badgio 1987; Virzi and Egeth 1984; Wolfe, Cave, and Franzel 1989; among others). Based on these, alternative theoretical accounts have been put forward (e.g., Duncan and Humphreys 1989; Humphreys and Müller, in press; Prinzmetal and Keysar 1989; Watt 1988). Evidence that feature conjunctions can be correctly coded in parallel, at least over small groups of search stimuli (Pashler 1987; Chmiel 1989), undermines the a priori argument for an intrinsic binding problem, necessitating a one-at-a-time solution, which was one of the theory's principal attractions. Treisman and Sato (1990) have recently suggested that the hypothesized attentional scan may in effect be a back up in conjunction search combined with a *nonserial* (i.e., spatially parallel) process of interactive, single-feature-based inhibition of nontarget locations (cf. Wolfe, Cave, and Franzel 1989; Phaf, van der Heijden, and Hudson 1990).

6. The sense intended here is related to the attentional functions of Gray's (1982) postulated "behavioral inhibition" system.

7. Martha J. Farah put forward this idea at the Attention and Performance XIV meeting, Ann Arbor, July 1990.

8. The term "simultanagnosia" has been applied also to a rather different disorder, associated with left inferior, occipito-temporal damage (e.g., Kinsbourne and Warrington 1962). For a careful discussion of the contrasting characteristics of these different disorders ("dorsal" versus "ventral" simultanagnosia), see Farah (1990). It is clearly possible that "dorsal" simultanagnosia also includes separable subtypes (e.g., Rizzo and Hurtig 1987).

9. Except, of course, in cases with accompanying field defects.

10. On the importance of keeping separate the problems of spatial selectivity in vision and audition, see Neumann, van der Heijden, and Allport (1986).

11. For example, Broadbent (1971): "The existence of a limit on capacity does not mean that messages must be dealt with one by one, but merely that ... parallel streams of messages will reduce the speed at which each can be processed" (314). "The selection of the category state is an operation that loads the capacity of the system, and which therefore cannot be carried out as fast for two simultaneous processes as for one. This is undoubtedly the explanation of the delay to the second of closely successive reactions" (Broadbent 1971, 318).

12. Pashler, however, proposes a "two component" theory of divided attention.

13. That is, a theory of the ecological *purposes*, and constraints, of attentional control. For some further discussion see Allport (1989).

REFERENCES

Alexander, G. E., DeLong, M. R., and Strick, P. L. (1986). Parallel organization of functionally segregated circuits linking basal ganglia and cortex. *Annual Review of Neuroscience, 9,* 357–382.

Allport, A. (1980). Attention and performance. In G. Claxton (Ed.), *Cognitive Psychology: New directions,* 112–153. London: Routledge and Kegan Paul.

Allport, A. (1987). Selection-for-action: Some behavioral and neurophysiological considerations of attention and action. In H. Heuer and A. F. Sanders (Eds.), *Perspectives on perception and action,* 395–419. Hillsdale, NJ: Erlbaum.

Allport, A. (1989). Visual attention. In M. I. Posner (Ed.), *Foundations of cognitive science,* 631–682. Cambridge, MA: MIT Press.

Allport, A. and Styles, E. A. (1990). Multiple executive functions, multiple resources? Experiments in shifting attentional control of tasks. Unpublished manuscript, University of Oxford.

Allport, A., Tipper, S. P., and Chmiel, N. (1985). Perceptual integration and post-categorical filtering. In M. I. Posner and O. S. M. Marin (Eds.), *Attention and performance XI,* 107–132. Hillsdale, NJ: Erlbaum.

Andersen, R. A. (1987). The role of the inferior parietal lobule in spatial perception and visual-motor integration. In F. Plum, V. B. Mountcastle, and S. R. Geiger (Eds.), *Handbook of physiology: The nervous system. Vol. 5, Higher functions of the brain.* Bethesda, MD: American Physiological Society.

Andersen, R. A. (1989). Visual and eye movement functions of the posterior parietal cortex. *Annual Review of Neuroscience, 12,* 377–403.

Baddeley, A. (1986). *Working memory.* Oxford: Oxford University Press.

Baddeley, A. (1990). *Human memory: Theory and practice.* London: Erlbaum.

Barbas, H. (1988). Anatomic organization of basoventral and medio-dorsal visual recipient prefrontal regions in the rhesus monkey. *Journal of Comparative Neurology, 276,* 313–342.

Barbas, H., and Pandya, D. N. (1989). Architecture and intrinsic connections of the prefrontal cortex in the rhesus monkey. *Journal of Comparative Neurology, 286,* 353–375.

Baynes, K, Holtzman, J. D., and Volpe, B. T. (1986). Components of visual attention: Alterations in response pattern to visual stimuli following parietal lobe infarction. *Brain, 109,* 99–114.

Bellugi, U., Poizner, H., and Klima, E. S. (1989). Language, modality, and the brain. *Trends in Neurosciences, 12,* 380–388.

Bisiach, E., Capitani, E., Luzzati, C., and Perani, D. (1981). Brain and conscious representation of outside reality. *Neuropsychologia, 19,* 543–551.

Bisiach, E., Capitani, E., and Porta, E. (1985). Two basic properties of space representation in the brain. *Journal of Neurology, Neurosurgery and Psychiatry, 48,* 141–144.

Bisiach, E., and Luzzati, C. (1978). Unilateral neglect of representational space. *Cortex, 14,* 129–133.

Bisiach, E., Perani, D., Vallar, G., and Berti, A. (1986). Unilateral neglect: Personal and extra-personal. *Neuropsychologia, 24, 759–767.*

Boussaoud, D., Ungerleider, L. G., and Desimone, R. (1990). Pathways for motion analysis: Cortical connections of the medial superior temporal and fundus of the superior temporal visual areas in the macaque. *Journal of Comparative Neurology, 296, 462–495.*

Broadbent, D. E. (1958). *Perception and communication.* London: Pergamon Press.

Broadbent, D. E. (1971). *Decision and stress.* London: Academic Press.

Broadbent, D. E. (1982). Task combination and selective intake of information. *Acta Psychologica, 50, 253–290.*

Brunn, J. L., and Farah, M. J. (1991). The relation between spatial attention and reading: Evidence from the neglect syndrome. *Cognitive Neuropsychology, 8, 59–75.*

Bundesen, C. (1990). A theory of visual attention. *Psychological Review, 97, 523–547.*

Butler, B. E., and Currie, A. (1986). On the nature of perceptual limits in vision: A new look at lateral masking. *Psychological Research, 48, 201–209.*

Calvanio, R., Petrone, P. N., and Levine, D. N. (1987). Left visual spatial neglect is both environment centered and body centered. *Neurology, 37, 1179–1183.*

Cappa, S., Sterzi, R., Vallar, G., and Bisiach, E. (1987). Remission of hemineglect and anosognosia during vestibular stimulation. *Neuropsychologia, 25, 775–782.*

Caramazza, A., and Hillis, A. E. (1990a). Internal spatial representation of words: Evidence from unilateral neglect. *Nature, 346, 267–269.*

Caramazza, A., and Hillis, A. E. (1990b). Levels of representation, coordinate frames, and unilateral neglect. *Cognitive Neuropsychology, 7, 391–445.*

Cheng, P. W. (1985). Restructuring versus automaticity: Alternative accounts of skill acquisition. *Psychological Review, 92, 414–423.*

Cherry, E. C. (1957). *On human communication: A review, a survey, and a criticism.* New York: John Wiley.

Chmiel, N. (1989). Response effects in the perception of conjunctions of colour and form. *Psychological Research, 51, 117–122.*

Cohen, J. D., Dunbar, K., and McClelland, J. L. (1990). On the control of automatic processes: A parallel distributed processing account of the Stroop effect. *Psychological Review, 97, 332–361.*

Cohen, R. M., Semple, W. E., Gross, M., Holcomb, H. J., Dowling, S. M., and Nordahl, T. E. (1988). Functional localization of sustained attention. *Neuropsychiatry, Neuropsychology, and Behavioral Neurology, 1, 3–20.*

Coslett, H. B., Bowers, D., Fitzpatrick, E., Hans, B., and Heilman, K. M. (1986). Hemispatial kypokinesia and hemisensory inattention in neglect. *Neurology, 36* (suppl. 1), 334.

Coslett, H. B., and Saffran, E. M. (1991). Simultanagnosia: To see but not two see. *Brain, 114,* 1523–1545.

Costello, A. D. C., and Warrington, E. K. (1987). The dissociation of visuospatial neglect and neglect dyslexia. *Journal of Neurology, Neurosurgery and Psychiatry, 50, 1110–1116.*

Creutzfeldt, O. (1985). Multiple visual areas: Multiple sensorimotor links. In D. Rose and V. G. Dobson (Eds.), *Models of visual cortex,* 54–61. New York: John Wiley.

Creutzfeldt, O. (1988). The integrative function of the neocortex (Group report). In P. Rakic and W. Singer (Eds.), *Neurobiology of neocortex*, 434. Chichester and New York: John Wiley.

Crick, F., and Koch, C. (1990). Towards a neurobiological theory of consciousness. *Seminars in the Neurosciences, 2*, 263–275.

Deiber, M.-P., Passingham, R. E., Colebatch, J. G., Friston, K. J., Nixon, P. D., and Frackowiack, R. S. J. (1991). Cortical areas and the selection of movement: a study with PET. *Experimental Brain Research, 84*, 393–402.

DeRenzi, E. (1982). *Disorders of space exploration and cognition.* New York: John Wiley.

Desimone, R., and Moran, J. (1987). Mechanisms for selective attention in area V4 and inferior temporal cortex of the macaque. *Society for Neuroscience Abstracts, 11*, 1245.

Desimone, R., and Ungerleider, L. G. (1989). Neural mechanisms of visual processing in monkeys. In F. Boller and J. Grafman (Eds.), *Handbook of neuropsychology.* Vol. 2, 267–299. Amsterdam: Elsevier.

Deutsch, J. A., and Deutsch, D. (1963). Attention: some theoretical considerations. *Psychological Review, 70*, 80–90.

DeYoe, E. A., and Van Essen, D. C. (1988). Concurrent processing streams in monkey visual cortex. *Trends in Neurosciences, 11*, 219–226.

Driver, J., and Halligan, P. W. (1991). Can visual neglect operate in object-centered co-ordinates? An affirmative single-case study. *Cognitive Neuropsychology, 8*, 475–496.

Driver, J., and Tipper, S. P. (1989). On the nonselectivity of "selective seeing": Contrasts between interference and priming in selective attention. *Journal of Experimental Psychology: Human Perception and Performance, 15*, 304–314.

Duhamel, J.-R., and Brouchon, M. (1990). Sensorimotor aspects of unilateral neglect: A single case analysis. *Cognitive Neuropsychology, 7*, 57–74.

Duncan, J. (1980). The locus of interference in the perception of simultaneous stimuli. *Psychological Review, 87*, 272–300.

Duncan, J. (1985). Visual search and visual attention. In M. I. Posner and O. S. M. Marin (Eds.), *Attention and performance XI*, 85–105. Hillsdale, NJ: Erlbaum.

Duncan, J. (1987). Attention and reading: Wholes and parts in shape recognition—A tutorial review. In M. Coltheart (Ed.), *Attention and performance XII: The psychology of reading*, 39–61. Hillsdale, NJ: Erlbaum.

Duncan, J., and Humphreys, G. W. (1989). Visual search and stimulus similarity. *Psychological Review, 96*, 433–458.

Ellis, A. W., Flude, B., and Young, A. W. (1987). "Neglect dyslexia" and the early visual processing of letters in words and nonwords. *Cognitive Neuropsychology, 4*, 439–464.

Ellis, R., Allport, D. A., Humphreys, G. W., and Collis, J. (1989). Varieties of object constancy. *Quarterly Journal of Experimental Psychology, 41A*, 775–796.

Eslinger, P. J., and Damasio, A. R. (1985). Severe disturbance of higher cognition after bilateral frontal lobe ablation: Patient EVR. *Neurology, 35*, 1731–1741.

Farah, M. J. (1990). *Visual agnosia.* Cambridge, MA: MIT Press.

Farah, M. J., Brunn, J. L., Wong, A. B., Wallace, M. A., and Carpenter, P. A. (1990). Frames of reference for allocating attention to space: evidence from the neglect syndrome. *Neuropsychologia, 28*, 335–347.

Feldman, J. A. (1985). Four frames suffice: A provisional model of vision and space. *Behavioral and Brain Sciences, 8*, 265–289.

Fischer, B. (1986). The role of attention in visually guided eye movements in monkey and man. *Psychological Research, 48,* 251–257.

Fischer, B., and Breitmeyer, B. (1987). Mechanisms of visual attention revealed by saccadic eye movements. *Neuropsychologia, 25,* 73–84.

Fuster, J. M. (1989). *The prefrontal cortex: Anatomy, physiology and neuropsychology of the frontal lobe,* 2d ed. New York: Raven Press.

Gnadt, J. W., and Andersen, R. A. (1988). Memory related motor planning activity in posterior parietal cortex of macaque. *Experimental Brain Research, 70,* 216–220.

Goldberg, M. E., and Bruce, C. J. (1985). Cerebral cortical activity associated with the orientation of visual attention in the rhesus monkey. *Vision Research, 25,* 471–481.

Goldberg, M. E., and Colby, C. L. (1989). The neuropsychology of spatial vision. In F. Boller and J. Grafman (Eds.), *Handbook of neuropsychology.* Vol. 2, 267–299. Amsterdam: Elsevier.

Goldberg, M. E., and Segraves, M. A. (1987). Visuospatial and motor attention in the monkey. *Neuropsychologia, 25,* 107–118.

Goldman-Rakic, P. S. (1987). Circuitry of primate prefrontal cortex and the regulation of behavior by representational memory. In F. Plum, V. B. Mountcastle, and S. R. Geiger (Eds.), *Handbook of physiology: The nervous system. Vol. 5, Higher-functions of the brain.* Bethesda, MD: American Physiological Society.

Goldman-Rakic, P. S. (1988a). Changing concepts of cortical connectivity: Parallel distributed cortical networks. In P. Rakic and W. Singer (Eds.), *Neurobiology of Neocortex,* 177–202. New York: John Wiley.

Goldman-Rakic, P. S. (1988b). Topography of cognition: Parallel distributed networks in primate association cortex. *Annual Review of Neuroscience, 11,* 137–156.

Gray, J. A. (1982). *The neuropsychology of anxiety: An enquiry into the functions of the septohippocampal system.* Oxford: Oxford University Press.

Hecaen, H., and de Ajuriaguerra, J. (1956). Agnosie visuelle pour les objets inanimes par lesion unilaterale gauche. *Revue Neurologique, 94,* 222–233.

Helfman, G. S. (1990). Mode selection and mode switching in foraging animals. In P. B. Slater, J. S. Rosenblatt, and C. Beer (Eds.), *Advances in the Study of Behaviour, 19,* 249–298.

Hillyard, S. A., Munte, T. F., and Neville, H. J. (1985). Visual-spatial attention, orienting, and brain physiology. In M. I. Posner and O. S. M. Marin (Eds.), *Attention and performance XI,* 63–84. Hillsdale, NJ: Erlbaum.

Hinton, G. E., McClelland, J. L., and Rumelhart, D. E. (1986). Distributed representations. In D. E. Rumelhart and J. L. McClelland (Eds.), *Parallel distributed processing: Explorations in the microstructure of cognition. Vol. 1, Foundations,* 77–109. Cambridge, MA: MIT Press.

Hinton, G. E., and Parsons, L. M. (1988). Scene-based and viewer-centred representations for comparing shapes. *Cognition, 30,* 1–35.

Hirst, W. (1986). The psychology of attention. In J. E. LeDoux and W. Hirst (Eds.), *Mind and brain: Dialogues in cognitive neuroscience,* 105–141. Cambridge: Cambridge University Press.

Hirst, W., Spelke, E., Reaves, C., Caharack, G., and Neisser, U. (1980). Dividing attention without alternation or automaticity. *Journal of Experimental Psychology: General, 109,* 98–117.

Hoffman, J. E. (1979). A two-stage model of visual search. *Perception & Psychophysics, 25,* 319–327.

Hoffman, J. E. (1986). Spatial attention in vision: Evidence for early selection. *Psychological Research, 48,* 221–229.

Hoffmann, J. (1987). Semantic control of selective attention. *Psychological Research, 4*, 123–129.

Holmes, G., and Horrax, G. (1919). Disturbances of spatial orientation and visual attention with loss of stereoscopic vision. *Archives of Neurology and Psychiatry, 1*, 385–407.

Houck, M. R., and Hoffman, J. E. (1986). Conjunction of color and form without attention. *Journal of Experimental Psychology: Human Perception and Performance, 12*, 186–199.

Humphreys, G. W., and Müller, H. M. (N.d.). Search via Recursive Rejection (SERR): A connectionist model of visual search. *Cognitive Psychology*. In press.

Jeannerod, M. (Ed.). (1987). *Neurophysiological and neuropsychological aspects of spatial neglect*. Amsterdam: North-Holland.

Jeannerod, M., and Biguer, B. (1987). The directional coding of reaching movements: A visuomotor conception of spatial neglect. In M. Jeannerod (Ed.), *Neurophysiological and neuropsychological aspects of spatial neglect*, 87–113. Amsterdam: North-Holland.

Joannette, Y., Brouchon, M., Gauthier, L., and Samson, M. (1986). Pointing with left versus right hand in left visual field neglect. *Neuropsychologia, 24*, 391–396.

Johnston, J. C., and Pashler. H. (1990). Close binding of identity and location in visual feature perception. *Journal of Experimental Psychology: Human Perception and Performance, 16*, 843–856.

Johnston, W. A., and Dark, V. J. (1986). Selective attention. *Annual Review of Psychology, 37*, 43–75.

Kahneman, D. (1973). *Attention and effort*. Englewood Cliffs, NJ: Prentice-Hall.

Kahneman, D., and Treisman, A. M. (1984). Changing views of attention and automaticity. In R. Parasuraman and D. R. Davies (Eds.), *Varieties ot attention*, 29–61. New York: Academic Press.

Kartsounis, L. D., and Warrington, E. K. (1989). Unilateral visual neglect overcome by cues implicit in stimulus arrays. *Journal of Neurology, Neurosurgery and Psychiatry, 52*, 1253–1259.

Keele, S. W., and Neill, W. T. (1979). Mechanisms of attention. In E. C. Carterette and M. P. Friedman (Eds.), *Handbook of perception*. Vol. 9. New York: Academic Press.

Kinsbourne, M. (1977). Hemi-neglect and hemispheric rivalry. In E. A. Weinstein and R. P. Friedland (Eds.), *Hemi-inattention and hemispheric specialization*. New York: Raven Press.

Kinsbourne, M. (1987). Mechanisms of unilateral neglect. In M. Jeannerod (Ed.), *Neurophysiological and neuropsychological aspects of spatial neglect*, 69–86. Amsterdam: North-Holland.

Kinsbourne, M., and Warrington, E. K. (1962). A disorder of simultaneous form perception. *Brain, 85*, 461–486.

Làdavas, E. (1987). Is the hemispatial deficit produced by right parietal lobe damage associated with retinal or gravitational coordinates? *Brain, 110*, 167–180.

Làdavas, E. (1990). Selective spatial attention in patients with visual extinction. *Brain, 113*, 1527–1538.

Levine, D. N., Warach, J., and Farah, M. (1985). Two visual systems in mental imagery: Dissociations of "what" and "where" in imagery disorders due to bilateral posterior lesions. *Neurology, 35*, 1010–1018.

Levy, J. (1990). Regulation and generation of perception in the asymmetric brain. In C. Trevarthen (Ed.), *Brain circuits and functions of the mind*. Cambridge: Cambridge University Press.

Logan, G. D. (1978). Attention in character-classification tasks: evidence for the automaticity of component stages. *Journal of Experimental Psychology: General, 107*, 32–63.

Logan, G. D. (1988). Toward an instance theory of automatization. *Psychological Review, 95*, 492–527.

Logan, G. D. (1990). Repetition priming and automaticity: Common underlying mechanisms? *Cognitive Psychology, 22*, 1–35.

Luria, A. R. (1959). Disorders of "simultaneous perception" in a case of bilateral occipitoparietal brain injury. *Brain, 83*, 437–449.

Luria, A. R., Pravdina-Vinarskaya, E. N., and Yarbuss, A. L. (1963). Disorders of ocular movement in a case of simultanagnosia. *Brain, 86*, 219–228.

McClelland, J. L., and Mozer, M. C. (1986). Perceptual interactions in two-word displays: Familiarity and similarity effects. *Journal of Experimental Psychology: Human Perception and Performance, 12*, 18–35.

McLeod, P. D. (1978). Does probe RT measure central processing demand? *Quarterly Journal of Experimental Psychology, 30*, 83–89.

McLeod, P. D., Driver, J., and Crisp, J. (1988). Visual search for a conjunction of movement and form is parallel. *Nature, 332*, 154–155.

McLeod, P. D., and Posner, M. I. (1984). Privileged loops from percept to act. In H. Bouma and D. G. Bouwhuis (Eds.), *Attention and performance X: Control of language processes*, 55–66. Hillsdale, NJ: Erlbaum.

Marcel, A. J. (1980). Conscious and preconscious recognition of polysemous words: Locating the selective effects of prior verbal context. In R. S. Nickerson (Ed.), *Attention and performance VIII*. Hillsdale, NJ: Erlbaum.

Marcel, A. J. (1983). Conscious and unconscious perception: An approach to the relations between phenomenal experience and perceptual processes. *Cognitive Psychology, 15*, 238–330.

Marr, D. (1982). *Vision*. San Francisco: Freeman.

Marshall, J. C., and Halligan, P. W. (1988). Blindsight and insight in visual spatial neglect. *Nature, 336*, 766–767.

Matelli, M., Olivieri, M. F., Saccani, A., and Rizolatti, G. (1983). Upper visual space neglect and motor deficits after section of the midbrain commissures in the cat. *Behavioural and Brain Research, 10*, 263–285.

Maunsell, J. H. R., and Newsome, W. T. (1987). Visual processing in monkey extrastriate cortex. *Annual Review of Neuroscience, 10*, 363–401.

Mesulam, M. M. (1985). Attention, confusional states, and neglect. In M. M. Mesulam (Ed.), *Principles of behavioral neurology*, 125–168. Philadelphia: F. A. Davis.

Milner, A. D. (1987). Animal models for the syndrome of spatial neglect. In M. Jeannerod (Ed.), *Neurophysiological and neuropsychological aspects of spatial neglect*, 259–288. Amsterdam: North-Holland.

Moran, J., and Desimone, R. (1985). Selective attention gates visual processing in the extrastriate cortex. *Science, 229*, 782–784.

Morrow, L. A., and Ratcliff, G. (1988). The disengagement of covert attention and the neglect syndrome. *Psychobiology, 3*, 261–269.

Mozer, M. C. (1987). Early parallel processing in reading: A connectionist approach. In M. Coltheart (Ed.), *Attention and performance XII: The psychology of reading*, 83–104. Hillsdale, NJ: Erlbaum.

Nakayama. K., and Silverman, G. H. (1986). Serial and parallel processing of visual feature conjunctions. *Nature, 320*, 264–265.

Navon, D. (1984). Resources—a theoretical soup stone? *Psychological Review, 91*, 216–234.

Navon, D. (1990). The locus of attentional selection: Is it early, late, or neither? *European, Journal of Cognitive Psychology*.

Neisser, U. (1967). *Cognitive Psychology*. New York: Appleton-Century-Crofts.

Neisser, U., Hirst, W., and Spelke, E. S. (1981). Limited capacity theories and the notion of automaticity: Reply to Lucas and Bub. *Journal of Experimental Psychology: General, 110*, 499–500.

Neumann, O. (1987). Beyond capacity: A functional view of attention. In H. Heuer and A. F. Sanders (Eds.), *Perspectives on perception and action*, 361–394. Hillsdale, NJ: Erlbaum.

Neumann, O., van der Heijden, A. H. C., and Allport, A. (1986). Visual selective attention: Introductory remarks. *Psychological Research, 48*, 185–188.

Newcombe, F., Ratcliff, G., and Damasio, A. (1987). Dissociable visual and spatial impairments following right posterior cerebral lesions: Clinical, neuropsychological and anatomical evidence. *Neuropsychologia, 25*, 149–161.

Nicoletti, R., and Umiltà, C. (1989). Splitting visual space with attention. *Journal of Experimental Psychology: Human Perception and Performance, 15*, 164–169.

Nissen, M. J. (1985). Accessing features and objects: is location special? In M. I. Posner and O. S. M. Marin (Eds.), *Attention and performance XI*, 205–219. Hillsdale, NJ: Erlbaum.

Norman, D. A. (1968). Toward a theory of memory and attention. *Psychological Review, 75*, 522–536.

Norman, D. A., and Bobrow, D. G. (1975). On data-limited and resource-limited processes. *Cognitive Psycology, 7*, 44–64.

Norman, D. A., and Shallice, T. (1986). Attention to action: Willed and automatic control of behavior. In R. J. Davidson, G. E. Schwartz, and D. Shapiro (Eds.), *Consciousness and self-regulation*. Vol. 4. New York: Plenum Press.

Ogden, J. A. (1985). Contralesional neglect of constructed visual images in right and left brain-damaged patients. *Neuropsychologia, 23*, 273–277.

Pardo, J. V., Pardo, P. J., Janer, K. W., and Raichle, M. E. (1990). The anterior cingulate cortex mediates processing selection in the Stroop attentional conflict paradigm. *Proceedings of the National Academy of Science, USA, 87*, 256–259.

Pashler, H. (1984). Processing stages in overlapping tasks: Evidence for a central bottleneck. *Journal of Experimental Psychology: Human Perception and Performance, 10*, 358–377.

Pashler, H. (1987). Detecting conjunctions of color and form: reassessing the serial search hypothesis. *Perception & Psychophysics, 41*, 191–201.

Pashler, H. (1991). Shifting visual attention and selecting motor responses: Distinct attentional mechanisms. *Journal of Experimental Psychology: Human Perception and Performance, 17*, 1023–1040.

Pashler, H., and Badgio, P. C. (1985). Visual attention and stimulus identification. *Journal of Experimental Psychology: Human Perception and Performance, 11*, 105–121.

Pashler, H., and Badgio, P. C. (1987). Attentional issues in the identification of alphanumeric characters. In M. Coltheart (Ed.), *Attention and performance XII: The psychology of reading*, 63–81. Hillsdale, NJ: Erlbaum.

Pashler, H., and Johnston, J. C. (1989). Chronometric evidence of central postponement in temporally overlapping tasks. *Quarterly Journal of Experimental Psychology, 41A*, 19–45.

Petersen, S. E., Fox, P. T., Posner, M. I., Mintun, M., and Raichle, M. E. (1989). Positron emission topographic studies of the processing of single words. *Journal of Cognitive Neuroscience, 1*, 153–170.

Petersen, S. E., Robinson, D. L., and Morris, J. D. (1987). Contributions of the pulvinar to visual spatial attention. *Neuropsychologia, 25,* 97–105.

Phaf, R. H., van der Heijden, A. H. C., and Hudson, P. T. W. (1990). SLAM: A connectionist model for attention in visual selection tasks. *Cognitive Psychology, 22,* 273–341.

Playford, E. D., Passingham, R. E., and Nutt, J. (1991). Impaired activation of medial frontal areas during movement in Parkinson's Disease: A PET study. *Journal of Cerbral Blood Flow Metabolism, 11* (suppl. 2) S.1. (Abstract).

Poizner, H., Bellugi, U., and Klima, E. S. (1990). Biological foundations of language: Clues from sign language. *Annual Review of Neuroscience, 13,* 283–307.

Posner, M. I. (1978). *Chronometric explorations of mind.* Hillsdale, NJ: Erlbaum.

Posner, M. I. (1982). Cumulative development of attentional theory. *American Psychologist, 37,* 168–179.

Posner, M. I. (1988). Structures and functions of selective attention. In T. Boll and B. K. Bryant (Eds.), *Clinical neuropsychology and brain function.* Washington, DC: American Psychological Association.

Posner, M. I., Inhoff, A. W., Friedrich, F. J., and Cohen, A. (1987). Isolating attentional systems: A cognitive-anatomical analysis. *Psychobiology, 15,* 107–121.

Posner, M. I., Petersen, S. E. (1990). The attention system of the human brain. *Annual Review of Neuroscience, 13,* 25–42.

Posner, M. I., Petersen, S. E., Fox, P.T., and Raichle. M. E. (1988). Localization of cognitive operations in the human brain. *Science, 240,* 1627–1631.

Posner, M. I., and Rothbart, M. K. (1991). Attentional mechanisms and conscious experience. In A. D. Milner and M. D. Rugg (Eds.), *The neuropsychology of consciousness.* London: Academic Press.

Presson, C. C., DeLange, N., and Hazelrigg, M. D. (1989). Orientation specificity in spatial memory: What makes a path different from a map of the path? *Journal of Experimental Psychology: Learning, Memory and Cognition, 15,* 887–897.

Prinzmetal, W., and Keysar, B. (1989). Functional theory of illusory conjunctions and neon colors. *Journal of Experimental Psychology: General, 118,* 165–190.

Requin, J., Riehle, A., and Seal, J. (1988). Neuronal activity and information processing in motor control: From stages to continuous flow. *Biological Psychology, 26,* 179–198.

Riddoch, M. J., and Humphreys, G. W. (1987). Perceptual and action systems in unilateral visual neglect. In M. Jeannerod (Ed.), *Neurophysiological and neuropsychological aspects of spatial neglect,* 151–181. Amsterdam: North-Holland.

Rizzo, M., and Hurtig, R. (1987). Looking but not seeing: Attention, perception and eye movements in simultanagnosia. *Neurology, 37,* 1642–1648.

Rizzolatti, G., and Camarda, R. (1987). Neural circuits for spatial attention and unilateral neglect. In M. Jeannerod (Ed.), *Neurophysiological and neuropsychological aspects of spatial neglect,* 289–313. Amsterdam: North-Holland.

Rizzolatti, G., Camarda, R., Fogassi, L., Gentilucci, M., Luppino, G., and Matelli, M. (1988). Functional organization of inferior area 6 in the macaque monkey. *Experimental Brain Research, 71,* 491–507.

Rizolatti, G., and Gallese, V. (1988). Mechanisms and theories of spatial neglect. In F. Boller and J. Grafman (Eds.), *Handbook of Neuropsychology.* Vol. 1, 223–246. Amsterdam: Elsevier.

Rizzolatti, G., and Gentilucci, M. (1988). Motor and visual-motor functions of the premotor cortex. In P. Rakic and W. Singer (Eds.), *Neurobiology of neocortex*. New York: John Wiley.

Rizzolatti, G., Gentilucci, M., and Matelli, M. (1985). Selective spatial attention: one center, one circuit, or many circuits? In M. I. Posner and O. S. M. Marin (Eds.), *Attention and performance XI*, 251–265. Hillsdale, NJ: Erlbaum.

Robinson, D. W., and Petersen, S. W. (1986). The neurobiology of attention. In J. E. LeDoux and W. Hirst (Eds.), *Mind and brain: Dialogues in cognitive neuroscience*, 142–171. Cambridge: Cambridge University Press.

Roland, P. E. (1985). Cortical organization of voluntary behavior in man. *Human Neurobiology*, 4, 115–167.

Rubens, A. B. (1985). Caloric stimulation and unilateral visual neglect. *Neurology*, 35, 1019–1024.

Rugg, M. D., Milner, A. D., Lines, C. R., and Phalp, R. (1987). Modulation of visual event-related potentials by spatial and non-spatial visual selective attention. *Neuropsychologia*, 25, 85–96.

Ryan, C. (1983). Reassessing the automaticity-control distinction: item recognition as a paradigm case. *Psychological Review*, 90, 171–178

Sanders, A. F. (1967). Attention and performance 1. *Acta Psychologica*, 27,

Shallice, T. (1988). *From neuropsychology to mental structure*. Cambridge: Cambridge University Press.

Shallice, T., and Burgess, P. (N.d.). Higher-order cognitive impairments and frontal lobe lesions in man. In H. Levin, H. M. Eisenberg, and A. L. Benton (Eds.), *Frontal lobe function and injury*. Oxford: Oxford University Press. In press.

Shiffrin, R. M. (1988). Attention. In R. C. Atkinson, R. J. Hernstein, G. Lindzey, and R. D. Luce (Eds.), *Stevens' handbook of experimental psychology. Vol. 2, Learning and cognition*. 2d ed., 739–811. New York: John Wiley.

Shiffrin, R. M., and Schneider, W. (1977). Controlled and automatic human information processing: II. Perceptual learning, automatic attending and a general theory. *Psychological Review*, 84, 127–190.

Sieroff, E., Pollatsek, A., and Posner, M. I. (1988). Recognition of visual letter strings following injury to the posterior visual spatial attention system. *Cognitive Neuropsychology*, 5, 427–449.

Smith, M. C. (1967). Theories of the psychological refractory period. *Psychological Bulletin*, 67, 202–213.

Smith, W. S., and Fetz, E. E. (1987). Non-invasive brain imaging and the study of higher brain function in humans. In S. P. Wise (Ed.), *Higher brain functions: Recent explorations of the brain's emergent functions*. New York: John Wiley.

Soechting, J. F., Tillery, S. I. H., and Flanders, M. (1990). Transformation from head- to shoulder-centered representation of target direction in arm movements. *Journal of Cognitive Neuroscience*, 2, 32–43.

Spitzer, H., Desimone, R., and Moran, J. (1988). Increased attention enhances both behavioral and neuronal performance. *Science*, 240, 338–340.

Styles, E. A., and Allport, D. A. (1988). Perceptual integration of identity, location and colour. *Psychological Research*, 48, 189–200.

Tipper, S. P. (1985). The negative priming effect: Inhibitory effects of ignored primes. *Quarterly Journal of Experimental Psychology*, 37A, 571–590.

Tipper, S. P., and Driver, J. (1988). Negative priming between pictures and words: Evidence for semantic analysis of ignored stimuli. *Memory and Cognition, 16,* 64–70.

Tipper, S. P., MacQueen, G. M., and Brehaut, J. C. (1988). Negative priming between response modalities: Evidence for the central locus of inhibition in selective attention. *Perception and Psychophysics, 43,* 45–52.

Treisman, A. M. (1960). Contextual cues in selective listening. *Quarterly Journal of Experimental Psychology, 12,* 242–248.

Treisman, A. M. (1969). Strategies and models of selective attention. *Psychological Review, 76,* 282–299.

Treisman, A. M. (1988). Features and objects: The fourteenth Bartlett memorial lecture. *Quarterly Journal of Experimental Psychology, 40A,* 201–237.

Treisman, A. M., and Gelade, G. (1980). A feature integration theory of attention. *Cognitive Psychology, 12,* 97–136.

Treisman, A. M., and Sato, A. (1990). Conjunction search revisited. *Journal of Experimental Psychology: Human Perception and Performance, 16,* 459–478.

Treisman, A. M., and Schmidt, R. A. (1982). Illusory conjunctions in the perception of objects. *Cognitive Psychology, 14,* 107–141.

Ungerleider, L. G., and Mishkin, M. (1982). Two cortical visual systems. In D. J. Ingle, M. A. Goodale, and R. J. W. Mansfield (Eds.), *Analysis of visual behavior.* Cambridge, MA: MIT Press.

Vallar, G., and Perani, D. (1987). The anatomy of spatial neglect in humans. In M. Jeannerod (Ed.), *Neurophysiological and neuropsychological aspects of spatial neglect,* 235–258. Amsterdam: North-Holland.

van der Heijden, A. H. C. (1981). *Short-term visual information forgetting.* London: Routledge and Kegan Paul.

van der Heijden, A. H. C. (1987). Central selection in vision. In H. Heuer and A. F. Sanders (Eds.), *Perspectives on perception and action.* Hillsdale, NJ: Erlbaum.

van der Heijden, A. H. C. (1991). *Selective attention in vision.* London: Routledge.

van der Heijden, A. H. C., Hagenaar, R., and Bloem, W. (1984). Two stages in postcategorical filtering and selection. *Memory and Cognition, 12,* 458–469.

Virzi, R. A., and Egeth, H. E. (1984). Is meaning implicated in illusory conjunctions? *Journal of Experimental Psychology: Human Perception and Performance, 10,* 573–580.

Watt, R. (1988). *Visual processing: Computational, psychophysical and cognitive research.* Hove, UK: Erlbaum.

Welford, A. T. (1952). The "psychological refractory period" and the timing of high speed performance—A review and a theory. *British Journal of Psychology, 43,* 2–19.

Williams, M. (1970). *Brain damage and the mind.* Harmondsworth, UK: Penguin Books.

Wolfe, J. M., Cave, K. R., and Franzel, S. L. (1989). Guided search: An alternative to the modified feature integration model for visual search. *Journal of Experimental Psychology: Human Perception and Performance, 15,* 419–433.

Wurtz, R. H., Goldberg, M. E., and Robinson, D. L. (1980). Behavioral modulation of visual responses in the monkey: Stimulus selection for attention and movement. In J. M. Sprague and A. M. Epstein (Eds.), *Progress in psychobiology and physiological psychology.* Vol. 9. New York: Academic Press.

Yantis, S., and Johnston, J. C. (1990). On the locus of visual selection: Evidence from focused attention tasks. *Journal of Experimental Psychology: Human Perception and Performance, 16,* 135–149.

Zipser, D., and Andersen, R. A. (1988). A back propagation programmed network that simulates response properties of a subset of posterior parietal neurons. *Nature, 331,* 679–684.

10 Electrocortical Substrates of Visual Selective Attention

George R. Mangun, Steven A. Hillyard, and
Steven J. Luck

10.1 INTRODUCTION

Research on visual attention over the past few decades has attempted to specify the levels of processing at which different kinds of sensory information are selected for further analysis (e.g., Hoffman 1986; Johnston and Dark 1986). This "levels-of-selection" issue can be formulated in both psychological and physiological terms. Within a psychological framework, one can ask whether paying attention affects the quality of sensory information that is extracted from attended versus unattended inputs (early selection), or whether the influence is upon subsequent stages of decision, categorization, or response selection (late selection). In support of early selection mechanisms, human psychophysical studies have identified attentional influences on processes of feature registration (Prinzmetal, Presti, and Posner 1986), visual encoding (Reinitz 1990), and threshold-level luminance detection (Hawkins et al. 1990). In an analogous fashion, neurophysiological studies in animals have begun to define the specific anatomical levels of the visual pathways at which attention modulates the responsiveness of neurons that encode form, color, and spatial information (e.g., Wurtz, Goldberg, and Robinson 1980; Yin and Medjbeur 1988; Desimone and Ungerleider 1989).

In humans, physiological and psychological aspects of selection may be studied concurrently by noninvasively recording event-related brain potentials (ERPs) to attended and unattended stimuli (e.g., Hillyard and Picton 1987). ERPs are voltage fluctuations in the ongoing EEG that can be extracted by signal-averaging techniques; these field potentials reflect synchronous neuronal activity associated with sensory, motor, or cognitive events. The successive positive and negative voltage deflections (components) in an ERP waveform have latencies that reveal the time course of activation of the contributing neuronal populations, and scalp distributions that are determined by the anatomical position and geometry of those active neurons. Because of these properties, ERP recordings can yield information about the timing, sequential order, and anatomical location of attentional selection processes.

The ERPs elicited by briefly flashed visual stimuli include a series of positive (P) and negative (N) components over the posterior scalp that begins as early as 35–40 msec poststimulus and continues for hundreds of milliseconds thereafter (e.g., Hackley, Woldorff, and Hillyard 1990). Typically, however, the stimuli used in psychological experiments are of relatively low intensity, such that only the larger, more prominent of these ERP components can be readily observed. These include the P1 (peaking between 90 and 140 msec), N1 (160–190 msec), P2 (200–250 msec), and N2 (260–300 msec) components (fig. 10.1).[1] All of these latter ERP components are sensitive to spatial attention and are typically enlarged in amplitude when attention is directed to the location of the evoking stimulus (Eason, Harter, and White 1969; Harter, Aine, and Schroeder 1982; Hillyard and Munte 1984; Mangun and Hillyard 1987; Neville and Lawson 1987; Van Voorhis and Hillyard 1977). The amplitude enhancements of the earliest of these components (P1 and N1) over visual cortical areas have been interpreted as manifesting an attentional mechanism that operates as a sensory "gain control" in the visual pathways (Mangun and Hillyard 1988); such early modulation of the sensory signals arising from

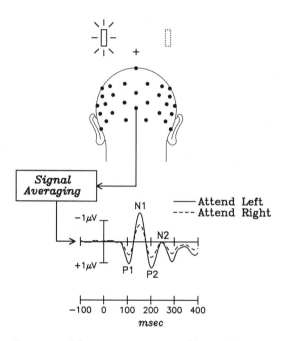

Figure 10.1 Schematic representation of the visual ERP components in a typical spatial attention experiment. In this example, left and right stimuli are shown being presented one at a time to the left and right visual fields. While continuously maintaining fixation on a central point (+), the subjects are instructed to attend to one stimulus position while ignoring the other; the goal is to detect target stimuli embedded within the sequence of target and nontarget stimuli at the attended location. The effects of attention are most validly assessed by comparing the ERPs elicited by the stimuli at a given position when that position was attended as compared to when attention was directed to the opposite visual field location: ERPs to left-field stimuli are indicated at bottom. The ERP waveform consists of a sequence of positive and negative deflections (components) labeled P1, N1, P2, and N2 (positive is plotted downward). These components are sensitive to the direction of attention and are typically larger in amplitude when the evoking stimulus is attended. Since these ERP components are relatively small in comparison to the ongoing EEG, signal averaging of the responses to many stimulus presentations is required to obtain a reliable waveform.

attended locations may underlie improvements in perceptual accuracy and response speed for those stimuli.

Interestingly, the concurrent amplitude enhancements of the early P1 and N1 components are uniquely associated with visual-spatial attention. Very different patterns of attention-related ERP components emerge when selection is based upon other stimulus attributes such as color, orientation, or feature conjunctions. In these cases, the most prominent component elicited by attended stimuli is typically a broad "selection negativity" that begins at 140–200 msec and may extend for several hundred milliseconds thereafter (Harter, Aine, and Schroeder 1982; Harter and Aine 1984; Wijers et al. 1987). Based on differences in the latency of this negativity, Harter, Aine, and Schroeder (1982) proposed that the selection of different attributes occurs in the following order: location, contour, color, spatial frequency, orientation, and feature conjunctions. Moreover, under certain circumstances, the selection of stimuli on the basis of color appears to be hierarchically dependent upon the prior selection for location (Hillyard and Munte 1984). Together, these results reinforce the hypotheses that location has a unique status as a cue for visual selection (e.g., Treisman 1988) and that spatial attention can modulate the registration of simple feature information (e.g., Prinzmetal, Presti, and Posner 1986).

10.2 NEURAL SUBSTRATES OF SPATIAL ATTENTION

Our understanding of the neural mechanisms involved in the attention-related changes in human ERPs can be advanced by considering the information about visual processes that is available from animal experiments. Studies of the anatomy and neurophysiology of the central visual pathways in monkeys have identified separate dorsal and ventral processing systems or "streams" that originate in primary visual (striate) cortex and mediate different aspects of visual perception (e.g., Desimone and Ungerleider 1989). The dorsal stream projects through prestriate area V2 to the posterior parietal lobe and is important for encoding the spatial aspects of visual inputs and for guiding visuomotor performance. In contrast, the ventral stream relays through prestriate areas V2, V3, and V4 of the occipital lobe and conveys information about stimulus form, color, and pattern to the inferior temporal lobe. Single-cell recordings from these visual cortical areas have shown that spatial selective attention exerts a strong influence on visually evoked neuronal activity in both the dorsal (posterior parietal lobe) and ventral (area V4 and inferior temporal lobe) streams, but not in prestriate area V2 or the striate cortex itself (Wurtz, Goldberg, and Robinson 1980; Desimone and Ungerleider 1989).

The anatomical and functional segregation of the visual pathways with respect to selective attention has been studied in humans with both neurometabolic and electrophysiological mapping techniques (Corbetta et al. 1990; Harter and Aine 1984; Mangun and Hillyard 1990b). As noted earlier, ERP recordings have revealed separate components over posterior cortical areas that are enhanced in response to stimuli presented at attended locations. The earliest attention-sensitive ERP component (the P1 wave beginning at 70–90 msec) has an amplitude maximum over the lateral occipital scalp, approximately overlying the ventrolateral prestriate cortex (Mangun and Hillyard 1987, 1988, 1990a). In contrast, the subsequent negative deflection (the N1 wave at 140–190 msec) is of maximal amplitude over parietal scalp sites for stimuli at attended locations (Harter, Aine, and Schroeder 1982; Mangun and Hillyard 1987, 1990a; Neville and Lawson 1987). Harter and Aine (1984) proposed that this negativity reflects the initial selection of stimulus location in the posterior parietal cortex.

The objective of the first experiment presented in this chapter was to localize the brain generators of the attention-sensitive P1 and N1 components of the human ERP with greater accuracy than previous studies had achieved. We wanted to determine whether the attentional modulation of the P1 and N1 components could indeed be assigned to separate cortical areas, perhaps in different functional streams of visual processing. The first step was to investigate whether the P1 component is actually generated in the lateral prestriate cortex itself, as suggested by Mangun and Hillyard (1990b), or in the more mesial striate cortex that provides input to both the dorsal and ventral streams.

To address this question, we recorded ERPs from a closely spaced array of electrode sites over the posterior scalp while subjects performed a visual-spatial attention task. The electrode array allowed a detailed mapping of voltage and current density distributions to be obtained for the P1 and N1 attention effects. Separate stimuli were presented in each of the four quadrants of the visual field in order to activate discrete zones of the primary visual (striate) cortex.

The striate cortex has a unique anatomical organization that results in characteristic ERP patterns for stimuli presented to the four visual field quadrants. Specifically, the striate cortex is folded within the depths of the calcarine fissure on the mesial aspect of the contralateral visual cortex. As a result, portions of the upper and lower visual half-fields are mapped upon separate, opposing sheets of cortical tissue facing each other across the calcarine fissure (fig. 10.2). Because of the opposed orientation of these cortical slabs, ERP components generated in striate cortex can be identified by observing polarity reversals on the scalp for upper- versus lower-field stimuli (Jeffreys and Axford 1972; Butler et al. 1987). The present study exploited this unique situation in order to distinguish between striate and prestriate generators of attention-sensitive ERP activity.

Methods

Eight university students participated in the experiment as paid volunteers. Subjects reclined in comfortable chairs facing video monitors. They were required to maintain fixation of their eyes upon a central cross while white rectangular bars were flashed in random order to the four visual field quadrants (fig. 10.3, top). The subjects' task was to attend exclusively to the bars in one

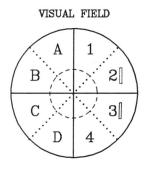

VISUAL FIELD

CORONAL SECTION
THROUGH OCCIPITAL CORTEX

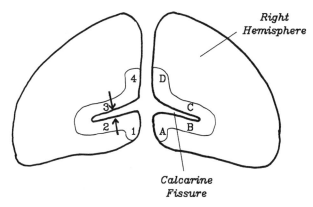

Figure 10.2 Diagrammatic representation of the visual field (top) and its projection onto the striate cortex (bottom). The figure at bottom is a posterior view of a coronal section taken through the occipital pole. The left and right hemispheres are shown with the calcarine fissure as indicated. The striate cortex is represented in outline surrounding the left and right calcarine fissures. The numbers correspond to those on the visual field map (top) and indicate the regions of striate cortex that receive inputs from a given contralateral zone of visual space. Stimuli in the upper- and lower-right visual field quadrants (near positions 2 and 3) would produce activation of cortical neurons that were oppositely oriented with respect to one another within the depths of the calcarine fissure in the left hemisphere (arrows). Adapted after Butler et al. (1987).

selected quadrant (ignoring the other three) and to press a button upon detecting each of the occasional, shorter "target" bars presented there. Each quadrant was selectively attended in different runs of 50 sec duration each; a total of twelve runs was presented under each of the four attention conditions.

The bars were flashed to the four quadrants in random order at intervals varying randomly from 250–550 msec for 67 msec duration each. The bars were either 3.75 (standard) or 3.25 (target) degrees in height. In each quadrant, the centers of the bars were positioned 5.8 degrees lateral to the fixation point and 3.5 degrees above or below the horizontal meridian. Thus, the horizontal separation between the stimuli was greater than the vertical separation (fig. 10.3, top). The probabilities of the standard and target stimuli in each quadrant were 0.83 and 0.17, respectively. The stimulus sequences included single bars flashed to only one of the four quadrants at a time (two-thirds of the stimuli),

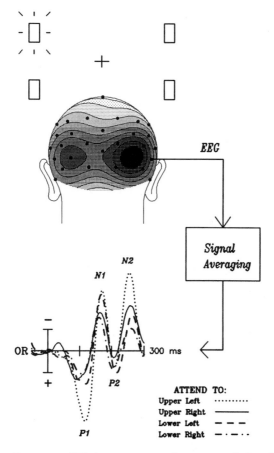

Figure 10.3 ERP changes in a spatial-attention task. Stimuli were presented in random order to the four quadrants of the visual field while subjects focussed attention on one of the quadrants at a time for runs of 50 sec each. ERPs were recorded from 30 scalp sites (dots on the schematic head) and computer-averaged separately for each stimulus and attention condition. ERP waveforms are grand averages over all eight subjects in response to upper-left flashes under the four conditions of attention. The scalp distribution of the P1 component for attended upper-left flashes (measured at 108 msec) is shown on the rear view of the head with darker areas representing greater positive voltages. Interpolation between recording sites was done by the spherical spline method of Perrin et al. (1989).

and bilateral bars flashed to left and right quadrants simultaneously, either both above or both below the horizontal meridian. Only ERPs to the single-position, nontarget stimuli will be considered here; the averages computed from these trials yielded waveforms with the highest signal-to-noise ratios and were also free from motor-related potentials, since no overt responses were made to these stimuli. For each subject, ERPs were averaged over approximately 240 nontarget stimuli per quadrant for each attention condition.

ERPs were recorded from thirty scalp sites using tin electrodes mounted in an elastic cap. Eye movements and blinks were monitored by recordings of the vertical and horizontal EOG; eye fixation was additionally verified by horizontal and vertical infrared corneal reflectance. The half-amplitude recording

Table 10.1 Amplitudes of P1 and N1 Components for Standard Stimuli in Each of the Four Quadrants as a Function of Attention Condition. Mean Amplitudes (Base-to-peak Measures in Microvolts) over Eight Subjects

P1 Amplitude

| *Attended Location* | Stimulus Location | | | |
	Upper Left	Upper Right	Lower Left	Lower Right
Upper Left	1.34	0.68	1.38	0.32
Upper Right	0.40	1.29	1.04	0.65
Lower Left	0.70	0.49	1.82	0.24
Lower Right	0.35	0.75	1.02	0.98

N1 Amplitude

| *Attended Location* | Stimulus Location | | | |
	Upper Left	Upper Right	Lower Left	Lower Right
Upper Left	−1.62	−0.80	−1.69	−1.31
Upper Right	−1.15	−1.24	−1.56	−2.10
Lower Left	−1.10	−0.48	−2.88	−1.90
Lower Right	−0.82	−0.91	−1.95	−2.71

bandpass for all sites was 0.01–100 hz. ERPs were computer-averaged for each stimulus type over epochs beginning 200 msec before stimulus onset and lasting for 1200 msec thereafter.

Results and Discussion

Grand average ERPs elicited by the bars flashed to the upper-left position are shown in figure 10.3 (bottom). As in previous studies, the amplitudes of the contralateral P1, N1, and N2 components increased when the subjects' attention was directed to the location of the evoking stimuli (Eason 1981; Harter, Aine, and Schroeder 1982; Hillyard and Munte 1984; Mangun and Hillyard 1987, 1988, 1990a; Neville and Lawson 1987; Rugg et al. 1987; Van Voorhis and Hillyard 1977). The lines and shaded areas on the schematic head show iso-voltage contours for the P1 component. The locus of maximum P1 amplitude for the left-field stimuli was over the lateral occipital scalp of the right (contralateral) hemisphere. A smaller, mirror-image focus arose over the left (ipsilateral) scalp some 15–20 msec after the contralateral P1 maximum and most likely represents activation of the ipsilateral hemisphere via the corpus callosum (Mangun and Hillyard 1988; Rugg, Milner, and Lines 1985; Saron and Davidson 1989).

Table 10.1 presents the P1 and N1 amplitudes for all four stimulus positions and attention conditions. The tabled values were measured at the scalp site where each component was largest (lateral occipital for P1; occipitoparietal for N1). For the P1 component, the mean amplitude in response to the bars when in the attended quadrant was larger (1.36 uV) than the amplitude of the responses they elicited when attention was directed to any other quadrant; this difference was significant when attention was directed away from the evoking stimulus and to the other quadrant in the same visual half-field (0.87 uV, $p < .05$), the opposite visual field at the same elevation (0.59 uV, $p < .005$), and the diagonally opposite position (0.55 uV, $p < .005$). For the N1 wave, the attended amplitude (-2.11 uV) was similarly larger (more negative) than unattended amplitudes for the same-field (-1.45 uV, $p < .001$), opposite-field (-1.50 uV, $p < .005$), and diagonal (-1.04 uV, $p < .001$) quadrants.

To localize the cortical generator(s) of the P1 component more precisely, voltage maps like those in figure 10.3 were transformed into current source density (CSD) maps. The CSD is calculated as the second spatial derivative of the voltage across the scalp. It provides a reference-free estimate of the instantaneous electrical currents flowing from the brain perpendicular to the scalp at each location at the specified time point (Nunez 1981). In comparison with voltage topographies, the CSD distributions emphasize superficial current sources, thus allowing more accurate localization of cortical ERP generators (Pernier, Perrin, and Bertrand 1988). Both the voltage and CSD maps shown here were calculated using the spherical spline interpolation algorithm developed by Perrin et al. (1989).

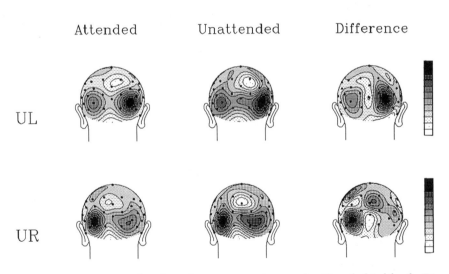

Figure 10.4 Scalp topography of grand average current source densities calculated for the P1 component (at 108 msec) in response to upper-left (UL) and upper-right (UR) stimuli. Separate CSD maps are shown for the P1 component elicited by those flashes when attended and when unattended (averaged over the 3 other attention conditions). At far right is the CSD distribution of the attention-related P1 difference formed by subtracting the ERPs in the unattended condition from those those in the attended. The darkest zones represent current sources (currents flowing out of the head), whereas the lightest zones represent current sinks. Each map is individually scaled to indicate 10 levels of CSD between the minimum and maximum values observed for that map.

The CSD maps for the P1 component reveal a narrowly focused current source over the contralateral occipital scalp (fig. 10.4), with a maximum situated about 6 cm lateral to the midsaggital plane. The location of this source in response to a given stimulus remained the same whether it was attended or unattended. Accordingly, the location on the scalp of the current source in the attention-difference map (attended—minus unattended CSD maps) was similar to that of the sensory-evoked P1 component (i.e., the unattended P1 current source). This equivalence supports the "sensory gain" hypothesis (Mangun and Hillyard 1988, 1990b) that spatial attention acts to regulate the amplitude of sensory evoked activity in the visual pathways without engaging additional neural generators (in the latency range of the P1 wave).

Figure 10.5 shows that maximal current density for the P1 attention effect remained unchanged in polarity and was highly similar in location for upper- versus lower-quadrant stimuli; this was also true for the P1 distributions for the attended and unattended stimuli. Such an invariance suggests that the P1 effect is not generated in striate cortex, because according to the model illustrated in figure 10.2, a striate generator for P1 would lead to a marked shift in CSD distribution and/or polarity due to the opposed orientation of active cortical neurons for the upper versus lower visual field stimuli. Instead, these relatively invariant and sharply localized CSD distributions suggest a generator in lateral prestriate cortex.

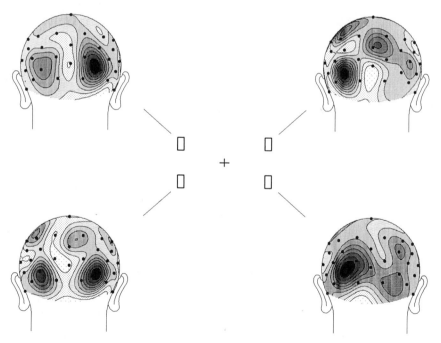

Figure 10.5 Current source density maps for the P1 difference wave (attended minus unattended) for stimuli in each of the four quadrants. The location of the CSD maximum is most affected by the left or right visual field position of the stimulus, in accordance with the contralateral projection of the visual pathways. In contrast, upper versus lower field stimulus position had little, if any, effect on the locus of maximal CSD for the P1 component.

Electrocortical Substrates of Visual Selective Attention

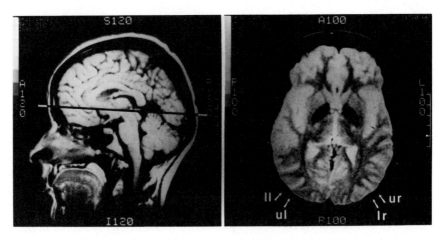

Figure 10.6 MRI scans of subject K.S.M. Image of midsaggital plane (left) shows depressions over posterior scalp where oil capsules were attached to identify midline electrode sites. Line through saggital section indicates plane of horizontal section (right) that passes through lateral occipital electrode sites where the current sources of the P1 attention effect were maximal. Arrows indicate locations of maximum CSD for the P1 attention effect elicited by flashes in lower-left (ll), upper-left (ul), lower-right (lr), and upper-right (ur) quadrants. Note that the horizontal brain section is right-left reversed, as is conventional for MRI scans.

The relation of the CSD distributions at the scalp to the underlying cortical anatomy was studied further by obtaining magnetic resonance images (MR scans) of the experimental subjects' brains. During the MR procedure, several electrode sites were marked on the subjects' heads by attaching small oil capsules that could be visualized in the obtained images. This procedure allowed the surface CSD maps to be brought into register with specific cortical gyri and sulci visible in the MR images.

Figure 10.6 (right panel) shows an MR section from one subject in a near-horizontal plane passing through the locus of maximum current density for the P1 attention effect. The maximum CSD locus for upper-left (ul) and lower-left (ll) stimuli are similar to one another, as are those for upper-right (ur) and lower-right (lr) stimuli. The indicated areas are situated over the ventrolateral prestriate cortex, which contains areas 18 and 19 of the occipital lobe.

The relative locations of the CSD maxima for the P1 and N1 attention effects (averaged over all subjects) are shown in a lateral view of the left hemisphere in figure 10.7. The P1 current source was situated ventrolaterally relative to the N1 maximum (a current sink), which lay near the border of the occipital and posterior parietal lobes. This difference in distribution is in line with the idea that the P1 attention effect reflects modulation of information flow along the ventral prestriate stream of visual processing (Mangun and Hillyard 1990b), whereas the N1 enhancement may be a sign of stimulus selection processes in the more dorsal pathways directed towards the parietal lobe (Harter and Aine 1984). Consistent with this proposal, the onset latency of the P1 effect corresponds well with the average latency of evoked unit

Scalp Current Density

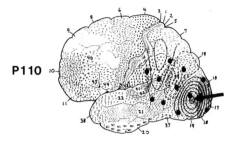

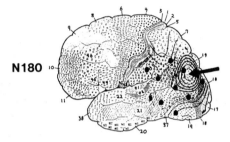

Figure 10.7 Superimposition of grand average CSD contours for P1 (P110) and N1 (N180) attention effects to upper-right stimuli upon a "classic" cytoarchitectonic map of the left hemisphere. The maximum CSD sink for the N1 effect is situated dorsally in relation to the CSD source of the P1 effect. This correspondence between the surface CSD and the underlying cortical areas must be considered approximate at present, since group-averaged ERP data were used and the relationship of electrode sites to Brodmann's areas was based on the averaged radiographic data of Homan, Herman, and Purdy (1987).

discharge in monkey prestriate area V4, reported to be in the 70–80 msec range (Robinson and Rugg 1988; Fischer and Boch 1985; Moran and Desimone 1985), whereas the average latencies of posterior parietal units are some 10–15 msec longer. Given our current lack of knowledge about the functional neuroanatomy of the prestriate cortex in humans, however, the hypothesis that the P1 and N1 effects are indices of attentional processes in separate processing streams must be regarded as tentative.

Although the results presented in figures 10.3 to 10.6 are strongly supportive of the view that the attention-related enhancement of the P1 wave is generated in prestriate rather than striate cortex, the question remains as to whether the underlying stimulus selection process takes place within the prestriate cortex itself or at an earlier level of the visual pathways. Given the retinotopic organization of the visual afferent structures, attentional selection of inputs based on stimulus location could, in principle, be accomplished in primary visual cortex or even at subcortical levels and "passed along" to prestriate levels to become manifest as an amplitude modulation of the P1 component. Such a subcortical selection mechanism was proposed by Yingling and Skinner (1976) on the basis of their finding (in cats) that thalamo-cortical

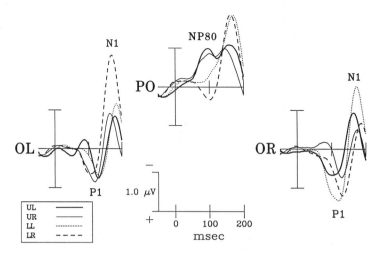

Figure 10.8 Grand average ERPs to stimuli in the four visual field quadrants when they were not attended. Recordings are from lateral left (OL) and right (OR) occipital sites and from a midline parieto-occipital site (PO). At site PO, the NP80 component can be seen to invert in polarity for upper- versus lower-field stimuli. In contrast, the longer-latency P1 and N1 components remain invariant in polarity.

transmission of sensory information could be controlled via inhibitory inputs from the thalamic reticular nucleus onto the thalamic relay neurons (see also Eason 1981; Crick 1984).

To gain further information about the anatomical level(s) at which spatial attention affects visual processing, the ERP waveforms of the present study were further examined for components showing polarity inversions for upper versus lower visual field stimuli that would be indicative of a striate cortex generator. As shown in figure 10.8, such a component was identified and was found to have a shorter latency than the P1 wave (onset at 50–60 msec, peak at 80–90 msec). This component, termed the NP80 wave, reversed its polarity from negative for upper-field stimuli to positive for lower-field stimuli. Further, its maximal amplitude was over parieto-occipital scalp sites near the midline, dropping off in amplitude toward the lateral occipital scalp sites where the P1 wave was largest. These characteristics of the NP80 are all consistent with a striate cortex generator; this wave probably corresponds to the Cl wave that was hypothesized by Jeffreys and Axford (1972) to originate in striate cortex.

Under the conditions of the present experiment, no attention-related amplitude enhancements could be observed for the NP80 component ($p > .10$ at parieto-occipital sites). Moreover, whereas the polarity of NP80 was inverted for upper- versus lower-field unattended stimuli ($p < .05$), the only effects of attention in this latency range (nonsignificant) could be ascribed to the leading edge of the positive-going enhancement of the P1 wave that began about 20 msec after the onset of the NP80 and was distributed more laterally on the scalp; in no case did the attention effect itself show a polarity inversion indicative of a striate cortex generator. Accordingly, these results are not supportive of an attentional gating mechanism at the level of the lateral

Mangun, Hillyard, and Luck

geniculate nucleus, since a subcortical modulation of visual input should affect striate cortex ERPs as well as subsequent prestriate activity. Rather, it appears that the earliest level where spatial attention modulates visual processing is in the prestriate cortex. This conclusion is consistent with studies in monkeys that found no evidence for attentional modulation of single-unit activity in primary visual cortex (Wurtz, Goldberg, and Robinson 1980; Moran and Desimone 1985). A recent study by Oakley and Eason (1990), however, did report significant changes in the time range prior to P1 in a spatial-attention paradigm, which suggests that the question of striate cortex involvement may need further study.

Although the present study obtained no evidence that spatial attention affects transmission through the lateral geniculate relay, this does not rule out an important role for the thalamus in the brain's attentional systems. Several lines of evidence have implicated the pulvinar nucleus in particular as playing a key role in stimulus selection processes in both monkeys (Desimone et al., in press; Peterson, Robinson, and Morris 1987) and humans (LaBerge 1990; Rafal and Posner 1987). According to recent proposals (Desimone et al., in press), projections from the pulvinar to prestriate cortex would have the capability of modifying visual processing at higher cortical levels without necessarily affecting transmission through the lateral geniculate relay. Such a mechanism would fit well with the present ERP results.

10.3 SPATIAL CUEING PARADIGMS

In order to test the generality of the ERP findings reported above, it was important to make comparable recordings from subjects performing in the spatial-attention paradigms most widely studied in the behavioral literature, which involve trial-by-trial cueing or priming procedures. In such designs, an initial cue or prime stimulus indicates the most likely location at which a subsequent test stimulus will occur (e.g., Posner 1980; Eriksen and Yeh 1985). Test stimuli presented to the precued (attended) location are generally detected and discriminated with greater speed and/or accuracy than are those at unattended locations. These behavioral effects have been attributed to improved sensory/perceptual processing by some authors (Posner 1980; Downing 1988) and to postperceptual factors such as decision bias by others (Shaw 1984; Sperling 1984).

Recordings of ERPs provide information relevant to this controversy. If the early, modality-specific ERP components could be shown to vary with spatial cueing, this would suggest an attention effect at the sensory/perceptual level. Although an early study of this type failed to observe significant effects on the P1 component during spatial cueing (Hillyard, Munte, and Neville 1985), that result may have been due to the somewhat long interval (1.8 sec) between the cues and targets that was used. More recent studies that employed cue-target intervals of 600–800 msec have indeed shown robust enhancement of the P1 component to targets at precued locations (Mangun, Hansen, and Hillyard 1987; Mangun and Hillyard 1991).

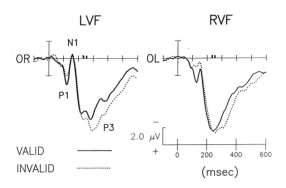

	Cue/Target Combination	Probability
Valid Left	[] $\underset{+}{<}$	.375
Invalid Left	[] $\underset{+}{>}$	.125
Valid Right	$\underset{+}{>}$ []	.375
Invalid Right	$\underset{+}{<}$ []	.125

Figure 10.9 Grand average ERPs for six subjects in a spatial cueing task in which subjects made simple reaction-time responses to both valid ($p = 0.75$) and invalid ($p = 0.25$) targets. ERPs were averaged separately for valid and invalid targets in left (LVF) and right (RVF) visual fields; the ERPs shown were recorded from the contralateral occipital scalp. Lateral eye movements were monitored by a high-gain EOG to ensure that subjects did not move their eyes toward the cued location. Data from Mangun and Hillyard (1991).

The effect of spatial cueing on P1 amplitude is illustrated in figure 10.9 for a simple reaction-time task (Mangun and Hillyard 1991). Each trial consisted of a cue and subsequent target stimuli. The cue (an arrow) appeared at fixation and indicated the most likely ($p = 0.75$) location of a subsequent target bar that was flashed to either the right or left visual field. The subjects had to make a speeded right-hand button press to all targets regardless of whether they occurred on the cued (valid) or uncued (invalid) side. Validly cued targets elicited significantly larger P1 components and shorter reaction times (230 vs. 254 msec). The later positive deflection that occurred 200–500 msec after the onset of the target stimulus is most likely a composite of a P3 (P300) component associated with the subjects' detection of the task-relevant target and the return to baseline of a prior negativity (CNV).

A similar enhancement of P1 amplitude for valid flashes has also been observed in a choice reaction-time task (fig. 10.10). The design of this experiment was equivalent to that illustrated in figure 10.9, except that subjects made a choice response based on the height of the target bar, pressing with the right hand for tall bars (2.1 degrees) and the left hand for short bars (1.9 degrees).

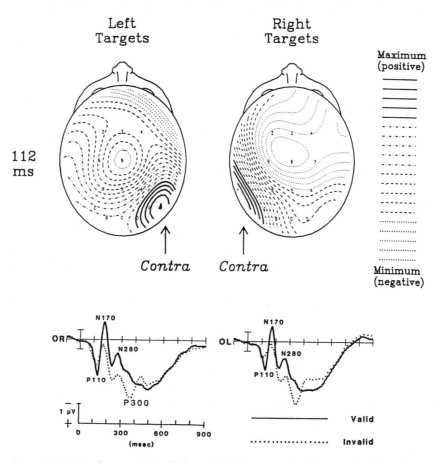

Figure 10.10 Grand average ERPs for fourteen subjects in a spatial cueing task where subjects made choice reaction-time responses to the target bars. Bars at both valid ($p < 0.75$) and invalid ($p = .025$) locations could be either "tall" or "short" (equiprobably), and subjects responded differentially according to bar height. ERPs were averaged over both tall and short bars and displayed as in figure 10.9. Topographic voltage maps (top view) are for the P1 validity effect measured as the P1 amplitude (112 msec) in the valid minus invalid difference wave. Maximum P1 enhancement for valid cues is over contralateral occipital scalp. Data from Mangun and Hillyard (1991).

In this choice task, unlike the simple reaction-time task, valid flashes elicited enlarged N1 as well as P1 components in association with faster reaction times (Mangun and Hillyard 1991). The voltage topography maps for the P1 attention effect show that the enhanced positivity was maximal over the same lateral occipital scalp sites as in the sustained attention tasks described in the previous section.

Harter and colleagues have observed similarly enhanced P1/N1 components for targets occurring at cued locations in a related design (Harter et al. 1989; Harter and Anllo-Vento 1991). In their task, a central arrow cue was followed 600 msec later by a target presented equiprobably to the left or right visual field; the subjects had to respond (finger-lift) to targets in the cued field but not to targets in the uncued field. The P1 and N1 amplitudes (measured peak-to-peak) were again most enlarged over the occipital scalp contralateral to the field of the attended target.

Importantly, Harter and his colleagues also identified slow lateralized ERPs within the cue-target interval. At around 200 msec postcue, a negative component appeared over the contralateral centroparietal scalp, which was interpreted as a sign of executive processes involved in directing attention in space. A later positive component (400 msec) was seen over the contralateral occipital scalp and was hypothesized to reflect the differential excitability of the visual projection pathways receiving input from relevant versus irrelevant visual fields.

The consistent finding in all these cueing studies of an enlarged P1 component over visual cortex for valid targets indicates that precueing of target location can facilitate sensory processing and does not act solely by biasing decision processes. This accords with recent observations that symbolic precues (e.g., arrows) can improve the detectability of near-threshold luminance targets at cued peripheral locations, an effect that cannot be accounted for by changes in decision bias (Downing 1988; Hawkins et al. 1990).

10.4 ATTENTION TO MULTI-ELEMENT STIMULUS ARRAYS

All of the ERP studies considered in the preceding sections used experimental designs in which single, isolated stimuli were presented to either attended or unattended locations in the visual fields. Although such designs do allow for the ready comparison of ERPs to attended versus unattended stimuli, they may not provide optimal conditions for spatial selection. There is considerable evidence, for example, that solitary stimuli presented in an "empty" visual field tend to draw attention to their locations automatically, regardless of whether or not they are supposed to be attended (Jonides 1981; Muller and Rabbitt 1989). In contrast, the selective processing of attended locations is generally facilitated when multiple stimuli are presented to different regions of the visual field simultaneously, and a subset of those stimuli is cued to receive attention (e.g., Jonides 1981; Eriksen and Yeh 1985). Experiments using multielement arrays have also revealed strong effects of spatial precueing on neural activity in monkey prestriate cortex (Moran and Desimone 1985), which adds incentive to search for corresponding effects in human scalp recordings.

In several recent ERP studies, we have investigated the differential processing of attended and unattended subregions within multielement displays (Luck and Hillyard 1989; Heinze et al. 1990; Heinze, Mangun, and Hillyard 1990; Luck et al. 1990). These experiments exploit the predominantly contralateral organization of the projections of the left and right visual fields onto the cerebral hemispheres. Because of this organization, the early visual ERPs (P1 and N1) are generally largest over the hemisphere contralateral to the visual field of a lateralized stimulus. Thus, the two hemispheres would be activated approximately equally by a bilateral stimulus with equal physical energy in the left and right visual fields. However, if attention is directed selectively to one side of a bilateral display, and if attention acts by increasing the gain of the sensory pathways that carry information from the attended half-field, a relative enlargement should occur in the early ERPs over the hemisphere contralateral to the direction of attention.

In one experiment that followed this approach (Heinze et al. 1990), two pairs of letters were presented simultaneously on each trial, one pair on each side of the fixation point (see fig. 10.11, top). These bilateral arrays were presented at a varying rate (280–520 msec) and contained random letter combinations from the set *E, L, T, F*. Subjects were instructed to attend to the left or right side during a 30-sec stimulus sequence and to press a button whenever the two letters on the attended side were identical (targets); identical letter pairs could also occur on the unattended side but did not require a response.

Figure 10.11 (bottom) shows the ERPs recorded over the visual areas of the left and right hemispheres when subjects attend to either the left or right half of such displays.[2] The amplitude of the P1 component over a given hemisphere was significantly larger ($p < .001$) when the contralateral visual hemifield was being attended. This effect is further illustrated by the CSD maps of the P1 component shown in figure 10.11 (middle). The bilateral stimuli produced a current source in both hemispheres, overlying the prestriate visual cortex, but the source was stronger over the hemisphere contralateral to the direction of attention. In contrast to the P1 component, however, there was no tendency for the N1 component to be enlarged over the contralateral hemisphere. Rather, during the N1 latency range the waveforms obtained over the scalp site contralateral to the attended field remain more positive.

As a further index of lateralized attention to these displays, ERPs were recorded to irrelevant, unilateral rectangular "probe" flashes randomly interspersed within the sequences of bilateral letter stimuli. These white probes were flashed to either the right or left letter-pair locations but did not disrupt the assigned task of detecting letter matches. Again, the P1 component was considerably enlarged over the contralateral occipital scalp ($p < .005$) for probes presented to the attended versus unattended half-fields (fig. 10.12, top). This finding strongly supports the hypothesis that P1 modulation reflects an

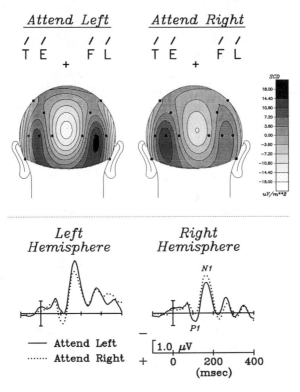

Figure 10.11 ERPs to sequences of bilateral arrays of letters recorded while subjects attended to either the left or right half of the display. The grand average waveforms (bottom) were elicited by nontarget letter pairs in a design equivalent to that of Heinze et al. (1990). The P1 wave was larger over the right hemisphere during the attend-left runs and larger over the left hemisphere during the attend-right runs. Topographic maps of CSD for the P1 wave (110 msec) show a stronger source over the lateral occipital scalp contralateral to the attended hemifield.

early selection for location that is applied equally to task-irrelevant probes and task-relevant letters. Once again, however, there was a conspicuous absence of any enhancement of N1 amplitudes to attended-field probes. As in figure 10.11, the waveform for attended-side probes remained more positive throughout the P1 and N1 latency ranges.

The strong spatial selection produced in this task was also evident in the ERPs to the letter-match stimuli (fig. 10.12, bottom). Letter matches (targets) in the attended field elicited an enlarged contralateral N2 wave at 250–350 msec followed by a P3 or P300 component at 400–600 msec. However, these late endogenous components were greatly reduced when letter matches occurred in the unattended field. The diminished N2 amplitude is of particular interest, since the visual N2 component has been interpreted as a sign of stimulus classification processes that may proceed automatically outside the focus of attention (Ritter, Vaughan, and Simson 1983; Wijers et al. 1987). Yet in the present study, there was little sign of any automatic classification of stimuli (targets vs. nontargets) at the unattended location. We consider this as evidence for the efficiency of the early spatial selection in preventing the

Mangun, Hillyard, and Luck

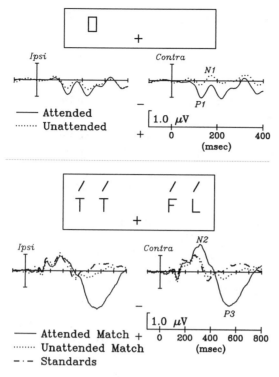

Figure 10.12 Grand average ERPs to unilateral probe flashes (top) and to targets with matching letters in one visual field (bottom) that were randomly interspersed among the nonmatching letter arrays in the study of Heinze et al. (1990). For the probe ERPs, the overlapped waveforms were recorded from an occipital scalp site (01/02), contralateral (right) or ipsilateral (left) to the probe location. Thus, the contralateral ERPs were obtained by averaging together the left field/right hemisphere and right field/left hemisphere responses. Solid tracings are ERPs to probes occurring in the attended half-field. The ERPs to targets (lower waveforms) were similarly collapsed according to whether the recording site was contralateral or ipsilateral to the half-field in which the letter match occurred.

transmission of information from the unattended half of the display to higher levels of pattern analysis and target classification indexed by the N2 and P3 components.

A further study was undertaken to examine the perceptual correlates of this focusing of attention upon one-half of a bilateral array (Heinze, Mangun, and Hillyard 1990). In this study, bilateral arrays of four "nonsense" symbols (two in each half-field) were flashed in rapid succession. The subjects had to focus attention on the symbol pairs on one side and make a match/mismatch judgment about occasional unilateral "target" symbols that would occur on one side or the other at random. As before, the unilateral target elicited a much larger P1 component when they occurred on the attended side. In conjunction with this P1 enhancement was a marked improvement in sensitivity (d') for matching targets to the preceding symbols; no significant attention effects were observed in decision criterion (Beta). These results support the view that the contralateral P1 enhancement observed for bilateral arrays and unilateral probes is associated with improved perceptual information from the attended locations.

10.5 GENERAL DISCUSSION

The ERP data described here strongly support the hypothesis that early selection in modality-specific cortex is a basic property of human visual-spatial attention. In three different types of paradigms, involving either sustained or precued focusing of attention upon a designated location, it was found that attended stimuli elicit an enlarged P1 component over the contralateral occipital scalp. The short latency of this P1 effect (onset at 70–90 msec) and its localization over ventrolateral prestriate cortex are consistent with an attentional process that modulates the flow of information arising from attended versus unattended locations (Eason 1981; Mangun and Hillyard 1990b). The stability of the earlier NP80 component attributed to the striate cortex suggests that spatial attention does not affect transmission through the lateral geniculate nucleus or the primary visual cortex but acts instead at higher, prestriate levels.

The finding that the contralateral P1 component was similarly enlarged for both relevant (patterned) and irrelevant (bar probe) stimuli flashed to the attended side of a bilateral display provides further evidence for an early selection process based solely on location (Heinze et al. 1990). The consequences of this early selection process were evident in both the reduced perceptual accuracy for detecting targets at unattended locations and in the diminished amplitudes of later, decision-related ERP components observed for unattended targets (Heinze, Mangun, and Hillyard 1990; Mangun and Hillyard 1990a, 1990b). These ERP findings converge with recent behavioral evidence indicating that spatial attention can affect the quality of sensory/perceptual information in the visual pathways (Downing 1988; Hawkins et al. 1990; Reinitz 1990).

The dissociation of the P1 and N1 attention effects observed in different task conditions raise the possibility that these ERPs index the operation of different attentional systems. Whereas the P1 effect was present in all of the spatial-attention paradigms considered here, the N1 effect was found to be greatly reduced or absent under conditions where (1) the target at a precued location did not need to be discriminated, (2) the stimulus sequence consisted mainly of bilateral arrays, and (3) a unilateral attended stimulus was immediately preceded by another stimulus at the same location (Luck et al. 1990). One possible interpretation would be that the N1 component is enlarged under conditions in which a stimulus calls for a switching or additional allocation of attention to its location, thereby allowing a further analysis of its features and properties. This interpretation of the N1 effect fits with evidence from single-unit recordings (Wurtz, Goldberg, and Robinson 1980) and studies of human patients (Posner et al. 1984, 1987), which point to a key role for the dorsal (posterior parietal) pathways in redirecting attention in space. Thus, while the

P1 attention effect is interpreted to be a reflection of preset changes in the gain of certain prestriate neurons during spatial attention, the N1 attention effect may signify the operation of a partially or completely independent parallel system that acts to allocate further attentional resources to the processing of the task-relevant stimulus.

Topographical CSD analyses indicated that the N1 attention effect arose from generators situated more dorsally than those of the P1 effect. This anatomical segregation suggests the intriguing possibility that the P1 effect may reflect attention-related modulation of activity along the ventral stream of visual processing that projects to the inferior temporal lobe and carries out object recognition functions. In contrast, the N1 effect may reflect the spatially selective functions of the dorsal stream that projects to the inferior parietal lobe. Such a correspondence is consistent with findings that spatial attention modulates neuronal responsiveness in monkeys along both the ventral (area V4, temporal lobe) and dorsal (posterior parietal lobe) pathways at latencies analogous to the human P1 and N1 components (Desimone and Ungerleider 1989; Robinson and Rugg 1988; Wurtz, Goldberg, and Robinson 1980).

While the above considerations conform well with the proposed assignment of the P1 and N1 attention effects to different attentional subsystems, additional work is also required to link them specifically with the ventral and dorsal processing streams identified from studies in monkeys. In particular, studies that combine the several imaging technologies now available for human research (ERPs, MEG, PET, and MRI) with neurophysiological and anatomical tracing studies in animals are required to expand and refine these proposals.

NOTES

This work has been supported by O.N.R. Contract N00014-89-J-1806 and by grants from N.I.M.H. (2 R01 MH25594 and 1 K21 MH00930) and N.I.H. (NS 2 P0117778-09). We thank Dr. Jonathan C. Hansen for superb scientific and engineering support, Dr. Eric Courchesne and Vince Clark for aid in obtaining the MR images, and Carol Montejano for manuscript preparation. We also acknowledge the significant contributions of our colleague Dr. Hans-Jochen Heinze to portions of the work reviewed here.

1. There is no uniform nomenclature used in the ERP literature. However, many authors label their ERP components using "P" or "N" to indicate positive or negative polarity components, respectively, and either a latency value or digit to indicate the time or order of appearance of the component within the waveform. Thus, "P1" designates a component that is the first major positive deflection in the visual ERP under the present conditions. The reader is cautioned not to assume that the P1 component defined here is necessarily the same as the P100 component elicited by pattern-reversal stimuli, or the C1 component described in early visual ERP studies (e.g., Jeffreys and Axford 1972; see text). The relationships among the various ERP components described in the literature can only be established by careful comparisons of their behavior over a range of stimulus and task parameters.

2. The data presented in figure 10.11 are actually from a related study (Heinze, Mangun, and Hillyard 1990) that utilized a similar design to that of Heinze et al. (1990). The effects described were identical in the two studies. These data were used in figure 10.11 because more scalp sites were recorded, and thus, it was more valid to plot the data as topographic CSD maps.

REFERENCES

Butler, S. R., Georgiou, G. A., Glass, A., Hancox, R. J., Hopper, J. M., and Smith, K. R. H. (1987). Cortical generators of the Cl component of the pattern-onset visual evoked potential. *Electroencephalography and Clinical Neurophysiology, 68,* 256–267.

Corbetta, M., Miezin, F. M., Dobmeyer, S., Shulman, G. L., and Petersen, S. E. (1990). Attentional modulation of neural processing of shape, color, and velocity in humans. *Science, 248,* 1556–1559.

Crick, F. (1984). The function of the thalamic reticular complex: The searchlight hypothesis. *Proceedings of the National Academy of Sciences, 81,* 4586–4590.

Desimone, R., and Ungerleider, L. G. (1989). Neural mechanisms of visual processing in monkeys. In F. Boller and J. Grafman (Eds.), *Handbook of Neuropsychology.* Vol. 2, 267–299. Amsterdam: Elsevier Science Pub. V.B.

Desimone, R., Wessinger, M., Thomas, L., and Schneider, W. (N.d.). Attentional control of visual perception: Cortical and subcortical mechanisms. *Cold Spring Harbor Symposium.* In press.

Downing, C. J. (1988). Expectancy and visual-spatial attention: Effects on perceptual quality. *Journal of Experimental Psychology: Human Perception and Performance, 14,* 188–202.

Eason, R. G. (1981). Visual evoked potential correlates of early neural filtering during selective attention. *Bulletin of the Psychonomic Society, 18,* 203–206.

Eason, R., Harter, M., and White, C. (1969). Effects of attention and arousal on visually evoked cortical potentials and reaction time in man. *Physiology and Behavior, 4,* 283–289.

Eriksen, C. W., and Yeh, Y. Y. (1985). Allocation of attention in the visual field. *Journal of Experimental Psychology: Human Perception and Performance, 11,* 583–597.

Fischer, B., and Boch, R. (1985). Peripheral attention versus central fixation: Modulation of the visual activity of prelunate cortical cells of the rhesus monkey. *Brain Research, 345,* 111–123.

Hackley, S. A., Woldorff, M., and Hillyard, S. A. (1990). Cross-modal selective attention effects on retinal, myogenic, brainstem, and cerebral evoked potentials. *Psychophysiology, 27,* 195–208.

Harter, M. R., and Anllo-Vento, L. (1991). Visual-spatial attention: Preparation and selection in children and adults. In C. Brunia, G. Mulder, and M. Verbaten (Eds.), *Event-Related Brain Research,* 183–194. Amsterdam: Elsevier.

Harter, M. R., and Aine, C. J. (1984). Brain mechanisms of visual selective attention. In R. Parasuraman and D. R. Davies (Eds.), *Varieties of Attention,* 293–321. Academic Press.

Harter, M. R., Aine, C., and Schroeder, C. (1982). Hemispheric differences in the neural processing of stimulus location and type: Effects of selective attention on visual evoked potentials. *Neuropsychologia, 20,* 421–438.

Harter, M. R., Miller, S. L., Price, N. J., LaLonde, M. E., and Keyes, A. L. (1989). Neural processes involved in directing attention. *Journal of Cognitive Neuroscience, 1,* 223–237.

Hawkins, H. L., Hillyard, S. A., Luck, S. J., Mouloua, M., Downing, C. J., and Woodward, D. P. (1990). Visual attention modulates signal detectability. *Journal of Experimental Psychology: Human Perception and Performance, 16,* 802–811.

Heinze, H. J., Luck, S. J., Mangun, G. R., and Hillyard, S. A. (1990). Visual event-related potentials index focused attention within bilateral stimulus arrays: I. Evidence for early selection. *Electroencephalography and Clinical Neurophysiology, 75,* 511–527.

Heinze, H. J., Mangun, G. R., and Hillyard, S. A. (1990). Visual event-related potentials index perceptual accuracy during attention to bilateral stimuli. In C. Brunia, A. Gaillard, and A. Kok, (Eds.), *Psychophysiological Brain Research.* Vol. 1, 196–202. Tilburg University Press.

Hillyard, S. A., and Munte, T. F. (1984). Selective attention to color and locational cues: An analysis with event-related brain potentials. *Perception & Psychophysics, 36*, 185–198.

Hillyard, S. A., Munte, T. F., and Neville, H. J. (1985). Visual-spatial attention, orienting and brain physiology. In M. I. Posner and O. S. Marin (Eds.), *Attention and Performance XI*, 63–84. Hillsdale, NJ: Erlbaum.

Hillyard, S. A., and Picton, T. W. (1987). Electrophysiology of cognition. In F. Plum (Ed.), *Handbook of Physiology Higher Functions of the Nervous System, Section 1: The Nervous System. Vol. V, Higher Functions of the Brain*, Part 2, 519–584. American Physiological Society.

Hoffman, J. E. (1986). Spatial attention in vision. *Psychological Research, 48*, 221–229.

Homan, R. W., Herman, J., and Purdy, P. (1987). Cerebral location of international 10–20 system electrode placement. *Electroencephalography and Clinical Neurophysiology, 66*, 376–382.

Jeffreys, D. A., and Axford, J. G. (1972). Source locations of pattern-specific components of human visual evoked potentials. I: Components of striate cortical origin. *Experimental Brain Research, 16*, 1–21.

Johnston, W. A., and Dark, V. J. (1986). Selective attention. *Annual Review of Psychology, 37*, 43–75.

Jonides, J. (1981). Voluntary versus automatic control over the mind's eye's movement. In J. B. Long and A. D. Baddeley (Eds.), *Attention and Performance IX*, 187–203. Hillsdale, NJ: Erlbaum.

LaBerge, D. (1990). Thalamic and cortical mechanisms of attention suggested by recent positron emission tomographic experiments. *Journal of Cognitive Neuroscience, 2*, 358–372.

Luck, S. J., Heinze, H. J., Mangun, G. R., and Hillyard, S. A. (1990). Visual event-related potentials index focused attention within bilateral stimulus arrays: II. Functional dissociation of P1 and N1 components. *Electroencephalography and Clinical Neurophysiology, 75*, 528–542.

Luck, S. J., Hillyard, S. A. (1989). On the automatic detection of visual popouts. Paper presented at the Annual Meeting of the Society for Psychophysiological Research, New Orleans, LA.

Mangun, G. R., Hansen, J. C., and Hillyard, S. A. (1987). The spatial orienting of attention: Sensory facilitation or response bias? In R. Johnson, Jr., J. W. Rohrbaugh, and R. Parasuraman (Eds.), *Current Trends in Event-Related Potential Research*, 118–124. Amsterdam: Elsevier.

Mangun, G. R., and Hillyard, S. A. (1987). The spatial allocation of visual attention as indexed by event-related brain potentials. *Human Factors, 29*, 195–211.

Mangun, G. R., and Hillyard, S. A. (1988). Spatial gradients of visual attention: Behavioral and electrophysiological evidence. *Electroencephalography and Clinical Neurophysiology, 70*, 417–428.

Mangun, G. R., and Hillyard, S. A. (1990a). Allocation of visual attention to spatial location: Event-related brain potentials and detection performance. *Perception & Psychophysics, 47*, 532–550.

Mangun, G. R., and Hillyard, S. A. (1990b). Electrophysiological studies of visual selective attention in humans. In A. B. Scheibel and A. F. Wechsler (Eds.), *Neurobiology of Higher Cognitive Function*, 271–295. New York: Guilford.

Mangun, G. R., and Hillyard, S. A. (1991). Modulations of sensory-evoked brain potentials indicate changes in perceptual processing during visual-spatial priming. *Journal of Experimental Psychology: Human Perception and Performance, 17*, 1057–1074.

Moran, J., and Desimone, R. (1985). Selective attention gates visual processing in the extrastriate cortex. *Science, 229*, 782–784.

Muller, H. J., and Rabbit, P. M. A. (1989). Reflexive and voluntary orienting of visual attention: Time course of activation and resistance to interruption. *Journal of Experimental Psychology: Human Perception and Performance, 15*, 315–330.

Neville, H. J., and Lawson, D. (1987). Attention to central and peripheral visual space in a movement detection task. I. Normal hearing adults. *Brain Research, 405,* 253–267.

Nunez, P. L. (1981). *Electric Fields of the Brain.* New York: Oxford University Press.

Oakley, M. T., and Eason, R. G. (1990). The conjoint influence of spatial selective attention and motor set on very short latency VERs. *Neuropsycholgia, 28,* 487–497.

Pernier, J., Perrin, F., and Bertrand, O. (1988). Scalp current density fields: Concept and properties. *Electroencephalography and Clinical Neurophysiology, 69,* 385–389.

Perrin, F., Pernier, J., Bertrand, O., and Echallier, J. F. (1989). Spherical splines for scalp potential and current density mapping. *Electroencephalography and Clinical Neurophysiology, 72,* 184–187.

Petersen, S. E., Robinson, D. L., and Morris, J. D. (1987). Contributions of the pulvinar to visual spatial attention. *Neuropsychologica, 25,* 97–105.

Posner, M. I. (1980). Orienting of attention. *Quarterly Journal of Experimental Psychology, 32,* 3–25.

Posner, M. I., Walker, J. A., Friedrich, F. J., Rafal, R. D. (1984). Effects of parietal lobe injury on covert orienting of visual attention. *Journal of Neurosciences, 4,* 1863–1874.

Posner, M. I., Walker, J. A., Friedrich, F. A., and Rafal, R. D. (1987). How do the parietal lobes direct covert attention. *Neuropsychologia, 25,* 135–145.

Prinzmetal, W., Presti, D. E., and Posner, M. I. (1986). Does attention affect visual feature integration. *Journal of Experimental Psychology: Human Perception and Performance, 12,* 361–369.

Rafal, R. D., and Posner, M. I. (1987). Deficits in human visual spatial attention following thalamic lesions. *Proceedings of the National Academy of Sciences* (USA) *84,* 7349–7353.

Reinitz, M. T. (1990). The effects of spatially directed attention on visual encoding. *Perception & Psychophysics, 47,* 497–505.

Ritter, W., Vaughan, H. G., Jr., and Simson, R. (1983). On relating event-related potential components to stages of information processing. In A. W. K. Gaillard and W. Ritter (Eds.), *Tutorials in ERP Research: Endogenous Components,* 143–158. Amsterdam: Elsevier/North-Holland Publishing Company.

Robinson, D. L., and Rugg, M. D. (1988). Latencies of visually responsive neurons in various regions of the Rhesus monkey brain and their relation to human visual responses. *Biological Psychology, 26,* 111–116.

Rugg, M. D., Milner, A. D., and Lines, C. R. (1985). Visual evoked potentials to lateralized stimuli in two cases of callosal agenesis. *Journal of Neurology. Neurosurgery and Psychiatry, 48,* 367–373.

Rugg, M. D., Milner, A. D., Lines, C. R., and Phalp, R. (1987). Modulation of visual event-related potentials by spatial and non-spatial visual selective attention. *Neuropsychologia, 25,* 85–96.

Saron, C. D., and Davidson, R. J. (1989). Visual evoked potential measures of interhemispheric transfer time in humans. *Behavioral Neuroscience, 103,* 1115–1138.

Shaw, M. L. (1984). Division of attention among spatial locations: A fundamental difference between detection of letters and detection of luminance increments. In H. Bouma and D. G. Bouwhuis (Eds.), *Attention and Performance X: Control of Language Processes,* 109–121. Hillsdale, NJ: Erlbaum.

Sperling, G. (1984). A unified theory of attention and signal detection. In R. Parasuraman and D. R. Davies (Eds.), *Varieties of Attention,* 103–181. London: Academic Press.

Treisman, A. (1988). Features and objects: The fourteenth Bartlett memorial lecture. *Quarterly Journal of Experimental Psychology, 40,* 201–237.

Van Voorhis, S., and Hillyard, S. A. (1977). Visual evoked potentials and selective attention to points in space. *Perception and Psychophysics, 22, 54–62.*

Wijers, A. A., Okita, T., Mulder, G., Mulder, L. J. M., Lorist, M. M., Poiesz, R., and Scheffers, M. K. (1987). Visual search and spatial attention: ERPs in focussed and divided attention conditions. *Biological Psychology, 25, 33–60.*

Wurtz, R. H., Goldberg, M. E., and Robinson, D. L. (1980). Behavioral modulation of visual responses in the monkey. In J. M. Sprague and A. N. Epstein (Eds.), *Progress in Psychobiology and Physiological Psychology, 9, 43–83.* New York: Academic Press.

Yin, T. C. T., and Medjbeur, S. (1988). Cortical association areas and visual attention. In *Comparative Primate Biology. Vol. 4: Neurosciences, 393–419.* Alan R. Liss, Inc.

Yingling, C. D., and Skinner, J. E. (1976). Selective regulation of thalamic sensory relay nuclei by nucleus reticularis thalami. *Electroencephalography and Clinical Neurophysiology, 41, 476–482.*

11 Dual-Task Interference and Elementary Mental Mechanisms

Harold Pashler

Human beings can perform an extraordinary variety of tasks involving coordinated perceptual, cognitive, and motor activity. In the psychological laboratory, people readily comply with even quite bizarre task instructions and successfully configure their mental machinery to produce arbitrary behaviors in response to the stimuli presented to them. Understanding how particular tasks are performed is often of theoretical and practical interest, but a scientifically deep understanding of human cognition and performance also requires uncovering essential constraints and mechanisms that underlie the extraordinary flexibility that we tend to take for granted.

This chapter summarizes recent work directed at revealing basic mental mechanisms by examining what happens when people attempt to perform more than one task concurrently. The goal of such "dual-task" research is one that has been useful in various fields: to reveal the basic components of a system and how they function together by examining how the system breaks down when it is overloaded in some way. Important facts about the overall structure and control of a complex system are often hidden when the system is functioning smoothly and little is demanded of it, but when it is challenged, important constraints may become evident.

Dual-task interference has been studied with a variety of different methods. The approach taken here starts with very basic (e.g., tachistoscopic and choice reaction time) tasks, studying performance on a trial-by-trial basis, adding additional components one by one, and focusing on the relative timing of particular stages of processing. This contrasts with much dual-task research of the past twenty years, which has often employed complex and temporally extended tasks, while assuming particular theoretical concepts (such as shared resources) in advance. I will argue that our results require postulation of several discrete attentional mechanisms. In general, our results tend to support some of the suggestions made by the investigators who first examined dual-task interference (notably Welford), while falsifying many hypotheses that have been advanced more recently.

11.1 DUAL-TASK INTERFERENCE

The simplest experimental situation that demands concurrent performance of two basic tasks is the *psychological refractory period (PRP)* paradigm. Here, two stimuli (*S1* and *S2*) are presented, separated by some stimulus onset asynchrony (*SOA*), and the subject makes a separate speeded response to each (*R1* and *R2*). Early investigators using manual responses to visual stimuli (e.g., Vince 1949) reported a marked slowing of the second response (the *PRP effect*) as the SOA decreased. In some cases, the slope of the function relating R2 latency to SOA was about minus one for short SOAs (Welford 1952).

Given the simplicity of the tasks employed, this interference is rather remarkable. It is also strikingly robust. Interference does not depend upon using two visual stimuli, as in the earliest studies. Davis (1959) found a PRP effect with a tone and a visual stimulus, for example. Nor does it depend upon requiring concurrent manual responses. For example, classic PRP functions have been observed with various manual and vocal response combinations (e.g., Pashler 1989, 1990), and even with manual and foot responses (Osman and Moore 1990).

Studies of divided attention that require the (unspeeded) report of brief visual displays have frequently observed better performance when the two stimuli are attributes of the same object (e.g., Duncan 1984). However, Clark Fagot and I have found that the classic PRP effect persists under these conditions. For example, in one experiment, we had subjects make a manual choice response to the identity of a character and name the color of the character aloud (the character—S1—started out grey and then turned to the target color—S2—after a variable SOA). In another experiment, subjects made a push-button response to the color of a character and named aloud its direction of motion (up vs. down). In both cases, the usual PRP effects were observed (Fagot and Pashler, in press).

It has been suggested that extensive practice with a consistent stimulus-response mapping allows performance to become independent of "attentional resources." This conclusion is based mostly on studies in which subjects perform a visual search task at the same time as they maintain a memory load (Schneider and Shiffrin 1977). However, practice does not generally seem to eliminate the PRP effect, despite the use of completely consistent mappings throughout. For example, James Johnston and I required subjects to perform more than 10,000 trials of practice with a pair of overlapping choice tasks; the PRP effect remained (Johnston and Pashler 1984; see also Gottsdanker and Stelmach 1971). Common sense would suggest that maintaining a memory load may simply not require continuous mental operations, in which case the usual interpretation of the "automaticity" studies is not demanded by the data (see below).

While the PRP paradigm is an elegantly simple model for dual-task interference, it is artificial in requiring the subject to deal with only two punctate events. This requirement is rather rare outside the laboratory, where one task is typically performed for a while, and then another task intrudes more or less unexpectedly. In principle, protracted performance might either increase interference (because of poor temporal warning) or decrease it (if performing a task for some time allows the processing machinery to organize itself so as to carry out the task autonomously). Johnston and I examined this question by having subjects perform a manual choice response to a tone either once or repeatedly, followed by a visual signal calling for a response with the other hand. The repeated first-task condition showed improved performance on that task, but the interference with the visual (second) task was actually *greater* than usual (Pashler and Johnston 1991). Extensive practice did not alter this, but providing an extra warning signal for the arrival of S2 mitigated the extra interference somewhat. Thus, so far we have found no reason to believe that the PRP effect is an artifact of performing two tasks in temporal isolation.

There is, however, at least one case in which the PRP effect seems to be largely eliminated. This occurs when one of the tasks involves a saccadic eye movement. Mark Carrier, Jim Hoffman, and I had subjects perform a manual response to a tone (high vs. low pitch) and, after a variable SOA, a saccadic eye movement cued by a visual stimulus (Pashler, Carrier, and Hoffman 1991). When the saccade task simply required subjects to move their eyes to a patch that appeared by itself on the left or right side of the screen, saccade latencies were not much affected by the SOA, and other indices of interference were virtually absent. The same was true when a red patch and a green patch were presented to either side of fixation, and subjects moved their eyes to the patch with a prespecified color. However, when a *central* color patch was presented, and subjects moved their eyes in one direction if it was red and in the other direction if it was green, the eye movement was clearly delayed by the first task. Clear-cut interference also occurred when the subject had to make a saccade toward the numerically higher of two large digits presented off fixation.

It appears, then, that under certain conditions, at least one response system (the oculomotor system) can be triggered to operate independently of other mental activities. This might be related to the fact that eye movements are mediated by several partially redundant brain systems. The response of shadowing verbal input may also be exempt from PRP-type interference (McLeod and Posner 1984). We are currently looking for other cases of interference-free behaviors (such as manual reaching), but even if there are several more of them, they would seem to represent the exception rather than the rule.

11.2   CAUSES OF DUAL-TASK INTERFERENCE

What causes the dual-task interference described so far? A wide range of theories have been proposed since the PRP effect was first observed. Early suggestions that the effect might stem simply from temporal uncertainty about the arrival of S2 were easily rejected. Instead, several workers proposed a "bottleneck" such that some stages of performance in each task require a common mechanism. According to this proposal, these stages in the second task cannot begin until the corresponding ones in the first task are complete.

This has the virtue of predicting in a straightforward way the minus one slopes noted above. Different researchers suggested different accounts of what stages constituted this bottleneck. A bottleneck in perceptual processing was considered (Broadbent 1958), while Welford (1952, 1980) suggested that a central mechanism was required to determine what response should be made (which he termed the "translation" mechanism).

Some early reviews favored Welford's proposals (e.g., Smith 1967), but the evidence was not compelling, and in the following years, still further alternatives were advanced. These included the possibility of a bottleneck in the actual initiation or execution of responses (Keele 1973), or graded sharing of capacity between tasks (Kahneman 1973; McLeod 1977). The latter suggestion was motivated primarily by the observation that R1 as well as R2 was sometimes slowed in the dual-task situation. For reasons that are not entirely clear, the main focus of dual-task research turned to other procedures involving more continuous types of tasks. The consequence of this shift was that the dual-task situation most amenable to detailed analysis was relatively neglected for more than a decade.

11.3 RECENT ANALYSES OF DUAL-TASK INTERFERENCE

Chronometric Methods

In recent studies, we have focused on the PRP effect once again, using methods that enable the various candidate theories to be distinguished. One method we have used involves manipulating the duration of component stages of the second task (cf. Sternberg 1969) to test the predictions of bottleneck models.

Figure 11.1 illustrates the time course of dual task performance assuming a bottleneck in response selection. Various predictions can be derived from such a model. If an experimental factor is manipulated to retard stages of the

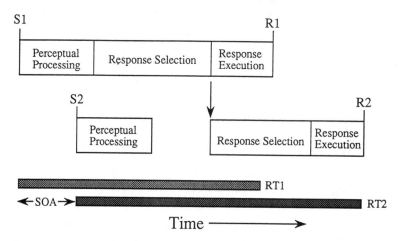

Figure 11.1 The response-selection queuing account for the psychological refractory effect.

second task *at* or *after* the bottleneck (i.e., response selection or execution), then this factor should slow the response correspondingly, whatever the SOA. Thus, at all SOAs, a 50-msec slowing of response selection in task 2 will increase RTs by 50 msec in both the single-task condition and the dual-task condition (whatever the SOA). On the other hand, if a stage of the second task located *before* the bottleneck (e.g., perceptual processing) is retarded, then some particularly diagnostic interactions are predicted. In the single-task condition, and at very long SOAs, the full slowing should be manifest in the R2 latency. However, when the SOAs are reduced, completion of the second task is increasingly likely to have to wait for the completion of the bottleneck stage of the *first* task, rather than for the completion of the stage of the second task that is slowed by the manipulation (fig. 11.1 shows just such a short SOA). For that reason, the effect of the manipulation should be progressively reduced as SOA is shortened.

It can be seen, then, that different bottleneck models make quite distinctive predictions about effects of S2 factors: (1) additive effects of dual-task slowing (i.e., dual-task short SOA vs. long SOA; or dual- vs. single-task) and factors affecting stages of task 2 *beyond* the bottleneck stage, and (2) *underadditive* interactions of SOA with factors affecting stages of task 2 *before* the bottleneck should be observed. By contrast, there is no particular reason to expect such a pattern if there is graded sharing of central capacity between tasks (e.g., Kahneman 1973; see Pashler 1984).

A number of PRP experiments have been analyzed in more or less this way over the years. Both Keele (1973) and Schweickert (1978) analyzed previously published PRP experiments that compared simple and choice RT2s, looking for signs of processing "slack." However, it appears that choice and simple RT do not differ merely in the duration of one particular single stage, rendering conclusions about dual-task interference from such analyses very uncertain (Sternberg 1969).

In the past several years, however, we have examined a wide range of task-2 factors that seem very likely to affect the duration of specific stages of processing, and the results have been quite consistent. When perceptual processing is slowed by reducing the intensity of a visual S2, the RT2 is increased less in the dual-task than in the single-task condition (Pashler 1984); furthermore, in the dual-task condition, intensity effects are reduced as SOA is shortened (Pashler and Johnston 1989). Similarly, display-size effects in a secondary visual search task are underadditive with dual-task slowing (Pashler 1984), and taper off with SOA (Pashler 1990). These effects indicate that a bottleneck exists beyond the perceptual processing which these manipulations retard. Manipulations that affect the speed of response selection generally have additive effects with dual-task slowing. For example, when the stimulus is repeated from trial to trial in a choice reaction-time experiment, response selection operates faster; this effect is *additive* with dual-task slowing, and with SOA (Pashler and Johnston 1989). Similarly, McCann and Johnston (1992) have found that the effect of S-R compatibility in a second task was also additive with SOA.

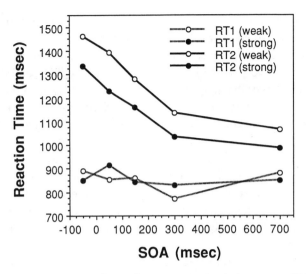

Figure 11.2 Dependency of RT2 on RT1. Graph shows mean RT2 as a function of the relative magnitude of RT1 on the corresponding trial (by quintile within the RT1 distribution for that SOA).

The results support a response-selection bottleneck. They also rule out the hypothesis that *producing* R2 is the first or only stage of processing that is delayed (as proposed by Keele 1973, and Norman and Shallice 1985). If no stage in task 2 before response production were delayed, then R2 latencies would not be affected by "cognitive" factors such as S-R compatibility at short SOAs. These findings also lend no support to capacity-sharing accounts either (see Pashler 1984 for a discussion).

Dual-Task Performance Dependencies

Further evidence for bottleneck models comes from analyzing the dependencies between R1 and R2 latencies. If processing required to produce R2 waits for completion of the major portion of the first task (where most of the variability in latency originates), then most trial-to-trial variance in R1 latency should propagate into the second task. Consistent with this, Welford (1967) noted positive correlations between response times in the two tasks. Positive correlations of this sort might be consistent with other possibilities, however, such as a positive dependency between the degree to which the subject has prepared each task in advance.

Bottleneck models predict a much more specific pattern of dependency between R2 and R1 latency, interacting with SOA. For our analyses, we generally divide the trials by quintiles, according to the relative speed of R1 within a condition. Figure 11.2 shows the mean R2 latency as a function of the relative R1 latency in a representative PRP experiment (similar to that described below and shown in fig. 11.3). At the long SOAs, there is little relationship (flat slope). As the SOA is reduced, R2 depends more positively upon R1 (upward tilt), and this dependency begins earlier and earlier in the R1

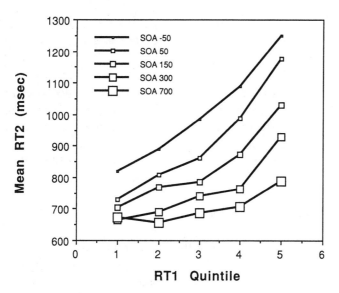

Figure 11.3 Effects of SOA and associative strength on RT1 and RT2 for speeded manual responses to a tone (R1) and speeded retrieval of a paired associate (R2). From Carrier and Pashler (1992).

distribution. Postponement of task-2 response selection predicts just this form of interaction between SOA and quintile. We have observed it repeatedly in PRP experiments with varying tasks, response modalities, and levels of practice (e.g., Pashler 1989, 1991; Pashler and Johnston 1991; Fagot and Pashler, in press).

Tachistoscopic Second Tasks

The evidence presented thus far supports a response-selection bottleneck and indicates that at least some perceptual processing in the second task proceeds unhindered by the first task. If this account is correct, certain additional predictions should also hold. For example, one should also find that the likelihood of completing perceptual processing of S2 within any given period of time after the onset of S2 should not be reduced when the two tasks overlap (i.e., at short SOAs) as opposed to when they do not overlap.

This prediction was tested by masking S2 and observing the accuracy of an *unspeeded* R2 (R1 was still speeded) as a function of SOA. Pashler (1989) reported several studies of this type. Subjects made a manual choice response to a tone, and after a variable SOA (50, 150, and 650 msec) a visual display was presented and then masked (display-mask interval was fixed in each block). To be sure that subjects had to complete perceptual processing before the mask in order to make an accurate response (rather than storing the contents of the display), the displays exceeded the span of immediate memory. In one experiment, the displays consisted of eight digits, and subjects named the highest of these digits; in another experiment, there were eight green and red O's and T's, and the subject decided whether a green T was present (feature-conjunction search). Accuracy of performance on the second task was impaired by only a few percent as SOA decreased from 650 (longer than most R1s) to 50 msec.

However, when exactly the same pair of tasks was used and both responses were speeded (with S2 not masked), the usual PRP effect occurred, as did the usual pattern of dependencies between R1 and R2. So these results further support the existence of a bottleneck beyond perceptual recognition, at least for stimuli such as letters and digits (and arbitrary conjunctions of features as well). The full extent of stimulus analysis that can operate without the bottleneck mechanism remains to be determined.

What Counts as a Response?

Thus far, we have spoken of the selection of a particular response without defining what is selected. This leaves open a very interesting issue. Studies of bimanual coordination (e.g., Kelso, Southard, and Goodman 1979) indicate that movements of both arms are sometimes temporally synchronized, suggesting some form of coupled control. Can two actions be selected as a couplet without employing the bottleneck mechanism twice? To answer this question, Clark Fagot and I have examined situations in which two responses must be produced—one manual and one vocal—but both are *redundantly* signaled by the same stimulus (Fagot and Pashler, in press). For example, in one experiment, subjects named the color of a stimulus and made a manual response that also depended upon its color. In the dual-task condition, only the vocal response showed any slowing compared to a single-task control, and this slowing was very small (about 30 msec). Correlations between R1 and R2 latencies were extremely high. Together, these results suggest that a single mental operation selected a response *couplet*. By themselves, however, the data cannot rule out the possibility that manual and vocal responses were selected independently and simultaneously.

To analyze the time course of processing further, we introduced a manipulation that slowed the single-task manual response but had no effect on the single-task vocal response (namely, compatibility of stimulus position and manual response, or the *Simon effect*). In the dual-task condition, the Simon effect extended the vocal RTs, slowing them to about the same degree as the manual RTs. This clearly rules out independent response selections, and suggests that the response-selection mechanism underlying the bottleneck effect can be "set" to generate essentially arbitrary assemblages of motor behaviors as a single response. Further experimentation involving two response-selection manipulations also confirmed these conclusions.

11.4 EXTENT OF THE BOTTLENECK

The results discussed thus far have supported Welford's early proposal that a bottleneck in selecting responses underlies the robust dual-task interference observed with pairs of sensorimotor tasks. The most natural interpretation of the existence of such a bottleneck would be that the brain possesses only a single mechanism that must perform the relevant stages in each task. (Note that it would be functionally equivalent if the "mechanism" consisted of physically distinct systems or networks that mutually inhibited each other's operation.) To understand the general significance of this mechanism for human performance and cognition, we must determine whether it is involved only in the choice of *action* per se, or if it is in fact responsible for a wider range of cognitive operations.

This is plainly a very broad issue, and thus far we have only begun to scratch its surface. Mark Carrier and I started with the case of memory retrieval in cued recall. While this sort of memory retrieval is effortful and sensitive to nonspecific stressors like fatigue and intoxication, dual-task researchers have not had much to say about its possible reliance on general-purpose central mechanisms. Baddeley et al. (1984) claimed that memory retrieval does *not* rely on general "capacity," based on small effects of a concurrent task on memory-retrieval accuracy. Large effects on retrieval latency were observed, but they were attributed to response-related interference (although there was really no way of telling where the interference lay in these studies).

Carrier and I have approached this issue with two converging methods (Carrier and Pashler 1992). The first involves manipulating second-task stages in a PRP study, as described above. Subjects were pretrained on a set of paired associates, half of which were easy to learn (because of high prior association), and half of which were difficult. Subjects then performed a PRP procedure: here, the first task was the tone task with manual response, and the second task involved standard paired-associate retrieval (with vocal responses). Figure 11.3 shows the results: an additive effect of SOA and retrieval difficulty. As described above, such data indicate that the memory retrieval requires the same mechanism as the tone task; otherwise the effect of associative strength should have been "swallowed up" as SOA decreased.

Our second approach involved more time-consuming memory retrievals. Subjects attempted a relatively difficult cued semantic memory recall task (category-letter cue, e.g., "VEGETABLE A" yielding "asparagus"). In one condition, this task was performed alone for 30 sec. In another condition, the subject performed the usual tone task over and over (with essentially zero response-stimulus interval) for 10 sec after the category-letter cue was presented, and then continued the retrieval task by itself. During the 10 sec when the tone task was performed, rather little was accomplished on the memory retrieval. This was true even if the tone task did not begin until 1 sec after the retrieval cue. Thus, it appears that these semantic memory retrievals may require the same mechanism as that used for response selection in the tone task.

McCann and Johnston (1989) reported chronometric results indicating that certain *noncategorical* perceptual judgments with visual stimuli (e.g., line-length comparison) also exhibit the bottleneck limitation, based on additive effects of SOA and comparison difficulty. This is further evidence that the bottleneck does not only arise in the process of selecting motor actions per se.

11.5   VISUAL ATTENTION SHIFTS AND THE BOTTLENECK

Thus far, I have used the rather quaint term *bottleneck* to describe the cognitive processes subject to postponement in the PRP situation, while avoiding the term *attention*, which is notoriously laden with a variety of different meanings. Nonetheless, the results described do suggest that a surprisingly wide range of mental processes rely on a single general-purpose mechanism. Therefore, it seemed worth inquiring whether this central serial mechanism can be identified with what is most commonly referred to as attention.

The paradigmatic form of attention arises in the selection of sensory stimuli for further processing. It has long been known that people can voluntarily attend to just a particular subset of their sensory input, with the consequence that they have little awareness or memory of the remaining stimuli. In the case of vision, attention shifts can be triggered by a wide range of cues (e.g., von Wright 1968) and do not depend upon eye movements.

This raises the question of whether shifts in visual selective attention involve the bottleneck mechanism previously described. Posner et al. (1989) suggested that attention shifts require an "anterior attention system" (a concept rather close to the response-selection bottleneck) on the basis of experiments that combined shadowing with cued visual simple RT. Furthermore, Rizzollati and Camarda (1987) claimed that control of motor movements and attention movements must involve the same neural system, based on patterns of associated symptoms observed in unilateral neglect patients. None of these results seemed conclusive, so the tachistoscopic second-task method described earlier was adapted to pursue the question (Pashler 1991). Subjects first performed the usual tone task with manual response, and after a variable SOA, a display of eight letters and a probe was presented; the probe indicated which letter should be attended to and reported. After a delay, the letters were masked. If the shift of attention to the probed letter was delayed by the tone task (as selection of a motor response would be), then task-2 errors should increase drastically as tone-display SOA is reduced. In fact, however, there was very little effect of SOA, even when the cueing was purely symbolic (an arrow in the center of the display pointing toward the cued letter). A control experiment provided direct evidence that a delay in the attention shift really would have produced a drastic increase in errors, because when the *probe* was delayed by 200 msec in a single-task condition, the error rate increased by more than 30 percent.

In summary, although a tone task reliably produced dramatic delays of speeded second-task responses, it did not delay a second-task attention shift more than a tiny amount. Thus, shifts of visual attention apparently do not involve the mechanism that underlies the bottleneck effects described earlier. More generally, one is forced to conclude that the form of attention responsible for selectivity in vision, and the form responsible for limitations in concurrent sensorimotor performance, are not the same. For this reason, it might be advisable to reserve the term attention for the former (if the term cannot be avoided altogether).

11.6 STORING INFORMATION IN VISUAL SHORT-TERM MEMORY

The technique used to separate selective attention from the central bottleneck can be extended to determine whether the bottleneck affects a variety of mental operations. Here we report some new empirical results that apply the technique to a previously unstudied mental operation: storing information in visual short-term memory (VSTM).

This is an important mental operation to examine in this context, because various intimate relationships between attention and short-term memory storage have been proposed over the years. For example, Shiffrin (1976) equated the limits on short-term storage with general attentional capacity. Baddeley, on the other hand, distinguished between a "central executive" and various "slave systems" used to store information in working memory. In principle, a central executive might play many different critical roles in short-term storage, retention, and retrieval. We focus on visual short-term storage because (1) the time during which visual stimuli are available can be carefully controlled, and (2) evidence concerning the identity and properties of visual short-term storage has been carefully analyzed at least for one particular kind of stimulus (used in the experiment reported here).

In particular, Phillips conducted a systematic investigation of VSTM, using short-term recognition of matrices composed of squares, stimuli that do not lend themselves to verbal description (summarized in Phillips 1983). A long series of elegant experiments provided converging evidence for a schematic memory (VSTM) that is not destroyed by masking, can maintain a spatiotopic representation of patterns, and clearly differs from both iconic memory and visual long-term memory. Phillips and Christie (1977) showed that nonvisual cognitive tasks lasting several seconds (e.g., adding auditorily presented digits) during the retention interval impair visual recognition performance quite substantially. To explain the latter result, they suggested that a central executive must intermittently refresh VSTM for optimal retention.

However, the Phillips experiments have not addressed whether *storing* information in VSTM requires intervention of this central executive. While memory for *unattended* stimuli is known to be very poor (e.g., Broadbent 1958), the preceding section indicates that visual selective attention, and the bottleneck mechanism investigated here, are quite distinct. Thus, storage in VSTM could well require appropriate deployment of visual attention even if it did not depend at all on the response-selection mechanism.

11.7 METHOD

Sixteen subjects from the UCSD subject pool participated for credit in a one-hour session. The experiment was controlled by IBM PC microcomputers, and stimuli were presented on NEC VGA monitors. The procedure is shown in figure 11.4. The first stimulus was a tone, which lasted 150 msec. Subjects

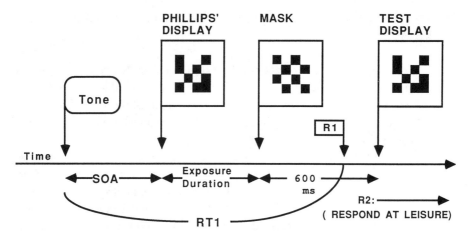

Figure 11.4 Procedure used on each trial in the VSTM experiment.

responded immediately by pressing the z key or the x key for tones of 300 hz or 900 hz, respectively. The speed of this response was strongly emphasized. After an SOA of 50, 150, or 650 msec, a visual stimulus was presented against a black background. The stimulus consisted of a random 4 × 4 matrix of squares (total width and length approximately 3.8 degree; squares were red or black with probability .5). The display was presented for either 100 msec or 300 msec. At the end of this interval, the display was masked with a 4 × 4 interleave pattern, which lasted for 100 msec. After an interval of 500 msec, a test stimulus was presented. On half the trials, this stimulus was identical to the study pattern; otherwise, one square was randomly flipped from red to black or vice versa. The subject responded by pressing the period key for same, and slash key for different. The second response was *unspeeded*.

The session began with forty-eight practice trials, followed by ten blocks of forty-eight test trials. Within a given block, each combination of SOA, exposure duration, and response type (same/different) was represented equally often.

Results

Trials on which RT1 fell below 150 msec or exceeded 1000 msec were discarded. Figure 11.5 shows the results as a function of SOA. RT1s were faster for the 50- and 150-msec SOA (452 and 455 msec, respectively) than for the 650 SOAs (485 msec), $F(2, 30) = 9.1, p < .001$. RT1s were also slightly longer for the 300 msec exposure duration (467 msec) than for the 100 msec exposure duration (461 msec), $F(1, 15) = 4.6, p < .05$. Other effects and interactions were nonsignificant.

The key results concern accuracy of second-task responses. These were analyzed as a function of response type (same/different), SOA, exposure duration, and the relative speed of R1. Error rates were lower for 300-msec exposures (.130) than for 100-ms exposures (.260), $F(1, 15) = 87.5, p < .001$.

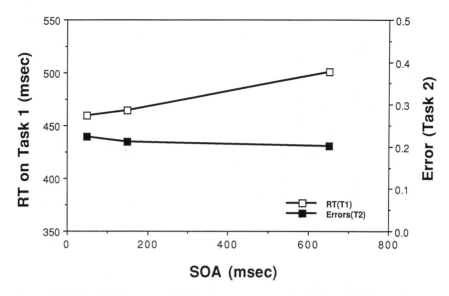

Figure 11.5 Mean RT for tone task (T1) and mean error rate for Phillips task (T2), as a function of SOA.

The error rates for SOAs of 50, 150, and 650 were .209, .190, and .186, respectively. This difference was not significant.

Thus, a 200-msec reduction in exposure duration increased error rates by 13 percent, whereas the SOA manipulation (contrasting extreme vs. minimal overlap with the first task) produced only a nonsignificant, approximately 2 percent difference. In many previous studies (e.g., Pashler 1989, 1991), the same tone task delayed *speeded* R2 responses by over 200 msec. Plainly, then, this first task was not delaying the storage of these patterns in visual STM nearly as much as it would delay selection of a second response. The effect of exposure duration also shows that the tiny effects of dual-task overlap do not reflect saturation of VSTM that could potentially introduce a sort of ceiling effect caused by the limited capacity of that memory system.

The R1 quintile effects (fig. 11.6) provide a check on this conclusion. If storage were delayed by task 1, then (increasingly at short SOAs) slow R1s should be associated with higher R2 error rates. For R1 quintiles 1–5, the R2 error rates were .178, .178, .191, .196, and .233. This modest correlation between performance on the two tasks was significant, $F(4, 60) = 3.6, p < .05$, but its relatively small size is not consistent with postponement of storage. Furthermore, the quintile effect was not larger for the short SOAs than for the long SOAs: the interaction between SOA and quintile was nonsignificant, $F(8, 120) = .21, p > .90$. The main effect of quintile probably stems from subjects being better prepared for both tasks on some trials compared to others. By contrast, the delay of response selection in a *speeded* second task produces a dramatic effect of quintile on R2 latency, interacting with SOA (compare fig. 11.2 with fig. 11.6).

(There was also an unexpected and, to the author, quite uninterpretable interaction between R1 quintile and exposure duration, $F(4, 60) = 3.6, p <$

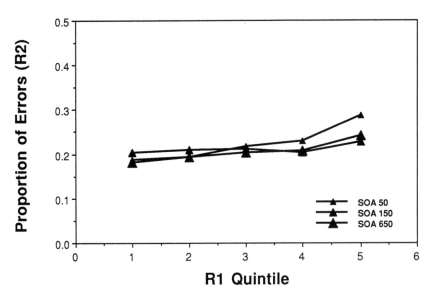

Figure 11.6 Mean error rate in the Phillips task (R2) as a function of the quintile in which RT1 belonged within its distribution.

.05. The interaction was nonmonotonic in character and mostly reflected a greater exposure-duration effect for quintile 2.)

Discussion

This experiment demonstrates that storage of information in visual short-term memory does not depend on the bottleneck mechanism associated with response selection, memory retrieval, and other mental operations. These results are especially interesting in light of Phillips and Christie's (1977) finding that adding auditory digits reduced the amount available from VSTM. Putting these conclusions together, it appears that the role of the bottleneck mechanism in visual short-term memory is probably restricted to intermittently refreshing fading temporary representations.

While of course we cannot generalize these conclusions to other forms of short-term storage with any confidence, they may apply there as well. If so, there would be clear implications for the many studies that have employed auditory memory loads to "deplete capacity." Perhaps subjects in such experiments did nothing whatsoever with the memory load while performing the punctate primary task. The effects of memory load may instead be attributable to interference with preparation for the primary tasks (see also Logan 1978).

In considering the generality of the results reported here, it is also worth noting that the present procedure required VSTM storage of information derived directly from perceptual input. However, this is not the only way that information can get into short-term storage: people are remarkably flexible in transferring information *between* different short-term stores (Broadbent 1989). The present results leave open the possibility that the bottleneck mechanism may be necessary for *recoding* information into formats that do not match the sensory input.

11.8 CONCLUSIONS

The work reviewed here bears on various different approaches to dual-task interference that have arisen over the past twenty-five years or so. But it is not possible to discuss these approaches comprehensively here. However, we conclude with some brief comments about these other perspectives.

Capacity Sharing

The idea that dual-task performance commonly depends on a graded sharing of mental "resources" has been frequently suggested and—much more commonly—simply assumed. Yet, in the situation where performance can be studied in most detail (the PRP experiment), there is little evidence for this. It is true that slowing of R1 is sometimes observed, and this certainly might seem to suggest capacity sharing. However, when Johnston and I encouraged subjects to delay R1, the results showed clearly that subjects complied by withholding R1 until R2 was ready to be produced; the pattern of factor effects indicated that the response-selection bottleneck was still present (Pashler and Johnston 1989). When instructions do not clearly emphasize first-task speed, then this sort of "grouping" will probably occur on some trials, for some subjects, yielding moderate slowing of the mean RT1. It would be a mistake to infer from this slowing that capacity sharing must be occurring.

Another phenomenon generally taken to support capacity sharing occurs when subjects are instructed to vary their relative emphasis on two extended tasks (e.g., tracking and sentence comprehension). Typically, there is a tradeoff between performance in the two tasks. However, this trade-off could have many causes, some of which are consistent with an underlying bottleneck. For example, subjects may simply shift the proportion of *time* allocated to the two tasks by the bottleneck mechanism. Subjects may also vary the degree to which they prepare for the two tasks in advance; thus, the trade-off may occur over the several seconds *preceding* the trial, not during the trial.

Nonetheless, graded capacity sharing has been assumed much more often than it has been argued for, and not only by students of divided attention per se, but also by researchers exploring a great variety of mental processes (ranging even into clinical and developmental psychology). In particular, many investigators have used the Posner and Boies (1971) simple RT probe technique to "measure how much capacity" some particular mental process requires. As noted above, the assumption that there is actually a graded sharing of capacity between tasks is questionable to start with. Slowing in probe tasks may often reflect the same discrete queuing argued to underlie the PRP effect. In addition, very fast simple RTs seem to require a "hair-trigger" state of preparation, which is difficult to maintain while extraneous stimuli are presented. Thus, even a to be-ignored stimulus immediately preceding an imperative signal can produce a marked slowing of simple RTs (Davis 1959), which does not generally occur in choice tasks such as visual search (Pashler and Johnston 1989). For reasons such as these, supposed measurements of "capacity demands" should be viewed somewhat skeptically.

Various multiple-resource theories that have been considered in recent years (e.g., Wickens 1983) are also based on the assumption of graded allocation of resources. For the most part, these theories have been supported by rather coarse-grained observations (e.g., aggregated error over many seconds or minutes). Such measures cannot distinguish between different possible underlying sources of interference, including bottlenecks, capacity sharing, preparation effects, reliance on common memory stores, and so forth. This is not to deny that multiple resource theories may offer a useful way of describing human performance limitations for practical purposes. However, one would hope that a theory describing the detailed time course of dual-task interference will ultimately do a better job.

Multiple Processors and Task Similarity

Over the years, several investigators contested Welford's original suggestion of a central bottleneck by pointing to cases where the use of very dissimilar response modalities seemed to reduce interference (e.g., McLeod 1978). Pashler (1990) reexamined this issue, comparing vocal-manual to manual-manual response combinations. In the usual PRP paradigm, clear-cut interference was observed with both combinations, with only slightly more interference for manual-manual combinations. However, when the experiment was modified so that the order of stimulus onset was not known to the subject before the trial (as in McLeod's experiments), then the manual-manual combination showed much more interference than did the manual-vocal. This previously unnoticed interaction between knowledge of stimulus order and response modality seems to have led to the mistaken impression that response modality is the main determinant of task interference, which it is not. (The question of how to interpret this interaction was discussed by Pashler 1990).

Closely related to the multiprocessor idea is the proposal that the the two cerebral hemispheres control or comprise separate pools of processing resources (e.g., Friedman and Polson 1981). The evidence for this view comes mostly from studies that use tasks like tapping, holding verbal memory loads, and other activities that may not demand constant central processing at all. For this reason, Shannon O'Brien and I have recently begun examining hemispheric factors in PRP experiments, using tasks that seem likely to depend relatively more upon one hemisphere than upon the other (e.g., responding with the left hand to a stimulus in the left hemifield, producing vocal responses, etc.). So far, we have found no sign that the PRP effect, or the R2/R1 dependencies, differ depending upon whether the same hemisphere or different hemispheres carry out the tasks. At the moment, this conclusion remains tentative; if it holds up, it may have interesting implications about the neural basis for the central bottleneck.

Directions for Further Research

It might appear from the preceding discussion that the similarity of two tasks is claimed to have no effects on the interference they produce for each other. This is plainly false. Especially in tasks that last several seconds or more, similarity can greatly exacerbate interference. There are several reasons why this could happen that would be perfectly consistent with the theoretical claims made above. For example, if two tasks both depend upon short-term retention over the same time period, then if the material to be remembered in the two tasks is highly similar, performance may break down due to well-known interference effects in memory. The results of Hirst and Kalmar (1987) can be readily interpreted in this way. In addition, when one task involves stimuli that could potentially trigger responses in the other task, this may necessitate preparation of more complex and specific response-selection routines. Neither of these factors need contradict or supplant the fundamental bottleneck argued for above. At present, though, similarity effects in dual-task performance are not well understood.

Another important area for future research pertains to some provocative findings of situations where seemingly very demanding continuous tasks, each involving response selection and production, show virtually *no* interference (e.g., Allport, Antonis, and Reynolds 1972; Shaffer 1975). The lack of interference may simply be, as Broadbent (1982) noted, because continuous tasks offer previews of stimuli and involve long stimulus-response lags. For that reason, central mechanisms may switch between tasks, buffering stimuli at input and response sequences at output. Another possible factor is that the studies cited used shadowing as one of the tasks; as noted earlier, shadowing may simply bypass the usual dual-task limitations (McLeod and Posner 1984). Finally, the high degree of practice these subjects had in performing some of these activities might also be a factor.

At the moment, these interesting observations demand further, more systematic study. The conclusions described in this article stem from studies that have deliberately focused on very austere and simplified tasks. To develop these ideas further so that they can encompass more of the enormous range of human mentation and behavior remains an exciting challenge for the future.

NOTE

The author is grateful to Mark Carrier, John Duncan, Clark Fagot, Jim Johnston, Jeff Miller, and Allen Osman for many useful discussions of these issues, and to Alann Lopes for excellent technical assistance. David Meyer and Mike Mozer provided many helpful comments on the manuscript. Lisa Kroenen, Haven Cloward, and Shannon O'Brien assisted in data collection. Funding was provided by NASA under Interchange NCA2-414, by the Office of Naval Research under contract N00014-88-K-0281, and by NIMH under grant 1-R29-MH45584-01.

REFERENCES

Allport, D. A., Antonis, B., and Reynolds, P. (1972). On the division of attention: A disproof of the single-channel hypothesis. *Quarterly Journal of Experimental Psychology, 24,* 225–235.

Baddeley, A., Lewis, V., Eldridge, M., and Thomson, N. (1984). Attention and retrieval from long-term memory. *Journal of Experimental Psychology: General, 113,* 518–540.

Bertelson, P. (1966). Central intermittency twenty years later. *Quarterly Journal of Experimental Psychology, 18,* 153–163.

Broadbent, D. E. (1958). *Perception and Communication.* London: Pergamon Press.

Broadbent, D. E. (1982). Task combination and the selective intake of information. *Acta Psychologica, 50,* 253–290.

Broadbent, D. E. (1989). Lasting representations and temporary processes. In Roediger, H., and Craik, F. I. (eds.), *Varieties of Memory and Consciousness,* 211–228. Hillsdale, NJ: Erlbaum.

Carrier, M., and Pashler, H. (1992). The attention demands of memory retrieval. Manuscript.

Davis, R. (1959). The role of "attention" in the psychological refractory period. *Quarterly Journal of Experimental Psychology, 11,* 211–220.

Duncan, J. (1984). Selective attention and the organization of visual information. *Journal of Experimental Psychology: General, 113,* 501–517.

Fagot, C., and Pashler, H. (N.d.). Making two responses to a single object: Exploring the central bottleneck. *Journal of Experimental Psychology: Human Perception and Performance.* In press.

Friedman, A., and Polson, M. C. (1981). Hemispheres as independent resource systems: Limited-capacity processing and cerebral specialization. *Journal of Experimental Psychology: Human Perception and Performance, 7,* 1031–1058.

Gottsdanker, R., and Stelmach, G. E (1971). The persistence of psychological refractoriness. *Journal of Motor Behavior, 3,* 301–312.

Hirst, W., and Kalmar, D. (1987). Characterizing attentional resources. *Journal of Experimental Psychology: General, 116,* 68–81.

Johnston, J. C., and Pashler, H. E. (1984). Can two decision processes operate simultaneously? Paper presented at the annual meeting of the Psychonomics Society, Austin, Texas.

Kahneman, D. (1973). *Attention and effort.* New York: Prentice Hall.

Keele, S. W. (1973). *Attention and human performance.* Pacific Palisades, CA: Goodyear.

Kelso, J. A. S., Southard, D. L., and Goodman, D. (1979). On the coordination of two handed movements. *Journal of Experimental Psychology: Human Perception & Performance, 5,* 229–238.

Logan, G. D. (1978). Attention in character classification tasks: Evidence for the automaticity of component stages. *Journal of Experimental Psychology: General, 107,* 32–63.

Logan, G. D., and Burkell, J. (1986). Dependence and independence in responding to double stimulation: A comparison of stop, change and dual-task paradigms. *Journal of Experimental Psychology: Human Perception & Performance, 12,* 549–563.

McCann, R. S., and Johnston, J. C. (1989). The locus of processing bottlenecks in the overlapping tasks paradigm. Paper presented at the annual meeting of the Psychonomics Society, Atlanta, GA.

McCann, R. S., and Johnston, J. C. (1992). The locus of the single-channel bottleneck in dual task interference. *Journal of Experimental Psychology: Human Perception and Performance, 18,* 471–484.

McLeod, P. (1977). Parallel processing and the psychological refractory period. *Acta Psychologica, 41,* 381–391.

McLeod, P. (1978). Does probe RT measure central processing demand? *Quarterly Journal of Experimental Psychology, 30,* 83–89.

McLeod, P., and Posner, M. I. (1984). Privileged loops from percept to act. In H. Bouma and D. G. Bouwhuis (eds.), *Attention and Performance X.* London: Lawrence Erlbaum Associates.

Norman, D. A., and Shallice, T. (1985). Attention to action: Willed and automatic control of behavior. In R. J. Davidson, G. E. Schwartz, and D. Shapiro (eds.), *Consciousness and self-regulation,* Vol 4. New York: Plenum.

Osman, A., and Moore, C. (1990). The effects of dual-task interference on movement related potentials. Paper presented at the Journal meeting of the Psychonomics Society, New Orleans, LA.

Pashler, H. (1984). Processing stages in overlapping tasks: Evidence for a central bottleneck. *Journal of Experimental Psychology: Human Perception and Performance, 10,* 358–377.

Pashler, H. (1989). Dissociations and dependencies between speed and accuracy: Evidence for a two-component theory of divided attention in simple tasks. *Cognitive Psychology, 21,* 469–514.

Pashler, H. (1990). Do response modality effects support multiprocessor models of divided attention? *Journal of Experimental Psychology: Human Perception and Performance.*

Pashler, H. (1991). Shifting visual attention and selecting motor responses: Distinct attentional mechanisms. *Journal of Experimental Psychology. Human Perception and Performance, 17,* 1023–1040.

Pashler, H., Carrier, M., and Hoffman, J. E. (N.d.). Saccadic eye movements and dual task interference. *Quarterly Journal of Experimental Psychology.* In press.

Pashler, H., and Johnston, J. C. (1989). Interference between temporally overlapping tasks: Chronometric evidence for central postponement with or without response grouping. *Quarterly Journal of Experimental Psychology, 41A,* 19–45.

Pashler, H., and Johnston, J. C. (1991). Continuous task performance and dual-task interference: Chronometric studies. Manuscript.

Phillips, W. A. (1983). Short-term visual memory. *Phil. Trans. Royal Soc. London, B302,* 295–309.

Phillips, W. A., and Christie, F. M. (1977). Interference with visualization. *Quarterly Journal of Experimental Psychology, 29,* 637–650.

Posner, M. I., and Boies, S. J. (1971). Components Of attention. *Psychological Review, 78,* 391–408.

Posner, M. I., Sandson, J., Dhawan, M., and Shulman, G. (1989). Is word recognition automatic? A cognitive-anatomical approach. *Journal of Cognitive Neuroscience, 1,* 50–60.

Rizzolatti, G., and Camarda, R. (1987). Neural circuits for spatial attention and unilateral neglect. In M. Jeannerod (ed.), *Neurophysiological and Neuropsychological Aspects of Spatial Neglect,* 289–313. Paris: Elsevier.

Schneider, W., and Shiffrin, R. M. (1977). Controlled and automatic human information processing: I. Detection, search and attention. *Psychological Review, 84,* 1–66.

Schweickert, R. (1978). A critical path generalization of the additive factor method: Analysis of a Stroop task. *Journal of Mathematical Psychology, 18,* 105–139.

Shaffer, L. H. (1975). Multiple attention in continuous verbal tasks. In P. M. A. Rabbitt and S. Dornic (eds.), *Attention and Performance V,* 157–167. New York: Academic Press.

Shiffrin, R. M. (1976). Capacity limitations in information processing, attention and memory. In W. K. Estes (ed.), *Handbook of learning and cognitive processes: Attention and Memory,* Vol. 4, 177–236. Hillsdale, NJ: Erlbaum.

Smith, M. C. (1967). Theories of the psychological refractory period. *Psychological Bulletin, 67,* 202–213.

Sternberg, S. (1969). The discovery of processing stages: Extensions of Donders' method. In W. G. Koster (ed.), *Attention and Performance II,* 276–315. Amsterdam: North Holland.

Vince, M. (1949). Rapid response sequences and the psychological refractory period. *British Journal of Psychology, 40,* 23–40.

von Wright, J. M. (1968). Selection in immediate visual memory. *Quarterly Journal of Experimental Psychology, 20,* 62–68.

Welford, A. T. (1952). The "psychological refractory period" and the timing of high speed performance—A review and a theory. *British Journal of Psychology, 43,* 2–19.

Welford, A. T. (1967). Single-channel operation in the brain. *Acta Psychologica, 27,* 5–22.

Welford, A. T. (1980). The single-channel hypothesis. In A. T. Welford (ed.), *Reaction Time,* 215–252. New York: Academic Press.

Wickens, C. D. (1983). Processing resources in attention, dual task performance, and workload assessment. In R. Parasuraman and R. Davies (eds.), *Varieties of Attention,* 63–102. New York: Academic Press.

12 Using Repetition Detection to Define and Localize the Processes of Selective Attention

George Sperling, Stephen A. Wurst, and Zhong-Lin Lu

12.1 INTRODUCTION

Overview

In our repetition-detection task, subjects search a rapid sequence of thirty frames for a stimulus that is repeated within four frames. Successful detection implies that a match occurs between an incoming item and a recent item retained in short-term visual repetition memory (STVRM).

We test selective attention to physical features in a single location within which successive items alternate in color, size, or spatial frequency. For example, in the size condition, large and small items strictly alternate, and subjects attend selectively to *small* (or to *large*) items. Selective attention to *small* facilitates detecting small-small repetitions and impairs detection of large-large repetitions (the benefit and cost of selective attention). In a control condition, the *large* items are replaced by blanks. The size of the attention benefit for small relative to the control performance gives the efficiency of attentional filtering relative to perfect optical filtering.

Whereas selective attention (relative to equal attention) facilitates homogeneous (e.g., small-small) repetition detections, it usually impairs heterogeneous detections (large-small or small-large). Comparisons of attention costs and benefits for homogeneous and for heterogeneous detections admit the following inferences: physical features are represented in STVRM; attentional filtering occurs before stimuli are recorded in STVRM; in some conditions, some subjects use strategies that encode the attention state of an item in STVRM.

Background: Early versus Late Selective Filtering

Theories of selective attention postulate that the human information processing system is limited in its capacity and that attention serves to select information to be processed from other, competing information (e.g., Broadbent 1958; Deutsch and Deutsch 1963; Norman 1968). Indeed, selective filtering of unattended information has been proposed as a mechanism in numerous visual processing tasks.

There is abundant evidence that selective attention can function as a mechanism to differentially filter information from different spatial locations (see reviews by Sperling and Dosher 1986; Sperling and Weichselgartner 1993). However, we find no convincing evidence that attention can function as a mechanism for selecting information on the basis of physical features when items containing different constellations of features occur at the same location. Rather, the data are consistent with a theory that asserts that stimulus features serve only to guide spatial attention. That is, whenever selection appears on the basis of the physical features of visual stimuli (such as color, spatial frequency content, size, etc.), these features serve to bring attention to a particular location, but the attentional filtering is on the basis of location rather than on the basis of feature. To test this theory, it is critical to present more information than can be successfully processed at a single location, and to observe whether, at this single location, attentional filtering is possible on the basis of physical features.

Selection from Streams

It is trivial to demonstrate that attentional filtering can occur within a given spatial location. Consider, for example, the following gedanken experiment. Subjects view a stream of alternating black and white digits on a gray background. Subjects are asked to compute the sum of the white digits and to ignore the black digits. Obviously, subjects can perform this task when the stream is slow enough, but this would not be profoundly revealing about selective attentional processes because we already know that selection can occur at a cognitive or a decision level of processing. The interesting questions about selective attention concern whether it can operate at an earlier sensory or perceptual level (reviewed in Sperling and Dosher 1986).

Search Procedures   A useful technique for studying attentional selection at a single location is to present a rapid stream of items at a location too rapidly to permit all items to be processed perfectly. Attentional selection can then be used to determine which items are processed. There are a number of tasks that involve items that are presented in a rapid visual stream at a single location. For example, Sperling et al. (1971) studied rapid visual search as a function of the number of locations in which streams of items were presented. However, the problem with search experiments is that, so far, no procedure has been developed to determine whether attentional selection (i.e., rejection of nontarget items) occurs at the perceptual or at the decision level of processing. Indeed, recent theories of selective filtering (Cave and Wolfe 1990; Duncan and Humphreys 1989; Pavel 1991; Wright and Main 1991; cf. Hoffman 1979) propose various cue-weighting algorithms to determine the sequence of attentional selections in visual search. Such weighting processes are typical of decision processes, although the algorithms themselves are neutral with regard to whether they operate at a perceptual or a decision level of processing.

Feature-based Partial Reports from Streams Another task involving a stream is the selective recall of items according to their physical characteristics. The procedure involves the selection of items from a rapid stream according to whether or not the target items have a distinguishing characteristic such as a ring around them, or whether they are brighter than their neighbors. Subjects can extract single target items from a rapid stream (Intraub 1985; Weichselgartner and Sperling 1987), or even a short sequence of four targets (Weichselgartner 1984). In fact, such experiments are partial report experiments in which the many items (from among which a few are selected for a partial report) are arrayed in time rather than in space as in the more usual procedure (Sperling 1960).

Feature-based Partial Reports from Spatial Arrays In spatial arrays, subjects can select items for partial report that have a ring around them (Averbach and Sperling 1961) or items that merely are pointed at by a short bar marker—a minimal feature for selection. When subjects are required to report only items of a particular color from briefly exposed letter matrices, these partial reports are not much better than whole reports (von Wright 1968). Similarly, when subjects are required to report only digits from mixed arrays of letters and digits, subjects do not report more digits than when they must report both letters and digits (e.g., Sperling 1960). Both of these studies required subjects to extract both item-identity and location information from briefly exposed arrays. When subjects are required only to report the item identities and not locations, partial reports according to feature easily surpass whole reports (e.g., selecting solid from outline characters; Merikle 1980). Thus, with comparable response requirements, feature-cued partial reports are comparably successful in temporal streams and in spatial arrays.

Partial Reports according to Spatial or Purely Temporal (versus Featural) Cues Originally, partial reports were studied in spatial arrays, and the selection cue designated one of several rows of characters—purely spatial selection (e.g., Sperling 1960, 1963). With spatial cues, there is a large and consistent partial-report advantage. When subjects must use a temporal cue to make a partial-report selection of four items from a rapid temporal stream, item selection appears to be based on a temporal window of attention (Sperling and Reeves 1980; Reeves and Sperling 1986; Weichselgartner and Sperling 1987). The subject's temporal window for selection from temporal streams is perfectly analogous to the spatial window for selection from spatial arrays (e.g., LaBerge and Brown 1989).

The Locus of Feature-based Attentional Selection Partial-report paradigms primarily focus on the process whereby information is selected for inclusion in short-term memory. That feature-based attentional selection of information for partial reports can occur in streams and in arrays merely places the level of attentional selection below the level of short-term memory. This constraint is unremarkable. Therefore, it is search tasks that seem most often to have been called forth to resolve the issue of early versus late selection on the basis of physical features (recent examples include Nakayama and Silverman 1986; Neisser 1967; Treisman 1977; Treisman 1986; Treisman and Gelade 1980; see Folk and Egeth 1989 for a review). Closely related issues are automatic versus controlled processing (Shiffrin and Schneider 1977), speeded classification (e.g., Felfoldy and Garner 1971; Garner 1978) and auditory selective attention (Swets 1984). The ambiguity of current search theories concerning the level of attentional selection was noted above. This is not the place for a review and critique of the many other approaches to these problems in the visual and auditory domains. Instead, we offer new variations of a repetition-detection task and new analyses that are particularly well suited to defining the locus of feature-based attentional selection (i.e.. perceptual filtering according to physical properties).

Repetition-Detection Paradigm

The repetition-detection paradigm (Kaufman 1978; Wurst 1989; Sperling and Kaufman 1991) seems particularly well suited for the study of attentional selection based on physical features. In this paradigm (fig. 12.1), a stream of thirty digits is presented rapidly (typically, 9.1 digits per sec). Within this stream, every digit is repeated three times, but only one digit is repeated within four sequence positions (lag 4 or less); all other digits are repeated with lags of nine or more. The subject is instructed to detect the recently repeated digit. Successful performance of this task obviously depends on the subject's ability to match incoming digits with previously presented digits in memory. Because all digits are repeated exactly three times within a list, only memory

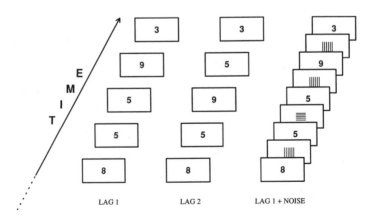

Figure 12.1 The repetition-detection paradigm. The leftmost sequence (lag 1) represents five consecutive frames from the middle of a longer sequence of frames. The target repetition is the digit 5. The middle sequence illustrates repetition of the digit 5 with lag 2. The rightmost sequence illustrates Kaufman's (1978) noise condition with lag 1. A grid of randomly chosen vertical or horizontal lines is interposed between each digit frame; repetition-detection performance was unimpaired.

that discriminates short-lag repetitions from long-lag repetitions is useful for performing this task.

In previous research (Kaufman 1978; Sperling and Kaufman 1991), it was found that, at lag 1, repetition detection was typically better than 80 percent correct, and that by lag 4 it had dropped below 30 or 40 percent. Adding a noise field between successive frames (fig. 12.1) did not impair performance, even when the noise field was so intense that, if it were simultaneous with digit presentations, it would have rendered them illegible. This immunity to visual masking suggests a central memory locus for short-term visual repetition memory (STVRM), even at lag 1.

In another adaptation of the task (Kaufman 1978; Sperling and Kaufman 1991), it was found that using nonsense shapes as stimuli instead of digits yielded equivalent results. This suggests that STVRM is visual rather than verbal or semantic.

Wurst (1989) used dicoptic presentations to demonstrate that the locus of short-term visual repetition memory (STVRM) was after the locus of binocular combination. A particularly interesting finding in Wurst's dicoptic viewing procedure was that one eye was given priority over the other eye. Thus, a filtering of items by the eye of presentation may have been occurring even though items were presented alternately (never simultaneously) to the two eyes and though, in control conditions, monocular performance was the same for both eyes. The present study was undertaken to determine whether selection could occur by varying stimulus attributes other than the eye of presentation.

Plan of the Experiments

To investigate the role of attention in the short-term visual repetition memory task, as in the previous studies, digits are presented in the same spatial location while being viewed binocularly. Two levels of a dimension are employed (e.g., large and small sizes of digits), and digits alternate between the levels. We will call a level of a dimension a *feature*. For example, *small* and *large* are features within the size dimension. In this study, five stimulus dimensions that have typically been employed in attention research (e.g., Nakayama and Silverman 1986; Treisman 1982; Sagi 1988)—size, angular orientation, spatial bandpass filtering, contrast polarity (black-on-gray vs. white-on-gray), and color—are examined separately. Additionally, we examine one feature pair (small black vs. large white). Digits with a different feature (e.g., large and small size) are alternated at the same location. We determine the ability of subjects to attend selectively to items with one feature (or feature pair) while ignoring items with the other feature (or feature pair).

12.2 METHOD

Experiment 1 examines five individual stimulus dimensions—orientation, size, contrast polarity, color, and spatial bandpass filtering—and one dimensional pair (small black vs. large white). Experiment 2 investigates three sets of stimulus characters and will be described more fully below.

A stimulus sequence consists of thirty consecutive digits. A position in the sequence is called a *frame*; thus we say the ith digit occurs in the ith frame. Stimuli in a sequence alternately exhibit one level A of a dimension on odd-numbered frames, and the other level B of the same dimension on even-numbered frames. We call such as sequence $\frac{1}{2}A + \frac{1}{2}B$. If subjects were completely successful in selectively filtering out unattended B stimuli on the even-numbered frames, detection of the repetitions of the attended-to-feature in a $\frac{1}{2}A + \frac{1}{2}B$ sequence would be similar to a control condition ($\frac{1}{2}A$) in which the even-numbered frames were simply blank. If the selection were totally unsuccessful, for example, if the features were indiscriminable, then the alternating feature sequence should be as difficult as a same-feature sequence (A). Consider performance in the two control conditions $\frac{1}{2}A$ and A. The point between these two performances where performance with $\frac{1}{2}A + \frac{1}{2}B$ falls indicates the success of attentional filtering. This is the broad plan of the experiments. Additional complications will become apparent as the story unfolds.

Stimulus Generation

Frames   The repetition-detection procedure (Kaufman 1978; Sperling and Kaufman 1991), was used in this experiment. Each trial consisted of a stream of thirty digits displayed on a video monitor. A digit was painted three times (three refreshes), followed by six refreshes of a blank, gray screen, all at sixty refreshes per second. The sequence of nine refreshes (digit plus subsequent blank screen) is called a *frame*. The frame duration is 150 msec; equivalently, the digit-to-digit stimulus onset asynchrony (SOA) is 150 msec. A digit sequence was composed of thirty frames: the ten digits, each presented three times.

Lag   To distinguish the different types of repetitions that occur, we use the term *lag*. When a digit occurs in frame i of the sequence, and then again in frame j, $1 \leq i < j \leq 30$, the digit is defined as being repeated with lag $j - i$ (see fig. 12.1). Only the target digit was repeated within a lag of 4 or less; all other repetitions of the digits were separated by eight or more intervening digits (lag ≥ 9). To generate a stimulus sequence, the first digit is chosen randomly. Subsequently, at any point in sequence generation, the requirement that no digit be repeated with lag ≤ 8 restricts the number of digits eligible to be chosen. At each point (except the critical repetition), the new digit was chosen with equal probability from among the eligible digits. The critical repetition was embedded at a random location in the sequence, so that (1) the first member of the repetition pair occurred between sequence positions 11 and 20, and (2) all other sequence constraints remained satisfied. Each sequence was generated by a new random draw.

Figure 12.2a shows a typical sequence of thirty digits. Figure 12.2b shows the expected distribution of lags in such a sequence. A single lag of 1, 2, 3, or

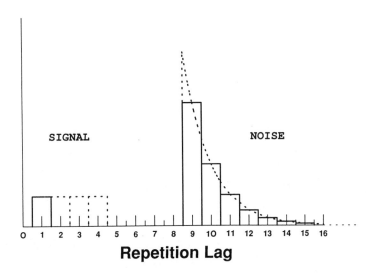

8 5 2 7 6 0 3 9 1 8 4 2 5 6 0 7 9 3 1 1 4 5 2 0 8 9 7 3 6 4

SIGNAL   NOISE

Repetition Lag

Figure 12.2 *Top:* A stimulus sequence in the repetition-detection experiment. *Bottom:* The expected frequency distribution of signal (target) and noise repetitions. Signal indicates that, on each trial, there is exactly one signal repetition; its lag is either 1, 2, 3, or 4. Nontarget digits are constrained to repeat only with lags of 9 or more (noise repetitions). The numbers 10 and 20 (top) demark the middle ten positions of the sequence within which the initial element of the target repetition is constrained to occur. These two constraints determine the expected frequency distribution of noise repetitions, indicated as NOISE.

4 represents the to-be-detected repetition—the signal. All the other repetitions have lag ≥ 9 and represent the noise. The distribution of noise lags is approximately exponential; it is truncated because repetition lags greater than 21 are impossible. While the actual noise distribution of lags is well defined, the *effective* noise distribution depends somewhat on how precisely, in such a rapid sequence, subjects can use their knowledge of constraints on the frames in which repeated pairs are permitted to occur (see below).

Procedures   Subjects were instructed to detect the repetition of lag 4 or less, and not to respond to any of the other stimuli. No masking stimuli were interleaved between the digits. All digits were presented in the same spatial location, centered on the CRT screen.

    A trial began with a centrally located fixation square. When the subject was ready to begin the trial, the subject pressed any key on the computer keyboard. After a repetition was detected, the subject pressed the return key as quickly as possible. After the end of the sequence, a message was presented on the monitor that cued the subject to enter the repeated digit and to enter a confidence rating between 0 (very low confidence that the response was the repetition) and 4 (very high confidence that the response was the correct repetition). The actual repeated digit was then presented on the screen to give the subject complete accuracy feedback information. A message to press the Return key was displayed, following which, the fixation square for the next trial appeared.

Stimulus Sets

Subjects viewed all stimuli at a distance of 93 cm. The square fixation box was 2.46 × 2.46 degree visual angle. The digits 0 to 9 were used in the Times Roman font. The background of all displays and blank intervals was set at 50 cd/m². Unless otherwise specified, digits were white on gray, with a digit height of 0.74 degree.

Six stimulus dimensions were investigated separately in the experiments. There were two levels (feature values) for each of the six dimensions. The stimulus sets are shown in figure 12.3. The six dimensions (and the two feature values of each, A and B, respectively) were

1. *Size* (large, 0.74 degree visual angle versus small, 0.49 degree visual angle).

2. *Orientation* (slanted 45 degrees up-to-the-left versus slanted 45 degrees right).

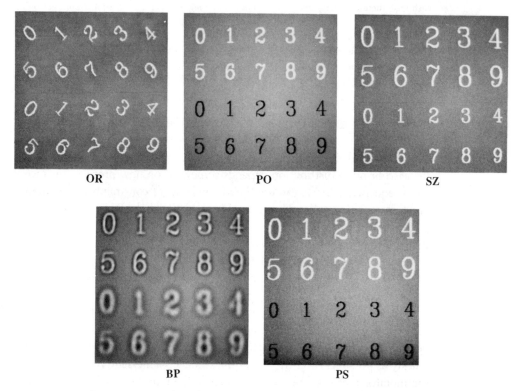

Figure 12.3 Stimuli used in the experiments. In each panel, the top ten digits are the type *A* stimulus of the indicated dimensions (orientation, polarity, size, bandpass, polarity and size). The bottom ten digits are the type *B* stimuli. Color (not shown) is similar to PO.

3. *Contrast Polarity* (white digits on gray background versus black digits on gray). The luminance level of the white digits was 101.50 cd/m², and the luminance level of the black digits was 0.40 cd/m² against a background of 50 cd/m².

4. *Color* (red digits on gray background vs. green digits on gray). Both red and green digits were 68 cd/m²; saturation was chosen such that red and green were perceived as "equally different" from the background of 50 cd/m².

5. *Bandpass Filter* (high spatial bandpass vs. low spatial bandpass). The mean luminance level for all bandpass-filtered stimuli was 50 cd/m². The high bandpass digits had a mean two-dimensional frequency of 5.77 cycles per letter height, and the low bandpass digits had a frequency of 2.92 cycles per letter height. (See Parish and Sperling 1991 for a description of the filters.)

6. *Polarity and Size* Large white digits represented feature type *A*; small black digits were type *B*. All were presented against the gray background. (Large, small, light, dark, gray were as defined above.)

Blocks of Trials

Figure 12.4 illustrates the design of experimental and control stimulus sequences and presents examples. A block of trials contained only one of the six stimulus transformations (fig. 12.3). The experimental blocks all were of type $(\frac{1}{2}A + \frac{1}{2}B)$ in which streams of strictly alternating *A*, *B* stimulus features were presented. There were three kinds of experimental blocks for a given transformation that differed in the attentional conditions: attend to *A*, equal attention, attend to *B*). In addition to experimental blocks, which consisted of sequences that alternated two feature values (*A* and *B*), there were control blocks, which consisted of digits having the same feature value throughout.

Experimental blocks contained 100 trials, and control blocks contained 150 trials. Every subject ran at least four blocks in every condition (2400 trials per transformation). Each of the trials was classified according to lag 1, 2, 3, or 4. In the experimental $(\frac{1}{2}A + \frac{1}{2}B)$ blocks, trials were classified according to whether the repetition pair was *aa*, *ab*, *ba*, or *bb*. We use *A* and *B* to denote features or streams that contain the features (e.g., *A* = large and *B* = small). We use *a*, *b*, respectively, to denote target digits—members of the repetition pair—that contain features *A* and *B*, respectively.

Attention Conditions

The three experimental blocks are distinguished by the attentional instructions, the probability of the different types of repetitions presented, and the payoffs for correct responses. For the Attend-*A* experimental block the subject was instructed to devote 80 percent of attention to feature *A* (e.g., large) and 20 percent to feature *B* (e.g., small); for the Attend-*B* experimental block, the subject was instructed to devote 80 percent of attention to feature *B* (e.g., small) and 20 percent to feature *A* (e.g., large). In equal-attention experimental

(a)

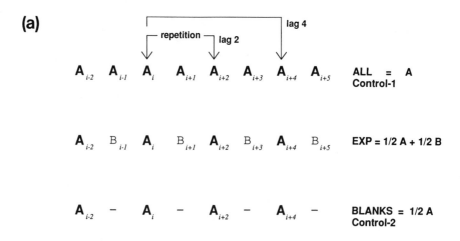

(b)

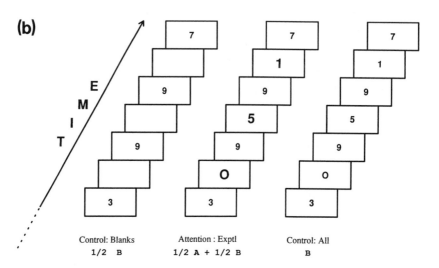

Figure 12.4 Experimental and control presentation sequences used to estimate the effectiveness of attentional filtering. (a) The middle row indicates the experimental condition, an alternating sequence of type A and type B stimuli, designated as $\frac{1}{2}A + \frac{1}{2}B$. If the subject could not discriminate the features that distinguished the type A and type B stimuli, the subject would perform equivalently in the $\frac{1}{2}A + \frac{1}{2}B$ and in the All control, which consists entirely of A stimuli, designated simply as A. On the other hand, if the subject were able to perfectly ignore the unattended-B feature in the $\frac{1}{2}A + \frac{1}{2}B$ stream, experimental performance would be equivalent to the Blanks control, designated as $\frac{1}{2}A$. This would be true for repetitions at lag 2 and at lag 4 (indicated above). (b) Graphical illustration of the three types of displays. The dimension is size. Type A stimuli are large, type B are small; the example illustrates bb targets.

Table 12.1 Probability of Each Condition within Each Block of Trials

Blocks of Alternating-Feature Sequences (AB)

Target =	Attend-A		Attend-B		Attend-equal	
	A	B	A	B	A	B
Lag 1*	.05	.05	.05	.05	.07	.07
Lag 2	.35	.05	.05	.35	.18	.18
Lag 3*	.05	.05	.05	.05	.07	.07
Lag 4	.35	.05	.05	.35	.18	.18

Blocks of Single-Feature Sequences

Stim. =	Feature A		Feature B	
	AA	A—	BB	B—
Lag 1	.167	—	.167	—
Lag 2	.167	.167	.167	.167
Lag 3	.167	—	.167	—
Lag 4	.167	.167	.167	.167

*Mixed-feature repetition pairs; "Target" indicates the feature of the first element of the pair.

blocks, the subject was instructed to devote 50 percent of attention to feature A and 50 percent to feature B. The probabilities of different trial types for the Attend-A, Attend-B, and Attend-equal blocks are shown in table 12.1. Note that when attending to feature A, 70 percent of the trials in the selective attention blocks are pure (aa) repetitions (35 percent at lag 2, 35 percent at lag 4). The remaining trials consist of mixed repetitions at lags 1 and 3, (ab) 10 percent, (ba) 10 percent, and of pure unattended-feature repetitions at lags 2 and 4, (bb) 10 percent. The converse holds when attending to feature B.

The attention instructions served only to define the initial conditions for the subjects. The steady-state behavior of subjects was controlled by carefully defined rewards to enforce the attention conditions. For every stimulus repetition in the attended-to stream that the subject detected correctly (that is, an aa or bb pair), the subject received five points. The subject received only one point for detecting repetitions in the unattended stream, and zero points for for the heterogeneous ab and ba repetitions. The paid subjects were paid 1 cent per point (in addition to their usual hourly wage for participation). The maximum expected payoff per trial for detecting targets with the attended feature is their probability of occurrence (0.7, table 12.1) times their value (5 cents), a net of 3.5 cents. The maximum expected earnings from detecting targets with the unattended feature is 0.1×1 cent = 0.1 cent. Thus, the expected value of detecting repetitions with the attended-to feature was thirty-five times greater than the value of unattended-feature repetitions. The 35 : 1 attended/unattended ratio of maximum possible earnings exerted a potent control over attention, although some of the effects of attention were unanticipated.

100 Percent–0 Percent Attention Conditions   Even the extreme divided attention conditions (nominally 80 percent–20 percent) involve divided attention because, when the subject notices repetitions involving the unattended feature, they are reported. Why not include experimental conditions in which the subjects are told to give 100 percent (rather than 80 percent) of their attention to the attended feature, and to give 0 percent (rather than 20 percent) to the unattended feature, and are paid only for detecting attended-feature repetitions? In previous research, Sperling and Melchner (1978a, 1978b) compared 100 percent–0 percent attention to a range of divided attention conditions similar to the nominal 80 percent–20 percent range used here. Sperling and Melchner's attentional manipulation involved only instructions; in contrast to the present study, their instructions were unenhanced by differential probabilities of occurrence of or by differential rewards for detecting attended targets. Nevertheless, in one-third of their cases, Sperling and Melchner's (1978b) divided-attention conditions spanned a range of performances that was fully as great as the extremes of the 100 percent–0 percent control conditions, and their remaining divided-attention cases spanned most of the 100 percent–0 percent performance range. Thus, while 100 percent–0 percent conditions might (or might not) slightly expand the range of performances observed here, the added conditions would not be expected to produce any qualitatively different data.

Controls $(A, B, \frac{1}{2}A, \frac{1}{2}B)$ Control blocks were run for each feature, as indicated in figure 12.4 and in table 12.1. In the control-All trials (A and B), all thirty digits have the same feature value, and lags 1, 2, 3, and 4 occur equally often. Control-All trials were interleaved with control-Blanks trials ($\frac{1}{2}A$ and $\frac{1}{2}B$) in which every other digit in the sequence was replaced by enough blank frames to permit the remaining digits to retain their precise temporal positions in the sequence. Therefore, for control-Blanks, only fifteen digits were presented, and repetitions only occurred at what, in the All sequence, would have been called lags 2 and 4 (since blanks occurred at lags 1 and 3). As indicated in table 12.1, the six control conditions with feature A (or feature B) had an equal probability of occurring (i.e., twenty-five trials for each condition in the control blocks).

Altogether, there were thirty-six different kinds of trials for each of the six stimulus transformations (fig. 12.3). There were twenty-four experimental conditions: 4 lags (1, 2, 3, 4) × 3 attentional instructions (80%, 50%, 20%) × two kinds of targets (aa, bb at lags 2, 4; ab, ba at lags 1, 3). And there were twelve control conditions: control-All contained 4 lags (1, 2, 3, 4) × 2 features (A, B), whereas control-Blanks contained 2 lags (2, 4) × 2 features ($\frac{1}{2}A$, $\frac{1}{2}B$).

Apparatus

A desktop computer (an IBM-compatible AT personal computer) was used to present stimuli and collect subjects' responses. Stimuli were created with HIPS image-processing software (Landy, Cohen, and Sperling 1984a, b) and displayed using a software package (Runtime Library for Psychology Experiments 1988) designed to drive an AT-Vista Videographics Adapter that produced black-and-white and color images on a NEC Multisync-Plus monitor (with horizontal resolution of 960 dots, vertical resolution of 720 lines, and short persistence phosphors).

Subjects

Two female and three male New York University graduate students and staff with normal or corrected-to-normal vision participated in this research. Three of these subjects were paid for their participation, and two were experimenters. All subjects were well practiced on the repetition-detection procedure before the formal experiments began.

Experiment 2

In the procedure described so far, there are twenty repetitions (three occurrences of each digit) with only the target repetition having a lag of 1, 2, 3 or 4 and all the others having lags of 9 or greater. Experiment 2 was designed to investigate whether this aspect of the procedure was critical to the results. Three character sets were created.

1. Ten digits (as used in experiment 1).

2. Twenty-nine unique characters consisting of the ten digits plus nineteen letters. (The letters B, I, O, Q, S, V and Z were eliminated because of their similarity to digits or other letters.) When using this character set, only the critical item is repeated.

3. A set of ten randomly chosen characters from among the twenty-nine, with a new random selection being made on each trial. Sequences were composed as for the digit stream.

The physical characteristics of the stimuli were the same as in the white-on-gray transformation. On each trial, the character set (1, 2, 3) and the lag (1, 2, 3, 4) were chosen randomly and independently. There were six sessions of 100 trials for subject SW, twelve sessions for subject ZL.

12.3 RESULTS AND DISCUSSION

Experiment 2: Different Character Sets

Figure 12.5 shows the data of experiment 2. There is a typical drop of performance with increasing lag but absolutely no indication of any systematic difference in the results for the three different character sets. Most theories of memory would suggest that, by eliminating the noise repetitions, the twenty-nine-element set would greatly improve performance. However, this effect is insignificant. The robust invariance of the data despite variations in the

Defining and Localizing the Processes of Selective Attention

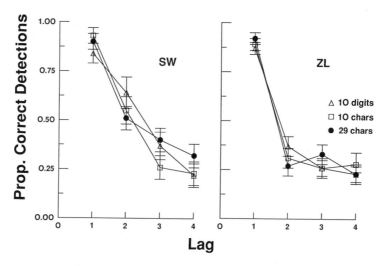

Figure 12.5 Results of variations in the character set (experiment 2). Data are shown for two subjects (SW, ZL). Lag is plotted on the abscissa, and proportion of correct detections on the ordinate. All stimulus streams contained thirty items; the curve parameter indicates the character set from which they were chosen. Open triangles—ten digits; filled circles—twenty nine characters (ten digits plus nineteen letters); open squares—a new set of ten characters chosen randomly on each trial from among the twenty nine.

nature and number of repetitions suggests that the immediate temporal environment of a repetition is the main determiner of whether or not it will be detected, and that variations in the more distant environment of a repetition are unimportant.

Experiment 1: Phenomena Illustrated with Selected Data

In the main experiment, there are thirty-six data points for each of the six types of stimuli. Therefore, presentation of the results is quite complex. We use three types of graphs. The first shows the attention conditions relative to the controls; the second shows attention-operating characteristics; and the third shows all thirty-six conditions on a single graph. We also table the benefits conferred by feature interleaving and by attentional manipulations.

Figures 12.6a, b, c show data from subject JW viewing the contrast polarity stimuli. Figure 12.6a shows detections of aa (white-white) repetitions in three stimulus contexts: two control stimuli ($\frac{1}{2}A$ and A, white-on-gray stimuli) and the experimental stimuli ($\frac{1}{2}A + \frac{1}{2}B$, alternating white and black stimuli). Consider first the control conditions $\frac{1}{2}A$ and A. The condition $\frac{1}{2}A$ represents a plausible upper bound on the attention conditions because it corresponds to what would be expected if the subject succeeded in ignoring B stimuli completely. The control A represents a plausible lower bound in which the B stimuli are indiscriminable from A stimuli. The projection of the diagonal line of figure 12.6a on the vertical axis (from 0.60 to 1.00) indicates the plausible bounds on the range of attention effects.

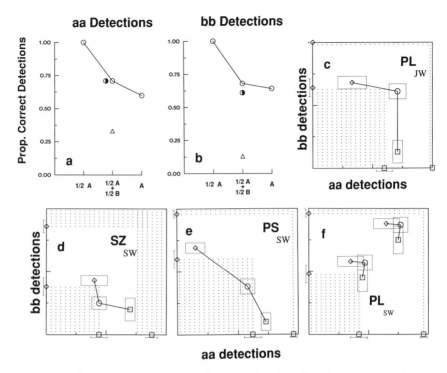

Figure 12.6 Illustrative results. (a, b, c) Polarity stimuli at lag 2 for subject JW. A = white-on-gray, B = black-on-gray. (a) The proportion correct in detecting aa (white-white) repetitions. Abscissa indicates the three types of stimuli (see text). The $\frac{1}{2}A + \frac{1}{2}B$ stimuli serve three attention conditions: the open circle indicates Attend-A, and it is connected by lines to the control conditions (which involve only aa repetitions); the half-filled point represents equal attention; the triangle indicates detecting aa while attending B. (b) Data for detecting type bb (black-black) repetitions. The open circle represents Attend-B; the half-filled point represents equal attention; the triangle indicates detecting bb while attending A. (c) Attention-operating characteristic (AOC) derived from the data of panels (a) and (b). The abscissa and ordinate both range from 0 to 1.0 and represent the proportions of correct aa and bb detections. The inner shaded area indicates performance worse than the corresponding All controls (A, B) for both aa and bb detections. The concave-down curve is the AOC derived from the $\frac{1}{2}A + \frac{1}{2}B$ stimulus with the points representing, from left-to-right, Attend-A, equal attention, and Attend-B. The error bars indicate one standard error of the mean; the relative sizes of the errors derive from the inverse square root of the number of observations. The concave-down curve of this AOC corresponds to costs but no benefits from selective attention. (d, e, f) Examples of different types of performance. (d) AOC for subject SW at lag 2 with size stimuli (A = large; type B = small). The concave-up shape of the AOC indicates benefits from selective attention without costs. The outer shaded area indicates performance better than a $Blanks$ control ($\frac{1}{2}A + \frac{1}{2}B$) for one or both of the two types of targets (aa, bb). (e) AOC for subject SW at lag 2 with polarity-and-size stimuli (A = large-white, B = small-black). The AOC with slope ≈ -1 indicates symmetrical trade-offs of costs and benefits of selective attention. (f) Two AOCs are plotted: the lower-left AOC is the AOC for subject SW at lag 2 with polarity stimuli (A = white, B = black). This real AOC is "enhanced" by adding 0.3 to each coordinate to produce the "enhanced" AOC at the upper right. The real AOC indicates a small stimulus differentiation benefit; the "enhanced" AOC indicates a large benefit; attention effects are identical for both AOCs.

In the experimental conditions, $\frac{1}{2}A + \frac{1}{2}B$, full attention to feature A while ignoring B is represented by the middle point on the diagonal line of figure 12.6a. Full attention to A shows a benefit relative to the control-All-A condition but not nearly as great a benefit as occurs when the B stimuli are replaced with blanks.

Two unconnected data points are shown in figure 12.6a. The half-shaded point adjacent to the full-attention point in figure 12.6a indicates equal attention. Equal attention in an alternating $\frac{1}{2}A + \frac{1}{2}B$ stream yields better performance than in the All-A stream because mixing two features in the stream (instead of only one) makes the stimuli more discriminable. Attention to B stimuli leads to poor performance on aa repetitions (0.25), and this is indicated by the triangle in figure 12.6a.

We expect good symmetry between features A and B (white-on-gray, black-on-gray). Indeed, figure 12.6b, generated for detections of bb repetitions, is basically similar to figure 12.6a.

Generating Attention-Operating Characteristics (AOCs)   The $\frac{1}{2}A + \frac{1}{2}B$ points in figures 12.6a and 12.6b generate the AOC (Kinchla 1980; Sperling and Melchner 1978b) of figure 12.6c. The lower-right square of figure 12.6c indicates joint performance on aa and bb repetitions when attention is directed to A. The rectangle around the square indicates one standard error of the mean in each dimension. The rectangle is extended in the B dimension because, in the Attend-A condition, there are seven times more aa repetition trials than bb trials, and this increases the standard error of bb detections relative to aa. The circle in figure 12.6c indicates equal-attention performance, and the diamond at the upper-left end of the AOC indicates Attend-B performance. Based on the data of figures 12.6a and 12.6b, the shape of the AOC is concave down, the limbs forming almost a right angle. The severe concave-down shape indicates that, relative to equal attention, selective attention yields negligible benefits but significant losses.

Additionally, figure 12.6c indicates a shaded area that represents excluded performances. Regardless of the state of attention, we expect performance in $\frac{1}{2}A + \frac{1}{2}B$ to equal or exceed performance in the All-A and All-B control conditions. This constraint excludes data from the lower-left rectangle of the AOC graph.

Figure 12.6d indicates an AOC derived from subject SW viewing the *size* stimuli. Here, the AOC is concave up. It indicates that, relative to equal attention, paying selective attention to large (A) stimuli improves detection of aa repetitions with only an insignificant loss of detectability of bb repetitions. Similarly, attending to small (B) stimuli significantly improves detection of bb repetitions but does not significantly penalize aa detections. A right-angle concave-up shape of AOC indicates benefits of selective attention with no costs.

Figure 12.6d illustrates a second shaded region that was absent in figure 12.6c because of that subject's perfect performance in the control conditions. Regardless of the state of attention, we expect the subject to perform worse in any experimental $\frac{1}{2}A + \frac{1}{2}B$ condition than in the corresponding $\frac{1}{2}A$ or $\frac{1}{2}B$ control condition. This excludes data from the shaded area in the outer rim of the AOC graph.

The pure costs and pure benefits indicated by the AOCs of figures 12.6c and 12.6d are somewhat unusual. Figure 12.6e (subject SW, polarity-and-size stimuli) illustrates a more typical AOC. The slope of -1 suggests a symmetrical trade-off between the costs and benefits of selective attention. The most common interpretation of linear AOCs is that the subject can perform only one task or the other, and that the equal-attention point represents a mixture of these two strategies (Sperling and Dosher 1986; Sperling and Melchner 1978a). Such a switching strategy could cause the AOC to traverse the excluded region and influence the equal-attention point to lie within it.

AOCs for the Data

Figure 12.7 shows all the AOCs from the experiments. The twenty-eight AOCs represent six stimulus transformations, each with lags 2 and 4. There are two subjects for each of the first four conditions and three subjects for the two remaining. Overall, the AOCs look similar to those illustrated in figure 12.6. Performance is consistently better for lag 2 than for lag 4.

Several AOCs show pure costs: for example, polarity (SW, JW, lag 2), and size (JW, lag 2), and many AOCs have a purely vertical or horizontal leg to indicate that one of the two selective-attention conditions results in pure costs. All in all, there are very few examples of AOCs that can be interpreted as yielding a continuum of trade-offs. We defer further discussion of these graphs until we consider the full range of data and additional summary statistics.

Consolidated Graphs of All Experimental and Control Conditions

Each panel of figure 12.8 shows mean data for each of the thirty-six kinds of repetition detections for one subject and one set of features. Except for variances and tests of significance, these graphs represent the entire data of the experiments. The plan of figure 12.8 is to indicate the data of control conditions by two sets of connected lines that form upper and lower reference bounds for four clusters of points that represent the data of the experimental conditions. We begin by making some general observations.

The Effects of Lag and SOA   The effects of lag on repetition-detection performance are indicated in figure 12.8 by the sloping connecting lines that indicate performance in the control-All-A and All-B conditions. Performance with the control-All stimuli is at or above 75 percent at lag 1 for nearly all subjects and types of stimulus transformation. There are clear individual differences. For example, in the polarity-and-size conditions, subject ZL performs better at lag 1 than does subject SW, although SW had much more practice. These lag data are completely consistent with earlier observations (Kaufman 1978).

LAG 2 **LAG 4**

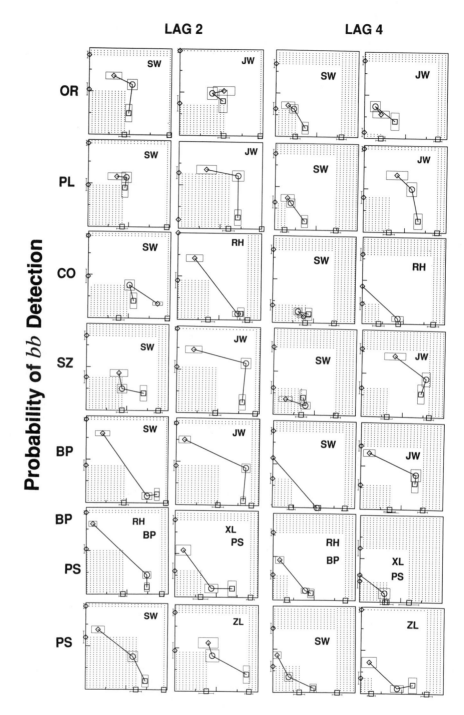

Probability of *bb* **Detection**

Probability of *aa* **Detection**

Figure 12.7 Attention-Operating Characteristics (AOC) for all subjects, stimulus transformations, and lags. Rows indicate different stimulus transformations (see figure 12.3) except row 6, which is shared by two different stimuli. The abscissa is the probability of detecting *aa* targets, the ordinate indicates *bb* detections. Coordinates range from 0 to 1.0. Symbols repre-

The effect of SOA is derived from the sloping lines labeled $A/2$ that represent data for the control-Blanks conditions ($\frac{1}{2}A$, $\frac{1}{2}B$), and which appear above lags 2 and 4. Performance in control-Blanks is better than the corresponding control-All (A, B) data. Alternatively, the control-Blanks conditions with lags 2 and 4 might be described as lags 1 and 2 of a stream with a doubled SOA (stimulus onset asynchrony—the time from the onset of one digit to the next). However, the control-Blanks is not quite equivalent to a slower sequence because it has only fifteen instead of the thirty items that would be produced by simply slowing the stream. The combined manipulation of slowing and shortening the sequence produces (except for ceiling effects) better performance for the control-Blanks than the comparable control-All conditions: control-Blanks, lag 2, surpasses control-All, lag 1, and control-Blanks, lag 4, surpasses control-All, lag 2.

The obvious interpretation of these data is that the main cause of the decline of performance with lag is retroactive interference (versus passive decay). Increasing the SOA increases the amount of time that the items must be retained but actually improves performance. (We know this also from unpublished observations in our laboratory in which sequence length was controlled.)

Repetition Blindness   The improvement of detection with shorter lags is different from another phenomenon discovered recently by using superficially similar procedures. "Repetition blindness" (Kanwisher 1987) is the reduced ability of subjects to report both occurrences of a repeated word embedded in a rapid sequence (approximately 4 to 9 per second) relative to the reportability of two independent words. In contrast to the present research, reportability of both occurrences of the word increases with increasing lag. There are several differences between our repetition-detection procedure and the procedure Kanwisher used. Repeated items are discriminated from unrepeated items in Kanwisher's studies rather than from other equally-often-repeated items, as in ours. However, the equivalence of the twenty-nine-element character set of experiment 2 (in which all noncritical repetitions were eliminated) to the other character sets shows that multiple repetitions are not the cause of the difference in results.

The repetition-blindness paradigm tests the tendency of subjects to report both occurrences of repeated items rather than their ability to discriminate repeated from unrepeated items. Moreover, repetition-blindness experiments typically have used linguistic stimuli (words) in the stimulus sequence, in some instances varying the context in which these words were presented (Kanwisher 1987; Kanwisher and Potter 1989), and in other in-

---

◀ sent attention conditions: squares = Attend-A, circles = equal attention, diamonds = Attend-B. One standard error is indicated around each point. A and $\frac{1}{2}A$ control conditions are shown on the abscissa, B and $\frac{1}{2}B$ on the ordinate. The clear area defines the reasonable bounds on performance. SW, JW, RH, XL, and ZL indicate subjects; other abbreviations indicate transformations.

Defining and Localizing the Processes of Selective Attention

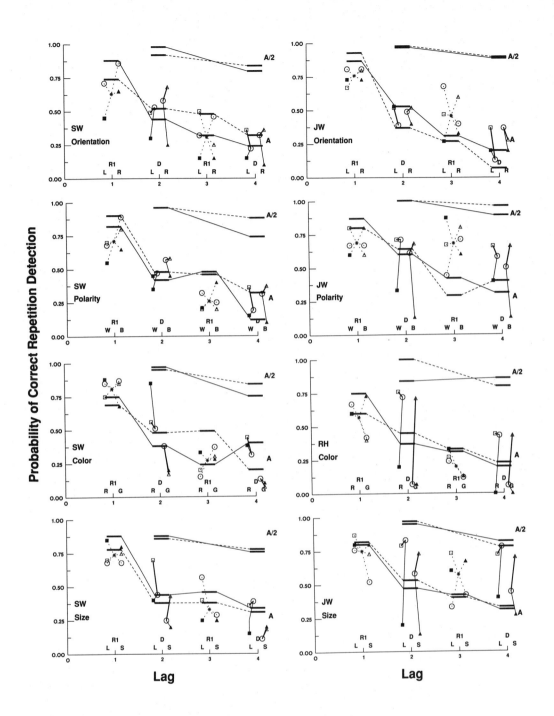

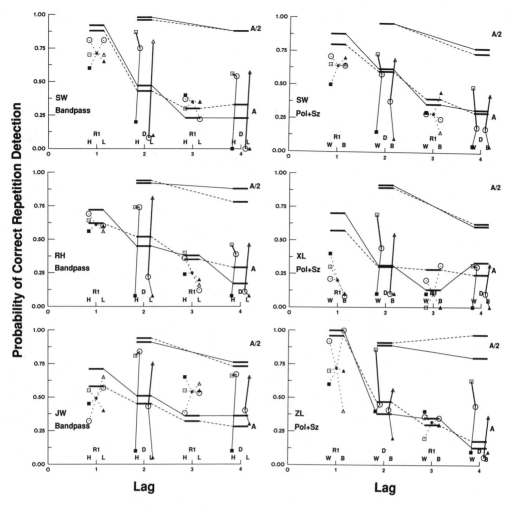

Figure 12.8 Data of all thirty-six trial types for each subject and type of stimulus transformation. In each panel, frame lag is plotted on the abscissa, and proportion of correct detections is plotted on the ordinate. Horizontal bars connected by continuous lines labeled A/2, A, represent control conditions $\frac{1}{2}A$ (control-Blanks) and A (control-All). $\frac{1}{2}B$ and B conditions are indicated by bars connected by dashed lines (not labeled). The data points at each of the frame lags represent the different attention conditions and targets in $\frac{1}{2}A + \frac{1}{2}B$ stimuli. Frame lags 2 and 4 indicate aa and bb detections; frame lags 1 and 3 indicate heterogeneous ab and ba detections. Open circles indicate equal attention. At frame lags 2 and 4, data points for the detection of aa repetitions are displaced to the left and detections of bb to the right, as indicated by dimension labels below (D indicates "detection"). At frame lags 1 and 3, detections of ab repetitions are displaced to the left and detections of ba repetitions to the right. R1 indicates the first occurring feature in a heterogeneous-repetition pair, indicated by the dimension label below R1. Open symbols indicate detection of the attended feature (even lags) or detection of heterogeneous-repetition pairs in which the attended feature occurred first. Filled symbols indicate reports of unattended features or, in heterogeneous pairs, that the attended feature occurred second. Reports of aa (bb) under different attention conditions are linked by lines; the heavier line indicates the attended feature. The asterisks at frame lags 1 and 3 indicate the means for the six heterogeneous-repetition types.

Defining and Localizing the Processes of Selective Attention

stances varying the case of the repetition without incurring a performance detriment (Marohn and Hochaus 1988). These procedural and stimulus differences suggest that repetition-blindness and repetition-detection paradigms may elicit different information-processing strategies and may reflect different levels of processing.

Equivalence of the Opposed Features within a Dimension   A glimpse at the control data in figure 12.8 shows that performance on the A and B control streams is essentially equivalent in all conditions. None of the differences approaches statistical significance.

Feature equivalence means that differential attentional effects exhibited in the $\frac{1}{2}A + \frac{1}{2}B$ conditions are due to factors other than differential discriminability of the streams. Further, we note that attentional effects cannot be due to cross-stream masking in which an item from $\frac{1}{2}A$ masks one from $\frac{1}{2}B$. We refer again to an earlier result that interposing noise fields between successive frames has minimal effects on performance (Kaufman 1978; Wurst, Sperling, and Dosher 1991).

Dominance Relations of Opposed Features within a Dimension   Whereas the opposed A and B features are equivalent when viewed in pure stimulus streams, when they are interleaved in a $\frac{1}{2}A + \frac{1}{2}B$ stream, in the unsymmetric dimensions, one feature may dominate completely. For example, in the color dimension, red is dominant over green. When subject RH attempts to pay equal attention to both colors, she performs exactly as she does when paying selective attention to red (figure 12.7). For subject SW, the color transformation is even more problematical. He is able to selectively attend to red. However, when he attempts to selectively attend to green, his performance on green deteriorates and his performance on red improves. This result was so unexpected that extra sessions were conducted. But the additional trials merely produced more of the same kind of data.

Other examples of dominance are high bandpass over low (subjects SW, RH) and large-white over small-black (subject ZL). The dominance of one feature over another is quite similar to the dominance of one eye over another: Alone, each eye or feature may be equivalent; dominance is observed only when they are placed into competition.

Heterogeneous Detections, *ab* and *ba*   In figure 12.8, heterogeneous detections are represented as clusters of points that lie above lags 1 and 3. Because of the strict feature alternation in the $\frac{1}{2}A + \frac{1}{2}B$ stream, different-feature (heterogeneous) repetitions can occur only at lags 1 and 3. The probabilities of these repetitions were quite low, $P = 0.1$ in the selective-attention conditions and $P = 0.14$ in the equal-attention condition (table 12.1). At each of these lags, there are six heterogeneous-detection types: three attentional states × two feature sequences (*ab*, *ba*). All six detection types are illustrated in figure 12.8 for each stimulus transformation, subject, and lag.

Because a heterogeneous repetition involves a feature difference, we expect heterogeneous repetitions to be more poorly detected than same-feature repetitions in all conditions (e.g., Posner et al. 1969, name vs. physical identity matching). The mean of all six heterogeneous-repetition types for lag 1 is below the level of same-feature repetitions in most instances, and dramatically below the same-feature level in some instances (with the exception of subject JW). Further characterization of heterogeneous-detection performance requires a more computational approach; we begin by developing some descriptive statistics of homogeneous detections.

Benefits and Costs in Homogeneous-Repetition Detections

A Computation Example   The goal is to characterize selective attention in terms of the efficiency of attentional filtering relative to perfect optical filtering. However, selective attention is studied in the alternating stimulus $\frac{1}{2}A + \frac{1}{2}B$ in which two features are alternated. Feature alternation alone, independent of attention, may have some positive effect on performance relative to All-A or All-B controls. Therefore, we first consider the stimulus benefit of alternating features.

We begin with an illustrative computation on the data of figures 12.6a and b. Consider the range defined by the two control conditions A and $\frac{1}{2}A$. The bottom end of this range represents a point where the A and B stimuli cannot be discriminated and so performance on $\frac{1}{2}A + \frac{1}{2}B$ is equivalent to performance in either of the controls. The upper end of this range $\frac{1}{2}A$ represents the point where A and B are discriminated perfectly, and one of them can be ignored perfectly. Therefore, we expect to find attentional effects confined to this range. In figure 12.6a, the range within which benefits might be reasonably be expected to occur extends from .60 to 1.00, a range of 0.40. The equal-attention condition yields a fraction correct of .71, which is $(.71 - .60)/(1.00 - .60) = 0.28$. Attending selectively to A also yields a score of 0.71; obviously, there is no additional benefit of selective attention over equal attention. Thus we might conclude that, in detecting aa repetitions, there is a stimulus differentiation advantage in the $\frac{1}{2}A + \frac{1}{2}B$ stimuli relative to the All-A controls, but no advantage of selective attention.

The detection computations made on aa detections in figure 12.6a can be repeated for bb detections in figure 12.6b. There is a stimulus differentiation advantage of $(.61 - .64)/(1.00 - .64) = -0.08$, that is, a small cost. The attentional benefit $(.68 - .64)/(1.00 - .64) = +0.10$ also is small.

Finally, we average the aa and bb results to obtain a stimulus-differentiation benefit of .10 and a selective-attention benefit of 0.05; both of these differ insignificantly from zero by a t test. The conclusion is that, for these data, the performance differences between control and experimental stimuli are too small to reach statistical significance. Applying the same computations to the data of figure 12.6d yields an insignificant stimulus-differentiation benefit but a highly significant selective-attention benefit of 0.49.

In summary, the alternating-feature stream, $\frac{1}{2}A + \frac{1}{2}B$, confers two possible benefits: *stimulus discrimination* in equal-attention conditions and *attentional filtering* in selective-attention conditions. To estimate these benefits, it was useful to average the two types of detections (*aa, bb*).

Stimulus-Discrimination Benefit   We define the *normalized stimulus-discrimination benefit* as the improvement in equal-attention conditions (equal attention minus control-All) compared to the maximum possible range of improvement (control Banks minus control-All). To compute the stimulus-discrimination benefit (Stim Disc Benefit), the following definitions are needed. Let $P(aa|\frac{1}{2}A + \frac{1}{2}B)_{Attn=A}$ be the probability of correct detections of *aa* repetitions given the $\frac{1}{2}A + \frac{1}{2}B$ stream with attention directed to the A feature. Let A indicate the All-A condition and $\frac{1}{2}A$ indicate the A blanks control condition. Then,

$$
\text{Stim Disc Benefit} = \frac{1}{2}\left[\frac{P(aa|\frac{1}{2}A + \frac{1}{2}B)_{Attn=AB} - P(aa|A)}{P(aa|\frac{1}{2}A) - P(aa|A)}\right]
$$
$$
+ \frac{1}{2}\left[\frac{P(bb|\frac{1}{2}A + \frac{1}{2}B)_{Attn=AB} - P(bb|B)}{P(bb|\frac{1}{2}B) - P(bb|B)}\right]
\tag{1}
$$

Selective-Attention Benefits and Costs   Similarly, the *normalized selective-attention benefit*, abbreviated here simply to Sel Attn Benefit, is

$$
\text{Sel Attn Benefit} = \frac{1}{2}\left[\frac{P(aa|\frac{1}{2}A + \frac{1}{2}B)_{Attn=A} - P(aa|\frac{1}{2}A + \frac{1}{2}B)_{Attn=AB}}{P(aa|\frac{1}{2}A) - P(aa|A)}\right]
$$
$$
+ \frac{1}{2}\left[\frac{P(bb|\frac{1}{2}A + \frac{1}{2}B)_{Attn=B} - P(bb|\frac{1}{2}A + \frac{1}{2}B)_{Attn=AB}}{P(bb|\frac{1}{2}B) - P(bb|B)}\right]
\tag{2}
$$

where $Attn = AB$ denotes the equal-attention condition.

The selective-attention cost is defined exactly like the benefit in equation 2 except that the subscripts $Attn = A$ and $Attn = B$ are interchanged.

In terms of AOCs, the stimulus-discrimination benefit describes where the equal-attention point lies relative to the two forbidden areas. For example, figure 12.6f shows the AOC derived from subject SW with the polarity stimuli and the same AOC translated up and to the right. The stimulus-differentiation benefit for the real data is 0.14; for the translated data it is .67.

In terms of AOCs, the attention benefit describes how far the arms of the AOC extend outward from the equal-attention point toward the upper and far-right boundaries. For selective-attention conditions, the stimulus and attention benefits sum. Stimulus discrimination measures the extent to which the physical attributes of the items aid in making them discriminable. The selective-attention benefit measures the efficiency of attentional filtering of the unattended items. Together these factors determine how closely attention performance in $\frac{1}{2}A + \frac{1}{2}B$ approaches control performance in $\frac{1}{2}A$ and $\frac{1}{2}B$.

Benefits and Costs in Heterogeneous-Repetition Detections

Heterogeneous-Repetition Cost   An alternating stimulus $\frac{1}{2}A + \frac{1}{2}B$ facilitates detections of homogeneous repetitions *aa* and *bb* because the elements of the repetition pair share a common A or B feature, and this helps to discriminate them from all the other possible pairs, half of which differ in this feature. The benefit of the $\frac{1}{2}A + \frac{1}{2}B$ stimulus becomes a cost when a heterogeneous repetition *ab* or *ba* must be detected.

To estimate the cost of heterogeneous detections, we use a computation similar to the estimation of the homogeneous stimulus-differentiation benefit. In term of the representation in figure 12.8, we measure the distance from the center of gravity of a heterogeneous cluster (the asterisk) to the mean of lower set of curves, divided by the distance between the two sets of curves. There are two complications in locating the appropriate point on the upper curve. At lag 3, we use the average of the upper curve at lags 2 and 4. At lag 1, there is no upper curve, so we simply use 1.0.

$$Hetero\ Rep\ Cost = \frac{\frac{1}{2}(P(ab|\frac{1}{2}A + \frac{1}{2}B) + P(ba|\frac{1}{2}A + \frac{1}{2}B)) - X}{Y - X} \tag{3}$$

where

$$X = \tfrac{1}{2}(P(aa|A) + P(bb|B))$$

$$Y_{Lag\ 3} = \tfrac{1}{4}\{(P(aa|A) + P(bb|B))_{Lag\ 2} + (P(aa|A) + P(bb|B))_{Lag\ 4}\}$$

and

$$Y_{Lag\ 1} = 1$$

For strict comparability with the homogeneous stimulus-discrimination benefit, $P(ab)$ and $P(ba)$ should be computed only for equal-attention conditions. However, there was so little systematic difference in heterogeneous detections between conditions that the computation is aggregated over all attention conditions.

Heterogeneous Equal-Attention Benefit   In homogeneous-repetition detections, *aa*, *bb*, equal attention was, on the whole, a cost relative to selective attention. Selective attention could filter unattended stimuli prior to STVRM, thereby simplifying the task of repetition detection. Alternatively, attention could operate at the level of memory by tagging the stimuli in STVRM as "attended" or "unattended." Insofar as attention operates prior to storage in memory, attended items are benefited, and unattended items are handicapped. If attention were to operate at the level of memory, either an attended tag or an unattended tag would benefit homogeneous detections relative to heterogeneous detections. As we shall see, there were widespread costs to misdirected attention, and these costs imply an early locus for selective attention.

On the other hand, heterogeneous detections are relatively neutral to an early locus of attention because positively directed attention favors one member of the repetition pair but impairs the other, and the two effects would tend to cancel. But, if attention acted at the level of memory coding, selective attention would impair heterogeneous detections because one member of the pair would be tagged as attended and the other as unattended. Whereas selective attention either at the perceptual or the memorial level would facilitate homogeneous detections, selective attention at the memorial level would be harmful to heterogeneous detections. To quantify this effect, we measure the performance difference between heterogeneous detections with selective attention and with equal attention. This difference is normalized by the same factor as the heterogeneous repetition cost. A positive equal-attention benefit for heterogeneous detections suggests a memorial locus for attention.

Tabulation of Attention Benefits and Costs

Table 12.2 presents the values of five different costs and benefits computed individually for every subject and stimulus transformation. To determine whether an effect was statistically significantly different from zero, a t-test was conducted on the numerator of the expression that defines the effect (equations 1–3), and these results also were tabulated. In analyzing the data we concentrate first on the regularities in the data, keeping in mind the very considerable individual differences.

Stimulus-Discrimination Benefits   Overall stimulus benefits are quite small. In figure 12.7 this was indicated by the closeness of the AOCs to the lower-left forbidden area. In figure 12.8, it is indicated by tendency of the open circles that represent equal attention to fall on or near the lower curve. Nevertheless there are exceptions: six of twenty-eight stimulus-discrimination benefits are statistically significant; these occur for size, contrast polarity, and bandpass stimuli. There are significant costs for subject SW viewing polarity-and-size.

A stimulus benefit indicates that homogeneous discriminations are facilitated by common features. A cost suggests a significant inability to simultaneously attend to the opposed features, even with equal attention. Apparently, SW can attend either to large-white or to small-black stimuli, but not to both, and therefore performance in an alternating stream suffers relative to the control. (This is further borne out by the large benefits and costs he shows with selective attention for these stimuli.) On the whole, stimulus benefits are small.

Heterogeneous-Repetition Costs   Stimulus benefits in homogeneous detections imply stimulus costs in heterogeneous detections. If a common physical feature aids an *aa* detection, the feature difference should impair an *ab* detection. As noted, common features aid homogeneous detections by increasing the distance of the target repetition (which has common features) from the nontarget repetitions that have differing features. This is a relatively small benefit because half of the nontarget repetitions have similar features, and these cause the interference. On the other hand, differing features impair a

Table 12.2 Benefits and Costs Achieved in Equal-Attention and in Selective-Attention Conditions

		Homog Repetition[a]: *aa, bb*						Heterog Rep: *ab, ba*					
		Stimulus		Selective		Selective		Heterog		Equal		Attn Type	
Stim	Sub	Discr	Benf	Attn	Benf[b]	Attn	Cost[b]	Rep	Cost	Attn	Benf	1/2	3/4
		lag=2	4	2	4	2	4	1	3	1	3		
OR	SW	.16	−.02	.09	.17*	−.58‡	−.27†	.85‡	−.18*	1.2†	.27*	s	s
	JW	−.06	.13*	.17	.12	.04	−.05	1.4†	.26*	.80	.18	o	o
PO	SW	.14	.05	−.01	.21†	−.24	−.22*	1.1†	−.50‡	.79	.09	o	p
	JW	.10	.32†	.09	.21*	−1.1‡	−.48†	.94†	.53‡	−.19	−.27*	o	r
CO	SW	.03	−.30	−.22*	.02	.29	−.09	.07	−.01	.25	−.03	r	o
	RH	.02	.03	.63‡	.33‡	−.57‡	−.38‡	−.28	−.21	−.09	−.07	p	p
SZ	SW	−.15	−.14	.49‡	.03	−.12	−.18	−.53	−.23*	−.59	.35†	p	s
	JW	.43‡	.58‡	.13	.23*	−1.2‡	−.54†	−.32	.34†	−.84*	−.62‡	r	r
BP	SW	.06	−.06	.67‡	.53‡	−.52‡	−.42‡	1.9†	.12	1.5*	−.08	b	p
	JW	.39†	.52‡	.29‡	.27‡	−1.3‡	−.80‡	.46†	.40‡	−.17	−.24	p	p
	RH	−.05	.00	.70‡	.41‡	−.87‡	−.25†	−.18	−.24†	.15	−.02	p	p
PS	SW	−.36*	−.28*	.65‡	.61‡	−.91‡	−.30†	1.3‡	−.19*	.31	−.06	p	p
	ZL	.00	.16	.57†	.33*	−.26	−.23	−.13‡	−.02	.18‡	.11	b	b
	XL	−.06	−.24	.58‡	.30*	−.28*	−.69‡	1.2‡	−.20*	−.22	.42†	p	b

* Statistically significant at: * .05; † .01; ‡ .001
a. Benefits and costs averaged over *aa* and *bb* repetitions.
b. Averaged over selective attention conditions.

heterogeneous target repetition relative to the half of nontarget repetitions that have similar features. This is a large cost because it brings the nearest neighbors closer. Nineteen of twenty-eight cells show significant heterogeneous repetition costs; most of these are highly significant. At lag 1, thirteen of fourteen cells show a cost, and nine of fourteen are highly significant. These data indicate that the physical feature is represented in STVRM, and that this feature representation figures prominently in repetition detection. The color dimension is an exception: color similarity seems not to play a significant role in repetition detection.

Feature similarity is a bigger effect for lag 1 than for lag 3. This is consistent with earlier observations (Kaufman 1978) that STVRM for lag 1 seems to be more iconic (less abstract) than for lag 3.

Finally, we note four significant benefits of feature dissimilarity in heterogeneous detections. These all occur for subject JW at lag 3 and characterize all his performances at this lag. Indeed, his performance with heterogeneous repetitions surpasses that of other subjects and at lag 3 surpasses his own for homogeneous repetitions. These data differ profoundly from all our other data and require a different explanation. One possibility that occurred to us is that JW uses the same repetition-detection mechanism that is used in the Kanwisher paradigm (in which longer lags aid repetition detection). If so, making the repeated item different in some physical feature might aid it in surviving repetition blindness. Of the many subjects who have run in our paradigm, JW is the only one who exhibits this effect.

Selective-Attention Benefits All subjects show highly significant attentional benefits for bandpass and polarity-and-size stimuli, and, for each of the other transformations, at least one subject shows a significant attentional benefit. The filtering efficiency of attentional filtering in the bandpass and polarity-and-size stimuli is very high. At lag 2, five of the six cells show a benefit that is 57 to 70 percent of the benefit produced by perfect optical filtering (i.e., the $\frac{1}{2}A$ and $\frac{1}{2}B$ control stimuli).

In multilocation search paradigms, it is not clear whether features merely draw attention to a location or whether information can be filtered according to physical features. In our paradigm, the data indicate that efficient attentional filtering according to physical features occurs within a single location.

Selective-Attention Costs Twenty-six of twenty-eight cells show attention costs for unattended items; nineteen of these costs are statistically significant, and there are no significant exceptions. There is, on the whole, a high correlation between attentional benefits for attended homogeneous repetitions and costs for unattended repetitions. Indeed, if detections of unattended repetitions were not correspondingly impaired, we would have to conclude that attentional selection occurred at a later stage where both attended and unattended items were available for selection.

In spite of the overall correlation between benefits for attended repetitions and costs for unattended ones, there are some obvious exceptions. Subject SW does not have an attentional benefit at lag 2 for orientation or for polarity stimuli but shows a large cost. Subject JW shows a similar effect for polarity stimuli. These observations are consistent with right-angled, concave-down AOCs (figure 12.7) for these conditions that indicate costs without benefits for selective attention.

If unattended items are filtered to the point where detection of unattended repetitions is significantly impaired, should there not be a benefit for the attended repetitions? Finding one but not both of these effects suggests that the unattended items are absent in some contexts (detecting unattended repetitions) but present in others (interfering with detection of attended repetitions). This is one of several indications in our data that attention may operate at more than one level: at a perceptual filtering level before STVRM and at the level of coding information within STVRM itself.

Equal-Attention Benefits in Heterogeneous Detections   If the state of attention were coded in STVRM, then we would expect equal-attention conditions to have an advantage in heterogeneous repetitions. On the whole, equal-attention benefits are small; only nine of twenty-eight cells show statistically significant benefits. Of these, three are negative (representing costs). Costs arise in subject JW's data, and the explanation is similar to that considered for JW's heterogeneous-repetition costs. Differentiating repeated items (in this case by the state of attention) facilitates JW's repetition detection.

Patterns of Attentional Benefits

Here we consider joint attentional benefits in detection of homogeneous and heterogeneous repetitions. Figure 12.9 illustrates the four combinations of small or large selective-attention benefits in homogeneous detections with small or large equal-attention benefits in heterogeneous detections. We con-

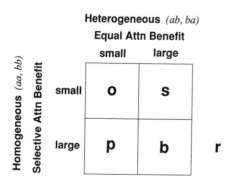

Figure 12.9 Types of attention performance, according to the joint magnitude of selective-attention benefits in homogeneous-repetition detections and equal-attention benefits in heterogeneous-repetition detections. The letters merely suggest causes: o = no attention benefits, p = perceptual benefits, s = benefits in STVRM (short-term visual repetition memory), b = both. The r outside the 2 × 2 table indicates reversed effects—impaired performance due to selective attention.

sider an attentional benefit to be large if it is greater than 0.20 and if it is statistically significant. Otherwise it is small. An attentional benefit that is significantly negative indicates impaired performance due to selective attention. Such effects are unexpected and are categorized separately as *r* (reversed). The last two columns of Table 12.2 use a code letter to represent the join distribution of benefits.

No Attention Benefits (*o*)   There are five instances of small-homogeneous with small-heterogeneous benefits. These occur in the orientation, polarity, and color stimuli but not in any of the other conditions. The first four of these *o*'s occur in conditions in which there are very large heterogeneous-repetition costs. This demonstrates that these features are highly discriminable; the absence of an attention effect must be attributed to something else. The fifth *o* occurs for subject SW color, which we have already noted is aberrant with respect to attention: attending to green impairs SW's performance for green stimuli but improves performance for red.

Selective-Attention Benefit (*p*); Both (*b*)   A selective-attention benefit implies attentional selection of attended items. Perhaps the strongest result in these experiments is the ubiquity of selective-attentional selection in certain stimulus transformations, most notably bandpass and polarity-and-size. For both of these stimuli, all three subjects, at both lags, show a strong selective-attentional benefit (twelve of twelve cells), and in three of these conditions there is also a strong equal-attention benefit (*b*). Even subjects such as JW and SW, who deal quite differently with other classes of stimuli, come together here to show strong attentional effects. Of sixteen remaining cells, only four show a *p* benefit. Clearly, the stimulus dimension strongly influences the ability of subjects to select items according to attentional instructions.

A benefit of selective attention for homogeneous detections without a corresponding penalty in heterogeneous detections (the *p* classification) suggests that attention operates prior to coding in STVRM. The *b* (both) category is ambiguous as to where attentional selection might be operating.

Equal-Attention Benefit for Heterogeneous Repetitions without a Selective-Attention Benefit for Homogeneous Repetitions (*s*)   A selective-attention cost for heterogeneous pairs without a selection benefit for homogeneous pairs suggests that attentional selection is occurring in or after STVRM. (If early attentional filtering had occurred, it would have yielded a selective-attention benefit.) The three *s* cells occur when subject SW views orientation or size stimuli. These are additionally coupled with significant heterogeneous repetition cost, indicating that the physical features are represented in memory to the point of interfering with heterogeneous detections. The equal-attention benefit is, alternatively phrased, a selective-attention cost over and above the stimulus heterogeneity cost. For this subject and these stimuli, the evidence quite consistently implies that both features and the attentional state of input items are stored in STVRM.

It is noteworthy that there are significant costs of selective attention connected with two of the three *s* cells and almost significant costs in the third instance. This suggests that selective-attention costs may be occurring at the level of STVRM as well as at an earlier stage.

Reversed Effects of Selective Attention (*r*)   These have already received much discussion: subject JW benefits from stimulus heterogeneity, especially at lag 3; and subject SW cannot selectively attend to green (among alternating red and green stimuli).

12.4   SUMMARY AND CONCLUSIONS

Detection of visual repetitions in a rapid stream of items depends on a short-term visual repetition memory (STVRM) that is indifferent to eye of origin and to interposed masking fields, and which functions as well for nonsense shapes as for digits. STVRM is visual, not verbal or semantic. It is governed by interference from new items; it does not suffer passive decay within the short interstimulus intervals under which it has been tested.

Using selective-attention instructions with the repetition-detection task permitted us to test the extent to which, at a single location, subjects could filter rapidly successive items according to their physical characteristics. By presenting all the items at the same location, only attentional selection according to features (and not according to location) is effective. Our subjects selectively attended to subsets of characters based on physical differences of orientation, contrast polarity, color, size, spatial bandpass filtering, and polarity-and-size combined.

Efficiency of attentional selection was determined by comparing performance in a stream of characters that alternated a physical feature with performance in two control conditions: one in which the to-be-unattended characters were optically filtered and another in which all chatacters shared the same physical feature. Selection efficiency in bandpass-filtered streams and in the polarity-and-size streams was greater than 50 percent. Attentional selection based on the other physical features was less effective or ineffective.

Corresponding to the benefits of attentional selection in detecting to-be-attended repetitions, there were large costs in the detection of unattended features. Costs were more ubiquitous than benefits.

In addition to studying repetitions of items that shared a physical feature (homogeneous repetitions), we studied heterogeneous repetitions. Costs for detecting heterogeneous repetitions (relative to homogeneous repetitions) were widespread, indicating that physical features are represented in STVRM. The corresponding stimulus benefits of detecting homogeneous repetitions in feature-alternating streams (under equal attention) were small and only occasionally significant.

If the state of attention were represented in STVRM, we would expect a cost in the detection of heterogeneous repetitions with selective-attention instructions (because the attentional state would differ for the two elements of the pair). Such costs were observed, and in some instances they occurred even when there was no corresponding benefit for selective attention in homogeneous detections. This was interpreted as a lack of early attentional filtering compensated by a memory tag representing whether or not an item was attended.

We conclude that the largest attentional effects occur at the level of attentional selection prior to encoding in STVRM (for bandpass and polarity-and-size stimuli) but that, even when early attentional filtering fails, it can still occur in STVRM.

ACKNOWLEDGMENTS

The experimental work was supported by Office of Naval Research, Cognitive and Neural Sciences Division, Grant N00014-88-K-0569; the theoretical work and preparation of the manuscript was supported by AFOSR, Life Science Directorate, Visual Information Processing Program; Grant No. 91-0178.

REFERENCES

Averbach, E., and Sperling, G. (1961). Short term storage of information in vision. In C. Cherry (Ed.), *Information Theory*, 196–211. Washington, D.C.: Butterworths.

Broadbent, D. E. (1958). *Perception and Communication*. London: Pergamon Press.

Cave, K. R., and Wolfe, J. M. (1990). Modelling the role of parallel processing in visual search. *Cognitive Psychology, 22,* 225–271.

Deutsch, J. A., and Deutsch, D. (1963). Attention: Some theoretical considerations. *Psychological Review, 70,* 80–90.

Duncan, J., and Humphreys, G. W. (1989). Visual search and stimulus similarity. *Psychological Review, 96,* 433–458.

Felfoldy, G. L., and Garner, W. R. (1971). The effects on speeded classification of implicit and explicit instructions regarding redundant dimensions. *Perception and Psychophysics, 9,* 289–292.

Folk, C. L., and Egeth, H. (1989). Does the identification of simple features require serial processing? *Journal of Experimental Psychology: Human Perception and Performance, 15,* 97–110.

Garner, W. R. (1978). Selective attention to attributes and to stimuli. *Journal of Experimental Psychology: General, 107,* 287–308.

Hoffman, J. E. (1979). A two-stage model of visual search. *Perception and Psychophysics, 25,* 319–327.

Intraub, H. (1985). Visual dissociation: An illusory conjunction of pictures and forms. *Journal of Experimental Psychology: Human Perception and Performance, 11,* 431–442.

Kanwisher, N. G. (1987). Repetition blindness: Type recognition without token individuation. *Cognition, 27,* 117–143.

Kanwisher, N. G., and Potter, M. C. (1989). Repetition blindness: The effects of stimulus modality and spatial displacement. *Memory and Cognition, 17,* 117–124.

Kaufman, J. (1978). *Visual repetition detection.* Unpublished doctoral dissertation, Department of Psychology, New York University.

Kinchla, R. A. (1980). The measurement of attention. In R. S. Nickerson (ed.), *Attention and Performance VIII*, 213–238. Hillsdale, NJ: Erlbaum.

LaBerge, D., and Brown, V. (1989). Theory of attentional operations in shape identification. *Psychological Review, 96,* 101–124.

Landy, M. S., Cohen, Y., and Sperling, G. (1984a). HIPS: Image processing under Unix. Software and applications. *Behavior Research Methods and Instrumentation, 16,* 199–216.

Landy, M. S., Cohen, Y., and Sperling, G. (1984b). HIPS: A Unix-based image processing system. *Computer Vision, Graphics, and Image Processing, 25,* 331–347.

Marohn, K. M., and Hochhaus, L. (1988). Different case repetition still leads to perceptual blindness. *Bulletin of the Psychonomic Society, 26,* 29–31.

Merikle, P. M. (1980). Selection from visual persistence by perceptual groups and category membership. *Journal of Experimental Psychology: General, 109,* 279–295.

Nakayama, K., and Silverman, G. H. (1986). Serial and parallel processing of visual feature conjunctions. *Nature, 320,* 264–265.

Neisser, U. (1967). *Cognitive psychology.* New York: Appleton-Century-Crofts.

Norman, D. A. (1968). Towards a theory of memory and attention. *Psychological Review, 75,* 522–536.

Parish, D. H., and Sperling, G. (1991). Object spatial frequencies, retinal spatial frequencies, noise, and the efficiency of letter discrimination. *Vision Research, 31,* 1399–1410.

Pavel, M. (1991). Model of preattentive search. *Mathematical Studies in Perception and Cognition, 91–4,* New York University, Department of Psychology.

Posner, M. I., Poies, S. J., Eichelman, W., and Taylor, R. L. (1969). Retention of visual and name codes of single letters. *J. Exptl. Psychol. Monograph, 70,* 1–16.

Reeves, A., and Sperling, G. (1986). Attention gating in short-term visual memory. *Psychological Review, 93,* 180–206.

Runtime Library for Psychology Experiments. (1988). New York: HIP Lab.

Sagi, D. (1988). The combination of spatial frequency and orientation is effortlessly perceived. *Perception and Psychophysics, 43,* 601–603.

Shiffrin, R. M., and Schneider, W. (1977). Controlled and automatic human information processing: II. Perceptual learning, automatic attending, and a general theory. *Psychological Review, 84,* 127–190.

Sperling, G. (1960). The information available in brief visual presentation. *Psychological Monographs, 74* (11, Whole No. 498).

Sperling, G. (1963). A model for visual memory tasks. *Human Factors, 5,* 19–31.

Sperling, G., Budiansky, J., Spivak, J. G., and Johnson, M. C. (1971). Extremely rapid visual search: The maximum rate of scanning letters for the presence of a numeral. *Science, 174,* 307–311.

Sperling, G., and Dosher, B. A. (1986). Strategy and optimization in human information processing. In K. Boff, L. Kaufman, and J. Thomas (eds.), *Handbook of Perception and Performance.* Vol. 1, 2-1–2-65. New York: Wiley.

Sperling, G., and Kaufman, J. (1978). Three kinds of visual short-term memory. Talk presented at Attention and Performance VIII, Educational Testing Service, Princeton, NJ, August 22.

Sperling, G., and Kaufman, J. (1991). Visual repetition detection. *Mathematical Studies in Perception and Cognition, 91–1,* New York University, Department of Psychology.

Sperling, G., and Melchner, M. J. (1978a). Visual search, visual attention, and the attention operating characteristic. In J. Requin (ed.), *Attention and Performance VII*, 675–686. Hillsdale, NJ: Erlbaum.

Sperling, G., and Melchner, M. J. (1978b). The attention operating characteristic: Examples from visual search. *Science, 202*, 315–318.

Sperling, G., and Reeves, A. (1980). Measuring the reaction time of a shift of visual attention. In R. Nickerson (ed.), *Attention and Performance VIII*, 347–360. Hillsdale, NJ: Erlbaum.

Sperling, G., and Weichselgartner, E. (1993). Episodic theory of the dynamics of spatial attention. *Psychological Review*. In press.

Swets, J. (1984). In R. Parasuraman and D. R. Davies (eds.), *Varieties of Attention*, 183–242. New York: Academic Press.

Treisman, A. M. (1977). Focused attention in the perception and retrieval of multidimensional stimuli. *Perception and Psychophysics, 22*, 1–11.

Treisman, A. M. (1982). Perceptual grouping and attention in visual search for features and for objects. *Journal of Experimental Psychology: Human Perception and Performance, 2*, 194–214.

Treisman, A. M. (1986). Properties, parts, and objects. In K. R. Boff, L. Kaufman, and J. P. Thomas (eds.), *Handbook of Perception and Human Performance, Vol. 2*, New York: Wiley.

Treisman, A. M., and Gelade, G. (1980). A feature-integration theory of attention. *Cognitive Psychology, 12*, 97–136.

von Wright, J. M. (1968). Selection in visual immediate memory. *Quarterly Journal of Experimental Psychology, 20*, 62–68.

Weichselgartner, E. (1984). Two processes in visual attention. Unpublished doctoral dissertation. Department of Psychology, New York University.

Weichselgartner, E., and Sperling, G. (1987). Dynamics of automatic and controlled visual attention. *Science, 238*, 778–780.

Wright, C. E., and Main, A. M. (1991). Selective search for conjunctively defined visual targets. Unpublished manuscript.

Wurst, S. A. (1989). Investigations of short-term visual repetition memory. Unpublished doctoral dissertation, Department of Psychology, New York University.

Wurst, S. A., Sperling, G., and Dosher, B. A. (1991). The locus and process of visual repetition detection. *Mathematical Studies in Perception and Cognition, 91–2*, New York University, Department of Psychology.

13 The Skill of Attention Control: Acquisition and Execution of Attention Strategies

Daniel Gopher

13.1 PROBLEM AND SCOPE

How able and efficient are humans in controlling and utilizing their limited mental resources? Can they be taught to improve their attention management skills? Can attention control be treated as a basic skill component? These are the main questions that will be examined in the present chapter. To support the notion of attention management as a trainable skill, we need evidence to show (1) the existence of behavioral potential, namely, control over the allocation of attention, (2) difficulties and failure in fulfilling this potential, and (3) ability to overcome or diminish these difficulties with proper training.

We seek data that bear upon the ability of performers to cope efficiently with tasks that require them to divide attention and processing efforts among multiple, dynamically varying elements. Such requirements are common in many daily tasks of intermediate and high complexity, where multiple dynamic elements have to be monitored, responded to, and interacted with to achieve a common general goal. For example, car drivers are required to divide attention among the manual control of the vehicle, monitoring the road, the traffic signs, and the behavior of other vehicles, while also attempting to locate themselves geographically in the environment. A similar task with much-elevated demands is that of a pilot who moves at high speed through six degrees of freedom space. Other examples include the task of a process controller in the control room of a modern power plant and a basketball player running with the ball while looking for the best opportunity to attempt a shot or pass, while also trying to anticipate defensive moves.

Common to all these tasks is that the performer would gain most if he or she could fully attend and respond to all elements at all times. However, such full attention is not possible. Hence, some trade-offs and priorities must be established along with attention-allocation strategies. Setting priorities is a common human experience; the question is how competent we are in establishing attention strategies and allocating processing efforts among concurrently changing task elements.

A *strategy* in this context is defined as a vector of differential weights or attention biases assigned to task elements. It influences the performer's mode of response to the requirements of the task (see also Logan 1985). A strategy represents the solution developed by the performer to cope better with task demands and performance objectives, within the boundaries of his or her processing and response limitations.

For example, several subcomponents of driving were listed, all of which covary concurrently and should be attended to while driving. However, their relative importance changes considerably (i.e., a different strategy has to be adopted) when the driver tries to arrive earlier at his destination, searches for an address in an unfamiliar territory, or pays extra caution to driving regulations after noticing a police car parked at the side of the road. Moreover, there are several ways in which each of these objectives can be pursued, and each may require a different attention strategy. Also, strategies and the importance of elements may vary in the course of driving, as the situation or the intentions of the driver change.

Two major questions can be posed regarding the adoption and execution of attention strategies. One concerns how cognizant performers are about the efficiency of their investments, and about the benefits and costs of alternative strategies. A second question concerns how able humans are in the control and mobilization of their processing efforts. Related to these questions are issues such as the trainability of attention control and the best methods of training.

With few exceptions (e.g., Logan 1985), strategic control of attention along the lines described in the previous examples has never been a main and independent topic of research in experimental psychology. Although fuzzy notions of a central executive and attention-control mechanism have been incorporated in many models of the human processing system (Gopher and Sanders 1984; Kahneman 1973; Norman and Shallice 1981), little systematic research has been conducted to explore the nature and capabilities of such a controller. Manipulations and evidence bearing on the issue of control have been embedded in the pursuit of other interests, such as unitary limited capacity, processing resources, mental workload, and modes of processing. Nonetheless, the literature is quite rich with experimental paradigms and data demonstrating successful strategic control. There is also ample evidence for control failures and deficient knowledge about the efficiency of investments.

A major claim of the present chapter is that from both theoretical and practical vantage points, strategic control of attention is an important topic that merits independent status in experimental psychology. To support this claim I will first briefly review evidence portraying successful control and problems of attention control. This review is followed by a description of the main results from two lines of experiments conducted in our laboratory, where acquisition and transfer of attention management skills have been studied in the context of performing complex tasks. The final section draws some principles and conclusions, outlining directions for future research.

13.2 EVIDENCE ABOUT ATTENTION CONTROL

Demonstrations of Successful Control

Experimental data demonstrating successful voluntary control of attention include results from the tasks of focusing, dividing, and switching attention together with investing graded amounts of processing efforts.

Focusing Attention   The most widely researched and documented aspect of voluntary attention control is the ability of humans to adopt a selective attention set and combat interference from irrelevant information. Research over the last four decades has shown that subjects can focus, lock on, and prioritize almost any feature that distinguishes one string of stimuli from another consistently. Although some features of the stimulus such as its spatial location and physical characteristics appear to be easier to focus upon and follow, voluntary selection is highly flexible and strategic. Throughout the years, this has led researchers to theoretical debates concerning early versus late selection models of attention limitations (Kahneman 1973; Kahneman and Treisman 1984). It is possible that evidence for one or more of these models may reflect the strategic freedom of the central executive in the selection of information.

For example, recent experiments on visual attention have provided elegant demonstrations of the separation between the "physical eye," dominated by the physical properties of the stimuli and the anatomy and physiology of the eye, versus the top-down selective-attention processes controlling the "mind's eye" (e.g., Posner, Snyder, and Davidson 1980). Contemporary research instigated by spotlight and zoom lens metaphors of visual attention has further demonstrated two strategic modes of focusing in the visual field, one general and the other specific mode (Castiliano and Umiltà 1990; Egeth 1977; Ericksen and St. James 1986; Jonides 1983). Under the general mode, attention is allocated evenly, in parallel, across the whole visual field. Under the specific mode, attention is focused on one display location, facilitating processing there, while inhibiting it at all others. Similar distinctions have been proposed by Kahneman (1973) for the auditory modality, when studying the behavior of subjects in dichotic listening tasks of selective attention.

Dividing Attention   Data that demonstrate the successful division of attention come primarily from experiments with the dual-task paradigm (Gopher and Donchin 1986). Within this paradigm, subjects have to cope with the demands of concurrently presented tasks. In different versions of the paradigm, two time-shared tasks have to be treated as equally important, or one is designated as primary and the other secondary. A secondary task should be attended to only insofar as performance of the primary task is fully achieved.

The dual-task paradigm has been a major methodological tool in experiments on processing and response limitations, and on the properties of tasks that interfere or can be time-shared in concurrent performance (Gopher 1990;

Wickens 1980). The study of voluntary control of attention has been incidental to this research. Nonetheless, successful compliance with the equal-importance and secondary-task emphases are clear examples of attention control.

Switching Attention   Switching attention from one task to another is an additional aspect of voluntary control that has been widely employed in the study of attention limitations. As before, the main interest in most studies has not been in the properties and control of switching, but rather in contrasting serial and parallel models of the human processing system. Isolated studies over the years attest to the significance of studying switching behavior and its control. One line of studies has documented consistent individual differences in attention-switching capabilities as a factor distinguishing between good and bad performers of complex tasks (Gopher 1982; Gopher and Kahneman 1971; Kahneman, Ben Ishai, and Lotan 1974; North and Gopher 1976).

Other support comes from the studies conducted by Posner and his colleagues (Posner and Rothbart 1986). They substantiate a distinction between two processes: focusing attention on a location in the visual field and processing information at that location, and disengaging and moving attention from one target to another. Experiments with brain-damaged subjects have led these researchers to identify different brain regions for the two processes. Most recently, Allport and Styles (1990) have conducted a series of experiments to test the ability of subjects to alternate and switch attention between tasks progressing serially through a single stimulus string. Their subjects demonstrated impressive ability to switch and adopt new processing and response sets in a wide variety of situations, while also exhibiting some difficulties that will be discussed in the next section.

Investing Graded Levels of Effort   The evidence most related to a notion of attention strategies comes from experiments in which attention control was manipulated as part of empirical efforts to construct Performance Operating Characteristic (POC) functions. A POC is a curve depicting all possible levels of joint performance in two concurrent tasks, which arise by dividing into different priorities a limited resource that they must share. The theoretical analysis of POCs was proposed by Norman and Bobrow (1975) and elaborated by Navon and Gopher (1979) to distinguish between data and resource constraints on the human processing system. The main objective has been to characterize performance decrements under time-sharing conditions not only in terms of task parameters and structure, but also the allocation policy adopted by a performer and the availability of resources. Moreover, manipulation of strategic control has emerged as an important source of information about the nature and limitations of the central processor.

Empirical POCs have been constructed by manipulating the relative emphasis on two concurrent tasks through verbal instructions, payoff matrices, and on-line augmented feedback (e.g., Gopher, Brickner, and Navon 1982; Sperling and Melchner 1978; Spitz 1988; Strayer and Kramer 1990; Wickens and

Gopher 1977). Although, as before, the focus of this research was not the ability to control attention, but rather the mapping of central-processor limitations, it has produced monotonic POCs comprising three, five, and seven different intertask priority levels. This evidence supports the ability of subjects to adopt and successfully apply graded levels of investment.

Summary   Although attention control has rarely been a direct topic of systematic research, several lines of experimental data support the ability of performers to adopt a selective set, divide and switch attention at will, and produce graded priority levels for two concurrently performed tasks.

Control Problems and Failures

Along with the positive evidence on voluntary attention control, there have been several reports that point to problems, failures, and limits of control.

Failure to Protect Primary-Task Performance   A frequent finding in dual-task experiments, with one task as primary, is that subjects fail, despite clear instruction, to protect its performance. The introduction of a secondary task and responses to it are accompanied by performance decrements on the primary task. Such decrements have usually been interpreted to reflect capacity overload or structural interference between tasks (Gopher and Donchin 1986). However, they may also be manifestations of deficient control. Subjects may not have adequate knowledge about the attention costs of performing each of the tasks, or they may be unable to exercise sufficient attention control such that only "spare capacity" is allocated to the secondary task, leaving primary task performance intact. Also, these two types of control deficiencies may not be mutually exclusive.

Dissociation between Subjective Estimates and Performance Measures of Workload   Research on the issue of measuring mental workload in demanding tasks has documented many cases of dissociation between the difficulty and demand estimates given by subjects, and the measures of load and demands derived from their actual task performance (Gopher and Braune 1984; Ye and Wickens 1988). The distribution of dissociations is quite symmetrical. Cases in which subjective estimates are higher than performance-based measures are as prevalent as the reverse order. Assuming that subjects made their best effort to perform the tasks, these dissociations may again imply either that subjects are not aware of the attention requirements of performance or that they invest their efforts inefficiently.

The Need for Augmented Feedback   Although within the POC paradigm subjects have been shown to produce five and seven step monotonic POCs through investing graded levels of effort, these demonstrations have depended on the use of augmented feedback. Instructions for graded priority adjustments had to be accompanied by special, on-line, augmented feedback, displaying the consequences of emphasis changes (e.g., Gopher, Brickner, and Navon 1982). Without such feedback or sufficient training, subjects were unable to perform multistep adjustments (Spitz 1986, 1988).

Attention Capture by Automatic Components In their study of controlled and automatic processes, Schneider and Fisk (1982) reported that under time-sharing conditions, task elements that were automated after prolonged training still captured attention, although controlled attention was not required to assure performance. Dedicated training efforts were needed to teach subjects to relax and release attention. This is another indication that either voluntary control or knowledge were deficient.

The Ability to Release Resources Voluntarily The problem hinted at by Schneider and Fisk (1982) has been revealed in a different form by our experiments with the POC paradigm. We have found that in many dual-task situations, subjects had as much difficulty lowering their standard of performance for the task for which priority was reduced as they had in improving performance for the task on which priority was increased. This phenomena was examined experimentally by Spitz (1986, 1988).

For example, when performing a tracking task concurrently with a letter-typing task, his subjects had difficulty complying with the requirement to lower their typing performance when the priority of this task was reduced, thereby allowing higher performance on the tracking task for which priority was increased. This phenomenon was equally powerful in difficult and easy tasks, precluding interpretations based on floor effects. Moreover, similar problems have been revealed in single-task conditions where emphasis instructions were given without any simultaneous competing task. Elsewhere we labeled this phenomena the problem of maintaining "minimal control levels" (Gopher 1982). It appears that subjects have difficulties lowering performance and reducing efforts on one task. They cannot easily release resources for the performance of another high-priority task, while still maintaining minimal control over the low-priority task.

Summary We have reviewed five types of problems and failures in the control of attention. In all types, the sources of difficulty appear to stem from insufficient knowledge about the efficiency of allocation or from deficient control capabilities. These deficits constitute clear targets for training.

Effects of Practice

Evidence concerning the contribution of practice to the improvement of attention control is scattered throughout the experimental literature. Most relevant studies have been conducted within the dual-task paradigm, using tasks whose performance posed a difficult or impossible mission for novice performers. With practice, time-sharing performance of the same tasks approximated the single-task levels of each. Typical examples are studies on the ability of subjects to read while taking oral dictations (Hirst et al. 1980), on simultaneous piano playing and reading (Allport, Antonis, and Reynolds 1972), and on performing two independent search tasks (Schneider and Fisk 1984).

All these studies have been concerned primarily with the effects of practice on time-sharing performance. Improved attention control was not among the factors considered. Practice effects were primarily attributed to a general reduction of attention costs and to improved integration and organization of the tasks. Nonetheless, it is reasonable to assume, based on the evidence presented in the previous section, that control problems contributed to subjects' initial degraded performance, and improved control was part of the effects of training.

More support for the effects of practice on improved attention control comes from the experiments of Spitz (1986, 1988) on the POC paradigm. He showed that subjects can improve their minimal control levels through practice under both single- and dual-task conditions. That is, with practice, subjects are better able to comply with a requirement to lower their standard of performance and release resources for the performance of a concurrent task under time-sharing conditions. Other direct support, using a different experimental paradigm, comes from the work of Allport and Styles (1990). They reported effects of practice on improving the efficiency of attention switching to alternate continually between two or four tasks.

In conclusion, this review of recent studies substantiates the three prerequisites for a skill-oriented approach to study attention control. We have seen positive evidence for the existence of behavioral potential, several types of control difficulties, and indications (both direct and indirect) for improvement of control with practice. The following sections review two lines of studies conducted in our laboratory to investigate training of attention control and management.

13.3   DEVELOPING THE SKILL OF ATTENTION CONTROL

Methodology and Theoretical Approach

Our approach to the training of attention control relies on observations of subjects' time-sharing performance in the POC paradigm. Mainly, their difficulties lie in establishing multiple emphasis levels and in failing to adapt comfortably to the consequences of minimal control levels. We have found numerous direct and indirect indications of deficient knowledge and attention-control problems (e.g., Gopher and North 1977; Wickens and Gopher 1977). They have led us to reason that the capability of subjects to cope with concurrent task demands can be improved if they are taken through a well-designed sequence of relative priority changes. With such experience, they may acquire better representations for the value of differential investments and improve their ability to control them. These abilities may be applied in later

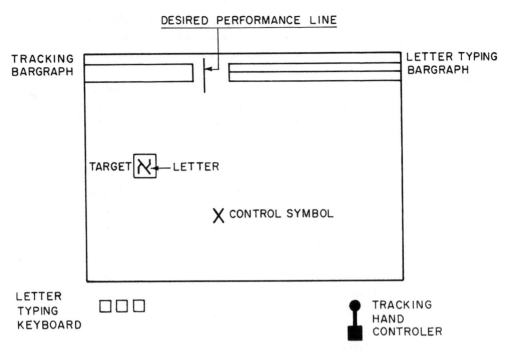

Figure 13.1 Subjects' display in concurrent performance of tracking and letter typing (from Brickner and Gopher 1981).

situations to optimize selected response strategies and enhance concurrent task performance.

A brief description of the techniques used to study these suggestions is in order before the main results of the experiments are presented. Figure 13.1 (Brickner and Gopher 1981) depicts one of our typical task situations (also see Gopher, Brickner, and Navon 1982; Gopher and Navon 1980; Navon et al. 1984). Subjects were presented with concurrent tracking and typing tasks. The tracking task required them to follow the movements of a computer-manipulated square by controlling the movement of an X symbol with a right-hand stick. For the typing task, subjects had to enter the corresponding chordic codes of letters presented within the tracking square, using a left-hand three-key keyboard. The upper portion of the screen displayed on-line dynamic feedback about their performance. Feedback indicators comprised a short vertical line representing desired performance levels, and two moving horizontal bar graphs representing actual performance levels. Desired performance was determined relative to normalized baseline performance distributions obtained for each subject. The distance between the bar graph of each task and the desired performance line reflected the momentary difference between actual and desired performance. This difference was computed continuously by subtracting the momentary error score (for tracking) and RT (for typing) from the desired score and dividing the outcome by the standard deviation of the subject's baseline distribution.

Task priorities were manipulated by moving the desired performance line from the center (equal priorities) to the left side (high priority for letter typing, low for tracking) or to the right side (high priority for tracking, low for typing). A priority level of, say, 70 percent for tracking corresponded to a level of performance that assumed the seventieth percentile in the baseline distribution of tracking performance by that subject. Instructions to put priority at 0.70 was actually a requirement to perform at a level better than the lowest 70 percent of the baseline performance levels. Other priority levels were determined in the same manner. Priority manipulations were complementary, so that when one task was increased, the other decreased, and vice versa.

Training under Variable Priorities

Brickner and Gopher (1981) investigated the effects of training under variable priorities in two dual-task experiments. In the first experiment, subjects performed concurrently the tracking and typing tasks presented in figure 13.1. In the second experiment, typing was paired with a discrete, self-paced, digit-classification task. Variable priority training was administered during two training sessions, comprising fifty three-minute trials, thirty-five of which fell under the relevant training conditions. Every trial was performed under one of five different relative priority levels (0.25, 0.35, 0.5, 0.65, 0.75).

Dual-task performance of the variable-priority group (VP) was compared with the performance of two other groups: an equal-priority (EP) group and a no-priority (NP) group. The EP group received the same augmented-feedback indicators as the VP group but performed all trials under the 0.5 equal-priority condition. The NP group received only verbal instructions with no augmented-feedback indicators. These subjects were instructed to consider both tasks as equally important, and they were given target performance levels similar to those of the EP group. Before the two training sessions, all groups had one session of practice under single-task conditions and dual-task conditions without feedback. Assignment of subjects to groups was determined at the end of this session.

The experimental results showed a large performance advantage for the variable-priority group over the other two groups. Moreover, the main differences were between the VP group and the other two groups that did not differ significantly from each other. Figures 13.2 and 13.3 depict the typing and tracking performance of the three groups on seven trials of the two training sessions. These were the trials in which the VP group performed under equal-priority instructions. For the EP and NP groups that performed only under equal-priority conditions, the plotted results are based on the trials that match in their sequential position those of the VP group. The advantage of the VP group is clear, despite the fact that unlike the other two groups, the equal-priority condition was practiced by this group in only 20 percent of the trials. The superiority of the VP group cannot be accounted for by the presence of augmented feedback. Performance levels of the EP group, which

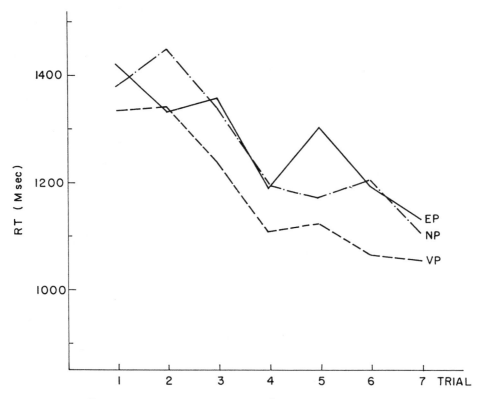

Figure 13.2 Letter-typing time (msec) during seven equal-priority trials, for each of three experimental groups (from Brickner and Gopher 1981).

was equally able to benefit from this feedback, were not significantly different from those of the NP group.

To further test the influence of variable-priority training, we gave subjects an additional (fourth) experimental session. In this session, the feedback indicators were removed from all groups. Instead, on each trial, the difficulty of the tracking and typing tasks was varied. There were three levels of difficulty for each task, and these levels were changed in a complementary manner; when the difficulty of typing increased, tracking difficulty decreased, and vice versa. There were four replications of the three commensurate difficulty combinations. Subjects were not given advance information about the change in difficulty. They were instructed to assign equal priority to tasks and to maintain a constant level of performance on both tasks during all trials. We reasoned that in order to maintain constant performance levels, subjects had to shift resources from performing the task that was made easy to performing the task whose difficulty was increased. Such adjustment had to be accomplished without prior information about the forthcoming changes, and augmented feedback was not available to help them supervise their performances.

The experimental data showed a clear superiority of the variable-priority group over the equal- and no-priority groups in maintaining a constant level of performance on both tracking and typing. Performance levels of the VP

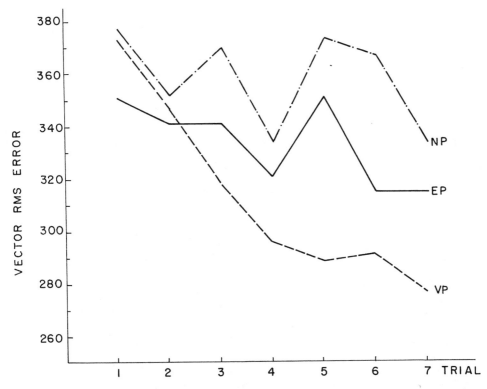

Figure 13.3 Tracking performance (RMS error) during seven equal-priority trials, for each of three experimental groups (from Brickner and Gopher 1981).

group were also much better than those of the other two groups. The EP and NP groups did not differ in their general performance levels, or in their ability to maintain performance despite the difficulty changes. The advantage of the VP group was smaller during the first two cycles of the new condition, but it gradually increased and stabilized over time (the Group × Replication interaction was highly significant).

Figure 13.4 depicts these results for the typing task; tracking errors had a very similar pattern. All groups were better and about equal in their single-task performance during this session, exhibiting similar performance slopes over the difficulty manipulation. It thus appears that the higher ability of the VP group in shifting efforts and maintaining performance under dual-task conditions does not stem simply from improved ability to perform each of the concurrent tasks. Rather, it stems from the control of behavior in the dual-task condition and the ability to detect changes and adjust efforts to cope with task demands.

A final test of the influence of variable-priority training was conducted in a fifth session. Subjects were required to pair one of the already-trained tasks with a new task of digit classification. Half of each of the original groups performed this task with tracking, the other half with typing. Additional superiority of VP training was revealed for the combination of tracking and

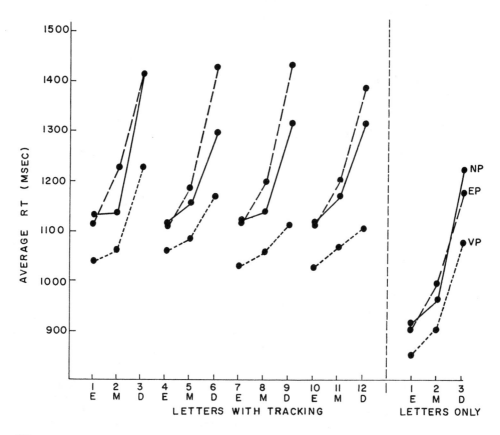

TRAINING PROCEDURE

NP NO PRIORITIES

EP EQUAL PRIORITIES

VP VARIABLE PRIORITIES

TASK DIFFICULTY

E - EASY

M - MEDIUM

D - DIFFICULT

Figure 13.4 Four replications of dual-task letter-typing time (msec) and average single-task performance levels of the three training groups, under varying difficulty conditions (from Brickner and Gopher 1981).

digit classification, but not for the pairing of typing and digit classification (though there was a trend in the expected direction). One source of the difference between tracking and typing in this condition, as well as in the earlier training sessions, may be the better inherent feedback in the typing task. When typing, subjects receive immediate feedback about the accuracy of their responses. The feedback is much more indirect and obscure in the tracking task. Of the two classes of attention-control difficulties, tracking may have been deficient in both knowledge and control, while typing was deficient mainly in control.

The general pattern of results of the first experiment was replicated in a second experiment that investigated dual-task performance of typing and digit classification. A follow-up study by Spitz (1986, 1988) supported the findings of Brickner and Gopher (1981) with a new set of tasks. It also demonstrated the importance of the performance range over which priority changes are made.

Another aspect studied by Spitz was the influence of single-task training with variable priorities on dual-task performance. He reasoned that if part of the attention-control problem is the inability of subjects to establish graded standards of performance so as to release resources, then this ability should improve even with training under single-task conditions. He had two experimental groups practice in four single-task training sessions, using the same typing task as Brickner and Gopher (1981) and a different two-dimensional tracking task (size matching; cf. Navon et al. 1984).

A variable-priority (VP) group practiced each of the individual tasks under five different emphasis levels with augmented feedback. Another fixed-priority (FP) group practiced each task only under one emphasis level with the on-line augmented feedback. Following single-task training, subjects performed in a dual-task session of tracking and typing. During the first part of this session, they performed twelve three-minute dual-task trials in which they were instructed verbally to maximize their performance, assigning equal importance to both tasks. In the second part of the session, they were asked to maintain constant performance on both tasks, while undergoing the same sequence of subtle, complementary, difficulty changes as in Brickner and Gopher (1981).

Average performance levels at the end of single-task training showed no difference between the two experimental groups. In contrast, dual-task performance levels of subjects trained under variable emphasis were significantly better on both experimental tasks, as compared with fixed-priority training. The variable-priority group was also significantly better in coping with the difficulty-change conditions and in obeying the constant-performance instructions. A final comparison of importance in this context showed that despite the magnitude and significance of these effects, the absolute dual-task performance levels and maintenance ability after single-task variable-priority training were significantly lower than those obtained by a group trained in the same tasks with variable priorities under dual-task conditions.

It can thus be concluded that under dual-task conditions, one part of the control problem stems from the inability to establish, supervise, and maintain graded control levels on each of the component tasks. Another part stems from the concurrency requirements, which account for the larger impact of variable-priority training under dual-task as compared with single-task conditions.

The knowledge and abilities that were acquired through variable-priority training have been shown to be present, influence, and benefit performance beyond the specific situation in which they are acquired. They affected performance without feedback indicators, when subtle implicit allocation adjustments were required, and when a new concurrent task was introduced. Such capabilities are the building blocks of attention strategies. They are the elements of an independent skill that can generalize and transfer beyond the specific situation in which it was originally trained.

Training through Emphasis Change on Subcomponents of Complex Tasks

During the last five years, we have continued to study the development of attention strategies in a more complex and dynamic situation, much closer to the task environments of driving, flying, and playing basketball discussed in section 13.1. The experiments at the Technion started as part of an international research collaboration conducted by twelve laboratories in four countries. It investigated the development of learning strategies to improve the behavior of trainees who practiced a highly complex and demanding computer game, which was designed jointly by the participating laboratories (Donchin, Fabiani, and Sanders 1989). The companion projects differed only in their proposed approach to training. Our project concentrated on the development of attention strategies to help performers cope with the high workload of the task.

We used an experimental game named Space Fortress, which was designed to simulate a complex and dynamic aviation environment. Players must control the movement of a spaceship on the display, fire missiles, and destroy a fortress. The fortress itself rotates, tracks, and fires at the spaceship. Other hostile elements are mines that appear every four seconds and actively chase the ship to damage it. There are two types of mines and different weapon systems to explode them. A large set of complex regulations specifies the rules of the game and the legal modes, intervals, and rates of responses. Another set of rules details point rewards and penalties. The subjects' main objective is to maximize their number of points during each three-minute game.

Figure 13.5 illustrates the game display. The game was carefully designed to include a representative sample of demand components. It combined a difficult, continuous manual-control task, several discrete and timed motor responses, visual monitoring, short-term and long-term memory load, dynamic division of attention, decision making, and resource management (Logie et al. 1989; Mane and Donchin 1989). Though comprising many dynamic elements and appearing cartoonlike to the naive eye, the game provided a rich and

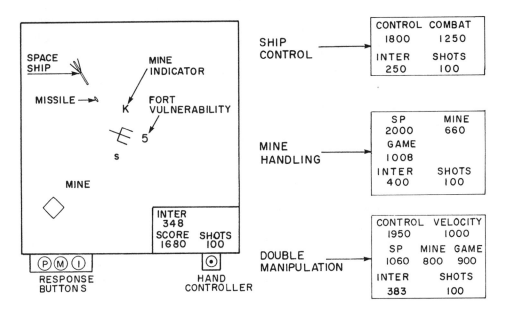

Figure 13.5 Subjects' display for the Space Fortress game. The three boxes on the right depict the special counters that were added in each of the emphasis manipulations. They replaced the information box presented for the standard game (from Gopher, Weil, and Siegal 1989).

highly controlled experimental environment in which parameters and manipulations were well specified.

Panic was the dominant first reaction of novice performers introduced to the game. Typical complaints were that "demands are too high; things happen too fast; too many events occur simultaneously; the situation is out of control." Performance scores during the first training session were all high negatives. However, with continuing experience, each control-group subject (who played the game with no special training) converged on a strategy that allowed him or her to survive and progress. The strategies differed among subjects. Still, given the algorithms and heuristics of the game, and the basic ability of subjects, the vast majority of them selected suboptimal strategies. Moreover, once a strategy was selected, it was never changed. After extensive practice, subjects just became more persistent and consistent in the application of their selected strategy. They progressed, but only within the limits and constraints that this strategy imposed (Foss et al. 1989; Gopher, Weil, and Siegal 1989).

This is yet another and more realistic manifestation of an attention-control and management problem. It emerged in the early phases of practice and continued to influence subjects' performance all the way through advanced stages of proficiency. Given the difficulty of the task, the emotional stress, and the lack of experience and skill, all of which typify the early stages of performance, it is hardly surprising that selected strategies were suboptimal. Less expected is the fact that new strategies were never explored.

Our approach to training in this difficult situation was based on leading subjects through a sequence of emphasis changes for subcomponents of the game. It embodied a direct outgrowth of the variable-priority method. Two emphasis-change manipulations were developed, following a pilot study and task analysis. One focused on the control of the ship, the other on the handling of mines (Gopher, Weil, and Siegal 1989).

When an emphasis manipulation was introduced, subjects were instructed to concentrate on the selected aspect of the task and respond to others only insofar as the selected element was not neglected. Specific feedback indicators and score counters were added to inform and reward subjects about the success of their emphasis change, but none of the physical parameters of the standard game were eliminated or changed. The only changes were in the instruction to focus attention and in the score value for different types of responses.

The emphasis changes can be construed to have created a different figure-ground relationship among game components, but they did not influence their physical properties. This approach represents a radical change from a traditional part-task training philosophy that has guided other participants in the project (e.g., Fredriksen and White 1989; Newell et al. 1989). Rather than decomposing the task into simpler elements and training subjects on isolated parts before transferring to the whole, our method created different loci of emphasis within the whole without decomposing it into parts.

Several premises provided the foundations for our approach. Through emphasis changes, subjects are guided to play the game from different perspectives. Consequently, they are forced to explore alternatives rather than to commit themselves early to a single strategy. They are led, for example, to explore the value and the costs of different strategies. Such exploration may improve their attention control, equip them with alternative response strategies to meet dynamic changes of demands, and help them achieve a better match between their basic ability and the parameters of the task. Equally important is the fact that while focusing on an emphasized task component, subjects can also evaluate their peripheral attention abilities and improve their minimal control levels. This important opportunity does not arise if parts are trained in isolation, as in the traditional part-training approach.

Four groups of subjects were trained on the Space Fortress game for ten one-hour sessions. One group served as a control and did not receive any special training. Two groups experienced a single emphasis manipulation. One was given the ship's control, the other the mine-handling manipulation. A fourth group received both manipulations in alternation. All groups experienced the standard game in the first session. Emphasis training was conducted during sessions 2 through 6. From sessions 7 to 10, all special counters were removed and all groups returned to play the standard game, in which all task components had equal importance.

Figure 13.6 presents the average game scores of the four groups during the ten sessions of training. While all groups progressed with practice, the double-manipulation group had a substantial advantage over all other groups. Single-emphasis training was better than no emphasis change (control condition). However, the effect of double manipulation was much more pronounced and larger than the additive contributions of each individual emphasis manipula-

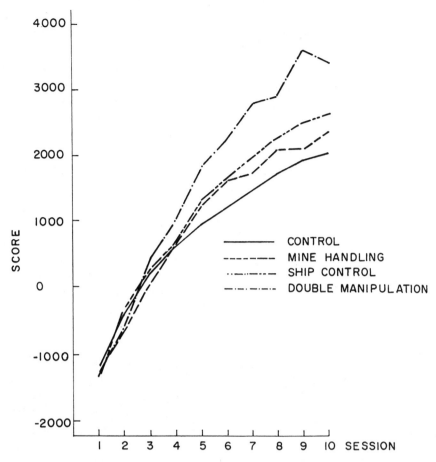

Figure 13.6 Learning curves of the four experimental groups. Performance is described in terms of total game scores. Special emphasis training was discontinued after session 6 (from Gopher, Weil, and Siegal 1989).

tion. Note also that there were no performance decrements when the special training was discontinued after the sixth session, and all auxiliary information was removed. The differences between groups continued to grow. It appears that by the seventh session subjects had already internalized their specialized knowledge and gained sufficient control to continue to improve on their own. Significant differences in the rates of progress indicated that the point of maximal difference between groups was yet to be reached.

Analysis of secondary performance indices demonstrated the differential influence of these emphasis manipulations. Thus, subjects were able to follow the instructions and shift their focus of attention. Although the overall scores of the two single-manipulation groups were not significantly different from each other, they were obtained by following different patterns of behavior. By comparison, the double-manipulation group was better able to progress in parallel on a wider range of game elements.

The Transfer of Skill

A second method of training that distinguished itself in the collaborative project was a hierarchical part-training approach developed by Fredriksen and White (1989). Based on an initial analysis of expert players in terms of game objectives, performance goals, and subgoals, they identified an inventory of twenty-seven part games. When practiced in isolation, part tasks were structured to lead subjects to gradually practice larger segments of the standard game. They were also given verbal tips and response recommedations derived from the analysis of expert behavior.

In a subsequent study, Fabiani et al. (1989) conducted an experiment to compare the relative effects of the emphasis change with the hierarchical part-training method. The experiment replicated the original ten-hour training schedules of the two methods but added five one-hour transfer sessions. During transfer, subjects were required to play the standard game while being given in each three-minute game trial one of seven secondary tasks. Secondary tasks were chosen from a battery developed in the original study by Logie et al. (1989) to investigate the load structure of the standard game. Thus, transfer sessions assessed the ability of subjects to cope with the additional load of a new concurrent task.

At the end of training, both groups were better than a control group that received no special instruction. Also, part-training subjects were significantly better than the emphasis-change group. In contrast, during transfer sessions, the effects were reversed. As during the variable priority experiments, subjects who trained under emphasis changes were better at coping with the additional secondary load, maintaining their original level of performance on the standard game and responding to secondary-task demands. Performance by the part-training group deteriorated markedly, declining on some task pairs to the control-group performance levels. The transfer superiority of emphasis-change training appeared both in proportional and absolute terms. It was largest on tasks imposing high working-memory load. A follow-up experiment showed that the advantage of the emphasis-training method persisted after fifteen additional hours of performing transfer tasks (Fabiani, Buckley, and Donchin, in press).

Recent research at the Technion employed a different set of secondary tasks and transfer conditions (Bareket 1990). This study generally replicated the results of Fabiani et al. (1989). Moreover, it showed that the advantage of the part-training method during the initial training period, which was observed in the Fabiani et al. study, completely disappeared when subjects in the emphasis-change group were given the same extra verbal tips.

One of the transfer conditions used by Bareket (1990) manipulated only the control dynamics of the ship without adding a secondary task. The control was changed from velocity to acceleration control, which required a radical change in subjects' response style. Subjects trained under emphasis change were significantly better in responding to this requirement than was the part-training group. It is clear from both studies (Fabiani et al. 1989; Bareket 1990) that emphasis-change training under high-load conditions not only improved the ability of trainees to handle the specific task requirements, but also prepared them more generally to handle additional and new demands, and to reorganize an already acquired skill. These cases all imply reconfiguration of attention-control strategies.

Finally, perhaps the most daring test of our hypotheses has been conducted over the last three years at the flight-training school of the Israeli Airforce (Gopher et al. 1988). Problems of attention division, attention control, and coping with the load of a flight task have been a frequently cited cause of failure and washout from flight training. To address this difficulty, we gave a group of thirty-three flight cadets ten hours of emphasis-change training on a slightly modified version of Space Fortress. These modifications followed an analysis of the flight-training program to improve the face validity and organization of the game display. Game training was administered after the completion of a four-month period of ground school and flight training on a light aircraft, but before moving to a high-performance jet trainer.

The effects of game training were evaluated in eight subsequent test flights. They were compared with the flight performance of a matched control group of flight cadets having no game experience. The eight flights were part of the regular training program and a major decision point. At the end of this period, trainees either dropped out or were assigned to specialty programs (fighter, helicopter, or transport planes). Control and experimental subjects were matched by school psychologists based on their initial-selection battery scores and on flight performance in the light aircraft. The experimenters did not know subjects' initial ability scores. The whole project was presented to the subjects and instructor pilots as a study of individual differences, directed at developing a computerized test battery for flight selection. The experimental group comprised only a small part of two consecutive classes, but the flight instructors completed special evaluation forms for all trainees in both classes.

Flight performance scores showed large and significant advantages for trainees who received emphasis-change game training. As in the laboratory experiments, the differences between experimental and control groups increased across flights and were largest on the eighth flight. The average flight score of the experimental group was increased from 6 to 7, which represents a 30 percent increase in the probability of program completion. The advantage of game-trained subjects was largest in high-load maneuvers that required integration of several elements. A year and a half later, the actual percentage of graduates in the experimental group was twice as high as in the control group.

When considering the significance of these results, it is important to recognize certain key points. Although the game and flight situations have been construed to impose similar demands and to promote the development of similar skill components, the physical fidelity of the game is very low, and the general load of flight is higher by an order of magnitude. The game is not a flight simulator. At best, it constitutes a specific skill trainer. Nonetheless, the lessons learned and the skills acquired while playing the game helped trainees to cope with the demands of flight, influencing their long-term approach to the acquisition of this complex and demanding skill.

13.4 CONCLUDING REMARKS

Our experiments have shown that while the potential to control attention and develop attention strategies exists, there are many difficulties and failures in realizing this potential when subjects have to cope with high-load, attention-demanding tasks. Nevertheless, through directed experience with different attention strategies, both task performance and attention control improve. Furthermore, these acquired capabilities and execution skills can be generalized; they may transfer to new situations and task demands, influencing the behavior of performers over extended time periods.

While ample evidence documents the effects and trainability of attention-management skills, the basic theoretical issues and empirical questions about them remained unresolved. We have proposed a working definition of attention strategies and a method for their development and manipulation, but this is a long way from uncovering the elements and structure of strategies, the modes in which they are represented in memory, and the linkage between them and the other skill components of a given task. In an earlier paper (Gopher, Weil, and Siegel 1989), we proposed that the response schemas associated with proficient behavior are the automated "hard-wired" products of early attention strategies.

To follow this line of thinking, attention strategies, previously defined as vectors of differential attention biases, may be alternately represented as vectors that combine performance objectives for elements of a complex task, in the service of a higher-level goal. Structurally, they can be construed as a set of production rules with attached gains and probability values binding together the elements of a complex task for the attainment of a specific objective. This suggestion may provide a framework with which to describe the process of moving from controlled strategies to automated schemas, consistent with contemporary views of skill training (Anderson 1981). However, even if the present view is accepted, we still lack knowledge about the building blocks and mechanisms that represent strategies and about the forces that drive them.

One approach toward closing this gap would be to further investigate what special propensity is acquired and generalized when subjects are trained under variable rather than fixed-priority conditions. Our results clearly demonstrate that the benifit of variable-priority training yields more than just an improved ability to perform the elements of a trained task. There is an additional and more general ability factor that develops independently of the specific factors governing task performance. Such capability may involve higher-level coordination and control functions that execute strategies and supervise behavior (e.g., Kahneman 1973; Logan 1985). Another possibility is that variable-priority training influences the form in which skill elements are organized and represented in memory, allowing greater flexibility in the incorporation of new demands or reconfiguration of old elements.

Our present state of knowledge does not yet favor one of these alternatives over the other. However, they may be differentiated further through a better understanding of the context in which the acquired skill factors generalize. The success of the computer game training in flight school attests to the crucial importance of this research. We have already noted the low physical fidelity between the game trainer and the flight task, and the large gap between the two in complexity and task demands. What then could have been the commonalities that paved the way for their inclusion in our studies?

Part of the answer to this question may stem from the fact that both airplane piloting and our computer game training involved a difficult manual-control component, several discrete motor responses, visual orientation and scanning, long- and short-term memory load, decision making, and resource management, all interacting dynamically under high time pressure. These components are based on an analysis in terms of crude and generic constructs adopted from the information-processing literature (e.g., Gopher and Sanders 1984; Wickens 1984). Nonetheless, this framework may provide sufficient clarity and constraints to enable a valid comparative analysis of task demands. If so, then the prospects for human-performance models based on these constructs are brighter than expected. This framework may also define a viable manipulation environment for studying the architecture and generality of attention-control skills.

With an eye on growing needs for theoretical efforts to model the processing and response limitations of the human processing system, our experiments underscore the importance of considering attention-control problems as a new and major contributing source of performance decrements under time-sharing conditions. Previous models of attention control have contrasted data and resource limitations (Norman and Bobrow 1975), and resource scarcity versus output conflict (Navon and Gopher 1979). Some performance deficits previously associated with one or more of these factors should be reexamined to assess the likelihood of deficient control. The strong influence of training on the control of attention should also concern us from a methodological viewpoint. Instructions to subjects and experimental procedures should take into consideration more carefully the possible influence of attention strategies and control problems.

Finally, the relationship between attention control and consciousness requires examination. We construe attention strategies to be driven by a voluntary intent, but how many of these strategies, bits of knowledge, and control efforts are open to awareness or supervised consciously? The study of attention strategies along the lines proposed in this chapter may constitute a new and powerful vehicle for the study of the long-sought, but yet missing, formal link between consciousness and behavior. In contemporary scientific zeitgeist, so heavily biased towards connectionist and neural network modeling of bottom-up, emerging, and self-organizing patterns of behavior (Rumelhart and McClelland 1986; McClelland and Rumelhart 1986), a systematic study of the power, properties, and operation rules of the top-down central executive may balance our prespective. Despite the fact that the notion of a central executive has a key position in many contemporary models of the human processing system, there has been little direct research on it. The present line of studies is a modest contribution in this direction.

NOTE

The preparation of this manuscript and our recent work in this area were supported by a grant from NASA, Ames Research Center.

REFERENCES

Allport, D. A., Antonis, B., and Reynolds, P. (1972). On the division of attention: A disproof of the single-channel hypothesis. *Journal of Experimental Psychology, 24,* 225–235.

Allport, D. A., and Styles, E. A. (1990). Multiple executive functions, multiple resources? Experiments in shifting attentional control of tasks. Unpublished manuscript.

Anderson, J. R. (1981). *Cognitive skills and their acquisition.* Hillsdale, NJ: Lawrence Erlbaum Associates.

Bareket, T. (1990). The comparative effects of different training methods on the acquisition and transfer of complex skills. Master's thesis, Faculty of Industrial Engineering and Management, Technion, Haifa, Israel.

Brickner, M., and Gopher, D. (1981). Improving time-sharing performance by enhancing voluntary control on processing resources. Research Report, Technion, Research Centre for Work Safety and Human Engineering, HEIS-81-3, February.

Castiliano, U., and Umiltà, C. (1990). Size of attentional focus and efficiency of processing. *Acta Psychologica, 73,* 195–209.

Donchin, E., Fabiani, M., and Sanders, A. (Eds.) (1989). The learning strategies program: An examination of the strategies of skill acquisition. *Acta Psychologica, 71,* 1–312.

Egeth, H. (1977). Attention and preattention. In G. H. Bower (Ed.). *The Psychology of learning and motivation,* Vol. 11, 277–320.

Ericksen, C. W., and St. James, J. D. (1986). Visual attention within and around the field of focal attention: A zoom lens model. *Perception and Psychophysics, 40,* 225–240.

Fabiani, M., Buckley, J., Gratton, G., Coles, M., and Donchin, E. (1989). The training of complex task performance. *Acta Psychologica, 71,* 259–300.

Fabiani M., Buckley, J., and Donchin, E. (N.d.). The effect of extended training on the performance of complex tasks. In press.

Foss, M. A., Fabiani, M., Mane, A., and Donchin, E. (1989). Unsupervised practice: The performance of the control group. *Acta Psychologica, 71,* 23–52.

Fredriksen, J. R., and White, B. Y. (1989). An approach to training based upon principal-task decomposition. *Acta Psychologica, 71,* 89–146.

Gopher, D. (1981). Performance tradeoffs under time-sharing conditions: The ability of human operators to release resources by lowering their standards of performance. In *Proceedings of the 1981 International Conference on Cybernetics and Society,* 609–613. Atlanta, GA.

Gopher, D. (1982). A selective attention test as a predictor of success in flight training. *Human Factors, 24,* 173–183.

Gopher, D. (1990). Dual-tasks. In N. Eysenk (Ed.), *The Blackwell Dictionary of Cognitive Psychology*, 23–28. Oxford: Basil-Blackwell.

Gopher, D., and Braune, R. (1984). On the psychophysics of workload: Why bother with subjective measures. *Human Factors, 26*, 519–532.

Gopher, D., Brickner, M., and Navon, D. (1982). Different difficulty manipulations interact differently with task emphasis: Evidence for multiple resources. *Journal of Experimental Psychology: Human Perception and Performance, 8*, 146–157.

Gopher, D., and Donchin, E. (1986). Workload: An examination of the concept. In K. Boff and L. Kaufman (Eds.), *Handbook of human perception and performance*, 1–49. New York: John Wiley.

Gopher, D., and Kahneman, D. (1971). Individual differences in attention and the prediction of flight criteria. *Perceptual and Motor Skills, 33*, 1335–1342.

Gopher, D., and Navon, D. (1980). How is performance limited: Testing the notion of central capacity. *Acta Psychologica, 46*, 161–180.

Gopher, D., and North, R. N. (1977). Manipulating the conditions of training in time-sharing performance. *Human Factors, 19*, 583–593.

Gopher, D., and Sanders, A. F. (1984). S-Oh-R: Oh stages! Oh resources. In W. Printz and A. F. Sanders (Eds.), *Cognition and motor processes*, 231–254. Berlin: Springer-Verlag.

Gopher, D., Weil, M., Bareket, T., and Caspi, S. (1988). Fidelity of task structure as a guiding principle in the development of skill trainers based upon complex computer games. In *Proceedings of the 32nd Annual Meeting of the Human Factors Society*, 1266–1270. Anaheim, CA.

Gopher, D., Weil, M., and Siegel, D. (1989). Practice under changing priorities: An approach to training of complex skills. *Acta Psychologica, 71*, 147–179.

Hirst, W., Spelke, E. S., Reaves, C. C., Caharack, G., and Neisser, U. (1980). Dividing attention without alternation or automaticity. *Journal of Experimental Psychology: General, 109*, 98–117.

Jonides, J. (1983). Further towards a model of the mind's eye-movements. *Bulletin of The Psychonomic Society, 21*, 247–250.

Kahneman, D. (1973). *Attention and Effort*. Englewood Cliffs, NJ: Prentice-Hall.

Kahneman, D., Ben Ishai, R., and Lotan, M. (1973). Relation of a test of attention to road accidents. *Journal of Applied Psychology, 58*, 113–115.

Kahneman, D., and Treisman, A. (1984). Changing views of attention and automaticity. In R. Parasuraman and D. Davis (Eds.), *Varieties of attention*, 29–63. Orlando, FL: Academic Press.

Logan, G. D. (1985). Executive control of thought and action. *Acta Psychologica, 60*, 193–210.

Logie, R., Baddeley, A., Mane, A., Donchin, E., and Sheptak, R. (1989). Working memory in the acquisition of complex cognitive skills. *Acta Psychologica, 71*, 53–88.

Mane, A., and Donchin, E. (1989). The space fortress game. *Acta Psychologica, 71*, 17–22.

McClelland, J. L., and Rumelhart, D. E., (Eds). (1986). *Parallel Distributed Processing: Explorations in the microstructure of cognition. Vol. 2: Applications*. Cambridge, MA: Bradford Books/MIT Press.

Navon, D., and Gopher, D. (1979). On the economy of the human processing system. *Psychological Review, 86*, 214–253.

Navon, D., Gopher, D., Chillag, M., and Spitz, G. (1984). On separability of and interference between tracking dimensions in dual-axis tracking. *Journal of Motor Behavior, 16*, 364–392.

Newell, K. M., Carlton, M. J., Fisher, A. T., and Rutter, B. G. (1989). Whole-part training in the acquisition of a complex perceptual-motor skill. *Acta Psychologica, 71*, 197–216.

Norman, D. A., and Bobrow, D. J. (1975). On data limited and resource limited processes. *Cognitive Psychology, 7,* 44–64.

Norman, D. A., and Shallice, T. (1981). Attention to action: Willed and automatic control of behavior. In M. Lansman and E. Hunt (Eds.), *Proceedings of the Lake Wilderness Attention Conference.* N-25, Department of Psychology, University of Washington, Seattle, WA.

North, R. A., and Gopher, D. (1976). Measures of attention as predictors of flight performance, *Human Factors, 18,* 1–14.

Posner, M. I., and Rothbart, M. K. (1986). The concept of energy in psychological theory. In R. J. Hockey, A. W. Gaillard, and M. G. H. Coles (Eds.). *Energetics and human information processing,* 23–42. *Dordrecht: Martinus* Nijhoff Publishers.

Posner, M. I., Snyder, C. R. R., and Davidson, B. J. (1980). Attention and the detection of signals. *Journal of Experimental Psychology: General, 109,* 160–174.

Rumelhart, D. E., and McClelland, J. L. (Eds.) (1986). *Parallel Distributed Processing: Explorations in the microstructure of cognition. Vol. I: Foundations.* Cambridge. MA: Bradford Books/MIT Press.

Schneider, W., and Fisk, A. D. (1982). Dual task automatic and control processing: Can it be done without cost? *Journal of Experimental psychology: Learning, Memory, and Cognition, 8,* 261–278.

Schneider, W., and Fisk, A. D. (1984). Automatic category search and its transfer. *Journal of Experimental Psychology: Learning, Memory, and Cognition, 10,* 1–13.

Sperling, G., and Melchner, M. J. (1978). The attention operating characteristic: Some examples from visual search. *Science, 202,* 315–318.

Spitz, G. (1986). Voluntary control of mental resource allocation. Ph.D. diss., Faculty of Industrial Engineering and Management, Technion, Haifa, Israel.

Spitz, G. (1988). Flexibility in resource allocation and the performance of time-sharing tasks. (1988). *Proceedings of the 32nd Annual Meeting of the Human Factors Society,* 1466–1469. Anaheim, CA.

Strayer, D. L., and Kramer, A. F. (1990). Attentional requirements of automatic and controlled processing. *Journal of Experimental Psychology: Learning, Memory and Cognition, 16,* 291–304.

Wickens, C. D. (1980). The structure of attentional resources. In R. S. Nickerson (Ed.), *Attention and Performance VIII,* 239–257. Hillsdale, NJ: Lawrence Erlbaum Associates.

Wickens, C. D. (1984). Processing resources in attention. In R. Parasuraman and D. R. Davis (Eds.), *Varieties of Attention.* Orlando, FL: Academic Press.

Wickens, C. D., and Gopher, D. (1977). Control theory measures of tracking as indices attention allocation strategies. *Human Factors, 19,* 349–365.

Ye, Y. Y., and Wickens, C. D. (1988). Dissociation of performance and subjective measures of workload. *Human Factors, 30,* 111–120.

14 The Control of Skilled Behavior: Learning, Intelligence, and Distraction

John Duncan, Phyllis Williams, Ian Nimmo-Smith, and Ivan Brown

This chapter concerns the relationship between two rather different phenomena: "general intelligence" or Spearman's *g*, and "divided-attention decrement" or the conflict that can occur between concurrent tasks. We develop a method to ask how closely these two are related and apply it to study a familiar skill, driving a car in traffic.

When any battery of performance tests is given to a broad sample of people, it will usually be found that all or nearly all of the resulting (between-test) correlations are positive: No matter how weakly, better performance on one test is associated with better performance on another. As pointed out by Spearman (1927), one obvious interpretation is that most or all performance scores receive a contribution from some "general" or *g* factor. In modern terms, we might think of this as a particular psychological system making at least some contribution to the control of many different activities. Thus even very dissimilar tasks may be expected to show some positive correlation, reflecting their shared reliance on the *g* factor.

Assuming this model, it is easy to show how strongly any particular score correlates with *g*. Roughly speaking, a score's *g* correlation reflects its average correlation with all other scores in the matrix (Spearman 1927). It turns out that the highest *g* correlations belong to typical "intelligence tests" like Raven's Matrices or the WAIS.

While the experimental method is very different, similar conclusions are suggested by the study of divided attention. Interference between concurrent tasks is greatest when they share obvious content, for example, when they share modality of input (Treisman and Davies 1973) or output (McLeod 1977). (Similarly the correlation between two tests increases with shared content, presumably reflecting shared reliance on specific knowledge sources, processing systems, etc.) Some interference generally remains, however, even when concurrent tasks appear very dissimilar (e.g., McLeod 1977; McLeod and Posner 1984). Again one interpretation is that interference between very dissimilar tasks might reflect shared demands on some rather general-purpose psychological system, important in controlling many different kinds of activity (Broadbent 1958; Kahneman 1973). An obvious hypothesis, raised already by Spearman (1927) himself, is that this might be the same system (or set of systems) that is reflected in g. To keep it distinct from Spearman's g proper, we shall refer to this as the *common g system* hypothesis.

Perhaps the best evidence for this hypothesis comes from the effects of practice. At least if a task is simple and consistent, practice tends to reduce its correlation with g (e.g., Ackerman 1988; for a counterexample with a more complex task, see Woodrow 1939). Practice tends also to reduce interference between concurrent tasks (e.g., James 1890; Schneider and Shiffrin, 1977). While most experimental studies of this effect have used concurrent tasks with much shared content, everyday experience strongly suggests the same conclusion even for quite dissimilar activities.

Beyond this direct suggestion of a link between g correlations and dual-task decrements, practice also provides a clue to the role any common g system might play in the control of behavior. Commonly, "executive" or "supervisory" functions have been implicated in both Spearman's g (e.g., Snow and Lohman 1984) and dual-task interference (e.g., Baddeley 1986; McLeod 1977). While their precise function has proved hard to define, there is widespread agreement in outline over certain changes in the way that behavior is controlled with increasing practice. Early in practice, there is substantial problem solving, or search through the space of possible lines of action (the problem space) (see Newell and Simon 1972) for the ideal solution to task demands. Late in practice, large sequences of behavior are combined into "units" or "chunks"; the parts are interconnected such that initiating a sequence (or receiving an appropriate triggering input) tends automatically to bring forth the whole (Bryan and Harter 1899; James 1890; Laird, Newell, and Rosenbloom 1987; Schneider and Shiffrin 1977), allowing more and more complex behavior to arise through the hierarchical combination of increasingly large and complex familiar parts. If practice diminishes the importance of a general-purpose behavioral control system, it seems likely that this system is especially significant in the early process of search through the problem space, or weighing alternative lines of action in the absence of a single dominant path (Duncan 1990; Norman and Shallice 1980).

Interestingly, consistent practice may also diminish the effects of damage to the frontal lobes of the brain (e.g., Walsh 1978), which have again been said to concern executive or supervisory functions (Luria 1966; Norman and Shallice 1980). It is tempting to suggest that here too we are dealing with impairment of a common g system (Duncan 1990).

14.1 THE GENERAL METHOD

It has sometimes been suggested that g correlations increase under dual-task conditions (e.g., Stankov 1983). While at first sight this might be taken to support the common g system hypothesis, on reflection it is really not clear that the hypothesis makes any such prediction. Consider that the (between-subject) variance of any performance score will receive contributions from several different psychological sources, and that the proportion of variance attributable to g is reflected in the squared g correlation. Certainly competition for the common *g* system predicts that performance will *decline* under dual-task conditions, but does this mean that individual differences in *g* should make a greater proportional contribution to total between-subject variance? The question cannot be answered without a detailed theory of how the variance of some performance score arises from the combined contributions of its different psychological components.

The real prediction of the common *g* system hypothesis concerns the relationship between *single-task g* correlations and *dual-task* performance decrements. In simple terms, a task that is very reliant on the common *g* system should show both a strong *g* correlation and a substantial decrement when paired with a (dissimilar) concurrent task; while a task that is rather independent of this system should show neither. Tasks or skills that correlate strongly with *g* should also be those most sensitive to dual-task interference.

To put the prediction more formally, we need only recall that the correlation[1] coefficient *r* is the slope of the best-fitting straight line relating z-scores on two variables. Thus the correlation of any variable *X* with *g* indicates the expected change in *X* per unit change in *g* (both expressed as z-scores). If we assume (or accept as an approximation) that the effect of a concurrent task can be modeled as a simple reduction in *g*, then across different tasks or skill measures, dual-task decrements expressed as z-scores should be exactly proportional to *g* correlations.

While the prediction follows clearly from the hypothesis of a common *g* system, we should also note the classical alternative, proposed originally by Thomson (see, e.g., Thomson 1951). Though correlations in a matrix are generally positive, there may be no single *g* factor contributing somewhat to all scores. A different model is that each score receives a contribution from many independent psychological sources or variables (e.g., processing systems); to the extent that two scores receive contributions from the same variables, they will show a positive correlation, but such positive correlations reflect chance overlap in the sets of variables sampled by pairs of tests, not any single variable contributing to all of them. Similarly for dual-task interference, even when tasks on the surface appear "dissimilar," there may be many unsuspected sources of local conflict between them. In this model, there would be no general-purpose psychological system responsible for many different cases of interference between apparently "dissimilar" pairs of tasks. Instead, interference between any particular pair of tasks would reflect the set (perhaps large) of particular special-purpose processing systems they happened to share (Allport 1980).

According to this theory, a test's apparent correlation with *g* reflects how *broadly* it samples the total population of internal variables or processing systems (Thomson 1951). Tests sampling more variables have higher measured *g* correlations. Would a test sampling more processing systems also be expected to show a greater dual-task decrement? Suppose that in total there are *p* separate processing systems, with any one task receiving a contribution from some subset of size *n*. The *probability* of interference from a concurrent task (the probability of shared processing systems) will obviously be a direct function of n. While the average *size* of such interference (expressed as a z-score) depends on the exact way that different systems combine to produce the measured total score, there are certainly plausible models predicting greater average interference as n increases. In the Appendix, this prediction is derived from a simple linear model; there are many more complex (and plausible) cases that could give the same result. For example, the more separate processing systems there are to coordinate in a task, the more serious might be the consequences of disturbing any particular one. Though the hypothesis of a common g system is particularly clear in predicting a close relationship between g correlations and dual-task decrements, we should note that it is not unique in this prediction.

14.2 SPECIFICITY AFTER PRACTICE

In principle, the predicted relationship between g correlations and dual-task decrements should hold for any set of performance scores. We chose to use the component skills of a familiar task—driving a car in traffic. The choice allows us to address a second issue concerning practice and skill.

According to the view outlined above, the role of practice is in part to build a novel control structure for each familiar skill, formed by linking together its parts into new "chunks" or "units." As practice progresses, accordingly, the control of behavior is gradually transferred from the common g system to a new structure of chunks that learning creates. Since such a novel control structure must be entirely specific to the particular skill that is learned, individual differences in skill might become increasing dependent on specific learning as practice progresses, rather than on any preexisting "ability" or characteristic. Not only should we observe reduced g correlations, but also increasing independence from all other psychological measures. The same conclusion follows from the familiar idea that experts and novices in domains such as computer programming and chess differ mainly in the extensive but domain-specific knowledge that experts acquire (Lesgold 1984).

The issue is important both theoretically and practically. Theoretically, the study of individual differences has often been seen as an attempt to map out the "geography" of mental abilities (Cattell 1971)—namely, to discover some ultimate taxonomy of mental variables along which people can differ. This effort is misguided if new dimensions of individual differences are created each time a new task is learned (Buss 1973). In practical terms, selection tests administered before a skill is trained are unlikely to be useful if eventual performance depends almost entirely on the new learning that subsequently takes place (Reynolds 1952).

In fact, it has often been suggested that practicing simple laboratory skills produces increasingly task-specific individual differences (Fleishman and Hempel 1955; Reynolds 1952). Recently, however, both new findings and reanalyses of old data have cast considerable doubt on this conclusion (Ackerman 1987, 1988). In our study, we examine the specificity of skills acquired over many years in the learning conditions of the outside world.

14.3 OUTLINE OF THE STUDY

The experiment involved an instrumented car driven over a fixed test route under reasonably normal conditions. Subjects were all drivers with many years of experience. The route was chosen to allow reliable measurement of twelve separate components of driving skill, including aspects of car control, scanning, and setting a safety margin. A group of 90 normal drivers took part in the study of individual differences. In addition to driving the test route, they were given a set of laboratory tasks including a standard test of g. Dual-task decrements were assessed in a separate group of 24 drivers. They drove the test route twice, once with and once without a concurrent task.

Various considerations guided our choice of which driving skills to assess. Though we wished to include standard perceptual-motor skills such as steering and gear changing, these are perhaps not the most important in producing a safe driving style (Näätänen and Summala 1976). Scanning patterns—in particular, mirror checking—and safety margin were chosen on the basis of several lines of evidence relating them to accident avoidance (Quenault 1967; Staughton and Storie 1977).

For the dual-task study, we needed a secondary task that shares no obvious content with driving but should make significant demands on a common g system. Following our previous reasoning, this suggests a task that cannot easily be learned as a set of consistent behavioral stereotypes. The task we chose was Baddeley's (1986) random letter generation. The subject is simply asked to generate letter names in random order, speaking them into a tape recorder in time with a metronome. The task has only auditory input and vocal output, but despite its simplicity, it is subjectively taxing because, by definition, no regular or familiar pattern of behavior is appropriate.

Since in driving we were measuring fairly simple, consistent components of a very familiar skill, we expected both g correlations and dual-task decrements to be modest. The main prediction, however, was that across driving skills, the profiles of g correlation and dual-task decrement should be in close agreement. It should be emphasized at the outset that the data we present provide only a preliminary test of the common g system hypothesis. Various difficulties associated with the use of measures from a real skill will be considered later. At the same time, some benefits will also emerge.

14.4 METHOD

The Experimental Car

The experiment was conducted in a new Vauxhall Astra 1600L with manual gear change. Full details of instrumentation appear in Duncan, Williams, and Brown (1991). Our goal was to minimize disturbance to the driver while measuring the chosen range of driving skills.

Movements of steering wheel, pedals, and gearstick were recorded on magnetic tape, using electronic sensors built onto the corresponding control linkages in the engine compartment. Each movement was recorded as a discrete event, along with its time of occurrence to the nearest msec. In the main body of the car, the front passenger seat was replaced by a small table. Above the table was a still camera, aimed through the windshield at the road ahead. Out of sight beneath the table was a video camera, aimed through a hole cut in the bottom of the passenger door at the passing roadside. In the rear sat the experimenter, giving directions and taking notes. By watching the driver's eyes in the rearview mirror, she was able to detect selected gross deviations of gaze (Quenault 1967), which she registered by pressing a button. Each button press was recorded on magnetic tape, along with the continuous record of control movements, and also lit a small lamp in the field of view of the video camera.

The Test Route

Car control skills and mirror use were assessed on a 2.8-km urban circuit, consisting simply of driving four times counterclockwise round the block in a quiet, residential area. (Recall that in Britain, *left* turns are made without crossing the line of oncoming traffic.) Approaches to roundabouts (rotaries) and overtaking (passing) were assessed on a 61-km rural circuit, including both two-lane roads and a six-lane freeway. The whole was preceded by a 9.6-km practice drive to familiarize the subject with the vehicle.

The route was chosen to balance the merits of road and track testing. While real driving conditions were preserved, traffic density was light to medium, so that all drivers could be expected to undertake much the same maneuvers in much the same way. Instructions emphasized that subjects should try to drive in their usual manner, not as they would in a test.

Measures of Component Skills

Six of our skill measures concerned scanning, five concerned car control, and one concerned safety margins (see table 14.1). The experiment was designed so that each skill would be assessed on multiple occasions, allowing direct estimates of within-subject reliability. Where appropriate, we used detailed criteria for excluding instances of a maneuver that could have been distorted by unpredictable traffic events. For a more complete description and justification of each measure, see Duncan, Williams, and Brown (1991).

Mirror Checking: Urban Circuit   The first three measures concerned mirror use on the urban circuit. The first was simply the total number of mirror checks recorded during the four laps. The second was the probability of at least one check during the 5 seconds before entering a corner (16 occurrences). The third was a more complex measure designed to reflect modulation of the overall checking rate by relevant driving events. The most appropriate period for mirror checking was defined as the 5 seconds preceding any change of direction, use of the brake, or gear change, and the modulation index was defined

Table 14.1 Measures of Driving Skills, with Mean Scores and Standard Deviations (in parentheses) from the Main Driver Sample ($N = 90$)

	Mean	(s.d.)
Scanning patterns		
1 Mirror checks: Total on urban circuit	16.5	(10.9)
2 Mirror checks: Probability at intersection	.41	(.24)
3 Mirror checks: Modulation index	.79	(.41)
4 Roundabouts: Right looks per approach	2.86	(.65)
5 Overtake pass phase: Probability of left look	.20	(.23)
6 Overtake pull-in phase: Probability of rear look	.91	(.18)
Car control		
7 Intersections: Time of braking on entry (sec)	4.65	(.89)
8 Intersections: Time of acceleration on exit (sec)	1.28	(.53)
9 Intersections: Divergence from curb (distance ratio)	1.10	(.24)
10 Intersections: Consistency of path (cm)	11.1	(3.4)
11 Gear changing: Duration of movement (sec)	.573	(.101)
Safety margin		
12 Overtakes: Following distance (m)	64.0	(17.4)

as follows:

$$\frac{\text{checks/sec during less appropriate periods}}{\text{total checks/sec}}$$

The closer the score to zero, the more clearly was mirror use confined to the most appropriate times.

Roundabouts: Rightward Looks Approach to a roundabout typically requires several anticipatory fixations to the right, as the driver judges how best to merge into the approaching traffic. Such fixations were assessed at nine roundabouts. The experimenter pressed her button each time a rightward look was detected, and all such looks in the range 100–20m before entering the roundabout were later counted from the video record of the approach. The score was the mean number of looks per roundabout.

Overtakes The last two scanning measures were made during overtaking on the freeway. Following the usual convention in Britain, drivers were asked to remain in the inner lane except when passing. Both scanning measures concerned monitoring the behavior of the vehicle being overtaken, expressed as the probabilities of (a) a look (left) towards that vehicle while the test car was passing, and (b) a look back (either in the mirror or over the shoulder) before returning to the inner lane.

Cornering: Urban Circuit The next four measures, taken on the urban circuit, concerned early braking heading into an intersection, prompt acceleration heading away, and steering smoothly around. Early braking (an aspect of anticipation) was measured simply as the mean interval between the midpoint of the bend (maximum steering angle) and the preceding onset of braking. Prompt acceleration was measured by the mean interval between the midpoint of the bend and the first subsequent depression of the accelerator. These two measures were taken only at the two intersections at which the driver turned from a major to a minor road, so that there was no need to give way to other traffic. There were two measures of steering. A characteristic of novices is understeering, or divergence from the curb while progressing around a bend (Duncan, Williams, and Brown 1991). From the video record, we measured distance from the curb at 3 points round each intersection on the urban circuit, one 7.7 m before the midpoint, one at the midpoint, one 7.7 m after. Based on our novice data, understeering was measured by the ratio of mean distance at the second and third measurement points over mean distance at the first. Finally, we measured *consistency* of steering path across occasions, since consistency is one of the hallmarks of skill. Four laps of the urban circuit gave four distance measurements for each of 12 measurement points (4 intersections × 3 points/intersection). Across-lap standard deviations were calculated separately for each point, and then averaged to give the overall consistency score.

Gear Changing   Speed of movement in gear changing was measured by the interval between leaving the initial gear and entering the target gear. Again using data from the urban circuit, mean intervals were calculated for changes from second to third and from third to second gear, and the overall score was the mean of the two means. Rapid gear changing is of course especially important in changing up, since one wishes to minimize the accompanying period of deceleration.

Overtakes: Following Distance   The last measure concerned one aspect of safety margins. Each time the driver pulled out to overtake another vehicle on the freeway, the experimenter took a still photograph of the road ahead and noted the current speed. Distance from the vehicle ahead (following distance) was later calculated from the photograph and corrected to a speed of 70 mph (the speed limit), using the average within-subject regression of distance on speed. (Results using uncorrected following distances were very similar.)

Individual-Differences Study

The individual-differences study involved 90 normal drivers, 53 of whom were women. They were obtained through employment centers, with the requirement that they should have held a full driving license for at least five years. The mean age was 41 years (range 29–57), and the mean time of holding a license was 20 years (range 5–38).

Subjects attended for two sessions of $1\frac{1}{2}$ to 2 hours each. One session was devoted to the test drive; subjects also completed a questionnaire concerning driving experience, annual mileage, and accident history. The second session was devoted to laboratory tests. Our main measure of g was Cattell's Culture Fair Test (Institute for Personality and Ability Testing 1959; Scale 2, Form A), which has four timed sets of problems (series completions, odd-man-out, matrices, topology) based on geometric figures. As a check on this, however, we took advantage of Spearman's (1927) "indifference of the indicator": No matter what their particular content, average performance on *any* broad set of tasks should give a reasonable approximation to *g*. We used seven tasks:

National adult reading test (Nelson 1982): Pronouncing irregularly spelled words.

Group embedded figures test (Witkin et al. 1971): Finding target shapes camouflaged by the dominant perceptual organization of the background.

Random letter generation: Random letters were generated for 4 minutes, at a rate of 40/min in time with a metronome. Various scores of nonrandomness give similar results (Baddeley 1966); one strong tendency is to generate letters in alphabetical order, and we chose a performance score reflecting this (the proportion of all digrams generated that were in strict alphabetical order). (In a control study, 25 subjects were asked to speak a single letter as fast as possible in response to one spoken by the experimenter. They were told that any letter would do, but that they must not choose it until hearing the stimulus letter. Thirteen out of 25 responses were the next letter after the stimulus in the alphabet.)

Matching (2 forms): One form required a standard physical-identity match between two uppercase letters (Posner and Mitchell 1967). In the other, subjects decided which of a set of geometric figures differed from the others according to a specified one of five possible attributes (e.g., shape, texture). In both cases, responses were manual, and the score was mean reaction time (RT) of correct responses.

Monitoring (2 forms): Rapidly presented streams of visual stimuli were monitored for the presence of occasional targets. In one case, there was a single stream of words, and the score was simply the proportion of correct target (first name) detections. In the other case, there were two separate streams of mixed letters and digits, and the emphasis was on switching from one stream to the other on receipt of a symbolic cue (cf. Gopher and Kahneman 1971).

Scores on each of the seven tasks were transformed to *z*-scores, then reflected where necessary so that lower scores always indicated better performance. The mean of the resulting seven *z*-scores was used as our second, "composite," measure of *g*.

Dual-Task Study

Twenty-four new subjects from the same source took part in the dual-task study. The test route was divided into five sections of 10–15 minutes each. Subjects drove the whole route twice, alternating from section to section between single- and dual-task conditions so that, by the end, each part of the route had been driven once under each condition. In the dual-task case, random letters again had to be generated at a rate of 40/min, insofar as the subject judged this compatible with driving safely. In fact, it was very rare for subjects to stop speaking altogether, though they did occasionally resort to highly stereotyped sequences.

14.5 Results

Individual-Differences Study

Means and between-subject standard deviations for the twelve driving measures appear in table 14.1. Data are taken from the main sample of 90 drivers. On the Culture Fair Test of g, the mean number of errors/uncompleted items was 14.6 (equivalent IQ = 98), standard deviation 5.1, range 30 to 4 (equivalent IQ range 66–145). These figures indicate a reasonably representative sample from the normal population.

Before calculating correlations, we reflected variables such that a numerically lower score always indicated better performance. Thus, positive correlations always mean that better performance on one measure is associated with better performance on another. While in the laboratory good performance can be defined arbitrarily, in a real skill the problem is less straightforward. A priori we defined better performance as *more* frequent looking at the mirror or other relevant parts of the environment (measures 1–2, 4–6), mirror checking *more strongly* differentiating appropriate and less appropriate times (3), *earlier* braking into and acceleration away from an intersection (7–8), *lower* divergence from the curb and variability while cornering (9–10), *faster* gear changing (11), and *greater* following distance (12).

Three subsequent observations supported these a priori definitions. First, we compared groups of experts and novices with our main sample of 90 normal drivers (Duncan, Williams, and Brown 1991). Except for measures 5 and 12, experts always differed from the mean of the other two groups in the expected direction. Second, while our driving measures showed only weak correlations (−.08 to .25) with annual mileage driven, these correlations were positive (using the reflected scores) for all but 8 and 12. Third, the correlation matrix based on reflected scores shows the usual property of positive manifold: The average of each measure's correlations with all the others is positive. Measure 12 is the only one whose directionality seems unclear, and reflecting it would change none of our conclusions.

Correlations between all scores appear in table 14.2. Reliabilities (diagonal) were calculated by the standard ANOVA procedure (Winer 1962), across either laps of the urban circuit (measures 1 and 3) or instances of each maneuver (remainder). The results suggest three conclusions. First, reliabilities on the whole were adequate (.56 to .91). Thus, the way that a person carries out a particular driving action is fairly stable from one occasion to the next, in line with the view that skilled behavior is rather stereotyped. Second, intercorrelations between different driving skills were remarkably low. Neglecting the correlation between measures 1 and 2 (which were based partly on the same data), the median correlation was .09, with a range from −.26 to .30.

Table 14.2 Reliabilities (diagonal), Intercorrelations, and Correlations with the Culture Fair Test (bottom row) for the 12 Driving Variables

	1	2	3	4	5	6	7	8	9	10	11	12
1	.89											
2	.76	.75										
3	−.07	.30	.56									
4	.02	.13	.24	.73								
5	.13	.02	−.05	.04	.65							
6	.16	.16	.04	.16	.11	.77						
7	−.07	−.03	.19	.24	.11	.09	.65					
8	−.20	−.08	.10	.04	.11	−.02	.27	.75				
9	−.07	−.10	.05	.26	.04	.07	.09	.14	.72			
10	.08	.12	.13	−.04	.06	.04	.29	.09	.10	.66		
11	.11	.18	.06	.01	.15	−.02	.03	.15	.16	.14	.91	
12	.13	.22	.12	.06	−.10	.12	−.07	−.26	−.11	.09	−.13	.63
Culture Fair	−.02	.01	.23	.11	−.03	.07	.17	.12	−.03	.00	−.12	−.06

Note: Numbering of driving skills follows table 14.1.

Even looking at closely related skills changes this picture very little. For example, the median correlation between the six scanning measures was .12, the same as the median correlation between the four cornering measures. These findings suggest that, after many years of driving experience, individual differences in component skills are extremely specific. There is only a very weak tendency for one person to be *in general* a better or worse driver than another; instead, each individual skill is almost independent of the others, and it seems safe to assume that independence from measures external to driving would be even clearer. Finally, and in line with this conclusion, correlations with *g* were extremely low (−.12 to .23). This result confirms our expectation for simple, consistent components of a highly practiced skill.

Subjects varied widely in their reports of annual mileage driven (100 to 70,000 miles per annum). Partialing out this factor, however, left findings essentially unchanged.

The correlation between the Culture Fair Test of *g* and our laboratory composite score was .67, with correlations between the Culture Fair Test and individual laboratory tasks ranging from .18 (word monitoring) to .61 (group embedded figures test). The correlation of .37 with random letter generation is important in showing that the latter does have a *g* component. The results confirm that the Culture Fair Test measures much the same factor as the average of a diverse set of other tests. The eighty-four correlations between driving variables and individual tasks in the laboratory composite ranged from −.33 to .40 (median .04), supporting again the conclusion of extreme specificity in driving skills.

Table 14.3 Dual-Task Study: Mean Scores in Single- and Dual-Task Conditions for the 12 Driving Variables

	Scores	
Skill	Single Task	Dual Task
1	15.8[a]	19.2[a]
2	.46	.40
3	.76[b]	.94[b]
4	2.62	2.59
5	.21	.27
6	.97	.90
7	4.77[a]	4.50[a]
8	1.26	1.33
9	1.08	1.05
10	11.3	11.7
11	.611	.594
12	62.5	59.8

Notes: Indicated differences between conditions significant at [a]$p < .05$, [b]$p < .01$ by analysis of variance. Numbering of driving skills and units for each follow table 14.1.

Dual-Task Study

Table 14.3 shows mean raw scores for all variables in the dual-task study. To transform dual-task decrements to z-scores, mean differences between single- and dual-task scores were each divided by the corresponding between-subjects standard deviation from the main sample of 90 drivers (see table 14.1). Signs were set so that, following our previous definitions, positive scores indicated better performance without the secondary task. Expressed as z-scores, dual-task decrements ranged from $-.34$ to $.43$. Decrements were individually significant only for measures 3 and 7; measure 1 showed a significant *improvement* under dual-task conditions. Again, this picture of generally modest effects is what we should expect for simple components of a familiar skill.

Comparison of g Correlations and Dual-Task Decrements

The main prediction in our study is tested in figure 14.1, which compares profiles of g correlation (as measured by the Culture Fair Test) and dual-task decrement across driving skills. The two profiles are in excellent agreement, with a correlation between them of .67.[2] Even though both g correlations and dual-task decrements were generally low and nonsignificant, the results support the hypothesis that the two are roughly proportional.

One way to put the results is in terms of the equivalent IQ reduction produced by concurrent random letter generation. Recall again that the correlation of any variable X with g reflects the expected change in X per unit change in g, both expressed as z-scores. In the present study, the slope of the

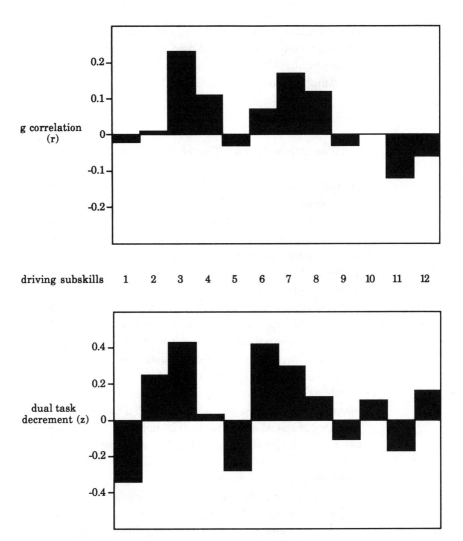

Figure 14.1 Profiles of g correlation (r) and dual-task decrement (z) across driving skills. Numbering of skills follows table 14.1.

linear regression relating dual-task decrements to g correlations was 1.2.[3] On average, generating random letters reduces driving scores by 1.2 times their g correlation, suggesting a reduction in g of 1.2 standard deviations. Using our observed g distribution, this may be translated into an equivalent IQ loss of about 16 points.

Results were a little less clear when the laboratory composite score was substituted for the Culture Fair Test as our measure of g. In this case, profiles of g correlation and dual-task decrement were correlated .51 across driving skills.

In a final analysis, dual-task decrements were reconverted to z-scores using, instead of the between-subjects standard deviation estimated from the main driver sample, the equivalent estimate from the twenty-four subjects in the dual-task study itself. In this way we wished to avoid the possibility of having built correlated errors into our estimates of g correlation and (z-score) decrement, by using the same standard deviation estimate in both. Results were again only a little less clear, with a correlation of .59 between profiles of g correlation and dual-task decrement.

14.6   DISCUSSION

Relationship between g Correlations and Dual-Task Decrements

From the common g system hypothesis we derived the prediction that *single-task* g correlations should be roughly proportional to *dual-task* performance decrements. With a correlation of .67 between profiles of g correlation and dual-task decrement, the data are in good accord with this prediction. Of the twelve measured driving skills, five (2, 3, 6, 7, and 8) were among the top six in terms of both g correlation and decrement. According to the hypothesis, these would be the skills most dependent on the common g system; it is perhaps worth noting that three concerned scanning, while the remaining two (early braking and prompt acceleration) might be taken to reflect anticipation. Considering the entirely different methods used to measure (between-subject) g correlations and (within-subject) dual-task decrements, the agreement between them is really rather remarkable.

While these are promising results, however, we must also emphasize several reasons to regard them as preliminary. First, individual correlations and decrements were almost all so low as to be nonsignificant. In some ways, this makes the result all the more remarkable: Any "signal" in the two profiles was evidently little greater than the "noise" contributed by sampling variability in each individual point; or to put it another way, the correlation between profiles should have been attenuated by severe restriction of range owing to the low g correlations/dual-task decrements seen throughout. On the other hand, the possible contribution of noise to the positive findings is also of concern. For example, of five skills whose g correlation was measured as negative, four also showed a negative measured dual-task "decrement," a result that could only be due to noise if we are right in the way measures have been scored. To offset such concerns, the results need to be replicated using tasks selected to give a wider range of g correlations/dual-task decrements.

The second concern is perhaps the most important and stems from our having used components of a real-world skill for this research. There are problems that this choice may have helped us to avoid; for example, verbal coding of task demands, strategies, and so forth, may always be important in unfamiliar tasks, perhaps introducing a specific source of conflict with any verbal secondary task like random letter generation. As we have said, however, the problem with real-world behavior is that the experimenter cannot arbitrarily define ideal performance. Though our definitions of "superior" driving skills seemed reasonable a priori, and though they were supported by various separate lines of evidence, they may only be approximations to the truth. Suppose, for example, that for some measure, performance, in the *middle* of the observed range was the ideal, with departures from this ideal equally likely in either direction. Scored unidirectionally, such a measure would be unlikely to correlate with anything, since people who performed poorly would be equally likely to make "errors" in either direction; and similarly, we should be unlikely to see any net dual-task "decrement" in one direction or the other. The same holds if some aspect of behavior has *no* ideal—or perhaps several different ideals dictated by different driving styles—and each person chooses more or less at random (though perhaps consistently) how to carry it out.

It should be noted that the key point is not whether a measure's ideal lies at one end of the *possible* range, but whether it lies at one end of the *observed* range. For example, though it is not correct to look an indefinitely large number of times to the right when approaching a roundabout, it does seem likely that in actual driving, looking too little rather than too much is the rule. Of the twelve measures we took, the most obviously "unidirectional" are perhaps 2 (mirror checking at corners), 6 (looking back after overtaking), 10 (consistency of steering path), and 11 (speed of gear change)—evidently, these were not those with conspicuously the greatest g correlations or dual-task decrements. Again, however, replication with laboratory tasks is essential to put our conclusions on sounder footing.

The last concern is that in our study, the range of ages was rather broad (29–57), and age was correlated with both g and some driving measures. Partialing out its effect reduces the correlation between profiles of g correlation and dual-task decrement to .45. This is immaterial if the effect of age can be understood as a simple reduction in g, which for many purposes it probably can (Rabbitt and Goward, in press), since age has little or no effect on performance scores once g is partialed out. In this case, age is simply contributing to the spread of our g distribution. However, if age has additional effects—for example, if people of different ages were taught different driving styles—then its contribution may be distorting our findings.

To summarize, we have obtained promising support for the predicted relationship between single-task g correlations and dual-task performance decrements. At the same time, there are good reasons for caution. Stronger conclusions must await replication.

Skill Specificity

Regarding skill specificity, our results are much stronger. The finding of low g correlations and modest dual-task decrements confirms the general expectation for simple stereotyped components of a familiar skill. Beyond this, the results show extreme specificity of these skill components; intercorrelations between even similar skills were uniformly low. The results are in line with the idea that contributions from a common g system decline as practice develops novel control structures tailored rather exactly to the particular sequences of action that are learned.

Consider as an example skills 2 and 6, mirror checking/looking back before respectively turning at an intersection and pulling back to the inner lane after overtaking. Reliabilities of .75 and .77 confirm that (at least for looking behind), each maneuver is reasonably stereotyped; a correlation of .16, on the other hand, shows that whether or not a person has learned reliably to check the mirror in one maneuver does not at all predict checking in another. There is little or no tendency to be a "reliable mirror checker" in general. Instead, quite separate control structures appear to be learned to coordinate sequences of behavior in different maneuvers, with the appearance of a mirror check in any particular sequence being almost independent of others.

In this context, it is interesting that, even in rather simple skills and even after many years of experience, our results suggest *some* remaining role for a common g system. Correlations between driving skills and g have two obvious interpretations: either some general-purpose control system still makes a small contribution to behavior even after many years of experience, or people with higher g scores originally learned slightly superior skills (cf. "crystallized intelligence," Cattell 1971). Only the former, however, can account for dual-task decrements. Though a common g system may be especially important in the early problem-solving phase of skill acquisition, it seems likely that its role never completely disappears.

A possible concern over our findings is that we may have measured aspects of driving skills so local as to be unimportant. For example, there might be many different ways to carry out a particular driving maneuver safely and successfully, involving very different local components; hence, correlations measured at too local a level could always be low, even though at a higher level there are important general dimensions of driving ability or style. While we would not wish to discount the possibility of such general dimensions, it does seem unlikely that the local components that we measured are all in themselves unimportant. In-depth analyses of individual accidents, for example, reveal numerous cases caused by failure to check an important feature of the environment or by following too closely (Staughton and Storie 1977). Irrespective of any general driving "style," failure to check behind before changing lanes on the freeway, and following the vehicle ahead too closely, increase accident probability in and of themselves.

As we have noted, recent findings cast serious doubt on the idea that individual differences become increasingly specific with practice in simple laboratory tasks (Ackerman 1987, 1988). There may be a real difference between results in the laboratory and the outside world. For example, learning conditions will be more variable in the outside world, and perhaps most important, people are more at liberty to set their own goals. Here may be one reason for the study of real skills as well as laboratory tasks: in real skills, specific learning history may really be paramount in determining individual differences.

One implication, as we have noted, is that learning itself creates innumerable new dimensions of individual differences, so that there is no fixed taxonomy of "mental abilities" (Buss 1973). Though the skills examined here are far more local than those appearing in standard taxonomies, even in those it seems evident that such dimensions as "verbal ability" and "numerical ability" must also be largely the products of specific learning. The results also have a practical implication: at least for skills like driving, selection tests given before a task is learned hold little promise (Reynolds 1952); and indeed, the long history of such selection tests has been disappointing (Ghiselli 1966).

14.7 CONCLUSION

Reservations notwithstanding, the close relationship between g correlations and dual-task decrements predicted by the hypothesis of a common g system was confirmed in our experiment. As we have pointed out, this hypothesis is only one interpretation of such findings, which in principle might also be explained by the view that both g correlations and dual-task decrements reflect chance sampling by different tasks from a large pool of internal variables (e.g., processing systems) with no true g component. But whether or not the interpretation in terms of a common g system is correct, the results do suggest that studies of (between-subject) individual differences and (within-subject) dual task interference may converge to define the same g factor.

APPENDIX

Consider a model with a total of p separate independent processing systems, n of which contribute to a task T. Further, let a person's score s on T be equal to his or her summed z-scores on each processing component:

$$s = z(1) + z(2) \ldots + z(n) \tag{1}$$

A concurrent task C involves a second, randomly selected set of m processing components. The expected number of components shared between T and C is $(mn)/p$ (Feller 1968). Let each person's effective z-score on a given component be reduced by a fixed amount d whenever this component is shared between tasks.

The expected dual-task decrement in s is given by $(dmn)/p$. To transform this to a z-score, it must be divided by the (between-subjects) standard deviation of s. The variance of s is equal to n (the summed variances of the component z-scores), the standard deviation is $n^{1/2}$, and the expected dual-task decrement expressed as a z-score is $(dmn^{1/2})/p$. Like the g correlation, the expected dual-task decrement increases monotonically with n. The result holds for any model in which addition of a processing component has an effect on expected dual-task decrement that is proportionally greater than its effect on the between-subjects standard deviation.

NOTES

Financial support was provided under contract 9652/32 from the Transport and Road Research Laboratory. We are extremely grateful for the encouragement and support of the project officer, Geoff Maycock.

1. Whenever we speak of a correlation in this chapter we refer to the product-moment correlation (r).

2. One might object to inclusion of measure 2 in this calculation since it is necessarily related to both 1 and 3. Increasing 2 increases 1 directly, and increases the denominator of 3. Omitting 2, however, only increases the correlation between profiles to .70.

3. For this purpose, g correlations for all driving measures were recalculated after translating each individual's score on the Culture Fair Test into an equivalent IQ. Though of course this has scarcely any effect, it is strictly correct for a desired answer in terms of IQ points.

REFERENCES

Ackerman, P. L. (1987). Individual differences in skill learning: An integration of psychometric and information processing perspectives. *Psychological Bulletin, 102*, 3–27.

Ackerman, P. L. (1988). Determinants of individual differences during skill acquisition: Cognitive abilities and information processing. *Journal of Experimental Psychology: General, 117*, 288–318.

Allport, D. A. (1980). Attention and performance. In G. Claxton (Ed.), *Cognitive psychology: New directions*, 112–153. London: Routledge and Kegan Paul.

Baddeley, A. D. (1966). The capacity for generating information by randomization. *Quarterly Journal of Experimental Psychology, 18*, 119–129.

Baddeley, A. D. (1986). *Working memory*. Oxford: Oxford University Press.

Broadbent, D. E. (1958). *Perception and communication*. London: Pergamon.

Bryan, W. L., and Harter, N. (1899). Studies on the telegraphic language: The acquisition of a hierarchy of habits. *Psychological Review, 6*, 345–375.

Buss, A. R. (1973). Learning, transfer, and changes in ability factors: A multivariate model. *Psychological Bulletin, 80*, 106–112.

Cattell, R. B. (1971). *Abilities: Their structure, growth and action*. Boston: Houghton Mifflin.

Duncan, J. (1990). Goal weighting and the choice of behaviour in a complex world. *Ergonomics, 33*, 1265–1279.

Duncan, J., Williams, P., and Brown, I. D. (1991). Components of driving skill: Experience does not mean expertise. *Ergonomics, 34*, 919–937.

Feller, W. (1968). *An introduction to probability theory and its application, Vol. 2*. New York: Wiley.

Fleishman, E. A., and Hempel, W. E. (1955). The relation between abilities and improvement with practice in a visual discrimination reaction task. *Journal of Experimental Psychology, 49*, 301–312.

Ghiselli, E. E. (1966). *The validity of occupational aptitude tests*. New York: Wiley.

Gopher, D., and Kahneman, D. (1971). Individual differences in attention and the prediction of flight criteria. *Perceptual and Motor Skills, 33*, 1335–1342.

Institute for Personality and Ability Testing. (1959). *Measuring intelligence with the Culture Fair Tests*. Champaign, IL: The Institute for Personality and Ability Testing.

James, W. (1890). *The principles of psychology*. New York: Holt.

Kahneman, D. (1973). *Attention and effort*. Englewood Cliffs, NJ: Prentice-Hall.

Laird, J., Newell, A., and Rosenbloom, P. (1987). SOAR: An architecture for general intelligence. *Artificial Intelligence, 33*, 1–64.

Lesgold, A. M. (1984). Acquiring expertise. In J. R. Anderson and S. M. Kosslyn (Eds.), *Tutorials in learning and memory: Essays in honor of Gordon Bower*, 31–60. New York: Freeman.

Luria, A. R. (1966). *Higher cortical functions in man*. London: Tavistock.

McLeod, P. (1977). A dual task response modality effect: Support for multiprocessor models of attention. *Quarterly Journal of Experimental Psychology, 29*, 651–667.

McLeod, P., and Posner, M. I. (1984). Privileged loops from percept to act. In H. Bouma and D. G. Bouwhuis (Eds.), *Attention and performance X*, 55–56. Hillsdale: Erlbaum.

Näätänen, R., and Summala, H. (1976). *Road user behaviour and traffic accidents*. Oxford: North-Holland.

Nelson, H. E. (1982). *National adult reading test manual*. Windsor, UK: NFER-Nelson.

Newell, A., and Simon, H. A. (1972). *Human problem solving*. Englewood Cliffs, NJ: Prentice-Hall.

Norman, D. A., and Shallice, T. (1980). *Attention to action: Willed and automatic control of behavior (Report No. 8006)*. San Diego: University of California, Center for Human Information Processing.

Posner, M. I., and Mitchell, R. F. (1967). Chronometric analysis of classification. *Psychological Review, 74*, 392–409.

Quenault, S. W. (1967). *Driver behaviour—safe and unsafe drivers (RRL Report LR70)*. Crowthorne, UK: Transport and Road Research Laboratory.

Rabbitt, P. M. A., and Goward, L. (N.d.). Age, intelligence and reaction time. *Quarterly Journal of Experimental Psychology*. In press.

Reynolds, B. (1952). The effect of learning on the predictability of psychomotor performance. *Journal of Experimental Psychology, 44*, 189–198.

Schneider, W., and Shiffrin, R. M. (1977). Controlled and automatic human information processing: I. Detection, search, and attention. *Psychological Review, 84*, 1–66.

Snow, R. E., and Lohman, D. F. (1984). Toward a theory of cognitive aptitude from learning for instruction. *Journal of Educational Psychology, 76*, 347–376.

Spearman, C. (1927). *The abilities of man*. New York: Macmillan.

Stankov, L. (1983). The role of competition in human abilities revealed through auditory tests. *Multivariate Behavioral Research Monographs*, no. 83–1, 1–63.

Staughton, G. C., and Storie, V. J. (1977). *Methodology of an in-depth accident investigation survey (TRRL Report LR 762)*. Crowthorne, UK: Transport and Road Research Laboratory.

Thomson, G.S. (1951). *The factorial analysis of human ability*, 5th ed. London: University of London Press.

Treisman, A. M., and Davies, A. (1973). Divided attention to ear and eye. In S. Kornblum (Ed.), *Attention and performance IV*, 101–117. London: Academic.

Walsh, K. W. (1978). *Neuropsychology: A clinical approach*. New York: Churchill Livingstone.

Winer, B. J. (1962). *Statistical principles in experimental design*. New York: McGraw-Hill.

Witkin, H. A., Oltman, P. K., Raskin, E., and Karp, S. A. (1971). *A manual for the embedded figures tests*. Palo Alto, CA: Consulting Psychologists Press.

Woodrow, H. (1939). The relation of verbal ability to improvement with practice in verbal tests. *Journal of Educational Psychology, 30*, 179–186.

15 Attention before and during the Decade of the Brain

Michael I. Posner

15.1 ENDURING ISSUES

Allport's tutorial lecture (chap. 9) discusses two enduring issues in the study of attention. The first issue is about early versus late selection and the second, automatic versus controlled processing. These two issues have been central throughout the modern history of attention. They enter explicitly or implicitly in each of the chapters presented here. Both Gopher (chap. 13) and Duncan et al. (chap. 14) are concerned with control. Mangun, Hillyard, and Luck (chap. 10) and Sperling and Wurst (chap. 12) are concerned with early selection, and Pashler (chap. 11) with both selection and control in relation to dual-task performance. One implication of the Allport tutorial is that attention may be performed by such a large number of different mechanisms that its study as a coherent topic may be obsolete. In contrast, I feel that recent work on brain systems serves to illuminate the enduring issues. This work suggests that there may be a limited number of networks underlying attention (Posner and Petersen 1990) making its study as a brain system central in the decade to come.

In this commentary, I would like to examine the issues of selection and control in light of the more than thirty years of work since Broadbent's 1958 filter model of attention. I will break this work into three historical periods with different emphases: human performance, cognition, and cognitive neuroscience. However, it would be wrong to consider each of these eras as an epoch followed by a paradigm shift. Rather, they seem to me to involve a continual growth in the tools available to study attention and in the questions we are able to ask. Congress has declared the 1990s as the decade of the brain. No doubt such a proclamation has a large element of public relations. Nonetheless, it does correspond to an expanded role for neuroscience in the study of concepts which, like attention, were once purely behavioral or cognitive. The Allport and Mangun, Hillyard, and Luck chapters both indicate this trend. A clearer analysis of where we have been in the eras of human performance and cognition may be helpful in indicating what unique aspects psychologists might bring to the exciting decade we have just entered.

In 1966, following the untimely death of Paul Fitts, I finished a book that he had started called *Human Performance*. A major theme of this book was that the human information-processing system was limited in its capacity to transform information from input either to output or to memory. When the first meeting of Attention and Performance symposium was held that year, human performance was its focus. The major attentional concept was the view of the human as a single-channel information processor. Eleven chapters of *Attention and Performance I* (Sanders 1967) were grouped under that title. Naturalistic tasks of vigilance, and maintenance of information in short-term memory were also strongly represented in *Attention and Performance I*.

The enduring nature of attentional control over information processing is illustrated by three chapters at the present symposium: those of Duncan, Gopher, and Sperling and Wurst. Gopher and Duncan both study aspects of tracking skills, which were also popular in *Attention and Performance I*.

Gopher summarizes a series of training studies and shows how practice stabilizes the application of particular strategies. The idea of attention as the source of highly specific strategies brought from old skills to new ones was a major idea in the study of human performance. Fitts viewed learning as involving several stages, the first of which required assembly of the relevant skills. He thought of this as a highly deliberate effortful process of attending to what had been acquired in previous learning. Indeed, Fitts believed that the power law relating practice to time required to perform a task was a result of the stabilization of strategies. Later, Newell and Rosenbloom (1981) derived the power function from the idea of chunking.

Duncan et al. (chap. 14) emphasizes another aspect of the use of well-practiced strategies—namely, that they lead to low correlations between even similar-appearing skills. However, Duncan argues that there is a common thread running through these low correlations that he attributes to underlying executive mechanisms related to dual-task performance. This idea suggests that high-level control via executive routines remains present throughout skilled performance. I will return to this aspect of his chapter later in the commentary.

Pashler's chapter concerns the psychological refractory period. In human performance theory, refractoriness was mainly related to the operation of a single channel. Pashler, however, uses refractoriness as a tool for studies of the relationship between internal modules. He first determines that there is some sort of common central overlap in a wide variety of tasks. Some forms of visual short-term memory and perceptual categorization take place without this bottleneck, but the bottleneck seems involved in memory retrieval, some forms of perceptual comparison, and all the types of cognitive judgment that Pashler has studied. This central bottleneck appears to be related to a form of control and hence to one aspect of attention.

Pashler identifies the bottleneck with response selection and, in a passing phrase, with the anatomy of what Posner and Petersen (1990) call the "anterior attention system." However, switching attention (orienting) to visual locations does not seem to involve the bottleneck. Thus, Pashler's data suggest two forms of attention. A similar separation between orienting and detecting underlies the anatomical distinctions between the anterior and posterior attention systems. It suggests that the cognitive psychology of attention may come to fit quite well with the developing anatomy of attention.

In one respect, however, Pashler's cognitive experiments are not in complete agreement with our own (Posner et al. 1989). We found occupying the anterior attention system by shadowing had effects on the speed at which a right visual-field cue summons attention. On the other hand, Pashler reports very slight, if any, influence. Of course, our differences need to be worked out in appropriate cognitive experiments. In many of Pashler's experiments, the use of a nonspeeded task causes a loss of interference effects, and this may be one reason for the difference.

Nevertheless, it does appear clear that if one identifies Pashler's results with our suggested anatomy, there must be communication between the anterior and posterior attention systems. This is because people can use high-level cognitive strategies to direct spatial attention and because the anatomical connections between the two systems are quite strong. However, Pashler's cognitive experiments inform us that this potential interaction may be largely, if not entirely, bypassed in some forms of performance.

15.3 COGNITION

The 1970s and 1980s reflected an emphasis on questions of internal representations and cognitive control. *Attention and performance IV* (Kornblum 1973) stressed internal mental representations in studies of priming, memory scanning, and binary classification. The distinction between automatic and controlled processes also began to emerge, and with it came a new concentration on multiple strategies for focal and divided attention.

The view of attention found in the human performance era, with a single channel connecting input to output, became outdated as cognitive psychology began to provide a basis for studying internal modules that performed operations during tasks. It was no longer enough for attention to serve as a bottleneck to block unwanted input, but its coordinative role began to be stressed. Allport contributed the idea that attention was more involved in preventing unwanted output than in the selection of competing signals.

During the cognitive era, much of our thinking was related to particular tasks, but the conclusions were often phrased as universals. For example, Shiffrin studied target-detection tasks, in which subjects had to detect a target that might arise from one or many sources. He found no evidence that performance was improved by monitoring fewer sources, and he concluded that attention must not affect perception (e.g., see Shiffrin and Grantham 1974). In retrospect, Shiffrin's finding seems to reflect the relative ease with which uncommitted attention can be summoned to a target even when one is uncertain in advance about which channel it will be on. If instead a subject's attention is first fixed on one target event, very large losses are found in the processing of other events (Duncan 1980). Similarly, Mangun, Hillyard, and Luck (chap. 10) show a very clear effect of attention on prestrate areas that is often accompanied by improvement in d' and reaction time, as well as increased cellular activity. On the other hand, Sperling and Wurst show that under the conditions of their task, attention does not alter the storage of information in short-term visual memory. There are many reasons why this might be so. However, as their chapter indicates, the most likely is the fact that their subjects' task requires selection by spatial frequency or form, while the one in Hillyard's study uses spatial location. Many results suggest that spatial location is the best means of selection for the visual system; indeed, the posterior attention system appears to be specialized for selection by location. When selection is by color or form, there is no evidence for activation of the posterior system (Corbetta et al. 1991). Once again, knowledge of the neural system involved helps support the cognitive results.

15.4 COGNITIVE NEUROSCIENCE

Attention and Performance XI (Posner and Marin 1985) emphasized the cognitive neuroscience link and included studies of feature integration in visual search, the mechanisms of orienting attention to visual locations, and anatomical and single-cell approaches to attentional networks. For the first time in the Attention and Performance series, physiologists, neurologists, and anatomists were all present in person as well as through their studies.

Three of the chapters in this volume reflect this theme. Allport deals with the study of lesioned patients. In cognitive neuropsychology the goal has been to dissociate internal modules. In the study of attention, much of this work has centered around lesions of the posterior parietal lobe. Lesions of the left parietal lobe tend to affect processing of stimuli in the right visual field. They affect the allocation of attention to local features more than to the global outline of an object, while lesions of the right parietal lobe affect the left side of space and the global outline. This neuropsychology of what we (Posner and Petersen 1990) call the posterior attention system fits well with the general idea of a zoom lens that has found considerable support in cognitive studies.

Mangun, Hillyard, and Luck (chap. 10) take the neuropsychology of attention a step further by attempting to localize the areas of the brain affected by an instruction to attend to a particular location. There has been a strong myth within cognitive neuropsychology that localization was not useful in trying to understand cognition. Nevertheless, Mangun, Hillyard, and Luck find an electrophysiological localization in prestriate areas of the hemisphere contralateral to a presented stimulus. Moreover, this localization fits very well with recent blood-flow studies that show attending to the velocity, form, or color of a stimulus activates separate prestriate areas presumably related to the attended dimension (Corbetta et al. 1991). Both the blood-flow and electrophysiological studies illustrate a common principle; namely, attention can operate by enhancing activity within sensory systems. I regard this evidence as important for the issue of whether attention affects perception. If attention boosts activity within a sensory area, it is very likely that later subjective experience will also be affected, as has been demonstrated by the many studies of spatial location that Mangun, Hillyard, and Luck cite. It seems to me that both these studies and those on blood flow show that one site at which attention operates is within prestriate cortex.

15.5 THE COMING DECADE

The study of attention should be greatly accelerated by our recently improved understanding of the anatomical systems that support it. In addition, the use of computational methods that have some analogy with the brain's connectivity also enhances the prospects for integration.

Do these new anatomical ideas contribute to a solution of the two enduring questions raised by Allport? The anatomy suggests at least two somewhat separate networks supporting selective attention. The posterior network is related to early sensory selection, for example, by location in the visual system. The anterior network is more related to late selection by semantic content and other higher-level variables. How these systems cooperate in particular tasks is under current investigation. However, the very existence of this anatomy suggests that selection can be either early or late, which fits well with the emerging cognitive view that only some forms of perceptual processing rest upon attentional selection (see Pashler, chap. 11; Sperling and Wurst, chap. 12).

There are complex data processing systems that operate to greater or lesser degrees without attention. This is the anatomical basis for the distinction between automatic and controlled processing. For example, the chunking of individual letters into a word appears to take place in the ventral occipital lobe and does not seem to require the posterior attention system (Petersen et al. 1990). On the other hand, the efficiency with which we obtain the meaning of a visual chunk is influenced by the availability of the anterior attention system, although perhaps some of it is automatic. Once again anatomy can contribute to the solution of enduring questions of function (Posner et al. 1989).

The coming decade will see a great enhancement in our knowledge of the anatomy of attentional networks. Refined methods using radionuclides, noninvasive recording methods to find generators of electrical and magnetic activity, and cellular and transmitter studies with animals should enhance our understanding of the general regions of the brain that support attention. Doubtless, there will be many surprises that we cannot anticipate, but it is certainly clear already that this level of analysis could have profound effects upon what we dare hope to know about attention by the turn of the century. In this, I believe there is agreement between Allport and myself.

In the next decade, it is likely that the brain's attentional system will be viewed in much the same way that we now view vision or audition. In these areas, psychological studies (often using psychophysical techniques) and physiological studies are combined to enhance our understanding of the computations performed. No one argues about whether there is an anatomy of the visual system. Instead studies focus on the rules and anatomy of its computations. The attentional system can be examined through the use of cognitive experiments as well as through simulations. These methods are important to guide the neuroscience work on attention into areas that are important to cognitive and human performance questions. The utility of viewing attention as a system of several networks seems to be at the heart of the differences between the tutorial and this commentary. Allport seems to feel that the uses of the term are so disparate that no unified system can incorporate them, while I think that the view of attention as a system is useful in relating cognitive and neuroscience conceptions.

The chapter by Duncan et al. illustrates the magnitude of the problem we face. Duncan et al. (chap. 14) relate frontal-lobe activity to aspects of general intelligence. This is just barely a start toward the kind of analysis we must develop. We need to determine what the computations are that underlie this general ability we call intelligence, and then we need to relate such computations to the enormous territory represented by the frontal lobes. One approach to this problem is to demonstrate that connectionist models can use brain-style computation to approach problems of higher-level cognition. While these studies are useful, it will not be sufficient to develop models of brain-style computation if they ignore the evidence for highly restricted anatomical localization of components of higher cognitive function. This type of a combined cognitive-anatomical analysis has been successful in more limited problems such as how visual orienting occurs, and it may well provide a basis for pursuing these more general issues of control. Even if a completely distributed model could carry out mental life, it does not seem to be the way humans do it. This means we have to divide the anterior attention system and its complex functions of awareness and control into more tractable elements.

Let me take two examples that may give us a start toward associating attentional functions with frontal areas. In sleep, we maintain the ability to be aware, as during dreaming. Recent advances in neuroscience provide specific computational ideas about the nature of information processing in the dream state (Mamelak and Hobson 1989). Dreams appear to dissociate voluntary control from awareness. The ideas present in sleep are not the result of thinking guided by attention. During sleep, attention in the sense of control is suspended, while attention in the sense of awareness is maintained. What changes in brain function produce this dissociation? We don't yet know, but there is progress in attempting to find out (see Mamelak and Hobson 1989).

A second example comes from studies of development in infancy. At age four months, infants are little looking machines. They are in a stage where the posterior attention system is rapidly developing. It makes them the organism of choice in visual studies; once hooked, they eagerly look at each of an experimenter's vacation slides sometimes until they are exhausted. By twelve months, they quickly turn to other things; infants by this age have their own agenda. An agenda is what artificial intelligence researchers have sometimes called a goal tree (Carbonnell 1981). Frontal patients often lack a goal tree, and clearly we all lack a goal tree during the sleep state. The goal tree is a kind of memory, and perhaps one of the most important for the study of cognitive control. I believe it has a location in the frontal lobes and a connection to the anterior attention system that can be switched off without the loss of awareness. These are the types of speculations that require a cognitive-anatomical analysis.

Two other applications of the cognitive-neuroscience approach to attention are already developing and should advance further during the next decade. These are the study of development and of psychopathology. Recently, Mark Johnson (1990) has written an important article tracing the neural systems underlying eye movements in infants over the first three months of life. What is remarkable about this topic is that specific visual behavior of infants reflects the maturation of particular layers of the visual system that give rise to individual pathways. For example, between 1 and 3 months, infants show a form of obligatory looking that occurs in the period following the maturation of a frontal to collicular pathway, which insures successful fixation and emerges before the parietal systems mature. We (Clohessy, Posner, and Rothbart 1991; Johnson, Posner, and Rothbart 1991; Rothbart, Posner, and Boylan 1990) have pursued this work, showing that many of the computations of the posterior attention system mature between three and six months of age. Many studies suggest 9–12 months as an important time for the anterior system. Future studies also need to examine the relation of attentional development to controls over action, language, and memory.

There are many so-called disorders of attention, just as there are many visual disorders. In the past, the term *attention* has been applied to many disorders possibly as a label for our failure to understand them. This situation is changing as we develop ideas about attention that are both biological and cognitive. In the last several years, I have been involved in the study of neurological disorders such as neglect from unilateral strokes, closed head injuries, and AIDS dementia, along with psychiatric disorders such as schizophrenia, attention deficit disorder, and depression (Posner 1988). In studying several of these disorders, we have been able to learn something about the operation of the posterior and anterior attention systems, and at the same time make modest contributions to a better grasp of each disorder. With a more refined analysis of the anterior attention system, the next decade may see much more progress along these lines.

Attention has played a central role in the psychology of the last twenty-five years. I think we have potential solutions to some of the enduring questions that Allport raised in his tutorial. More exciting, however, are the many new questions and techniques that are available for use in the decade ahead.

NOTE

This research was supported by ONR contract 89-N00014-89J and by a grant from the James S. McDonnell Foundation and the Pew Charitable Trusts.

REFERENCES

Broadbent, D. E. (1958). *Perception and Communication*. London: Pergamon.

Carbonnell, J. (1981). *Subiective Understanding of Belief Systems*. Ann Arbor Michigan: UMI Research Press.

Clohessy, A. B., Posner, M. I., and Rothbart, M. K. (1991). The development of inhibition of return in early infancy. *Journal of Cognitive Neuroscience, 3*, 345–350.

Corbetta, M., Miezin, F., Dobmeyer, S., Shulman, G. L., and Petersen, S. E. (1991). Attentional modulation of neural processing of shape, color, and velocity in humans. *Journal of Neuroscience, 11*, 2383–2402.

Duncan, J. (1980). The locus of interference in the perception of simultaneous stimuli. *Psychology Review, 87*, 272–300.

Eriksen, C. W., and St. James, J. D. (1986). Visual attention within and around the field of focal attention: A zoom lens model. *Perception and Psychophysics, 40*, 225–240.

Fitts, P. M., and Posner, M. I. (1967). *Human Performance*. Belmont, CA: Brooks/Cole.

Harter, M. R., Miller, S. L., Price, N. J., LaLonde, M. E., and Keyes, A. L. (1989). Neural processes involved in directing attention. *Journal of Cognitive Neuroscience, 1*, 223–237.

Johnson, M. H. (1990). Cortical maturation and the development of visual attention in early infancy. *Journal of Cognitive Neuroscience, 2*, 81–95.

Johnson, M., Posner, M. I., and Rothbart, M. K. (1991). The development of visual attention in infancy: Contingency learning, anticipations, and disengaging. *Journal of Cognitive Neuroscience, 3*, 335–344.

Kornblum, S. (1973). *Attention and Performance IV*. New York: Academic Press.

Mamelak, A. N., and Hobson, J. A. (1989). Dream bizarreness as the cognitive correlate of altered neuronal behavior in REM sleep. *Journal of Cognitive Neuroscience, 1*, 201–222.

Newell, A., and Rosenbloom, P. S. (1981). Mechanisms of skill acquisition and law of practice. In J. R. Anderson (Ed.), *Cognitive Skills and their Acquisition*. Hillsdale, NJ: Erlbaum.

Petersen, S. E., Fox, P. T., Snyder, A. Z., and Raichle, M. E. (1990). Activation of extrastriate and frontal cortical areas by visual words and word-like stimuli. *Science, 249*, 1041–1044.

Posner, M. I. (1988). Structures and function of selective attention. In T. Boll and B. Bryant (Eds.), *Master Lectures in Clinical Neuropsychology and Brain Function*. Washington D.C.: American Psychological Association.

Posner, M. I., and Marin, O. S. M. (Eds.). (1985). *Attention and Performance XI: Mechanisms of Attention*. Hillsdale, NJ: Erlbaum.

Posner, M. I., and Petersen, S. E. (1990). The attention system of the human brain. *Annual Review of Neuroscience, 13*, 25–42.

Posner, M. I., Sandson, J., Dhawan, M., and Shulman, G. L. (1989). Is word recognition automatic? A cognitive anatomical approach. *Journal of Cognitive Neuroscience, 1*, 50–60.

Rothbart, M. K., Posner, M. I., and Boylan, A. (1990). Regulatory mechanisms in infant temperament. In J. Enns (Ed.), *The Development of Attention: Research and Theory*. Amsterdam: North-Holland.

Sanders, A. (1967). *Attention and Performance I*. Amsterdam: North-Holland.

Shiffrin, R. M., and Grantham, D. W. (1974). Can attention be allocated to a sensory modality. *Perception and Psychophysics, 15*, 460–474.

IV Learning and Memory

Introduction

Like attention and mental chronometry, the topics of learning and memory have been classical ones in empirical and theoretical research on human performance. With respect to learning, for example, researchers have maintained a long-standing interest in how people acquire the procedural skills needed to perform various mental and physical tasks (Fitts 1964). The experimental study of skill acquisition dates back about a century to the era of Bryan and Harter (1899), who examined changes in the proficiency of telegraph operators as they practiced sending and receiving Morse code. Interest in specific aspects of memory, such as the distinction between short-term (primary) and long-term (secondary) storage, likewise has an extensive history (e.g., see James 1890). The relevance of short-term storage to information processing was clearly recognized at the first Attention and Performance symposium, following the influential ideas of Broadbent (1958) about this matter. Moreover, since the decade of the 1960s, in which the series of Attention and Performance symposia began, research on learning and memory has undergone a vibrant upsurge, thereby advancing performance theory even further.

One important advance during the past twenty-five years concerns the architecture of the human memory system. Around the time of *Attention and Performance I* (Sanders 1967), many researchers believed that this system might consist of three interrelated components: sensory store, short-term store, and long-term store (Atkinson and Shiffrin 1968; Sperling 1967; Waugh and Norman 1965). Little was known, however, about the substrates of these components. In contrast, our ideas about them—though still open to substantial debate (cf. Craik and Lockhart 1972)—now seem much more detailed. It appears that the short-term store actually includes several modality-specific "working memories" (Baddeley 1986), each of which has its own set of subcomponents and serves a variety of complementary processing functions. For example, there may be an articulatory loop that contributes to language comprehension, verbal learning, and subvocal reasoning through interactions with a phonological short-term store, motor-program buffer, central executive, and other ancillary components. Similarly, the long-term store has been analyzed with considerable care. In particular, memory theorists have made concerted efforts toward analyzing its verbal subcomponent into distinct lexicons that mediate the inputs and outputs of visual and auditory language (e.g., see Monsell 1987).

A second major advance involves the representation of knowledge in long-term store. Memory theorists now appreciate much more fully than ever before that they must deal precisely with several related dichotomies, including the distinctions between "propositional" versus "analog" codes (Kosslyn 1980), "declarative" versus "procedural" knowledge (Anderson 1976), "episodic" versus "semantic" memory (Tulving 1972), and "explicit" versus "implicit" memory (Schacter 1987). Powerful formalisms have been developed to characterize various types of knowledge within the contexts of these distinctions. For example, through efforts of cognitive psychologists (e.g., Anderson and Bower 1973; Collins and Quillian 1969; Kintsch 1974; Meyer 1970; Norman and Rumelhart 1975; Rumelhart 1975; Schank and Abelson 1977) and computer scientists (e.g., Quillian 1969; Schank 1975), tremendous progress has occurred in specifying how declarative knowledge may be represented with propositional networks, schemas, and scripts. Tremendous progress has likewise occurred in specifying how procedural knowledge may be represented with production systems (Anderson 1976, 1983; Newell 1973).

Third, important developments have taken place in describing the processes that mediate memory performance, such as encoding, priming, retrieval, retention, and forgetting. An influential product of research on encoding operations is the levels-of-processing framework, which Craik and Lockhart (1972) introduced to characterize how retention and retrieval processes depend on the nature of initial stimulus-analysis operations. Augmenting their research, there has been intensive work on rehearsal operations, including maintenance (type I) and elaborative (type II) rehearsal. Ideas about priming and retrieval have been elaborated in studies of spreading activation (e.g., Collins and Loftus 1975; Meyer and Schvaneveldt 1971), serial versus parallel search (e.g., Sternberg 1975), and direct-access mechanisms (e.g., Humphreys, Bain, and Pike 1989; Murdock 1982). Because of these developments, recognition, recall, and other types of retrieval are better understood than ever before.

We believe that a substantial amount of the progress summarized here is attributable to contributions made possible by two beneficial approaches. One involves formal mathematical modeling (e.g., Atkinson and Shiffrin 1968; Eich 1982; Gillund and Shiffrin 1984; Hintzman 1986; Humphreys, Bain, and Pike 1989; Murdock 1982; Raaijmakers and Shiffrin 1981) and computer simulation (e.g., Anderson 1976, 1983). Another beneficial approach involves exploring the mind-body interface through the techniques of neuropsychology and cognitive neuroscience (e.g., Squire 1987). Consequently, these approaches and their recent products constitute a major focus of *Attention and Performance XIV*. We combine them here by also including the perspective of connectionism (e.g., see Rumelhart and Todd, chap. 1), which integrates facets of formal mathematical/simulation modeling with those of cognitive neuroscience (Rumelhart and McClelland 1986).

Setting the stage for the remainder of part IV, Hintzman begins with a thoughtful, stimulating, contentious tutorial review of the past twenty-five year's research on human learning and memory. His main question concerns whether, on balance, the cognitive perspective that dominated this era has been all for the best. Readers of *Attention and Performance XIV* will have an opportunity to decide the answer themselves by contemplating what Hintzman has to say and then examining, among other items, the chapters that follow. There, Raaijmakers discusses the extent to which the original Atkinson and Shiffrin (1968) memory model remains viable despite the many theoretical onslaughts that it has encountered along the way (e.g., see Craik and Lockhart 1972). Interestingly, given Raaijmakers's arguments, one might conclude that this model, along with offspring such as the SAM model (Gillund and Shiffrin 1984; Raaijmakers and Shiffrin 1981), is still more alive and well than some current memory textbooks would have us believe. Also, in a similar vein, Humphreys, Wiles, and Bain (chap. 21) show how some concepts related to those of the SAM model can be extended to deal with recognition and recall tasks that involve complex combinations of retrieval cues. To what extent their model will ultimately prove different from previous ones is an intriguing question for future theoretical research.

Meanwhile, the chapters by Squire et al., Howard and Franklin, and Sartori, Job, and Coltheart take us into the realms of neuropsychology and cognitive neuroscience as they bear on learning and memory performance. Squire et al. present a cogent overview of their extensive research program on amnesia, different forms of memory, and the memorial functions of various brain structures, including the hippocampus, amygdala, and medial temporal lobe system. Consistent with Squire et al.'s conclusion that memory performance can be profitably analyzed through the cognitive-neuroscience approach, Howard and Franklin's chapter examines the component mechanisms of short-term working memory. Their results, which manifest a number of striking dissociations among the deficits of brain-damaged patients, impressively illustrate how some previous analyses of working memory (e.g., Monsell 1987) may be substantiated empirically and extended theoretically. The value of the cognitive-neuroscience approach is likewise demonstrated by Sartori, Job, and Coltheart's chapter, which deals with long-term memory. Here we find that not all semantic information in long-term memory is stored or represented equally. Rather, it appears that knowledge about animate objects may be selectively impaired in some patients, suggesting that the memory system perhaps includes a categorically organized object knowledge base, where information about animate objects has a unique status separate from information about inanimate objects. How such discoveries through cognitive neuroscience may mesh with those from formal mathematical modeling and computer simulation thus becomes the challenging question confronted by Roediger, part IV's discussant. His answer, witty and satisfying to dyed-in-the-wool fans of traditional experimental psychology, is that further emphasis on the systematic collection of behavioral data in various sophisticated laboratory paradigms may provide a sturdy bridge between the neuroscience and formal-model approaches.

REFERENCES

Anderson, J. R. (1976). *Language, memory, and thought*. Hillsdale, NJ: Lawrence Erlbaum Associates.

Anderson, J. R. (1983). *The architecture of cognition*. Cambridge, MA: Harvard University Press.

Anderson, J. R., and Bower, G. (1973). *Human associative memory*. Washington, D.C.: Winston and Sons.

Atkinson, R., and Shiffrin, R. (1968). Human memory: A proposed system and its control processes. In K. W. Spence and J. T. Spence (Eds.), *The psychology of learning and motivation*, vol. 2, 89–105. New York: Academic Press.

Baddeley, A. D. (1986). *Working memory*. Oxford, UK: Oxford University Press.

Broadbent, D. E. (1958). *Perception and communication*. London: Pergamon Press.

Bryan, W. L., and Harter, N. (1899). Studies on the telegraphic language: The acquisition of a hierarchy of habits. *Psychological Review, 6*, 345–375.

Collins, A. M., and Loftus, E. F. (1975). A spreading-activation theory of semantic memory. *Psychological Review, 82*, 407–428.

Collins, A. M., and Quillian, M. R. (1969). Retrieval time from semantic memory. *Journal of Verbal Learning and Verbal Behavior, 8*, 240–247.

Craik, F. I. M., and Lockhart, R. S. (1972). Levels of processing: A framework for memory research. *Journal of Verbal Learning and Verbal Behavior, 11*, 671–684.

Eich, J. M. (1982). A composite holographic associative recall model. *Psychological Review, 89*, 627–661.

Fitts, P. M. (1964). Perceptual-motor skill learning. In A. W. Melton (Ed.), *Categories of human learning*. New York: Academic Press.

Gillund, G., and Shiffrin, R. M. (1984). A retrieval model for both recognition and recall. *Psychological Review, 91*, 1–67.

Hintzman, D. L. (1986). "Schema abstraction" in a multiple-trace memory model. *Psychological Review, 93*, 411–428.

Humphreys, M. S., Bain, J. D., and Pike, R. (1989). Different ways to cue a coherent memory system: A theory for episodic, semantic, and procedural tasks. *Psychological Review, 96*, 208–233.

James, W. (1890). *The principles of psychology*. New York: Holt.

Kintsch, W. (1974). *The representation of meaning in memory*. Hillsdale, NJ: Lawrence Erlbaum Associates.

Kosslyn, S. (1980). *Image and mind*. Cambridge, MA: Harvard University Press.

Meyer, D. E. (1970). On the representation and retrieval of stored semantic information. *Cognitive Psychology, 1*, 243–299.

Meyer, D. E., and Schvaneveldt, R. W. (1971). Facilitation in recognizing pairs of words: Evidence of a dependence between retrieval operations. *Journal of Experimental Psychology, 90*, 227–234.

Monsell, S. (1987). On the relation between lexical input and output pathways for speech. In A. Allport, D. MacKay, W. Prinz, and E. Scheerer (Eds.), *Language perception and production: Relationships between listening, speaking, reading, and writing*. London: Academic Press.

Murdock, B. B., Jr. (1982). A theory for the storage and retrieval of item and associative information. *Psychological Review, 89*, 609–626.

Newell, A. (1973). Production systems: Models of control structures. In W. G. Chase (Ed.), *Visual information processing*, 463–526. New York: Academic Press.

Norman, D. A., and Rumelhart, D. E. (1975). *Explorations in cognition*. San Francisco, CA: W. H. Freeman.

Quillian, M. R. (1969). The teachable language comprehender: A simulation program and theory of language. *Communications of The Association for Computing Machinery, 12*, 459–476.

Raaijmakers, J. G. W., and Shiffrin, R. M. (1981). Search of associative memory. *Psychological Review, 88*, 93–134.

Rumelhart, D. E. (1975). Notes on a schema for stories. In D. G. Bobrow and A. M. Collins (Eds.), *Representation and understanding*. New York: Academic Press.

Rumelhart, D. E., and McClelland, J. L. (1986). *Parallel distributed processing*. Vol. 1, *Foundations*. Cambridge, MA: MIT Press.

Sanders, A. F. (Ed.) (1967). *Attention and performance*. Amsterdam: North-Holland Publishing Co.

Schacter, D. L. (1987). Implicit memory: History and current status. *Journal of Experimental Psychology: Learning, Memory, and Cognition, 13*, 501–518.

Schank, R. C. (1975). *Conceptual information processing*. Amsterdam: North-Holland Publishing Co.

Schank, R. C., and Abelson, R. (1977). *Scripts, plans, goals and understanding*. Hillsdale, NJ: Lawrence Erlbaum Associates.

Sperling, G. S. (1967). Successive approximations to a model of short-term memory. *Acta Psychologica, 27*, 285–292.

Squire, L. R. (1987). *Memory and brain*. Oxford, UK: Oxford University Press.

Sternberg, S. (1975). Memory scanning: New findings and current controversies. *Quarterly Journal of Experimental Psychology, 27*, 1–32.

Tulving, E. (1972). Episodic and semantic memory. In E. Tulving and W. Donaldson (Eds.), *Organization and memory*. New York: Academic Press.

Waugh, N. C., and Norman, D. A. (1965). Primary memory. *Psychological Review, 72*, 89–104.

Winograd, T. (1975). Frame representations and the declarative-procedural controversy. In D. G. Bobrow and A. Collins (Eds.), *Representation and understanding*, 185–210. New York: Academic Press.

16 Twenty-Five Years of Learning and Memory: Was the Cognitive Revolution a Mistake?

Douglas L. Hintzman

The first Attention and Performance symposium was held in 1966, when I was a graduate student (Sanders 1967). It is clear in hindsight that a scientific revolution was underway—indeed, the founding of the Attention and Performance association can be seen as a sign of the revolution's success. My fellow students and I were cognitive psychologists, although we did not know it at the time, because Neisser's book hadn't been published yet (Neisser 1967). What we *did* know was that exciting things were happening. New memory tasks were being invented and old ones reinvented, and new theoretical questions were being asked and long-abandoned ones revived. Tasks that had dominated the study of human learning for decades because they lent themselves easily to an S-R analysis—particularly serial and paired-associate learning—were being replaced by tasks such as recognition memory and free recall, which did not lend themselves easily to such analysis. Once-taboo concepts such as memory, attention, and image were discussed without embarrassment. It was easy to invent new and interesting experimental hypotheses (and also to do the experiments, since human-subjects review boards didn't exist). In both human and animal research, there was a growing belief that the "running dogs of behaviorism" had been barking up the wrong tree, and a flexible new device—the computer—was replacing the telephone switchboard as the metaphor of choice.

How did the cognitive revolution come about? Lachman, Lachman, and Butterfield (1979) discuss several precursors of the revolution, but single out as the seminal event a 1958 conference conducted by Newell and Simon, which was attended by several figures who were to become "the giants of information-processing psychology" (Lachman, Lachman, and Butterfield, 98). These future giants, it seems, saw immediately how the computer analogy could be applied to verbal learning, memory, perception, and attention, and left the conference to spread the word. The Lachman, Lachman, and Butterfield view might be characterized as the big bang theory. My own reading of history is that questions raised earlier by the Gestalt psychologists were central (the term *Gestalt* and the names of Köhler, Koffka, and Wertheimer do not appear in the index of Lachman, Lachman, and Butterfield 1979).

Big bang or no, a new order was ascending, and—as is usual in revolutions—the outgoing incumbents were the targets of revenge. They may have brought some of this unpleasantness on themselves. I recall finding aspects of the Hull-Spence theory amusing as an undergraduate—particularly the insistence on calling unobservable events "responses" and "stimuli"—and Skinner's attempts to explain virtually every aspect of human behavior as though we were all hungry pigeons confined in little boxes (e.g., Skinner 1974) struck me as absurd. Others tell me that they had similar reactions. So behaviorism may have died as much of self-inflicted wounds as of stabs in the back by the upstart rebels (e.g., Chomsky 1959). Maybe it didn't give itself a chance.

Two stimuli occasioned my emitting these responses. One is a book I read recently on the effects of the cognitive revolution in animal learning, by an unreconstructed neobehaviorist, Abram Amsel (1989). To my surprise, I found myself agreeing with most of what Amsel had to say. The other was a letter from the organizers of this symposium reminding me of my deadline. Searching in panic for a theme for my talk, I came up with a phrase, undoubtedly primed by Amsel's book: "The cognitive revolution was a mistake." This seemed provocative, and possibly worthy of a couple of jokes, but it was obviously too outrageous to be sustained for a full presentation. But after some thinking and reading, I began to see the basic thesis as far less amusing and outrageous than I had at the start.

I will return to this point later, after reviewing some of the main topics in the field over the past twenty-five years or so. For now, however, I want to make an observation that is brought out forcefully in Amsel's book: the "behaviorism" that modern cognitive science castigates as witless or worse is a caricature. It is drawn primarily from the more extreme polemical writings of Watson and Skinner and bears only superficial resemblance to the sober explanatory attempts of such neobehaviorists as Hull (e.g., 1943), Spence (1956), Mowrer (1960), Osgood (1953), and N. E. Miller (1959). Prerevolutionary psychology was in many ways more "cognitive" than most of our textbooks admit, and as I will argue, it had other virtues as well.

In what follows I first consider several empirical issues in the field of learning and memory, then I note some striking similarities between present theoretical frameworks and prerevolutionary ones, and finally I discuss attitudes toward empirical and theoretical methodology. I will not be so perverse as to argue that no good at all came from the cognitive revolution. I will, however, lament the collective amnesia for prerevolutionary psychology that the revolution seems to have caused. It is useful, in covering half-explored territory, to know where the pioneers found the going easy, where they stumbled, and where they found quicksand. Such lessons are lost if one thinks the pioneers were fools or, worse, doesn't even know there were pioneers.

16.1 EMPIRICAL ISSUES

In this section, I argue that learning and memory researchers, collectively, seem to be conducting a gigantic, double-blind "conceptual replication." The dominant positions on several central issues in our field have returned to points that would have given the neobehaviorists and functionalists well-founded feelings of déjà vu.

All-or-None Learning

I start with incremental versus all-or-none learning, because this was a lively topic around the time I was a student. The traditional view was that, in learning, associative strength gradually increases through repetition. (Contrary to the picture held by most cognitive psychologists, the role of reinforcement was usually downplayed where humans were concerned. For example, reinforcement played no role in the theory of human rote learning proposed by Hull et al. 1940.) This standard "continuity" or "incremental" view of learning contrasted with Gestalt theory, which saw learning as a matter of sudden reorganization, as illustrated by "insight" in Köhler's (1925) apes and by so-called hypothesis testing in Krechevsky's (1932) rats. The idea that learning is discontinuous did not acquire real respectability, however, until the late 1950s and early 1960s. This change may have been partly due to the growing influence of the computer metaphor in psychology. All-or-none learning is supported by the computer metaphor, because the elementary symbol-processing operations of a digital computer—storing, comparing, copying, and manipulating symbols—are discrete events.

The incremental versus all-or-none learning controversy marked the end of a long tradition in the study of learning, in that the crucial data on a central theoretical issue came from human beings instead of from animals such as rats. The results of certain paired-associate learning experiments seemed to support the view that learning is all-or-none: For example, changing pairs when subjects got them wrong did not seem to retard learning (e.g., Rock 1957), and when two test trials were given following a single study trial, an error on the first test trial was almost always followed by an error on the second (e.g., Estes 1960). These studies, however, were severely criticized for problems of subject and item selection. Underwood and Keppel (1962) argued that the data could be explained by such selection, combined with an assumption borrowed from Clark Hull's theory: that subthreshold changes in associative strength do not affect overt performance. In response, Estes (1962) disparaged the threshold construct as an "outcast stepchild of psychophysics" (23), and it virtually disappeared from learning theory for some twenty years.

The idea of sudden learning was captured most simply by Markov learning models that assumed discrete states, and characterized learning and forgetting as all-or-none jumps from state to state. Bower's (1961) one-element model, for example, had only two states (learned vs. unlearned), no forgetting, and a single learning parameter. This model accounted for quantitative characteristics of the data from certain paired-associate experiments with astonishing precision, and occasioned either great excitement or disbelief, depending on one's theoretical orientation. However, subsequent work revealed serious problems for the one-element model. The model implies that, on all trials prior to the last error on a pair, the pair must have been in the unlearned state. But performance gradually improves over such precriterion trials if the list contains more than two response alternatives (Bower 1967). Moreover, second attempts after errors are right more often than expected by chance (e.g., Bower 1967), and subjects can discriminate precriterion correct responses from precriterion errors (Hintzman 1967). Contrary to the idea of a discrete learned state, response latencies decrease gradually after the last error on a pair (Millward 1964), and overlearning is revealed on delayed retention tests (e.g., Runquist 1957). Modelers responded to such predictive failures by proposing Markov systems with more than two states (e.g., unlearned, partially learned, and learned), but these never had the appeal of the one-element model, and different models of this general type often made identical predictions (see Murdock 1974, chap. 4, for a summary).

Textbooks suggest that the question of all-or-none learning was not settled, if they discuss it at all (e.g., Crowder 1976). Strictly speaking, that may be true. But the all-or-none hypothesis was implausible a priori, on biological grounds (because, for example, neural firing rates vary continuously), and advocates of the all-or-none position never made a convincing case. While learning functions may show discontinuities when subjects find helpful mediators, few theorists today would suggest that human memory has the all-or-none property that computer memory has. Current models of associative learning assume the gradual learning of associations, as the prerevolutionary theories did (e.g., chap. 21, this volume; Mensink and Raaijmakers 1988; Murdock 1982; chap. 20, this volume); and Estes's "outcast stepchild"—the threshold—has been warmly embraced by modern connectionism. A similar retreat from discrete, all-or-none processing back to continuous processing can be seen in theoretical treatments of the Sternberg (1966) memory-scanning task (e.g., Ratcliff 1978).

Mnemonics

A second cognitivist attack on associative learning was spurred by the subversive writings of Miller, Galanter, and Pribram (1960), who (among less successful heresies, such as the TOTE unit) promoted interest in imagery mnemonics. The power of such methods was dramatically illustrated by the peg-word, or "one is a bun," technique. Experimenters soon showed that the strategy of forming bizarre, interacting visual images can dramatically enhance the associative learning of pairs of concrete words (e.g., Bugelski, Kidd, and Segmen 1968). The effect was so striking that it seemed to call for some new explanatory principle—or at least one outside of the functionalists' stock in trade.

One prominent early hypothesis held that the imagery advantage derives from redundancy: Subjects following imagery instructions have both a verbal and a visual memory code for each pair (Paivio 1969). Several lines of evidence, however, suggested that the specifically visual nature of the images was not important. For example, congenitally blind subjects benefit from imagery instructions (Jonides, Kahn, and Rozin 1975), and imagining two objects side by side is no more effective for learning than just rehearsing the word pair aloud (Bower 1970a). Using pictures to control their subjects' images, Wollen, Weber, and Lowry (1972) concluded that interaction was crucial, but bizarreness was not. This suggests that it is the formation of a unitary, configural representation that is essential, which fits nicely with what the Gestaltists believed.

A graduate student at the University of Oregon, Steve Buggie, had a different hypothesis. He noted that previous work had confounded the type of relation (noninteracting vs. interacting) with the number of relations used in the list as a whole. That is, in the static image condition the relation *side by side* was the same for all pairs, but in the interacting image condition, subjects were free to make up different relations for the different pairs. Buggie attacked this problem by having subjects learn incidentally, by rating the vividness of the images evoked by verbal descriptions. Each description included two concrete nouns linked by a relation (e.g., apple *jammed into a* window, parakeet *crushing* a goblet). In one condition, a single static relation (*beside a*) was used for all 28 of the pairs. In three other conditions, either 1, 4, or 28 different interactive relations were used for the 28 pairs.

Because Buggie never published his dissertation (Buggie 1974), I present the recall data from his experiment 1 in figure 16.1. The results show that it is the number of relations used in the list that is crucial, not the type of relation. A single interactive relation used for all 28 pairs was no better than imagining all 28 pairs side by side.

Buggie's (1974) results suggest that the effect of imagery on memory, which once seemed so special, may instead represent one more example of a venerable and commonplace law. Effects of intralist similarity on learning were a staple topic of functionalist research and neobehaviorist theory long before the

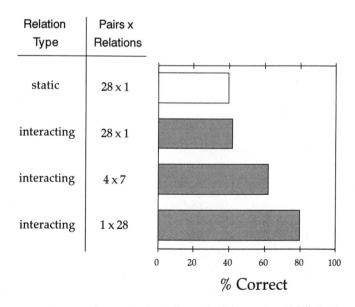

Figure 16.1 Recall percentage as a function of the number of different imagined relations in a 28-pair list, from Buggie's (1974) experiment 1.

Twenty-Five Years of Learning and Memory

cognitive revolution occurred (e.g., Gibson 1940). Recent work on imagery mnemonics invokes concepts from the past in a way consistent with Buggie's study. For example, in exploring the question of when and why bizarreness aids memory, Einstein, McDaniel, and Lackey (1989) offer an updated version of the interference theory of forgetting (e.g., Postman 1961; Postman and Underwood 1973). They report experiments on retroactive interference, suggesting that bizarre images endure because they are less similar to intervening events than nonbizarre images are.

Memory Span

One of the cornerstones of the cognitive revolution was the constancy of the memory span as measured in familiar units or "chunks" (Miller 1956). This view was sanctioned by the computer metaphor, which suggests a temporary memory buffer with a limited number of addresses, or slots. Seemingly contrary evidence, showing that different materials yield different spans, was accommodated by assuming that the size of a chunk varies with different materials, thus preserving the presumed constancy of the span (e.g., Simon 1974).

Studies of the memory span, however, display properties that are very difficult for a fixed-slot model to explain (e.g., Baddeley 1986). The span is smaller for items that take a long time to pronounce than for items that are pronounced quickly (the word-length effect); it is smaller for lists whose members have similar pronunciations than for dissimilar lists (the phonological-similarity effect); and confusion errors tend to be items that resemble the target items in the way they are pronounced. Transpositions of phonologically similar items (e.g., BP for PB) are especially likely. All this happens even when initial presentation is visual, so auditory input is not required.

Baddeley and his colleagues have proposed that such findings reflect the operation of an "articulatory loop"—a kind of peripheral "slave system" of working memory, used to retain speech-based information for short periods of time (e.g., Baddeley 1986). Support for this explanation comes from studies of articulatory suppression, which reduces the memory span, and—more important—eliminates both the phonological-similarity effect and the word-length effect. (This description holds for visual input; when input is auditory, the results are more complex.)

An important question is whether subjects have a harder time articulating phonologically similar lists than dissimilar lists—that is, whether the similarity effect is mediated by pronunciation rate. Schweickert, Guentert, and Hersberger (1990) found that it is not; they are independent effects. Reisberg, Rappaport, and O'Shaughnessy (1984) showed that the memory span for digits could be expanded almost 50 percent, by training subjects to use their fingers to code digits—an advantage that disappeared when they were required to drum their fingers. Reisberg, Rappaport, and O'Shaughnessy argued that the articulatory loop is not a part of working memory, as suggested by Baddeley. Rather, they write, "When we use the articulatory loop ... we are *creating* a temporary memory component by taking an activity that is not intrinsically memorial, and recruiting that activity for short-term storage" (203–204).

This begins to sound like a system that a behaviorist would love—recall that Watson (1930) related thinking to subvocal speech. A neobehaviorist like Hull might have explained such findings in terms of fractional (subvocal) articulatory responses (r's), produced at study by preestablished reading habits. In Hull's (e.g., 1930) system, such r's produced kinesthetic feedback, leaving stimulus traces (s's) that decayed over time. Suppose that the recall phase of a trial consists of overt responses to the traces of these response-produced stimuli. Generalization among the traces, based on articulatory similarity, would produce phonemic confusions and the phonological-similarity effect. Decay of a given stimulus trace would be a function of the pronunciation times of the intervening items, so recall would display a word-length effect. Such a model would predict that phonological similarity and word length are independent factors, as Schweickert, Guentert, and Hersberger (1990) found. Of course, additional assumptions would be needed to deal with serial order—a problem with which Hull was concerned. Perhaps such a model of the memory span would not be completely successful; but it seems better than the computer-inspired fixed-slot model was. And imagine the fun Hull or one of his students could have had modeling the memory span—especially if they'd had a Sun workstation to run simulations on.

Compatibility and Transfer Effects

The rise of the computer metaphor gave us multistore memory models, with sensory buffers, small-capacity short-term stores, and large-capacity long-term stores (chap. 20, this volume). However, these models soon gave way—in our journals, if not in our textbooks—to a broad-based fascination with differential effects of encoding tasks. More than twenty years ago, Hyde and Jenkins (1969) reported that free recall was much poorer following an incidental learning task that focused attention on visual characteristics of the words than it was following a semantic orienting task. Such findings provided lumber for the levels-of-processing framework (Craik and Lockhart 1972), which quickly became one of the dominant theoretical structures of the field. The basic idea was that the processing of information can terminate at any of several levels, ranging from shallow (e.g., visual information) to deep (e.g., semantic elaboration), and that the longevity of the resulting trace is directly related to its initial processing depth. Thus, semantic traces are not just qualitatively different from visual traces in the kind of information they hold; somehow, because of this qualitative difference, they are longer-lasting.

Subsequent research surrounded the question of whether the best metaphor was "depth" of processing or something else, such as "distinctiveness," "richness," or "breadth" (see Cermak and Craik 1979). An important challenge to all these views was reported by Morris, Bransford, and Franks (1977), who obtained an interaction between the encoding task and the retrieval task. Semantic (deep) encoding was superior to rhyme (shallow) encoding for standard recognition memory, but the opposite was true when subjects had to recognize rhymes of the words they had seen. This study thus emphasized the relationship (i.e., the compatibility) between the encoding task and the retrieval task, rather than the encoding task per se.

This emphasis on compatibility or transfer has become increasingly popular in the past few years. For example, Roediger, Weldon, and Challis (1989) argue that so-called dissociations in the effects of encoding tasks on different retrieval tasks can be explained in terms of the similarity of the operations that the tasks require. McDaniel, Waddill, and Einstein (1988) argue for a compatibility explanation of what has been called the "generation effect." And Glass, Krejci, and Goldman (1989), who obtained differential effects of several study conditions on three different measures of memory for digit strings, conclude that their results supported "an emerging framework in which memory is viewed as the product of a large number of individual processing operations ... which may be altered by their use" (197).

Such transfer or compatibility effects, of course, should be particularly apparent when the encoding and retrieval tasks are identical, as they are in so-called long-term priming tasks such as naming latency and—more generally—in any task that is acquired through repeated practice. To put it differently, all demonstrations of learning and memory involve transfer. Despite the functionalists' and behaviorists' recognition of the topic's central importance—or perhaps because of it—the term *transfer* virtually disappeared from the active literature when the cognitive revolution took place. It is now making a belated comeback (e.g., Singley and Anderson 1989).

My argument is that differential encoding effects, which appeared so puzzling to the cognitive revolutionaries, might have been readily assimilated as another example of transfer of training, if the cognitive revolution had not been so complete. (Perhaps the cognitivist coding of the problem was so different from the prerevolutionary one that no transfer occurred.) The Osgood (1949) transfer surface was developed primarily to deal with paired-associate learning, but it might help current workers understand compatibility effects. The surface is an empirical generalization relating the amount and direction of transfer to the similarity of the stimuli and of the responses in initial and transfer tasks (see fig. 16.2). One could think of different encoding tasks as strengthening different responses to the stimulus word (e.g., generating a rhyme might strengthen a pronunciation response, while categorization might strengthen the response of naming the superordinate), and one could think of different retrieval or transfer tasks as varying in how much they benefit from each type of response. A detailed theory would be required, describing how such responses mediate performance in the different tasks, and I have none to offer here. But such an approach might help to clarify what it means to say that subjects do not store information, but rather learn mental "operations" or "procedures" (e.g., Kolers and Roediger 1984). The Osgood surface also raises the interesting question of whether encoding-retrieval interactions can yield negative transfer. To my knowledge, no one has looked for that.

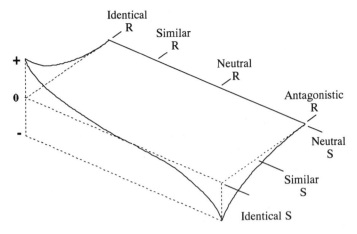

Figure 16.2 Osgood's transfer and retroaction surface (adapted from Osgood 1949).

There would also be a supreme irony in a transfer-surface account of encoding effects: A paper by Jenkins, focusing on the puzzling nature of the initial orienting-task results, was entitled "Remember that old theory of memory? Well forget it!" (Jenkins 1974). A belated rejoinder may be in order, which could be titled "You probably don't remember this, but Jenkins told you to forget an old theory of memory. Now it's time to remember it again!" Bob Bjork could write the rejoinder (see Bjork 1972).

Consciousness and Learning

Cognitivists may have neglected transfer, in part, because the term smacks of unconscious determinants of behavior. It was an article of faith of the cognitive revolution that learning and retrieval are conscious acts. According to the revolutionaries, paired-associate acquisition is not a matter of "rote learning"; rather, subjects learn pairs by discovering suitable verbal mediators or constructing relational images. In the early two-store memory models (e.g., Atkinson and Shiffrin 1968), nothing could get into the long-term store without passing through the short-term store (often seen as the seat of consciousness), and nothing in the long-term store could affect behavior without first being copied back into the short-term store (but see chap. 20).

A review paper by Brewer (1974) claimed that all behavior purported to reflect classical and operant conditioning in adult humans is actually mediated by subjects' conscious hypotheses about the experimental situation. Brewer's main point was a good one, and it served to counter common misconceptions about the automatic effects of contiguity and reward that were especially popular in introductory textbooks and in behavior therapy, even if his conclusion did go too far. In general, human subjects have been seen as not only *cognitive*, but also *cognizant*. There is little room in such a conception for either past or present events to affect behavior without the person being aware of it. Behaviorism had rejected a general prejudice against subconscious determinants of behavior inherited from folk psychology ("I know why I do things"); but after the revolution, the once-rejected prejudice was back.

The first challenge to the prejudice from within cognitive psychology may have been provided by associative priming, in which behavior is influenced by information that has been subconsciously activated (Meyer and Schvaneveldt 1971). Then there was evidence suggesting that one does not even have to be aware of the retrieval cue (Marcel 1983). There were also amnesics, who showed evidence of having learned even though they didn't consciously remember doing so; and then experiments on normal subjects showed the same thing.

Legions of psychologists now study this exciting "implicit" kind of memory and contrast it with the drab and boring "explicit" kind (Schacter 1987). Most recently, subjects have been shown to *learn* without realizing it. The most convincing of the demonstrations involve the learning of skills (Hayes and Broadbent 1988; Lewicki, Czyzewska, and Hoffman 1987; Willingham, Nissen, and Bullemer 1989). Yet such findings would have been unsurprising to the behaviorists, with their emphasis on automatic habits. A recent demonstration that memory can unconsciously bias perceptual judgment (Jacoby and Whitehouse 1989) harkens back even further to Helmholtz's ([1910] 1962) concept of "unconscious inference." So these recent discoveries may not be as new as they seem.

Memory Systems

Disinterest in unconscious processes went hand in hand with disinterest in animals. Behaviorism and functionalism were devoted to the concepts of adaptation and evolution—hence the presumption that experiments on rats and pigeons can yield information relevant to the behavior of human beings. When the cognitivist revolutionaries finished their victory celebration, evolutionary considerations—among other valuables—had been thrown in the trash. Chomsky (1968) argued that the mechanisms underlying language syntax are unique to humans, and it was often assumed that much more is uniquely human as well. Cognitivists were half-jokingly said to believe that humans and computers are more closely related than are humans and chimps. Students of human learning and memory, who had once read the animal-learning literature for inspiration, stopped; animal researchers began reading the human literature instead. Of course, the theory of evolution explains not only why species are alike but also why they are different, and the behaviorists had overemphasized the first of these and neglected the second. The "biological constraints" movement among animal researchers helped to correct that bias, although its advocates often went to the opposite extreme and (in agreement with the attitude in cognitive psychology) assumed that each species' learning abilities are unique (e.g., Johnston 1981).

It is only recently, with the growing interest in separate memory systems, that students of human memory have returned to the idea that something of value can be learned from animal research. Efforts to establish different memory systems with normal human subjects by finding functional dissociations and stochastic independence suffer from theoretical and methodological flaws (Hintzman 1990a; Hintzman and Hartry 1990). Better evidence for the multiple-systems approach comes from research on amnesics with medial-temporal and diencephalic damage, who display a fascinating pattern of impaired and preserved learning abilities (e.g., Shimamura 1989; Squire 1987). Certain kinds of fast cognitive learning, typically involving conscious awareness, appear to require intact medial temporal structures—most prominently, the hippocampus. Slower and presumably more primitive kinds of learning appear to depend on other brain areas. It is noteworthy that these conclusions derive not only from experiments with human amnesics, but also from studies of animal preparations using monkeys (Mishkin, Malamut, and Bachevalier 1984; chap. 17, this volume; Squire and Zola-Morgan 1988) and rats (Hirsch 1974; Oakley 1981).

But an earlier comparative psychology literature supports the hypothesis of different learning and memory systems, as well. The Russian-born psychologist, Gregory Razran, reviewed over fifteen hundred publications on learning in the Russian, German, and English scientific literature, identifying several types of learning and relating them to the evolutionary stage where they first appear (Razran 1971). He identified four "superlevels" of learning, each (a) emerging from lower levels, (b) dominating lower levels, and (c) coexisting with lower levels in phylogenetically later species.

A slightly modified version of Razran's system is shown in figure 16.3. Of particular interest are two dividing lines. The first is between lower and higher vertebrates. Higher vertebrates have brains roughly ten times as large as those of lower vertebrates when body size is taken into account (Jerison 1973), and their learning abilities seem to be considerably more sophisticated. Razran places special emphasis on *configuring* in classical conditioning, which requires that an animal respond differently to a compound stimulus than to its components—for example, food may follow a bell, and follow a light, but not follow the bell-light combination. (In his theory of learning and memory

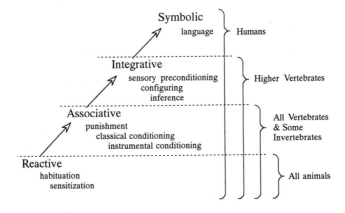

Figure 16.3 A modified version of Razran's (1971) learning hierarchy.

phenomena, including amnesia, Wickelgren 1979 related configuring to chunking.) According to Razran's review, lower vertebrates cannot learn this type of discrimination.

Other evidence that lower vertebrates learn about arbitrary events in a more primitive way than do higher vertebrates comes from the work of Bitterman (1975). Today, one might say that higher vertebrates, but not lower vertebrates, have the ability to form representations. The learning phenomena that distinguish higher vertebrates appear to depend on the hippocampus and, in young rats, to emerge as this structure develops (Amsel and Stanton 1980).

Razran's second major dividing line—between humans and other animals —corresponds to another jump in brain size relative to body size, and involves learning through (and, presumably, about) language. It is interesting to note that Razran's hierarchy allows for the laws of language to differ from those for other types of behavior. Thus, biological considerations lead to the reasonable conclusion that the essentially unique linguistic ability of humans, which Pavlov ([1934] 1955) called the "second signal system," lies on a continuum with, and interacts with, cognitive abilities that we share with other species. Razran's proposal that higher systems dominate lower ones is also consistent with the ubiquitous effects of hypothesis and instruction on conditioning, as revealed by Brewer's (1974) review.

Organization versus Association

The rejection of animal research as irrelevant to human learning was predicated on the assumption that the doctrines of associationism would have to be replaced. Bower (1970b) wrote, "A modest revolution is afoot today within the field of human learning, and the rebels are marching under the banner of 'cognitive organization'" (18). A page later he admitted that organization was "a slogan, a rallying cry, with clearer emotional than denotative meaning" (19). It was never entirely clear just what the term referred to, except that it meant more than mere "association." Champions of organization preferred to study memory using methods such as free recall, which allowed subject-imposed, as opposed to experimenter-imposed, organization to reveal itself (e.g., Tulving 1968).

The change in the field of memory was dramatic. In just five years, between 1967 and 1972, the ratio of paired-associate studies to free-recall studies in the index of the *Journal of Verbal Learning and Verbal Behavior* dropped from 31:9 to 2:32. In today's literature, however, free recall is on the list of endangered tasks and paired associates is making a comeback. At a recent memory conference, I did not hear the word "organization" once, but terms from the heyday of interference theory, such as "A-B, A-B' paradigm" and "A-B, A-B$_r$ paradigm," popped up several times. Classic studies from that era (e.g., Barnes and Underwood 1959; Melton and Irwin 1940; Postman 1961; Underwood 1957) are being dusted off and read with interest, as directly relevant to current theoretical concerns (e.g., Mensink and Raaijmakers 1988).

The banner of organization fluttered over the study of semantic memory, as well as over free recall. In considering ways to retrieve information from a complex database, artificial intelligence (AI) workers concluded that two-term relations, such as simple associations, are not up to the job, and that different types of relationships, such as *superordinate*, *property*, and *opposite* need to be distinguished. This can be accomplished with three-term relations, as realized in labeled associations—an idea first proposed by Otto Selz in 1913 (see Mandler 1985). Psychological models of the organization of semantic memory employed various types of associative labels in various ways, together with complex rules of inference, to explain our ability to answer a variety of questions about the real world (see Johnson-Laird, Herrmann, and Chaffin 1984).

Most such models, however, described a static structure and made no allowance for adding information—particularly, information requiring an organizational change. Two creators of one of these models commented, "It is somehow strange that throughout the recent work on semantic memory, the study of learning has been slighted. The term *learning* has fallen into disuse, replaced by vague references to 'acquisition of information in memory'" (Rumelhart and Norman 1978, 37).

Higher-order structures called "schemas," adapted from Bartlett (1932), were invoked to deal with this problem and enjoyed great popularity in verbally stated theories. For example, Mandler (1985) described schemas as "a category of mental structures that stores and organizes past experience and guides our subsequent perception and experience" (36). He claimed that they "vary from the most concrete to the most abstract; they organize the perceptual elements of an event, as well as its 'meaning' or gist" (37). Moreover, schemas interact and inhibit one another and "change, spin off new ones, are incorporated into others, and develop subordinate relations to each other" (109). The explanatory powers of schemas seemed as unlimited as those of homunculi, and they lacked the pejorative name.

Not surprisingly, attempts to derive all these properties of schemas from more basic assumptions have failed. One AI practitioner has suggested that memory must reorganize itself dynamically, using several different types of abstract structures called scripts, scenes, MOPS, meta-MOPS, and TOPS (Schank 1982). This takes the notion of the schema to its ultimate conclusion, in an elaborate system that seems impervious to empirical testing. Versions of schema theory that are more restricted appear inconsistent with a growing body of experimental evidence (Alba and Hasher 1983). Faced with this unsatisfying situation, cognitive theorists have largely abandoned models of semantic organization per se in favor of systems that learn.

16.2 THEORETICAL FRAMEWORKS

Cognitive psychologists and Skinnerians agree on very little, except that neobehaviorism was a misguided failure—an absolute dead end. Given this rare unanimity, it would be suprising if the new cognitive approaches to learning that have occasioned so much excitement turned out to resemble theories of neobehaviorists such as Hull. In this section, I briefly examine the connectionism and production-system approaches to learning, and conclude that the similarities to Hull's theory are strong. If the excitement over these new frameworks is justified, then perhaps the neobehaviorists were on the right track after all.

Connectionism

Connectionist, or parallel distributed processing (PDP) models (e.g., Hinton and Anderson 1981; Rumelhart and McClelland 1986), represent a radical change for cognitive theory in several respects—among them is a renewed focus on systems that learn. Modern connectionism builds on the earlier attempt by Rosenblatt (1958) to model biological intelligence as "perceptrons"—an effort that was abandoned after his death, in favor of the now-standard symbol manipulation style of AI. The roots of PDP models go back further, however. Thorndike's (1913) learning theory was known as "connectionism," and a diagram of a connectionist network and discussion of what is now called "Hebbian learning" can be found even earlier in the work of William James (1890, 569–570). James's diagram is shown in figure 16.4.

But the most striking parallels with modern connectionism are found in the writings of Hull, whose major theoretical statements appeared in two books (Hull 1943, 1952) and in a series of papers appearing in *Psychological Review* between 1929 and 1950 (Hull 1929, 1930, 1931, 1934a, 1934b, 1945; recently reprinted in Amsel and Rashotte 1984). Hull's ultimate goal was to describe a purely mechanical system—a robot—that would mimic the flexibility of human behavior. He often stated his theories in mathematical terms, using theoretical constructs called intervening variables, which he hoped ultimately to relate to processes in the brain. The basic elements were to be "small

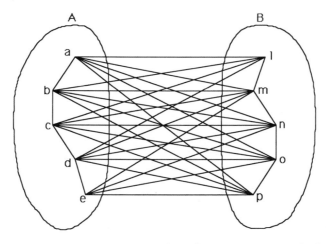

Figure 16.4 William James's one-layered connectionist network, illustrating the concept of "compound association" (James 1890, fig. 40).

unitary stimulus-response units, attached to *parts* of stimulus patterns, and these units being aggregated into larger and larger units always operating on the same general principle" (Hull, quoted in Amsel and Rashotte 1984, 3). Hull pursued his dream with an enormous grant to Yale's Institute of Human Relations from the Laura Spellman Rockefeller Memorial Fund (a kind of early-day Sloan Foundation), and with the help of a collection of psychologists, logicians, mathematicians, and others (Boakes 1984).

The top panel of figure 16.5 shows the basic unit of Hull's theory as it is usually depicted, alongside a simple PDP or connectionist network. The contrast of I and O (input and output) with S and R is obviously just labeling. The distributed PDP representation could reflect a more fundamental difference, but as the preceding quote from Hull shows, he saw the stimulus as made up of components. Further, his spatial depictions of stimulus generalization suggest that a stimulus might be represented as a point in multidimensional space. The PDP diagram simply breaks the stimulus down into components, or (alternatively) represents each dimension separately, so Hull would have felt quite comfortable with a distributed representation of S. He also wrote about response generalization and fractional responses, both of which suggest a componential, or distributed, representation of R.

Connecting all stimulus components to all response components gives the PDP diagram at the right. Like PDP models, which allow for both excitatory and inhibitory connections, Hull's theory included both positive (habit strength)

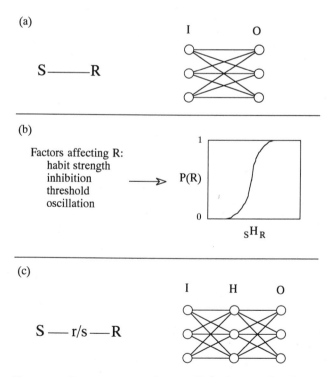

Figure 16.5 Some comparisons between Hull's theory and modern connectionism.

and negative associations (conditioned inhibition). Hull also assumed a threshold for response production, which, when combined with normally distributed oscillation, made the probability of R an ogive function of habit strength (panel b of fig. 16.5). Thresholds and quasi-threshold functions similar to that of figure 16.5b are routine assumptions in the PDP approach (Rumelhart and McClelland 1986).

What contrasts modern connectionism with early perceptrons, of course, is the use of hidden units to construct distributed representations that mediate between input and output. Hull had hidden units too, in his fractional response mechanism (fig. 16.5, panel c). In some of his writings, the fractional response (r) was incipient muscle activity and its stimulus consequences were peripheral feedback (e.g., Hull 1931); but in others, r was completely internal, serving no function except to control behavior through its production of the internal s. Such r's were variously called "cortical responses" or "pure stimulus acts" (Hull 1930). One difference from PDP modeling practice is that Hull's S-r bonds were learned independently of the s-R ones. No backpropagation was needed; the r/s mechanism either transferred from previous learning or migrated into its place as a mediating mechanism according to conditioning and generalization rules. "Backprop" would have been pointless in any case, because in most of the learning situations Hull considered there was no "teacher." Feedback did not indicate what the response should have been—it was binary: reward versus no reward. Such impoverished feedback poses problems for backpropagation using the delta rule (Munro 1987).

It may be worth mentioning that one advantage of hidden units is to allow a PDP model to master the "exclusive or" problem, which is identical to the configuring problem in classical conditioning. Not having a way to tune hidden units to represent conjunctions of stimuli, Hull had a difficult time with configuring. He proposed that stimuli change when they are combined with other stimuli—a process called "afferent neural interaction" (Hull 1945). A different approach would have been to assume that units representing conjunctions already exist, so that they do not have to be learned. This is how the configural-cue model of Gluck and Bower (1988) works. Those authors also discuss the identity of the delta rule of PDP modeling with the learning rule used in Rescorla and Wagner's (1972) model of classical conditioning. Despite occasional claims that it embodies "expectancy" and "surprise," the Rescorla-Wagner model is clearly in the Hullian tradition. Hull assumed that habit strength increases by a fixed proportion of the distance to asymptote, and in one version of the theory the asymptote increased with the size of reward (Hull 1943). What was missing from Hull's learning rule was the idea of credit assignment—namely, that components of a stimulus compete for habit strength (cf. Amsel and Rashotte 1984).

A further similarity between Hull's theory and the current PDP approach lies in his use of multiplicative functions to determine the strength of R. In Hull's system, the multipliers were purely motivational (drive and incentive multiplied habit strength), but PDP modelers have used the same idea to enable connections to modulate other connections—in effect, turning them on and off. Among other things, this allows the equivalent of labeled associations in PDP networks (e.g., McClelland 1986). It can also be used to create units that will respond only to configurations of inputs. Hull would have found this a natural addition to his theoretical bag of tricks, which was already well filled. As Amsel and Rashotte (1984) comment: While [Hull's papers] are brilliant in many respects, for the modern reader they raise once again the nagging question of whether an analytical S-R account of complex behaviors is viable. … The sheer number of individual associative bonds, and the problem of quantifying their individual and combined momentary status to predict behavior is mind-boggling" (53).

Hull's theory was criticized for inconsistencies (e.g., Koch 1954), so this complexity may have been partly responsible for its downfall. Today's connectionists can use powerful computers to keep track of large numbers of variables and to systematically explore the implications of structural and parametric changes in their models. The Hullians did not invent modern PDP systems, of course. But they might have, if they had owned Sun workstations or a Cray.

Production Systems

Another current approach to the learning problem, which is more in touch with mainstream AI, is that based on production systems (e.g., Anderson 1983; Newell 1990). Others have noted that productions are similar to S-R units; I elaborate on this observation by comparing production systems with Hull's theory (see fig. 16.6). A production has two parts: (1) a condition that, when satisfied will activate the production, and (2) an action to be taken if the condition is met. The condition may be a complex configuration of the states of several variables, and the action can either be overt or a change in an internal variable, like Hull's "pure stimulus act."

A central problem for production systems is conflict resolution (response competition, to Hull)—that is, determining which production will fire next. Anderson (1983) discusses several conflict-resolution rules that have been used, all of which have analogs in Hull's system. They include refractoriness (Hull's reactive inhibition), the recency with which a condition element was last satisfied (Hull's decaying stimulus trace), the number of condition matches or specificity (Hull's stimulus generalization), ordering (Hull's S-R chain), production strength (Hull's habit strength), and the primacy of goals (Hull's drive stimulus and fractional goal response).

Learning rules in production systems also resemble those of Hull. For example, in Anderson's (1983) ACT* model, learning occurs in multiple ways: A production's strength increases if its firing is followed by success (reward to Hull, or more generally, the Law of Effect). The conditions for a production's firing can be tuned (discrimination learning to Hull), and new productions can be compiled out of old ones—a process called "chunking" by Newell (1990). Compilation or chunking has no direct parallel in Hull's system, but some close analogues include the habit-family hierarchy, in which an entire S-R sequence

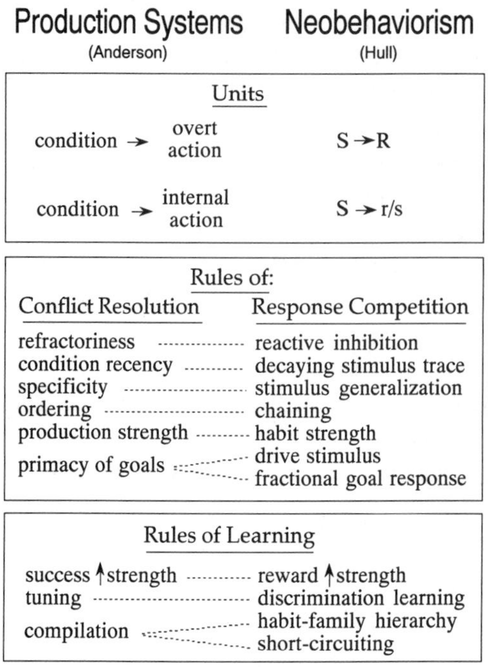

Production Systems (Anderson)	Neobehaviorism (Hull)

Units

condition → overt action	S → R
condition → internal action	S → r/s

Rules of:

Conflict Resolution	Response Competition
refractoriness	reactive inhibition
condition recency	decaying stimulus trace
specificity	stimulus generalization
ordering	chaining
production strength	habit strength
primacy of goals	drive stimulus
	fractional goal response

Rules of Learning

success ↑strength	reward ↑strength
tuning	discrimination learning
compilation	habit-family hierarchy
	short-circuiting

Figure 16.6 Some correspondences between production systems and Hull's theory.

becomes an operative unit (Hull 1934a,b), and "short-circuiting," in which superfluous S-R habits drop out of a chain (Hull 1929). Hull did not assume, as Anderson does, that skill learning always begins with a verbal or declarative representation—but then Hull's subjects were usually rats. (As mentioned earlier, humans do seem able to learn some kinds of skills unconsciously, contrary to Anderson's hypothesis.)

Again, I do not mean to imply that Hull invented production-system models. Certainly, the systems of Anderson (1983) and Newell (1990) are much more powerful than Hull's. Nevertheless, to my eye they resemble Hull's system more than their more immediate symbol-processing ancestors, such as Simon and Feigenbaum's (1964) EPAM. If one squints to blur the details, it is not hard to imagine both PDP models and production systems as picking up the threads of Hull's theoretical program after a hiatus of forty to fifty years.

16.3 METHODOLOGY

In the preceding sections I have tried to show that, during the past several years, a largely unrecognized counterrevolution has been underway. Empirical problems from prerevolutionary days have quietly retaken central positions, and old theoretical ideas have reemerged in disguise. But the revolution also encouraged wholesale rejection of a kind of methodological moral code that had gradually won acceptance in the preceding decades. In this section, I argue that the rejection of these methodological strictures has had negative effects.

Empirical Methodology

Functionalism and behaviorism rejected anecdotal evidence, insisted on objective measures, and endorsed experimentation as the fundamental method of science. What went on in psychology experiments looked as artificial as what went on in the chemistry lab. Some cognitive revolutionaries complained about all the artificiality, saying that learning a list of nonsense syllables bore little resemblance to learning in everyday life. They felt more kinship to Bartlett (1932), with his naturalistic materials and poor controls, than to Ebbinghaus (1885), with his nonsense syllables, randomization, and rigorous experimental techniques. Unconstrained by the old rules, some cognitivists have made liberal use of anecdote and subjective observation. Even those who stick to objective data sometimes treat experimental control with indifference, if not something to be deplored.

Anecdote and intuition fed Schank's growing system of scripts, scenes, MOPs, meta-MOPs, and TOPs. These devices were invented to explain "remindings"—for example: Why did an increase in the price of marijuana after a period of unavailability remind someone of a previous shortage of gasoline that cleared up after the price had risen (Schank 1982, 120)? Mandler (1985) seems to have had this style of research in mind when he wrote: "Intuition, anecdotal examples, striking exemplars, and singular demonstrations of complex processes are poor substitutes for hard evidence. Free association in response to interesting problems may be a good way of revealing underlying motives, but it is not (and has not been in the past) a particularly edifying way of doing science" (1985, 14).

The empirical study of semantic memory illustrates the dangers of lack of experimental control. As a student, I was a subject in one of the first semantic memory studies (Landauer and Freedman 1968). In such experiments, category-verification reaction times (RTs) are measured for statements like "A canary is a dwelling." These RTs were once thought to show how knowledge is organized, either by reflecting the time to search the category or by revealing directly the "distances" between concepts, in terms of number of links. The logic of this procedure and its relationship to a labeled-association model were laid out in a seminal paper by Collins and Quillian (1969), and the experimental literature on semantic memory boomed; but today, it has almost disappeared. As one lonely author complained, "Few areas of psychological inquiry have shown as spectacular a rise and decline as that of semantic memory" (Chang 1986, 199).

What happened? A great service might be rendered if scientists who give up a line of research were to write articles explaining why, but they seldom do ("I got interested in something else" is not very revealing, in any case). My own view as an outsider is that the downfall of the semantic memory paradigm began with an article by Collins and Loftus (1975), which argued that the model that had provided the initial impetus for the RT experiments didn't really make the predictions people thought it made. Collins and Loftus presented a more complex version of the model, allowing for category-verification decisions to be made in several different ways. In deciding whether a bat is a bird, for example, subjects might use a direct negative link (bat not-a bird), or match on the basis of properties. In the latter case, they have the option of giving special weight to certain "criterial" properties of the category (e.g., feathers, wings). Alternatively, they might note that a bat is a mammal and that the mammal and bird categories are mutually exclusive. For other sorts of questions (e.g., "All lawyers are politicians"), subjects might try to generate counterexamples. Collins and Loftus noted that any of these types of evidence might be used to make a particular decision and that the method might vary from person to person, adding that there were still more methods that people could use, which they didn't have space to describe.

The arguments of Collins and Loftus (1975) made intuitive sense but suggested that an adequate model of semantic memory would be too complex to test. Their article brought to the surface (or *near* to the surface, since the point was not explicitly made) a fundamental problem with semantic memory experiments: Since the conditions of learning are uncontrolled, there is no way to know what the recency and frequency of exposure have been, or even to know what information any particular subject has learned. (Of the University of Texas students queried by Gernsbacher and Goldsmith 1983, 31.6% said that bats *are* birds.)

This is not to say that semantic memory experiments produced only unreliable findings. One—the "typicality effect"—is very robust. But there are several ways to measure typicality, which are not perfectly correlated (Rosch and Mervis 1975), and the core variable may be our old friend, similarity (Kintsch 1980). Moreover, a large body of research on choice RT suggests that similarity affects the duration of the decision process, not the retrieval time, making the RT measure largely irrelevant to the question of how knowledge is organized.

The semantic memory paradigm has largely disappeared, but some of its concerns live on, in the study of "concepts." Researchers in this area have attempted to use simple models of conceptual structure and combination to explain subjects' judgments about natural concepts and their relations (RTs are not a central concern). These efforts seem to have foundered on complexity, just as the study of semantic memory did. Medin and Shoben (1988) provide some examples of the problems that theorists face: (1) *Wooden spoon* is judged to be a worse example of *spoon*, but a better example of *large spoon* than *metal spoon* is; (2) *Gray* is judged more similar to *white* in the context of *hair*, but more similar to *black* in the context of *cloud*; (3) A *straight banana* is judged to be a fairly typical banana, but a *straight boomerang* is seen as a poor boomerang.

An influential article by Murphy and Medin (1985) argued that all extant models of conceptual coherence were inadequate. They did not present a substitute model, but proposed a general approach based on people's theories about the concepts. This approach emphasizes the "structure-function relationships" internal to each concept, and "the position of the concept in the complete knowledge base" (313). Another way to put this might be to say that conceptual judgments tell us little about psychology per se (i.e., about the processes that operate on the database and the principles of its organization), because they primarily reflect what the knowledge is *about*. Of course, one might achieve some control over the content of the knowledge by teaching subjects artificial concepts, and thus tease the contributing factors apart. But to many psychologists this harkens back to the nonsense syllable. Such research is viewed as too artificial to reveal how "real" concepts are known.

Lack of control also plagues the study of "everyday memory" (a.k.a. "autobiographical memory")—though some devotees see this as a good thing. The seminal event in the study of everyday memory, as current accounts have it, was a talk by Ulric Neisser at a meeting in Wales (Neisser 1978). (This meeting might be called the "little bang.") In his talk, Neisser praised schema theory, cried out for more ecological validity, said that third-graders, if not kindergartners, knew most of what psychologists knew about memory, argued that memory researchers had never studied anything important or interesting (giving, as an example, the causes of forgetting), provided a misleading capsule history of the field of animal learning with the admonishment to learn from it, and told his audience what the really important memory problems were (these included the Catholic confessional, sex differences in early memories, and verbatim memory for the Koran). According to one source, "Neisser's ideas had an enthusiastic reception and the wind of change has blown strongly since 1978" (Cohen 1989, 3).

At least one member of that audience, however, wondered whether the speaker shouldn't see a psychologist. A recent assessment of research on everyday memory vindicates my reaction. Banaji and Crowder (1989) criticize naturalistic studies that abandon control over the learning and test situations, argue that no new principles have been uncovered in such studies, and point out that—contrary to the intent—ecological validity can be an impediment to generalizability, because variation among real-world situations is so great.

Banaji and Crowder's article triggered a furious reaction (see the January 1991 issue of *American Psychologist*), including a response by Bahrick (1991). Bahrick admits that there has been bad research in naturalistic settings, but cites as an exception his own work on retention of Spanish learned in school (Bahrick 1984). Indeed, that work has been highly praised. According to Neisser, "Bahrick's careful and statistically sophisticated study of Spanish produced a major discovery—one of the most important yet made in the ecological study of memory. Some of the material that people learn in classroom settings is essentially immune to forgetting" (1988, 359).

The basis for this claim is a correlational analysis of scores on a Spanish test, earned by people who had taken Spanish from zero to fifty years before. Since this was a cross-sectional study, Bahrick tried to control statistically for various factors that would correlate with original learning, such as the subject's average Spanish grade (as recalled by the subject). However, he did not correct for the wrenching changes in academic standards that hit American education in the late 1960s and early 1970s. Symptoms included grade inflation, easier homework, "dumbed down" textbooks, and the dropping of requirements, including foreign-language requirements, by many colleges. When Bahrick's data are adjusted for grade inflation and for different grading standards in high school and college, the evidence for permanent memory disappears (Hintzman 1990b). This steady decline of memory over time is, of course, consistent with a large body of other evidence (e.g., Ebbinghaus 1885; Squire 1989).

Undoubtedly, naturalistic data such as Bahrick's contain many unidentified sources of variance and bias. One can control for a variable in a correlational study only to the extent that one can identify and accurately measure it. Naturalistic studies can suggest phenomena for further investigation in the laboratory, but provide a flimsy basis for proclaiming a general law. Banaji and Crowder's (1989) objection is upheld.

I am not saying that everyday memory should be ignored. Our functionalist and behaviorist forebears were concerned with the relation between experimental findings and phenomena found outside the laboratory. There are two ways that the study of everyday memory can contribute to the general psychology of memory. First, as was just indicated, it can suggest phenomena for experimentation—the experimental analysis of mnemonic techniques is a good case in point. It may be true that some variables cannot be manipulated experimentally, but most probably can. For example, effects on learning of stress or drugs or hippocampal damage can be studied by using animals (e.g., McGaugh 1973; Zola-Morgan and Squire 1990). Even the elusive tip-of-the-tongue phenomenon has been brought into the lab (e.g., Brown and McNeill 1966). Second, both everyday memory and laboratory research may be needed to learn how principles uncovered in basic research apply in the real world. Applications of these principles may not be immediately obvious. (To give an example from outside psychology, wind-tunnel experiments have been crucial in showing how principles of aerodynamics apply to automobile design.) But Neisser's (1978) call for practical memory research went too far—first by suggesting that ecological validity is somehow an end in itself, and second by implying that one could safely ignore decades of laboratory-based research and theory on memory because, being unnatural, it had been a waste of time.

Theoretical Methodology

If there has been backsliding in empirical methodology since the cognitive revolution, theoretical methodology seems to have suffered a setback as well. The prerevolutionary period is sometimes seen as an era of grand theories, Hull's (1943, 1952) being the best example. Although it was based primarily on experiments on maze learning in rats, Hull's theory was meant to apply broadly to mammalian learning. What set Hull's approach apart from others of the time was not its supposed breadth, however, but the insistence on the hypotheticodeductive method. Taking Newtonian mechanics as his model, Hull set out the basic principles of his theory, and showed how various empirical phenomena could be derived from them. At times, he spelled out (and numbered) the postulates, theorems, and corollaries of his theory in a ponderous and unfamiliar style. His aim was to pressure his opponents into doing the same, thereby bringing the intuitive and sometimes anthropomorphic nature of their explanations to light. For the most part, they did not follow his lead (but see Tolman 1959).

Hull's preference for formal theory was accepted by many of the cognitive revolutionaries, but they preferred the starkly elegant style of Estes (1950) to that of Hull. This meant concentrating on a single task or phenomenon at a time and constructing an extremely simple model of it, rather than trying to derive all manner of learned behavior from a single set of postulates. As the preferred strategy was described by Levine and Burke (1972):

The new theories for which mathematical models have been developed generally address themselves to single paradigms or to clearly circumscribed theoretical questions. It is possible to compare sets of assumptions as predictors, for some one paradigm, asking what smallest set of assumptions yields the most accurate predictions. Armed with the best predicting set of assumptions, the issue of further generality to other paradigms and to broadened theoretical issues, with or without additional axioms, can be faced. (P. 3)

This strategy led to quantitative models that were overly simple in obvious ways—Bower's (1961) one-element model, discussed earlier, being a case in point—and of course the hoped-for generality never was obtained. The models produced were like the blind philosophers' descriptions of the elephant—precise down to the last wrinkle, but lacking any conception of the beast's overall shape. Moreover, in the postrevolutionary climate, there were so many interesting intuitive hunches to check out that formal models sometimes seemed more of a hindrance than a boon to research. Compared to the experimental side of research, the theoretical side has suffered from neglect. One trend has been to resort to pseudoexplanations such as schemas, whose elaborate abilities are essentially unexplained (e.g., Mandler 1985). Another has been to seek data patterns that are somehow believed to be diagnostic of fundamental theoretical postulates. For example, an interaction was once thought to indicate that two independent variables affect the same processing stage (Sternberg 1969). More recently, functional dissociations and stochastic independence between memory tasks have been taken as evidence that different memory systems underlie the tasks (Dunn and Kirsner 1988; Tulving and Schacter 1990)—but both functional dissociations and stochastic independence can be easily derived from models assuming a single memory system, so their diagnosticity is an illusion (Hintzman 1990a). As Broadbent observed, "the standard of precision in theoretical statements in the experimental journals is now markedly lower than it was at the height of the Hullian movement 40–50 years ago" (1987, 169–170).

In graduate school, I worked with a computer-simulation model and learned to distrust my intuitions about how even a few simple interacting processes will behave. If someone had told me then that by 1990 psychologists would all have powerful desktop computers, I might have believed it. But I would not have believed that they would just use the computer as a substitute for the typewriter, calculator, and telephone. The capacity to explore the behavior of theoretical systems by doing experiments on working models of those systems—*not* the computer metaphor—is the great gift to psychological theory of the electronic age.

It is surprising and disappointing that psychologists have been so slow to take advantage of that gift, but this will certainly change. It is encouraging that several recent theoretical efforts in human learning and memory use computer simulation, and seek to explain behavior in a variety of tasks using a single set of core assumptions, much as Hull tried to do. Examples include Anderson's (1983) ACT*, the SAM model (e.g., Gillund and Shiffrin 1984; Mensink and Raaijmakers 1988; chap. 20, this volume), and convolution-correlation model (e.g., Eich 1982; Murdock 1982).

16.4   CONCLUSIONS

Was the cognitive revolution a mistake, or do revolutions, as the term suggests, really go around? Were those "running dogs" of behaviorism barking up the right tree after all, or will this once-extinguished response just have to be extinguished again? Is our big bang expansion collapsing into a cognitively impenetrable black hole, or is it just setting the conditions for another inevitable big bang?

One might defend the thesis that the revolution was a mistake by asking what the field would be like if the revolution had never occurred. By this I mean, what if some key elements had been missing—not if all progress had stopped. What if Skinner had decided to stick to science, instead of writing wildly speculative books? Then Chomsky wouldn't have reviewed *Verbal Behavior*, and behaviorists and neobehaviorists would not have all been tainted with Skinner's sins in a review that a generation of graduate students read (Chomsky 1959). What if the neobehaviorists had called the unobservable events they postulated "representations," "units," or (even more vaguely) "processes," instead of s's and r's? Countless budding psychologists like me would have been less ready to scoff. What if Newell and Simon had decided to put off their big bang conference until after they had done a little reading on what was known about the brain? Or if Frank Rosenblatt had lived, and had convinced Minsky and Papert that AI on digital computers was *too* artificial because the nervous system works in a completely different way? We might have been spared a loveless marriage to the computer metaphor, which was too forced—too nonorganic—to really be believed. What if we hadn't all taken Kuhn's (1962) book on scientific revolutions as a license to treat the past with disrespect? We might have been less willing to discard valuable notions like motivation, evolution, generalization, transfer, inhibition, association, and unconscious learning, and to yield to the temptation of loose theory and poor experimental control. A good case could be made that, if the cognitive revolution had never occurred, we would have gotten where we are considerably earlier than we did.

As a counterargument, the revolution can be seen as a badly needed stimulant. It is difficult to thumb through the journals of the 1950s and early 1960s without feeling that learning and memory researchers were in a deep rut. An astonishing percentage seem to have been laboring to fill in the cells of a gigantic matrix of paired-associate transfer paradigms (Tulving and Madigan 1970). Although some of that work again appears relevant, one can only wonder how broad an empirical foundation our theories would rest on today if workers hadn't been shaken out of that rut by a cataclysmic event. How much would we know about recognition memory, recency judgments, frequency judgments, priming, prose understanding, strategies, and the role of metacognitive beliefs? Fad and fashion surely would have led us from pasture to pasture bleating excitedly, as always; but herds don't scatter over such a wide range without a stampede. We may have drifted back to near where the stampede started, but our collective knowledge of the neighboring territory has greatly increased.

The problem with stampedes (and big bangs) is that they tend to wipe out evidence of what went before. The typical cognitive psychologist's view of history is: William James ... the Dark Ages (except for Bartlett) ... and the Renaissance (or big bang). But if revolutions do go around, one would like it to be in spirals, not in circles; and (I refuse to quote Santayana here) the only way to ensure this is to remember the past. We have been perverse, and even stupid, to ignore our predecessors' good ideas solely because they labeled their theoretical constructs with s's and r's. The similarities between neobehaviorist theory and modern connectionism suggest that it might be worthwhile to take another look at Hull's theory—particularly as it was liberalized and applied to human cognition by Berlyne (1965). Connectionism needs to give more attention to motivation, to learning through reward, and to the ways in which dynamically interacting PDP modules might organize themselves. The Hullians lacked computers to verify their reasoning, but some of the spade-work on these problems may already have been done.

But progress delayed is only one risk of ignorance. If we don't understand where prerevolutionary psychology took the right turns, we may also visit their old cul-de-sacs. Two examples come to mind. The first concerns current models of human learning and memory. They are like early associationist theories in that they tend to focus only on the formation of direct associations (e.g., Eich 1982; Mensink and Raaijmakers 1988; Murdock 1982). Thus, they essentially ignore the overwhelming evidence for mediation based on previous learning (e.g., Prytulak 1971) and sidestep the question of how such mediation works. Current models likewise tend to represent information in simple feature lists, or vectors (e.g., Hinton and Anderson 1981; Hintzman 1986; Humphreys, Bain, and Pike 1989; Murdock 1982; Rumelhart and McClelland 1986). But despite the claim by some that their models are concerned with problems of representation (e.g., Rumelhart and McClelland 1986), it is not clear that associations among vectors can accommodate the flexibility of information retrieval, the complex hierarchical structure, or the apparent isomorphisms between representing and represented systems (Gallistel 1990) that animal and human cognition display.

The second example concerns language. Perhaps the best-aimed shots of the revolution concerned inadequacies of S-R theory in dealing with grammar or syntax (Bever, Fodor, and Garrett 1968; Fodor 1965). Some of the same arguments are being made against PDP models today (Fodor and Pylyshyn 1988; Pinker and Prince 1988), though the emphasis has shifted: Connectionist models are not said to be inadequate in principle, as was claimed of S-R models, but to fall at the "wrong level of description." The proper level presumably describes the software, not the hardware; and the software involves computer-like manipulation of symbols. A further argument is that the proper level for syntax is the proper level for cognition in general. The argument regarding syntax seems compelling, but the evidence I have reviewed here suggests that symbol manipulation may be the wrong level for explaining many aspects of learning and memory. If there are different interacting systems (fig. 16.3), these two conclusions need not be in conflict.

So, was the cognitive revolution a mistake? A good case could be made on either side, but I will argue that it was. My objection is not to the *cognitive* part of the phrase—that is, to the study of attention, memory, imagery, comprehension, decision making, and the like. Indeed, the behaviorist revolution, by banning such concepts outright, was a mistake in the same way the cognitive revolution was. The problem is with the *revolution* part of "cognitive revolution," and all the excess that term implies. There was no looting or mayhem, perhaps; but we did, in effect, burn the old regime's books. Such mob behavior is inappropriate among scholars and inimical to progress. It is to be deplored.

NOTE

Preparation of this paper was supported by National Science Foundation grant BNS-87-11218. Deborah Frisch, Tom Carr, Peter Jusczyk, Myron Rothbart, Henry Roediger, and David Meyer improved the paper with their thoughtful comments, but neither they nor the NSF are responsible for any heresies it may contain.

REFERENCES

Alba, J. W., and Hasher, L. (1983). Is memory schematic? *Psychological Bulletin, 93,* 203–231.

Amsel, A. (1989). *Behaviorism, Neobehaviorism and Cognitivism in Learning Theory: Historical and Contemporary Perspectives.* Hillsdale, NJ: Lawrence Erlbaum Associates.

Amsel, A., and Rashotte, M. E. (1984). *Mechanisms of Adaptive Behavior: Clark Hull's Theoretical Papers, with Commentary.* New York: Columbia University Press.

Amsel, A., and Stanton, M. (1980). Ontogeny and phylogeny of paradoxical reward effects. In J. S. Rosenblatt, R. A. Hinde, C. Beer, and M. Busnel (Eds.), *Advances in the Study of Behavior.* New York: Academic Press.

Anderson, J. R. (1983). *The Architecture of Cognition.* Cambridge, MA: Harvard University Press.

Atkinson, R. C., and Shiffrin, R. M. (1968). Human memory: A proposed system and its control processes. In K. W. Spence and J. T. Spence (Eds.), *The Psychology of Learning and Motivation.* New York: Academic Press.

Baddeley, A. (1986). *Working Memory.* Oxford, UK: Clarendon Press.

Bahrick, H. P. (1984). Semantic memory content in permastore: Fifty years of memory for Spanish learned in school. *Journal of Experimental Psychology: General, 113,* 1–29.

Bahrick, H. P. (1991). A speedy recovery from bankruptcy for ecological memory research. *American Psychologist, 46,* 76–77.

Banaji, M. R., and Crowder, R. G. (1989). The bankruptcy of everyday memory. *American Psychologist, 44,* 1185–1193.

Barnes, J. M., and Underwood, B. J. (1959). Fate of first-list associations in transfer theory. *Journal of Experimental Psychology, 58,* 97–105.

Bartlett, F. C. (1932). *Remembering: A Study in Experimental and Social Psychology.* Cambridge, UK: Cambridge University Press.

Berlyne, D. E. (1965). *Structure and Direction in Thinking.* New York: John Wiley & Sons.

Bever, T. G., Fodor, J. A., and Garrett, M. G. (1968). A formal limitation of associationism. In T. R. Dixon and D. L. Horton (Eds.), *Verbal Behavior and General Behavior Theory.* Englewood Cliffs, NJ: Prentice-Hall.

Bitterman, M. E. (1975). The comparative analysis of learning. *Science, 188,* 699–709.

Bjork, R. A. (1972). Theoretical implications of directed forgetting. In A. W. Melton and E. Martin (Eds.), *Coding Processes in Human Memory,* 217–235. Washington, DC: V. H. Winston & Sons.

Boakes, R. (1984). *From Darwin to Behaviorism: Psychology and the Minds of Animals.* Cambridge, UK: Cambridge University Press.

Bower, G. H. (1961). Application of a model to paired-associate learning. *Psychometrika, 26,* 255–280.

Bower, G. H. (1967). A descriptive theory of memory. In D. P. Kimble (Ed.), *The Organization of Recall,* 112–185. New York: New York Academy of Science.

Bower, G. H. (1970a). Imagery as a relational organizer in associative learning. *Journal of Verbal Learning and Verbal Behavior, 9,* 529–533.

Bower, G. H. (1970b). Organizational factors in memory. *Cognitive Psychology, 1,* 18–46.

Brewer, W. F. (1974). There is no convincing evidence for operant or classical conditioning in adult humans. In W. Weimer and D. Palermo (Ed.), *Cognition and the Symbolic Processes.* Hillsdale, NJ: Lawrence Erlbaum Associates.

Broadbent, D. (1987). Simple models for experimental situations. In P. Morris (Ed.), *Modelling Cognition,* 169–185. London: John Wiley & Sons.

Brown, R., and McNeill, D. (1966). The "tip of the tongue" phenomenon. *Journal of Verbal Learning and Verbal Behavior, 5,* 325–337.

Bugelski, B. R., Kidd, E., and Segmen, J. (1968). Image as a mediator in one-trial paired-associate learning. *Journal of Experimental Psychology, 76,* 69–73.

Buggie, S. E. (1974). *Imagery and Relational Variety in Associative Learning.* Unpublished Ph.D. diss., University of Oregon, Eugene, OR.

Cermak, L. S., and Craik, F. I. M. (1979). *Levels of Processing in Human Memory.* Hillsdale, NJ: Lawrence Erlbaum Associates.

Chang, T. M. (1986). Semantic memory: Facts and models. *Psychological Review, 99,* 199–220.

Chomsky, N. (1959). A review of Skinner's *Verbal Behavior. Language, 35,* 26–58.

Chomsky, N. (1968). *Language and Mind.* New York: Harcourt, Brace & World.

Cohen, G. (1989). *Memory in the Real World.* Hove, UK: Lawrence Erlbaum Associates.

Collins, A. M., and Loftus, E. F. (1975). A spreading-activation theory of semantic processing. *Psychological Review, 82,* 407–428.

Collins, A. M., and Quillian, M. R. (1969). Retrieval time from semantic memory. *Journal of Verbal Learning and Verbal Behavior, 8*, 240–247.

Craik, F. I. M., and Lockhart, R. S. (1972). Levels of processing: A framework for memory research. *Journal of Verbal Learning and Verbal Behavior, 11*, 671–684.

Crowder, R. G. (1976). *Principles of Learning and Memory*. Hillsdale NJ: Lawrence Erlbaum Associates.

Dunn, J. C., and Kirsner, K. (1988). Discovering functionally independent mental processes: The principle of reversed association. *Psychological Review, 95*, 91–101.

Ebbinghaus, H. (1885). *Über das Gedächtnis*. Leipzig: Duncker & Humbolt.

Eich, J. M. (1982). A composite holographic associative recall model. *Psychological Review, 89*, 627–661.

Einstein, G. O., McDaniel, M. A., and Lackey, S. (1989). Bizarre imagery, interference, and distinctiveness. *Journal of Experimental Psychology: Learning, Memory, and Cognition, 15*, 137–146.

Estes, W. K. (1950). Toward a statistical theory of learning. *Psychological Review, 57*, 94–107.

Estes, W. K. (1960). Learning theory and the new "mental chemistry." *Psychological Review, 67*, 207–223.

Estes, W. K. (1962). Learning theory. *Annual Review of Psychology, 12*, 107–144.

Fodor, J. A. (1965). Could meaning be an r_m? *Journal of Verbal Learning and Verbal Behavior, 4*, 73–81.

Fodor, J. A., and Pylyshyn, Z. W. (1988). Connectionism and cognitive architecture: A critical analysis. *Cognition, 28*, 3–71.

Gallistel, C. R. (1990). Representations in animal cognition: An introduction. *Cognition, 37*, 1–22.

Gernsbacher, M. A., and Goldsmith, H. H. (1983). Evaluating cognitive constructs using structural equation modeling. *Proceedings of the Cognitive Science Society, 5*, 133–145.

Gibson, E. J. (1940). A systematic application of the concepts of generalization and differentiation to verbal learning. *Psychological Review, 47*, 196–229.

Gillund, G., and Shiffrin, R. M. (1984). A retrieval model for both recognition and recall. *Psychological Review, 91*, 1–67.

Glass, A. L., Krejci, J., and Goldman, J. (1989). The necessary and sufficient conditions for motor learning, recognition, and recall. *Journal of Memory and Language, 28*, 189–199.

Gluck, M. A., and Bower, G. H. (1988). Evaluating an adaptive network model of human learning. *Journal of Memory and Language, 27*, 166–195.

Hayes, N. A., and Broadbent, D. E. (1988). Two modes of learning for interactive tasks. *Cognition, 28*, 249–276.

Helmholtz, H. von. ([1910] 1962). *Helmholtz's Physiological Optics*. Ed. and trans. J. P. C. Southall. New York: Dover.

Hinton, G. E., and Anderson, J. A. (1981). *Parallel Models of Associative Memory*. Hillsdale, NJ: Lawrence Erlbaum Associates.

Hintzman, D. L. (1967). Some tests of a discrimination net theory: Paired-associate learning as a function of stimulus similarity and number of responses. *Journal of Verbal Learning and Verbal Behavior, 6*, 809–816.

Hintzman, D. L. (1986). "Schema abstraction" in a multiple-trace memory model. *Psychological Review, 93*, 411–428.

Hintzman, D. L. (1990a). Human learning and memory: Connections and dissociations. *Annual Review of Psychology, 41,* 109–139.

Hintzman, D. L. (1990b). *Permastore or grade inflation? Adjusting Bahrick's data for changes in academic standards.* (Report No. 90–15). Eugene, OR: University of Oregon Institute of Cognitive and Decision Sciences.

Hintzman, D. L., and Hartry, A. L. (1990). Item effects in recognition and fragment completion: Contingency relations vary for different subsets of words. *Journal of Experimental Psychology: Learning, Memory, and Cognition, 16,* 955–969.

Hirsch, R. (1974). The hippocampus and contextual retrieval of information from memory: A theory. *Behavioral Biology, 12,* 421–444.

Hull, C. L. (1929). A functional interpretation of the conditioned reflex. *Psychological Review, 36,* 498–511.

Hull, C. L. (1930). Knowledge and purpose as habit mechanisms. *Psychological Review, 37,* 511–525.

Hull, C. L. (1931). Goal attraction and directing ideas conceived as habit phenomena. *Psychological Review, 38,* 487–506.

Hull, C. L. (1934a). The concept of the habit-family hierarchy and maze learning: Part 1. *Psychological Review, 41,* 33–54.

Hull, C. L. (1934b). The concept of the habit-family hierarchy and maze learning: Part 2. *Psychological Review, 41,* 134–152.

Hull, C. L. (1943). *Principles of Behavior.* New York: Appleton-Century-Crofts.

Hull, C. L. (1945). The discrimination of stimulus configurations and the hypothesis of afferent neural interaction. *Psychological Review, 52,* 133–142.

Hull, C. L. (1952). *A Behavior System: An Introduction to Behavior Theory Concerning the Individual Organism.* New Haven, CT: Yale University Press.

Hull, C. L., Hovland, C. I., Ross, R. T., Hall, M., Perkins, D. T., and Fitch, F. B. (1940). *Mathematico-deductive Theory of Rote Learning.* New Haven, CT: Yale University Press.

Humphreys, M. S., Bain, J. D., and Pike, R. (1989). Different ways to cue a coherent memory system: A theory for episodic, semantic, and procedural tasks. *Psychological Review, 96,* 208–233.

Hyde, T. S., and Jenkins, J. J. (1969). Differential effects of incidental tasks on the organization of recall of a list of highly associated words. *Journal of Experimental Psychology, 82,* 472–481.

Jacoby, L. L., and Whitehouse, K. (1989). An illusion of memory: False recognition influenced by unconscious perception. *Journal of Experimental Psychology: General, 118,* 126–135.

James, W. (1890). *The Principles of Psychology,* vol. 1. New York: Henry Holt & Co.

Jenkins, J. J. (1974). Remember that old theory of memory? Well, forget it! *American Psychologist, 29,* 785–795.

Jerison, H. (1973). *Evolution of the Brain and Intelligence.* New York: Academic Press.

Johnson-Laird, P. N., Herrmann, D. J., and Chaffin, R. (1984). Only connections: A critique of semantic networks. *Psychological Bulletin, 96,* 292–315.

Johnston, T. D. (1981). Contrasting approaches to a theory of learning. *The Behavioral and Brain Sciences, 4,* 125–173.

Jonides, J., Kahn, R., and Rozin, P. (1975). Imagery instruction improves memory in blind subjects. *The Bulletin of the Psychonomic Society, 5,* 424–426.

Kintsch, W. (1980). Semantic memory: A tutorial. In R. S. Nickerson (Ed.), *Attention and Performance VII*. Hillsdale, NJ: Lawrence Erlbaum Associates.

Koch, S. (1954). Clark L. Hull. In W. K. Estes, S. Koch, K. McCorquodale, P. E. Meehl, C. G. Mueller, W. N. Schoenfeld, and W. S. Verplanck, *Modern Learning Theory*, 1–176. New York: Appleton-Century-Crofts.

Köhler, W. (1925). *The Mentality of Apes*. Trans. E. Winter. New York: Harcourt, Brace & World.

Kolers, P. A., and Roediger, H. L. (1984). Procedures of mind. *Journal of Verbal Learning and Verbal Behavior, 23*, 425–449.

Krechevsky, I. (1932). "Hypotheses" in rats. *Psychological Review, 39*, 516–532.

Kuhn, T. S. (1962). *The Structure of Scientific Revolutions*. Chicago: University of Chicago Press.

Lachman, R., Lachman, J. L., and Butterfield, E. C. (1979). *Cognitive Psychology and Information Processing: An Introduction*. Hillsdale, NJ: Lawrence Erlbaum Associates.

Landauer, T. K., and Freedman, J. L. (1968). Information retrieval from long-term memory: Category size and recognition time. *Journal of Verbal Learning and Verbal Behavior, 7*, 291–295.

Levine, G., and Burke, C. J. (1972). *Mathematical Model Techniques for Learning Theories*. New York: Academic Press.

Lewicki, P., Czyzewska, M., and Hoffman, H. (1987). Unconscious acquisition of complex procedural knowledge. *Journal of Experimental Psychology: Learning, Memory, and Cognition, 13*, 523–530.

McClelland, J. L. (1986). The programmable blackboard model of reading. In J. L. McClelland and D. E. Rumelhart (Eds.), *Parallel Distributed Processing*. Vol. 2, *Psychological and Biological Models*, 122–169. Cambridge, MA: MIT Press.

McDaniel, M. A., Waddill, P. J., and Einstein, G. O. (1988). A contextual account of the generation effect: A three-factor theory. *Journal of Memory and Language, 27*, 521–536.

McGaugh, J. L. (1973). Drug facilitation of learning and memory. *Annual Review of Pharmacology and Toxicology, 13*, 229–241.

Mandler, G. (1985). *Cognitive Psychology: An Essay in Cognitive Science*. Hillsdale, NJ: Lawrence Erlbaum Associates.

Marcel, A. J. (1983). Conscious and unconscious perception: Experiments on visual masking and word recognition. *Cognitive Psychology, 15*, 197–237.

Medin, D. L., and Shoben, E. J. (1988). Context and structure in conceptual combination. *Cognitive Psychology, 20*, 158–190.

Melton, A. W., and Irwin, J. McQ. (1949). The influence of degree of interpolated learning on retroactive inhibition and the overt transfer of specific responses. *American Journal of Psychology, 53*, 173–203.

Mensink, G. J., and Raaijmakers, J. G. W. (1988). A model of interference and forgetting. *Psychological Review, 95*, 434–455.

Meyer, D. E., and Schvaneveldt, R. W. (1971). Facilitation in recognizing pairs of words: Evidence of a dependence between retrieval operations. *Journal of Experimental Psychology, 90*, 227–234.

Miller, G. A. (1956). The magical number seven, plus or minus two: Some limits on our capacity for processing information. *Psychological Review, 63*, 81–97.

Miller, G. A., Galanter, E., and Pribram, K. H. (1960). *Plans and the Structure of Behavior*. New York: Henry Holt & Co.

Miller, N. E. (1959). Liberalization of basic S-R concepts: Extensions to conflict behavior, motivation and social learning. In S. Koch (Ed.), *Psychology: A Study of a Science*, vol. 2, 196–202. New York: McGraw-Hill.

Millward, R. (1964). Latency in a modified paired-associate learning experiment. *Journal of Verbal Learning and Verbal Behavior, 3,* 309–316.

Mishkin, M., Malamut, B., and Bachevalier, J. (1984). Memories and habits: Two neural systems. In G. Lynch, J. L. McGaugh, and N. M. Weinberger (Eds.), *Neurobiology of Learning and Memory.* New York: Guilford.

Morris, C. D., Bransford, J. D., and Franks, J. J. (1977). Levels of processing versus transfer appropriate processing. *Journal of Verbal Learning and Verbal Behavior, 16,* 519–533.

Mowrer, O. H. (1960). *Learning Theory and Behavior.* New York: John Wiley & Sons.

Munro, P. (1987). A dual back-propagation scheme for scalar reward learning. Paper presented at the Ninth Annual Conference of the Cognitive Science Society, Seattle, Washington, July 16–18.

Murdock, B. B., Jr. (1974). *Human Memory: Theory and Data.* Potomac, MD: Lawrence Erlbaum Associates.

Murdock, B. B., Jr. (1982). A theory for the storage and retrieval of item and associative information. *Psychological Review, 89,* 609–626.

Murphy, G. L., and Medin, D. L. (1985). The role of theories in conceptual coherence. *Psychological Review, 92,* 289–316.

Neisser, U. (1967). *Cognitive Psychology.* New York: Appleton-Century Crofts.

Neisser, U. (1978). Memory: What are the important questions? In M. M. Gruneberg, P. E. Morris and R. N. Sykes (Eds.), *Practical Aspects of Memory,* 3–24. London: Academic Press.

Neisser, U. (1988). What is ordinary memory the memory of? In U. Neisser and E. Winograd (Eds.), *Remembering Reconsidered: Ethological and Traditional Approaches to the Study of Memory.* Cambridge, UK: Cambridge University Press.

Newell, A. (1990). *Unified theories of cognition.* Cambridge, MA: Harvard University Press.

Oakley, D. A. (1981). Brain mechanisms of mammalian memory. *British Medical Bulletin, 37,* 175–180.

Osgood, C. E. (1949). The similarity paradox in human learning: A resolution. *Psychological Review, 56,* 132–143.

Osgood, C. E. (1953). *Method and Theory in Experimental Psychology.* New York: Oxford University Press.

Paivio, A. (1969). Mental imagery in associative learning and memory. *Psychological Review, 76,* 241–263.

Pavlov, I. P. ([1934] 1955). *Selected Works.* Moscow: Foreign Languages Publishing House.

Pinker, S., and Prince, A. (1988). On language and connectionism: Analysis of a parallel distributed model of language acquisition. *Cognition, 28,* 73–193.

Postman, L. (1961). The present status of interference theory. In C. Cofer (Ed.), *Verbal Learning and Verbal Behavior,* 152–179. New York: McGraw-Hill.

Postman, L., and Underwood, B. J. (1973). Critical issues in interference theory. *Memory & Cognition, 1,* 19–40.

Prytulak, L. S. (1971). Natural language mediation. *Cognitive Psychology, 2,* 1–56.

Ratcliff, R. (1978). A theory of memory retrieval. *Psychological Review, 85,* 59–108.

Razran, G. (1971). *Mind in Evolution*. Boston, MA: Houghton Mifflin.

Reisberg, D., Rappaport, I., and O'Shaughnessy, M. (1984). Limits of working memory: The digit digit-span. *Journal of Experimental Psychology: Learning, Memory, and Cognition, 10*, 203–221.

Rescorla, R. A., and Wagner, A. R. (1972). A theory of Pavlovian conditioning: Variations in the effectiveness of reinforcement and nonreinforcement. In A. H. Black and W. F. Prokasy (Eds.), *Classical Conditioning II: Current Research and Theory*. New York: Appleton-Century-Crofts.

Rock, I. (1957). The role of repetition in associative learning. *American Journal of Psychology, 70*, 186–190.

Roediger, H. L. I., Weldon, M. S., and Challis, B. H. (1989). Explaining dissociations between implicit and explicit measures of retention: A processing account. In H. L. Roediger and F. I. M. Craik (Eds.), *Varieties of Memory and Consciousness: Essays in Honour of Endel Tulving*. Hillsdale, NJ: Lawrence Erlbaum Associates.

Rosch, E., and Mervis, C. B. (1975). Family resemblances: Studies in the internal structure of categories. *Cognitive Psychology, 7*, 573–605.

Rosenblatt, F. (1958). The perceptron: A probabilistic model for information storage and organization in the brain. *Psychological Review, 65*, 386–408.

Rumelhart, D. E., and McClelland, J. L. (1986). *Parallel Distributed Processing*. Vol. 1, *Foundations*. Cambridge, MA: MIT Press.

Rumelhart, D. E., and Norman, D. A. (1978). Accretion, tuning, and restructuring: Three modes of learning. In J. W. Cotton and R. L. Klatzky (Eds.), *Semantic Factors in Cognition*, 37–53. Hillsdale, NJ: Lawrence Erlbaum Associates.

Runquist, W. N. (1957). Retention of verbal associates as a function of strength. *Journal of Experimental Psychology, 54*, 369–375.

Sanders, A. F. (1967). *Attention and Performance I*. Amsterdam: North-Holland.

Schacter, D. L. (1987). Implicit memory: History and current status. *Journal of Experimental Psychology: Learning, Memory, and Cognition, 13*, 501–518.

Schank, R. C. (1982). *Dynamic Memory*. Cambridge, UK: Cambridge University Press.

Schweickert, R., Guentert, L., and Hersberger, L. (1990). Phonological similarity, pronunciation rate, and memory span. *Psychological Science, 1*, 74–77.

Shimamura, A. P. (1989). Disorders of memory: The cognitive science perspective. In F. Boller and J. Grafman (Eds.), *Handbook of Neuropsychology*. Amsterdam: Elsevier Press.

Simon, H. A. (1974). How big is a chunk? *Science, 183*, 482–488.

Simon, H. A., and Feigenbaum, E. A. (1964). An information-processing theory of some effects of similarity, familiarity, and meaningfulness in verbal learning. *Journal of Verbal Learning and Verbal Behavior, 3*, 385–396.

Singley, M. K., and Anderson, J. R. (1989). *The Transfer of Cognitive Skill*. Cambridge, MA: Harvard University Press.

Skinner, B. F. (1974). *About Behaviorism*. New York: Alfred A. Knopf.

Spence, K. W. (1956). *Behavior Theory and Conditioning*. New Haven, CT: Yale University Press.

Squire, L. R. (1987). *Memory and Brain*. New York: Oxford University Press.

Squire, L. R. (1989). On the course of forgetting in very long-term memory. *Journal of Experimental Psychology: Learning, Memory, and Cognition, 15*, 241–245.

Squire, L. R., and Zola-Morgan, S. (1988). Memory: Brain systems and behavior. *Trends in Neuroscience, 11,* 170–175.

Sternberg, S. (1966). High-speed scanning in human memory. *Science, 153,* 652–654.

Sternberg, S. (1969). The discovery of processing stages: Extensions of Donders' method. *Acta Psychologica, 30,* 276–315.

Thorndike, E. L. (1913). *The Psychology of Learning.* New York: Teachers College.

Tolman, E. C. (1959). Principles of purposive behavior. In S. Koch (Ed.), *Psychology: A Study of a Science.* New York: McGraw-Hill.

Tulving, E. (1968). Theoretical issues in free recall. In T. R. Dixon and D. L. Horton (Eds.), *Verbal Behavior and General Behavior Theory.* Englewood Cliffs, NJ: Prentice-Hall.

Tulving, E., and Madigan, S. A. (1970). Memory and verbal learning. *Annual Review of Psychology, 21,* 437–484.

Tulving, E., and Schacter, D. L. (1990). Priming and human memory systems. *Science, 247,* 301–306.

Underwood, B. J. (1957). Interference and forgetting. *Psychological Review, 64,* 49–60.

Underwood, B. J., and Keppel, G. (1962). One-trial learning? *Journal of Verbal Learning and Verbal Behavior, 1,* 1–13.

Watson, J. B. (1930). *Behaviorism.* New York: W. W. Norton & Co.

Wickelgren, W. A. (1979). Chunking and consolidation: A theoretical synthesis of semantic networks, configuring in conditioning, S-R versus cognitive learning, normal forgetting, the amnesic syndrome, and the hippocampal arousal system. *Psychological Review, 86,* 44–60.

Willingham, D. B., Nissen, M. J., and Bullemer, P. (1989). On the development of procedural knowledge. *Journal of Experimental Psychology: Learning, Memory, and Cognition, 15,* 1047–1060.

Wollen, K. A., Weber, A., and Lowry, D. H. (1972). Bizarreness versus interaction of mental images as determinants of learning. *Cognitive Psychology, 3,* 518–523.

Zola-Morgan, L. M., and Squire, L. R. (1990). The primate hippocampal formation: Evidence for a time-limited role in memory storage. *Science, 250,* 288–290.

17 Memory: Organization of Brain Systems and Cognition

Larry R. Squire, S. Zola-Morgan, C. B. Cave,
F. Haist, G. Musen, and W. A. Suzuki

Cognitive neuroscience is that part of the brain sciences concerned with the functional organization and neural substrates of higher cortical functions, namely, perception, attention, language, memory, problem solving, and the organization of action. Among these diverse topics, the topic of memory has been a particularly fruitful target of experimental inquiry. Work on memory is currently benefiting from approaches at many levels of analysis: from studies of cellular and molecular mechanisms underlying synaptic plasticity to studies of brain systems and behavior. Cellular and molecular approaches address questions about how neurons exhibit history-dependent activity. Systems-level questions address a more global level of analysis: How is memory organized? Is there one kind of memory or many? Where are memories stored? What are the structures and connections involved in memory, and what jobs do they do?

One useful strategy for asking systems-level questions about memory is to study instances of relatively selective memory impairment. In such cases, particularly in human patients, an analysis of the deficit can provide useful information about the normal function of the damaged system and about the organization of normal memory. In addition, study of animal models of human memory impairment, especially a recently developed model of amnesia in the monkey (Mahut, Zola-Morgan, and Moss 1982, Mishkin 1982; Squire and Zola-Morgan 1983), can identify the anatomical structures and connections that comprise the damaged system.

The sections that follow summarize what has been learned from such an approach. First, we consider the nature of the primary deficit in global human amnesia, namely, impaired ability to learn new material. Second, we discuss what has been learned about memory from the analysis of retrograde amnesia, namely, the loss of material acquired before the onset of memory impairment. Third, we review the scope and limits of human memory impairment, focusing on the important finding that even severely amnesic patients are entirely normal at some kinds of learning and memory. Finally, we consider recent work in monkeys, which has been successful during the past decade in establishing an animal model of human amnesia. With this animal model, it has been possible to identify the structures and connections that comprise the medial temporal lobe memory system.

17.1 ANTEROGRADE AMNESIA

Global amnesia is a severe deficit in the ability to learn new facts and events (anterograde amnesia), which occurs against a background of otherwise intact intellectual ability (fig. 17.1) (Cermak 1982; Hirst 1982; Mayes 1988; Milner 1972; Schacter 1985; Squire 1987; Weiskrantz 1987). The deficit extends to both verbal and nonverbal material and to material presented in any sensory modality. Memory for facts and events from the period prior to the onset of amnesia is also affected. Language, social skills, and personality can be intact, as well as memory for material acquired very early in life.

Patients with amnesia are also able to perform normally on memory tasks in which the material to be retained is within the capacity of immediate memory (usually on the order of 7 items). For example, the ability to repeat strings of digits is generally normal. The difficulty that amnesic patients have is in placing new information into *long-term memory*, which can be demonstrated with any number of standardized neuropsychological tests (Squire and Shimamura 1986). Figure 17.1 illustrates the performance of amnesic patients on three conventional measures of new learning ability (paired associate learning, story recall, and diagram recall).

In amnesia the new learning of both events and facts is affected, namely, both episodic and semantic memory (cf. Tulving 1983). Indeed, amnesic patients seem to have about as much difficulty acquiring new semantic knowledge (facts) as event-specific (episodic) knowledge. Nevertheless, some new semantic knowledge can usually be acquired through repeated exposures to factual material. Such an ability to acquire new information through repetition, albeit at an impaired rate, would be expected to exceed the ability to acquire episodic knowledge, because episodic knowledge is by definition unique to time and place and cannot be repeated. In other words, repeated material is always easier to learn than material that is not repeated (see Ostergaard and Squire 1990). The issue then is not that amnesic patients can accumulate some semantic knowledge over time without acquiring episodic knowledge (Tulving and Schacter 1990). The issue is whether their ability to acquire semantic knowledge is disproportionately spared, namely, is it special in some way (e.g., outside the province of the structures and functions damaged in amnesia)? Or does it reflect simply the residual learning capacity of a partially damaged system? This important question has not yet been adequately addressed.

Recall and Recognition Memory in Amnesia

When amnesic patients are tested for their memory of recently presented material, they perform poorly whether they are requested to recall the material or to recognize it, that is, choose the correct answers from among alternatives. An important, though difficult question to address experimentally is whether recall and recognition are affected similarly. Free recall is usually considered more dependent upon retrieval processes than is recognition. Accordingly, if recall were more impaired than recognition, one might suppose that amnesia

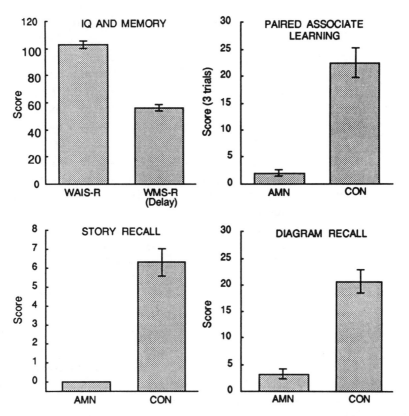

Figure 17.1 *Upper left:* Performance of patients with amnesia (N = 14) on a standard intelligence test (Full Scale WAIS-R [Wechsler Adult Intelligence Scale-Revised]) and on a standard memory test (WMS-R [Wechsler Memory Scale-Revised] Delay Index). In the normal population, both tests yield average scores of 100 with a standard deviation of 15. The amnesic patients are 7 with alcoholic Korsakoff's syndrome, 6 with confirmed or suspected damage to the hippocampal formation, and 1 with a bilateral medial thalamic infarction. Also shown is performance of the same 14 patients with amnesia (AMN) and 8 control subjects (CON) on three tests of new learning ability. *Upper right:* Paired-associate learning measures the ability to learn unrelated word pairs by reporting the second word in a pair when cued with the first word (10 pairs, 3 trials, maximum score = 30). *Lower left:* Story recall measures retention of a short prose passage consisting of 21 meaning segments (maximum score = 21). *Lower right:* Diagram recall measures the ability to reconstruct a complex line drawing (the Rey Osterreith figure) from memory (maximum score = 36). Brackets show standard error of the mean. See Squire and Shimamura (1986) for additional description of these tests.

is due to faulty retrieval processes. Alternatively, if recall and recognition were affected similarly, one would suppose that amnesia is due to an impairment in functions that are equally important for recall and recognition. The best way to compare performance in recall and recognition is to obtain both kinds of measures at several times after learning, and then to compare the forgetting functions produced by both normal subjects and amnesic patients (Haist, Shimamura, and Squire, in press).

Figure 17.2 shows the results of such an experiment. On each of twelve occasions, a different list of twenty common words was presented for learning. Then after a delay that ranged from fifteen second to eight weeks, retention was tested either by free recall or by recognition (6 different delays for recall and 6 delays for recognition). The free recall test required subjects to report as many of the words from the list as they could remember. The recognition test (two-alternative, forced-choice) required subjects to choose which word they had seen before. Amnesic patients performed overall much worse than did the normal subjects. However, recall and recognition were similarly affected. Specifically, the free recall scores obtained by the two subject groups (amnesic patients and control subjects) matched each other at exactly the same retention intervals at which the recognition scores matched. (Amnesic performance at delays from 15 seconds to 10 minutes matched control performance at delays from 1 day to 8 weeks.) Thus, although recall and recognition tests differ in their sensitivity for detecting memory, the same difference in sensitivity was observed in amnesia that was observed in normal memory during the course of forgetting. These results provide strong evidence that recall and recognition memory are similarly dependent on the structures and functions damaged in amnesia. The findings are consistent with the idea that the structures damaged in amnesia are essential for establishing representations in long-term memory. An imperfectly or incompletely established representation should result in both poor recall and poor recognition.

It should be noted that Hirst and his colleagues (Hirst et al. 1986; Hirst et al. 1988) have suggested, on the basis of work with a different group of memory-impaired patients, and on the basis of tests done at single retention intervals, that free recall can be somewhat more impaired in amnesia than can recognition memory. We have been unable to replicate this result using their procedure with our study population. Differences among patients may be important. For example, damage to the frontal lobes might affect recall more than recognition because recall should be affected more than recognition by impaired search strategies and impaired ability to organize new information.

Associated and Dissociated Deficits: Identifying the Essential Components of Amnesia

Some deficits that occur commonly in memory-impaired patients are not essential to the memory impairment. As these deficits are identified, a more accurate picture develops about which deficits are inextricably a part of memory impairment and which ones are related only incidentally. One major

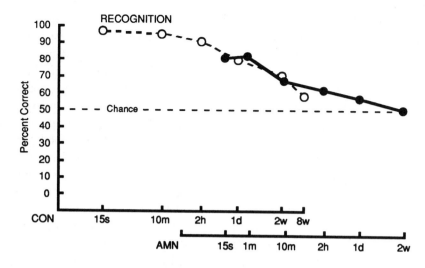

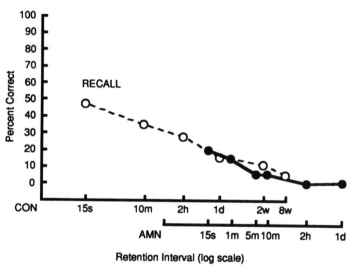

Figure 17.2 Performance of patients with amnesia (closed circles, N = 12) and control subjects (open circles, N = 20), who were tested for either recognition (two-alternative, forced-choice) or free recall of different groups of 20 words at one of the indicated delays after learning. Control subjects were tested at relatively long intervals after learning, so that their performance could be evaluated at a time when it was as poor as that of the amnesic patients. The performance of control subjects tested about 1 day after learning matched the performance of amnesic patients who were tested 15 sec after learning. The forgetting curves continued to match at longer delays following learning. The correspondence between control and amnesic performance was the same when memory was measured by recognition (top) as when memory was measured by recall (bottom). Accordingly, recall and recognition memory appear to be similarly affected in amnesia.

Memory: Organization of Brain Systems and Cognition

strategy for identifying the essential nature of amnesia has been to carry out comparative studies of patients with alcoholic Korsakoff's syndrome, patients with confirmed or suspected damage to the hippocampal formation (non-Korsakoff amnesic patients), and patients with radiographically confirmed lesions restricted to the frontal lobe. These three groups have different lesions and different patterns of cognitive impairment. Amnesic patients with Korsakoff's syndrome have midline diencephalic lesions (which are known to be sufficient to cause amnesia), and they also have frontal lobe damage, as demonstrated by quantitative analysis of computed tomography (CT) scans (Jacobson and Lishman 1987; Shimamura, Jernigan, and Squire 1988). The non-Korsakoff amnesic patients studied in this context have medial temporal lobe lesions, but do not have detectable frontal lobe lesions. Finally, the patients with frontal lobe lesions have no known pathology outside the frontal lobes and are not amnesic (Janowsky et al. 1989).

The logic of this approach is to suppose that deficits observed only in the two amnesic groups are reflections of memory impairment due to medial temporal lobe or diencephalic pathology, whereas deficits observed in both patients with Korsakoff's syndrome and frontal patients, but not in other amnesic patients, are due to frontal lobe dysfunction. Table 17.1 summarizes some of the findings from this approach.

The comparisons summarized in table 17.1 suggest that many deficits exhibited by patients with Korsakoff's syndrome are due to frontal lobe damage and are dissociable from amnesia. Consider, for example, the finding that patients with Korsakoff's syndrome are poor at making judgments and predictions about their own memory ability, namely, they have impaired

Table 17.1 Associated and Dissociated Deficits in Amnesia

Test	Amnesia	Korsakoff's Syndrome	Frontal Lobe Damage
Delayed Recall	+	+	−
Dementia Rating Scale: Memory Index	+	+	−
Dementia Rating Scale: Initiation/Perseveration Index	−	+	+
Wisconsin Card Sort	−	+	+
Temporal Order Memory	+	+ +	+ +
Metamemory	−	+	+
Release from Proactive Interference	−	+	−

Constructed from data in Janowsky et al. 1989; Shimamura, Janowsky, and Squire 1990; Janowsky, Shimamura, and Squire 1989; Shimamura and Squire 1986; Amnesia = amnesic patients with confirmed or suspected damage to the hippocampal formation; Korsakoff's Syndrome = amnesic patients with diencephalic lesions and confirmed frontal lobe atrophy; Frontal Lobe Damage = patients with lesions restricted to the frontal lobes. + = deficit; − = no deficit; + + = disproportionally impaired relative to item memory.

metamemory. In the absence of other information, one might suppose that impaired metamemory is an inextricable part of disordered memory. One might even suspect that an impairment in the ability to monitor and to be aware of one's own memory abilities could be a cause of disordered memory. However, impaired metamemory abilities are not observed in non-Korsakoff amnesic patients, even when the severity of their amnesia is similar to the severity of memory impairment in patients with Korsakoff's syndrome (Shimamura and Squire 1986). Moreover, patients with frontal lobe lesions exhibit metamemory deficits in the absence of amnesia (Janowsky, Shimamura, and Squire et al. 1989). These findings indicate that metamemory functions are separately organized from memory ability itself. Memory ability depends on the integrity of the medial temporal lobe and midline diencephalon. Metamemory functions depend importantly on the frontal lobe.

As table 17.1 shows, patients with amnesia can have somewhat heterogeneous patterns of symptoms, which vary depending on what anatomical damage has occurred. Certain deficits are found in virtually all amnesic patients and likely reflect damage to the medial temporal lobe or midline diencephalon. These include difficulty in learning new facts and events, as measured by tests of both recall and recognition. Other deficits are sometimes present as well that are not obligatory to memory impairment. These include deficits in problem solving (Janowsky et al. 1989a; Oscar-Berman 1980), temporal order memory (Meudell et al. 1985; Milner 1971; Shimamura, Janowsky, and Squire 1990; Squire 1982), metamemory (Shimamura and Squire 1986), and sensitivity to proactive interference, namely, failure to show the normal improvement in performance when attempting to learn words belonging to a new category after attempting several word lists from another category (Cermak, Butters, and Moreines 1974; Squire 1982). These deficits are associated with frontal lobe dysfunction, which occurs in some cases of amnesia but not in others.

17.2 RETROGRADE AMNESIA

Retrograde amnesia refers to impaired memory for information that was acquired prior to the onset of amnesia. It has long been recognized that the status of retrograde amnesia has important implications for understanding both the organization of normal memory and the function of the damaged brain structures. In 1881, Theodule Ribot brought together a large number of clinical case reports indicating that recent memory is typically lost more readily than remote memory (Ribot [1881] 1882). These case reports formed the basis of his Law of Regression, which stated that in memory "the new perishes before the old," an idea that has been confirmed repeatedly by clinical observers during this century. Considering the limitations of informal observation, it is surprising that quantitative studies of retrograde amnesia were initiated only twenty years ago (Sanders and Warrington 1971). Since that time a great deal has been learned, despite the fact that most methods for assessing retrograde amnesia in humans are imperfect in a number of ways (Squire 1975; Squire and Cohen 1982). Indeed, the most decisive tests of

Ribot's Law, which distinguish between alternative interpretations of his basic observation, have been carried out prospectively with experimental animals.

Useful descriptions of retrograde amnesia have come from formal studies of groups of amnesic patients (fig. 17.3), including patients with Korsakoff's syndrome (Albert, Butters, and Levin 1979; Cohen and Squire 1981; Meudell et al. 1980; Squire et al. 1989), patients with confirmed or suspected hippocampal damage (Squire, Haist, and Shimamura 1989), and patients with transient global amnesia (TGA) (Kritchevsky and Squire 1989). For these patients, remote memory impairment is extensive and temporally graded, affecting the most recent decades more than remote decades. Indeed, very remote memory can be intact, even when the test items are so difficult that they can be answered by fewer than 20 percent of normal subjects (Squire, Haist, and Shimamura 1989). The findings from the (non-Korsakoff) amnesic patients and the patients with TGA are particularly useful, because these patients became amnesic on a known calendar day. In this circumstance, there can be no ambiguity about which test items measure retrograde amnesia. In contrast, patients with Korsakoff's syndrome often develop amnesia gradually and have learning deficits that could later affect performance on a remote memory test.

The time period affected in retrograde amnesia can be quite limited when damage is limited to the hippocampus and when anterograde amnesia is only moderately severe (e.g., patient R.B., who had bilateral lesions limited to the CA1 region of the hippocampus and retrograde amnesia of a few years at the most; see Zola-Morgan, Squire, and Amaral 1986). Retrograde amnesia may be more extensive when anterograde amnesia is more severe, as was the case for the patients whose data appear in figure 17.3: the Korsakoff patients, the (non-Korsakoff) amnesic patients, and the patients with TGA. Thus, retrograde amnesia may vary in its severity and extent as a function of the severity of anterograde amnesia. Moreover, both medial temporal lobe and diencephalic damage can produce similarly extensive and temporally graded retrograde amnesia. These ideas replace an earlier proposal that distinguished two different types of retrograde amnesia—a brief, temporally limited impairment and a more extensive impairment—depending on whether the locus of damage is medial temporal or diencephalic (Cohen and Squire 1981).

What accounts for the finding that the four (non-Korsakoff) amnesic cases in figure 17.3, who became amnesic following an anoxic or ischemic event, have more severe anterograde and retrograde amnesia than R.B.? One would expect that their pathology is more extensive than what was found in R.B., namely, that it is not restricted to the CA1 region of the hippocampus. Two of these four patients have been examined recently with an improved protocol for imaging the human hippocampus with magnetic resonance (Press, Amaral, and Squire 1989). In both patients, the hippocampal formation was markedly reduced in size bilaterally, apparently affecting all the fields of the hippocampus including the CA1 region, together with the dentate gyrus and the subicular complex.

It is important to note that some memory-impaired patients have extensive remote memory impairment covering many decades with no evidence of a

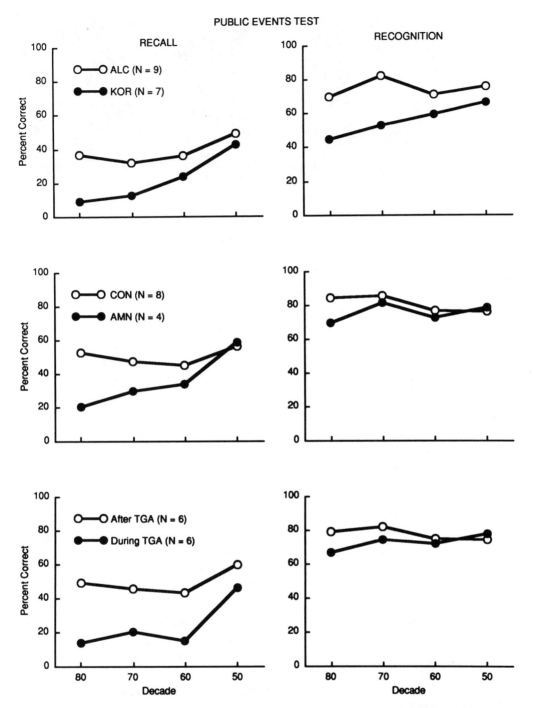

Figure 17.3 Remote memory performance of amnesic patients with Korsakoff's syndrome (KOR N = 7), alcoholic control subjects (ALC N = 9), amnesic patients with confirmed or suspected damage to the hippocampal formation (AMN N = 4), healthy control subjects (CON N = 8), and patients with transient global amnesia (TGA N = 6). *Left:* Recall of past public events that had occurred in one of the four decades from 1950 to 1985. *Right:* Performance on a multiple-choice test (4 alternatives) involving the same public events (from Squire, Haist, and Shimamura 1989 and Kritchevsky and Squire 1989).

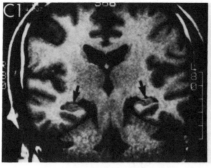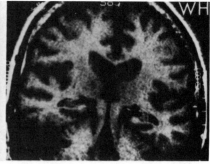

Figure 17.4 *Left panel:* Magnetic resonance scan of a normal subject (resolution = .625 mm). Several anatomical features of the hippocampal formation can be distinguished. *Right panel:* Magnetic resonance scan of amnesic patient W.H. using the same protocol. The hippocampal formation is markedly reduced in size. The calibration bars to the right represent 5 cm in 1-cm increments. From Press, Amaral, and Squire 1989.

temporal gradient (for discussion, see Squire, Haist, and Shimamura 1989). It is not clear whether this extreme form of retrograde amnesia is always accompanied by a correspondingly more severe form of anterograde amnesia, namely, an impairment that would be more severe than is found in the patients contributing to figure 17.3. While this is a possibility, an alternative is that severe, ungraded retrograde amnesia requires damage beyond the medial temporal lobe and midline diencephalic structures usually associated with circumscribed amnesia, and that this damage impairs performance on remote memory tests without producing a proportional impairment of new learning. This possibility appears tenable because most of the clinical conditions in which severe, ungraded retrograde amnesia is observed are conditions in which additional damage is known to have occurred, especially in the neo-cortex, which is a likely repository of permanent memory (Mishkin 1982; Squire 1987).

In correspondence with their performance on tests of remote memory for factual material, amnesic patients also exhibit retrograde amnesia on tests that assess autobiographical memory for specific episodes (Butters and Cermak 1986; see also Beatty et al. 1987; Gabrieli, Cohen, and Corkin 1988; Kopelman 1989; MacKinnon and Squire 1989). Across individual patients, the severity of the impairment is similar for autobiographical memory and fact memory. The work reviewed to this point suggests that extensive, temporally graded retro-grade amnesia for facts and personal events is a common feature of memory impairment. In addition, repeated testing across a period of years has shown that retrograde amnesia can be highly stable (Squire, Haist, and Shimamura 1989).

Recently, a single-case report suggested that retrograde amnesia can be severe and extensive when assessed with standard tests, but that it is not observed at all when the same tests are redesigned as semantic memory tests, namely, when one assesses simple familiarity for famous names or name completion ability rather than associative memory (Warrington and McCarthy

1988). However, such tests could be too easy to discriminate between normal and impaired performance; that is, retrograde amnesia might be obscured by a ceiling effect. To explore these issues further, we constructed similar tests of simple familiarity and name completion ability but made the tests more difficult. We tested two amnesic patients who have severe and extensive retrograde amnesia, as assessed by standard tests of remote memory, namely, Boswell (Damasio et al. 1985) and WI (Squire, Amaral, and Press 1990). The first test asked subjects to select the famous name from a group of nonfamous names (e.g., Arthur Elliot, David Conner, Richard Daley). The second test asked subjects to complete a fragment to form a famous name (e.g., Adlai Stev__). The famous names for both tests spanned the time period 1940–1985 and were taken from a standard famous faces test. On the new tests, both patients performed better than on more conventional remote memory tests. However, they still scored outside the range of control subjects for every decade, and at every decade scored more than two standard deviations below the control mean (fig. 17.5; Haist, Squire, and Damasio 1990). Thus, there seems little basis for generalizing from the case report to the general conclusion that retrograde amnesia can be mitigated by simple changes in test procedure.

There are two possible interpretations of the important finding that amnesia affects recent memory for facts and events more than it does remote memory. One possibility is that the structures damaged in amnesia are necessary for the retrieval of components or features of memory that are ordinarily short-lasting. These memories will be abundant in recent memory and relatively uncommon in remote memory. According to this interpretation, amnesia will always affect recent memory more than it will remote memory. However, there is no transformation or consolidation of information across time, only differential attrition of memory by type. A second possibility is that information is reorganized or consolidated with the passage of time after learning. Memory initially depends on the integrity of the structures damaged in amnesia. As time passes after learning, memory is gradually reorganized and becomes independent of these structures.

These two alternatives can be distinguished by determining the precise shape of the performance curve in retrograde amnesia. The difficulty is that the precise shape of the temporal gradient of retrograde amnesia cannot be established with certainty using the available methods for testing remote memory retrospectively in humans. One can imagine two possibilities (figs. 17.6A and 17.6B). The critical feature of the data illustrated in the right panel is that scores for more remote periods are actually better than scores for more recent periods. Only this pattern of data requires that active reorganization or consolidation occur in memory (for discussion, see Zola-Morgan and Squire 1990).

Findings from patients prescribed electroconvulsive therapy (ECT) (Squire, Slater, and Chace 1975), using a specially constructed test that permitted equivalent sampling of past time periods, and findings from mice given electro-

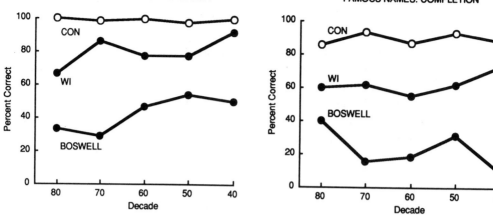

FAMOUS NAMES: FAMILIARITY   **FAMOUS NAMES: COMPLETION**

Figure 17.5 Performance of amnesic patients W.I. and Boswell on two tests of remote memory that were redesigned as semantic memory tests. In one case, subjects selected the famous names from two nonfamous names. In the other case, subjects attempted to complete the famous name when given the first name and a fragment of the last name. Performance of both amnesic patients was severely impaired. CON = 8 control subjects.

convulsive shock (ECS) (Squire and Spanis 1984) have shown unequivocally (in accordance with fig. 17.6B) that a consolidation process must occur in very long-term memory. However, treatments like ECT and ECS cannot be usefully related to neuroanatomy. Accordingly, these gradients of retrograde amnesia do not reveal how the structures damaged in amnesia participate in the maintenance and consolidation of memory. The findings are useful primarily in showing that long-term memory retains considerable dynamism and that changes continue in memory storage for a long time after learning.

Recently, retrograde amnesia was assessed prospectively in monkeys with bilateral lesions of the hippocampal formation (Zola-Morgan and Squire 1990). The key finding was that operated monkeys remembered object discriminations learned twelve weeks previously significantly better than object discriminations learned two weeks previously (fig. 17.6C). In addition, the scores of the operated monkeys increased monotonically, and there was a significant trend across the two-week to twelve-week time period ($p < .01$). Only one operated monkey obtained a lower score for object pairs learned twelve weeks before surgery than for object pairs learned two weeks before surgery. These results provide unequivocal evidence for a gradual process of reorganization or consolidation in memory. Similar results were also reported recently for rats given hippocampal lesions, though the gradient of retrograde amnesia extended across a period of only 2–5 days (Winocur 1990). The hippocampal formation is essential for memory storage for a limited period of time. As time passes after learning, the contribution of the hippocampal formation gradually diminishes and a more permanent memory system develops, presumably in the neocortex, which is independent of the hippocampal formation. A temporary memory in the hippocampal formation (a simple memory, a

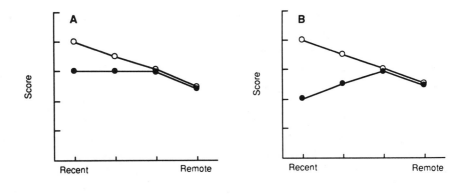

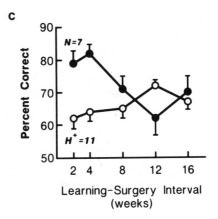

Figure 17.6 (A, B). Hypothetical retrograde amnesia data for normal subjects (open circles) and amnesic patients (closed circles), assuming an optimal remote memory test, that is, a test for which the information sampled from each time period is known to have been learned to the same level and the forgotten at the same rate. Only the curves shown in panel B require the hypothesis that memory is actively reorganized or consolidated across time. (C). Temporally graded retrograde amnesia in monkeys with bilateral lesions of the hippocampal formation (H⁺). Monkeys were trained on 20 different object-discrimination problems on each of five occasions, beginning 16, 12, 8, 4, and 2 weeks prior to surgery. Two weeks after surgery, retention for all 100 pairs was tested by presenting each object pair for a single trial. The results were similar to the hypothetical data in panel B. At the 12-week time period, the data for normal animals was quite variable, and the comparison between normal and operated monkeys was not significant ($p = 0.12$) (from Zola-Morgan and Squire 1990).

conjunction, or an index; see Marr 1971; Squire, Shimamura, and Amaral 1989; Teyler and Discenna 1986) is eventually replaced by a gradually developing, more permanent memory elsewhere (for further discussion, see Squire 1992).

A considerable amount has been learned about the organization of normal memory since quantitative studies of retrograde amnesia were undertaken beginning twenty years ago. Extensive and temporally graded amnesia can occur across a decade or more, even in patients with well-circumscribed amnesia. Very remote memory can be preserved. Similar findings are obtained for tests based on factual information and tests based on autobiographical, event-specific information. When damage is limited to the CA1 region of the human hippocampus, retrograde amnesia is limited to a period of only a few years at most. Retrograde amnesia is more extensive when the anatomical damage is more extensive, and it increases in severity as anterograde amnesia increases. The memory loss represents a loss of usable knowledge that cannot be mitigated in any known way by altering the manner in which remote memory questions are presented. Finally, a prospective study in monkeys has provided the first direct evidence in primates for the dynamic role of the hippocampal formation in memory storage. The hippocampal formation is initially essential for the storage and retrieval of memory, but its contribution diminishes and a more permanent memory develops elsewhere that is independent of the hippocampal formation. In order for memory to be established and then maintained in a usable form, the hippocampal formation must interact with the neocortex during a lengthy period of reorganization and consolidation.

17.3 MULTIPLE FORMS OF MEMORY

The evidence from anterograde and retrograde amnesia indicates that the system that is damaged in amnesia is essential for establishing long-term memory at the time of learning, and that it remains essential during a lengthy period of reorganization. Eventually, a more permanent memory develops that is independent of this system. The important finding to be considered in this section is that this sequence of events involves only one kind of memory. The kind of memory that is impaired in amnesia, which is dependent on the integrity of the damaged system, has been termed declarative (explicit) memory. Declarative memory refers to information about previously encountered facts and events, the kind of information that is ordinarily available as conscious recollections.

Although amnesic patients are gravely disabled by their disorder in declarative memory, performance on some learning and memory tasks is entirely intact. The kinds of learning and memory that are spared are a heterogeneous group of abilities, collectively termed nondeclarative (implicit) memory (see fig. 17.7). Examples of preserved learning include perceptuo-motor skills (Brooks and Baddeley 1976; Milner 1962), perceptual and cognitive skills (Cohen and Squire 1980; Nissen and Bullemer 1987; Squire and Frambach

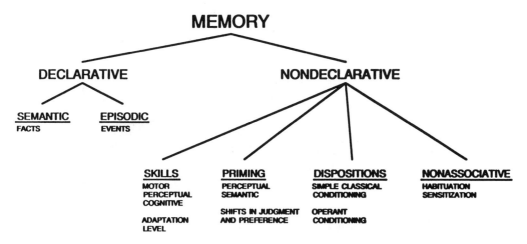

Figure 17.7 A tentative memory taxonomy. Declarative memory is available as conscious recollection. Nondeclarative memory refers to a large number of separable learning and memory abilities where performance changes but without affording access to the original experience or to any memory content.

1990), and priming (Graf, Squire, and Mandler 1984; Shimamura 1986; Tulving and Schacter 1990). Priming refers to an increased facility for identifying words or other perceptual objects, which is caused by their recent presentation. Amnesic patients also show normal shifts in preference after exposure to novel material (Johnson, Kim, and Risse 1985), normal adaptation-level effects (Benzing and Squire 1989), and successful acquisition and extinction in simple classical conditioning (Daum, Channon, and Canavar 1989; Weiskrantz and Warrington 1979). Taken together, these findings have provided the best evidence for the important idea that memory is not a unitary mental function, but a collection of different abilities.

Skill Learning

Early work showed that amnesic patients could learn perceptuo-motor skills such as mirror drawing (Milner 1962) and could improve on a rotary pursuit tracking task (Brooks and Baddeley 1976; Corkin 1968). Subsequently, it became clear that perceptual skills and cognitive skills can also be learned normally, even when there is no motor component to the acquired skill. Thus, amnesic patients improved as rapidly as did normal subjects at the skill of reading mirror-reversed words and exhibited normal retention after a three-month interval (Cohen and Squire 1980). They were also normal during the early phase of learning a cognitive skill task, which required subjects to interact with a computer to maintain a specific target value across trials (Squire and Frambach 1990). In these cases normal learning occurred, but the amnesic patients could not answer simple factual questions about the learning task, even when the questions were presented in a multiple-choice test. One important feature of these tasks is that memory is tested implicitly. That

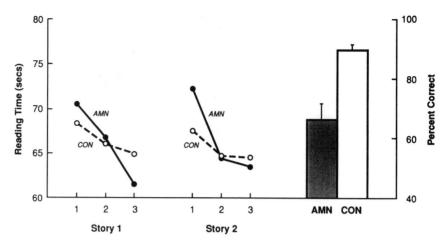

Figure 17.8 Time required to read aloud two different stories, each presented three times in succession (AMN = amnesic patients, N = 8; CON = control subjects, N = 9). The bars show the performance of each group on a test of story content given immediately after the final reading of the second story (chance = 33%). Brackets show standard error of the mean (from Musen, Shimamura, and Squire 1990).

is, performance is based on speed or proficiency and does not depend on explicit reference to any previously presented information.

Acquired skills could potentially depend on generic information, which is acquired cumulatively across many study trials, or skills could depend on specific information that is based on the particular items that are encountered. For example, in the case of mirror reading, a skill could be general (i.e., a subject improves at reading any reversed letters or words), or a skill could be specific to the particular letters or words that were practiced. If item-specific information is retained, a further question is whether such information is non-declarative, that is, whether amnesic patients are entirely intact at acquiring item-specific information that is part of a skill.

One experimental approach to these questions has focused on the reading of normal text. The phenomenon of interest is that, when subjects reread a passage of text, they tend to read it faster on the second reading than on the first. Studies of normal subjects have shown that this facilitation is specific to familiar passages and is not a nonspecific improvement in reading ability (Kolers 1975). To determine whether amnesic patients can acquire and retain text-specific reading skills, patients were asked to read a text passage aloud three times in succession and were then given a second text to read three times (Musen, Shimamura, and Squire 1990). The results were that reading speed improved at a similar rate in both amnesic patients and normal subjects, and was specific to the text that was read (fig. 17.8). After improving at reading the first passage, both groups read the second passage at the same slower speed with which they had initially read the first passage. In both groups the facilitation persisted for about ten minutes and disappeared within two hours. These results, and similar findings obtained in other studies (Moscovitch,

Winocur, and McLachlan 1986), show clearly that very specific skill-based information (e.g., information about the words and ideas presented in text) can be supported by nondeclarative (implicit) memory.

Priming

Priming occurs when performance is facilitated or biased by recently encountered information (Shimamura 1986; Tulving and Schacter 1990). For example, in perceptual identification tasks, subjects try to identify words or pictures that are presented very briefly (for about 50 msec). Priming is indicated by more accurate identification or by faster response times for previously presented items compared to new items. In word-stem completion tasks, subjects are given word stems (e.g, MOT_) and asked to form the first words that come to mind. Priming is indicated by an increased tendency to complete the stems to form recently presented words (e.g., MOTEL), compared with a condition when words were not presented first. Amnesic patients exhibit fully intact priming effects (Cermak et al. 1985; Graf, Squire, and Mandler 1984; Schacter 1985). Some forms of priming are rather short-lived, disappearing within two hours. In these cases, the duration of priming is identical for normal subjects and amnesic patients (Graf, Squire, and Mandler 1984; Shimamura and Squire 1984). Longer-lasting priming effects (e.g., days or weeks) have also been reported in normal subjects (see Tulving, Schacter, and Stark 1982), and amnesic patients also show long-lasting effects under some circumstances (Cave and Squire, in press; McAndrews, Glisky, and Schacter 1987; Moscovitch, Winocur, and McLachlan 1986; but see Squire, Shimamura, and Graf 1987).

One way to understand priming is to suppose that preexisting representations are transiently activated, thereby influencing behavior for a period of time. The difficulty with this view is that in normal subjects priming-like effects have been found for novel stimuli including pronounceable nonwords (Cermak et al. 1985; Feustel, Shiffrin, and Salasoo 1983; Smith and Oscar-Berman 1990) and novel patterns and objects (Gabrieli et al. 1990; Musen and Treisman 1990; Schacter et al. 1990). These observations suggest that priming may operate at early stages of perceptual processing, prior to the analysis of meaning. A recent study of priming using positron emission tomography supports this idea (Squire et al. 1992). Thus, priming of novel material may be supported entirely by nondeclarative memory and may be intact in amnesic patients. Recently, this view has been confirmed by finding fully intact performance by amnesic patients on tasks involving nonwords (Haist, Musen, and Squire 1991; Musen and Squire 1991) and on priming tasks involving novel nonverbal material (Gabrieli et al. 1990; Musen and Squire, in press; Schacter et al. 1991).

One interesting possibility is that there are two forms of priming: perceptual and semantic (Gabrieli 1991; Schacter 1990; Tulving and Schacter 1990). Perceptual priming operates on early-stage perceptual systems (e.g., a pre-semantic word-form system), and semantic priming depends on access to word meanings. Perceptual priming is illustrated in word-identification or object-identification tasks that do not require access to meaning. Semantic priming is illustrated by the increased tendency of amnesic patients and normal subjects to produce recently presented words (e.g, BABY) when they are asked to "free associate" to semantically related words (e.g., CHILD, see Shimamura and Squire 1984).

This distinction between perceptual and semantic priming might illuminate the issue of whether the acquisition of entirely novel information can be supported by nondeclarative memory. Amnesic patients may be able to acquire novel information only when the information does not require access to or integration into meaning systems. For example, when normal subjects study WINDOW-REASON, they are later more likely to produce the word REASON when given WINDOW-REA than when given OFFICER-REA (Graf and Schacter 1985). This effect of context depends on forming a meaningful link between the two words at the time of study. Amnesic patients do not show this effect (Cermak, Bleich, and Blackford 1988; Shimamura and Squire 1989), perhaps because they lack the ability to join the two words into a unitized representation at the time the words are initially studied. Similarly, priming of pronounceable nonwords may occur in amnesic patients only when the task requires that items be read aloud, but not when items must be identified as words or nonwords. For example, in one study a lexical-decision task was used in which subjects needed to decide rapidly whether a previously presented letter string was a real word or not (Smith and Oscar-Berman 1990). Normal subjects showed priming for both words and nonwords in this task; namely, they made the lexical decision faster when either a word or nonword had been presented recently. Amnesic patients also showed priming of words, but they showed no priming of nonwords. By contrast, in a reading-speed task, which did not require access to meaning, amnesic patients and normal subjects showed a similar ability to acquire information about nonwords (Musen and Squire 1991). Further study of priming and the perceptual-semantic distinction should be useful in order to clarify what kinds of new knowledge can be supported by nondeclarative memory.

Figure 17.7 illustrates a taxonomic organization of memory. Declarative memory is impaired in amnesia. It includes memory for both facts and events, which are represented such that learned information can be brought to mind as a conscious recollection. Declarative memory is flexible, available to multiple response systems, and is adapted for rapid, even one-trial, learning. Nondeclarative memory includes a wide variety of examples in which behavior changes with experience but without conscious access to what has been learned. Information is embedded in specific procedures or stored as tunings, biases, or activations. The knowledge gained occurs as changes in particular perceptual systems and response systems, or as the development of specific production rules. The knowledge is inflexible and is best expressed by the same response systems that were used for its acquisition (Eichenbaum,

Matthews, and Cohen 1989; Glisky, Schacter, and Tulving 1986; Saunders and Weiskrantz 1989).

Declarative memory depends on the integrity of the structures and connections that are damaged in amnesia. These structures provide a mechanism for forming new relationships rapidly in long-term memory, such as when a stimulus is associated to its spatial-temporal context (thus representing a new event) or when names and terms are associated to a semantic context (thus representing a new concept). Nondeclarative memory depends on anatomical structures and connections specific to what is being acquired. The striatum may be important for some kinds of nondeclarative memory, especially where a habit is acquired incrementally (Packard, Hirsh, and White 1989), but pathways in the cerebellum (Thompson 1988) and amygdala (LeDoux et al. 1988) are also important, as for example in classical conditioning of skeletal musculature and in the conditioning of emotional responses. These and other observations are consistent with the idea that nondeclarative memory is heterogeneous (Butters, Heindel, and Salmon 1990; Squire 1987). For example. Heindel et al. (1989) found that word-completion priming was impaired in patients with Alzheimer's disease but that skill learning was intact. Patients with Huntington's disease showed the opposite pattern. For additional discussion of distinctions between memory systems, see Squire (1992b).

17.4 THE NEUROANATOMY OF MEMORY: RECENT FINDINGS FROM ANIMAL MODELS OF HUMAN AMNESIA

Careful neuropsychological descriptions of amnesic patients have contributed enormously to understanding how memory is organized in the brain. An important related issue is to identify the structures that, when damaged, produce amnesia. One promising approach to identifying these structures has taken advantage of an animal model of human amnesia in the nonhuman primate. The following sections describe a series of studies that used this approach to identify the structural components of the medial temporal lobe memory system.

Evaluating Memory Function in the Nonhuman Primate

Memory function in monkeys can be evaluated using a number of behavioral tasks that assess memory in a variety of ways (Zola-Morgan and Squire 1990). Some of the tests are identical to ones failed by amnesic patients (delayed nonmatching to sample, delayed retention of object discriminations, and concurrent discrimination; Squire, Zola-Morgan, and Chen 1988), and others are analogous to ones that amnesic patients do not fail (motor skill learning and pattern discrimination learning; Zola-Morgan and Squire 1984). These tasks, taken together, provide useful measures of the severity, the scope (impaired versus spared memory functions), and the duration of memory deficit.

The Contribution of the Medial Temporal Lobe to Memory Function

It is established in the monkey that large bilateral lesions of the medial temporal lobe, which include the structures thought to have been removed in amnesic patient H.M. (Scoville and Milner 1957), produce severe memory impairment (Mahut, Zola-Morgan, and Moss 1982; Mishkin 1978; Zola-Morgan and Squire 1985). In the monkey, this lesion involves the hippocampal formation (i.e., the dentate gyrus, the hippocampus proper, the subicular complex, and the entorhinal cortex), the amygdala, and the surrounding perirhinal and parahippocampal cortices. The lesion is termed the $H^+ A^+$ lesion, where H refers to the hippocampus, A to the amygdala, and $^+$ to the respective, adjacent cortical regions (Squire and Zola-Morgan 1988; Zola-Morgan, Squire, and Amaral 1989b). The memory deficit in monkeys produced by the $H^+ A^+$ lesion (fig. 17.9) parallels the deficit in human amnesia in several important ways (see Zola-Morgan and Squire 1990): the deficit increases as the delay interval increases between acquisition and retention; it is severe and enduring; short-term memory is spared; it is modality general; and skill-based learning is spared. These parallels provide strong evidence that monkeys with the $H^+ A^+$ lesion provide a good animal model of medial temporal lobe amnesia in humans. The work to be described next assesses the importance to memory functions of the components of the $H^+ A^+$ lesion.

The Hippocampal Formation and the Parahippocampal Cortex

As shown in figure 17.9, the $H^+ A^+$ removal is not required to produce significant memory impairment. A substantial, though less severe memory deficit is observed in monkeys following a lesion limited to the hippocampal formation and parahippocampal cortex (referred to as the H^+ lesion; the anterior portion of the entorhinal cortex is spared in this lesion, see Zola-Morgan, Squire, and Amaral 1989a). This deficit is also enduring and appears to be qualitatively similar to the deficit associated with $H^+ A^+$ lesions. One possibility for the more severe memory deficit associated with the $H^+ A^+$ lesion could be that the amygdala is included in the $H^+ A^+$ lesion but not in the H^+ lesion.

The Amygdaloid Complex

Recent findings suggest that amygdala damage does not contribute to the severe memory deficit exhibited by monkeys with $H^+ A^+$ lesions. Lesions of the amygdaloid complex that spared the surrounding perirhinal and entorhinal cortex (the A lesion) produced no detectable memory impairment on any of four amnesia-sensitive tasks (figure 17.9; Zola-Morgan, Squire, and Amaral 1989b). Moreover, adding an amygdala lesion to the H^+ lesion ($H^+ A$ lesion) did not exacerbate the level of memory deficit exhibited after the H^+ lesion alone (fig. 17.9).

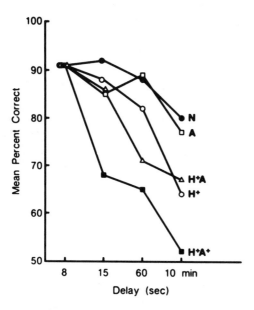

Figure 17.9 Performance on the delayed nonmatching to sample task by normal monkeys (N), monkeys with lesions of the amygdala (A), monkeys with damage to the hippocampal formation (H+), monkeys with conjoint lesions of the hippocampal formation and the amygdala (H+A), and monkeys with large medial temporal lobe resections (H+A+). Each operated group consisted of either 3 or 4 monkeys.

The Perirhinal and Parahippocampal Cortices

Recently, reevaluation of the extent of damage to the components of the original H^+A^+ lesion revealed that the perirhinal cortex (areas 35 and 36; Brodmann 1909) was more extensively damaged than had previously been appreciated (Zola-Morgan et al. 1989). Neuroanatomical studies had already identified the perirhinal cortex, and the closely associated parahippocampal cortex (areas TH and TF, see Bonin and Bailey 1947), as important links between the polymodal and unimodal associational areas of the neocortex and the hippocampal formation (fig. 17.10A). Specifically, the perirhinal and para-hippocampal cortices provide the major source of cortical input to the hippo-campal formation, by way of the entorhinal cortex (Insausti, Amaral, and Cowan 1987; Van Hoesen 1982). These anatomical considerations suggest that lesions limited to the perirhinal and parahippocampal cortices, which spare the hippocampal formation and the amygdala (the PRPH lesion), should pro-duce a severe memory deficit. Recently, monkeys with PRPH lesions were found to be severely impaired on three amnesia-sensitive tasks (Zola-Morgan et al. 1989). On the delayed nonmatching to sample task, the PRPH group exhibited a more severe impairment than either the H^+ group or the H^+A^+ group (fig 17.10B). Neuroanatomical studies of the brains of the PRPH mon-keys showed that the PRPH lesion eliminated most of the cortical inputs to the entorhinal cortex that arise from structures other than perirhinal and parahippocampal cortices. In contrast, the cortical inputs to the amygdala were

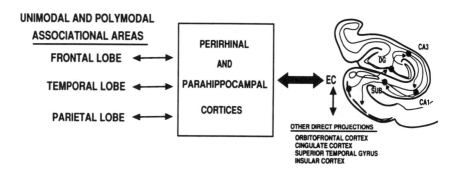

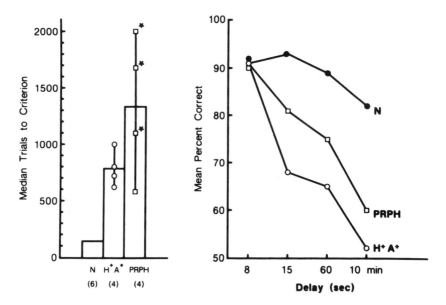

Figure 17.10 *Top:* Schematic representation of the connectivity of the perirhinal and the parahippocampal cortices in the monkey brain. The width of the arrows corresponds to the relative proportion of cortical inputs arising from the areas indicated. Abbreviations: EC, entorhinal cortex; DG, dentate gyrus; SUB, subicular complex; CA3 and CA1, fields of the hippocampus proper. *Bottom:* Performance on the delayed nonmatching to sample task by normal monkeys (N), monkeys with conjoint lesions of the perirhinal and parahippocampal cortices (PRPH), and monkeys with large medial temporal lobe resections (H⁺A⁺). *Left:* Initial learning of this task with a delay of 8 sec. Symbols show trials required to reach learning criterion for individual animals. Asterisk indicates animals for which the task was made easier by providing two presentations of the sample object on each trial, instead of one (double-sample presentation). One monkey was performing at only 56 percent correct when testing was discontinued after 2000 trials. *Right:* Performance across delays for the same groups. The curve for the PRPH animals underestimates the severity of impairment, because 2 of the 3 monkeys required double-sample presentation during this portion of the task. Indeed, when the single-sample procedure was used, performance of these 2 PRPH monkeys was even poorer than the performance of the H⁺A⁺ monkeys (8 sec: 70%; 15 sec: 60%; 60 sec: 55%).

largely intact. The latter finding was consistent with the observation that monkeys with PRPH lesions showed none of the changes in emotionality that have invariably occurred following direct damage to the amygdala, even when damage to the amygdala is incomplete (Zola-Morgan, Squire, Alvarez-Royo, and Clower 1991).

Three conclusions can be reached from the findings described to this point. First, damage to the amygdala does not appear to contribute to the memory deficit exhibited by monkeys with either H^+A^+ lesions or PRPH lesions. Second, the hippocampal formation and the anatomically related perirhinal and parahippocampal cortices are critical for normal memory function. Consistent with this view, in another operated group (the H^{++} lesion), damage to the perirhinal cortex, sparing the amygdala, exacerbated the memory impairment associated with damage to the hippocampal formation (Zola-Morgan, Squire, Clower, and Rempel, in press). This finding contrasts sharply with the finding that amygdala damage did not increase the deficit associated with H^+ lesions. Third, the PRPH lesion produced more severe impairment than the H^+ lesion.

One difference between the PRPH and H^+ lesion was that the perirhinal cortex was included in the PRPH lesion but not in the H^+ lesion. A second difference was that the PRPH lesion substantially deafferented the entorhinal cortex from cortical input, whereas the H^+ lesion damaged only the posterior portion of entorhinal cortex. Accordingly, either or both of these two differences could have contributed to the more severe impairment produced by the PRPH lesion, as compared to the H^+ lesion. The important point is that the structures and connections damaged in the PRPH lesion, but not in the H^+ lesion, must make a contribution to memory functions. Other studies will be needed to identify separate contributions to memory function of the perirhinal cortex, the entorhinal cortex, the parahippocampal gyrus, and other cortical areas whose projections to entorhinal cortex were damaged by the PRPH lesion. In summary, the results strongly suggest that the severe memory impairment resulting from the H^+A^+ lesion depends not on conjoint damage to the hippocampus and the amygdala but on conjoint damage to the hippocampal formation and the surrounding perirhinal and parahippocampal cortices.

The Hippocampus Proper

An additional issue is whether lesions limited to the hippocampus proper produce a significant memory deficit, or whether additional cortical damage is required. Valuable evidence pertaining to this point comes from patient R.B. who, as the result of an ischemic episode, sustained a lesion involving the entire CA1 field of the hippocampus bilaterally. The perirhinal, entorhinal, and parahippocampal cortices were spared. R.B. exhibited a significant and enduring memory impairment (Zola-Morgan, Squire, and Amaral 1986). This case showed that damage limited to the hippocampus proper is sufficient to cause a clinically significant and enduring memory deficit.

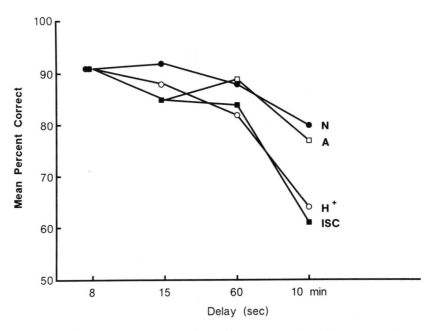

Figure 17.11 Performance on the delayed nonmatching to sample task by normal monkeys (N), monkeys with lesions of the amygdala (A), monkeys with lesions of the hippocampal formation (H$^+$), and monkeys with ischemic lesions of the hippocampus (ISC).

Monkeys that underwent a noninvasive procedure to produce cerebral ischemia (the ISC lesion) sustained substantial, bilateral loss of CA1 pyramidal cells in the hippocampus and were as impaired on the delayed nonmatching to sample task as monkeys with H$^+$ lesions (fig. 17.11; Zola-Morgan, Squire, Rempel, Clower, and Amaral, in press). Moreover, the memory deficit exhibited by the ISC group was enduring. Across the three tasks that were given, the ISC group was less impaired than the H$^+$ group, in keeping with the fact that the ISC lesion involved less damage to the hippocampal formation than did the H$^+$ lesion.

The findings from the ISC group make several points: First, the procedure used to produce global ischemia in the monkey consistently resulted in selective damage to the hippocampal formation sufficient to cause memory impairment. Second, lesions of either the hippocampal formation (H$^+$) or incomplete hippocampal lesions (ISC) produced significant and long-lasting amnesia in the monkey. Third, the finding of significant and enduring memory impairment following even partial damage to the hippocampus (in the ISC group) contrasts with the lack of impairment that followed complete amygdala (A) damage.

The Medial Temporal Lobe Memory System

Cumulative and systematic work in monkeys has identified structures and connections important for memory function. The findings to date suggest that the hippocampal formation, and the closely related perirhinal and parahippocampal cortices, comprise the medial temporal lobe memory system. Importantly, the perirhinal and parahippocampal cortex, and possibly other cortical areas projecting to entorhinal cortex, do not serve simply as a connecting route to the hippocampus but must themselves contribute to memory functions. The amygdala does not appear to be an essential component of this memory system, though it has been implicated in other kinds of cognitive functions, namely, ones that involve the association between a stimulus and its affective component (Gaffan and Harrison 1987; Mishkin and Aggleton 1981).

17.5. CONCLUSION

This chapter has reviewed recent progress in understanding the organization of memory and its neurological foundations. Parallel study of memory-impaired patients and an animal model of human memory impairment has illuminated the function of a medial temporal lobe/diencephalic system that is essential for the establishment of long-term memory. The role of this system is temporary, however, and a temporary memory supported by this system is eventually replaced by a gradually developing, more permanent memory elsewhere, probably in the neocortex. Other work has led to the proposal that multiple forms of memory must be distinguished. The kind of memory that depends on the integrity of the medial temporal lobe/diencephalic system has been termed declarative (or explicit) memory. This kind of memory stores representations about facts and events and is accessible to conscious recollection. Nondeclarative (or implicit) memory is a heterogeneous collection of memory abilities, including the capacity for skill learning, priming, conditioning, and other instances in which memory is expressed through performance without access to prior encounters or to memory content. Nondeclarative memory depends on anatomical structures and connections that vary depending on what is being learned. Declarative memory depends on the neocortex and on specific medial temporal lobe and diencephalic structures. Based on work with monkeys, the critical structures in the medial temporal lobe are the hippocampal formation and adjacent, anatomically related structures, especially the perirhinal and parahippocampal cortices.

NOTES

This chapter is a revised version of one that appeared originally in *Cold Spring Symp. Quant., Biol. 55.,* 1991.

We thank Dr. Antonio Damasio for permission to test his patient Boswell. Supported by the Medical Research Service of the Department of Veterans Affairs, NIMH Grant MH24600, NIH Grant 19063, the Office of Naval Research, the McKnight Foundation, a Bioscience Grant for International Joint Research from NEDO, Japan, and National Institute of Mental Health (NIMH) postdoctoral fellowships to C. B. C. and G. M.

REFERENCES

Albert, M. S., Butters, N., and Levin, J. (1979). Temporal gradients in the retrograde amnesia of patients with alcoholic Korsakoff's disease. *Archives of Neurology, 36,* 211–216.

Beatty, W. W., Salmon, D. P., Bernstein, N., and Butters, N. (1987). Remote memories in a patient with amnesia due to hypoxia. *Psychological Medicine, 17,* 657–665.

Benzing, W. C., and Squire, L. R. (1989). Preserved learning and memory in amnesia: Intact adaptation-level effects and learning of stereoscopic depth. *Behavioral Neuroscience, 103,* 548–547.

Bonin, G., and Bailey, P. (1947). *The Neocortex of Macaca Mulatta.* Urbana: University of Illinois Press.

Brodmann, K. (1909). *Vergleichende Lokalizationslehre der Grosshirnrinde.* Leipzig: Barth.

Brooks, D., and Baddeley, A. (1976). What can amnesic patients learn. *Neuropsychologia, 14,* 111–122.

Butters, N., and Cermak, L. S. (1986). A case study of the forgetting of autobiographical knowledge: Implications for the study of retrograde amnesia. In *Autobiographical Memory,* edited by D. Ruben, 253–272. New York: Cambridge University Press.

Butters, N., Heindel, W. C., and Salmon, D. P. (1990). Dissociation of implicit memory in dementia: Neurological implications. *Bulletin Psychonomic Society, 28,* 359–366.

Cave, C. B., and Squire, L. R. (1992). Intact and long-lasting visual object priming in amnesic patients. *Journal of Experimental Psychology, Learning, Memory, and Cognition, 18,* 509–520.

Cermak, L. S. (Ed). 1982. *Human Memory and Amnesia.* Hillsdale, NJ.: Erlbaum.

Cermak, L. S., Bleich, R. P., and Blackford, S. P. (1988). Deficits in implicit retention of new associates by alcoholic Korsakoff patients. *Brain and Cognition, 7,* 312–323.

Cermak, L. R., Butters, N., and Moreines, J. (1974). Some analyses of the verbal encoding deficit of alcoholic Korsakoff patients. *Brain and Language, 1,* 141–1150.

Cermak, L. S., Talbot, N., Chandler, K., and Wolbarst, L. R. (1985). The perceptual priming phenomenon in amnesia. *Neuropsychologia, 23,* 615–622.

Clower, R. P., Zola-Morgan, S., and Squire, L. R. (1990). Lesions of perirhinal cortex, but not lesions of the amygdala, exacerbate memory impairment in monkeys following lesions of the hippocampal formation. *Society for Neuroscience Abstracts, 16,* 616.

Cohen, N. J., and Squire, L. R. (1980). Preserved learning and retention of pattern analyzing skill in amnesic patients: Dissociation of knowing how and knowing that. *Science, 210,* 207–209.

Cohen, N. J., and Squire, L. R. (1981). Retrograde amnesia and remote memory impairment. *Neuropsychologia, 19,* 337–356.

Corkin, S. (1968). Acquisition of motor skill after bilateral medial temporal lobe excision. *Neuropsychologia, 6,* 225–265.

Damasio, A. R., Graff-Radford, N. R., Eslinger, P. J., Damasio, H., and Kassell, N. (1985). Amnesia following basal forebrain lesions. *Archives of Neurology, 42,* 263–271.

Daum, I., Channon, S., and Canavar, A. (1989). Classical conditioning in patients with severe memory problems. *Journal of Neurology and Neurosurgery Psychiatry, 52,* 47–51.

Eichenbaum, H., Matthews, P., and Cohen, N. J. (1989). Further studies of hippocampal representation during odor discrimination learning. *Behavioral Neuroscience, 6,* 1207–1216.

Feustel, T. C., Shiffrin, R. M., and Salasoo, A. (1983). Episodic and lexical contributions to the repetition effect in word identification. *Journal of Experimental Psychology: General, 112,* 309–316.

Gabrieli, J. D. E. (1991). Differential effects of aging and age-related neurological diseases on memory subsystems of the brain. In *The Handbook of Neuropsychology*, edited by F. Boller and J. Grafman, 149–166. New York: Elsevier.

Gabrieli, J. D. E., Cohen, N. J., and Corkin, S. (1988). The impaired learning of semantic knowledge following medial temporal-lobe resection. *Brain and Cognition, 7*, 157–177.

Gabrieli, J. D. E., Milberg, W., Keane, M. M., and Corkin, S. (1990). Intact priming of patterns despite impaired memory. *Neuropsychologia, 28*, 417–427.

Gaffan, D., and Harrison, S. (1987). Amygdalectomy and disconnection in visual learning for auditory secondary reinforcement by monkeys. *Journal Neuroscience, 7*, 2285–2292.

Glisky, E. L., Schacter, D. L., and Tulving, E. (1986). Computer learning by memory-impaired patients: Acquisition and retention of complex knowledge. *Neuropsychologia, 24*, 313–328.

Graf, P., and Schacter, D. L. (1985). Implicit and explicit memory for new associations in normal and amnesic subjects. *Journal of Experimental Psychology, Learning, Memory, and Cognition, 13*, 45–53.

Graf, P., Squire, L. R., and Mandler, G. (1984). The information that amnesic patients do not forget. *Journal of Experimental Psychology, Learning, Memory, and Cognition, 10*, 164–178.

Haist, F., Musen, G., and Squire, L. R. (1991). Intact priming of nonwords in amnesia. *Psychobiology, 19*, 275–285.

Haist, F., Shimamura, A. P., Squire, L. R. (N.d.). On the relation between recall and recognition memory. *Journal of Experimental Psychology: Learning, Memory, and Cognition.* In press.

Haist, F., Squire, L. R., and Damasio, A. R. (1990). Extensive retrograde amnesia on tests of familiarity and name completion ability. *Society for Neuroscience Abstracts, 16*, 287.

Heindel, W. C., Salmon, D. P., Shults, C. W., Walicke, P. A., and Butters, N. (1989). Neuropsychological evidence for multiple implicit memory systems: A comparison of Alzheimer's, Huntington's, and Parkinson's disease patients. *Journal of Neuroscience, 9*, 582–587.

Hirst, W. (1982). The amnesic syndrome: Descriptions and explanations. *Psychological Bulletin, 91*, 435–460.

Hirst, W., Johnson, M., Kim, J., Phelps, E., Risse, G., and Volpe, B. (1986). Recognition and recall in amnesics. *Journal of Experimental Psychology, Learning, Memory, and Cognition, 12*, 445–451.

Hirst, W., Johnson, M. K., Phelps, E. A., and Volpe, B. T. (1988). More on recognition and recall in amnesics. *Journal of Experimental Psychology, Learning, Memory, and Cognition, 14*, 758–762.

Insausti, R., Amaral, D. G., and Cowan, W. M. (1987). The entorhinal cortex of the monkey: II. Cortical afferents. *Journal of Comparative Neurology, 264*, 356–395.

Jacobson, R. R., and Lishman, W. A. (1987). Selective memory loss and global intellectual deficits in alcoholic Korsakoff's syndrome. *Psychological Medicine, 17*, 649–655.

Janowsky, J. S., Shimamura, A. P., Kritchevsky, M., and Squire, L. R. (1989). Cognitive impairment following frontal lobe damage and its relevance to human amnesia. *Behavioral Neuroscience, 103*, 548–560.

Janowsky, J. S., Shimamura, A. P., and Squire, L. R. (1989). Memory and metamemory: Comparisons between patients with frontal lobe lesions and amnesic patients. *Psychobiology, 17*, 3–11.

Johnson, M. J., Kim, J. K., and Risse, G. (1985). Do alcoholic Korsakoff's syndrome patients acquire affective reactions? *Journal of Experimental Psychology, Learning, Memory, and Cognition, 11*, 22–36.

Kolers, P. A. (1975). Specificity of operations in sentence recognition. *Cognitive Psychology, 7*, 289–366.

Kopelman, M. D. (1989). Remote and autobiographical memory, temporal context memory and frontal atrophy in Korsakoff and Alzheimer patients. *Neuropsychologia, 27,* 437–460.

Kritchevsky, M., and Squire, L. R. (1989). Transient global amnesia: Evidence for extensive, temporally graded retrograde amnesia. *Neurology, 39,* 213–218.

LeDoux, J. E., Iwata, J., Cicchetti, P., and Reis, D. J. (1988). Different projections of the central amygdaloid nucleus mediate autonomic and behavioral correlates of conditioned fear. *Journal of Neuroscience, 8,* 2517–2529.

McAndrews, M. P., Glisky, E. L., and Schacter, D. L. (1987). When priming persists: Long-lasting implicit memory for a single episode in amnesic patients. *Neuropsychologia, 25,* 2497–2506.

MacKinnon, D. F., and Squire, L. R. (1989). Autobiographical memory and amnesia. *Psychobiology, 17,* 247–256.

Mahut, H., Zola-Morgan, S., and Moss, M. (1982). Hippocampal resections impair associative learning and recognition memory in the monkey. *Journal of Neuroscience, 2,* 1214–1229.

Marr, D. (1971). Simple memory: A theory of archicortex. *The Philosophical Transactions of the Royal Society of London Series B, 262,* 23–81.

Mayes, A. R. (1988). *Human Organic Memory Disorders.* Cambridge: Cambridge University Press.

Meudell, P. R., Mayes, A. R., Ostergaard, A., and Pickering, A. (1985). Recency and frequency judgments in alcoholic amnesics and normal people with poor memory. *Cortex, 21,* 487.

Meudell, P. R., Northern, B., Snowden, J. S., and Neary, D. (1980). Long-term memory for famous voices in amnesia and normal subjects. *Neuropsychologia, 18,* 133–139.

Milner, B. (1962). Les troubles de la memoire accompagnant des lesions hippocampiques bilaterales [Memory impairment accompanying bilateral hippocampal lesions]. In *Physiologie de l'hippocampe.* Paris: Centre National de la Recherche Scientifique.

Milner, B. (1971). Interhemispheric differences in the localization of psychological processes in man. *British Medical Bulletin, 127,* 272–277.

Milner, B. (1972). Disorders of memory after temporal lobe lesions in man. *Clinical Neurosurgery, 19,* 421–466.

Mishkin, M. (1978). Memory in monkeys severely impaired by combined but not by separate removal of amygdala and hippocampus. *Nature, 273,* 297–298.

Mishkin, M. (1982). A memory system in the monkey. *Philosophical Transactions of the Royal Society of London, [Biology], 298,* 85–92.

Mishkin, M., and Aggleton, J. P. (1981). Multiple functional contributions of the amygdala in the monkey. In *The Amygdaloid Complex,* edited by Y. Ben-Ari. Amsterdam: Elsevier.

Moscovitch, M., Winocur, G., and McLachlan, D. (1986). Memory as assessed by recognition and reading time in normal and memory-impaired people with Alzheimer's disease and other neurological disorders. *Journal of Experimental Psychology, General, 115,* 331–347.

Musen, G., Shimamura, A. P., and Squire, L. R. (1990). Intact text-specific reading skill in amnesia. *Journal of Experimental Psychology, Learning, Memory, and Cognition, 16,* 1068–1076.

Musen, G., and Squire, L. R. (1991). Normal reading skill for words and nonwords in amnesia. *Journal of Experimental Psychology, Learning, Memory, and Cognition, 17,* 1095–1104.

Musen, G. and Squire, L. R. (1992). Nonverbal Priming in amnesia. *Memory & Cognition.* In press.

Musen, G., and Treisman, A. (1990). Implicit and explicit memory for visual patterns. *Journal of Experimental Psychology, Learning, Memory, and Cognition, 16,* 127–137.

Nissen, M. M., and Bullemer, P. (1987). Attentional requirements of learning: Evidence from performance measures. *Cognitive Psychology, 19,* 1–32.

Oscar-Berman, M. (1980). The neuropsychological consequences of long-term chronic alcoholism. *American Scientist, 68,* 410–419.

Ostergaard, A. L., and Squire, L. R. (1990). Childhood amnesia and distinctions between form of memory. A comment on Wood, Brown and Felton, *Brain and Cognition, 14,* 127–133.

Packard, M. F., Hirsh, R., and White, N. M. (1989). Differential effects of fornix and caudate nucleus lesions on two radial maze tasks: Evidence for multiple memory systems. *Journal of Neuroscience, 9,* 1465–1472.

Press, G., Amaral, D. G., and Squire, L. R. (1989). Hippocampal abnormalities in amnesic patients revealed by high-resolution magnetic resonance imaging. *Nature, 341,* 54–57.

Ribot, T. ([1881] 1882). *Diseases of Memory.* Translated by W. H. Smith. New York: Appleton-Century-Crofts.

Sanders, H. I., and Warrington, E. K. (1971) . Memory for remote events in amnesic patients. *Brain, 94,* 661–668.

Saunders, R. C., and Weiskrantz, L. (1989). The effects of fornix transection and combined fornix transection, mammillary body lesions and hippocampal ablations on object-pair association memory in rhesus monkey. *Behavioral Brain Research, 2,* 85–94.

Schacter, D. L. (1990). Perceptual representation systems and implicit memory: Toward a resolution of the multiple memory systems debate. In *Development and Neural Bases of High Cognitive Function,* edited by A. Diamond, 543–567. New York: Annals of the New York Academy of Science.

Schacter, D. L. (1985). Multiple forms of memory in humans and animals. In *Memory Systems of the Brain: Animal and Human Cognitive Processes,* edited by N. Weinberger, G. Lynch, and J. McGaugh, 351–379. New York: Guilford Press.

Schacter, D. L., Cooper, L. A., and Delaney, S. M. (1990). Implicit memory for unfamiliar objects depends on access to structural descriptions. *Journal of Experimental Psychology, General, 119,* 5–24.

Schacter, D. L., Cooper, L. A., Tharan, M., and Rubens, A. B. (1991). Preserved priming of novel objects in patients with memory disorders. *Journal of Cognitive Neuroscience, 3,* 118–131.

Scoville, W. B., and Milner, B. (1957). Loss of recent memory after bilateral hippocampal lesions. *Journal of Neurology, Neurosurgery, and Psychiatry, 20,* 11–21.

Shimamura, A. P. (1986). Priming effects in amnesia: Evidence for a dissociable memory function. *Quarterly Journal of Experimental Psychology, 38A,* 619–644.

Shimamura, A. P., Janowsky, J. S., and Squire, L. R. (1990). Memory for the temporal order of events in patients with frontal lobe lesions and amnesic patients. *Neuropsychologia, 28,* 803–814.

Shimamura, A. P., Jernigan, T. L., and Squire, L. R. (1988). Korsakoff's syndrome: Radiological (CT) findings and neuropsychological correlates. *Journal of Neuroscience, 8,* 4400–4410.

Shimamura, A. P., and Squire, L. R. (1984). Paired-associate learning and priming effects in amnesia: A neuropsychological study. *Journal of Experimental Psychology, General, 113,* 556–570.

Shimamura, A. P., and Squire, L. R. (1986). Memory and metamemory: A study of the feeling-of-knowing phenomenon in amnesic patients. *Journal of Experimental Psychology, Learning, Memory, and Cognition, 12,* 452–460.

Shimamura, A. P., and Squire, L. R. (1987). A neuropsychological study of fact memory and source amnesia. *Journal of Experimental Psychology, Learning, Memory, and Cognition, 13,* 464–473.

Shimamura, A. P., and Squire, L. R. (1989). Impaired priming of new associations in amnesia. *Journal of Experimental Psychology, Learning, Memory, and Cognition, 15*, 721–728.

Smith, M. E., and Oscar-Berman, M. (1990). Activation and the repetition priming of words and pseudowords in normal memory and amnesia. *Journal of Experimental Psychology, Learning, Memory, and Cognition, 16*, 1033–1042.

Squire, L. R. (1975). A stable impairment in remote memory following electroconvulsive therapy. *Neuropsychologia, 13*, 51–58.

Squire, L. R. (1982). Comparisons between forms of amnesia: Some deficits are unique to Korsakoff's syndrome. *Journal of Experimental Psychology, Learning, Memory, and Cognition, 8*, 560–571.

Squire, L. R. (1987). *Memory and Brain*. New York: Oxford University Press.

Squire, L. R. (1992a). Memory and the hippocampus: A synthesis from findings with rats, monkeys, and humans. *Psychol. Rev., 99*, 195–231.

Squire, L. R. (1992b). Declarative and nondeclarative memory: Multiple brain systems supporting learning and memory. *Journal of Cognitive Neuroscience*. In press.

Squire, L. R., Amaral, D. G., and Press, G. (1990). Magnetic resonance measurements of hippocampal formation and mammillary nuclei distinguish medial temporal lobe and diencephalic amnesia. *Journal of Neuroscience, 10*, 3106–3117.

Squire, L. R., and Cohen, N. J. (1982). Remote memory, retrograde amnesia, and the neuropsychology of memory. In *Human Memory and Amnesia*, edited by L. Cermak, 275–303, Hillsdale, NJ: Erlbaum.

Squire, L. R., and Frambach, M. (1990). Cognitive skill learning in amnesia. *Psychobiology, 18*, 109–117.

Squire, L. R., Haist, F., and Shimamura, A. P. (1989). The neurology of memory: Quantitative assessment of retrograde amnesia in two groups of amnesic patients. *Journal of Neuroscience, 9*, 828–839.

Squire, L. R., Ojemann, J. G., Miezin, F. M., Petersen, S. E., Videen, T. O., and Raichle, M. E. (1992). Activation of the hippocampus in normal humans: A functional anatomical study of memory. *Proceedings of the National Academy of Sciences, 89*, 1837–1841.

Squire, L. R., and Shimamura, A. P. (1986). Characterizing amnesic patients for neurobehavioral study. *Behavioral Neuroscience, 100*, 866–877.

Squire, L. R., Shimamura, A. P., and Amaral, D. G. (1989). Memory and the hippocampus. In *Neural Models of Plasticity*, edited by J. Byrne and W. Berry, 208–230. New York: Academic Press.

Squire, L. R., Shimamura, A. P., and Graf, P. (1987). Strength and duration of priming effects in normal subjects and amnesic patients. *Neuropsychologia, 25*, 195–210.

Squire, L. R., Slater, P. C., and Chace, P. M. (1975). Retrograde amnesia: Temporal gradient in very long-term memory following electroconvulsive therapy. *Science, 187*, 77–79.

Squire, L. R., and Spanis, C. W. (1984). Long gradient of retrograde amnesia in mice: Continuity with the findings in humans. *Behavorial Neuroscience, 98*, 345–348.

Squire, L. R., and Zola-Morgan, S. (1983). The neurology of memory: The case for correspondence between the findings for man and nonhuman primate. In *The Physiological Basis of Memory*, edited by J. A. Deutsch, 199–268. New York: Academic Press.

Squire, L. R., and Zola-Morgan, S. (1988). Memory: Brain systems and behavior. *Trends in Neurosciences, 11*, 170–175.

Squire, L. R., Zola-Morgan, S., and Chen, K. (1988). Human amnesia and animal models of amnesia: Performance of amnesic patients on tests designed for the monkey. *Behavioral Neuroscience, 102*, 210–221.

Teyler, T. J., and DiScenna, P. (1986). The hippocampal memory indexing theory. *Behavioral Neuroscience, 100*, 147–154.

Thompson, R. F. (1988). The neural basis of basic associative learning of discrete behavioral responses. *Trends in Neuroscience, 4*, 152–155.

Tulving, E. (1983). *Elements of Episodic Memory.* New York: Oxford University Press.

Tulving, E., and Schacter, D. L. (1990). Priming and human memory systems. *Science, 247*, 301–396.

Tulving, E., Schacter, D., and Stark, H. A. (1982). Priming effects in word-fragment completion are independent of recognition memory. *Journal of Experimental Psychology, Learning, Memory, and Cognition, 8*, 336–342.

Van Hoesen, G. (1982). The parahippocampal gyrus. *Trends in Neuroscience, 5*, 345–350.

Warrington, E. K., and McCarthy, R. A. (1988). The fractionation of retrograde amnesia. *Brain and Cognition, 7*, 184–200.

Weiskrantz, L. (1987). Neuroanatomy of memory and amnesia: A case for multiple memory systems. *Human Neurobiology, 6*, 93–105.

Weiskrantz, L., and Warrington, E. K. (1979). Conditioning in amnesic patients. *Neuropsychologia, 17*, 187–194.

Winocur, G. (1990). Anterograde and retrograde amnesia in rats with dorsal hippocampal or dorsomedial thalamic lesions. *Behavioral Brain Research, 38*, 145–154.

Zola-Morgan, S., and Squire, L. R. (1984). Preserved learning in monkeys with medial temporal lesions: Sparing of motor and cognitive skills. *Journal of Neuroscience, 4*, 1072–1085.

Zola-Morgan, S., and Squire, L. R. (1985). Medial temporal lesions in monkeys impair memory on a variety of tasks sensitive to human amnesia. *Behavioral Neuroscience, 99*, 22–34.

Zola-Morgan, S., and Squire, L. R. (1990). The primate hippocampal formation: Evidence for a time-limited role in memory storage. *Science, 250*, 288–290.

Zola-Morgan, S., and Squire, L. R. (1990). Neuropsychological investigations of memory and amnesia: Findings from humans and nonhuman primates. In *The Development and Neural Bases of Higher Cognitive Functions*, edited by A. Diamond. Cambridge: MIT/Bradford Press.

Zola-Morgan, S., Squire, L. R., Alvarez-Royo, P., and Clower, R. (1991). Independence of memory functions and emotional behavior: Separate contributions of the hippocampal formation and the amygdala. *Hippocampus, 1*, 207–220.

Zola-Morgan, S., Squire, L. R., and Amaral, D. G. (1986). Human amnesia and the medial temporal region: Enduring memory impairment following a bilateral lesion limited to field CA1 of the hippocampus. *Journal of Neuroscience, 6*, 2950–2967.

Zola-Morgan, S., Squire, L. R., and Amaral, D. G. (1989a). Lesions of the hippocampal formation but not lesions of the fornix or the mammillary nuclei produce long-lasting memory impairments in monkeys. *Journal of Neuroscience, 9*, 898–913.

Zola-Morgan, S., Squire, L. R., and Amaral, D. G. (1989b). Lesions of the amygdala that spare adjacent cortical regions do not impair memory or exacerbate the impairment following lesions of the hippocampal formation. *Journal of Neuroscience, 9*, 1922–1936.

Zola-Morgan, S., Squire, L. R., Clower, R. P., and Rempel, N. (1992). Damage to the perirhinal cortex exacerbates memory impairment following lesions to the hippocampal formation. *Journal of Neuroscience*. In press.

Zola-Morgan, S., Squire, L. R., Rempel, N. L., Clower, R. P., and Amaral, D. G. (1992). Enduring memory impairment in monkeys after ischemic damage to the hippocampus. *Journal of Neuroscience*. In press.

Zola-Morgan, S., Squire, L. R., Amaral, D. G., and Suzuki, W. A. (1989). Lesions of the perirhinal and parahippocampal cortex that spare the amygdala and hippocampal formation produce severe memory impairment. *Journal of Neuroscience, 9*, 4355–4380.

18 Dissociations between Component Mechanisms in Short-Term Memory: Evidence from Brain-Damaged Patients

David Howard and Sue Franklin

18.1 INTRODUCTION

People, when trying to hold some set of words temporarily in memory, will often say the words, either aloud or under their breath. When they are prevented from rehearsing (for instance by irrelevant vocalization), the short-term memories are more fragile and less easily retained (e.g., Murray 1968).

Rehearsal may, of course, have other uses. Repetition has often been thought necessary in building long-term memory traces; indeed, in the Waugh and Norman (1965) memory model rehearsal is supposedly the way in which material is transferred from short-term to long-term memory (see also Atkinson and Shiffrin 1968). Neuropsychological data in the early 1970s raised an obstacle to such accounts; in particular, Shallice and Warrington (1970) demonstrated that long-term memory could be normal in patients who, following brain damage, had severely restricted short-term memory. More recently, it has been suggested that phonological short-term (working) memory may be important for setting up long-term phonological representations: short-term memory patients may be severely impaired in learning new words (Baddeley, Papagno, and Vallar 1988).

In this chapter, we report on two aphasic patients, who appear to have specific deficits in the processes necessary for rehearsal of auditorily presented material. Our aim is to use their pattern of performance in a variety of tasks involving short-term memory and phonological processing to evaluate models of short-term memory. We will argue that their deficits can be most readily interpreted in terms of models of performance that distinguish between an input phonological buffer and an output phonological buffer, linked by the processes of rehearsal. First, we briefly review some accounts of the structure of the cognitive mechanisms involved in short-term memory tasks, and some of the arguments for distinguishing between different kinds of short-term storage. Then, we turn to our investigations of the patients' performance.

Short-term Memory and Concurrent Articulation

In laboratory experiments with normal subjects, the role of rehearsal has been examined in dual-task experiments, which investigate whether various secondary tasks interfere with short-term memory functions. Much interest has centerd on concurrent articulation of irrelevant material (Levy 1971; Murray 1968). In particular, Baddeley's (1986) model of working memory is based on evidence about the interactions between the effects of concurrent articulation, phonological similarity, word length, and irrelevant heard speech on immediate serial recall. The model supposes a single phonological buffer into which auditory information is encoded directly and automatically. Visually presented material must be recoded into phonological form to access the phonological buffer. Information in the buffer may be refreshed, to prevent its loss through decay, by a rehearsal process, which involves articulatory coding of the material. Both recoding from vision and rehearsal are assumed to depend on the same articulatory process; together this process and the phonological buffer comprise the "articulatory loop."

Recall of phonologically similar items, whether presented visually or auditorily, is worse than recall of phonologically unrelated items (Conrad and Hull 1964). This seems to indicate that the material is held in a phonologically coded buffer, with the result that rhyming items can be confused. Moreover, lists of long words are recalled less accurately than lists of short words with either auditory or visual presentation (Baddeley, Thomson, and Buchanan 1975). Baddeley attributes the word-length effect to the articulatory rehearsal system. Because long words take longer to say, fewer of them can be rehearsed within the time interval determined by the trace decay, and thereby maintained in short-term memory. With concurrent articulation, the phonological similarity effect disappears when the list is presented visually but is unaffected when presentation is auditory (Baddeley, Thomson, and Buchanan 1975; Besner and Davelaar 1982; Murray 1968). The interpretation of this is that visually presented items can only be recoded into phonological form via the articulatory rehearsal loop, whose operation is prevented by concurrent articulation; auditorily presented items can directly enter the phonological short-term store (PSTS), which receives input both from the rehearsal loop and the ears. The word-length effect is eliminated by concurrent articulation during both presentation and recall of visual and auditory lists (Baddeley, Lewis, and Vallar 1984); this occurs because concurrent articulation interferes with maintenance of information in the buffer via the articulatory loop.

The pattern of interaction between the effects of concurrent articulation, phonological similarity, and word length is therefore consistent with a system in which there is a PSTS, whose contents have a phonological form and are rehearsed by a process involving articulation. Without rehearsal the contents of the PSTS rapidly decay. Visually presented items can only access the PSTS via an articulatory rehearsal loop (Baddeley 1986).

Short-term Memory, Articulation, and Articulation Disorders

Baddeley's working memory model identifies rehearsal directly with the process of articulation. It is supported by certain properties of short-term memory span. For example, Baddeley (1986) has noted that memory span is inversely related to the time taken to articulate material—the mean span is the amount of material that can be said in around 1.5 seconds. In Welsh-English bilingual children, digit span is smaller for Welsh where the digit names have more syllables than for English (Ellis and Hennelley 1980). Even with material matched for the number of syllables and phonemes, memory span is less for words that take longer to say, because they have long vowels (e.g., harpoon, Friday) than for words with short vowels (e.g., bishop, wicket) (Baddeley, Thomson, and Buchanan 1975).

The close identification of rehearsal with the process of articulation led to a prediction that brain-damaged patients with disorders of articulation should act, in immediate serial list recall, as if rehearsal processes are disturbed. These patients should behave like normal subjects in whom rehearsal is prevented by concurrent articulation. However, when Baddeley and Wilson (1985) examined short-term memory performance in several anarthric patients using written recall, they found that contrary to expectation, performance was essentially normal; the phenomena that had been attributed to articulatory rehearsal (e.g., the word-length effect, and the phonological-similarity effect with visual presentation) were unaffected (see also Vallar and Cappa 1987).

One possible explanation for this unanticipated result is that more central aspects of articulation might be essential for rehearsal. Articulatory apraxia is classically described as a disorder of articulatory planning and organization in the absence of impairments to the organs of articulation or their innervation (e.g., Wertz, LaPointe, and Rosenbek 1984). Recently Waters, Rochon, and Caplan (1989) have investigated adults with acquired articulatory apraxia. They found that while all these patients had reduced short-term memory span, the pattern of impairments was not consistent across patients, nor was it the pattern that would be expected if rehearsal were always selectively impaired.

We will argue that the two patients reported in his chapter have a disorder of short-term memory that can be most readily understood as a loss in the ability to rehearse. They are not, however, impaired in speech production or articulation. No simple explanation of these patients is possible in a model that identifies rehearsal with articulation. We turn, now, to a discussion of models of short-term memory that distinguish between different levels of phonological storage, thus opening different interpretations of the process of rehearsal.

Evidence for Separate Input and Output Phonological Stores

Evidence for more than one kind of phonological code that can be accessed from visually presented material comes from the effects of concurrent articulation on different kinds of tasks (see Besner 1987). One set of tasks shows interference with phonological recoding by concurrent articulation. For instance, as we have seen, in immediate serial list recall, the phonological similarity effect disappears under concurrent articulation (Murray 1968). Furthermore, judgments of whether pairs of visually presented words rhyme are also significantly impeded by concurrent articulation (Besner, Davies, and Daniels 1981;

Brown 1987; Johnston and McDermott 1986; Wilding and White 1985). On the other hand, judging whether two visually presented words are homophones is unaffected by suppression (Baddeley and Lewis 1981; Brown 1987; Richardson 1987). There is clearly some level of phonological representation sufficient for comparing the phonology of two whole strings that can be accessed under concurrent articulation, which cannot be used to perform the additional process of segmentation involved in rhyme judgments.

Other lines of evidence point towards two different levels of phonological representation, where access to only one of these is interfered with by concurrent articulation. Besner and Davelaar (1982) showed that recall of visually presented nonwords was better for pseudohomophones than control nonwords, and was worse when the nonwords rhymed (i.e., a phonological-similarity effect). Concurrent articulation abolished the effects of phonological similarity but left the advantage for pseudohomophones intact. In addition, Klapp, Greim, and Marshburn (1981) demonstrated that assembly of an articulatory output program from visual presentation was unaffected by concurrent articulation.

An obvious interpretation of these findings is that there are two phonological stores, one an input buffer and the other an output store. The output buffer, which holds information in phonological form, can be accessed from visual presentation even under concurrent articulation. This can hold material and can be used for homophone judgments, and is used for preparation of an articulatory program, including assembly of the phonology for nonwords.

Monsell (1987) develops an account of auditory-verbal short-term memory processes that incorporates separate input and output phonological buffers, and relates these processes to those involved in language production and comprehension. The form of his model is shown in figure 18.1. The input buffer is a prelexical phonological store, and the output buffer is, like Morton's (1970) "response buffer," a postlexical phonological store that precedes the creation of an articulatory program. The process of rehearsal is achieved by the use of the "inner loop" that sublexically cycles information between these two buffers. The links between these buffers play other roles: the link from input to output is used in nonword repetition (and possibly in word repetition although this can also be done lexically). The link from output phonology to input phonology is needed for phonological lexical decision, as well as other "inner ear" functions such as transfer of material from visually presented lists into the input buffer, and for visual rhyme judgments.

Central to this chapter is the claim that the auditory-verbal short-term memory is not a separate system, but is rather an emergent property of systems used in the comprehension and production of spoken language (cf. Morton 1970; Monsell 1987). Under this interpretation, the links between the phonological input buffer and the phonological output buffer should be involved in other language tasks. The link from input to output must be involved in the repetition of materials that cannot access lexical representations—that is, nonwords. The link from an output buffer to an input buffer should be involved in tasks that require lexical access from output phonology; evidence

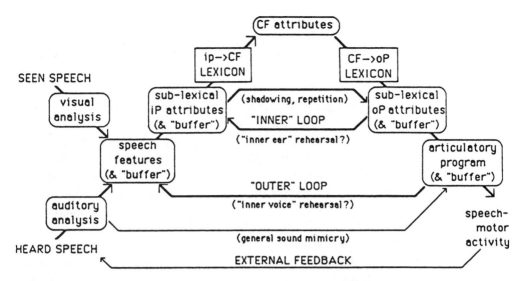

Figure 18.1 Monsell's (1987) model of auditory-verbal short-term memory and lexical processing. The Input lexicon performs word-specific mappings from input phonology representations (iP) to central conceptual/functional (CF) attributes. The output lexicon similarly maps from CF attributes to output phonology (oP). The input and output phonological buffers store sublexical phonological information. Rehearsal is via the "inner loop" cycling information between the input and output prelexical phonological buffers. The "outer loop" is primarily responsible for (mouthed and spoken) suffix effects in list recall.

from priming tasks indicates that phonological-lexical decisions (deciding whether pseudohomophones or control nonwords sound like real words) involve access to input phonology. Gipson (1986) showed that detecting a pseudohomophone primes subsequent auditory identification of the corresponding real word. The obvious interpretation of this result is that the (output) phonology of the pseudohomophone has to be silently generated from print and then transferred via the output-to-input link for lexical access. If this is so, we should predict that phonological lexical decision will be interfered with by concurrent articulation (which, it has already been suggested, interferes with the transfer of information between input and output phonology); evidence on this from normal subjects is not clear-cut, but there is interference at least with rapid concurrent articulation (Besner, Davies, and Daniels 1981).

In the light of the performance of our patients one further aspect of Monsell's model deserves mention. As can be seen in figure 18.1, the phonological input buffer can be accessed both from audition and from seen, lip-read speech. This implies that, at the level of the input buffer, information from both sources is equivalent. In general, information from a speaker's lips can improve the perception of speech in normal subjects when the signal is degraded (see Campbell 1990 for a review). Where stimuli are drawn from a restricted set, so that lipreading alone can support unambiguous word recognition (as with digit lists), recall is equal for lists presented auditorily and by lipreading (Campbell 1990). Anecdotal accounts of patients with difficulties in spoken word perception and comprehension suggest that some of these subjects may benefit from the opportunity to supplement the auditory signal with information from the speaker's lips (e.g., Miceli 1982). However, as far as we know, there are no experimental investigations of the effects of lipreading in short-term memory tasks with brain-damaged patients.

Neuropsychological evidence also supports a distinction between two phonological stores. On the basis of a double dissociation between patients with impaired short-term memory, Allport (1984) argued for separate input and output stores. One of Allport's patients, R.C., was unable to repeat more than two digits but was able to perform perfectly in a matching-span task with lists of four digits, where he had to judge whether the two lists had the digits in exactly the same order or had adjacent items transposed. Allport argued that an intact input buffer could be used for the matching-span task. Evidence for an impairment to R.C.'s output buffer came from both her poor performance in list repetition and her sparse, laborious, and agrammatic speech production. Allport contrasted this pattern with a second patient, J.D., whose speech was fluent and well formed, suggesting that he had access to an output buffer. His digit span was, however, only three items, and Allport argued that J.D.'s recall depended on the immediate transfer of the auditorily presented material to the output buffer. In support of this, he demonstrated that J.D.'s list repetition was facilitated by slow presentation (allowing more efficient transfer of information to the output code) and severely affected by concurrent articulation during list presentation (which prevents access to the output buffer).

This chapter attempts to account for the patterns of performance of two brain-damaged patients, M.K. and D.R.B., in a variety of tasks involving phonological processing and short-term memory in terms of a model, which like Monsell's (1987), distinguishes between a phonological input store, a separate output buffer, and the transcoding processes that link them in the process of rehearsal. In normal subjects, access to the input phonological buffer from the output buffer is prevented by concurrent articulation. The input phonological store holds ordered items. Phonological manipulations, including the segmentation required for rhyme judgments, can be done at this level. Phonologically similar items are confused at the level of input phonology, causing the phonological-similarity effect. The process of rehearsal consists of the cycling of information between the input and output stores; the operation of this rehearsal loop is interfered with by articulatory rehearsal.

The experimental section of this chapter is in two halves: first, we use a variety of tasks to establish whether the components of the short-term memory system are intact in these subjects. It will be argued that one subject, D.R.B., has a selective impairment of the phonological input store, while the second, M.K., has a specific loss of the processes that transcode between the input and output buffers. In the second part of the chapter, we use the model to develop predictions for their patterns of performance in rhyme judgments and the effect of variables on auditory-verbal short-term memory, which we put to empirical test.

18.2 THE PATIENTS

The two patients D.R.B. and M.K. became aphasic following left-hemisphere cerebrovascular accidents; a detailed case study for M.K. can be found in Howard and Franklin (1988) and for D.R.B. in Franklin, Howard, and Patterson (in press). For the purposes of this chapter, only their repetition performance is directly relevant. Here they share a disorder in repetition of single words that has the following characteristics as shown in table 18.1:

1. Repetition of nonwords is impossible; word repetition, while impaired, is very much better.

2. High-imageability words are repeated better than low-imageability words.

3. A substantial number of errors are semantically related to the targets.

These characteristics show that both patients can only transcode between input phonology and output phonology via a lexical routine, which frequently involves semantic mediation. The difficulty in repeating nonwords is not due to any difficulty in their perception. Both patients perform within the range of normal control subjects in judging whether pairs of spoken nonwords, half of which differ in a single phoneme, sound the same (table 18.1, section 3). Also, their difficulty in nonword repetition cannot be attributed to impairment in nonword assembly and production. Both patients read short nonwords aloud with reasonable accuracy (on single-syllable nonwords: M.K. 100%, D.R.B. 85%).

The two patients differ in the level of their impairment in understanding spoken words. M.K. performs poorly in auditory lexical decision; this appears to reflect an impairment to representations in an input lexicon (Howard and Franklin 1988). D.R.B., on the other hand, is extremely accurate in auditory lexical decision when unable to use lip-read information, even for words that he does not understand (Franklin, Howard, and Patterson, in press). His difficulty in word comprehension results from an impairment to the processes of

Table 18.1 Performance in Word and Nonword Repetition and Minimal-Pair Judgments for Patients M.K. and D.R.B.

Type of Task	Item Type	Number of Items	Proportion Correct	
			M.K.	D.R.B.
Word repetition	High-frequency words	40	0.40	0.43
	Low-frequency words	40	0.50	0.38
	High-imageability words	100	0.61	0.93
	Low-imageability words	100	0.29	0.49
Nonword repetition	Nonwords	20	0.00	0.00
Minimal-pair judgments	CV (e.g., /ka/ /ga/)	40	0.90	0.98
	CVC (e.g., /pub/ /pum/)	72	0.94	0.88

Note: On the CVC minimal-pair judgments, age-matched normal control subjects scored on average 0.95 correct (range 0.86–1.00).

Table 18.2 Accuracy of Homophone Judgments (proportion correct) for Patients M.K. and D.R.B. and Ten Normal Age-Matched Controls

Stimulus Type	Examples	Patients		Normal Controls	
		M.K.	D.R.B.	Mean	Range
Regular words	LAX LACKS	0.94	0.90	0.96	0.86–1.00
Irregular words	BEAR BARE	0.90	0.90	0.96	0.86–1.00
Nonwords	NAX NACKS	0.94	0.80	0.91	0.68–1.00

access to central semantic information after the lexicon has been appropriately activated.

In list repetition, both patients are profoundly impaired. M.K. cannot repeat a single digit reliably, and his span for high frequency concrete nouns is only one. D.R.B. has a repetition span of two digits and only one concrete noun. In the following section, we examine the status of different components of the short-term memory system, in order to identify the reasons for the severe limitation in span in both these patients.

Evidence for an Intact Output Phonological Buffer

We have argued that evidence from normal subjects with concurrent articulation indicates that representations in the output buffer are sufficient for visual homophone judgments.

With Coltheart's (1980) homophone judgment tasks (shown in table 18.2), both these patients performed accurately, and within the range of normal controls for regular words, irregular words, and nonwords. As these materials are designed so that correct performance must be achieved on the basis of homophony and not on the basis of visual-letter similarity, both patients clearly have access to phonology from written presentation that is sufficient for comparing whole phonological strings.

A similar conclusion can be drawn from the patients' speech production. Morton (1970) and Allport (1984) argue that the output buffer is needed for assembly of fluent, well-articulated speech. Both patients show fluent and well-articulated production despite some word-finding difficulty, and despite M.K. showing some paragrammatic difficulties in sentence construction.

A third role for an output buffer has been suggested by Caramazza, Miceli, and Villa (1986), and Bub et al. (1987), who argue that an output buffer is needed for assembling nonwords in reading. Again, consistent with the claim that these patients both have an intact output buffer, they are relatively good at reading simple nonwords (table 18.3), although they are totally unable to repeat them.

In all three of the preceding tasks (homophone judgments, speech production, and nonword reading), both M.K. and D.R.B. perform relatively well. If,

Table 18.3 Accuracy of Patients in Reading and Repeating Twenty Simple Nonwords (e.g., TROB VIKE)

	Proportion Correct	
Task	M.K.	D.R.B.
Reading	1.00	0.85
Repetition	0.00	0.00

as we have argued, these tasks require representations in a phonological output buffer, for both patients the buffer is intact (or nearly so). It is, of course, impossible for us to demonstrate that the patients have an entirely normal output buffer, because we know of no serious estimates of its capacity in isolation from other components of the language system. Nevertheless, we can demonstrate that, in tasks whose performance should involve the output buffer, the patients show normal or near-normal levels of performance.

Testing the Input Buffer

Some evidence from M.K. and D.R.B. might, at first, be taken to indicate their lack of a phonological input buffer. As already indicated, both patients have extremely limited memory spans. However, because both patients also have a profound impairment of single-word repetition, such results do not provide a reliable test for the presence of an input phonological buffer.

More reliable evidence for an input buffer comes from other types of task. Allport (1984) has argued that in patients with repetition disturbances, matching span is the appropriate task for assessing the status of an input buffer. Here a patient has to judge whether two consecutively presented spoken strings are the same or different. In half the trials the strings are the same, and in half they are different. Differences between the strings occur in each letter position an equal number of times.

Some results on this task for M.K. and D.R.B. appear in table 18.4. The results at the top relate to nonmatching lists generated by substitution of an item by another item (e.g., 3 1 4 8–3 1 6 8); lists of digits, words and nonwords with list length varied from three to five items were tested in this way. Presentation was blocked by list length and type of materials. In the bottom part of the table, nonmatching lists have adjacent items switched (e.g., 3 1 4 8–3 4 1 8); only digit lists were tested in this way.

The performance of the two patients dissociate in matching-span tasks. For the item-substitution lists, M.K. performed with reasonable accuracy on digits, words, and nonwords up to lists of length 4. On the other hand, D.R.B. was significantly worse than M.K. for lists of every length (McNemar's test, combining over materials: length 3, $p = .01$; length 4, $p = .0004$; length 5, $p = .029$). With these lists, D.R.B. only scored above chance because he consistently detected changes in the final item of a list, regardless of its length;

Table 18.4 Proportion Correct Judgments by Patients in Matching-Span Tasks
(i) Matching span where nonmatching lists have substituted items

Stimulus Type	List Length	Proportion Correct	
		M.K.	D.R.B.
Digits	3	0.93	0.77
	4	1.00	0.68
	5	0.80	0.74
Concrete nouns	3	0.97	0.90
	4	0.85	0.70
	5	0.78	0.60
Nonwords	3	0.93	0.80
	4	0.85	0.70
	5	—	0.58

(ii) Matching span where nonmatching lists have adjacent items transposed

Stimulus Type	List Length	Proportion Correct	
		M.K.	D.R.B.
Digits	3	—	0.65
	4	0.92	0.55

he had minimal knowledge about items at earlier positions in the lists. If a record of the first list has to be held in the phonological buffer in order to compare it with the second heard list, these findings suggest that, while M.K. has a relatively intact phonological input buffer, D.R.B.'s is severely impaired.

For digit lists where nonmatching strings are generated by switching adjacent items, information about the order of the items is necessary to perform correctly. Here M.K. performed with a high level of accuracy, while D.R.B. was scarcely above chance, even on pairs of three digit strings. Again, this is consistent with D.R.B. having a severe impairment to a phonological input store that codes item order, whereas M.K.'s buffer appears to be intact.

Converting Output Phonology to Input Phonology

Apart from the input and output phonological buffers, Monsell's model of the normal short-term memory system requires the ability to transfer material by sublexical conversion systems between these buffers. In this section, we use phonological judgment tasks to assess whether these patients are able to translate phonological information in an output buffer into the input buffer.

In the Introduction, it was argued that phonological lexical decisions require assembly of a phonological code in an output buffer, conversion of this to an input code, and then lexical access. We have seen already that both M.K. and D.R.B. can assemble an output code for written letter strings. However, D.R.B.

Table 18.5 Detection of Written Pseudohomophones: Performance of the Patients, M.K. and D.R.B., and of Age-Matched Normal Controls (n = 10 for forced-choice selection, and n = 5 for phonological lexical decision)

Type of Task	Number of Items	Outcome Measure	Patients		Normal Controls	
			M.K.	D.R.B.	Mean	Range
Forced-choice selection	39	Ppn correct	0.62	0.62	0.92	0.85–0.97
Phonological lexical decision	100	Ppn correct	0.63	0.57	0.88	0.78–0.94
		Mean correct RT (msecs)	5493	4143	1775	1268–2608

has an impaired input buffer, so he should therefore be impaired in performing the phonological lexical decision task. In contrast, M.K. has a (relatively) intact input buffer. Whether he can make phonological lexical decisions therefore depends on whether he can transcode from an output buffer to a phonological input buffer. The phonological lexical decision task therefore provides a further test of the adequacy of the short-term memory model in describing these patients' performance.

Both patients were given a forced-choice pseudohomophone detection test: for each of 39 pairs of nonwords (e.g., *stawn–stawk*, *floo–froo*), they had to select the ones that sounded like real words. They also performed a timed phonological lexical decision task, with 50 control nonwords and 50 pseudohomophones matched for mean positional bigram frequency and word proximity (i.e., N-ness—the number of real-word neighbors that can be created by substituting a single letter).

Table 18.5 shows the results. In forced-choice pseudohomophone selection, both M.K. and D.R.B. performed much worse than normal controls, and neither patient reached at a level significantly better than chance. In phonological lexical decision, D.R.B. performed no better than chance; M.K.'s accuracy score was just above chance (binomial test, $p < .05$), but was still massively impaired relative to the normal controls, both in terms of accuracy and response latency.

M.K.'s poor performance in detection of pseudohomophones suggests that he could not convert an output phonological code into an input phonological code. On the assumption that phonological lexical decision requires the assembly of a representation in the input buffer for lexical access, D.R.B.'s inability to detect pseudohomophones can be explained simply by an impairment to the input buffer.

An Interim Summary

The results considered thus far provide some support for a multicomponent STM model that distinguishes between input and output phonological buffers (cf. fig. 18.1). Both M.K. and D.R.B. have (relatively) intact phonological output buffers. M.K. performed well in matching-span tasks both for lists where mismatches were generated by item substitution and with lists where the mismatches were created by swapping adjacent items. His input buffer can hold four items (words, digits, or nonwords) with reasonable accuracy. However, in tasks that require sublexical transfer of phonological information from input to output (nonword repetition) and from output to input (phonological lexical decision), M.K. was very severely impaired.

Relative to M.K., D.R.B. was impaired in matching-span tasks, particularly for lists where knowledge of item order is necessary. This suggests that he has an impaired phonological input buffer, which is needed for coding order information. His poor performance in phonological lexical decision and nonword repetition may therefore be explained by an impairment to the phonological input buffer.

The next section of this chapter concerns the patients' ability to make rhyme judgments, and the effects of phonological similarity and word length on their STM performance. We test whether their patterns of performance are consistent with the predictions made by a model of auditory-verbal STM incorporating phonological input and output buffers, where the process of rehearsal involves cycling (sublexical) phonological information between the two.

Rhyme Judgments

As we discussed in the Introduction, in normal subjects, rhyme judgments on written words are disrupted by concurrent articulation. It has been argued that this occurs because these judgments require access to the input buffer for phonological segmentation, and the secondary task disrupts transfer of information to input phonology. However, with auditory presentation words can access the input buffer directly, and so concurrent articulation has no effect.

This proposal makes clear predictions that can be tested against the performance of the two patients. M.K. who has an intact input buffer, should be able to perform auditory rhyme judgments, but because of his impairment in transcoding from output phonology to input phonology, he should be impaired in rhyme judgments about written words. D.R.B. has an impairment in his phonological input buffer, and should therefore be impaired in rhyme judgments about words presented in both the auditory and visual modalities.

Table 18.6 shows results that test these predictions. Here the pattern of performance is as expected. M.K. achieved a normal level of accuracy with pairs of auditorily presented words, but was at chance with visually presented words. On the other hand, D.R.B. was equally impaired with auditory and visual presentation. These results, therefore, are consistent with the hypothesis that rhyme judgments are performed on the basis of representations held in the phonological input buffer, which is specialized for phonological segmentation. That rhyme judgments by normal subjects are impaired by concurrent articulation suggests that this secondary task may interfere with the transfer of information from output to input phonology.

Table 18.6 Accuracy of Patients and Age-Matched Normal Controls (n = 10) in Rhyme Judgments; Proportions Correct (fifteen judgments of each type)

| Stimulus Type | Proportion Correct Judgments | | | | | |
| | M.K. | | D.R.B. | | Normal Controls | |
	Auditory	Visual	Auditory	Visual	Auditory	Visual
Visually similar rhymes e.g., CREAM TEAM	1.00	0.53	0.80	1.00	1.00	0.95
Visually dissimilar rhymes e.g., COME SUM	0.87	0.53	0.87	1.00	0.99	0.94
Visually similar nonrhymes e.g., FOOT BOOT	1.00	0.33	0.40	0.33	0.97	0.94
Visually dissimilar nonrhymes e.g., SHOUT LOOT	1.00	0.80	0.80	0.73	1.00	0.98
Total	0.97	0.55	0.72	0.76	0.99	0.95
(Range)					(0.97–1.00)	(0.87–1.00)

The Effects of Phonological Similarity and Word Length on Short-term Memory: Patient M.K.

This model of short-term memory makes predictions about the pattern of effects of phonological similarity and word length for patient M.K. If the ability to rehearse depends on the ability to transcode between input and output phonological codes, M.K. should be unable to rehearse. His performance in single-item repetition (see table 18.1) indicates that he can only transcode from input to output lexically. His inability to detect pseudo-homophones shows that he cannot transcode from output to input phonology. On the other hand, both input and output phonological buffers appear to be (relatively) intact. For short-term memory span, M.K. should therefore show the same pattern of performance as a normal subject in whom rehearsal is disrupted by concurrent articulation; that is, there should be a phonological-similarity effect with auditory but not visual presentation, and no word-length effects with either presentation method.

To assess these predictions, M.K. was tested in a matching-span task. The phonological similarity effect was measured with lists of rhyming and non-rhyming letters. Half the lists matched; with each nonmatching list, one pair of adjacent letters was transposed. Each possible pair of items was transposed on an equal number of trials. The word-length effects were tested in exactly the same way with lists of one- and three-syllable concrete nouns.

The results appear in figure 18.2. They show the pattern we would expect. With auditory presentation, M.K. had a phonological-similarity effect, but there was no effect with lists presented visually. Also, there was no effect of word length with either presentation mode. Performance given visual presentation was somewhat better than with auditorily presented lists. In all four tasks accuracy declines with increasing list length.

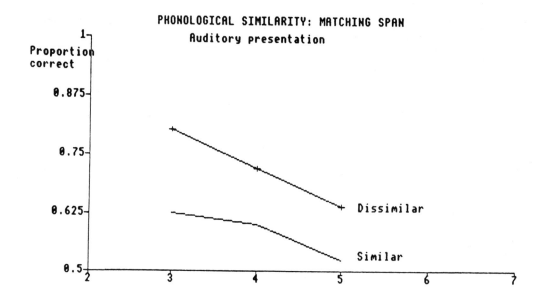

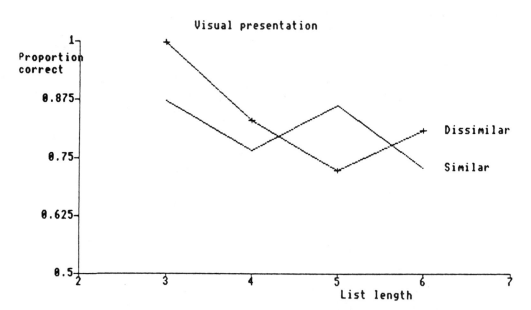

Figure 18.2 The effects of phonological similarity and word length on M.K.'s performance in a matching-span task. The left-hand panel shows the effects of phonological similarity with auditory and visual presentation. The right-hand panel shows the effects of word length (one syllable vs. three syllables) with auditory and visual presentation.

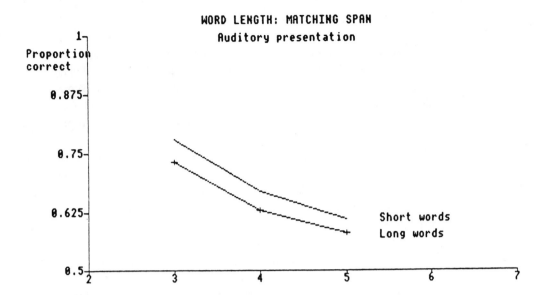

WORD LENGTH: MATCHING SPAN
Auditory presentation

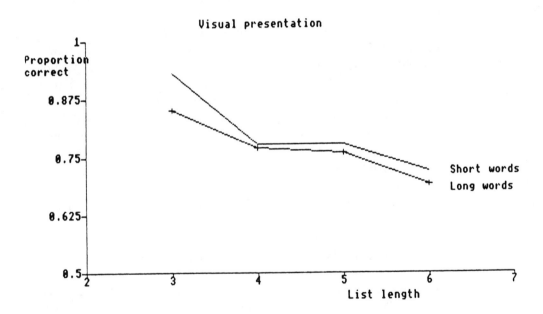

Visual presentation

Dissociations between Component Mechanisms

The Effects of Lipreading in Repetition: Patient D.R.B.

Descriptions of patients with difficulties in spoken-word recognition some-times mention that performance is improved by lipreading (e.g., Buchman et al. 1986). As we saw in the Introduction to this chapter, normal subjects are able to use lipreading to supplement auditory information, and in short-term memory tasks information from the speaker's lips has the same properties as heard speech (Campbell 1990).

In order to further examine the properties of these patients' short-term memory systems, we examined whether the availability of supplementary information from the speaker's lips had any effect on spoken-word repetition.

The results of a number of such experiments are shown in table 18.7. In single-word repetition, additional information from lipreading has no effect on M.K.'s performance. In contrast, D.R.B. improves in word repetition with lipreading. A number of further experiments investigate how, with patient D.R.B., the effects of lipreading interact with properties of the words to be repeated. The results show that information from the speaker's lips benefits both high and low imageability words, but improves performance only with shorter words. Without lipreading, D.R.B. can repeat no nonwords and can rarely hazard even an approximate guess; with lipreading, his responses con-tain 49 percent of the phonemes in the stimuli. The final section of table 18.7 shows for D.R.B.'s repetition of nonwords with lipreading how the probability that phonemes are present in the response depends on their serial position in the stimulus item. The results indicate that he is more likely to represent phonemes at the beginning of the nonword than at the end.

In the Introduction, we suggested that nonword repetition may depend on holding the item in a phonological input buffer. It appears that when lip-read information is available, D.R.B. has a more durable representation in the input buffer. That it benefits only repetition of short words, and the initial phonemes of nonwords, suggests that even with lipreading D.R.B. has an impaired phonological input buffer, which is either subject to rapid decay or is very limited in its capacity.

Further Evidence for a Limited Phonological Representation

The serial-position effect in nonword repetition is found in a task that involves both holding the phonological string and producing it in articulatory output. So, if the effect stems from impairment to an *input* buffer, the same position effects should occur in tasks that do not require spoken output. We tested this prediction by giving D.R.B. two tasks requiring segmentation of auditorily presented items:

Phonological Segmentation Test   (from Kay, Lesser, and Coltheart 1989) D.R.B. was presented with a spoken word, and had to indicate from a choice of four letters either the first sound or the last sound in the word. For the first

Table 18.7 The Effects of Lipreading on Patients' Spoken-Word Repetition

(i) Effects of lipreading on word repetition: patients M.K. and D.R.B.

Type of Input	Proportion Correct	
	M.K.	D.R.B.
Without lipreading	0.29	0.43
With lipreading	0.29	0.73

(ii) Lipreading and word imageability: patient D.R.B. (proportion correct; n = 100 in each cell)

Type of Input	Imageability	
	High	Low
Without lipreading	0.77	0.07
With lipreading	0.95	0.50

(iii) Lipreading and word length: patient D.R.B. (proportion correct; n = 60 in each cell)

Type of Input	Number of Syllables			Total
	One	Two	Three	
Without lipreading	0.70	0.67	0.70	0.69
With lipreading	0.93	0.83	0.73	0.83

(iv) Lipreading and nonword repetition: patient D.R.B. (proportion correct)

Type of Input	Nonwords n = 50	Phonemes n = 220
Without lipreading	0.00	0.08
With lipreading	0.04	0.49

(v) Proportion correct at different positions in nonword repetition with lipreading: patient D.R.B.

	Phoneme Position				
	1	2	3	4	5
Proportion of phonemes correct	0.73	0.46	0.47	0.55	0.24

sound, D.R.B. was correct on 38/45 items (.84). He is much worse in segmenting the final sounds (21/45 0.46 where chance is 0.25). The difference is significant (Fisher Exact Test, $z = 6.34$, $p < .001$). This result is consistent with an impairment to the phonological representation at input.

Binary Phonological Judgments A second experiment attempted to eliminate the possibility that D.R.B. used phonological information at an output level in the phonological segmentation task, by requiring phonological judgments only on items where he was unable to access output phonology. D.R.B. was given a sequence of monosyllabic words to repeat. When he could not repeat an item, he was given a choice of two letters and asked to indicate either the first or last sound in the word. The distractors differed from the target in a single feature of voice, manner, or place of articulation. When indicating initial phonemes, D.R.B. scored 23/31 (.74 correct); for final phonemes, his performance fell to chance (12/25; .48 where chance $= 0.5$). This difference is significant (Fisher Exact Test, $z = 1.72$; $p < .05$). These results confirm the view that D.R.B. has an impairment to the input buffer that leaves him with reliable information about sounds at the beginning of stimuli.

Lipreading and Short-term Memory

The lip-reading data suggest that when D.R.B. can lip-read he is able to maintain a limited representation in a phonological input buffer. Therefore, his performance in memory-span tasks should improve with lipreading. In addition, as storage in the input buffer is responsible for the phonological similarity effect, there should be a phonological similarity effect with lip-read lists.

To examine the effects of lipreading on short-term memory span, D.R.B. was presented with a list of sixty three-digit lists for immediate serial recall under three conditions. In the first condition, he heard the lists but was unable to lip-read; in the second condition, lip-read and auditory input were combined; in the third condition, digits were silently mouthed by the experimenter, so that only information from lipreading was available.

The results both for the proportion of lists repeated correctly in order, and the proportion of items repeated correctly, are shown in table 18.8. Both methods of scoring revealed the same pattern. D.R.B.'s recall was much worse

Table 18.8 Results from Digit List Repetition and Lipreading: Patient D.R.B. (3 digit lists)

Type of Input	Proportion Correct Recall	
	Lists (n = 60)	Items (n = 180)
Heard lists	0.05	0.53
Heard with lipreading	0.40	0.63
Lipreading alone	0.45	0.65

in the condition where lists were presented by audition alone, than in either of the other two conditions, in both of which lip-read information was available (for lists correct, chi squared (2) = 27.14, $p < .001$). Performance in the second condition, where information is available from both audition and lips, did not differ from list recall with lipreading alone, indicating that audition provided D.R.B. with no useful additional information over that available from lipreading. Even with lipreading, D.R.B.'s performance was very severely impaired relative to normal subjects, who have essentially equal spans for lip-read and heard digits (Campbell 1990). D.R.B.'s digit span, although it improves with lipreading, is still less than three.

The results of this experiment are consistent with the prediction that, with lipreading, D.R.B. can access a more durable representation to support list recall, although even then the representation is limited in capacity. The phonological similarity effect, which is found in recall of auditory lists by normal subjects, is attributed to interference between items in the input buffer. Thus, if D.R.B. is using a representation in an input buffer with lip-read information, then performance should be affected by phonological similarity between list items. This prediction was tested in a further experiment, by presenting lists of three letters for immediate serial spoken recall under two conditions. In the first condition, lists were presented auditorily without information from lips; in the second condition, D.R.B. was encouraged to attend to the speaker's lips. Half of the lists comprised rhyming letter names (e.g., CBD), and half letter names with no phonological similarity (e.g., JSH).

D.R.B.'s performance, scored both by the number of lists repeated correctly in the correct serial order and the proportion of items correctly recalled, is shown in table 18.9. As predicted there was a significant effect of phonological similarity on recall when D.R.B. was able to lip-read (on lists correct, Fisher Exact Test, $z = 2.32$, $p = .01$); without lipreading, his performance is at floor in terms of the number of lists correct, but the proportion of items correctly recalled shows no effect of phonological similarity. As in the previous experiment in digit list recall, D.R.B.'s overall performance is improved by lipreading but remains severely impaired relative to normal subjects.

Lipreading improved D.R.B.'s performance in list recall tasks, as well as in single-word repetition. The emergence of a phonological similarity effect only with lipreading suggests that, in this condition, D.R.B. is able to use a representation in an input buffer for immediate serial recall.

Table 18.9 The Effects of Phonological Similarity and Lipreading on the Spoken Recall of Auditorily Presented Lists of Three Letters: Patient D.R.B.

| Type of Input | Ppn. of Lists Correct | | Ppn. of Items Correct | |
	Similar (n = 50)	Dissimilar (n = 50)	Similar (n = 150)	Dissimilar (n = 150)
Without lipreading	0.00	0.00	0.17	0.20
With lipreading	0.02	0.18	0.27	0.47

The Effects of Phonological Similarity in Visual List Recall; Patient D.R.B.

Normal subjects show effects of phonological similarity on recall of visually presented lists. This shows that the items are recoded into phonological form. We have demonstrated that, at least when he was able to lip-read, D.R.B. was able to use some phonological storage in immediate recall of auditorily presented lists. Is there evidence that he recodes visually presented material into phonological form in recall?

Like patients with selective impairment to auditory-verbal STM, D.R.B. has better recall of visually presented than auditorily presented lists (cf. Vallar and Shallice 1990). Given visual presentation, D.R.B. has a digit span of 4.5 items, which is much better than his span of 2 with auditory presentation. Clearly, D.R.B. cannot be relying only on phonological storage for short-term retention of visually presented lists; some other form of storage, possibly visually based, must be playing a role. If the phonological buffer is playing no role in recall of visual lists, D.R.B. should show no phonological similarity effect with visual presentation. This was tested by requiring spoken recall of visually presented lists that varied from three to six letters in length. Half the lists at each length were made of letters with phonologically similar (rhyming) names; the other half as made up of letters with phonologically dissimilar names.

Table 18.10 shows the results of this experiment. When scored either by the total number of lists repeated in the correct order, or by the number of items correctly recalled, there was no effect of phonological similarity on D.R.B.'s spoken recall of visually presented lists. His level of performance was, however, very much better than with auditory list presentation.

The results of this experiment show that D.R.B. is not using phonological storage in the recall of visually presented lists. There are two possible reasons for this outcome: either he is unable to recode the visual material into the phonological input buffer, or he is able to access the buffer, but because it has very restricted capacity, it can play no useful role. The second explanation is the most plausible; a number of lines of evidence show that D.R.B.'s phonological input buffer has very restricted capacity.

Table 18.10 The Effect of Phonological Similarity on the Spoken Recall of Visually Presented Lists: Patient D.R.B. (ten lists of each type at each length)

List Length	Ppn. of Lists Correct		Ppn. of Items Correct	
	Similar	Dissimilar	Similar	Dissimilar
3	1.0	1.0	1.0	1.0
4	0.6	0.7	0.78	0.83
5	0.2	0.4	0.68	0.68
6	0.1	0.0	0.57	0.47
Total	0.38	0.43	0.72	0.69

18.3   DISCUSSION

Most neuropsychological studies of short-term memory have concentrated on subjects who show impairment in tasks that involve auditory-verbal STM, while performance in other language domains is relatively intact. This chapter takes a rather different approach. We have focused on two patients who have severe impairments in word repetition, and we have examined how their performance in tasks that involve STM are related to their impairments in language tasks.

Our data support models having two phonological stores, one located at input and the other at output (e.g., Monsell 1987). Consistent with such models, M.K. has relatively good access to a phonological input store, which can hold around four items in matching-span tasks. Patient D.R.B. performed much less accurately in matching-span tasks; he could only reliably indicate changes involving the final item in a list. In tasks that tap output phonological representations, however, both patients performed well. This seems inconsistent with any theory, such as Baddeley's 1986 "working memory" model, that postulates only a single level of phonological storage.

More precisely, M.K.'s performance suggests specific impairments in both the nonlexical conversion of input phonology to output phonology and the conversion of output to input phonology. The input-to-output impairment explains his difficulties in nonword repetition. The output-to-input impairment explains his difficulty both in phonological lexical decision and in rhyme judgments about written words. Overall, this qualitative pattern of performance is almost identical to that found with normal subjects under conditions of concurrent articulation (cf. Baddeley 1986). Yet M.K.'s output processes and articulation are essentially unimpaired. So, while rehearsal in normal subjects may involve articulation, the essential aspects of rehearsal can be impaired through a central disruption in transcoding between input and output phonology.

Unlike M.K., D.R.B. has a much more severely impaired phonological input buffer. As a result, D.R.B.'s memory span is very poor both when tested in matching-span tasks and with list repetition. However, when he is able to lip-read, he can attain a somewhat more durable representation in the input buffer, but one that is still severely impaired. Consequently, D.R.B. performs poorly in all tasks that require segmentation of phonological strings, both when input is spoken (auditory rhyme judgments and auditory segmentation tasks) and when it is written (visual rhyme judgments). Also, in tasks involving list retention, D.R.B. is severely impaired when knowledge of item order is required. However, his ability to compare whole unsegmented phonological strings in homophone judgments on visually presented stimuli is, by contrast, unimpaired.

These results support Monsell's 1984 suggestion that a phonological input buffer is specialized for coding of item order information. The pattern of performance across M.K. and D.R.B. in rhyme judgments, and the characteristics of D.R.B.'s segmentation ability, suggest that the phonological input buffer is also specialized for segmentation of phonological strings. Yet, in both patients the output buffer is relatively well preserved. It can still be used to assemble nonword strings for spoken output (hence the patients' relatively good nonword reading), for comparing whole phonological strings (hence their relatively good performance in written homophone judgments), and for fluent speech production.

Perhaps the most surprising result from patient D.R.B. is the way in which his performance is improved by lipreading both in word (and nonword) repetition and in spoken list recall. In normal subjects information from the lips has no effect on word recognition or short-term memory, when the heard stimuli are not auditorily degraded (Campbell 1990). This might suggest that D.R.B. has a peripheral difficulty in auditory perception, resulting in degraded input to both word recognition systems and the phonological input buffer. However, there is good evidence that both word-sound perception and word recognition from audition alone are unimpaired; D.R.B. performs normally in minimal pair judgments on spoken strings, and achieves very high levels of accuracy in auditory lexical decision, even for abstract words that he cannot understand (Franklin, Howard, and Patterson, in press). This pattern of performance is not readily explicable in terms of models, such as Monsell's (1987), where the word-recognition system receives its input from the phonological input buffer (see fig. 18.1). The results seem to imply independent access of auditory information to the phonological buffer and the lexicon. D.R.B.'s lexical system receives auditory input sufficient to support accurate lexical decision; his phonological input buffer is only able to store more than rudimentary information when information from visual information from the speaker's lips is available.

There is some additional support for the distinction between input and output phonological buffers from case reports of brain-damaged patients in whom the phonological output buffer is selectively impaired. For instance, Bub et al. (1987) described a patient (M.V.) who was equally impaired in nonword repetition (0.53) and nonword reading (0.48). Her output was nonfluent and halting, and with any nonredundant word sequences she produced no more than one word every two seconds. So, if rehearsal depends on cycling information between the input buffer and the output buffer, M.V. should behave in list recall as if she were unable to rehearse. That is, she should show a phonological-similarity effect given auditory but not visual presentation, and she should show no word-length effect. And this is the pattern of performance that Bub et al. (1987) reported.

In conclusion, the claim of this chapter is that there are different components of the short-term memory system, and they are not devoted exclusively to short-term memory but also play roles in a variety of language tasks. We have discussed a role for the "inner ear" (the system that transcodes from output phonology to input phonology) in rhyme judgments, phonological lexical decision, recall of visually presented lists, and rehearsal. The inner ear may play a role in other tasks as well; for instance, Levelt (1983, 1989) has argued that this system is used for monitoring speech output. We have yet to test whether the errors that our patients make in speech production conform to Levelt's account. Nevertheless, while a great deal of detail in the operation of the components of our model remain to be specified, the convergence between the results of this study and experimental investigations of short-term memory performance in normal subjects gives us some confidence that we can analyze the functional architecture of the systems used in auditory-verbal short-term memory.

REFERENCES

Allport, D. A. (1984). Auditory-verbal short-term memory and aphasia. In H. Bouma and D. G. Bouwhuis (Eds.), *Attention and performance X: Control of language processes*, 313–326. London: Lawrence Erlbaum.

Atkinson, R. C., and Shiffrin, R. M. (1968). Human memory: A proposed system and its control processes. In K. W. Spence and J. T. Spence (Eds.), *The psychology of learning and motivation: Advances in research and theory* vol. 2, 89–195. New York: Academic Press.

Baddeley, A. D. (1986). *Working memory*. Oxford: Oxford University Press.

Baddeley, A. D., and Lewis, V. J. (1981). Inner active processes in reading: The inner voice the inner ear and the inner eye. In A. M. Lesgold and C. M. Perfetti (Eds.), *Interactive processes in reading*, 107–129. Hillsdale, NJ: Lawrence Erlbaum.

Baddeley, A. D., Lewis, V. J., and Vallar, G. (1984). Exploring the articulatory loop. *Quarterly Journal of Experimental Psychology, 36*, 233–252.

Baddeley, A. D., Papagno, C., and Vallar, G. (1988). When long-term learning depends on short-term storage. *Journal of Memory and Language, 27*, 586–595.

Baddeley, A. D., Thomson, N., and Buchanan, M. (1975). Word length and the structure of short-term memory. *Journal of Verbal Learning and Verbal Behaviour, 14*, 575–589.

Baddeley, A. D., and Wilson, B. (1985). Phonological coding and short-term memory in patients without speech. *Journal of Memory and Language, 24*, 490–502.

Besner, D. (1987). Phonology, lexical access in reading, and articulatory suppression: A critical review. *Quarterly Journal of Experimental Psychology, 39A*, 467–478.

Besner, D., and Davelaar, E. (1982). Basic processes in reading: Two phonological codes. *Canadian Journal of Psychology, 36*, 701–711.

Besner, D., Davies, J., and Daniels, S. (1981). Reading for meaning: The effects of concurrent articulation. *Quarterly Journal of Experimental Psychology, 33A*, 415–437.

Brown, G. D. A. (1987). Phonological coding in rhyme and homophony judgement. *Acta Psychologica, 65*, 247–262.

Bub, D., Black, S., Howell, J., and Kertesz, A. (1987). Speech output processes and reading. In M. Coltheart, G. Sartori, and R. Job (Eds.), *The cognitive neuropsychology of language*, 79–110. London: Lawrence Erlbaum.

Buchman, A., Garron, D., Trost-Cardamone, J., Wichter, M., and Schwartz, M. (1986). Word deafness: One hundred years later. *Journal of Neurology, Neurosurgery and Psychiatry, 49*, 489–499.

Campbell, R. (1990). Lipreading, neuropsychology and immediate memory. In G. Vallar and T. Shallice (Eds.), *Neuropsychological impairments of short-term memory*, 268–286. Cambridge, UK: Cambridge University Press.

Caramazza, A., Miceli, G., and Villa, G. (1986). The role of the (output) phonological buffer in reading, writing and repetition. *Cognitive Neuropsychology, 3*, 37–76.

Coltheart, M. (1980). Analysing acquired disorders of reading. Unpublished manuscript, Birkbeck College, London.

Conrad, R., and Hull, A. J. (1964). Information, acoustic confusion and memory span. *British Journal of Psychology, 55*, 429–432.

Ellis, N. C., and Hennelley, R. A. (1980). A bilingual word length effect: Implications for intelligence testing and the relative ease of mental calculation in Welsh and English. *British Journal of Psychology, 71*, 43–52.

Franklin, S., Howard, D., and Patterson, K. E. (N.d.). Abstract word meaning deafness. *Cognitive Neuropsychology*. In press.

Gipson, P. (1986). The production of phonology and auditory priming. *British Journal of Psychology, 77*, 359–375.

Howard, D., and Franklin, S. (1988). *Missing the meaning? A cognitive neuropsychological analysis of single word processing in an aphasic patient.* Cambridge, MA: MIT Press.

Johnston, R. S., and McDermott, E. A. (1986). Suppression effects in rhyme judgement tasks. *Quarterly Journal of Experimental Psychology, 38A*, 111–124.

Kay, J., Lesser, R., and Coltheart, M. (1989). Psycholinguistic assessments of language processes in aphasia. Unpublished manuscript, University of Exeter, Exeter, UK.

Klapp, S. T., Greim, D. M., and Marshburn, E. A. (1981). Buffer storage of programmed articulation and articulatory loop: Two names for the same mechanism or two distinct components of short-term memory? In J. Long and A. D. Baddeley (Eds.), *Attention and performance IX*, 459–472. Hillsdale, NJ: Lawrence Erlbaum.

Levelt, W. J. M. (1988). Monitoring and self-repair in speech. *Cognition, 14*, 41–104.

Levelt, W. J. M. (1989). *Speaking: From intention to articulation.* Cambridge, MA: MIT Press.

Levy, B. A. (1971). The role of articulation in auditory and visual short-term memory. *Journal of Verbal Learning and Verbal Behaviour, 10*, 123–132.

Miceli, G. (1982). The processing of speech sounds in a patient with cortical auditory disorder. *Neuropsychologia, 20*, 5–20.

Monsell, S. (1981). Components of the working memory system underlying verbal skills: A 'distributed capacities' view. In H. Bouma and D. G. Bouwhuis (Eds.), *Attention and performance X: Control of language processes*, 327–350. London: Lawrence Erlbaum.

Monsell, S. (1987). On the relation between lexical input and output pathways for speech. In D. A. Allport, D. MacKay, W. Prinz, and E. Scheerer (Eds.), *Language perception and production: Common processes in listening, speaking, reading and writing*, 273–312. London: Academic Press.

Morton, J. (1970). A functional model of memory. In D. A. Norman (Ed.), *Models of human memory*, 203–254. New York: Academic Press.

Murray, D. J. (1968). Articulation and acoustic confusability in short-term memory. *Journal of Experimental Psychology, 78*, 679–684.

Richardson, J. T. E. (1987). Phonology and reading: The effects of articulatory suppression upon homophony and rhyme judgements. *Language and Cognitive Processes, 2*, 229–244.

Shallice, T., and Warrington, E. K. (1970). Independent functioning of the verbal memory stores: A neuropsychological study. *Quarterly Journal of Experimental Psychology, 22*, 261–273.

Vallar, G., and Cappa, S. F. (1987). Articulation and verbal short term memory: Evidence from anarthria. *Cognitive Neuropsychology, 4*, 55–77.

Vallar, G., and Shallice, T. (Eds.). (1990). *Neuropsychological impairments of short-term memory*. Cambridge, UK: Cambridge University Press.

Waters, G. A., Rochon, E., and Caplan, D. (1989). Short term memory: The effects of articulatory apraxia. Paper delivered at the International Conference on Cognitive Neuropsychology, Harrogate, UK.

Waugh, N. C., and Norman, D. A. (1965). Primary memory. *Psychological Review, 72,* 89–104.

Wertz, R. T., LaPointe, L. L., and Rosenbek, J. C. (1984). *Apraxia of speech in adults: The disorder and its management*. Orlando. FL: Grune and Stratton.

Wilding, J., and White, W. (1985). Impairments of rhyme judgement by silent and overt articulatory suppression. *Quarterly Journal of Experimental Psychology, 37A,* 95–107.

19 The Organization of Object Knowledge: Evidence from Neuropsychology

Giuseppe Sartori, Remo Job, and Max Coltheart

19.1 INTRODUCTION

We are concerned in this chapter with the nature of object knowledge and with how such knowledge is represented mentally. Four facts about object knowledge that provide a useful starting point are the following:

The knowledge we possess about objects is of various kinds. There is abstract functional information ("Is this object used for writing?"). There is perceptual information ("Does this object make a noise? Is it round? Does it have a smell?"). There is information about the object's relations to other concepts ("Would you spread this on bread?").

The knowledge we possess about objects is accessible from various input modalities. Suppose X is an object that we know to be edible. We can answer the question "Is X edible?" when we see a picture of the object X, or when we see or read the object's name, or when we identify it by sound or touch or smell.

The objects about which we possess knowledge are of various categories. Consider animate objects and inanimate objects, for example.

The knowledge we possess about objects is needed for various object-oriented tasks. Visual-object recognition must depend upon access to some kind of knowledge of the structural description of the object; so must the task of drawing the object, spontaneously or to dictation; so must the task of answering questions about what the object looks like.

These basic facts about the nature of object knowledge lead to a variety of questions that can be raised concerning the organization of the mental representation of object knowledge. The simplest model would be this: we have a single system of object knowledge, with an entry for each object, animate or inanimate, that we know about. In this system, the entry for object X contains all the different types of knowledge we possess about X, is accessible from all the relevant sensory modalities, and is used for performing various object-oriented tasks like those described above.

The results of many neuropsychological investigations of the breakdown of object knowledge after brain damage show that this model cannot be correct. These investigations have revealed many different ways in which the disruption of object knowledge can be *selective*. In some patients, one type of object knowledge is impaired far more than other types. In other patients, access to object knowledge is impaired far more from one sensory modality than from others even when that sensory modality is itself unimpaired. In still other patients, object knowledge can be used normally for some object-oriented tasks while other such tasks are performed very poorly. To give just one example: McCarthy and Warrington (1988) presented their patient with two classes of object's (animate objects and inanimate objects) using two input modalities (spoken names or pictures) and asked the patient to say what he knew about each object. The patient performed well with both types of objects when the objects were presented as pictures; he performed well in response to the spoken names of inanimate objects; but when responding to the spoken names of animals, his responses were extremely impoverished. For example, in response to a picture of a dolphin, he said, "Dolphin lives in water ... they are trained to jump up and come out.... In America during the war they started to get this particular animal to go through to look into ships"; but in response to the spoken word *dolphin* all he could say was "A fish or a bird." Hence his performance varied as a function both of modality of input and of type of object.

Studies of such selective impairments of object knowledge have led cognitive neuropsychologists to explore various theoretical issues concerning how such knowledge is represented, including the following four questions:

1. *Are there separate systems of object knowledge for the different types of such knowledge?* Both Basso, Capitani, and Laiacona (1988) and Silveri and Gainotti (1988) have described patients who were much worse at accessing knowledge of visual attributes of objects than at accessing nonperceptual knowledge concerning the same objects; Silveri and Gainotti have therefore proposed a model of semantic memory in which there are separate semantic subsystems for visual knowledge and for nonperceptual knowledge.

2. *Do the different input modalities have their own dedicated separate systems of object knowledge?* Warrington and co-workers have adopted the view that there is one semantic system ("visual semantics") accessible from pictures and seen objects, and a separate semantic system ("verbal semantics") accessible from (written or spoken) words. For example, Warrington (1975) compared two patients who showed impairments on tasks requiring access to semantic memory. One patient was worse when the stimuli were pictures than when they were spoken words, and the other patient showed the reverse effect, which, Warrington noted, "raises the possibility of structurally and presumably functionally partially distinct modality-specific meaning systems. That is, a particular concept, say 'canary', would be represented in two semantic memory systems, the one primarily visual and the other primarily verbal" (Warrington 1975, 656). More recently, Warrington and McCarthy (1987, 1287) refer to the view put forward by Warrington and Shallice (1984) as postulating "complete autonomy" of the verbal and visual semantic systems. In contrast, Silveri and Gainotti (1988) and Riddoch et al. (1988) have taken the view that the comprehension of pictures, seen objects, printed words, and spoken words

depends upon access to a single semantic system that is indifferent to modality of stimulus input.

3. *Are there separate systems of object knowledge for different categories of objects?* The important object categories here are animate and inanimate objects. Numerous studies of semantic memory impairment (Warrington and Shallice 1984; Hillis and Caramazza 1990; Hanley, Young, and Pearson 1989; Pietrini et al. 1988; Basso, Capitani, and Laiacona 1988; Silveri and Gainotti 1988; Farah et al. 1988; Farah, McMullen, and Meyer 1991) have documented patients whose comprehension performance is worse with animate than with inanimate objects, and the opposite result has been reported by Warrington and McCarthy (1983), Warrington and McCarthy (1987), and Hillis and Caramazza (1990).

4. *Do different object-oriented tasks (e.g., recognizing an object vs. answering questions about its appearance vs. drawing it from memory) depend upon different systems of object knowledge?* Both Riddoch et al. (1988) and van Sommers (1989) have proposed models in which such tasks call upon a single system of knowledge about visual attributes of objects.

Since the answers to these four questions are independent of each other, and since each question has a number of different possible answers, the number of different possible models of the organization of object knowledge is rather large. No one has yet attempted to build a model from the neuropsychological data that addresses all four of the questions set out above, and we will not be attempting this either. However, in the neuropsychological investigations of impairment of object knowledge that we describe here, data have been collected that are germane to each of these four questions; our hope is that this will assist the eventual development of a comprehensive model of the organization of object knowledge.

Deficits of Representation versus Deficits of Access

A neurological patient who can no longer answer a question such as "Are parrots colored?" may have lost the representation of this fact; or, instead, the representation may have survived while the procedures by which it is accessed are no longer reliable. Shallice (1987) has explored possible ways of distinguishing between these two different forms of deficit. He suggests that, if some but not all representations have been lost from the relevant system, the patient should both be *consistent* (that is, he should fail with the same items and pass with the same items across different testing occasions in which the same items are presented) and *frequency sensitive* (it is plausible that if a system of representations is damaged, the more frequently used a representation is the more resistant to damage it is). If the patient's difficulty is, instead, due to unreliability of the procedures by which the system of representations is accessed, with the representations in the system still intact, one might expect inconsistency across repeated testing and an absence of frequency effects. These inferences depend to a considerable extent upon particular theoretical conceptions about the nature of semantic representations and about the procedures by which they are accessed. Nevertheless, the basic idea is proving a useful analytic tool in cognitive neuropsychology. Certainly, the phenomenon of item-specific consistency is shown by some patients to an impressive degree. For example, the patient studied by Pietrini et al. (1988), who was selectively impaired at naming animals, scored 18/39 correct when tested in 1985; when retested by us with the same items in 1989, he scored 19/39 correct. Every item that was correct in 1985 was again correct in 1989, and only one of the 21 items that was wrong in 1985 was correct in 1989.

The study of item-specific consistency is of particular importance for a number of the theoretical issues we have raised. Suppose, for example, one observed a patient with a selective deficit of object recognition for animate objects in comparison to inanimate objects. One might then make the following argument: if the system we use for recognizing objects is the same as the system we use for drawing them from memory, this patient should also be worse at drawing animate object from memory than at drawing inanimate objects. If this result is not observed, one might then conclude that object recognition and drawing depend upon different systems.

But when one distinguishes representation deficits from access deficits, one lays bare the fallacy in this reasoning. Suppose a patient's problem with object recognition were due to a defect in the procedures by which visual input accesses "visual semantics," with this visual semantic system still intact. Such a patient could exhibit defective object recognition with intact drawing, even if these two tasks do in fact use a common system of representations.

What one must do here is to show first that the object-recognition problem is a representation problem—for example, by demonstrating that there is a high degree of consistency across testing sessions, in which objects the patient recognizes successfully and which he fails to recognize. Such consistency implies that, when an object cannot be recognized, it is because the object's representation has been lost from the representation system. If this can be shown, then it *is* required that the patient will also be impaired at drawing objects from memory, if recognition and drawing use a common system of representations (and, indeed, that there should be close correspondence between the set of objects that the patient fails to recognize and the set of objects that he fails to draw). In other words, as long as there is within-task consistency, one can then study between-task consistency to obtain data that could adjudicate between different theories about how object knowledge is represented.

19.2 SUBJECTS

The patients whose data we report here we refer to as Michelangelo and Dante. General neuropsychological details concerning them are provided in the Appendix. Both had inferotemporal lesions. Both were profoundly amnesic. Both showed an impairment in picture naming that was worse for animate than for inanimate objects (though we demonstrate below that this selective deficit arose for quite different reasons in the two patients). Clinical testing of language comprehension and language production revealed no obvious deficits of either ability in either patient (apart, of course, from the difficulties with animal names).

19.3   NAMING TASKS

Picture Naming

Sixty-four pictures, 32 of living things and 32 of inanimate objects, were selected from a larger pool on the basis of ratings of picture familiarity, picture complexity, and name frequency. These ratings had been collected using a group of 20 normal subjects as raters. The two sets of 32 pictures were matched on the potentially confounding variables of familiarity, complexity, and frequency. This matching is essential since Stewart, Parkin, and Hunkin (1992) have reported a case where differences in accuracy of naming living and nonliving things vanished when visual complexity was controlled. These 64 pictures were then administered to 47 normal subjects for naming. Their score for the living pictures was 27/32 (sd .89), and for the nonliving pictures 27.6/32 (sd 1.35).

Two different control groups of normal subjects (ten subjects per group) were then selected, one group for each patient and matched to the patient by age. *Throughout this chapter, the performance of each patient on any task is assessed by calculating the Z-score of the patient in relation to the performance of his individual control group on that task.* The patients and their control groups were given the 64 pictures to name, and the results are shown in table 19.1. It is clear that both patients were far more successful at naming nonliving things than living things (although Dante is also somewhat impaired at the latter task).

Of Michelangelo's 18 naming errors, 16 were visual and semantic (that is, the response was an item that was similar in appearance *and* in meaning to the stimulus picture, such as naming a lemon "orange" or a squirrel "rabbit"), 1 was a visual error, and 1 was an omission. Of Dante's 23 errors, 16 were superordinate responses (such as naming a seahorse "animal"—Michelangelo never produced errors of this kind), 3 were visual and semantic, 3 were visual, and 1 was semantic.

Table 19.1 Percent Correct Picture Naming by the Two Patients, and z-Score Comparisons with Each Patient's Control Group

Type of Object	Michelangelo	Dante
Animate	46.9% ($z = -14.7$)	46.9% ($z = -33.9$)
Inanimate	93.8% ($z = -0.27$)	81.2% ($z = -5.4$)

Table 19.2 Effect of Phonemic Cueing on Picture Naming by the Two Patients (precue percent correct before arrow, postcue after arrow)

Type of Object	Michelangelo	Dante
Animate	46.9% → 53.1%	46.9% → 93.8%
Inanimate	93.8% → 93.8%	81.2% → 93.8%

Effects of Phonemic Cueing in Naming Accuracy

After any failure to name, each patient was given a phonemic cue (the initial phoneme of the correct name), and he then attempted to produce the correct name with the help of this cue. The results are reported in table 19.2.

It is obvious that phonemic cueing assisted Dante's naming greatly, while giving Michelangelo no help. This outcome may be interpreted by proposing that sensitivity to phonemic cueing distinguishes between a naming deficit that arises within the phonological output lexicon (impaired access to a representation in this lexicon being aided by the partial phonological information provided by a phonemic cue) and a naming deficit that is caused by an impairment within the semantic system (a difficulty there would not be aided by providing nonsemantic cueing). Note that this suggestion depends upon the idea that the normal naming system does *not* include a processing route direct from the recognition of a picture to the phonological output lexicon; to get from the recognition system to the naming system, it is obligatory to traverse the semantic system. If there were such a nonsemantic naming route, one could observe patients who could name pictures that they could not understand; no convincing evidence of such a phenomenon has yet been reported. We conclude that, although Michelangelo and Dante not only have a naming difficulty but also specifically a selective difficulty in naming living things, they nevertheless have different deficits. Michelangelo's naming impairment is due to a semantic deficit. Dante's naming impairment is due to difficulties of retrieval within the phonological output lexicon.[1]

Item-specific Consistency of Naming Performance

The two patients were given the same 64 pictures to name again, 10 days after the original naming test. Michelangelo was highly consistent, achieving the same correctness on the two occasions (that is, being right both times, or wrong both times) to 90 percent of the living things and 84 percent of the nonliving things. In contrast, Dante was highly inconsistent, the corresponding figures for him being 33 percent and 41 percent. We conclude not only that the two patients have problems at different stages of the naming process, but also, following the logic of Shallice (1987) discussed earlier, that they have different types of problems at these stages. Michelangelo's semantic deficit is one in which some semantic representations (particularly those for living things) have been deleted from the semantic system. Dante's phonological

Table 19.3 Part-Whole Matching: Number Correct by the Two Patients, plus Mean and Standard Deviation of Performance by Each Patient's Control Group, and Patient's z-Score Relative to Control

Type of Object	Michelangelo	Dante
Animate	5/16 (31.3%)	13/16 (81.3%)
$N = 16$; chance $= 4/16$	14.7; 1.2	15.2; 0.7
	$z = -8.16$	$z = -3.14$
Inanimate	41/50 (82.0%)	47/50 (94.0%)
$N = 50$; chance $= 25/50$	44; 1.5	49; 0.9
	$z = -2.00$	$z = -1.39$

deficit arises because the procedures for accessing representations within the phonological output lexicon are no longer working reliably, even if the representations themselves are still intact.

19.4 VISUAL-KNOWLEDGE TASKS

Tasks with Visual Input

Part-Whole Matching   We developed a test involving 50 inanimate objects and 16 animals. Each of the 66 trials in this test consisted of a card showing a drawing of a target with a part missing plus drawings of two or four alternatives, the task being to choose which of the alternatives was the part missing from the target. For the animals, the target might, for example, be a headless body with four alternative heads, one correct; or a beak, with four different beakless bodies as alternatives. For the nonliving objects, the procedure was similar except only two alternatives were used. Both patients, and their two control groups, were given this test with the results shown in table 19.3.

Here for Dante there is no selective difficulty with living objects. His performance is very good for both categories, if not quite normal. Michelangelo, on the other hand, continues to show much worse performance on living than on nonliving objects—indeed, he was at chance on the former, while well above chance on the latter.

Object-Decision   This is the pictorial equivalent of the lexical decision task. Subjects are shown pictures of real objects and of plausible but nonexistent objects, and asked to classify the stimuli as real or not (Kroll and Potter 1984; Riddoch and Humphreys 1987). Our version of the task used 24 pictures of real things (16 animals, 8 inanimate objects) and 24 pictures of unreal things. Of the latter, 16 were constructed by conjoining appropriate parts from two different animals to produce a plausible but nonexistent nonanimal, and the remaining 8 were analogously constructed plausible nonobjects. Examples are given in figure 19.1.

Figure 19.1 Examples of stimuli used in the object-decision task.

The task is to respond Yes or No (real or unreal) to each stimulus. The test was first given to 50 normal subjects. Mean percent correct was 87.4 percent correct on the animals and 89.8 percent on the objects, confirming that the test is not too easy, and the two stimulus categories do not differ in difficulty. The test was then administered to the two patients and their two control groups. The results are shown in table 19.4.

Dante's performance is almost flawless, with both types of stimuli. Michelangelo is normal with the inanimate stimuli, but he makes a very large number of false acceptances with the animate stimuli.

Tasks with Neither Visual Input nor Visual Output: Deciding about Perceptual Properties

A set of 10 animal names and 10 names of inanimate objects was chosen. For each of these 20 names, 8 statements attributing particular perceptual properties to the animal or object (four true, four false) were composed. Examples of these statements are: "A motorcycle has a rearview mirror"; "A motorcycle has a steering wheel"; "A rabbit has long ears"; "A rabbit has a curved beak." A group of 90 normal control subjects averaged 71/80 correct for the animal statements and 70/80 correct for the nonliving object statements. The results for the two patients and their controls are given in table 19.5.

Dante performed within the normal range for both types of stimulus. Michelangelo was normal for inanimate stimuli but very impaired for animate stimuli. Five more tasks of this kind were devised, as described in table 19.6, and administered to Michelangelo and controls, with the results also shown in table 19.6. Once again, for inanimate stimuli he performed normally but was very impaired when asked questions about animals—except that he was able to judge the relative sizes of animals.

Table 19.4 Object Decision Test: Number of Correct Responses for Real and Unreal Stimuli for the Two Patients, plus Mean and Standard Deviation of Performance by Each Patient's Control Group, and Patient's z-Score Relative to Control

Type of Object	Michelangelo	Dante
Animate		
Real ($N = 16$)	16	16
	14.4; 0.8	15.6; 0.8
	$z = 2.05$	$z = 0.51$
Unreal ($N = 16$)	4	16
	14.1; 1.5	14.9; 0.8
	$z = -6.5$	$z = 1.3$
Inanimate		
Real ($N = 8$)	8	6
	7.4; 1.7	7.8; 0.7
	$z = 0.35$	$z = -2.5$
Unreal ($N = 8$)	7	8
	7.2; 1.3	7.9; 0.8
	$z = -0.15$	$z = 0.11$

Table 19.5 Perceptual, Attribute Decision: Number Correct by the Two Patients, plus Mean and Standard Deviation of Performance by Each Patient's Control Group, and Patient's z-Score Relative to Control

Type of Object	Michelangelo	Dante
Animate	48/80 (60%)	72/80 (90%)
$N = 80$; chance $= 40/80$	69.5; 4.1	70.5; 4.5
	$z = -5.24$	$z = 0.32$
Inanimate	71/80 (88.8%)	7/80 (88.8%)
$N = 80$; chance $= 40/80$	72.6; 2.9	72.2; 4.2
	$z = -0.18$	$z = -0.26$

A Task with Visual Output: Drawing to Dictation

Figure 19.2 gives examples of Michelangelo's output when drawing in response to spoken names of animals or inanimate objects. His drawings of animals exhibit the same kinds of errors he makes in the other kinds of visual-knowledge tasks: just as he accepts as real animals incorrect combinations of animal parts, or answers "Yes" to the question "Does an oyster have legs?" so he *draws* an oyster with legs, an eel with ears (and legs), a squid with quills, and so on. In contrast, his drawings of inanimate objects, though imperfectly executed, contain no incorrect information.

Specific versus Generic Visual Knowledge

When Michelangelo was shown drawings of isolated parts of animal's bodies and asked to name these parts, he performed relatively well—32/42 (76.2%)

Table 19.6 Attribute Decision Test: Performance by Michelangelo and by His Control Group (percent). Chance Performance 50 Percent

	Straight/curved letter judgment (N = 40)[a]	
Michelangelo	98	
Controls	91	

	Size comparison[b]	
	Animals (N = 20)	Inanimate objects (N = 20)
Michelangelo	100	94
Controls	95	95

	Visual details	
	Animals (N = 18)[c]	Inanimate objects (N = 18)[d]
Michelangelo	50	94
Controls	90	93

a. E.g., has uppercase A any curved lines?
b. E.g., is an X larger than a Y?
c. E.g., does a rabbit have floppy ears?
d. E.g., has an igloo sharp or round ends?

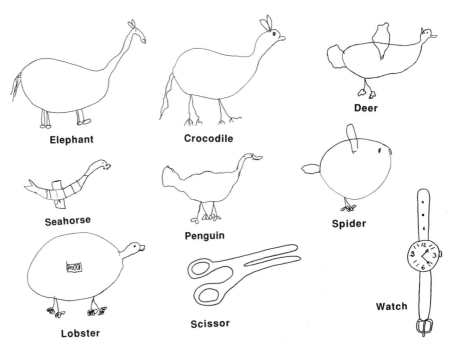

Figure 19.2 Examples of Michelangelo's drawings of animate and inanimate objects.

correct—and when shown a stick figure of an animal plus a detailed picture of a specific part of a specific animal (e.g., the muzzle of a cow), he could usually position the body part on the appropriate part of the stick figure—35/42 (83.3%) correct. So he knows that a nose is a nose, and where it goes.

However, this knowledge is only *generic*. When shown a drawing of a highly characteristic part of an animal and asked to name the animal, he performed very poorly, scoring only 4/42 (9.5%) correct; and when shown stick figures of animals in which one body part was replaced by a detailed picture of that part (e.g., a stick figure with the head of a cow), he could name the relevant animal only rarely, scoring 3/20 (15%) correct.

Tests of Visual Knowledge: Summary

In these various test of visual knowledge, then, Dante was essentially normal and, for inanimate items, Michelangelo was normal or nearly normal too. But with animate items, Michelangelo performed very poorly, whether the task required recognizing visual input or producing visual output—or even in tasks where there was neither visual input nor visual output involved.

19.5 CONCLUSIONS

At the beginning of this chapter we raised four questions about the organization of object knowledge. We conclude by offering answers to each of these questions.

1. *Are there separate systems of object knowledge for the different types of such knowledge?* Data from Sartori and Job (1988) suggest that this is so. Their (rather limited) testing of Michelangelo indicated that he retains knowledge about animals as long as this is nonvisual knowledge, from which one might argue that there are separate subsystems of semantic memory for visual and for nonvisual knowledge. The same conclusion has been reached by Basso, Capitani, and Laiacona (1988) and Silveri and Gainotti (1988).

2. *Do the different input modalities have their own dedicated separate systems of object knowledge?* Our inclination is to deny this, on the ground that Michelangelo behaves in exactly the same way when the stimulus is a picture as when it is a spoken word: he performs less well with animals than with inanimate objects, and across the two tasks there is considerable consistency in which animals he succeeds with and which he fails with, two results that strongly suggest he is using the same system of representations in these two tasks.

3. *Are there separate systems of object knowledge for different categories of objects?* We believe so; even when the confounding variables of familiarity, complexity, and name frequency are controlled, Michelangelo is worse at naming animate objects than inanimate objects, and this selective inferiority with animals extends to tasks not involving naming, such as comprehension of spoken words and drawing. We infer from this that knowledge about animate objects is stored separately from knowledge about inanimate objects.

4. *Do different object-oriented tasks (e.g., recognizing an object vs. answering questions about its appearance vs. drawing it from memory) depend upon distinct systems of object knowledge?* We think not. If there were separate systems of representations used for these three tasks, why should Michelangelo be bad at all three? One could reply to this by proposing that he simply has three different impairments. But why should all three impairments selectively affect living things, if they are separate impairments? We can see no reason why this would be expected. An even stronger counterargument comes from intertask consistency: when he is bad at naming an animal, he is generally bad at drawing it, and vice versa. Why should this be so if these two tasks use different systems of visual representations?

Our general conclusion, then, is that there is a system of knowledge about objects that is categorically organized (containing, for example, separate subsystems for animate objects and inanimate objects); that all the different types of knowledge we have about objects are stored together in this system; that the representations in this system are accessible from all modes of input (spoken words, printed words, and pictures, for example); and that these representations are required for all modes of output (spoken object naming, written object naming, and drawing from memory, for example).

APPENDIX: CASE HISTORIES

Michelangelo

Michelangelo, a 38-year-old Italian man, was an employee, as well as an active member, of the World Wildlife Fund. As such, according to his wife and colleagues, he used to know a huge number of different fish, birds, etc. In May 1984 he suddenly developed temporospatial disorientation and a severe amnesia, which were, in the first place, wrongly interpreted as a consequence of an alcoholic syndrome. A few days postonset, he was admitted to the Neurological Department of Treviso Hospital. His EEG was normal, but the CT scan showed two areas of hypodensity in both the right and the left anterior temporal lobes. Increase of intratecal herpes antibodies was found via serial analysis of the liquor and serum. He was immediately treated with Acyclovir.

The basic neuropsychological results that are here summarized may be found in a more extensive and detailed form in Sartori and Job (1988). At the first neuropsychological examination, conducted at the bedside, the patient was found to be severely anomic with comprehension disorders, anterograde amnesia, and anosognosia. A more formal examination was conducted twenty days postonset. WAIS verbal IQ was 82, performance IQ was 76, and overall IQ was 78. On the Wechsler Memory Scale he scored 57. His condition remained essentially stable until 1989, the period in which the data reported in this chapter were collected. Performance in a retrograde memory test was clearly related to the temporal distance from onset. Tested on four-alternative forced-choice questions about events that happened in 1983–1984, he scored

12.5 percent correct (mean of controls = 79%) while for events that happened in 1966–1967 his accuracy was 50 percent (mean of controls = 73.3). In a recognition memory test, he scored 26/50 ($z = -2.23$; chance = 25/50) for faces and 38/50 ($z = -1.3$) for words. He was able to recall only 1/10 of a list of words presented to him. Comprehension, as tested with the Token Test, was fairly good (33/36), showing that the initial comprehension disorder recovered very quickly. Experimental testing of naming ability pinpointed a specific disorder for items belonging to the category of animals and vegetables, with inanimate objects relatively spared. A set of stimuli was presented for naming in two different sessions and a very high consistency of response across sessions was found. Michelangelo was also at chance in deciding if a given perceptual attribute belongs to a given concept when the attributes presented to him were his own errors collected in a previous session. The patient failed also in carrying out visual recognition tests such as reality judgments on pictures of animals (i.e., discriminating real animals from unreal ones), almost invariably accepting unreal animals as real ones. Reality judgments on objects were, in contrast, perfect.

These symptoms occurred in the absence of any deficit of early visual processing. He was 100 percent correct in naming overlapping figures, provided that they did not represent living things. He was very good at identifying objects depicted in unusual views; he named 17/20 of unusual and 19/20 of usual views of inanimate objects. When presented with a target object seen from an unusual view, he could choose the correct alternative representing the same object from a prototypical view even when this was presented with a visually similar foil. His drawing from memory was worse for animals than for inanimate objects.

Dante

Dante, a 22-year-old Italian-speaking man, was, for over a month, in a comatose state with insufficient respiratory function and frequent convulsive states. A meningoencephalitis was suspected. The EEG showed major irritative abnormalities diffusely present in the right frontotemporal areas. A CT scan showed a nonhomogeneous superficial hypodensity located in fronto-temporo-parietal regions. After a positive liquor examination, the diagnosis was of an encephalitis of unknown origin with postencephalitic epilepsy.

At neuropsychological examination, carried out a month postonset, the WAIS verbal IQ was 50, performance IQ was 40, and full-scale IQ was 52. On the Wechsler Memory Scale the MQ score was 50. His speech was fluent and, when required to describe three complex pictures taken from Goodglass and Kaplan (1972), Ellis and Young (1988), and Bisiach, Cappa, and Vallar (1983), he made two anomic errors and one phonemic paraphasia, three *conduits d'approche*, and two circumlocutions. Three times out of three when prompted with the first phoneme of the target word his response was correct. On the Token Test he scored 32/36, thus showing no comprehension disorder. In contrast, a marked naming difficulty was detected: he named only 59/150 (39%) of the pictures shown to him.

NOTES

We thank Karalyn Patterson and David Meyer for their patient and valuable comments upon a previous draft of this chapter.

1. It seems strange that a phonological deficit could depend upon a nonphonological stimulus variable. It is indeed strange, but true. Semenza and Zettin (1988) described a patient who had a selective naming deficit for proper nouns. They showed convincingly that their patient could comprehend proper and common nouns, and could produce as names common nouns but not proper nouns. So their patient had a phonological deficit selective for proper nouns, even though the category "proper noun" is not a phonological category. And Caramazza and Hillis (1991) reported a case of a naming deficit that was restricted to the production of verbs—a naming deficit that depends upon a nonphonological (here syntactic) variable.

REFERENCES

Basso, A., Capitani, E., and Laiacona, M. (1988). Progressive language impairment without dementia: A case with isolated category specific semantic defect. *Journal of Neurology, Neurosurgery and Psychiatry, 51*, 1201–1207.

Bisiach, E., Cappa, S., and Vallar, G. (1983). *L'Esame Neuropsicologico*. Milano: Cortina.

Caramazza, A., and Hillis, A. (1991). Lexical organization of nouns and verbs in the brain. *Nature, 349*, 788–790.

Dennis, M. (1976). Dissociated naming and locating of body parts after anterior lobe resection: An experimental case study. *Brain and Language, 3*, 147–163.

Ellis, A. W., and Young, A. W. (1988). *Human cognitive neuropsychology*. London: Lawrence Erlbaum Associates.

Farah, M. J., Hammond, K. M., Mehta, Z., and Ratcliff, G. (1988). Category-specificity and modality-specificity in semantic memory. *Neuropsychologia, 27*, 193–200.

Farah, M. J.. McMullen, P. A., and Meyer, M. M. (1991). Can recognition of living things be selectively impaired? *Neuropsychologia, 29*, 185–194.

Goodglass, H., and Kaplan, E. (1972). *The assessment of aphasia and related disorders*. Philadelphia: Lea & Febiger.

Hanley, J. R., Young, A. W., and Pearson, N. A. (1989). Defective recognition of familiar people. *Cognitive Neuropsychology, 6*, 179–210.

Hillis, A., and Caramazza, A. (1990). Category-specific naming and comprehension impairment: A double dissociation. *Report 90–6, Cognitive Neuropsychology Laboratory*, Johns Hopkins University.

Kroll, J. F., and Potter, M. (1984). Recognising words, pictures and concepts: A comparison of lexical, object and reality decisions. *Journal of Verbal Learning and Verbal Behavior, 23*, 39–66.

McCarthy, R. A., and Warrington, E. K. (1988). Evidence for modality-specific meaning systems in the brain. *Nature, 334*, 428–340.

Pietrini, V., Nertempi, P., Vaglia, A., Revello, M. G., Pinna, V., and Ferro-Milone, F. (1988). Recovery from herpes simplex encephalitis: Selective impairment of specific semantic categories with neuroradiological correlation. *Journal of Neurology, Neurosurgery and Psychiatry, 51*, 1284–1293.

Riddoch, M. J., and Humphreys, G. W. (1987). Visual object processing in optic aphasia: A case of semantic access agnosia. *Cognitive Neuropsychology, 4,* 131–185.

Riddoch, M. J., Humphreys, G. W., Coltheart, M., and Funnell, E. (1988). Semantic systems or system? Neuropsychological evidence re-examined. *Cognitive Neuropsychology, 5,* 3–26.

Sartori, G., and Job, R. (1988). The oyster with four legs: a neuropsychological study on the interaction of visual and semantic information. *Cognitive Neuropsychology, 5,* 105–132.

Semenza, C., and Zettin, M. (1988). Generating proper names: A case of selective inability. *Cognitive Neuropsychology, 5,* 711–722.

Shallice, T. (1987). Impairments of semantic processing: Multiple dissociations. In M. Coltheart, G. Sartori, and R. Job (eds.), *The cognitive neuropsychology of language,* 111–128. London: Lawrence Erlbaum Associates.

Silveri, M. C., Gainotti, G. (1988). Interactions between vision and language in category-specific semantic impairment. *Cognitive Neuropsychology, 5,* 677–710.

Stewart, F., Parkin, A. J., and Hunkin, N. M. (1992). Naming impairments following recovery from herpes simplex encephalitis: Category-specific? *Quarterly Journal of Experimental Psychology, 44A,* 261–284.

Van Sommers, P. (1989). A system for drawing and drawing-related neuropsychology. *Cognitive Neuropsychology, 6,* 117–164.

Warrington, E. K. (1975). The selective impairment of semantic memory. *Quarterly Journal of Experimental Psychology, 27,* 635–657.

Warrington, E. K., and McCarthy, R. A. (1983). Category-specific access dysphasia. *Brain, 106,* 859–878.

Warrington, E. K., and McCarthy, R. A. (1987). Categories of knowledge: Further fractionation and an attempted integration. *Brain, 110,* 1273–1296.

Warrington, E. K., and Shallice, T. (1984). Category-specific semantic impairment. *Brain, 107,* 829–853.

20 The Story of the Two-Store Model of Memory: Past Criticisms, Current Status, and Future Directions

Jeroen G. W. Raaijmakers

20.1 INTRODUCTION

About twenty-five years ago, Atkinson and Shiffrin (1965, 1968) introduced the so-called two-store model of memory. It proposed a distinction between a temporary short-term store (STS) and a more permanent long-term store (LTS). A basic assumption of the model was that storage of information in LTS is determined by the processing of information in STS. The two-store model quickly became quite popular, and for a number of years dominated the field of memory research.

In the early 1970s, however, it was claimed that a number of phenomena were difficult to explain within this model. These included a dissociation between the time that an item resides in STS and the strength of the LTS trace, and recency effects observed in situations where STS does not play any role. As a result, alternative theories were presented that could handle these findings better, the best-known ones being the levels-of-processing framework proposed by Craik and Lockhart (1972) and the working-memory model proposed by Baddeley and Hitch (1974).

The preceding brief historical account, or something quite similar, appears in many current textbooks on human memory. I will argue, however, that this account is wrong, and that current versions of the two-store model are in fact quite capable of handling many problematic memory phenomena.[1] It is my hope that the present argument will lead to a reappraisal of the two-store model.

Following my reexamination of the two-store model, I will discuss a few aspects of the SAM (search of associative memory) model originally proposed by Richard Shiffrin and myself (Raaijmakers and Shiffrin 1980, 1981), which developed out of the two-store model. I will present some new applications of SAM that illustrate its usefulness as a general framework for analyzing memory processes.

20.2 EVALUATING THE CRITICISMS OF THE TWO-STORE MODEL

Basic Principles of the Two-Store Model

The Atkinson and Shiffrin (1968) version of the two-store model emphasized a distinction between permanent, structural aspects of memory and flexible control processes. They originally proposed a division of memory into three stores: the sensory registers, short-term store, and long-term store. In more recent versions (Atkinson and Shiffrin 1971; Shiffrin 1975, 1976), the sensory registers have been combined with STS into a single component, also termed STS. Furthermore, it is emphasized that STS should not be viewed as a physiologically separate structure. Rather, it should be thought of as the temporarily activated portion of LTS. This STS is a kind of working memory that serves the dual purpose of maintaining information in a readily accessible state and of transferring information to LTS. What gets stored in LTS is determined by the type of processing (coding, rehearsal, and attention) that is carried out in STS.

Rehearsal or coding processes in STS are control processes whose nature is determined by task constraints, prior experience, and so forth. Atkinson and Shiffrin (1968) presented a specific quantitative "buffer model" that incorporated one such control process, rehearsal. It was used to give a precise explanation of performance in a particular type of experimental paradigm, the continuous short-term memory task. One frequent misunderstanding seems to be the idea that this rehearsal buffer is equivalent to STS itself. However, Atkinson and Shiffrin (1968) explicitly did not view the rehearsal buffer as a structural aspect of the memory system:

In our view, the maintenance and use of the buffer is a process entirely under the control of the subject. Presumably a buffer is set up and used in an attempt to maximize performance in certain situations. In setting up a maximal-sized buffer, however, the subject is devoting all his effort to rehearsal and not engaging in other processes such as coding and hypothesis testing. In situations, therefore, where coding, long-term search, hypothesis testing, and other mechanisms appreciably improve performance, it is likely that a trade-off will occur in which the buffer size will be reduced and rehearsal may even become somewhat random while coding and other strategies increase. (P. 113)

This shows that Atkinson and Shiffrin saw the buffer as a control process, and not as a structural aspect of the memory system. That is, STS does not consist of a fixed number of slots such that once the slots are filled STS is full. The buffer model was only a way of modeling the rehearsal process, namely, describing which items are rehearsed at a particular time. The preceding quotation also shows that they did not regard this type of rehearsal as particularly effective with respect to storage of information in LTS.

Atkinson and Shiffrin distinguished between two aspects of STS control processes: *rehearsal*, maintaining the information in STS, and *coding*, storing information in LTS. These two aspects, rehearsal and coding, should in most practical situations be regarded as the end points of a continuum: even a "pure" rehearsal process will lead to storage of some information in LTS, and a "pure" coding process will similarly keep some of the information in an active state, and hence in STS.

What probably confused many people was that Atkinson and Shiffrin (1968) in their original paper presented a model that focused on rehearsal but did assume some storage in LTS as a function of the length of the rehearsal period. As a result, rehearsal came to be viewed as *the* mechanism for transfer of information from STS to LTS. In later analyses (Shiffrin 1975), this aspect was clarified by replacing the terms "rehearsal" and "coding" with "maintenance rehearsal" and "elaborative rehearsal," respectively. Maintenance rehearsal has the primary function of keeping the information in a readily accessible state while elaborative rehearsal has the primary function of storing information in LTS. Hence, according to the two-store model, it is not the amount of rehearsal per se that determines recall, but rather the amount of elaborative rehearsal. Only in those cases where the emphasis is on elaborative coding into long-term memory (e.g., in a free recall situation) would it be appropriate to assume a direct relationship between length of rehearsal and storage in long-term memory.

The Levels-of-Processing Framework

Following the introduction of the two-store model, Craik and Lockhart (1972) proposed "an alternative framework for human memory research." They assumed that memory performance is determined by the level of processing given to the to-be-remembered material. They distinguished between type-I and type-II processing. Type-I processing refers to continued processing at a level that serves to maintain the information in what they termed "primary memory." Type-II processing, on the other hand, involves a "deeper" analysis of the information that should lead to improved memory performance.

Their analysis received considerable support from a large number of experiments that showed that simply keeping the information in an active state (type-I processing) has no effect on recall performance, but that type-II processing strongly affects the probability of recalling information. Even though later experiments showed that type-I processing has some effects on long-term storage, especially if a recognition measure is used (Dark and Loftus 1976; Nelson 1977), the finding that long periods of type-I processing had little effect on recall performance was considered by Craik and Lockhart (1972) and others as crucial evidence against the two-store model. Ever since, this conclusion has been echoed in many review articles (e.g., Postman 1975; Crowder 1982; Baddeley 1983) and textbooks.

However, over the years there have also been many instances where this conclusion was rejected (Bjork 1975; Glanzer 1977; Shiffrin 1977). As mentioned previously, the two-store model does not assume that every type of rehearsal is equally effective for long-term storage. In fact, the distinction between type-I and type-II processing is virtually the same as the earlier distinction between the control processes of rehearsal and coding, respectively, or maintenance and elaborative rehearsal. Hence, the previous results taken as evidence against the two-store model by no means invalidate it. If anything, they provide strong evidence for the role of control processes in memory.

In hindsight, it is difficult to understand why so many researchers rejected the two-store model. This rejection is even more surprising since a casual look at the Craik and Lockhart (1972) article shows that they did in fact propose a kind of two-store model. That is, they made a distinction between primary and secondary memory, where primary memory has the function of maintaining information in an active state for further processing. It is unfortunate that proponents of the levels-of-processing framework have never put their model in a quantitative form. I believe that such an exercise would have demonstrated the close similarity between it and the two-store model of Atkinson and Shiffrin (1968).

The Working-Memory Model

The second criticism that I want to discuss briefly derives from the working-memory model proposed by Baddeley and Hitch (1974). Whereas the levels-of-processing framework focused on the nature of the relation between STS and LTS, the working-memory model entails a detailed analysis of STS itself. For the present discussion, two types of results are most relevant. The first is that concurrent memory load has a strong effect on the prerecency part of the serial position curve but not the recency part. According to Baddeley and Hitch (1974), this result is inconsistent with the two-store model. Although their exact reasoning has never been spelled out in great detail, the basic idea seems to be that the concurrent memory load should have kept STS fully occupied, leaving little room for additional items presented on the free-recall list.

The second type of result thought to be incompatible with the two-store model is that recency effects also occur in certain types of long-term memory tasks. This long-term recency effect is interpreted by Baddeley and Hitch (1974, 1977) and others as the result of an ordinal retrieval strategy. Since the two-store model attributes recency effects in free recall to retrieval from STS, it supposedly cannot accommodate long-term recency effects other than ones based on STS.

However, the criticisms derived from the working-memory model are based on an incorrect assumption that the rehearsal buffer proposed in Atkinson and Shiffrin's model is a structural aspect of memory and that it is more or less coincident with STS. In their 1971 paper on the properties of the short-term store, Atkinson and Shiffrin already argued that STS and the rehearsal buffer should not be equated. For example, they showed that particular rehearsal strategies (i.e., rehearsing only a single item at a time) did affect the primacy part of the serial-position curve but did not affect the recency part. A similar assumption has to be made in order to explain recency effects in single-trial paired-associate recall. In such a paradigm, there is no primacy effect but there is a recency effect (see Murdock 1974). According to the two-store model, the absence of a primacy effect indicates a one-item rehearsal strategy (in other words, a one-item buffer), namely, at any time only a single item is actively rehearsed. If the buffer and STS were equivalent, a one-item recency effect would be predicted.

The recency effect is assumed to depend on recall from STS (i.e., those items that are still in an active state at the time of recall). Which items are still in STS at the time of recall is determined by both the rehearsal strategy and the forgetting properties of STS. Rehearsal may be thought of as reactivating an item's representation in STS (Schweickert and Boruff 1986). If an item is not rehearsed, some time will be taken before it is really forgotten from STS. In fact, if every item was immediately forgotten once attention was taken away from it, it would be difficult to successfully implement a rehearsal strategy.

Consider now the finding that the recency effect is not attenuated by concurrent memory load, while recall from LTS is. Such a result is not incompatible with a two-store model. To explain it, one may assume that the items do enter STS, even though STS is kept busy by the concurrent memory load. Although the memory load may make it difficult to actively rehearse the items in STS (using elaborative coding strategies to store information in LTS), they need not immediately disappear once the next item on the list is presented. If the items do enter STS, the recent ones should still be retrievable from STS once recall starts.

The preceding interpretation seems reasonably plausible. Even the working-memory model has to assume that items do enter working memory in the first place; otherwise an ordinal retrieval strategy would not work, and there would not be any recall possible. Second, the serial-position curves presented by Baddeley and Hitch (1974) show some recall for earlier items, even in the memory-load condition. Hence, at least in a two-store model, this is consistent with an assumption that the task leaves spare capacity for coding processes, and that these items have indeed entered STS. Finally, it is of some interest to note that the exact pattern of results can in fact be generated by the two-store model by setting the LTS-storage parameter to a very small value while maintaining all other parameters (including buffer size) at their typical value.

What about long-term recency effects? The two-store model assumes that in a free-recall task, the subject first tries to recall those items still in STS. This, to me at least, seems a very sensible strategy. These items are easily accessible and easily lost, so why not recall them right away? This recall from STS leads to a recency effect, since the items that are still active in STS most likely come from the end of the list. However, no one would deny that other factors could also lead to a recency effect. For instance, suppose that the items at the end of the list are much easier than the other items. This too would lead to a recency effect.

The criticism of the two-store model based on long-term recency effects makes a logical error. The two-store model assumes that recall from STS leads to recency, or in symbolic form: A → B. It does not follow that the reverse, B → A, is also true. That is, the model does not assume that all recency effects are based on recall from STS. In fact, as I will show later, modern versions of the two-store model, such as the SAM model, predict that retrieval from LTS is based on contextual retrieval cues. Such contextual retrieval will, everything else being equal, lead to an advantage for more recent items if the context stored in the memory images varies.

This analysis is supported by findings that short-term and long-term recency effects are differentially susceptible to the effects of various experimental factors. For example, long-term recency is not sensitive to output order while short-term recency is (Dalezman 1976; Whitten 1978). Moreover, interresponse times in regular free recall show an abrupt increase after the first three or four items (Metcalfe and Murdock 1981). Although I am not aware of similar data in long-term recency paradigms, I expect that the results will be quite different.

20.3 THE SAM MODEL

In the previous sections, I have argued that the framework of the two-store model is still viable. Nevertheless, there have been several new theoretical developments since the original paper by Atkinson and Shiffrin (1968). For example, one of these is the search of associative memory (SAM) model proposed about a decade ago by Raaijmakers and Shiffrin (1980, 1981). This latter model, which is a contemporary version of the two-store model, has been extended to a large number of memory paradigms, including paired-associate recall, recognition, and interference paradigms (Gillund and Shiffrin 1984; Mensink and Raaijmakers 1988, 1989).

In this section, I will describe the basic elements of the SAM model, both the general framework and the way in which it has been applied to several memory paradigms. This seems appropriate, not only because SAM grew out of the two-store model, but also because it emphasizes the cumulative nature of this theoretical approach.

The Basic Framework

The basic framework of the SAM model assumes that during storage, information is represented in "memory images," which contain item, associative, and contextual information. The amount and type of information stored is determined by coding processes in STS (elaborative rehearsal). In most intentional-learning paradigms the amount of information stored is a function of the length of time that the item is studied while in STS.

According to the SAM model, retrieval from LTS is based on cues. These cues may be words from the studied list, category cues, contextual cues, or any other type of information that the subject uses in attempting to retrieve information from LTS. Whether an image is retrieved or not depends on the associative strengths of the retrieval cues to that image. These strengths are a function of the overlap of the cue information and the information stored in the image. In most applications, the simplifying assumption is made that the strengths are a linear function of the amount of elaborative rehearsal (the amount of time that the item is actively rehearsed).

An important property of the SAM model is that it incorporates a rule to describe the overall strength of a set of probe cues to a particular image. For example, let $S(Q_j, I_i)$ be the strength of association between cue Q_j and image I_i. Then the combined strength or activation of image I_i, $A(i)$, for a probe set consisting of $Q_1, Q_2, \ldots, Q_m$ is given by

$$A(i) = \prod_{j=1}^{m} S(Q_j, I_i)^{W_j}.$$ (1)

The W_j in this equation are weights assigned to the different cues, representing their relative salience or importance. These weights are used to model the limited capacity of STS in retrieval. The sum of the weights is assumed to be limited (Raaijmakers and Shiffrin 1981; Gronlund and Shiffrin 1986): adding extra cues takes attention away from the other cues. However, the key feature of equation (1) is that the individual cue strengths are combined multiplicatively into a single activation measure. This multiplicative feature focuses the search process on those images that are strongly associated to *all* cues.

Application to Recall Tasks

In recall tasks, the search process of the SAM model is based on a series of elementary retrieval attempts. Each attempt involves selecting or sampling one image based on the activation strengths A_i. The probability of sampling image I_i equals the relative strength of that image compared to the other images in LTS:

$$P_S(I_i) = \frac{A(i)}{\sum A(k)}.$$ (2)

Sampling an image allows recovery of information from it. For simple recall tasks where a single word has to be recalled, the probability of successfully recovering the name of the encoded word after sampling the image I_i is assumed to be an exponential function of the sum of the weighted strengths of the probe set to the sampled image:

$$P_R(I_i) = 1 - \exp\left[-\sum_{j=1}^{m} W_j S(Q_j, I_i) \right].$$ (3)

The probability of recall, assuming L_{max} retrieval attempts with the same set of cues, is given by the probability that the item was sampled at least once, times the probability that recovery was successful:

$$P_{recall}(I_i) = [1 - (1 - P_S(I_i))^{L_{max}}]P_R(I_i).$$ (4)

Special assumptions are necessary when an image has previously been sampled using one or more of the present cues but its recovery did not lead to successful recall. In that case, recovery is based only on the "new" components of the sum in equation (3), corresponding to cues that were not involved in the earlier unsuccessful retrieval attempts (see Gronlund and Shiffrin 1986).

If the retrieval attempt is successful, the associative connections between the probe cues and the sampled image are strengthened. Thus, SAM assumes that learning occurs during retrieval as well as during study. This assumption leads to a kind of retrieval inhibition, because it decreases the probability of sampling other images. If the retrieval attempt is not successful, a decision is made about whether to continue, either with the same set of cues or with some other set of cues. The decision to terminate the search process is usually based on the number of unsuccessful searches, although other types of stop rule are also possible.

Application to Recognition Tasks

Although the SAM model assumes that the process of activating information is basically the same in recall and recognition, there are some important differences between these two processes. Gillund and Shiffrin (1984) proposed that old-new recognition decisions are based on the overall activation induced by the probe cues. That is, the overall activation, $\sum A(k)$, defines a familiarity value that is used in the manner of signal-detection theory to determine the probability of recognition. In order to derive predictions, some assumption is also needed about the variance of the strength distributions. Typically, the standard deviation is assumed to be proportional to the mean strength value (Gillund and Shiffrin 1984; Shiffrin, Ratcliff, and Clark 1990).

However, within the SAM framework, other types of models are also possible. For example, I believe that it would be worthwhile to consider an alternative version that assumes instead that recognition is based on a comparison of the overall activation with both context and the item as cues versus the item cue alone. Such an alternative has not yet been worked out.[2] For most predictions, this probably would not make much difference. However, it might handle word frequency effects in recognition tasks more easily than the Gillund and Shiffrin (1984) version did.

Contextual Fluctuation

The SAM model assumes that for typical episodic-memory tasks, contextual information is always encoded in the memory image and context is one of the retrieval cues. Context and changes in context play an important role in the prediction of forgetting phenomena. Changes in context may be discrete or occur in a more gradual way. Discrete changes are typical for studies that explicitly manipulate the test context (e.g., Godden and Baddeley 1975; Smith 1979). On the other hand, gradual changes may occur when the experimental paradigm is homogeneous (as in continuous paired-associate learning). In such cases, context similarity will be a decreasing function of delay.

Mensink and Raaijmakers (1988, 1989) recently proposed an extension of the SAM model to handle time-dependent changes in context. The basic idea, adapted from stimulus sampling theory (Estes 1955), is that a random fluctuation of elements occurs between two sets, a set of available context elements and a set of (temporarily) unavailable context elements. Performance is a function of the relationship between sets of available elements at different points in time (viz., study and test trials).

In this version of the SAM model, the experimental context is represented as a set of contextual elements. At any given time, only a part of this set is "perceived" by the subject, and this subset is denoted the current context. Elements in this set are said to be in the active state. All other elements are inactive. With the passage of time, the current context changes through a fluctuation process: some inactive elements become active and some active ones become inactive. At storage, only active elements are encoded in the memory image. If there are multiple study trials, each study trial gives a new opportunity for encoding a particular element in the image. The context strength at test is assumed to be proportional to the overlap between the set of context elements encoded in the image and the set of context elements that are active at the time of testing. Mensink and Raaijmakers (1989) show how some simple assumptions concerning the fluctuation process yield equations for computing the probability that any given element is active both at the time of storage and at the time of retrieval.

20.4 IMPORTANT APPLICATIONS

The SAM model was proposed to integrate phenomena from various memory paradigms within a single theoretical framework. As such, the model has been quite successful. With it, quantitative accounts have been developed for free recall, paired-associate recall, interference paradigms, and various recognition paradigms. In this chapter, I will briefly review these applications, focusing attention on those results that are most intriguing and that best illustrate the usefulness of a formal framework such as SAM. Special attention will be given to some new developments concerning spacing and repetition phenomena.

Free Recall and the Part-List Cuing Effect

SAM was initially developed as a model for free recall. Although the first version of the model was conceptually simple, the predictions that follow from it have been quite complicated to analyze. This is because they involve a large number of dependencies that make it difficult to intuit what may happen as the result of a particular experimental manipulation.

Raaijmakers and Shiffrin (1980, 1981) demonstrated that SAM predicts many findings from free-recall paradigms. For example, one important prediction is the list-length effect: the longer the list, the lower the probability of recalling any particular item. This follows because the rules for terminating search imply that *relatively* fewer samples are made from a longer list than from a shorter list. In fact, it seems to be a general characteristic of retrieval processes that *the larger the number of items associated with a cue, the smaller the probability that any one of those items will be recalled*. This *cue-overload principle* has been used by Watkins to explain a number of empirical phenomena (Mueller and Watkins 1977; Watkins 1975; Watkins and Watkins, 1976). Thus, it is of some interest to note that the cue-overload principle can be derived from the SAM model.

Probably the most intriguing aspect of the SAM model for free recall is its prediction of the *part-list cuing effect*, a *decrease* in the probability of recall when, at test, some of the list items are given as cues. This effect has generally been considered problematic for any model that assumes the use of interitem associations in recall. It seems that giving some items as cues should aid recall of the remaining items (the target items).

However, application of the SAM model has revealed that the logic under-lying this latter prediction is not correct. We showed that it is important to consider the nature of the cues used during retrieval. Experimenter-provided cues (used by the cued group in a part-list cuing experiment) are inferior to self-generated cues, because experimenter-provided cues slightly bias the sampling process in favor of cue items. For any given cue, the model predicts that there is some probability of sampling the cue item itself. By definition, the cued group starts its retrieval using the experimenter-provided cues. For the non-cued or control condition, there is no such bias since this group starts retrieval with a self-generated cue. Hence, the images sampled by the cued group are less likely to come from the set of target items.

We recently completed a study in which the SAM model's explanation for the part-list cuing effect was tested against a class of theories that attribute the negative cuing effect to storage factors (e.g., Roediger and Neely 1982). In this study, subjects were presented lists of unrelated words. They were tested either immediately or after a delay filled with learning a list of paired associates. It is assumed that the delay leads to a decrease in the strength of the contextual associations. The SAM model predicts that the usual negative effect will be obtained in the immediate-recall condition but that a positive effect will be obtained in the delayed-testing condition. The reason is that the part-list cues will help in conditions where subjects are not able to recall many items without any cues. On the other hand, most other explanations that attribute the part-list cuing effect to storage factors predict no difference in it for immediate and delayed testing. Our results (fig. 20.1) support the SAM model: there was a negative effect of cuing in the immediate-testing condition and a positive effect in the delay condition.

Recognition and the List-Strength Effect

The SAM model for recognition developed by Gillund and Shiffrin (1984) has been quite successful in predicting a large number of well-known findings. Recently, attention has been focused on the so-called *list-strength effect* (Ratcliff, Clark, and Shiffrin 1990; Shiffrin, Ratcliff, and Clark 1990), which concerns the

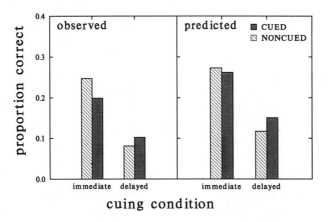

Figure 20.1 Proportion correct in free recall with and without part-list cues for immediate and delayed testing. The left panel gives observed data from an unpublished experiment; the right panel gives simulated results from the SAM model for free recall.

effects of strengthening (or weakening) some list items upon memory for other list items. Ratcliff, Clark, and Shiffrin (1990) showed that strengthening some items in the list decreases recall of the remaining list items but has no or even a positive effect on recognition performance. This contrasts with the list-length effect: adding items to a list decreases both recall and recognition performance. Thus, the number of irrelevant items, but not their strength, affects recognition.

Shiffrin, Ratcliff, and Clark (1990) showed that many current models (including the original SAM model) cannot predict both the presence of a list-length effect and the absence (or reversal) of a list-strength effect. However, a simple modification of SAM can handle these results. To explain them, a number of assumptions are required. First, different items are stored in separate traces but repetitions of an item within a list are stored in a single memory trace (under the conditions of these experiments). Second, the variance of activation of each separate trace, when the cue item is unrelated to the item(s) encoded in the trace, is constant regardless of the strength of the trace. Third, recall and recognition operate differently, with recognition based on the combined activation of all traces and recall based on access to a single trace.

The problematic assumption is the second one. In the SAM model for recognition (Gillund and Shiffrin 1984), the variance of the activation for an unrelated item was assumed to increase with the strength of the context association. Since the interitem associative strength for unrelated items was always set equal to a constant residual value (d), the combined variance for such unrelated items is larger for the stronger items. In contrast, Shiffrin, Ratcliff, and Clark (1990) propose that the residual strength is not a constant but decreases as a function of the strength of the image. Yet while this assumption seems ad hoc, it can be defended using a *differentiation* argument: the better the image is encoded, the clearer are the differences between it and the test item, and hence the lower the activation. In this way, a constant or even decreasing variance may be predicted, depending on the weighting of context and item cues.

A crucial aspect of this explanation is that repetitions of an item are assumed to be stored in a single memory image. To evaluate it further, Murnane and Shiffrin (1989) tested whether a reversal of the list-strength effect in recognition occurs if repetitions are presented in such a way that they are likely to be encoded in separate images. They found that repetitions of words in different sentences produced a list-strength effect whereas repetitions of entire sentences did not. This demonstrates that the nature of the encoding of a repeated item is a crucial factor.

Clearly, we now need a more detailed model of how the relation between the information in a cue item and a stored image determines associative strength, not only for items studied separately but also for items studied together. In addition, some older theoretical analyses should be repeated to see whether the extended SAM model's predictions are still the same.

Interference and Forgetting

Mensink and Raaijmakers (1988) applied the SAM model with the contextual-fluctuation assumption to several classic findings on interference and forgetting. The model can handle most of the findings on retroactive and proactive interference and transfer relations between lists in a straightforward way, including results that were problematic for classical interference theories.

A crucial requirement for many of these predictions is that recall performance depends on both the relative and absolute strengths of the memory images. In the SAM model, the sampling process is a function of the relative strength of the target image compared to the other images, whereas the recovery process is a function of the absolute strength. For example, if one equates recall in the interference and control conditions by giving the interference condition more study trials, this does not imply that the respective associative strengths are also equal. Instead, the model predicts that if the probability of recall is equalized, the absolute strength will be higher and hence the relative strength lower for the interference condition (otherwise recall would not be equal). This enables us to account for a number of results, including the differential effects of interference on accuracy and latency measures (Anderson 1981).

Spacing of Repetitions in Continuous Paired-Associate Recall

Recently, we have also used the SAM model to explain results concerning the spacing of repetitions. Suppose an item is presented twice for study (at times P_1 and P_2) and tested at a later time T. If the retention interval (i.e., the interval $P_2 - T$) is relatively long, the probability of recall increases as a function of the spacing between the two presentations (the interval $P_1 - P_2$). With short retention intervals, however, the probability of recall decreases as a function of the spacing between the presentations. With intermediate retention intervals, the results are more complicated, often showing a nonmonotonic effect of spacing (Glenberg 1976, 1979).

Recent work by Raaijmakers and van Winsum-Westra shows that this complicated state of affairs is predicted by the SAM model through its assumptions concerning contextual fluctuation. As the spacing interval increases, the context at P_2 will include more new, not yet encoded, elements that may be added to the memory image. Encoding more elements in the image increases the expected overlap between the test context and the contextual elements in the image.

Although the basic principle is quite straightforward, the full SAM model requires supplementary assumptions that complicate matters. Crucial here is what happens on the second presentation, P_2. It is assumed that at P_2, an implicit automatic retrieval attempt is made for the image stored at P_1 (a study-phase retrieval assumption). New context elements that are present at P_2 are only added to the image formed at P_1 if that image is retrieved at P_2. If it is not retrieved, a new storage attempt is made, based only on the information present at P_2. Also, to accommodate effects of differential storage strengths, it is assumed that each storage attempt either succeeds or fails. If it is not successful, the probability of sampling that image on a future retrieval attempt is zero. It is further assumed that no new storage takes place for any item still in STS at P_2.

According to this model, spacing of repetitions has a number of effects. As mentioned, due to context fluctuation, more new context elements are stored when an item is "recognized" at P_2. As the spacing interval increases, the probability that the item is still in STS at P_2 decreases. Both of these effects lead to an increase in the probability of recall at test (i.e., they increase the likelihood that new information is added to the trace at P_2). However, spacing also has a negative effect. The longer the spacing interval, the lower the probability that the image is successfully retrieved at P_2. This is a simple forgetting effect: as the interval increases, the expected overlap between the contexts at P_1 and P_2 decreases, and this decreases the strength of the context cue at P_2. Together, these factors produce a nonmonotonic effect of spacing. The spacing effect has an initial increase followed by a decrease, the maximum point depending on the length of the retention interval (P_2 to T).

The present extension of the SAM model has been used successfully to fit the results of a number of well-known experiments (e.g., Glenberg 1976; Rumelhart 1967; Young 1971). The most clear demonstration of the nonmonotonic effect of spacing is provided by Young (1971). Figure 20.2 shows the observed data and the SAM model's predictions. We have also fit this model to the results of a multitrial learning experiment reported by Rumelhart (1967) in which the spacing between repetitions was varied (fig. 20.3). This demonstrates that SAM can handle the basic learning data that were the main focus of the Markov models in the 1960s.

Another particularly interesting aspect of the present model is that it provides an explanation for the intriguing results of Ross and Landauer (1978). According to their analysis, most theories of spacing effects based on encoding

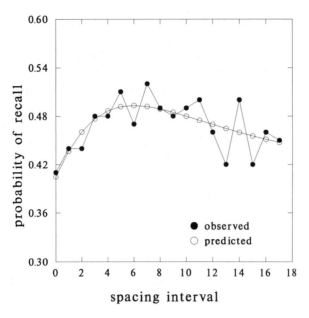

Figure 20.2 Observed and predicted probabilities of recall as a function of spacing interval (number of intervening items). Data from Young (1971).

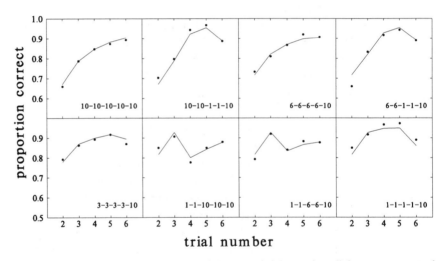

Figure 20.3 Observed (dots) and predicted (lines) probabilities of recall for experiment I of Rumelhart (1967). Each graph gives the spacing (number of intervening items) between successive presentations.

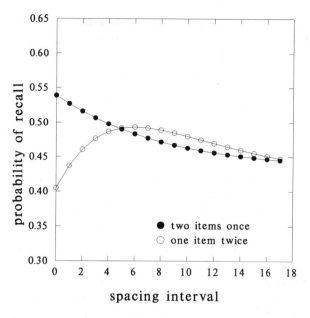

Figure 20.4 Predictions of the SAM model for the probability of recalling one or both of two items each presented once, and for the probability of recall of a single item presented twice, as a function of the spacing interval (number of intervening items) between the two presentations. Parameter estimates and experimental design are based on the SAM model applied to the experiment of Young (1971).

or contextual-variability assumptions predict beneficial effects of spacing for both two presentations of the same item and for two presentations of two different items. That is, the probability of recalling either of the two items should increase. However, Ross and Landauer showed that such a result is not obtained: a typical spacing effect only occurs for one item presented twice, not for two items presented once each.

The SAM model can handle this result because it treats these two situations quite differently. For the one-item case, it predicts that new information is often added to the same memory trace (if the item is recognized). In the two-item case, it predicts that two different images are formed. Since recall depends on the overlap in elements with each image separately, the spacing of the presentations by and large only matters for the single-item case. This is illustrated in figure 20.4, which shows predicted patterns of results for these two types of items.

To explain these results, the SAM model must assume that repetitions of an item are often encoded in the same memory image. This assumption, which we have also used in the analysis of interference data, agrees with one that Shiffrin, Ratcliff, and Clark (1990) have found necessary to account for the list-strength effects in recognition. That the same assumption is needed in quite different applications provides additional evidence for it.

The preceding account of spacing effects is in many respects quite similar to the components-levels theory proposed by Glenberg (1979), although he did not present a quantitative analysis. Interestingly, Glenberg and Smith (1981) mention the Ross-Landauer result as the one result that the component-levels theory cannot explain. Our analysis of the SAM model shows that their conclusion may not have been correct and that their theory can probably handle more data than they are aware of. This illustrates, once again, the usefulness of quantitative modeling of memory phenomena.

20.5 SOME IMPORTANT THEORETICAL ISSUES

The preceding applications show that the SAM model is a quite powerful framework for analyzing memory experiments. Perhaps the most significant aspect of a model such as SAM is that it provides a tool for the analysis of various complex and/or problematic memory phenomena. Quantitative predictions for specific designs can be obtained quite easily, and such analyses may lead to novel insights into the conditions under which particular phenomena are obtained. This has been true, for example, concerning the part-list cuing effect, the list-strength effect, various interference effects, and the Ross-Landauer results for spacing of repetitions.

Even though the SAM model has been applied to many results in the memory literature, there are still a number of issues that need to be dealt with. In this final section, I will discuss a few of these for which there are some preliminary ideas.

The Nature of the Units of Memory

The first issue concerns the nature of the units in memory. In the original SAM model for free recall, it was assumed that the units in memory, the memory images, corresponded to single words presented on the list. However, the SAM model does not restrict images to single words. Indeed, in our recent accounts of paired-associate recall, we have assumed that images correspond to the word pairs presented on the list. The nature of the units in memory is of course not an issue unique to the SAM model. Other theories will also, at some time, have to consider it.

In principle, then, the SAM model has great flexibility for representing memory images. Does this mean that there is complete freedom to choose whatever units one likes? The answer is, not surprisingly, no. Several constraints follow from the functional rules in the SAM model (Raaijmakers and Shiffrin 1981; Shiffrin et al. 1989). These constraints are

1. An image is unitized in the sense that the encoded information can be recovered from that image without further sampling.

2. Information encoded in other, nonsampled images does not contribute to the recovery process.

3. To recover the core information in an image other than the sampled one requires that image to be sampled on a subsequent retrieval attempt.

The general framework of the SAM model assumes that what gets stored in LTS is what gets attended to in STS. A corollary of this assumption is that the nature of the stored units depends on coding processes in STS. For example, if a subject focuses on sentences, the memory images might be sentences, whereas if the focus is on single words, the memory images would correspond to words. This does not deny that the images themselves might be structured in some way. For example, if they correspond to sentences, a complete theory might specify how specific words are retrieved from them. However, such retrieval is assumed to be qualitatively different from retrieval of the image itself. In SAM, retrieval of information from within an image is part of the recovery process and is independent of the information in the other, nonsampled memory images.

Shiffrin et al. (1989) describe some experiments to investigate the nature of the units in memory when subjects are presented at study with sentences and are cued at test with some words from those sentences to recall the remaining words. In their analysis, they not only investigated the nature of the units in memory but also the nature of the units in retrieval. The data clearly favored a model that posits the use of sentence-level units in storage and retrieval.

Semantic Memory

As described in this chapter, the SAM model has been applied to the major episodic memory paradigms. What has not been done yet is to a specify how the model would handle retrieval from semantic memory (e.g., in word-association tasks). Although a complete model has not yet been developed for this latter process, I would like to propose some ideas that may serve as a useful starting point.

The basic idea here is that semantic memory represents an accumulation of many specific episodic memories. That is, an episodic memory image is characterized by the inclusion of contextual information. Recalling a particular episodic image requires an appropriate context cue. However, if a particular association is stored in a large number of different contexts, its retrieval will become more or less independent of any specific contextual retrieval information. Hence, it will acquire "semantic" properties. Thus, a semantic association is not stored as one very strong image but is represented by a large number of images. This implies that the semantic-episodic distinction should be viewed as a continuum, with some associations completely context-bound, some completely context-free, and others in between. The extent to which an association is context-free would then depend not just on the total number of times it has been stored but also on the total number of different contexts in which it has been stored.

Retrieval of semantic associates would be context-free in more than one sense. First, they would tend to become activated regardless of the particular context at the time of retrieval. Second, even when context is not used as a cue, they would still be activated because retrieval probability depends simply on the relative number of images (more accurately, the strengths of the images) that incorporate them as opposed to other associations.

Such an account of semantic memory may be used to answer a criticism raised by Humphreys, Bain, and Pike (1989) against several memory models including the SAM model. This involves the so-called crossed associates problem, which stems from the fact that subjects do not suffer overwhelming interference when presented with a paired-associates list containing semantic associates in different pairs such as *bread-queen* and *king-butter*. Humphreys, Bain, and Pike claimed that SAM could not handle this result. According to them, the model would predict the retrieval of *butter* in response to the cue *bread*, since *butter* is strongly associated to both the context and the item cue.

This claim is not correct, however. In SAM, cues are associated to images, not to more or less abstract (semantic) representations of individual words. As a result, one possibility is that each memory image may correspond to a single word. We assume that semantic memory consists of a large number of episodic images. So the cue *bread* will be associated to a number of images containing the word *butter*, whether or not *butter* was on the list. If the pair *king-butter* was on the list, a new image containing *butter* will be formed. The cue *bread* will not be strongly associated to this image, since the image contains no interitem information with both *bread* and *butter*. The SAM model does not assume a single memory representation for *butter*. The strong preexperimental association between *bread* and *butter* is not due to one strong link between *bread* and *butter* but to the fact that both items have co-occurred many times and this information is reflected in a large number of images.

Another possibility is that each image corresponds to a pair of words. This is the usual assumption in SAM for lists of paired associates. In this case, the cue *bread* is associated to a number of preexisting images containing both *bread* and *butter* but not to the experimental image representing the pair *king-butter*. The result is that SAM does not predict strong interference. The explanation by SAM is in this case basically the same as that of Humphreys, Bain, and Pike.

Implicit Memory

Another topic that we have not yet dealt with is "implicit memory." One fruitful idea to explore with the SAM model is that tasks may differ in how much retrieval relies on the use of context cues. This idea, which is similar to one adopted by Humphreys, Bain, and Pike (1989), assumes that in implicit or indirect memory tasks, subjects do not rely much on specific contextual cues.

Even though context is not explicitly used as a cue, recent exposure to an item may still affect the probability of retrieval on a subsequent implicit memory test. For example, certain types of amnesic patients who show little or no memory on an explicit memory task perform quite well on implicit memory tasks (Graf and Schacter 1985; Moscovitch 1984). Such results might be explained by assuming that amnesics are impaired in the use of context information for retrieval. This implies that they will show impairments on explicit memory tests but much less on implicit tests, since on such tests, both amnesic and normal subjects do not explicitly use contextual retrieval cues.

This account of the amnesic deficit is still sketchy but has obvious similarities to many other explanations (see Squire and Butters 1984). In my view, a more adequate theoretical analysis, using formal modeling techniques, could prove very helpful in deciding between these various explanations.

20.6 CONCLUSION

The results reviewed in this chapter show that the SAM model provides a useful framework for the analysis of memory phenomena. Since SAM is based on the general two-store model described by Atkinson and Shiffrin (1968), one may conclude as well that the two-store model is far from obsolete, contrary to suggestions by some critics (e.g., Crowder 1982). The distinction between a temporary limited-capacity memory (active memory, working memory, or STS) and a more permanent memory (LTS) is an almost universal aspect of contemporary models of memory, even in ones that claim to be alternatives to a two-store model. Perhaps this stems from a requirement that any reasonable model of memory must have a way of retaining information for brief periods of time.

NOTES

I thank Jan Maarten Schraagen, Richard Shiffrin, Robert Nahinsky, Janet Metcalfe, Douglas Hintzman, and David Meyer for their comments and sugestions.

1. The observation that a levels-of-processing account is quite compatible with the STS/LTS framework has been made several times in the past (e.g., see Bjork 1975; Shiffrin 1977), although this does not seem to have had any influence on the typical textbook presentation.

2. A similar assumption is made by Humphreys, Bain, and Pike (1989).

REFERENCES

Anderson, J. R. (1981). Interference: The relationship between response latency and response accuracy. *Journal of Experimental Psychology: Human Learning and Memory, 7,* 326–343.

Atkinson, R. C., and Shiffrin, R. M. (1965). Mathematical models for memory and learning. Technical report 79. Institute for Mathematical Studies in Social Sciences, Stanford University.

Atkinson, R. C., and Shiffrin, R. M. (1968). Human memory: A proposed system and its control processes. In K. W. Spence and J. T. Spence (Eds.), *The psychology of learning and motivation: Advances in research and theory,* vol. 2, 742–775. New York: Academic Press.

Atkinson, R. C., and Shiffrin, R. M. (1971). The control of short-term memory. *Scientific American, 224,* 82–90.

Baddeley, A. D. (1983). Working memory. *Philosophical Transactions of the Royal Society of London, Series B, 302,* 237–436.

Baddeley, A. D., and Hitch, G. J. (1974). Working memory. In G. H. Bower (Ed.), *The psychology of learning and motivation: Advances in research and theory,* vol. 8, 742–775. New York: Academic Press.

Baddeley, A. D., and Hitch, G. J. (1977). Recency reexamined. In S. Dornic (Ed.), *Attention and Performance VI*, 647–667. Hillsdale, NJ: Erlbaum.

Bjork, R. A. (1975). Short-term storage: The ordered output of a central processor. In F. Restle, R. M. Shiffrin, N. J. Castellan, H. R. Lindman, and D. B. Pisoni (Eds.), *Cognitive theory*, vol. 1, 151–171. Hillsdale, NJ: Erlbaum.

Craik, F. I. M., and Lockhart, R. S. (1972). Levels of processing: A framework for memory research. *Journal of Verbal Learning and Verbal Behavior, 11*, 671–684.

Crowder, R. G. (1982). The demise of short-term memory. *Acta Psychologica, 50*, 291–323.

Dalezman, J. J. (1976). Effects of output order on immediate, delayed and final recall performance. *Journal of Experimental Psychology: Human Learning and Memory, 2*, 597–608.

Dark, V. J., and Loftus, G. R. (1976). The role of rehearsal in long-term memory performance. *Journal of Verbal Learning and Verbal Behavior, 15*, 479–490.

Estes, W. K. (1955). Statistical theory of spontaneous recovery and regression. *Psychological Review, 62*, 145–154.

Gillund, G., and Shiffrin, R. M. (1984). A retrieval model for both recognition and recall. *Psychological Review, 91*, 1–67.

Glanzer, M. (1977). Commentary on "Storage mechanisms in recall." In G. Bower (Ed.), *Human memory: Basic processes*, 115–124. New York: Academic Press.

Glenberg, A. M. (1976). Monotonic and nonmonotonic lag effects in paired-associate and recognition memory paradigms. *Journal of Verbal Learning and Verbal Behavior, 15*, 1–16.

Glenberg, A. M. (1979). Component-levels theory of the effects of spacing of repetitions on recall and recognition. *Memory and Cognition, 7*, 95–112.

Glenberg, A. M., and Smith, S. M. (1981). Spacing repetitions and solving problems are not the same. *Journal of Verbal Learning and Verbal Behavior, 20*, 110–119.

Godden, D. R., and Baddeley, A. D. (1975). Context-dependent memory in two natural environments: On land and underwater. *British Journal of Psychology, 66*, 325–331.

Graf, P., and Schacter, D. L. (1985). Implicit and explicit memory for new associations in normal and amnesic subjects. *Journal of Experimental Psychology: Learning, Memory, and Cognition, 11*, 501–518.

Gronlund, S. D., and Shiffrin, R. M. (1986). Retrieval strategies in recall of natural categories and categorized lists. *Journal of Experimental Psychology: Learning, Memory, and Cognition, 12*, 550–561.

Humphreys, M. S., Bain, J. D., and Pike, R. (1989). Different ways to cue a coherent memory system: A theory for episodic, semantic, and procedural tasks. *Psychological Review, 96*, 208–233.

Mensink, G. J., and Raaijmakers, J. G. W. (1988). A model for interference and forgetting. *Psychological Review, 95*, 434–455.

Mensink, G. J. M., and Raaijmakers, J. G. W. (1989). A model of contextual fluctuation. *Journal of Mathematical Psychology, 33*, 172–186.

Metcalfe, J., and Murdock, B. B. (1981). An encoding and retrieval model for single-trial free recall. *Journal of Verbal Learning and Verbal Behavior, 20*, 161–189.

Moscovitch, M. (1984). The sufficient conditions for demonstrating preserved memory in amnesia: A task analysis. In L. R. Squire and N. Butters (Eds.), *Neuropsychology of memory*, 104–114. New York: Guilford Press.

Mueller, C. W., and Watkins, M. J. (1977). Inhibition from part-set cuing: A cue-overload interpretation. *Journal of Verbal Learning and Verbal Behavior, 16*, 699–709.

Murdock, B. B., Jr. (1974). *Human memory: Theory and data*. Potomac, MD: Erlbaum.

Murnane, K., and Shiffrin, R. M. (1989). Word repetitions in sentence recognition. Research Report 8, Cognitive Science Program, Indiana University, Bloomington, IN.

Nelson, T. O. (1977). Repetition and depth of processing. *Journal of Verbal Learning and Verbal Behavior, 16*, 151–172.

Postman, L. (1975). Verbal learning and memory. *Annual Review of Psychology, 26*, 291–335.

Raaijmakers, J. G. W., and Shiffrin, R. M. (1980). SAM: A theory of probabilistic search of associative memory. In G. H. Bower (Ed.), *The psychology of learning and motivation: Advances in research and theory*, vol. 14, 207–262. New York: Academic Press.

Raaijmakers, J. G. W., and Shiffrin, R. M. (1981). Search of associative memory. *Psychological Review, 88*, 93–134.

Ratcliff, R., Clark, S., and Shiffrin, R. M. (1990). The list-strength effect: I. Data and discussion. *Journal of Experimental Psychology: Learning, Memory, and Cognition, 16*, 163–178.

Roediger, H. L., and Neely, J. H. (1982). Retrieval blocks in episodic and semantic memory. *Canadian Journal of Psychology, 36*, 231–242.

Ross, B. H., and Landauer, T. K. (1978). Memory for at least one of two items: test and failure of several theories of spacing effects. *Journal of Verbal Learning and Verbal Behavior, 17*, 669–680.

Rumelhart, D. E. (1967). The effects of interpresentation intervals on performance in a continuous paired-associate task. Technical report 16. Institute for mathematical studies in social sciences, Stanford University.

Schweickert, R., and Boruff, B. (1986). Short-term memory capacity: Magic number or magic spell? *Journal of Experimental Psychology: Learning, Memory, and Cognition, 12*, 419–425.

Shiffrin, R. M. (1975). Short-term store: The basis for a memory system. In F. Restle, R. M. Shiffrin, N. J. Castellan, H. Lindman, and D. B. Pisoni (Eds.), *Cognitive theory*, vol. 1, 193–218. Hillsdale, NJ: Erlbaum.

Shiffrin, R. M. (1976). Capacity limitations in information processing, attention and memory. In W. K. Estes (Ed.), *Handbook of learning and cognitive processes. Vol. 4: Memory processes*, 177–236. Hillsdale, NJ: Erlbaum.

Shiffrin, R. M. (1977). Commentary on "Human memory: A proposed system and its control processes." In G. Bower (Ed.), *Human memory: Basic processes*, 1–5. New York: Academic Press.

Shiffrin, R. M., Murnane, K., Gronlund, S., and Roth, M. (1989). On units of storage and retrieval. In C. Izawa (Ed.), *Current issues in cognitive processes: The Tulane Flowerree Symposium on cognition*, 25–68. Hillsdale, NJ: Erlbaum.

Shiffrin, R. M., Ratcliff, R., and Clark, S. (1990). The list-strength effect: II. Theoretical mechanisms. *Journal of Experimental Psychology: Learning, Memory, and Cognition, 16*, 179–195.

Smith, S. M. (1979). Remembering in and out of context. *Journal of Experimental Psychology: Human Learning and Memory, 5*, 460–471.

Squire, L. R., and Butters, N. (1984). *Neuropsychology of memory*. New York: Guilford Press.

Watkins, M. J. (1975). Inhibition in recall with extralist "cues." *Journal of Verbal Learning and Verbal Behavior, 14*, 294–303.

Watkins, M. J., and Watkins, O. C. (1976). Cue-overload theory and the method of interpolated attributes. *Bulletin of the Psychonomic Society, 7*, 289–291.

Whitten, W. B., II. (1978). Output interference and long-term serial position effects. *Journal of Experimental Psychology: Human Learning and Memory, 4,* 685–692.

Young, J. L. (1971). Reinforcement-test intervals in paired-associate learning. *Journal of Mathematical Psychology, 8,* 58–81.

21 Memory Retrieval with Two Cues: Think of Intersecting Sets

Michael S. Humphreys, Janet Wiles, and John D. Bain

The biennial Attention and Performance symposia have played a substantial role in the emergence of the information processing approach to cognition. There have been many benefits of this approach, including the shift away from stimulus-response analysis to underlying processes. However, this shift has not come without its costs (Watkins 1990), and the two with which we are most concerned are (1) deemphasis of the cue-dependent nature of trace access, and (2) overuse of search and decision processes (rather than direct access) in explanations of memory phenomena.

For example, Sternberg's (1966) proposal about a serial-exhaustive search has dominated thinking about how subjects identify items held in short-term memory. Search has also been proposed as a component of long-term recognition (Atkinson and Juola 1973) and as a means of lexical access (Forster and Bednall 1976). In the early 1970s several influential models of free recall emphasized search processes (e.g., Kintsch 1970).

In recent years there has been an increased emphasis on direct access. Nevertheless, search processes continue to be popular, especially when memory processes are of secondary concern as in models of impression formation (Srull and Wyer 1989) and mental addition (Widaman et al. 1989). Search processes are also popular in situations where cues are poorly specified as in models for the retrieval of historical or autobiographical memories (Brown 1990). More important, from the viewpoint of this chapter, search processes continue to be popular when information from two or more sources must be combined as in priming of lexical decisions (Becker 1985) and in cued recall with extralist cues (Nelson 1989).

In this chapter we argue for direct access as the most prevalent memory-retrieval process. Of course, we will not be able to reject search models universally. First of all, as Tulving (1976) has pointed out, many discussions of search have failed to distinguish between two very different kinds of search processes: rapid search through preecphoric (unconscious) memories and decisions applied to postecphoric (consciously retrieved) memories. As Tulving noted, there is universal agreement that postecphoric decision processes occur. The dispute is over whether rapid search processes occur that are not open to introspection. In addition, the idea of search coupled with a sophisticated decision mechanism is such a general-purpose computational device that it seems difficult to reject purely on behavioral grounds. Nevertheless, in our opinion, search models have not produced the kind of cross-paradigm generality that should be the goal of cognitive theories. Though explicit models of direct access are in their early stages of development, we will attempt to show that they may eventually produce this cross-paradigm generality. To do so, we first must distinguish between tasks that require three-way information (the cues have a joint history in relation to a retrieval target) and tasks that only require pairwise information (the cues have separate histories in relation to a retrieval target).

21.1 CUE HISTORY IN RELATION TO RETRIEVAL TARGETS

When pairs of cues are involved, some memory-retrieval tasks (cued recall with a list associate, production of an antonym, or recall of the meaning of an idiom) are purely recall tasks. That is, information linking the conjunction of the cues and the target (three-way information) has been stored and is used to retrieve the target. Other tasks (cued recall with an extralist associate, semantic priming, and lexical priming) require accessing information using novel combinations of cues. In the last mentioned tasks, pairwise information linking each cue separately to the target is used, not three-way information linking the cues and the target. In the following sections, we will first show how some tasks may be performed using pairwise information whereas other tasks require the use of three-way information. Search explanations are probably somewhat more common for tasks that use pairwise information than for tasks which use three-way information. Thus, for our argument, it is especially important to show that direct access will work for tasks that use pairwise information. With these tasks we can also show that a common direct-access mechanism is likely and a common search mechanism is unlikely.

Cues with Separate Histories

Our starting point is a discussion by Rubin and Wallace (1989) of how two cues might be combined to elicit a retrieval target. They asked whether the observed probability of producing a target T given two cues X and Y is expressible as a function of the pairwise probabilities of producing the target in response to the separate cues, using equation (1):

$$P(T|X \text{ and } Y) = f[P(T|X), P(T|Y)]. \tag{1}$$

To address this question, they examined the responses produced to combinations of weak category and rhyming cues, where a single target was contained in the intersection of the associative sets of targets subsumed under each of the two cues (e.g., *a mythical being that rhymes with post*). For these cue combinations, the average probabilities of producing the target in response to the definition and to the rhyming cue were estimated as .03 and .003, respectively. The probability of producing the target to the combination of the two cues was 1.0.

Humphreys, Wiles, and Bain

Rubin and Wallace also examined recall performance with stronger cues, where two or more targets were contained in the intersection of the cues' associative sets (e.g., *a four-footed animal that rhymes with spat*). In this latter case, the average probabilities of producing the target for the definition and for the rhyming cues were .29 and .25, respectively. However, the probability of producing the target in response to the combination of the two cues was only .74.

Rubin and Wallace (1989) therefore concluded that the joint probability (left side of equation (1) could not be written as a monotonic function of the separate probabilities. We agree with this conclusion. However, it does not follow from these results that more than pairwise cue-target relationships are involved in a subject's recall performance in this task. As Rubin and Wallace (1989) showed, the joint probability depends not just on the separate probabilities of producing the target for each of the two cues, but also on the number of targets in the intersection of the cue's associative sets. So we suggest a modification to equation (1) where the pairwise relationships between each cue and all possible targets are included, as expressed by equation (2):

$$P(T_i | X \text{ and } Y) = f[\{g(T_j, X), g(T_j, Y)\}]. \tag{2}$$

In equation (2) the function $g(T_i, X)$ represents the strength of the relationship between the cue X and the target T_i. When only a single cue is used, or when the contribution of the second cue does not differ between two targets T_i and T_j, the function g would have the characteristic that $P(T_i|X) > P(T_j|X)$ if and only if $g(T_i, X) > g(T_j, X)$. The function f is defined over the set of all possible targets T_j; it is a monotonically increasing function of $g(T_i|X)$ and $g(T_i|Y)$, a monotonically decreasing function of $g(T_j|X)$ and $g(T_j|Y)$, where $j \neq i$. In other words the joint probability of producing T_i given X and Y as cues would increase with the amount of evidence linking the separate cues to T_i and decrease with the amount of evidence linking the separate cues to targets other than T_i.

Equation (2) thus represents a generic way by which a pairwise associative memory could combine information from two cues. Before considering the kind of models that satisfy equation (2) and how such a memory could account for Rubin and Wallace's data, it will be instructive to consider phenomena that, by contrast, cannot be handled by pairwise associations.

Cues with a Joint History

When a subject studies a cue-target pair in an experimental list there is an obvious opportunity to learn three-way information about the occurrence of the pair in that list or context. Furthermore, it can be shown that this information is necessary to avoid massive negative transfer and retroactive interference in an *AB ABr* paradigm. In this paradigm, a subject first learns one list of pairs, and then learns a second list that contains repairings of the list-1 members resulting in each cue (*A*) having one target (*B*) in list 1 and a another target (*D*) in list 2. In addition both targets occur in both lists. The amount of negative transfer (slower learning of list 2) and retroactive interference (forgetting of list 1) produced by this paradigm is often compared to the amount produced by the *AB AD* paradigm (in which the cue terms are the same in list 1 and list 2, but the targets differ). For example, Jung (1962) reported that with a low level of list-1 learning, less negative transfer occurred in the *AB ABr* paradigm than in the *AB AD* paradigm. Barnes and Underwood (1959) found almost no difference in the amount of retroactive interference produced by the *AB ABr* and *AB AD* paradigms. The general assumption has been that this relative lack of interference stems from the greater availability of targets (stronger context-to-target associations) in the *AB ABr* paradigm.

We agree that context is involved, but wish to point out that context and the list cue cannot be used in the pairwise manner required by equation (2). The reason is that the pairwise relationships are the same between the hypothetical contextual cue and the list-1 and list-2 targets. With context "neutralized" in this way, performance should be a function of the strengths of the associations between the cue and each of the targets. However, the relatively small amounts of observed negative transfer and retroactive interference suggest that this does not happen. Targets strongly linked with the cue (the list-1 target during the initial stages of learning list 2, and the list-2 target when the subject is asked, after learning list 2, to recall list 1) are not always produced in preference to targets weakly linked to the cue. The same argument applies to the crossed-associates paradigm (Humphreys, Bain, and Pike 1989), which exemplifies an *AB ABr* paradigm where preexisting semantic associations serve as the list-1 associations.

What is required to learn an *AB ABr* and a crossed-associates paradigm is information about the occurrence of the cue and the target *in conjunction* with the list or experimental context. Humphreys, Bain, and Pike (1989) used the tensor product of three vectors representing the context, the cue, and the target to represent this information. It can also be represented if memories that are unique to the experimental context are stored. This difference between pairwise and three-way representations can be illustrated by considering two alternative interpretations of the SAM model (Raaijmakers and Shiffrin 1981; Shiffrin, Ratcliff, and Clark 1990). Suppose list 1 contains the pairs *AB* and *CD* and list 2 contains the pairs *AD* and *CB*. In one interpretation of the SAM model the image for a target does not change between presentations (Shiffrin, Ratcliff, and Clark 1990). If the image for the target is the same in list 1 and list 2, there would be a strong association between *A* and the image for *B* and between *A* and the image for *D*. There would also be strong and equal associations between the list-2 context and the images for both *B* and *D*. The probability of sampling the image for *B* is proportional to the product of the strengths of the associations between *A* and *B* and context and *B* ($S(A, B)S(X_2, B)$ where X_2 represents the list-2 context) and the probability of sampling the image for *D* is proportional to the product of the strengths of the associations between *A* and *D* and context and *D* ($S(A, D)S(X_2, D)$). This interpretation of the SAM model is subsumed under equation (2) because only pairwise information is available. Since the contextual association does not differentiate between the list-1 and the list-2 target it (wrongly) predicts substantial negative transfer and retroactive interference. As we will show later, this interpretation of the SAM model is essentially equivalent to the model we propose for cued recall with an extralist associate.

In a second version of the SAM model, different images for the targets are stored for each list (Raaijmakers and Shiffrin, 1981). In this version of the model when we cue with A and the list-2 context the probability of retrieving the list-2 image for D is proportional to the product of two strong associations $(S(A, D_2)S(X_2, D_2)$, where D_2 is the list-2 image for D). However, the probabilities of retrieving the list-1 image for B or the list-2 image for B are both proportional to the product of one strong and one weak association, $S(A, B_1)$ $S(X_2, B_1)$ and $S(A, B_2)S(X_2, B_2)$, respectively. Thus, in principle, this version of the SAM model can learn an AB ABr or a crossed-associates paradigm without large amounts of negative transfer and retroactive interference. It can do this because the image of the target is unique to each list and the sampling probability is a function of the strength of the associations between cues and these episodically unique images (rather than cue-to-target strengths). Thus, it is not compatible with equation (2).

Another example involving the use of three-way information comes from Selz (translated in Mandler and Mandler 1964). He asked how a subject could produce the antonym of a word such as *dark* when the strength of the association between *dark* and *night* equals the strength of the association between *dark* and *light*, and both *night* and *light* are antonyms, though not of each other. This question was raised as an argument against associationism, but we can now see it as an argument against treating the concept of an antonym as a cue and combining it with another cue as in equation (2). In essence, Selz's argument boils down to the assertion that the pairwise relationships between the cues and the targets are equal. That is, $g(light, dark) = g(night, dark)$, and $g(light, antonym) = g(night, antonym)$. Under these conditions equation (2) predicts that the probability of producing *light* as the response to the cues *dark* and *antonym* should equal the probability of producing *night* as the response to the same cues. However, this prediction is clearly wrong, invalidating the assumption that antonym production can be explained by pairwise relationships. Indeed it seems likely that the concept of antonym cannot be treated as a cue which can be used separately from other cues. A labeled association (Anderson and Bower 1973) is one way to represent this.

Similarly, retrieving the meaning of an idiom such as *hot dog* probably requires using information about the three-way relationship between the cues and the target (the meaning). One way to do this is to treat *hot dog* as a "unified" representation, not as a pair of cues.

21.2 DIRECT ACCESS OF ASSOCIATIVE-SET INTERSECTIONS FOR CUES WITH SEPARATE HISTORIES

Given this distinction between pairwise and three-way information we can now consider the kinds of models that can solve the Rubin and Wallace (1989) task. Their demonstration that two weak cues can produce a stronger joint effect than obtained with two moderate cues does not require information about the three-way relationship between the two cues and the target. Instead, as we will show, the only requirement is a mechanism that retrieves the intersection of the two cues' associative sets. This could be accomplished with search, but Wiles et al. (1990) have shown that it can be accomplished in a direct-access connectionist model as well.

One constraint imposed by Wiles et al. (1990) in their demonstrations was that word cues must be represented either simultaneously or sequentially on the same set of units. They did this because if two word cues are represented on different sets of units, it would also be necessary to store the same association in different sets of connections. Given this constraint the most robust model (the one least sensitive to the number of cues and to assumptions about associative strengths and thresholds) was a multiplicative model with sequential use of cues.

This model was adopted for the case where both cues are words and for all other cases (e.g., a word plus a part-word cue) as well. Here the presentation of the first cue (e.g., *a mythical being*) is assumed to activate the representations of all of the targets associated with it. Then the second cue (e.g., *rhymes with post*) is presented and it also activates the representations of all targets associated with it. The activation produced by the second cue multiplies the activation remaining from the presentation of the first cue. This yields strongly activated representations of the target or targets associated with both cues, while representations of targets only associated with one of the cues are suppressed.

When a local representation is used (that is, each cue and target is represented by a single node in the network), it is easy to show that this process results in the activation of the intersection of the associative sets. Because subjects are assumed to split their responses among the activated set of targets, the likelihood of recalling a particular target will depend on the number of targets in the intersection. Thus, this model is incompatible with equation (1). However, it is compatible with equation (2) because only pairwise information is used. The probability of producing a target increases with the strength of the relationship between the cues and the target, and decreases with the strength of the relationship between the cues and other targets.

With a distributed representation additional processes are required to retrieve the associative intersection (Wiles et al. 1990). This is because when the representations of the targets overlap to a significant extent, spurious intersections are created. Still, most of the complications introduced by these additional processes can be avoided by using a sparse distributed representation. In our simulations of this model a small number of randomly chosen units are set equal to 1.0 and all the other units are set equal to .00 (Humphreys et al. 1990). With these assumptions most of the words that are in one associative set and not the other will be suppressed. However, there is still some overlap in the representations of words so there will be some noise in our retrieval process. The amount of noise will depend on the amount of overlap (the average number of active units) and the product of the number of targets in the two associative sets. Each target in one set has a chance of overlapping with each target in the other set, so the total number of potential spurious overlaps equals the number of targets in the first set times the number of targets in the second minus the number of true overlaps. The potential for multiple targets to be in the intersection, and the presence of noise from spurious overlaps, require a procedure to select a particular response. For example, a specialized module might be employed to suppress units that do not form part of a coherent pattern and to turn on units that do.

In the next sections, we will discuss the cues used in semantic retrieval, semantic priming, lexical priming, cued recall, and recognition showing that the retrieval of the intersection of two sets can plausibly account for results from all these paradigms. We will also show that search explanations for these paradigms are cumbersome and inconsistent across paradigms. Another relevant issue concerns whether or not subjects may have a significant opportunity to acquire information about the joint occurrence of the two cues with the target. The occurrence of such an opportunity would not preclude the use of pairwise (cue-target) associations, as in our sequential-activation model, but the absence of it does rule out competing models in some paradigms.

21.3 APPLICATIONS OF THE SEQUENTIAL-ACTIVATION MODEL

Semantic Retrieval

The task used by Rubin and Wallace (1989), in which subjects were given a definition and an ending cue to retrieve a target, is one example of a semantic-retrieval task. As already indicated, we agree with Rubin and Wallace that the two cues are used jointly for retrieval. This possibility is consistent with our sequential-activation model.

However, another possibility must be considered as well. Rubin and Wallace's subjects may have generated multiple responses to one of the cues, checking whether each response was consistent with the other cue (a variant of search and decision). For example, in informal demonstrations, we have noted that some individuals suppress the response *ghost* because they regard it as a supernatural, not a mythical being. As Tulving (1976) has pointed out, however, introspective support for such a decision process does not also support a high-speed search through preecphoric memories. It is the latter kind of search that would be required in this situation, because subjects would probably have to generate many instances to one of the cues if they were to have a reasonable probability of producing *ghost* (given the very low estimated probabilities of producing the target in response to either of the separate cues). In our view the direct-access mechanisms of our sequential-activation model are more plausible than such a high-speed, covert search/generation process.

Semantic Priming

When subjects are unable to answer a general knowledge question, they can still, with above chance accuracy, indicate their likelihood of being able to recognize the correct answer (Hart 1967). Nelson, Gerler, and Narens (1984) used a priming paradigm to explore this "feeling of knowing" (FOK). They first collected FOK judgments and then presented their subjects with the question, followed by a brief display of the answer, which in turn was followed by a visual mask. Under these presentation conditions, the answer would not have been identifiable when presented by itself. Nevertheless, the presentation of the masked answer increased the probability that it would be produced in response to the question. This result also depended on the FOK rating. Subjects were more likely to benefit from the presentation of the masked answer if they had indicated on the prior test that they thought they would be able to recognize the answer.

All that is required to explain this result is the assumption that the FOK rating reflects the subject's general familiarity with the subject matter of the question; we do not have to assume that subjects are aware of the contents of a partially retrieved answer although that may occur occasionally. If the subjects are familiar with the subject matter there is likely to be some association between the cue and the answer. When such an association exists, the answer will be in the intersection of the target sets produced by the question and the masked answer.

By contrast to a direct access process, a search process capable of explaining this result would have to be even faster and more complicated than the one required to explain Rubin and Wallace's (1989) results. There is so little information provided by the masked presentation of the answer that it is unlikely to be used to generate possible hypotheses to be compared with the question. Likewise there may not be enough information in the masked answer to facilitate selection of an answer from possibilities generated to the question.

Lexical Priming

Under this subhead we first consider the relationship between our model and Morton's (1969) logogen model for the identification of a physically degraded word in context. We then consider the relationship between these models and Ratcliff and McKoon's (1988) compound-cue theory for priming in a lexical decision task.

In the logogen model, the prime activates a set of related logogens. These logogens stay activated for a limited amount of time, preserving the information derived from the prime. In our model, this corresponds to the activation of all the associates of the first cue. In the logogen model, when the target word is presented the information derived from it summates with the persisting activation of the logogens. If a logogen exceeds threshold, it fires and all other logogens are suppressed. In our model, for each output unit, we multiply the activation produced by the second cue by the activation remaining from the presentation of the first cue. This process selects the intersection of the set activated by the prime and the set activated by the sensory information.

Morton (1969) did not indicate that an objective of his theory was to select the intersection of the items activated by the prime and the items activated by the sensory information. Furthermore, his choice of parameter values for the mathematical model of his theory does not produce a close approximation to this intersection because he set the residual strength between the sensory information and items other than the target item equal to 1.0. In his multiplicative model, this value will not suppress an item that is strongly activated by the prime. However, McClelland and O'Regan (1981) discuss a version of the logogen model that is specifically designed to focus on this intersection. In their version items that are activated by the prime but not the target or vice versa are suppressed, leaving only the item that is activated by both. Thus, both McClelland and O'Regan's version of the logogen model and our sequential-activation model can be seen to be using information activated by the prime to suppress the noise in the representation that is produced by a physically degraded word.

Our sequential-activation model can also be used for semantic pair recognition (a decision is required about whether two words such as *train* and *black* are related). Here the set activated by one member of the pair is intersected with the representation of the other member of the pair. If the two words have a preexisting associative relationship, the second word will be in the associative set of the first word and the intersection will be nonempty. There are two basic options for making a decision about whether or not the intersection is nonempty. One option is to base this decision on the total amount of activation (the sum of the activity levels for all units). In our sequential-intersection model, this is identical to the dot product that was used for pair recognition in the Matrix model (Humphreys et al. 1989). The other option is to use some measure of the coherency of the pattern. For example, the decision might be based on the time needed for the cleaning-up process to stabilize.

This ability to conceptualize both the use of context to suppress noise and pair recognition as intersections links Ratcliff and McKoon's (1988) cue-combination model with the logogen and our sequential-activation model. Ratcliff and McKoon used the pair-recognition process proposed by Gillund and Shiffrin (1984) to model priming in lexical decision. However, they did not explain why a pair-recognition process would be used for primed lexical decisions. We believe the answer to this question comes from thinking in terms of intersections. That is, when one thinks in this fashion, Ratcliff and McKoon's pair-recognition process can be seen to be an extension of the process that people normally use to identify a physically degraded word in context.

To demonstrate this relationship between these models we start with Raaijmakers and Shiffrin's (1981) explanation of why they used a product rule in their retrieval model. Their justification was that it allowed the retrieval cues to focus on images that were subsumed under all the cues. Furthermore, they set the residual value between a cue and an unrelated image to .02 so images that are subsumed under one cue but not another cue are suppressed. The pair-recognition process proposed by Gillund and Shiffrin (1984) follows from this work. It sums across all cross-product terms to produce an overall measure of familiarity or matching strength. Although Gillund and Shiffrin (1984) did not present their model in these terms, it can also be thought of as a measure of the total amount of activation in the intersection (this interpretation would require minor modifications to the recognition equation in order to indicate which item is being intersected with the associative set of the other item). Thus, identifying a noisy word in context and a primed lexical decision can be seen to involve the same retrieval process. They differ, in that word identification requires the selection of a response from the pattern of activity in the intersection whereas primed lexical decision requires a judgment about whether or not the intersection is empty.

For primed lexical decisions, the total amount of activation in the intersection may be a relatively crude measure of whether a word or a nonword is present. In some situations (e.g., the nonwords are very wordlike and there is little time pressure) a decision based on the coherency of the pattern in the intersection may be better. It appears to be possible to implement this within our framework and it should also be possible to do it within the SAM framework. In the latter case, the decision would be based on the retrieval of an image (Gillund and Shiffrin 1984).

It is also possible in our framework to distinguish between similarity relationships and associative relationships (Humphreys, Bain, and Pike 1989; Humphreys et al. 1990). For lexical priming, the most important implication of this distinction concerns the difference between identity priming (where the target is the same as the prime) and associative priming (where the target is an associate of the prime). In identity priming, we assume that only a representation of the prime has to be active, whereas in associative priming we assume that a representation of the prime has to activate its associates. The extra step required with associative priming suggests that it may be more subject to strategic influences than is identity priming.

Burt (1990) has provided some evidence supporting this conjecture. She studied both identity and associative priming using Warren's (1972) version of the Stroop task. In keeping with Warren, she found that associative priming slows color naming. However, this only occurs if subjects are required to remember the prime or to make a lexical decision about it, but not if they simply have to read it. Unlike in previous work (McClain 1983), Burt found that identity priming speeds color naming and that this occurs regardless of how the subjects have to process the prime. These results establish that there is a difference between identity and associative priming; identity priming is less subject to strategic influences than is associative priming.

Further support for a distinction between identity and associative priming has been provided by Snow and Neely (1987). They reported that including a large number of identity primes in the lexical decision task reduced associative priming. Apparently the large number of identical primes reduced a bias towards using the prime as a retrieval cue.

Although the SAM framework has some difficulties in representing both associative and similarity relationships (this issue will be discussed later) it can probably accommodate the difference between identity and associative priming. To do so requires that the use of the self-association (the association from an item to an image of that item) and of interitem associations be treated as control processes. This would be similar to our use of an item to activate its own representation or to activate representations of its associates.

Cued Recall with an Extralist Associate

Perhaps the most popular explanation for cued recall with an extralist associate (the cue is a preexisting associate of the target but was not studied with the target in the list) has been to treat it as being the same as cued recall with a list associate (the cue and the target were studied together in the list). For this treatment to work it must be assumed that the three-way association is stored: that is, the subject must *covertly* generate the cue (encode the relationship between the cue and the target) while studying the target in the experimental context (Tulving and Thomson 1973). This appears to be the explanation proposed by Raaijmakers and Shiffrin (1981) for the use of category cues. It is certainly plausible that such an encoding process occurs in a categorized list, especially if the items within a category are presented in a block. However, it is less plausible with associative cues, for which there are a large number of possible cue-target relationships and the target may not even elicit the cue in free association (Humphreys and Gailbraith 1975).

In addition to the implausibility of the encoding assumption we can now see that three-way information linking the cue, the target, and the context is not necessary. Instead, the use of pairwise information to access the intersection of the list and the associative set of the cue is all that is required. This alternative not only explains the basic phenomenon, namely that strong preexisting associates are effective as extralist retrieval cues, but also many of the findings of Nelson and his colleagues (Nelson 1989; Nelson and McEvoy 1979; Nelson, McEvoy, and Friedrich 1982).

The general procedure of Nelson and his colleagues involves having large numbers of subjects free-associate to word cues, produce a category instance for taxonomic labels, and produce a rhyme for both word and ending cues. From these data, they have calculated the relative number of subjects producing a target in response to a given cue (the associative strength). They have also calculated the number of different targets produced for a given cue (the cue set size). Cued-recall performance has been assessed by providing a unique extralist, rhyme, or ending cue for each item in a study list, with the instruction to use the cue to help recall a word from the list. There are three well-replicated results from this procedure that concern us now:

1. Cued recall is an increasing function of associative strength to the target for ending, extralist associate, taxonomic, and rhyme cues.

2. Among the nonsemantic cues, ending cues are more effective than rhyming cues even when target strength and cue set size are controlled.

3. Cued recall is inversely related to the cue set size for ending, extralist associate, taxonomic, and rhyming cues.

Our sequential-activation model can easily explain these results. It assumes that a representation of the experimental setting is used as a cue along with the nominal cue (the word, rhyme, or ending supplied by the experimenter). The result is the retrieval of the intersection of the list and the associative set of the cue so that the probability of retrieving the target is greater than the associative strength with the nominal cue (the probability of producing the target to the cue in free or controlled association).

Better cued recall with endings than with rhymes presumably indicates that there is a tendency for rhyme cues to elicit associates which interfere with recall. In a direct test of this idea, Nelson, McEvoy, and Friedrich (1982) had subjects study either a rhyme and an associate of each test cue, or just a single target for each cue. Studying two targets produced interference in the retrieval of rhymes when the test required the subjects to switch between retrieving rhymes and associates. There was no interference. however, when the test required the subject to use all the cues to retrieve rhymes. Most important, this finding shows that subjects in cued-recall experiments have difficulty in suppressing the retrieval of associates to word cues just as do subjects in priming experiments.

Our explanation for the cue set size effect in cued recall is also straightforward. Even when the experimenter has arranged conditions so there is only a single target in the intersection of the associative sets of two cues (e.g., context and a part-word cue), the amount of noise in the system will be a function of the product of the total number of targets in the two associative sets and recall will be degraded accordingly. That is, with a sparse representation, the representation of each target in one set has some chance of overlapping with the representation of each target in the other set. The amount of noise in the system will depend on the total number of these spurious intersections. This noise may block the production of the item that is in the intersection of the associative sets and it may even result in the retrieval of a word that was not in the list. Of course, an increase in list length would also increase the number of spurious intersections. Thus, our explanation for the cue set size effect is the same as our explanation for the list-length effect.

We also predict a list-strength effect (Ratcliff, Clark, and Shiffrin 1990; Shiffrin, Ratcliff, and Clark 1990). That is, if the context-to-item associations are strengthened for some items in a list (they are presented more often or for a longer period of time) the probability of recalling the strengthened items should increase and the probability of recalling the nonstrengthened items should decrease. To understand how this occurs, consider the situation where the context-to-item association is strengthened for *every* item in the list. Here we will have increased the activation of both the signal and noise component in the intersection by the same amount. In fact, the model predicts that there will be no improvement in performance in this case unless a probabilistic learning rule is used or the increase in associative strength between the context and the list items reduces noise from previous memories. In contrast, if context-to-item associations are strengthened for *some* items and a non-strengthened (weak) item is cued, there will be an increase in the noise component of the intersection without a corresponding increase in the signal component resulting in poorer performance for the weak items, relative to the case where all items are weak (the list-strength effect).

Our model also predicts an increase in interference when the target and an interfering word have similar representations as compared to a situation where they have dissimilar representations. At this time we do not have a compelling example of such an effect. However, Tehan (1991) reported a finding that may be explicable in terms of target similarity, plus assumptions about the temporal course of interference. Tehan examined interference effects using cues in a short-term memory paradigm. His procedure requires subjects to study two four-item lists. He then cues, either immediately or after a two-second filled delay, for one of the list-2 words. In different experiments, the cue has been either a taxonomic cue (*tool* is used as a cue for *wrench*) or an ending cue (*_ench* is used as a cue for *wrench*). In addition, proactive interference is manipulated by the presence or absence of an associate of the cue in list 1 (*hammer* is the interfering word for the taxonomic cue *tool* and *bench* is the interfering word for the ending cue *_ench*). He finds that proactive interference is stronger for ending cues, especially on an immediate test.

To explain this finding, we assume that on the immediate test the context cue elicits a strong representation of the list-2 target and a weaker representation of the list-1 interfering word, as well as representations of other items in the lists. The representations of the target and the interfering word are assumed to be more nearly equal after a delay, producing the increase in interference in the delay conditions. The taxonomic and ending cues are also assumed to elicit representations that include both the target and the interfering word. On an immediate test, when the intersection of these two associative sets is taken, there should be a strong representation of the target and a weaker representation of the interfering word. When the representations of the target and the interfering word have a large number of common units (e.g., they have the same ending), then the burden of discrimination will fall on a few unique elements. If some of these unique elements are corrupted by the noise then the retrieval of the target may be blocked and the interfering word may even be produced. Thus, there should be more interference with greater amounts of overlap in the representations of the target and the interfering word.

As we have indicated, the SAM framework can be used to construct a model for cued recall with an extralist associate using pairwise information that is very similar to our model. When an extralist cue and a context cue are used, the multiplicative rule in the SAM model will focus the retrieval process on those items that are in the associative set of the cue and are in the list. The cross-product terms, between items subsumed under one cue but not the other, will produce noise just as do spurious intersections in our model. The predictions for these two models with respect to cue set size, list length, and list-strength effects should be almost identical.

However, the two frameworks are not identical in all respects. In particular, it may not be possible to introduce a target-similarity effect into the SAM model. In addition, the use of both episodically unique and pairwise information causes problems for the SAM model. For example, if episodically unique images are used in the SAM model, then an explanation for the association between the extralist cue and the image is required. On the other hand, if only pairwise information is used, then an explanation for cued recall with a list associate is required. If both pairwise and episodically unique information are to be represented in the SAM model, there will have to be a theory about when a repetition produces the same image and when it produces a different image. In our framework (Humphreys, Bain, and Pike 1989) we can store an episodically unique memory (the tensor product of the context, the list cue, and the list target vectors) and extract both episodically unique information (the cue is the vector product of the context and list cue) or pairwise information (the list cue alone is used as a cue).

Thus far we have shown that cued recall with an extralist or a part-word cue plausibly involves the use of two cues with separate histories relative to the target. The next point to consider is whether these cues are used together for (direct) memory access, or whether they are only combined at a later decision stage that is preceded by a search process.

There are two possibilities here. One is that subjects *search* through the *list* until they find a word that that is related (e.g., rhymes with or is associated with) the cue. Although such a possibility often appeals to psychologists working with other paradigms, it is not being considered seriously by those working with cued recall. There are several reasons for this. Firstly, a list-search process explains neither the cue set size effect nor the fact that some rhyme cues are better than other rhyme cues (e.g., the accuracy of the decision that *bench* has the ending *ench* should not depend on the number of different words with that ending). Secondly, cued recall seems to be very different from free recall: cued recall is frequently better than free recall (Bilodeau, Fox, and Blick 1963); serial-position effects are often very different (Humphreys 1976); and free recall takes a substantial amount of time, whereas cued recall can be quite rapid.

Another possibility is that the search process may start with the cue. That is, subjects may *generate associates* to the cue, selecting one that they recognize as having occurred on the list (generation recognition). However, most psychologists working with cued recall also find this possibility implausible. In our view, there are even more reasons for rejecting generation recognition as an important part of cued recall than were available when Tulving (1976) wrote his classic critique of it.

The most important addition to the argument is that we now have an example of a retrieval task in which an increase in performance occurs without a postretrieval recognition check. Subjects who are asked, after a study trial, to complete a part-word cue with the first word that comes to mind produce a studied word at an above-baseline rate. If these subjects are following instructions, then the study experience must have affected memory access, not a postaccess process. Moreover, if we have to assume an effect on memory access in one situation (production instructions), then it is certainly plausible that there is such an effect in other situations (cued-recall instructions).

Evidence against a major role for generation recognition in cued-recall performance also comes from a study by Jacoby and Hollingshead (1990). They used word stems as cues and directly compared cued-recall, generate-recognize, and stem-completion instructions. Some of the word stems could be completed with an old word and some could not. The probability of completing one of the new stems was .94 for the stem-completion instructions, .48 for the cued-recall instructions and .14 for the generate-recognize instructions. They also found significant interactions between their instructional conditions and study conditions that differentially affected the retrieval and recognition processes. They concluded that subjects who were given cued-recall instructions "often output items as recalled without benefit of a recognition check" (Jacoby and Hollingshead 1990, 445).

A complete generation-recognition theory would also have to explain how list memories are isolated from preexisting memories and why recognition cues directly access memories while endings or extralist associates do not. Note that theories of lexical access frequently assume that sensory cues, which may be similar to ending cues, provide direct access to lexical memories. Thus it may not be possible to develop a coherent account of both cued recall and lexical access using search concepts.

Recognition

There are only two components to a recognition memory (context and the item) so, by default, only pairwise information is available. In our model for recognition we take the intersection of the representation of the to-be-recognized item and the associative set of the context cue. A decision about whether or not the item was in the list is then based either on the total amount of activity in the intersection or on a measure of how wordlike it is (the coherency of the pattern in the intersection). The former corresponds to the decision process used in both the Matrix model (Humphreys et al. 1989) and in the SAM model (Gillund and Shiffrin 1984).

On the other hand, basing the decision on the coherency of the pattern in the intersection is attractive because Ratcliff, Clark, and Shiffrin (1990) have reported that there is no list-strength effect for recognition. That is, strengthening some items in a list does not appear to weaken the ability to discriminate between nonstrengthened items and new items. Repeating some items will not make the intersection between the list and a new item more wordlike; it will simply increase the activation of units that are already active. That is, if the intersection between the list and a new item contains k active units before a word is repeated it will still contain only k active units after a word is repeated. If subjects require $k + 1$ active units before they will say that an intersection contains a word then there will be no effect on discriminability.

21.4 CONCLUSIONS

We have distinguished between memory tasks that require the use of three-way information (e.g., cued recall with a list associate, production of an antonym, or recall of the meaning of an idiom) and tasks that may be solved using only pairwise information (e.g., the retrieval of a word in response to a combination of a definition and rhyming cue, semantic and lexical priming, cued recall with an extralist associate, and recognition). We have shown that the solution to the tasks that use pairwise information can be viewed as finding the intersection of two sets. This conclusion is independent of the algorithm that is used to find the intersection. It can be found using our sequential-activation model, the SAM model, or via search, among other ways.

There are three corollaries to the proposal that these tasks are intersection tasks. The first is based on the assumption that, for any biological organism, memory codes will not be perfectly orthogonal. The consequence is that in an intersection task there will be noise produced by the relationships between the items in one set and the items in the other set. In a multiplicative model, such as our sequential-activation model, noise will also be produced by cross-product terms, even if the representations are orthogonal. Thus, it seems very likely that a major component of the noise in these tasks will come about through the interactions of the items in the two sets.

The second corollary is that, in accordance with task demands, a cue can either activate its own representation or the representation of items associated with it. The third corollary is that some tasks require the selection of a response from the noisy intersection, whereas others require a judgment about whether or not the intersection is nonempty.

In modeling psychological processes, it will be necessary to go beyond this computational analysis to specify the memory representations and the algorithms that operate on those representations. This will be difficult because it should be possible to create a search model, a connectionist model, or a SAM-based model that fits the data for almost any task. We doubt, however, that search will produce a coherent explanation of these tasks. The problem is not just in the different search rates that would have to be postulated. A theory based on search would also have to provide a coherent account of the noise in the system and why some cues can and others cannot directly access memories. We think that the prospects of producing a coherent account are better for the other two approaches, which are generally similar. There are, however, some advantages to our connectionist framework as compared to the SAM framework. These include the demonstrated ability to incorporate both three-way (episodically unique) and pairwise information in the same memory and to accommodate target-similarity effects.

NOTE

This work was supported from a grant from the Australian Research Council to the authors. We would like to thank J. S. Burt, J. L. McClelland, D. E. Meyer, and J. G. W. Raaijmakers for their helpful comments.

REFERENCES

Anderson, J. R., and Bower, G. H. (1973). *Human associative memory*. Washington, DC: V. H. Winston & Sons.

Atkinson, R. C., and Juola, J. F. (1973). Factors influencing speed and accuracy of word recognition. In S. Kornblum (Ed.), *Attention and performance IV*, 583–612. New York: Academic Press.

Barnes, J. M., and Underwood, B. J. (1959). "Fate" of first-list associations in transfer theory. *Journal of Experimental Psychology, 58*, 97–105.

Becker, C. A. (1985). What do we really know about semantic context effects during reading? In D. Besner, T. G. Waller, and E. H. MacKinnon (Eds.) *Reading research: Advances in theory and practice*, vol. 5, 125–166. Toronto: Academic Press.

Bilodeau, E. A., Fox, P. W., and Blick, K. A. (1963). Simulated verbal recall and analysis of sources of recall. *Journal of Verbal Learning and Verbal Behavior, 2*, 422–428.

Brown, N. R. (1990). Organization of public events in long-term memory. *Journal of Experimental Psychology: General, 119*, 297–314.

Burt, J. S. (1990). Identity priming produces facilitation in a colour naming task. Unpublished manuscript, University of Queensland.

Forster, K. I., and Bednall, E. S. (1976). Terminating and exhaustive search in lexical access. *Memory & Cognition, 4*, 53–61.

Gillund, G., and Shiffrin, R. M. (1984). A retrieval model for both recognition and recall. *Psychological Review, 91*, 1–67.

Hart, J. T. (1967). Second-try recall, recognition, and the memory-monitoring process. *Journal of Educational Psychology, 58*, 193–197.

Humphreys, M. S. (1976). Frequency and recency in cued recall: Interaction of old and new learning. *Journal of Experimental Psychology: Human Learning and Memory, 2*, 413–422.

Humphreys, M. S., Bain, J. D., and Pike, R. (1989). Different ways to cue a coherent memory system: A theory for episodic, semantic and procedural tasks. *Psychological Review, 96*, 208–233.

Humphreys, M. S., Burt, J., Bain, J. D., and Dennis, S. J. (1990). The distributed representation of words. Paper presented at the conference on The Connectionist Approach to Memory, Reasoning, and Language, University of Queensland, August.

Humphreys, M. S., and Gailbraith, R. C. (1975). Forward and backward associations in cued recall: Predictions from the encoding specificity principle. *Journal of Experimental Psychology: Human Learning and Memory, 1*, 702–710.

Humphreys, M. S., Pike, R., Bain, J. D., and Tehan, G. (1989). Global matching: A comparison of the SAM, Minerva II, Matrix, and TODAM models. *Journal of Mathematical Psychology, 33*, 36–67.

Jacoby, L. L., and Hollingshead, A. (1990). Toward a generate/recognize model of performance on direct and indirect tests of memory. *Journal of Memory and Language, 29*, 433–454.

Jung, J. (1962). Transfer of training as a function of degree of first-list learning. *Journal of Verbal Learning and Verbal Behavior, 1,* 197–199.

Kintsch, W. (1970). Models for free recall and recognition. In D. A. Norman (Ed.). *Models of human memory,* 333–373. New York: Academic Press.

McClain, L. (1983). Color priming affects Stroop interference. *Perceptual and Motor Skills, 56,* 643–651.

McClelland, J. L., and O'Regan, J. K. (1981). Expectations increase the benefit derived from parafoveal visual information in reading words aloud. *Journal of Experimental Psychology: Human Perception and Performance, 7,* 634–644.

Mandler, J. M., and Mandler, G. (1964). *Thinking: From association to gestalt.* New York: Wiley.

Morton, J. (1969). Interaction of information in word recognition. *Psychological Review, 76,* 165–178.

Nelson, D. L. (1989). Implicitly activated knowledge and memory. In C. Izawa (Ed.). *Current Issues in Cognitive Psychology: The Tulane Flowerree Symposium on Cognition,* 369–388. Hillsdale, NJ: Erlbaum.

Nelson, D. L., and McEvoy, C. L. (1979). Encoding context and set size. *Journal of Experimental Psychology: Human Learning and Memory, 5,* 292–314.

Nelson, D. L., McEvoy, C. L., and Friedrich, M. A. (1982). Extralist cueing and retrieval inhibition. *Journal of Experimental Psychology: Learning, Memory, and Cognition, 8,* 89–105.

Nelson, T. O., Gerler, D., and Narens, L. (1984). Accuracy of feeling of knowing judgments for predicting perceptual identification and relearning. *Journal of Experimental Psychology: General, 113,* 282–300.

Raaijmakers, J. G. W., and Shiffrin, R. M. (1981). Search of associative memory. *Psychological Review, 88,* 93–134.

Ratcliff, R., and McKoon, G. (1988). A retrieval theory of priming in memory. *Psychological Review, 95,* 385–408.

Ratcliff, R., Clark, S. E., and Shiffrin, R. M. (1990). List-strength effect I: Data and discussion. *Journal of Experimental Psychology: Learning, Memory, and Cognition, 16,* 163–178.

Rubin, D. C., and Wallace, W. T. (1989). Rhyme and reason: Analysis of dual retrieval cues. *Journal of Experimental Psychology: Learning, Memory, and Cognition, 15,* 698–709.

Shiffrin, R. M., Ratcliff, R., and Clark, S. E. (1990). List-strength effect II: Theoretical Mechanisms. *Journal of Experimental Psychology: Learning, Memory, and Cognition, 16,* 179–195.

Snow, N., and Neely, J. H. (1987). Reduction of semantic priming from inclusion of physically or nominally related prime-target pairs. Paper presented at the 28th Annual Meeting of the Psychonomic Society, Seattle, WA, November.

Srull, T. K., and Wyer, R. S., Jr. (1989). Person memory and judgement. *Psychological Review, 96,* 58–83.

Sternberg, S. (1966). High speed scanning in human memory. *Science, 153,* 652–654.

Tehan, G. (1991). A cueing framework for short-term recall. Ph.D. diss., University of Queensland.

Tulving, E. (1976). Ecphoric processes in recall and recognition. In J. Brown (Ed.). *Recall and Recognition.* London: Wiley.

Tulving, E., and Thomson, D. M. (1973). Encoding specificity and retrieval processes in episodic memory. *Psychological Review, 80,* 352–373.

Warren, R. E. (1972). Stimulus encoding and memory. *Journal of Experimental Psychology, 94,* 90–100.

Watkins, M. J. (1990). Mediationism and the obfuscation of memory. *American Psychologist, 45,* 328–335.

Widaman, K. F., Geary, D. C., Cormier, P., and Little, T. D. (1989). A componential model for mental addition. *Journal of Experimental Psychology: Learning, Memory, and Cognition, 15,* 898–919.

Wiles, J., Humphreys, M. S., Bain, J. D., and Dennis, S. J. (1990). Control combinations and cue combinations in a connectionist model of human memory. Department of Computer Science Technical Report #186, University of Queensland.

22 Learning and Memory: Progress and Challenge

Henry L. Roediger III

22.1 LEARNING AND MEMORY: PROGRESS AND CHALLENGE

The chapters on learning and memory in this volume provide a balance between the strengths of traditional approaches to these topics in experimental psychology and the innovations that we have witnessed in the past twenty-five years through cognitive science and neuroscience. As Hintzman forcefully points out here, the field has been dominated by the cognitive revolution, whose origins date from around the same time as the Attention and Performance symposium series began. After Hintzman's provocative tutorial review (chap. 16), the other contributions in *Attention and Performance XIV* can be divided into two groups, with two chapters on mathematical/computer simulation models of learning and memory (chaps. 20 and 21), and three on cognitive neuropsychology (chaps. 17, 18, 19). My selection as the discussant of these particular chapters may be considered somewhat unusual, because I think that I am widely known as having never contributed to either the mathematical psychology/computational modeling approach or the neuropsychology of memory. Perhaps I can be impartial as a result, if not especially informed.

22.2 THE COGNITIVE REVOLUTION

Hintzman's tutorial review (see chap. 16) of the cognitive revolution's influence on the field of learning and memory makes compelling reading. Many topics that seemed banished from human experimental psychology, such as transfer of training, have recently returned to the fore. Hintzman argues that in many (maybe most) cases the revolutionaries went too far. This argument may have some merit, but certainly the cognitive revolution opened up the field to topics, ideas, and approaches that were largely absent from the discipline of human experimental psychology before the revolt.

Historians of science may marvel at the cognitive revolution for many reasons; whatever else it accomplished, it certainly has been a public relations bonanza. Currently North American universities are racing against one another to establish programs in cognitive science. The race is so swift that one wonders whether the university administrators have a good grasp on exactly what the field represents. Indeed, I am not sure I have a good grasp, because cognitive science has many different meanings even for those in the field; it ranges from single-cell recording in behavioral neuroscience, through experimental/cognitive psychology, to anthropology, linguistics, computer science, and philosophy (Gardner 1985). Unfortunately, as my colleague Michael Watkins (1991) points out, one should be suspicious of any field that feels a need to append *science* to its name. In many cases, such as *culinary science, social science, creation science*, or *Christian science*, the appellation indicates that the field is none too sure of its scientific status. Similarly, contemporary cognitive science encompasses all sorts of fanciful ideas drawn from many disciplines, and at the moment the field seems incoherent, with opposing views battling among one another for acceptability.

Given this state of affairs, Hintzman is surely right that many theoretical concepts, such as schemas, scripts, MOPS, and so forth, are vague and have added little precision to our thinking. In my opinion, we have seen few original ideas about the mind develop from modern cognitive science. By this I mean ideas that might have made (say) William James raise his eyebrows. (According to Hintzman, James even had a connectionist model). Presumably this is where experimental cognitive psychologists can make a contribution. The genius of experimental psychologists has been in creating clever laboratory techniques to study vague concepts and to make them more precise. Virtually all fields of cognitive science are informed by hard-won insights from the experimentalists' laboratories. One scenario for the next twenty-five years is that cognitive psychologists may take the speculative ideas decried by Hintzman and turn them into concrete, testable, laboratory phenomena. Careful experimental analyses, in the end, could yet carry the day and cement the success (or failure) of the cognitive revolution. I now turn to some observations on the two areas represented by the chapters, memory models and neuropsychological approaches to memory.

22.3 MEMORY THEORIES

The contributions by Raaijmakers (chap. 20) and Humphreys, Wiles, and Bain (chap. 21) illustrate well the types of memory theories available to modern cognitive psychologists. Raaijmakers does a great service by resurrecting the traditional two-store model of memory and showing how many of its alleged problems evaporate if the formulation of Atkinson and Shiffrin (1968) is carefully applied. He makes a good case that the "standard" version of the model rejected by many researchers was oversimplified. Part of the reason for this oversimplification may be that several versions of the two-store model became amalgamated as the "modal model" (Murdock 1974). Although Raaijmakers (chap. 20) writes as if Atkinson and Shiffrin invented the two-store model, there were other developments before them (Crowder 1976). The models of Waugh and Norman (1965) and Glanzer and Cunitz (1966) preceded the Atkinson and Shiffrin (1968) theory and its briefer, more popularized version (Atkinson and Shiffrin 1971). It seems to me that the empirical complaints and contradictions registered against "two-store theory" are apt when applied to the other (simpler) versions and to what became known as the modal model, even if they do not apply to the full-blown 1968 version.

Nevertheless, the two-store model has been one of the theoretical success stories in the past twenty-five years. This fact, combined with the reflective mood occasioned by the Silver Jubilee of the Attention and Performance series, leads me to ask: What other theories have been particularly successful over the same time span? To answer this question, we must first define what we mean by a theory and by a theory's success. By a theory, I mean any set of coherent conceptual ideas designed (in this context) to account for phenomena of learning and memory. By successful, I mean that people used it, talked about it, did research on it—in short, that it guided the field.

These criteria are certainly not incontestable, but if adopted they lead to one interesting conclusion: the levels of processing framework may be cognitive psychology's most successful theory of learning and memory over the past twenty-five years. Craik and Lockhart (1972), drawing on ideas prevalent in the study of attention (Treisman 1964) and on experimental observations provided by Jenkins and his collaborators (e.g., Hyde and Jenkins 1969; Jenkins 1974) "suggested that the memory trace could be thought of simply as the record of those analyses that had been carried out primarily for the purposes of perception and comprehension and that deeper, more semantic, analyses yielded records that were more durable" (Lockhart and Craik 1990, 88). This idea, and its corollaries, are my candidate for the most successful theory.

Now, at this point, many readers may think I have taken leave of my senses. After all, the levels of processing framework came in for some of the most stinging criticism of the last twenty-five years, applied by T. O. Nelson (1977), Eysenck (1978), Baddeley (1978), D. L. Nelson (1979), and Kolers (1979), among many others (see Cermak and Craik 1979). Isn't this the theory that was variously charged as (a) vague, (b) circular, (c) untestable, (d) tautological, and (e) empirically wrong? (Never mind that some of these charges—such as being untestable and empirically wrong—are mutually contradictory and yet were raised by the same critic.) Yes, this is precisely the theory I nominate.

My criterion for success is amount of use, indexed by citations. Since 1972 the original Craik and Lockhart (1972) paper has been cited 1,758 times, through 1989, in the *Social Sciences Citation Index*. The cumulative citations are shown in figure 22.1, compared to citations of two other influential works published at about the same time (Anderson and Bower's 1973 book on human associative memory and Tulving's 1972 chapter on the distinction between episodic and semantic memory). Even though these other contributions were are highly influential, the cumulative citations to the levels of processing paper greatly outpace the other contributions. In fact, I suspect that only Miller's (1956) "magical number 7 $\pm$ 2" paper comes close to being as heavily cited in the field.[1]

A complete analysis of the reasons for the success of the levels of processing theory would be interesting. Among my hypotheses are the following: The theory was simple, having few postulates; it was directly applicable to experi-

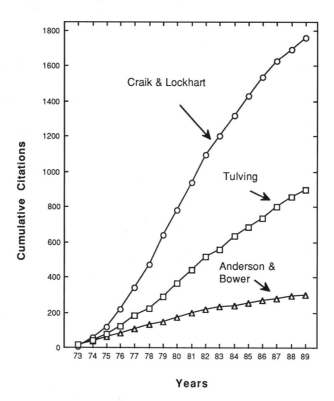

Figure 22.1 Cumulative citations to three important theoretical statements made in 1972 or 1973.

mental data; it proposed a new framework, emphasizing processing over memory structure; it had implications for other fields, such as educational psychology and developmental psychology; the experimental techniques needed for investigations within the framework were straightforward; and finally, the theory was at least partly wrong, and showing this is always fun. Only a handful of years after the theory had been proposed, enough evidence had been collected to show how it did not hold for some types of memory tests (e.g., Morris, Bransford, and Franks 1977; see also Fisher and Craik 1977, and McDaniel, Friedman, and Bourne 1978). The theory gave way in some quarters to an approach known as transfer appropriate processing (Morris Bransford, and Franks 1977; Stein 1978), which has been widely influential in explaining differences found on various memory tests (e.g., Blaxton 1989).

Perhaps the main flaw of the levels-of processing framework was that it was too simple. It was a main effect theory—deep processing is better than shallow processing—and thus it could not account for interactions between study and test. In addition, levels-of-processing was a pure encoding theory and neglected retrieval processes. These related deficits are rectified in the newer transfer-appropriate processing approaches. However, what is praiseworthy in the original "levels" approach is that the theory started off by making straightforward assumptions that were closely tied to experimental operations.

Table 22.1 Ten Parameters of the Original (1981) SAM Model

a	context-cue-to-image strength
b	word-cue-to-image strength
c	word-cue-to-self-image strength
d	residual-word-cue-to-image strength
e	context-to-image increment
f	word-cue-to-image increment
g	word-cue-to-self-image increment
Kmax	total failure stopping criterion
Lmax	stopping criterion for a word cue
r	buffer size

It is informative to contrast a theory like levels of processing with those outlined in some of the present chapters. For example, the successor to the two-store theory is Raaijmakers and Shiffrin's (1980, 1981) SAM model, which has been elaborated in various directions in the past decade, including Raaijmakers's current chapter (see chap. 20). The virtues of the SAM model are several. It is clearly articulated, it relies on traditional (popular) assumptions about associative storage and memory search, it attempts to explain data from many paradigms, and it has been applied to both recall and recognition. The model has been quite influential; certainly I have used it (albeit in a qualitative fashion) in my own work (e.g., Roediger et al. 1982; Roediger and Neely 1982). SAM, however, has some drawbacks. These include (at least to my way of thinking) the model's complexity and the fact that most of its constructs are not tied to direct observables, and in principle probably cannot be.

Listed in table 22.1 are the ten parameters of the original SAM model (Raaijmakers and Shiffrin 1981). There are probably another half dozen by now, but these will suffice to make the point. The first four represent different aspects of memory strength, the next three refer to types of enhancement owing to retrieval from memory, then two more correspond to different stopping rules for when search is terminated, and so forth. These do not exhaust the model's constructs, even in the 1981 version, because other important processes are not represented as formal parameters (see fig. 22.2 for a schematic outline of retrieval processes in the model). One such is the concept of *rechecking*. After search has been completed (K_{max} been reached), then the subject is assumed to use each previously recalled word and its context in an attempt to recall more words. Words recalled during rechecking are used for further rechecking, and so on.

An interesting property of the hypothetical constructs listed in table 22.1 and shown in figure 22.2 is that few are tied to observable behavior. There is, and probably cannot be, an external check on the reality of the model's operation at the level of individual processes. All the parameters operate together to produce probability of recall or recognition, or some other overall performance measure. The performance measure is affected by manipulation

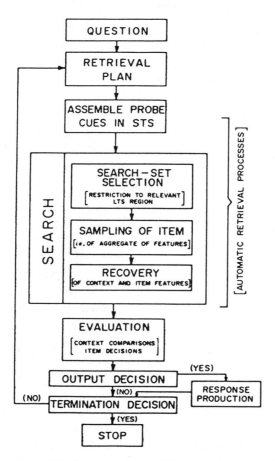

Figure 22.2 The phases of retrieval instantiated in the SAM model. All these processes, and the parameters listed in table 22.1, combine in leading to "response production," the only observable consequence and the only reality check in the model's operation.

of some independent variable and its operation can be accounted for in various ways by the model, but usually the model is rich enough to explain observed effects in several different ways. Raaijmakers (chap. 20) notes that such is the case for the phenomenon of part-list cueing inhibition (Slamecka 1968); with the plethora of hypothetical mechanisms, the phenomenon can be explained in several different ways. Determining the plausibility of any particular version of the SAM model is usually accomplished by computer simulations, not by examining subjects' performance. If some overall difference in recall is explained within the model by appealing (say) to the c parameter (residual-word-cue-to-image-strength), there is no way to test this assumption against behavior, because no behavioral index for the parameter exists.

In the 1950s, when experimental psychologists were first gingerly reintroducing hypothetical constructs to explain behavior, such constructs were carefully tied to a set of measuring operations; ideally, a set of experimental operations should converge on the construct (Garner, Hake, and Ericksen 1956). Such an idea seems quaint today, where modern "cognitive scientists" introduce constructs such as schemas, MOPS, and so forth on little better than introspective grounds, a development that Hintzman (chap. 16) properly deplores. However, it seems to me that the same charge can be made against some of the computer simulation/mathematical models of learning and memory that he favors. Their constructs may be realized in a concrete fashion in computer programs, but they are not similarly tied to observable behavior. Given the richness of the models, some way can usually be found to accommodate unexpected experimental results. The models' complexities often make true testability all but impossible. For example, the retrieval assumptions built into Raaijmakers's (chap. 20) SAM model are built on the idea of memory search; on the other hand, Humphreys, Wiles, and Bain (chap. 21) assume that search is not needed and that cues provide "direct access" to memories. Despite starting from diametrically opposite assumptions, both models account well for many of the same data. This leads me to suspect that the complexity of the models prevents a direct test of their basic competing assumptions.

Today at least some behaviorists are willing to admit hypothetical constructs into explanations of behavior; indeed, some argue that even behavioristic concepts such as reinforcement are in a sense no less hypothetical (e.g., Williams 1986). Yet behaviorists still follow the dictum of William of Occam, "Entities should not be multiplied unnecessarily." Occam's razor has been dulled or lost in modern cognitive psychology of most any variety. Consider, for example, the second of five "guiding principles" of the original SAM model: "Long term memory is a richly interconnected network, with numerous levels, frames and associations. Roughly speaking, all elements of memory are connected to all others, directly or indirectly (though perhaps quite weakly)" (Raaijmakers and Shiffrin 1981, 120). In fact, in some ways the approach used in SAM is the opposite of Occam's—the mind is stuffed with numerous mechanisms and these are abandoned only if and when they are not needed. Raaijmakers and Shiffrin (1981) state this explicitly in defending the number of parameters in their model. It is worth quoting a few lines of their logic:

At first glance, 10 parameters seems quite a high number to fit the results from free recall studies, especially since Shiffrin (1970) used a much simpler search model with just three parameters to fit a great deal of free recall data. This objection is ameliorated by the following factors. We can show that most of the present parameters, and their precise values, are not essential for the fit of the model to most of the data. The parameters are listed above for generality, even though some are never varied and others are equated before fits to the data are begun. Some of the parameters are given nonzero values and included in the fit merely to demonstrate that the presence of the processes they represent will not harm the ability of the model to predict the data. In fact, we have set many of these parameters to zero, and no harm to the model's predictions has resulted. However, each of these parameters represents processes that we feel are needed on logical grounds, or needed to deal with data that will not be discussed in detail in this article. (Pp. 97–98)

The logic, then, is to introduce numerous hypothetical mechanisms into the mind for potential explanatory function and then abandon them if they are not needed. In fairness, the unused parameters in one situation may become critical in another, but this leads back to the question of the model's overall testability at the level of individual processes. If an experimental result is explained by (say) appealing to a greater degree of a certain type of "incrementing" in one experimental condition rather than another, one would ideally like to have a behavioral index of the assumed change to check the theory. However, in most cases, no such index exists.

I have quite possibly overstated the problems with the SAM model (and by extension, other complex models) in the foregoing paragraphs. After all, the model is tied to the aggregate behavior of the subjects and not all parameters in models need necessarily to correspond to psychological constructs to be realized (even potentially) in behavior. However, at least for my tastes, there is a high number of explanatory concepts and parameters that are only indirectly tied to subjects' behavior.

A decade ago I advocated the following: "At a bare minimum, it should be necessary before proposing any mental construct to specify the operations by which the construct can be observed, or at least to point to several lines of evidence that support the usefulness of the construct. It seems fair to say that even this simple requirement would eliminate a great proportion of the theoretical hypothetical mechanisms discussed in cognitive psychology, which are now often introduced on intuitive, logical, or rational grounds" (Roediger 1980, 244). Surveying the current scene, it is apparent that few have heeded this advice. But at some point we must return to ground our observations more directly in behavior, or else quite literally be accused of producing nonsense models and theories. In advocating the use of computer simulation models, Hintzman (1990) noted that "to have one's hunches about how a simple combination of processes will behave repeatedly dashed by one's own computer program is a humbling experience that no experimental psychologist should miss" (111).

I am sure this is a bracing experience, but I would prefer cognitive psychologists to have the experience of having their theoretical ideas dashed on the shoals of behavioral evidence. Of course, both experiences could occur, yet at the moment computer simulation/mathematical modelers seem more concerned with introducing constructs that can be realized in computer programs and in equations than in supplying constructs that correspond to behavior. Certainly I am all for mathematical/computer simulation models, if the constructs put into those models are realized concretely in behavior. Hintzman (1991) provides an excellent case for formal modeling in psychology. Formal models have proved invaluable in other sciences and have greatly advanced understanding in many areas of psychology—sensation, perception, animal learning, and others. We can hope for the same happy outcome in the study of learning and memory, but this state of affairs seems unlikely to occur until modelers employ fewer constructs more directly tied to behavior.

The levels-of-processing framework was simple relative to fancy modern models, but it captured the imagination of a generation of researchers who disputed, tested, refined, and extended it. It led to great progress in the field. Raaijmakers (chap. 20) believes that "it is unfortunate that proponents of the levels-of-processing framework have never put their model in a quantitative form" (470). Actually, it is probably fortunate for all of us that they did not. Extraneous processes added in realizing the theory in a computer simulation may have greatly weakened its testability, so that its defects would likely not have been uncovered so easily. Formal models are often credited with greater testability through their precision, but this seems only to be the case when the models' constructs are grounded firmly in behavior. Although it is popular to call for mathematical, computer-simulation models, a case could be made for the reverse: at the present state of our knowledge about memory, we are better off proposing straightforward verbal theories that make direct predictions and that are closely tied to behavior in experimental paradigms. These theories excite researchers, lead to clever experiments, and advance the field more quickly. Levels-of-processing is a good example. Only a few years after it was proposed, the deficiencies in the theory were clearly identified by reference to behavioral evidence, and we knew conditions to which the theory applied as well as its limitations (see Lockhart and Craik 1990).

22.4 COGNITIVE NEUROPSYCHOLOGY OF MEMORY

A popular theme of this Silver Jubilee symposium has been to wonder what reaction a Rip van Winkle might have upon awakening after a twenty-five-year hiatus and viewing the contemporary scene. The answer for a cognitive psychologist interested in learning and memory would be clear: the influence of cognitive neuropsychology would startle old Rip. The idea of using brain-damaged patients to discover important principles and processes in memory was as foreign in 1965 as is tying theoretical constructs to observable behavior today. In his 1975 *Annual Review of Psychology* chapter, in a section on two-store theories, Postman wrote: "We have not considered the results obtained with brain-damaged patients which continue to be cited as evidence for dual-process theory.... The existing data do not strike us as unequivocal; more important, extrapolations from pathological deficits to the structure of normal memory are of uncertain validity" (1975, 308). Most experimental psychologists probably agreed with Postman's assertions then.

Today the situation is quite different. It is no longer the case that neuropsychologists take a cognitive paradigm that is five years old and see how patients of various sorts perform on it. Now advances in cognitive neuropsychology often lead experimental psychologists to new insights and in new directions, as has happened in the study of implicit memory (Schacter 1987). The contributions by Squire et al. (chap. 17) by Howard and Franklin (chap. 18), and by Sartori, Job, and Coltheart (chap. 19) represent excellent examples of the best research in this field, dealing (respectively) with short-term memory, long-term memory, and general knowledge systems. However, the logic of extrapolating results from "pathological deficits" to normal memory functioning remains a vexing issue.

My own knowledge of this field is much greater than it was only a short while ago, owing to my coteaching a seminar on cognitive neuropsychology with a colleague, Randi Martin. Besides numerous journal articles, the primary sources for the course were excellent books by Ellis and Young (1988) and by Shallice (1988). The knowledge gained was edifying, but I must admit to feeling, occasionally, a bit like Alice, having slipped into a wonderland that was not so different as to be unrecognizable for a traditional cognitive/experimental psychologist, but that was off-kilter enough to seem a bit strange, nonetheless. I strived to comprehend terms like *neologistic jargonaphasia* and was led to wonder if the theorist inventing the name didn't suffer from the disease.

Besides terminology, the practices of these psychologists are a bit different, too. Important research is known by the initials of the patients involved (J.S., H.M., K.F., K.C., etc.) rather than (or in addition to) the names of the authors of the reports about them. (Learning to associate patients' initials with the experimental results and conclusions drawn from them lends ecological validity to the often maligned tactic of studying associative processes with nonsense syllables.) Also, despite the *neuro* in cognitive neuropsychology, many leading practitioners of this approach really do not care much about neural processes or even their localization. Brain damage is treated as a powerful "independent" variable and its effects are observed in a more or less functional analysis. (More properly, the manipulation should be considered a subject variable, being out of experimental control and hence correlational in nature). On the other hand, neuropsychologists interested in memory are much more likely to be interested in neural processes and in localization of function than are those who study the neuropsychology of language, as exemplified by Squire et al.'s (chapter 17) chapter describing the neural circuitry of declarative memory.

The chapter by Howard and Franklin (chap. 18) provides an excellent analysis of impairments of short-term memory and their interpretation. Following others, especially Monsell (1987), these authors argue for "the claim that the auditory-verbal short-term memory is not a separate system, but is rather an emergent property of systems used in the comprehension and production of spoken language" (428). In particular, the data from patients D.R.B. and M.K. are interpreted as further evidence for separate input and output phonological stores that operate in comprehending and speaking, respectively.

Patient data such as those reported by Howard and Franklin speak importantly to the role of short-term memory in language use. Another series of studies on this issue was conducted by my colleague Martin (1990). She recently studied two interesting cases that also bear on the role of short-term memory in comprehending and speaking. Short-term memory (as measured by memory span and other related tasks) has generally been considered to be essential for understanding speech, for reading, and (through the phonological output buffer) for speaking, as implied in the quote above. Martin's (1990) results call these assumptions into question, because her patients have very impaired short-term memory abilities by the usual measures (such as memory span), yet nonetheless perform at normal levels on many language comprehension tasks, especially those involving complex syntax. Subjects often cannot repeat words back but are shown to understand them perfectly well on other measures. The repetition difficulties cannot be ascribed to difficulties with an output buffer, because at least one of the patients speaks fluently.

If traditional articulatory/phonological short-term memory is not essential for language comprehension and production, as Martin's data suggest, then what function does it serve? Following Gardner (1974) and others, Martin (1990) suggests that short-term memory plays a critical role in language acquisition, because children may need to repeat words after hearing them in order for language learning to progress. She writes: "Thus, the child may have a need to hang on to a phonological representation of a sentence longer than an adult while trying to derive the underlying meaning. If so, then the phonological memory abilities of an adult may represent the residual of a system that was once vital to language processing but that only comes into play in exceptional situations in adult language" (Martin 1990, 424). Of course, remembering telephone numbers and other instances requiring verbatim repetition are not *that* exceptional in adult life—we probably need to repeat something verbatim fairly frequently. Nonetheless, cognitive psychologists may well have overestimated the role of short-term memory in language comprehension. This is the sort of insight that can be derived from cognitive neuropsychological analyses of patients with impaired short-term memories, but which seems unlikely to have emerged from studies of normals where the critical role of short-term memory in cognition (and especially language processing) has generally gone unquestioned.

Raaijmakers (chap. 20) defends the two-store theory of yesteryear, but it is clear that, as with Postman (1975), the neuropsychological evidence has not influenced his thinking on this point. The idea of two stores in cognitive neuropsychology is as extinct as the dodo. As Howard and Franklin (chap. 18) argue, we need two stores (the phonological input and output buffers) just for verbal short-term memory. Turning to Squire et al.'s (chap. 17) description of memory as embodied in their figure 22.7, we see some thirteen different stores or systems (assuming each entry is so counted), and Squire et al. do not even treat the short-term memory systems in this scheme. In a recent review (Roediger 1990), I counted some twenty to twenty-five stores or systems based mostly on neuropsychological evidence, so perhaps in a few years someone will have to defend the twenty-two-store model.

Squire's theory, both in this volume and elsewhere, serves the important function of reminding us that many forms of learning and memory exist simultaneously in the organism and all should be studied. A few cognitive psychologists, in particular, have expressed the belief that nothing much has been (or could be) gained in understanding human cognition from studying animal learning and memory (e.g., Lachman, Lachman, and Butterfield 1979; Neisser 1978). Squire et al.'s (chap. 17) and Hintzman's (chap. 16) contributions in this volume provide convincing reminders to the contrary.

Returning to the issue of theory in cognitive neuropsychology, even a quick glance at the field shows that the number of memory stores or systems postulated by neuropsychologists is growing at a rapid pace, fueled by the discovery of numerous dissociations between measures of memory as a function of subject variables (such as brain damage or age) and of variables under experimental control. Elsewhere I have argued that we need to adhere to more rigorous criteria for postulating systems or stores, with converging evidence for such ideas (Roediger, Rajaram, and Srinivas 1990). I will not rehearse those arguments here, but note instead that we certainly have excellent evidence for at least one such system, which Squire et al. (chap. 17) refer to as the declarative-episodic system. We have converging evidence from animal work (e.g., Mishkin and Appenzeller 1987), and from numerous patients with hippocampal damage (e.g., H.M., as studied by Milner, Corkin, and Teuber 1968, and the many newer data cited by Squire et al. (chap. 17) with other patients). The neural pathways involved are well worked out, at least relative to neural underpinnings of other putative memory systems, which are largely unknown.

There is still debate about whether damage to the limbic system impairs semantic memory as well as episodic memory. Squire et al. (chap. 17) maintain that the semantic system is impaired by damage to the hippocampus and related structures, because amnesic patients never show normal learning of meaningful facts after their injuries. On the other hand, Tulving, Hayman, and MacDonald (1991) maintain that semantic memory is at least partially (and perhaps completely) spared, because amnesic patients show intact priming of semantic information in some paradigms. Tulving, Hayman, and MacDonald's patient, K.C., showed intact semantic priming from multiple exposures of information a year after learning, although he had no conscious recollection of the learning episodes. Presumably Squire et al. would attribute this feat to a "semantic priming" subsystem of nondeclarative memory, but this leads to the puzzle of how one could obtain intact semantic priming with a gravely damaged declarative/semantic system. It is just these sorts of problems that should lead us to be cautious about postulating some new system to solve every theoretical difficulty.

I predict that the coming years will see the "discovery" of many more memory systems, unless we agree upon tightened criteria. At the moment, the primary requirement is to produce experimental observations in which a measure that seems plausibly to reflect one system is dissociated from a measure that seems to reflect a different system. The dissociation can occur a function of either a subject variable or an independent variable under experimental control. Such observations underlie the proposed collection of systems seen on the right-hand side of Squire et al.'s figure 17.7. Sherry and Schacter (1987) have proposed stricter criteria for postulating memory systems, but their recommendations have not been adopted by students of the field.

If we continue to use the traditional dissociation criteria for proposing memory systems, then we may soon have (if we don't already) an overabundance of such systems identified with memory. To confirm my prediction of increasing systems, I will add one more possible memory system, with some supporting evidence: the female reproductive system. Obstetricians and nurses have long noted a phenomenon that we may call *reproductive priming*, the fact that labor proceeds more quickly when women bear later children than when they bear their first child. I discovered the form of priming reflecting this new memory system on May 22, 1986, when my daughter Rebecca was born. I noticed that events were moving much more rapidly than they had during the birth of my son, 14 months earlier. Upon my inquiring, the nurse told me that labor for second children usually occurs more rapidly than for first children. "Priming," I thought. Sure enough, my daughter was born after two hours of labor, whereas my son had been born after eight hours, constituting a savings of six hours. Now a six-hour priming effect is obviously something to be taken seriously (it represents 21,600,000 milliseconds for those of you accustomed to working with faster reaction times), so I have investigated the matter more closely. Reproductive priming is a real phenomenon, I have discovered, and data exist documenting the effect over large samples of women.

Presented in table 22.2 are data based on a textbook on labor and its clinical management (Friedman 1978). They are based on a large sample of women giving birth either for the first time or for a subsequent time. The figures are divided into a latent phase (dilation of the cervix) and an active phase (the rapid finish of dilation and the descent of the fetus). The data given are for women experiencing no complications during labor and represent means and standard deviations of the latencies for the two phases of labor, as well as a composite number. (Adding births in which there were complications lengthens the times and increases the variability, but the relation between numbers remains.) The data clearly show priming in both the latent and active phases of labor, with a composite showing just under three hours of reproductive priming.

Table 22.2 Selected Data on Duration of Labor for First-Born and Latter-Born Children during Labors in which There Were No Medical Complications (mean data are presented in hours, with standard deviations in parentheses)

	Phase of Labor		
	Latent	Active	Total
First born	6.1	3.4	9.5
	(4.0)	(1.5)	
Later born	4.5	2.1	6.6
	(4.2)	(2.0)	
Savings	1.6	1.3	2.9

Adapted from data in table 3 (p. 49) of *Labor: Clinical evaluation and management* by E. A. Friedman. New York: Appleton-Century-Crofts, 1978.

One might therefore claim that reproductive priming reflects the operation of a subsystem of procedural memory, the female reproductive system. As far as I can tell, the data supporting this claim meet most of the criteria suggested by Sherry and Schacter (1987) for postulation of memory systems, such as functional incompatibility of operation between this system and others (i.e., they evolved for different reasons). Surely the underlying neural and physical systems that lead to this kind of priming are quite distinct from those that produce, say, episodic memory and perceptual priming. So using the broad definition of memory suggested by Tulving (1983, 7)—"Memory has to do with the after-effects of stimulation at one time that manifest themselves subsequently at another time"—reproductive priming would clearly seem to be an instance of memory.

Some may object to calling the female reproductive system a memory system, but is there any essential difference between reproductive priming and many of the phenomena studied under the rubric of implicit memory, such as learning of motor skills, adaptation-level effects, McCollough effects, or, for that matter, perceptual priming (see Benzing and Squire 1989; Corkin 1968; Savoy and Gabrieli 1991)? I think not, because all these phenomena meet the broad definition of memory cited above. However, if all persisting "after-effects of stimulation" are to be classified as memory, then most biological systems possess memories—the circulatory system, the respiratory system, the perceptual system, the immune system, and so forth. To avoid the Pandora's box created by this fact, perhaps we need to define memory more narrowly, to encompass only the hippocampally mediated system, and then simply note that most cognitive and biological systems show priming, the facilitating effects of a process on its later reapplication.

The fractioning of knowledge systems is the focus of the chapter by Sartori, Job, and Coltheart (chap. 19). They explore another fascinating new set of problems, dissociations between different forms of knowledge. In particular, they present cases supporting a distinction between specific perceptual knowledge and more general (amodal) knowledge. This evidence converges nicely with other proposals maintaining that certain types of priming depend on a structural description system (Schacter 1990). It would be interesting to test the patients Dante and Michelangelo on various types of priming tasks, including ones requiring the word-form system, the structural description system, and the semantic system. The analysis of knowledge systems through neuropsychological analyses are just beginning, but the early dividends as reported here are quite interesting. These studies may even provide new life to the study of semantic memory in normal subjects, a field noted by Hintzman to be dormant. (Making up names for patients, as Sartori, Job, and Coltheart do, also strikes me as an important advance over use of initials, as it renders the information more memorable.)

In the course I taught with Martin, we covered many different topics, and the authors of our texts dutifully provided information-processing models (with boxes and arrows) for different parts of the cognitive system (reading, talking, remembering, etc.). However, none of the authors ever put together all the parts into a coherent cognitive system, which led us to wonder what such a system would be like. Therefore, we assigned a term project to our students in which they had to design a model of the mind from the perspective of contemporary cognitive neuropsychology.

I think our students enjoyed this task, especially since it was apparently unprecedented in the field. Such model building can be a lot of fun. We received projects on large poster boards, others on large sheets of paper, and in some cases the sheets were hooked together with tape. Figure 22.3 displays the model proposed by Ed Cuttrell (1990), a perspicacious undergraduate in the course. I include it here to provide a flavor of what the mind is like in

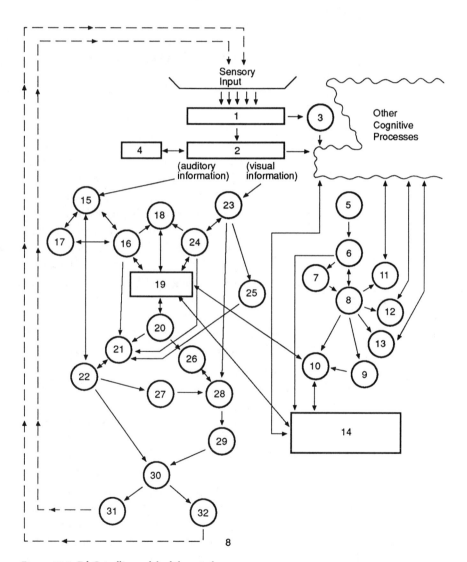

Figure 22.3 Ed Cutrell's model of the mind.

contemporary cognitive neuropsychology; Cuttrell was the only student able to confine his model to a single $8\frac{1}{2}'' \times 11''$ sheet of paper. Each box represents a store (or system or module) and arrows indicate information flow. The numbers in the boxes refer to a legend, not presented here, in which the names of the various modules are provided. For example, 16 is the auditory input lexicon, 14 is episodic memory, and 19 represents semantic memory.

Lest any reader assume that the model in figure 22.3 is the result of youthful exuberance, I can assure you that this sort of model pervades modern cognitive neuropsychology. In fact, Cuttrell's model is an expansion of one provided in Ellis and Young (1988, 222), although theirs was confined only to recognition and production of spoken and written words. (Their model had 22 entries, and the caption explaining them ran for 6.5 pages.) If anything, Cuttrell's model underestimates the complexity of the "cognitive system," because boxes (such as those involving episodic and semantic memory) likely need to be further fractionated. Although Hintzman (chap. 16) argues that the computer metaphor is dead, it is clear that the information-processing approach to explaining cognition is alive and well (and perhaps even running amuck).

As implied in earlier parts of my discussion, I have some misgivings about this approach to explaining the interesting phenomena of cognitive neuropsychology. The increasing fractionation of mind into little components or modules—a new one for each new dissociation—will quickly lead to an explosion of little boxes. In some ways, the modular approach assumed in cognitive neuropsychology resembles the eighteenth-century approach of faculty psychologists, with a different mental faculty postulated for each human ability. Fodor (1983) makes this link directly in his book on the modularity of mind, with the picture on the front resembling (in surface appearance) the model in figure 22.3. (See Boring 1950, 55, for a more extensive faculty psychology model.)

The fate of this earlier enterprise—faculty psychology and phrenology—is well known. It fell of its own weight shortly after the turn of the century. As Boring (1950, 207) comments, "People have always accepted readily such contentions as that . . . a good memory depends on having a good faculty of memory. Such naming is word magic. . . ." Of course, the basis of modern cognitive neuropsychology is on much more certain ground than was phrenology and faculty psychology, but it strikes me that a good deal of "explanation by naming" still occurs. Campbell (1990) comments, in her review of the Ellis and Young text, that "Box and arrow diagrams cannot capture many of the important aspects of what is going on. . . . Cognitive neuropsychology is growing too big for its boxes. . ." (637). It will be interesting to see what theoretical ideas take hold to supplant the box-and-arrow diagrams so prevalent now. Cognitive neuropsychologists are making excellent empirical progress in studying various cognitive malfunctions caused by brain damage; the stage is now set for comparable theoretical advances in understanding these provocative phenomena.

22.5 CONCLUDING REMARKS

Reviewing the set of six chapters in the learning and memory sections of this volume provides some interesting contrasts. Despite the surface similarity in theorizing between computational modellers and cognitive neuropsychologists—a complex chain of unseen events postulated in the mind—there has been surprisingly little cross-fertilization of thought between the two disciplines. Formal modelers rarely rely on, or even consult, neuropsychological evidence to bolster or disconfirm their cases; similarly, cognitive neuropsychologists usually do not provide formal models, relying instead on verbal or pictorial ones. Perhaps the next twenty-five years of symposia in the Attention and Performance series will see developments in which the hypothetical constructs embedded in both types of models become more closely tied to converging operations supplied by experimental data. A melding of these fields in the future, if grounded in behavioral methods from experimental psychology, could lead to exciting progress in understanding learning and memory.

NOTES

The author is grateful to Dr. Tina Whitworth for guiding him to the literature on labor of first -and later-born children, to Kathleen McDermott for providing the citation data contained in figure 22.1 and the text, and to Denny LeCompte for creating figure 22.1. The chapter was improved by comments from Derek Besner, Fergus Craik, Mary Czerwinski, Mark McDaniel, James Neely, and especially David Meyer.

1. Citations to Miller's (1956) paper since 1972 are 1492, whereas 885 citations accrued to Atkinson and Shiffrin's (1968) paper in the same period. Since 1969, when the SSCI was initiated, the totals for the two papers are 1797 and 1020.

REFERENCES

Anderson, J. R., and Bower, G. H. (1973). *Human associative memory.* Washington, DC: V. H. Winston & Sons.

Atkinson, R. C., and Shiffrin, R. M. (1968). Human memory: A proposed system and its control processes. In K. W. Spence and J. T. Spence (Eds.). *The psychology of learning and motivation: Advances in research and theory,* vol. 2, 89–125. New York: Academic Press.

Atkinson, R. C., and Shiffrin, R. M. (1971). The control of short-term memory. *Scientific American, 224,* 82–89.

Baddeley, A. D. (1978). The trouble with levels: A re-examination of Craik and Lockhart's framework for memory research. *Psychological Review, 85,* 139–52.

Benzing, W. E., and Squire, L. R. (1989). Preserved learning and memory in amnesia: Intact adaptation-level effects and learning of stereoscopic depth. *Behavioral Neuroscience, 103,* 538–547.

Blaxton, T. A. (1989). Investigating dissociations among memory measures: Support for a transfer appropriate processing framework. *Journal of Experimental Psychology: Learning, Memory and Cognition, 15,* 657–668.

Boring, E. G. (1950). *A history of experimental psychology*, 2d ed. New York: Appleton-Century-Crofts.

Campbell, R. (1990). Review of *Human cognitive neuropsychology*. *Quarterly Journal of Experimental Psychology, 42A,* 636–638.

Cermak, L. S. and Craik, F. I. M. (Eds.). (1979). *Levels of processing in human memory.* Hillsdale, NJ: Erlbaum.

Corkin, S. (1968). Acquisition of motor skill after bilateral medial tempural excision. *Neuropsychologia, 6,* 255–265.

Craik, F. I. M., and Lockhart, R. S. (1972). Levels of processing: A framework for memory research. *Journal of Verbal Learning and Verbal Behavior, 11,* 671–684.

Crowder, R. G. (1976). *Principles of learning and memory.* Hillsdale, NJ: Erlbaum.

Cuttrell, E. B. (1990). A (very) abbreviated model of modular cognition. Unpublished term paper, Rice University.

Ellis, A. W., and Young, A. W. (1988). *Human cognitive neuropsychology.* Hillsdale, NJ: Erlbaum.

Eysenck, M. W. (1978). Levels of processing: A critique. *British Journal of Psychology, 68,* 157–169.

Fisher, R. P., and Craik, F. I. M. (1977). Interaction between encoding and retrieval operations in cued recall. *Journal of Experimental Psychology: Human Learning and Memory, 3,* 701–711.

Fodor, J. A. (1983). *The modularity of mind: An essay on faculty psychology.* Cambridge, MA: MIT Press.

Friedman, E. A. (1978). *Labor: Clinical evaluation and management.* New York: Appleton-Century-Crofts.

Gardner, H. (1974). *The shattered mind.* New York: Random House.

Gardner. H. (1985). *The mind's new science.* New York: Basic Books.

Garner, W. R., Hake, H. W., and Ericksen, C. N. (1956). Operationism and the concept of perception. *Psychological Review, 63,* 149–159.

Glanzer, M., and Cunitz, A. R. (1966). Two storage mechanisms in free recall. *Journal of Verbal Learning and Verbal Behavior, 5,* 351–360.

Hintzman, D. L. (1990). Human learning and memory: Connections and dissociations. *Annual Review of Psychology, 41,* 109–139.

Hintzman, D. L. (1991). Why are formal models useful in psychology? In. W. E. Hockley and S. Lewandowsky (Eds.), *Relating theory and data: Essays on human memory in honor of Bennet B. Murdock.* Hillsdale, NJ: Erlbaum.

Humphreys, M. S., Bain, J. D., and Pike, R. (1989). Different ways to cue a coherent memory system: A theory for episodic, semantic, and procedural tasks. *Psychological Review, 96,* 208–233.

Hyde, T. S., and Jenkins, J. J. (1969). Differential effects of incidental tasks on the organization of recall of a list of highly associated words. *Journal of Experimental Psychology, 82,* 472–481.

Jenkins, J. J. (1974). Remember that old theory of memory? Well, forget it! *American Psychologist, 1974,* 785–795.

Kolers, P. A. (1979). A pattern-analyzing basis of recognition. In L. S. Cermak and F. I. M. Craik (Eds.), *Levels of processing in human memory,* 363–384. Hillsdale, NJ: Erlbaum.

Lachman, R., Lachman, J. L., and Butterfield, E. C. (1979). *Cognitive psychology and information processing: An introduction.* Hillsdale, NJ: Erlbaum.

Lockhart, R. S., and Craik, F. I. M. (1990). Levels of processing: A retrospective commentary on a framework for memory research. *Canadian Journal of Psychology, 44,* 87–112.

McDaniel, M. A., Friedman, A., and Bourne, L. E. (1978). Remembering the levels of information in words. *Memory & Cognition, 6,* 156–164.

Martin, R. C. (1990). Neuropsychological evidence on the role of short term memory in sentence processing. In G. Vallar and T. Shallice (Eds.), *Neuropsychological impairments of short-term memory.* Cambridge: Cambridge University Press.

Miller, G. A. (1956). The magical number seven plus or minus two: Some limits on our capacity for processing information. *Psychological Review, 63,* 81–97.

Milner, B., Corkin, S., and Teuber, H. L. (1968). Further analysis of the hippocampal amnesia syndrome: 14 year follow-up study of H.M. *Neuropsychologia, 6,* 215–234.

Mishkin, M., and T. Appenzeller. (1987). The anatomy of memory. *Scientific American, 256,* 80–90.

Monsell, S. (1987). On the relation between lexical input and output pathways for speech. In A. Allport, D. G. Mackay, W. Pring, and E. Scheerer (Eds.), *Language perception production: Relationships between listening, speaking, reading, and writing.* London: Academic Press.

Morris, C. D., Bransford, J. D., and Franks, J. J. (1977). Levels of processing versus transfer appropriate processing. *Journal of Verbal Learning Behavior, 16,* 519–533.

Murdock, B. B., Jr. (1974). *Human memory: Theory and data.* Potomac, MD: Erlbaum.

Neisser, U. (1978). Memory: What are the important questions? In M. M. Gruneberg, P. E. Morris, and R. N. Sykes (Eds.), *Practical aspects of memory,* 3–24. London: Academic Press.

Nelson, D. L. (1979). Remembering pictures and words: Appearance, significance, and name. In L. S. Cermak and F. I. M. Craik (Eds.), *Levels of processing in human memory,* 45–76. Hillsdale, NJ: Erlbaum.

Nelson, T. O. (1977). Repetition and levels of processing. *Journal of Verbal Learning and Verbal Behavior, 16,* 151–171.

Postman, L. (1975). Verbal learning and memory. *Annual Review of Psychology, 26,* 291–235.

Raaijmakers, J. G. W., and Shiffrin, R. M. (1980). SAM: A theory of probabilistic search of associative memory. In G. Bower (Ed.), *The psychology of learning and motivation,* vol. 14. New York: Academic Press.

Raaijmakers, J. G. W., and Shiffrin, R. M. (1981). Search of associative memory. *Psychological Review, 88,* 93–134.

Roediger, H. L. (1980). Memory metaphors in cognitive psychology. *Memory & Cognition, 8,* 231–246.

Roediger, H. L. (1990). Implicit memory: A commentary. *Bulletin of the Psychonomic Society, 28,* 373–380.

Roediger, H. L., and Neely, J. H. (1982). Retrieval blocks in episodic and semantic memory. *Canadian Journal of Psychology, 36,* 213–242.

Roediger, H. L., Payne, D. G., Gillespie, G. L., and Lean, D. (1982). Hypermnesia as determined by level of recall. *Journal of Verbal Learning and Verbal Behavior, 21,* 635–655

Roediger, H. L., Rajaram, S., and Srinivas, K. (1990). Specifying criteria for memory systems. In A. Diamond (Ed.), *Development and neural bases of higher cognitive functions. Annals of the New York Academy of Sciences, 608,* 572–589.

Sanders, A. F. (Ed.). (1967). *Attention and performance, vol 1.* Amsterdam: North-Holland.

Savoy, R. L., and Gabrieli, J. D. E. (1991). Normal McCollough effect in Alzheimer's disease and global amnesia. *Perception & Psychophysics, 49,* 448–455.

Schacter, D. L. (1987). Implicit memory: History and current status. *Journal of Experimental Psychology: Learning, Memory, and Cognition, 13,* 501–518.

Schacter, D. L. (1990). Perceptual representation systems and implicit memory: Toward a resolution of the multiple memory systems debate. In A. Diamond (Ed.), *Development and neural bases of higher cognitive functions. Annals of the New York Academy of Sciences, 608,* 543–571.

Shallice, T. (1988). *From neuropsychology to mental structure.* Cambridge, England: Cambridge University Press.

Sherry, D. F. and Schacter, D. L. 1987. The evolution of multiple memory systems. *Psychological Review, 94,* 439–454.

Shiffrin, R. M. (1970). Memory search. In D. A. Norman (Ed.), *Models of human memory,* 375–447. New York: Academic Press.

Slamecka, N. J. (1968). An examination of trace storage in free recall. *Journal of Experimental Psychology, 76,* 504–513.

Stein, B. S. (1978). Depth of processing reexamined: The effects of precision of encoding and test appropriateness. *Journal of Verbal Learning and Verbal Behavior, 17,* 165–174.

Treisman, A. (1964). Selective attention in man. *British Medical Bulletin, 20,* 12–16.

Tulving, E. (1983). *Elements of episodic memory.* New York: Oxford University Press.

Tulving, E. (1972). Episodic and semantic memory. In E. Tulving and W. Donaldson, (Eds.), *Organization and Memory.* New York: Academic Press.

Tulving, E., Hayman, C. A. G., and MacDonald, C. (1991). Long-lasting perceptual priming and semantic learning in amnesia: A case experiment. *Journal of Experimental Psychology: Learning, Memory and Cognition, 17,* 595–617.

Watkins, M. J. (1991). An experimental psychologist's view of cognitive science. In R. G. Lister and H. H. Weingartner (Eds.), *Perspectives in cognitive neuroscience,* 132–144. New York: Oxford University Press.

Waugh, N. C., and Norman, D. A. (1965). Primary memory. *Psychological Review, 72,* 89–104.

Williams, B. A. (1986). On the role of theory in behavior analysis. *Behaviorism, 14,* 111–124.

V Mental Chronometry and Processing Dynamics

Introduction

Among the dependent variables that experimental psychologists have measured in order to study human attention and performance, response accuracy and reaction time are by far the most widespread. Indeed, the use of reaction time for making inferences about mental and physical processes dates back more than a century to the advent of experimental psychology, when pioneers like Helmholtz (1850) and Donders ([1868] 1969) introduced the simple-reaction and choice-reaction procedures, respectively. Following their lead, many researchers were later attracted by the prospect that mental processes could be analyzed into underlying discrete, temporally separate stages. Thus, although serious doubts about the feasibility of this enterprise were raised along the way (e.g., Külpe 1909), from the time of Donders's work to the first Attention and Performance symposium (Sanders 1967) mental chronometry has remained a hot topic, particularly in the latter part of this period.

Research on mental chronometry and on the dynamics of human information processing that followed Attention and Performance I may be viewed as an attempt to bolster Donders's (1868) original theoretical framework and to answer several related questions raised by it (Meyer, Irwin, Osman, and Kounios 1988; Miller 1988). For example, are there distinct component mental processes that mediate overt responses to external stimuli and that take measurable amounts of time to be completed? If so, how many different processes are there? What function does each process perform, and how much time does it take? Do these processes proceed in a strict serial fashion, with no temporal overlap among them, or do they operate at least somewhat in parallel? Is information transmitted in discrete packets or as continuously varying activation?

To help answer such questions, Sternberg (1969) formulated the so-called additive-factor method, which he presented at Attention and Performance II. It provided a simple, elegant test of whether discrete serial stages mediate the performance of various cognitive tasks, thereby bolstering Donders's ([1868] 1969) earlier subtraction method for estimating stage durations. Many investigators who participated in subsequent symposia of the Attention and Performance series began using the additive-factor method in their research (for a review, see Broadbent 1986). At the same time, however, other investigators were developing alternative accounts of reaction-time data based on temporally overlapping parallel processes and continous accumulation of partial information (e.g., Eriksen and Schultz 1979; Link 1975; McClelland 1979; Ratcliff 1978; Townsend 1974; for a review, see Luce 1986). Unlike the discrete stage model introduced by Donders and later championed by Sternberg, these alternative accounts explain additive-factor effects on mean reaction times without assuming temporally separate processes whose outputs are all-or-none information packets. In turn, this explanation stimulated the development of more powerful empirical methods for distinguishing between discrete stage and continuous parallel models (e.g., Coles, Gratton, Bashore, Eriksen, and Donchin 1985; Meyer, Irwin, Osman, and Kounios 1988; Miller 1982, 1983; Schweickert 1978; Townsend and Ashby 1983). Among these methods, some noteworthy ones combine reaction time and response accuracy with psychophysiological measures of event-related brain potentials and electromyographic activity (e.g., Coles et al. 1985), thus laying some of the groundwork for the interdisciplinary themes of the Attention and Performance XIV symposium.

Part V of the present volume summarizes the state of the art in mental chronometry and provides goals toward which future research on the dynamics of human information processing may proceed. A scholarly tutorial review by Schweickert begins this section. In it, he highlights alternative classes of models whose predictions about reaction times and speed-accuracy trade-offs are virtually equivalent, but whose properties can be tested further by means of other complementary dependent variables, such as ones derived from some psychophysiological measures.

Reinforcing many of Schweickert's main points, four additional chapters outline recent approaches that augment the additive-factor method for the discovery and analysis of processing stages. Specifically, Mulder et al. report results from a research program in which an intriguing brainwave component, the lateralized readiness potential (LRP), has inspired inferences about the transmission of partial information between stimulus-evaluation and response-preparation processes. Another promising approach is introduced by Roberts, who shows how correlations among multiple dependent variables (e.g., the maximum rate of operant responding and the time at which this maximum occurs) may allow distinct component processes to be discovered. Roberts's work is likewise of note because it illustrates how studies of animal behavior and performance can both draw from and go beyond traditional aspects of human information-processing research. Similarly, the chapter by Roberts and Sternberg contains a wealth of new detailed quantitative tests whereby investigators may analyze reaction-time distributions in order to test alternative processing models. As their analyses reveal, discrete stage models, continuous-flow (e.g., cascade) models, and hybrid mixture models have many testable properties that complement those involving mean reaction times. It will be interesting to see whether the new GRAIN model developed by McClelland in his chapter fares well under the scrutiny of Roberts and Sternberg's tests. In that McClelland has combined and extended many attractive features of the earlier cascade model (McClelland 1979) and interactive-activation model

(McClelland and Rumelhart 1981), the GRAIN model is certainly worthy of further careful pursuit.

Where this sort of pursuit could lead us in the future is the topic of Sanders's final discussion chapter. Consistent with his astute assessments and admonitions, the field must continue seeking fruitful combinations of behavioral and psychophysiological methods, while not exceeding the inferential bounds that the assumptions of these methods permit.

REFERENCES

Broadbent, D. E. (1986). The enterprise of performance. Review of *Attention and performance X*, by H. Bouma and D. Bouwhuis (Eds.). *Quarterly Journal of Experimental Psychology, 38A*, 151–162.

Coles, M. G. H., Gratton, G., Bashore, T. R., Eriksen, C. W., and Donchin, E. (1985). A psychophysiological investigation of the continuous flow model of information processing. *Journal of Experimental Psychology: Human Perception and Performance, 11*, 529–553.

Donders, F. C. ([1868] 1969). On the speed of mental processes. Translation by W. G. Koster in W. G. Koster (Ed.), *Attention and performance II*, 412–431. Amsterdam: North-Holland. Original work published in *Onderzoekingen gedann in het Psychologisch Laboratorium der Utrechtsche Hoogeschool*, Tweede reeks, 1868–1869, *II*, 92–120.

Eriksen, C. W., and Schultz, D. (1979). Information processing in visual search: A continuous flow conception and experimental results. *Perception and Psychophysics, 25*, 249–263.

Helmholtz, H. L. F. von. (1950). Über die Methoden, kleinste Zeittheile zu messen, und ihre Anwendung für physiologische Zwecke. Original work translated in *Philosophical Magazine*, 1853, *6* (section 4), 313–325.

Külpe, O. (1909). *Outlines of psychology*. 3d ed. New York: MacMillan. Translation of original work published in 1893.

Link, S. W. (1975). The relative judgment theory of two-choice reaction time. *Journal of Mathematical Psychology, 12*, 114–136.

Luce, R. D. (1986). *Response times: Their role in inferring elementary mental organization*. New York: Oxford University Press.

McClelland, J. L. (1979). On the time relations of mental processes in cascade. *Psychological Review, 86*, 287–330.

McClelland, J. L., and Rumelhart, D. E. (1981). An interactive activation model of context effects in letter perception, Part I: An account of basic findings. *Psychological Review, 88*, 375–407.

Meyer, D. E., Irwin, D. E., Osman, A. M., and Kounios, J. (1988). The dynamics of cognition and action: Mental processes inferred from speed-accuracy decomposition. *Psychological Review, 95*, 183–237.

Meyer, D. E., Osman, A. M., Yantis, S. G., and Irwin, D. E. (1988). Modern mental chronometry. *Biological Psychology, 26*, 3–67.

Miller, J. O. (1982). Discrete versus continuous stage models of human information processing: In search of partial output. *Journal of Experimental Psychology: Human Perception and Performance, 8*, 273–296.

Miller, J. O. (1983). Can response preparation begin before stimulus recognition finishes? *Journal of Experimental Psychology: Human Perception and Performance, 9*, 161–182.

Miller, J. O. (1988). Discrete and continuous models of human information processing: Theoretical distinctions and empirical results. *Acta Psychologica, 67*, 191–257.

Ratcliff, R. (1978). A theory of memory retrieval. *Psychological Review, 85*, 59–108.

Sanders, A. (1967). *Attention and performance*. Amsterdam: North-Holland.

Schweickert, R. (1978). A critical path generalization of the additive factor method: Analysis of a Stroop task. *Journal of Mathematical Psychology, 18*, 105–139.

Sternberg, S. (1969). The discovery of processing stages: Extensions of Donders' method. In W. G. Koster (Ed.), *Attention and performance II*, 276–315. Amsterdam: North-Holland.

Townsend, J. T. (1974). Issues and models concerning the processing of a finite number of inputs. In B. H. Kantowitz (Ed.), *Human information processing: Tutorials in performance and cognition*, 133–185. Hillsdale, NJ: Erlbaum.

Townsend, J. T., and Ashby, F. G. (1983). *Stochastic modeling of elementary psychological processes*. Cambridge, England: Cambridge University Press.

23 Information, Time, and the Structure of Mental Events: A Twenty-Five-Year Review

Richard Schweickert

A coherent explanation of choice reaction time and accuracy could be given twenty-five years ago with Hick's (1952) law,

$$RT = a + bH.$$

Reaction time, RT, was considered to be a linear function of Shannon's (1948) measure of information, H, because the stimulus was assumed to be identified in a series of binary decisions, each taking the same amount of time. Accuracy was included in the information transmitted, H, which depended on stimulus presentation probability. The rate of gain of information, the time to process one bit, was given by the slope, b. It decreased as stimulus-response compatibility increased. The time, a, for processes other than the decision was assumed to be affected by uncertainty in when the stimulus was presented. This time was added to the decision time in accord with Donders's (1869) hypothesis that reaction time is the sum of the durations of component processes.

An electrophysiological parallel was readily available. The amplitude and timing of the P300 component of the evoked potential was discovered to depend on stimulus probability, that is, on information (Sutton et al. 1965).

Dual choice reaction time could also be explained. When two stimuli occur close together in time, the response time for the second is longer than if it occurred alone (Telford 1931). Broadbent (1958) and Welford (1952, 1967) explained this psychological refractory period by saying the two stimuli use a central channel with limited capacity for processing information.

According to Broadbent (1958), more than one stimulus could be processed at a time if the total bits per second did not exceed the limit. Welford's (1952, 1967) hypothesis was that the central channel could process only one stimulus at a time. If a second stimulus arrived while the central mechanism was busy, the stimulus had to wait, causing a refractory delay. Hick and Welford (1956) proposed that the duration of central processing increased with stimulus information according to Hick's law. Since this duration could not be measured directly, Welford estimated the central processing time of the first stimulus by the processing time remaining for the first stimulus after the second stimulus arrived. This strong version of Welford's model assumed processing was serial, that is, the first stimulus was processed completely before processing of the second stimulus began. It accounts for many aspects of the data (Bertelson 1966; Kantowitz 1974).

Twenty-five years ago the cognitive revolution was underway, and the concept of information helped reify the contents of cognition. But the synthesis based on a single channel limited in ability to transmit information had problems. An experiment by Karlin and Kestenbaum (1968) manipulating the number of alternatives and the interstimulus interval, together with additional analyses by Kantowitz (1974) and Ollman (1968) showed the predictions to be wrong in several details (see Luce 1986 for a review). The rejection of this strong version of Welford's single channel hypothesis was important because it demonstrated that concurrent processing occurs.

As for Hick's law, Crossman (1953) showed that discriminability affected response time. Discriminability is often confounded with the number of alternatives. For three or more alternatives, multidimensional stimuli must be used if they are to be equidistant. Discriminability and multidimensionality are not represented in Hick's law (Laming 1968; Welford 1960). Another problem was that response times are not linear in the logarithm of stimulus probability for stimuli considered individually (Hyman 1953). Further, when the number of alternative stimuli is changed, the information, H, changes, but so does the probability that a given stimulus follows itself from trial to trial. Kornblum (1969) showed that some, although not all, of the effect attributed by Hick's law to information was in fact due to sequential effects.

Finally, the channel capacity theorem, an important part of information theory, was never supported quantitatively. The theorem predicts that the upper limit of the channel's rate of transmission of information would be a constant number of bits per second. While it is clear there is a limit, as postulated by Broadbent (1958), no constant ever emerged as the human channel capacity. As Moray (1967) pointed out, the "channel" actually operates on the stimuli, and is more like a computer than a passive channel. We would now say that the number of steps required for a response, the complexity of the task, is as important as channel capacity. Complexity is studied in computer science, but typically for a Turing machine, which is a serial digital computer, while the computing parts of the brain include parallel and analog processing.

Twenty-five years ago, the short-lived synthesis based on the single limited channel was known to be wrong. Many advances have occurred since. To trace their growth, the components of Hick's law will be considered one by one, followed by a discussion of the limited channel. Unfortunately, there is no new synthesis. The offshoots of one approach do not often merge with those of another, so the theory is like a tree with separate branches. The facts trim away a few hypotheses, but allow many to thrive.

A review of mental chronometry is more concerned with what can be revealed than what has been revealed. Reporting is from a special viewpoint, like surveying architecture through advances in girders. In the production of a report rather than a catalog in the space available, only a few developments can be mentioned, and much important work by colleagues and friends has to be neglected. Fortunately, there are excellent surveys of chronometry by Posner (1978), Welford (1980), Townsend and Ashby (1983), and Luce (1986) and of event-related potentials by Coles, Gratton, and Fabiani (in press).

23.1   WHAT BECAME OF *H*, THE INFORMATION TRANSMITTED?

Alternatives to Hick's conception assumed that information accrues from a sequence of samples (LaBerge 1962; Stone 1960). Sequential sampling models have steadily improved through readjustments. The term *information* has often been replaced by *activation* or *evidence*. Work by Burbeck and Luce introduces some key notions.

In the visual and auditory systems, one type of neuron gives a transient response to stimuli, while another gives a sustained response. Burbeck and Luce supposed that either type might initiate a response in a simple reaction time task, in which a subject responds as soon as he detects the stimulus (Burbeck 1979; see also Luce 1986). The transient cells would be used when stimuli are turned on abruptly, while the sustained cells would be used when there is gradual onset. In intermediate conditions, the response would be initiated by whichever type of cell responded first, that is, via a race between the two types. The model gives a good account of log survivor functions, and Poisson parameters that were expected to vary with stimulus intensity indeed did so. We will see that the gradual and abrupt changes discussed by Burbeck and Luce for simple reactions have analogs at all levels of processing.

In their model, response time is determined by the faster of two processes in a race. Work by Marley and Colonius (in press), Townsend (1976), and Vorberg (see Luce 1986) shows that for a fixed finite set of response alternatives to a stimulus in a fixed experimental condition, stochastically independent races among the response alternatives are sufficient to account for virtually any pattern of response times and response probabilities. Marley and Colonius describe the conditions under which such a race model would lead to the Luce choice rule. The Luce choice rule may provide a way to incorporate discriminability in Hick's law, since it leads to a similar prediction (Luce 1986).

Current alternatives to Hick's conception can be classified as applying to abrupt or gradual accrual of information.

Large Signal-to-Noise Ratios: Abrupt Accrual

Fast Guesses   With highly discriminable stimuli, a sample size of one could provide all the information required for a correct stimulus-controlled response, although an error may arise in response execution. If the subject responds before a sample is taken, he or she guesses. With the fast guess model (Ollman 1966; Yellott 1971) the guessing probability can be estimated from properties of mixture distributions (see also Falmagne 1965).

Payoff and stimulus probability are assumed to affect the proportion of guesses and their latencies, but not the stimulus-controlled processes. In

Yellott's (1971) experiments, using highly discriminable stimuli, the mean latency of the stimulus-controlled responses was invariant over payoff and stimulus probability. Estimated mean latencies of the stimulus-controlled responses were quite fast, typically about 300 ms.

Yellott (1971) also discussed a deadline model in which a stimulus-controlled process races against a deadline estimation process. If the subject estimates that the deadline has passed, he makes a fast guess, otherwise he makes a stimulus controlled response. This model predicts the invariance in latency for stimulus-controlled responses Ollman and Yellott found (see Thomas 1974), but can also predict variation in the latency with payoff, depending on the situation. Fast guess and deadline models reappear in recent work on response preparation, discussed later.

Small Signal-to-Noise Ratios: Gradual Accrual

The major classes of models when detection or discrimination is difficult are general accumulator models and random walk models. In a random walk, information about the alternatives is combined before the decision is made, while in an accumulator, it is kept separate.

Accumulator Models   In general accumulator models, evidence favoring each response accrues and that response whose criterion is reached first is emitted. LaBerge (1962) and Audley and Pike (1965) proposed that evidence accrues in discrete time. This predicts that response time distributions are symmetrical when a large number of units are accrued. More typical skewed distributions are predicted by models that assume evidence is produced by a Poisson process (e.g., Pike 1973; Rumelhart 1970; Townsend and Ashby 1983, 272–289).

In an accumulator system, it is likely that evidence favoring the correct response would accrue at a faster average rate than evidence favoring an incorrect response. This predicts that an error would take longer, on the average, than the same response made correctly, if the criterion were the same for all responses. The facts are different, but complicated. A rule of thumb was suggested by Swensson (1972; Luce 1986, 233): Incorrect responses are faster than correct ones when discriminability is high and speed is important; incorrect responses are slower than correct ones when discriminability is low and accuracy is important.

Some of the fast incorrect responses may be fast guesses. Pike (1973) gave an alternative explanation. If the criterion for each response varied randomly from trial to trial, low criterion values would often result in fast errors. Smith and Vickers (1988) extended the accumulator model of Vickers (1970) by allowing such criterion variability. A good description of the data was obtained when criterion variability was assumed to follow a principle proposed by Vickers (1970) that subjects attempt to maintain a set level of confidence by increasing their response criteria when discriminability is low.

Random Walks   A random walk with two alternatives, A and B, subtracts the evidence favoring B at any instant from that favoring A. If and when the net evidence reaches the criterion for A, the response for A is made; the response for B is made similarly. If step sizes are small, so that the walk hits one of the criteria exactly, then an equation, Wald's identity, can be solved. It gives the decision time distributions (via moment generating functions) and the probabilities of making one response or the other to a given stimulus.

Stone (1960) proposed a particular random walk model, the sequential probability ratio test (Wald 1947). It mistakenly predicts that for a given response, reaction times are the same whether or not that response is correct for the given stimulus. A general random walk model, unfortunately, has too many parameters for Wald's identity to be useful if only mean response times and response probabilities are available (Luce 1986, 328–331).

Luce lists four ways to proceed. Two make simplifying assumptions about how the moment generating function for one stimulus is obtained from that of the other. In the first, Laming's (1968) "information theory" (not the usual sense of the term), the moment generating functions are related by a shift. In the second, the relative judgment theory of Link and Heath (1975; Link 1975), they are related by a reflection. According to Laming (1979), these are only two tractable assumptions about moment-generating functions. Each accounts for some, although not all, differences between correct and erroneous response times.

The third approach assumes a known form for the response time distribution, the convolution of a normal and an exponential distribution. In Ratcliff's (1978) model for search, comparisons of the probe with items in the search set go on in parallel. Each comparison is a random walk (diffusion) process. A positive response is initiated when any one of the comparison processes reaches the criterion for a match, and a negative response is initiated when all comparison processes reach the criterion for a nonmatch. The criteria can be adjusted strategically by the subject. The model gives a unified account of response time and accuracy in several item recognition paradigms.

Luce (1986) lists, but does not pursue, a fourth approach to random walk models, manipulating experimental factors that affect the parameters. There is a simple empirical test using this approach for general random walk models.[1] In the Appendix, the expected decision time is written as a linear function of the probability of making response A when stimulus s_i is presented, under the usual assumptions for random walk models. The deadline is shown to affect only the slope of this function, while stimulus probability affects only the intercept. The result is a testable model with fewer parameters than observations.

Guesses and Sampling   According to sequential sampling models, the subject can spend more or less time sampling during a stimulus-controlled response, depending on the payoffs. The invariance Yellott (1971) found for stimulus-controlled processes in the fast-guess experiment poses a problem. Swensson (1972) reconciled the two kinds of models. He showed that when the guessing responses have been removed, it is still possible to obtain a trade-off between speed and accuracy, when (a) stimuli are not easy to discriminate and (b) the payoff explicitly exchanges accuracy and latency.

Electrophysiological Correlates   A tantalizing recent development is the possibility of electrophysiological manifestations of the accrual of evidence. The P300 is sensitive to changes in stimulus probability, but analysis shows it to be influenced by the subject's expectation, rather than stimulus information per se. In a recent discussion, Donchin and Coles (1988) say the P300 is not a direct manifestation of accrual of information, but is the product of a subsystem of strategic processes executed in parallel with the processes extracting stimulus information.

Another candidate is the lateralized readiness potential. Just prior to hand movement, a negative potential occurs over the motor cortex on the side contralateral to the limb (Kornhuber and Deecke 1965). The lateralized readiness potential corresponding to a movement is obtained by subtracting the potential of the ipsilateral side of the scalp from that of the contralateral side. Gratton et al. (1988) found that response initiation—namely, EMG onset— occurs when the lateralized readiness potential reaches a certain critical value, regardless of when that value is reached. This suggests a role for the motor system in decisions.

23.2   WHAT BECAME OF *b*, THE RATE OF GAIN OF INFORMATION?

The slope in Hick's (1956) law increases as stimulus-response compatibility decreases (Alluisi, Muller, and Fitts 1957). This is puzzling if the slope is interpreted as "the rate of gain of information." Why should information about a stimulus accrue at a different rate depending on the response assigned to it and to the other stimuli? A different conception is suggested by tasks such as naming the successor to a digit, in which response selection is the translation of the stimulus code into another code. Then, the time for response selection is the time to carry out operations in some computation. The number of operations and their difficulty would depend on the entire stimulus-response mapping.

Compatibility and its effects are subtle and difficult to characterize (see Proctor and Reeve 1990 for a survey). The problem is to characterize the degree of compatibility without appealing unduly to intuition or case-by-case analysis.

Reeve and Proctor (1990) proposed the salient-features coding principle. The stimulus set is coded in terms of its salient features, such as spatial locations, and the response set is also coded in terms of its salient features. Responses are selected fastest when the salient features of each set correspond, that is, when salient features of the stimulus set can be used to discriminate among salient features of the response set.

Kornblum, Hasbroucq, and Osman (1990) proposed that stimulus-response compatibility depends on "overlap" between dimensions in the stimulus set and response set. They say the stimuli form a relational system, that is, a set of items together with a set of relations on the items. The responses also form a relational system. The stimulus system and the response system are homomorphic if there is a mapping from stimulus items to responses that preserves the relations of both sets. They conjecture that the more relations preserved by a mapping, the greater the dimensional overlap. The degree of overlap is also determined by the similarity of the dimensions (also see Garner interference below). Reeve and Proctor (1990) and Kornblum, Hasbroucq, and Osman (1990) both emphasize the mapping of the structure of the stimulus set to the structure of the response set.

What Does the Slope Mean?

Hick's notion that response time increased with the number of branches in a binary decision tree was ruled out because response time is not a linear function of the information in bits for individual stimuli (Hyman 1953). Further investigations of computational complexity required some other means of manipulating the number of operations to be executed. A fruitful approach was to manipulate the number of items to be processed in search tasks. The function relating response time to the number of items is typically linear, so its slope, the number of items processed per second, is a measure of capacity. We now consider what the slope means and why it is sometimes zero.

In a memory search task, the subject is given a set of items to remember. On each trial, a probe is presented and the subject indicates whether or not the probe is in the memory set. Sternberg (1966, 1967, 1969) found response time to increase linearly with set size, with the same slope for presence and absence trials. He explained the results with a serial and exhaustive search. Items in the memory set are processed one after the other, accounting for the linear increases in response time. Every item in the memory set is processed, even when the probe is present, thus accounting for the equal slopes of the presence and absence trials. Later studies sometimes found the slope for the presence trials to be half that for the absence trials (see Sternberg 1975 for a review), a natural outcome for a self-terminating search.

Is Search Serial? Unfortunately, the question is still disputed. In the study of cognition the chances are good that two logically distinct systems will not make distinguishable predictions about the few variables available for measurement. Theories can be more easily proposed than disposed. Townsend's (1971, 1976) demonstrations that serial and parallel systems often mimic each other showed how serious the problem could be. Suppose there is a separate process for each item, and all processes must be completed for the response to be made. If processes are parallel, and processing times are random variables, then the more items to be processed, the longer the response time would be. If items are processed in series, each additional item would take some extra time as well. One might think that the response time density functions produced by the serial and parallel systems would be somehow different. Townsend (1976) showed, however, that if the times between the completions of the items are independent, then any set of density functions produced by a parallel model could also be produced by an equivalent serial model. Many, although not all, sets of density functions produced by a serial model could be produced by an equivalent parallel model. Sternberg's data were clear, and his model was elegant, but it was not the only possible explanation.

A model quite different from Sternberg's, but accounting for many of the same results, was proposed by Anderson (1973). It was an early example of a parallel neural network model. Anderson assumed that memory traces were vectors, and that memory is searched by constructing a matched filter for the positive set and another for the negative set. Using the matched filter requires finding the weighted sum of the inputs to each neural unit multiplied by the filter coefficient for that unit. By assuming that the summation proceeded at a fixed rate, and that subjects maintained a constant signal-to-noise ratio as memory set size changes, Anderson accounted for the typical memory scanning response times, including the linear increase in response time with the size of the memory set. The model fit data by Theios (1973) well. It also accounted for sequential effects by assuming that trace strength decayed exponentially after stimulus presentation, and gave a reasonable fit to Remington's (1969) sequential effects data.

Is Search Exhaustive? When response time is plotted as a function of load, parallel presence and absence functions do not necessarily imply exhaustive search. A general self-terminating model can produce such parallel functions as well as target position effects (Townsend and Roos 1973). Other outcomes are more diagnostic. Estes (1972) found that the time for a presence response in visual search decreased as the number of targets increased. This is inconsistent with an exhaustive search (see later remarks about redundant stimuli, however).

Townsend and Van Zandt (1990) showed that for a very general class of serial models, exhaustive processing cannot produce strong position effects unless response times are a nonlinear function of display size, and nontarget processes are supercapacity. Supercapacity processes speed up when the load increases, and are implausible for most tasks. Townsend and Van Zandt also considered the ability of parallel exhaustive models to produce a difference between slopes for presence and absence response times. They concluded, after reviewing the literature, that self-terminating searches, serial or parallel, can produce all results typically found, while exhaustive searches can only produce a small subset of them.

When Is the Slope Zero?

Response time functions that do not increase with load are important, because it is hard for serial models to explain them when processing is exhaustive

(Townsend 1974). Response times invariant with load have depended mainly upon four things: categories of targets and distractors, similarity of targets and distractors, practice, and the number of items displayed.

Categorical Search The time to search through a display of items and to respond that a target item is present or absent typically increases linearly with the number of items in the display (Atkinson, Holmgren, and Juola 1969; Nickerson 1969). The slope is often the same for present and absent trials. When the target is from one category, say, digits, and the nontargets are from another category, say, letters, searching is very rapid (Sperling et al. 1971; Brand 1971). Is the slope zero? Early studies found that the slopes decrease with practice (Egeth, Jonides, and Wall 1972) and are nearly flat for both presence and absence responses (Jonides and Gleitman 1972). However, Duncan (1983) failed to replicate the latter result. He reviewed previous between-category search experiments, and found that slopes near zero, although positive, were not uncommon for presence responses, but were uncommon for absence responses.

Similarity Treisman and Gelade (1980) found nearly flat functions for both presence and absence trials when subjects searched for a target that differed from nontargets by only one feature, for example, a pink letter among brown and purple ones. They proposed that a single feature difference is required for such flat functions. Recently, however, Treisman and Gormican (1988) found, contrary to the earlier hypothesis, that response time increases linearly and appreciably with display size when a target differs from the nontargets by a slight change in only one feature. Further, flat functions are more likely to occur if the target has more of some property than the nontargets, rather than less.

Duncan and Humphreys (1989) summarize the search data, including their own, by saying response time increases with the similarity between the target and the nontargets, and decreases with the similarity among the nontargets.

Practice and Automaticity For choice response time, with high compatibility and practice, the slope b in Hick's Law approached zero (Leonard 1959; Mowbray and Rhoades 1959). In 1982, Ten Hoopen, Akerboom, and Raaymakers replicated Leonard's results but only for large intensities. They found an appreciable slope for intensities weaker than those Leonard used.

For search, Swanson and Briggs (1969) found that extended practice with the same memory set led to response times that increased nonlinearly, and only slightly, with set size. Later, Schneider and Shiffrin established that in addition to practice, an important condition for response times and errors to increase little with load in a combined visual and memory search task is a consistent mapping of stimuli to responses. An item is consistently mapped if it is always a target, or always a distractor; otherwise, it has a varied mapping (Schneider and Shiffrin 1977; Shiffrin and Schneider 1977). With practice, processing of consistently mapped items becomes automatic, as evidenced by little or no effect of load on performance. Even with practice, elements with a varied mapping require controlled processing, which demands attention, has limited capacity, and is governed by the subject's strategy.

One of Schneider and Shiffrin's many findings was that with varied mapping, response time variances increased more rapidly with load on presence trials than on absence trials. Their analysis showed this to be inconsistent with an exhaustive search, which predicts the same variances for presence and absence trials. It is predicted by their serial self-terminating search model for controlled search, however. Further analysis is in Townsend and Ashby (1983, 198).

Small Display Size   Fisher et al. (1988) noted that even with highly practiced subjects using consistent mappings, effects of load sometimes occur in visual search, but sometimes do not. The limited channel model (Fisher 1982) explains this by saying the number, k, of concurrent comparison processes is greater than one, but not large. Parallel processing is possible when the number of comparisons does not exceed k. After items are encoded, attempts are made to assign each item, one by one, to an available comparison processor. If all comparison processors are busy, the item is lost; otherwise the comparison processor determines whether the item is a target or not. When a target is found, a response is made.

An important feature of the steady-state model is that the number of comparison processors can be estimated through an equation known as Erlang's loss formula, if the items arrive with a Poisson distribution. The model gives good fits to reaction time and accuracy from several experiments from the literature, and several new ones (Fisher et al. 1988). The best fitting estimate of k is surprisingly consistent, between 3 and 5, indicating that the number of processors is about 4.

Summary

Current models of decisions involve sequential sampling, perhaps combined with fast guesses. They account well for response time and accuracy, although not in all details, and are little developed for more than two alternatives. They are mute about stimulus-response compatibility, even though its effects are thought to arise in the decision process.

Investigations of decision time often examine how two variables, response time and accuracy, change as a function of one other variable. This was powerful enough to falsify Hick's original explanation for his law. But one independent variable is not enough to distinguish serial from parallel processing, except in the rare case of flat response time functions. More independent variables give better resolution. For example, exhaustive search cannot account for the known effects of both search set size and target position.

23.3 WHAT BECAME OF THE PERIPHERAL TIME, a?

The a in Hick's law is the time for everything but the decision. This section discusses three questions. Once a decision starts, is the response inevitable? If the decision stops early, what information is available to response processing? Is information available to response processing all at once or piecemeal?

External Response Signals

Stopping the Response   Hick preferred an alternate version of his law which omitted the term a, and increased H by one bit to account for the decision of whether or not to respond. The option not to respond is explicit in the stop-signal paradigm, where a signal cues the subject to inhibit the response on some trials. Subjects do so provided the interval between the primary stimulus and the stop signal is not too long. Logan and Cowan (1984) found experimental support for a model of stopping with two processes in series for the primary stimulus, an early one that can be stopped and a later one that cannot. These race against the parallel processing of the stop signal, if one is presented. The response is stopped if stop-signal processing is completed before the stoppable early process is completed.

The unstoppable later process may be very short, if it exists at all. De Jong et al. (1990) found electrophysiological evidence that the response can be inhibited even after response activity has begun. A procedure for estimating the distribution of the unobservable processing of the stop signal was developed by Colonius (1990a).

Gradual or Abrupt Response Preparation   In a more complicated paradigm, a secondary signal tells the subject to stop the current processes and respond immediately. Recall that in the fast-guess model of Ollman (1966) and Yellott (1971), the subject either responded with no information from the stimulus, or else made a more accurate stimulus-controlled response. The response time distribution is a mixture of guesses and stimulus-controlled responses. What if response priming were not all or none, so that graded information could be available to the stimulus-controlled response?

The question can be answered using a newer method for analyzing mixture distributions developed by Smith et al. (1982). It allows an investigator to test the hypothesis that an observed response time distribution is a mixture of other observed distributions. The mixing probabilities are estimated and a test of goodness of fit is produced.

Evidence for all-or-none priming was found with the technique in one situation and not in another. In the first situation, Meyer et al. (1984) presented subjects with a letter string, followed by an arrow. If the string was a word, the arrow pointed right; if the string was a nonword, the arrow pointed left. Three values of stimulus onset asynchrony (SOA) were used. With the SOA of 0, no advance preparation was possible, so all responses were produced in an unprepared state. With the SOA of 700, subjects had enough time to completely decide whether the string was a word or not, so all responses to the arrow were produced in a completely prepared state. The interesting trials are those for the intermediate SOA. It might be expected that priming is all or none in this situation, since letter strings and arrows do not occur together naturally. Thus, response times for the intermediate SOA should be a mixture of responses from the unprepared and prepared states. This was found to be the case.

The second situation involved more conventional priming in a lexical decision task. Yantis and Meyer (1988) presented a prime word, followed after an SOA by a target string, either a word or a pronounceable nonword. If the target was a word, it was highly related to the prime. Once again, there were three SOAs—short, intermediate, and long. This time, the hypothesis that the response times for the intermediate SOAs were a mixture of times from unprepared and completely prepared states was rejected. Evidently, in this situation activation does not spread in an all-or-none fashion, but spreads gradually.

Internal Response Signals

Gradual or Abrupt Transmission of Output   Donders (1869) implicitly assumed that a process does not produce output before it is completed. Such a process is called a *complete-output* process here; otherwise it is a *partial-output* process (Miller 1982a). Miller (1982a) introduced a paradigm to study the evidence that response preparation could begin before stimulus identification was complete. Each stimulus had two attributes, such as size and letter name. Responses were made with the middle and index fingers of each hand. The value of the more discriminable (or salient) stimulus attribute sometimes specified which hand to use in responding and sometimes specified which finger type, middle or index, to use.

The following assumptions lead to Miller's prediction:

1. To respond, the values of the two stimulus attributes must be encoded.

2. The value of one attribute is encoded faster than the value of the other.

3. The value encoded faster is available to the response preparation process before the value encoded more slowly, and prepares whatever limb part it specifies.

4. Preparation of a hand, but not a finger type, decreases response time more than preparation of a finger type, but not a hand. Therefore,

5. Response time will be shorter if the faster encoded value specifies the hand than if it specifies the finger type.

The assumptions are supported in that the predicted hand advantage has been found in several experiments (see Miller 1988 for a review).

There are two problems: other quite different assumptions lead to the same conclusion, (5), and some key terms are only implicitly defined. The assumption of interest here is (3). It says partial output occurs, if the stimulus identification process is defined to include encoding of both attributes. But by using only the ordinal properties of response time and accuracy, it is hard, if not impossible, to tell whether two attributes become available at different times or become available at the same time but with, say, different signal strengths.

Reeve and Proctor (1984) proposed an alternative, saying the attributes arrive at the translation process rather than the response-preparation process. The attributes may or may not arrive at the same time, but one attribute is more salient than the other. They showed that the apparent hand advantage could be explained as an advantage for specific pairs of response locations. This was demonstrated by varying hand placements. The effects did not depend on whether the fingers were from the same or different hands. This finding is consistent with results from studies of stimulus-response compatibility, which typically are attributed to nonmotoric translation processes rather than to response-preparation processes (e.g., Teichner and Krebs 1974). The duration of the translation process varies as a function of the relation between stimuli and responses. This creates a difficulty. It is unclear whether an advantage for a particular assignment is due to one attribute arriving before the other, as input for some process, or is due to compatibility effects. Complete understanding of the results of Miller and those of Reeve and Proctor awaits resolution of other issues in the argument.

Better resolution through electrophysiology looks promising. Coles et al. (1985) presented strings such as *SSHSS* and *SSSSS* The task was to squeeze a dynamometer with one hand if the center letter was an *S* and with the other if the center letter was an *H*. Five quantities were measured: evoked potentials, electromyographic activity (EMG), the force on the dynamometer, the response time for the force to exceed a preset criterion, and accuracy.

In about half of the trials, either EMG or force activity was present in both arms. Such activity was not inconsequential, because when activity was present in both arms, indicating response competition, the EMG and force onsets were delayed for the response that was eventually made. Effects of target and flanker incompatibility were not confined to one locus. Incompatibility delayed the P300 and the EMG onset, prolonged the interval between EMG onset and force onset, delayed the onset of the force, and increased the time until the force reached the criterion, which would be the conventional response time. It seems that at no place in the stream of processing was evidence for one of the responses eliminated, except at the end.

If the entire string is considered to be the stimulus, if stimulus identification determines the unique response required by the stimulus, and if deviation from baseline activity in the arms is taken as evidence for response preparation, then the data indicate that stimulus identification is not complete before response preparation begins. It is still possible that there is complete-output processing at a lower level. Miller (1988) provides an account of the results in which identification of each letter is a complete-output process.

Summary

Subjects can stop a response even after processing has begun. When a decision is stopped early, sometimes the response is partially prepared and sometimes preparation is all or none. The question of whether a process must stop before it sends output to its successors is logically clear, but hard to answer with response time and accuracy alone. It is a good example of a question now addressed through electrophysiology.

23.4   WHAT BECAME OF THE PLUS SIGN?

The failure of the strong version of Welford's single channel theory ruled out serial processing for double stimulation tasks, but not for single stimulus tasks. In 1969 Sternberg pointed out that if response time is the sum of the durations of a series of stages, then the combined effect of prolonging two stages would be the sum of the effects of prolonging them individually. His additive-factor method is based on two converse statements. If two experimental factors have additive effects on response time, then it is likely that each affects a different stage in a series of stages; and if two factors have interactive effects, then it is likely that they each affect the same stage. Sternberg (1967) found, for example, that the effect of degrading the stimulus with a superimposed checkerboard pattern was additive with the effect of increasing the set size. His interpretation was that stimulus encoding and memory comparison are separate processes.

Applications have been plentiful and many examples of factors having additive effects on response time have been found. The additive-factor method systematically considers effects of two independent variables rather than one, giving it considerable resolving power. In a recent review Sanders (1990) found thirteen factors having consistently additive or interactive effects on response time. He proposed seven stages to account for the effects: preprocessing, feature extraction, identification, response selection, motor programming, program loading, and motor adjustment.

Do Additive Factors Imply Abrupt Transitions between Processes?

Are There Components to Add?   It seems obvious that if two factors have additive effects on reaction time, then the processing time is divided into two intervals; during the first interval one factor alone has an effect and during the second interval the other factor alone has an effect. This beguiling conclusion was refuted by counterexamples constructed by McClelland (1979) and Townsend and Ashby (1983).

Many results for McClelland's (1979) cascade model were originally based on simulations. Ashby (1982a), on the other hand, derived exact expressions for response times from McClelland's model. He found it predicted that sometimes no response would be made. For those trials on which a response would be made, he found two further problems: reaction time variance does not change as the mean changes (a minor change in the assumptions might mend this), and the model cannot predict the exponentially distributed inter-completion times sometimes found (Ashby and Townsend 1980; Ashby 1982b). Ashby found that the model does indeed predict approximate additivity for mean response times when two factors selectively influence the rates of two different processes.

In each counterexample, the output of one process is the input to another, but processing does not satisfy Donders's assumption that a process must be completed before its successor is started. The counterexamples show that factors with additive effects on response time do not rule out partial-output processing.

Additivity for Time and Accuracy: Complete Output   Evidence for complete-output processing is obtained if factors have additive effects on reaction time and also on some function of time, such as accuracy. Additive effects of factors on accuracy arise naturally in complete output models. Suppose the times allocated to processes 1 and 2 are t_1 and t_2, respectively. Let the probability that process 1 produces the correct output, given its input, be $p_1(t_1)$ and let the analogous probability for process 2 be $p_2(t_2)$. Suppose that the response is correct when and only when both processes are correct (see Luce 1986, 484; Ollman 1982; Schweickert 1985). Then the probability $p(t_1, t_2)$ of a correct response is approximately $p_1(t_1) \times p_2(t_2)$, and

$$\log p(t_1, t_2) = \log p_1(t_1) + \log p_2(t_2).$$

From the equation above, factors affecting separate processes will have additive effects on log percent correct, if the process durations t_1 and t_2 are stochastically independent. Furthermore, for low error rates, factors having additive effects on log percent correct will have approximately additive effects on errors (Schweickert 1985).

Examples   In a lexical decision task Schuberth, Spoehr, and Lane (1981) presented a sentence context, (e.g., "The tailor mended the ...") followed by a target string (e.g., soup). When the target was a word, three factors were manipulated: stimulus degradation, word frequency, and whether or not the target word was congruent with the context. The three factors had additive effects on response time and on log percent correct.

Further examples of factors having additive effects on both response time and log percent correct have occurred in identification (Shwartz, Pomerantz, and Egeth 1977), memory scanning (Lively 1972), geometric figure matching (Dickman and Meyer 1988), and dual choice reactions (Pashler and Johnston 1989).

Additivity for Time and Accuracy: Partial Output   In a system without distinct stages, accuracy would be a function of the total processing time, t. Accuracy measured as log percent correct would then be written $\log p(t)$. It is clear that if accuracy is a linear function of time, $\log p(t) = a + bt$, then two factors having additive effects on time would also have additive effects on accuracy. What may be surprising is that if accuracy is a nonlinear function of the total processing time, then two factors cannot have additive effects on both time and accuracy (see Schweickert 1989 for details). If log percent correct is not a linear function of time, then the examples above are evidence against systems without distinct stages. Note, however, that accuracy functions sometimes are linear (see Luce 1986).

What Do Interactive Factors Imply about Processing Structure?

The processes involved in a simple task may all be in series, but for complex tasks it is more realistic to suppose that sequential and concurrent processes occur, perhaps with feedback. It is also realistic to suppose that some processes operate on information, while others provide support. A model incorporating these features is Sanders's (1983) cognitive-energetic model for performance under stress. In that model a strategic subsystem concerned with evaluation and resource allocation accompanies the subsystem of information processing stages. Sanders argued that there are multiple sources of energy, each serving specific processes. Energy and resources for early processing stages are supplied by the arousal system, and those for late stages are supplied by the activation system. Energy and resources for the central stage, response choice, are supplied by effort, which also controls the other two energy systems. The evaluation mechanism receives energetic feedback from the arousal and activation systems, and performance feedback via the responses made. The evaluation mechanism optimizes the entire system by controlling effort. The duration of a process is determined by the computational work it does, and by its allocation of energy. The model explains results such as those of Frowein (1981), who found that amphetamine had additive effects with such input variables as stimulus intensity and signal quality, while barbiturate had additive effects with the computational variables he examined, except for signal quality.

Precedence Networks The need for such complicated models indicates a need for ways to analyze them. Predictions for complex models often require simulations. But if there is no feedback, sequential and concurrent processes can be represented in a precedence network (see figs. 23.1, 23.2). The network structure can be determined with latent network theory (Schweickert 1978, 1983) and response time predictions can be made with an algorithm of Fisher and Goldstein (1983).

Each process in a precedence network has a starting point and an ending point. When all the processes are complete-output processes, a process begins execution when all its immediate predecessors have finished. Certain partial-output processes can also be represented in such a network. Suppose that x is a partial-output process transmitting input to y. This is represented by drawing an arc to indicate that the starting point of x precedes the starting point of y, and drawing another arc to indicate that the finishing point of x precedes the finishing point of y. Two processes are *sequential* if there is a path directed from the head of one to the tail of the other; otherwise they are *concurrent*.

The duration of a process is a nonnegative random variable. On any given trial, one of the paths from stimulus onset to the response will be the longest. This path is called the *critical path*, and the sum of the durations of the processes on it is the response time for the trial.

Latent Network Theory A key idea of Sternberg's (1969) additive-factor method was to examine the effects of prolonging processes. Such effects are surprisingly informative about precedence networks. In particular, sequential and concurrent processes can be distinguished, and it turns out that this is enough information to construct a precedence network representing the task (Schweickert 1978, 1980, 1983; Schweickert, Fisher and Goldstein 1991; Schweickert and Townsend 1989; Townsend and Schweickert 1989).

If each of two factors affects a different process, their combined effects on response time may interact. The results are therefore not as simple as in the serial case considered by Sternberg (1969). Nonetheless, the interactions often have a simple form. These will be discussed as they arise in the topics to follow.

Sanders's Cognitive-Energetic Model Molenaar and van der Molen (1986) constructed both a neural network representation of Sanders's (1983) model and a precedence network representation of a version of the model without feedback. They investigated the theoretical effects of prolonging processes in each network. (They actually prolonged transmissions between processes, rather than the processes themselves, but that does not matter here.) Simulations of the neural network representation demonstrated once again that factors affecting different processes in a McClelland's (1979) cascade model can have additive effects on response time.

The precedence network representation was investigated without simulations, using an algorithm by Fisher and Goldstein (1983). It gives exact expressions for the mean, variance, and distribution function of the response time when the process durations have independent exponential distributions.

Suppose two factors prolong two processes in a precedence network. Let T_{ij} be the mean response time when one factor is at level i and the other is at level j, with the factor levels numbered in order of increasing prolongations. The interaction contrast for the combination (i, j) is

$$T_{ij} - T_{1j} - T_{i1} + T_{11}.$$

The following three results are predicted (a special network, an embellished Wheatstone bridge, may be an exception): (a) Effects of factors are monotonic with the factor levels, (b) interaction contrasts all have the same sign, and (c) they too are monotonic with the factor levels. If the interaction contrasts are positive, the processes are sequential. If they are negative, the processes are concurrent, or in a Wheatstone bridge (Schweickert 1978; Schweickert, Fisher and Goldstein 1991; Schweickert and Townsend 1989).

Molenaar and van der Molen (1986) considered the effects of two hypothetical factors prolonging two different processes in Sanders's (1983) model. They considered one concurrent pair of processes and one sequential pair of processes. For the concurrent processes, expected values of response times monotonically increased with the prolongations. The effects of the prolongations were not additive, but the interaction contrasts were all negative and they were monotonic with the factor levels.

For the sequential processes, expected values of response times monotonically increased with factor levels. For the parameters chosen, the interaction contrasts were small. Nonetheless, the pattern described above occurred again, that is, interaction contrasts had the same sign, positive in this case, and increased monotonically with the factor levels. All results were as predicted.

Visual Search Egeth and Dagenbach (1991) investigated concurrent and sequential processes in visual search. Subjects searched for a target letter in a display of two letters. Two levels of luminance contrast were available for each of the two characters. In one experiment, subjects searched for an O among Xs, or an X among Os, arranged to produce efficient search according to the criteria of Duncan and Humphreys (1989). The absence trials are of interest because to respond correctly a subject must process every item, that is, processing is exhaustive. Decreasing contrast for either letter alone increased absence response time. The combined effect of decreasing contrast for both characters equaled the effect of decreasing contrast for either one alone. This subadditivity is exactly what would be predicted for a parallel search (Egeth and Dagenbach 1991; Schweickert 1978).

In the second experiment, subjects searched for rotated Ls among rotated Ts, or rotated Ts, among rotated Ls which would be difficult according to the criteria of Duncan and Humphreys (1989). In this case, on absence trials, there was no effect of decreasing contrast for either nontarget individually, but there was an effect when contrast was decreased for both. This superadditive effect would be predicted if processing of the nontargets were sequential and could not occur if processing were parallel.

Stages and Additive Factors Reconsidered Suppose two factors prolong two different processes in a precedence network. It is clear that if all the processes are in series, the combined effect of the two factors will be the sum of their individual effects. However, the two factors can have additive effects on response time even though the processes they prolong are not in series, as is apparent from figure 23.1.

The vertex p is called a cut-point, because if it were removed the network would have two parts. Schweickert, Fisher, and Goldstein (1991) showed that two factors prolonging different processes in a precedence network invariably have additive effects on response time if and only if the two processes are on

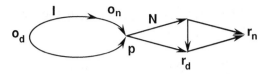

Figure 23.1 A precedence network representing the double stimulation task of Becker (1976). The digit is presented at o_d, followed after interval I by the tone at o_n. Responses to them are at r_d and r_n. Process N is prolonged by increasing the number of alternative responses to the tone. Point p is a cut-point.

opposite sides of a cut-point. Of course, if all the processes are in series, every vertex is a cut-point.

The theorem can be interpreted in the following way. Processing between stimulus onset and the first cut-point can be thought of as a superprocess. Then processing between the first cut-point and the second cut-point is also a superprocess, and so on. Now, the theorem says that two factors prolonging processes invariably have additive effects on response time if and only if they affect processes in different superprocesses. If two factors affect different processes in the same superprocess, they can be made to interact. This recapitulates Sternberg's (1969) original logic for the additive-factors method.

Effects of Factors on Physiological Variables

A neglected measure probably useful in conjunction with speed and accuracy is force. It is sensitive to manipulations of interest. For example, Abrams and Balota (1990) found that when responses were made by moving a lever, the force exerted at response onset increased with set size in a memory scanning task, and with word frequency in a lexical decision task.

Cognitive psychologists have given more attention to evoked potentials. Suppose by volume conduction, electrodes pick up signals from groups of neurons whose geometry is suitable (see, e.g., Coles, Gratton, and Fabiani, in press). These groups generate electrical potentials, $c_1(t), \ldots, c_k(t)$, called components. An electrode placed at location 1 on the scalp will register a potential $x(t, 1)$ at time t. The potential depends on the component potentials according to an approximation, described in Mocks (1988). Suppose "there are $k = 1$, ..., K basic functions of time, say, $c_k(t)$, which are common to all electrodes, and there is a set of coefficients $b_k(1)$ independent of time measuring the strength of the presence of the component $c_k(t)$ at the electrode at 1. All contributions add up to approximate the data

$$x(t, 1) = \sum_{k=1}^{K} c_k(t) b_k(1)."$$

The equation indicates that if each of two experimental factors altered a different component potential, without changing the coefficient, they would have additive effects on the potential recorded at each electrode. If component potentials were produced by dipoles it would be important that their orienta-

Information, Time, and the Structure of Mental Events

tions not change as the factor levels change, to keep the coefficients unchanged as the factors change.

An Application to Semantic Relatedness   Kutas and Hillyard (1980) discovered a negative peak, the N400, in the event-related potential at about 400 ms, which is sensitive to semantic anomaly. An experiment by Holcomb and Kounios (1990) found additive effects of two factors on the N400. They displayed a sentence such as *no dogs are animals* and subjects indicated whether it was true or false. To avoid eye movements, the first three words were presented first, followed 300 ms later by the predicate word. The following three factors were manipulated:

1. The quantifier was *all, some,* or *no.*

2. The subject was either related to the predicate or unrelated.

3. In a superset sentence, the subject was more general or abstract than the predicate. In a subset sentence, the subject was less general or abstract.

The results relevant here are that the ERP was significantly more negative when the subject and predicate were unrelated, and significantly more negative for the superset than the subset sentences. There was no interaction. The effects of the factors on the potential were additive at all times relevant to the N400, not just for the peaks. Holcomb and Kounios explain the additive effects by saying "these two factors could affect independent, parallel processes that are somehow time-locked or synchronized."

Summary

Donders proposed stages with processing executed between discrete beginning and ending events. Sternberg's additive-factor method interprets additive effects of two factors on response time as evidence that each factor affects a different stage in a series of stages. An interaction is interpreted as evidence that the two factors affect the same stage. Counterexamples show that additive factors do not imply stages as Donders conceived them, but factors with additive effects on both response time and log percent correct rule out certain non-Donderian models.

Factors prolonging different processes in a precedence network often have interactive effects, so the additive-factor method does not apply to the processes. However, if a stage in a precedence network is defined as the processing between two consecutive cut-points, then Sternberg's additive-factor-method applies to the stages. Factors having additive effects on evoked potentials have been found, but this outcome is not often reported.

23.5   WHAT BECAME OF THE LIMITED CHANNEL?

Double stimulation can have two effects when compared with single stimulation, facilitation, and inhibition. Each will be discussed.

Facilitation: The Redundant Signals Effect

Suppose on some trials two signals are presented, on others, one signal is presented, and on still others none is presented. The subject is to respond as soon as any signal is detected. Detection is usually faster for two signals than one. In the race model (Raab 1962), there is a process for each signal, and as soon as a signal is detected by either of these parallel processes, the subject responds. Miller (1982b) noted that the race model makes another prediction. Let S_i denote the event that a signal is present on channel i, $i = 1, 2$; let T_i be the processing time for signal i, assumed to be the same whether or not the other signal is also present, and let RT denote the reaction time. Then $RT = \min\{T_1, T_2\}$ when both signals are present. Then

$$P(RT \leq t \mid S_1 \text{ and } S_2)$$

$$= P(RT \leq t \mid S_1) + P(RT \leq t \mid S_2) - P(T_1 \leq t \text{ and } T_2 \leq t \mid S_1 \text{ and } S_2)$$

$$\leq P(RT \leq t \mid S_1) + P(RT \leq t \mid S_2).$$

(Colonius 1990b found a smaller upper bound based on Frechet bounds.) Miller found significant violations of the inequality in his own data, and those of others, so the race model can be rejected.

Schwarz (1989) accounted for the redundant signals effect by supposing each signal produces events that are counted. When the total count reaches a criterion, the response is made. When both signals are present, the events they produce are interleaved, and all events are counted. Even though there is a process for each signal, they are not racing. Schwarz was able to account for mean response times by postulating a Poisson counter. The model does not account for the variances, however (Diederich and Colonius 1991).

Inhibition: Psychological Refractoriness and Garner Interference

Psychological Refractory Period   The strong version of Welford's (1967) single channel hypothesis assumed all processing of the second stimulus followed that of the first, and this was shown to be false. A precedence network model by Davis (1957) allowed concurrent execution of sensory and motor processes, and sequential execution of central ones, but it was not clear how to test it at the time. Such models can be tested by prolonging processes, and suitable data were obtained in an experiment by Smith (1969). (It is noteworthy that these data were presented at the Attention and Performance symposium where Sternberg 1969 proposed the idea of prolonging processes.)

The first stimulus was a digit on a red or green background, and the response was manual. The second stimulus was a 1 or a 2 on a gray background, and the response was vocal. The number of alternatives for the first stimulus was varied, as was the interstimulus interval (ISI).

Response times to the first stimulus were unaffected by the size of the interstimulus interval, and so are not of interest here. Response times to the second stimulus, read from a graph in Smith (1969), are in table 23.1. For

Table 23.1 Responses to Second Stimulus; Smith (1969)

Number of S1 Alternatives			
ISI	2	4	8
Response Times (msec)			
50	665	766	835
150	680	769	836
300	750	809	889
500	913	929	963
Interaction Contrasts			
50	—	—	—
150	—	−12	−14
300	—	−42	−31
500	—	−85	−120

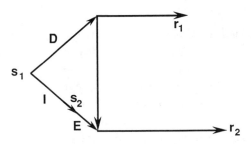

Figure 23.2 A precedence network representing the double stimulation task of Smith. s_1 and s_2 are the first and second stimulus, separated by the interstimulus interval, I. Process D is prolonged by increasing the number of alternatives for s_1. Process E is encoding of the second stimulus. r_1 and r_2 are responses to s_1 and s_2.

analysis, these response times are all measured with respect to the same starting point, the onset of the first stimulus.

The times monotonically increase with the number of alternatives and with the ISI, as predicted when processes are prolonged in a precedence network. Further, the interaction contrasts are also monotonic, and have the same sign. There is one exception, the −31 in the second row, an error of 11 ms. The negative interactions would be expected if the ISI and the decision about the first stimulus were concurrent.

A precedence network for the task is in figure 23.2. Expected values of response times were derived using the Fisher-Goldstein (1983) algorithm, assuming independent exponential process durations. The model accounts for 99.4 percent of the variance. Further details are in Schweickert, Fisher, and Goldstein (1990).

In a double stimulation task by Becker (1976), a digit was followed by a tone. The subject pressed a button with one hand to identify the digit, and with the other to identify the tone. The ISI was either 90 or 190 ms. The number of alternative responses to the tone was either one or two. Increasing the ISI and increasing the response alternatives had additive effects on both the response time to the digit and the response time to the tone. Additivity indicates that ISI and the decision about the tone are sequential (fig. 23.1).

Pashler and Johnston (1989) varied the intensity of the second stimulus and the ISI. Interaction contrasts were positive and monotonic with ISI, indicating that the ISI and the process affected by intensity are sequential.

Garner Interference A phenomenon closely related to, if not identical to, psychological refractoriness is *Garner interference*. Refractoriness investigations often use an ISI of 0 as a special case, sometimes require a response to only one of the stimuli, and sometimes vary the number of alternatives of one of the stimuli, with one alternative as a special case. These conditions in the refractory period paradigm form the Garner interference paradigm. Although the phenomena are not ordinarily linked, their paradigms are remarkably similar.

In one experiment, Pomerantz and Garner (1973) asked subjects to classify stimuli made of two parentheses according to the orientation of one of them, say, the left one. The number of alternatives for the relevant left parenthesis was always two. In the single-dimension task, the irrelevant right parenthesis was always the same; it had one alternative. In the orthogonal-dimensions filtering task, the irrelevant right parenthesis had two alternatives. Performance was worse in the two-alternative filtering orthogonal-dimensions task than in the one-alternative single-dimension task. The difference between performance in these two conditions is called Garner interference. If it is not zero, it indicates that values on the irrelevant dimension prolong the decision about the stimulus, and the dimensions are said to be not separable.

One might think that dimensions of stimuli in different modalities would be separable. But Melara and O'Brien (1987), noting that normal individuals and synesthetes associate high pitch with high vertical position, found Garner interference for compound stimuli made with those dimensions. A single channel explanation of Garner interference would say a decision is required for the irrelevant dimension, and delays the decision about the relevant dimension by occupying the channel.

Summary

Race models account for performance for a given stimulus, but do not account for effects of redundant stimuli. A generalized version of single channel theory allowing both concurrent and sequential processing accounts for some aspects of refractoriness. A complete explanation of refractoriness would also explain Garner interference.

23.6 WHAT COMES NEXT?

Figure 23.3, from Churchland and Sejnowski (1988), illustrates the spatial and temporal resolution of techniques now used for investigation of brain

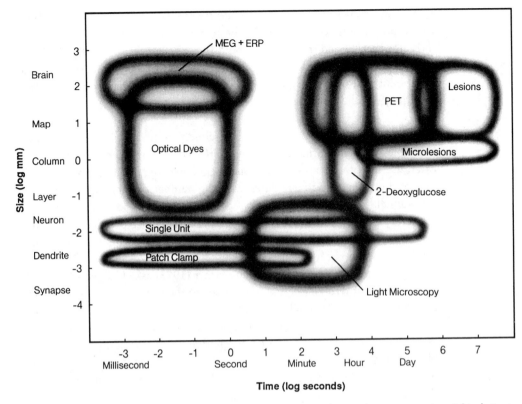

Figure 23.3 Illustration of temporal and spatial resolution of various experimental techniques for investigating brain function. From Churchland and Sejnowski (1988). © 1988 by the AAAS.

functioning. Most tasks studied by cognitive psychologists take from 1/4 second (simple reaction time) to about 10 seconds (problem solving), with tasks on the order of a second (memory scanning, lexical decision, sentence verification) providing the base for most cognitive theory. There is a conspicuous gap in the figure for this time interval. A single neuron is not the crucial structure for these tasks, while optical dyes skirt the temporal range of interest. Some years from now it may be feasible, painlessly and without surgery, to apply a magnetic field directly to a small region of cortex and observe the effects in an awake human.[2] For now, evoked response potentials and magnetoencephalography are the key technologies for supplementing response time to understand these tasks.

To locate response time in the figure, note that RT includes all processing from sensation to movement, that is, the entire brain and often the spinal cord and beyond. If response time could be fractionated into the time spent in perception, motor preparation, and so on, the spatial resolution would automatically improve considerably, since the location of these components is known, often at the level of cortical maps. It has been hard to apportion the response time to various components, because their processing overlaps in time. We are pursuing a long detour through processing structure, before continuing with Donders's goal of measuring the time for a single stage. I think we are starting to separate structural components right now, and the fractionation will not be far behind. Surely we will make great progress on this in the next twenty-five years.

After that? A typical neural network might represent a region about a millimeter in diameter, roughly the size of a cortical column. These are the bottom level constituents of cognition. Churchland and Sejnowski (1988) say, "It is apparent that we lack detailed information about processing in neural networks within cortical layers and columns over a wide range of time scales, from milliseconds to hours." Would response times be useful for structures this small? As anyone measuring response times knows, equipment precision is no limitation and statistical variation could be overcome by increasing sample size, if the quantity to be estimated were not kept in motion by poorly understood sequential and practice effects. These are exactly the effects neural networks might illuminate, but better data awaits better theory and vice versa, surely a sign of excitement to come.

APPENDIX: A FACTORIAL TEST FOR GENERAL RANDOM WALKS

Let N be the number of observations required to reach a decision, X_N be the sum of the evidence from N observations, and u_i be the drift rate with stimulus s_i. From Cox and Miller (1965, 57), for a general random walk, no matter what the distribution of the increments,

$E[X_N|s_i]/u_i = E[N|s_i].$

Let $P_i(R_A)$ be the probability response A is made when stimulus s_i is presented. The usual approximation for small steps is

$E[X_N|s_i] = AP_i(R_A) - BP_i(R_B),$

where A and $-B$ are the upper and lower criteria. After substitution into the first equation,

$$E[N|s_i] = \frac{A + B}{u_i} \left[P_i(R_A) - \frac{B}{A + B} \right].$$

Suppose the deadline affects the distance between the two criteria, $A + B$, without affecting the ratio $B/(A + B)$, while the stimulus probability affects the ratio without affecting the distance. For deadline j let d_j be the distance, and for prior probability level k, let r_k be the ratio. Then

$$E[N_{jk}|s_i] = \frac{d_j}{u_i} [P_{ijk}(R_A) - r_k],$$

and

$E[T_{ijk}] = cE[N_{jk}|s_i] + t,$

where $P_{ijk}(R_A)$ is the probability of responding A when stimulus s_i is presented and $E[T_{ijk}]$ is the expected response time, c is a scale factor and t is the time for processes other than the decision. With two stimuli, J levels for the deadline, K levels for prior probability, and two responses, there are $2 \times J \times K \times 2$ expected response times to account for. The number of parameters is smaller (two values of u_i, J of d_j, K of r_k, c and t), so the model can be rejected.

NOTES

I thank Jerome Busemeyer, Michael Coles, Hans Colonius, Ritske de Jong, Donald Fisher, Leslie Geddes, Gordon Logan, Robert Melara, Jeff Miller, James Neely, Robert Proctor, and Patricia Van Zandt for helpful discussions.

1. Suggested to me by Jerome Busemeyer.

2. Leslie Geddes, personal communication, May 16, 1990.

REFERENCES

Abrams, R. A., and Balota, D. A. (1991). Mental chronometry: Beyond reaction time. *Psychological Science, 2,* 153–157.

Alluisi, E. A., Muller, P. F., and Fitts, P. M. (1957). An information analysis of verbal and motor responses in a forced-paced serial task. *Journal of Experimental Psychology, 53,* 153–158.

Anderson, J. A. (1973). A theory for the recognition of items from short memorized lists. *Psychological Review, 80,* 417–438.

Ashby, F. G. (1982a). Deriving exact predictions from the cascade model. *Psychological Review, 89,* 599–607.

Ashby, F. G. (1982b). Testing the assumptions of exponential additive reaction-time models. *Memory and Cognition, 10,* 125–134.

Ashby, F. G., and Townsend, J. T. (1980). Decomposing the reaction time distribution: Pure insertion and selective influence revisited. *Journal of Mathematical Psychology, 21,* 93–123.

Atkinson, R. C., Holmgren, J. E., and Juola, J. F. (1969). Processing time as influenced by the number of elements in a visual display. *Perception and Psychophysics, 6,* 321–326.

Audley, R. J., and Pike, A. R. (1965). Some alternative stochastic models of choice. *The British Journal of Mathematical and Statistical Psychology, 18,* 207–225.

Becker, C. A. (1976). Allocation of attention during visual word recognition. *Journal of Experimental Psychology: Human Perception and Performance, 2,* 556–566.

Bertelson, P. (1966). Central intermittency twenty years later. *Quarterly Journal of Experimental Psychology, 18,* 153–163.

Brand, J. (1971). Classification without identification in visual search. *Quarterly Journal of Experimental Psychology, 23,* 178–186.

Broadbent, D. E. (1958). *Perception and communication.* London: Pergamon.

Burbeck, S. L. (1979). Change and level detectors inferred from simple reaction times. University of California at Irvine, Ph.D. dissertation.

Churchland, P. S., and Sejnowski, T. J. (1988). Perspectives on cognitive neuroscience. *Science, 242,* 741–745.

Coles, M. G. H., Gratton, G., Bashore, T. R., Eriksen, C. W., and Donchin, E. (1985). A psychophysiological investigation of the continuous flow model of human information processing. *Journal of Experimental Psychology: Human Perception and Performance, 11,* 529–553.

Coles, M. G. H, Gratton, G., and Fabiani, M. (N.d.). Event-related brain potentials. In J. T. Cacioppo and L. G. Tassinary (Eds.), *Principles of psychophysiology: Physical, social, and inferential elements*. Cambridge, UK: Cambridge University Press. In press.

Colonius, H. (1990a). A note on the stop-signal paradigm, or how to observe the unobservable. *Psychological Review, 97,* 309–312.

Colonius, H. (1990b). Possibly dependent probability summation of reaction time. *Journal of Mathematical Psychology, 34,* 253–275.

Cox, D. R., and Miller, H. D. (1965). *The theory of stochastic processes*. London: Methuen.

Crossman, E. R. F. W. (1953). Entropy and choice time: The effect of frequency unbalance on choice-response. *Quarterly Journal of Experimental Psychology, 5,* 41–52.

Davis, R. (1957). The human operator as a single channel information system. *Quarterly Journal of Experimental Psychology, 9,* 119–129.

de Jong, R., Coles, M. G. H., Logan, G. D., and Gratton, G. (1990). In search of the point of no return: The control of response processes in speeded choice reaction performance. *Journal of Experimental Psychology: Human Perception and Performance, 16,* 164–182.

Dickman, S. J., and Meyer, D. E. (1988). Impulsivity and speed-accuracy tradeoffs in information processing. *Journal of Personality and Social Psychology, 54,* 274–290.

Diederich, A., and Colonius, H. (1991). A further test of the superposition model for the redundant signals effect in bimodal detection. *Perception & Psychophysics, 50,* 83–86.

Donchin, E., and Coles, M. G. H. (1988). Is the P300 component a manifestation of context updating? *Behavioral and Brain Sciences, 11,* 357–374.

Donders, F. C. (1869). Over de snelheid van psychische processen [On the speed of mental processes]. *Onder-zoekingen degaan in het physiologisch Laboratorium der Ugtrechtsche Hoogeschool, 1868–69,* Tweede reeks, *11,* 92–130. In W. G. Koster (Ed. and Trans.), *Attention and Performance II*. (Reprinted from *Acta Psychologica* 1969, *30,* 412–431.)

Duncan, J. (1983). Category effects in visual search: A failure to replicate the "oh-zero" phenomenon. *Perception and Psychophysics, 34,* 221–232.

Duncan, J., and Humphreys, G. W. (1989). Visual search and stimulus similarity. *Psychological Review, 96,* 433–458.

Egeth, H., and Dagenbach, D. (1991). Parallel versus serial processing in visual search: Further evidence from subadditive effects of visual quality. *Journal of Experimental Psychology: Human Perception and Performance. 17,* 551–560.

Egeth, H., Jonides, J., and Wall, S. (1972). Parallel processing of multielement displays. *Cognitive Psychology, 3,* 674–698.

Estes, W. K. (1972). Interactions of signal and background variables in visual processing. *Perception and Psychophysics, 12,* 278–286.

Falmagne, J. C. (1965). Stochastic models for choice reaction time with applications to experimental results. *Journal of Mathematical Psychology, 2,* 77–124.

Fisher, D. L. (1982). Limited channel models of automatic detection: Capacity and scanning in visual search. *Psychological Review, 89,* 662–692.

Fisher, D. L., Duffy, S. A., Young, C., and Pollatsek, A. (1988). Understanding the central processing limit in consistent-mapping visual search tasks. *Journal of Experimental Psychology: Human Perception and Performance, 14,* 253–266.

Fisher, D. L., and Goldstein, W. M. (1983). Stochastic PERT networks as models of cognition: Derivation of the mean, variance, and distribution of reaction time using order-of-processing (OP) diagrams. *Journal of Mathematical Psychology, 27,* 121–151.

Information, Time, and the Structure of Mental Events

Frowein, H. W. (1981). Selective effects of barbiturate and amphetamine on information processing and response execution. *Acta Psychologica, 47,* 105–115.

Gratton, G., Coles, M. G. H., Sirevaag, E., Eriksen, C. W., and Donchin, E. (1988). Pre- and post-stimulus activation of response channels: A psychophysiological analysis. *Journal of Experimental Psychology: Human Perception and Performance, 14,* 331–344.

Hick, W. E. (1952). On the rate of gain of information. *Quarterly Journal of Experimental Psychology, 4,* 11–26.

Hick, W. E., and Welford, A. T. (1956). Comments on "Central inhibition: Some refractory observations," by A. Elithorn and C. Lawrence. *Quarterly Journal of Experimental Psychology, 8,* 39–41.

Holcomb, P. J., and Kounios, J. (1990). Structure and process in semantic memory (II): Evidence from event-related brain potentials and reaction times. Manuscript submitted for publication.

Hyman, R. (1953). Stimulus information as a determinant of reaction time. *Journal of Experimental Psychology, 45,* 188–196.

Jonides, J., and Gleitman, H. (1972). A conceptual category effect in visual search: O as letter or as digit. *Perception and Psychophysics, 12,* 457–460.

Kantowitz, B. H. (1974). Double stimulation. In B. H. Kantowitz (Ed.), *Human information processing: Tutorials in performance and cognition,* 83–131. Hillsdale, NJ: Erlbaum.

Karlin, L., and Kestenbaum, R. (1968). Effects of number of alternatives on the psychological refractory period. *Quarterly Journal of Experimental Psychology, 20,* 167–178.

Kornblum, S. (1969). Sequential determinants of information processing in serial and discrete choice reaction time. *Psychological Review, 76,* 113–131.

Kornblum, S., Hasbroucq, T., and Osman, A. (1990). Dimensional overlap: A cognitive basis for stimulus-response compatibility—A model and a taxonomy. *Psychological Review, 97,* 253–270.

Kornhuber, H. H., and Deecke, L. (1965). Hirnpotentialanderungen bei Willkurbewegungen und passiven Bewegungen des Menchen: Bereitschaftpotential und reaffarente Potentiale. *Pflugers Archives fur die gesammte Physiologie, 284,* 1–17.

Kutas, M., and Hillyard, S. A. (1980). Reading senseless sentences: Brain potentials reflect semantic incongruity. *Science, 207,* 203–205.

LaBerge, D. (1962). A recruitment theory of simple behavior. *Psychometrika, 27,* 375–396.

Laming, D. R. J. (1968). *Information theory of choice-reaction times.* London: Academic Press.

Laming, D. R. J. (1979). A critical comparison of two random-walk models for two-choice reaction time. *Acta Psychologica, 43,* 431–453.

Leonard, J. A. (1959). Tactual reactions: I *Quarterly Journal of Experimental Psychology, 11,* 76–83.

Link, S. W. (1975). The relative judgment theory of two-choice response time. *Journal of Mathematical Psychology, 12,* 114–135.

Link, S. W., and Heath, R. A. (1975). A sequential theory of psychological discrimination. *Psychometrika, 40,* 77–105.

Lively, B. L. (1972). Speed/accuracy trade-off and practice as determinants of stage durations in a memory-search task. *Journal of Experimental Psychology, 96,* 97–103.

Logan, G. D., and Cowan, W. B. (1984). On the ability to inhibit thought and action: A theory of an act of control. *Psychological Review, 91,* 295–327.

Luce, R. D. (1986). *Response times: Their role in inferring elementary mental organization.* New York: Oxford University Press.

Marley, A. A. J., and Colonius, H. (N.d.). The "horse race" random utility model for choice probabilities and reaction times, and its competing risks interpretation. *Journal of Mathematical Psychology*. In press.

McClelland, J. L. (1979). On the time relations of mental processes: An examination of systems of processes in cascade. *Psychological Review, 86,* 287–330.

Melara, R. D., and O'Brien, T. P. (1987). Interaction between synesthetically corresponding dimensions. *Journal of Experimental Psychology: General, 116,* 323–336.

Meyer, D. E., Yantis, S., Osman, A., and Smith, J. E. K. (1984). Discrete versus continuous models of response preparation: A reaction time analysis. In S. Kornblum and J. Requin (Eds.), *Preparatory states and processes,* 69–94. Hillsdale, NJ: Lawrence Erlbaum.

Miller, J. C. (1982a). Discrete versus continuous stage models of human information processing: In search of partial output. *Journal of Experimental Psychology: Human Perception and Performance, 8,* 273–296.

Miller, J. O. (1982b). Divided attention: Evidence for coactivation with redundant signals. *Cognitive Psychology, 14,* 247–279.

Miller, J. O. (1988). Discrete and continuous models of human information processing: Theoretical distinctions and empirical results. *Acta Psychologica, 67,* 191–257.

Mocks, J. (1988). Decomposing event-related potentials: A new topographic components model. *Biological Psychology, 26,* 199–215.

Molenaar, P. C. M., and van der Molen, M. W. (1986). Steps to a formal analysis of the cognitive-energetic model of stress and human performance. *Acta Psychologica, 62,* 237–261.

Moray, N. (1967). Where is capacity limited? A survey and a model. *Acta Psychologica, 27,* 84–92.

Mowbray, G. H., and Rhoades, M. V. (1959). On the reduction of choice reaction times with practice. *Quarterly Journal of Experimental Psychology, 11,* 16–23.

Nickerson, R. S. (1969). "Same"-"different" response times: A model and a preliminary test. *Acta Psychologica, 30,* 257–275.

Ollman, R. T. (1966). Fast guesses in choice-reaction time. *Psychonomic Science, 6,* 155–156.

Ollman, R. T. (1968). Central refractoriness in simple reaction time: The deferred processing model. *Journal of Mathematical Psychology, 5,* 49–60.

Ollman, R. T. (1982). Additive factors and the speed accuracy trade-off. Paper presented at the Mathematical Psychology Meeting, Princeton, NJ.

Pashler, H., and Johnston, J. C. (1989). Chronometric evidence for central postponement in temporally overlapping tasks. *Quarterly Journal of Experimental Psychology, 41(A),* 19–45.

Pike, A. R. (1973). Response latency models for signal detection. *Psychological Review, 80,* 53–68.

Pomerantz, J. R., and Garner, W. R. (1973). Stimulus configurations in selective attention tasks. *Perception and Psychophysics, 14,* 565–569.

Posner, M. I. (1978). *Chronometric explorations of mind.* Hillsdale, NJ: Erlbaum.

Proctor, R. W., and Reeve, T. G. (Eds.) (1990). *Stimulus-response compatibility.* Amsterdam: Elsevier.

Raab, D. (1962). Statistical facilitation of simple reaction times. *Transactions of the New York Academy of Sciences, 24,* 574–590.

Ratcliff, R. (1978). A theory of memory retrieval. *Psychological Review, 85,* 59–108.

Reeve, T. G., and Proctor, R. W. (1984). On the advance preparation of discrete finger responses. *Journal of Experimental Psychology: Human Perception and Performance, 10,* 541–553.

Reeve, T. G., and Proctor, R. W. (1990). The salient-features coding principle for spatial- and symbolic-compatibility effects. In R. W. Proctor and T. G. Reeve (Eds.), *Stimulus-response compatibility.* Amsterdam: Elsevier.

Remington, R. J. (1969). Analysis of sequential effects in choice reaction times. *Journal of Experimental Psychology, 82,* 250–275.

Rumelhart, D. E. (1970). A multicomponent theory of the perception of briefly exposed visual displays. *Journal of Mathematical Psychology, 7,* 191–218.

Sanders, A. F. (1983). Towards a model of stress and human performance. *Acta Psychologica, 53,* 61–97.

Sanders, A. F. (1990). Issues and trends in the debate on discrete versus continuous processing of information. *Acta Psychologica. 74,* 123–167.

Schneider, W., and Shiffrin, R. M. (1977). Controlled and automatic human information processing: I. Detection, search, and attention. *Psychological Review, 84,* 1–66.

Schuberth, R. E., Spoehr, K. T., and Lane, D. M. (1981). Effects of stimulus and contextual information on the lexical decision process. *Memory and Cognition, 9,* 68–77.

Schwarz, W. (1989). A new model to explain the redundant-signals effect. *Perception and Psychophysics, 46,* 498–500.

Schweickert, R. (1978). A critical path generalization of the additive factor method: Analysis of a Stroop task. *Journal of Mathematical Psychology, 18,* 105–139.

Schweickert, R. (1980). Critical path scheduling of mental processes in a dual task. *Science, 209,* 704–706.

Schweickert, R. (1983). Latent network theory: Scheduling of processes in sentence verification and the Stroop effect. *Journal of Experimental Psychology: Learning, Memory, and Cognition, 9,* 353–383.

Schweickert, R. (1985). Separable effects of factors on speed and accuracy: Memory scanning, lexical decision, and choice tasks. *Psychological Bulletin, 97,* 530–546.

Schweickert, R. (1989). Separable effects of factors on activation functions in discrete and continuous models: d' and evoked potentials. *Psychological Bulletin, 106,* 318–328.

Schweickert, R., Fisher, D. L., and Goldstein, W. M. (1991). Structural and quantitative analysis of network representations of cognition. Unpublished manuscript.

Schweickert, R., and Townsend, J. T. (1989). A trichotomy: Interactions of factors prolonging sequential and concurrent mental processes in stochastic discrete mental (PERT) networks. *Journal of Mathematical Psychology, 33,* 328–347.

Shannon, C. E. (1948). A mathematical theory of communication. *Bell System Technical Journal, 27,* 379-423, 623-565.

Shiffrin, R. M., and Schneider, W. (1977). Controlled and automatic human information processing: II. Perceptual learning, automatic attending and a general theory. *Psychological Review, 84,* 127–190.

Shwartz, S. P., Pomerantz, J. R., and Egeth, H. (1977). State and process limitations in information processing: An additive factor analysis. *Journal of Experimental Psychology: Human Perception and Performance, 3,* 402–410.

Smith, J. E. K., Meyer, D. E., Yantis, S., and Osman, A. (1982). Finite-state models of reaction time: Estimation of latency distributions. Paper presented at the meeting of the Society for Mathematical Psychology. Princeton, NJ.

Smith, M. C. (1969). The effect of varying information on the psychological refractory period. In W. G. Koster (Ed.), *Attention and Performance II. Acta Psychologica, 30,* 220–231.

Smith, P. L., and Vickers, D. (1988). The accumulator model of two-choice discrimination. *Journal of Mathematical Psychology, 32,* 135–168.

Sperling, G., Budiansky, J., Spivak, J. G., and Johnson, M. C. (1971). Extremely rapid visual search: The maximum rate of scanning letters for the presence of a numeral. *Science, 174,* 307–311.

Sternberg, S. (1966). High-speed scanning in human memory. *Science, 153,* 652–657.

Sternberg, S. (1967). Two operations in character recognition: Some evidence from reaction-time measurements. *Perception and Psychophysics, 2,* 45–53.

Sternberg, S. (1969). The discovery of processing stages: Extensions of Donders' method. In W. G. Koster (Ed.), *Attention and Performance II,* 276–315. Amsterdam: Elsevier-North Holland.

Sternberg, S. (1975). Memory scanning: New findings and current controversies. *Quarterly Journal of Experimental Psychology 17,* 1–2.

Stone, M. (1960). Models for choice-reaction time. *Psychometrika, 25,* 251–260.

Sutton, S., Braren, M., Zubin, J., and John, E. R. (1965). Evoked potential correlates of stimulus uncertainty. *Science, 150,* 1187–1188.

Swanson, J. M., and Briggs, G. E. (1969). Information processing as a function of speed versus accuracy. *Journal of Experimental Psychology 81,* 223–229.

Swensson, R. G. (1972). The elusive tradeoff: Speed versus accuracy in visual discrimination tasks. *Perception and Psychophysics, 12,* 16–32.

Teichner, W. H., and Krebs, M. J. (1974). Laws of visual choice reaction time. *Psychological Review, 81,* 75–98.

Telford, C. W. (1931). The refractory phase of voluntary and associative responses. *Journal of Experimental Psychology, 14,* 1–36.

Ten Hoopen, G., Akerboom, G., and Raaymakers, E. (1982). Vibrotactual choice reaction time, tactile receptor systems and ideomotor compatibility. *Acta Psychologica, 50,* 143–157.

Theios, J. (1973). Reaction time measurements in the study of memory processes: Theory and data. In G. H. Bower (Ed.), *The psychology of learning and motivation.* Vol. 7, 43–85. New York: Academic Press.

Thomas, E. A. C. (1974). The selectivity of preparation. *Psychological Review, 81,* 442–464.

Townsend, J. T. (1971). A note on the identifiability of parallel and serial processes. *Perception and Psychophysics, 10,* 161–163.

Townsend, J. T. (1974). Issues and models concerning the processing of a finite number of inputs. In B. H. Kantowitz (Ed.), *Human information processing: Tutorials in performance and cognition,* 133–185. New York: Wiley.

Townsend, J. T. (1976). Serial and within-stage independent parallel model equivalence on the minimum completion time. *Journal of Mathematical Psychology, 14,* 219–238.

Townsend, J. T., and Ashby, F. G. (1983). *Stochastic modeling of elementary psychological processes.* Cambridge, England: Cambridge University Press.

Townsend, J. T., and Roos, R. N. (1973). Search reaction time for single targets in multiletter stimuli with brief visual displays. *Memory and Cognition, 1,* 319–332.

Townsend, J. T., and Schweickert, R. (1989). Toward the trichotomy method of reaction times: Laying the foundation of stochastic mental networks. *Journal of Mathematical Psychology, 33,* 309–327.

Townsend, J. T., and Van Zandt, T. (1990). New theoretical results on testing self-terminating versus exhaustive processing in rapid search experiments. In H. G. Geissler (Ed.), *Psychophysical explorations of mental structures*. Toronto: Hogrefe and Huber.

Treisman, A., and Gelade, G. (1980). A feature-integration theory of attention. *Cognitive Psychology 12*, 97–136.

Treisman, A., and Gormican, S. (1988). Feature analysis in early vision: Evidence from search asymmetries. *Psychological Review, 95*, 15–48.

Vickers, D. (1970). Evidence for an accumulator model of psychophysical discrimination. *Ergonomics, 13*, 37–58.

Wald, A. (1947). *Sequential analysis*. New York: Wiley.

Welford, A. T. (1952). The "psychological refractory period" and the timing of high-speed performance—A review and a theory. *British Journal of Psychology, 43*, 2–19.

Welford, A. T. (1960). The measurement of sensory-motor performance. *Ergonomics, 3*, 189–230.

Welford, A. T. (1967). Single channel operation in the brain. *Acta Psychologica, 27*, 5–22.

Welford, A. T. (Ed.). (1980). *Reaction times*. London: Academic Press.

Yantis, S., and Meyer, D. E. (1983). Dynamics of activation in semantic and episodic memory. *Journal of Experimental Psychology: General, 117*, 130–147.

Yellott, J. I. (1971). Correction for fast guessing and the speed-accuracy trade-off in choice reaction time. *Journal of Mathematical Psychology, 8*, 159–199.

24 On the Transfer of Partial Information between Perception and Action

Gijsbertus Mulder, H. G. O. M. Smid, and
L. J. M. Mulder

24.1 INTRODUCTION

Mental chronometry is concerned with the time course of human information processing and with the architecture of cognition. In studies of mental chronometry, response time and errors are the main dependent variables. Important issues in the study of mental chronometry (Meyer et al. 1988) are:

1. the existence of separable processing stages;

2. the degree to which various stages of processing produce partial outputs before they are completed;

3. the discrete versus continuous form of the outputs.

An important approach in the study of mental chronometry is the subtraction method which was introduced by Donders ([1868] 1969). This method assumes that component processes are strictly successive stages whose durations combine additively and that stages of processing may be inserted and deleted without changing the time course of other concomitant processes. About a century later, Sternberg (1969) introduced his additive-factor method. Though this method avoids the dubious assumption of pure insertion, it assumes that the stages of processing do not overlap, that the outputs of the stages are always discrete quanta of information, and finally that task variables can selectively influence the durations of different stages.

In our previous research we tried to obtain converging evidence for the existence of processing stages by recording, in addition to classical performance measures (response time and errors), event-related brain potentials (ERPs), using visual or memory search tasks. The subjects are required to attend selectively to a certain spatial location or to a specific color or to a particular size of the stimulus or to a conjunction of these attributes. Relevant and irrelevant information is presented, but only the relevant information should be further processed. Further processing is manipulated by requiring the subject to determine whether stimuli with relevant attributes belong to a memorized category and/or to mentally rotate the relevant stimuli.

The results of these experiments showed that the onset of ERP components associated with early and late selection and further controlled processing (memory search and rotation) are sequentially organized, that insertion of search processes did not affect the timing of the ERP components associated with selective attention, and that the insertion of the process of rotation did not affect the timing of the ERP components associated with selective attention or memory search (Okita et al. 1985; Wijers et al. 1987; Wijers et al. 1989a; Wijers et al. 1989b; Wijers et al. 1989; Wijers 1989). These data indicate that (inferred) stages of information processing occur in a consistent serial order. However, these data are not conclusive with regard to the question whether information transfer between these processes occurs in a discrete fashion. Thus, the question whether these processes can be regarded as independent stages in the sense of the additive-factor method (AFM) could not be answered on the basis of these results.

Shortly after the introduction of the additive-factor method, the continuous flow conception of human visual information processing was introduced (Eriksen and Schultz 1979). This conception does not postulate the existence of processing stages. In contrast, it assumes that stimuli impinging on the visual system activate a large pool of perceptual and motor processes. Perceptual processes gradually accumulate evidence (over about 200 ms) as the percept develops. As soon as evidence comes available it is transmitted to the motor level, where it activates associated response channels. A response channel receiving activation produces its overt response when the activation reaches a criterion level. Among other sources of activation, such as response bias, the accumulation of a critical amount of perceptual output determines when this level will be reached. Response channels communicate in a competitive fashion; that is, when activation of one channel increases, it decreases (inhibits) activation of other channels. This represents response competition. Competition may apply not only to motor processes but also to stimulus recognition processes (Eriksen and Schultz 1979).

The serial stage and continuous flow conceptions are two extremes of a complex multidimensional model space (Miller 1988). Information processing models can take intermediate positions between the two offered here. That is, models may be relatively discrete in some respects, and relatively continuous in others. Miller proposes that such models should be analyzed according to at least three different functions, each of which can be relatively discrete or continuous. Information processing modules represent information in a code, transform an input code into an output code, and transmit the output code to other modules.

On the basis of this analysis, Miller (1988) proposed two criteria for evaluating evidence that challenges an explanation in terms of serial stages. If it can be shown that (1) a module transmits partial output of transformation, which (2) serves as input for the transformation by a contingent module, these modules cannot be stages. This means that modules cannot be stages when transmission from module N to module $N + 1$ consists of an incompletely transformed code, while a complete code is transmitted some time later. Other assumptions on which the applicability of the AFM is based are that (1) the stages form a unidimensional chain so that each stage transmits output to only one other, contingent stage; and (2) transformation of information in a particular stage is not affected by selective outputs from any later stage (i.e., "on-line" feedback does not occur). Violation of any of these assumptions can be used to outline the limits of the applicability of the AFM.

We tried to obtain evidence for the validity of these assumptions by combining behavioral data with ERP data in response priming tasks and visual search tasks (Smid et al. 1991; Smid, Mulder, and Mulder 1987, 1990; Smid et al. 1992).

24.2 ELECTROPHYSIOLOGICAL MEASURES

In addition to reaction time, three electrophysiological measures were used. Two of these are based on event-related brain potentials (ERPs), which were obtained by averaging the electrical activity at the scalp of the subjects following the presentation of a stimulus. The third concerns the electromyographic activity in the muscles producing the overt responses.

A Central Measure of Response Activation: The LRP

We designed and used the lateralized readiness potential (LRP) as an index of central response activation. The LRP is derived from the readiness potential (Deecke, Grozinger, and Kornhuber 1976). The readiness potential (RP) refers to premovement potentials related to voluntary hand movements. The RP is a gradually increasing negative shift, beginning one second or more prior to movement onset. Some variable time before movement onset the RP starts to lateralize, with larger amplitudes above the hemisphere contralateral to the side of the activated response (Kutas and Donchin 1977, 1980). This lateralization, however, is confounded by other processing and structural asymmetries. These asymmetries are assumed to be equal for left- and right-hand responses. Thus, lateralization of the RP can be corrected for the nonmotor asymmetries by subtracting right-hand asymmetries from left-hand asymmetries, resulting in a difference potential consisting of "pure" motor-related activity (de Jong et al. 1988; Gratton et al. 1988) (see also fig. 24.1 for additional explanation). This difference potential is called the LRP.

The logic of the derivation of the LRP implies, therefore, that it reflects only motor-related activity. De Jong et al. (1988) showed that the LRP is a highly sensitive index of selective motor activation, both in the absence of an overt response (i.e., in the interval between an informative precue and the imperative signal) and preceding the overt response (i.e., after the imperative signal).

Osman et al. (1988) presented evidence that lateralization can occur to a multiattribute NOGO stimulus (a relevant stimulus to which no response should be made), of which one attribute is associated with a response and the other with the inhibition of that response. This lateralization occurred in the absence of peripheral activation. De Jong et al. (1990) showed that lateralization of the LRP in response to a response choice stimulus occurred, but that this lateralization could be prevented from producing more peripheral activation (of EMG and squeeze activity) when a stop signal followed the choice signal at some critical delay. These results indicate that the onset of significant lateralization of the LRP can be interpreted as evidence that at that time a response has at least been selected.

An important issue is the onset latency of the LRP. To determine LRP onset latency, first a Wilcoxon ranksum test was performed, at each sample point, on the amplitude difference between C3' − C4' (i.e., the difference in electrical brain activity above the relevant parts of the motor cortex) on left-hand response trials and C3' − C4' on right-hand trials. Prestimulus differences were corrected by subtracting a baseline voltage averaged over the 100-ms interval prior to stimulus onset. The Wilcoxon tests were performed on a matrix of trials by sample points for each subject and category. This way, for each subject and category a new time series was obtained, consisting of Wilcoxon W-statistics for the one hundred sample points following stimulus onset. The W-statistic is used to obtain an index of difference that is less sensitive to noise than the amplitude of the difference (note that the LRP shown in the figures is still expressed in amplitude differences).

Next, we compute the onset latency of the LRP across subjects on the basis of their W-statistics. This involves performing a t-test at each sample point in each condition, in which the null hypothesis of zero average Wilcoxon W-statistics across subjects is tested (van Dellen, Brookhuis, Mulder, Okita and Mulder 1985; de Jong et al. 1988, 1990; Smid et al. 1990, 1991). The latency at which the Wilcoxon W-statistic starts to differ significantly from zero is called LRP onset ($p < .01$, one tailed). When the LRP accompanies an overt response, the t-statistic is usually found to be significantly different from zero for more than 200 ms. The t-test in this procedure is performed in a one-tailed version, because the W-statistics are expected to have values in a predefined direction, that is, they should be negative when accompanying a correct response and positive when accompanying an incorrect response (see fig. 24.1).

A Peripheral Measure of Response Activation: The EMG

A second important measure concerns the electromyogram (EMG) recorded from the muscles activated prior to a response (when a button press is required these muscles involve the flexor digitorum). This measure is important for several reasons. In many choice RT tasks subjects have to choose between a left and a right hand criterion response (such as a button press or a criterion squeeze), only one of which is correct. It has been shown that on a number of trials (from 10% to 40%) the incorrect response muscle is activated although only a correct criterion response was registered (Coles et al. 1985; Gratton et al. 1988; Smid et al. 1990, 1991). These incorrect EMG responses were found to be related to such factors as flanker identity in the response priming

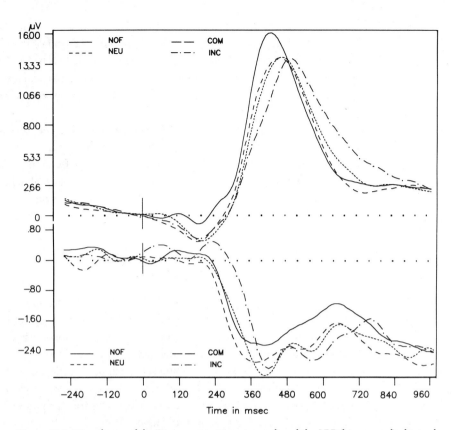

Figure 24.1 Waveforms of the P3 component (upper panel) and the LRP (lower panel) obtained on no flanker trials (NOF), trials with compatible flankers (COM), neutral flankers (NEU), and incompatible flankers (INC). Stimulus onset was at time 0. Note that the P3 component peaks later in COM and NEU trials than in the no-flanker trials, and that it peaks later in INC than in all other trial types. The LRP can change in two directions. An upward change (positive amplitudes) indicates incorrect response activation, whereas a downward change (negative amplitudes) indicates correct response activation. Note that there is a small positive LRP in INC trials (the dash-dot waveform) starting significantly around 200 msec poststimulus (the small positive deflection starting at stimulus onset in these trials is an artifact of outliers because it disappeared in the *t*-tests; see sec. 24.2). The LRP changes in the negative direction at about 300 msec poststimulus. Note also that the LRP in COM trials (the dashed waveform) starts to activate the correct response (downward deflection) earlier than in all other trial types (amplitude is in microvolt).

task designed by Eriksen and Eriksen (1974, see also the following) and to response bias. On these trials, there was also lateralization of the LRP towards the incorrect response. If such trials are not discarded from the LRP analysis to establish the onset time of correct lateralization in a particular experimental condition, the onset time is confounded (delayed) by incorrect lateralization. Thus, LRP analysis requires EMG analysis.

From these observations it also follows that the EMG measure is important because it provides a more sensitive measure of the occurrence of errors than counting the number of incorrect criterion responses. Even more importantly, the EMG onset time can be used as an index of the time at which response processes related to actual execution of the response become manifest at the peripheral level. If no incorrect EMG activation occurs on a trial, this time point can be taken as a more sensitive index for the timing of the ultimate response than criterion RT, because aspects of the choice signal and response bias have been shown to affect the interval between EMG onset and criterion RT (Coles et al. 1985; Smid et al. 1990).

It has been shown (Requin 1985) that there is a constant time interval between central initiation of a response and onset of EMG activation. Also, Bullock and Grossberg (1988) reviewed evidence indicating that response production is mediated by two distinct processes. One process, cortically located, "computes" response parameters such as direction of movement; the other, more peripherally located, provides for parameters such as force and speed of the response. With a typical chronometric technique as the stop-signal task, Osman, Kornblum, and Meyer (1990) using RT, and de Jong et al. (1990) using the LRP and EMG measures, presented evidence that supports this model of response production. It seems, therefore, that it is not unwarranted to interpret EMG onset time as a relative index of response initiation, that is, differences in EMG onset between experimental conditions reflect differences in response initiation times although the absolute time of initiation is unknown.

To summarize: These measures then, in combination with RT, provide powerful tools to observe the chronometric aspects of response production, since they show consistent and selective effects of the main variables affecting choice reaction time (CRT).

A Central Index of Stimulus Categorization: P3

A third measure concerns the P3 peak latency derived from the ERP. This latency is considered as a relative index of the duration of stimulus categorization processes. Many investigators have shown that the latency of this component is relatively independent of response selection and execution processes, and in general they consider the peak latency of the component as a relative index of the stimulus evaluation process (Donchin 1981; Magliero et al. 1984; Mulder et al. 1984; Donchin and Coles 1988).

24.3 PARTIAL INFORMATION ARISING FROM MULTIPLE STIMULUS DISPLAYS

Introduction

In the first experiment (Smid, Mulder, and Mulder 1990) we applied the choice reaction time paradigm designed by Eriksen and Eriksen (1974). In this paradigm the subject should only respond to either an *H* or a *D* (targets) with different hands. Four different types of trials are presented to the subject:

1. No flanker (NOF) trials. In these trials only one of the two target letters is presented.

2. Compatible flanker (COM) trials. During these trials the target letter is presented with letters which may call for the same response as the target (e.g., "*DDDDDDD*").

3. Neutral flanker (NEU) trials. During these trials the target is presented together with letters which are not associated with a response (e.g., "*XXXDXXX*").

4. Incompatible flanker (INC) trials. In these trials the flankers may call for the opposite response (e.g., "*HHHDHHH*").

According to the continuous flow conception, any information in the display associated with a response hand will activate that channel. If a particular stimulus display contains information that activates two different response channels, the concurrent activation of these channels produces mutual inhibition (response competition). This would occur at least on incompatible trials. If, on the other hand, a stimulus array contains redundant information associated with a response channel, it will activate it earlier and to a higher degree. Thus, in the case of compatible displays, response facilitation may occur.

We tried to obtain evidence for response facilitation by comparing performance on compatible trials with target alone trials. Continuous flow mechanisms predict that compatible flankers activate their associated response channel earlier than if only one target is present. In that case the LRP would show earlier lateralization to compatible displays than on target alone trials, and later lateralization on neutral and incompatible trials. On incompatible trials, the incorrect response may initially be activated. The P3 peak latency was used to index the duration of stimulus evaluation. We expected that stimulus evaluation would take longer on neutral, compatible and incompatible trials as compared to no flanker trials. Finally, by measuring the onset of response activation at the EMG level we were able to infer peripheral response execution duration and its accuracy.

We defined four error categories based on the sequence of correct and incorrect EMG activation, and incorrect button presses. No-error trials (NOE) contained only correct EMG activation, followed by a correct button response. Correct-incorrect-error trials (CIE) contained two EMG responses: first a correct EMG response that produced a button press, followed by an incorrect

EMG response that did not result in a button press. Incorrect-correct-error trials (ICE) also contained dual EMG responses, but in the reverse order. First, incorrect EMG activation occurred that did not result in a button press, followed by correct EMG activation that did produce a button press. Finally, the button-press-error category consisted of trials on which an incorrect button press was made (the traditional RT error).

Results and Discussion

The behavioral and psychophysiological data replicated the findings by Eriksen et al. (1985) and Coles et al. (1985) and provided additional evidence for the mechanisms postulated by the continuous flow conception. RTs to targets alone did not differ from RTs to compatible arrays. The latter were faster than RTs to neutral arrays, which were faster than RTs to incompatible arrays. P3 peak latencies were longer on incompatible than on neutral trials, and longer on compatible than on target alone trials. The LRP indicated that incorrect central response activation on incompatible trials, and correct central response activation on compatible trials, both began at approximately the same time as on target alone trials. More incompatible but less compatible trials than neutral ones exhibited incorrect peripheral (EMG) response activation. Peripheral response execution (the time interval between EMG onset and overt responding) was faster and more accurate on compatible than on target alone trials, while it was slower and less accurate on incompatible than on neutral trials. ICE responses were mainly present in INC trials.

These results indicate that flankers activate their associated response before the target has been identified, and, possibly as a result of this, that response facilitation and competition occur. After applying the criteria proposed by Miller (1988), it was concluded that the set of stimulus recognition processes consisting of letter identity analysis and location analysis and the set of response activation processes cannot be regarded as independent stages of processing. Our data strongly suggest that before the target is located and identified, central response activation on the basis of the identity of the flankers has already begun. This means that partial output of stimulus recognition processes (i.e., flanker identity) is transmitted and serves as input for transformation by response activation processes. It follows that these sets of processes cannot have a stage relationship.

In the next section we shall explore whether partial information can be transmitted and used in tasks in which only a single stimulus is presented.

24.4 PARTIAL INFORMATION ARISING FROM SINGLE STIMULUS DISPLAYS

Introduction

The task we used in this experiment (Smid et al. 1992) is a variation of a task introduced by Miller (1982). This task is based on a method of precueing subsets of a set of relevant responses. The subjects had to respond with one of four fingers that consisted of the index and middle fingers on the left and right hand. Miller (1982) observed that if two fingers on the same hand are precued, RTs are faster than if two fingers on different hands are precued. This same-hand benefit suggests that response preparation is more efficient if the precue signals two fingers on the same hand. Miller (1982) further reasoned that stimuli that can be coded on two dimensions (e.g., colored letters) might serve both as a precue and as an imperative stimulus, if the possible values of one of the dimensions (e.g., red and green) are easier to discriminate than the possible values of the other dimension (e.g., M and N). However, a necessary condition for this to happen is that partial information about the color dimension (the precue) be transmitted to contingent motor processes before information about the letter dimension (the imperative stimulus) has been processed. Thus, if two letters in the same color are assigned to two fingers on the same hand, preparation of response hand might begin on the basis of color information before letter information is available. If same-colored letters are assigned to two fingers on different hands, no advance preparation on the basis of color would be possible.

The LRP measure seems perfectly suited for study of whether this is the case, because it reflects the differential activation of response hands. If color can be used to discriminate between hands before letter information is available, LRP onset should be earlier than if no stimulus dimension discriminates between hands. We combined this task with a method introduced by Osman et al. (1988) that makes it possible to obtain an LRP in response to partial information in trials in which no overt response occurs. To achieve this, easily discriminable stimulus features (e.g., red and green) must signal the hand with which a response has to be made, whereas features difficult to discriminate (e.g., M and N) indicate whether a response has to be made (the GO response) or not (the NOGO response). If information about color can be used to prepare the response hand before information about the letter has been fully processed, the motor system would initially begin to prepare the response hand, both on GO and NOGO response trials. Next, after the letter has been fully processed, the response would either be executed with the prepared hand (on GO trials), or the advance preparation would be cancelled (on NOGO trials). Thus, if on NOGO trials an LRP occurs, it would strongly support the idea that partial information is transmitted and used for advance preparation of the response hand.

We combined the GO/NOGO technique with the four-choice task introduced by Miller (1982) in the following way. Three conditions were designed, in which four letters appeared that were difficult to discriminate (e.g., the GO letters M and N, and the NOGO letters H and W). These letters appeared in two colors which were easy to discriminate (e.g., red and green). A sample of these conditions is shown in table 24.1. In one condition, called the "hand:color" condition (the H:C condition in table 24.1), the color of the letter signaled two response fingers on the same hand, while the identity of the letter signaled two fingers on different hands or that no response should

Table 24.1 A Sample Mapping of Colored Letters onto the Responses in the Miller Task

Responses:								
Hand	GO-LH		NOGO				GO-RH	
Finger	M	I					I	M
H:N	M1	N2	H1	W2	H2	W1	M2	N1
H:L	W1	W2	N1	N2	M1	M2	H2	H1
H:C	G4	C4	D4	Q4	Q3	D3	C3	G3

Notes: Digits denote colors (e.g., 1 means a red letter, 2 means a green letter, 3 a white letter, and 4 a blue one). Numbered letters denote colored letter stimuli. Abbreviation: M denotes middle finger, I denotes index finger, LH denotes left hand, RH denotes right hand, GO denotes GO stimuli and NOGO denotes NOGO stimuli. H:N denotes Hand:Neither, H:L denotes Hand:Letter, H:C denotes Hand:Color.

be made. We reasoned that if color is available before letter identity and is used to initially select the response hand associated with it, there would appear an LRP on both GO and NOGO trials. Next, when letter identity comes available and this identity represents a NOGO letter, it would be used to cancel the initial activation of the selected hand. If it represents a GO letter, it would be used to select one of the two fingers on the hand already selected, which would subsequently execute the required response.

In the second condition, called the "hand:letter" condition (the H:L condition in table 24.1), the identity of the letter either signaled two response fingers on the same hand or that no response should be made, while the color of the letter signaled two fingers on different hands. On NOGO trials in this condition there is no information which permits discrimination between hands. Therefore, no LRP can occur on NOGO trials. In the third condition, called the "hand:neither" condition (the H:N condition in table 24.1), both color and letter identity signaled two responses on different hands, while the GO/NOGO decision again depended on the identity of the letter. In this case also, there is no information on the basis of which an LRP can occur in NOGO trials.

These latter two conditions should provide baseline controls. The psychophysiological response latencies obtained in the hand:letter and hand:neither conditions would be diagnostic for the occurrence of a same-hand benefit in the hand:color condition. Selection of response hand in these two conditions would not occur before at least letter identity had been processed, so if color can be used to select a response earlier than letter identity there should be a same-hand benefit in LRP onset on the GO trials of the hand:color condition. Since on all trials of all three conditions both the color and the identity of the stimulus letter have to be recognized, P3 latency should not differ across the S-R mapping conditions. This would rule out the possibility that the same-hand benefit might be the result of faster stimulus recognition. For these three mapping conditions the probability of a NOGO trial was .50.

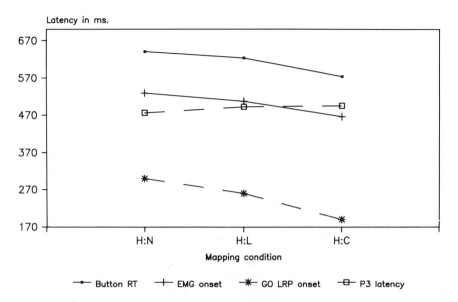

NO—ERROR TRIALS
RT, CEMG, LRP, P3

Figure 24.2 Latencies in ms of button presses (RT), correct EMG onset (CEMG), onset of lateralization of the RP (LRP), and peak of the P3 component (P3) in the GO trials of the three S-R mapping conditions. H:N denotes hand:neither, H:L denotes hand:letter and H:C denotes hand:color. Note that there are clear effects of S-R mapping on LRP onset, EMG onset, and RT, but not on P3 latency.

Results and Discussion

Figure 24.2 depicts the latencies of (a) the overt button press response, (b) the onset of the response at the EMG level, (c) the peak of the P3 component, and (d) the onset of the LRP. As can be seen, a clear and statistically significant same-hand benefit (70 ms) in the hand:color condition was obtained at the RT level. This result is consistent with earlier findings of Miller (1982), Proctor and Reeve (1985) and de Jong et al. (1988). This indicates that responses are faster when color can be used to discriminate between hands. Moreover, the EMG and LRP onset latencies also showed a clear same-hand benefit, indicating that the same-hand benefit was present even at the central motor level.

The peak latencies of the P3 component were not affected by S-R assignment, nor by the interaction of processing GO or NOGO stimuli with S-R mapping. These results are consistent with those obtained by de Jong et al. (1988), and suggest that the time at which full information about the stimulus becomes available was not affected by how the four finger responses were assigned to the stimuli. This makes it rather unlikely that the same-hand benefit obtained when color discriminated between hands is the result of faster stimulus identification.

Figure 24.3 depicts the LRP waveforms that were obtained in the GO trials of the three S-R mapping conditions together with the LRP obtained in the

Transfer of Partial Information between Perception and Action

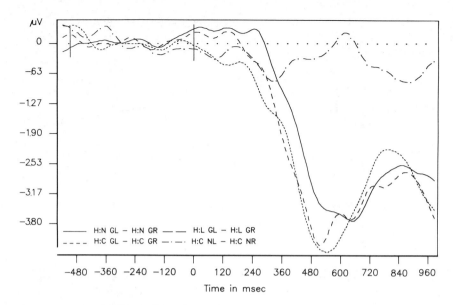

Figure 24.3 LRP waveforms obtained in the hand:neither (H:N), hand:letter (H:L), and hand:
color (H:C) conditions. Stimulus presentation occurred at time 0 (second vertical line). A
warning signal occurred 500 msec before onset of the stimulus (first vertical line at time −500).
In the H:C condition two LRPs were found: one in the GO trials and one in the NOGO trials.
In the GO trials in this condition the LRP was obtained by subtracting the C3′ − C4′ waveforms
accompanying right-hand responses from those accompanying left-hand responses (thus, in
"H:C GL − H:C GR," H:C denotes Hand:color, GL denotes the left-hand responses in the Go
trials, and GR denotes the right-hand responses in the GO trials). In the NOGO trials the LRP
was obtained by subtracting the C3′ − C4′ waveforms evoked by the color signaling a right
hand response from those evoked by the color signaling a left-hand response (thus, in "H:C
NL − H:C NR," H:C again denotes the hand:color condition, NL denotes the left-hand color
in NOGO trials, and NR denotes the right-hand color in NOGO trials. Summarized. "H:C
GL − H:C GR" stands for hand:color GO left minus hand:color GO right (the dotted waveform), whereas "H:C NL − H:C NR" stands for hand:color NOGO left minus hand:color
NOGO right (the dash-dot waveform). In the same vein, the LRPs in the other conditions
are denoted. "H:N GL − H:N GR" stands for hand:neither GO left minus hand:neither go
right (the continuous waveform), and "H:L GL − H:L GR" means hand:letter GO left minus
hand:letter GO right (the dashed waveform). The amplitudes are in microvolts.

NOGO trials of the hand:color condition. In this latter condition, LRP waveforms were derived on GO and NOGO trials by subtracting the C3′ − C4′
ERPs evoked by the color indicating a right hand response from those evoked
by the color indicating a left hand response. As can be seen in the figure, there
is a clear LRP present on NOGO trials in the hand:color condition, which was
significantly present from 260 ms until 350 ms poststimulus. This NOGO LRP
reached highly significant amplitudes as tested by the combined Wilcoxon-t-
test (ts (23) > 3.49, ps < .001). NOGO trials on which increased EMG activity
was observed were practically absent (less than 1%), and were removed from
the analyses, so that we were sure that the subjects had always processed both
stimulus attributes.

Note that if in NOGO trials color *and* letter identity had been recognized prior to response activation there would have been no reason for activating the response hand. Thus, the presence of the NOGO LRP strongly suggests that in the hand:color condition, partial information concerning the color of the stimulus is transmitted and used by central motor processes before information concerning letter identity is available. Since the LRP represents differential *motoric* activation of the two hands, the LRP data indicate that this partial information affects motoric processes. This finding supports the interpretation of Miller (1982) that the same-hand benefit is the end result of advance selection of response hand on the basis of partial information. That is, advance selection of response hand may lead to advance preparation or programming of the response, which, in turn, may produce the same-hand benefit. Evidence suggesting that response preparation is involved comes from the finding that the interval between EMG onset and RT was shorter in the hand:color condition than in the hand:letter and hand:neither conditions. A similar decrease of this interval was observed by Smid et al. (1990) when flankers in the Eriksen task were identical to the target letter (i.e., in compatible trials). When flankers consisted of repetitions of the conflicting target, the EMG–RT interval was found to be increased (see also Coles et al. 1985).

Several other conditions were applied in this experiment; these yielded similar and consistent results. The hand:color task was used in three versions, either with 50%, 25%, or no NOGO trials. Whether there were NOGO trials did not affect LRP onset to color, but P3 latency was increased and EMG onset delayed when NOGO trials occurred. These results suggest that insertion of NOGO trials (i.e., increasing the number of S-R alternatives) increased the time to identify the letter, but not the color of it. An LRP was also found on the NOGO trials when the relative frequency of NOGO trials in the hand:color condition was 25%.

Furthermore, a hand:letter condition was used which was a mirror image of the hand:color condition. In this hand:letter task, one of two letters appeared, each signaling two fingers on one hand (e.g., *M* signaled two fingers on the left hand and *Q* signaled two fingers on the right hand). These two letters could appear in one of four colors. Two of the colors signaled that no response had to be made (e.g., white and blue), whereas two other colors each signaled two fingers on different hands (e.g., green signaled both middle fingers and red, both index fingers). As in the hand:color condition, an LRP was found in the NOGO trials of this condition. This finding suggests that letter identity can also be used to prepare response hand before full stimulus information has been processed.

In summary, the results of this experiment strongly suggest that perceptual analysis of a single two-dimensional stimulus may transmit information about one dimension (i.e., partial information) before it has finished analyzing the other dimension. They further suggest that motor processes receiving partial information subsequently use this information to prepare a response in advance.

24.5 ON THE GRAIN SIZE OF PARTIAL INFORMATION

Introduction

Visual search tasks are used to study how people detect a prespecified piece of information in highly varying visual environments. In such tasks, displays are presented that contain several elements and the subject has to choose one response when a specific target form is present among them, and another response when it is absent.

As a starting point for our study (Smid et al. 1991), we used Duncan and Humphreys's theory of visual search (Duncan and Humphreys 1989). This theory incorporates the main mechanisms of earlier theories and is able to explain a wide range of experimental data. Duncan and Humphreys propose three processes enabling the detection of a target among nontargets. One process produces a parallel, hierarchically structured representation of the visual field at several levels of spatial scale. This is accomplished by segmenting and organizing the visual input into structural units according to Gestalt principles. Another process matches input descriptions against an internal template of the information searched for. Nonmatching elements lead to a lower, and matching elements to a higher probability of being selected for further processing. The third process transfers the selected elements to visual short term memory (VSTM), where an eventual target enters awareness and can become input for cognitive and/or motor processes.

However, as the results in the response priming paradigm of Eriksen and Eriksen (1974) indicate, it might be that a response is already selected and prepared before search is completed. A positive response may be selected and prepared prematurely on the basis of features that nontargets currently processed share with the target (e.g., when the target is a Q and nontargets in the display are Cs and Ds). A negative response may be selected prematurely on the basis of features that nontargets currently processed do not share with the target(s) (e.g., when the target is Q and the current nontargets are Ws and Ns).

If preliminary response activation on the basis of features of letter symbols occurs, it would suggest that information transmission between the search process and response-activation processes occurs in a continuous fashion and not discretely. That is, response activation would be based initially on information having a very small grain size (Miller 1988). This information might represent a yet unfinished percept of the contents of the display. Later, when perceptual analysis has detected and identified a target (or has found no target), response activation would be based on the identity of this target (or on the absence of a target).

To test this prediction of the continuous flow conception, a task was constructed based on the response-competition paradigm (Eriksen and Eriksen 1974), which ensured that search would have to be carried out. The search task consisted of detecting a target which could appear in any one of the four corners of an imaginary square, with equal probability. On two-thirds of the trials nontargets were present on the other three corners of the square, and on one-third the target appeared alone. Two targets were used, one (e.g., *Q*) as the target for a left hand response and another one (e.g., *H*) as the target for a right-hand response.

When nontargets were present in the display, they had physical features in common with one of the targets—either with the one in the display or with the one not in the display. Thus the nontargets used were neutral with regard to their relevance for a response on the level of a letter, but compatible or incompatible on the level of the features they were composed of. This procedure produced response compatible displays (e.g., a *Q* with nontargets *D*, *G*, and *C*), response incompatible displays (e.g., a *Q* with nontargets *N*, *W*, and *M*) and target alone displays (e.g., a *Q* on one of the four corners). There was always a target present, thus, there were no target absent displays.

Several psychophysiological measures were used in addition to RT. As a relative index for the duration of the set of visual search processes, the peak latency of the P3 component was used. In the present task, duration of visual search consists of the time needed for target detection and identification. Brookhuis, Mulder, Mulder, Gloerich, van Dellen, van der Meere, and Ellerman (1981); Hoffman, Simons, and Houck (1983); Kramer and Strayer (1988); and van Dellen et al. (1985), using a similar task as the present one, showed that P3 latency is a reliable index for the duration of visual search. Perceptual processing of the target alone displays consists only of the time needed for target identification, because no nontargets are present. Perceptual processing of compatible and incompatible displays consists of search plus target identification. It was therefore expected that P3 latencies and of course RTs would be longer to these latter displays than to target alone displays.

The P3 latency measure seems to be especially useful here because it makes it possible to distinguish between effects on search duration and effects on response processes. Smid et al. (1990) observed that the presentation of a target together with incompatible targets on irrelevant locations delayed both P3 latency and RT, compared to the presentation of a target together with neutral letters. The authors attributed the effect on P3 latency to competition among letter identities which are candidates for recognition. The effect on RT was attributed to response competition, as evidenced by speed-accuracy functions and preliminary incorrect response activation (at the LRP and EMG level) produced by the incompatible targets. Since in the present study the distractors used are nontargets (comparable to the neutral letters in the Smid et al. 1990 study), it was expected that P3 latencies produced by compatible and incompatible displays would be about equal, while RTs to incompatible displays would be delayed as a result of response competition.

As an index of the start of selective response preparation the lateralized readiness potential (LRP) was used. If selective response preparation begins before the target has been detected and identified, the compatible and incompatible displays should activate the correct and the incorrect response, respectively, at about the same time as target alone displays would activate the correct response. Moreover, this would indicate that there is continuous information transmission between search processes and response processes. First, information about the features the nontargets share with one of the two targets would activate a response. Next, information about the target actually present in the display would activate a response. If selective response activation begins only after a target has been detected, compatible and incompatible displays should activate the correct response only and at a much later time than target alone displays. As an index for the beginning of peripheral response execution, the electromyographic activity (EMG) of the muscles responsible for the response was measured.

Results and Discussion

We found that RTs and P3 latencies were longer in trials on which a target with nontargets appeared than in trials on which only a target was presented (see fig. 24.4). This indicates that on target alone trials the target only had to be identified, whereas on trials on which also nontargets appeared it took additional time to detect the target among the nontargets. Thus, visual search delayed both P3 latencies and RTs if nontargets were presented. These results are consistent with previous results presented by Brookhuis et al. (1981), Hoffman et al. (1983), Kramer and Strayer (1988), and Van Dellen et al. (1985). In all these studies P3 latency and RT were found to be positively related to the number of nontargets in a display.

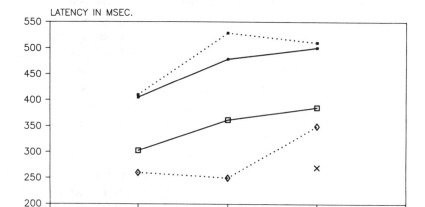

Figure 24.4 P3 peak latencies, correct EMG (CEMG) onset, correct LRP (CLRP) onset, and incorrect LRP (ILRP) onset latencies, and RTs in msec averaged across no-error trials as a function of display type (TGA = TarGet Alone, COM = COMpatible, and INC = INCompatible displays).

Mulder, Smid, and Mulder

If nontargets were present, they could have features that were either compatible or incompatible with the target in the display. The P3 waveforms obtained in target alone, compatible and incompatible trials are shown in the upper panel of figure 24.5. As can be seen in figures 24.4 and 24.5, P3 latencies to displays with compatible nontargets were not different from those to displays with incompatible nontargets. However, RTs were slower and EMG onsets were later to incompatible displays than to compatible ones. Furthermore, the number of overt button press errors and covert EMG errors produced was also larger on incompatible than on compatible trials.

Significant lateralization of the RP began at about the same time for all display types and concerned the response (correct or incorrect) signaled by the majority of the physical features in the display (see fig. 24.4; X denotes the onset latency of incorrect lateralization). In the lower panel of figure 24.5, the averaged LRP waveforms are shown. On incompatible trials the incorrect response channel was activated first at about the same time as the correct channel was activated on compatible and target alone trials. In this figure,

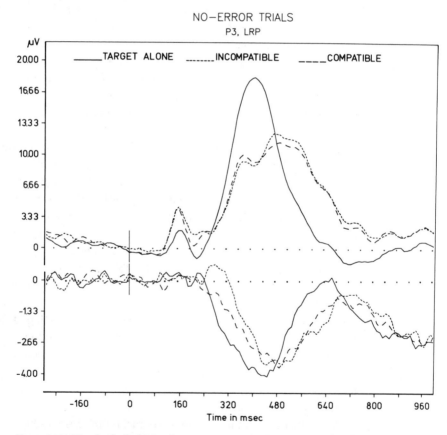

Figure 24.5 Stimulus-locked (stimulus onset is at time 0) P3 (upper panel) and LRP (lower panel) waveforms averaged across no-error trials as a function of display type. Note that the P3 waveforms in compatible trials (dashed waveforms) are nearly identical to those in incompatible trials (dotted waveforms). Amplitudes are in microvolts.

activation of the incorrect response in incompatible trials is visible as a small positive LRP (the dotted waveform) between 250 and 320 ms poststimulus. It can also be seen in this figure that at the same time there is a small negative LRP (the dashed waveform), indicating activation of the correct response on compatible trials. On both types of trials the waveforms accelerate negatively after 320 ms, indicating increased activation and execution of the correct response. Note the remarkable similarity of these LRPs with the LRPs obtained in the response priming paradigm discussed earlier and which were shown in figure 24.1.

These results are consistent with and extend the previous findings of Gratton et al. (1988) and Smid et al. (1990). In combination, the findings presented here confirm that response competition took place. If the incompatible response is activated first, activation of the correct response has to compete with it. This conflict has to be resolved, which delays activation of the correct response and RT in addition to the time needed for visual search.

The LRP results not only suggest that response competition produced delayed EMG onsets and RTs, but also that selective response preparation began before the target was detected and fully identified. The preliminary character of selective response preparation follows from two observations. On incompatible trials, central activation of the incorrect response was not accompanied by peripheral (EMG) response activation, but was followed by central activation of the correct response. On compatible trials, activation of the correct response began at the same time as on target alone trials, but peripheral (EMG) activation of that response was postponed and began much later than on target alone trials.

On the basis of these findings we concluded that partial information about nontarget letters was transmitted to, and served as input for the response activation processes. The findings suggest that letter identification produced output of such a small grain size that it may best be characterized as continuous instead of discrete. This is strong evidence for the continuous flow conception of information processing. It seems reasonable, therefore, to conclude that the AFM is limited in its application to visual search tasks.

However, one may think about plausible alternative explanations. One alternative could be that a letter that looks like a target activates the representation of the identity of that target. Next, this representation sends a discrete output (i.e., a guess) to its associated response, activating it below some criterion level. The problem with this alternative explanation is that the motor system receives no information about the correctness of the output it is sent. The result would be that it would always produce an incorrect response when incompatible nontargets are present in the display. This alternative therefore needs to postulate additional assumptions.

Another alternative is that the perceptual output responsible for preliminary response selection does not arise from the letter identification process. It might stem from a global feature analysis process like that proposed by Hoffman (1975) and Treisman and Gelade (1980). This process might send a low-level discrete output (representing either "roundness" or "angledness" of features in the display), which activates a response always below its criterion level (e.g., only at the LRP level). Only output from the higher-level letter identification process can activate it above its criterion level (e.g., at the EMG level). The problem with this alternative explanation is that we found that the incorrect responses to nontargets are not activated at only one level (e.g., LRP), but also very frequently at other levels (e.g., EMG). Thus, the initial output does not seem to be as discrete as it should be in discrete models.

Our results suggest effects on response selection of elementary products of perceptual processes which are hard to model in a discrete conception of human information processing.

24.6 CONCLUSIONS

In the studies we have reviewed, several tasks were used, each with its own characteristic stimuli and response requirements. In addition to overt response time we used indices of central (LRP) and peripheral response activation (EMG), and of stimulus recognition time (P3). In the response-priming task designed by Eriksen and Eriksen (1974), targets are presented at a fixated location flanked by identical, different or no other letters. We found central responses to be activated first by the flankers and next by the target.

In the response-priming tasks designed by Miller (1982) and Osman et al. (1988), single, two-dimensional stimuli were presented. Subjects had to select one out of several possible responses (including a NOGO response) on the basis of certain combinations of values on the two dimensions of the stimuli. Central responses appeared to be activated initially by partial information consisting of one dimension of the stimulus.

In the visual search task, displays were presented that contained one target or one target plus three other characters. Responses were found to be activated by elementary features of nontargets that the nontargets shared with one of the possible targets.

These results indicate that across a number of paradigms, information transmission between perceptual and motor processes may consist of at least two steps. The letter identification process even seems to transmit continuous output. This leads to the conclusion that, for a number of important paradigms, it is questionable whether the AFM can be applied, because its requirements of discrete output and one-dimensionality seem not to be satisfied. Thus, RTs obtained with these tasks can not be taken simply to be the sum of the durations of the processes engaged in their production.

Central response activation can occur very early, in some conditions by around 170 ms, while overt responding occurs about 400 ms later. EMG onset precedes overt responding by about 100 ms. Thus, in these conditions motor processes are selectively active more than half the time required for producing an overt response. Of course, this does not mean that stimulus recognition processes are only active during the other half of the RT interval; stimulus recognition and motor selection seem to occur in parallel.

A large proportion of correct overt responses appear to be accompanied by EMG errors, resulting in increased response times. Speed-accuracy trade-off procedures should take errors of this type into account.

Our future research efforts will focus on the determination of the stochastic properties of the onset times of these different psychophysiological indices (this requires single trial analysis) and on the localization in time and space of the cerebral sources underlying the observed brain activity. The moment at which a dipole (a source) starts to contribute to the observed brain activity is probably a better index of the moment a certain psychological process is initiated, as it circumvents the problem facing ERP research—that many distinct sources contribute to, and overlap with, the phenomena observed at the surface of the scalp.

The AFM logic has been shown to be a fruitful and powerful tool for mental chronometric research, although our results suggest that it has its limits when applied to the RT measure alone. A systematic research program in which behavioral and neuroimaging methods are simultaneously used is necessary to identify the conditions under which the assumptions of this method are valid.

NOTES

Preparation of this article was supported in part by the Netherlands Organization of Pure Research and PSYCHON. Grant 560-265-040 to Gijsbertus Mulder and Cees Brunia. We gratefully acknowledge the thoughtful comments of Allen Osman, Jean Requin, Sylvan Kornblum, and Cees Brunia on an earlier draft of this article.

REFERENCES

Brookhuis, K. A., Mulder, G., Mulder, L. J. M., Gloerich, A. B. M., van Dellen, H. J., van der Meere, J. J., and Ellerman, H. H. (1981). Late positive components and stimulus evaluation time. *Biological Psychology, 30* 107–123.

Brookhuis, K. A., Mulder, G., and Gloerich, A. B. M. (1983). The P3 component as an index of information processing: The effects of response probability. *Biological Psychology, 17,* 277–296.

Bullock, D., and Grossberg, S. (1988). Neural dynamics of planned arm movements: Emergent invariants and speed accuracy properties during trajectory formation. *Psychological Review, 95,* 49–90.

Coles, M. G. H., Gratton, G., Bashore, T. R., Eriksen, C. W., and Donchin, E. (1985). A psychological investigation of the continuous flow model of human information processing. *Journal of Experimental Psychology: Human Perception and Performance, 11,* 529–553.

Deecke, L., Grozinger, B., and Kornhuber, H. H. (1976). Voluntary finger movements in man: Cerebral potentials and theory. *Biological Cybernetics, 23,* 99–119.

de Jong, R., Wierda, M., Mulder, G., and Mulder, L. J. M. (1988). The use of partial information in response preparation. *Journal of Experimental Psychology: Human Perception and Performance, 14,* 682–692.

de Jong, R., Coles, M. G. H., Logan, G. D., and Gratton, G. (1990). In search of the point of no return: The control of response processes. *Journal of Experimental Psychology: Human Perception and Performance, 16,* 164–182.

Donders, F. C. ([1868] 1969). On the speed of mental processes. Translation by W. G. Koster in W. G. Koster (Ed.), *Attention and Performance II*, 412–431. Amsterdam: North-Holland.

Donchin, E. (1981). Surprise! ... Surprise? *Psychophysiology, 18*, 493–515.

Donchin, E., and Coles, M. G. H. (1988). Is the P300 component a manifestation of context updating? *The Behavioral and Brain Sciences, 11*, 355–372.

Duncan, J., and Humphreys, G. W. (1989). Visual search and stimulus similarity. *Psychological Review, 96*, 433–458.

Eriksen, B. A., and Eriksen, C. W. (1974). Effects of noise letters upon the identification of a target letter in a nonsearch task. *Perception and Psychophysics, 16*, 143–149.

Eriksen, C. W., and Schultz, D. W. (1979). Information processing in visual search: A continuous flow conception and experimental results. *Perception and Psychophysics, 25*, 249–263.

Eriksen, C. W., Coles, M. G. H., Morris, L. R., and O'Hara, W. P. (1985). An electromyographic examination of response competition. *Bulletin of the Psychonomic Society, 23*, 165–168.

Gratton, G., Coles, M. G. H., Sirevaag, E., Eriksen, C. W., and Donchin, E. (1988). Pre- and poststimulus activation of response channels; A psychophysiological analysis. *Journal of Experimental Psychology: Human Perception and Performance, 14*, 331–344.

Hoffman, J. E. (1979). A two-stage model of visual search. *Perception and Psychophysics, 25*, 319–327.

Hoffman, J. E., Simons, R. F., and Houck, M. R. (1983). Event-related potentials during controlled and automatic target detection. *Psychophysiology, 20*, 625–632.

Kramer, A. F., and Strayer, D. L. (1988). Assessing the development of automatic processing: An application of dual-task and event-related brain potential methodologies. *Biological Psychology, 26*, 231–267.

Kutas, M., and Donchin, E. (1977). The effects of handedness, of responding hand, and of response force on the contralateral dominance of the readiness potential. In J. Desmedt (Ed.), *Attention, voluntary contraction and event-related cerebral potentials*, 189–210. Basel, Switzerland: Karger.

Kutas, M., and Donchin, E. (1980). Preparation to respond as manifested by movement-related brain potential. *Brain Research, 202*, 95–115.

Magliero, A., Bashore, T. R., Coles, M. G. H., and Donchin, E. (1984). On the dependence of P300 latency on stimulus evaluation processes. *Psychophysiology, 21*, 171–186.

Meyer, D. E., Osman, A. M., Irwin, D. E., and Yantis, S. (1988). Modern mental chronometry. *Biological Psychology, 26*, 3–67.

Miller, J. O. (1982). Discrete versus continuous stage models of human information processing: In search of partial output. *Journal of Experimental Psychology: Human Perception and Performance, 8*, 273–296.

Miller, J. O. (1988). Discrete and continuous models of human information processing: Theoretical distinctions and empirical results. *Acta Psychologica, 67*, 191–257.

Mulder, G., Gloerich, A. B. M., Brookhuis, K. A., van Dellen, H. J. and Mulder, L. J. M. (1984). Stage analysis of the reaction process using brain evoked potentials and reaction time. *Psychological Research, 46*, 15–32.

Okita, T., Wijers, A. A., Mulder, G., and Mulder, L. J. M. (1985). Memory search and visual spatial attention: An event-related brain potential analysis. *Acta Psychologica, 60*, 263–292.

Osman, A., Bashore, T. R., Coles, M. G. H., Donchin, E., and Meyer, D. E. (1988). A psychophysiological study of response preparation based on partial information. *Psychophysiology, 25*, 426.

Osman, A., Kornblum, S., and Meyer, D. E. (1990). Does motor programming necessitate response execution? *Journal of Experimental Psychology: Human Perception and Performance, 16,* 183–198.

Proctor, R. W., and Reeve, T. G. (1985). Compatibility effects in the assignment of symbolic stimuli to discrete finger responses. *Journal of Experimental Psychology: Human Perception and Performance, 11, 623–639.*

Requin, J. (1985). Looking forward to moving soon: Ante factum selective processes in motor control. In M. I. Posner and O. S. M. Marin (Eds.), *Attention and performance XI,* 147–169. Hillsdale, NJ: Lawrence Erlbaum.

Smid, H. G. O. M., Lamain, W., Hogeboom, M. M., Mulder, G., and Mulder, L. J. M. (1991). Psychophysiological evidence for continuous information transmission between visual search and response processes. *Journal of Experimental Psychology: Human Perception and Performance, 17.* 696–714.

Smid, H. G. O. M., Mulder, G., and Mulder, L. J. M. (1987). The continuous flow model revisited: Perceptual and motor aspects. In R. Johnson, Jr., J. W. Rohrbaugh, and R. Parasuraman (Eds.), *Current trends in event-related potential research,* 270–278. *Electroencephalography and Clinical Neurophysiology* (Suppl. 40). Amsterdam: Elsevier.

Smid, H. G. O. M., Mulder, G., and Mulder, L. J. M. (1990). Selective response activation can begin before stimulus recognition is complete: A psychophysiological and error analysis of continuous flow. *Acta Psychologica, 74,* 169–201.

Smid, H. G. O. M., Mulder, G., Mulder, L. J. M., and Brands, G. J. (1992). A psychophysiological study of the use of partial information in stimulus-response translation. *Journal of Experimental Psychology: Human Perception and Performance, 18.*

Sternberg, S. (1969). The discovery of processing stages: Extensions of Donders' method. *Acta Psychologica, 30,* 276–315.

Treisman, A., and Gelade, G. (1980). A feature integration theory of attention. *Cognitive Psychology, 12,* 97–136.

Van Dellen, H. J., Brookhuis, K. A., Mulder, G., Okita, T., and Mulder, L. J. M. (1985). Evoked potential correlates of practice in a visual search task. In D. Papakoustopoulos, S. Butler, and I. Martin (Eds.), *Clinical and experimental neurophysiology,* 132–155. Beckenham, England: Croomhelm.

Wijers, A. A. (1989). *Visual selective attention: An electrophysiological approach.* Unpublished doctoral dissertation. University of Groningen, Groningen.

Wijers, A. A., Mulder, G., Okita, T., Mulder, L. J. M., and Scheffers, M. K. (1989a). Attention to color: An analysis of selection, controlled search and motor activation, using event-related potentials. *Psychophysiology, 26,* 89–109.

Wijers, A. A., Mulder, G., Okita, T., and Mulder, L. J. M. (1989b). Event-related potentials during memory search and selective attention to letter size and conjunctions of letter size and color. *Psychophysiology, 26,* 529–547.

Wijers, A. A., Okita, T., Mulder, G., Mulder, L. J. M., Lorist, M. M., Poiesz, R., and Scheffers, M. K. (1987). Visual search and spatial attention: ERP's in focussed and divided attention conditions. *Biological Psychology, 25,* 33–60.

Wijers, A. A., Otten, L. J., Feenstra, S., Mulder, G., and Mulder, L. J. M. (1989). Brain potentials during selective attention, memory search and mental rotation. *Psychophysiology, 26,* 452–467.

25 Use of Independent and Correlated Measures to Divide a Time-Discrimination Mechanism into Parts

Seth Roberts

25.1 INTRODUCTION

For most tasks, performance of the task probably involves many parts of the brain (many = four or more). Some of the evidence for this is anatomical: most neuronal paths from input to output go through many brain areas. Some is physiological: metabolic maps of human brain activity during a variety of tasks have shown that, for almost every task studied, many areas of the brain become more active while the person does the task (e.g., Ingvar 1976; Roland and Friberg 1985; Roland and Skinhoj 1981). And some is behavioral: lesion experiments with rats, using a wide range of tasks, have found that damage in a number of areas impairs performance on a single task (e.g., Thompson 1978). The best-known example is Lashley's (1929) "mass action" result: damage to many different cortical areas interfered with maze-running.

Along with the evidence that, for many tasks, the underlying mechanism has a number of *physically* different parts, there is also evidence that the underlying mechanism of many tasks can be divided into *functionally* different parts, different in the sense that they are separately changeable. The first evidence came from signal-detection experiments in the 1950s that observed a change in a measure of bias without a change in a measure of sensitivity. This result suggested, of course, that the underlying mechanism could be divided into at least two parts, and that one part (a comparison process, reflected in the bias measure) could be changed without changing the other part (a detection process, reflected in the sensitivity measure). Other evidence has come from reaction time experiments with humans via the additive-factor method (Sanders 1980; Sternberg 1967, 1969) and response rate experiments with rats, pigeons, and goldfish via the multiplicative-factor method (Roberts 1987). For example, the result that reward density and hours of deprivation had multiplicative effects in a bar-pressing experiment with rats suggests that the underlying mechanism can be divided into a reward-sensitive stage and a hunger-sensitive stage.

The physical and functional analyses are probably related: the separately changeable parts suggested by signal-detection experiments, and so forth, probably correspond to different parts of the brain, just as the separately heritable parts (genes) first suggested by breeding experiments were eventually linked to different parts of the cell. But it has been unclear how to make the connection. The two types of evidence—for multiple physical parts and for multiple functional parts—have come from entirely different tasks. In both cases, the tasks involved are so diverse that the conclusion probably holds for most tasks; however, there has been no one situation where one could do both types of experiments. For example, metabolic mapping experiments have required tasks that the subject does continuously for many minutes; reaction time experiments have generally used tasks that the subject does quickly (in under two seconds) in widely separated trials.

This chapter describes a situation where both types of experiments are possible—where one can both (a) divide a mechanism into separately changeable parts, and (b) try to locate those parts in the brain. It outlines one way of dividing a mechanism into separately changeable parts—the *independent measures method*—and applies it to one task—the *peak procedure*, a duration-discrimination task with rat subjects. The method is not new; similar ideas were part of the reasoning behind signal-detection theories of the fifties. But this chapter takes it further than previous uses, with more detailed conclusions, more measures, a wider range of factors, interpretation of between-measure correlations, and novel data analyses.

In the next sections, I describe the independent measures method and the peak procedure. Then I use the method to interpret some peak procedure experiments with a wide range of factors. Finally, I use the theory based on that work to interpret a lesion experiment.

The Independent-Measures Method

Most psychologists are familiar with *double dissociations*, which usually refers to the result that one factor changed a measure based on one set of responses (e.g., percent correct on task A) but not a measure based on another set of responses (e.g., percent correct on task B) and a second factor changed the second measure but not the first. The usual interpretation, of course, is that separately changeable mechanisms control the two sets of responses. Double dissociations are a main ingredient of recent neuropsychological and memory research (e.g., Richardson-Klavehn and Bjork 1988; Shallice 1988).

Much rarer is what I call *independent measures*: the result that two measures of one set of responses can be changed separately. For example, the signal-detection result that a measure of bias and a measure of sensitivity were separately changed is a case of independent measures because both bias and sensitivity are computed from exactly the same responses (responses = "present" and "absent"). In contrast, the observation that, in a free-recall task, the beginning and end of the serial-position curve (showing percent correct as a function of list position) were separately changed is *not* a case of independent measures, because the two measures—percent correct at the beginning of the list and percent correct at the end of the list—are derived from different responses.

The *independent-measures method* is a way of moving from examples of independent measures to theory and new experiments (Roberts 1981, 1985, 1987).

Reasoning   The method is based on two assumptions: (1) The mechanism contains two separately changeable parts (i.e., regions, subsections): one changed by F but not G; one changed by G but not F; and (2) measure X reflects changes in the F part but not the G part; measure Y reflects changes in the G part but not the F part.

Given these assumptions, factor F should change measure X but not measure Y, and factor G should change Y but not X. If this pattern of results (independent measures) occurs, it suggests that the assumptions are true—in particular, that the mechanism contains two separately changeable parts.

In some cases, it can be concluded that the two parts are serially arranged. Let us say that a particular response (e.g., a particular bar press) was *influenced* by a factor if part of the mechanism that generated that response was sensitive to that factor. Two factors that change two measures based on the same responses do not necessarily influence the same responses. In a signal-detection experiment, for example, suppose that a random half of a subject's responses are pure guesses, generated by a process unaffected by the signal, and that the rest of his responses are generated by a process that *is* sensitive to the signal. Suppose factor F changes the guessing process and factor G changes the signal-sensitive process. Then F will influence only the guesses, and G will influence only the non-guesses—two nonoverlapping sets of responses.

Suppose F and G produce independent measures (F changes one measure, G changes the other). This alone suggests two parts. If, in addition, it can be shown that factors F and G influenced to some extent the same responses— that there were some responses influenced by both—then, in addition, it can be argued that the mechanism that produced those responses contains two serially arranged parts. The argument is based on a consideration of the possibilities. That the parts are serially arranged means that the mechanism, however complicated, must contain at least one path leading to the response for which the signal that follows that path is affected first by one factor, then by the other. Figure 25.1 shows three possible arrangements. In the top model, F and G (a) influence the same responses, and (b) act sequentially. In the middle model, F and G (a) influence different responses, and (b) do not act sequentially. The bottom model is ambiguous. Whether it resembles the top model or the middle model depends on the nature of the processing at the junction of the two paths (marked with a circle). Suppose the junction is like an OR gate: a signal from either the upper branch or the lower branch passes though the junction unchanged, and triggers a response. Then the bottom model is equivalent to the middle model. On the other hand, suppose that information from the upper and lower branches is in some way combined at the junction. Then the bottom model is equivalent to the top model. Consider a signal that starts on the lower branch. It is first affected by G; then it reaches the junction,

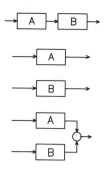

Figure 25.1 Three possible explanations of independent measures.

where it is affected by F (because every response is influenced by both factors); and finally it triggers a response. F and G have acted sequentially on that signal.

The argument can also be made less formally. Suppose a memo, after circulating around the office, emerges with the signatures of both F and G (= influenced by both F and G). If they signed it at separate times, they must have signed it sequentially.

Independent measures resemble additive factors with reaction time; in both cases, the result apparently implies serial processing only if the two factors influenced the same responses. (Roberts and Sternberg, chap. 26, show that a result of additive factors does *not* imply serial processing if the two factors influence nonoverlapping responses.)

Examples   In the 1970s, Hoffman and his colleagues found that in some situations the latency and amplitude of a rat's acoustic startle reflex could be changed separately (e.g., Stitt, Hoffman, and Marsh 1976); they took this to suggest that the mechanism had two separately changeable parts. This conclusion is supported by the observation of additive effects on the latency of the reflex (Roberts 1987). Ivry, Keele, and Diener (1988) used a model of human timing developed by Wing and Kristofferson (1973) to divide total variability in a tapping task into a clock component and a response component. Both components were computed from the same responses. Lateral cerebellar lesions increased the clock variability; medial cerebellar lesions increased the response variability. In a fixed-interval schedule with two signals and two responses (lever press and chain pull), Roberts (1983) found that response ratio (local response rate divided by overall response rate) and the proportion of chain responses, two measures of the same responses, were separately changeable, suggesting a time-measurement stage followed by a response-choice stage. The changes in response ratio were large enough to imply that at least some responses were influenced by both factors, suggesting a serial arrangement. Other evidence for serial processing in this situation comes from the observation of multiplicative factors with rate in a number of other fixed-interval-schedule experiments (Roberts 1987).

A case of independent measures that does *not* imply a serial arrangement comes from Roberts and Holder (1985), who trained rats to press one lever ("short") after a 2-s signal and another lever ("long") after an 8-s signal. The two durations were equally likely. The separately changeable measures were: (a) percent correct with the 2-s signal (short accuracy), and (b) percent correct with the 2-s signal *minus* percent correct with the 8-s signal ("short" bias). Like most animal discrimination experiments, and like the hypothetical signal-detection example described earlier, the observed responses probably came from two sources: one sensitive to signal duration, the other insensitive to signal duration ("guesses"). Some responses come from one source; some come from the other; none come from both. Factors that changed "short" bias without changing short accuracy apparently changed the mapping between physical time and perceived time—changing the time-sensitive source. Factors that changed short accuracy without changing "short" bias apparently changed the probability of a guess.

The Peak Procedure

My interest in independent measures was stimulated by results from an animal time-discrimination task called the *peak procedure*, first used by Catania (1970). It is a type of discrete trials, fixed-interval schedule. Trials begin when a signal (say, light) is turned on; they end when the signal is turned off. There are two kinds of trials, randomly mixed: *food* trials, where the first response after a fixed time from the start of the trial produces food, and the trial ends; and much longer *empty* trials, where no food is given, and the trial ends regardless of responding. The procedure has been used extensively with rats (e.g., Roberts 1981, 1982) and pigeons (e.g., Cheng and Roberts 1989) as subjects.

The experiments described here used ten to eighteen rats per experiment. Figure 25.2 shows their typical performance after a few weeks of training. In this experiment, the fixed interval was 40 s; that is, on food trials, food was *primed* at second 40 (i.e., given for the first response more than 40 s from the start of the trial). Figure 25.2 shows that response rate was low when the trial began, reached a peak at about the time that food was sometimes given, and then declined symmetrically. Response rates after the peak are only observed on empty trials; on food trials, the trial ends at about the time of the peak.

To measure performance, we compute a function like the function shown in figure 25.2—response rate as a function of time into the trial—for each rat. Then we compute five numbers from each function:

• *Peak time*, the time of the maximum response rate measured from the start of the trial (in fig. 25.2, 49 s). This is computed by treating the response rate function as if it were a frequency distribution, and finding its mean.

• *Spread*, a measure of the width of the response rate function (22 s). As with peak time, the response rate function is treated like a frequency distribution; in this case, its standard deviation is computed.

• *Relative spread*, defined as spread divided by peak time (22/49).

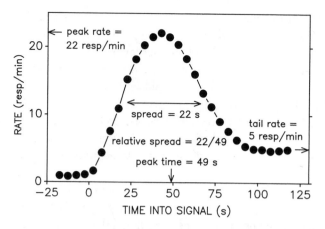

Figure 25.2 Typical peak-procedure results and 5 measures of performance.

- *Peak rate*, the maximum response rate (22 responses/min).
- *Tail rate*, the rate to which response rate drops late in the trial (5 responses/min).

We use four of the numbers—peak time, relative spread, peak rate, and tail rate—to summarize behavior. An equation with four adjustable parameters corresponding to peak time, relative spread, peak rate, and tail rate was able to closely fit about 20 response-rate functions, one per treatment, from five experiments (median variance described = 99.8%; Roberts 1981). So these four measures capture most of the between-treatment variation in performance. Peak time, relative spread, and peak rate are based on the same responses (responses within 100 s of the start of the signal); tail rate is based on later responses.

Early Results   The first peak procedure experiments stressed that peak time and peak rate could be separately changed. Catania (1970) reported that, for one pigeon, changing the probability of food trials changed peak rate but not peak time. My first experiment with the peak procedure (Roberts 1981, experiment 1) went further along these lines. During phase 1 of the experiment, the time of food was varied. Food was primed at second 20 during one signal (light or sound) and at second 40 during the other signal. With both signals, the mix of trials was 80 percent food, 20 percent empty. During phase 2 of the experiment, the probability of food was varied. Trials with one signal were 80 percent food, 20 percent empty; with the other signal, 20 percent food, 80 percent empty. During both signals, food was given (on food trials) for the first response after second 20. Figure 25.3 shows the results of this experiment. Changing the time of food changed peak time, but not peak rate; changing the probability of food changed peak rate, but not peak time. Peak time and peak rate were also changed separately in a number of other experiments (Roberts 1981, experiments 2 and 5; Roberts and Holder 1984, experiment 5).

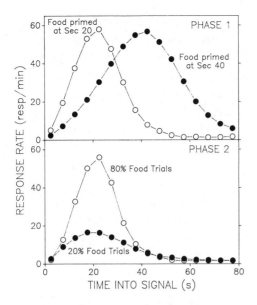

Figure 25.3 The independence of peak time and peak rate. (Redrawn from Roberts 1981.)

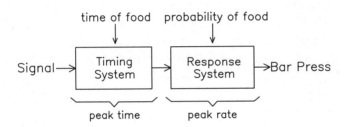

Figure 25.4 A theory of peak-procedure performance based on the independence of peak time and peak rate.

These results suggested the theory shown in figure 25.4 (Roberts 1981). It assumes (a) the mechanism that controls peak procedure performance can be divided into *two separately changeable parts*, one of them changed by time of food ("timing system"), the other changed by probability of food ("response system"); and (b) *selective measurement*, namely, that peak time selectively measures the timing system and peak rate selectively measures the response system. That the parts were serially arranged came from other considerations. The conclusion that peak time selectively measured part of the mechanism led to many experiments (e.g., Holder and Roberts 1985; Maricq, Roberts, and Church 1981; Meck and Church 1987; Roberts 1981, 1982; Roberts and Holder 1984).

Questions The model of figure 25.4 seemed like a good start. It raised a number of questions:

1. Could the mechanism be divided into more than two parts? Roberts (1982) found that relative spread could be changed without changing peak time and

peak rate, and vice versa. This suggested that the mechanism could be divided into at least three parts, each associated with a different measure. But it was unclear what relative spread was measuring. And what about tail rate?

2. Was the model of figure 25.4 overstated? It assumes that peak time and peak rate do not overlap in what they measure; but what was observed were merely a few examples where factors changed one measure but not the other. Other factors might change both. How could the overlap of the two measures be determined?

3. To conclude that one measure changed and another did not is in part to accept the null hypothesis. Can this conclusion be strengthened, at least in situations where it deserves strengthening? The absence of a statistically reliable difference might be due, of course, either to (a) little or no effect or (b) imprecise measurement. The hypothesis of little or no effect would become more plausible if the hypothesis of imprecise measurement became less plausible.

25.2 USE OF A WIDE RANGE OF FACTORS

To try to divide the mechanism into more parts, and determine the overlap between different measures, I studied the effect of a relatively large, diverse set of factors on peak procedure performance. If the set were large and diverse enough, then at least one of the factors should selectively change each separately changeable part of the mechanism.

Factors

Sometimes using experiments done for other purposes, I measured the effect of the following treatments:

1. *Time of food.* This was done in the experiment described earlier (fig. 25.3).

2. *Probability of food.* This was also done in the experiment described earlier (fig. 25.3).

3. *Extinction.* During the last three hours of a four-hour session, all food trials were eliminated (Roberts and Holder 1984, experiment 5).

4. *Amount of training,* e.g., early in training versus late in training.

5. *Hunger,* varied by sometimes feeding the rats prior to the daily session (Roberts 1981, experiment 3).

6. *Time elapsed in session* (Roberts and Holder 1984, experiment 5). Results from the first hour of the session were compared to the results from the last (fourth) hour.

7. *Signal,* namely, the difference between light and sound.

8. *Box type,* a comparison between ten older Skinner boxes and eight newer ones.

9. *Limited hold* of primed food. Some rats had to respond within a limited period of time after food was primed (say, second 40 to second 50) in order to collect the food pellet.

10. *Delayed end* of empty trials. For some rats, empty trials did not end if the rat had recently made a response.

11. *Vacation.* The rats were not run for three weeks, during which time they had unlimited food.

12. *Sham surgery,* namely, surgery that duplicated brain-lesion surgery except that the lesion maker was not turned on.

In addition, during these experiments, there were two occasions where performance changed dramatically even though the experimental conditions were supposedly constant. In one case (called *dip* in table 25.1), there was a sharp drop in peak rate and tail rate that lasted only a few days (fig. 25.9). In the other case (called *DC change* in table 25.1), peak rate and tail rate both dropped at the same time and stayed at the lower level for many days (fig. 25.8). Although these changes were not experimenter-produced, it can be asked whether they were selective.

Re-expression of the Data

Re-expression (transformation) of data can often simplify its description, for example, by increasing the symmetry of single batches or equalizing the variance of different batches (Tukey 1977). To decide how to express peak procedure data, I examined distributions of peak times, relative spreads, peak rates, and tail rates. Each of the four batches contained 126 numbers (7 experiments × 18 rats/experiment). A logarithmic transformation increased the symmetry of peak rates and tail rates, and had little effect on the symmetry of peak times and relative spreads. For consistency, then, it seemed worth using logs of all four measures.

When all four measures were expressed in the same units (log units), their variability could be compared. This comparison is shown by the leftmost four boxplots of figure 25.5. Log peak time and log relative spread varied much less than log peak rate and log tail rate. This is probably because the measures had different limits. Peak rate and tail rate could be no less than zero. In contrast, peak time was unlikely to be less than 40 s because, in the experiments that provided the data of figure 25.5, food was given for the first response after second 40. And relative spread, unlike the other measures, had an upper limit. A flat response rate function—zero discrimination—would have a relative spread of 0.58, and the discrimination was unlikely to be less than zero.

The existence of these limits suggests adjusting for them before taking logs. (In a similar way, Tukey 1977 gives an example in which radiation counts are adjusted for background level before taking logs.) Peak time would be measured relative to second 40 (e.g., a peak time of 45 s becomes 5 s) and relative spread would be measured relative to 0.58 (e.g., 0.47 becomes 0.11). To

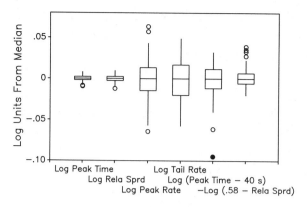

Figure 25.5 Distributions of the performance measures with various transformations (Rela Sprd = relative spread).

preserve order, the negative of the logs of relative spread were used. For example, a relative spread of 0.47 is transformed to 0.33 because $0.58 - 0.47 = 0.11$ and $\log 0.11 = -0.33$. With these adjustments, the spreads of the four measures were much closer. The rightmost two boxplots of figure 25.5 show adjusted peak times and relative spreads.

The rightmost four transformations of figure 25.5—log peak rate, log tail rate, log (peak time − 40 s), and −log (.58 − relative spread)—were used in all of the data analyses described here. Although they were chosen for conventional reasons (to increase symmetry and equate spread), their use had two important, unplanned benefits:

1. *Easy comparison of measures.* Different measures could be plotted on the same graph. After adjusting for level (e.g., by subtracting medians), it was easy to compare the time courses of different measures. Sometimes this revealed that two measures changed by roughly the same amount (in log units) at roughly the same time—conclusive evidence that the changes in the two measures were due to the same internal change.

2. *Quality control.* As mentioned earlier, a problem with the method was the need, in some cases, to accept the null hypothesis—conclude that a factor did not change a measure—simply because there was no reliable effect. The use of logs led to an improvement. It happened that three pairs of measures sometimes had a one-to-one relation, that is, the two measures changed at the same time by equal log unit amounts: peak rate and tail rate (figs. 25.8 and 25.9), relative spread and tail rate (fig. 25.6), and peak time and peak rate (figs. 25.6 and 25.7). (The peak time/peak rate correlation was negative; the other two correlations were positive.) Therefore, to support the hypothesis of independence—that one measure changed and another measure did not—it was reasonable to take a one-to-one change as the null hypothesis; that is, to ask if what was observed was reliably less than a one-to-one change. For example, given a case where peak rate changed reliably and tail rate did not, one would, in addition, ask if the log unit change in peak rate produced by the treatment exceeded the log unit change in tail rate. To qualify as an example

of independent measures, then, three conditions had to be met: (1) The change in measure A exceeded zero ($p < .05$); (2) the change in measure B did not differ from zero; and (3) the change in measure A exceeded the change in measure B in the direction expected from other results, such as simple or partial correlations (a one-tailed test). The third condition ensured that A and B would not be considered independent simply because B was imprecisely measured.

Results

Independent Measures   Thirty-six cases fulfilled the three criteria for independence. Table 25.1 gives the details. For example, the entry *food time* in the cell with row = Peak Time, column = Relative Spread, means that food time changed peak time, did not change relative spread, and the change in peak time was reliably larger than the change in relative spread. Except for the factor Box Type, which changed all four measures, and the factor Delayed End, which had no effect, every factor changed some but not all of the measures.

One interesting feature of table 25.1 is that two nondiagonal cells are empty. In one case (peak time changed, tail rate unchanged), the cause is

Table 25.1 Cases of Independent Measures

Changed Measure	Unchanged Measure			
	Peak Time	Relative Spread	Peak Rate	Tail Rate
Peak Time		food time prefeeding session time sham surg.—l.l.	food time	(none)
Relative Spread	food prob. training vacation—s.l. sham surg.—s.l.		training signal vacation—s.l.	(none)
Peak Rate	food prob. extinction DC change vacation—l.l.	prefeeding session time extinction limited hold DC change vacation—l.l. sham surg.—l.l. dip		vacation—l.l. sham surg.—l.l.
Tail Rate	food prob. training signal DC change sham surg.—s.l. dip	DC change dip	training signal	

Note: The vacation and sham surgery caused both short-lived (s.l.) and long-lived (l.l.) changes in performance.

Dividing a Time-Discrimination Mechanism into Parts

probably artifactual: that no treatments changed peak time but not tail rate is probably because there were few experiments where peak time was changed and tail rate was measured. But this cannot explain the other empty cell (relative spread changed, tail rate unchanged)—there were many experiments where relative spread changed and tail rate was measured. Apparently it is impossible, or at least difficult, to change relative spread without changing tail rate. Quality control was essential in revealing this connection because, in two instances, there *was* a reliable change in relative spread and no reliable change in tail rate. For example, the effect of training seen in figure 25.3 (between the second-20 signal in phase 1 and the same signal—80 percent-food—in phase 2) was, for relative spread, .08 ± .02 log units; for tail rate, .02 ± .20 log units. It is clear that the change in tail rate is not reliably less than the change in relative spread.

With a single pair of independent measures, the interpretation is obvious—something like the model of figure 25.4. With many pairs, and one missing pair, the interpretation is not so obvious. Three other aspects of the results help choose between the possibilities: evidence for serial arrangement, time-course correlations between measures, and between-measure correlation coefficients based on rat-to-rat variation.

Evidence for Serial Arrangement   Did factors with selective effects influence the same responses? For tail rate, the answer is easy. Tail rate is computed from different responses (responses late in the trial) than the other three measures. A factor that, say, changed tail rate but not peak time and a factor that changed peak time and not tail rate could plainly have influenced entirely different responses. So examples of independence involving tail rate cannot suggest a serial arrangement.

In contrast, factors with selective effects on the other three measures do appear to have influenced the same responses. An example is the data of figure 25.3. Figure 25.3 shows a case of almost *three*-way independence. During phase 1, time of food changed peak time, but not peak rate or relative spread; during phase 2, the probability of food changed peak rate and relative spread, but not peak time; and, comparing across phases, the difference between the second-20 signal of phase 1 and the 80 percent-food signal of phase 2 (which were physically the same signal) changed relative spread but not peak time or peak rate. The difference between the similar conditions (second-20 and 80 percent-food) in the two phases was probably due to a difference in training; phase 1 ended before the rats were completely trained.

In figure 25.3, food time changed peak time; training (or whatever) changed relative spread; and food probability changed peak rate. The conclusion that these three factors—food time, training, and food probability—influenced overlapping responses rests on two results:

1. *Size of effects.* Food probability and food time both had large effects—so large that they must have influenced almost every response. Food probability, when varied by a factor of 4 during phase 2, changed peak rate by a factor of 4; if food probability was reduced to zero, then, plainly, *all* responses would

disappear. Because any particular response could have been eliminated by the right choice of food probability, the mechanism of every response must contain something sensitive to food probability. Food time was almost as powerful. The upper panel of figure 25.3 shows that a change in peak time shifted the distribution of all of the responses except perhaps those in the tail of the function—roughly 95 percent of all responses. Almost any particular response could have been eliminated by the right choice of food time; so food time must have influenced almost every response. Training—the difference between the corresponding conditions of phases 1 and 2—had a much weaker effect, but it must have influenced at least 15 percent of the responses during phase 1 because the average rate during the 80 percent-food signal of phase 2 is 15 percent less than during the second-20 signal of phase 1. If food probability influenced 100 percent of the responses, food time influenced 95 percent, and training influenced 15 percent, then at least 10 percent of the responses must have been influenced by all three.

2. *Shape of response-rate functions.* In all four conditions of figure 25.3, the response-rate functions, omitting the tails, resemble Gaussian ("normal") density functions. If a substantial fraction of the responses were *not* influenced by the various factors, this result is highly unlikely. Suppose, for example, that in phase 1, half of the responses in the second-20 condition were uninfluenced by food time. Then the change in food time to second 40 would leave half of the area under the second-20 function unaffected. Food at second 40 would produce a bimodal function with one peak at second 20 and another peak at second 40. (For an actual example of something similar, see Blough 1978.) But there is no trace of bimodality in the second-40 function. More generally, if a substantial fraction of the responses were not influenced by even one of the factors, it is unlikely, and probably impossible, that the response rate functions would have the same simple shape in all four conditions. Part of the distribution (the influenced responses) would disappear or shift from one condition to the next, and part of the distribution would remain the same (the uninfluenced responses).

The first result (effect sizes) suggests that at least a few responses were produced by a serial arrangement; the second result (shape of functions) suggests that almost all of the responses, except maybe those in the tail of the function, were produced by a serial arrangement.

Time-Course Correlations   In a number of cases, one treatment changed two measures. In some of these instances, the changes had similar time course, implying that both were due to the same internal change.

One example, the effect of training, is shown in figure 25.6. In three experiments, tail rate and relative spread changed together over a remarkably large range. Peak time and peak rate also changed together, although over a much smaller range (to show the peak time/peak rate correlation, which is negative, the peak times are sign-reversed—e.g., 1 plotted as -1).

Figure 25.7 shows the effect of sham surgery. As in figure 25.6, tail rate and relative spread changed with the same time course although, in this case, by

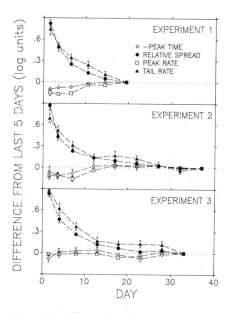

Figure 25.6 Effect of training. (The functions were adjusted vertically so that they would be equated for the final 5-day block. To show the negative correlation with peak rate, the negatives of the transformed values of peak time are plotted. For example, 0.2 is plotted instead of −0.2. Error bars show standard errors based on between-rat variance; when no bar is visible, it was smaller than the point.)

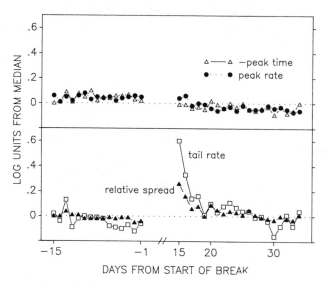

Figure 25.7 Effect of sham surgery. (As in fig. 25.6, the negatives of the transformed values of peak time are plotted. For each measure, plotted points are deviations from the median of all values of that measure.)

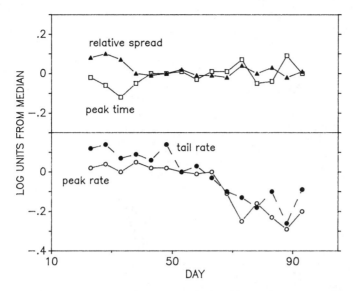

Figure 25.8 A naturally occurring change. (Conditions were supposedly constant during the days shown here. For each measure, plotted points are deviations from the median of all values of that measure.)

different amounts; and peak time and peak rate changed with the same time course and by the same amount.

In two cases, the correlated changes occurred when the conditions of the experiment were supposedly constant. Figure 25.8 shows data averaged over five-day blocks; the lower panel shows that peak rate and tail rate changed together. Another example is shown in figure 25.9. The rats took a three-week vacation (no work and unlimited food); and shortly after the vacation ended, something caused peak rate and tail rate to dip sharply.

All of these examples of parallel time courses (figs. 25.6, 25.7, 25.8, and 25.9) suggest the same conclusions: (a) the changes in the two correlated measures were due to a single internal cause; and, therefore, (b) the two measures overlap in what they measure.

Within-Rat Correlation Coefficients   The existence of a few examples of time-course correlations raises the possibility that if enough data were examined, all pairs of measures would turn out to be correlated on occasion. One way to assess this possibility is to measure correlation coefficients based on between-rat variation. Does a rat with, say, high peak time tend to have high relative spread? Assume that the mechanism has multiple separately change-able parts, that all parts vary from rat to rat, and that within a single rat, the variation in one part is independent of the variation in other parts. Then if two measures reflect exactly the same parts, they will have a correlation of 1 (or −1); if they reflect entirely different parts, they will have a correlation of 0; and if they reflect different but overlapping parts, they will have a correlation between 0 and 1 or 0 and −1 (Tulving 1985). If these assumptions are reasonable, then correlation coefficients based on between-rat variation are an

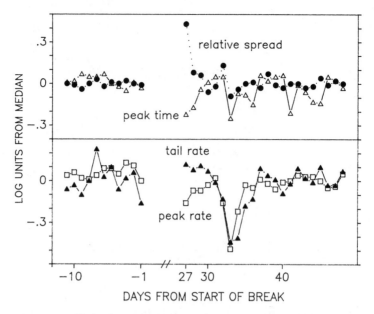

Figure 25.9 Effect of a vacation. (For each measure, plotted points are deviations from the median of all values of that measure.)

unbiased way to determine the overlap between two measures—unbiased in the sense that they do not depend on the treatments that the experimenter happens to study.

Table 25.2 gives Pearson correlation coefficients based on between-rat variation. They suggest the same conclusions as the treatment effects. Three pairs of measures apparently overlap a fair amount: peak time and peak rate ($r = -.5$), relative spread and tail rate ($r = .5$), and peak rate and tail rate ($r = .3$). The other three pairs of measures apparently overlap little or not at all (r's = near 0).

Interpretation

Most of the results are explained by the three-part model of figure 25.10. The existence of three parts is based on the pairwise independence of peak time, relative spread, and tail rate; for each pair, there were at least five cases where one was changed without changing the other (table 25.1). Selective effects, such as those of table 25.1, occur when a treatment changes only one or two parts; for example, a treatment that changed the final stage would change peak rate and tail rate, but not relative spread and peak time. The lack of instances where relative spread changed without changing tail rate is, according to the model, because there is no part measured by relative spread but not tail rate. Time-course correlations (e.g., fig. 25.8) and nonzero within-rat correlations (table 25.2) are explained by overlap in what the measures reflect; for example, the correlation during training of relative spread and tail rate (fig. 25.6) is due to changes in a part measured by both. The serial arrangement of the parts is

Table 25.2 Within-Rat Correlations between Measures

Measures	Correlation
peak time and peak rate	$-.5 \pm .1$
relative spread and tail rate	$.5 \pm .1$
peak rate and tail rate	$.3 \pm .1$
other pairs	$.1 \pm .1, .0 \pm .1, -.1 \pm .1$

Note: Each correlation is based on ten experiments. They were computed by (a) finding the simple Pearson correlation for each experiment, and (b) taking the mean across experiments. The standard errors are based on between-experiment variation.

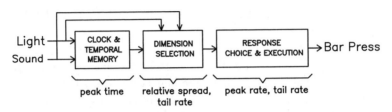

Figure 25.10 Model of the underlying mechanism suggested by the results.

based on the conclusion that, as explained above, in some cases, at least some of the responses were influenced by three factors with selective effects on peak time, relative spread, and peak rate.

The most interesting feature of the model of figure 25.10 is the existence of a separate dimension-selection stage. Learning theorists have often posited a dimension-selection process based on less convincing evidence (Bitterman 1979; Sutherland and Mackintosh 1971). That the function of the part selectively measured by relative spread is dimension selection is suggested by the close connection between relative spread and tail rate, especially the fact that they changed together during training (fig. 25.6). The rat has a problem: it needs to learn what features of the situation predict food. When it presses the bar during light and gets food, it is unclear with what the food should be linked: the presence of light or the duration of the light. Over the course of training, the rat gradually learns that a specific duration of light is a better predictor of food than the mere presence of light. Relative spread, a measure of time discrimination, should reflect how much attention the rat pays to the duration of light; tail rate, measured long after the time that food is sometimes given, should reflect how much the rat expects food based on only the presence of light. In the beginning of experiments, relative spread and tail rate are both high, suggesting that, initially, food is mainly attributed to the presence of the light rather than to its duration. As the rat pays less attention to the presence/absence of light, tail rate decreases; as it pays more attention to duration, relative spread decreases. The same shift in guidance—away from presence/absence, toward duration—causes both measures to change; when the shift is complete, both measures stop changing. (This does not explain why the two measures changed by the same *amount* during training.) The existence of a dimension-selection process is not obvious; the model of Gibbon and Church (1984) does not include one.

The model of figure 25.10 does not explain all of the results. It does not explain: (a) Correlations between peak time and peak rate (figs. 25.6 and 25.7, table 25.2). This is probably an artifact: When peak rate declines, food is actually given later, because there is a longer delay between when food is primed and the next response. This artifact would produce a one-to-minus-one correlation in log units, which is what was observed (figs. 25.6 and 25.7). (b) Two cases where peak rate changed and tail rate did not (figs. 25.7 and 25.9). This may indicate another part of the mechanism.

25.3   APPLICATION: WHAT DOES THE STRIATUM DO?

The theory of figure 25.10 can be used to interpret lesion experiments—in particular, an experiment done by Jamie Eberling and me and described by her in her doctoral dissertation (Eberling 1989). Its goal was to locate the parts of the model of figure 25.10 in the brain. We chose to lesion the striatum, part of the basal ganglia, for a number of reasons, especially its size (very large) and the fact that striatal lesions often interfere with learning in bar-pressing experiments.

Our design was simple: We trained some rats, divided them into two groups—one group, of twelve rats, got bilateral striatum lesions, the other, of six rats, got sham surgery—and, finally, gave them more training. Figure 25.11 shows the daily results. The lesions changed relative spread and tail rate, but had no obvious effect on peak time and peak rate. The relative spread and tail-rate changes lasted at least 100 days.

Figure 25.12 summarizes the effect of the lesions. Both soon after and long after surgery, the changes in relative spread and tail rate were the same size in log units—just like the changes observed during training (fig. 25.6), attributed to changes in dimension selection. A change in the dimension-selection stage of our model (fig. 25.10) would change both measures; changing other parts of the model would not produce this result.

Thus the striatum apparently corresponds to at least some of the dimension-selection stage, the part of the model that learns which dimensions predict food. This conclusion makes sense in terms of other data. Anatomical study of the striatum has shown that it receives input from many modalities, all over the cortex (e.g., Nauta and Domesick 1984). In order to decide which dimensions are most relevant, the dimensions must be compared, so a structure that does this must physically receive input from many of them. In addition, electrophysiological recordings from the striatum show that it contains cells whose firing properties vary with the predictive value of the trigger stimulus (e.g., Kimura, Rajkowski, and Evarts 1984). For example, in some cases a cell would fire in response to a click if the click signaled food, but not if the click did not signal food.

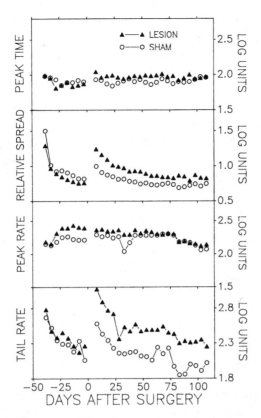

Figure 25.11 Effect of striatum lesions day by day.

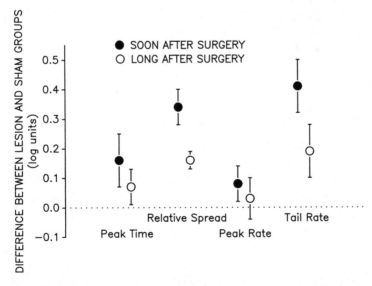

Figure 25.12 Effect of striatum lesions summarized. (Soon after surgery = the first 5 days of testing after surgery. Long after surgery = the last 20 days of testing after surgery. Error bars show standard errors based on between-subject variance.)

Dividing a Time-Discrimination Mechanism into Parts

That anatomy and physiology fit nicely with conclusions from behavior is good support for our approach. Lesion experiments are notoriously difficult to interpret much beyond the conclusion that, if a lesion in place X changes performance, then place X must be part of the mechanism guiding performance. For example, Hansing, Schwartzbaum, and Thompson (1968) observed results much like ours: Using rats trained with a fixed-interval schedule, they found that bilateral striatum lesions increased response rate early in the interval, but had little effect on response rate late in the interval. They concluded that the striatum was involved in "inhibitory regulation of behavior" (p. 378). Our work shows one way that more specific conclusions can be reached.

25.4 CONCLUSIONS

The novelty of this work is not the extension of the idea of double dissociations to multiple measures of the same responses; it is that the reasoning can be taken further than this, in three main ways:

1. *Structure.* If the two factors that separately change two measures influence the same responses, it suggests that the two inferred parts are serially arranged.

2. *Data analysis.* Logarithmic transformations can make it easier to compare the effects of one treatment on different measures, especially the time courses of the effects. In at least some situations, log transformations can make possible a certain amount of quality control, detecting cases of independent measures due to imprecise measurement.

3. *Correlations.* Correlation coefficients (zero or nonzero) computed from between-subject variation can give an unbiased idea of how much two measures overlap (Tulving 1985 makes a similar point). Time-course correlations (nonzero) due to treatment effects can help determine what a selectively measured part does.

Interpretation of the striatal-lesion experiment benefited from these extensions. The conclusion that the part measured by relative spread was serially arranged with other parts makes more plausible the idea that its function is dimension selection because a dimension-selection process must be serially arranged with other processes. It must receive input from various analyzers, each with information about a different dimension, and its output must be used to choose and make a response (Sutherland and Mackintosh 1971). Logarithmic transformations made it much easier to see that relative spread and tail rate changed together during training (fig 25.6). This is the most important fact suggesting that relative spread measured dimension selection. The transformations also made it easier to see that the lesion effects—equal-sized changes in relative spread and tail rate (fig. 25.12)—resembled the effects of training (fig. 25.6); this strengthens the conclusion that the striatum learns. The quality control made possible by the transformations led to the elimination of two cases where relative spread changed and tail rate did not, strengthening the connection between the two measures. Other correlations (fig. 25.7 and table 25.2) also strengthened the connection between relative spread and tail rate. The extensions, not the independent measures alone, led to the conclusion that there was a separately changeable, serially arranged part of the mechanism that learns which dimensions are relevant. Without the extensions, the lesion experiment would merely connect the striatum with relative spread and tail rate—much less of a clue to its function.

NOTE

This work was supported by a grant from the Sloan Foundation. I thank Richard Ivry for comments on the manuscript.

REFERENCES

Bitterman, M. E. (1979). Attention. In M. E. Bitterman, V. M. LoLordo, J. B. Overmier, and M. E. Rashotte, *Animal learning: Survey and analysis*, 445–471. New York: Plenum.

Blough, D. S. (1978). Reaction times of pigeons on a wavelength discrimination task. *Journal of the Experimental Analysis of Behavior, 30*, 163–167.

Catania, A. C. (1970). Reinforcement schedules and psychophysical judgments: A study of some temporal properties of behavior. In W. N. Schoenfeld (Ed.), *The theory of reinforcement schedules*, 1–42. New York: Appleton-Century-Crofts.

Cheng, K., and Roberts, W. A. (1989). Timing multimodal events in pigeons. *Journal of the Experimental Analysis of Behavior, 52*, 363–376.

Eberling, J. L. (1989). The striatum and temporal discrimination: Use of a new method to localize cognitive processes in rat brain. Unpublished doctoral dissertation. University of California at Berkeley.

Gibbon, J., and Church, R. M. (1984). Sources of variance in an information-processing theory of timing. In H. L. Roitblat, T. G. Bever, and H. S. Terrace (Eds.), *Animal cognition*, 465–488. Hillsdale, NJ: Lawrence Erlbaum.

Hansing, R. A., Schwartzbaum, J. S., and Thompson, J. B. (1968). Operant behavior following unilateral and bilateral caudate lesion in the rat. *Journal of Comparative and Physiological Psychology, 66*, 378–388.

Holder, M. D., and Roberts, S. (1985). Comparison of timing and classical conditioning. *Journal of Experimental Psychology: Animal Behavior Processes, 11*, 172–193.

Ingvar, D. H. (1976). Functional landscapes of the dominant hemisphere. *Brain Research, 107*, 181–197.

Ivry, R. B., Keele, S. W., and Diener, H. C. (1988). Dissociation of the lateral and medial cerebellum in movement timing and movement execution. *Experimental Brain Research, 73*, 167–180.

Kimura, M., Rajkowski, J., and Evarts, E. (1984). Tonically discharging putamen neurons exhibit set-dependent responses. *Proceedings of the National Academy of Sciences, 81*, 4998–5001.

Lashley, K. S. (1929). *Brain mechanisms and intelligence; a quantitative study of injuries to the brain.* Chicago: University of Chicago Press.

Maricq, A. V., Roberts, S., and Church, R. M. (1981). Methamphetamine and time estimation. *Journal of Experimental Psychology: Animal Behavior Processes, 7*, 18–30.

Meck, W. H., and Church, R. M. (1987). Nutrients that modify the speed of internal clock and memory storage processes. *Behavioral Neuroscience, 101,* 465–475.

Nauta, W. J. H., and Domesick, V. B. (1984). Afferent and efferent relationships of the basal ganglia. In D. Evered and M. O'Connor (Eds.), *Functions of the basal ganglia,* 3–23. London: Pitman.

Richardson-Klavehn, A., and Bjork, R. A. (1988). Measures of memory. *Annual Review of Psychology, 39,* 475–543.

Roberts, S. (1981). Isolation of an internal clock. *Journal of Experimental Psychology: Animal Behavior Processes, 7,* 242–268.

Roberts, S. (1982). Cross-modal use of an internal clock. *Journal of Experimental Psychology: Animal Behavior Processes, 8,* 2–22.

Roberts, S. (1983). Properties and function of an internal clock. In R. L. Mellgren (Ed.), *Animal cognition and behavior.* Amsterdam: North-Holland.

Roberts, S. (1987). Evidence for distinct serial processes in animals: The multiplicative-factors method. *Animal Learning and Behavior, 15,* 135–173.

Roberts, S., and Holder, M. D. (1984). What starts an internal clock? *Journal of Experimental Psychology: Animal Behavior Processes, 10,* 273–296.

Roberts, S., and Holder, M. D. (1985). Effect of classical conditioning on an internal clock. *Journal of Experimental Psychology: Animal Behavior Processes, 11,* 194–214.

Roland, P. E., and Friberg, L. (1985). Localization of cortical areas activated by thinking. *Journal of Neurophysiology, 53,* 1219–1243.

Roland, P. E., and Skinhoj, E. (1981). Extrastriate cortical areas activated during visual discrimination in man. *Brain Research, 222,* 166–171.

Sanders, A. F. (1980). Stage analysis of reaction processes. In G. E. Stelmach and J. Requin (Eds.), *Tutorials in motor behavior,* 331–354. Amsterdam: North-Holland.

Shallice, T. (1988). *From neuropsychology to mental structure.* Cambridge, England: Cambridge University Press.

Sternberg, S. (1967). Two operations in character recognition: Some evidence from reaction-time measurements. *Perception and Psychophysics, 2,* 45–53.

Sternberg, S. (1969). The discovery of processing stages: Extensions of Donders' method. In W. G. Koster (Ed.), *Attention and Performance II.* Amsterdam: North-Holland. Reprinted from *Acta Psychologica, 30.*

Stitt, C. L., Hoffman, H. S., and Marsh, R. (1976). Interaction versus independence of startle-modification processes in the rat. *Journal of Experimental Psychology: Animal Behavior Processes, 2,* 260–265.

Sutherland, N. S., and Mackintosh, N. J. (1971). *Mechanisms of animal discrimination learning.* New York: Academic Press.

Thompson, R. (1978). *A behavioral atlas of the rat brain.* New York: Oxford University Press.

Tukey, J. W. (1977). *Exploratory data analysis.* Reading, MA: Addison-Wesley.

Tulving, E. (1985). How many memory systems are there? *American Psychologist, 40,* 385–398.

Wing, A., and Kristofferson, A. (1973). Response delays and the timing of discrete motor responses. *Perception and Psychophysics, 14,* 5–12.

26 The Meaning of Additive Reaction-Time Effects: Tests of Three Alternatives

Seth Roberts and Saul Sternberg

26.1 INTRODUCTION

At Attention and Performance II, Sternberg (1969) introduced the additive-factor method, for interpreting reaction-time (RT) data from factorial experiments. In that method, additivity of the effects of experimental treatments on mean RT is taken to suggest that the underlying mechanism can be divided into independently changeable, serially arranged operations (stage model). In this chapter we consider two other explanations of additive means: a model with independently changeable alternate pathways and the McClelland-Ashby cascade model. In all three models, experimental factors that influence different operations can have additive effects. To choose among these models we develop several tests, including comparisons of entire RT distributions. Applied to the results of four diverse experiments, the tests support the stage model and contradict the alternate-pathways and cascade models. In particular, the results of one distributional test, based on a suggestion by Ashby and Townsend (1980), support the stage model remarkably well.

Some of the examples of additivity in Sternberg (1969) were remarkably precise. In a numeral-naming experiment, for example, main effects of about 50 and 100 ms were additive with a precision of about 1 ms. Since then, many more examples of impressive additivity have been observed (Roberts 1987; Sanders 1980, 1990; Sternberg 1971). These results were unexpected; there is no obvious reason why behavior should be so simple. Nothing in the anatomy or physiology of the brain would lead one to expect such simplicity, and there is almost no precedent in other observations of behavior. Unlike the few other well-established cases where behavior has a simple quantitative structure, such as Stevens's power law, or receiver operating characteristics (ROCs) that are linear in normalized coordinates (e.g., Swets 1986), RT additivity is comparatively general, found in a large range of experiments, with diverse factors. Whatever the mechanism that produces additivity, it must be widespread.

What is the mechanism? The proposal that additivity reflects stages of processing has gained some support. Sanders (1980; 1990, especially fig. 1) has shown how existing examples of additivity, taken together and interpreted in terms of processing stages, make a consistent picture. Roberts (1987) showed that with some modification, the stages explanation of RT additivity also explained multiplicative effects of factors on response rate in animal experiments, and that this explanation made sense in terms of other knowledge.

The proposal has also faced both specific challenges and general skepticism. As an example of a specific challenge, Pieters (1983) questioned the use of analysis of variance to test additivity. Other critics include Taylor (1976), Townsend (1984), Townsend and Ashby (1983), and Wickelgren (1977). For a summary, see Luce (1986, 481–483), who states that "many of those who have commented on the matter very strongly question the existence of stages at all, at least as conceived by Sternberg" (482). (Miller 1988 argues that some of the evidence regarded as negative is unpersuasive, however.) For examples of general skepticism see Broadbent (1984, 56–58) and Gardner (1985, 120–124). Such skepticism may reflect the belief that stage models are too simple; Broadbent, for example, calls them "simplistic" (55). But additivity is simple.

Alternative Explanations of Additive Effects

Regardless of current theories and beliefs, additivity as a phenomenon is too widespread to be ignored. Here we consider Sternberg's (1969) explanation together with two alternatives. The first, which produces exact additivity, is a mechanism with alternate pathways; the response is generated by one or the other pathway with a fixed mixing probability. The second, which produces approximate additivity, is McClelland's (1979) cascade model as further developed by Ashby (1982). See also Townsend and Ashby (1983, chap. 12).

Suppose that factors A and B have additive effects on mean RT. In all three of the explanations we consider, the mechanism is modular (Shallice 1988, sec. 2.1) in the sense that it is composed of processes a and b that can be changed independently. Additivity in an experiment with factors A and B is explained by the mechanism together with an assumption of selective influence: factor A influences process a but not b, whereas factor B influences process b but not a. Hence, for purposes of the present chapter, we incorporate an assumption of selective influence among the defining features of each model, from which we derive properties that permit it to be tested. The models differ in the arrangement of processes a and b, and in the nature of the communication between them.[1] In a *stage model* the processes are arranged sequentially, with one beginning when its predecessor is complete; both are required for response initiation. In the *alternate-pathways model*, process a is used on some occasions while process b is used on the remaining occasions; on no trials are they both used. In the *cascade model* both processes are used on all trials, but process a provides output continuously to process b ("partial output") which thus operates concurrently with a.[2]

Implications for the Additive-Factor Method

That radically different mechanisms are capable of producing additive effects of experimental manipulations on mean RT has important implications for the additive-factor method. First, insofar as approximations to these mechanisms exist, it widens the domain within which the method can be used to discover and determine the properties of independently changeable (modular) processes.[3] But second, although a finding of additivity still supports such modularity, it does not support a stage model without additional evidence, contrary to Sternberg (1969). In what follows we provide such evidence, based on tests that distinguish among the three mechanisms.

26.2 GENERAL AND STOCHASTICALLY-INDEPENDENT STAGE MODELS

Definition of the Models

In the stage model, processes a and b operate in sequence, possibly concatenated with other operations; one process begins when its predecessor is complete (discrete transmission; see, e.g., Meyer, Yantis, Osman, and Smith 1984; Miller 1988, 1990; and Sanders 1990). For a description of three relations between processes that would produce such seriality, see Sternberg 1984. According to the model, the stream of processes between stimulus and response can be cut at some point, defining two processing stages, "stage a" the processes before the cut (including process a), and "stage b" the processes after the cut (including process b). The cut is temporal; it may or may not be spatial (anatomical). We make two assumptions, the first of which follows from the sequential arrangement of stages:

1. *Stages*: RT is the sum of stage durations: $T = T_a + T_b$.

2. *Selective Influence*: Factor A influences the duration of stage a, but not b; factor B influences the duration of stage b, but not a.

In other words, factor A acts only before the cut; factor B acts only after the cut. A third assumption strengthens the model considerably:

3. *Stochastic Independence (SI)*: Durations T_a and T_b are stochastically independent. We refer to a model with this property as an *SIstage model*, to distinguish it from a general stage model (Gstage model) for which assumption (3) is not made. Of course, any evidence that favors the SIstage model also supports a fortiori the Gstage model.

Additivity of Factor Effects on Mean and Variance

Suppose each factor can have two levels, indexed by $i = 1, 2$ for factor A and $j = 1, 2$ for factor B. Given selective influence we can then write T_{ai} for the duration of stage a when factor A is at level A_i, and T_{bj} for the duration of stage b when factor B is at level B_j, so that we have for the RT, T_{ij}, at levels A_i and B_j,

$$T_{ij} = T_{ai} + T_{bj}. \tag{1}$$

We shall assume that increasing an index i or j corresponds to increasing the mean RT; we refer to such a change in level as "raising the level" of the factor. As we shall be considering the two-way interaction contrast of various quantities in what follows, it is convenient to define it symbolically: For any function or quantity S_{ij}, where $i = 1, 2$ and $j = 1, 2$ we let

$$I\{S_{ij}\} \equiv S_{11} - S_{12} - S_{21} + S_{22}. \tag{2}$$

The central property of the stage model is then[4]

$$I\{\mu_{ij}\} = 0. \tag{3}$$

To make similar statements about higher-order moments, we must know or assume something about the stochastic dependence of stage durations. For example, relations among the RT variances under the four conditions in a 2×2 experiment depend on the set of covariances $\gamma_{ij} \equiv \mathrm{cov}(T_{ai}, T_{bj})$. If we invoke the SI assumption, then because this implies that all four covariances are zero, we have variance additivity:

$$I\{\sigma_{ij}^2\} = 0. \tag{4}$$

Equation (4) characterizes the stage model under conditions more general than stochastic independence of stage durations, however. By using the relation $\sigma_{ij}^2 = \sigma_{ai}^2 + \sigma_{bj}^2 + 2\gamma_{ij}$ we see that $I\{\sigma_{ij}^2\} = 2I\{\gamma_{ij}\}$. Equation (4) will thus be satisfied not only if the stage-duration covariances are all zero (required in the SIstage model), but also if they are nonzero but constant (which also implies $I\{\gamma_{ij}\} = 0$), or nonconstant but additive. The last two possibilities are implausible, however: let $D_a = T_{a2} - T_{a1}$ and $D_b = T_{b2} - T_{b1}$ be the increments in stage duration produced by raising the respective factor levels. Richard Schweickert pointed out to us that equation (4) (additive variances) obtains if and only if $\mathrm{cov}(D_a, D_b) = 0$ (uncorrelated increments). It is implausible that we would have uncorrelated increments but correlated base durations, T_{a1}, T_{b1}. This observation leaves zero covariance of stage durations as the favored explanation of additive RT variance and renders such additivity even more important.

The Summation Test

Further implications of the SI property are expressed informally by

$$F_{T_{11}+T_{22}}(t) = F_{T_{12}+T_{21}}(t), \qquad (t \geq 0), \tag{5}$$

which asserts the stochastic equality of the two sums: $T_{11,22} \equiv T_{11} + T_{22}$ and $T_{12,21} \equiv T_{12} + T_{21}$, where $F_X(t) \equiv F_X$ is the cumulative distribution function (CDF) of the random variable X. The idea of directly comparing the two CDFs of equation (5) to test the SIstage model in a 2×2 experiment was first proposed by Ashby and Townsend (1980), who proved the equality of convolutions equivalent to equation (5): $F_{T_{11}} * f_{T_{22}} = F_{T_{12}} * f_{T_{21}}$, where the $\{f_{T_{ij}}\}$ and $\{F_{T_{ij}}\}$ are the density functions and CDFs, respectively, of the $\{T_{ij}\}$, and $*$ represents convolution. To use the relation in the way they advocate, however, requires estimating density functions (Silverman 1986) and then performing numerical convolution. We prefer the simpler method of approximating the convolutions that is embodied in the *summation test*, and that is suggested by equation (5) and its constructive proof (see Appendix). Instead of numerical convolution, one creates samples from $T_{11} + T_{22}$ and $T_{12} + T_{21}$ by simply summing RTs from each of the two pairs of conditions, and then determines the empirical CDFs of the two sums.

Because the summation distributions $T_{11,22}$ and $T_{12,21}$ must be identical (except for sampling error) given the SIstage model, any arbitrary property of the distributions must be identical. Thus, one advantage over testing the additivity of cumulants of the four component distributions (a property theoretically equivalent to the distributional equality) is that measures of scale and shape of the summation distributions can be used that may be more stable, robust, and resistant than the sample cumulants (Mosteller and Tukey 1977; Ratcliff 1979), even if such measures are biased.

While sufficient for the summation test to work, stochastic independence of stage durations is not necessary. This is shown by the following example, for which we are indebted to Frank Norman: Let $T_{ai} = t_{ai} + z$ and $T_{bj} = t_{bj} - z$, and assume that t_{a1}, t_{a2}, t_{b1}, t_{b2}, and z are mutually independent. Then the summation test is satisfied, even though stage durations T_{ai} and T_{bj} are not independent. Here $\mathrm{cov}(T_{ai}, T_{bj}) = \sigma_z^2$, an instance of nonzero but constant covariance that satisfies equation (4), as described above. Necessary conditions for the summation test—which must be stronger than the Gstage model, but weaker than the SIstage model—have yet to be discovered.[5]

Another sufficient condition for equation (5), noted by Frank Norman, can be described as a translation condition among the distributions of the $\{T_{ij}\}$, and does not require stochastic independence of the stage durations that contribute to T_{ij}. Under this condition the distributions differ by translation only; the distributions of the centered RTs, $t_{ij} \equiv T_{ij} - \mu_{ij}$ are therefore identical:

$$F_{t_{ij}} \equiv F_{T_{ij} - \mu_{ij}} = F, \qquad (i = 1, 2; j = 1, 2). \tag{6}$$

The translation condition is approximated by a stage mechanism in which the durations of stages a and b display little variability from trial to trial, so that most of the variability is contributed by stages other than those influenced by factors A and B; an increase in factor level then only adds a constant to the RT. (Although it differs in detail, we shall see that such a mechanism is similar in spirit to the cascade model, in which the units influenced by experimental factors are not inherently stochastic, so that the required variability is grafted onto a deterministic mechanism.) Given the translation condition, the summation test would not be particularly helpful, since it would require only means additivity (equation 3) in addition. For the test to be interesting, therefore, the RT distributions for different conditions should differ by more than just their means. In sections 26.7 and 26.8 we show this to be dramatically true for the data sets we consider.

26.3 THE ALTERNATE-PATHWAYS (AP) MODEL

Definition of the Model

In the second model we consider that generates additive RT effects, the task is accomplished by process a on a proportion p of the trials, and by process b on the remaining trials. We call the processes "pathways" to suggest the possibility of distinct anatomical substrates. We make three assumptions:

1. *Alternate Pathways*: With probability p the response is produced by pathway a; with probability $1 - p$ by pathway b.

2. *Selective Influence*: Factor A influences the duration of pathway a, but not b; factor B influences the duration of pathway b, but not a.

3. *Fixed Probability*: Neither A nor B influences the pathway probabilities, p and $1 - p$.

Generality: Embedded AP Structure   Suppose the AP mechanism is preceded and followed by one or more other processes (stages c and d). The resulting mechanism can be regarded as an AP model with one pathway containing stages c, a, and d, and the other containing c, b, and d. For all properties of the AP model to apply, however, we must assume that factors A and B do not influence stages c or d.

Generality: Multiple Pathways   Suppose multiple alternate pathways, with one subset $\{a_k\}$ of pathways influenced by factor A, a second subset $\{b_l\}$ by factor B, and a third subset $\{c_m\}$ influenced by neither A nor B. This is equivalent to a two-pathway model with pathway a a probability mixture of the $\{a_k\}$ and pathway b a probability mixture of the $\{b_l\}$ and the $\{c_m\}$. The important constraint is that no subset of pathways be influenced by *both* A and B. Thus, unlike the SIstage model, in which a third factor C that interacts with both A and B cannot be permitted to vary freely without inducing a spurious correlation between stage durations, such free variation in an AP model does not alter any of its properties; different levels of C can be regarded as corresponding to different members of pathway a and pathway b subsets.

Plausibility   The AP model deserves serious consideration for several reasons. The alternate processing pathways of the model may correspond to different physical paths: the brain contains multiple anatomical pathways along the route from input to output. An argument from anatomy that has been used to support parallel and connectionist processes (Rumelhart and McClelland 1986) thus also lends plausibility to the AP model.[6] Different paths may correspond to different subsets of stimuli: In Atkinson and Juola's (1974) theory of memory recognition, for example, decisions about some items are based on familiarity while decisions about others require an extended search. According to some models of choice that have been successfully applied to data, RTs are a mixture of responses from different pathways, determined by fluctuations in the subject's state: In the fast-guess model of Ollman (1966) and Yellott (1971), for example, some responses are stimulus-controlled, others guesses, and factors that influence the former do not influence the guessing probability, consistent with assumption 3. In an RT experiment with pigeons, Blough (1978; see also Luce 1986, sec. 6.3) found that on some trials the response was not controlled by the wavelength of the stimulus while on the others it was; again consistent with assumption 3, the proportion was unaffected by wavelength. The naming of printed words is believed to be accomplished by more than one route, not all requiring graphemic-phonemic conversion (Coltheart 1985). Assumption 3 would be plausible in this context if, for example, the choice of pathway were governed by a fixed attribute of the word, unknown to the experimenter, and independent of the factors manipulated explicitly. For a review of multiple-pathway models of human information processing, methods for their analysis, and supporting data, see Yantis, Meyer, and Smith (1991). They consider experiments in which the manipulations are believed to alter the pathway probabilities but have no effect on the pathways, complementary assumptions to those of the AP model.

The Central Property and the Mixture Test

Let $G_i(t)$ be the CDF of the duration T_{ai} when factor A is at level i, and let $H_j(t)$ be the CDF of the duration T_{bj} when factor B is at level j. With this notation the observed reaction time T_{ij} is a mixture of T_{ai} and T_{bj} with mixing probability p; the CDF is the weighted sum,

$$F_{ij}(t) = pG_i(t) + (1 - p)H_j(t), \qquad (t \geq 0). \tag{7}$$

This leads to the central property of the AP model

$$I\{F_{ij}(t)\} = 0, \qquad (t \geq 0), \tag{8}$$

which is equivalent to

$$\tfrac{1}{2}[F_{11}(t) + F_{22}(t)] = \tfrac{1}{2}[F_{12}(t) + F_{21}(t)], \qquad (t \geq 0); \tag{9}$$

we multiply by $\tfrac{1}{2}$ so that each side of equation (9) is a CDF. The power of equations (8) and (9) resides in their independence of the pathway probability, p. Because each side of equation (9) is the distribution of an *equal-probability mixture* of two populations of RTs, it can also be written

$$F_{\text{mix}(T_{11}, T_{22})}(t) = F_{\text{mix}(T_{12}, T_{21})}(t), \qquad (t \geq 0), \tag{10}$$

where mix(X, Y) denotes such a mixture of random variables X and Y; this equation can be contrasted with equation (5) in which each side is the distribution of the *sum* of the same RTs. Corresponding to the summation test for the stage model we thus have a *mixture test* for the AP model. If sample sizes are equal in paired conditions, the model asserts that pooling the RTs from conditions 11 and 22, and from conditions 12 and 21, should produce two samples with the same population distribution. If sample sizes are unequal, then comparison of the means of pairs of corresponding empirical CDFs may be preferable.

Meaning of Additive Reaction-Time Effects

Two sets of implications of equation (8) lead to tests of special interest: one concerned with means and variances, useful where distributions are not available, the other concerned with relations among the distributions.

Additivity of Factor Effects on the Mean and Other Raw Moments

Unlike the stage model, the AP model constrains the relations among the means and higher-order moments across the conditions of a factorial experiment without added assumptions comparable to stochastic independence of stage durations. Because estimates of moments of increasing order are increasingly unstable, we focus on first and second moments. From equation (8) it is easy to show that for the raw moments of order r, $\{\mu'_{rij}\}$,

$$I\{\mu'_{rij}\} = 0, \qquad (r \geq 1). \tag{11}$$

When $r = 1$ we have additivity of means, $I\{\mu_{ij}\} = 0$, the property we are trying to explain. When $r = 2$ we have additivity of the second raw moments (not the variances):

$$I\{\mu'_{2ij}\} = 0. \tag{12}$$

Because $\mu'_2 = \sigma^2 + \mu^2$, equation (12) becomes

$$I\{\sigma_{ij}^2\} = -I\{\mu_{ij}^2\}. \tag{13}$$

It is convenient to introduce two notational conventions for the means in 2×2 experiments. First, let a dot subscript represent averaging over levels of the corresponding index; for example, $\mu_{\cdot 1} \equiv \frac{1}{2}(\mu_{11} + \mu_{21})$. Second, let a d subscript represent a difference between levels of the corresponding index, subtracting lower from higher; for example, $\mu_{d1} \equiv \mu_{21} - \mu_{11}$; we also define $\mu_{dd} \equiv \mu_{22} - \mu_{11} = \mu_{d\cdot} + \mu_{\cdot d}$. We choose indices for factor levels such that the main effects of both factors are nonnegative: $\mu_{d\cdot} = \mu_{2\cdot} - \mu_{1\cdot} \geq 0$, and $\mu_{\cdot d} = \mu_{\cdot 2} - \mu_{\cdot 1} \geq 0$. In what follows we assume that both main effects are nonzero. Given means additivity,

$$I\{\mu_{ij}^2\} = 2\mu_{d\cdot}\mu_{\cdot d}; \tag{14}$$

from equation (13) we then have

$$I\{\sigma_{ij}^2\} = -2\mu_{d\cdot}\mu_{\cdot d}. \tag{15}$$

Because $\mu_{d\cdot}$ and $\mu_{\cdot d}$ are both positive, the right-hand side of equation (15) is negative. The AP model thus requires that rather than being additive, as in equation (4), the effects of the two factors on the variance interact, with $2\mu_{d\cdot}\mu_{\cdot d}$ being the magnitude of the (negative) interaction contrast. If the main effects of A and B on the variance are in the same direction as their effects on the mean (often but not always the case; compare $na = 2$ and $na = 8$ in tables 26.2 and 26.3), then the interaction is negative (underadditivity).

The contrast between equations (4) and (15) implies that no set of distributions $\{F_{ij}\}$ can satisfy both the mixture and summation tests: For any distributions that satisfy the summation test, variance effects are additive (equation 4);

for any distributions that satisfy the mixture test, variance effects interact (equation 15). Furthermore, equation (15) indicates how the summation test should fail, given the AP model: Because $\sigma_{11}^2 + \sigma_{22}^2 < \sigma_{12}^2 + \sigma_{21}^2$, $F_{T_{12}+T_{21}}$ will be flatter than $F_{T_{11}+T_{22}}$, and, to the extent that the two distributions are symmetric, the CDFs will cross close to their medians ($F \approx 0.5$). It is also of interest how the mixture test will fail, given a stage model. We need assume only variance additivity (equation 4), not full stochastic independence, to show that

$$\sigma_{\text{mix}\{T_{11}, T_{22}\}}^2 - \sigma_{\text{mix}\{T_{12}, T_{21}\}}^2 = 4\mu_{d.}\mu_{.d}. \tag{16}$$

Thus $F_{\text{mix}\{T_{12}, T_{21}\}}$ will be steeper than $F_{\text{mix}\{T_{11}, T_{22}\}}$; again, to the extent that the two distributions are symmetric, the CDFs will cross close to $F = 0.5$. The pattern expected in failures of the mixture test is further discussed below.

The expected failure of variance additivity produced by the AP model can be dramatic, sometimes a *crossover interaction*, in which the *direction* of the effect of one factor (not merely its magnitude) depends on the level of the other. Thus, let an "*i*-crossover" in a 2×2 experiment be an interaction in which the sign of the *i*-effect on a statistic S_{ij} depends on the *j* level, and let a "*j*-crossover" be defined similarly. It is easy to show that we have an *i*-crossover if and only if $|I\{S_{ij}\}| > 2S_{d.}$ and a *j*-crossover if and only if $|I\{S_{ij}\}| > 2S_{.d}$. For example, in experiment 2, $na = 8$, the mean predicted variance interaction contrast $(-2\mu_{d.}\mu_{.d})$ is $-10{,}824 \pm 1{,}894$ ms^2; this value can be compared to the main effects on RT variance (438 ± 166 ms^2 for factor A and 841 ± 297 ms^2 for factor B), after doubling them.[7] Both crossover conditions are satisfied; if the model is correct the variances must therefore display both kinds of crossover interaction.

The AP Model as a Special Stage Mechanism

That the AP model is a special case of the Gstage model (but different from the SIstage model) can be seen as follows: Suppose a stage model with stages *a* and *b* and corresponding factors A and B. Now suppose there is a third factor, C, that influences both stages so as to interact powerfully with factors A and B in a special way: At level C_1 of C the effect of A on *a* is nullified; at level C_2 of C the effect of B on *b* is nullified. If data are pooled over levels of C, we have an AP model in which the pathway on a trial is determined by C level. (The means additivity of the AP model thus follows from its being a stage model; the failure of variance additivity shows that this special stage model cannot be an SIstage model.) The AP and SIstage models are thus at the ends of a continuum of joint influence: Let an "A-influenced process" be a process whose duration depends on A. In the AP model there are no trials on which A-influenced and B-influenced processes both operate; in the SIstage model A-influenced and B-influenced processes operate on all trials. (Roberts, chap. 25, 600–601, describes two ways of distinguishing these possibilities in other situations.)

Tails of the RT Distribution and Mixture-Test Failures

It is helpful to consider how the mixture test might be expected to fail, given a stage model; we do so by supposing processes with minimum and maximum durations.[8] It is plausible for most psychological processes that their minimum durations are greater than zero: even the fastest output cannot be produced in arbitrarily short time. (Cf. Donders's ([1868] 1969) application of the subtraction method to the minimum RT.) With some important exceptions it also seems plausible that a change in factor level that increases the mean duration of a process also increases its minimum duration. (We shall see that neither of these properties applies to the cascade model, however.) In an SIstage model any change in factor A that increases $\min(T_a)$ will increase the minimum RT, $\min(T)$ to the same extent. (A corollary is that factors will have *additive* effects on the minimum, such that $I\{\min(T_{ij})\} = 0$, mirroring the additivity of μ_{ij}.) Finally, this property will be robust in the face of all except extreme forms of stochastic dependence (such as that embodied in the AP model), so we can expect it in many cases of the Gstage model. For the AP model, however, the property need not obtain, even though additivity in the mean does: Suppose that the shortest times are produced by pathway a. An increase in the level of factor B will then not change the minimum RT. In this respect the AP model acts like a (self-terminating) pair of parallel processes, in which the one with the shortest duration is reflected in the RT. In short, for a Gstage model it is possible (but not necessary) that increasing the level of *either* of two factors will increase the minimum RT; for an AP model *both* levels must be increased. A similar contrast between the models holds for the relation between maximum process durations and the maximum RT.

These intuitions about extreme RTs are captured by two corollaries of equation (8) that may focus analyses on aspects of the AP and stage models that are especially useful in model discrimination. The first is interesting in relation to short RTs:

$$F_{11}(t) \leq F_{12}(t) + F_{21}(t), \qquad (t \geq 0). \tag{17}$$

For small t, where $F_{22}(t)$ is small, equation (17) captures the intuition that, depending on which pathway contains the shortest times in condition 11, either F_{12} or F_{21} will contain RTs that are as short as the shortest in F_{11}. In contrast, increasing the level of either factor alone in a stage model can increase $\min(T)$; the short times in condition 11 would then be too abundant for equation (17) to be satisfied, and the left side of equation (9) would exceed the right, for small t. The second corollary is interesting in relation to long RTs. Let $\bar{F}_{ij}(t) \equiv 1 - F_{ij}(t) = Pr\{T_{ij} > t\}$. Then,

$$\bar{F}_{22}(t) \leq \bar{F}_{12}(t) + \bar{F}_{21}(t), \qquad (t \geq 0). \tag{18}$$

For large t, where $\bar{F}_{11}(t)$ is small, equation (18) captures the intuition that either F_{12} or F_{21} will contain RTs as long as the longest in F_{22}. In contrast, decreasing the level of either factor alone in a stage model can reduce $\max(T)$; the long times in condition 22 would then be too abundant for equation (18) to be satisfied, and the right side of equation (9) would exceed the left, for large t.

This pattern of mixture test failures expected for some stage models corresponds to what we expect from the behavior of the variance of the SIstage model, discussed above.

26.4   THE MCCLELLAND-ASHBY CASCADE MODEL

Definition of the Model

The third model we consider, the cascade model, was introduced by McClelland (1979) and further developed by Ashby (1982). Even assuming selective influence of factors on processes, it does not invariably generate additive RT effects, but with some parameter settings additivity is approximated well. This model is of interest partly because it is a precursor of more complex connectionist models, which often incorporate some of its features (Rumelhart and McClelland 1982).

The model contains a set of $k = 1, 2, \ldots, n$ processing units, each with an input and an output. The output from unit k is the input to unit $k + 1$. The amount of its work accomplished by unit k by a given time t after stimulus onset is measured by its level of output activation $a_k(t)$ at that time; this grows continuously and at a rate proportional to the instantaneous difference between its current input and output levels (a linear integrator), divided by its time constant, τ_k. Thus, in response to a step-function input at time $t = 0$ the output grows exponentially to an asymptote, α: $a_k(t) = \alpha(1 - e^{-t/\tau_k})$. Stimulus onset provides such a step-function input to unit 1. The response mechanism is triggered when the output of unit n exceeds an activation criterion. RTs vary from trial to trial because of variability in the time added by the response mechanism, and because of noise in the final output activation level or, equivalently, in the criterion; the units themselves function deterministically.[9]

In the model's initial formulation, experimental manipulations could influence the asymptotic activation level as well as the time constants. Because of this feature, as well as the choice of noise distribution, there could be too many trials on which the criterion exceeded the asymptotic activation level, precluding a response. To eliminate this problem, Ashby (1982) permitted experimental factors to influence only the time constants, and adjusted the noise distribution slightly, truncating it at $+2.5\sigma$, so that the criterion never exceeds the asymptotic activation level. With these adjustments and a few others Ashby derived the RT CDF that we have used in our explorations.

The cascade model is much more specific than the stage and AP models; for example, it does not share their virtue of being distribution free. It is not obvious how best to characterize its many features, nor is it yet clear which features are essential for its interesting properties. For example, it is not known how important are the particular shape, location, and spread of the criterion distribution, nor the particular law for the growth of activation. On the other hand, not all such laws are consistent with the spirit of the model, since some could transmute it into a stage model. One consequence of our current ignorance about which features are critical is that evidence against the model, which may result from an incorrect choice of particular features or parameter values, is relatively less important than evidence for it, which is unlikely to result from a combination of such incorrect choices. By testing this particular model we hope to learn one way to approach the more interesting goal of testing a larger class of models of which it is a member. One possible description of the model is as follows; the first four assumptions refer to quantitative features that must be specified precisely.

1. *Processes in Cascade*: Processing is gradual, with the current results of one process immediately available to the next.

2. *Unit Time Course*: A linear integrator relates $a_k(t)$ to $a_{k-1}(t)$, as described above.

3. *Response Actuation*: A response is triggered when $a_n(t)$ reaches criterion.

4. *Noise Distribution*: Here is specified the criterion (or activation) noise distribution and the assumption that the mechanism is affected by just one sample from this distribution per trial.

5. *Selective Influence*: Factor A influences only process a; factor B influences only process b.

6. *Influence Mechanism*: A factor influences a process by altering its time constant, τ_k.

The processing units in the cascade model are ordered structurally by their input-output relations. Only in some senses are they ordered temporally. For example, a given level of activation must be achieved by unit k before it can be achieved by unit $k + 1$, but activation begins to rise at the output of the final unit as soon as the stimulus is applied, and responses can be triggered before any process is close to its asymptote. Furthermore, the output activation function $a_n(t)$ is independent of unit order, evident in equation (19). In addition to its relevance to connectionist models, the cascade model is interesting because, as we shall see, it is capable of producing approximately additive factor effects on both mean and variance, like the SIstage model, and because it embodies an interesting and plausible idea—that information is passed continuously from one process to the next. The idea of "partial output," of which this is one realization, has been tested (with mixed conclusions) by devising special experimental procedures or using measures other than RT; see, for example, Osman, Bashore, Coles, Donchin, and Meyer (1992), Meyer, Irwin, Osman, and Kounios (1988), Meyer, Osman, Irwin, and Yantis (1988), Miller (1988), Miller and Hackley (in press), and Schweickert (1989). Testing of the cascade model is an additional approach.

The Processing-Time Distribution

Activation level at the output of unit n, as a proportion of the asymptotic value, behaves according to the cascade equation:

$$E_n(t) = 1 - \sum_{k=1}^{n} \left[\prod_{\substack{m=1 \\ m \neq k}}^{n} \frac{\rho_m}{\rho_m - \rho_k} \right] e^{-\rho_k t}, \qquad (0 \leq t < \infty, n \geq 2), \qquad (19)$$

where $\rho_k = \tau_k^{-1}$ is the rate constant of unit k. As t grows from 0 to ∞, $E_n(t)$ grows from 0 to 1. Time, t, is in arbitrary units; to connect the model to data requires either using statistics in which the time unit is eliminated, or specifying t_u ms, the duration of a time unit, and multiplying t in equations (19) and (20) by t_u. Following Ashby (1982) we set the asymptotic activation level at 5 units and the mode of the adjusted criterion distribution at 2.5 units; the distribution of the time to reach criterion is then:

$$G_n(t) = \frac{\Phi(5E_n(t) - 2.5)}{\Phi(2.5)}, \qquad (0 \leq t < \infty), \tag{20}$$

where $\Phi(\cdot)$ is the standard normal CDF. The numerator is $\Phi(-2.5)$ when $t = 0$, and approaches $\Phi(2.5)$, or about 0.994, for large t; the term in the denominator normalizes the truncated distribution.

Additivity of Factor Effects on the Mean and Variance

Given a specification of the number of units and their time constants, one can use the CDF, $G_n(t)$, to compute any statistic one wishes. Sufficiently little is known about the model, however, so that one must perform such computations over a subspace of parameters, rather than determining statistics analytically as functions of the set of time constants, or independently of them. One consequence is that the generality of our conclusions may be limited. In considering the implications of the computed statistics for observed RTs one must also keep in mind that the assumed cascade process may be concatenated with other components, such as other cascade units or processing stages.

To investigate the model, we had to decide on a plausible range of values for the set of time constants τ_a and τ_b that we manipulated. Given that the time unit, t_u is free to vary, only the *ratios* of time constants matter, so no loss of generality results from specifying one arbitrarily; we thus defined 1.0 time unit as the largest value. We chose 20:1 as the maximum ratio of time constants to examine, as did Ashby (1982), so that in most calculations, τ ranged downward to about .05. (In supplementary calculations we worked with ratios of time constants up to 100:1, and found that our conclusions were not altered, as will be seen in section 26.10.) Some considerations that might justify the choice of 20:1 are as follows: (a) The contribution of a cascade unit to $\overline{RT}$ is proportional to its time constant. Even if the highest factor level (longest time constant, i.e., 1.0) is associated with as much as 300 ms, the lowest level would then be associated with only 15 ms. Given what we know about elementary cerebral events it seems unlikely that anything one would call the same process could take both as much as 300 and as little as 15 ms. (b) A unit is eliminated from the model when its time constant is set to zero. The time constant associated with the lowest attainable factor level may thus be small, but cannot be zero, as we don't wish to permit the lowest attainable level of a factor to entirely eliminate the process it influences. (c) It is likely that the lowest level of a factor in an actual experiment is higher than the lowest attainable level of that factor.

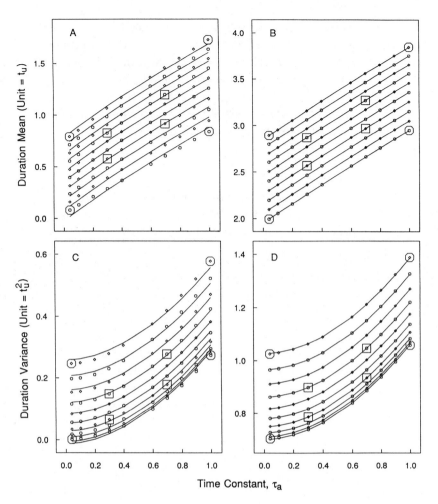

Figure 26.1 Behavior of the mean and variance in two cascade models (see table 26.1). In each panel the statistic is shown as a set of points plotted as a function of τ_a, with τ_b as the parameter distinguishing the sets of points. The values of τ_a are 0.04, 0.1, 0.2, 0.3, 0.4, 0.6, 0.7, 0.8, 0.9, and 1.0; the ten increasing values for each τ_a are generated by $\tau_b = .05, .15, \ldots, .95$. The ten curves in each panel are parallel, the least squares fit of an additive model to the set of 100 points. *Panel A:* Means for model 2.1 in arbitrary units, t_u. *Panel B:* Means for model 4.3. *Panel C:* Variances for model 2.1 in arbitrary units, t_u^2. *Panel D:* Variances for model 4.3. The subsets of points marked by large squares and large hexagons indicate values used for the interaction measures given in table 26.1.

Table 26.1 Interaction of Effects on Mean and Variance in Six Cascade Models

Model	τ_c	τ_d	$\dfrac{100\,I\{\mu_{ij}\}}{\sqrt{\mu_{d\cdot}\,\mu_{\cdot d}}}$ Large Effects	Small Effects	$\dfrac{100\,I\{\sigma_{ij}^2\}}{\sqrt{\sigma_{d\cdot}^2\,\sigma_{\cdot d}^2}}$ Large Effects	Small Effects
2	0	0	21.5	10.0	20.6	13.8
3.1	0.32	0	11.6	7.2	17.6	11.4
3.2	1.05	0	0.4	0.8	3.0	0.0
4.1	0.32	0.73	3.4	2.3	7.7	3.3
4.2	1.05	0.32	1.1	0.8	3.4	0.5
4.3	1.05	1.10	−0.1	−0.1	2.9	0.1

For each model are shown values of the time constants τ_c and τ_d of units uninfluenced by factors A and B. (A zero time constant is equivalent to absence of the corresponding unit; the first digit of the model's designation is the number of units with nonzero time constants.) The interactions are those obtained by orthogonal combination of $\tau_a = 0.04$, 1.0 with $\tau_b = 0.05$, 0.95 (large effects), and $\tau_a = 0.3$, 0.7 with $\tau_b = 0.35$, 0.65 (small effects). Corresponding points for two of the models are emphasized in figure 26.1. The interaction measure is the interaction contrast as a percentage of the geometric mean of the main effects. (Normalizing in this way has little theoretical justification and, because main effects are similar across models, does not alter the relative sizes of interactions. Because the measure is dimensionless, however, it permits comparison of interactions of effects on means and variances, and also permits comparisons to data.) The models illustrated in figure 26.1 are models 2 and 4.3.

In figure 26.1 are shown the means and variances generated in two factorial simulations in which τ_a and τ_b were varied over the one hundred points in the orthogonal grid described in the caption.[10] Panels A and B show the means we obtained (points) together with a fitted additive model (parallel curves). Results in panel A, from a two-process cascade, show an overadditive (positive) interaction. Consistent with earlier findings, the results in panel B, from a four-process cascade in which processes a and b were joined by fixed slow processes c ($\tau_c = 1.05$) and d ($\tau_d = 1.1$), show a remarkably good approximation to additivity. In panels C and D are shown the variances for the same pair of models. Again the two-process model shows overadditivity, while effects in the four-process model are remarkably additive. Table 26.1 provides descriptions of six different cascade models, including those in figure 26.1, together with measures of $I\{\mu_{ij}\}$ and $I\{\sigma_{ij}^2\}$. Confirming McClelland's (1979) suggestion for means, the interaction for both means and variances is negligible if the model contains a unit with a long time constant that is unaffected by factors A or B.[11] When fixed slow processing units are incorporated in a cascade model, the pattern of factor effects on both the mean and variance of the processing time can thus mimic the pattern produced by a stage model with uncorrelated stage durations, a remarkable feature of the cascade model given its dependence, in the stage model, on the RT being a sum of stage durations, and given that units in a cascade model operate concurrently.[12]

Figure 26.1 also shows that the increase in mean processing duration with τ is approximately linear, and that as the level of a factor increases, the variance considered as a function of the mean will accelerate. To test this property requires a one-factor experiment that is precise (because the contrast incorporates three sample variances and three means) in which performance is measured at three or more levels of that factor.[13]

26.5 FOUR EXPERIMENTS

We tested the three models with five sets of RTs for correct responses from four experiments, selected because they produced additive effects of two factors on mean RT, and because RT distributions, or at least variances, were available for individual subjects and for each combination of factor levels. Factors we shall call "A" and "B" are indicated below. Where factors had more than two levels, we selected pairs of levels (four conditions) for 2 × 2 analyses; where not otherwise stated, analyses depend on only those pairs for which mean RTs differed the most ("corners" of the design). For experiments 1 and 2 individual trials data were available, permitting distributional tests: for experiments 3 and 4 we used only means and variances. Sizes n of data sets are given as approximate mean observations per subject per condition. For experiments 1 and 2 we tried to reduce effects of heterogeneity by performing computations (such as moment calculations) within subsets of the data within each condition, and then averaging the results. The factor used to partition the data to form such subsets is indicated.

Experiment 1: Detection

Seven subjects produced simple reaction times, responding to a flash at one of four locations by pulling a lever (Backus and Sternberg 1988, experiment 1). Stimulus probability was high (.6) in one location and low (.05) in each of the other three; the remaining probability (.25) represents catch trials. The high-probability location changed from trial to trial, and was indicated by a central visual cue. The four locations were corners of an imaginary rectangle centered on a fixation point and separated from it by about 9 degrees of visual angle. The factors we consider are *foreperiod* (A) and *intensity* (B): the interval from warning signal to flash was one of six values: 750, 950, 1150, 1350, 1550, or 1750 ms; flash intensity was high, medium, or low. Levels of both factors varied randomly from trial to trial. Data were collected in six one-hour sessions after three hours of practice. For the present tests we restricted our analysis to responses to flashes in high-probability locations, and to trials on which the intensity was either high or low. The effect of foreperiod on mean RT is U-shaped, and is more convincingly additive with intensity for short than long foreperiods; we therefore used 750, 950, and 1150 ms as levels of A, and high and low as levels of B. We excluded data for one subject, for whom the main effect of A was markedly and significantly smaller than its effect on the other six subjects, but with no effect on conclusions. Calculations were done separately for each session (there were six sessions) and then averaged over sessions; $n \approx 96$.

Experiment 2: Identification

Five subjects saw numerals and responded with spoken digits (Sternberg 1969, experiment V). The number of alternative stimulus-response pairs (na) was either 2 or 8. Within each of these there was a 2×2 factorial design, with factors *stimulus quality* (intact, or degraded by a superimposed checkerboard pattern; A) and *S-R compatibility* (name x, name $x + 1$; B). Data were collected from each subject in seven one-hour sessions, after five hours of practice. We have conducted separate tests for each of the two levels of na. We rejected seven of the observations (0.2%) for $na = 2$ and 14 (0.3%) for $na = 8$ as outliers, because each differed by more than 4 SDs from the mean of the remaining observations for that subject and condition. For $na = 2$ we reversed the sense of the compatibility factor for one subject whose main effect was opposite to the other subjects. Because of changes in analysis, means and variances differ slightly from those reported by Sternberg (1969). For $na = 2$, calculations were done separately for each numeral-repetition combination (two numerals × repeat/nonrepeat of the prior stimulus), then averaged over the four combinations; $n \approx 204$. For $na = 8$, calculations were done separately for each numeral (eight numerals), then averaged over numerals; there were no immediate repeats; $n \approx 245$.

Experiment 3: Classification

Twelve subjects served in an item-recognition experiment (Sternberg 1967). The stimulus was a numeral, and the response pulling a lever. One lever ("positive") was correct if the stimulus was contained in a memorized set of one, two, or four elements; otherwise the "negative" lever was correct. Positive responses were required on about 27% of the trials. Factors were *stimulus quality* (intact, or degraded by a superimposed checkerboard pattern, A) and *set size* (B). The analyses below are based on only the data from the more frequent negative responses, and only from the second of two sessions, during which an interaction between A and B present during the first session had disappeared; $n \approx 22$.

Experiment 4: Overlapping Tasks

Twenty-two subjects performed two binary-choice tasks on each trial (McCann and Johnston 1989). Task 1 was pitch discrimination: The stimulus was a tone of one of two frequencies, with "high" the correct response for the high tone, and "low" for the low tone. Task 2 was size discrimination: the stimulus was a rectangle of one of four sizes; the correct response was a button press with one hand for "very small" (S1) and "small" (S2), and with the other hand for "large" (S3) and "very large" (S4). We analyze the RTs in task 2.

Table 26.2 Statistics Based on Means in Four Experiments

Experiment	$m_{..}$	$m_{d.}$	$m_{.d}$	$I\{m_{ij}\} \pm SE_b(SE_p)$
1	222	15	36	$-0.6 \pm 2.1\ (1.9)$
2 ($na = 2$)	354	30	21	$3.2 \pm 3.7\ (4.5)$
2 ($na = 8$)	449	53	102	$1.4 \pm 3.8\ (2.7)$
3	458	69	121	4.5 ± 12.2
4	648	264	59	-4.0 ± 14.7

The unit is 1 ms. Data for each experiment are from a 2×2 set of conditions. $m_{..}$ represents the overall mean RT, $m_{d.}$ the main effect of factor A on the mean, and $m_{.d}$ the main effect of factor B. All main effects are statistically significant across subjects. $I\{m_{ij}\}$ is the interaction contrast of means (see equation 3). SE_b is based on between-subject variation; where available we also show SE_p, based on variation pooled over data subsets and subjects. For experiment 1, with six subjects, each with six data subsets, SE_b is based on 5 df and SE_p is based on 35 df. Corresponding degrees of freedom for experiment 2 are 4 df and 15 df for $na = 2$, and 4 df and 39 df for $na = 8$.

Factors were *stimulus onset asynchrony* (SOA; the time between onsets of tone and rectangle: 50, 150, 300, or 800 ms; A) and *discriminability* (the closeness of the rectangle to the classification boundary: near, for S2 and S3, or far, for S1 and S4; B). Levels of both factors varied randomly from trial to trial. Data are from the final 384 trials of the single session, following 128 practice trials. Trials were excluded if (a) either response was an error, (b) $RT_1 > 1000$ ms, (c) $RT_2 > 1500$ ms, or (d) either RT departed from its cell mean by more than 3 SDs. For these reasons 2.5% of the trials were excluded; $n \approx 47$. See Pashler and Johnston (1989) for discussion of overlapping tasks experiments.

26.6 ADDITIVITY OF FACTOR EFFECTS ON THE MEAN

In most of our tests we replace theoretical quantities by corresponding sample estimates, and base our estimates of precision on differences between subjects. Here we provide tests of the property shared by all three models, $I\{\mu_{ij}\} = 0$, by evaluating $I\{m_{ij}\}$; results are shown in table 26.2, together with the overall mean RT for the four experimental conditions considered, and the mean sizes of the two main effects. The interactions are all small compared to the main effects, and nonsignificant.[14] SE_b is sufficiently close to SE_p so as to indicate no important individual differences in $I\{m_{ij}\}$.

26.7 RELATIONS AMONG THE VARIANCES

Additivity of Factor Effects

Here we provide tests of variance additivity, $I\{\sigma_{ij}^2\} = 0$, which is expected from the SIstage model and weaker variants, and is well approximated by some variants of the cascade model. Results of evaluating $I\{s_{ij}^2\}$ are shown in the

Table 26.3 Statistics Based on Variances in Four Experiments

Experiment	$s_{..}^2$	$s_{d.}^2$	$s_{.d}^2$	$I\{s_{ij}^2\} \pm SE_b(SE_p)$	$I\{s_{ij}^2\} + 2m_{d.}m_{.d} \pm SE_b$
1	6.1	2.8	3.1	$-1.2 \pm 2.2\ (2.0)$	$10.1 \pm 3.0\ (p = .02)$
2 (na = 2)	26	9.2	4.0^{ns}	$-0.2 \pm 3.5\ (3.8)$	$14.7 \pm 2.0\ (p = .002)$
2 (na = 8)	13	4.4	8.4	$1.8 \pm 0.8\ (1.4)$	$116 \pm 21\ (p = .005)$
3	57	21^{ns}	53	18 ± 27	$180 \pm 47\ (p = .003)$
4	258	140	42	-40 ± 52	$279 \pm 69\ (p = .0005)$

The unit is $100\ ms^2$. Data for each experiment are from a 2×2 set of conditions. Where possible (experiments 1 and 2), we calculated variances for subsets of the data and then averaged within subjects. $s_{..}^2$ represents the overall mean variance of the RT, $s_{d.}^2$ the main effect of factor A on the variance, and $s_{.d}^2$ the main effect of factor B. All main effects are statistically significant except those with the superscript ns. $I\{s_{ij}^2\}$ is the interaction contrast of variances (see equation 4). $I\{s_{ij}^2\} + 2m_{d.}m_{.d}$ is the variance contrast whose expectation is zero, given the AP model (see equation 15). See table 26.2 for definitions of SE_b and SE_p. The p-values in the final column are based on two-tailed t-tests of the AP variance contrast versus zero; the df is one less than the number of subjects.

fifth column of table 26.3. Also shown are basic variance data for the four experiments: mean variances over the four conditions considered, and mean sizes of the main effects of factors A and B on the variance. The interaction contrasts are uniformly nonsignificant. SE_b and SE_p tend to be large, however—often as large as the smaller of the two main effects. Although these data are consistent with variance additivity, they are less convincing than the means additivity results.

Evidence against the Alternate-Pathways Model

Results of the variance test for the AP model are shown for all five data sets in the final column of table 26.3. Because $m_{d.}$ and $m_{.d}$ are orthogonal, we can assume that $E(m_{d.}m_{.d}) = \mu_{d.}\mu_{.d}$; we are therefore justified in substituting sample moments for theoretical quantities in equation (15). The differences between the two sides of that equation, which should be zero, are substantially and significantly positive in every case. For all the data sets except experiment 2, $na = 2$, the expected interaction contrast is so large relative to the main effects of both factors on the variance that both an i-crossover and j-crossover are required.

26.8   THE SUMMATION TEST: FURTHER SUPPORT FOR THE STAGE MODEL

We regard the summation test and the remarkable support it provides for the stage model as the most important contribution of the present chapter; we therefore describe the test and results in some detail for the three data sets to which we could apply it.

Violation of the Translation Condition

As discussed in section 26.2, if the translation condition (equation 6) were satisfied by the T_{ij}, then the summation test would add nothing to means additivity. Conversely, given means additivity, the degree to which one is impressed by success of the summation test should increase with the extent to which the T_{ij} distributions differ in more than location. That there are significant main effects on the variance (table 26.3) is one indication that the condition is violated, but the failure is more pervasive: in each of the three data sets, each of the second, third, and fourth moments about the mean, $\hat{\mu}_2$, $\hat{\mu}_3$, and $\hat{\mu}_4$, increases from condition 11 to condition 22 for every subject. The effect is significant (by two-tailed t-test) for all four moments in experiment 1 and experiment 2, $na = 2$. For experiment 2, $na = 8$, there is sufficient variation in the magnitude of the increase of the third and fourth moments so that the same test produces p-values of $p = .05$ and $p = .08$, respectively. The increases are also large: over the three data sets, $\hat{\mu}_2^{1/2}$ increases by an average factor of 1.5, $\hat{\mu}_3^{1/3}$ increases by an average factor of 2.1, and $\hat{\mu}_4^{1/4}$ increases by an average factor of 1.7.

The Test Procedure

Partitioning of Data   Suppose that factor A influences stage a, and factor B influences stage b, and that the SIstage model is valid. If the data include a mixture of levels of a third factor, C, that influences both stages (as level of practice or particular stimulus-response pair might), then this can induce a nonzero covariance of stage durations and cause the test to fail. If the level of C on each trial is known, however, the data can be partitioned into subsets within which the level of C is fixed, and the test applied separately to each subset, eliminating the problem, at least for that factor. This is the approach we took: In the $na = 8$ condition of experiment 2, for example, we noted that stimulus numeral had a systematic effect on mean RT, and used it as the partitioning factor, performing the test separately for the trials involving each of the eight numerals, in each of the four conditions within each subject. An incidental advantage of this approach is that it provided eight separate summation-test comparisons per subject, permitting within-subject measures of precision and tests of significance.

The Cartesian-Product Sums   The summation test requires estimation of the two distributions, $T_{11,22}$ and $T_{12,21}$. Consider the first of these, for example. To obtain an estimate we created a sample by forming the Cartesian product of the sets of observations in conditions 11 and 22, and, for each pair in the product, determining the sum of its two members.[15] Thus in experiment 2, $na = 8$, an observation set in each of the four conditions for a particular numeral and subject contained about 31 RTs; the Cartesian-product sum that provided the sample of $T_{11,22}$ for that numeral and subject thus contained about $31^2 = 961$ values,[16] as did the sample of $T_{12,21}$ for that numeral and subject. We use $\hat{F}_{11,22}(t, k)$ and $\hat{F}_{12,21}(t, k)$, respectively, to denote the empirical CDFs of these *summation sets* (*summation CDFs*), where k ranges over the data subsets in an analysis; thus, for eight subsets per subject and five subjects, $k = 1, 2, \ldots, 40$.

Adjustment of Distributions   For each pair of summation CDFs we computed several statistics to be compared. However, before doing so we adjusted the locations and scales of each pair. To make statements about the data for each subject separately we planned to average the computed statistics over data subsets within subjects and use subset differences as a basis for variability estimates. To make statements about the group data and inferences about the population of subjects, we planned to average the computed statistics over subjects as well, and to base variability estimates on subject differences. The adjustment prior to averaging is based on the idea that any systematic failures of the summation test are more likely to occur at points with equal p-values in different pairs of distributions, than, for example, at points with equal time values. Another reason for adjustment was graphical: to increase the similarity of the shape of the average distribution to the shapes of the distributions being averaged.

For each pair of summation distributions we let a location parameter λ_k be the mean of their medians, and a scale parameter ξ_k be the mean of their interquartile ranges. We then determined the means, $\lambda.$ and $\xi.$ of these parameters over all data sets and performed the same linear transformation on all the values (X) in the kth pair of summation distributions:

$$X^* = \lambda. + \left(\frac{\xi.}{\xi_k}\right)(X - \lambda_k) \tag{21}$$

The result is that $\lambda_k^* = \lambda.$ and $\xi_k^* = \xi.$ for all k. For graphical purposes it was important to perform a corresponding adjustment to create the transformed component distributions T_{11}^*, T_{12}^*, T_{21}^*, and T_{22}^*, such that the summation property would be preserved (e.g., $T_{11,22}^* = T_{11}^* + T_{22}^*$), as well as the relative differences among the locations of the components. We accomplished this by using the same transformation (equation 21), but with $\lambda.$ and λ_k replaced by $\frac{1}{2}\lambda.$ and $\frac{1}{2}\lambda_k$, respectively.

Results of the Test

After forming the four adjusted component CDFs, $\{\hat{F}_{ij}^*(t, k)\}$, and the two adjusted summation CDFs, $\hat{F}_{11,22}^*(t, k)$ and $\hat{F}_{12,21}^*(t, k)$, for each data subset, we computed their means over data subsets to obtain CDFs for individual subjects. Means of the resulting CDFs over subjects are shown in figure 26.2. In all three data sets, the agreement between the two summation CDFs is remarkably good.

It is not obvious in which way the summation test will fail, if it fails. We therefore examined three different sets of statistics of the adjusted distributions in each pair, $\hat{F}_{11,22}^*(t, k)$ and $\hat{F}_{12,21}^*(t, k)$: proportions; quantiles and quantile-

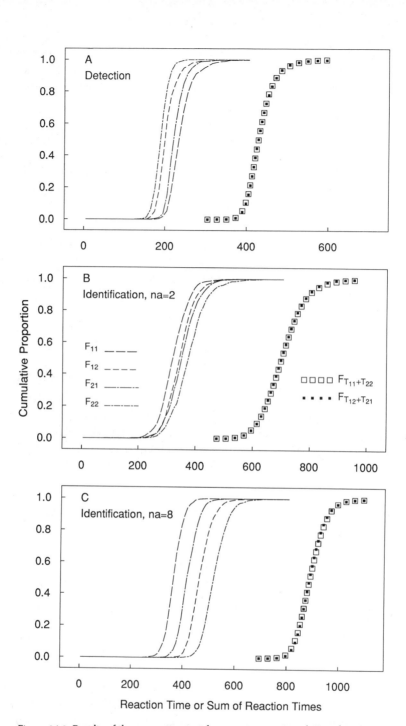

Figure 26.2 Results of the summation test for experiment 1 (panel A) and experiment 2 (panels B, C). CDFs were adjusted and averaged as described in the text. At the left of each panel are the average CDFs for each of the four conditions. At the right of each panel are the two summation CDFs; to enhance the visibility of the small differences we use symbols instead of curves. The scaling of the x-axis varies from panel to panel.

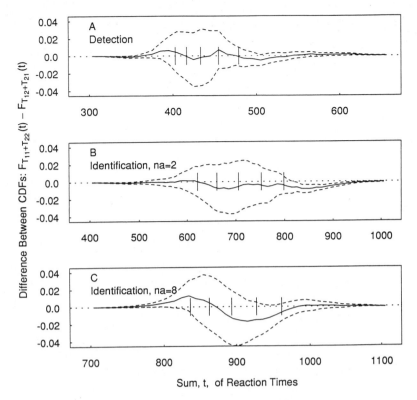

Figure 26.3 Deviations from CDF equality in the summation test for experiment 1 (panel A) and experiment 2 (panels B, C). On a greatly enlarged ordinate scale, each panel shows differences (continuous curve) between the two summation CDFs shown in the corresponding panel of figure 26.2. Broken curves show the standard errors of the differences, based on between-subject variation, and computed at each 10-ms interval. In each panel the vertical line segments mark the means over the two summation CDFs of five quantiles, $t_{.10}$, $t_{.25}$, $t_{.50}$, $t_{.75}$, and $t_{.90}$, to facilitate comparison across data sets.

based measures of location, spread, skewness, and kurtosis; and moments. For details of the calculation method, see the discussion of equation (21) in the Appendix.

Comparison of Proportions   For proportions, we compared the values of each pair of empirical CDFs by determining their difference at each 10-ms interval. To facilitate seeing pattern in the deviations, we display the differences in figure 26.3, together with pointwise $\pm SE$ bands based on between-subject variation. There is a suggestion of a difference that is positive at low p-values and negative at high p-values, but the differences are small, and not consistent among subjects. The impression of excellent agreement is confirmed by tests: at each 10-ms time value we performed a t-test on the difference between mean proportions, using the SEs shown in figure 26.3; none of the tests was significant. Such tests can of course be performed only where the SE is nonzero, which excludes any time value at which there is a zero difference between summation CDFs for all subjects. The number of tests performed is

Table 26.4 Summation Test: Quantile Measures of Location, Scale, and Shape

Experiment	MED		IQR		SK		KR	
	$Diff \pm SE_b$	Mean	$Diff \pm SE_b$	Mean	$Diff \pm SE_b$	Mean	$Diff \pm SE_b$	Mean
1	0.2 ± 0.9	434	-0.2 ± 2.6	38	1.3 ± 7.2	30	0.9 ± 1.9	18
2 ($na = 2$)	0.9 ± 5.0	705	0.1 ± 2.9	91	3.7 ± 5.5	18	0.8 ± 0.5	16
2 ($na = 8$)	1.2 ± 3.8	894	3.2 ± 2.1	64	-5.3 ± 7.4	18	-0.4 ± 0.5	16

We estimated quantiles for $T_{11,22}$ and $T_{12,21}$, and combined them to provide robust measures of location (median, MED), scale (interquartile range, IQR), and shape (skewness, SK, and kurtosis, KR) for each distribution. For each statistic is shown the difference between the two estimates ($Diff$), a standard error SE_b of the difference based on between-subject variation, and the mean of the two estimates. See the text for definitions of SK and KR. The unit is 1 ms.

thus a conservative estimate of the number of opportunities for the SIstage model to fail. For experiments 1, 2, $na = 2$, and 2, $na = 8$, respectively, there were 42, 66, and 61 tests; they are unlikely to be independent, of course.

We also did hundreds of exploratory tests on the differences between the summation distribution proportions for individual subjects. P-values were not corrected for numbers of tests (Miller 1986; Johnson and Tukey 1987), so they should be taken as indications only. Among all the statistics of the CDFs we examined (proportions, quantiles, and moments), the closest we came to finding systematic deviations was in t-tests of the differences between proportions at each 10-ms time value for which the SE was nonzero. In experiment 1, none of the 173 tests was significant. In experiment 2, $na = 2$, 18 of the 318 tests were significant; in experiment 2, $na = 8$, 15 of the 241 tests were significant. These numbers would of course be consistent with the hypothesis of no difference if the tests were independent, but they are not, and the similarity of the patterns suggests that although minor, the deviations may be meaningful.[17]

Comparison of Quantiles   We compared each of a set of quantiles of the two distributions, t_p for $p = .05, .10, .25, .50, .75, .90, .95$. We also compared three different functions of those quantiles, a robust measure of spread, $IQR \equiv t_{.75} - t_{.25}$, a robust measure of skewness, $SK \equiv t_{.95} + t_{.05} - 2t_{.5}$, and a robust measure of kurtosis, $KR \equiv 10(t_{.95} - t_{.75} + t_{.25} - t_{.05})/IQR$. In each case we determined differences between corresponding values for $\hat{F}^*_{11,22}$ and $\hat{F}^*_{12,21}$. Table 26.4 shows that in no case were the differences between distributions in location, spread, or shape measures significant, and in most cases the differences were small relative to the size of the quantities compared. Within-subject tests, based on between-session (experiment 1) or between-stimulus (experiment 2) variation, also failed to find significant ($p < .05$) differences between members of any of the four pairs of measures.

Comparison of Moments   The interaction contrasts of means and variances, in tables 26.2 and 26.3, respectively, are equivalent to testing the differences between the first two moments of $\hat{F}^*_{11,22}$ and $\hat{F}^*_{12,21}$; we also examined the third and fourth moments and found none of the differences to be significant, in either within-subject or between-subject tests.

26.9 THE MIXTURE TEST: FURTHER EVIDENCE AGAINST THE ALTERNATE-PATHWAYS MODEL

Based on the variance test, we noted in section 26.7 that the AP model can be decisively rejected for these data. For two reasons, however, we shall discuss application of the mixture test to the data from experiments 1 and 2: first, because the mixture test appears to be more powerful in cases where the model is wrong but where the variance test is not decisive, the mixture test would be more persuasive where the model is correct; and, second, because the pattern of deviations is instructive.

The Test Procedure

Adjustment of Distributions Variation in a factor that interacts with both A and B will not cause the mixture test to fail (section 26.3), as it could the summation test; hence we did not divide the data into subsets within subjects. For each subject we estimated the four component CDFs and averaged them in pairs to obtain $F_{\text{mix}(T_{11}, T_{22})}(t) = \frac{1}{2}[F_{11}(t) + F_{22}(t)]$ and $F_{\text{mix}(T_{12}, T_{21})}(t) = \frac{1}{2}[F_{12}(t) + F_{21}(t)]$. To average the CDFs over subjects for a graphical display free of artifacts (features in the averages but not in the individual distributions) we eliminated between-subject differences in location and scale before averaging. To do this while preserving the relation between the two mixture distributions we applied the same transformation to the two mixture distributions for each subject, a transformation defined for each subject so as to equate the mean locations and mean scales of the two distributions across subjects.[18] We then averaged the transformed CDFs to obtain those shown in figure 26.4.

Results of the Test

All three data sets show the same systematic pattern of differences between the two mixture distributions: instead of being equal, the left side of equation (9) exceeds the right for short RTs, and the right side exceeds the left for long RTs. As discussed in section 26.3, this is the pattern expected from a stage model in which the duration of each stage responds to an increase in level of the corresponding factor by lower frequencies of short durations and higher frequencies of long ones, and in which, unlike the AP model, both stages contribute to all trials.

In all three cases shown in figure 26.4, the spread appears to be greater for $F_{\text{mix}(T_{11}, T_{22})}$ than for $F_{\text{mix}(T_{12}, T_{21})}$; indeed, it can be shown that the difference between the two variances is the same as the statistic used in the variance test. However, because the mixture distributions must be identical in every respect, according to the AP model, determination of the mixture distributions provides the opportunity of using robust estimates of spread. We found, for

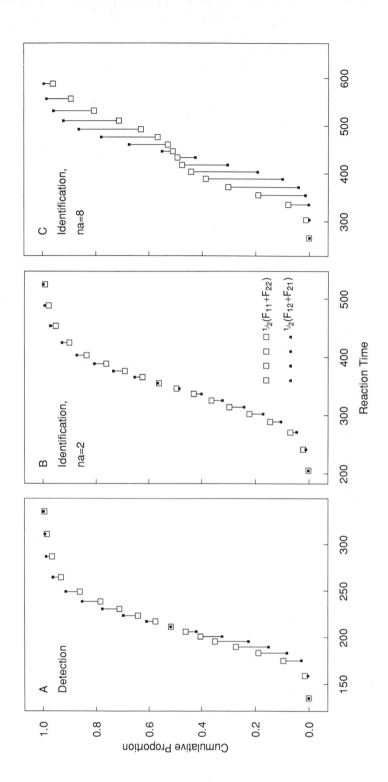

Figure 26.4 Results of the mixture test for experiment 1 (panel A) and experiment 2 (panels B, C). Mixture CDFs were adjusted and averaged as described in the text.

Table 26.5 Mixture Test: Integrated Differences between Two Mixture Distributions

Experiment	Small-RT Statistic	Large-RT Statistic	All-RT Statistic
1	$.926 \pm .054$ ($p < .0001$)	$-.854 \pm .094$ ($p = .0003$)	$.901 \pm .051$ ($p < .0001$)
2 ($na = 2$)	$.480 \pm .248$ (ns)	$-.793 \pm .130$ ($p = .004$)	$.757 \pm .057$ ($p = .0002$)
2 ($na = 8$)	$.996 \pm .003$ ($p < .0001$)	$-.999 \pm .001$ ($p < .0001$)	$.997 \pm .002$ ($p < .0001$)

The three statistics are defined in the text. In each case the mean $\pm SE_b$ is shown, with values of SE_b based on between-subject variation; p-values are based on two-tailed t-tests of the means versus the zeros expected from the AP model. Normalization requires all three statistics to lie within the $[-1, +1]$ interval.

example, that s_{bi}^2, a measure of spread based on the biweight (Mosteller and Tukey 1977, 208), is substantially more powerful than the sample variance, for all three data sets. We prefer, however, a test that we devised for the present purpose that would permit separate testing of conditions 17 and 18 and would be especially sensitive to the pattern of deviations from the AP model that would be expected from a stage model in which factor levels influenced the frequencies of short and long stage durations, as discussed in section 26.3.

Consider the difference between the two mixtures, $\Delta(t) \equiv F_{\text{mix}(T_{11}, T_{22})}(t) - F_{\text{mix}(T_{12}, T_{21})}(t)$. For a stage model in which minimum stage duration varies with factor level it is possible that $\Delta(t)$ will be positive for small RT and negative for large RT (sec. 26.3). The numerator of the *small-RT statistic* is the integrated (signed) difference $\Delta(t)$ for $0 \leq RT \leq \overline{RT}_{.5}$, where $\overline{RT}_{.5}$ is the mean of the medians of the two mixtures. If the mixtures were identical except for sampling error (AP model) then the average magnitudes of positive and negative deviations $\Delta(t)$ would be expected to be equal, so that the integrated or averaged $\Delta(t)$ taken over any interval would have zero expectation. The normalizing denominator of the small-RT statistic is the absolute difference $|\Delta(t)|$ over the same RT-range. If all the deviations were positive (negative) then the statistic would take on its maximum (minimum) value of $+1$ (-1). According to the AP model the small-RT statistic should thus be close to zero; according to the stage model and the argument associated with equation (17) it may be positive. The *large-RT statistic* is the integrated signed difference $\Delta(t)$ over the complementary interval $RT > \overline{RT}_{.5}$, similarly normalized by the integrated absolute difference over the same RT-interval. According to the AP model this also has a zero expectation; according to the stage model and the argument associated with equation (18) it may be negative. The *all-RT statistic* is the difference (small-RT statistic) − (large-RT statistic), normalized by the integrated absolute difference over the entire RT range. According to the AP model this has a zero expectation; according to the stage model it may be positive. Values of these statistics are unaffected by the distributional adjustment that we performed for purposes of graphical display.

We computed the three statistics for each subject and each of the three sets of data, with the results shown in table 26.5. Mean values of the statistics over subjects are remarkably close to their maximum possible values in several cases. The strength of the evidence against the AP model from the mixture test is substantially greater than from the variance test (table 26.3, last column; compare significance levels); furthermore, the pattern of deviations is consistent with expectations from an SIstage model (sec. 26.3). Because they appeared to be especially sensitive, we applied the same three integrated-differences comparisons to each of the three pairs of summation CDFs (fig. 26.2). None of the nine comparisons even approached significance; the largest t value was 1.6 (with 4 df).

26.10 EVIDENCE AGAINST THE CASCADE MODEL

That several features of the SIstage model could be approximately mimicked by variants of the cascade model (sec. 26.4) led us to consider in what ways its behavior might be constrained. Instead of trying to derive such additional properties analytically, we searched for them by exploring its parameter space. We did this for each of the six models described in table 26.1. For each model, τ_c and τ_d are fixed, while τ_a and τ_b are permitted to vary. By assigning values to τ_a and τ_b we specify the model for one condition in a hypothetical experiment sufficiently well to be able to compute its distribution of cascade durations. We can then generate a random sample of the durations, or determine the expected value of any statistic. We limited ourselves to the mean and variance; for two of the models, results are illustrated in figure 26.1.

The four conditions in any 2 × 2 experiment that can be described by the model correspond to points at the corners of a rectangle in the (τ_a, τ_b) space: (τ_{a1}, τ_{b1}), (τ_{a1}, τ_{b2}), (τ_{a2}, τ_{b1}), and (τ_{a2}, τ_{b2}). For any such set of four points we can determine the expected values of four means and four variances; these eight *condition statistics* can be selected and combined in different ways to produce a single number for the experiment, an *experiment statistic*. A set of eight such condition statistics for one model is represented by the eight points given emphasis by large squares in figures 26.1B and 26.1D. Examples of experiment statistics that we have already seen are the interaction contrasts $I\{\mu_{ij}\}$ and $I\{\sigma_{ij}^2\}$.

Allowed and Forbidden Regions in a Statistic Space

For present purposes we used two new statistics, described below. With two such statistics, each hypothetical experiment is mapped onto a point in a two-dimensional *statistic space*, where each statistic is represented by a value on one dimension. In such a space the model's capabilities are represented by an *allowed region*, defined by the set of such points for all possible experiments, given the model. Results that the model cannot generate are represented by the unoccupied or *forbidden region*. Any real 2 × 2 experiment produces a single point in the two-dimensional statistic space; to test the model one asks whether this point falls into the allowed or forbidden region, taking sampling error into account.

Roberts and Sternberg

Dimensions of the Statistic Space

Figure 26.1 (as well as Ashby's 1982 work) suggests that the cascade model may constrain the relation between location and spread, which is reflected in our choice of one of the experiment statistics. (Conditions that slow the model's response tend to do so by slowing the rate at which activation grows, and a slower growth rate increases the RT spread induced by the fixed criterion variance.)

Examination of the relation between location and spread requires some care in the choice of measures. First, because the time unit in the model is arbitrary, we must either estimate it or use measures that don't depend on it. Second, we must allow for the possibility that in generating the observed RTs the postulated cascade mechanism, influenced by factors A and B, is concatenated with other processes not influenced by those factors, such as the response mechanism assumed by McClelland (1979) and Ashby (1982) or supplementary stages or cascade units, processes that might contribute, along with the cascade mechanism, to both location and spread. Our measures should reflect the cascade mechanism alone, whether or not such supplementary processes are present.

To avoid distortion due to such supplementary processes we use statistics defined as factor effects, i.e., as differences between RT measures at different factor levels, exploiting the assumption that the supplementary processes are unaffected by factors A and B. Not all measures will serve, however. Thus, if RT_1 and RT_2 are RTs obtained in conditions 1 and 2, M is a measure of location or spread, and T_{C1} and T_{C2} are the contributions to the RT from the cascade mechanism, then we require that $M(RT_2) - M(RT_1) = M(T_{C2}) - M(T_{C1})$. If T_S represents the duration of the supplementary processes, this condition in turn requires that any measure be additive, in the sense that $M(RT) = M(T_C) + M(T_S)$. The mean satisfies this requirement for the location measure, but an additional assumption is needed to select an appropriate measure of spread. One possibility is the variance; another that has been applied in testing the cascade model (Ashby 1982) is the standard deviation. The variance is additive if $\text{cov}(T_C, T_S)$ is zero or constant, or if the supplementary processes consist of one or more additional cascade units. Additivity of the standard deviation requires that $|\text{cov}(T_C, T_S)| = \sigma_{T_C}\sigma_{T_S}$, its maximum possible value. We believe that variance additivity is more likely, so we chose the variance as our measure of variability. (Our conclusions may depend on the validity of this assumption.) Let η_{ij} and θ_{ij}^2 be the mean and variance of the cascade duration under factor levels i and j, μ_S and σ_S^2 be the mean and variance of T_S, and t_u be the scale factor expressing the model's time unit in ms. We can then write $\mu_{ij} = t_u\eta_{ij} + \mu_S$ and $\sigma_{ij}^2 = t_u^2\theta_{ij}^2 + \sigma_S^2$. To link the cascade process under study to the data, we constructed statistics that eliminated μ_S and σ_S^2 (by taking differences of quantities assumed to be additive), and eliminated t_u (by forming dimensionless ratios of these differences). The first statistic relates the change in variance to the corresponding change in mean, as both factor levels are increased:

$$\text{variance-change statistic} \equiv \frac{\sigma_{22}^2 - \sigma_{11}^2}{(\mu_{22} - \mu_{11})^2} = \frac{\theta_{22}^2 - \theta_{11}^2}{(\eta_{22} - \eta_{11})^2}. \tag{22}$$

Our explorations suggest, for example, that the values of the variance-change statistic that the cascade model can produce are bounded below. The second statistic is the difference between the two main effects, normalized by their sum:

$$\text{main-effect difference statistic} \equiv \frac{|\mu_{d.} - \mu_{.d}|}{\mu_{d.} + \mu_{.d}} = \frac{|\eta_{d.} - \eta_{.d}|}{\eta_{d.} + \eta_{.d}} = \frac{|\eta_{21} - \eta_{12}|}{\eta_{22} - \eta_{11}}, \tag{23}$$

which can range from zero to one. We shall see that larger main-effect differences are associated with more severe bounds on values that the model can produce for the variance-change statistic.

The Test Procedure

We studied each of the six models described in table 26.1. For each model we determined the mean and variance of the processing time for each of the 100 points in the two-parameter grid used to create figure 26.1. Within this grid there are 2025 possible simulated 2×2 experiments in which both factors have nonzero effects; for each of these we computed the variance-change statistic and the main-effect difference statistic. Results of these computations for model 3.1 are shown as an example in figure 26.5A; each plotted point represents the outcome of one simulated experiment, and the allowed region of the model is included within the surrounding contour, the convex hull of the set of points. The figure, which shows the left-hand portion of this region, reveals that values of the variance-change statistic that can be achieved by the model are bounded below, and that the bound varies with the main-effect difference. The allowed regions are similar for the six models, as shown by figure 26.5B, where the contours for three of them are displayed on an expanded abscissa. The similarity suggests that this feature of the cascade model depends little on values of the fixed time constants, and is thus quite general.

We took this analysis further in three ways. First, we determined whether the quantization of the parameter grid contributed to the constraints, by sampling parameter values in .01-unit steps in the range (.05, 1.00). This caused the allowed region (dotted in fig. 26.5B) to expand upwards, but not to the left. Second, we extended the parameter range in model 3.2 to encompass a 100:1 ratio, despite its implausibility as discussed in section 26.4, again using a sampling method. The result is the leftmost contour in figure 26.5B, which reveals only a mild relaxation of the lower bound. Finally we examined the small-sample properties of the main-effect difference and variance-change statistics by using model 3.2 with several pairs of (τ_a, τ_b) values to generate random samples of the same size as in our experiments, to check for bias; we found no evidence of bias.

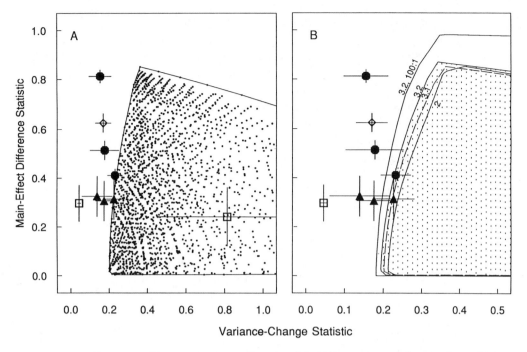

Figure 26.5 Data points versus allowed and forbidden regions of the cascade model in a two-dimensional statistic space. *Panel A:* Each of the numerous small points represents the expected values of the two statistics for one simulated experiment generated by model 3.1 (See table 26.1.) The set of 2025 points continues off the plot to the right. Surrounding the points is the contour defined by their convex hull, which includes the allowed region of the model, subject to considerations discussed in the text. Also shown by larger points are data from the four real experiments, together with lines marking $\pm SE_b$ for each statistic, based on between-subject variation. For each of experiments 1 and 3 (2 × 3 designs), there are three points, one for the corners of the design (also discussed elsewhere in this chapter), and one each for the two other possible 2 × 2 experiments. Experiment 1: filled octagons, the top point for levels of factor B (foreperiod) of 950 and 1150 ms, the middle point for 750 and 950 ms, and the bottom point for the corners, 750 and 1150 ms. Experiment 2: unfilled squares, $na = 8$ to the left, $na = 2$ to the right. Experiment 3: filled triangles, the left point for levels of factor B (set size, s) of $s = 2$ and $s = 4$, the right point for $s = 1$ and $s = 2$, and the middle point for the corners, $s = 1$ and $s = 4$. Experiment 4: unfilled diamond. *Panel B:* Note the expanded abscissa scale. Contours abutting and within the dotted area mark the allowed regions for models 2, 3.1, and 3.2, all with time-constant ratios no greater than 20:1. The contours for models 4.1, 4.2, and 4.3, with the same 20:1 constraint, fall almost entirely between those for models 3.1 and 3.2. The contour labeled "3.2, 100:1" shows the allowed region when time-constant ratios are permitted to increase to 100:1. Data points as in panel A; experiment 2, $na = 2$, is now off scale.

Test Results: Data versus Allowed Region

Also shown in figures 26.5A and 26.5B are points that represent the same pair of statistics for each of the four experiments, together with lines indicating $\pm SE$ based on between-subject variability. For the detection and classification experiments, in which one of the factors had three levels, the figure shows the statistics for each of the three possible 2×2 designs. (Within each of these two sets of three, values are not independent.) For most of the data points the variance-change statistic is too small for the model.

Excess Model Variance in the Best-Fitting Case

To gain further insight into the cascade model we considered the version of model 4.3 ($\tau_a = 0.04, 0.4$; $\tau_b = 0.05, 0.95$) that provided the best fit within the two-dimensional statistic space (fig. 26.5) to the data from experiment 1 with levels of factor A of 750 and 1150 ms. When we adjusted the time unit t_u in the model by forcing it to produce agreement with the separation between the means of conditions 11 and 22, we found that the average variance of the distributions produced by the model is about twice as great as the variance in the data. Thus the variances in the model are too large relative to the main effects on the means. This can be seen by comparing the simulated distributions on the left side of figure 26.6 with the actual distributions in figure 26.2A. Both the upper and lower tails of the four distributions tend to be more separated in the data than in the model, where they appear to fan out from common points. This property may reflect an essential feature of the cascade model: its continuous transmission of activation. Because activation in the nth unit starts rising immediately when the stimulus is presented, the increment in activation that triggers the response occasionally occurs shortly after the stimulus is applied, even in the slowest condition. And because activation in the fixed slow process needed for additivity continues to rise for a long time, the model produces a few slow responses, even in the fastest condition. Adjustments of the model that might reduce the discrepancy include reducing the spread of the criterion distribution, or changing its shape so as to introduce a high threshold for triggering the response.

Application of the Summation Test to a Cascade Mechanism

On the right side of figure 26.6 is shown the result of applying the summation test to the four simulated distributions.[19] Consistent with Ashby's (1982) findings, the test works remarkably well. Thus, just as mean and variance additivity fail to discriminate cascade and stage models, so does the summation test (though this is known only under limited conditions); this observation emphasizes the importance of discovering necessary conditions for that test.

One possibility is that the conditions that permit the cascade model to emulate a stage model (the incorporation of one or more fixed units with long time constants) are also ones under which it approximates a stage model in

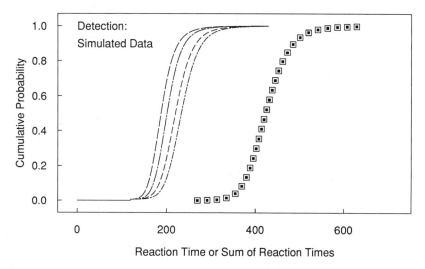

Figure 26.6 Summation test applied to the cascade model. Results of simulation by cascade model 4.3 of the data from experiment 1 (detection) shown in figure 26.2A. Simulated RT distributions from the four conditions are shown on the left, with a constant (121 ms) added to all simulated times; the two convolutions of these distributions, obtained by applying numerical convolution to the pairs of density functions $\{f_{T_{11}}, f_{T_{22}}\}$ and $\{f_{T_{12}}, f_{T_{21}}\}$ are shown on the right. The maximum (vertical) separation between the two functions on the right is .001.

function. In the defining conditions of a stage model, process a has completed its work before process b starts, and, assuming selective influence, the time required by process b is independent of systematic changes in the rate of process a. If we think of the slow unit in a cascade model as placed between units a and b, then it seems possible that its presence causes these two stage-model conditions to be approximately satisfied. This conjecture is encouraged by some exploratory comparisons of the activation functions of unit a alone, and of units a, b, and c together, using several different proportions of asymptotic level to define a process having "completed" its work; the two conditions were approximately satisfied.

Future Tests

Quantitative analyses of the cascade model, such as those above, may help to guide future tests. For example, reference to figure 26.1 will suggest why experiments with more than two levels per factor may challenge the cascade model more severely: Suppose that an increase in level of factor A induces a given change in mean RT by changing τ_a from τ_{a2} to τ_{a3}. Because the function relating variance to τ accelerates, the corresponding change in variance is greater if τ_{a2} is greater. Requiring the model to fit a third, faster condition (yielding τ_{a1}) as well, will force τ_{a2} and τ_{a3} to increase, which in turn will increase the variance-change statistic associated with levels 2 and 3, and hence perhaps the disparity between model and data. Future tests using 2×2 designs can also be guided by figure 26.5, which shows that the model is challenged more by experiments with unequal main effects. (Shaw 1984 provides another example of the use of quantitative theory to guide experimental design.)

26.11 DISCUSSION

Additivity of the effects of experimental factors on mean RT has often been taken to suggest the existence of stages. In this chapter we have considered two alternative explanations of additivity, one new (the alternate-pathways model) and one developed earlier (the cascade model). That additivity has more than one possible explanation has long been taken for granted, at least by critics of the additive-factor method, and is hardly surprising. Nevertheless, the AP model is the first alternative to the stage model we know of that produces exact additivity; the cascade model approximates additivity with some parameter values but not others. The AP model has the virtue of being simple and plausible, yet readily testable because it strongly constrains the data. It is noteworthy that three models so different in spirit can explain the same pattern of means. Because of this, discriminating among the models has required analysis of other aspects of the data. Thus we have tried to discover what the models predict about variances and entire distributions, and have confronted these predictions with five sets of data from a wide range of RT experiments.

The most important feature of this work is the new evidence for stage models. This consists of: the dramatic failures of the AP model for all five data sets (tables 26.3, 26.5; fig. 26.4); failures of the cascade model (figs. 26.5, 26.6); and successes of the SIstage model (tables 26.3, 26.4; figs. 26.2, 26.3, 26.4). The successes of the summation test (table 26.4; figs. 26.2, 26.3) seem especially persuasive.[20] It should be kept in mind that the summation test was applied to only two experiments (detection and identification), which, moreover, have features in common, such as verbal instructions and visual stimuli. However, the two experiments also differ in several ways, such as the meaningfulness of the stimuli, the number of possible responses, the nature of the responses (the muscles used, for example), and the ranges of RTs.

One important limitation of the present work is that it is not altogether clear what success of the summation test implies: the necessary conditions—stronger than the Gstage model, but weaker than the SIstage model—have yet to be discovered. We do not know why the cascade model satisfies the test under some parameter settings; perhaps it is because with those parameters it resembles a stage model. Another important limitation of this work lies in our uncertainty about how to interpret the failures of the cascade model. They may reflect fundamental constraints of an interesting class of models of which it is a member, or may depend on details, such as the criterion distribution or the law that governs the growth of activation. Rejection of the cascade model for these data may thus be less interesting than rejection of the much simpler, and in that sense, weaker AP model. One interesting issue here is how the failure of the AP model bears on the validity of the complementary set of mixture models (Yantis, Meyer, and Smith 1991) in which the pathway probabilities vary while the pathways remain fixed. A final limitation worthy of mention is that the "off the shelf" experiments that provided the data we used had not been designed to discriminate among the three models. It seems likely that future work will suggest better experiments for this purpose; factors with more than two levels, and experiments with more than two factors, for example, are likely to be helpful.[21]

When alternatives to the stage model have been proposed in the past, it has not been clear how they constrain the data, that is, what they predict. Nor has it been clear what the stages explanation of additivity predicts, although the work of Meyer et al. (1984, 1988), Miller (1988), and Schweickert (1985), for example, has taken important steps in that direction. If an explanation is based only on the result that suggested it, it may not be especially convincing, and a preference for that explanation over competitors may be only a matter of taste. For example, Taylor (1976) proposed that additivity may arise because the factors changed one stage "in an additive way" (181). Because it resembles the fact it explains, and predicts nothing, this is not a satisfying explanation. However, as long as competing explanations also predict nothing, it is hard to dismiss. It is much easier to dismiss when a competing explanation makes a successful prediction. In particular, the summation test, based on Ashby and Townsend's (1980) suggestion, will help compare stage models to competitors. A traditional difficulty associated with testing the properties of RT distributions other than their locations is the large sampling error associated with the variance and higher moments, especially given the high tails and outliers of some distributions. Along with the mixture test developed for the AP model, the summation test permits the use of robust measures of spread, skewness, and so forth, which are likely to be less variable than the sample moments.

The evidence for the existence of something like stages (independently changeable, serially arranged operations) is now both deep and broad. It is deep—relatively extensive and persuasive—for the detection and identification experiments. It is broad—relatively general—because Roberts (1987) found evidence for stages in animal response-rate experiments, which have little in common with human RT experiments beyond the use of vertebrate subjects.

The improvements in the evidence have come at roughly the same time that theorizing in human experimental psychology has shifted toward models of high complexity. Astrophysicists have a joke: Never propose a theory that can be tested in your lifetime. By proposing complicated theories with many free parameters, psychologists seem to be moving in all seriousness quite close to this ideal. Complex models are usually "tested" by asking if they can fit another data set. The virtue of such models, in the eyes of their proponents, is often the range of the data they can fit. This is indeed a virtue; a model that explains only one result is not very interesting. Such tests are incomplete, however. They should increase our belief in the model only if they are sufficiently extensive to identify forbidden as well as allowed regions in the statistic space. This requires knowing what the model cannot do, as well as what it can (cf. Massaro 1988). And determination of what a complex model cannot do may require a vast amount of computation.

The shift toward relatively complex models has been motivated, at least in part, by considerations of plausibility. When choosing a theory, this is a good place to start. The message of this chapter, however, is that something implausible is apparently true: The vertebrate brain, in a wide range of situations, has a simple functional structure.

APPENDIX: PROOFS AND COMMENTS ON EQUATIONS

Equation (3): Additivity of factor effects follows from additivity of stage durations and its preservation under expectation, and from the selective influence of factors A and B on T_{ai} and T_{bj}, respectively. Take expectations in equation (1), replace the μ_{ij} in equation (3), and collect terms. (See Sternberg 1969.)

Equation (5): In a proof by construction, which also suggests a method of testing, note that $T_{11} + T_{22}$ and $T_{12} + T_{21}$ can each be regarded as the sum of RTs that results from concatenating two stage models; the two sums are the same because the two concatenations contain the same stages at the same factor levels, just differently ordered. To elaborate, $T_{11} + T_{22} = T_{a1}[+]T_{b1} + T_{a2}[+]T_{b2}$, and $T_{12} + T_{21} = T_{a1}[+]T_{b2} + T_{a2}[+]T_{b1}$. Here, "+" represents summation of RTs from different conditions, which are stochastically independent by construction (sec. 26.8). In the first sum, for example, the construction method implies that T_{a1} and T_{b1} are each independent of T_{a2} and T_{b2}. Summation of stage durations that contribute to the same RT is represented by "[+]." Given stochastic independence of stage durations, the two kinds of summation are equivalent. Because the two sums are composed of the same independent random variables, they have the same distribution.

In a more formal proof, we note that summation of random variables (RVs) requires them to be defined over the same sample space. For the original RVs, $\{T_{ai}\}$ and $\{T_{bj}\}$, there are, instead, four different sample spaces, one each for conditions 11, 12, 21, and 22. For example, T_{a1} corresponds to two RVs, one in condition 11 and one in condition 12; let us call them T_{a11} and T_{a12}, respectively. By the assumption of selective influence, factor B has no effect on T_{a1}; hence T_{a11} and T_{a12} are identically distributed. To permit the desired summation we first replace each of these identically distributed pairs of original RVs by a new RV with the same distribution, such that the four new RVs are mutually independent and are defined over the same sample space. For example, we replace T_{a11} and T_{a12} by T'_{a1}. (It is well known that such new RVs whose distributions are the same as the marginal distributions of the original RVs can be defined.) Because of the assumed stochastic independence of the original RVs (such as T_{a11} and T_{b11}, which sum to T_{11}), the sum of each pair of new RVs (such as $T'_{a1} + T'_{b1}$) has the same distribution as the sum of the corresponding pair of original RVs. Now, however, T_{11} and T_{22}, for example, are defined over the same sample space, thus permitting us to define their sum, which we write as above, except that the $\{T_{ai}\}$ and $\{T_{bj}\}$ are replaced by the $\{T'_{ai}\}$ and $\{T'_{bj}\}$.

Given the independence of the $\{T_{ij}\}$, equation (5) is equivalent to additivity of cumulants of all orders: $I\{\kappa_{rij}\} = 0$, $r \geq 1$ (Sternberg 1969). However, because of instability of their estimates, testing equation (5) by using the higher cumulants is less attractive than using other aspects of the distributions, which the summation test makes possible.

Equation (6): To show that equation (5) is implied by this translation condition plus means additivity, observe that the condition implies $T_{11} + T_{22} = \mu_{11} + \mu_{22} + t + t$ and $T_{12} + T_{21} = \mu_{12} + \mu_{21} + t + t$, where the subscripts on the $\{t_{ij}\}$ are dropped to emphasize the equality of their distributions. Given means additivity, $\mu_{11} + \mu_{22} = \mu_{12} + \mu_{21}$, so the two sums have the same distribution.

Equation (8): Use equation (7) to expand each term, and collect terms. As for equation (5) of the SIstage model, there is a proof by construction that also suggests a method of testing. Write equation (8) as equation (9), to which it is equivalent. The left side of this equation is the CDF of an equal-probability mixture of the processes that generate T_{11} and T_{22}, and the right side similarly for T_{12} and T_{21}. The two corresponding mechanisms each have four alternate pathways with pathway probabilities $\frac{1}{2}p$, $\frac{1}{2}(1 - p)$, $\frac{1}{2}p$, and $\frac{1}{2}(1 - p)$; the two mechanisms are equivalent because they differ only in the ordering of the same four pathways. The suggested *mixture test* is to pool equal-size samples from T_{11} and T_{22}, and from T_{12} and T_{21}; CDFs of the resulting data sets should be equal, except for sampling error. If sample sizes are unequal, then comparison of the means of pairs of corresponding CDFs permits better use of the information in the data. As in the summation test, equality of CDFs implies identity of any statistic, so that one can choose measures with desirable sampling properties, for example.

Equation (11): Differentiate equation (8) with respect to t to get density functions, multiply by t^r, and integrate with respect to t.

Equation (14): Additivity of the means ($I\{\mu_{ij}\} = 0$) permits us to replace μ_{12}, μ_{21}, and μ_{22} in $I\{\mu_{ij}^2\}$ by $\mu_{11} + \mu_{1d}$, $\mu_{11} + \mu_{d1}$, and $\mu_{11} + \mu_{1d} + \mu_{d1}$, respectively. Do so, expand, and collect terms.

Equation (15): This failure of variance additivity for the four component distributions is equivalent to equality of variances of the two mixture distributions specified in equation (9), the latter, however, can be tested by using measures of spread that may have more desirable sampling properties than the variance.

Equation (16): The variance of an equal-probability mixture of X and Y is $(\sigma_X^2 + \sigma_Y^2)/2 + (\mu_X - \mu_Y)^2/4$. Use this to rewrite the terms on the left, and use variance additivity to eliminate the terms in σ^2. Now expand, and use equation (14) and its method of proof.

Equation (17): From equation (8), $F_{12}(t) + F_{21}(t) = F_{11}(t) + F_{22}(t)$. Now note that $F_{22}(t) \geq 0$, $(t \geq 0)$.

Equation (18): From equation (8), $\bar{F}_{12}(t) + \bar{F}_{21}(t) = \bar{F}_{11}(t) + \bar{F}_{22}(t)$. Now note that $\bar{F}_{11}(t) \geq 0$, $(t \geq 0)$.

Equation (19): See McClelland (1979).

Equation (20): See Ashby (1982) for proof of an equivalent result. To generalize from a criterion distribution with unit variance to one with variance σ_c^2, replace $\Phi(x)$ by $\Phi(x/\sigma_c)$ in both numerator and denominator. Because the normal criterion distribution has nonzero probability when $t < 0$, $G_n(t)$ has accumulated probability .006 at $t = 0$. In our computations we have set $G_n(0) = 0$. To compute the expected mean and variance we used a discrete approximation of equation (20), truncated at a t-value great enough for sufficient accuracy, then differentiated numerically to obtain the density function, then summed after multiplying by t^r for the rth raw moment. For a random sample from the $G_n(t)$ distribution we used $G_n^{-1}(U)$, where U is the value of a random variable distributed uniformly on the [0, 1] interval.

Equation (21): Calculations for the summation test, including this adjustment, were performed in the following order: (a) the data were divided into subsets within each subject, each subset containing RTs from four conditions, and indexed by k as described in the text. Then, for each subset, (b1) the Cartesian product method (see text) was used to provide two summation sets; (b2) the median and interquartile range were computed for each summation set, and averaged over the two summation sets, giving λ_k and ξ_k; (b3) λ_k and ξ_k were used in equation (21) to adjust each value in the two summation sets, providing two *adjusted summation sets*; (b4) the statistic—proportion, quantile-based measure, or moment—was computed for each of the two adjusted summation sets; (b5) the difference between the two values of the statistic (one for each summation set) was found. Finally, (c1) for each subject the differences were combined over subsets to provide a mean and a within-subject SE; (c2) for the set of subjects, the subject means were combined to provide a final mean and a between-subject SE.

Equations (22) and (23): Replace the μ_{ij} and σ_{ij}^2 by their equivalents in η_{ij}, θ_{ij}^2, μ_S, σ_S^2, and t_u, and combine terms.

NOTES

Supported in part by Grant AFOSR-91-0015 from the Air Force Office of Scientific Research to the University of Pennsylvania, and by a Sloan Foundation Research Fellowship to Seth Roberts. We thank Sylvan Kornblum and David E. Meyer for encouragement and helpful comments. We are grateful to Paul Rosenbaum and Frank Norman for statistical and mathematical guidance, to Benjamin T. Backus, James C. Johnston, and Robert S. McCann for their generosity in permitting us to use unpublished details of their data, and to F. Gregory Ashby, David H. Krantz, Richard Schweickert, James T. Townsend, and Dirk Vorberg for comments on an earlier draft.

1. The theory below is limited to situations in which there are just two factors and two underlying processes, and where each factor has just two levels. It is straightforward to extend these developments to cover experiments with more than two factors, and/or more than two levels per factor. This is done to some extent in the data analyses that follow.

2. Given two or more mechanisms, each of which produces additive effects of the same pair of factors on mean RT, hybrid mechanisms can be created for which that property is preserved. One type of hybrid is the serial concatenation of two such mechanisms; another is a probability mixture. Consideration of such hybrids is an interesting problem for future work.

3. Miller, van der Ham, and Sanders (unpublished manuscript) have drawn the same conclusion.

4. See the Appendix for proofs and comments on equations.

5. The summation test is a stronger test of the stage model than merely the additivity of means and variances. That is, equations (3) and (4) are not sufficient for equation (5). Again we thank Frank Norman for an example: Suppose that both of two factors have nonzero effects, and that F_{11}, F_{12}, F_{21}, and F_{22} satisfy equations (3) and (4). Then if the F_{ij} are all Gaussian distributions, equation (5) is satisfied. But if the F_{ij} are all gamma distributions, equation (5) also requires that the differences among them are limited to their shape parameters; their scale parameters cannot differ.

6. Alternative pathways should be distinguished from parallel processes. However, an AP mechanism could result from a pair of self-terminating parallel processes if there were fluctuating dominance of one process over the other, with no overlap between completion times of the dominant and nondominant process, and if the probability of dominance was unaffected by factors A and B. Alternating cerebral dominance (Weintz et al. 1983) exemplifies a mechanism that might produce such fluctuating dominance of processes.

7. Unless stated otherwise, the u in $u \pm v$ represents the mean over subjects, and the v represents SE_b, the standard error based on between-subject variation.

8. The present discussion is concerned with population minima and maxima and is intended for heuristic purposes; we do not consider tests based on sample extrema.

9. McClelland (1979) assumed that the noise in the final output activation level was distributed as a standard normal distribution ($\mu = 0, \sigma^2 = 1$). Such noise can alternatively be associated with the criterion, as in Grice's (1972) account of response evocation (see also Grice, Canham, and Boroughs 1984; and Luce 1986, section 4.3); the criterion is then normally distributed with unit variance $\sigma_c^2 = 1$ about its mean. The important constraints in either interpretation are that the variance of the noise distribution is independent of the time constants, and that only one sample from the distribution is used per trial. The time added by the response mechanism is assumed to be stochastically independent of the other component of RT, and is not included in the calculations that lead to equations (19) and (20).

10. The choice of values was constrained by the cascade equation's (19) requirement that all rate parameters be distinct.

11. If the slow unit is influenced by factor C, then a test is provided by lowering the level of C, which may convert an additive relation between A and B into an overadditive one.

12. Ashby (1982, table 2) also found indications of good means additivity, but parameter values in most of his examples caused one of the main effects to be substantially smaller than the other, which tends to be associated with small interactions, and interactions were not measured relative to main effect sizes. Ashby also reported that under some conditions the cascade model could approximately satisfy the summation test. As discussed in section 26.3, this implies failure of the mixture test.

13. For $\mu_1 < \mu_2 < \mu_3$ the model requires that $(\mu_3 - \mu_1)/(\mu_2 - \mu_1) < (\sigma_3^2 - \sigma_1^2)/(\sigma_2^2 - \sigma_1^2)$.

14. Unless stated otherwise the significance level is $p = .05$.

15. The Cartesian product of two sets consists of all possible pairs containing one member of each set. If one set has m members, and the other, n, the Cartesian product consists of $m \times n$ pairs.

16. The Kolmogorov-Smirnov (K-S) test of distributional equality would be applicable if the summation set for $T_{11,22}$, for example, contained just the 31 statistically independent values obtained from one of the 31^2 possible random pairings of the observations in conditions 11 and 22. The Cartesian-product summation set uses more of the information in the data, but the resulting 961 values do not meet the K-S test's requirement of statistical independence. The

summation CDFs can be regarded as smoothed versions of the estimates based on single random pairings, for which sampling properties of the K-S test statistic are likely to differ. As Grayson (1983) observed, the same concern about applicability of the K-S test applies to empirical CDFs generated by density estimation and numerical convolution (Ashby and Townsend 1980). At this writing, unfortunately, there appears to be no appropriate replacement test. A test of the identity of the two Cartesian-product CDFs is needed that is especially sensitive to likely departures, such as the differences in spread expected from the AP model, rather than broad-gauge and sensitive to location differences, as is the K-S test.

17. The deviations were shown by the same two of the five subjects in the $na = 2$ and $na = 8$ conditions. In each case the significant tests were located at a set of contiguous time values (separated by 10 ms). They were of the same sign within subjects, but different between subjects. For one subject the ten (six) significant tests for $na = 2$ ($na = 8$) were associated with mean summation CDF values from about .02 to .29 (.12 to .47); the median significance level was .003 (.03); and the differences $\hat{F}^*_{11,22}(t, k) - \hat{F}^*_{12,21}(t, k)$ were negative, with a mean of $-.04$ ($-.08$). For the second subject the eight (nine) significant tests for $na = 2$ ($na = 8$) were associated with mean summation CDF values from about .04 to .25 (.01 to .38); the median significance level was .03 (.004); and the differences were positive, with a mean of .06 (.06).

18. We first estimated the median and interquartile range of each of the mixture CDFs for each subject. Let λ_k and ξ_k be the means of these medians and IQRs, respectively, for subject k; let $\lambda_.$ and $\xi_.$ be their means over subjects; and define $t^*_k \equiv \lambda_k + (\xi_k / \xi_.)(t - \lambda_.)$, a linear transformation of t. The pair of transformed mixture distributions for each subject, $F^*_{\text{mix}(T_{11}, T_{22})}(t)$ and $F^*_{\text{mix}(T_{12}, T_{21})}(t)$, produced by applying the same transformation $F^*_k(t) \equiv F_k(t^*_k)$, then has the desired property of having $\lambda_.$ as their mean median and $\xi_.$ as their mean IQR for all subjects.

19. For the method (convolution by fft), see Press, Flannery, Teukolsky, and Vetterling 1988, section 12.4.

20. Note added in proof: To strengthen the summation test we have extended the search for differences between $F_{T_{11}+T_{22}}(t)$ and $F_{T_{12}+T_{21}}(t)$ to histograms and density estimates, to supplement what we had already done for CDFs, and we have fitted orthogonal polynomials to the CDF differences to render the tests independent. These new tests strengthen our conclusions. We have also begun to explore the sensitivity of the summation test to violations of the SIstage model by applying it to data that simulate the AP model, thereby introducing stochastic dependence of stage durations. In an attempt to be realistic we created such data from experiment 1, experiment 2, $na = 2$, and experiment 2, $na = 8$, by retaining the T_{11} and T_{22} values in each data set, but replacing T_{12} and T_{21} by random halves of the values obtained by pooling T_{11} and T_{22}. The summation test failed dramatically for all three simulations. For example, in comparisons of proportions (analogous to those in fig. 26.3, where there were no significant differences among 169 tests) there were 39, 69, and 91 tests for the three data sets, of which 29, 37, and 57 were significant, respectively. In the IQR comparisons (analogous to those in table 26.4) the differences and means were (24.0 $\pm$ 2.6, 51.8), (16.7 $\pm$ 5.0, 97.9), and (102.4 $\pm$ 1.9, 116.9), with corresponding significance levels $p = .0002$, $p = .03$, and $p < .0001$, respectively. These results show that our procedures are sensitive to at least one type of violation of the SIstage model of a size that might be observed in actual experiments.

21. Consider a three-factor experiment with each factor at two levels and assume that the effects of the factors on mean RT are pairwise additive. The eight conditions can be represented as vertices of a cube, where the three dimensions (x, y, z) are levels of the three factors. Each of the six faces of the cube provides one two-dimensional summation test. For example, the front face, where $z = 1$, provides $T_{111} + T_{221}$ and $T_{121} + T_{211}$ (which should have the same distribution). Similarly the right face, where $x = 2$, provides $T_{211} + T_{222}$ and $T_{212} + T_{221}$. These are just particular cases of the test we have already used. In addition, there are six distributional equality relations among four sums of RTs for conditions represented as vertices of oblique planes within the cube, such as $T_{111} + T_{222}$ and $T_{112} + T_{221}$. The proof that these two sums (and two other similar pairs, $T_{121} + T_{212}$ and $T_{122} + T_{211}$) all have the same distribution, given the SIstage

model, is similar to the proof of equation (5). These twelve summation tests reflect a basis containing four orthogonal tests. One such set of four are those corresponding to the left, front, right, and bottom faces of the cube. Thus the extra additive factor provides a disproportionate increase in the number of possible summation tests of the SIstage model: One $2 \times 2 \times 2$ experiment provides twice as many independent tests as two 2×2 experiments.

REFERENCES

Ashby, F. G. (1982). Deriving exact predictions from the cascade model. *Psychological Review, 89*, 599–607.

Ashby, F. G., and Townsend. J. T. (1980). Decomposing the reaction time distribution: Pure insertion and selective influence revisited. *Journal of Mathematical Psychology, 21*, 93–123.

Atkinson, R. C., and Juola, J. F. (1974). Search and decision processes in recognition memory. In Krantz, D. H., Atkinson, R. C., Luce, R. D., and Suppes, P. (Eds.), *Contemporary developments in mathematical psychology*. Vol. 1, 242–93. San Francisco: W. H. Freeman.

Backus, B. T., and Sternberg, S. (1988). Attentional tradeoff across space early in visual processing: New evidence. Paper presented at the meeting of the Psychonomic Society, Chicago.

Blough, D. (1978). Reaction times of pigeons on a wavelength discrimination task. *Journal of the Experimental Analysis of Behavior, 30*, 163–167.

Broadbent, D. E. (1984). The Maltese cross: A new simplistic model for memory. *The Behavioral and Brain Sciences, 7*, 55–94.

Coltheart, M. (1985). Cognitive neuropsychology and the study of reading. In M. I. Posner and O. S. M. Marin (Eds.), *Attention and performance XI*, 3–37. Hillsdale, NJ: Lawrence Erlbaum.

Donders, F. C. ([1868] 1969). On the speed of mental processes. Translation by W. G. Koster. In W. G. Koster (Ed.), *Attention and performance II. Acta Psychologica, 30*, 412–431.

Gardner, H. (1985). *The mind's new science: A history of the cognitive revolution*. New York: Basic Books.

Grayson, D. A. (1983). *The role of the response stage in stochastic models of simple reaction time*. Unpublished doctoral dissertation, University of Sydney, Australia.

Grice, G. R. (1972). Application of a variable criterion model to auditory reaction time as a function of the type of catch trial. *Perception & Psychophysics, 12*, 103–107.

Grice, G. R., Canham, L., and Boroughs, J. M. (1984). Combination rule for redundant information in reaction time tasks with divided attention. *Perception & Psychophysics, 35*, 451–463.

Johnson, E. G., and Tukey, J. W. (1987). Graphical exploratory analysis of variance illustrated on a splitting of the Johnson and Tsao data. In C. L. Mallows (Ed.), *Design, data, and analysis*, 171–244. New York: John Wiley and Sons.

Luce, R. D. (1986). *Response times: Their role in inferring elementary mental organization*. Oxford: Oxford University Press.

McCann, R. S., and Johnston, J. C. (1989). The locus of processing bottlenecks in the overlapping-tasks paradigm. Paper presented at the meeting of the Psychonomic Society, Atlanta.

McClelland, J. L. (1979). On the time relations of mental processes: An examination of systems of processes in cascade. *Psychological Review, 86*, 287–330.

Massaro, D. W. (1988). Some criticisms of connectionist models of human performance. *Journal of Memory and Language, 27*, 213–234.

Meyer, D. E., Irwin, D. E., Osman, A. M., and Kounios, J. (1988). The dynamics of cognition and action: Mental processes inferred from speed-accuracy decomposition. *Psychological Review*, 95, 183–237.

Meyer, D. E., Osman, A. M., Irwin, D. E., and Yantis, S. (1988). Modern mental chronometry. *Biological Psychology*, 26, 3–67.

Meyer, D. E., Yantis, S., Osman, A., and Smith, J. E. K. (1984). Discrete versus continuous models of response preparation: A reaction-time analysis. In S. Kornblum and J. Requin (Eds.), *Preparatory states and processes*, 69–94. Hillsdale, NJ: Lawrence Erlbaum.

Miller, J. (1988). Discrete and continuous models of human information processing: Theoretical distinctions and empirical results. *Acta Psychologica*, 67, 191–257.

Miller, J. (1990). Discreteness and continuity in models of human information processing. *Acta Psychologica*, 74, 297–318.

Miller, J., and Hackley, S. A. (N.d.). Electrophysiological evidence for temporal overlap among contingent mental processes. *Journal of Experimental Psychology: General*. In press.

Miller, J., van der Ham, F., and Sanders, A. F. (N.d.). Overlapping stage models and the additive factor method: A simulation study. Unpublished manuscript.

Miller, R. G., Jr. (1986). *Simultaneous statistical inference*. New York: Springer-Verlag.

Mosteller, F., and Tukey, J. W. (1977). *Data analysis and regression: A second course in statistics*. Reading, Massachusetts: Addison-Wesley.

Ollman, R. T. (1966). Fast guesses in choice-reaction time. *Psychonomic Science*, 6, 155–156.

Osman, A., Bashore, T. R., Coles, M. G. H., Donchin, E., and Meyer, D. E. (1992). On the transmission of partial information: Inferences from movement-related brain potentials. *Journal of Experimental Psychology: Human Perception and Performance*, 18, 217–232.

Pashler, H., and Johnston, J. C. (1989). Chronometric evidence for central postponement in temporally overlapping tasks. *Quarterly Journal of Experimental Psychology*, 41A, 19–45.

Pieters, J. P. M. (1983). Sternberg's additive factor method and underlying psychological processes: Some theoretical considerations. *Psychological Bulletin*, 93, 411–426.

Press, W. H., Flannery, B. P., Teukolsky, S. A., and Vetterling, W. T. (1988). *Numerical recipes in C: The art of scientific computing*. Cambridge, England: Cambridge University Press.

Ratcliff, R. (1979). Group reaction time distributions and an analysis of distribution statistics. *Psychological Bulletin*, 86, 446–461.

Roberts, S. (1987). Evidence for distinct serial processes in animals: The multiplicative-factors method. *Animal Learning and Behavior*, 15, 135–173.

Rumelhart, D. E., and McClelland, J. L. (1982). An interactive activation model of context effects in letter perception: Part 2. The contextual enhancement effect and some tests and extensions of the model. *Psychological Review*, 89, 60–94.

Rumelhart, D. E., and McClelland. J. L. (1986). PDP models and general issues in cognitive science. In Rumelhart, D. E. and McClelland, J. L. (Eds.), *Parallel distributed processing. Vol. 1: Foundations*. Cambridge, MA: MIT Press.

Sanders, A. F. (1980). Stage analysis of reaction processes. In G. E. Stelmach and J. Requin (Eds.), *Tutorials in motor behavior*, 331–354. Amsterdam: North-Holland.

Sanders, A. F. (1990). Issues and trends in the debate on discrete versus continuous processing of information. *Acta Psychologica*, 74, 123–167.

Schweickert, R. (1985). Separable effects of factors on speed and accuracy: Memory scanning, lexical decision, and choice tasks. *Psychological Bulletin*, 97, 530–546.

Schweickert, R. (1989). Separable effects of factors on activation functions in discrete and continuous models: d' and evoked potentials. *Psychological Bulletin, 106*, 318–328.

Shallice, T. (1988). *From neuropsychology to mental structure*. Cambridge, England: Cambridge University Press.

Shaw, M. L. (1984). Division of attention among spatial locations: A fundamental difference between detection of letters and detection of luminance increments. In H. Bouma and D. G. Bouwhuis (Eds.), *Attention and performance X: Control of language processes*, 109–121. Hillsdale, NJ: Lawrence Erlbaum.

Silverman, B. W. (1986). *Density estimation*. London: Chapman and Hall.

Sternberg, S. (1967). Two operations in character recognition: Some evidence from reaction-time measurements. *Perception & Psychophysics, 2*, 45–53.

Sternberg, S. (1969). The discovery of processing stages: Extensions of Donders' method. In W. G. Koster (Ed.), *Attention and performance II, Acta Psychologica, 30*, 276–315.

Sternberg, S. (1971). Decomposing mental processes with reaction-time data. Invited address, Midwestern Psychological Association Annual Meeting, Detroit.

Sternberg, S. (1984). Stage models of mental processing and the additive-factor method. *The Behavioral and Brain Sciences, 7*, 82–84.

Swets, J. A. (1986). Form of empirical ROCs in discrimination and diagnostic tasks: Implications for theory and measurement of performance. *Psychological Bulletin, 99*, 181–198.

Taylor, D. A. (1976). Stage analysis of reaction time. *Psychological Bulletin, 83*, 161–191.

Townsend, J. T. (1984). Uncovering mental processes with factorial experiments. *Journal of Mathematical Psychology, 28*, 363–400.

Townsend, J. T., and Ashby, F. G. (1983). *The stochastic modeling of elementary psychological processes*. London: Cambridge University Press.

Weintz, D. A., Bickford, R. G., Bloom, F. E., and Shannahoff-Khalsa, D. S. (1983). Alternating cerebral hemispheric activity and the lateralization of autonomic nervous function. *Human Neurobiology, 2*, 39–43.

Wickelgren, W. A. (1977). Speed-accuracy tradeoff and information processing dynamics. *Acta Psychologica, 41*, 67–85.

Yantis, S., Meyer, D. E., and Smith, J. E. K. (1991). Analyses of multinomial mixture distributions: New tests for stochastic models of cognition and action. *Psychological Bulletin, 110*, 350–374.

Yellott, J. I. (1971). Correction for fast guessing and the speed-accuracy tradeoff in choice reaction time. *Journal of Mathematical Psychology, 8*, 159–199.

27 Toward a Theory of Information Processing in Graded, Random, and Interactive Networks

James L. McClelland

This chapter describes some initial steps toward a theory of the asymptotic and dynamic properties of systems in which information processing adheres to the principles of graded, gradual, random, interactive, and competitive processing. The goals for the theory are (1) to unify the results of a number of different experimental paradigms with a single theoretical framework; (2) to examine the conditions under which adherence to the principles will give rise to simple general regularities of information processing, and to examine whether the framework makes it possible to explain or predict cases in which these regularities will not hold; and (3) to examine interdependencies among the principles.

The principles, their motivation, and some of their general computational properties are described first. Then the three goals are discussed. Following this, two case studies are reviewed in which progress is made toward each of the three goals. A concluding discussion indicates directions for further development of the theory.

The principles are very general, but their examination will presuppose that information processing takes place in a parallel-distributed processing (PDP) system (Rumelhart, Hinton, and McClelland 1986). A *PDP system* is simply a system in which processing occurs through the interactions of a large number of simple, interconnected processing elements called units. These elements may be organized into modules, each containing a number of units; sets of modules may be organized into pathways, each containing a set of interconnected modules. Pathways may overlap, in that they may contain modules in common. Processing in a PDP system occurs by the propagation of activation among the units, via weighted connections. The knowledge that governs processing is stored in the weights of the connections, and the effects of experience on information processing are captured by changes to the connection weights.

The PDP framework is an extremely broad framework and can be used to address a very wide range of different modeling goals, from efforts to capture the detailed properties of specific neural circuits to efforts to solve problems in artificial intelligence that have not yielded to more traditional symbolic approaches. The PDP framework has also been used for psychological modeling, and it has been very useful in this regard; but it is really best construed as a framework providing tools with which to construct a theory, and not as a theory in and of itself. For the general framework is so broad that it does not provide much guidance or constraint without further assumptions.

27.1 PRINCIPLES

The following list of principles begins to provide such a constraining framework. While each of the principles has been used in previous work by the present author, none of the principles can easily be attributed to any particular source, since each is in extremely common use.

1. The activation of each unit is a graded, sigmoid function of its summed input.

2. Activation propagates gradually in time.

3. Between-module connections are mutual and excitatory, so that processing is interactive.

4. Within-module connections are mutual and inhibitory, so that processing is competitive.

5. The activation process is intrinsically variable.

It should be stressed that this set of principles is provisional. They should be viewed as a starting place and guide for research. No doubt there are other principles in addition to these, and no doubt, some or all of the principles will require further refinement.

Taken together with the basic characteristics of PDP, these principles define a modeling framework called the GRAIN model. GRAIN stands for graded, random, adaptive, interactive, (nonlinear) network. The framework encompasses adaptation or learning as well as the principles enumerated above, but the principles of adaptation are not yet fully clear and will not be considered further here. For a discussion of learning in GRAIN networks, see Movellan and McClelland (1991) and Cohen, Servan-Schreiber, and McClelland (in press).

Also missing from the list above are principles of representation. Although distributed representations have considerable advantages (see McClelland and Rumelhart 1985; Hinton, McClelland, and Rumelhart 1986) the particular models that will be the focus of interest in what follows, and the motivations for them, are couched in localist terms. That is, each processing unit stands for a specific choice that might be made in interpreting an input at a particular level of description. This feature arises not as a matter of principle but as a simplification. Of course, further work is required to examine the extent to which the results obtained for localist networks actually transfer to systems using distributed representations.

In this connection it is worth noting that models based on the above principles should not be construed as models of the neuronal processes underlying cognition. The units do not correspond to individual neurons, nor do the connections correspond to individual synapses. Rather, activations of units represent representational states of a processing system and connections capture constraints that hold among these representational states. A discussion of the relation between such models cast at this rather cognitive level and models of the underlying neural substrate may be found in Smolensky (1986).

The reader will note that the principles are stated in qualitative terms, without specific detailed quantitative assumptions. While particular simulation models must be formulated in terms of specific quantitative assumptions, it can often be shown that these details are relatively unimportant. It does not appear to matter, for example, what the exact form of the graded sigmoid function is, or whether the intrinsic noise is Gaussian or uniformly distributed in a bounded interval.

Discussion of the Principles

The motivations for the principles are complex and interdependent, and to do full justice to each would require much more space than is available here. In what follows, direct and basic psychological motivations are given for each principle. Sometimes, however, the motivation for one principle arises primarily from its interaction with others. These interactions are addressed more fully in the later parts of this chapter, but forward pointers to some of the most important interactions are given at the end of this section. In general, the principles and their motivations are attributable to a number of sources; no claim for priority is intended by listing them here.

In what follows some basic theoretical results concerning networks that adhere to the principles are also noted. More details can be found in a number of sources; the most up-to-date review is given in Hertz, Krogh, and Palmer (1990).

Graded, Sigmoid Activation Function The use of a graded activation function of summed input allows a variable to exert a continuous or graded influence on processing outcomes, while leaving these outcomes open to other influences. Graded influences on cognitive outcomes are ubiquitous. To mention just one key example, category membership appears to be a graded function of similarity to typical exemplars. Openness to additional influences allows for factors such as contextual or attentional inputs to influence the outcome of processing. Graded influences allow for collaboration and competition of cues, and play a role in a number of basic approaches to processing (Oden and Massaro 1978; MacWhinney 1987).

A sigmoid activation function is simply a continuous activation function that is monotonically increasing, has a single point of inflection, and levels off at both extremes (fig. 27.1). Such a function is used to characterize the asymptotic activation produced by a fixed net input to a unit. The motivation for the use of a sigmoid activation function, as opposed to a completely linear activation function, is basic: multilayer networks that use linear activation functions are computationally trivial. They cannot compute anything that

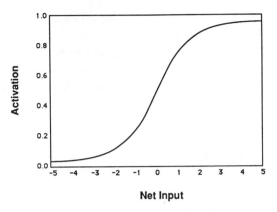

Figure 27.1 A sigmoid function of the type used in many connectionist models.

cannot be computed with a single layer of units, and what can be computed by a single layer of units is very limited indeed (Minsky and Pappert 1969).

Furthermore, linear networks with bidirectional connections, as required by the interactivity principle, can easily exhibit explosive growth of activations. The use of a sigmoid activation function prevents this. On the other hand, the sigmoid is a very simple function; it is, for example, monotonic in each of its inputs, independently of all the others (Williams 1986).

Once a sigmoid function is used, the effect of an input on the outcome of processing depends on other inputs. Each input (excitatory or inhibitory) tends to push the activation of each unit in a particular direction, but the magnitude of the effect depends critically on the other inputs to the unit. This allows us to understand, for example, how a cue can influence response probabilities when other cues are relatively neutral but fail to have much influence when other cues strongly favor one particular response.

Once sigmoid functions are used in multilayer systems, arbitrarily complex patterns of activation through time can arise. Further constraints are crucial. The use of bidirectional connections helps a great deal, as will be discussed below.

Gradual Propagation of Activation   The assumption of gradual propagation arose in the context of efforts to study the dynamics of information processing and of contextual influences on processing (McClelland 1979; Rumelhart and McClelland 1981). One key observation here is that it often takes subjects less time to recognize a stimulus when they use more information to do so. Thus recognition may be both more accurate and faster when a stimulus occurs in a predictive context (e.g., a word appearing in a sentence context) than when it appears alone. In many such experiments (e.g., McClelland and O'Regan 1981) context alone is not sufficient for recognition, so information from both the stimulus and the context must be used. A very natural and direct way to account for such effects is to assume that information about both the stimulus and the context accumulates gradually over time, so that when both sources of information are accumulating at the same time a response threshold is reached more quickly.

Interactive Processing   The idea that processing is interactive arose in the author's thinking from Rumelhart's (1977) seminal paper, "The Interactive Model of Reading." (Grossberg 1978a also explored this idea, though mostly for different reasons, at around the same time.) The key point of Rumelhart (1977) was to argue that in reading (as in speech perception and other perceptual processes) decisions at each level—in this case feature, letter, word identity, word meaning, syntactic structure, role assignment, anaphoric reference, etc.—reflected influences from all other levels. McClelland and Rumelhart (1981; Rumelhart and McClelland 1981, 1982) developed a model that applied this assumption to visual letter recognition. This work was motivated by the fact that the perception of a letter in a word is facilitated more when it occurs in context (Reicher 1969) than when it occurs in isolation. The account for this was simply that partial activations of context and target letters could give rise to activations of words and these in turn could feed back activation to the letters, increasing their activation compared to cases in which a single letter was presented in isolation. Elman and McClelland (1988) confirmed a key prediction of this same model in a speech perception context by showing that phonemes whose identification depended on lexical context could trigger coarticulatory influences on the identification of other phonemes. Such influences have long been studied in the speech perception literature, and they are generally interpreted as operating at or below the phoneme level. The finding that these coarticulatory influences could be triggered by lexical context was predicted from the principle of interactivity, and contradicts feed forward models in which lexical influences do not feed back to the phoneme level.

Mutual Competition   Competitive interactions among units have been used by many investigators (e.g., Feldman and Ballard 1982; Grossberg 1976, 1978a,b). They allow contrast enhancement and the suppression of weak activations. They also allow the activation of each alternative to be influenced by the extent to which there is input that favors other alternatives. Response choices reflect this weighing of alternatives relative to others (Luce 1959), and mutual inhibition can implement this relative weighting process (Grossberg 1978b). In McClelland and Rumelhart (1981), the use of this idea at each of several levels of processing was motivated originally by the desire to distribute decision making throughout information processing systems, rather than to centralize this function in a limited capacity executive.

The general principles of interactivity and competition are consistent with a specific network constraint, called symmetry, in which for all pairs of units A and B, the connection from A to B has the same value as the connection from B to A. Obviously interactive and competitive networks need not be strictly symmetric, but they can be. Symmetric networks have a very important property, which is that there exists some function (known as a Liapunov function) whose value changes monotonically as processing proceeds through time. Hopfield (1982) was the first to point this out. His symmetric networks monotonically decrease the value of what Hopfield called an energy function; alternatively the minus sign may be removed, and the function, which is now monotonically increasing, may be called a goodness function (Rumelhart et al. 1986). Choosing the latter formulation, it can be shown that symmetric networks always proceed uphill in goodness as processing continues, where goodness is defined as the extent to which the activations in the network satisfy the constraints represented by the inputs to the network and the connection weights (see Rumelhart et al. 1986 for a full discussion). When activations are bounded, as they are in GRAIN networks, the activations and thus the goodness eventually stop increasing as processing continues. This point will have higher goodness than any neighboring points. Such a point is called a local maximum.

The fact that networks are monotonically adjusting the value of some function as the activation process proceeds from a starting point does not mean that the activation of each unit will vary monotonically with time. Such nonmonotonicities in the time course of activation arise from the changing pattern of activation surrounding each unit, sometimes causing units that receive net excitation at the beginning of processing to receive net inhibition at a later point. Examples of this were discussed in McClelland and Rumelhart (1981) and a different example will be considered again below.

Variability   That human performance is variable cannot really be subject to much doubt, and in fact most models of information processing dynamics are stochastic models (see Luce 1986 for a review). Some authors (e.g., Anderson 1991) have stressed that manifest variability in reaction times across different test items (e.g., in a recall experiment) may in fact reflect differences among items rather than actual variability in the processing itself, and there are surely many other factors (mood, context, motor preparation, accommodation of the eye, etc.) that introduce trial-to-trial variation. What is of interest here is that incorporating some source of variability, either in the input to processing or intrinsic to processing activity itself, improves our ability to model human information processing, relative to a deterministic model in which variability is introduced only at the response selection stage. This matter will be considered at great length in a subsequent section. Here we consider a very general characteristic of stochastic symmetric networks.

Stochastic symmetric networks, like deterministic ones, are minimizing a Liapunov function, but this function characterizes distributions of states rather than individual states. Over time they settle to a particular distribution over possible states of activation, independent of the starting point of the settling process (this is a basic general fact; see Movellan and McClelland 1991 for a fuller discussion). Note that the actual pattern of activation does not stabilize; what stabilizes is the probability that the network will be in each possible activation state. At the beginning of settling, the distribution of states of the network will be determined largely by the initial pattern of activation. But as time goes on, the distribution eventually becomes independent of the starting point. Note that initial patterns of activation should not be confused with fixed inputs that remain on throughout the settling process. These do affect the equilibrium distribution, making some patterns more probable at the expense of others.

It is actually possible to write down the equilibrium probability distributions of some stochastic symmetric networks as a function of their fixed inputs and of the connection strengths. This fact will be used below in discussing derivations of asymptotic choice probabilities.

27.2 GOALS FOR A THEORY OF INFORMATION PROCESSING

There are many possible goals that we may have for a theory of information processing. For the present we will focus on the three goals that were mentioned at the beginning of this chapter: (1) synthesis of the results of a range of different experimental paradigms, (2) exploration of the conditions under which systems that adhere to the principles can be characterized by simple general laws, and (3) analysis of the interdependencies among the principles.

Synthesis

One goal for a theory of information processing is to bring together in a single model results from a variety of different paradigms. The three main classes of paradigms of interest here will be designated (1) the asymptotic choice paradigm, (2) the reaction-time paradigm, and (3) the time-accuracy paradigm. Though the paradigms will be familiar to most readers, a brief review of their characteristics and their relation to the present approach will be worthwhile.

The asymptotic choice paradigm encompasses experiments in which subjects are asked to make choice responses (or yes-no responses) without time pressure, and the assumption is that they wait until there is nothing further to be gained from waiting. The dependent measure is the distribution of responses over alternatives. Such situations are the easiest to model, since as already noted it is often possible in connectionist systems to characterize the distributions of asymptotic states mathematically as functions of inputs and connections.

The reaction-time paradigm encompasses experiments in which subjects are asked to make responses as rapidly as possible without sacrificing accuracy. Ordinarily the main dependent variable is simply mean reaction time. From the point of view of graded, stochastic systems that adhere to the principles outlined above, this paradigm is the least satisfactory. First of all, while models based on the above principles can in principle model mean reaction times, there is one main difficulty. This is simply that in systems where there is a gradual accumulation of graded information, the instruction to respond as rapidly as possible without sacrificing accuracy is not well defined (Wickelgren 1977;

Pachella 1974; Ratcliff 1978). All else being equal, it is very commonly observed that accuracy is lowest in conditions producing the longest reaction times. While this fact arises naturally from some continuous models (see Ratcliff 1978) in which a fixed evidence criterion is used, it is also very likely that the criteria themselves may slip, as the subject becomes impatient to respond. To model the data requires complex assumptions about criteria which can be both extraneous to the theory and difficult to check.

It is true that some researchers (e.g., Ratcliff 1978) make extensive use of dependent measures other than mean reaction time. These include error rates and properties of reaction-time distributions that characterize their form and spread. When such properties are available for both correct and error responses, for each of several conditions, the overall pattern of data certainly imposes a considerable degree of constraint. However even here assumptions about criteria remain, and considerable information about the actual time course of processing is lost.

The time-accuracy paradigm encompasses a variety of procedures that attempt to relate accuracy to elapsed time since the onset of a stimulus. This can be done in a variety of ways. Sometimes different deadlines are used in different blocks of trials (Pachella 1974). Sometimes a response signal is used, and subjects are trained to respond very shortly after the occurrence of the signal (Wickelgren 1977). In these cases, accuracy is typically plotted as a function of mean reaction time in each deadline or response signal condition. Such curves are called time-accuracy curves. In other variants, subjects are simply told to go so fast that overall accuracy falls to something like 70–80% (Lappin and Disch 1973; Gratton et al. 1988). This often induces a broad distribution of reaction times for each experimental condition, with relatively low accuracy for short reaction times. The RT distribution can be divided into bins, and accuracy for responses falling in each bin can be plotted, yielding what Gratton et al have called a "conditional accuracy function." Although time-accuracy curves and conditional accuracy functions are not the same, both can provide information about the accumulation of information through the changing distribution of responses over time. Thus both are useful tools for studying graded, stochastic processes.

A theory of information processing dynamics like the present one ought to be able to provide insight not only into asymptotic choice behavior, but also into the time course of change in response-choice probabilities. Although the time course of nonlinear stochastic dynamical systems is known to be difficult to analyze mathematically (Cox and Miller 1965), the hope is that simulations, supplemented where possible by mathematical analyses of boundary conditions, can provide some insight into various qualitative aspects of these systems.

Because of the ubiquity of reaction-time experiments, any reasonable theory must address results from this paradigm as well. However in the present chapter there is room to cover only a limited range of results, so the focus will be on recent analytic progress characterizing effects of variables on asymptotic choice probabilities and on simulations addressing aspects of the time course of processing as revealed through time-accuracy studies.

Complex Systems, Simple Laws

The principles stated above are remarkably simple, but processing systems that adhere to them can be very complex, both in terms of their structure and in terms of their behavior. Yet often the data produced in information processing tasks can be captured by very simple laws. This chapter will be concerned with two examples.

Morton's Independence Law for Effects of Context and Stimulus Information in Perception It has been repeatedly observed that context and stimulus information produce additive, or independent, effects on the z-transform of stimulus identification response probabilities. The generality of this pattern was first noted by Morton (1969), and has been stressed by Massaro (e.g., Massaro 1989). It is illustrated in graphical form in figure 27.2.

Wickelgren's Law for Time-Accuracy Curves In studies where response accuracy is measured at different times after stimulus onset, a simple general pattern is typically observed (fig. 27.3). Responses that occur immediately after stimulus onset are essentially random, and unrelated to the stimulus. At a later point, accuracy begins to rise rapidly above chance, then gradually levels off. The overall pattern of performance can generally be described as a shifted exponential approach to asymptote, as Wickelgren (1977) was the first to point out. These regularities will be called Morton's independence law and

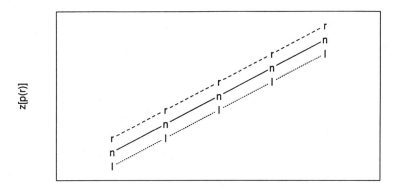

/l/ - /r/ continuum

Figure 27.2 Idealized pattern of results expected in the Massaro and Cohen experiment if the independence law holds. The stimulus conditions are ordered from *l*-like to *r*-like on the x-axis. The y-axis represents the z-score of the probability of the *r* response. This is plotted for each of three context conditions. Curves are labeled *r*, *l*, and *n* for contexts favoring *r*, *l*, and *n*, respectively. Reprinted with permission from McClelland (1991).

Toward a Theory of Information Processing

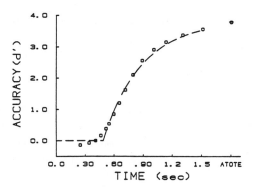

Figure 27.3 The dashed line depicts the shifted-exponential curve proposed by Wickelgren (1977) that characterizes the time-accuracy curves that have been obtained in a large number of different experiments. A composite of data from a number of different experiments demonstrates the close correspondence. Reprinted with permission from McClelland (1979).

Wickelgren's law for ease of reference. In calling them laws, no claim is made that either actually always holds, and indeed we shall be concerned with cases where they do not hold; they are, however, robust empirical regularities that do hold under a wide range of circumstances.

Typically, such simple regularities in information processing have led to simple models. Morton's (1969) model of context effects in perception, and the more recent model of Oden and Massaro (1978) are clearly cases in point. In the Oden and Massaro model, for example, it is assumed that independent sources of evidence are evaluated independently, then combined according to a simple combination rule, to yield response strengths for each alternative. These response strengths then enter into a decision process which selects an alternative probabilistically based on the Luce (1959) choice rule.

One of the central goals of the present work is to understand whether, and under what circumstances, these (and eventually other) simple laws might arise from processing systems that adhere to the principles described above. A related and equally important goal is to delineate circumstances in which these simple patterns of data break down. The hope is that it will be possible to see just what additional constraints beyond the basic principles themselves are needed for the simple laws to hold, and what the consequences of violations of these assumptions may be.

The goal of subsuming empirical regularities under a set of general principles is one that the present work shares with Newell's (1990) work on unified theories of cognition. The goal of going beyond merely subsuming these regularities to giving some account of cases where they hold and do not hold is curiously absent from Newell's approach. The view taken here is that the utility of the general principles is perhaps most strongly established when they can lead us beyond general laws that usually hold, to an understanding of how they might fail and what it might mean when this happens. We will see that two sources of information do not always exert independent effects on performance, and that time-accuracy curves are not even always monotonic; and we will see that these cases can be understood in terms of violations of architectural constraints on the structure of GRAIN networks.

Interdependencies of the Principles

As shall become evident below, there are cases in which models that adhere to only four of the five principles produce poor fits to data, but models that adhere to all five produce excellent fits. This kind of discovery argues strongly in favor of the effort to articulate and evaluate an entire *set* of principles, rather than to try to evaluate the validity of the principles one-by-one (Newell 1973, 1990). For if there are interdependencies, any finding we might obtain about the validity of one of the principles will change with changes in other assumptions. For this reason, an effort to understand interdependencies among the principles is among the central goals of the theory.

27.3 CASE STUDIES

In this section, two case studies are reviewed. In each case we will see that GRAIN networks exhibit correspondence to well-known general laws—but only under certain boundary conditions. In the first case study, the analysis is somewhat more developed. Here it has been possible to use mathematics to analyze asymptotic choice performance, to relate the parameters of the GRAIN model to parameters of classical models of asymptotic choice performance, and to generate and confirm a prediction that arises from the mathematical analysis for a case in which the general laws will not hold. The second case study illustrates one future direction for the work with simulation studies of performance in the time-accuracy paradigm. Here we find that the GRAIN model can produce curves that approximate Wickelgren's time-accuracy law, while also providing a framework for developing a plausible account of one case in which this law fails.

27.3.1 ASYMPTOTIC PERFORMANCE IN PERCEPTUAL IDENTIFICATION TASKS

The Problem

A basic assumption of the GRAIN model is the principle of interactivity, or bidirectional influence between mutually consistent units at different processing levels. However, Massaro (1989) called this principle into question. He pointed out that the interactive activation model (McClelland and Rumelhart 1981), which embodied this principle, violated the independence law mentioned above. Here we consider the independence law in the context of a particular experiment: the determination of the identity of an ambiguous consonant under the influence of perceptual and contextual information. In this experiment (Massaro 1989) perceptual information was varied by creating seven tokens of an ambiguous segment on a continuum from /l/ to /r/.

Original IA Assumptions

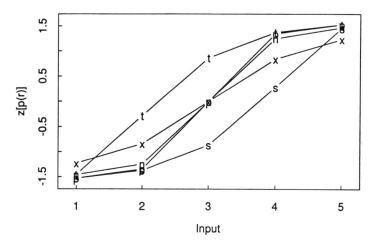

Figure 27.4 Simulation results from the interactive activation network shown in figure 27.5. Reprinted with permission from McClelland (1991).

Context was varied by presenting each token in a context in which both /r/ and /l/ can appear (/p_i/ as in *pre* or *plea*), a context where /r/ can appear (/t_i/ as in *tree*), a context where /l/ can appear (/s_i/ as in many words such as *sleep, sleet*, etc.) and finally a context in which neither actually occurs in English (/v_i/). Subjects must simply identify the ambiguous token as /r/ or /l/, without time pressure.

The independence law states that we should be able to space the seven input conditions along the x-axis of a graph (representing a log-likelihood continuum from /l/ to /r/) in such a way that the results from the 28 conditions of the experiment form four (straight and) parallel lines, one for all seven of the points in each of the four contexts (fig. 27.2). In fact the data from a large number of similar experiments can indeed be fit fairly closely in just this way.

What Massaro noted was that the interactive activation model as originally formulated failed to produce the required straight lines. The actual curves produced in a simulation of a simplified network appropriate for modeling the Massaro data is shown in figure 27.4. The network is shown in figure 27.5. It consists of two target units, one for /r/ and one for /l/; three context-input units, for the initial phonemes /s/, /p/, and /t/ from the Thompson and Massaro experiment; and four higher-level units, one for each of the legal combinations of context and target letters. Thus there are higher-level units for *pr, pl, tr,* and *sl* but not for *sr, tl, vr* or *vl.* (A fourth context input unit for /v/ would not have been helpful since /v/ is not connected to anything.) Five steps along the /r/–/l/ continuum were considered, varying the input to the /r/ unit from 0.3 to 0.7 in steps of 0.1. The input to the /l/ unit was set equal to one minus the input to the /r/ unit. The four context conditions were simulated by supplying an input of 1.0 to the appropriate context unit (or to

McClelland

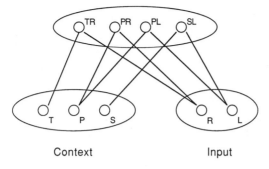

Context   Input

Figure 27.5 The network used in the simulations of the joint effects of context and stimulus information in phoneme identification. Reprinted with permission from McClelland (1991). Lines indicate bidirectional excitatory connections. All units within the same enclosed region are mutually inhibitory.

no unit at all, in the case of the /v/). Each simulated trial began with activations of all units set to rest ($-.1$), and appropriate inputs were turned on and left on.

Processing occurred according to the specific activation assumptions of the interactive activation model (using the **iac** program of McClelland and Rumelhart 1988). These assumptions are consistent with the GRAIN model in most respects. The activation function is a graded sigmoid function; gradual propagation of activation is assumed; between-level connections are bidirectional and excitatory, and within level connections are bidirectional and inhibitory. But there is no variability; processing itself is completely deterministic. Probabilistic performance is "tacked on at the end," to use a phrase from Luce (1986): At the end of 60 cycles activations of the /r/ and /l/ units were used to determine response probabilities according to the Luce choice rule applied to the exponential of the activation of each unit, as in McClelland and Rumelhart (1981).

As figure 27.4 indicates, the interactive activation model did not produce parallel lines in this simulation. While it is possible to space the points on the x axis to make *one* of the curves a straight line, no transformation can make all the lines parallel, since some of them actually cross.

Massaro's (1989) claim was not simply that the interactive activation model failed in particular cases to produce the right pattern of results. Rather, the claim was that the principle of interactivity itself was incompatible with independence. He based this claim on the following intuitively appealing argument. The independence law states that each source of information makes an independent (additive) contribution to the evidence for or against each alternative. But in the interactive activation model, the effects of context and direct stimulus information on activations of letter detector units are not independent. That is, the effects of one source of evidence—direct stimulus input—are influenced by the presence of bidirectional connections between the letter and word level units. Bottom-up input can activate a letter unit, which can in turn feed upward and activate a word unit, and the word unit will in turn send activation back to the letter unit. This process seems to be sending back from the word level some of the activation that came up to it from the letter level. Further, and this is where independence is violated, the extent of the activation that is fed back depends on context; the context influences the activations of word level units, and if a particular context activates supporters of one target alternative rather than another, only the former will have the benefit of recurrent activation; the latter will not get this benefit. Thus, the context appears to modulate the extent of activation a letter gets from stimulus input, thereby violating the independence assumption.

The Role of Variability

Interestingly, this intuitively appealing argument only applies to the deterministic version of the interactive activation model studied by McClelland and Rumelhart; it does not hold when there is variability, either in the input or in the processing itself (McClelland 1991). The presence of variability actually permits a simplification of the model in one respect: When there is variability, responses can be made simply by settling until equilibrium is reached and then picking the most active alternative. Under these conditions, the network itself is in a real sense choosing the response, and the probabilistic character of these choices arises from the variability. Under these conditions, interactive activation models do behave in accordance with Morton's independence law.

Simulation results establishing the independence pattern for the network shown in figure 27.5 are shown in figures 27.6a and 27.6b. For figure 27.6a, variability was added to the input to the network. Specifically, the input to the /r/ unit was perturbed by a Gaussian random noise with 0 mean and standard deviation 0.14. Again the input to the /l/ unit was one minus the (perturbed) input to the /r/ unit. Each trial was run just as before; processing was completely deterministic. All of the variability was in the input, which stayed constant within a given trial. Response choices were made by simply selecting the alternative with the largest activation at the end of 60 cycles (other values were used in other runs with indistinguishable results). Of course, the variability in the input made performance probabilistic, and many runs are needed to establish the actual probabilities. The graphs are based on 10,000 independent simulation trials per data point.

For figure 27.6b, the external input to each unit was fixed as in the initial simulation; this time all of the variability was intrinsic to the processing in the network. On each time step, a sample of noise from a Gaussian distribution with mean 0 and standard deviation 0.14 was added into the net input of each unit. Again, after 60 cycles of processing, the network's response was determined by selecting the most active response unit.

Analysis The fact that the model conformed to the independence law can be established mathematically for the case where the variability occurred in the input. A formal presentation can be found in McClelland (1991). For the present, the following informal analysis is given. In the case under consideration, the network itself remains completely deterministic. This means that

Noise in Inputs

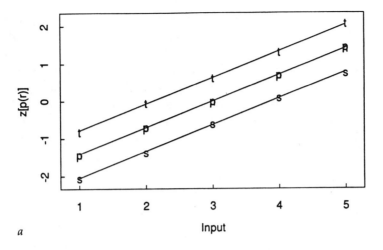

a

Intrinsic Noise

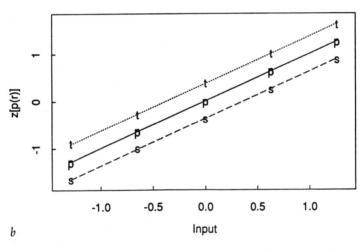

b

Figure 27.6 Simulations based on the network shown in figure 27.5 with perturbed inputs (*a*) and intrinsic variability (*b*). Reprinted with permission from McClelland (1991).

each particular choice of inputs (context plus direct input to /r/ and /l/) always produces the same output. Consider first a series of trials, without any contextual input, but with input to /l/ (denoted $i(l)$) increasing across trials in small steps from 0 to 1.0, while input to /r/ is decreasing correspondingly so that $i(l) + i(r) = 1$. The network is symmetric with respect to /l/ and /r/ in this case and so when $i(l) < i(r)$, $a(l)$ will be less than $a(r)$. So in this case, the network will choose /l/ whenever $i(l) > i(r)$, and will choose /r/ otherwise.

Now consider what would happen with some contextual input $c(a)$, and let us suppose that the contextual input in question favors /r/. Then in this case, when $i(r) = i(l)$, and even when $i(r)$ is slightly less than $i(l)$, $a(r)$ will be greater than $a(l)$, and so the subject will choose /r/. However, as we increase $i(l)$ and correspondingly decrease $i(r)$ there will come a point at which the disparity in the input is enough to overcome the differential effect of the context. At this point, $a(l)$ will be greater than $a(r)$ after settling, and the response chosen would be /l/. A similar argument can be given for another context, $c(b)$, that favors alternative /l/.

In short, when the network itself is deterministic, each context establishes a different cut-point along an axis that represents $i(l)-i(r)$. All values of $i(l)-i(r)$ that are less than this cut-point result in the /l/ response; all those above the cut-point result in /r/. Each different context establishes a different cut-point.

Figure 27.7 shows the distributions of $i(l)-i(r)$ for three different stimulus input conditions with Gaussian noise in the input. The figure also shows three cut-points, one for a context favoring /r/, one for a context favoring /l/, and

2-Choice Model (FLMP)

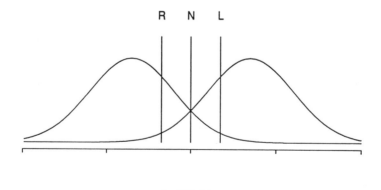

log(I(R)/I(L))

Figure 27.7 Distributions of $i(l)-i(r)$ for two different stimulus input conditions with Gaussian noise in the input, together with cut-points imposed by the interactive activation process for three different contexts. The cut-point labeled R represents a context favoring R; L represents a context favoring L; and N represents a neutral context. Reprinted with permission from McClelland (1991).

one for a neutral context. As the figure illustrates, the effect of context is simply to shift the criterion along the $i(l)-i(r)$ continuum. Now, the z-score of the probability of choosing the $/l/$ response is the distance, in units of the standard deviation of the noise, from the mean value of $i(l)-i(r)$ to the cut-point. Obviously changes in the input $(i(l)-i(r))$ or in the criterion, have independent, additive effects on this distance. Thus the model directly captures Morton's law.

This informal argument showing that the network of figure 27.5 captures Morton's law when variability is introduced in the inputs to an interactive activation network is presented more formally in McClelland (1991). However, for the case where the noise is intrinsic to processing, the result was established by simulation only. A formal derivation of the result was possible if the particular processing assumptions of the interactive activation model were replaced by those of the Boltzmann machine (Hinton and Sejnowski 1986).

The Boltzmann machine is inherently a stochastic and interactive model, but it makes use of binary, rather than graded, activations. Units are updated one at a time in random order, and activations are set to 1 with a probability given by the logistic function of the net input to each unit:

$$p(a_i = 1) = 1/(1 + e^{-net_i/T}).$$

This is the actual sigmoid function shown in figure 27.1: now it is being used to give the probability that the activation is 1, rather than the actual activation of the unit.

For present purposes T, a parameter called temperature, is taken to be a fixed parameter that simply scales the magnitude of the net input. As before, trials are run by presenting input plus context, leaving them on until equilibrium is reached; and then selecting, at some particular time t, the most active member of the alternative set as the network's response. There is one minor complication: In Boltzmann machines, units representing particular alternatives are either on or off; therefore when a choice must be made, a tie is possible. In case of a tie, it is necessary to resample at a later time, repeating until no tie occurs.

The Independence Constraint on Architecture

When the above choice procedure is used, it can be shown that Boltzmann machines (symmetric, stochastic networks using the above binary update function) will conform to Morton's law as long as the network adheres to a particular architectural constraint. This constraint can be stated as follows:

1. The network must be partitionable into three sets of units: one set representing the alternatives, one set representing the stimulus input to the alternatives, and one set representing the context relevant to the alternatives.

2. No connections are allowed between any of the units in the input set and any of the units in the context set. The only interactions among the sets occurs by way of the units representing the alternatives.

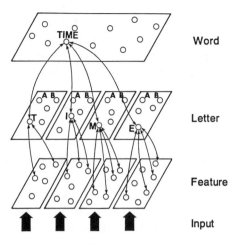

Figure 27.8 Architecture of the interactive activation model. Only selected connections are shown. All units within each enclosed region are mutually inhibitory. Reprinted from McClelland (1985).

The original interactive activation model, as formulated by McClelland and Rumelhart (1981) adhered to this architectural constraint, as shown in figure 27.8 (from McClelland 1985). For example, when the task is to identify the letter in a particular position (say, the second) the letter units in this position become the set representing the alternatives. The input set is the set of feature units for the second position, and the context set is all of the rest of the network, including the feature and letter units for other positions and including the word level units. There are no connections between any of the units in the input set and any of the context units, so the condition holds. Note that the condition holds simultaneously for all four letter positions. The crucial thing about this architectural constraint is that it preserves a kind of independence of the two sources of input. Neither source can influence the other—except by way of the units representing the alternatives. Therefore we will henceforth refer to this constraint as the independence constraint on network architecture, and we will refer to sources of input that are independent in this way as structurally independent.

To summarize, the analysis presented in McClelland (1991) shows that binary stochastic interactive networks that adhere to the independence constraint on architecture also adhere to the independence law of the effect of context on perceptual identification. Simulations suggest that the result holds for graded as well as binary activations.

Some readers may view the result of the analysis presented above as a minor matter, redressing an empirical inadequacy of the interactive activation model. But such a view misses the fact that the analysis actually represents an important advance in our understanding of the possible mechanistic basis of the independence law. This result shows that adherence to the independence law is an inherent characteristic of stochastic interactive networks that respect the architectural constraint. We need not conclude, as Massaro (1989) suggests we should, that data adhering to Morton's independence law requires a strictly feedforward processing system; rather we now can see that an interactive mechanism with the right architecture is consistent with—even bound to produce—independence.

Using the Independence Constraint to Test Claims about Network Architecture

This result also leads to empirical tests that can distinguish between alternative possible network architectures. The independence law should hold, not only between stimulus and context, but more generally between any two sources of input that are structurally independent. Given this, suppose we manipulate two inputs that affect choices among a set of alternatives. If the independence law does not hold, this would establish that these inputs are not structurally independent. In a more agnostic vein, we can just run experiments, manipulating different inputs, and see whether the independence law holds. Note that cases in which the independence law does hold cannot strictly be used to argue for strict structural independence. There may well be structurally dependent architectures that produce close approximations to independence.

The method is analogous to the additive-factors method of Sternberg (1969a,b). According to this method, one manipulates two experimental factors. If they have non-additive effects on mean reaction time, we conclude that they exert their effects on one or more stages of processing in common. In what we will call the structural independence method, one manipulates two sources of input that influence stimulus identification response probabilities. If they have nonindependent effects on the z-transform of the probability of choosing a particular response, then we can conclude that the influences each source exerts on activations of response alternatives are not structurally independent.

If the architecture postulated for the interactive activation model is correct, we may find a failure of independence for effects of two different context letters on the identification of a target letter in a word. In the interactive activation model, the individual letters in the context of a target letter are not structurally independent. Rather, the individual context letters exert their influence on the identification of a target letter by way of a unit at the word level (see fig. 27.8). The nonlinearities in the network mean that they need not in this case have independent effects. This makes it possible for the effects of joint manipulations of context letters to violate independence.

Consider, for concreteness, the choice between the alternatives *I* and *O* for the identity of the middle letter in the following contexts: *L_E W_G L_G W_E*. Here, the lexical constraints are such that *LIE* and *WIG* are words, but *LOE* and *WOG* are not; while *LOG* and *WOE* are words but *LIG* and *WIE* are not. If we look at any one context letter (say, *L*), the constraint it places on the identity of the target letter reverses as we manipulate the identity of the other letter in the context. When the last letter is *E*, initial *L* favors middle *I*; but when the last letter is *G*, initial *L* favors middle *O*. Thus the constraint imposed by one letter in the context is clearly dependent on the identity of the other letter. Now, if each context letter really does exert an independent effect on the identification of the target letter, then we expect no difference in the tendency to choose I in the contexts $W_{-}G$ and $L_{-}E$ compared to the contexts $L_{-}G$ and $W_{-}E$. In other words, we expect no advantage for cases in which the target letter makes a word with the context, compared to cases in which it does not. On the other hand, if, as in the interactive activation model, each letter (target or context) influences activations of word units, and these in turn feed activation back to the letter level, then particular combinations of context letters may have differential effects. A word advantage, then, would support the interactive activation model's claim that the influences of different context letters on target identification are not structurally independent. Movellan and McClelland (n.d.) carried out an experiment to test for nonindependence in this case. Their subjects viewed brief, masked presentations of three-letter strings, and were given a forced-choice between two alternatives for one of the letters. In each case, neither context letter alone favored one alternative over the other, as in the above example; but the two context letters together always formed a word with only one of the two alternatives. If the two context letters were exerting independent effects on the probability of target identification, we should not expect a word advantage; if, however, the effects of the two context letters were not independent, but actually influenced target identification by way of their conjunction at the word level, then a word superiority effect should be obtained. The results confirmed the prediction of the interactive activation model: an accuracy advantage for words relative to nonwords was in fact obtained. The effect was relatively small, but was statistically reliable at the .001 level over both items and subjects.

There are other network architectures besides the one embodied in the interactive activation model. The described experiment does not rule out all alternatives to the architecture of the interactive activation model. But it does place constraints on the architecture, just as interactive effects of two factors on reaction times placed constraints on discrete stage models in Sternberg (1969a,b).

Summary

The present section has described how independent effects of context and stimulus information can arise in a stochastic interactive processing system and has demonstrated that independence need not always hold between different sources of information relevant to a particular identification response. Much remains to be done, of course. One task is to return to the kinds of situations that motivated the interactive activation model in the first place: situations in which context actually facilitates the discrimination of alternative letters (Reicher 1969). Such situations typically involve very brief presentations followed by a masking pattern—conditions in which activations clearly do not reach asymptote. One of the key findings from this paradigm is the discovery that the relative timing of context and stimulus information has a big impact on performance; context must precede or be contemporaneous with the target for facilitation to occur. This and other aspects of the findings from this paradigm were accounted for by the original interactive activation model, and served to substantiate the claim that the phenomena required an account in terms of the detailed time course of information processing. For the present, though, the section has done three things relevant to the goals of the theory. First, it has illustrated how the principles described at the start are consistent with the effects of context and stimulus information on asymptotic choice responses; it has shown that the simple independence law can be an emergent result of processing systems that adhere to these principles; and it has made a first step toward using this result to begin establishing when independence will hold, and when it will not hold.

27.3.2 DYNAMICS OF PROCESSING: MONOTONIC AND NONMONOTONIC TIME-ACCURACY CURVES

This section will present some initial findings on the time-accuracy characteristics of information processing systems that are consistent with the principles of the GRAIN model. The theory is not as well developed for this case as for asymptotic activation; indeed it is generally easier to characterize the equilibrium states of nonlinear systems than it is to understand their time-dependent properties. In the absence of formal mathematical results, it is still possible to get some preliminary understanding of the variation of accuracy as a function of time in networks that adhere to the principles of the GRAIN model.

Wickelgren's Law

As in the previous section, we will consider a simple general regularity that has often been accounted for by simpler models, namely the fact that time-accuracy curves exhibit the shifted exponential form described by Wickelgren's law. Time-accuracy curves with approximately the right form arise naturally from models such as Ratcliff's diffusion model, in which there is a single continuous stochastic process. Such curves also arise when several gradual processes are organized in a feedforward cascade (McClelland 1979). Here we consider the case of multilayer graded, stochastic, processing systems with bidirectional excitatory connections between layers and bidirectional inhibitory connections within each layer.

The first point to note is the importance of distinguishing between propagation of activation and propagation of information in GRAIN networks. Let us think of the information propagation issue as follows. An experimenter selects one of n stimuli, and the subject's task is to indicate which it was through one of n corresponding responses. The stimulus is presented to the input layer of a multilayer GRAIN net, and begins a stochastic process of activation and inhibition that proceeds forward in time. For the sake of simplicity, we will consider a particular case in which there is one unit at each level corresponding

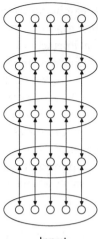

Input

Figure 27.9 A simple five-layer GRAIN network used for exploring accumulation of information and RT distribution properties of GRAIN networks. Lines indicate bidirectional connections between levels; all units within each oval are mutually inhibitory.

to each stimulus, and we will assume that stimulus identification responses might be generated from any level at any time by selecting the most active unit at that level as the response. The propagation of information then consists of a gradual change in the sensitivity (d') of the response choice at each successive level to the actual identity of the stimulus presented as input. Simulations of d' as a function of time were carried out using the network of figure 27.9. In this network, there are five levels, each with five units. Units at each level have bidirectional excitatory connections with corresponding units at the next level. Within each level, there are bidirectional inhibitory connections among all the units. The details of the simulation follow, since they are not reported elsewhere. Each trial began with all activations set to 0, and was followed by 200 initialization cycles, with no external input. Stimulus onset then occurred. This consisted of applying external input of 3.0 to the middle unit at the input level. Processing continued for 2000 cycles. On each cycle, net input to each unit was first computed, then all activations were updated. The net input consisted of a fixed negative bias of -3.0, external input if any, a sample of Gaussian noise with mean 0 and standard deviation 1.0, and the summed input from all other units. Between level excitatory weights were 5.0; within level inhibitory weights were -1.5. The activation of each unit was then incremented by an amount equal to $k_l(\text{logistic}(net) - act)$, where k_l represents a rate constant for all the units at a particular level, net represents the net input and act represents the activation of the unit from the previous time step.

In calculating d', we need to know the hit rate, or the probability that the correct alternative is the most active at each level at each time step. This is calculated simply by keeping a tally over many repeated trials. We also need a false alarm rate, which would ordinarily be the probability that the middle alternative is active when some other input is presented. Due to the fact that parameters are equivalent for all alternatives, the probability that the middle alternative would be most active when some other alternative is shown is equal to the probability that some other alternative is most active when the middle alternative is shown. So the false alarm rate was estimated from this latter probability.

The results of two simulation runs of 5000 trials each using the network of figure 27.9 are shown in figure 27.10. What we see in each case is that, even though activation flows both ways in this network, information in the sense of sensitivity to the stimulus propagates from the input forward. Each successive level exhibits a shifting and slowing of the growth of d', in approximate conformity to the cascade model. When all the levels have the same rate constant, the cascade model produces time-accuracy curves that converge to a sigmoid as more and more levels are added. The same thing happens in the GRAIN network, as shown in the upper panel, where the rate constant, k_l is set to 0.15 for all levels.

There are some differences between the behavior of GRAIN networks and the behavior of the cascade model. In the cascade model, when the rate constant of one level is slowed, it affects the time course of processing at that level and all subsequent levels. In the case where one level has a slower rate constant than all the others, the time-accuracy curves generated by the cascade model have a clear shifted exponential shape, with the slowest rate constant determining the rate constant of the curve, and the other rate constants determining merely the shift of the takeoff point (McClelland 1979). In the present GRAIN network, on the other hand, when the rate constant of one level is slowed relative to the rate constants of the others, the effect spreads throughout the network, and the results are difficult to distinguish from the case in which all of the levels have the same rate constants. This is seen in the lower panel of figure 27.10, where the rate constant of the third level is set to the slow value of 0.05, while the rate constants of all of the other levels are set to 0.30. In a cascade model these values would produce a very clearly marked change in the rate of rise of the third curve; the fourth and fifth curves would look almost exactly like the third, but just successively shifted over.

This simulation shows, then, that the conformity of the GRAIN model to Wickelgren's law is somewhat less exact than its conformity to Morton's law. The time-accuracy curves are not strictly or even closely shifted exponentials but are perhaps better described as slightly skewed sigmoids. Even so, the curves do obey the general qualitative form of the empirical findings. Accuracy starts at chance and, after a flat period, makes a transition to a relatively steep, then negatively accelerating, approach to asymptote. Whether the exact form of empirical time-accuracy curves is consistent with this pattern is not completely clear at this time. Furthermore, it seems quite possible that interactivity may not hold between perceptual and response selection processes. In that case, if response selection is a rate-limiting process, the overall resulting time-accuracy curve would look indistinguishable from the curves generated by the cascade model and would closely approximate Wickelgren's law.

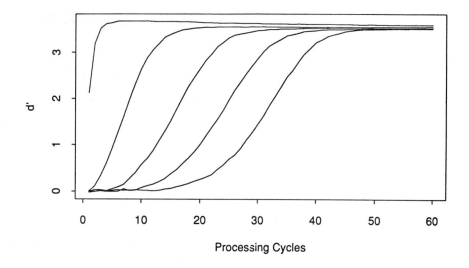

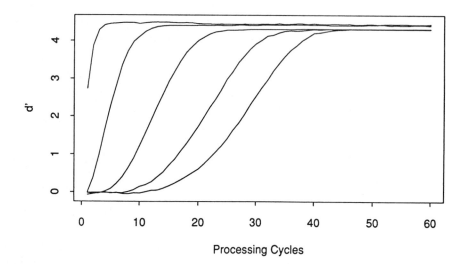

Figure 27.10 The buildup of sensitivity to the input at successive levels in the GRAIN network shown in figure 27.9, for four different values of the parameter lambda. Note that the same value of lambda applies to all of the units in the network in these simulations. Each panel shows d' at the first, second, third, fourth, and fifth level of the processing system shown in figure 27.9. In all cases the curves for successively deeper levels arrange themselves from left to right.

While GRAIN models can conform to the general form of Wickelgren's law, there are circumstances in which they will not. One factor that appears to be important is resting activation level, as determined in this case by the bias in the net input. A large negative bias is required, so that resting activations tend to be quite low, or else the network will exhibit a tendency to become relatively committed to a spurious pattern of activation prior to stimulus presentation. In such cases, information can propagate extremely slowly through the system, and the time-accuracy curves have a rather different shape.

Even when parameters are such that information propagates promptly through the system, a Wickelgren-like shape to time-accuracy curves is not strictly ensured; indeed, the curve need not even by monotonic, as will be seen below. A statement of the conditions under which approximate conformity to an exponential approach to asymptote can be obtained is beyond the reach of the present analysis. However it is possible to offer one observation concerning conditions that may lead to violations of monotonicity. The observation is simply that time-accuracy curves may fail to be monotonic when the ordering of expected values of asymptotic activations of units would be different without lateral inhibition than with lateral inhibition. In the simulation reported below, lateral inhibition does change the ordering of expected values of asymptotic activations of response units in one experimental condition, and a U-shaped time-accuracy curve is obtained.

A U-shaped Time-Accuracy Curve

It is one thing to know that a process model adhering to a set of principles can account for data that exhibit a general regularity. This state of affairs allows us to suppose that the principles in question may in fact be part of a useful description of the underlying processes. But the question arises, what does the process model buy us, if we already have a general law that we can refer to that correctly characterizes the outcomes of experiments? One answer to this question is that it may allow us to give straightforward accounts for results obtained in cases where existing data actually violates the general regularities.

Such a case is provided by the interesting experiment of Gratton et al. (1988). In this experiment, subjects viewed target letters flanked by two letters on each side. The task was to indicate whether the target was S or H. The two targets (S and H) could be flanked either by the congruent letter (as in SSSSS and HHHHH) or by the other letter (SSHSS and HHSHH). Subjects were induced to respond so quickly that they produced about 15 percent errors over all. When Gratton et al. looked at accuracy in the two conditions, conditional on response time, they found a Wickelgren-like conditional accuracy function in the congruent condition, but a U-shaped curve in the incongruent condition. The results are shown in figure 27.11 (top). The conditional accuracy functions are shown along with the distribution of response times by bin, for each condition. (Actually the graph shows time and accuracy for electromyographically detected muscle activity that precedes the response. The actual RT data

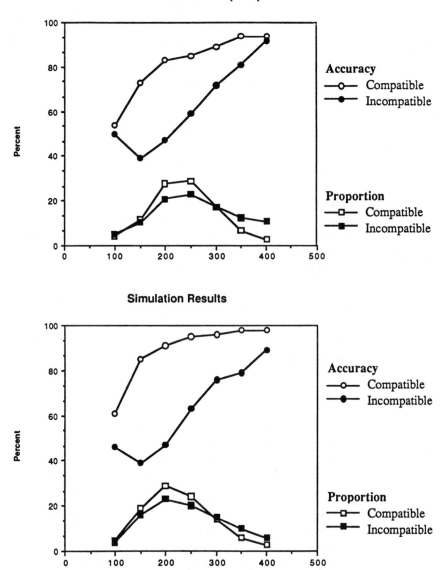

EMG Data from Gratton et al. (1988)

Simulation Results

Figure 27.11 Data and simulation of Gratton et al. (1988). RTs are actually time from stimulus onset to the detection of electromyogram (EMG) activity in the muscles innervating the executed response, though actual RTs show the same effects. The top panel represents the experimental data; the bottom panel represents the results of the simulation. Within each panel, the top two curves represent accuracy in each time interval; the bottom two curves represent the proportion of trials falling in each bin. Reprinted with permission from Cohen, Servan-Schreiber, and McClelland (1992).

looks much the same, except that all times are somewhat longer). Gratton et al. interpreted their results in the following way. They suggested that there are two letter identification pathways, one, which is fast, for identification of letters without regard to position; and another, slower one, for position-specific identification. Their idea was that the fast pathway will report the predominant identity present in the display, and this will lead to the dip if a response is initiated before target-specific information arrives from the position-specific pathway.

The GRAIN framework provides us with an opportunity to propose an alternative interpretation. In accord with the observation made at the end of the preceding section, it can be proposed that the U-shaped curve reflects the resolution of a competition process driven by mutual inhibition. Servan-Schreiber (1990) has developed a GRAIN model that captures this notion and provides a nice account of the pattern of data obtained in the experiment.

The model begins with the idea, common to many recent connectionist models of spatial attention (e.g., Cohen, Dunbar, and McClelland 1990; Phaf, van der Heiden, and Hudson 1990; Mozer 1991; LaBerge and Brown 1989) that attention serves to prime feature detectors for attended locations. This gives the detectors for the attended location a very slight initial advantage over detectors in other locations. Early in processing, features in the target location have only a slight advantage over features in non-target locations, allowing them to conspire against the target in incongruent displays. Mutual competition then causes this initial advantage to become accentuated as the detectors become activated by the stimulus.

The network Servan-Schreiber used to capture these ideas consists of three pools of units: A pool consisting of position-specific feature analyzer units (for features of letters in each of three positions), an output layer consisting of a response unit for each alternative, and an attention layer consisting of position-specific attention-to-location units (see fig. 27.12). While Gratton et al. used a target with two flankers on each side, the flanker effect can be captured easily enough with only one, for a total of three display positions. So there are only three positional attentional units (for left, center, and right locations). In the feature pool, there are feature analyzers for features of S and H in each position; for simplicity only one S-feature unit and one H-feature unit is included for each position. Within each pool, units are mutually inhibitory. Between pools, there are mutually excitatory connections between S features and the S output unit, and between H features and the H output unit. There are also mutually excitatory connections between the attentional unit for a particular position and the units for features in the corresponding position. A response is recorded as soon as one of the output units reaches a fixed threshold.

Consider, now, what happens when a display is presented containing an H flanked by an S on each side. Attention to the center position is implemented by external input to the position-specific attention unit for the target location. This input is turned on and the network is allowed to stabilize before the trial begins. During stabilization, some activation spreads to the corresponding

Toward a Theory of Information Processing

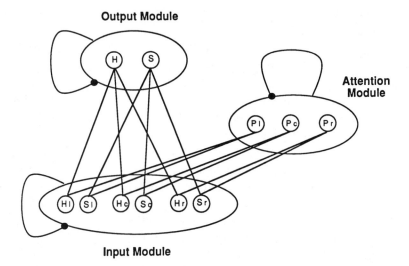

Figure 27.12 Network used to simulate the U-shaped time-accuracy curve of Gratton et al. (1988).

position-specific feature units, giving the detector for the features in the target location a very slight advantage over features in other positions. This slight advantage is maintained when the target is presented. However, since there are two nontargets but only one target, the aggregate activation for S features is almost twice as great as the aggregate activation for H features. Without mutual competition, this state of affairs would persist indefinitely in this network. But with mutual competition, the target features gradually gain the upper hand over the features of the nontargets. This happens because the features of each letter are in competition with the features of each other letter, and because of the slight initial advantage for the target features due to top-down activation from attention. The ability of items with a slight initial advantage to win out over a number of competing alternatives was examined by McClelland and Rumelhart (1981); in that model it allowed words with a very small advantage in resting activation level (due to higher frequency) to win out over other words of lower frequency.

The simulation results are shown below the data from Gratton et al. in figure 27.11. The simulation of the compatible condition follows the conventional gradual approach to asymptote, as found by Gratton et al. In the incompatible condition, the curve follows the U-shaped pattern seen in the empirical data. This occurs, not because of separate pathways for position-dependent and position-independent information, but because of an interactive activation and competition process that initially favors the flankers due to their greater number but eventually favors the letter in the attended position.

The simulation also captures several other aspects of the Gratton et al. data. One of these is the general shape of the reaction-time distributions found in each condition of the experiment (see fig. 27.11), and the effect of compatibility on these distributions. Another is a fact that emerged from the analysis by

Gratton et al. of ERP (event-related potential) data recorded from subjects in their experiment. They recorded ERPs over the motor area contralateral to each responding hand as well as EMGs in the muscles governing each response, and found that responses appeared to be triggered when the difference in the evoked response over the two motor cortices reached a particular threshold value. Even though the simulations of Servan-Schreiber (1991) actually used a fixed threshold, rather than a difference signal, to trigger the response, it turned out that the difference in activation of the two response units at the time the response was triggered exhibited the same constant difference that Gratton et al. found in their ERP data.

Let us now consider how the various principles of the GRAIN model contribute to the account for the data. Competitive inhibition at the position-specific feature level plays a crucial role in producing the U-shaped form of the time-accuracy curve in the incompatible condition, as already explained. A feature of competitive inhibition is that it only comes into effect after some initial activation; it is this initial activation that actually gives rise to the dip in the curve, and the competitive inhibition that ultimately results in the correct response dominating performance, correcting the dip. Competitive inhibition at the response level plays a role in another aspect of the model, as well. It causes a fixed activation threshold to actually correspond to a fixed difference in activation between the two alternatives. Both of these effects of competitive inhibition are, however, dependent on graded and gradual propagation of activation. Graded and gradual propagation allow the summed influences of the flankers to initially govern the preferred response, while also allowing the balance to swing gradually back in favor of the correct alternative as processing continues. Indeed, Coles (1989) argues that aspects of the findings of Gratton et al. actually demonstrate the propagation of graded information.

Intrinsic variability also plays an important enabling role. This variability has the effect of causing variability in the activation of response units at stimulus onset, and in the subsequent activation process. (Variability at time of onset may be crucial in the present simulations, since it alone would be sufficient to produce a broad distribution of reaction times.) The U-shaped time-accuracy curves arise primarily from trials in which the incorrect alternative happens to be relatively more active at the time of stimulus onset so that the slight early activation advantage of the incorrect alternative pushes the incorrect alternative over the threshold.

We have seen, then, that the model relies on competition, graded and gradual propagation of activation, and on variability. On the other hand, interactivity does not appear to contribute importantly to the account of the data. Servan-Schreiber (verbal communication, 1991) has found that in fact the data can be fit quite well in a network with only unidirectional connections between levels (input and position specific locations to position-specific features, position-specific features to responses). Interactivity is perfectly compatible with the findings, and there are many reasons to favor an interactive account of attention and perception (Cohen et al. in press), but this particular feature of GRAIN models appears not to be crucial in this case.

Summary

This second case study indicates, once again, some progress on each of the three goals of theory development. First, we have seen how the principles of GRAIN can begin to offer an account for aspects of data obtained within the time-accuracy paradigm. Second, we have seen how relatively complex processing systems (i.e. with as many as five levels) can in some cases give rise to time-accuracy curves that conform approximately to a simple general law, in this case Wickelgren's law. Correspondingly we have seen in another case how GRAIN provides a framework for understanding one particular case in which this simple general law breaks down. In the case in point, GRAIN appears to provide a fairly natural and direct account, without requiring that responses be based at different times on the output of different processing systems. Third, some small steps have been taken toward an understanding of which of the principles are responsible for the simulation of the experimental results, and which are merely compatible with them.

While these results are suggestive, it should be clear that we are far from a full account of the relation between GRAIN networks and time-accuracy curves. It is far from clear, for example whether the forms of typical empirical time-accuracy curves are really more accurately described by Wickelgren's shifted exponentials than by GRAIN's skewed sigmoids. Nor is it clear in any detail what conditions will lead even to monotonicity, and what conditions will produce U-shaped time-accuracy curves. These issues are among those that must be addressed, if the theory is to be advanced beyond its present suggestive but preliminary state.

27.4 DISCUSSION

Obviously, the initial steps taken here leave us far from a complete theory of the asymptotics and dynamics of information processing. Of the three information-processing paradigms that the theory is intended to unify, only two (the asymptotic accuracy paradigm and the time-accuracy paradigm) have really been considered at all. Analytic results are available only for asymptotic accuracy. Nevertheless we can begin to see three contributions emerging from these preliminary explorations.

First, this research has already begun to help us to see how general regularities of human performance data might arise as emergent properties of networks of simple computing elements that adhere to the principles of GRAIN. Morton's independence law and Wickelgren's characterization of time-accuracy curves are cases in point. As such, the work is a first step toward understanding how the mass of processing activity triggered by the presentation of a stimulus gives rise to the simple and regular outcomes that are typically observed in behavior.

Second, the work begins to give us ways of predicting violations of these simple regularities (in the case of the proposed test of nonindependent effects of context letters), and of providing a basis for accounting for observed deviations from typical outcomes (as in the case of the Gratton et al. U-shaped time-accuracy curves). Thus the theory allows a significant advance in our understanding beyond the simple statement of the regularities themselves.

Third, this research begins to provide a unification of the disparate literatures on the dynamics of information processing on the one hand and of the effects of context on asymptotic choice performance on the other. In this regard it may be worth noting that such a unification seems to be possible only because a common set of principles is used in both cases. Many models of asymptotic choice behavior use time-independent functions of graded variables (e.g., strengths), while many models of the time course of processing use time-dependent functions of discrete variables (e.g., subprocess X is or is not complete by time t). Of course, the present framework is not the first to consider the propagation of graded information; the point here is only that this may well be a necessary, though surely not a sufficient, condition for unifying the analysis of the dynamics and the asymptotics of information processing.

Next Steps for Experimental Research

If the unification of these disparate literatures is to be complete, and if the exploration of the detailed dynamics of processing is to be taken further, it will become necessary to conduct a greater number of studies exploring the time course of processing. Up to now relatively few such studies have been produced. One reason for this has been the apparent difficulty of collecting time-accuracy data. It may be, however, that the difficulty of time-accuracy studies is more apparent than real. In the author's laboratory we have recently been able to replicate the Gratton et al. study, complete with a dip below chance in the incongruent condition, in an experiment in which each of ten unpracticed subjects came into the lab and performed in 800 trials (400 per condition) in less than 45 minutes. The method is very simple. The subject is instructed to go as fast as possible, and is rewarded for fast correct responses (a penny for each RT less than 300 ms). RTs range from less than 100 to more than 500 ms, with the bulk between 150 and 400, which spans the dip in the Gratton et al. curve.

Given the simplicity of the method, it seems likely that it is feasible to trace more thoroughly than has typically been done in the past the relation between time since stimulus onset and response accuracy. If so, this should help us to see whether the GRAIN model, some refinement of it, or some completely different kind of account, ends up providing the best characterization of the time course and the outcome of information processing.

NOTES

The work reported here was supported by a NIMH Career Development Award MH-00385. Thanks for valuable comments on earlier drafts of this article are due to the editors, to two anonymous reviewers, and to Jonathan Cohen, Javier Movellan, and Leigh Nystrom. Address correspondence concerning this manuscript to the author at Department of Psychology, Carnegie-Mellon University, Pittsburgh, PA.

1. There is now a considerable body of work on learning rules that operate by making symmetric adjustments to training weights. Such networks may be initialized with non-symmetric weights, which are naturally symmetrized in the course of training (Hinton 1989; see Hertz, Krogh, and Palmer 1990 for a discussion of this issue). In practice it is generally found that it is not even strictly necessary for every unit to be connected to every other unit; networks that use distributed representations come to behave as though they were fully symmetric, even when the symmetry is not maintained on a unit-by-unit level.

2. Technically, this property holds only when the network is both Markovian (so that the next state depends only on the preceding state) and ergodic (so that every state can be reached from every other state.) GRAIN networks have both of these properties.

REFERENCES

Anderson, James A. (1991). Why, having so many neurons, do we have so few thoughts? In W. E. Hockley and S. Lewandowsky (Eds.), *Relating theory and data*. Hillsdale, NJ: Erlbaum.

Cohen, J. D., Dunbar, K., and McClelland, J. L. (1990). On the control of automatic processes: A parallel distributed processing account of the Stroop effect. *Psychological Review, 97*, 332–361

Cohen, J. D., Servan-Schreiber, D., and McClelland, J. L. (1992). A parallel distributed processing approach to automaticity. *American Journal of Psychology, 105*, 239–269.

Coles, Michael G. H. (1989). Modern mind-brain reading: psychophysiology, physiology, and cognition. *Psychophysiology, 26*, 251–269.

Cox, D. R., and Miller, H. D. (1965). *The theory of stochastic processes*. New York: Wiley

Elman, J. L., and McClelland, J. L. (1988). Cognitive penetration of the mechanisms of perception: Compensation for coarticulation of lexically restored phonemes. *Journal of Memory and Language, 27*, 143–165.

Feldman, J. A. and Ballard, D. H. (1982). Connectionist models and their properties. *Cognitive Science, 6*, 205–254.

Gratton, G., Coles, M. H., Sirevaag, E. J., Eriksen, C. W., and Donchin, E. (1988). Pre- and poststimulus activation of response channels: A psychophysiological analysis. *Journal of Experimental Psychology: Human Perception and Performance, 14*, 331–344.

Grossberg, S. (1976). Adaptive pattern classification and universal recoding: Part 1. Parallel development and coding of neural feature detectors. *Biological Cybernetics, 23*, 121–134.

Grossberg, S. (1978a). A theory of human memory: Self-organization and performance of sensory motor codes, maps and plans. In R. Rosen and F. Snell (Eds.), *Progress in theoretical biology*. Vol. 5, 233–374. New York: Academic Press.

Grossberg, S. (1978b). A theory of visual coding, memory, and development. In E. L. J. Leeuwenberg and H. F. J. M. Buffart (Eds.), *Formal theories of visual perception*. New York: Wiley.

Hertz, J. Krogh, A., and Palmer, R. (1990). *Introduction to the theory of neural computation*. Redwood City, CA: Addison-Wesley.

Hinton, G. E. (1989). Deterministic Boltzmann learning performs steepest descent in weight-space. *Neural Computation, 1*, 143–150.

Hinton, G. E., McClelland, J. L., and Rumelhart, D. E. (1986). Distributed representations. In D. E. Rumelhart, J. L. McClelland and the PDP research group (Eds.), *Parallel distributed processing: Explorations in the microstructures of cognition*. Cambridge, MA: MIT Press.

Hinton, G. E., and Sejnowski, T. J. (1986). Learning and relearning in Boltzmann machines. In D. E. Rumelhart, J. L. McClelland and the PDP research group (Eds.), *Parallel distributed processing: Explorations in the microstructure of cognition*. Vol. 1, *The PDP perspective*. Cambridge, MA: MIT Press.

Hopfield, J. J. (1982). Neural networks and physical systems with emergent collective computational abilities. *Proceedings of the National Academy of Sciences, USA, 79*, 2554–2558.

LaBerge, D., and Brown, V. (1989). Theory of attentional operations in shape identification. *Psychological Review, 96*, 101–124.

Lappin J. S. and Disch, K. (1973). The latency operating characteristic: 11. Effects of visual stimulus intensity on choice reaction time. *Journal of Experimental Psychology, 93*, 367–372.

Luce, R. D. (1959). *Individual choice behavior*. New York: Wiley.

Luce, R. D. (1986). *Response times*. New York: Oxford University Press.

McClelland, J. L. (1979). On the time relations of mental processes: An examination of systems of processes in cascade. *Psychological Review, 86*, 287–330.

McClelland, J. L. (1985). Putting knowledge in its place: A scheme for programming parallel processing structures on the fly. *Cognitive Science, 9*, 113–146.

McClelland, J. L. (1991). Stochastic interactive processes and the effect of context on perception. *Cognitive Psychology, 23*, 1–44.

McClelland, J. L., and O'Regan, J. K. (1981). Expectations increase the benefit derived from parafoveal visual information in reading words aloud. *Journal of Experimental Psychology: Human Perception and Performance, 7*, 634–644.

McClelland, J. L., and Rumelhart, D. E. (1981). An interactive activation model of context effects in letter perception, Part I: An account of basic findings. *Psychological Review, 88*, 375–407.

McClelland, J. L., and Rumelhart, D. E. (1985). Distributed memory and the representation of general and specific information. *Journal of Experimental Psychology: General, 114*, 159–188.

McClelland, J. L., and Rumelhart, D. E. (1988). *Explorations in parallel distributed processing. A handbook of models, programs, and exercises*. Cambridge, MA: MIT Press.

MacWhinney, B. (1987). The competition model. In B. MacWhinney (Ed), *Mechanisms of language acquisition*. Hillsdale, NJ: Erlbaum.

Massaro, D. W. (1989). Testing between the TRACE model and the fuzzy logical model of speech perception. *Cognitive Psychology, 21*, 398–421.

Minsky, M., and Pappert, S. (1969). *Perceptrons: An introduction to computational geometry*. Cambridge, MA: MIT Press.

Morton J. (1969). Interaction of information in word recognition. *Psychological Review, 76*, 165–178.

Movellan, J., and McClelland, J. L. (1991). Learning continuous probability distributions with the contrastive Hebbian algorithm. *Technical Report PDP-CNS-92-2*, Department of Psychology, Carnegie-Mellon University.

Movellan, J., and McClelland, J. L. (N.d.). Theoretical and empirical consequences of the stochastic interactive activation model. Unpublished.

Mozer, M. C. (1991). *The perception of multiple objects: A connectionist approach*. Cambridge, MA: MIT Press.

Newell, A. (1973) . You can't play 20 questions with nature and win: Projective comments on the papers of this symposium. In W. G. Chase (Ed.), *Visual information processing*. New York: Academic Press.

Newell, A. (1990). Metaphor for mind, theories of mind, should the humanities mind? In J. Sheehan and M. Sosna (Eds.), *Boundaries of humanity: Humans, animals and machines*. Berkeley, CA: University of California Press.

Oden, G. C., and Massaro, D. W. (1978). Integration of featural information in speech perception. *Psychological Review, 85*, 172–191.

Pachella, R. (1974). The interpretation of reaction time in information processing research. In B. Kantowitz (Ed.), *Human information processing: Tutorials in performance and cognition*. New York: Halstead.

Phaf, R. H., van der Heijden, A. H. C., and Hudson, P. T. W. (1990). SLAM: A connectionist model for attention in visual selection tasks. *Cognitive Psychology, 22*, 273–341.

Ratcliff, R. (1978). A theory of memory retrieval. *Psychological Review, 85*, 59–108

Reicher, G. M. (1969). Perceptual recognition as a function of meaningfulness of stimulus material. *Journal of Experimental Psychology, 81*, 274–280.

Rumelhart, D. E. (1977). Understanding and summarizing brief stories. In D. LaBerge and S. J. Samuels (Eds.), *Basic processes in reading: Perception and comprehension*, 265–303. Hillsdale, NJ: Erlbaum.

Rumelhart, D. E., Hinton, G. E., and McClelland, J. L. (1986). A general framework for parallel distributed processing. In D. E. Rumelhart, J. L. McClelland, and the PDP research group (Eds.), *Parallel distributed processing: Explorations in the microstructures of cognition*. Vol. 1, *Biological mechanisms*. Cambridge, MA: MIT Press.

Rumelhart, D. E., and McClelland, J. L. (1981). Interactive processing through spreading activation. In C. Perfetti and A. Lesgold (Eds.), *Interactive processes in reading*. Hillsdale, NJ: Erlbaum.

Rumelhart, D. E., and McClelland, J. L. (1982). An interactive activation model of context effects in letter perception. Part II: The contextual enhancement effect and some tests and extensions of the model. *Psychological Review, 89*, 60–94.

Rumelhart, D. E., Smolensky, P., McClelland, J. L., and Hinton, G. E. (1986). Schemata and sequential thought processes in PDP models. In D. E. Rumelhart, J. L. McClelland, and the PDP research group (Eds.), *Parallel distributed processing: Explorations in the microstructure of cognition*. Vol. 1, *Foundations*. Cambridge, MA: MIT Press.

Servan-Schreiber, D. (1990). From physiology to behavior: Computational models of catecholamine modulation of information processing (Ph.D. thesis). *Technical Report CMU-CS-90-167*, School of Computer Science, Carnegie-Mellon University.

Smolensky, P. (1986). Neural and conceptual interpretation of PDP models. In D. E. Rumelhart, J. L. McClelland, and the PDP research group (eds.), *Parallel distributed processing: Explorations in the microstructure of cognition*. Vol. 2, Psychological and Biological models. Cambridge, MA: MIT Press.

Sternberg, S. (1969a). The discovery of processing stages: Extensions of Donders' method. In W. G. Koster (Ed.), *Attention and performance*. Vol. 2. Amsterdam: North-Holland.

Sternberg, S. (1969b). Memory-scanning: Mental processes revealed by reaction time experiments. *American Scientist, 57*, 421–457.

Wickelgren, W. A. (1977). Speed accuracy tradeoff and information processing dynamics. *Acta Psychologica, 41*, 67–85.

Williams, R. J. (1986). The logic of activation functions. In D. E. Rumelhart, J. L. McClelland, and the PDP research group (Eds.), *Parallel distributed processing: Explorations in the microstructure of cognition*. Vol. 1, *Foundations*. Cambridge, MA: MIT Press.

28 Performance Theory and Measurement through Chronometric Analysis

Andries F. Sanders

28.1 RT: SCOPE AND LIMITATIONS

A discussion of chronometric analysis as a tool for measuring human performance might well start by delineating scope and limitations. In my view there are two essential points. First, reaction time (RT), or any of its related measures—for example, interresponse times, electrophysiological latency measures, duration of eye fixations, but also measures of timing and anticipation—is foremost a dependent variable. This may sound trivial, but is worth noting since RT has been often viewed as a research area in its own right. As a dependent variable, RT requires a well-defined starting and stopping point, or in other words, a well-defined stimulus and response in the broad sense of the word. Even if these conditions are met, there are some remaining measurement problems, (Pachella 1974), however, most of them seem technical rather than substantive.

Second, RT is seldom interesting when its value exceeds, say, two seconds. This relates to the major rationale for studying RT, which is to identify a set of elementary operations that characterize human information processing (Posner and McLeod 1982). The hope is that RT reflects a finite set of processes with some invariant properties. In fact this has been the main rationale for studying RT in its own right, and in this respect RT differs from error proportion as a dependent variable. The main difference between RT and error proportion is that the calculation of a proportion requires a number of trials instead of a single trial. In addition, errors do not delineate a set of processes but indicate that something went wrong in the course of processing.

It remains legitimate to ask whether analysis of mental processes through time measurement is at all possible. Perhaps it is as far-fetched as attempting to reconstruct parts of a computer program on the basis of changes in the duration of its operations, dependent on what the program must do. Yet, the best opportunities for such a reconstruction may be when a "program" is relatively small and not very time consuming. In that case there may be hope that the effects of experimental variables on processing time are sufficiently isolated to allow some inferences to be made about what is going on.

Together these limitations on RT imply that chronometric analysis is always tied to speeded performance in some type of S-R setting. To what extent does this exclude relevant aspects of cognitive processing? Some investigators do not see a potential problem here, witness for instance Hofstadter's (1981) view that "everything of interest in cognition happens below the 100 ms level—the time to recognize your mother." If this merely meant to say that mental processes are characterized by high-speed processing in the brain, I might perhaps endorse this view. But however valid it may be for individual processes, it remains quite questionable whether high speed is also typical for higher-level organization and control of information flow, and that might well be the most relevant cognitive aspect of a reaction process. Thus, legitimate doubts have been expressed about the relevance of RT studies, which are invariably conducted in elementary laboratory tasks, to descriptions of cognitive processing in the "richness of reality" (Allport 1980; Newell 1974).

Rather than speculating on this relevance, I tend to consider it as a major issue for research. Current computer techniques make it possible to simulate various real-life tasks in great detail and to record relevant output measures (see Sanders 1991 for a review). A great challenge for performance theory in the next few decades may well be to determine the extent to which theoretical descriptions based on studies in simple conditions hold in more complex conditions. It is important to distinguish between those that are relatively invariant over a wide range of complexity, and those that are limited to a relatively narrow range. In the case of the latter it is important to know *why* the range is so limited. A good example of research specifically aimed at addressing such questions is the "space fortress" project (Donchin, Fabiani, and Sanders 1989) in which subjects acquired the skill of playing a complex, specially constructed video game, the various actions of which combined elements of popular performance paradigms, like visual discrimination, visual search, memory search, emitting two responses in rapid succession, tracking, and strategic resource management by way of costs and benefits.

Like all techniques, chronometric analysis has its limitations. However, an a priori depreciation would be unwise. The observation that about 40 percent of the articles published in the *JEP-Human Perception and Performance* have used measures of RT (Meyer et al. 1988) attests to the value of the technique. Yet, it is experimental ingenuity together with an appropriate conceptual framework that determines what can ultimately be achieved. The framework defines the issues of major interest; experimental ingenuity is what develops the issues in greater detail.

28.2 THE INFORMATION-PROCESSING APPROACH

Without question, the information-processing approach to human performance—initiated by investigators like Garner, Broadbent, and Fitts during the 1950s—has served as the major framework during the last forty years. A large stream of research themes has emerged from this approach, some of which are discussed by Schweickert in detail, namely, models of RT; double stimulation; memory search; additive-factor techniques, including Schweickert's own important elaborations (Schweickert 1984, 1989), and the related issue of reaction processes, either by way of discrete linear stages, by way of continuous flow, or by way of utilizing partial discrete stage outputs (e.g., Miller 1988; Sanders 1990). Additional current issues of interest concern speed-accuracy trade-off (Meyer et al. 1988) and processes involved in same-different judgments, (e.g., Farell 1985). In the context of the latter the matching technique, as developed by Posner and associates (1978), has perhaps been especially fruitful.

Despite the considerable impact of the conceptual aspects of information theory, Schweickert correctly mentions the highly limited impact of the original serial dichotomization model of choice reaction time (Hick 1952), the only model that was really based on information theory. It was soon superseded by a host of other mathematical descriptions, among them accumulation, horse race, random walk, and stochastic diffusion. Some of these are briefly sketched, while, of course, reference is made to Luce's monumental book (Luce 1986).

Luce and Schweickert are both theoreticians, and I am an experimenter. I, therefore, recognize my bias when I express my doubts about the future of those mathematical models that do not, or at least do not effectively, lead to a program of experimental research. Mathematical models that are only designed to deal with existing data usually do not satisfy this criterion and, at least in my opinion, are liable to gradually fade away. A real problem arises when theoreticians and experimenters ignore or only selectively use each other's contributions. I myself became painfully aware of my shortcomings in this respect when I realized that in my recent review (Sanders 1990), I had ignored Schweickert's important elaborations of the additive-factors method of analyzing RT. Perhaps experimenters and theoreticians—this combination in one person seems rare—can only be really productive when working in close cooperation.

A problem of some mathematical models is that RT is treated as if, with the exception of peripheral afferent and efferent conduction, it reflected a single process. Thus, it is not unusual to find descriptions of RT as a process of information accrual that stops when some criterion is exceeded, without any specification of what "information" actually refers to—it is "uneventful" in Schweickert's words. In a similar vein, some continuous-flow models simply distinguish between stimulus evaluation and response processing (Eriksen and Schultz 1979). The major conceptual alternative is embodied in the processing stage approach (Donders 1868; Sternberg 1969), which defends the position that RT is composed of a set of processing stages, each of which requires a distinct theoretical analysis. One stage, commonly termed "memory search," has been the subject of a great deal of research, which is well summarized by Schweickert (chap. 23). In comparison the analysis of most other stages has been almost fully neglected, and this asks for considerable future research. Mathematical models, originally meant to cover the complete process, may well be proved valuable as characteristic of a single stage. I could mention random walk and accumulation models of choice RT. These are usually formulated in terms of acquisition of the relative perceptual evidence favoring the various response alternatives. In fact, they may be inappropriate as a characteristic for perceptual processing (Sanders and Rath, 1991), but might do well in modeling response selection.

28.3 THE AFM AND THE ISSUE OF DISCRETE VERSUS CONTINUOUS PROCESSING

Since Sternberg's (1969) publication, the additive-factor method (AFM) and its basic tenets of linear unidimensional stages with complete and constant stage output have been controversial. However, evoking controversy is better than neglect. The coin may have two sides: one side is that the AFM has been quite successful in that its application has delivered a generally consistent and robust picture (see Van Duren and Sanders 1988 for a recent example). There are exceptions but, usually, these can be reasonably argued (Sanders 1990). The other side is reflected in Schweickert's discussion of the various doubts that have been raised about the validity of the original assumptions of the AFM. The question whether a stimulus is discretely or continuously processed evolved from the debate about applying the AFM to choice reactions, and has become a lively research topic in its own right.

There are at least two issues at stake. The first concerns the extent to which an interpretation of choice reactions along the lines of the AFM really requires discrete processing in all respects. Miller (1988) has argued that this is only so for transmission between stages but neither for the transformation within a stage nor for the output code of a stage. In contrast, I have argued that a constant stage output is the only real constraint of the AFM, which is best guaranteed by a discrete output code. I will obviously not deny that discrete transmission between stages strengthens the case (Sanders 1990). Yet, McClelland's (1979) simulations suggested that, for all practical purposes, processes in cascade allow an AFM interpretation of additive and interactive effects of experimental variables. The main constraint for an AFM interpretation proved to be that, provided a response criterion within reasonable limits, the asymptotic values of the processes were not affected by experimental variables, which is equivalent to the constraint of constant stage output of the AFM.

Recently, Miller, van der Ham, and I (in preparation) carried out a number of cascade-type simulations in order to determine the extent to which McClelland's (1979) results are constrained by his assumptions that (1) all units at all stages of processing are linear integrators of information, albeit with different rate constants, and that (2) like in a capacitor, the rate of activation of a unit depends on the difference between the asymptotic level and the actual level of activation of a unit. The consequence of the latter assumption is that, in order to reach its asymptotic level, a next stage always uses all information from the previous one. In other words, processing at a later stage can never reach its asymptote before processing at the previous stage has reached its asymptote. This turns out to be crucial: if assumption (2) is removed and one allows that processing at a later stage is completed earlier than that at an earlier stage, the simulations show large interactions between the effects of variables, programmed to affect different stages. In human information processing this could happen if response processes finish before a signal's full identification—not incidentally, due to a risky speed-accuracy trade-off, but as a natural property of processing. If processing at a later stage is earlier completed, the implication is that not all information of an earlier stage is used by that later one, which violates the constant stage output assumption of the AFM.

In contrast, the simulations showed that McClelland's assumption that units are linear integrators of information is less crucial. A variety of other rules had surprisingly little effect on the outcome of the simulations. Thus the AFM seems less strictly tied to at least some of its original premises, and that may well be one reason for its empirical success. Let me at this point briefly mention Roberts's (1987) important work on *multiplicative* effects of variables when the dependent variable is rate of responding in animals instead of reaction time. The most interesting aspect of this work is that it supports a linear stage model from a different perspective. In the same way his argument on *independent measures* is at least intriguing, although I need more information and more direct comparisons between methods to become convinced that we are dealing here with convergent approaches. In particular, I am not yet convinced that the independence of measures necessarily implies a linear stage model.

The second issue concerns the debate on discrete versus continuous processing itself, about which Schweickert does not even reach a tentative conclusion. He does review some of his own theoretical work, showing that partial cascade type of output requires a linear relation between RT and accuracy, which is inconsistent with most empirical data. Again, various studies are reviewed which all show additive effects of variables on both RT and error proportions, which is consistent with the constant stage output assumption of discrete stage models. On the other hand, Schweickert cites data obtained with the EMG technique applied to an Eriksen focused-attention paradigm—e.g., *HHHSHHH*, with *S* and *H* as competing responses (Coles et al. 1985)—that favors continuous processing.

Here, Schweickert may be too hasty, however. Despite the elegance of the EMG technique there is the question of what constitutes the *functional* stimulus in the Eriksen focused-attention paradigm. It would be unjust to expect from a discrete stage model that an experimenter-defined nominal stimulus is always processed as a single stimulus. Thus, a nominal stimulus may consist of more than one functional stimulus, which are separately processed and transmitted. There is nothing in the AFM that requires serial processing of different functional stimuli like in the classical single-channel theory. Indeed, to avoid confusion, it is wise to strictly separate the notion of serial processing in discrete stages from that of serial processing of different stimuli. Different functional stimuli may compete at any processing level, and may do so particularly if only one response is allowed. But that does not imply continuous flow!

Miller's grain-size notion also suggests that a single nominal stimulus can contain more than one functional stimulus. A basic condition for Miller's asynchronous discrete processing is that there are separable stimulus dimensions, in the sense of Garner (1974), each of which constitutes a functional stimulus. Thus, the problem of the functional stimulus is essential to the debate; it appears indeed a major source of confusion, as seems also clear from Smid, Mulder, and Mulder's (1990) deductions in their psychophysiological analysis of the Eriksen paradigm with respect to serial versus continuous processing.

Roberts and Sternberg (chap. 26) are also directly concerned with the debate on discrete versus continuous processing: Their alternatives to linear stage processing do not only concern the cascade possibility but, interestingly, also an alternate-pathway notion. Yet, their findings suggest that a linear stage model explains their data best. Let me just add one possible limitation of the Roberts and Sternberg experiments, namely that they all are concerned with variables that are presumably related to perception and response selection. Most successes of the AFM stem from such studies, while motor stages have typically received much less attention (but see Sanders 1990). Without additional tests, the data of Roberts and Sternberg cannot be simply generalized to the total RT process.

As a further, more general comment on the discrete versus continuous processing issue, the controversy deals only with a preliminary question. It should be kept in mind that the notion of processing stages, whether discrete or continuous, does not say anything about what is going on within a stage. Thus, a processing stage is no more than a preliminary heuristic. The main advantage of the AFM is that it summarizes relations between experimental variables, on the basis of which one should proceed and attempt to formulate more precise process models. Obviously, the processing principles of these models need not be linear or discrete.

28.4   PSYCHOPHYSIOLOGICAL MEASURES

Before I return to the issue of stimuli competing for a response, I will express some of my biases about the contribution of the psychophysiological approach, and evoked potentials (EP) in particular, to the discrete versus continuous controversy. I have expressed recently (Sanders 1990) serious doubts about combining RT and components of the EP in a single measure—like subtracting peak P3 latency from RT—since different metrics are involved, and since it is not at all clear why peak latency should be psychologically relevant. For example, under some conditions the reaction appears to occur before the P3 peak: I consider it unwarranted to conclude from such data that the reaction is carried out without full perceptual analysis, or that perceptual and response processes occur in parallel (Coles and Gratton 1986). I should add that Mulder does not argue along these lines. Yet, I have problems with the way he and others (e.g., Coles 1989) a priori define EP components as "indices" for processes. For instance, Smid, Mulder, and Mulder (1990) use P3 peak latency as an index for the duration of stimulus evaluation, the onset of lateralized readiness potential (LRP) as an index of selective two-choice central motor activation, and the onset of EMG activity as an index of the start of peripheral motor activation. Intuitively this may not seem unreasonable, but it should be clear that these relations cannot simply be taken for granted. For example, Requin, Riehle and Seal (1990) have recently argued that exclusively assigning different parts of the cortex to perceptual or motor processing is not justified. There are probably "motor" cells with a perceptual function and vice versa.

I do not deny that EP data are reliable chronometric measures although their stopping points may be somewhat unclear, which should make one careful in comparing their mutual time relations. Mulder's present proposal to study which task variables have joint effects on a certain EP component at a particular location, and which variables affect different components, is certainly legitimate. It is also relevant to establishing more sophisticated notions about behavioral and brain measures, since consistent relations between EP components and experimental variables help to establish their functional significance. My point is that it is dangerous to reverse the reasoning: according to the reversed reasoning an LRP is defined a priori as reflecting central motor activation and, then, the effects of experimental variables are interpreted as affecting central motor activity. I object to this procedure, since I doubt that the measure is as "pure" as some proponents suggest. Why could the LRP not reflect a composite effect of response selection, motor programming, and program loading—to use some of the labels of the AFM literature?

In my view, determining relations between variables and EP components is *not*, as Mulder suggests, an application of the AFM. The basic difference remains that RT deals with an *overall characteristic* of the total duration of all processes involved, and that is required when applying the AFM. In contrast, the EP deals with a variety of *local components*. Thus, there is more than one EP feature whose occurrence time can be taken as a measure, and an EP feature may be generated by only a subset of the operations that produce the response. For instance the observed forms of EP negativity at different latencies—which are found to be correlated with various demands on selective attention—may well reflect a differential depth of processing, but do not necessarily reflect a serial sequence of processing stages in the sense of the AFM.

Let me immediately add that I am convinced that the availability of local brain correlates of information processing is and will prove to be an extremely valuable tool in the analysis of performance. I am, however, worried by premature claims—for instance about the issue of discrete versus continuous processing.

28.5   DISCRETE VERSUS CONTINUOUS AND THE PARADIGM OF THE FUNCTIONAL VISUAL FIELD

Scientific issues usually profit from results from new experimental approaches. I hope that the paradigm of the functional visual field (e.g., Sanders and Houtmans 1984) is a case in point with respect to the issue of discrete versus continuous processing (Sanders 1990). In this context I briefly discuss some new results obtained by Angela Rath and me (Sanders and Rath 1991). In the paradigm, two signals are always simultaneously presented, separated by a visual angle of 45 degrees. At the beginning of a trial a subject fixates the left signal (SL), shifts to the right, inspects the right signal (SR), and carries out some joint response to both signals (TR).

One aim of this paradigm is to study information processing during saccades: Is it possible to process SL during the eyeshift to SR? So far our data suggest that encoding SL is completed during the fixation time of SL (TL) (e.g., Sanders and Houtmans 1985; Hansen and Sanders 1988). If this is valid, TL would qualify as a candidate for Wundt's *d-reaction*, which aimed at separating discrimination time from decision time. Another question concerns invariance across RT paradigms. Are the perceptual processes during TL the same as those during a traditional choice reaction? This would require experimental effects of the same size in both cases. Again, TL should not be affected by the type of joint response, following fixation of SR. There might be special cases where the type of joint response requires extra processing of SL but that should be explicitly predicted. Provided this all works—and so far promising results have been obtained—the paradigm would enable a more refined analysis of perceptual processing. It would also support stage notions of processing in that the completion of a certain stage would be a convenient starting point to start a saccade.

It may be mentioned in passing that TL bears some resemblance to the latency of components of the EP in its role in performance analysis. Neither reflects the final response but at best a subset of the processes involved in the final response. Which processes are reflected in either measure cannot be stated a priori but should be empirically established. It is even unwarranted to assume unconditionally that either one is psychologically relevant. TL has perhaps two advantages: it has a better stopping point and RT and TL have the same metric. The components of the EP are perhaps more interesting since they belong to another domain of analysis, perhaps ultimately enabling more conclusions about the relations between brain and behavior.

As an example of a contribution to the issue of discrete versus continuous processing, Angela Rath and I studied the speed-accuracy trade-off (SAT) during TL. In accounting for SAT, the traditional "modal" model assumes some type of information accrual until a more or less risky response criterion is exceeded. They always start from the implicit, albeit in my view dated, assumption of a dichotomy of stimulus and response processing. Since TL is supposed to reflect perceptual processing of SL the models also suggest that a usual SAT function should be obtained in the case of TL. We attempted tests of this hypothesis by forcing subjects to leave SL very soon. SR was only briefly presented, which left only a limited time to inspect SL and to carry out the saccade. In order to avoid missing SR, the modal model would expect a single distribution of response times with a low criterion for information accrual about SL, and, hence, a short TL. However, the results showed two distributions, one of which seemed to reflect reactions—in which case SR was missed—and the other anticipations, in which case SL was missed while SR was seen. This could support Yellott's fast guessing, which has always been an alternative to the optional stopping notion of the modal model. Yet, this interpretation met the problem that the reactions were faster than those in a control condition without speed stress. Moreover, TL at the reactions was insensitive to an extra complication of SL like rotation. Together, the data suggest that subjects may leave SL at either one of three specific points in processing, each marking the completion of a perceptual processing stage. These stages are, respectively, *preprocessing*, a stored unanalyzed "picture" of the signal; *feature extraction*, a partially analyzed signal in the sense of a feature set; and *identification*, a fully interpreted signal. This constraint on SAT is consistent with that observed by Meyer et al. (1988). Processing can only be interrupted when a certain "result" has been obtained, which is at odds with continuous flow. Again, as SL was left at an earlier point, TR took longer, which suggests that, if certain operations on SL are not carried out during TL, they are postponed until SR is fixated. In turn, this implies that perceptual processing cannot continue during the saccade, a deduction that is also more in line with discrete than with continuous processing.

28.6 DOUBLE TASKS

As argued it is not self-evident what actually constitutes a functional "signal-unit" in processing information. Sometimes a nominal signal can consist of different functional ones and, on other occasions, multiple nominal signals may evoke a single response. Exemplary of the last possibility are phenomena of "grouping" in the classical paradigm of the psychological refractory period (e.g., Sanders and Keuss 1969), in which case the speed of processing is considerably enhanced in comparison to separate processing of each individual signal. There is more interest in these phenomena due to the rise of models from connectionism and operations research, which tend to describe mental processing in terms of interactive activation and waiting, rather than of capacity allocation (see McClelland, chap. 27, this volume). When engaged in simultaneous processing, the analysis of interference patterns has become an important research issue and, witness the chapters by Schweickert and by McClelland, connectionism and operations research offer splendid methodological tools. However, as argued earlier in this chapter, the basic question with respect to the ultimate success of the exciting endeavor remains whether there will be a fruitful cooperation between connectionist models, which are now flourishing everywhere, and newly developed experimental paradigms that are capable of testing the particular models. Sometimes I fear that the present enthusiasm for connectionist models hides the need for showing how they can be proven wrong, both as individual cases and as a general framework. Or is connectionism nothing but a tool for analysis?

REFERENCES

Allport, D. A. (1980). The state of cognitive psychology: A critical note of W. G. Chase (Ed.), *Visual information processing. Quarterly Journal of Experimental Psychology: 31*, 41–152.

Coles, M. G. H. (1989). Modern mind-brain reading: psychophysiology, physiology and cognition. *Psychophysiology, 26,* 251−269.

Coles, M. G. H., and Gratton, G. (1986). Cognitive psychophysiology and the study of states and processes. In G. R. J. Hockey, A. W. K. Gaillard, and M. G. H. Coles (Eds.), *Energetics and human information processing.* Dordrecht: Nijhoff.

Coles, M. G. H., Gratton, G. Bashore, T. R. Eriksen, C. W., and Donchin, E. (1985). A psychophysiological investigation of the continuous flow model of human information processing. *Journal of Experimental Psychology. Human Perception and Performance 11,* 529−553.

Donchin, E., Fabiani, M., and Sanders, A. F. (Eds.). (1989). The learning strategies program: An examination of the strategies in skill acquisition. *Acta Psychologica, 71.*

Donders, F. C. (1868). Die Schnelligkeit psychischer Prozesse. *Archive fuer Anatomie und Physiologie 8,* 657−681.

Eriksen, C. W., and Schultz, D. W. (1979). Information processing in visual search: A continuous flow conception and experimental results. *Perception and Psychophysics, 25,* 249−263.

Farell, B. (1985). Same-different judgements: A review of current controversies in perceptual comparisons. *Psychological Bulletin, 98,* 419−456.

Garner, W. R. (1974). *The processing of information and structure.* Hillsdale, NJ: Erlbaum.

Hansen, W., and Sanders, A. F. (1988). On the output of encoding during stimulus fixation. *Acta Psychologica 69,* 83−94.

Hick, W. E. (1952). On the rate of gain of information. *Quarterly Journal of Experimental Psychology, 1,* 36−51.

Hofstadter, D. R. (1981). *Metamagical themas: Questing for the essence of mind and pattern.* London: Penguin.

Luce, R. D. (1986). *Response times.* New York: Oxford University Press.

McClelland, J. L. (1979). On the time relations between mental processes: a framework for analysing processes in cascade. *Psychological Review, 86,* 287−330.

Meyer, D. E., Osman, A. M., Irwin, D. E., and Kounios, J. (1988). The dynamics of cognition and action: Mental processes inferred from speed-accuracy decomposition. *Psychological Review, 95,* 183−237.

Miller, J. O. (1988). Discrete and continuous models of human information processing: Theoretical distinctions and empirical results. *Acta Psychologica, 67,* 191−257.

Newell, A. (1974). You can't play 20 questions with nature and win. In W. G. Chase (Ed.), *Visual information processing.* New York: Academic Press.

Pachella, R. G. (1974). The interpretation of reaction time in information processing. In B. Kantowitz, (ed.), *Human information processing.* Hillsdale NJ: Erlbaum.

Posner, M. I. (1978). *Chronometric explorations of mind.* New York: Academic Press.

Posner, M. I., and McLeod, S. (1982). Information processing models: In search of elementary operations. *Annual Review of Psychology, 30,* 363−396.

Requin, J., Riehle, A., and Seal, J. (1990). Cognitive neuroscience studies of movement planning. Paper presented at the symposium on Sequencing and Timing of Human Movement, Netherlands Institute for Advanced Studies (NIAS), Wassenaar, June 10−13.

Roberts, S. (1987). Evidence for distinct serial processes in animals: The multiplicative-factors method. *Animal Learning and Behavior, 15,* 135−173.

Sanders, A. F. (1990). Issues and trends in the debate on discrete versus continuous processing of information. *Acta Psychologica, 74,* 123−168.

Sanders, A. F. (1991). Simulation as a tool in the measurement of human performance. *Ergonomics, 34*, 995–1025.

Sanders, A. F., and Houtmans, M. J. M. (1984). The functional visual field revisited. In A. J. van Doorn, W. A. van der Grind and J. J. Koenderink (Eds.), *Limits in perception*. Utrecht: VNU Science Press.

Sanders, A. F., and Houtmans, M. J. M. (1985). There is no central stimulus encoding during saccadic eye shifts: A case against parallel processing models. *Acta Psychologica, 60*, 323–338.

Sanders, A. F., and Keuss, P. J. G. (1969). Grouping and refractoriness in multiple selective responses. *Acta Psychologica, 30*, 177–194.

Sanders, A. F., and Rath, A. (1991). Perceptual processing and speed-accuracy trade-off. *Acta Psychologica, 77*, 275–291.

Schweickert, R. (1989). Separable effects of factors on activation functions in discrete and continuous models, d' and evoked potentials. *Psychological Bulletin, 106*, 318–328.

Schweickert, R. (1984). The representation of mental activities in critical path networks. *Annals of the New York Academy of Sciences, 423*, 82–95.

Smid, H. G. O. M., Mulder, G., and Mulder, L. J. M. (1990). Selective response activation can begin before stimulus recognition is complete: A Psychophysiological and error analysis of continuous flow. *Acta Psychologica, 74*, 169–203.

Sternberg, S. (1969). The discovery of processing stages. *Acta Psychologica, 30*, 276–315.

Van Duren, L. L., and Sanders, A. F. (1988). On the robustness of the additive factors stage structure in blocked and mixed choice reaction designs. *Acta Psychologica, 69*, 83–94.

VI Motor Control and Action

Introduction

The final major theme of *Attention and Performance XIV* encompasses the topics of movement production and action. By putting them last, however, we do not mean to imply that these topics are either conceptually least important or chronologically most recent in performance theory. Quite the contrary. As Allport (1987) and others (e.g., Broadbent, chap. 35) have stressed already, mental processes like those treated in prior sections of the present volume (e.g., visual information processing, attention, learning, and memory) are all presumably devoted to promoting successful goal-directed action. Thus, in order to understand these processes fully and to characterize their ultimate functions, one should carefully consider the nature of action and the physical movements on which it depends.

Further substantiating the primacy of movement production and action, it should be recalled that they have preoccupied some of our field's historically most influential investigators. For example, R. S. Woodworth (1899), a leading pioneer of experimental psychology, wrote his doctoral dissertation—still widely cited and germane—on speed-accuracy trade-offs in voluntary rapid aimed movements. Following Woodworth's lead, Karl Lashley (1917, 1951), the revered biopsychologist and psychophysiologist, broke new ground with his innovative explorations of motor programs and hierarchical control of serially ordered behavior. In another related vein, K. J. W. Craik (1947, 1963), who before his untimely death was a principal progenitor of the attention and performance movement, helped popularize servomechanisms as models of manual tracking behavior. And Paul Fitts (1954), who had he not also died prematurely might stand together with Broadbent as today's co-godfather of Attention and Performance, carried Woodworth's (1899) tradition forward by further exploring the basis of movement speed-accuracy trade-offs.

Consistent with these precedents, the Attention and Performance symposium series has put movement production and action high on its agenda. Although the first symposium of the series (Sanders 1967) did not include any presentations on movement per se, subsequent symposia did—increasingly so. This trend culminated in *Attention and Performance XIII* (Jeannerod 1990), which constituted a whole volume devoted to motor representation and control. What motivated such emphasis on a single theme for an Attention and Performance symposium was an explosion of activity by researchers from the allied disciplines of experimental psychology, physical education, kinesiology, neurophysiology, biomechanics, and robotics, each of which has contributed greatly over the past twenty-five years to our current understanding of the mental and physical processes that together mediate human movement.

The fruits of these contributions can be summarized in terms of new findings about how the human motor system solves several interrelated problems of motor control (Rosenbaum 1991). For example, much has been discovered recently about the motor system's solution to the so-called serial-order problem, originally formulated by Lashley (1951). It concerns the fact that overt behaviors typically consist of concatenated elementary movements having particular serial orders and temporal arrangements directed toward achieving various goals. Because the same movement elements are used in generating different behaviors, the motor system must have flexible ways of specifying their changing orders and controlling the amounts of time between them. Regarding this requirement, researchers now know that the needed specificity and control may entail the preparation and execution of elaborate "motor programs" that provide organized multilevel plans whereby sequences of movements proceed once their initiation has commenced. At relatively high levels of organization, movement sequences appear to be planned and executed through hierarchical structures whose nodes and branches dictate the arrangements of intermediate movement-element groups (e.g., see Rosenbaum, Inhoff, and Gordon 1984; Rosenbaum, Kenny, and Derr 1983). Supplementing these hierarchical structures, lower levels of organization may rely on linear structures (viz., motor-program buffers) to store fully-prepared programs for movement sequences immediately before overt action begins (e.g., see Sternberg et al. 1978).

Much has likewise been discovered recently about how individual elementary movements are represented within a motor program. Under at least some circumstances, the behavioral data (e.g., movement latency and duration) imply that a rapid movement from an initial starting position to a final target position is represented in terms of parameter values for the movement's effector, direction, extent, force, and overall travel time (see Ghez, Hening, and Favilla 1990; Meyer, Smith, and Wright 1982; Rosenbaum 1980; Schmidt et al. 1979). This implication is strengthened by neurophysiological data, which have revealed evidence of such parameterization in records of electromyographic (EMG) activity (e.g., Hallett, Shahani, and Young 1975; Wadman et al. 1979; Wallace 1981) and neural firing rates (e.g., Evarts 1981; Georgopoulos 1990).

On what principled bases are the parameter values for individual movements chosen? Current answers to this question stem from solutions that the human motor system adopts as part of coping with other related problems that confront it. In particular, among these problems is one involving the multiplicity of biomechanical "degrees of freedom" that the body has. The degrees-of-freedom problem has been cogently articulated by Bernstein (1967). As he pointed out, there are many different possible movements among which a person may choose in order to achieve a particular end result at a particular time. This abundance of possibilities exists because the space around us is three-dimensional, whereas many of the body's effectors have more than three degrees of freedom. For example, the human arm has seven mechanical degrees of freedom, including three around the shoulder, one around the elbow, and three around the wrist (Soechting and Terzuolo 1990). Consequently, there are many different paths that in principle the arm could take to reach a given target object. Yet in analyzing the movements that people actually produce, researchers have found that the human motor system is quite selective among its options. Instead of haphazardly using all the available degrees of freedom, it typically programs and executes movements according to certain heuristics whose implementation may help maximize the efficiency and effectiveness of action. In particular, arm movements may be constrained so that their paths are essentially straight lines (see Abend, Bizzi, and Morasso 1982; Morasso 1981), and so that their velocity-versus-time profiles minimize physical quantities such as changes in acceleration and muscle torque (Hogan and Flash 1987; Nelson 1983; Uno, Kawato, and Suzuki 1989).

Also related to the degrees-of-freedom problem are speed-accuracy trade-offs. As Woodworth (1899) found originally, overt movements suffer from the same "haste makes waste" syndrome as do covert mental processes; moving very quickly accrues a cost in reduced accuracy, and moving very accurately accrues a cost in reduced speed. Thus, like other aspects of performance efficiency, trade-offs between movement speed and accuracy may be taken into account to constrain the motor system's degrees of freedom. Indeed, our understanding about the importance of this latter constraint has grown substantially since the first Attention and Performance symposium (Sanders 1967). New theoretical accounts have been developed for various forms of movement speed-accuracy trade-offs (e.g., Schmidt et al. 1979; Meyer et al. 1988; Meyer et al. 1990), and concerted attempts have been made to integrate relevant classical research (e.g., Fitts 1954; Woodworth 1899) with contemporary approaches to the degrees-of-freedom problem (see, e.g., Kawato, chap. 33).

Of course, this by no means exhausts all of the problems with which the human motor system has to deal (see for example Rosenbaum 1991). Besides the serial-order and degrees-of-freedom problems, there are other major ones, including: (1) the "current-control problem"—how do people correct movement errors based on feedforward and feedback signals during movement execution? (2) the "perceptual-motor integration problem"—how are perceptual representations of the environment converted into motor codes useful for movement execution? And how are motor codes manifested in perceptual representations? (3) the "skill-acquisition problem"—how are complex movement tasks mastered through extensive systematic practice? Though space does not permit us to describe more fully what general solution/answers have emerged regarding these latter problem/questions, we hope that part VI of this book will at least give a flavor of where the field is presently headed with each of them.

Specifically, part VI begins with a tutorial chapter by Wing in which he addresses issues raised by the inherent variability of the human motor system. This variability poses yet another problem for movement production. As Wing makes clear, motor-system variability may in part influence how people solve the serial-order, degrees-of-freedom, perceptual-motor integration, and skill-acquisition problems. Next, Requin, Riehle, and Seal outline a program of research that further considers these problems and their interrelationships from a neurophysiological perspective. Breaking the mold of classical stage models (cf. Sternberg et al. 1978), they argue—based on single-cell recordings in various cortical areas—that motor programming, perceptual-motor integration, and other precursors of action may be much more intertwined than previously conceived. As Ivry and Gopal report subsequently, however, the perceptual and motor components of action may still be at least somewhat separable when viewed through the lens of cognitive neuropsychology. Their studies focus on the internal mechanisms used to perceive and produce voice-onset times. In patients with certain types of cerebellar brain damage, it appears that these mechanisms are selectively impaired, and that one of them can remain intact even though another no longer functions normally.

Shifting back from the perceptual-motor integration problem to the degrees-of-freedom problem, the subsequent chapter by Rosenbaum, Vaughan, Jorgensen, Barnes, and Stewart discusses manual movement production. A major contribution of their research is to identify new constraints through which objects are manipulated spatially while reducing the otherwise over-abundant movements available to the arm. Whether these constraints—which involve the goal of attaining comfortable final effector postures—apply equally well to speech production remains an open question for future studies of tongue twisters. Meanwhile, what can be said at the moment is that Kawato's chapter nicely complements the prior ones on several fronts. Here Kawato shows how a combination of behavioral, neurophysiological, and connectionist-modeling approaches can yield explanations of numerous movement phenomena while solving the degrees-of-freedom problem with useful movement-efficiency requirements. Also, an extra benefit of these combined approaches is that they lend themselves to some neat solutions for the skill-acquisition and perceptual-motor integration problems. Thus, readers should find it an enticing exercise to discover how Viviani, the discussant of this section, deftly weaves Kawato's approaches together with those of our other contributors through a clever series of twists and turns about motor-system variability, neural firing rates, vocal timing mechanisms, and manual object manipulation.

REFERENCES

Abend, W., Bizzi, E., and Morasso, P. (1982). Human arm trajectory formation. *Brain, 105,* 331–345.

Allport, A. (1987). Selection-for-action: Some behavioral and neurophysiological considerations of attention. In H. Heuer and A. F. Sanders (Eds.), *Perspectives on perception and attention*, 395–419. Hillsdale, NJ: Erlbaum.

Bernstein, N. (1967). *The coordination and regulation of movements*. London: Pergamon.

Craik, K. J. W. (1947). Theory of the human operator in control systems. Part I: The operator as an engineering system. *British Journal of Psychology, 38*, 56–61.

Craik, K. J. W. (1963). Psychological and physiological aspects of control mechanisms with special reference to tank gunnery, Part I: *Ergonomics, 6*, 1–33. Original work reported in 1943.

Evarts, E. V. (1981). Role of motor cortex in voluntary movements in primates. In V. B. Brooks (Ed.), *Handbook of physiology*. Vol. 2, section 1, 1083–1120. Bethesda, MD: American Physiological Society.

Fitts, P. M. (1954). The information capacity of the human motor system in controlling the amplitude of movement. *Journal of Experimental Psychology, 47*, 381–391.

Georgopoulos, A. P. (1990). Neurophysiology of reaching. In M. Jeannerod (Ed.), *Attention and performance XIII: Motor representation and control*, 227–263. Hillsdale, NJ: Erlbaum.

Ghez, C., Hening, W., and Favilla, M. (1990). Parallel interacting channels in the initiation and specification of motor response features. In M. Jeannerod (Ed.), *Attention and performance XIII: Motor representation and control*, 265–293. Hillsdale, NJ: Erlbaum.

Hallett, M., Shahani, B. T., and Young, R. R. (1975). EMG analysis of stereotyped voluntary movements in man. *Journal of Neurology, Neurosurgery, and Psychiatry, 38*, 1154–1162.

Hogan, N., and Flash, T. (1987). Moving gracefully: Quantitative theories of motor control. *Trends in Neuroscience, 10* (4), 170–174.

Jeannerod, M. (1990). *Attention and performance XIII. Motor representation and control*. Hillsdale, NJ: Erlbaum.

Lashley, K. (1917). The accuracy of movement in the absence of excitation from the moving organ. *American Journal of Physiology, 43*, 169–194.

Lashley, K. (1951). The problem of serial order in behavior. In L. A. Jeffress (Ed.), *Cerebral mechanisms in behavior*, 112–131. New York: Wiley.

Meyer, D. E., Abrams, R. A., Kornblum, S., Wright, C. E., and Smith, J. E. K. (1988). Optimality in human motor performance: Ideal control of rapid aimed movements. *Psychological Review, 95*, 340–370.

Meyer, D. E., Smith, J. E. K., Kornblum, S., Abrams, R. A., and Wright, C. E. (1990). Speed-accuracy tradeoffs in rapid aimed movements: Toward a theory of rapid voluntary action. In M. Jeannerod (Ed.), *Attention and performance XIII: Motor representation and control*, 173–226. Hillsdale, NJ: Erlbaum.

Meyer, D. E., Smith, J. E. K., and Wright, C. E. (1982). Models for the speed and accuracy of aimed movements. *Psychological Review, 89*, 449–482.

Morasso, P. (1981). Spatial control of arm movements. *Experimental Brain Research, 42*, 223–227.

Nelson, W. L. (1983). Physical principles for economics of skilled movements. *Biological Cybernetics, 46*, 135–147

Rosenbaum, D. A. (1980). Human movement initiation: Specification of arm, direction, and extent. *Journal of Experimental Psychology: General, 109*, 444–474.

Rosenbaum, D. A. (1991). *Human motor control*. San Diego, CA: Academic Press.

Rosenbaum, D. A., Inhoff, A. W., and Gordon, A. M. (1984). Choosing between movement sequences: A hierarchical editor model. *Journal of Experimental Psychology: General, 113*, 372–393.

Rosenbaum, D. A., Kenny, S., and Derr, M. A. (1983). Hierarchical control of rapid movement sequences. *Journal of Experimental Psychology: Human Perception and Performance, 9,* 86–102.

Sanders, A. F. (1967). *Attention and performance.* Amsterdam: North-Holland.

Schmidt, R. A., Zelaznik, H., Hawkins, B., Frank, J. S., and Quinn, J. T., Jr. (1979). Motor-output variability: A theory for the accuracy of rapid motor acts. *Psychological Review, 86,* 415–451.

Soechting, J. F. and Terzuolo, C. A. (1990). Sensorimotor transformations and the kinematics of arm movements in three-dimensional space. In M. Jeannerod (Ed.), *Attention and performance XIII: Motor representation and control,* 479–494. Hillsdale, NJ: Erlbaum.

Sternberg, S., Monsell, S., Knoll, R. L., and Wright, C. E. (1978). The latency and duration of rapid movement sequences: Comparisons of speech and typewriting. In G. E. Stelmach (Ed.), *Information processing in motor control and learning,* 117–152. New York: Academic Press.

Uno, Y., Kawato, M., and Suzuki, R. (1989). Formation and control of optimal trajectory in human multijoint arm movement: Minimum torque-change model. *Biological Cybernetics, 61,* 89–101.

Wadman, W. J., Denier van der Gon, J. J., Geuze, R. H., and Mol, C. R. (1979). Control of fast goal-directed arm movements. *Journal of Human Movement Studies, 6,* 19–37.

Wallace, S. A. (1981). An impulse-timing theory for reciprocal control of muscular activity. *Journal of Motor Behavior, 13,* 144–160.

Woodworth, R. S. (1899). The accuracy of voluntary movement. *Psychological Review, 3* (Whole No. 13), 1–114.

29 The Uncertain Motor System: Perspectives on the Variability of Movement

Alan M. Wing

29.1 INTRODUCTION

Human movement, unlike that of most machines, is extraordinarily adaptable; many everyday actions can be performed in a variety of ways. We can, for example, sign our names in all kinds of different situations. We can hold a variety of writing implements in all manner of grips on a range of writing surfaces oriented horizontally or vertically. The act of signing may require quite different patterns of upper limb movement. Yet, whether we write using mostly movements of the hand or movements of the whole arm, the written product is likely to be similar in form and identifiably our own. We can even make a passable attempt at writing with the other hand, even though the movements required are the mirror image of those used with the preferred hand. However, there are likely to be a number of points of difference in the writing produced by the two hands (Wright 1990).

By contrast, a machine for performing the task of writing would likely be restricted to one particular pen held in a certain way. Moreover, the machine would most likely be special purpose. If it were capable of the repeated fine movements required of writing, it would be unlikely to have the power, the range of movement or the strength to use hammer and chisel to carve letters in wood or stone. However, offsetting the greater flexibility of human movement, a machine such as a computer pen-plotter would be far more consistent and exhibit less variability over repetitions of an action such as writing a particular letter of the alphabet. The mechanical redundancy of the human motor system, which allows it to be so general-purpose in nature, carries a cost. The redundancy must be controlled. The very flexibility that makes humans capable of variety of action also makes any single action liable to variability.

Flexibility, or choice, in action is both a function of the mechanics of the effector system and of the organization of control. People can use effectors that are mechanically separate in movement combinations and sequences that are often quite arbitrary. However, this is typically a function of skill. It may take considerable practice to make certain combinations of movements with any degree of consistency. Again, the very flexibility of the organization of the human motor system seems to make the execution of any particular action less simple than it would be for a special-purpose machine, and so liable to be more variable.

In this tutorial review of twenty-five years of studies in the area of movement control published in the Attention and Performance symposia proceedings, the theme is variability. Taking the Attention and Performance proceedings as representative of the field, we will consider how the study of movement variability, that is, the measurement and analysis of apparently random errors around an intended performance, can yield valuable theoretical insights into underlying control processes.

It can be tempting to see variability of movement as no more than "a cloud ready to obscure highlights in data" (Welford 1967) especially if the reason for taking measures of movement is to provide a window on higher cognitive functioning (as for example, in the use of eye movements to look at processes in reading; Rayner and Pollatsek 1987). However, with the goal of understanding the nature of human movement, our thesis is that the analysis of variability in movement provides a powerful tool in pointing to the underlying functional organization of the motor system.

Nearly a quarter of a century has passed since the first Attention and Performance symposium was held in the Netherlands in 1966. The volume of proceedings that emerged from it (Sanders 1967) was dedicated to the memory of Paul Fitts, who had been invited to the meeting, but died before it took place. In the context of the present review, this dedication may now be seen as particularly apposite for two reasons. First, Fitts provided an analysis of motor behavior that focused on a tradeoff between the speed and accuracy of aimed movement (Fitts 1954). The essence of this trade-off is that movements covering larger distances require more time in their execution than do smaller movements, if the spread of their endpoints is not to be greater. Fitts's concern was thus with the variability of movement. Second, Fitts's work in this area has, over the last twenty-five years, been one of the most cited studies in the field of movement control. Indeed, to date, the relation that Fitts established between speed and accuracy is the only body of data concerning the psychology of human movement to be designated a law.

But just how far have we progressed in understanding the nature of movement variability since Fitts's pioneering work? Do we now have better characterizations of the nature of this variability? Do we have descriptions of variability for tasks other than that used by Fitts, namely, repetitive movement of the hand between two arbitrary points in space? Can we identify different sources of variability that are, for example, subject to the influence of different internal or external factors? Have there been attempts to identify structure within the variability? Insofar as movement is variable, do we know how the motor system copes with the uncertainty that this creates on the progress and outcome of a particular movement? The claim made here is that questions such as these can be answered in the affirmative. As part of the progress made in the field of motor control over the last twenty-five years, researchers have been documenting variability in movement and/or advancing theoretical accounts with implications for motor variability. Notably absent, however, has been any attempt at an integrative review of these developments.

The theme of the present chapter will be pursued by referring to the many chapters under the broad heading of motor behavior that have appeared in the thirteen published volumes of Attention and Performance symposia proceedings. This source provides an eclectic assortment of studies ranging widely over methodological details such as movement task (laboratory versus real-world), effector system (not only the arms, but also speech articulators, eyes, etc.) and performance measures (discrete versus continuous) as well as theoretical orientation. Such a variety of approaches might be seen as appropriate to our variability theme. One problem in limiting ourselves to chapters published in the Attention and Performance proceedings is that many do not treat movement variability explicitly. However, it is probably fair to say that this is a common limitation throughout studies of motor behavior and not just in Attention and Performance symposia proceedings. Indeed, such failures of previous work to adequately document an aspect of behavior provide opportunities for further work rather than a reason for avoiding central issues in movement control.

Our review of variability in movement starts with a section on how movement is recorded and analyzed. There then follow results from individual studies grouped on three dimensions. The first dimension has a statistical basis; whether the variability is treated as a unitary measure or whether structure is sought within variability by cross-relating observations from more than one measure at a time. The second and third classificatory dimensions relate to task definition; the research is subdivided according to whether the task takes place in a constant, static environment or in a dynamically changing environment, and also according to whether performance involves a single action or several distinct actions in an extended sequence. In the conclusion, we then draw together the results into the broad theme that the study of variability can afford useful theoretical insights into the nature of the control of movement.

29.2 LOOKING AT MOVEMENT

Since our interest is in the variability of movement, it is natural that we should be concerned that inaccurate or "noisy" movement recording techniques do not mask the focus of our interest. Measurement accuracy may be considered under two headings: *bias* and *consistency*. Over repeated measurements of some aspect of movement, we would like the estimated average to be unbiased and correspond to the true mean. We would also like the variance of the measurements to reflect only the variability of the subject's performance. If there is measurement variability, it will inflate our estimates of performance variability. Such variability may arise in unreliable equipment and sensitivity to artifacts. In addition, measurement variability may stem from limited resolution on the physical dimension of interest. This may arise through the design of the equipment or through the way measures are derived from recordings (that are otherwise sufficiently accurate). In this section, we consider some of the alternative means employed to represent human movement and the implications of these methods for assessing movement variability.

Perhaps the most obvious way of capturing movements for subsequent analysis is to use cine film (Jeannerod 1981), its close relative, stroboscopic photography (Prablanc and Pelisson 1990), or video recording (Craske 1981; Larochelle 1984; Butterworth and Grover 1990). Each of these methods can give a full and readily interpretable view of task performance in terms that may be easily related to the movement of individual body parts. For example, an ingenious use of video was Larochelle's inclusion of a mirror mounted at 45 degrees to the horizontal within the field of view of an overhead camera. In this way, he observed both horizontal and vertical components of fingertip movements associated with typing. He examined individual video fields (occurring at 20-ms intervals) to identify the times of occurrence of certain features of finger trajectories, such as movement onset and key contact. This method of measurement has the disadvantage of being extremely time-consuming. However, as a method of charting movement trajectories, it has another potential problem. The experimenter may unwittingly introduce both systematic bias and random error in identifying the positions of the points of interest in each successive video field.

The extent of judgmental bias in video analysis may be checked through two independent observers (see Butterworth and Grover 1990). However, there exist various alternatives for recording movement objectively that avoid the problem of bias and have the advantage of circumventing the labor-intensive aspects of measuring trajectories from film or video. One approach is to instrument the apparatus. If the movement being studied is relatively simple, nothing more complicated than switch contacts may be needed to register the time and position of an effector at the start and end of movement. Examples of this in the Attention and Performance symposia proceedings include the many studies of reaction time (RT) for finger movements producing button depression (e.g., Rabbitt 1967) or release (e.g., Glencross 1980) as well as onset of voicing (e.g., Cooper and Ehrlich 1981). Examples are also provided by studies of aiming movements with registration of movement endpoint (e.g., Welford, Norris, and Shock 1969) and computer-keyboard timing of keystrokes in typing (e.g., Shaffer 1973).

If the microstructure of a movement (and not just its outcome) is of interest, other methods of instrumenting the apparatus are necessary. For example, Ghez, Hening, and Favilla (1990), Johansson and Westling (1990), and Sanes (1990), who studied isometric contractions of elbow and hand muscles, have used strain gauges to register force acting on a manipulandum. Gottsdanker (1967) used an accelerometer attached to a sliding manipulandum to characterize subjects' movement corrections during rapid changes of hand position in one dimension (see fig. 29.1). Manipulandum position has been recorded in two dimensions by Georgopoulos (1990) and Wright (1990). Angular position of a manipulandum was recorded by MacKenzie and van Eerd (1990), Meyer

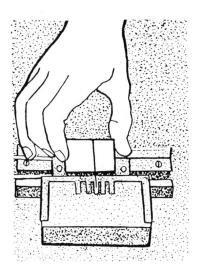

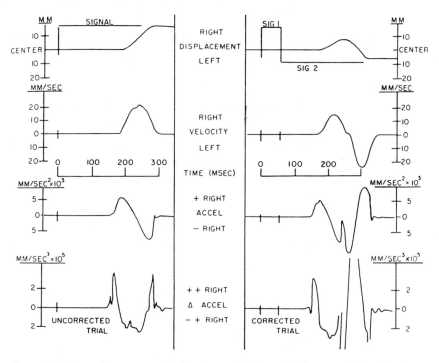

Figure 29.1 Measuring movement. Subjects moved a linear slide from a central position to one of four possible nearby positions. The target was indicated by an illuminated lamp. In the movement recordings below, a normal trial (left) is contrasted with a trial (right) on which the illuminated light changed (from SIG 1 to SIG 2). The switching of the target caused an amendment to the movement as revealed by the traces based on the outputs of a linear potentiometer (position and its derivative, velocity) and an accelerometer (acceleration and its derivative, jerk). (From Gottsdanker 1967.)

et al. (1990), Trumbo (1970), and Young and Schmidt (1990). Angular position measures have the potential advantage that they can be directly related to body movement if the measurement axis of rotation corresponds to a joint axis. This contrasts with the complex relations between movements of the speech articulators and their acoustic consequences, captured by the microphone as fluctuations of pressure with time (e.g., Huggins 1978; Fowler and Tassinary 1981; MacNeilage and Davis 1990).

In situations where contact with the manipulandum is discontinuous or unreliable, direct recording of the position of parts of the body is desirable. For three-dimensional recording of fingertip position during typing, Sternberg, Knoll, and Turock (1990) used three potentiometers linked mechanically to the fingernail. A system for tracking the position of an ultrasonic sound source attached to the hand has been used by Georgopoulos (1990). For situations in which coordination of the relative movement of two or more body segments is of interest, optoelectronic techniques have been used in which special cameras track infrared light-emitting diodes placed on relevant parts of the anatomy (Lee et al. 1990; von Hofsten 1990; Tuller and Kelso 1990). Both types of tracking system have the advantage that they are less likely to interfere with a subject's movement than a mechanically attached device. However, they are prone to introduce spurious measurements, and these may result in inflated estimates of variability.

Once a set of continuous records on one or more dimensions of movement has been obtained, a difficulty arises if the data from several trials (e.g., from a number of repetitions of a particular condition) are to be combined. Even a relatively stereotyped movement is likely to fluctuate in duration over trials. This will introduce differences in times of the individual features relative to key temporal landmarks (e.g., movement onset). As a result, features identifiable in the individual record may be smeared if different records are averaged with respect to movement onset. In such cases, the average would be considered a most unsatisfactory representation of performance.

Estimates of the variability at successive points in time for data pooled by averaging can also be misleading. They may reflect both variation in temporal alignment and fluctuations on other measured dimensions of movement. However, if, for example, movement is paced or driven by an external tracking signal, timing variations may be sufficiently small that averaging across movement records may provide a meaningful picture (Viviani 1990). In other cases, duration differences across trials may reflect fluctuations in time scale taken over the whole movement. Rescaling all the trials to have unit duration before averaging can then yield more interpretable time functions (Gottsdanker 1967). Nevertheless, the latter approach does embody certain theoretical assumptions, which will be discussed in a later section.

The difficulties of combining continuous-record data over trials may be sidestepped if the investigator's interest is in certain distinct features in the movement trajectory. Thus, for example, Larochelle (1984) was only concerned with using video records to identify the times of onset and termination

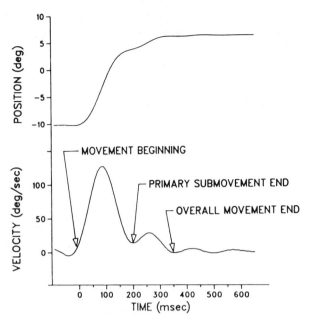

Figure 29.2 Position and velocity records for a wrist-rotation movement to a target of 6.3 deg angular width at an angular distance of 15.8 deg from the starting position. The movement has been parsed into primary and secondary submovements. (From Meyer et al. 1990; fig. 6.9.)

of finger movements in typing. In studies of speech, the spectrogram (a continuous record of the changing distribution of frequency components in the speech acoustic waveform) may be used simply to identify phonemes and their onset times (Huggins 1978; Fowler and Tassinary 1981). Similarly, for upper limb movements, Meyer et al. (1990) limited their use of continuous movement recordings to identifying and describing submovements in terms of their duration and amplitude (see fig. 29.2).

Three points, two methodological and one conceptual, should be mentioned here. These concern the reduction of a continuous movement record to a series of discrete features whose parameters (mean, variance, etc.) are then studied. All of them have implications for interpreting estimates of movement variability.

The first methodological point is that supposedly continuous movement records have necessarily limited resolution. This limitation may, for example, occur in the temporal dimension as a result of a relatively low sampling frequency. Suppose measurement points are spaced at intervals of t units so that the timing of an event can only be measured to an accuracy of $+/-t/2$. Over repetitions, this can yield measurements for which an interval will be estimated correctly in the mean, but will have measurement variability distributed uniformly about the mean. The practice of taking first and second derivatives of position as a function of time to obtain velocity and acceleration also contributes a limit to sampling resolution. Each stage of differencing effectively halves the maximum possible time resolution (MacKenzie and van Eerd

1990; Meyer et al. 1990; Young and Schmidt 1990). To preserve the temporal resolution it is preferable to measure velocity or acceleration directly.

Limitations in measurement resolution may also arise from the criteria used for identifying the movement feature of interest. In Larochelle's (1984) case, where the interest was in the durations of keystrokes, using video with its limited temporal and spatial resolution relative to the small and rapid movements of typing is likely to have introduced appreciable measurement variability. Although not a direct problem for his study (which was primarily concerned with mean data), it might have caused difficulties if the aim had been to characterize variability.

A second, related point concerns the method used to determine the discrete features from the continuous record. For example, Larochelle's (1984) identification of finger-movement onset in typing involved subjective judgments based on predefined criteria. With this approach, it is quite possible for a judge to make both systematic and random errors in applying the criteria. Such errors could introduce measurement variability that would be confounded with the nature of the movement of interest. In contrast, Meyer et al. (1990) used computer algorithms to parse their movement recordings according to predefined criteria such as a local minima in the velocity/time function (see also Gottsdanker 1967; Sternberg et al. 1990). These investigators were thus able to avoid potential confounding caused by errors of judgment in manual scoring versus systematic effects (or variability) in the performance itself.

There is also a third, conceptual point to consider about treating continuous movement in terms of discrete features. The psychological validity of a feature has an important bearing on the strength of inferences made about movement control based on the variability of that feature. Some investigators might argue that movement is essentially continuous, even oscillatory (Kelso 1981). They would, for example, fault an analysis in terms of movement features that has as its goal the identification of a mechanism that regulates the temporal sequence of those features. Yet, even if one is committed to the view that ostensibly continuous action streams are fundamentally discrete (Sternberg et al. 1990), there are few a priori grounds for assuming that an arbitrary aspect of movement has any particular relevance to the motor system. So, caution must be exercised in choosing appropriate features for study. There may be considerable variability in arbitrarily selected features, but their inconsistency will be quite uninformative compared with the variability of a feature truly relevant to, and regulated by, the motor system.

29.3 VARIABILITY OF MOVEMENT

In the previous section, we have seen various approaches to measuring movement that, it is hoped, capture the spirit of the behavior. After collection of the data, the next stage is to summarize them. Describing movement often entails using averages as a measure of central tendency to say what constitutes typical behavior. However, with our theme that the degree of movement consistency is a hallmark of the underlying control processes, we want to go beyond this. We now consider some of the various measures that are available for quantifying motor variability.

The range between the minimum and maximum observations provides a very direct measure of the scatter in a set of data. A historically significant treatment of minimum observations appears in Donders (1869). He represented the latency of movement onset in response to a stimulus (RT) as the sum of delays taken up by a succession of processing stages (also see Sternberg 1969). In a footnote on unwanted fluctuations of RT caused by effects such as distraction, Donders (1869) emphasized the importance of the minimum RT, suggesting that it represents "the smoothest and most undisturbed course of the process." He also suggested that, under changes of experimental conditions that caused alterations in mean RT, it was useful to examine differences between the minimum and the mean. His idea was that this might provide "clear insight into the deviations from ideal regularity, and from this something may no doubt be deduced about the cause of the deviations."

A century later, Welford (1969) also argued for using measures of range, but this time the focus was on the scatter of movement endpoints around a target in Fitts's (1954) tapping task, rather than on RT. Here, Welford suggested that in estimating the scatter, extreme outlying values or "wild deviants" should be discarded. A problem with this suggestion is that there may be arbitrariness in the identification of such outliers. To overcome it, one might examine the full distribution of values in the form of a histogram. Indeed, the shape of the histogram could itself indicate mechanisms that generate the outlying values, as suggested by Shaffer (1973) for keystroke intervals in typing.

Because it is a single number, the range offers a more convenient way to represent the variability in a set of data than does the histogram. However, since the range is a statistic based on only two observations, it is an unreliable and wasteful way of indicating the scatter of a set of observations. The variance, defined as the average squared deviation about the mean, does a far better job of representing all the data, and it is the most commonly used index of movement variability. In movement research, the variance is often called *variable error*, or VE (Stelmach and Kelso 1977; Stelmach and McCracken 1978; Meyer et al. 1990).

In addition to employing variance as an index of motor performance, it is of course usual to report the mean. Sometimes the variance (or more usually its square root, the standard deviation) is scaled relative to the mean and reported as the *coefficient of variation* (MacKenzie and van Eerd 1990; Young and Schmidt 1990). If the mean is reported as a difference from the target value, it is commonly called the *constant error*, CE. Movement researchers sometimes also report *absolute error*, AE, which indicates the average unsigned departure from the target. This last statistic and, its close relative, the root mean-square error represent linear combinations of the information contained in VE and CE (Lee et al. 1990). However, because AE cannot be unambiguously related to variance (Meyer et al. 1990), we will not consider it further in this review.

Static Environment

In the next two subsections, we look at movement that takes place in a static environment. Under the heading single action, we start with studies that examine the control of movements aimed at a target. Examination of the factors governing movement variability provides insight into the processes underlying the control of movement. In these studies, although the subject's task is defined in terms of spatial accuracy, timing of movement is an important aspect of performance. Next, we will turn from single action to serial action. Here, timing becomes an explicit component of the tasks in the studies that we review. However, the theme remains the same, namely, that variability provides useful clues to the organization of human movement control.

Single Action   As mentioned earlier, Fitts (1954) observed that movements aimed at a target require more time as the target distance increases, if the spread of movement endpoints is to be kept within the bounds set by the width of the target. Welford et al. (1969) investigated this speed-accuracy tradeoff by running a wide age-range of subjects on a task where a stylus had to be moved alternately between two targets. In regressing movement time (MT) on the measured scatter of endpoints and the experimenter-determined distance between the targets, Welford et al. identified a dissociation between the effect of age on two regression parameters. One of the parameters, which Welford et al. identified with control over an initial ballistic distance-covering phase of movement, was at its maximum in the youngest age group. The other parameter, which was taken to reflect visually guided control of the approach to the target at the end of movement, attained its zenith in the forty-year-old group. The analysis by Welford et al. therefore suggests that the variability of movement in any given individual reflects a balance between two different modes of control exerted in the initial and end phases of movement.

A formalized theory of the speed-accuracy trade-off, also based on such a two-phase view of rapid aiming movements, is reviewed in Meyer et al. (1990). These authors supposed that subjects adjust the initial distance covering movement by taking a prototypical force-time function and scaling parameters that determine the function's duration and amplitude. Meyer et al. also assumed that the scaling of the parameters is inherently noisy, so that there are errors in setting duration or amplitude. Over trials, this results in a scatter of endpoints for any given target distance. They showed that Fitts's law (and other forms of trade-off between movement duration and accuracy) may occur because subjects allow for increases in the variability of movement with larger values of the two scale parameters by introducing one or more secondary, compensating submovements. An optimal performance model developed by Meyer et al. (1990) predicts that, for a given MT, greater relative accuracy would be expected with increasing numbers of corrective submovements, n. However, the gains decline with n and Fitts's law emerges as a limiting case with very large n (see fig. 29.3).

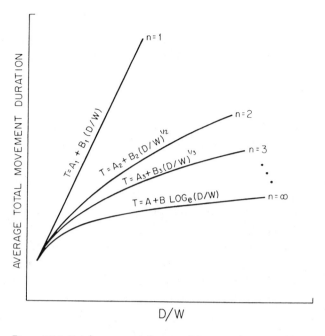

Figure 29.3 Total movement duration (T) versus the ratio of target distance to width (D/W) predicted by an optimized multiple submovement model for different maximum numbers of submovements, n. (From Meyer et al. 1990; fig. 6.13.)

One important component of the Meyer et al. (1990) model is the noisy scaling of the prototypical force-time function. Some support for the hypothesis of scaled fluctuations as a source of variability in aiming appeared in an earlier report by Gottsdanker (1967). He contrasted various methods for averaging accelerometer recordings from repeated movements to a fixed target. His goal was to determine the times at which corrections to movement occurred when a target changed its position. He suggested that averaging after time-scaling yielded a picture more indicative of individual acceleration functions. This would be expected if the variability of aiming movements arises from scale fluctuations in a single underlying prototypical force-time function.

What might be the sources of the variability assumed by Meyer et al. (1990)? One possibility is inaccuracy in selecting the appropriate values for the scaling parameters. Resetting of the scaling parameters (either for each submovement in the course of approaching a particular target, or for the return movement back to the start position) may be prone to error. However, studies in which subjects must reproduce a movement after a delay show that variable (as well as constant) error increases with time (Stelmach and McCracken 1978), especially if there is some intervening task competing for memory (Stelmach and Kelso 1977). Although movement durations in this delayed-response paradigm were not controlled, these results suggest that a second source of variability in the scaling parameters of the Meyer et al. (1990) model may be random fluctuations after parameter selection has occurred. Yet another potential source of variability is the use of sensory information in the setting of movement parameters. Soechting and Terzuolo (1990), for example, discussed the role of sensorimotor transformations mediating between localization of the visual target, proprioceptive information about current hand position, and specification of motor commands. However, to date, research on this topic has emphasized systematic rather than random error.

Serial Action   In turning from single aimed movements to serial action, our focus shifts from the positional inaccuracy of movement to variability in timing the component movements of a sequence. The regulated timing of a succession of movements is a feature of the performance in both trained skills such as music (Shaffer 1984) and of everyday activities such as speech (Fowler and Tassinary 1981). In this section we ask what is known about timing variability in such performance.

It is generally accepted that longer time intervals are produced with greater variability (but see MacKenzie and van Eerd 1990, as discussed below). A study by Rosenbaum and Patashnik (1980) had the novel feature of manipulating required temporal accuracy (somewhat analogous to varying the target width for a positioning movement). On each trial, subjects produced a brief time interval by making two key-press responses in quick succession, the first with the left index finger, the second with the right. The time interval, or rather the first key-press, was produced in response to an auditory signal (which also allowed RT to be measured). The target interresponse interval, which ranged from 0 (when the two keys had to be pressed simultaneously) to 1050 ms, was constant over a block of trials.

Rosenbaum and Patashnik (1980) found a linear increasing relation between the variability and the mean of the interresponse intervals (see fig. 29.4). One possible mechanism that would produce this result is a timing device (a "mental clock") that waits until a predetermined count of random neural events (a Poisson source) has accrued. A key feature of such a stochastic timer is that the variance of the times taken to reach a given count is directly proportional to the mean. This was just what Rosenbaum and Patashnik observed, and it was also the relation assumed by Meyer et al. (1990) in their model of aimed movements.

Rosenbaum and Patashnik's (1980) experiment included a manipulation of knowledge of results (KR): subjects in one condition ("stringent") were encouraged to be more accurate and received more detailed KR than in the other ("relaxed") condition. In the stringent condition, RTs were generally longer but the intervals were less variable than in the relaxed condition. A steeper-sloped (but equally linear) function was obtained in the relaxed condition. Under the stochastic-timer model, this may be interpreted as the result of a lowering in the rate of the random event source.

Another particularly important result of the accuracy manipulation by Rosenbaum and Patashnik (1980) was that it left the variance function's intercept (corresponding to zero mean interresponse interval) virtually unchanged. This is interesting because if there were a random delay in response execution caused by motor delays at the beginning and at the end of the

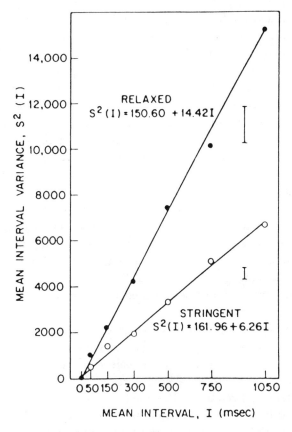

Figure 29.4 Interresponse interval variance ($S^2(I)$) versus mean interval (I) between two key-press responses made under relaxed or stringent interval accuracy requirements. Estimates of $+/-SE$ based on mean square fits of mean functions to the individual data of three subjects. (From Rosenbaum and Patashnik 1980; fig. 5.2.)

interval timed by the mental clock, then the sum of their variances would result in the observed intercept. However, for such an interpretation to hold, variability in the motor delays would have to be independent of clock variability. The constancy of the intercept (attributed to the motor delays) with changes in the slope of the function (attributed to the clock) is consistent with this assumption.

Variability of interresponse intervals in multiple-response sequences has been reported by MacKenzie and van Eerd (1990), who studied pianists as they performed scales (with the goal of playing as regularly as possible). The motivation for their study was to test whether, for any particular scale, there might be a single internal representation of the motor commands required to play it (a motor program), such that producing the note sequence faster or slower involves a scaling of the time values. This would correspond to the time scaling proposed by Meyer et al. (1990), except that in the piano playing example the force dimension would be replaced by representations of finger responses as discrete events on an elastic timeline.

MacKenzie and van Eerd (1990) argued that the pattern of departures from regularity, which by assumption would reflect the temporal structure of the underlying motor program, should be maintained in proportional terms when playing at different speeds. Moreover, if in playing slower, for example, the intervals were all scaled longer, there would be a corresponding increase in their variance. However, data from a number of concert-level performers who played scales at various rates failed to support these predictions. MacKenzie and van Eerd (1990) found that as tempo increased from four to twelve notes per second, namely, as the intervals between notes got shorter, the timing pattern of performances changed, and a monotonic increase occurred in the standard deviation of internote intervals.

How, then, can we square Rosenbaum and Patashnik's (1980) finding of greater variance at longer intervals with these new data? One possible answer is that in piano playing, the control of timing is not the only, perhaps not even the principal, source of variability. If peripheral anatomical interactions increase as internote intervals get shorter, regulation of the movements per se may require more control and cause increased variability in peripheral execution delays.

An interaction between effectors reported by Tuller and Kelso (1990) is possibly relevant here. They found that, as subjects increased their rate of producing a repetitive utterance, the movements of the two speech articulators tended to be drawn into an altered phase relationship. This changed the resulting utterance. Even before this point, the interval between given phases of movement by the two articulators became more variable as the interval between successive repetitions got shorter. This last point may underline the seemingly anomalous increase in variance at shorter intervals in the piano-playing study. Suppose in playing scales there was a tendency for the movements of the two hands to move into some inappropriate phase relation. If this tendency increased with rate, it might have introduced additional variability of a peripheral nature that could have masked any reduction in variability associated with a central timing device.

In order to interpret differences between the findings in piano-playing and finger-tapping, we have appealed to separate sources of variability in higher- and lower-level processes. Sternberg et al. (1990) have reported other evidence of a dissociation between lower and higher levels of control in typing. Under conditions that loaded a high-level response specification process and resulted in slowing of overall typing rate, the microstructure of individual finger movements revealed that only one movement component (the late lift immediately before key attack) increased in duration. The other component phases of movement exhibited low-level invariance with respect to changes in the high-level process. However, there are other data on mean intervals in serial tasks that raise doubts about a strict division of control between higher and lower levels. For example, typing might be thought to be limited by peripheral mechanical interactions between the fingers moving with various degrees of overlap to successive keys. Larochelle (1984) showed that timing is sensitive to lexical aspects (word versus non-word) of the typed material even though these would normally be considered as acting at a high level.

Changing Environment

In the previous sections on actions in a static environment, we have seen how changes in variability in time-based measures of performance may be understood in terms of the variability of hypothetical component processes. Variability of movement is "explained" by decomposing it into distinct sources that are subject to separate influences. In the next two subsections, we turn to studies of movements that are made in relation to changes in the environment. An understanding of movement variability in such situations requires an appreciation of the degree to which the variability depends on the input to which the action relates.

Over the last twenty-five years, a very common psychological research paradigm has involved the analysis of the latency (RT) between an abrupt change in the environment and a movement made in response to that change. A majority of the RT studies in past Attention and Performance symposia volumes have sought to examine the nature of perceptual processes by the effects on RT of experimental manipulations of the stimulus. However, some have had as their focus the organization of movement and, in particular, the nature of the preparation that occurs before movement and allows a movement to be initiated more or less rapidly according to the movement demands. In turning to consider these and other studies of movements made in a changing environment, we will again see how movement variability is identified with various underlying processes, each providing a separate source of variance.

Single Action   An important element in motor preparation is the role of uncertainty. Clearly, if a subject is not sure until the very last moment which of two alternate movements is required, the result is likely to be greater variability in movement outcome (e.g., Ghez et al. 1990). But, even in simple RT tasks where the subject knows in advance exactly what movement is required (usually a button press), he or she may be uncertain about the time at which the imperative signal to respond will occur. This temporal uncertainty may be either because the foreperiod between warning and imperative signals is made to vary over trials by the experimenter, or because the subject's temporal judgment is inherently unreliable.

Gottsdanker (1975) suggested that RTs are longer with greater temporal uncertainty because maintaining full motor readiness over an extended period requires effort which subjects would prefer to avoid. Instead, they judge the time when they think the imperative signal will occur and set readiness to peak at that point. If the signal then occurs at a different time, they will be slower to initiate their response. Näätänen and Merisalo (1977) argued that the most important determinant of simple RT is the subjective probability of immediate delivery of the imperative stimulus, and that this is affected both by the distribution of foreperiod times and the stimulus probability on a given trial.

Variability of movement timing in a task that required action related to continuous environmental change (as opposed to the abrupt onset of a signal light typical of RT paradigms) has been documented by McLeod, McLaughlin and Nimmo-Smith (1985). The basic tenet of their work was that an approaching object (e.g., a ball) generates a characteristic optic-flow field whose physics provides very direct cues about the object's time of arrival at the observer (see also Lee et al. 1990). Given this fact, the visual information may afford simplicity of movement timing when the observer has to swing a bat across the ball's trajectory and hit it.

To test this idea, McLeod et al. (1985) contrasted temporal variability of movement in batting a ball dropped down a fixed path toward the subject versus variability in another task (coincidence timing) in which the optic-flow field could not provide a cue for timing movement. They found remarkably low variability in the batting task. For a ball flight time of approximately 0.5 s, the standard deviation of the interception time was only 5 ms. This was approximately six times less than for the coincidence-timing task and some five times lower than the timing variability in the two-response task of Rosenbaum and Patashnik (1980) that we considered earlier.

On the basis of these results, McLeod et al. (1985) suggested that low temporal variability is a characteristic of a computational process performed by a "specific, dedicated processor, uninfluenced by other cognitive activities," a concept that corresponds to that of modularity as discussed by Keele, Cohen, and Ivry (1990). McLeod et al. further suggested that if perceptual-motor skill acquisition proceeds by the selection of a fast route to action, the study of shortened latencies resulting from the elimination of intervening processing stages would be usefully complemented by examining the variability of performance. There should be a close correspondence between changes in mean and changes in variance.

In simple RT paradigms, the only uncertainty concerns the time at which the movement is required, and this is resolved by the imperative signal. In choice RT procedures, the imperative signal not only indicates the time at which the subject should respond, it also provides information about which of two or more alternative movements should be made. (An intermediate case is the precue RT paradigm in which, before the imperative signal, the subject is partially informed about the required response in terms of a subset of the dimensions of movement that distinguish the alternate responses (for a review, see Requin 1985).

A two-choice RT study described by Frowein, Reitsma, and Aquarius (1981) provides an interesting example because it includes data on both RT and MT. Each trial started with the subject resting a hand-held stylus on a central start plate. At a variable interval after a visual warning signal, one of two lamps was illuminated to indicate whether the subject should move the stylus to a target plate on the right or on the left. RT was measured as the time between illumination of this lamp and movement off the start plate. MT

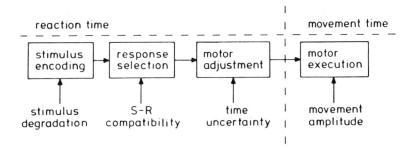

Figure 29.5 A model of the reaction process in which latency is assumed to arise as the sum of the times taken by each of a series of discrete information-processing stages. Each stage is liable to the influence of the experimental factor shown. (From Frowein, Reitsma, and Aquarius 1981; fig. 33.1.)

was defined by the time between start-plate release and arrival at the target plate.

Frowein et al. were interested in using the effects of various experimental factors to evaluate the relationship between processes underlying the preparation and execution of movement. Figure 29.5 provides a schematic representation of their theoretical model, which was based on Sternberg's (1969) additive-factor approach. Latencies are assumed to arise as a summation of times taken by a series of discrete information-processing stages. Each stage is liable to the influence of one or more experimental factors. Where two factors act on separate stages, their effects on RT will be additive. Thus, the figure represents time uncertainty and stimulus degradation as affecting separate stages because other research (e.g., Sanders 1980) had shown additive effects of these two factors on RT. An interaction between two factors is taken to indicate that they act on a stage in common. Sanders (1980), for example, concluded that instructed muscle tension (tense or relaxed) and time uncertainty (a foreperiod of 1 or 10 seconds) affected a common motor-adjustment process because a significant slowing of RT in the relaxed condition was greater at the short foreperiod than at the long foreperiod.

The factors treated by Frowein et al. were movement amplitude (target distance either 10 or 30 cm), time uncertainty (foreperiod either fixed at 1 s or variable in the range 4 to 6 s), sleep deprivation (half the subjects lost one night's sleep before testing), and administration of amphetamine (one hour before testing, subjects received either an amphetamine derivative or a placebo in double-blind fashion). Sleep deprivation, amphetamine and time uncertainty had interactive effects on RT, and these were interpreted as arising in the motor-adjustment stage. Movement amplitude also had a small effect on RT. However, its effect on RT did not interact with the other factors, so that additive-factor logic would suggest its effect occurred through some process other than the motor-adjustment process affected by time uncertainty.

MT was, not surprisingly, affected by movement amplitude. The more interesting result was that sleep deprivation and amphetamine affected MT, but in an additive rather than interactive fashion. This led Frowein et al. (1981) to suggest (according to the logic of the additive-factor method) that two different mechanisms in movement execution were being affected by the physiological stressors. With our interest in movement control, it is tempting to speculate that these two putative processes might be identified with the ballistic and guided phases of aimed movement mentioned in an earlier section.

In his original exposition of the additive-factor method, Sternberg (1969) pointed out that, provided certain additional assumptions were met, the implication of additivity for separate underlying stages applied not only to the mean (first cumulant) but also to higher cumulants, including variance (the second cumulant). The additional assumption required for additivity of variance is that the stages be stochastically independent. In that case, for example, if two different factors each separately increase the variance by some amount, and they have interactive effects on variance when applied together, this would be taken as evidence of their influencing a common processing stage. Additivity of variance would obtain if the factors were to affect separate stages. However, there are no reports of the method being successively applied to variability data. This probably reflects the unwillingness of researchers to accept the necessary independence assumption. Sternberg (1969) provided some arguments about why it might be problematic. Findings such as Meyer and Gordon's (1984) demonstration that vocal RT is faster if an aural stimulus shared voicing as a feature in common with the vocal response also call into question the validity of the assumptions of the additive-factor method.

Serial Action   Having considered variability in single, isolated actions related to a changing environment, we now turn to consider variability in sequences of actions. In the earlier section on serial action in a static environment, we referred to the work of Rosenbaum and Patashnik (1980). Their results suggested that the variability observed in the interval between two successive responses arises from two distinct sources: a timing mechanism, and delays in implementing movement. In that study, Rosenbaum and Patashnik also collected RT data. The first of each pair of responses that produced the variability data was made in response to an auditory imperative signal. With our present focus on variability, a particularly interesting aspect of the RT data was that lower interresponse-interval variability was associated with longer RTs. Thus, RTs for the stringent condition were longer than for the relaxed condition. Moreover, RTs were shorter in a control condition where subjects produced only a single response without any timing requirements. This suggests that timing is an element of the preparatory processes that are precursors to action.

In fact, a number of empirical studies (Glencross 1980; Klapp, Greim and Marshburn 1981; Semjen and Gottsdanker 1990) and a review chapter (Marteniuk and MacKenzie 1980) have been devoted to the nature of latency effects in the initiation of response sequences of varying length and complexity. So it would be naive to suppose that absence of timing demands was the only factor contributing to the reduction of RT in Rosenbaum and Patashnik's single response condition. However, the importance of timing regulation in movement sequences made in response to environmental input also emerges in a study of typing by Shaffer (1973). Shaffer required subjects to type words or random letter strings that were presented on a visual display. Of particular interest was the effect of varying preview (the number of letters displayed ahead of the letter currently being typed). In typing prose, he found that the mean and variability of the interkeystroke intervals produced by the subjects increased with decreasing preview.

The form of the distribution of intervals led Shaffer to suggest that typing involves temporally regulated output (specifying individual target keys) from a storage buffer containing batches of material awaiting execution. With material comprising preformed lexical units, given sufficient preview, larger groups of keystrokes may be loaded into the buffer, and the output may then be paced at a higher rate without risk of the buffer being emptied, which would force an idle period. The buffer thus serves to "insulate" the production of keystrokes from the vagaries of earlier processing stages. With the pacing rate adjusted to suit the difficulty of incoming material, the variability of keystrokes would normally only reflect the processes of movement production. To the extent that the timer controls the pacing rate, the variability (or even the form of the distribution) of the interkeystroke intervals may be taken as characterizing the two sources—the timer, and the implementation delays. If movements are invariant with changes in rate, then changes in variability might be attributed to the timer.

Despite the "insulating" function of the output buffer, Shaffer (1973) did consider that perceptual processes might also contribute to timing variability. This view has parallels with earlier work on serial RT with short interstimulus intervals (comparable to transcription with one-item preview). Rabbitt (1967) and Welford (1967) both speculated that processing of KR for one trial might affect the RT on the next trial because "any high point of kinaesthetic, tactile or other stimulation arising during a response might capture the decision mechanism ... the end of a movement often provides such a high point" (Welford 1967).

Subsequently, Shaffer (1984) revised his view of timing regulation in typing to allow for the fact that early phases of keystroke movements exhibit greater timing variability than do the keystrikes. A finger movement towards a particular target key may even be initiated before the movement of another finger to a target that is actually struck later (also see Larochelle 1984). Shaffer suggested that the pacing of output applies to a later phase of movement (e.g., that resulting in key depression). Earlier phases, such as departure of a finger from the previously struck key, may be determined in common with a number of other simultaneously active finger movements as a compound movement trajectory for a larger linguistic unit.

29.4 STRUCTURE IN MOVEMENT VARIABILITY

Up to this point, we have looked at variability in a global manner, as though it were a matter of indifference regarding which particular observations had been taken into account. Yet, hidden within what might appear to be completely random data sets, there may be subtle patterns due to statistical dependence within or between measures. We now turn, in the second half of this chapter, to review a number of studies that illustrate how such "structure within variation" can extend our understanding of the processes underlying motor control. The identification of patterns of dependence between distinct measures can reveal functional links between the elements giving rise to those measures.

The covariance between two measures is usually employed to summarize the statistical association between the measures that would, for example, be evident in a scatterplot. *Covariance* is defined as the expected value of the product of two terms; the deviation of each individual value about the mean on one measure and the deviation of the corresponding value of a second measure around its mean. Taking pairs of values, if departures from the mean on one measure have the same sign as departures from the mean on the other more often than would be expected by chance, the covariance is positive. If departures from the mean tend to have opposite signs more often than chance, the covariance is negative. To facilitate comparison of statistical dependence between various pairs of measures which, individually, might have quite different degrees of variability, the product-moment correlation may be used. The *correlation* between two variables equals their covariance normalized by the product of the square root of their variances. Correlation values are bounded by plus and minus one. If two variables are independent the expected value of their correlation is zero.

Often, in the study of movement, a set of paired observations will be ordered in time. For example, changes in the angular position of the elbow may be recorded along with shoulder-angle changes over the course of a series of oscillating movements that take the hand repetitively between two positions in space. In such cases, it may be important to recognize differences in covariance between two measures as a function of their relative phase. Different *cross-covariance* terms may be computed for pairs of observations separated by different intervals, or phase lags (e.g., Lee et al. 1990). Often the cross-covariance term at zero phase lag will have the greatest absolute value, but if one measure "drives" the other with some delay, then the cross-covariance will be at a maximum at a phase lag corresponding to that delay. At this delay, the variation in the second, "driven" measure will be most closely related to the first, "dominant" measure. In our example, if shoulder movement serves as a trigger for elbow movement, changes in shoulder angle will lead elbow-angle changes. If a cross-covariance function is computed it will be an asymmetric function of phase lag, with a maximum at a lag reflecting the shoulder's lead. Patterns of covariation can thus suggest the existence of a functional linkage between measures varying as a function of time.

Finally, it is necessary to mention a special case of cross-covariance in which the two values, whose cross-product is taken at some lag, are defined on the same measure (e.g., Vorberg and Hambuch 1978). Termed the *auto-* or *serial covariance*, it describes the dependence as a function of lag within a series of observations of a single variable. Two points to note about serial covariance are that it is a symmetric function of lag and that the serial covariance at lag zero corresponds to the variance.

Static Environment

In the next section, we look at simultaneous changes in various components cooperating in a single action such as reaching and grasping an object. Then we turn in the subsequent section to serial action, where we will be concerned with the dependence within a series of observations of a single measure taken repeatedly. In both cases, we will see how structure within variability illuminates the nature of movement control.

Single Action Many studies of movement variability, such as those reviewed earlier in this chapter, have involved no more than simple positioning of the hand. However, in real life, hand positioning most often subserves the ultimate goal of grasping an object to move or manipulate it. To achieve a successful grasp, positioning and orienting by the arm (hand transport) must be accompanied by appropriate shaping of the fingers (hand aperture). The covariation of these two components of movement represents a useful point of departure in our search for functional linkages revealed by constraints on variability.

A study by Jeannerod (1981) documented a temporal linkage between the transport and aperture components of reaching. Before the hand closed on the object, a maximum hand aperture was observed that allowed the fingers to encompass the object. Over a series of movements to the same object, the maximum aperture tended to coincide with the time at which there was deceleration of the transport component (see fig. 29.6). Had Jeannerod computed it, the correlation between these two components would have been positive. He did not do so, but he did report that the transport component was unaffected by quite major changes in hand aperture, occasioned, for example, by variation in object size, even when that change occurred during the hand's approach. He therefore reasoned that the control of aperture is influenced by visuo-motor processes associated with transport, but not the converse. This hierarchy or dominance relationship may also be seen in Arbib's (1990) schematic representation of the control of prehensile movement.

Two effector systems, the hand and the arm, capable of independent movement, thus appear to be used in a coordinated fashion. To the extent that one of these components exhibits variation over trials, there is a temporal constraint on the other, limiting its variation. The anticipatory hand-shaping component exhibits relative temporal invariance.

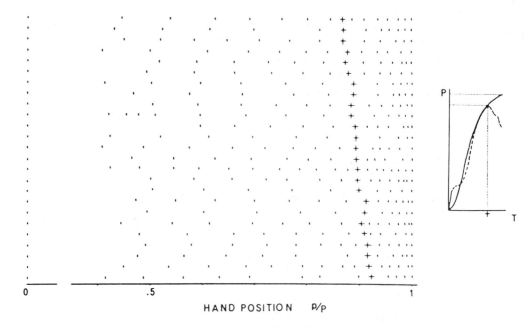

Figure 29.6 Hand position (normalized by total movement distance) at 40-msec intervals for a series of 25 reaching movements. Maximum grasp aperture (marked +) tends to co-occur with onset of the hand's slowing down. The diagram on the right shows an illustrative time plot of aperture (dashed line) superimposed on transport (solid line). (From Jeannerod 1981; fig. 9.6.)

This may be relevant to other work on coordination. For example, in discussing the coordination of elements in systems with several degrees of freedom, Turvey, Shaw, and Mace (1978) proposed a taxonomy of possible classes of interaction between the elements. One of their main themes was that there are limitations to hierarchical arrangements, in which one process dominates a number of others. They argued that heterarchical coalitions may play an important role in the coordination of movement. Jeannerod's work thus suggests a way in which correlational data might be used to distinguish between hierarchically or heterarchically organized component processes.

The linkage between hand aperture and transport has also been studied in infants. Von Hofsten (1990) showed that around the age of five months, infants exhibit onset of hand closure distributed evenly around the time of contact with an object they wish to grasp. However, the distribution of closure-onset times had changed in a group of thirteen-month-olds carrying out the same task. In the majority of these latter subjects, by the time of contact with the object, the hand had usually started to close. An interesting question is whether this increase in anticipatory shaping with age is accompanied by tighter temporal coupling of the kind demonstrated by Jeannerod (1981) in adults. A within-subject correlational analysis would be informative in this respect.

Coordination between the arm and hand has also been studied by Johansson and Westling (1990), but in the context of lifting a grasped object. Using an instrumented handle attached to loads of varying weight, Johansson and Westling obtained measures of grip force, load force, and position as a function of time. Their time plots suggested a tight coupling between the lifting action of the arm and the grip force exerted by the hand to prevent the object slipping from grasp. Although correlational analyses were not performed, scatter plots of grip force versus load force (taken at zero phase, i.e., at identical points in time) indicated a dependence between the gripping and lifting actions. As load force increased (indicating lifting by the hand), there was a concomitant increase in grip force such that the traces for different weights overlay one another even though the rates of change of force differed systematically across weights. Johansson and Westling's other graphs suggest that, had they computed correlations, for example, between peak rate of change in grip force and load force, these would have been strongly positive.

An important point made by Johansson and Westling (1990) was that the coupling of gripping and lifting was evident from the outset, which implies that the coordination pattern was specified in advance. Indeed, they reported that if the subject, having performed a series of lifts at one weight, was then given an unexpectedly heavy weight to lift, slipping occurred because the rate of increase in grip force with time was only sufficient (relative to a given lifting rate) for the lighter load. When such an object-slip occurred, feedback corrections to increase grip force were observed. Further commentary on the importance of feedback in such compensatory reactions may be found in Abbs and Winstein (1990). However, for present purposes, the important point is that grip-force changes are generally linked to load-force changes produced by the lifting action.

Serial Action We now turn from considering covariation over time between measures defined on two separate effectors to dependence between successive observations on a single-effector measure. In work by Vorberg and Hambuch (1978) the single measure of interest was the time interval between repetitive finger movements. Their procedure required subjects to tap a morse key at a fixed rate with period of either 300 or 500 ms. To set the rate, subjects initially synchronized their responses with a train of brief tones. These tones coincided either with every response, or, in three conditions designed to induce different subjective groupings, with every second, third or fourth response. This manipulation had the desired effect as evidenced by the serial covariance functions. In the last three conditions, the maximum serial covariance occurred at lags corresponding to the size of the experimenter-intended grouping.

Vorberg and Hambuch's (1978) important insight was that, assuming subjects did group their responses, they might have controlled response timing at a number of different levels. For example, in one model, it was hypothesized that a superordinate timer regulates a long interval taking in a whole response group, while a set of lower-level timers is responsible for timing the succession of short intervals within each group (see fig. 29.7). Vorberg and Hambuch

MODEL I

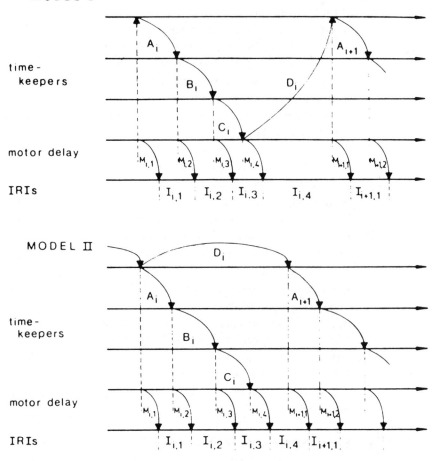

time-
keepers

motor delay

IRIs

MODEL II

time-
keepers

motor delay

IRIs

Figure 29.7 Two schematic models for the timing of responses grouped in fours. Model I: Serial succession of timekeepers. Model II: Hierarchically organized timing (the timekeeper responsible for interval D is superordinate to the other three). (From Vorberg and Hambuch 1978; fig. 4.)

contrasted various hierarchical structures of this kind with a model in which a series of timers works at a single level. For all their models, they assumed that the timers would have to operate through independently varying delays associated with motor execution processes (cf. Rosenbaum and Patashnik 1980).

This work is relevant to our present theme because Vorberg and Hambuch showed that these models, which differ in the linkages proposed between processing elements, make contrasting predictions about the within- and between-group structure of interresponse-interval variability. For example, consider the serial cross-covariance matrix (the serial covariances recognizing the position of the interval within the group). Vorberg and Hambuch showed that it would have negative off-diagonal elements for every model. However, in the case of single-level timing, just the off-diagonal elements would be negative and they would all be equal.

Also, a further interesting property involves the variance of the interval spanning the response group. With r responses in a group, the sum of any r successive interresponse intervals (a cycle) must have the same mean (assuming stationarity, i.e., no drift in the mean interresponse interval). However, the situation is different for variances. The cycle variance will be smaller if the component interresponse intervals all fall within one hierarchical group than if they span the boundary between two adjacent hierarchical groups. In contrast, a serial-timer model implies the cycle variance should not depend on how the cycle is chosen with respect to the group.

A number of analyses were performed by Vorberg and Hambuch (1978). For the most part, the results conformed to the latter prediction. The structure of the interresponse-interval variance did not support the concept of hierarchical timing.

Theoretically, this finding might seem somewhat puzzling. After all, the synchronization procedure of Vorberg and Hambuch introduced a grouping that was demonstrable in terms of the serial covariance functions. To account for such discrepancy, Vorberg and Hambuch suggested that the latter response grouping, which was primarily an effect on the mean of every nth interval, may have been associated with a hierarchical structure limited to setting up or planning the sequence. In contrast, execution may involve only serial timing. (For a similar distinction between hierarchical and sequential modes of controlling serial order in planning and execution, see Sternberg et al. 1990).

Although they found no evidence of hierarchical timing, Vorberg and Hambuch (1978) noted consistent support for a separation of timing variability into central timing functions and peripheral execution processes, as discussed earlier regarding Rosenbaum and Patashnik's (1980) work. Such a division was also suggested by Shaffer (1973) in his study of the variability of inter-keystroke intervals in typing. However, as pointed out earlier, Shaffer (1984) subsequently questioned the applicability of clock-like control of typing, at least in respect to the early phase of each keystroke. Instead he favored a view in which the regularity of interkeystroke intervals is a secondary consequence of movement logistics. In this later work he also questioned whether expressive timing in music is regulated by a movement system tightly linked to a central timekeeper. As an alternative, he sketched a system in which movements may exhibit considerable voluntary departures from an internal beat.

The concept that a performer is aware of motor output delays, and indeed can optionally vary them, perhaps by exaggerated movement, seems reasonable. Moreover, there seems to be a formal similarity with MacNeilage and Davis's (1990) view of the development of speech in infants. These authors suggested that infants move toward an adult organization of speech, in which syllable structure constraints provide a "frame" for segmental content elements, by local modification of a uniform oscillatory sequence. Still, it will be appreciated that such schemes also encourage scientific efforts to partition movement variance into component sources.

Changing Environment

In the previous two sections, we have seen how the variability of distinct elements (either spatially distinct in the sense of being simultaneously available to observation, or temporally distinct in comprising a series of successive observations) may exhibit underlying structure. In the next two sections, we further explore the connectedness in sets of movement observations, where the movements are related to environmental changes. In such cases, the environmental dynamics may drive the individual components into coordinated patterns of activity to give structure within variability.

Single Action The previous section described how a cycle-variance property was used by Vorberg and Hambuch (1978) as a test for a hierarchical control mechanism in the timing of interresponse intervals. Their models made contrasting predictions about the serial covariances of the intervals. A related approach to understanding the structural organization of interceptive timing in single actions has been described by Young and Schmidt (1990).

Young and Schmidt's procedure, which has a number of parallels with the ball-interception task of McLeod et al. (1985), required subjects to make a hand-positioning movement (elbow extension) coincident with an "approaching" train of sequentially pulsed lights arranged in a line (as if to hit the end light). The start position of the hand was aligned with the target, but the procedure required preliminary movement away (as in a backswing) before reversing to return to the target. The timing of various phases in this action was examined for two groups of subjects who had contrasting levels of movement proficiency. One group received KR on practice trials. They achieved coincident-timing performance superior to a group that received no KR. (The levels of performance were considerably lower than in the batting group studied by McLeod et al. and, for the KR group, more like those of Rosenbaum and Patashnik's subjects; this is probably because in Young and Schmidt's task, the visual array afforded a less direct cue to action than in McLeod's task).

To evaluate the temporal microstructure of the reversal movements, Young and Schmidt (1990) identified various features in the kinematic profiles (see fig. 29.8). They then computed cumulative times, first with respect to movement onset, then relative to the time of coincidence. As might be expected, they obtained a general trend of greater variability with longer intervals. However, while there was a simple monotonic increase for the no-KR group, the KR

Figure 29.8 Coincidence timing. *Top:* Position, velocity, and acceleration-time functions for a single trial from a subject in the KR group showing temporal location of landmarks *a–g*. *Middle:* Averaged within-subject standard deviations of intervals 1 through 6 defined between (left) time of movement onset and landmarks *b* through *g* and (right) landmarks *a* through *f* and target attainment. Data from KR (solid line) and no KR (broken line) groups. *Bottom:* Averaged within-subject correlations between (left) onset time and times of landmarks *b* through *g*, and (right) times of landmarks *a* through *f* and target-attainment time. (From Young and Schmidt 1990; figs. 28.4, 28.6, 28.7.)

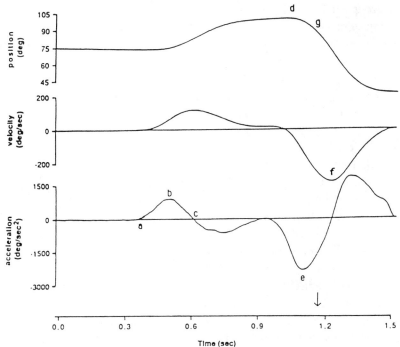

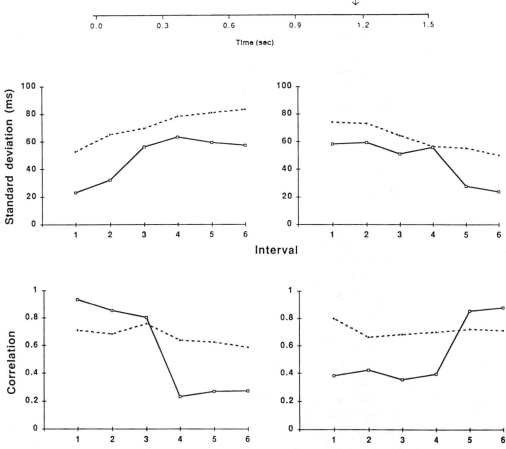

group exhibited a step increase in variance around a point in time corresponding to maximum outward excursion (*d* on the position trace).

Correlations between the onset or the coincidence-point times and the times of the intervening features also distinguished the two groups of subjects (see fig. 29.8). The KR group exhibited a clustering such that the movement-onset time correlated much more highly with time points up to maximum excursion than with later points. And, in complementary fashion, their coincidence times correlated much more highly with time points after maximum excursion than with earlier points. In contrast, for the no-KR group, the correlations were uniformly high.

To interpret the structure evident in the movement variability of the KR group, Young and Schmidt (1990) suggested that maximum excursion represents a transition between two separate action units. The groupings evident in the data may reflect a discontinuity imposed by higher-level patterning of an ostensibly continuous movement. Young and Schmidt also made a further suggestion for testing this idea. It rested on the fact that within one action unit, the coefficient of variation (normalized standard deviation) for intervals spanning two or more successive features might be expected to remain relatively constant. However, an interval spanning adjacent features that straddle a boundary between units not tightly controlled in time might be expected to exhibit a larger coefficient.

This was indeed the case for the KR group with a boundary defined by the maximum excursion. Since the identification of action segmentation is a perennial issue in motor control (e.g., see Viviani 1990 on arm movements; Fowler and Tassinary 1981 on speech), such a test appears to hold considerable promise. The payoff might be especially great if testing were carried out exhaustively, for example, by defining intervals across all potential boundaries with contrasting sets of kinematic features. This would circumvent the potential criticism of arbitrariness in time points chosen for analysis.

Serial Action At perhaps the highest level of complexity in the study of movement is the analysis of serial action that occurs relative to a changing environment. An example of such a situation is the synchronization component of the tapping procedure used by Vorberg and Hambuch (1978). Their subjects were required to produce key presses in tight temporal proximity to the pacing tone pulses. The pacing intervals and the intervals produced by the subject between successive responses may be considered as two time series of intervals.

Such time series have played a prominent role in previous related work. Michon and van der Valk (1967), for example, analyzed synchronization performance by treating the subject's task as one of temporal tracking. Their account of the effects of a step increase (or decrease) in the rate of the pacing stimulus was formulated in terms of a simple linear model relating input to output (cf. Viviani 1990). They hypothesized that the subject's current interresponse interval was determined by a weighted sum of the previous interval between pacing stimuli and the difference between the two previous stimulus intervals.

Although Michon and van der Valk's model accounts for input-output relations in a serial task, it does so only in terms of mean performance data. Nevertheless, other investigators have examined how data on variability in serial motor output may be related to variation in the environment. A good example of this appears in Lee et al. (1990). The focus of their study was the characterization of relations between movements of the head and a visual target. In some conditions, head movements were triggered by target movements and in other conditions, by movement of the observer's seat.

Lee et al. (1990) tested various groups of subjects, including 11-week-old infants, 29-week-old infants, and adults. Some relevant statistics from these tests concerned the general amount of movement of the head and of the eyes. The ratios of head-movement standard deviations to target-movement standard deviations were reported as 60 percent for both the 11-week-old infants and the adults, whereas, for 29-week-old infants, they were 100 percent. However, adults differed from the infants by the average root mean square deviations between their eye and target velocities, which were considerably less than at 11 and 29 weeks. Since we may assume that the adult visual system is accurately "geared" to foveate moving objects in the environment, the variability measures suggest a relatively greater contribution of eye movements for adults.

So far we have only a rather global characterization of variability in gaze. However, Lee et al. (1990) provided details of structure within the variability by computing cross-correlations between the subjects' movements and movements of the target and chair (see fig. 29.9). They found that the cross-correlation between head and target movements at zero lag was considerably higher in 29-week-old infants and adults (over 90%) than in 11-week-old infants (below 70%).

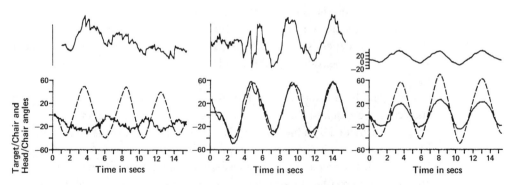

Figure 29.9 Illustrative gaze stablization records when the chair in which the subject was seated turned between +/−50 deg. *Left:* 11-week-old infant. *Middle:* Same infant, 29 weeks old. *Right:* Adult, 23 years old. Upper record is eye position (uncalibrated eog in the case of the infant data); in the lower record the broken line is the target/chair angle and the solid line, the head/chair angle. (From Lee et al. 1990; fig. 21.3a, b, e)

The correlation at lag zero corresponds to taking values for the head and target positions at the same points in time. If there is good correspondence between the two position waveforms, this implies predictive behavior. However, a low correlation at lag zero, as displayed by the 11-week-old infants, might be interpreted in various ways. For example, it could arise if they did not attend to the visual input, or if they controlled gaze with another (unanalyzed) movement. In the present case, this ambiguity can be resolved because Lee et al. (1990) computed correlations over a range of lags to determine whether peak correlations might be equally high in the very young and older infants, but at different lags (longer for the very young). They found that 11-week-old infants exhibited a peak cross-correlation of over 85% at a 350-ms lag (compared to values of around 95% at a lag below 100 ms in the older infants and the adults). This suggests a different, reactive rather than predictive, control mode in the 11-week-old infants.

While the work of Lee et al. (1990) concerned gaze, it also suggests interesting questions about the relative coordination between head and eye movements. Normally, rapid eye movements (saccades) are dominated by head movements. To achieve coordination in activities such as reaching, Prablanc and Pelisson (1990) suggested that when a common command invokes head and saccade movement generators, there is inhibition of the normal dominance relationship. Such linking of processes subserving head and eye movements is related to earlier observations by Biguer, Jeannerod, and Prablanc (1985). They noted that while there is an ordering of movement onset by eye, head, and lastly hand movement, EMG measures indicated a relative synchrony of command. Moreover, within trial-to-trial variability, there were positive correlations between the three systems consistent with informational links.

Most of the emphasis in this review has been on limb movements. Given the past tradition of motor behavior studies of pursuit tracking (e.g., Viviani 1990), it is perhaps appropriate to close with a cautionary note about using correlational analysis to relate sequential limb movements to a dynamic environment. Correlations must be computed over extended periods of time. Their interpretation depends on assuming that the processes under study remain stable over the period of interest. This assumption may not necessarily be valid.

For example, consider the work of Kelso, Colle, and Schoner (1990). Their subjects were required to synchronize finger-flexion movements either on or off a beat provided by a metronome. Depending on the relative phase and rate of the metronome, individual data records showed clear evidence of quantitative instability, or even qualitative change, in the relative phase of movement and metronome. One interpretation of such instabilities is that they arise through the interactions of two coupled oscillators (Kelso et al. 1990). Interestingly, this account predicts that certain relative phases should be more stable than others, and this was observed to be the case. Another virtue of this account is that it can also encompass apparent qualitative changes of behavior in moving from in-phase to out-of-phase patterns, as when animals change gait (Kelso 1981). However, in the present context, the point is that a correlational analysis would not be informative without allowing for the underlying drift.

29.5   CONCLUSIONS

In concluding this chapter we may contrast the uses of variance as a means to understanding movement control with the uses of variance in inferential statistics. Suppose that we must compare the means of two separate sets of data collected under different experimental conditions. Then it is customary to take account of the unreliability of sampled data by asking whether the difference between the means could have arisen by chance. This question is approached by comparing the variability of all the data, pooled over conditions, with the average variability within each condition. The latter constitutes a baseline against which the additional variability from changing the experimental conditions may be assessed.

In such comparisons of variance for inferential purposes, the estimates of baseline variance are not usually appropriate as indices of motor-system variability. To generalize conclusions about a difference between means across individuals, estimates of baseline variability must include differences between individuals performing under constant conditions. "Good" experimental design entails constraining the task so that subjects all behave in the same way, thereby minimizing baseline variability. The additional variance associated with an experimental effect will then stand out better against the low baseline variability. However, given the present review the emphasis changes if motor variability is the prime focus. It is then inappropriate for an experimenter to choose a task with minimal performance variability. Rather, experimental control is a matter of stabilizing the conditions so that, across subjects, estimates of within-subject variance may be consistent.

There are also other important aspects of using tasks that allow variability when we seek to characterize movement for our theorizing. We should recognize that the functional organization of movement may actively benefit from the presence of motor variability. A system that has intrinsic variability is likely to be more robust when faced with extrinsic sources of variability, whether the latter arise in the form of unexpected perturbations to intended movement, or as dynamic changes in environmentally-defined movement goals. A strategy that evolves to compensate for the inherent variability of ballistic movements in a static environment (Meyer et al. 1990) may well be adaptable to movement in a changing environment.

Intrinsic variability also affords versatility. Stereotyped movements can be difficult to change and adapt to suit different goals. If there is no information about how a movement can go wrong, there is no basis for improving movement. Subtle variation in movement over trials lends itself to opportunistic modification and improvement.

This point is underlined by neural network models. Jordan (1990), for example, described a connectionist network that learns to coordinate reaching movements of the upper limb. In the network, numerical weights determine the influence of underlying units on the movements of individual limb segments. The values of these "hidden" unit weights are incrementally changed according to an algorithm (backpropagation) that takes account of the rate of approach towards the desired outcome, namely, spatial coincidence of end-effector position with the target (see also Arbib 1990). A new movement is learned once a new set of hidden-unit weights has emerged. In such models it is commonly found that performance benefits from a degree of random variability in the weights. In this sense, therefore, variability is an important element in the learning of a coordinated action.

The introduction to this chapter raised several questions about the advancement, through the pages of Attention and Performance symposia proceedings, in our understanding of movement variability beyond Fitts's law. Over the years, there has been a steady growth of contributions to Attention and Performance dealing with movement variability. Fitts's (1954) original tapping task involved discrete movements occurring in a static environment, characterized only in terms of the speed and accuracy of the end points in the region of the target. Now the list of paradigms that have explored variability includes tasks requiring serial actions and actions related to a changing environment, with movements often being collected as continuous temporal records over several dimensions at once. Both observational and interventionist approaches have yielded a mass of data, largely concerned with temporal aspects of movement. Insights into underlying sources of variability have been derived from a widening repertoire of analysis techniques. These now include not only variance decomposition, but also the analysis of serial and cross-covariance. The latter afford descriptions of structure within variability that are particularly suggestive for future theorizing about the functional architecture of motor control.

NOTE

I thank David Meyer for many helpful comments in the course of preparation of this chapter and David Rosenbaum for reading an earlier version.

REFERENCES

Abbs, J. H. and Winstein, C. J. (1990). Functional contributions of rapid and automatic sensory-based adjustments to motor output. In M. Jeannerod (Ed.), *Attention and Performance XIII: Motor representation and control*, 627–652. Hillsdale, NJ: Erlbaum.

Arbib, M. A. (1990). Programs, schemas, and neural networks for control of hand movements: Beyond the RS framework. In M. Jeannerod (Ed.), *Attention and Performance XIII: Motor representation and control*, 111–138. Hillsdale, NJ: Erlbaum.

Biguer, B., Jeannerod, M., and Prablanc, C. (1985). The role of position of gaze in movement accuracy. In M. Posner and O. Marin (Eds.), *Attention and Performance XI*, 407–424. Hillsdale, NJ: Erlbaum.

Butterworth, G. and Grover, L. (1990). Joint visual attention, manual pointing, and preverbal communication in human infancy. In M. Jeannerod (Ed.), *Attention and Performance XIII: Motor representation and control*, 605–624. Hillsdale, NJ: Erlbaum.

Cooper, W. E. and Ehrlich, S. F. (1981). Planning speech: Studies in choice reaction time. In J. Long and A. Baddeley (Eds.), *Attention and Performance IX*, 537–552. Hillsdale, NJ: Erlbaum.

Craske, B. (1981). Programmed aftereffects following simple patterned movements of the eyes and limbs. In J. Long and A. Baddeley (Eds.), *Attention and Performance IX*, 473–485. Hillsdale, NJ: Erlbaum.

Donders, F. C. ([1869] 1969). On the speed of mental processes. Translation reprinted in W. G. Koster (Ed.), *Attention and Performance II. Acta Psychologica, 30*, 412–431.

Fitts, P. M. (1954). The information capacity of the human motor system in controlling the amplitude of movement. *Journal of Experimental Psychology, 47*, 381–391.

Fowler, C. A. and Tassinary, L. G. (1981). Natural measurement criteria for speech: The anisochrony illusion. In J. Long and A. Baddeley (Eds.), *Attention and Performance IX*, 521–535. Hillsdale, NJ: Erlbaum.

Frowein, H. W., Reitsma, D., and Aquarius, C. (1981). Effects of two counteracting stresses on the reaction process. In J. Long and A. Baddeley (Eds.), *Attention and Performance IX*, 575–589. Hillsdale, NJ: Erlbaum.

Georgopoulos, A. P. (1990). Neurophysiology of reaching. In M. Jeannerod (Ed.), *Attention and Performance XIII: Motor representation and control*, 227–263. Hillsdale, NJ: Erlbaum.

Ghez, C., Hening, W., and Favilla, M. (1990). Parallel interacting channels in the initiation and specification of motor response features. In M. Jeannerod (Ed.), *Attention and Performance XIII: Motor representation and control*, 265–293. Hillsdale, NJ: Erlbaum.

Glencross, D.J. (1980). Response planning and the organization of speed movements. In R. S. Nickerson (Ed.), *Attention and Performance VIII*, 108–125. Hillsdale, NJ: Erlbaum.

Gottsdanker, R. (1967). Computer determinations of the effect of superseding signals. In A. F. Sanders (Ed.), *Attention and Performance. Acta Psychologica, 27*, 35–44.

Gottsdanker, R. (1975). The attaining and maintaining of preparation. In P. M. A. Rabbitt and S. Dornic (Eds.), *Attention and Performance V*, 33–49. London: Academic Press.

Hofsten, C. von (1990). A perception-action perspective on the development of manual movements. In M. Jeannerod (Ed.), *Attention and Performance XIII: Motor representation and control*, 739–762. Hillsdale, NJ: Erlbaum.

Huggins, A. W. F. (1978). Speech timing and intelligibility. In J. Requin (Ed.), *Attention and Performance VII*, 279–297. Hillsdale, NJ: Erlbaum.

Jeannerod, M. (1981). Intersegmental coordination during reaching at natural visual objects. In J. Long and A. Baddeley (Eds.), *Attention and Performance IX*, 153–169. Hillsdale, NJ: Erlbaum.

Johansson, R. S., and Westling, G. (1990). Tactile afferent signals in the control of precision grip. In M. Jeannerod (Ed.), *Attention and Performance XIII: Motor representation and control*, 677–713. Hillsdale, NJ: Lawrence Erlbaum.

Jordan, M. I. (1990). Motor learning and the degrees of freedom problem. In M. Jeannerod (Ed.), *Attention and Performance XIII: Motor representation and control*, 796–836. Hillsdale, NJ: Erlbaum.

Keele, S. W., Cohen, A., and Ivry, R. (1990). Motor programs: Concepts and issues. In M. Jeannerod (Ed.), *Attention and Performance XIII: Motor representation and control*, 77–110. Hillsdale, NJ: Erlbaum.

Kelso, J. A. S. (1981). Contrasting perspectives on order and regulation in movement. In J. Long and A. Baddeley (Eds.), *Attention and Performance IX*, 437–457. Hillsdale, NJ: Erlbaum.

Kelso, J. A. S., Colle, J. D., and Schoner, G. (1990). Action-perception as a pattern formation process. In M. Jeannerod (Ed.), *Attention and Performance XIII: Motor representation and control*, 139–169. Hillsdale, NJ: Erlbaum.

Klapp, S. T., Greim, D. M., and Marshburn, E. A. (1981). Buffer storage of programmed articulation and articulatory loop: Two names for the same mechanism or two distinct components of short-term memory? In J. Long and A. Baddeley (Eds.), *Attention and Performance IX*, 459–472. Hillsdale, NJ: Erlbaum.

Larochelle, S. (1984). Some aspects of movements in skilled typewriting. In H. Bouma and D. G. Bouwhuis (Eds.), *Attention and Performance X*, 43–54. Hillsdale, NJ: Erlbaum.

Lee, D. N., Daniel, B. D., Turnbull, J., and Cook, M. L. (1990). Basic perceptuo-motor dysfunctions in cerebral palsy. In M. Jeannerod (Ed.), *Attention and Performance XIII: Motor representation and control*, 583–603. Hillsdale, NJ: Erlbaum.

MacKenzie, C. L. and van Eerd, D. L. (1990). Rhythmic precision in the performance of piano scales: Motor psychophysics and motor programming. In M. Jeannerod (Ed.), *Attention and Performance XIII: Motor representation and control*, 375–408. Hillsdale, NJ: Erlbaum.

McLeod, P., McLaughlin, C., and Nimmo-Smith, I. (1985). Information encapsulation and automaticity: Evidence from the visual control of finely timed actions. In M. Posner and O. Marin (Eds.), *Attention and Performance XI*, 391–406. Hillsdale, NJ: Erlbaum.

MacNeilage, P. F. and Davis, B. (1990). Acquisition of speech production: Frames, then content. In M. Jeannerod (Ed.), *Attention and Performance XIII: Motor representation and control*, 453–476. Hillsdale, NJ: Erlbaum.

Marteniuk, R. G. and MacKenzie, C. L. (1980). Information processing in movement organization and execution. In R. S. Nickerson (Ed.), *Attention and Performance VIII*, 29–57. Hillsdale, NJ: Erlbaum.

Meyer, D. E. and Gordon, P. C. (1984). Dependencies between rapid speech perception and production: Evidence for a shared sensorimotor voicing mechanism. In H. Bouma and D. G. Bouwhuis (Eds.), *Attention and Performance X*, 365–377. Hillsdale, NJ: Erlbaum.

Meyer, D. E., Smith, J. E. K., Kornblum, S., Abrams, R. A., and Wright, C.E. (1990). Speed-accuracy tradeoffs in aimed movements: Toward a theory of rapid voluntary action. In M. Jeannerod (Ed.), *Attention and Performance XIII: Motor representation and control*, 173–226. Hillsdale, NJ: Erlbaum.

Michon, J. A. and van der Valk, N. J. L. (1967). A dynamic model of timing behavior. In A. F. Sanders (Ed.), *Attention and Performance. Acta Psychologica*, 27, 204–212.

Näätänen, R. and Merisalo, A. (1977). Expectancy and preparation in simple reaction time. In S. Dornic (Ed.), *Attention and Performance VI*, 115–138. Hillsdale, NJ: Erlbaum.

Prablanc, C. and Pelisson, D. (1990). Gaze saccade orienting and hand pointing are locked to their goal by quick internal loops. In M. Jeannerod (Ed.), *Attention and Performance XIII: Motor representation and control*, 653–676. Hillsdale, NJ: Erlbaum.

Rabbitt, P. (1967). Time to detect errors as a function of factors affecting choice-response time. In A. F. Sanders (Ed.), *Attention and Performance. Acta Psychologica*, 27, 131–142.

Rayner, K. and Pollatsek, A. (1987). Eye movements in reading: A tutorial review. In M. Coltheart (Ed.), *Attention and Performance XII: The psychology of reading*, 327–362. Hillsdale, NJ: Erlbaum.

Requin, J. (1985). Looking forward to moving soon: Ante factum selective processes in motor control. In M. Posner and O. Marin (Eds.), *Attention and Performance XI*, 147–167. Hillsdale, NJ: Erlbaum.

Rosenbaum, D. A. and Patashnik, O. (1980). Time to time in the human motor system. In R. S. Nickerson (Ed.), *Attention and Performance VIII*, 93–106. Hillsdale, NJ: Erlbaum.

Sanders, A. F. (Ed) (1967). *Attention and Performance. Acta Psychologica, 27*.

Sanders, A. F. (1980). Some effects of instructed muscle tension on choice reaction time and movement time. In R. S. Nickerson (Ed.), *Attention and Performance VIII*, 59–74. Hillsdale, NJ: Erlbaum.

Sanes, J. N. (1990). Motor representations in deafferented humans: A mechanism for disordered movement performance. In M. Jeannerod (Ed.), *Attention and Performance XIII: Motor representation and control*, 714–735. Hillsdale, NJ: Erlbaum.

Semjen, A. and Gottsdanker, R. (1990). Rapid serial movements: Relation between the planning of sequential structure and effector selection. In M. Jeannerod (Ed.), *Attention and Performance XIII: Motor representation and control*, 409–427. Hillsdale, NJ: Erlbaum.

Shaffer, L. H. (1973). Latency mechanisms in transcription. In S. Kornblum (Ed.), *Attention and Performance IV*, 435–446. London: Academic Press.

Shaffer, L. H. (1984). Motor programming in language production: A tutorial review. In H. Bouma and D. G. Bouwhuis (Eds.), *Attention and Performance X*, 17–41. Hillsdale, NJ: Erlbaum.

Soechting, J. F. and Terzuolo, C. A. (1990). Sensorimotor transformations and the kinematics of arm movements in three-dimensional space. In M. Jeannerod (Ed.), *Attention and Performance XIII: Motor representation and control*, 479–494. Hillsdale, NJ: Erlbaum.

Stelmach, G. and Kelso, J. A. S. (1977). Memory processes in motor control. In S. Dornic (Ed.), *Attention and Performance VI*, 719–739. Hillsdale, NJ: Erlbaum.

Stelmach, G. and McCracken, H. D. (1978). Storage codes for movement information. In J. Requin (Ed.), *Attention and Performance VII*, 515–534. Hillsdale, NJ: Erlbaum.

Sternberg, S. (1969). The discovery of processing stages: Extensions of Donders' method. In W.G. Koster (Ed.), *Attention and Performance II. Acta Psychologica, 30*, 276–315.

Sternberg, S., Knoll, R. L. and Turock, D. L. (1990). Hierarchical control in the execution of action sequences: Tests of two invariance properties. In M. Jeannerod (Ed.), *Attention and Performance XIII: Motor representation and control*, 3–55. Hillsdale, NJ: Erlbaum.

Trumbo, D. (1970). Acquisition and performance as a function of structure and uncertainty in serial tracking tasks. In A. F. Sanders (Ed.), *Attention and Performance III. Acta Psychologica, 33*, 252–266.

Tuller, B. and Kelso, J. A. S. (1990). Phase transitions in speech production and their perceptual consequences. In M. Jeannerod (Ed.), *Attention and Performance XIII: Motor representation and control*, 429–452. Hillsdale, NJ: Erlbaum.

Turvey, M. T., Shaw, R. E., and Mace, W. (1978). Issues in the theory of action: Degrees of freedom, coordinative structures and coalitions. In J. Requin (Ed.), *Attention and Performance VII*, 557–595. Hillsdale, NJ: Erlbaum.

Viviani, P. (1990). Common factors in the control of free and constrained movements. In M. Jeannerod (Ed.), *Attention and Performance XIII: Motor representation and control*, 345–373. Hillsdale, NJ: Erlbaum.

Vorberg, D. and Hambuch, R. (1978). On the temporal control of rhythmic performance. In J. Requin (Ed.), *Attention and Performance VII*, 535–555. Hillsdale, NJ: Erlbaum.

Welford, A. T. (1967). Single-channel operation in the brain. In A. F. Sanders (Ed.), *Attention and Performance. Acta Psychologica, 27*, 5–22.

Welford, A. T., Norris, A. H., and Shock, N. W. (1969). Speed and accuracy of movement and their changes with age. In W.G. Koster (Ed.), *Attention and Performance II. Acta Psychologica, 30*, 3–15.

Wright, C. E. (1990). Generalized motor programs: Reexamining claims of effector independence in writing. In M. Jeannerod (Ed.), *Attention and Performance XIII: Motor representation and control*, 294–320. Hillsdale, NJ: Erlbaum.

Young, D. E. and Schmidt, R. A. (1990). Units of motor behavior: Modifications with practice and feedback. In M. Jeannerod (Ed.), *Attention and Performance XIII. Motor representation and control*, 763–795. Hillsdale, NJ: Erlbaum.

30 Neuronal Networks for Movement Preparation

Jean Requin, Alexa Riehle, and John Seal

30.1 INTRODUCTION

During the last fifteen years, advances in our knowledge of both the cognitive processes and the neural mechanisms by which motor actions are planned have made it realistic for this field of cognitive neuroscience to fulfill the long-held desire to understand higher brain functions (Mountcastle 1986). The basic research strategy proposed in this perspective was either to add physiological measurements such as ERP recordings to the experimental procedures designed in the field of human cognitive psychology (Meyer, Osman, Irwin, and Yantis 1988), or to adapt these procedures to nonhuman primates on which invasive techniques of studying brain activity can be used (see Evarts, Shinoda, and Wise 1984; Requin, Brener, and Ring 1991).

While this research strategy was made possible by the exciting opportunities offered by new methodological developments, its main justification was the existence of experimental paradigms that are shared by the two cooperating disciplines. Cognitive psychologists have developed models of information processing that are formalized as a series of independent, functionally specialized processing stages (Meyer et al. 1988; Miller 1988). These models have a structural isomorphism with those proposed by neuroscientists, in which brain organization is viewed as an ensemble of functionally specialized neuronal structures interconnected by unidirectional or looped input-output pathways (Requin, Riehle, and Seal 1988; Wiesendanger 1990). Such an isomorphism between the processing "boxology" concept and the brain "patchwork" concept was a convenient basis for designing combined neurophysiology/experimental psychology experiments (Mountcastle 1976) aimed at validating the functional correspondence between neuronal structures and processing stages. In brief, in a somewhat idealized study, when the manipulation of one experimental factor acts selectively on one processing stage and results in selective changes in the activity of a particular neural structure, one might infer that the process taking place within this stage is implemented by that neural structure.

This rationale was used with some success in most studies on preparation for action. Analysis of the data accumulated has led to the current views of motor planning which, disregarding a number of variations, can be summarized as follows (Keele, Cohen, and Ivry 1990; Schmidt 1988; Rosenbaum 1987; Sternberg et al. 1978; Wiesendanger 1990): Preparatory processes for motor activity require the extraction and utilization of pertinent information from multiple, hierarchically organized representations of motor actions. These representations, which are elaborated and stored during ontogenesis and learning, may be viewed as the language of the motor system and may therefore be defined by using the metaphor of linguistics.

At the highest, most abstract level, which may be called "semantic," the objective of action (the changes in the world that will result from acting) would be represented in a nonmotoric, holistic and symbolic form, which does not yet contain the spatiotemporal structure of the forthcoming motor act. In information processing models, the process by which this context-independent representation of action goal is extracted from memory is the response selection or determination stage. Data collected in combined experiments suggest that such a process would be implemented in the frontal and parietal association cortex areas (Andersen 1989).

At an intermediary level, which may be called "syntactic," the instructions of the motor program would be represented still in an abstract form that specifies the kinematics, dynamics and timing of the forthcoming movement or movement sequence. In information-processing models, the process by which these context-dependent representations of movement features are extracted and assembled is the motor programming stage. Analysis of the data collected in combined experiments suggests that such a process is implemented in the premotor cortex (Wise 1984).

At the lowest level, which can be called "phonemic," would be represented the basic motor units which are selected according to program instructions resulting in the pattern of neuromuscular activations. In information-processing models, the process by which these basic motor units are activated is the motor output stage. Neurophysiological studies have shown that this activation process is implemented in the neural pathways connecting motor cortical areas, directly or via subcortical structures, to spinal structures (Hepp-Reymond 1988). It is at some point of no return during this activation process that action planning may be considered as ending and movement execution as starting (Osman, Kornblum, and Meyer 1990).

However, for a number of years now, the paradigm that underlies the research strategy of combined experiments has come under increased scrutiny in both cognitive psychology and behavioral neuroscience. This challenge stems, in large part, from the two principal and complementary streams of the connectionist approach: attempts at modeling cognitive processes by networks of formal neurons on the one hand (e.g., McClelland and Rumelhart 1986; Jordan 1990), and attempts at modeling the architecture and functioning of the neuronal networks of real brains on the other hand (see, for example, Kawato, Furukawa, and Suzuki 1987; Kwan et al. 1990).

At the formal level, the functional, temporal, and structural aspects of serially organized information processing stages are being questioned (Miller 1988). First, the idea of the discreteness of information transformation within stages and of information transmission between stages now tends to be replaced by the notion of a continuous information flow. Second, the notion of seriality, and, consequently, of hierarchical processing operations now tends to be replaced by the notion of parallel processing. Third, the idea of the processing stage itself, as a functionally specialized part of an information-processing system, now tends to be replaced by that of a distributed organization in which the entire system is involved in implementing any particular function (Hopfield 1982; McClelland and Rumelhart 1986).

At the empirical level, classical views about the link between neural structures and behavioral functions are being seriously reconsidered because of the pressure of two emerging concepts. One is the functional heterogeneity of neural structures that is being found at the macroanatomical level of large areas: neurons involved in the implementation of the same behavioral function are found in several different areas, although in varying proportions. Thus, the notion of a rigid functional specialization of cortical areas appears to be suspect, not only when the complex cortical association areas are considered, but even in the primary sensory and motor areas: functional differences between cortical regions must be viewed as more quantitative than qualitative (Goldman-Rakic 1988; Requin, Riehle, and Seal 1988). The second concept that is emerging is the continuum of function for neuronal populations: the notion that each neuron is highly specialized for contributing to the implementation of a particular function, and, thus, that neurons can be classified into discrete functional categories, must be abandoned. Functional differences between neurons must similarly be viewed as more quantitative than qualitative, that is, a neuron may be more or less involved in implementing different functions (Bruce and Goldberg 1985; Requin, Riehle, and Seal 1988).

This progressive depreciation of the paradigm based on macroanatomical localization of serially organized and discrete functional processes will be illustrated in detail with the results of two research programs that have been in progress for several years. Both programs were based on the rationale of combined experiments and were aimed at identifying the neural structures that supposedly implement the processing stages responsible for movement planning. Single-neuron recording techniques were used in monkeys to analyze changes in activity in cortical areas—selected on the basis of classical anatomical and functional features—during the performance of reaction-time (RT) tasks. These tasks were designed to manipulate factors that acted specifically on either the response determination or the movement programming processes. The results of these experiments appear to be increasingly incompatible with current concepts concerning the links between neural structures and behavioral functions. However, before describing the data, it is useful to underline various biases in the design and the running of such studies that have hindered the reconsideration of the current concepts.

30.2 CONCEPTUAL AND METHODOLOGICAL BIASES FAVORING THE ONE STRUCTURE–ONE FUNCTION MAPPING CONCEPT

A first, paradigmatic bias results from studying the activity of a neural structure during the performance of a task that is supposed to specifically involve the behavioral function currently attributed to this structure. Most often this functional specification is based on data provided by previous studies conducted with methods such as clinical lesion studies and electrophysiology on anesthetized animals. Moreover, technical difficulties in training and testing animals restrict the number of control conditions. The overall effect is to increase the likelihood that the data obtained will support the hypothesis that the experiment was designed to test and, thus, to validate the concept of a functional specialization for the neural structure under investigation. For example, the posterior parietal cortex was initially thought to be responsible for associating stimuli from different modalities or stimulus features within the same modality. This was based on descriptive studies of neuronal activity observed in response to behaviorally irrelevant stimuli. When the neuronal activity of the posterior parietal cortex was studied in monkeys trained to perform ocular saccades, visual tracking or hand reaching movements to touch a visual target, it became clear that such a sensory association function could not encompass all the roles played by this cortical area. Analysis of these data showed that the posterior parietal cortex may be responsible for implementing multiple, complex behavioral functions, such as the higher, secondary processing of sensory inputs, the integration of information provided by different sensory modalities, the building of a flexible representation of extrapersonal and/or body space, the interfacing of sensory inputs and motor outputs, the initiation of a holistic command for motor actions, and so forth (see Lynch 1980 for a review). Thus it progressively seemed that functional heterogeneity was the most salient characteristic of this cortical region.

A second bias, this time methodological, contributing to maintain the brain "patchwork" concept is directly related to a central assumption that underlies the experiments conducted with single-cell recording techniques—that is, that the functional properties of a neural structure can be inferred from a necessarily small sample of neuronal activity. Unfortunately, the various constraints of these techniques (see Lemon 1984) often converge to change this supposedly random method of sampling into a biased selection. First, the unpredictable and limited period of time during which neuronal activity can be recorded from a neuron often leads to the recording of only neurons that appear to be task related, on the basis of a rapid examination of the first few trials. Second, often the cortical region to be studied is not systematically explored, which further adds to the inaccuracy of the anatomical localization of function; there is an obvious bias in the economical strategy of repeating electrode penetrations in the locations where task-related neurons have already been found. Lastly, and most importantly, the probability of recording the extracellular activity of a single neuron depends on the size of the electrical field generated by the neuron, and hence the recording of the larger-sized neurons within a cytologically heterogenous neural structure is favored.

An example of the cumulative effect of these biases is that our knowledge of the functions of the primary motor (MI) cortex was, until recently, based on recordings of the activity of about 5 to 10 percent of the whole neuronal population of this region (Humphrey and Corrie 1978). The current concept of the exclusively motor role played by MI and its rigid somatotopy led most workers to record only from neurons with clear movement-related changes in neuronal activity, in restricted cortical locations. Thus, investigations focused on the regions found to be most active. This, coupled with the high probability of recording from the large pyramidal tract cells, led to all of MI being assigned the functions of only a small neuronal population responsible for neuromuscular control. Here too, when variations in current experimental designs such as more rigorous methods for sampling neuronal activities were employed, it was shown that MI functions cannot be restricted to the activation of corticospinal pathways according to the instructions of a program. As we will show later, an increasing number of studies have provided evidence for neuronal populations in MI that are involved in the higher cognitive processes responsible for planning and updating motor actions according to the behavioral context (e.g., Evarts, Shinoda, and Wise 1984; Lecas et al. 1986; Riehle and Requin 1989) and that even participate in visual sensory processes (Kwan et al. 1985; Riehle 1991; Wannier, Maier, and Hepp-Reymond 1989).

A third bias in analyzing neuronal activity results from the practice of summarizing data by classifying neurons into clear-cut functional categories according to the temporal relationships between changes in neuronal activity and external events. Such classification procedures rest on and at the same time strengthen the assumption of an unequivocal functional differentiation between neurons—for example between "sensory" and "motor" neurons—thus extending the concept of anatomical separation of function from neural structures to neuronal units. Typically, a consistent temporal relation between an observable event, such as a sensory stimulus or movement onset, and a change in neuronal activity is considered sufficient information to draw inferences about the causal relationship between them. In particular, it is often concluded that a change in neuronal activity is related to stimulus processing, and not to movement control, when the time of this change is closer to stimulus presentation than to movement onset. Even when the variability of these temporal relationships is taken into account, the decision remains as to whether to attribute either a sensory or a motor function to the neuron. Finally, recent technical refinements to evaluate the strength of the temporal relationship between the activity of two neurons (cross-correlation) or between central and peripheral components of the motor system (spike-triggered EMG averaging) do not challenge the basic assumption that each neuron is functionally specialized— that is, it participates, as a member of a homogeneous population, in the implementation of a unique and unchanging behavioral function.

The difficulty in demonstrating unequivocally that these changes in neuronal activity are related to either stimulus presentation or movement onset may be overcome by abandoning the assumption of discrete specialization in neuronal function and conceding that a neuron may be involved in both sensory and motor processes. This new view has led to the following proposition. The role played by at least one population of parietal neurons is in the linkage between the perception of a behaviorally meaningful external event and the initiation of the motor action called for by that event (Andersen 1989; Crammond and Kalaska 1989; Seal and Requin 1987; Seal 1989). Moreover, such an interpretation fits in well with the emerging concept of quantitative rather than qualitative differences in function between neurons (Bruce and Goldberg 1985). Provided that the appropriate statistical techniques for data analysis are used, it now becomes possible, in principle, to locate each neuron on a sensorimotor continuum, or gradient (Seal and Commenges 1985; Requin, Riehle, and Seal 1988).

30.3 A COMBINED STUDY OF STIMULUS-TO-RESPONSE ASSOCIATION

The identification of a processing stage during which the response is selected in sensorimotor tasks resulted mainly from applying the logic of the additive-factor method (Sternberg 1969). With this method, several experimental factors were manipulated simultaneously and the resulting pattern of RT data was analyzed. At this stage, the response is selected as a holistic, context-independent representation of the action to be performed. For instance, the effects on choice RT of response probability and S-R compatibility were most often found to interact; therefore they were considered to act on the same stage (Kornblum, Hasbroucq, and Osman 1990 for a review). However, the effects of response probability and S-R compatibility were generally found to be additive—and therefore were considered to act on different stages—with the effects of factors modulating the earlier sensory and perceptual processes or the later motor programming and execution processes.

Independently, anatomical studies of the connections of the posterior parietal cortex, as well as lesion studies, suggested that this cortical region was involved in the initiation of intended actions, but not in specifying the spatio-temporal features of the forthcoming motor output. Such a hypothesis was elaborated by Mountcastle et al. (1975), who attributed a command function to a population of parietal neurons—the so-called early cells—which modified their activity prior to the onset of a visually-cued movement and for which there was no apparent visual receptive field. Although subsequently criticized this hypothesis was confirmed and the central origin of these "early" changes in neuronal activity was demonstrated by showing their presence when sensory feedback from the trained limb had been suppressed (Seal, Gross, and Bioulac 1982).

Principles and Methods

The comparison of the findings in behavioral and neurophysiological experiments has formed the basis for designing combined studies aimed at investigating the role of the posterior parietal cortex in the formation of sensorimotor associations. Two similar experimental designs were used. In the first experiment, monkeys were trained in three different conditions of a simple sensorimotor task. In the first, stimulus-movement condition, monkeys had to perform a choice RT task of extension or flexion of the forearm about the elbow in response to an auditory stimulus of either 400 Hz or 1000 Hz, respectively. The second, stimulus–no movement condition was obtained by rewarding nonexecution of forearm movements. The third, no stimulus–movement condition was obtained by rewarding the forearm movements when performed spontaneously. In the second experiment, monkeys were trained in a choice RT task in which the stimulus was a brief vibration delivered either to the fingers or to the thumb and the response was a press with the stimulated digit(s). These experiments were designed to differentiate between neuronal activities specifically related to sensory processes, motor processes and S-R association processes.

Standard surgical procedures, single-neuron recording techniques and methods for investigating neuronal activity were used (see Seal 1989 for details). Bearing in mind some of the experimental biases previously mentioned, recordings were made in four cortical areas—primary somaesthetic cortex (SI), area 5 of the posterior parietal cortex, premotor cortex (PM) and MI— although we were particularly interested in the role of area 5 in the mechanism of S-R association. Data obtained in the SI and motor areas of the brain were to serve as a reference for the comparison of data from area 5. In addition, all neurons were recorded in the three conditions regardless of whether, on examination of the initial trials, they appeared to be "sensory" or "motor." Finally, recorded data were analyzed using not only standard methods of peri-event histograms and raster displays, but also using a novel method that placed each neuron on a hypothetical sensorimotor gradient (Seal and Commenges 1986; Requin Riehle, and Seal 1988).

This quantitative index of the function of neurons was not based on the mean latency between external and internal events, as is traditionally done, but instead on the variance of this latency during a series of trials. The ratio of the variance of the interval (X), which is the time between the onset of the stimulus and the onset of a change in neuronal activity, and of the interval (Y), which is the time between this change and movement onset, is an estimation of the relative strength of the relationship between the external events and any change in neuronal activity. We say that the change in neuronal activity is variance-related to stimulus onset—and hence to sensory processes—when the ratio (Var Y/Var X) tends towards infinite, and is variance-related to movement onset—and hence to motor processes—when the ratio (Var Y/Var X) tends towards zero. The use of log (Var Y/Var X) gives a quantitative variable centered on 0 (where Var Y = Var X) and extending from $-\infty$ to $+\infty$. In terms of brain function, this measure provides a continuous gradation from pure sensory mechanisms, as seen at the level of the sensory receptor, to pure motor mechanisms, as seen at the level of the electromyogram.

Results and Discussion

We present here the results of both quantitative and qualitative analyses of the neuronal discharge data obtained in the two series of experiments. First, it will be shown that, qualitatively, the same characteristics of neuronal discharge can be described for neurons in different cortical areas and in different experimental protocols. Secondly, quantitative analysis of the data illustrates the continuous nature of the neural correlates of the stimulus-response process.

In the simple auditory RT task previously described, area 5 neurons were first recorded in the condition when the stimulus was followed by the behavioral response. Neurons that modified their activity during the RT ($n = 94$)—and, thus, could be implicated in the S-R association process—were subsequently recorded in the stimulus–no movement and no stimulus–movement conditions. The neurons were divided into three populations on the basis of the presence or absence of a neuronal response in each of the three experimental conditions. The sensory-type neurons (10%) showed a change in activity only when the auditory stimulus was presented. The motor-type neurons (56%) showed a change in activity only prior to movement onset. However, the occurrence and timing of these changes in activity for sensory and motor neurons were found to be labile with the repetition of trials in the stimulus-no movement condition and the no stimulus–movement condition, respectively. The change in neuronal activity of the sensory neurons gradually disappeared as the stimulus–no movement condition was repeated so that after about 50 trials, the change in neuronal activity was no longer detectable. For certain motor neurons, the time of change in neuronal activity gradually occurred earlier and earlier prior to the onset of movement in the no stimulus–movement condition. These observations suggest that the sensory and motor neurons process information in a particular behavioral context, that is, auditory stimulus–arm movement–reward.

The "sensorimotor" type neurons (34%) showed a modification of activity in all three conditions. There were two components to the modification in activity of these neurons in the stimulus-movement condition. The first component was a change in activity time-locked to stimulus onset and it had a similar time course to the change in neuronal activity observed in the stimulus–no movement condition. The second component was a change in activity time-locked to movement onset, with a time course similar to that of the change in neuronal activity observed in the no stimulus–movement condition. The mean latency of these changes in neuronal activity between stimulus presentation and the onset of the neuronal response increased significantly (see fig. 30.1) from "sensory" neurons (23 ms) to "sensorimotor" neurons (137 ms)

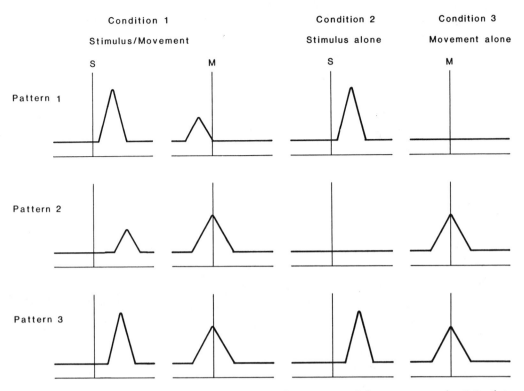

Figure 30.1 A schematic diagram of the three patterns of change in neuronal activity that were used to characterize area-5 cells as "sensory" (pattern 1), "motor" (pattern 2), and "sensorimotor" (pattern 3).

and, then, to "motor" neurons (264 ms). With respect to movement onset, these latencies were -314 ms, -135 ms, and -55 ms, respectively.

This temporal organization of sensory, sensorimotor and motor neurons has obvious similarities with a minimal model of information flow, such as stimulus perception—response selection—response execution, and it is tempting to attribute one of these functions to each of the three types of neurons. However, we observed a considerable degree of overlap when comparing the mean time of change in activity for the individual neurons recorded in these cortical areas (fig. 30.2, top and middle). The degree of such overlap is inconsistent with a serial stage model of information flow. There is also a certain degree of overlap for the values of log (Var Y/Var X) even for neurons that were apparently as "functionally" different as the "sensorimotor" and "motor" neurons (fig. 30.2, bottom), although neurons recorded in structures close to the source of sensory input and motor output showed close grouping of the values of log (Var Y/Var X). The presence of neurons in area 5 that modified their activity in all three conditions, and also had sensory and motor components, leads us to suggest that one function of area 5 is to associate the sensory response to a cue for movement with the motor activity necessary for the expression of that movement.

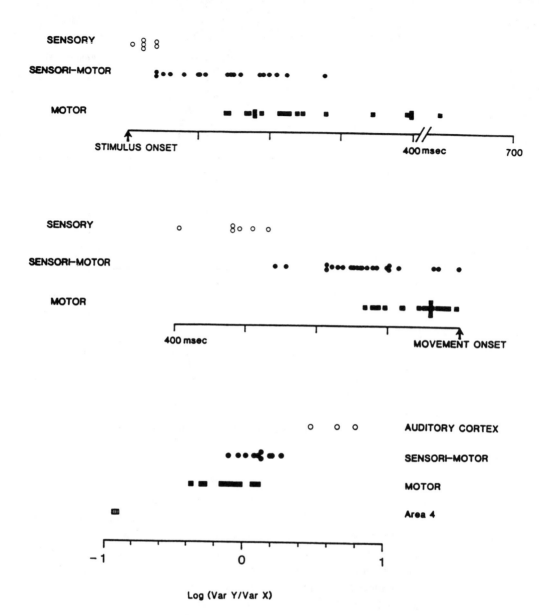

Figure 30.2 *Top and middle:* Distribution of mean time of change in activity with respect to the stimulus (top) and movement onset (middle) for "sensory", "sensorimotor," and "motor" neurons ($n = 64$) recorded in area 5 of a monkey. Although there is considerable overlap in time of change for each neuronal type, note that the timing of sensory cells is grouped around the onset of the stimulus and that of motor cells around the onset of movement while the timing of sensorimotor cells is equally distributed with respect to the stimulus and the movement.

Bottom: Representation of a sensorimotor continuum along a gradient defined by log(Var Y/Var X). Although the relative position of the different populations is clear, there is considerable overlap for the values of sensorimotor and motor cells recorded in area 5.

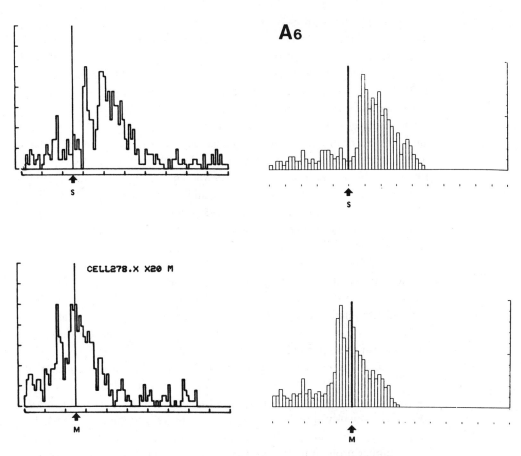

Figure 30.3 Examples of "sensorimotor" neurons, as defined by the presence of a change in neuronal activity in the three experimental conditions, in area 5 (left), and in PM (right). The two neurons have similar patterns of change in activity—one component related to the stimulus, a second related to the movement—although they were recorded in different experimental protocols. Bin width: 20 msec, S: stimulus onset, M: movement onset.

Similar observations were made for certain neurons recorded in a different cortical area, PM, during the second series of experiments (fig. 30.3) using a different sensory modality (tactile somaesthesia) and a different motor effector (finger or thumb presses). What functional interpretation can, or should, be made from such a description of the characteristics of a neuronal population? Is PM, like area 5, also a site for S-R association, but for a different sensory modality and different effectors? Clearly, the isomorphism between stage models of information flow and the localization of function within anatomically connected cortical areas is greatly weakened by such observations. However, these observations suggest a common mode of function within the cortex.

30.4   A COMBINED STUDY OF PROGRAMMING PROCESSES

The idea that the features of the motor activity needed to attain a predetermined goal are prescribed in some central representation is widely accepted in theories of motor control developed by cognitive psychologists (Keele, Cohen, and Ivry 1990; Requin, Semjen, and Bonnet 1984; Rosenbaum et al. 1990; Schmidt 1988). The notion of motor program is mainly supported by three kinds of evidence. First, skilled movements can be performed without proprioceptive feedback (Keele 1981; Schmidt 1988). Second, RT for initiating the first element of a movement sequence depends upon the length, ordering and temporal structure of the sequence as a whole (Semjen and Gottsdanker 1990; Sternberg, Knoll, and Turock 1990). Third, a number of RT studies, especially those conducted with precuing and priming techniques (Rosenbaum 1983; Lépine, Glencross, and Requin 1989) have shown that increasing the subject's expectancy about the features of the forthcoming movement results in an increase in the efficiency of the processing systems responsible for performing the movement.

The concept of motor programming has increasingly been challenged as being too complex and inflexible (Meijer and Roth 1988). First, the possibility of an infinite number of potential movements implies the need for an equally unlimited storage capacity in the program register. Second, controlling the large number of degrees of freedom involved in any movement would require an excessively high computational power. Third, the current concept of a program makes it difficult to understand how a well-learned motor action, such as writing, can be performed using an untrained body part such as the head or foot. Consequently, hierarchical models of motor programming have been proposed, in which at least two separate levels of processing are recognized. At the higher programming level, only the common structure of a large class of movements would be specified according to some abstract proto-program, plan or schema. Details to complete this schema would be filled in at the lower programming level according to contextual requirements and biomechanical constraints.

Within the conceptual framework of a hierarchical organization of the brain, anatomical and physiological studies have pointed to the privileged position of PM and supplementary motor area (SMA), i.e. the lateral and medial parts of area 6 respectively, in movement programming (Wiesendanger 1990). Both areas project to MI and are innervated by two association areas, prefrontal and posterior parietal cortex. Neurons in PM were found to show changes in activity that did not depend on the physical features of a preparatory signal, but on information that this signal provided about the features of the forthcoming movement (Wise and Mauritz 1985; Riehle and Requin 1989). Although the role of the SMA in motor control remains controversial (see Goldberg 1985; Wiesendanger 1986, for reviews), similar data have been collected in this cortical region (Kurata and Tanji 1985; Tanji and Kurata 1982), suggesting its close involvement in movement programming.

Once again, the comparison of data from the fields of cognitive psychology, on the one hand, and behavioral neuroscience, on the other, formed the grounding for combined experiments aimed at detailing the role of premotor cortical regions in the implementation of movement programming. The experimental design was based on the movement precuing method which requires the assumption that the programming process may be decomposed into separate operations, each of which has a measurable duration (see Rosenbaum 1983; Lépine, Glencross, and Requin 1989, for review). In this method, a specific movement is demanded by the response stimulus (RS), after partial information about one or more parameters of the forthcoming movement has been supplied by the preparatory stimulus (PS) or precue. If the programming system uses such partial information to program the corresponding movement parameter(s), then RT will be shortened when compared to conditions in which no prior information on movement parameter(s) is given. This shortening is attributed to the programming time(s) for the precued parameter(s) and it may differ according to the particular parameters. Furthermore, one can infer that the set of programming operations is serially processed if programming times for the precued parameters are additive. Finally, if the reduction in RT associated with the precuing of one movement parameter only occurs in the presence of another simultaneously precued parameter, one can infer that the programming processes are ordered, with the latter parameter being programmed before the former.

Principles and Methods

Monkeys were trained to grasp and to rotate a vertical handle by performing wrist flexion and extension movements in the horizontal plane. A rod fixed to the handle served as a pointer which the monkey moved in front of a semicircular, vertical panel on which two horizontal rows of five light-emitting diodes (LEDs) were displayed. Two centrally located yellow LEDs, one in each row, indicated the starting position for movements. Four green LEDs, two on the left and two on the right, formed the upper row and served as PS. Four similarly arranged red LEDs formed the lower row and served as RS and as targets to be pointed at.

A trial began by the monkey pointing to and maintaining the pointer at the starting position. After 1 second, information about the parameters of the forthcoming movement was provided by illuminating either one of the green LEDs for 1 s (complete information), two of the green LEDs (partial information: on movement direction, when either the two left or the two right LEDs were illuminated; on movement extent, when either the two distal or the two proximal LEDs were illuminated), or all four green LEDs (no information). This precue was followed by a preparatory period (PP) of variable duration (from 0.7 s to 1.3 s) that ended with the illumination of one red LED located at the same position as that of the green LED, or one of the green LEDs previously illuminated as the precue. The animal was required to point to the indicated target as quickly as possible in order to obtain a reward.

Standard surgical procedures, single-neuron recording techniques and methods for investigating neuronal activity were used (see Riehle and Requin 1989 for details). Similarly, as in previous experiments, recordings were made not only in PM, but also in MI and SI. No selection of the neuronal activities to be subsequently analyzed was made on the basis of task-related response properties. The timing of changes in neuronal activity and their sensitivity to information provided by the precue were analyzed and trial-by-trial correlations between changes in neuronal activity during the PP and RT were calculated systematically in the different conditions of prior information. Once again, although a correlation between the variations in the features of two events does not necessarily mean that these two events are causally related, the strength of such a correlation was considered as a variable defining a functional continuum on which each neuron could be located.

Results and Discussion

Behavioral data (see table 30.1) showed that prior information on movement direction reduced RT markedly (79 ms, 32 ms, and 30 ms, for monkeys 1, 2, and 3, respectively), while prior information on movement extent did not, except for monkey 3 in which a small (6 ms) but statistically significant reduction in RT was found. Since a virtually identical (7 ms) and significant decrease of RT was found between conditions of directional information and complete information, the data from this animal (monkey 3) fit perfectly with an additive pattern of programming times and, thus, with a serial organization of the corresponding processes. A significant RT reduction (12 ms) between conditions of directional information and complete information was also observed in monkey 2, while providing information on movement extent only did not affect RT: this underadditivity is consistent not only with a serial, but also with a hierarchical information-processing model in which movement extent is processed after movement direction. Reaction times of monkey 1 indicated that this animal did not use prior information on movement extent at all. The behavioral data, therefore, supported the hypothesis that the programming of the different movement parameters results from assembling processes of different duration. Moreover, they are consistent with a model in which these programming operations are serially, and in some cases, perhaps hierarchically ordered.

Table 30.1 RTs in the Different Precueing Conditions

Conditions	None		Extent		Direction		Complete
Monkey 1	262	*	256	*	232	*	225
Monkey 2	333		331	*	265	*	253
Monkey 3	600		600	*	521		518
mean	398		396		339		332

Note: * statistically significant differences between adjacent RTs

In accordance with the rationale of this experiment, we focused on the activity of PM neurons. Neurons were classified into three main types: (1) "execution-related" neurons, whose changes in activity were related only to the movement performed, (2) "preparation- and execution-related" neurons, and (3) "preparation-related" neurons, whose changes in activity were related only to information provided by the PS.

Changes in neuronal activity during the PP were analyzed as a function of information provided by the precue. While precuing movement direction resulted in significant changes—either an increase or a decrease—in neuronal activity for 40 percent of neurons, the precuing of movement extent did not result in any change in neuronal activity. However, some neurons (6%) were found that showed larger changes in activity when both direction and extent were known in advance than when only direction was precued; these changes disappeared when only extent was precued or when no dimensional information was provided (see fig. 30.4). Therefore, these physiological data were more compatible with a hierarchical than a serially nonordered model of motor programming, corresponding with the RT data for monkeys 2 and 3, respectively.

The predictive value of these changes in neuronal activity for RT was then evaluated in the different conditions of prior information by calculating trial-by-trial correlations between neuronal discharge frequency during the last 500 ms of the PP and RT. Statistically significant correlations were found for 39 percent of the task-related neurons in at least one condition. These percentages did not differ between conditions in which movement extent (8%) and no -movement parameter (6%) were precued, but increased significantly when either movement direction—flexion (17%) or extension (20%)—was precued. Moreover, the mean value of the correlation coefficients was significantly larger when direction was precued than when extent was precued. Correlations were always negative when neuronal discharge frequency increased (i.e., the higher the neuronal activity, the shorter the RT), and were always positive when neuronal discharge frequency decreased (i.e., the weaker the neuronal activity, the shorter the RT; fig. 30.5). This rule also applied to the few neurons that showed reciprocal preparatory changes in activity for the two precued directions.

When the behavioral and neuronal data are considered together, the hypotheses that first motivated this experiment appear to have been confirmed. Reaction time data are interpretable in the framework of a parametric model of motor programming in which separable programming operations of different duration are performed serially in a fixed order, with the programming of movement direction taking longer than, and occurring before, the programming of movement extent. Accordingly, different clusters of neurons were found in PM that changed their activity during the PP in a manner consistent with such a model. These changes in neuronal activity had a high predictive value for performance speed, which validated their functional significance as preparatory for motor action. Thus a good correspondence was observed between the programming processes inferred from the use of behavioral

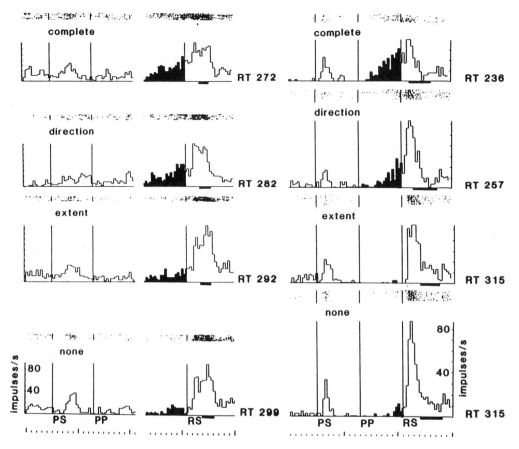

Figure 30.4 Changes in activity of two directionally selective, preparation-related neurons during the four precuing conditions when the same movement was to be performed. Neuronal activity is presented in the form of a raster display (each dot represents an action potential and each line a trial), trials being ordered from top to bottom according to increasing RT, and a peristimulus frequency histogram (bin width: 40 msec). Horizontal black bars indicate movement duration. Time base: 100 msec; PS: preparatory signal; PP: preparatory period; RS: response (imperative) signal. Note, on the left, that the PP was of variable duration and, hence, neuronal activity during the first and the last 800 msec of the PP is shown.

chronometric methods and neural activity in the structure presumed to be involved in these programming processes (i.e., in PM).

However, as was true in the first series of experiments, this conclusion is challenged when data collected in another cortical area (MI) are considered. Very similar patterns of results were found in both areas, so that the assumption of a specific and unique role for PM in motor programming is in doubt. First, changes in neuronal activity during the PP when the precue provided directional information were also found in MI (21% of the neurons), although to a lesser extent than in PM (40%). As in PM, there was no significant change in neuronal activity following the precuing of movement extent. Second, statistically significant correlations between RT and changes in neuronal activity during the PP were found in 48 percent of MI neurons in at least one

Requin, Riehle, and Seal

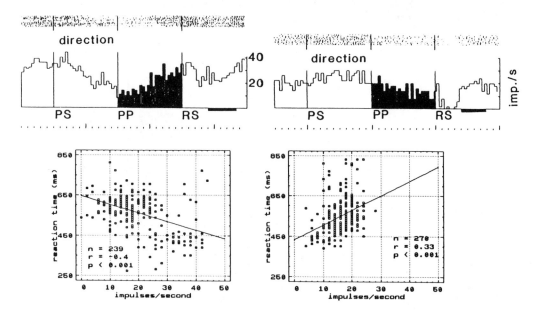

Figure 30.5 *Upper part:* changes in activity of two nonselective, preparation-related neurons. Same format as in figure 30.4. *Lower part:* diagrams of linear regression of RT on neuronal activity during the last 500 msec of the preparatory period, data for the four precuing conditions being pooled.

precuing condition—significantly more than in PM (39%). However, the distribution of these correlations in the different precuing conditions did not differ from that found in PM and, moreover, the mean absolute value of the significant correlation coefficients identical in both areas ($r = .40$ in MI and $r = .38$ in PM). Third, as in PM, negative correlations were associated with an increase and a positive sign with a decrease in activity. Finally, populations of "preparation-related" (5%) and "preparation- and execution-related" (16%) neurons were also found in MI, although in lesser proportions than PM (18% and 22%, respectively). In contrast, purely "execution-related" neurons were found more often in MI (47%) than in PM (28%).

To summarize, all the conclusions drawn from data collected in PM may also be drawn from the data collected in MI: only quantitative, but not qualitative differences were observed between the two areas. Both regions may be considered as equally involved in programming processes. Even the hypothesis that MI is more "motor," and PM more "preparatory," which was based on the differences in the proportions of "preparatory" and "motor" neurons in the two areas (Riehle and Requin 1989), may be challenged when the predictive value for RT of the changes in neuronal activity during the PP is considered. Figure 30.6 compares the distributions of the absolute values of correlations between preparatory neuronal activity and RT in conditions of directional precuing for both cortical areas. Not only the shape of these distributions, but also the proportions and mean values of the significant correlations are almost identical in both areas. Moreover, it is clear that when the strength of these correlations is taken as an index of the involvement of

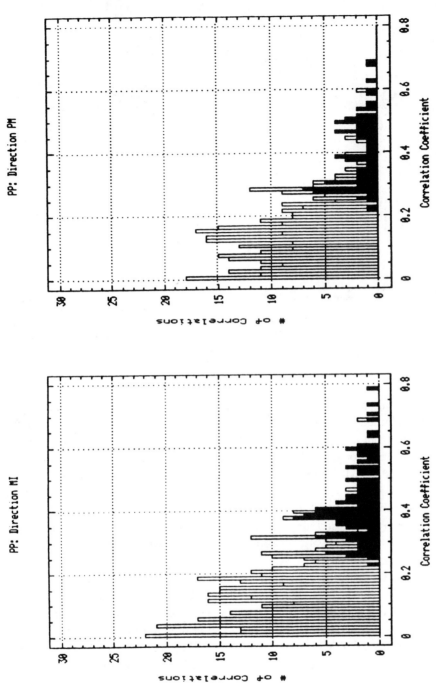

Figure 30.6 Histograms of correlation coefficients for all the neurons recorded in the premotor cortex (right) and in the primary motor cortex (left) in the condition of directional precuing. Black columns: statistically significant ($p < .05$) correlations; white columns: statistically nonsignificant correlations.

individual neurons in programming, neurons are continuously distributed along such an axis of functionality. Note, finally, that the position of each neuron on this continuum seems to depend stochastically upon its belonging to one of the neuronal types as defined by the timing of their changes in activity.

30.5 TOWARD THE NEW PARADIGM OF COGNITIVE NEUROSCIENCE

Data provided by both these studies of the neuronal correlates of planning for action add to the current reconsideration of classical views of the anatomical separation of behavioral functions, both at the macroanatomical level of neural structures and at the microanatomical level of neuronal units. Neither the concept of functional homogeneity of cortical areas, as defined by the cyto-architecture, nor the concept of functional specificity of neurons is tenable at this point. For some years, revised views of the relationship between the structural and functional aspects of the brain have been stimulated mainly by the influential conception of a modular organization of the neocortex (Mountcastle 1978). In the modular concept, all cortical areas consist of aggregates of similar units, or modules, having the same neuronal circuitry, and performing the same basic operation. Networks of modules are distributed and the functions—where function is used in the usual sense of the term—are implemented in different networks depending on the relative weighting of extramodular connections. The basic modular unit has an intrinsic mechanism that governs the connectivity between modular input and output and, consequently, controls the so-called functional structuring of modular networks (Phillips, Zeki, and Barlow 1984). This does not imply that the whole cerebral cortex is a homogeneous, modular structure, nor that each neuron is totally nonspecific in its functional involvement. Quantitatively different functions between neurons with limited course-coding properties (Ballard 1986), resulting in variations in the statistical parameters of neuronal populations (Requin, Riehle, and Seal 1988; Requin, Lecas, and Vitton 1990) make the existence of topographical differences in function between cortical regions consistent with the concept of a distributive parallel network (see Goldman-Rakic 1988).

Such a view of cortical organization appears to be particularly appropriate for interpreting the data we have obtained in our experiments. The three main aspects of these data—the existence of a sensorimotor gradient showing the temporal organization of sensorimotor function, the distribution of sensorimotor functioning over different cortical areas, and the description of three types of neuronal populations—are brought together in the model schematized in figure 30.7. Parallel networks of modules are distributed throughout the three cortical areas we have studied. Each network is responsible for processing a particular sensorimotor (S-R) function which is defined by its relative proximity to primary sensory and motor systems. In a particular S-R network, any neuron is characterized by two functional features. First, the

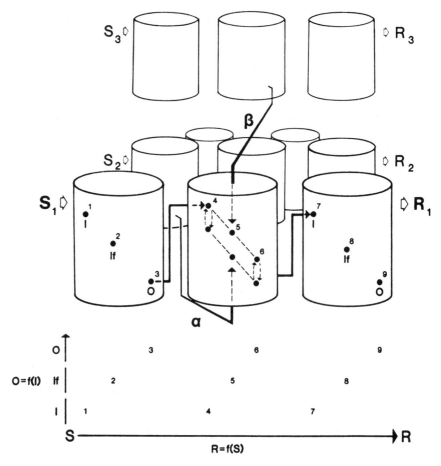

Figure 30.7 A modular network model of cortical organization; I = input neuron, O = output neuron, If = interfacing neuron, S = stimulus, R = response (see further explanations in the text).

specific location of the neuron within the architecture of the module itself, whether it be an "input" (I), "interfacing" (IF), or "output" (O) element, determines the action of this neuron in the basic processing operation implemented by the module. This operation would be to associate an input signal with an output signal. Both input and output signals are selected via the interplay of excitatory and inhibitory influences between neurons of the same module. Interfacing neurons would play the role of association controllers by governing this intramodular linking process. The interfacing neurons themselves receive extramodular influences from other networks in either a feedforward or feedback mode, with respect to the direction of information flow. Second, the position of the neuron within the network determines whether the neuron can be characterized, in purely descriptive terms, as being sensory or motor. These two arguments explain why we did not find a strict correlation between the type of neuron—defined by the discrete function $O = f(I)$—and the sensory or motor characteristics—as defined by the continuous $R = f(S)$.

For instance, neuron 7 (see fig. 30.7), which is a within-module input neuron, has a more "motor" behavioral function than neuron 3, which is a within-module output neuron.

In order to develop this conception further we need (1) to determine whether all the neurons within a module are members of a single class whose role in the module is probabilistic rather than discrete, or members of several distinct classes, each characterized by its specific role within the functioning of the module; (2) to describe the functional cooperation among the neurons in a module by studying their possible interconnectivity; (3) to confirm that the functions of the cortical areas involved in motor planning reflect only quantitative differences as indicated by the degree of overlap between populations of neurons in a continuous distribution of function; and (4) to understand how the cognitive processes underlying preparation for action are brought into play, either continuously or in sequence, by the type of organization of the neocortex that we have outlined.

When considering the increasing doubts and uncertainty surrounding one of the fundamental paradigms of cognitive neuroscience, one may suggest that the scientific community in this field is experiencing something of a paradigmatic crisis which heralds a scientific revolution. Several symptoms that characterize such a crisis can be identified. First is the increasing number of experimental facts that are no longer comprehensible in the context of the established paradigm—namely, the information processing "boxology" and the brain organization "patchwork" concept. Second is the attempt to maintain the general explanatory value of this established paradigm by progressively complicating it and adding piecemeal, ad hoc theoretical refinements. Examples of this trend may be found in the proliferation of new "stages," the subdivision of currently admitted stages, and the serial/parallel hybridization in the field of information-processing models (see Miller 1988), as well as the parceling of large cortical regions into increasingly smaller, functionally specialized micro-areas (see, for example, Baylis, Rolls, and Leonard 1987; Cavada and Goldman-Rakic 1989; Kaas 1987). Third is the blooming of competing theories, none of which has yet succeeded in replacing the established paradigm. For instance, in spite of their great potential interest, the concept of continuous flow of information processing (Miller 1988), the modular conception of brain organization (Phillips, Zeki, and Barlow 1984), the notion of parallel-distributed processing (McClelland and Rumelhart 1986), the revival of Bernstein's ideas in action science (Requin, Semjen, and Bonnet 1984), and the perspectives opened by nonlinear laws in biological systems (Arbib 1987; Skarda and Freeman 1987) do not have sufficient explanatory power to constitute a new paradigm for cognitive neuroscience. Most likely, the paradigmatic revolution will emerge from an unexpected synthesis of some of these influential new ideas with the old ones.

This unstable and presumably transitory state of uncertainty may be felt as either exciting or discouraging. The excitement is for those who believe that by exploring original conceptual approaches, they will accelerate the emergence of the new paradigm and who are willing to take the risk of not producing theoretically integrable data for some time. The discouragement would be for those waiting for the time when some new paradigm will be fruitful in producing testable hypotheses.

NOTE

This work was supported by ONR grant N00014 89 J1557.

REFERENCES

Andersen, R. A. (1989). Visual and eye movement functions of the posterior parietal cortex. *Annual Review of Neuroscience, 12,* 377–403.

Arbib, M. A. (1987). Levels of modeling of mechanisms of visually guided behavior. *Behavioral and Brain Sciences, 10,* 407–465.

Ballard, D. H. (1986). Cortical connections and parallel processing: Structure and function. *Behavioral and Brain Sciences, 9,* 67–120.

Baylis, G. C., Rolls, E. T., and Leonard, C. M. (1987) . Functional subdivisions of the temporal lobe neocortex. *Journal of Neuroscience, 7,* 330–342.

Bruce, C. J., and Goldberg, M. E. (1985). Primate frontal eye fields: I. Single neurons discharging before saccades. *Journal of Neurophysiology, 53,* 603–635.

Cavada, C., and Goldman-Rakic, P. S. (1989). Posterior parietal cortex in rhesus monkey: I. Parcellation of areas based on destructive limbic and sensory corticocortical connections. *The Journal of Comparative Neurology, 287,* 393–421.

Crammond, D. J., and Kalaska, J. F. (1989). Neuronal activity in primate parietal cortex area 5 varies with intended movement direction during an instructed-delay period. *Experimental Brain Research, 76,* 458–462.

Evarts, E. V., Shinoda, Y., and Wise, S. P. (1984). *Neurophysiological approaches to higher brain functions.* New York: Wiley.

Goldberg, G. (1985). Supplementary area structure and function: Review and hypotheses. *Behavioral Brain Sciences, 8,* 567–615.

Goldman-Rakic, P. S. (1988). Topography of cognition: Parallel distributed networks in primate associative cortex. *Annual Review of Neuroscience, 11,* 137–156.

Hepp-Reymond, M. C. (1988). Functional organization of motor cortex and its participation in voluntary movements. In H.D. Steklis and J. Erwin (Eds.), *Comparative primate biology.* Vol. 4, 501–624. New York: Liss.

Hopfield, J. J. (1982). Neural networks and physical systems with emerging collective computational abilities. *Proceedings of the National Academy of Sciences, 79,* 2554–2558

Humphrey, D. R., and Corrie, W. S. (1978) . Properties of pyramidal tract neuron system within a functionally defined subregion of primate motor cortex. *Journal of Neurophysiology, 41,* 216–243.

Jordan, M. (1990). Motor learning and the degrees-of-freedom problem. In M. Jeannerod (Ed.), *Attention and Performance XIII,* 796–836. Hillsdale, NJ: Erlbaum.

Kaas, I. H. (1987). The organization of neocortex in mammals: Implications for theories of brain function. *Annual Review of Psychology, 38,* 129–151.

Kawato, M., Furukawa, K., and Suzuki, R. (1987). A hierarchical neural-network model for control and learning of voluntary movements. *Biological Cybernetics, 57,* 169–185.

Keele, S. W. (1981). Behavioral analysis of motor control. In V. B. Brooks (Ed.), *Handbook of Physiology*. Vol. 2, part 2, 1391–1414. Bethesda, MD: American Physiological Society.

Keele, S. W., Cohen, A., and Ivry, R. (1990). Motor programs: Concepts and issues. In M. Jeannerod (Ed.), *Attention and Performance XIII*, 77–110. Hillsdale, NJ: Erlbaum.

Kornblum, S., Hasbroucq, T., and Osman, A. (1990). Dimensional overlap: Cognitive basis for stimulus-response compatibility: A model and taxonomy. *Psychological Review, 97*, 253–270.

Kurata, K., and Tanji, J. (1985). Contrasting neuronal activity in supplementary and precentral motor cortex of monkeys: II. Responses to movement triggering versus nontriggering sensory signals. *Journal of Neurophysiology, 53*, 142–152.

Kwan, H. C., MacKay, W. A., Murphy, J. T., and Wong, Y. C. (1985). Properties of visual cues responses in primate precentral cortex. *Brain Research, 343*, 24–35.

Kwan, H. C., Yeap, T. H., Jiang, B. C., and Borrett, D. (1990). Neural network control of simple limb movements. *Canadian Journal of Physiology and Pharmacology, 68*, 126–130.

Lecas, J. C., Requin, J., Anger, C., and Vitton, N. (1986). Changes in neuronal activity of the monkey precentral cortex during preparation for movement. *Journal of Neurophysiology, 56*, 1680–1702.

Lemon, R. N. (1984). Methods for neuronal recording in conscious animals. *IBRO Handbook series*, vol. 4. New York: Wiley.

Lépine, D., Glencross, D., and Requin, J. (1989). Some experimental evidence for and against a parametric conception of movement programming. *Journal of Experiment Psychology: HPP, 15*, 347–362.

Lynch, J. C. (1980). The functional organization of posterior parietal association cortex. *Behavioral and Brain Sciences, 3*, 485–534.

McClelland, J. L., and Rumelhart, D. E. (1986). *Parallel distributed processes*. Vols. 1 and 2. Cambridge: MIT Press.

Meijer, O. G., and Roth, K. (1988). *Complex movement behavior: The motor action controversy*. Amsterdam: North-Holland.

Meyer, D. E., Osman, A. M., Irwin, D. E., and Yantis, S. (1988) . Modern mental chronometry. In B. Renault, M. Kutas, M. G. M. Coles, and A. W. K. Gaillard (Eds.), *Event related potential investigations of cognition*, 3–67. Amsterdam: North-Holland.

Miller, J. O. (1988). Discrete and continuous models of human information processing: Theoretical distinctions and empirical results. *Acta Psychologica, 67*, 191–257.

Mountcastle, V. B. (1976). The world around us: Neural command functions for selective attention. *Neuroscience Research Progress Bulletin, 14*, suppl. 1, 1–47.

Mountcastle, V. B. (1978). An organizing principle for cerebral function: The unit module and the distributed system. In F. O. Schmitt and F. G. Worden (Eds.), *The Neurosciences. Fourth Study Program*, 21–42. Cambridge, MA: MIT Press.

Mountcastle, V. B. (1986). The neural mechanisms of cognitive functions can now be studied directly. *Trends in Neurosciences, 9*, 505–508.

Mountcastle, V. B., Lynch, J. C., Georgopoulos, A., Sakata, H., and Acuna, C. (1975). Posterior parietal association cortex of the monkey: command functions for operations within extrapersonal space. *Journal of Neurophysiology, 38*, 871–908.

Osman, A. M., Kornblum, S., and Meyer, D. E. (1990). Does motor programming necessitate response execution? *Journal of Experimental Psychology: HPP, 16*, 183–198.

Phillips, C. G., Zeki, S., and Barlow, H. B. (1984). Localization of function in the cerebral cortex. *Brain, 107*, 327–361.

Requin, J., Brener, J., and Ring, C. (1991). Preparation for action. In J. R. Jennings and M. G. H. Coles (Eds.), *Handbook of cognitive psychophysiology: Central and autonomic nervous system approaches*, 357–448. New York: Wiley.

Requin, J., Lecas, J. C., and Vitton, N. (1990). A comparison of preparation-related neuronal activity changes in the prefrontal, premotor, primary motor and posterior parietal areas of the monkey cortex: Preliminary results. *Neuroscience Letters, 111*, 151–156.

Requin, J., Riehle, A., and Seal, J. (1988). Neuronal activity and information processing in motor control: From stages to continuous flow. *Biological Psychology, 26*, 179–198.

Requin, J., Semjen, A., and Bonnet, M. (1984). Bernstein's purposeful brain. In H. T. A. Whiting (Ed.), *Human motor action: Bernstein reassessed*, 467–504. Amsterdam: North-Holland.

Riehle, A. (1991). Visually-induced signal-locked neuronal activity changes in precentral motor areas of the monkey: hierarchical progression of signal processing. *Brain Research, 540*, 131–137.

Riehle, A., and Requin, J. (1989). Monkey primary motor and premotor cortex: Single-cell activity related to prior information about direction and extent of an intended movement. *Journal of Neurophysiology, 61* (3), 534–549.

Rosenbaum, D. A. (1983). The movement precuing technique: Assumptions, applications and extensions. In R. A. Magill (Ed.), *Memory and control in motor behavior*, 231–274. Amsterdam: North-Holland.

Rosenbaum, D. A. (1987). Successive approximations to a model of human movement programming. In G. Bower (Ed.), *The psychology of learning and motivation*, 153–182. New York: Academic Press.

Rosenbaum, D. A., Marchak, F., Barnes, H. J., Vaughan, J., Slotta, J. D., and Jorgensen, M. J. (1990). Constraints for action selection: Overhand versus underhand grips. In M. Jeannerod (Ed.), *Attention and Performance XIII*, 321–342. Hillsdale, NJ: Erlbaum.

Schmidt, R. A. (1988). Motor and action perspectives in motor behavior. In O. G. Meijer and K. Roth (Eds.), *Complex movement behavior; The motor-action controversy*, 3–44. Amsterdam: North-Holland.

Seal, J. (1989). Sensory and motor functions of the superior parietal cortex of the monkey as revealed by single neuron recordings. *Brain, Behavior and Evolution, 33*, 113–117.

Seal, J., and Commenges, D. (1985). A quantitative analysis of stimulus- and movement-related responses in the posterior parietal cortex of the monkey. *Experimental Brain Research, 58*, 144–153.

Seal, J., and Commenges, D. (1986). Modeling of the stimulus-response process and the determination of function in the central nervous system. *Mathematical Modelling, 7*, 905–913.

Seal, J., and Requin, J. (1987). Sensory to motor transformation within area 5 of the posterior parietal cortex in the monkey. *Society for Neuroscience Abstracts 13*, part 1, 673.

Seal, J., Gross, C., and Bioulac, B. (1982). Activity of neurons in area 5 during a single arm movement in monkeys before and after deafferentation of the trained limb. *Brain Research, 280*, 229–243.

Semjen, A., and Gottsdanker, R. (1990). Rapid serial movements: Relation between the planning of sequential structure and effector selection. In M. Jeannerod (Ed.), *Attention and Performance XIII*, 409–427. Hillsdale, NJ: Erlbaum.

Skarda, C. A., and Freeman, W. J. (1987). How brains make chaos in order to make sense of the world. *Behavioral and Brain Sciences, 10*, 161–195.

Sternberg, S. (1969). The discovery of processing stages: extensions of Donder's method. *Acta Psychologica, 30*, 276–315.

Sternberg, S., Knoll, R. L., and Turock, D. L. (1990). Hierarchical control in the execution of action sequences: Tests of two invariance properties. In M. Jeannerod (Ed.), *Attention and Performance XIII*, 3–55. Hillsdale, NJ: Erlbaum.

Sternberg, S., Monsell, S., Knoll, R. L., and Wright, C. E. (1978). The latency and duration of rapid movement sequences: Comparisons of speech and typewriting. In G. E. Stelmach (Ed.), *Information processing in motor control and learning*, 117–152. New York: Academic Press.

Tanji, J., and Kurata, K. (1982). Comparison of movement-related activity in two cortical motor areas of primates. *Journal of Neurophysiology, 48*, 633–653.

Wannier, T. M. J., Maier, M. A., and Hepp-Reymond, M. C. (1989). Responses of motor cortex neurons to visual stimulation in the alert monkey. *Neuroscience Letters, 98*, 63–68.

Wiesendanger, M. (1986). Recent developments in studies of the supplementary motor area of primates. *Review of Physiology, Biochemistry and Pharmacology, 103*, 1–59.

Wiesendanger, M. (1990). The motor cortical areas and the problem of hierarchies. In M. Jeannerod (Ed.), *Attention and Performance XIII*, 59–75. Hillsdale, NJ: Erlbaum.

Wise, S. P. (1984). The non-primary motor cortex and its role in the cerebral control of movement. In G. Edelman, W. Cowan, and E. Gall (Eds.), *Dynamic aspects of cortical function*, 525–555. New York: Wiley.

Wise, S. P., and Mauritz, K. H. (1985). Set-related neuronal activity in the premotor cortex of rhesus monkey: Effects of changes in motor set. *Proceedings of the Royal society of London, B 223*, 331–354.

31 Speech Production and Perception in Patients with Cerebellar Lesions

Richard B. Ivry and H. S. Gopal

Over the past few years, we have sought to identify the elementary mental operations that underlie the performance of coordinated behavior. The putative operations studied here include ones related to the control of sequencing, force, and timing. A guiding hypothesis of our work is that success or failure in the execution of movements may, in part, reflect individual differences in these computations. Moreover, we have sought to determine whether these operations are independent of one another, or whether they should be construed as the unified computational focus of the motor control system (Keele and Ivry 1988).

Elucidating elementary mental operations in the study of motor control entails answering two central questions. Of primary concern is what the operations are and how these operations interact. In addition, a natural extension of this concern is to consider the generality of a hypothetical operation. For example, if the evidence suggests that timing is controlled independently from force in reaching movements, a logical question to ask is whether the same timing mechanism is used in other effector domains.

Figure 31.1 presents two ways to conceive of how elementary operations might be organized. They deal with a case in which the behavioral goal is invariant; an actor is trying to attract the attention of another person. Figure 31.1a sketches how a simplified model of the motor system might divide its functions in terms of effector systems. According to this view, many elementary computations must be performed for an action to occur, but the computations are specific to effector systems, perhaps because of their idiosyncratic constraints. Figure 31.1b retains the notion that there are elementary operations, but here the operations are shared across effector systems. Not only is a specialized module activated when a behavioral goal requires this module's particular computation, but the same module can be invoked by other effector systems when that computation is needed. In Fodor's (1983) terms, figure 31.1a embodies a system characterized by both vertical and horizontal modularity. Vertical modularity reflects the segregation of function across task domains, and horizontal modularity reflects the fact that within each domain there are distinct computational modules. Vertical modularity is violated in figure 31.1b because the same computational modules are shared across domains.

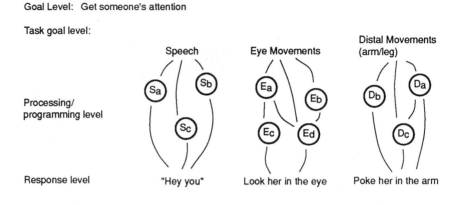

Task/Domain Specific Organization

Goal Level: Get someone's attention

Task goal level:

Speech   Eye Movements   Distal Movements (arm/leg)

Processing/programming level

Response level   "Hey you"   Look her in the eye   Poke her in the arm

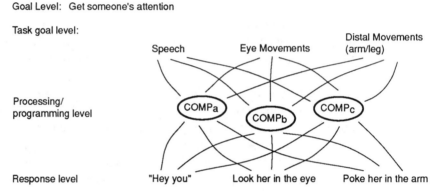

Shared Computation Organization

Goal Level: Get someone's attention

Task goal level:

Speech   Eye Movements   Distal Movements (arm/leg)

Processing/programming level   COMPa   COMPb   COMPc

Response level   "Hey you"   Look her in the eye   Poke her in the arm

Figure 31.1 Two hypothetical organizations of the motor system. Figure 31.1a entails vertical and horizontal modularity. Figure 31.1b entails only horizontal modularity.

Much past research in motor control has either ignored the notion of separable operations or assumed, perhaps for practical reasons, the organization depicted in figure 31.1a. For example, many researchers have sought to identify the minimal set of parameters needed to describe a movement trajectory (e.g., Flash and Hogan 1985; Hasan 1986; Lacquaniti and Soechting 1982). Generally, the computations of these parameters require joint information about forces and time, and they also frequently require knowledge about the specific effector system (Atkeson 1989). In addition, researchers have generally studied performance of specific tasks and, thus, have limited their attention to single effector systems.

By contrast, our research strategy has been to test directly the viability of the organization suggested in figure 31.1b. We have used a number of different methodologies to delineate a set of candidate elementary operations and to assess their generality. In correlational studies, we have found evidence that timing and force control might constitute two independent operations.

For example, Keele, Ivry, and Pokorny (1987) had subjects perform two tasks. The first task required subjects to produce a series of isochronous intervals by repetitive tapping. The second task assessed the subjects' ability to produce consistent force pulses. The movements were performed with either the finger or the forearm. Correlations were low between performance with the same effector for timing versus force production. However, the correlations were high within tasks. For example, a subject good at controlling force in finger flexions was also typically good at controlling force in forearm extensions. The same was observed for the timing task. In addition, we have found that timing precision on motoric tasks also correlates significantly with perceptual timing acuity (Keele et al. 1985).

Research with neurological patients has further supported this dissociation between timing and force control. In particular, we have found that patients with lesions of the cerebellum have difficulty producing a series of isochronous intervals (Ivry and Keele 1989). Moreover, an analysis of patients with focal lesions indicated that when the lesions include the neocerebellum, this difficulty stems from increased variability in a central timing process rather than from a deficit in implementing a central movement command (Ivry, Keele, and Diener 1988). On the other hand, patients with lesions of the basal ganglia are unimpaired in time production, but have difficulty in regulating the force of a movement (Hallett and Khoshbin 1980; Ivry 1990; Stelmach, Teasdale, Phillips, and Worringham 1989). Together, these studies indicate that the basal ganglia and cerebellum are involved in separable computations for the production of coordinated behavior, thus supporting modularity as depicted at the processing/programming level of figure 31.1 (also see Lundy-Ekman et al. 1991).

Additional studies lead us to believe that horizontal modularity (fig. 31.1b) provides a more parsimonious functional description of the motor system than does vertical modularity (fig. 31.1a). Of greatest interest and surprise is the finding that cerebellar lesions not only disrupt the production of periodic movements but also impair subjects' ability to estimate the duration of intervals demarcated by auditory clicks (Ivry and Keele 1989). This provides the first demonstration of a role played by the cerebellum in a non-motoric task. The duration-perception deficit is not generic; patients who show it are unimpaired in judging the loudness of similar stimuli. Thus, we have argued that one function of the cerebellum is to operate as an internal clock for both perception and production (Keele and Ivry 1991; cf. Gordon and Meyer 1984).

Given these results, we have recently examined the performance of cerebellar patients on a new perceptual task, velocity perception, which may require precise timing (Ivry and Diener in 1991). Here, each stimulus was composed of a line of dots that continuously moved across the field of view. The subjects judged whether the velocity of a test stimulus was faster or slower than the velocity of a standard stimulus. In three experiments sampling a range of velocities, patients with cerebellar lesions were impaired in making the velocity judgments. Control experiments indicated that the visual deficit was specific to velocity judgments and could not be explained by faulty eye movements. These results provide a second demonstration of the timing functions of the cerebellum in perception. The utilization of this computational capability in tasks as diverse as finger tapping, auditory time perception, and velocity perception corresponds to a violation of vertical modularity (Fodor 1983).

To further explore the generality of the cerebellar timing system, the present chapter reports new experiments that extend our cerebellar research into the linguistic domain. This extension is a natural outgrowth of earlier work. Temporal regularities are pervasive in speech perception and production. These phenomena have been studied at the level of phonemes (House 1961; Lisker and Abramson 1967; Miller and Liberman 1979), syllables (Kent and Moll 1975; Kozhenvnikov and Chistovich 1965), and larger segments of speech where rate and stress parameters vary (Kelso et al. 1985; Tuller and Kelso 1990; Weismer and Fennell 1985). The question of whether timing in speech is explicitly represented or is an indirect consequence of biomechanical and dynamical constraints has proven difficult to answer (see Fowler 1980; Tuller, Kelso, and Harris 1983).

Examining the performance of cerebellar patients with deficits in timing should prove useful in answering a number of questions related to this one. First, can the speech disorders observed in these patients be described by the hypothesis that the patients have suffered a selective deficit in temporally coordinating the numerous neuromuscular events involved in *producing* speech? Second, are the timing capabilities of the cerebellum involved in speech *perception*?

Evidence of a perceptual deficit would support the hypothesis that some psychological processes directly use the temporal information in speech and that these processes invoke the timing capabilities of the cerebellum. On the other hand, the psychological processes involved in speech perception may not directly exploit temporal cues identified through the acoustic analysis of speech. Temporal cues in the acoustic signal may be correlated with spectral cues (e.g., Port 1981) or other sources of information such as those defined at the level of the motoric actions that produce the sound (Abbs and Gracco 1983).

31.1 EXPERIMENT 1

Experiment 1 investigated the performance of cerebellar patients on two speech perception tasks. The stimuli for one task formed a temporal continuum; for the other task, the stimuli formed a spectral continuum. If the cerebellar timing system is required for processing temporal information in speech, we expected the patients to be impaired in judging the temporal continuum. The spectral continuum was included for control purposes.

The temporal continuum was established by varying the voice-onset time of stop consonants. All stop consonants in syllable initial positions are initiated by the rapid release of airflow from a point of constriction in the vocal tract.

One dimesion by which these consonants can be classified is voicing. For voiced stop consonants such as /b/, /d/, and /g/, the onset of vocal cord vibration (voicing) occurs at approximately the same time as the release of airflow. In contrast, voicing is delayed for an interval of time after the release of consonantal airflow for voiceless stops such as /p/, /t/, and /k/. The temporal difference between the release of airflow and the onset of voicing is the voice-onset time (VOT). For example, in English, VOT is generally less than 20 ms for voiced stop consonants and greater than 40 ms for voiceless stop consonants. Although many languages make a voiced/voiceless distinction, the mean values differ across languages and individuals (Lisker and Abramson 1964). Moreover, some languages contain consonants that are in a different region of the voicing continuum, namely, prevoiced such that vocalcord vibration precedes the release of air at the oral tract (Lisker and Abramson 1964; Strange and Jenkins 1978).

Discrimination between voiced, voiceless, and prevoiced consonants has been examined in studies of categorical perception (see Studdert-Kennedy 1976 for a review). For example, Abramson and Lisker (1968) generated three series of synthetic consonants that varied in VOT. Within each series, the frequencies were constant, simulating formants associated with one of three places of articulation: labial, alveolar, and velar consonants. Across all three continua, listeners produced identification and discrimination functions indicative of categorical perception. While the mean boundary was around 30 ms, the exact boundaries varied slightly as a function of place of articulation, Nonetheless, these results support the hypothesis that voicing is a salient feature in speech perception.

In the current experiment, patients with cerebellar lesions were tested on a series of consonants that differ in VOT. The cerebellum has proven critical for accurate timing in perceptual and motoric tasks. Thus, our primary interest was whether these patients would show evidence of categorical perception. If the cerebellar timing mechanism is involved in the computation of VOT, then damage to it should reduce the categorical effect. On the other hand, null results would suggest one of two interpretations. The psychological mechanism underlying categorical perception of the voicing dimension may not involve a temporal computation, or this computation may be outside the domain of the cerebellar timing system.

As in all patient research, we must be cautious in making claims about specific functional capabilities from the study of pathology. Patients are notorious for showing aberrant performance on a wide range of tasks, so an experimenter must provide a means to determine the specificity of a deficit. For example, an observed deficit may reflect impairment in a timing mechanism. However, it could also reflect a deficit in auditory processing or a general inability to follow directions for a psychophysical test.

To control for this possibility, the patients were also tested with a continuum of consonants that varied in place of articulation, ranging from /ba/ to /da/. Acoustically, this continuum is primarily formed by varying differences in the frequencies of the second and third formants during the transitional portion of the consonant. VOT is held constant. Thus, unlike the *ba-pa* series, there is no obvious temporal cue distinguishing the two categories of the *ba-da* series. Therefore, we expect cerebellar patients to be unimpaired in classifying these syllables if the deficit in VOT discrimination is a specific one. It should be kept in mind, though, that formant transitions convey both temporal and spectral information (e.g., Miller and Liberman 1979). So, the *ba-da* series provides only a partial control test. If the patients were to perform poorly on both continua, additional control tests would be needed.

Method

Subjects   All subjects were native speakers of German. The experiment was conducted at the Neurology Clinic of the Tuebingen University Medical School in Tuebingen, Germany. Fifteen patients with cerebellar disorders were tested. Many of them have been described in previous reports (Ivry and Keele 1989).

Two of the patients had focal lesions from stroke, and one had a bilateral ischemic lesion. The remaining patients had symptoms consistent with a diagnosis of cerebellar atrophy ($n = 8$) or olivopontocerebellar atrophy ($n = 4$). The difference between these latter two diagnoses is more a matter of degree than a reflection of distinct entities. In all of the cases, the diagnosis was consistent with neuroimaging results obtained with CT or MRI scans. The patients ranged in age from 22 to 75 years (mean = 51.6, SD = 16.7).

The patients received a clinical examination by a neurologist at the time of testing. The examination included tests of postural stability, oculomotor reflexes, voluntary movements with the upper and lower extremities, and speech. Though the patients varied in terms of their performance on these tests, all showed deficits on some part of the examination. Indeed, most of the patients had deficits in tests of postural and voluntary motor control.

Seven other people who had no history of disease of the central nervous system were recruited as control subjects. These subjects were clerical workers at the hospital ($n = 5$) or patients with back injuries ($n = 2$). They ranged in age from 24 to 56 years (mean = 44.4, SD = 13.0). Our only criteria in selecting the control subjects were that they were native German speakers and that the group spanned the approximate age range of the patients.

Stimuli   The stimuli were generated on a PDP 11/73 computer with the cascade-parallel synthesizer designed by Klatt (1980) and modified by Kewley-Port (1978). The synthesizer was set to cascade mode.

Each syllable had a total duration of 250 ms with identical frequencies during its steady-state portion. The steady-state formant frequencies were: F1 = 750 hz, F2 = 1200 hz, F3 = 2350 hz, F4 = 3300 hz, F5 = 3850 hz, and F6 = 4900 hz. The fundamental frequency for each syllable began at 121 Hz, rose to 125 Hz by 40 ms, and then fell linearly to 100 Hz at offset. All of the stimuli were made without release bursts.

There were two sets of nine stimuli each. One set formed the *ba-pa* continuum, and the other formed the *ba-da* continuum. Figure 31.2 shows examples of the stimuli, depicting the fundamental frequency and the first three formants. The *ba-pa* continuum was created by varying the energy onset for F0 and F1 relative to the onset of F2 and F3. For the end point /*ba*/, the onset of F0 and F1 preceded the onset at the higher frequencies by 10 ms. The onset of F0 and F1 was delayed 70 ms for the end point /*pa*/. The rest of the series was synthesized by varying the onset of F0 and F1 in steps of 10 ms, thus creating a continuum of VOT values ranging from -10 ms to $+70$ ms. The starting frequencies for F1, F2, and F3 were 200 Hz, 825 Hz, and 2000 Hz, respectively. The formants followed linear trajectories, achieving their steady-state values by 35 ms. There were no transitions for the higher formants.

For the *ba-da* series, the energy onset of all the formants occurred simultaneously. The onset frequency values of F2 and F3 were manipulated, while all other aspects of the syllable were held constant. The end point /*ba*/ was the same as the stimulus with VOT $= 0$ in the *ba-pa* series. The initial frequencies of F2 and F3 were 825 hz and 2000 hz. The initial frequencies of the end point /*da*/ were 1500 hz and 2630 hz. Thus, F2 and F3 had rising trajectories for the endpoint /*ba*/ and falling trajectories for the end point /*da*/. The series was created by varying F2 in steps of 84 hz, and F3 in steps of 79 hz.

Four blocks of stimuli were made for each series. Each block consisted of eight repetitions of the nine stimuli, yielding a total of 72 syllables. Stimulus order within a block was random. A four-second interstimulus interval separated the syllables. In addition, two training blocks were created with only the end point stimuli. These blocks contained ten repetitions of each end point.

Procedure Each subject was tested individually in a single session. The subject sat in a quiet room in front of an Apple IIe computer and monitor. After being instructed (in German), he or she was presented with a training block of stimuli from either the *ba-pa* series or the *ba-da* series. After each stimulus, the subject responded by pressing one of two keys. For the *ba-pa* series, the keys were labeled "*ba*" and "*pa*" whereas the second key was labeled "*da*" for the other series. Feedback was provided on the computer monitor during the training block.

Following the training block, the subjects were run on a test block for that series. No feedback was given during the test block. After completing the test block, the subjects were given a short rest before being tested on a training block and test block with the other series.

In summary, the first half of the experiment consisted of four blocks of trials, two training blocks and two test blocks. The second half of the experiment consisted of a second test block with each series. There was a lengthy pause between the two halves during which the subjects rested and performed in a different experiment. Half of the subjects were tested on the *ba-pa* series first and half were first tested on the *ba-da* series. The order was reversed for the second half of the experiment.

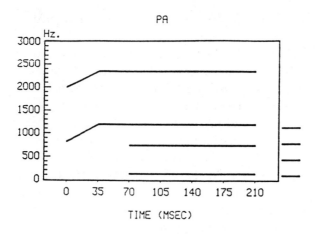

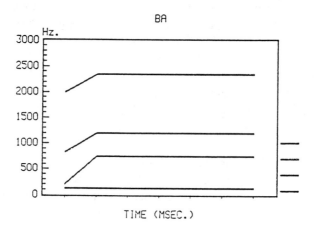

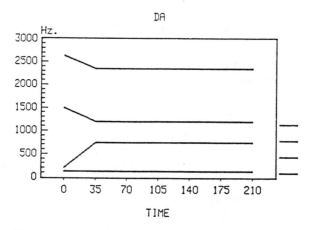

Figure 31.2 Primary formant trajectories for synthetic /ba/, /da/, and /pa/ syllables.

Results and Discussion

The mean number of *ba* responses was calculated for each of the nine stimuli from each continuum. One transformation was applied to the data before the averages were obtained. It took into account the fact that the point at which there is a shift from hearing *ba* to hearing either *pa* or *da* differs across subjects. For example, on the *ba-pa* series, six of the seven control subjects switched from *ba* responses to *pa* responses between stimulus 4 and stimulus 5. The 50 percent crossover point for the remaining subject was between stimulus 5 and stimulus 6. Similarly, the majority of responses to stimulus 4, VOT = 30 ms, were "*pa*" for one of the patients. Given these differences, the group functions would not appear as steep if the raw data were averaged across subjects without adjusting for individual differences in the crossover point. Thus, the data were realigned so that the crossover points for all of the subjects were the same stimulus. The crossover point could be unambiguously identified for all subjects. Note that by shifting the function in one direction, no entry was available for one of the tails. To correct this, a perfect score was entered there since subjects rarely made errors on the extreme stimuli.

This transformation was only required for the two subjects mentioned above on the *ba-pa* series. However, on the *ba-da* series, transformations were required for two control subjects and seven of the cerebellar patients. These centered the crossover point between stimulus 6 and stimulus 7. The direction of the transformation was to the right for the two control subjects and three of the patients. The remaining four patients required a leftward transformation. A transformation to the right indicates that the subject responded *da* more than average, whereas a transformation to the left indicates a relative bias to respond *ba*. The fact that so many subjects required transformations for this series points to a general problem encountered with the *ba-da* series. The stimuli in this series were more likely to be labeled *ba* than *da*. We chose our stimulus values on the basis of past research with American subjects (Reed 1984). These values may not have been ideal for German subjects, since the optimal stimulus set should lead to an equal distribution of responses between the two candidates.

Identification functions derived from the mean data for the cerebellar patients and control subjects are presented in figure 31.3. Results for the *ba-pa* series appear in the top half and results for the *ba-da* series appear on the bottom half. The functions indicate that the stimuli were generally perceived categorically. Qualitatively, the transition from one response category to the other appears similar to that obtained in previous studies of categorical perception in speech (e.g., Abramson and Lisker 1968). Within each category there is little change in performance.

For the *ba-pa* series, the patients tended to make a few more errors on each stimulus level. To assess this outcome further, we fit each subject's data with a normal ogive function and calculated the mean and standard deviation (Kling and Engen 1971). The mean of the standard deviations for each group on the two series appear in the top half of figure 31.4.

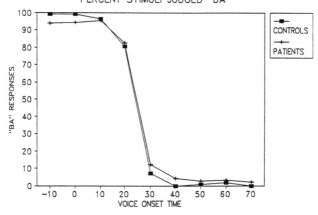

SPEECH PERCEPTION OF BA–PA SERIES
PERCENT STIMULI JUDGED "BA"

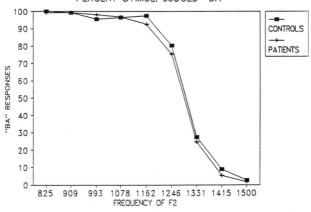

SPEECH PERCEPTION OF BA–DA SERIES
PERCENT STIMULI JUDGED "BA"

Figure 31.3 Identification functions on the *ba-pa* and *ba-da* continua for the cerebellar patients and control subjects.

These data were entered into a 2 × 2 ANOVA with one between-subjects factor (*group*: normal versus patient) and one within-subjects factor (*syllable*: *ba-pa* versus *ba-da*). A marginally significant effect of *syllable* emerged ($F(1, 20) = 4.08$, $p = .057$). Standard deviation estimates were higher for the *ba-da* continuum. However, the interaction depicted in figure 31.4 was not significant ($F(1, 20) = 2.29$, $p = .15$).

Although the preceding statistical procedure has been used to examine data in other experiments on categorical perception (e.g., Reed 1984), it may not be appropriate for theoretical and practical reasons. First, the data are fit to a normal ogive, the function assumed to describe most psychophysical data. However, functions interpreted as indicative of categorical perception are, by

Ivry and Gopal

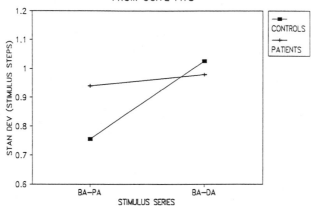

STANDARD DEVIATION ESTIMATES
FROM OGIVE FITS

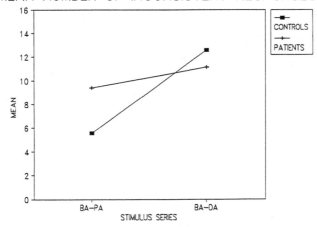

MEAN NUMBER OF INCONSISTENT RESPONSES

Figure 31.4 *Top:* Mean of the standard deviations for each subject group on the two continua. *Bottom:* Mean number of inconsistent responses made by each subject group on the two continua.

definition, poorly described by this function. Second, the estimation procedure requires that the raw data be transformed to z-scores. A decision must be made about what z-score to use when all sixteen presentations of a stimulus are assigned to the same category. We used a z-score of ±3.0 for such cases in the above analysis. Different values would alter the statistical outcome, although the interaction terms do not achieve significance when z-scores of either 2.2 or 4.0 are used for the perfect scores.

Given these problems, we designed a new measure of response inconsistency for each stimulus labeling function. Here, the total number of inconsistent responses was tallied. For example, if the number of *ba* responses by a subject for the nine stimuli of the *ba-pa* series was 16-16-16-15-13-1-0-0-0, then the number of inconsistent responses would be $0 + 0 + 0 + 1 + 3 + 1 + 0 + 0 + 0 = 5$. Two inconsistency scores were calculated for each subject, one per series.

The means of the inconsistency scores appear in the bottom half of figure 31.4. An analysis of them yielded results similar to those in the previous ANOVA. More inconsistent responses were obtained with the *ba-da* series ($F(1, 20) = 4.23$, $p = 0.053$), perhaps reflecting the greater similarity between /ba/ and /da/ than between /ba/ and /pa/ (Shepard 1980; Miller and Nicely 1955). Most important, there was no difference between the patients and controls ($F(1, 20) < 1.0$) and the syllable by group interaction was not significant ($F(1, 20) < 1.54$, $p = .23$).[1]

In summary, the evidence does not indicate that the cerebellar patients have a deficit in identifying speech syllables that differ in VOT. While the means in figure 31.4 show that the patients tended to be more variable in identifying the VOT continuum and performed slightly better than the control subjects on the frequency continuum, the interaction was not significant (but see note 1). Further research will be needed to determine if a subset of cerebellar patients are impaired in categorizing stimuli that vary in VOT.[2] For example, the four subjects who performed most inconsistently on the VOT task also produced poor scores on a duration-perception task with pure-tone stimuli (Ivry and Keele 1989). However, some of the patients who were perfect on the categorical-perception task were impaired on the time-perception task. Thus, at present, we favor the conservative interpretation that the psychological mechanisms involved in the categorical perception of speech do not utilize the cerebellar timing system.

31.2 EXPERIMENT 2

From the preceding experiment, we tentatively conclude that the cerebellar timing system is not involved in one speech perception task that might require a temporal computation, the perception of syllables differing in VOT. We cannot differentiate between two interpretations of our null results. One interpretation is that the neural systems involved in language are independent of the cerebellar timing system, a variant of vertical modularity. Alternatively, the essential cues underlying VOT perception may not require timing (see Miller, Weir, Pastore, Kelly, and Dooling 1976). In experiment 2, we further assess the role of the cerebellum in language processes by investigating whether the cerebellar timing system plays a role in speech production. Specifically, can the cerebellar timing hypothesis account for speech disorders associated with dysfunction of this neural structure?

Patients with cerebellar disorders frequently suffer from speech dysarthria. Their symptoms include irregular articulation, fluctuating pitch, irregular rate and stress, and erratic phonation (Darley, Aronson, and Brown 1969; Kluin et al. 1988). Such disturbances have been characterized as an ataxic dysarthria rather than a spastic dysarthria (Darley, Aronson, and Brown 1969; Kluin et al.

1988). Ataxia is generally associated with voluntary movements, whereas spasticity primarily reflects disturbances of posture.

Many deficits in the control of arm movements produced by patients with cerebellar lesions can be explained by the timing hypothesis. For instance, hypermetria and intentional tremor may reflect the inability to anticipate when the antagonist muscle needs to be activated to terminate a movement properly (see Ivry and Keele 1989). In experiment 2, we explore whether the timing hypothesis provides a useful description of cerebellar speech dysarthria. Specifically, we examine whether patients with speech dysarthria have difficulty in coordinating the articulatory actions that determine whether a consonant is voiced or voiceless.

Method

Subjects   Six male patients with diffuse cerebellar lesions and four age-matched control subjects (three males and one female) were tested. The subjects were all native German speakers, between the ages of 49 and 60. All of the patients had cerebellar atrophy, and all were identified by clinical examination as presenting symptoms of speech dysarthria. Four of them and two of the control subjects had participated in the perception tasks of experiment 1. Two new patients and two new control subjects were recruited.

Procedure   There were two different protocols used to obtain the speech samples. The subjects in protocol 1 were asked to alternate between saying the syllables *ba* and *pa*. The experimenter provided a pacing signal by moving his arm up and down. The syllables were produced at a rate of approximately one every 850 ms. Each trial contained between 12 and 15 alternations of the two syllables, yielding a total of 24 to 30 responses. If the subject became confused about which syllable was next in the sequence, the experimenter terminated the trial and began the procedure again. Subjects in protocol 1 were also tested on trials where they either repeated a single syllable or alternated between *ba* and *da*. The analysis of these trials is not included here.

Subjects in protocol 2 were tested more systematically. During testing, they sat in front of a computer monitor. Every four seconds, the computer generated a 50-ms warning tone, followed 500 ms later by the presentation of one of four printed nonsense syllables: *ba, pa, da,* or *ta*. The subjects were instructed to read the syllable in a normal voice. After the subject said the syllable, the experimenter triggered the computer to continue, and one second later the next trial began. On average, the subjects produced one syllable every 3.5 seconds.

Protocol 2 has two advantages over protocol 1. First, there was no rhythmicity to the subjects' responses and thus nonlinguistic temporal deficits should not be relevant. Second, since the subjects were presented with a target syllable, we could directly verify if their responses matched the stimuli.

The speech samples were recorded on high-quality metal cassette tapes. Subjects were tested in a quiet laboratory room.

Data Analysis   We analyzed all of the speech samples with the Interactive Laboratory Systems (ILS) software (Signal Technology, Inc.). The digitizing hardware, however, differed for the two protocols. For protocol 1, the output from the cassette recorder was low-pass filtered at 4.8 kHz and then sampled by a 12-bit analog-to-digital converter. For protocol 2, the recorder output was low-pass filtered at 9.6 kHz before conversion. The sampling rate for both protocols was set at 20 khz and the amplitude of the signal output was adjusted so that it spanned at least half the range of the A-D converter.

Analysis of Voice-Onset Time   The VOT values of subjects' responses were determined from a visual display of the acoustic waveform. The judges, one for protocol 1 and one for protocol 2, were unfamiliar with the purpose of the experiment. On each trial, the judge located a syllable and marked two points. The first deviation from the background signal was identified as the onset of the burst of the stop consonant. Then, the judge identified the point where clear periodicity in the signal was evident. This was taken as the onset of voicing. The difference between these two points was recorded as the VOT for the syllable. Both authors verified the judges' performance for a subset of the trials.

For protocol 1, the data were displayed with a temporal resolution of 1 pixel per 6.4 ms, constraining the recorded VOTs for each trial to be multiples of 6.4 ms. Response syllables were selected in random order for analysis, rather than being evaluated in the order spoken. Thus, the judge did not know the hypothesis being tested, the subject's group (patient or control), or the syllable being evaluated.

For protocol 2, the temporal resolution of the displays was increased to 1 ms. Examples of three response-waveform displays are presented in figure 31.5. The judge heard and identified each spoken syllable before determining its VOT onset and offset. He was naive about the purpose of the experiment and did not know the subject's neurological status. Nor did he know the typical VOTs of the four syllables.

Spectral Analysis   The judge for protocol 2 also performed a spectral analysis of the subjects' responses. In the waveform displays, he identified the midpoints of the vocalic portions of the syllables, defined as the points where their amplitudes were greatest. The formant frequencies around these points were then calculated by the ILS software. Frequency values were obtained for F1 and F2. These formants correlate roughly with the up-down and front-back positions of the articulators, respectively (Pickett 1980).

The spectral analysis was performed with a window spanning 5-ms intervals. Because data were sometimes missing from this analysis, an algorithm was used to calculate the frequencies for each trial. As part of it, F1 and F2 values were examined over a 30-ms epoch, spanning ± 15 ms around the midpoint. If values of F1 and F2 were present for at least four of the seven measured points (-15 ms to $+15$ ms in steps of 5 ms), then the average of these values was recorded for that syllable. If there were values present for

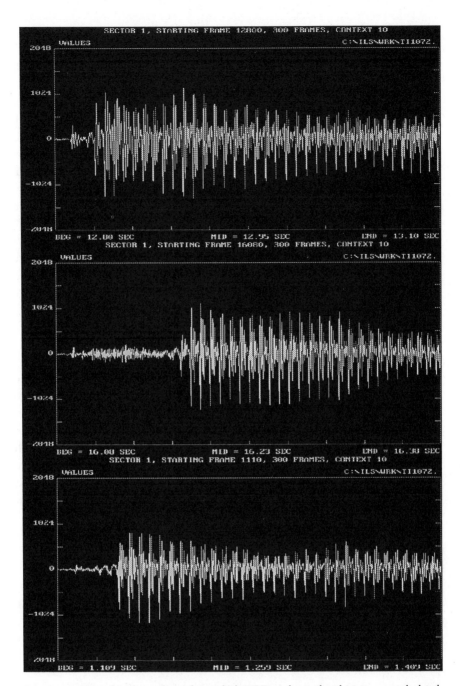

Figure 31.5 Examples of waveforms from which VOTs and vowel midpoints were calculated. Three syllables produced by patient B.U.C. The top trace is *da* with VOT = 9 msec. The middle trace is *pa* with VOT = 72 msec. The bottom trace is *pa* with VOT = 16 msec. All three traces are 300 msec in duration with burst onset at approximately 12 msec. Criterion for identifying onset of voicing was the first downward minimum of the periodic portion of the waveform. In all three examples shown, this point occurred one or two cycles prior to the large increase in signal amplitude.

fewer than four of the measured points, frequency data were not recorded. Spectral analyses were only performed on male speakers.

The VOT analysis provides an acoustic measure of articulatory events involved in the coordination between a consonant and a vowel. We hypothesize that timing control is essential during this dynamic phase. In contrast, we hypothesize that precise timing is less important during the relatively static portions of speech such as the steady-state segment of vowels. At normal speaking rates, the articulators maintain a stable configuration, however briefly, during the production of vowels; the need for timing control may be reduced during this relatively static phase of speech.

To summarize, we hypothesized that the cerebellar patients would be highly variable during the dynamic phases of speech. This should be observed in the VOT measure which presumably reflects the coordination of muscles involved in voicing and release of the consonantal burst. On the other hand, we expect that the patients will be relatively less variable during the steady-state portion of vowel production because timing demands are reduced there. This reduced variability should be revealed by the spectral analysis.

Results and Discussion

Protocol 1   The numbers of obtained VOT estimates differed across subjects because of variation in the quality of the recordings. Approximately ten productions of each syllable were analyzed per subject. The resulting data were averaged separately over the two control subjects and four patients.

The top half of figure 31.6 presents the mean VOTs for the *ba* and *pa* syllables when produced alternately. There was a large difference in the mean VOTs for the productions of the voiced *ba* and voiceless *pa*. As in previous research (Lisker and Abramson 1964), no overlap of VOTs occurred between the two distributions for the control subjects.

The bottom half of figure 31.6 presents the means of the individual standard deviations. The patients were much more variable in their VOTs. Given that the mean VOTs of the patients and control subjects were quite similar, especially for the voiceless *pa*, it appears that the patients produced VOTs both shorter and longer than the control subjects. For example, the measured VOTs of *pa* syllables produced by one patient ranged from 6.4 ms to 205 ms. The VOT variability was perceptually salient with the lower end of the continuum sounding like *ba* and the upper end like a *pa* with a loud, breathy burst.

All four patients produced at least one *pa* that sounded like *ba*. Two of them also produced at least one *ba* that sounded like *pa*. However, it should be noted that these auditory judgments of the German subjects' responses were made by American listeners.

Given the small number of subjects and violations of homogeneity of variance, statistical analyses were not performed. Nonetheless, the finding of increased variability in the patients was consistent. For example, the standard deviation of the voiceless syllables produced by the most consistent patient

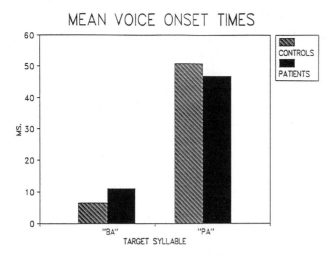

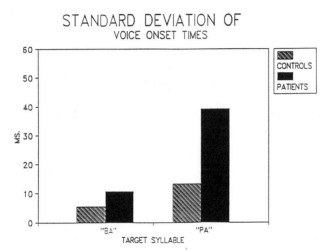

Figure 31.6 *Top:* Mean VOTs for the *ba* and *pa* syllables from protocol 1. *Bottom:* Mean standard deviations of the VOTs.

was 21.2 ms, whereas the comparable values for the control subjects were 12.0 and 14.3 ms.

Protocol 2, VOT Analysis   The preceding analysis indicates that cerebellar patients are more variable in producing the articulatory actions that underlie VOT. However, as noted earlier, there are two problems with the previous data. First, the resolution of the VOT measurement was only 6.4 ms. Second, protocol 1 does not provide a clear separation of errors that resulted from selection of the wrong goal and errors that occurred in the process of achieving that goal. For example, in trying to say *pa* while alternating between *ba* and *pa*, a token may have a short VOT. This could reflect selection of the wrong syllable to produce (*ba* instead of *pa*) or incorrect articulation of *pa*. Protocol 2 avoids these problems. Here, the measurement resolution was 1 ms and all of the stimuli were presented explicitly with an intertrial interval of approximately 3.5 seconds.

Figure 31.7 presents the mean VOTs and standard deviations for the patient and control groups. For simplification, we have combined the results over place of articulation: the results for *ba* and *da* were averaged together, as were the results for *pa* and *ta*. Thus, each data point represents approximately 48 productions per subject. With one exception, the mean values agree closely with the data in figure 31.6. The exception is the mean VOT for the control subjects on the voiceless syllables. The mean VOT was 43.5 ms for one control

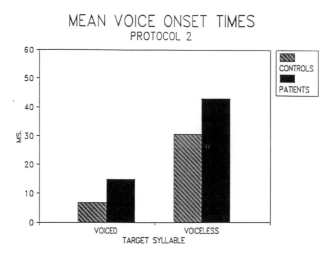

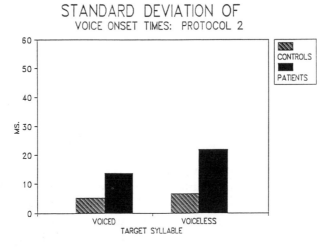

Figure 31.7 *Top:* Mean VOTs for the *ba* and *pa* syllables from protocol 2. *Bottom:* Mean standard deviations of the VOTs.

Ivry and Gopal

subject, but was only 17.8 ms for the other subject. Despite the short VOT, the productions were almost always perceived correctly by the rater.

As in protocol 1, the patients were more variable than the control subjects on both the voiced and the voiceless syllables. To analyze these results statistically, we performed a series of pairwise tests of homogeneity of variance, assessing the null hypothesis that the variability observed for a patient equaled the variability observed for a control subject. Rather than use standard F ratios, we used the q-statistic discussed by Zar (1984, 204). This provides a conservative test for comparing variances in which the overall Type I error probability is held constant by adjusting the critical value of q as a function of how many pairwise comparisons are involved. A q-value is calculated as

$$q = (\ln(\text{Var}_{patient}) - \ln(\text{Var}_{control}))/sqrt(2/n_{patient} + 2/n_{control})$$

when experimental conditions are compared to control conditions.

The q-values derived from these pairwise comparisons demonstrate the consistency of the differences in VOT variances between the two patients and two control subjects (table 31.1). All of the patients' variances were significantly greater than those of the control subjects at the .05 level.

The variance differences in the acoustic signals were also apparent perceptually. As the subjects' responses were analyzed, the judge tried to classify them. The misclassifications are summarized in table 31.2. Very few errors occurred for the control subjects. In contrast, 13 percent of the patients' responses were misclassified (26 errors divided by 200 productions), almost all of which involved confusions along the temporal dimension. The errors were as likely to involve a voiced syllable being labeled voiceless as the reverse. This result was obtained for both of the cerebellar patients.

Two final points concern the error data. First, there were no errors for either group in which the perceived syllable differed from the stimulus on both the place and VOT features. Second, to repeat our earlier caveat, the judge was a native American-English speaker whereas the patients were German. However, any language-specific artifacts would be apparent in the classifications of responses by both the controls and patients.

Protocol 2, Spectral Analysis The vowel midpoint occurred approximately 100 ms after the release of the voiced consonants and was slightly later for

Table 31.1 q Values from Pairwise Comparisons of Voice-Onset-Time Variances in Protocol 2

	Voiced Consonants		Voiceless Consonants	
Control	WER	SCC	WER	SCC
Patient				
BEN	7.72*	9.21*	7.14*	6.30*
BUC	3.77*	5.11*	10.14*	9.29*

* p < .01 (Critical value = 2.93 for eight comparisons; at alpha = 0.5, critical value = 2.34.)

Table 31.2 Errors in Perceptual Classifications from Protocol 2

	Stimulus	Response	Total
Controls			
	voiced	voiceless	2
	voiceless	voiced	0
		VOT errors	2
	labial	alveolar	3
	alveolar	labial	1
		place errors	4
Patients			
	voiced	voiceless	12
	voiceless	voiced	11
		VOT errors	23
	labial	alveolar	0
	alveolar	labial	3
		place errors	3

the voiceless consonants (98 ms versus 120 ms for voiced and voiceless consonants, respectively). Although the vowel was the same in all of the syllables, consistent differences were found between the labial and alveolar syllables: F1 was slightly lower for the alveolars than the labials (mean = 690 hz versus 707 hz) and F2 was higher for the alveolars (mean = 1280 hz versus 1173 hz). Thus, in the following analysis, we combined the results from *ba* and *pa* into one group, and *da* and *ta* into another.

The mean formant frequencies fell within the normal range for male speakers. More informative are the mean standard deviations of F1 and F2, which appear in the top and bottom halves of figure 31.8, respectively. As the figure shows, the formants produced by the patients tended to be more variable across trials.

To test the reliability of this result, we again conducted a series of pairwise comparisons on the spectral data using the *q*-statistic mentioned previously. As shown in table 31.3, the difference between the patients and control subjects for F1 and F2 variability was inconsistent. Nine of the sixteen pairwise comparisons were significant; the remaining seven were not. Moreover, the median *q* value for the nine significant comparisons involving the formant frequencies was 4.31, considerably lower than the median *q* value of 7.43 obtained for the comparisons involving VOTs (table 31.1).

In summary, patients with cerebellar dysarthria produced syllables with greater variability in VOTs. This effect occurred for both voiced and voiceless syllables produced alternately and in isolation. We believe that these results reflect a difficulty in temporally coordinating the neuromuscular events responsible for voicing and release of the stop consonant. This hypothesis is consistent with the cerebellar timing hypothesis.

However, other interpretations of these data are possible and cannot be ruled out given our current analyses. For example, VOT varies as a function

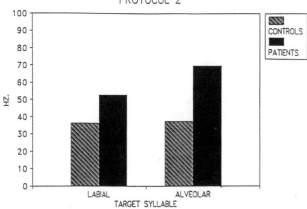

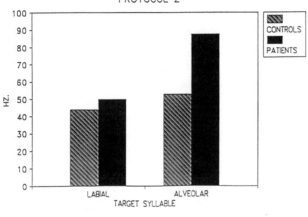

Figure 31.8 *Top:* Mean standard deviation of F1 at vowel midpoint from protocol 2. *Bottom:* Same for F2.

Table 31.3 *q* Values from Pairwise Comparisons of First and Second Formant Steady-State Frequency Measures in Protocol 2

F1	Labial Consonants		Alveolar Consonants	
Control *Patient*	WER	SCC	WER	SCC
BEN	5.41*	4.65*	6.74*	3.93*
BUC	− 2.21	− 2.37	4.30*	1.29
F2	Labial Consonants		Alveolar Consonants	
Control *Patient*	WER	SCC	WER	SCC
BEN	3.47*	− 1.25	4.31*	1.95
BUC	3.99*	− 1.00	4.62*	2.24

* p < .01 (Critical value = 2.93 for eight comparisons/meausre; at alpha = 0.5, critical value = 2.34.)

of speaking rate (Miller, Green, and Reeves 1986). Thus, the increased VOT variability may arise indirectly as a consequence of greater variability in terms of overall speaking rate. If the syllable durations were more variable for the patients' productions, it would then be necessary to compute a relative VOT measure that allows an adjustment for the duration of the individual syllable tokens. Syllable duration measurements were not made on the current data set, but will be obtained in future studies. This should allow stronger tests of whether the increased variability is manifest at the level of VOT, syllable duration, or both. In other words, at what level are speech deficits in patients with cerebellar lesions manifest—phonemic, syllabic, or suprasegmental? Moreover, if articulatory deficits are identified for linguistic phenomena spanning different temporal ranges, it will be of interest to determine whether the timing hypothesis can account for all or just a subset of these deficits.

The spectral analysis performed here (fig. 31.8 and table 31.3) was included as an initial attempt to obtain an acoustic measure independent of timing control. We anticipate that vowel formant frequencies may reflect the configuration of the articulators during steady-state speech. We hypothesized that a loss in timing control would be more marked during the dynamic period characteristic of consonant articulation. The results of experiment 2 provide mixed support for this prediction. The patients were generally more variable than the control subjects on the spectral measures, but this deficit was less consistent and quantitatively less robust than that observed in the production of VOT. The distinction between static and dynamic articulatory events may prove useful to researchers examining the underlying bases of different speech disorders.

31.3 EXPERIMENT 3

In what follows, we briefly present two additional experiments that explore a different temporal regularity in language. In certain written languages, word

Table 31.4 Sample Stimuli for Gemination Perception Experiment

	Stimulus Condition	
	Geminates	Controls
Examples:	seno/senno (breast/wisdom)	seno/seco (breast/with)
	seco/secco (with/arid)	secco/senno (arid, wisdom)
	sete/sette (thirst/seven)	sete/sere (thirst/evenings)

pairs exist in which the only orthographic difference is that the medial consonant is doubled for one member. This phenomenon, known as gemination, is found in Italian. Examples of Italian geminate pairs appear in table 31.4. As can be seen from them, there is no obvious connection between the word meanings within each pair. While the distinction between the two members of a pair is obvious orthographically, a different (acoustic) cue must be used to discriminate them in oral language.

One way that they are differentiated is to lengthen the duration of the word with the doubled consonant (referred to as the doublet). This lengthening occurs in the medial consonant (and sometimes in the vowel preceding this consonant). With some pairs, the difference in duration is the only salient perceptual cue; other pairs may differ on additional dimensions such as syllabic stress or vowel pronunciation.

As with categorical perception, the temporal difference in the acoustic signal between members of a geminate pair may or may not be directly exploited by psychological mechanisms. In experiment 3, we investigate whether patients with cerebellar lesions have difficulty discriminating between geminate-pair members that differ in duration.

Method

Subjects Six patients, four men and two women (mean age = 44.2 years, SD = 10.5), with atrophy of the cerebellum were tested. The patients included a family pair of mother and son. One of the patients, the mother of the familial pair, showed symptoms indicative of olivopontocerebellar atrophy. All of the patients were native Italian speakers. Four of the patients were born and lived within 100 km of Rome. Another was from Naples and one was from northern Italy, a region where gemination is less marked.

Two men and one woman served as control subjects (mean age = 38.3 years, SD = 14.4). Two of them were native Romans, and one was a native Venetian. In addition, two non-Italian control subjects were tested, a 40-year-old man born in Chile, and a 32-year-old Brazilian male. Both of these subjects were fluent in conversational Italian, although it was not their native language.

The subjects were tested at the Neurology Department of Catholic University in Rome.

Five of the patients and all of the Italian control subjects were tested on a version of the time-perception task reported in Ivry and Keele (1989). The mean standard deviations for the patients and control subjects were 74.4 ms and 29.3 ms, respectively, for a base interval of 600 ms. This difference is significant ($t(6) = 2.36$, $p < .05$), replicating our previous findings that cerebellar patients are impaired on the time-perception task.

Stimuli An Italian assistant, native to Rome, generated the pairs of geminate words for the experiment. During the course of two one-hour sessions, she produced 53 pairs (106 words). Twenty-eight of the stimulus words were digitized to verify that they embodied a difference in duration between the members of the geminate pairs. Non-negligible differences in duration occurred for the medial consonant and the vowel preceding the medial consonant (defined as the interval from vowel offset to vowel onset). Across the 14 pairs, the consonant was longer by 126 ms (SD = 58 ms) on average for the doublet. While the preceding vowel tended to differ between the two members of each pair, the direction of this difference was inconsistent: in half the cases, the vowel for the doublet was longer; in the other half, it was shorter.

In addition to the geminates, control words were selected for 76 of the geminates. These words differed from the corresponding geminates in that their medial consonants were changed. Here the differences were not temporal, but involved consonants that differed either in place, manner, or voicing of articulation or a combination of these three features. Some of the control words were also geminates, and some were new words (see table 31.4).

Through an oversight, one geminate word was omitted from the test stimuli, and thus the final stimulus set consisted of 181 words. These words were recorded individually on a cassette tape in random order, with an interstimulus interval of approximately 4 seconds. The set was divided into five blocks of between 35 and 38 words each. The words were spoken by the Italian assistant.

Procedure The subjects sat in front of a computer monitor. On each trial, a pair of words was displayed on the monitor. Then, a spoken stimulus, representing one of these words, was played from the tape recorder. The subject pressed one of two keys to indicate which word on the screen corresponded to the spoken stimulus.

There were 105 trials on which the displayed version of the spoken word and the alternative word formed a geminate pair. The two displayed words had different medial consonants on the remaining 76 trials. The spoken stimulus came from a geminate pair on half of the control trials and from the set of control words on the other half.

A short break occurred between test blocks.

Results and Discussion

As noted earlier, in addition to duration, spoken members of geminate pairs may differ from each other in terms of other acoustic cues such as syllabic stress or vowel pronunciation. However, a decomposition of the geminate pairs into two groups, those with non-temporal cues and those in which the only salient cue was medial consonant duration, showed no difference in performance. Thus, the trials involving geminate pairs were merged into a single condition.

The percentage of erroneous classifications is presented in table 31.5. Cerebellar patients did not have a selective deficit in discriminating between members of a geminate pair. While the error rate was higher on these trials for the patients than for the control subjects, the same pattern also occurred on the control pairs. Indeed, there were very few errors in this task. If the data from the cerebellar patient with olivopontocerebellar atrophy are excluded, the percentage of errors on the geminate pairs drops to 1.4 percent.

The two nonnative control speakers made errors on 16.5 percent of the geminate pairs. In contrast, one of these subjects was perfect on the control pairs, while the other made 7 percent errors, yielding a mean of 4.7 percent. This suggests that the gemination discrimination is perceptually difficult, at least for nonnative speakers. Nonetheless, the patients were generally successful at this discrimination.

Experiment 3 provides a second source of evidence indicating that the integrity of the cerebellum is not critical for the perception of linguistic differences that can be described temporally. It must be noted that, for both experiments 1 and 3, this conclusion is based on null results, the lack of any performance difference between the patients and control subjects. However, the same cerebellar patients producing these null results were impaired on the time-perception task with nonspeech, tone stimuli. These results suggest that the requisite psychological processes for perceiving differences in voice-onset time or discriminating between members of a geminate pair do not include the cerebellar timing system.

31.4 EXPERIMENT 4

In our final experiment, we examine the production side of the gemination phenomena. The issue here concerns whether cerebellar patients can produce the acoustic cues that underlie perceptual discriminations between the mem-

Table 31.5 Percent Errors in Geminate Perception Experiment

Subject Group	Geminate Pairs	Control Pairs
Controls	1.3	2.1
Cerebellars	4.4	6.2
Nonnative speakers	16.5	4.5

bers of geminate word pairs. The results of experiment 2 indicated that patients with cerebellar lesions were impaired in coordinating the articulatory gestures that produce consistent differences between voiced and voiceless consonants. This production deficit can be interpreted as a deficit in temporally coupling the muscular actions needed for consonantal release and voicing. In experiment 4, we look for converging evidence that cerebellar dysarthria can be characterized as a problem in temporally controlling articulatory actions.

Method

Subjects   The six patients with cerebellar atrophy and three native Italian control subjects from experiment 3 were tested. Given the difficulty in identifying patients with cerebellar lesions, we were unable to select only Italian patients with clinical evidence of speech dysarthria—the subjects who would be of most interest in a speech production study. When tested informally at the time of the experiment, four of the patients showed some signs of dysarthria. The speech of the other two patients appeared normal.

Stimuli   The same 181 words were used.

Procedure   Each subject again sat in front of the computer monitor. On each trial, a single word was presented on the monitor screen, and the subject read the word in a normal voice. The subjects' productions were recorded on cassette tape. The words were read in the same order as the stimulus words judged in experiment 3. There were five blocks of 35 to 38 words each.

Two new native Italian speakers were recruited to judge the taped productions. Each judge listened to each word that had been read, and then chose which of two alternatives it matched. Thus, the task for the judges was identical to the perception task of experiment 3, except that the judged words were produced by the patients and control subjects rather than by the Italian assistant.

As in experiment 3, on 105 trials the judged alternatives were geminate pairs, and on the other 76 trials the alternatives differed in terms of their medial consonants. The judges listened to the productions of all nine subjects. The order of listening to the subjects was random, and the judges did not know whether a subject was a patient or a control.

Results and Discussion

Except in one case, there was near-perfect agreement between the classifications of the two judges. The exception occurred for eight words in which the syllable stress was inconsistent across subjects. These words have been excluded from the analysis.

The top half of figure 31.9 depicts the mean percentage of errors in each condition for the two subject groups (patients versus controls). The figure indicates that, overall, the patients' syllables on both types of trials were more

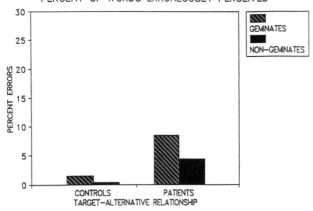

GEMINATE PRODUCTION EXPERIMENT
PERCENT OF WORDS ERRONEOUSLY PERCEIVED

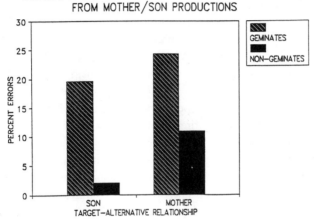

GEMINATES ERRONEOUSLY PERCEIVED
FROM MOTHER/SON PRODUCTIONS

Figure 31.9 *Top:* Mean number of productions erroneously classified for each subject group on the geminate and control words. *Bottom:* Mean number of productions erroneously classified for two patients, a mother and son.

likely to be misperceived than the syllables produced by the control subjects. The interaction suggested in figure 31.9 may result from a floor effect because very few of the syllables produced by the control subjects were misperceived.

While errors were obtained for the syllables produced by all of the patients, over 60 percent of the perceptual discrimination errors were made in judging the productions of the mother-son patient pair. These two patients showed the most marked speech dysarthria of all the patients. The percentage of errors for these two subjects is presented in the bottom half of figure 31.9. Errors by the mother were obtained with both types of word pairs (geminates and non-geminates). In contrast, the son's deficit appeared to be restricted to the geminate pairs. Almost 20 percent of these pairs produced a misperception for him whereas only 2 percent of the consonant pairs yielded errors. The mother's dysarthria and general disorder were much more marked.

These data raise an intriguing possibility: the articulatory actions that differentiate members of geminate-word pairs may be impaired during the early stages of cerebellar atrophy. This deficit perhaps reflects a reduced ability to temporally coordinate the requisite articulations. As the atrophy becomes more advanced, other articulatory deficits may emerge, perhaps because the atrophic process has spread to other neural systems. Further research is required to determine if the errors on the non-geminate trials can be explained by the timing hypothesis.

31.5 SUMMARY AND CONCLUSIONS

As reported in our previous research (Ivry et al. 1988; Ivry and Keele 1989; Ivry and Diener 1991), patients with cerebellar lesions are impaired on a variety of motor and perceptual tasks that require precise timing. These results have led us to propose that the cerebellum operates as an internal timing system. This hypothesis embraces the notion of horizontal modularity in that the same system is shared across task domains when temporal computations are needed. Such sharing constitutes a violation of vertical modularity.

Given that the cerebellar timing system is not restricted by vertical modularity, we are interested in determining the domain of this system. When are the temporal computations of the cerebellum needed? Over what temporal range do they apply? The experiments presented in this chapter provide our initial answers to whether timing phenomena in oral language involve the computational mechanisms of the cerebellum.

Two distinct linguistic phenomena have been studied here: the perception and production of voice-onset time in German, and the perception and production of gemination in Italian. There are obvious differences between these two linguistic phenomena including segment position (initial versus medial), and temporal range (VOT differences of approximately 40 ms versus geminate differences of 120 ms). Nonetheless, the results were similar. Cerebellar lesions did not produce consistent deficits in the perception of either VOT or gemination differences. Overall, VOT identification functions were similar for the patients and healthy subjects. Nor did the patients have a selective deficit in discriminating geminate pairs.

These null results suggest at least four plausible interpretations. First, although temporal features in the acoustic signal provide a salient means for describing voicing and gemination, the actual psychological processes may not exploit these cues, at least not in a direct manner. If the psychological mechanism does not require precise temporal computations, we would not expect the integrity of the cerebellum to be critical. Second, the psychological process may use the temporal information, but the process may not explicitly compute this information. Perhaps the temporal cue is derived implicitly. The cerebellar timing system may only be invoked for explicit temporal computations. Third, temporal information may be essential for VOT and gemination perception, but the time differences involved in these tasks may not be in the range encompassed by the cerebellar timing system (see Keele and Ivry, in press). Other neural systems may be essential for short-duration phenomena, and these may be essential for processing the temporal information associated with VOT and gemination. Fourth, there may be a timing module independent of the cerebellar timing system that is specialized for speech perception (Liberman Mattingly 1985). Of course, these interpretations are not mutually exclusive. Some combination of them may be the actual case.

In contrast to the null results obtained from our perception experiments, the timing hypothesis provides an interpretation of cerebellar speech dysarthria in production. The VOTs produced by the patients of experiment 2 were more variable, and led to perceptual errors along the voicing dimension. Similarly, the Italian patients, especially the familial mother/son pair, frequently failed to produce an unambiguous distinction between the two members of a geminate pair. These production deficits may reflect an inability to temporally coordinate events across different sets of articulators (e.g., those involved in the onset of voicing and the release of consonantal airflow). This type of control would, of course, be most needed during the dynamic portions of speech when the articulators are rapidly changing their configuration.

If this hypothesis is correct, then the cerebellar contribution to speech production would be less critical during the relatively stable periods of articulation, namely during steady-state vocalic segments. Instead, the primary control problems during these periods are more configural or static, rather than dynamic. The articulators must achieve and maintain the proper configuration to create certain target resonances. Muscular events are maintained rather than dynamically coordinated.

Our first test of this corollary hypothesis in experiment 2 has been inconclusive. While the differences between the patients and controls seemed less robust, the vocalic formant frequencies produced by the patients were generally more variable than those produced by the control subjects. Perhaps there is not really a true steady state in speech; all articulatory events may be dynamic. Our future research will continue to explore the usefulness of a dynamic/static distinction, both as it applies to understanding the role of the cerebellum in motor control, and as a way to contrast different disorders of speech.

NOTES

This research was supported by an Office of Naval Research Contract (N00014-87-K-0279) and a fellowship from the Alfred P. Sloan Foundation. The authors thank Steven Keele for his help throughout this project as well as David Meyer, Sylvan Kornblum, Peter Gordon and Herbert Heuer, and Al Liberman for helpful comments. H. C. Diener and G. Macchi graciously provided facilities and patient access for the experiments. Lori Kennedy and Warren Branson provided invaluable help in performing the acoustic analyses, and Paul Lebby assisted in the statistical analyses.

1. The inconsistency measure weights all stimuli equally. However, it might be argued that errors more distant from the crossover point should receive greater weight. Thus, linear integer

weights were employed in an analysis, with errors on the crossover stimulus given a weight of 0.0, errors on stimuli neighboring the crossover point given a weight of 1.0, errors on stimuli 2 steps from the crossover a weight of 2.0, and so forth. An ANOVA with this measure revealed a significant interaction of group X *syllable* (F(1, 20) = 5.56, p = 0.029). The patients were more inconsistent when identifying the stimuli from the *ba-pa* continuum.

2. This hypothesis would predict that there should be more variability across patients in comparison to variability across the control subjects. A test of heterogeneity of variance was performed on the standard deviations of the group means from the analysis of the ogive fits. The group standard deviations were not significantly different from each other for the *ba-pa* series (F(14, 6) = 2.16, p > .10). A similar test for the *ba-da* series was not conducted since the standard deviation of the control group mean was larger than that obtained for the patients.

REFERENCES

Abbs, J., and Gracco, V. (1983). Sensorimotor actions in the control of multi-movement speech gestures. *Trends in Neuroscience, 6*, 391–395.

Abramson, A., and Lisker, L. (1968). Voice timing: Cross-language experiments in identification and discrimination. Paper presented at the meeting of the Acoustical Society of America. Ottawa.

Atkeson, C. (1989). Learning arm kinematics and dynamics. *Annual Review of Neuroscience, 12*, 157–183.

Darley, F., Aronson, A., and Brown, J. (1969). Differential diagnostic patterns of dysarthria. *Journal of Speech and Hearing Research, 12*, 246–269.

Flash, T. and Hogan, N. (1985). The coordination of arm movements: An experimentally confirmed mathematical model. *Journal of Neuroscience, 5*, 1688–1703.

Fodor, J. (1983). *The modularity of mind.* Cambridge, MA: MIT Press.

Fowler, C. (1980). Coarticulation and theories of extrinsic timing. *Journal of Phonetics, 8*, 113–133.

Gordon, P., and Meyer, D. (1984). Perceptual-motor processing of phonetic features in speech. *Journal of Experimental Psychology: Human Perception and Performance, 10*, 153–178.

Hallett, M. and Khoshbin, 5. (1980). A physiological mechanism of bradykinesia. *Brain, 115*, 465–480.

Hasan, Z. (1986). Optimized movement trajectories and joint stiffness in unperturbed, inertially loaded movements. *Biological Cybernetics, 53*, 373–382.

House, A. (1961). On vowel duration in English. *Journal of the Acoustical Society of America, 33*, 1174–1178.

Ivry, R. (1990). Multi-task component analysis of movement and perception in normal and clinical populations. Paper presented at the annual meeting of North American Society for the Psychology of Sport and Physical Activity. Houston.

Ivry, R., and Diener, H. (1991). Impaired velocity perception in patients with lesions of the cerebellum. *Journal of Cognitive Neuroscience, 3*, 355–366.

Ivry, R., and Keele, S. (1989). Timing functions of the cerebellum. *Journal of Cognitive Neuroscience, 1*, 136–152.

Ivry, R., Keele, S., and Diener, H. (1988). Dissociation of the lateral and medial cerebellum in movement timing and movement execution. *Experimental Brain Research, 73*, 167–180.

Keele, S., and Ivry, R. (1988). Modular analysis of timing in motor skill. In G. Bower (Ed.), *The Psychology of learning and motivation.* Volume 21, 183–228. New York: Academic Press.

Keele, S., and Ivry, R. (1991). Does the cerebellum provide a common computation for diverse tasks: A timing hypothesis. In A. Diamond (Ed.), *Developmental and Neural Basis of Higher Cognitive Function*, 179–211. New York: Annals of the New York Academy of Sciences.

Keele, S., Ivry, R., and Pokorny, R. (1987). Force control and its relation to timing. *Journal of Motor Behavior, 19*, 96–114.

Keele, S., Pokorny, R., Corcos, D., and Ivry, R. (1985) . Do perception and motor production share common timing mechanisms? *Acta Psychologica, 60*, 173–193.

Kelso, J., Bateson, E., Saltzman, E., and Kay, B. (1985) . A qualitative dynamic analysis of reiterant speech production: Phase portraits, kinematics, and dynamic modelling. *Journal of the Acoustical Society of America, 77*, 266–280.

Kent, R., and Moll, K. (1975). Articulatory timing in selected consonant sequences. *Brain and Language, 2*, 304–323.

Kewley-Port, D. (1978). *Executive program to implement the Klatt software speech synthesizer.* (Progress Report 4, Research on Speech Perception.) Bloomington: Indiana University.

Klatt, D. (1980). Software for a cascade/parallel formant synthesizer. *Journal of the Acoustical Society, 67*, 971–995.

Kling, J., and Engen, T. (1971). *Experimental Psychology.* 3d ed. New York: Holt, Rinehart, and Winston.

Kluin, K., Gilman, S., Markel, D., Koeppe, R., Rosenthal, G., and Junck, L. (1988). Speech disorders in olivopontocerebellar atrophy correlate with positron emission tomography findings. *Annals of Neurology, 23*, 547–554.

Kozhenvnikov, V., and Chistovich, L. (1965). *Speech articulation and perception*, J.P.R.S. Washington D.C. #30543.

Lacquaniti, F., and Soechting, J. (1982). Coordination of arm and wrist motion during a reaching task. *Journal of Neuroscience, 2*, 399–408.

Liberman, A., and Mattingly, I. (1985). The motor theory of speech perception revised. *Cognition, 21*, 1–36.

Lisker, L., and Abramson, A. (1964). A cross-language study of voicing in initial stops: Acoustical measurements. *Word, 20*, 384–422.

Lisker, L., and Abramson, A. (1967). Some effects of context on voice-onset time in English stops. *Language and Speech, 10*, 1–28.

Lundy-Ekman, L., Ivry, R., Keele, S., and Woollacott, M. (1991). Timing and force control deficits in clumsy children. *Journal of Cognitive Neuroscience, 3*, 370–377.

Miller, G., and Nicely, P. (1955). Analysis of perceptual confusions among some English consonants. *Journal of the Acoustical Society of America, 27*, 338–353.

Miller, J., and Liberman, A. (1979). Some effects of later-occurring information on the perception of stop consonant and semivowel. *Perception and Psychophysics, 25*, 457–465.

Miller, J., Green, K., and Reeves, A. (1986). Speaking rate and segments: A look at the relation between speech production and speech perception for the voicing contrast. *Phonetica, 43*, 106–115.

Miller, J., Weir, L., Pastore, R., Kelly, W., and Dooling, R. (1976). Discrimination and labelling of noise-buzz sequences with varying noise-lead times: An example of categorical perception. *Journal of the Acoustical Society of America, 60*, 410–417.

Pickett, J. (1980). *The sounds of speech communication.* Baltimore: University Park.

Port, R. (1981). Linguistic timing factors in combination. *Journal of the Acoustical Society of America, 69*, 263–274.

Reed, M. (1984). Temporal processing and speech perception in readinq disabilities. Unpublished doctoral dissertation, University of Oregon.

Shepard, R. (1980). Multidimensional scaling, tree-fitting, and clustering. *Science, 210*, 390–398.

Stelmach, G., Teasdale, N., Phillips, J., and Worringham, C. (1989). Force production characteristics in Parkinson's disease. *Experimental Brain Research, 76*, 165–172.

Strange, W., and Jenkins, J. (1978). Role of linguistic experience in the perception of speech. In R. Walk and H. Pick (Eds.), *Perception and experience*. New York: Plenum.

Studdert-Kennedy, M. (1976). Speech perception. In N. Lass (Ed.), *Contemporary issues in experimental phonetics*, 243–293. New York: Academic Press.

Tuller, B., and Kelso, J. (1990). Phase transitions in speech production and their perceptual consequences. In M. Jeannerod (Ed.), *Attention and performance XIII*. Hillsdale, NJ: Erlbaum.

Tuller, B., Kelso, J., and Harris, K. (1983). Converging evidence for the role of relative timing in speech. *Journal of Experimental Psychology: Human Perception and Performance, 9*, 829–833.

Weismer, G. and Fennell, A. (1985). Constancy of (acoustic) relative timing measures in phrase-level utterances. *Journal of Acoustical Society of America, 78*, 49–57.

Zar, J. (1984). *Biostatistical analysis*. Englewood Cliffs, NJ: Prentice-Hall.

32 Plans For Object Manipulation

David A. Rosenbaum, Jonathan Vaughan, Matthew J. Jorgensen, Heather J. Barnes, and Erika Stewart

32.1 INTRODUCTION

The research described here is concerned with one of the central problems in human motor control and, more broadly, human behavior—the *degrees of freedom* problem. The problem can be understood by considering the simple act of touching a point in 3-space. Such a point, by definition, has 3 degrees of freedom (df). Yet the arm and hand (excluding the fingers) have 7 df: the shoulder can twist, move up and down, and move to the left and right (3 df); the elbow can bend up and down and twist (2 df); and the wrist can bend up and down and turn left and right (2 df). Thus, more degrees of freedom are associated with the arm and shoulder than with the point to be touched. The problem of selecting a movement for touching the point is therefore mathematically under-determined. Nonetheless, we instantly and effortlessly select particular configurations and trajectories. The question is how we do so.

The classical approach to this problem has been to identify interactions or dependencies within the motor system that effectively reduce the degrees of freedom to be controlled (Bernstein 1967). A familiar example is the difficulty encountered while simultaneously performing two tasks such as rubbing the stomach and patting the head. When one tries this ostensibly simple task, the head-patting movements tend to become circular though they are supposed to go straight up and down. This outcome is more than just a curiosity. It implies that the two arms are functionally interdependent. A broader implication is that there are fewer *effective* degrees of freedom in the motor system than would be expected from a simple count of the body's mechanical degrees of freedom (Kugler, Kelso, and Turvey 1980). The task of selecting movements may be simplified by such interdependencies.

The starting point for our work is a point of departure from Bernstein (1967). We believe that while it is useful to have interactions within the motor system, they cannot provide the only basis for solving the degrees-of-freedom problem. If one were asked to pick up a glass to one's left, for example, one would probably pick it up with the left hand. If the left hand were occupied—say, if one were holding a suitcase with the left hand—the glass would probably be picked up with the right hand. Similarly, if one were a thirsty hostage with one's hands tied behind one's back, one would probably pick up the glass with one's teeth. The point of these observations is that one can generally perform a wider range of movements to achieve a goal than are actually performed. The further conclusion is that constraints help limit movement choices. The goal of our work is to find out what these constraints are.

Before we turn to our empirical work, we wish to offer two general remarks about our search for constraints. First, in supposing that constraints exist, we do not assume that they are explicitly represented. In fact, we doubt that they are. Constraints can be thought of as kinds of solutions toward which a system converges. Second, the kinds of constraints we are interested in as psychologists are "soft" in the sense that they can be relaxed or even violated depending on one's intentional state. Soft constraints can be thought of as preferences rather than obligations. "Hard" constraints, by contrast, *require* one to perform particular movements. Examples of hard constraints are those imposed by gravity, tensile strengths of bones, and the maximum speed of muscle contraction. We are interested in soft constraints because we wish to understand the contributions of attention, perception, and computation to motor control. Our broader aim is to show that psychology has a key role to play in the understanding of action control.

32.2   BAR-TRANSPORT EXPERIMENTS

Our experiments have been inspired by observations of people in the everyday environment. When we see people consistently carrying out tasks in ways that could be performed in some other fashion, we wonder why they behave as they do and whether they are obeying (or behaving as if they are obeying) planning constraints. We then adapt the task to the laboratory and study it under controlled conditions.

Figure 32.1 illustrates the apparatus for the kind of study we have performed (Rosenbaum, Vaughan, Barnes, Marchak, and Slotta 1990). This setup consisted of a section of a broomstick handle (the "bar"), painted black on one end and white on the other. The bar lay on a "cradle" standing on a tabletop. Subjects in the experiment (all students at the University of Massachusetts, Amherst) could easily lift the bar from the cradle, using either an overhand grip (approaching the bar from above) or an underhand grip (approaching the bar from below). There were four tasks defined by placing either the left or right end of the bar squarely on the disk to the left or right of the cradle. For each task, subjects were asked to step forward and lift the bar from the cradle with the right hand. The question was: Which way would they spontaneously pick up the bar—with an overhand grip (that is, with the thumb pointing to the left end of the bar), or with an underhand grip (with the thumb pointing to the right end of the bar)? We assumed that if subjects consistently chose particular hand grips for particular tasks, a planning constraint applied.

As seen in figure 32.1, when the task was to place the left end of the bar on either the left or right disk, 12 out of 12 subjects picked up the bar with the overhand grip (with the thumb toward the black end), but when the task was to place the right end of the bar on either the left or right disk, 12 out of 12

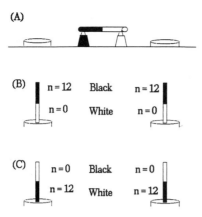

(A)

(B) n = 12 Black n = 12
    n = 0   White n = 0

(C) n = 0   Black n = 0
    n = 12 White n = 12

Figure 32.1 The bar-transport study of Rosenbaum et al. (1990) (A) Apparatus. (B) Number of subjects out of 12 who picked up the bar with the thumb toward the black end or white end when the white end of the bar was placed on the left or right disk. (C) Number of subjects out of 12 who picked up the bar with the thumb toward the black end or white end when the black end of the bar was placed on the left or right disk.

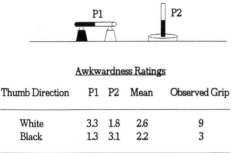

P1   P2

Awkwardness Ratings

Thumb Direction	P1	P2	Mean	Observed Grip
White	3.3	1.8	2.6	9
Black	1.3	3.1	2.2	3

Figure 32.2 Results of a replication of the main bar-transport study of Rosenbaum et al. (1990).

subjects picked up the bar with the underhand grip (with the thumb toward the white end). Thus all subjects switched strategies in the same way depending on which end of the bar was to be brought to the target disk. Why did subjects behave this way? A simple explanation is that they sought to complete the task with the hand and arm in a comfortable posture. We call this the *end-state comfort* effect.

In another study, we investigated a variety of tasks like the ones just described. In one task, shown in figure 32.2, subjects picked up the bar and placed the left end on the disk to the right, as in the first experiment. Now 9 out of 12 subjects (rather than 12 out of 12) picked up the bar with the underhand grip. As shown in figure 32.2, we also collected awkwardness ratings. These were obtained from an independent group of subjects who simply held the bar in each of the four possible starting and ending postures—holding the bar in the cradle with an underhand or overhand grip, or holding the bar vertically on the target disk (located to the right of the cradle) with the thumb (or the base of the thumb) pointing up or down. For each

Awkwardness Ratings

Thumb Direction	P1	P2	Mean	Observed Grip
White	1.8	3.3	2.6	4
Black	3.1	1.3	2.2	8

Figure 32.3 Results of a bar-transport task in which the bar began in the vertical position. (From Rosenbaum et al. (1990.)

posture, subjects gave a rating for how awkward it felt to maintain that posture, from 1, which meant least awkward, to 5, which meant most awkward. As shown in figure 32.2, the underhand grip was rated more awkward than the overhand grip, and the thumb-down posture was rated more awkward than the thumb-up posture. The most important outcome was that for the original subjects (the ones who performed the bar-transport task) the choice of grip was apparently not designed to minimize awkwardness at position 1 (P1), nor was it designed to minimize *mean* awkwardness (at positions 1 and 2); instead, it was designed to minimize awkwardness at position 2 (P2), the terminal position for the task.

This outcome was corroborated in another task that was the reverse of the one just described. As shown in figure 32.3, at the start of the trial, the bar stood vertically on the disk to the right of the cradle. Subjects stepped forward, picked up the bar and placed the black end, which was always on the bottom, onto the left end of the cradle. In this condition, two-thirds of the subjects picked up the bar with the thumb pointing *down*, which was the posture they *avoided* when the bar stood on end at the completion of the other task. Thus again, subjects' choices of initial hand grips allowed the hand to end in a comfortable *final* posture.

32.3 HANDLE-ROTATION EXPERIMENTS

The new experiments reported here were designed to test alternative hypotheses concerning the end-state comfort effect. A secondary aim was to allow for more fine-grained measures of subjects' performance than was possible in the bar-transport studies. The new apparatus is shown in figure 32.4. As shown in panel A, subjects were supposed to reach out and turn a handle with the right hand. What they saw (shown in panel B) was a handle connected to a disk. A small cardboard tab was attached to the disk, and when the handle was rotated, it turned the disk and the cardboard tab. Depending on the position of the tab, it could cover one of the eight target numbers that appeared just beyond the perimeter of the disk and just below the disk plane. In figure 32.4, the tab covers target 5. In a typical trial, the experimenter read

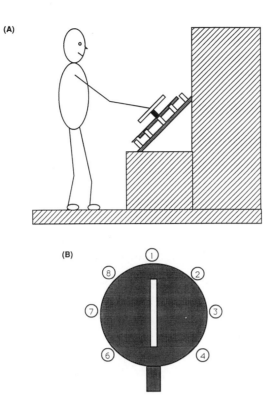

Figure 32.4 Handle-rotation task (A) and subject's view of the handle (B).

a target number, such as 1, and the subject reached out for the handle and turned the handle so the tab covered the announced number. Every possible pair of starting and ending positions was tested in a balanced order. The dependent variable was how subjects chose to take hold of the handle—with the thumb (or the base of the thumb) toward the tab or away from the tab. Subjects in the first experiment were asked to take hold of the handle with the right hand and to grip the handle firmly like a tennis racket, reaching out for the handle and turning it at a comfortable speed.

The data are shown in figure 32.5. The probability, $p(T)$, of grabbing the handle with the thumb toward the tab was systematically related to the tab's final position. The effect of final position was highly significant, as tested through analysis of variance. The results suggest that subjects in the handle-rotation task planned with respect to final position, as did subjects in the earlier bar-transport tasks. That subjects in the handle-rotation task sought to maximize end-state comfort is suggested by the fact that the minimum of the $p(T)$ function was at the position (position 4) which presumably was least comfortable for the right arm.

Figure 32.6 shows the results of a replication of the handle rotation task with the *left* hand. This experiment was conducted the same way as the previous study, except that subjects were told always to use the left hand. For these subjects, the minimum of the $p(T)$ function was at position 6. As the

Plans for Object Manipulation

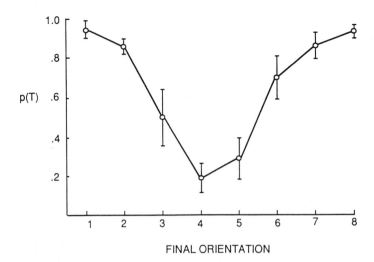

FINAL ORIENTATION

Figure 32.5 Probability, $p(T)$, of grabbing the handle with the thumb (or the base of the thumb) toward the tab as a function of the tab's final orientation. Standard error bars reflect variability associated with starting orientation. The task was performed with the right hand.

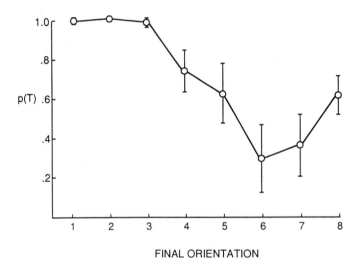

FINAL ORIENTATION

Figure 32.6 Probability, $p(T)$, of grabbing the handle with the thumb (or the base of the thumb) toward the tab as a function of the tab's final orientation when the task was performed with the left hand. Standard error bars reflect variability associated with starting orientation.

Rosenbaum et al.

Table 32.1 Factors Taken into Account according to the Two-Submovement Hypothesis*

Movement	Sequence A	Sequence B
1	Reach out, grabbing handle with thumb down	Reach out, grabbing handle with thumb up
2	Turn thumb to 1	Turn thumb to 5

* The example task is turning the handle from position 5 to position 1.

reader can demonstrate for him or herself, position 6 is an extremely uncomfortable position for the left hand, just as position 4 is an extremely uncomfortable position for the right hand. From these results, we conclude that subjects selected hand grips that ensured comfortable postures, both for the left hand and right.

32.4 MAXIMIZING EASE OF MOVEMENT

What is the source of the end-state comfort effect? One possibility is embodied in a *two-submovement* model (see table 32.1). To understand the model, consider the task of turning the handle with the right hand so the tab goes from position 5 to position 1 (see fig. 32.4 for reference). Recall that subjects generally adopted an awkward initial posture when performing this task: they turned the thumb *down* to take hold of the handle when it pointed to position 5 (P5), and then they turned the tab toward position 1 (P1) by rotating the thumb *up* to the more comfortable, vertical posture. According to the two-submovement model, subjects chose this method because they determined that the sequence of submovements they would have to perform would be easier if they initially took hold of the handle in an awkward posture than if they initially took hold of the handle in a comfortable posture.

Consider this claim in more detail. To complete the handle-rotation task, two submovements must be performed. One is reaching out and grabbing the handle; the other is turning the handle to its goal position. If the task is to turn the handle from P5 to P1, there are two possible submovement sequences. One, labeled A in table 32.1, involves reaching for the handle and grasping it with the thumb down, then twisting the arm so the thumb points up. The other, labeled B, involves reaching for the handle and grasping it with the thumb up, then twisting the arm so the thumb points down. Subjects could have taken hold of the handle with the thumb toward P5 when the tab had to be turned to P1 if they determined that sequence A was easier than sequence B. There is a plausible reason for preferring sequence A to sequence B: It may be easier to get into an uncomfortable posture if the arm can move freely through space on its way to that posture than if the arm can only twist to the uncomfortable posture within a plane. More degrees of freedom are available for the free movement, so it may be that the free movement makes it easier to avoid uncomfortable postures along the way.

Table 32.2 Tests of the Two-Submovement Hypothesis*

Task: Turn Pointer from 4 to 8					
Prediction: Ease[(Reach to 4) + (Twist 4 → 8)] > Ease[(Reach to 8) + (Twist 8 → 4)]					
Result:	1.4	+	3.5	<	5.0	+	1.8
		(4.9	<	6.8)	
Task: Turn Pointer from 5 to 1					
Prediction: Ease[(Reach to 5) + (Twist 5 → 1)] > Ease[(Reach to 1) + (Twist 1 → 5)]					
Result:	2.6	+	4.5	<	4.6	+	3.8
		(7.1	<	8.4)	

* Results concern ease-of-movement ratings, where 1 = hardest … 5 = easiest.

The two-submovement model assumes that movements rather than static postures are the primitives for motor decision making. Thus, evaluation of the two-submovement hypothesis can reveal whether decisions about motor performance are made on the basis of movements or static postures. To our knowledge, this issue has not been considered before in the motor-control literature.

To test the two-submovement model, we asked subjects to produce individual reaching and twisting movements and to provide a rating of the ease with which each movement could be performed. 1 meant hardest; 5 meant easiest. The results from the 12 University of Massachusetts students who served as subjects are shown in table 32.2.

First, consider the task of turning the tab from P5 to P1. The prediction was that the rated ease of movement for reaching to P5 (that is, grabbing the bar with the thumb toward P5) and then twisting to P1 would be higher than the rated ease of movement for reaching to P1 and then twisting to P5. In fact, the data went the other way. Reaching to P5 and then twisting to P1 had a total ease-of-movement rating of 7.1, whereas reaching to P1 and then twisting to P5 had a total ease-of-movement rating of 8.4. Thus, the ratings went opposite the prediction. Subjects found it easier to twist to P5 (rating = 3.8) than to reach for P5 (rating = 2.6), and they found it somewhat easier to reach for P1 (rating = 4.6) than to twist to P1 (rating = 4.5), although only the former difference was statistically significant.

The same outcome was obtained for the task of turning the tab from position 4 (P4) to position 8 (P8). This was the other task for which there was a marked tendency to adopt an initially awkward posture. The prediction of the two-submovement model was that reaching to P4 and then twisting to P8 would be rated easier than reaching to P8 and then twisting to P4. In fact, the results were the opposite, mainly because subjects found it easier to reach to P8 (rating = 5.0) than to twist to P8 (rating = 3.5); this difference was highly significant. Twisting to P4 (rating = 1.8) was somewhat easier than reaching to P4 (rating = 1.4), but this difference was not significant.

The above results argue against the two-submovement model. Moreover, they imply that subjects did not select hand grips by evaluating possible *movements*.[1]

32.5 EXPLOITING POTENTIAL ENERGY: ALLOWING THE ELBOW TO DROP

The evidence just reviewed suggests that decisions about initial hand grips were not based on considerations of the ease of the *pair* of submovements needed to complete the task (reaching for the handle and turning the handle). Nevertheless, it may be that subjects considered *one* of the submovements rather than two. A reason to take this possibility seriously is that in the rating study, when subjects twisted the thumb from P5 to P1, they gave that movement a rating of 4.5 (see table 32.2), but when they twisted the thumb from P1 to P5, they gave that movement a rating of 3.8 (recall that 5 is easiest). Thus, subjects found that moving from an uncomfortable position (P5) to a comfortable one (P1) was easier than moving from a comfortable position (P1) to an uncomfortable one (P5). Similarly, as shown in table 32.2, subjects found that moving from P4 to P8 was easier than moving from P8 to P4.

Based on these data, another hypothesis comes to mind: Subjects may have selected initially uncomfortable handgrips to exploit instability of the arm at its initial position, allowing the arm to move more or less passively toward the more stable (or more comfortable) final position. This strategy would be computationally efficient because, at least in theory, the arm's trajectory (after the handle was grabbed) would come "for free" by virtue of the arm's tendency to turn to its biomechanical attractor position. The idea that movement control is simplified by reliance on mechanical features of the musculoskeletal system has been advocated by several authors (e.g., Bizzi and Mussa-Ivaldi 1989; Rosenbaum 1991).

What biomechanical variables could underlie such a hypothesized "drift" to an attractor position? One possibility is suggested by the observation that when a person takes hold of the handle with the thumb pointing down, the elbow is high relative to the shoulder and hand. Some force is needed to maintain the elbow in this upward position, so when the force is removed, the elbow drops. It is possible, therefore, that subjects selected their initial handgrips so rotation of the handle would be aided by gravity.

To test this hypothesis, we placed the handle-rotation apparatus on the floor. Subjects performed the task while seated, with the right arm hanging down. Our aim was to make the axis of rotation of the arm parallel to the force of gravity rather than orthogonal (or roughly orthogonal) to it. The prediction was that if the end-state comfort effect was due to subjects' raising the elbow and letting it drop during handle rotation, the effect would disappear when the arm hung down.

As shown in figure 32.7, the results were virtually identical to those obtained before. This outcome argues against the "elbow-drop" hypothesis and attests to the robustness of the end-state comfort effect. Thus, it is unlikely that the source of the end-state comfort effect was dropping the elbow, even if in theory this strategy might have been biomechanically and computationally efficient.[2]

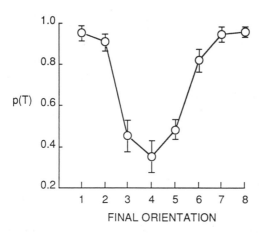

Figure 32.7 Probability, $p(T)$, of grabbing the handle with the thumb (or the base of the thumb) toward the tab as a function of the tab's final orientation when the task was performed with the right hand hanging straight down. Standard error bars reflect variability associated with starting orientation.

32.6 ELASTIC ENERGY

If dropping the elbow was not the source of the end-state comfort effect, was there some other mechanical basis for attraction toward the resting state? Another possibility is that subjects used *elastic energy*. Consider, as an analogy, the act of flying a toy airplane—the kind with a rubber band along its base. First, one winds up the propeller, storing elastic energy in the rubber band. Then one releases the propeller, allowing the stored elastic energy to be converted to kinetic energy, and the plane flies. It is possible that subjects did something similar with their arms. They might have "wound up" their arms when taking hold of the handle and then released their arms, allowing their arms to "unwind" toward the resting position. We call this the *elastic energy* strategy.

The elastic energy strategy, like the elbow-drop strategy, exploits mechanical features of the musculoskeletal system and so reduces the computational burdens on motor planning. Exploitation of elasticity for motor performance has been demonstrated for locomotion. When one jumps up, the first thing one usually does is bend down, allowing elastic energy to be stored to promote upward lift (Alexander and Bennet-Clark 1977; Bobbert, Huijing, and van Ingen Schenau 1986). Analysis of running also indicates that elasticity helps the foot rebound from the running surface (McMahon 1984). Running tracks have been designed with this principle in mind (McMahon 1984).

As appealing as the elastic energy strategy may be, we doubt that it underlies the end-state comfort effect, for the following reasons:

1. Patients with Parkinson's disease have high muscle rigidity (low muscle elasticity). Yet they exhibit the end-state comfort effect in the handle-rotation task (Rosenbaum and Rafal unpublished observations). If the source of the

end-state comfort effect were reliance on muscle elasticity, then when muscle elasticity is low, one would expect the end-state comfort effect to diminish.

2. Prolonged stretching of an elastic medium (e.g., a rubber band) reduces its elasticity (Lindsay 1933). In an informal study, we studied the effects of prolonged stretch of the muscles (and tendons) of the arm by asking subjects to hold the handle with the outstretched right arm in its most uncomfortable position (with the thumb toward position 4) for 3 minutes. Half the subjects brought the thumb to position 4 (or as near as possible to position 4) via clockwise arm rotation; half the subjects brought the thumb to position 4 (or as near as possible to position 4) via counterclockwise arm rotation. We assumed that for the clockwise group, the muscles and tendons responsible for counterclockwise rotation would become less elastic because those muscles and tendons were stretched. We likewise assumed that for the counterclockwise group, the muscles and tendons responsible for clockwise rotation would become less elastic because those muscles and tendons were stretched. The prediction of the elastic energy hypothesis was that subjects would be unlikely to place themselves in an uncomfortable posture if the subsequent movement toward a comfortable posture relied on stretched muscles and tendons. This prediction was not supported, however. Subjects in both groups displayed the usual end-state comfort effect for both directions of rotation.

3. If elasticity were the source of the end-state comfort effect, one would expect the effect to depend on the opportunity for elasticity to manifest itself during other biomechanical events. Presumably, it would be more difficult to rotate the arm via simple elastic recoil if the arm were bending at the elbow or being raised or lowered at the shoulder than if the arm were outstretched and otherwise immobile. If the end-state comfort effect was due to elastic energy, one would therefore expect the end-state comfort effect to be reduced or even eliminated during complex multijoint movements. In fact, the end-state comfort effect appears even for complex movements. For example, it appeared in the bar-transport experiments of Rosenbaum et al. (1990), where subjects lifted a bar, carried it to another location, and set it down again. End-state comfort was also demonstrated in a task where subjects lifted a bar from a cradle (at waist height) and brought one end to a target at a variable height above the floor (Rosenbaum and Jorgensen 1992). For some target heights, subjects had to bend at the knees, whereas for other target heights, subjects had to stretch as high as they could. Regardless of target height, subjects took hold of the bar in a way that ensured a comfortable posture when the bar was brought to the target.[3]

4. Observation of people engaging in everyday activities indicates that they often do not behave in a manner consistent with the elastic energy strategy. At the dinner table, for example, people pick up salt shakers, ketchup bottles, and containers from which liquids must be poured in such a way that the shaking, squeezing, or pouring operation is carried out with the arm in an uncomfortable orientation (with the thumb, or base of the thumb, pointing down). Because these tasks are similar to the bar transport and handle rotation

tasks, and because they could exploit elastic energy, the fact that they are completed with the arm in uncomfortable orientations suggests that people do not always exploit elastic energy to facilitate arm rotations. Nor, for that matter, do their movements always end in comfortable postures, a point to which we return later in this chapter.

5. A final difficulty with the elastic energy strategy is that one must still explain why people are content to climb an energy gradient as they "wind up the arm" when reaching for an object to be manipulated. Even if the elastic energy strategy explained the end-state comfort effect, it could not qualify as a complete explanation of the effect, for one would still need to explain why elastic energy is used for one part of the task but not the other.

32.7 PRECISION

How, then, can the end-state comfort effect be explained? We believe the effect is related to precision. The wheel used in the handle rotation task had a low moment of inertia, as well as low friction and viscosity. Consequently, precise control was needed to steady the wheel at the target location. In the bar-transport tasks of Rosenbaum et al. (1990) and Rosenbaum and Jorgensen (1992), fine control was needed to position the bar at its target location. We hypothesize that subjects determined that completing these tasks with the arm in a comfortable posture would ensure precise task completion. We call this the *precision* hypothesis.

Thus far, we have no direct evidence for the precision hypothesis. Nor do we know of data that serve to disconfirm it. The hypothesis makes at least two predictions, one of which can be said already to have been confirmed by the "dinner-table" observations outlined above. For tasks such as shaking salt out of a salt shaker or squeezing ketchup out of a ketchup bottle, the degree of required control is minimal, so according to the precision hypothesis, these tasks need not be performed in comfortable postures. The general prediction is that the likelihood of obtaining the end-state comfort effect should be inversely related to the degree of precision required for task completion. In an adaptation of the handle-rotation task, for example, if subjects did not have to precisely control the position of the handle, they would not attempt to complete the rotation in a comfortable posture.

The second prediction is that if subjects were required to keep the arm in the middle of its range of motion (the most comfortable part of the range), the degree of precision they could achieve would be greater than if they were required to keep the arm in an extreme part of its range of motion (the uncomfortable part of the range). An experimental context in which to test this prediction is tracking. Subjects could be asked to turn a handle to keep a cursor aligned with a target. The main independent variable would be the range of arm orientations that could be adopted—either in the middle of the range or only in an extreme portion of the range. According to the precision hypothesis, accuracy should be better in the middle of the range than at the extreme.[4]

32.8 THE THUMB-TOWARD BIAS

If subjects selected handgrips that ensured maximum precision during task completion, the handgrips they selected should have made it as easy as possible for them to use perceptual information to complete the task. A feature of subjects' grip choices bears out this expectation. Superimposed on the preference for end-state comfort was a preference for taking hold of the handle with the thumb, or the base of the thumb, on the same side of the handle as the tab. We call this the *thumb-toward bias*. As seen below, we believe this bias ensured visibility of the tab at or near the target.

To understand the thumb-toward bias, consider the way a physicist or engineer might design a system for reaching out and turning a handle. The physicist or engineer would probably recognize that if a handle must be turned through 180° so a massless pointer at one end must turn from position A to position B or from position B to position A, the same physical rotation of the handle could be used for both translations. Similarly, in the handle-rotation task, if the tab were initially at some position, such as P5, and had to be turned 180° to P1, or if the pointer were initially at P1 and had to be turned to P5, the identical sequence of arm movements could be carried out for both tab displacements.

This invariance was not exhibited by our subjects. As seen in table 32.3, when the tab was turned from P5 to P1, $p(T)$ was .93. If subjects had used the same movements to turn the handle from P1 to P5, the value of $p(T)$ when the tab first pointed to P1 should have been just $1 - .93$, or .07; instead it was .28. Similar discrepancies occurred for all the 180° turns. This outcome implies that subjects did not perform the same physical rotations of the handle with the same movements. In all cases, they were biased to take hold of the handle with the thumb toward rather than away from the pointer.[5]

What accounts for the thumb-toward bias? A possible *cognitive* explanation is based on notions of stimulus-response compatibility. When one turns a handle, the torque is applied principally by the thumb and index finger. If the thumb and index finger are not on the same side of the handle as the pointer,

Table 32.3 Use of Different Movements to Perform the Same 180° Handle Rotations

Task	$p(T)$*	$1 - p(T)$
5 → 1	.93	.07
1 → 5	.28	.72
6 → 2	.85	.15
2 → 6	.70	.30
7 → 3	.49	.51
3 → 7	.85	.15
8 → 4	.18	.82
4 → 8	.93	.07

* $p(T)$ denotes the probability of grabbing the handle with the thumb toward the tab.

the effect of the torque, as monitored at the pointer, has a different directional sign than the torque: If the torque is upward, the observed movement is downward; if the torque is to the right, the observed movement is to the left. However, if the thumb is on the *same* side as the tab, the effect of the torque, as monitored at the tab, has the same directional sign as the torque. If people prefer consistent directional relations, this preference could have led to the thumb-toward bias. Note that this explanation assumes that compatibility is defined with respect to rectilinear rather than rotational motion.

The *perceptual* explanation of the thumb-toward bias is simpler, and so we prefer it. Stretch out your right arm, keeping your hand at stomach level, and hold a pencil with your right hand, keeping the pencil pointed to four o'clock. You will not be able to see the pencil point unless you crane your neck; your forearm and wrist will be in the way. By contrast, if your arm is twisted so the thumb as well as the pencil point are aimed at four o'clock, your arm will be uncomfortable, but you will be able to see the pencil point. In the handle-rotation task subjects could always see the tab when they held the handle with the thumb pointing toward the tab. However, when they held the handle with the thumb away from tab, there was a range of positions in which the tab could only be seen by craning the neck. Thus, the thumb-toward bias was perceptually advantageous for this task, which, after all, required visual aiming. Hence, subjects may have favored the thumb-toward grip because it ensured visibility of the tab. Such continued visibility would have helped subjects complete the task accurately. This objective, we have argued, was also served by the end-state comfort constraint.

32.9 A COMPOSITE MODEL

As seen above, $p(T)$, the probability of grabbing the handle with the thumb (or the base of the thumb) toward the tab, reflected two constraints: end-state visibility and end-state comfort. We propose that the two constraints operated together as follows:

$$p(T) = \beta + \alpha\left(1 - \frac{|\theta_F - \theta_R|}{180°}\right), \qquad 0 \leq p(T) \leq 1 \qquad (1)$$

The model says that $p(T)$ has a minimum value of β, corresponding to the thumb-toward bias, and increases as the hand's final orientation, θ_F, comes closer to the resting orientation, θ_R, up to a maximum value of $p(T) = 1$. Note that the absolute difference $|\theta_F - \theta_R|$ is expressed in degrees and never exceeds 180°; that is, $|\theta_F - \theta_R|$ corresponds to the shortest angular path from the final orientation to the resting orientation. Dividing $|\theta_F - \theta_R|$ by 180° allows for a dimensionless value between 0 and 1. The model has three parameters: α, β, and θ_R.

We have fitted the model to the three sets of data shown in figures 32.5, 32.6, and 32.7, imposing the requirements that α and β must be constant for all three experiments, that θ_R must be the same for the two experiments in which subjects used the right hand, and that for the experiment in which subjects used the left hand, θ_R had to be the mirror image of θ_R for the right hand. Under these requirements, setting $\beta = .28$, $\alpha = .90$, and $\theta_R = 130°$ for the right hand (and $\theta_R = 50°$ for the left hand), the model accounted for 90.0% of the variance in the mean $p(T)$ data of the first right-hand experiment (fig. 32.5), 92.3% of the variance in the mean $p(T)$ data of the second right-hand experiment (fig. 32.7), and 93.0% of the variance in the mean $p(T)$ data of the left-hand experiment (fig. 32.6). The model therefore provides a satisfactory account of the mean $p(T)$ data from this set of experiments.[6]

32.10 SUMMARY AND CONCLUSIONS

Four main points emerge from these experiments. First, a profitable way to address the degrees-of-freedom problem is to posit planning constraints. This approach complements the search for interdependencies among motor segments, championed by Bernstein (1967). We are not alone in searching for planning constraints; other authors have pursued them as well (Cruse 1986; Hasan 1986; Hogan and Flash 1987; Kawato, chap. 33; Nelson, 1983; Uno, Kawato, and Suzuki 1989). However, whereas these authors have focused on relatively detailed aspects of movement kinematics and dynamics, we have concentrated on macroscopic, qualitative features of motor behavior. The latter topic has received little attention in the motor-control literature (Rosenbaum 1991).

Like other authors taking a constraint approach, we wish to find the smallest and most powerful set of constraints we can. Postulating a few general-purpose constraints provides a way of explaining how actors can perform adaptively in novel circumstances. In addition, identifying a small number of general-purpose constraints can help eliminate the need to assume massive memory loads, as in models requiring storage of extensive lists of condition-action pairs.

The second main point is that we have found, in the context of taking hold of an object to be turned, that an important planning constraint is end-state comfort. We observed behavior consistent with this constraint both in our earlier bar-transport studies and in the handle-rotation experiments described here. We considered several hypotheses to explain the end-state comfort effect. One hypothesis, which we rejected, was that subjects plan with respect to sequences of submovements rather than with respect to final postures. Another hypothesis was that subjects consider one submovement rather than a sequence of two and select handgrips that allow for easy rotations. We rejected one version of this hypothesis, according to which subjects exploit gravity to facilitate the hand-rotation movement. We also considered the hypothesis that subjects stored elastic energy in their muscles and tendons when first taking hold of the handle, allowing the arm to unwind passively during the handle rotation. Although this was an attractive hypothesis, both from a biomechanical and computational standpoint, it was found wanting. Ultimately, we were led to the view that the end-state comfort effect reflects an attempt to maximize precision. Completing the handle rotation with the arm as close as possible to its resting orientation (or equivalently, as far as possible from its extreme orientations) allows the forces acting on the arm to be consistent with, rather than opposed to, the tab-centering requirement. Moreover, finer adjustments may be possible in the middle of the range of motion than at the extremes.

The third main conclusion from our work is that we have discovered a bias to take hold of the handle with the thumb toward the tab. This bias might be related to stimulus-response compatibility, but we think it stems from simpler considerations of visibility. If the visibility interpretation is correct, it implies that people take into account the perceptual affordances of the movements they are about to perform. This conclusion accords with the claim that subjects choose ways of behaving that maximize accuracy when high accuracy is demanded.

The fourth and final point of this chapter is that psychology should play a central role in the study of movement selection. This point is worth mentioning because there has been prejudice against the view that psychologists can contribute to the study of motor control, particularly among neurophysiologists and roboticists. (We refrain from citing references to avoid *ad hominem* attacks.) We believe that if one hopes to simulate what people do—assuming that people are the among cleverest action systems around—it will be important to acknowledge that the ways people act are not always what physicists or engineers might expect. There were two ways in which our subjects behaved differently from what might be expected from a simple physical perspective. First, in trying to adopt comfortable postures at the end of the handle-rotation tasks, our subjects adopted uncomfortable postures when beginning the task, that is, when taking hold of the handle. This implies that some parsing mechanism divided up the task into components, and determined which components were primary and which were secondary. Second, our subjects showed a bias to take hold of the handle with the thumb toward the tab. As indicated above, we believe this bias ensured end-state visibility.

Physicists and engineers are not the only ones who have acted as if psychology and motor control should be separated. Psychologists are nearly as guilty. Psychologists historically have paid little attention to the mechanisms underlying the physical production of behavior. This is odd when it is recalled that psychology is the science of mental life and *behavior*. Why it is that psychology has historically ignored motor control is unclear. One reason may be the belief that movement control does not require much intelligence. When one studies how movements are selected, however, one recognizes that a great deal of intelligence is actually brought to bear, even for simple tasks.

NOTES

The research was supported by grants BNS-87-10933 and BNS-90-08665 from the National Science Foundation and a Research Career Development Award from the National Institute of Neurological Disease and Stroke (to the first author). The chapter was drafted while the first author was a Fellow at the Netherlands Institute For Advanced Study, Wassenaar, The Nether-

Rosenbaum et al.

lands. David Meyer, Sylvan Kornblum, Alan Wing, and Howard Zelaznik provided helpful comments on earlier versions of the text.

1. To be confident about this, one needs to be sure that the ratings reflected perceived ease of movement. We believe the ratings were movement-based because the ratings associated with particular final positions differed according to what movements were made to them. For example, twisting to P5 was rated easier than reaching to P5, and reaching to P8 was rated easier than twisting to P8.

2. In several conditions of the bar-transport studies of Rosenbaum et al. (1990), the elbow remained at about the same height throughout the task. Given that the end-state comfort effect appeared in those conditions, it is fitting that the elbow-drop hypothesis appears not to be the source of the end-state comfort effect.

3. An aim of the Rosenbaum and Jorgensen (1992) study was to see if the choice of handgrip on a given trial would be affected by handgrip choices on preceding trials. It was. Subjects persisted in grabbing the bar with an overhand grip when successive target heights got lower and lower, and persisted in grabbing the bar with an underhand grip when successive target heights got higher and higher.

4. There are several plausible reasons why positioning accuracy might be better in the middle than at the extremes of the arm's range of (twisting) motion. First, given the inverted-U-shaped relation between muscle length and tension (see McMahon 1984), more force can generally be produced by muscles at intermediate lengths than at extreme lengths. Hence, a broader range of muscle forces is available at intermediate lengths, which in turn may allow for more precise control. Second, it has been shown that positioning accuracy is higher at intermediate joint angles than at extreme joint angles, at least for the elbow and using constant error as the measure of accuracy (see Clark and Horch 1986, 13−14). Third, at midrange, the arm is free to turn in either direction and over a roughly equal amplitude, but at extreme positions the arm can only turn in one direction. Corrective movements should be easier, then, for the part of the range of motion in which movements are possible in both directions. Fourth, the forces acting on the arm near the middle of its range of motion are consistent with the goal of centering the tab on the target. When the arm is at or near an extreme angle, the forces acting on it pull it toward midrange and so should make it difficult to complete the tab-centering operation.

5. The thumb-toward bias can also be characterized as an elevation (above zero) of the minimum of the psychophysical function relating $p(T)$ to final position (see fig. 32.5, 32.6, and 32.7).

6. Although it is tempting to fit the model to individual subject data, we have not done so because each subject contributed relatively little data to the pooled data which are summarized in figure 32.5, 32.6, and 32.7. Each subject performed each non-180° rotation only once, and each 180° rotation six times. The 180° rotations were tested more often than non-180° rotations because they were a priori unbiased with respect to rotation direction.

REFERENCES

Alexander, R. M., and Bennet-Clark, H. C. (1977). Storage of elastic strain energy in muscle and other tissues. *Nature, 265,* 114−117.

Bernstein, N. (1967). *The coordination and regulation of movements.* London: Pergamon.

Bizzi, E., and Mussa-Ivaldi, F. A., (1989). Geometrical and mechanical issues in movement planning and control. In M. I. Posner (Ed.), *Handbook of cognitive science,* 769−792. Cambridge, MA: MIT Press.

Bobbert, M. F., Huijing, P. A., and van Ingen Schenau, G. J. (1986). An estimation of power output and work done by the human triceps surae muscle-tendon complex in jumping. *Journal of Biomechanics, 19,* 899−906.

Clark, F. J., and Horch, D. W. (1986). Kinesthesia. In K. R. Boff, L. Kaufman, and J. P. Thomas (Eds.), *Handbook of human perception and performance*. Vol. 1, *Sensory processes and perception*, 13–1 to 13–62. New York: Wiley.

Cruse, H. (1986). Constraints for joint angle control of the human arm. *Biological Cybernetics, 54*, 125–132.

Hasan, Z. (1986). Optimized movement trajectories and joint stiffness in unperturbed, inertially loaded movements. *Biological Cybernetics, 53*, 373–382.

Hogan, N., and Flash, T. (1987). Moving gracefully: Quantitative theories of motor coordination. *Trends in the Neurosciences, 10*, 170–174.

Kugler, P. N., Kelso, S., and Turvey, M. T. (1980). On the concept of coordinative structures as dissipative structures: I. Theoretical lines of convergence. In G. E. Stelmach and J. Requin (Eds.), *Tutorials in motor behavior*, 3–47. Amsterdam: North-Holland.

Lindsay, R. B. (1933). *Physical mechanics*. New York: Van Nostrand.

McMahon, T. A. (1984). *Muscles, reflexes, and locomotion*. Princeton, NJ: Princeton University Press.

Nelson, W. L. (1983). Physical principles for economies of skilled movements. *Biological Cybernetics, 46*, 135–147.

Rosenbaum, D. A. (1991). *Human motor control*. San Diego, CA: Academic Press.

Rosenbaum, D. A. and Jorgensen, M. J. (1992). Planning macroscopic aspects of manual control. *Human Movement Science, 11*, 61–69. Also appeared in A. Thomassen, D. A. Rosenbaum, and P. Wieringen (Eds.), *Sequencing and timing of movement*. Amsterdam: North-Holland.

Rosenbaum, D. A., Vaughan, J., Barnes, H. J., Marchak, F., and Slotta, J. (1990). Constraints on action selection: Overhand versus underhand grips. In M. Jeannerod (Ed.), *Attention and Performance XIII*, 321–342. Hillsdale, NJ: Erlbaum.

Uno, Y., Kawato, M., and Suzuki, R. (1989). Formation and control of optimal trajectory in human multijoint arm movement: Minimum torque-change model. *Biological Cybernetics, 61*, 89–101.

33 Optimization and Learning in Neural Networks for Formation and Control of Coordinated Movement

Mitsuo Kawato

33.1 INTRODUCTION

Studies of computational neuroscience and neural computing have increased exponentially in recent years. Marr (1982), a pioneer in this field, pointed out that an information-processing device (e.g., the brain) must be understood at the following different levels: (1) computational theory, (2) representation and algorithm, and (3) hardware implementation. Based on detailed knowledge of neural circuits, Marr (1969) and Albus (1971) proposed neural network models of the cerebellum. In these models, the efficacy of parallel-fiber/Purkinje-cell synapses was assumed to change when conjunction of the parallel-fiber input and the climbing-fiber input occurs. Subsequently, Ito (1984) demonstrated the presence of the putative heterosynaptic plasticity of Purkinje cells in the flocculus of the cerebellum, which plays an essential role in the adaptive control of the vestibulo-ocular reflex. Fujita (1982) expanded the Marr-Albus model into an adaptive filter model for the vestibulo-ocular reflex. Consequently, a comprehensive understanding of the adaptive control of the vestibulo-ocular reflex has been developed at all of the above three levels.

For several reasons, investigation of voluntary movement is much more difficult than investigation of the involuntary vestibulo-ocular reflex. First, the effectors of voluntary movements (e.g., a hand or leg) have highly nonlinear dynamics with multiple degrees of freedom. Second, many neural networks and pathways are hierarchically involved in the execution of voluntary movements (Allen and Tsukahara 1974). Third, volition participates at the highest level of control. Fourth, an understanding at the computational level is not trivial.

In this chapter, a computational theory of trajectory formation and supervised motor learning will be developed. I also describe corresponding neural network models and their simulated behaviors. Finally, I will propose a unified model in which the trajectory-formation problem and the supervised motor-learning problem are dealt with coherently.

Following the pioneering work of Saltzman (1979) and Hollerbach (1982), we have proposed a computational model of voluntary movement, as shown in figure 33.1, which deals with Marr's first level (Kawato, Furukawa, and Suzuki 1987). Our model implements a number of important control functions.

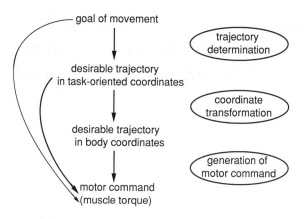

Figure 33.1 Computational models of information processing and internal information representation in the brain for sensory-motor control of voluntary movement.

For example, consider a thirsty person reaching for a glass of water on a table. Here the goal of the model would be to control the movements of the arm toward the glass to reduce thirst. To achieve this goal, one desirable trajectory in task-oriented coordinates is first selected by the model from the infinite number of possible trajectories that lead to the glass, whose spatial coordinates are provided by the visual system (determination of trajectory). Second, the spatial coordinates of the desired trajectory are transformed in terms of a corresponding set of body coordinates, such as joint angles or muscle lengths. Finally, motor commands are generated to coordinate the activity of many muscles so that the desired trajectory is realized.

Of course, we do not adhere strictly to the step-by-step information processing shown by the three straight arrows in figure 33.1. Rather, Uno, Kawato, and Suzuki (1989) proposed an optimization algorithm that calculates motor commands directly from the goal of a movement (thin curved arrow in fig. 33.1). Further, as shown by the thick curved arrow in figure 33.1, the motor commands can also be obtained directly from the desired trajectory represented in task-oriented coordinates (Kawato, Isobe, Maeda, and Suzuki 1988). In this respect, our model differs from the three-level hierarchical movement plan proposed by Hollerbach (1982). We will discuss later how the direct (bypassing) computations shown by the curved arrows and the serial, step-by-step computations shown by the straight arrows cooperate to take shared responsibility for the computational control of voluntary movement.

Before proceeding further, however, let us consider some evidence in favor of our model. Several lines of experimental evidence suggest that the various types of information in figure 33.1 are represented in the brain. Bizzi, Accornero, Chapple, and Hogan (1984) reported that a desired movement trajectory is explicitly planned in the brain. In their experiments, when the forearm of a deafferented monkey was quickly forced to a final target position early in a movement, the arm returned to some intermediate point between the initial and final positions, then gradually approached the final target position again.

This result is not consistent with the final-position control hypothesis proposed earlier by the same authors. Furthermore, Flash and Hogan (1985) also obtained strong evidence that movement is first planned in task-oriented (visual) coordinates rather than at the joint or muscle level. The presence of the transcortical loop (Evarts 1981), which is a negative-feedback loop via the cerebral cortex, indicates that the desired trajectory must be represented in body coordinates as well, since signals from proprioceptors are expressed in body coordinates. For example, tendon organs sense muscle tension, whereas the spindle organs sense both muscle length and the rate of change in length. Conrad, Matsunami, Meyer-Lohmann, Wiesendanger and Brooks (1974) showed activity modulation of motor cortex neurons that compensates load during voluntary elbow movements. Finally, Cheney and Fetz (1980) showed that discharge frequencies of primate corticomotoneuronal cells in the motor cortex are roughly proportional to active forces (torque). Consequently, the central nervous system must adopt, at least partly, a step-by-step computation strategy for the control of voluntary movement.

33.2 ILL-POSED MOTOR-CONTROL PROBLEMS

Unfortunately, voluntary-movement control is an "ill-posed" rather than "well-posed" problem. A problem is well-posed when its solution exists, is unique, and depends continuously on the initial data. Ill-posed problems fail to satisfy one or more of these criteria. Most motor-control problems are ill-posed in the sense that their solutions are not unique. Any computational theory or neural network model with biological or psychological relevance should possess capability to resolve ill-posedness of these problems. Models proposed in this chapter will be examined from this viewpoint. We list three ill-posed control problems in figure 33.2.

First, consider the trajectory-formation problem for a two-joint arm movement within a plane, where the starting point, the via-point, and the end point, as well as the movement time, are specified (fig. 33.2, top panel). There are an infinite number of possible trajectories satisfying these conditions. Thus, the solution for how to control the two-joint movement is not unique, and the problem is ill-posed.

A second ill-posed problem is the inverse-kinematics problem for controlling a redundant manipulator with excess degrees of freedom. For example, consider a three-degrees-of-freedom manipulator in a plane (fig. 33.2, middle panel). The inverse-kinematics problem is to determine the three joint angles (three degrees of freedom) when the hand position is given in Cartesian coordinates (two degrees of freedom). Because of system redundancy, even when the time course of the hand position is strictly determined, the time course of the three joint angles cannot be determined uniquely. In particular, human arms have such excess degrees of freedom.

A third ill-posed motor-control problem is the inverse-dynamics problem for controlling a manipulator with agonist and antagonist muscles (actuators). For example, consider a single joint manipulator with a pair of muscles (fig.

Trajectory Formation

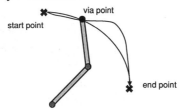

Inverse Kinematics in Redundant Manipulator

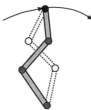

Inverse Dynamics in Redundant Manipulator

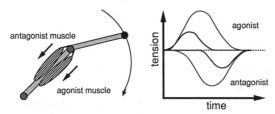

Figure 33.2 Three ill-posed problems in sensory-motor control.

33.2, bottom panel). The inverse-dynamics problem is to determine the time courses of agonist and antagonist muscle tensions when the joint-angle time course has been specified. Even when the time course of the joint angle has been specified, there are an infinite number of tension waveforms in the two muscles that can realize the same joint-angle time course, as indicated by the thick and thin curves at the bottom of figure 33.2.

At least two different approaches may be taken to resolve these ill-posed problems. The first approach is to utilize a feedback controller. The feedback controller may provide one specific motor command in the inverse-dynamics and inverse-kinematics problems even for redundant manipulators. The second approach is to introduce a performance index which requires smoothness.

Based on the first approach, we have proposed a feedback-error learning neural network model in which an inverse model of the controlled object (effector) is learned by using a feedback motor command as an error signal for training (Kawato, Furukawa, and Suzuki 1987; Kawato 1990). Because the feedback motor command is determined uniquely even for redundantly controlled objects, the inverse model can be acquired both for ill-posed and well-posed inverse-kinematics and inverse-dynamics problems. Applications of our model to learning trajectory control of redundant arms have been successful (Kano, Kawato, Uno, and Suzuki 1990; Katayama and Kawato 1991). This illustrates the first approach stated above.

As part of taking the second approach, we have also proposed the minimum torque-change model for computation (Uno, Kawato, and Suzuki 1989) and a cascade neural network model for its hardware implementation (Kawato, Maeda, Uno, and Suzuki 1990). This involves using a forward model of the controlled object in a relaxation calculation, and it can simultaneously resolve all three ill-posed problems shown in figure 33.2.

In this chapter, these two approaches and their relationship will be explained further. We will show that if a feedback controller with a Moore-Penrose pseudoinverse matrix is used, the feedback-error learning approach can approximately generate a minimum motor-command-change trajectory that is a natural extension of the minimum torque-change model. Finally, we will also propose a unified neural network model that integrates the two previous models. In our integrated model, trajectories for very skilled movements result from a relaxation computation using both forward and inverse models of the controlled object, however only the inverse model, acquired through feedback-error learning, is used for relatively difficult and less-skilled movements.

33.3 TRAJECTORY FORMATION BASED ON OPTIMIZATION PRINCIPLES

Minimum Motor-Command-Change Model

In this section, we outline two experimentally confirmed accounts of voluntary movements: the minimum-jerk model, and the minimum motor-command-change model. These models are intended to emulate certain important movement features.

One beautiful feature of human multijoint arm movements is that hand paths between two points are roughly straight, and hand-speed profiles are bell-shaped (Kelso, Southard, and Goodman 1979; Morasso 1981; Abend, Bizzi, and Morasso 1982; Atkeson and Hollerbach 1985; Flash and Hogan 1985; Uno, Kawato, and Suzuki 1989). To account for such features, Flash and Hogan (1985) proposed a mathematical model, the minimum-jerk model. It assumes that the trajectory followed by a subject's arm tends to minimize the square of the movement jerk (rate of change in acceleration), integrated over the entire movement:

$$C_J = 1/2 \int_0^{t_f} \left\{ \left(\frac{d^3X}{dt^3}\right)^2 + \left(\frac{d^3Y}{dt^3}\right)^2 \right\} dt. \tag{1}$$

Here, (X, Y) are Cartesian coordinates of the hand, and t_f is the movement duration.

Flash and Hogan (1985) showed that the unique trajectory predicted by this equation agreed with data on movements made in front of the body. However, their analysis was based solely on the kinematics of movement, independent of the dynamics of the musculoskeletal system. It was successful only when formulated in terms of the motion of the hand in extracorporeal space.

Based on the idea that movement optimization must be related to movement dynamics, Uno, Kawato, and Suzuki (1989) proposed the following alternative quadratic measure of performance:

$$C_T = 1/2 \int_0^{t_f} \sum_{i=1}^{m} \left(\frac{d\tau_i}{dt}\right)^2 dt, \tag{2}$$

where, τ_i is the torque fed to the ith of m actuators. Here the performance measure (objective function) is the sum of the square of the rate of change of the torque, integrated over the entire movement. One can see that C_T (equation 2) is related to C_J (equation 1) because the rate of change of torque is locally proportional to the jerk. However, it must be emphasized that C_T depends critically on the dynamics of the musculoskeletal system, not just kinematics.

For movements between pairs of targets in front of the body, predictions made by both these equations agree well with experimental data. However, movement trajectories under the minimum torque-change model (equation 2) are quite different from those under the minimum-jerk model (equation 1) in four other behavioral situations. In one situation, past data already support the minimum torque-change model (Atkeson and Hollerbach 1985). The other three situations have not been examined until recently. However, Uno, Kawato, and Suzuki (1989) recently dealt with them and found that the minimum torque-change model accounted for the data better than did the minimum-jerk model.

The first result of Uno, Kawato, and Suzuki (1989) concerned what happened when the starting point of an arm was on the side of the body and the end point was in front. Here the movement path was curved under the minimum torque-change model, but it was always straight under the minimum-jerk model. The hand paths of sixteen human subjects were all curved, supporting the minimum torque-change model.

A second result of Uno, Kawato, and Suzuki (1989) concerned movements between two points while resisting a spring, one end of which was attached to the hand while the other was fixed. Here the minimum-jerk model always predicts a straight movement path regardless of external forces. The minimum torque-change model predicts a curved path and an asymmetrical speed profile for the movement with the spring. The latter predictions again agreed closely with the data, further supporting the minimum-torque-change model.

Third, Uno, Kawato, and Suzuki (1989) examined vertical movements affected by gravity. For them, the minimum-jerk model always predicts a straight path between two points. The minimum torque-change model predicts curved paths for large up-and-down movements, but essentially straight paths for small fore-and-aft movements. The speed profiles were bell-shaped for both movements. This outcome agrees closely with data of Atkeson and Hollerbach (1985), as we would expect from the minimum torque-change model.

Finally, the most compelling evidence obtained by Uno, Kawato, and Suzuki (1989) concerns a pair of via-point movements. These movements involved two subcases, with identical start and end points, but with mirror-image via-points. Because the objective function C_J is invariant under translation, rotation, and roll, the minimum-jerk model predicts identical movement paths with respect to roll as well as identical speed profiles for the two subcases. On the other hand, the minimum torque-change model predicts two different paths. For the concave path, the speed profile should have two peaks. However, for the convex path, the speed profile should have only one peak. The latter predictions agree closely with the data (Uno, Kawato, and Suzuki 1989).

Summarizing these comparisons, we see that the trajectory derived from the minimum-jerk model is determined only by the geometric relationship of the initial, final, and intermediate points on the movement trajectory. The trajectory derived from the minimum torque-change model depends not only on the relationship among these three points but also on the arm posture (in other words, the relative location of the shoulder for the three points), and on external forces. Empirical data suggest that the latter dependence is in fact the case. Wann, Nimmo-Smith and Wing (1988) also found that the minimum-jerk model fails because of its lack of information about movement dynamics.

There are other conceptual reasons to favor the minimum torque-change model over the minimum-jerk model. The minimum-jerk model postulates the smoothest possible trajectory in task-oriented Cartesian coordinates, while the minimum torque-change model postulates the smoothest possible trajectory in the motor-command space. This induces a difference in the model's capability to resolve the ill-posed motor-control problems shown in figure 33.2. The minimum-jerk model can only determine the desired trajectory in task-oriented coordinates, and hence cannot resolve the ill-posed inverse-kinematics and inverse-dynamics problems for redundant manipulators. Thus, a combination of this approach and the feedback-control approach is needed to resolve all three ill-posed problems. The needed step-by-step computational approach was illustrated in figure 33.1. It has been taken recently by many researchers (Hogan 1984; Flash 1987; Mussa-Ivaldi, Morasso, and Zaccaria 1988; Massone and Bizzi 1989; Kano, Kawato, Uno, and Suzuki 1990). However, the minimum torque-change model can resolve all three of the ill-posed problems at the same time when the locations of the desired end point, desired via-points, and obstacles are given in task-oriented coordinates.

The minimum torque-change model has some important consequences. If we adopt it as a computational scheme, it leads to two important conceptual requirements. First, the brain needs to acquire, by training, an internal model of the controlled object and continuously use it for trajectory formation. This is because the smoothness criterion is applied to the motor-command space, which is more central than the task-oriented coordinates, so these two spaces must be connected. Second, the brain must simultaneously solve all three ill-posed problems shown in figure 33.2 by direct computations of the sort shown in figure 33.1 (curved arrows).

Considering that musculoskeletal systems possess muscle-tension sensors (Golgi tendon organs) but no direct torque sensors, Uno, Suzuki, and Kawato (1989) have developed a minimum muscle-tension-change model for a two-link manipulator with six muscles as a model of the human arm. We found that this model is better than the minimum torque-change model in that it can reproduce human data for a wider range of inertial parameters of the arm. Furthermore, I believe that a final solution to the trajectory-formation problem is a minimum motor-command-change model, since the motor command is information directly represented in the central nervous system.

Cascade Neural Network Model

How might the brain solve these problems? It has been reported that some neural network models can deal with computationally difficult nonlinear optimization such as the "traveling salesman problem" (Hopfield and Tank 1985) and constraint-satisfaction in early vision (Poggio, Torre, and Koch 1985). Since the dynamics of the human arm and robotic manipulators are nonlinear, finding the unique trajectory that minimizes C_T (equation 2) is a nonlinear optimization problem. This is a difficult problem because the smoothness criterion is represented in the motor-command space while movement conditions such as locations of target points, via-points, and obstacles are represented in task-oriented coordinates. To perform in the two spaces simultaneously, some model of the controlled object must be used to convert constraints from one space to constraints in the other.

We have proposed the cascade neural network model[1] shown in figure 33.3 to resolve all three ill-posed problems coherently (fig. 33.2) based on the minimum torque-change criterion (Kawato, Maeda, Uno, and Suzuki 1990). Our model calculates the minimum torque-change trajectory and the corresponding necessary torque from information about the locations of the target point, via-points, and obstacles, which are given by the higher motor center. The cascade structure of the model corresponds to the dynamic properties of the controlled object; it provides a forward model of the controlled object as a whole. The minimum torque-change criterion is embedded as hardware (electrical synapses) in the model. In use, the network first acquires a forward model of a controlled object by training, and then calculates motor commands by relaxation, utilizing the learned-forward model.

In a sense, the network first learns the energy that should be minimized, and then minimizes the learned energy. As part of this system, the minimum torque-change model is (1) a computational model for the trajectory-formation problem. The cascade neural network model provides a basis for (2) the representation and algorithm level, and also instantiates (3) the hardware level for the same problem. As Marr (1982) pointed out, a number of different hardware implementations can realize a single computational model. Actually, we will propose a different neural network model which realizes the minimum torque-change trajectory at the end of this chapter. Jordan (1990) also noted

Energy Minimization Phase
— Trajectory Formation —

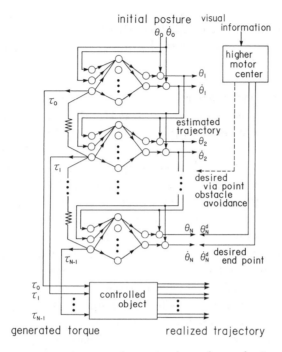

Figure 33.3 A repetitively structured cascade neural network model for trajectory formation based on the minimum torque-change criterion. For simplicity, a case with one degree of freedom and no kinematics problem is shown. All four-layer network units are identical. Operations of the model are divided into a learning phase and a trajectory-formation phase. Only the trajectory-formation phase is shown. In the trajectory-formation phase, the network relaxes its state to minimum-energy equilibrium based on backward propagation of errors through the acquired forward model.

that his forward-inverse sequential network can generate minimum-torque-change trajectory.

For simplicity, we explain the model in the case of a single-degree-of-freedom controlled object. Extension to the multiple-degrees-of-freedom case is straightforward. We need only to increase the number of neurons according to degrees of freedom in the motor command, the body space and the task space.

The controlled object in figure 33.3 could be body, arm, leg, speech articulator and so on. States of the controlled object, such as the joint angles of the arm, are denoted by θ. The time derivatives of the states such as angular velocities, are denoted by $\dot{\theta}$. The motor command is denoted by τ. Joint torque is a special case of the motor command. Generally, the controlled object is described by the following dynamical equations:

Optimization and Learning in Neural Networks

$$d\theta/dt = \dot{\theta} \tag{3}$$

$$d\dot{\theta}/dt = f(\theta, \dot{\theta}, \tau). \tag{4}$$

The cascade structure of the neural network model in figure 33.3 corresponds exactly to the temporal structure of the preceding dynamical equations. However, these equations are expressed in continuous time, while the network adopts a discrete-time representation. That is, the model consists of many identical four-layer network units; the jth network unit corresponds to time $j\Delta t$. If there are N network units, the model can generate a movement of duration up to $N\Delta t$.

The network units have four layers of neurons. The first layer represents the time course of the movement trajectory and torque. The third layer calculates the change of the trajectory within a unit of time, that is, $\Delta t \cdot f(\theta, \dot{\theta}, \tau)$. The second layer provides necessary representation of input for the third layer. The fourth layer and the output line on the right side of figure 33.3 represent the estimated time course of the trajectory. Neurons in the fourth layer calculate the next state by summing the previous state with its change during the current unit of time. In the preceding dynamical equations, the rate of change of state depends only on the current state, the current time derivative of the state, and the current value of the motor command. Correspondingly, each network unit only receives information about the current state, the current time derivative, and the current motor command.

Operations of the network are divided into a learning phase and a trajectory-formation phase. In the learning phase, the common input torque is fed to both the controlled object and the neural network model. The realized trajectory from the controlled object is used as a teaching signal to acquire the forward model between the first and third layers of the network. We use a backpropagation learning algorithm (Rumelhart, Hinton, and Williams 1986) during this phase. In the feedforward-calculation mode, the activation of each neuron is assumed simply to be a weighted linear summation of the synaptic inputs with a sigmoid nonlinear transformation, that is, "squashing function" (Rumelhart, Hinton, and Williams 1986).

Once learning has been completed, the cascade neural network provides a forward model of the controlled object. In the trajectory-formation phase (fig. 33.3), the cascade neural network model computes the torque that realizes the minimum-torque-change trajectory while satisfying various movement conditions by relaxation of its state variable τ. To guarantee the smoothness of the torque, electrical couplings[2] between neurons representing torques at neighboring times in the first layer are activated (see electrical resistance in fig. 33.3). The current flow through the gap junction tends to equalize torque values at neighboring times and decreases the criterion C_T (equation 2). The higher motor center gives information to the fourth layer of the network about locations of the desired target point, the desired via-point, and the locations of obstacles to be avoided. Satisfaction of these movement conditions requires information conversion, because they are represented in task-oriented coordinates, while the state variable τ of relaxation is in the motor-command space.

Our multilayer feedforward neural network model has several attractive features. For example, once it acquires the mapping from its input to its output it can calculate the partial derivative of its output with respect to its input in parallel, using learned synaptic weights based on the backpropagation algorithm (see Jordan 1990). The cascade neural network implements this feature as follows. First, errors in task-oriented coordinates are calculated in the fourth layer of the network as the difference between estimated hand positions and the desired target. That is, the desired target position plays the role of the "teaching signal" in a conventional learning procedure. Then backpropagation of these errors through the network is done with the algorithm of Rumelhart, Hinton, and Williams (1986). This converts the errors in task-oriented coordinates to errors in the motor-command space.

During the forward calculation through the network, information flows from the past to the future, from top to bottom in figure 33.3. On the other hand, during the error backpropagation, information flows from the future to the past, from bottom to top in figure 33.3. Thus, backpropagation in the cascade neural network model is "backpropagation through time" (Werbos 1988). The state of the torque neurons changes in proportion to the calculated error. This guarantees that the error in the movement conditions is decreased.

Although the state of the cascade neural network model changes continuously during the trajectory-generation phase, for ease of understanding, the network operations may be outlined serially as follows: (1) The operations began with initial torque values at n different times. (2) The forward model of the controlled object acquired in the cascade structure estimates the movement trajectory at n different times from the given torque time course and the initial state of the controlled object. (3) In the fourth layer of the network, the estimated position of the hand is compared with the desired target, desired via-points, and so forth, and errors in the task-oriented coordinates are calculated. (4) These errors are backpropagated throughout the cascade structure to calculate errors for the torque neurons. By this computation, the errors in the torque space are determined from the estimated error in the task-oriented coordinates. (5) Electric current flows from the neuron with the larger torque value to that with the smaller torque value. (6) Torque values of neurons in the first layer of the network change in proportion to the two forces calculated during steps (4) and (5) above. (7) Control returns to step (2) until the torque values reach equilibrium.

It can be shown mathematically that the cascade neural network will reach a stable equilibrium point where the summation of the smoothness criterion multiplied by the electrical conductance of the gap junction and the error in movement conditions is minimum. Consequently, the torque time course required to generate the minimum torque-change trajectory can be calculated by relaxation. An appropriate delay line should be inserted between the first layer of the cascade neural network and the controlled object in figure 33.3 so that the controlled object is moved by this calculated motor command.

Generation of Speed-Accuracy Trade-off

Our cascade neural network executes the steepest descent motion with respect to a weighted sum of the smoothness criterion C_T (equation 2) and the constraint regarding movement conditions. The value of the electrical conductance is the weight of the smoothness term. The electrical conductance must be slowly decreased to zero so that the movement-condition constraint is strictly satisfied. This embodies the well-known "penalty method" in optimal-control theory. Furthermore, for the cascade neural network model to calculate the exact minimum torque-change trajectory, the number of relaxation iterations must be sufficiently large. When the electrical conductance is fixed, and the number of iterations is rather small, the cascade neural network model cannot calculate the exact torque, and the hand will not reach the desired target using the feedforward control alone. Thus, one may observe an error between the final position of the controlled object and the desired target location.

Fortunately, this is not a weak point of our model but rather a virtue. First, the model reproduces the planning time–accuracy trade-off (Hirayama, Kawato, and Jordan 1990). That is, for a fixed electrical conductance, the final-position error of the object controlled by the cascade neural network decreases as the number of iterations increases. Second, the model yields a speed-accuracy trade-off in the arm movement, well known as Fitts's law (Fitts 1954).

We have examined the speed-accuracy trade-off in the cascade neural network model with a fixed electrical conductance of 0.001 and a fixed iteration number of 2,500 (Hirayama, Kawato, and Jordan 1990). Five different point-to-point movements were examined. The starting and target points (T1–T6) were the same as those in the experiments by Uno, Kawato, and Suzuki (1989).

Figure 33.4a shows the studied movements. Here the origin is the location of the shoulder. Figure 33.4a also shows the hand paths, and figure 33.4b shows the corresponding tangential hand velocities for five different movements with a 0.7-second duration. The hand paths are roughly straight, and the hand velocities are bell shaped. Thus, major qualitative features of human multijoint movement were reproduced, even though the conductance and the number of iterations were fixed.

Next, we used the cascade neural network to generate five trajectories for six different movement durations (0.5, 0.6, 0.7, 0.8, 0.9, and 1.0 s). This was done with a single network while changing the number of the network unit to which the target position was given. Figure 33.4c shows the resulting movement time, MT, as a function of Fitts's law equation:

Figure 33.4 (a) Five hand paths produced by the cascade neural network model with a fixed electrical conductance of 0.001 and a fixed iteration number 2500 for 0.7-sec movement durations. (b) Tangential velocity profiles for the hand paths shown in (a). (c) Movement time-accuracy trade-off predicted by the cascade neural network model.

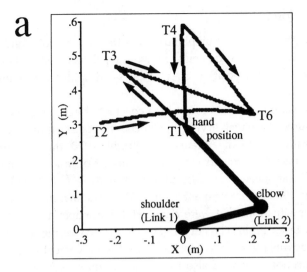

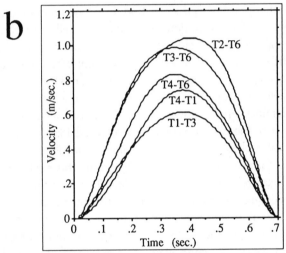

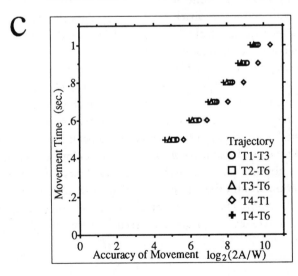

$$MT = a + b \log_2(2A/W), \tag{5}$$

where A is the movement amplitude, W is the target width, and a and b are constants. Here the cascade neural network reproduced Fitts's law quite well. In this case, the final position error of the hand is identified with the target width, W.

Our simulation held movement time constant at each of several values and then measured the variability of movement endpoints. In the classification of Meyer, Smith, Kornblum, Abrams, and Wright (1990) this is a time-matching movement task. Movements made under this set of task constraints typically exhibit a linear speed-accuracy trade-off $W = K_1 + K_2(A/MT)$ (see Wright and Meyer 1983 for experimental support). Fitts's law, in contrast, is usually observed in situations that were classified in that paper as time-minimization movement tasks. In this class of movements the goal of the subject is to move as fast as possible given the constraints on the movement end point. Thus if this classification is applied also to multijoint arm movement with relatively long movement durations, our simulation result should obey the linear speed-accuracy tradeoff. The simulation data was fairly well described by the linear law for a small range of velocity variation. However, for the total range simulated, the log law accounts better for our simulation result than the linear law. Consequently, we should examine whether our new neural network model proposed later in this chapter can reproduce linear speed-accuracy trade-off. Examination of single-degree-of-freedom controlled objects such as wrist or eye with the cascade neural network model is also interesting.

The classical explanation of Fitts's law invokes feedback corrections at long intervals (see, for example, Keele 1986). We think this explanation fails if one considers a relatively long feedback delay. The loop time, which includes sensory processing by photoreceptors in the retina, planning and motor-command generation, and activation of muscles, may exceed 100 ms (Evarts 1974). If one has experience with conventional real-time feedback control (for example using usual PID controllers), it is evident that control of a 700-ms movement with 100-ms feedback delay is very difficult. However, it must be noted that a feedback control with 100-ms delay could contribute adequately in slow movements or in posture control.

Even an elegant and comprehensive theory, the "stochastic optimized-submovement model" proposed by Meyer et al. (1990), relies on a feedback signal for starting a secondary corrective submovement in order to hit a target. If one assumes that the error signal for corrective submovements requires detecting the final position of the first submovement, there must exist at least 50 ms dead time due to somatosensory feedback before the second submovement. This is not the case because the typical oscillation of movement velocity and acceleration around the end of the first ballistic movement is continuous (Meyer et al. 1988). Thus, Meyer et al. (1988) assumed that feedback and feedforward (efference copy) are processed "on the fly" during movement production.

In our opinion, the submovements reported by Meyer et al. (1990) instead might be interpreted as physical oscillation caused by visco-elastic properties of the musculoskeletal system. It might be hypothesized that the initial ballistic part of a movement is controlled by a strictly feedforward mechanism like the cascade neural network, whereas the later part of the movement is executed by a posture controller that specifies levels of stationary motor commands for groups of muscles based on visual information about target location. Presumably, the use of visual feedback is stationary, as in the inverse-statics model described later. If the final position of a hand realized by the feedforward control coincides with the stationary posture commanded by the feedback mechanism (posture controller), no oscillation occurs. However, when these two positions are different, then damped oscillation which converges to the specified posture should be observed because of the spring-like dynamics of the musculoskeletal system in combination with the posture controller. Thus, this mechanism explains why and how this "passive" oscillation made the movements more accurate when there was visual feedback. Furthermore, when concurrent visual feedback of the current position is removed, the posture controller suffers from inaccurate coordinate transformation between the target visual location and necessary motor commands because of loss of the reference. Then, under this condition, our model predicts inaccurate final positioning and decrease of stiffness of the final posture (see Meyer et al. 1988 for related experimental results). We will later describe one candidate for this posture controller: the inverse-statics model (Katayama and Kawato 1991).

Nevertheless, we agree with the view that variability in motor-output processes mediates errors in rapid movements, which is the basic assumption of the stochastic optimized-submovement model (Meyer et al. 1990). This viewpoint was originally proposed in an impulse-variability model, and validated by behavioral experiments on controlling ballistic force pulses (Schmidt, Sherwood, Zelaznik, and Leikind 1985). Our own subsequent work provides one possible neural mechanism that explains the stochastic variability in the time course of feedforward motor commands. From simulations by Hirayama, Kawato, and Jordan (1990) and by Uno and Suzuki (1990), we infer that the calculated feedforward torque contains stochastic variability associated with variability in the number of iterations during relaxation computation, and with variability in electrical resistance values (Hirayama, Kawato, and Jordan 1990), or with variability in the learned-forward model (Uno and Suzuki 1990).

Furthermore, the cascade neural network model explains this variability for movements involving multiple degrees of freedom and a controlled object with realistic dynamics. These dynamics contain centripetal and Coriolis forces and frictional forces. The presence of such realistic forces violates basic assumptions of Meyer, Smith, and Wright (1982) about force-time rescalability and symmetry.

In summary, the movement speed-accuracy trade-off may be explained by difficulty in feedforward neural calculation of ballistic motor commands for a controlled object with multiple degrees of freedom. Our present study is less refined in several ways (especially treatment of "time-matching" versus "time-minimizing") than some others (for example, the elegant and comprehensive model proposed by Meyer et al., 1990). Nevertheless, for the first time, we have tried to explain motor-command variability based on a specific, neural model of motor-command generation. Furthermore, our model extends previous theories about movements with a single degree of freedom and oversimplified dynamics to coordinated movements with realistic dynamics. Perhaps the strongest virtue of the cascade neural network model is that it can reproduce both quantitative features of multi joint movements and motor-command variability.

33.4   COMPUTATIONAL SCHEMES FOR SUPERVISED MOTOR LEARNING

Three Learning Schemes

One of the features of the central nervous system (CNS) in its control of movement is the capability of motor learning. For higher mammals, especially humans, supervised learning is probably the most important class of motor learning. In nearly every case, the teacher cannot directly demonstrate the correct motor command to the student, but can only show the desired movement trajectory. For example, parents teach correct pronunciation of words to children in the sound space. However, they cannot directly present firing patterns of nerve fibers that innervate articulator muscles. Other such examples involve small children mimicking various movement patterns of older children, and beginners in sports learning by watching expert athletes.

How might such learning proceed? Perhaps the answer entails a neural network that receives a desired motor pattern and outputs a motor command to realize a desired movement. The motor command may be transmitted to the musculoskeletal system and some particular movement might be realized. The realized trajectory may be measured by various sensory systems. It would be logically possible to compare this realized trajectory with the desired movement pattern (teaching signal) and to calculate the error between the two patterns. So if a teacher were to able to give the difference between an ideal motor command and an actual motor command, then various supervised learning rules could be used to train the motor-control network.

However, this last step is not possible in practice, so the problem of converting errors from task-oriented coordinates to the motor-command space is an essential and difficult one. It has been addressed by Jordan and Rumelhart (Jordan 1990; Jordan and Rumelhart 1991), under the rubric "supervised learning with a distal teacher." They proposed a forward- and inverse-modeling approach for such learning. Their approach will be discussed later in connection with our own. Also, Barto (1990) has reviewed the topic and compared several different approaches.

Exploring such approaches further, we have proposed a *feedback-error learning* neural network as a model of the lateral cerebellum and the parvocellular part of the red nucleus (Tsukahara and Kawato 1982; Kawato, Furukawa, and

Suzuki 1987). Our model constitutes one possible solution to the preceding error-conversion problem. In the context of this model, three representative computational schemes to resolve the problem will be reviewed and compared here. The objective of these learning schemes is to develop a feedforward controller for an unknown controlled object. Perfect feedforward control can be realized if the controller provides an inverse model of the controlled object. An inverse-dynamics model and an inverse-kinematics model are formulated in what follows.

As part of these models, θ denotes an n-dimensional vector that represents body coordinates, such as joint angles or muscle lengths, of a controlled object. $\dot{\theta}$ represents the corresponding velocity vector. τ represents an m-dimensional vector of motor commands such as joint torque or muscle tension. The state change of the controlled object is described by the same ordinary differential equations introduced previously.

$$d\theta/dt = \dot{\theta}, \tag{6}$$

$$d\dot{\theta}/dt = f(\theta, \dot{\theta}, \tau),$$

where f is an n-dimensional nonlinear vector function. Given this representation, the forward-dynamics problem is to find the body-space trajectory $(\theta(t), \dot{\theta}(t))$ when the motor command $\tau(t)$ is given. Conversely, the inverse problem is to find the motor command $\tau(t)$ that realizes a special trajectory $(\theta(t), \dot{\theta}(t))$.

Before proceeding further, we must also formulate the forward-kinematics and inverse-kinematics problems. To do this, let x denote a k-dimensional vector of task-oriented coordinates for the controlled object, for example, retinal coordinates of hand position. Then x may be uniquely determined from θ according to the following nonlinear equation:

$$x = G(\theta), \tag{7}$$

where G is a k-dimensional nonlinear vector function. Given this representation, the forward-kinematics problem is to determine x from θ based on the above equations. The inverse-kinematics problem is to compute θ from x.

Now, more precisely, the problem of feedforward control is to find the motor command $\tau_d(t)$ that realizes the desired movement pattern $x_d(t)$. This may be done in two steps, solving the inverse-kinematics problem and then the inverse-dynamics problem. First, the desired trajectory in body space is calculated from that in task space: $\theta_d(t) = G^{-1}(x_d(t))$. Second, the necessary motor command is calculated from the desired trajectory, velocity, and acceleration $(\theta_d(t), \dot{\theta}_d(t), \ddot{\theta}_d(t))$ as a solution to the second equation in (6). Although this equation is implicit with respect to τ, it can be rewritten in an explicit form: $\tau_d(t) = h(\theta_d(t), \dot{\theta}_d(t), \ddot{\theta}_d(t))$. Consequently, in this case, the motor-learning problem is equivalent to acquisition of the conjoined inverse-kinematics model (IKM) and inverse-dynamics model (IDM) $h \cdot G^{-1}$ in the feedforward controller.

In figure 33.5, three computational approaches to learning the inverse model of a controlled object are compared. They are somewhat independent of the

a. direct inverse modeling

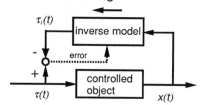

b. forward and inverse modeling

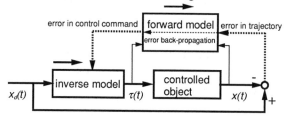

c. feedback error learning

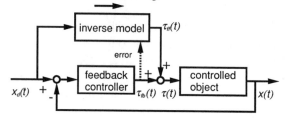

Figure 33.5 Three computational schemes for learning an inverse model of a controlled object: (a) direct inverse modeling, (b) forward and inverse modeling, and (c) feedback-error learning model.

neural-network models that actually constitute the inverse model. We will consider each possibility in turn.

The simplest approach is shown in figure 33.5a. Here, the controlled object receives the torque input $\tau(t)$ and outputs the resulting trajectory $x(t)$. The inverse model is oriented in the input-output direction opposite to that of the controlled object, as shown by the leftward top arrow. That is, the inverse model receives the trajectory as an input and outputs the torque $\tau_i(t)$. The error signal $s(t)$ consists of the difference between the actual torque and the estimated torque: $s(t) = \tau(t) - \tau_i(t)$. This approach to acquiring an inverse model was named "direct inverse modeling" (Jordan and Rosenbaum 1989). Direct inverse modeling has been proposed and used by Albus (1975), Miller, Glanz, and Kraft (1987), Kuperstein (1988), and Atkeson and Reinkensmeyer (1988).

Figure 33.5b shows a second method of combining a forward model and an inverse model proposed by Jordan and Rumelhart (Jordan 1990; Jordan and Rumelhart 1991). Here the forward model of the controlled object is first learned by monitoring both the input $\tau(t)$ and the output $x(t)$ of the controlled object. Next, the desired trajectory $x_d(t)$ is fed to the inverse model to calculate the feedforward motor command $\tau(t)$. The resulting error in the trajectory

$x_d(t) - x(t)$ is backpropagated through the forward model to calculate the error in the motor command, which is then used as the error signal for training the inverse model.

A third computational approach, which we have proposed and termed feedback-error learning (Kawato, Furukawa, and Suzuki 1987), appears in figure 33.5c. Here the total torque $\tau(t)$ fed to the controlled object is the sum of the feedback torque $\tau_{fb}(t)$ and the feedforward torque $\tau_{ff}(t)$ calculated by the inverse model. The inverse model receives the desired trajectory x_d and monitors the feedback torque $\tau_{fb}(t)$ for the error signal. As a result, the feedback signal will tend to zero as learning proceeds. This learning scheme is called feedback-error learning to emphasize the importance of using the feedback torque (motor command) as the error signal of the heterosynaptic learning.

In summary, the three approaches illustrated in figure 33.5 have various advantages and disadvantages. Direct inverse modeling (fig. 33.5a) avoids the error-conversion problem by reversing the input and output. Forward and inverse modeling (fig. 33.5b) converts the trajectory error into a motor-command error by backpropagation through the forward model. Feedback-error learning (fig. 33.5c) has the feedback controller convert trajectory error into motor-command error.

Stability of Feedback-Error Learning

Which of the three approaches to learning outlined in figure 33.5 do people take? Direct inverse modeling does not seem to be used by the central nervous system. The main reason is that after the inverse model has been acquired, large-scale connection changes must be carried out while preserving minute one-to-one correspondence, before it can be input from the desired trajectory instead of the actual trajectory. In engineering applications, another drawback of the direct inverse-modeling approach is that it does not necessarily achieve a particular target trajectory $x_d(t)$, even when the training period is long. In this sense, the learning is not "goal-directed" (Jordan and Rosenbaum 1989).

A more plausible approach is the one based on forward and inverse modeling (Jordan and Rumelhart 1991). It is goal-directed. This follows because the error for learning is defined as the square of the difference between the desired trajectory and the realized trajectory.

The approach based on feedback-error learning is also plausible. Its stability has been demonstrated mathematically by Kawato (1990). Here the feedback controller provides a linear approximation of the inverse-dynamics model. In this sense, the forward-and-inverse model of Jordan and Rumelhart (1991) and the feedback-error learning scheme contrast sharply with each other. Under the forward-and-inverse model, backpropagation through the forward model of the controlled object converts trajectory error into motor-command error. Under the feedback-error learning model, a linear approximation of the inverse model (i.e., feedback controller) converts trajectory error into motor-command error.

Feedback-Error Learning for Ill-posed Problems

In some simple cases where feedback-error learning may apply, the inverse kinematics and inverse dynamics are well-posed problems, that is, G^{-1} and h both exist. There are other cases, however, where these problems are ill-posed. For a kinematically-redundant controlled object with $n > k$, G^{-1} is one-to-many, and hence cannot be defined generally. For a dynamically redundant controlled object with $m > n$, $h(\theta, \dot{\theta}, \ddot{\theta})$ is one-to-many and hence can not generally be defined. Nevertheless, the feedback-error learning model can still resolve these ill-posed inverse-kinematics and inverse-dynamics problems, even for redundant controlled objects such as human arms. Furthermore, the obtained solution approximates the minimum motor-command-change trajectory, which is a natural extension of the minimum torque-change trajectory.

Another noteworthy point is that any feedback controller typically provides one specific motor command even for redundant controlled objects. However, the desired trajectory cannot be exactly realized by the feedback control alone. Because of this characteristic, a feedback-error learning model can learn to control redundant objects either at the kinematic or dynamic level (Kano, Kawato, Uno, and Suzuki 1990; Katayama and Kawato 1991).

For example, Kano et al. (1990) developed a successful model that learned trajectory control in stereo-camera coordinates even when an industrial manipulator (PUMA) was given an extra degree of freedom. In this study, the controller calculated the feedback motor command by multiplying the error in the visual coordinates by a Moore-Penrose pseudoinverse of the coordinate transformation. Because the pseudoinverse matrix finds the solution with the smallest norm, this calculation is closely related to our minimum torque-change model.

Similarly, Katayama and Kawato (1991) solved the ill-posed inverse-dynamics problem for an armlike manipulator (Bridgestone SoftArm) with "rubbertuators" that are air-driven, musclelike actuators. Because each joint contained agonist and antagonist rubbertuators, there was no unique solution for tensions to realize a particular joint-angle movement. Nevertheless, we obtained a roughly minimal muscle-tension-change trajectory with the feedback-error learning scheme.

Another characteristic of our work on SoftArm was that we have trained two inverse models automatically for trajectory control (Katayama and Kawato 1991). Part of this training involves the usual inverse-dynamics model (IDM) that compensates dynamic forces due to movements of links. The IDM was trained by using the feedback command as an error signal when the arm was moving. The training process also involved the inverse-statics model (ISM) that solves the static equilibrium problem between agonist and antagonist muscle groups. The ISM was trained while the arm was in a static posture. Given a desirable static posture, the ISM calculated motor commands for muscle groups to attain the posture while taking into account the nonlinear spring-like properties of muscles and the static equilibrium between opposing muscles. In essence, the IDM deals with the open-link architecture of the skeletal system, while the ISM deals with the closed-loop architecture of the muscle system.

Simultaneous Learning of Feedback and Feedforward Controller

As shown in the previous section, design of a feedback controller that calculates an optimal feedback command is not a trivial task for kinematically and dynamically redundant controlled objects. Thus, the feedback controller must itself be acquired by monitoring both the input and output from the controlled object. Here the learning should occur on line while monitoring the previous motor-command change as a function of the present state change. If synapse-modification rule contains a linear decay term proportional to strength of synaptic weights, the smallest norm solution is guaranteed for the feedback controller. Given this approach, simultaneous learning of the feedback and feedforward controller during real-time control will reach a unique solution that approximates the minimum motor-command-change trajectory for redundant controlled objects.

Feedback-Error Learning Neural Network Models for Different Parts of the Cerebellum

With network models based on feedback-error learning, it may be possible, in principle, to characterize structural features of the cerebellum. The cerebellum is divided into separate sagittal regions with distinctive anatomical connections. These divisions form three functionally distinct parts: the vestibulo-cerebellum, the spinocerebellum, and the cerebrocerebellum (Ito 1984). Given the histological uniformity of the cerebellar cortex with such different functional modules, Ito (1970) asked: "What is the role of the cerebellum should thus be asked in the following two ways; (1) common throughout the cerebellum, how does a given portion of the cerebellum process the incoming and outgoing information? (2) Specific to each part of the cerebellum, how is a given portion involved in regulation of a certain particular motor activity?" In this section, we will try to answer these questions coherently based on the feedback-error earning model.

To begin, we may note that the cerebrocerebellum is the lateral zone of the cerebellum. Its inputs originate in pontine nuclei that relay information from the cerebral cortex, and its output is conveyed by the dentate nucleus to the thalamus, and then to the motor cortex. The feedback-error learning neural network was originally proposed as a model for the cerebrocerebellum and the parvocellular part of the red nucleus (Tsukahara and Kawato 1982; Kawato, Furukawa, and Suzuki 1987), extending the pioneering work of Ito (1970).

Figure 33.6d shows this model of the lateral part of the cerebellar hemisphere. Here the feedback controller and the summation of the feedforward and feedback command reside in the motor cortex of the cerebrum. The feedback loop is the transcortical loop. A desired movement trajectory is sent

a. Adaptive Modification of Vestibulo-ocular Reflex

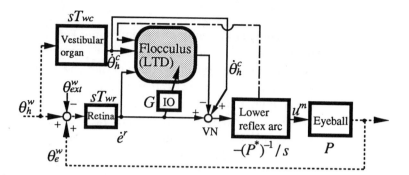

b. Adaptive Control for Posture

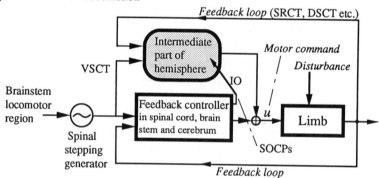

c. Adaptive Control for Locomotion

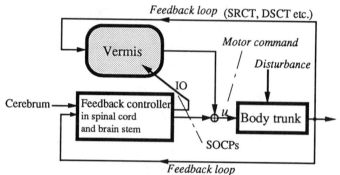

d. Learning Control for Voluntary Movement

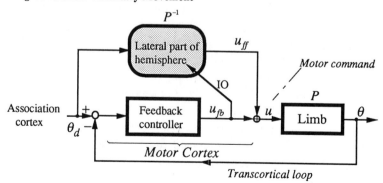

to the cerebellum and motor cortex from the association cortex. The output of the cerebellum is sent back to the motor cortex via the thalamus.

It should be noted as well that the spinocerebellum includes the vermis at the midline and the intermediate zone of the hemispheres. These two regions are the areas of the cerebellum that receive sensory information from the periphery. The vermis, for example, is related to control of posture. The intermediate part plays an adaptive role, for example, in control of locomotion.

Given these considerations, we have proposed a closed-loop control system based on the feedback-error learning scheme shown in figure 33.6b and 33.6c (Gomi and Kawato 1990). This system includes models of the vermis and the intermediate part zone of the cerebellum, respectively. In these closed-loop control systems, the feedback controller plays a threefold role. First, it converts the trajectory error into the motor-command error as a linear approximation of the inverse model of the controlled object. Second, it guarantees global trajectory stability like a typical feedback controller. Third, it defines an inverse-reference model.

For example, suppose that we prepare the PDA (proportional, derivative, and acceleration) feedback controller in Cartesian space. Then it will define the mechanical impedance of the hand tip in task-oriented coordinates. In this case, K_A determines the virtual inertia, K_D viscosity, and K_P stiffness. Consequently, the feedback-error learning scheme in the closed-loop system can perform Hogan's (1985) impedance control.

Our model also applies to other aspects of cerebellar function. For example, the vestibulocerebellum occupies the flocculonodular lobe. The flocculus is known to play a role in adaptive modification of the vestibulo-ocular reflex (Ito 1984). Its circuit diagram is shown in figure 33.6a.

Since this system does not contain any direct neural feedback loop, it first appears that its function cannot be understood in the feedback-error learning formulation. However, the visual system may play the role of feedback controller in learning. Maekawa and Simpson (1973) showed that the visual system, which provides climbing fiber input, calculates the negative of the summation of the head and eyeball velocities from retinal slip: $-\dot{\theta}_h - \dot{\theta}_e$. Because the head velocity $\dot{\theta}_h$ is the negative of the desired eyeball velocity for a perfect vestibulo-ocular reflex, the summation of the two velocities equals the differential negative feedback term: $e = -\dot{\theta}_h - \dot{\theta}_e = \dot{\theta}_{ed} - \dot{\theta}_e$. This negative feedback term is actually used in optokinetic eye movement responses. Consequently, the function of the flocculus can also be understood from the feedback-error learning concept.

We believe that the model shown in figure 33.6a has firm experimental support, whereas models shown in figure 33.6b and 33.6c are still speculative.

◀ Figure 33.6 Functional roles played by different parts of cerebellum interpreted according to the feedback-error learning scheme: (a) flocculus for adaptive modification of the vestibulo-ocular reflex, (b) vermis for adaptive control of posture, (c) intermediate zone for adaptive control of locomotion, and (d) lateral hemisphere for learning voluntary motor control.

33.5 UNIFIED NEURAL NETWORK MODEL FOR TRAJECTORY FORMATION AND LEARNING

We hypothesize that our cascade neural network (direct computation in fig. 33.1) is used for very skilled movements, while step-by-step computation is used for relatively difficult and less skilled movements. That is, the computational scheme adopted by the brain may change with motor learning. Some of our experimental data seem to support this idea. First, in human arm movements perturbed by external spring force (Uno, Kawato, and Suzuki 1989), subjects first tended to generate trajectories of various shapes when they were still not accustomed to the spring. After tens of repetitions, however, they consistently generated a curved hand path, which is the minimum torque-change trajectory. Second, Uno et al. (personal communication) have introduced a nonlinear coordinate transformation between the hand position on a two-dimensional position digitizer and the CRT coordinates where the end point, the start point, and the hand position are displayed. Because of the nonlinear transformation, a straight line on the CRT corresponds to a curve on the digitizer, and vice versa. Here subjects first generated roughly straight hand paths on the CRT approximating the minimum-jerk trajectory in visual task space (CRT coordinate). After several periods of training, however, they tended to generate roughly straight hand paths on the digitizer (i.e., curved paths on the CRT), conforming to the minimum torque-change trajectories.

These data suggested that step-by-step computation is replaced by direct computation in motor learning. In the first case, the forward-dynamics model of an arm in combination with the spring must be relearned. In the second case, the forward-kinematics model of an arm in combination with an imposed nonlinear transformation between the digitizer and the CRT must be relearned. Thus, step-by-step computation seems to be used temporarily until the forward model is relearned.

This is consistent with findings by some other investigators. Schneider and Zernicke (1989) reported a decrease of jerk cost during practice. Their results might be explained as improved control performance caused by an intensive learning of forward dynamics and kinematics of the arm for a special task. In contrast, some other motor-control schemes, such as the equilibrium-trajectory approach (Hogan 1984; Flash 1987), do not support efficient movement refinement during practice.

Although our cascade neural network model reproduces both the quantitative features of multijoint trajectories and Fitts's law, it has at least two weak points as a model of the brain. The first is the large number of iterations for relaxation calculations. When the initial torque is set at zero, there are typically several hundreds to thousands of iterations, although this can be reduced by moving a virtual target point in the course of relaxation (Kitano et al. 1990). A second weak point is the necessity of backpropagation during the relaxation calculation. Backpropagation is biologically implausible. However, backpropagation during the learning phase can be replaced by another learning

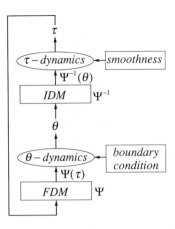

Figure 33.7 A unified neural network model for trajectory planning and trajectory learning. IDM is the inverse-dynamics model acquired by the feedback-error learning scheme. FDM is a forward-dynamics model equivalent to the cascade neural network used for forward calculation.

algorithm such as associative reward-penalty learning (Barto and Anandan 1985). Still, the backpropagation during relaxation calculations seems to be indispensable in the present form of the cascade neural network model.

Figure 33.7 shows a natural extension of the cascade neural network model to resolve these two weak points. We have achieved this resolution through a unified neural network model that integrates the feedback-error learning scheme and the cascade neural network model, thereby explaining the above-mentioned change of motor-control strategy with learning. Here IDM stands for the inverse-dynamics model acquired by feedback-error learning. FDM stands for the forward-dynamics model and is just the cascade neural network model that uses feedforward calculation to estimate the trajectory from the motor-command time course. Ψ and Ψ^{-1} are forward and inverse dynamics, respectively.

For a relatively difficult movement under this unified model, in which FDM is not accurate and movement planning time is not sufficient, one-shot calculation with only IDM from the minimum-jerk trajectory θ_J is used. This would yield a step-by-step control strategy. However, if FDM is quite accurate and the planning time is sufficient, the total network relaxes its states so that the minimum motor-command-change trajectory is generated. In this relaxation, both the motor command τ and the trajectory θ change somewhat independently. This constitutes a first point of essential difference between our unified model and the earlier cascade neural network model, in which only τ is the relaxation state. The smoothness criterion is imposed on dynamical change in τ, and boundary conditions such as the target point are imposed on dynamical change in θ. Thus, there is no need to transform one of the two constraints from the motor-command space to trajectory space or vice versa. Consequently, no backpropagation is necessary for relaxation in this model. This is a second essential difference between the original cascade neural network model and our unified model. Compatibility between τ and θ is doubly

Optimization and Learning in Neural Networks

guaranteed by the calculation of IDM and FDM. This follows because the τ-dynamics contains a force $\Psi^{-1}(\theta) - \tau$ that brings τ closer to the estimated $\tau = \Psi^{-1}(\theta)$ by IDM from θ. Similarly, θ-dynamics contains a term $\Psi(\tau) - \theta$. Because the initial condition of τ is not zero and realizes the minimum-jerk trajectory θ_J, the number of iterations required for relaxation is much smaller than in the cascade neural-network model.

From a broader viewpoint, FDM may be regarded as a model of a controlled object and an environment. Similarly, IDM may be regarded as a model of primitive action program. Thus relaxation computation using both FDM and IDM could be understood as internal simulation of action-response chain, which leads to better behavioral planning and motor control.

NOTES

I thank David E. Meyer, Charles E. Wright, and an anonymous reviewer for their useful comments on earlier drafts of this chapter.

1. Our cascade neural network model has some common features with the cascade model proposed by McClelland (1979) such as the cascade structure, that the dynamics is governed by differential equations, and that information flow is continuous rather than discrete. However, the cascade neural network model is specific to motor-control problems compared with the general cascade model of McClelland (1979).

2. Electrical couplings shown by electrical resistance in figure 33.3 are models of electrical synapses in biological nervous systems, while arrows in figure 33.3 show usual chemical-synapse connections.

REFERENCES

Abend, W., Bizzi, E., and Morasso, P. (1982). Human arm trajectory formation. *Brain, 105,* 331–348.

Albus, J. S. (1971). A theory of cerebellar functions. *Mathematical Bioscience, 10,* 25–61.

Albus, J. S. (1975). A new approach to manipulator control: The cerebellar model articulation controller (CMAC). *Transactions of the ASME, Journal of Dynamic Systems, Measurement, and Control, 97,* 220–227.

Allen, G. I., and Tsukahara, N. (1974). Cerebrocerebellar communication systems. *Physiological Review, 54,* 957–1006.

Atkeson, C. G. and Hollerbach, J. M. (1985). Kinematic features of unrestrained vertical arm movements. *Journal of Neuroscience, 5,* 2318–2330.

Atkeson, C. G., and Reinkensmeyer, D. J. (1988). Using associative content-addressable memories to control robots. *Proceedings of IEEE Conference on Decision and Control,* 792–797. Austin, Texas.

Barto, A. G. (1990). Connectionist learning for control: An overview. In T. Miller, R. Sutton, and P. Werbos (Eds.), *Neural networks for robotics and control.* Cambridge, MA: MIT Press.

Barto, A. G., and Anandan, P. (1985). Pattern-recognizing stochastic learning automata. *IEEE Transactions on Systems, Man, and Cybernetics, SMC-15,* 360–375.

Bizzi, E., Accornero, N., Chapple, W., and Hogan, N. (1984). Posture control and trajectory formation during arm movement. *Journal of Neuroscience, 4,* 2738–2744.

Cheney, P. D., and Fetz, E. E. (1980). Functional classes of primate corticomotoneuronal cells and their relation to active force. *Journal of Neurophysiology, 44*, 773–791.

Conrad, B., Matsunami, K., Meyer-Lohmann, J., Wiesendanger, M., and Brooks, V. B. (1974). Cortical load compensation during voluntary elbow movements. *Brain Research, 71*, 507–514.

Evarts, E. V. (1974). Precentral and postcentral cortical activity in association with visually triggered movement. *Journal of Neurophysiology, 37*, 373–381.

Evarts, E. V. (1981). Role of motor cortex in voluntary movements in primates. In V. B. Brooks (Ed.), *Handbook of physiology*, section 1: volume 2, part 2, 1083–1120. Bethesda: American Physiological Society.

Fitts, P. M. (1954). The information capacity of the human motor system in controlling the amplitude of moment. *Journal of Experimental Psychology, 47*, 381–391.

Flash, T. (1987). The control of hand equilibrium trajectories in multi-joint arm movements. *Biological Cybernetics, 57*, 257–274.

Flash, T., and Hogan, N. (1985). The coordination of arm movements: An experimentally confirmed mathematical model. *Journal of Neuroscience, 5*, 1688–1703.

Fujita, M. (1982). Adaptive filter model of the cerebellum. *Biological Cybernetics, 45*, 195–206.

Gomi, H., and Kawato, M. (1990). Learning control for a closed loop system using feedback-error-learning. *Proceedings of IEEE Conference on Decision and Control*, 3289–3294. Hawaii.

Hirayama, M., Kawato, M., and Jordan, M. I. (1990). Speed-accuracy trade-off of arm movement predicted by the cascade neural-network model. *Proceedings of IEEE International Conference on Systems, Man and Cybernetics*, 32–37. Los Angeles.

Hogan, N. (1984). An organizing principle for a class of voluntary movements. *Journal of Neuroscience, 4*, 2745–2754.

Hogan, N. (1985). Impedance control: An approach to manipulation. Part I: Theory. *Journal of Dynamics Systems, Measurement, and Control, 107*, 1–7.

Hollerbach, J. M. (1982). Computers, brains and the control of movement. *Trends in Neuroscience, 5*, 189–192.

Hopfield, J. J., and Tank, T. W. (1985). "Neural" computation of decisions in optimization problems. *Biological Cybernetics, 52*, 141–152.

Ito, M. (1970). Neurophysiological aspects of the cerebellar motor control system. *International Journal of Neurology, 7*, 162–176.

Ito, M. (1984). *The cerebellum and neural control*. New York: Raven.

Jordan, M. I. (1990). Motor learning and the degrees of freedom problem. In M. Jeannerod (Ed.), *Attention and Performance XIII*, 796–836. Hillsdale, NJ: Erlbaum.

Jordan, M. I., and Rosenbaum, D. A. (1989). Action. In M. I. Posner (Ed.), *Foundations of cognitive science*, 727–767. Cambridge, MA: MIT Press.

Jordan, M. I., and Rumelhart, D. E. (1991). Forward models: Supervised learning with a distal teacher. MIT Center for Cognitive Science Occasional Paper #40.

Kano, M., Kawato, M., Uno, Y., and Suzuki, R. (1990). Learning trajectory control of a redundant arm by feedback-error-learning. *Japan IEICE Technical Report, NC89-61*, 1–6 (in Japanese).

Katayama, M., and Kawato, M. (1991). Learning trajectory and force control of an artificial muscle arm by parallel-hierarchical neural network model. In R. P. Lippmann, J. E. Moody, D. S. Touretzky (Ed.), *Advances in neural information processing systems 3*. (436–442) San Mateo: Morgan Kaufmann.

Optimization and Learning in Neural Networks

Kawato, M. (1990). Feedback-error-learning neural network for supervised motor learning. In R. Eckmiller (Ed). *Advanced neural computers*, 365–372. Amsterdam: Elsevier.

Kawato, M., Furukawa, K., and Suzuki, R. (1987). A hierarchical neural-network model for control and learning of voluntary movement. *Biological Cybernetics, 57*, 169–185.

Kawato, M., Isobe, M., Maeda, Y., and Suzuki, R. (1988). Coordinates transformation and learning control for visually-guided voluntary movement with iteration: A Newton-like method in a function space. *Biological Cybernetics, 59*, 161–177.

Kawato, M., Maeda, M., Uno, Y., and Suzuki, R. (1990). Trajectory formation of arm movement by cascade neural-network model based on minimum torque-change criterion. *Biological Cybernetics, 62*, 275–288.

Keele, S. W. (1986). Motor control. In J. K. Boff, L. Kaufman, and J. P. Thomas (Eds.), *Handbook of perception and human performance*, vol. 2, 30–1 through 30–60. New York: Wiley.

Kelso, J. A. S., Southard, D. L., and Goodman, D. (1979). On the nature of human interlimb coordination. *Science, 203*, 1029–1031.

Kitano, M., Kawato, M., Uno, Y., and Suzuki, R. (1990). Optimal trajectory control by the cascade neural network model for industrial manipulator. *Japan IEICE Technical Report, NC89-64*, 19–24 (in Japanese).

Kuperstein, M. (1988). Neural model of adaptive hand-eye coordination for single postures. *Science, 239*, 1308–1311.

McClelland, J. L. (1979). On the time relations of mental processes: An examination of systems of processes in cascade. *Psychological Review, 86*, 287–330.

Maekawa, K., and Simpson, J. I. (1973) Climbing fiber responses evoked in vestibulocerebellum of rabbit from visual system. *Journal of Neurophysiology, 36*, 649–666.

Marr, D. (1969). A theory of cerebellar cortex. *Journal of Physiology, 202*, 437–470.

Marr, D. (1982). *Vision*. New York: Freeman.

Massone, L., and Bizzi, E. (1989). A neural network model for limb trajectory formation. *Biological Cybernetics, 61*, 417–425.

Meyer, D. E., Smith, J. E. K., and Wright, C. E. (1982). Models for the speed and accuracy of aimed movements. *Psychological Review, 89*, 449–482.

Meyer, D. E., Abrams, R. A., Kornblum, S., Wright, C. E., and Smith, J. E. K. (1988). Optimality in human motor performance: Ideal control of rapid aimed movements. *Psychological Review, 95*, 340–370.

Meyer, D. E., Smith, J. E. K., Kornblum, S., Abrams, R. A., and Wright, C. E. (1990). Speed-accuracy tradeoffs in aimed movement: Toward a theory of rapid voluntary action. In M. Jeannerod (Ed.), *Attention and Performance XIII*, 173–226. Hillsdale, NJ: Erlbaum.

Miller, W. T., Glanz, F. H., and Kraft, L. G. (1987). Application of a general learning algorithm to the control of robotic manipulators. *International Journal of Robotics Research, 6*, 84–98.

Morasso, P. (1981). Spatial control of arm movements. *Experimental Brain Research, 42*, 223–227.

Mussa-Ivaldi, F. A., Morasso, P., and Zaccaria, R. (1988). Kinematic networks: A distributed model for representing and regularizing motor redundancy. *Biological Cybernetics, 60*, 1–16.

Poggio, T., Torre, V., and Koch, C. (1985). Computational vision and regularization theory. *Nature, 317*, 314–319.

Rumelhart, D. E., Hinton, G. E., and Williams, R. J. (1986). Learning representations by back-propagating errors. *Nature, 323*, 533–536.

Saltzman, E. L. (1979). Levels of sensorimotor representation. *Journal of Mathematical Psychology, 20*, 91–163.

Schmidt, R. A., Sherwood, D. E., Zelaznik, H. N., and Leikind, B. J. (1985). Speed-accuracy trade-offs in motor behavior: Theories of impulse variability. In H. Heuer, U. Kleinbeck, and K. H. Schmidt (Eds.), *Motor behavior: Programming, control, and acquisition*, 79–123. Berlin: Springer-Verlag.

Schneider, K., and Zernicke, R. F. (1989). Jerk-cost modulations during the practice of rapid arm movements. *Biological Cybernetics, 60*, 221–230.

Tsukahara, N., and Kawato, M. (1982). Dynamic and plastic properties of the brain stem neuronal networks as the possible neuronal basis of learning and memory. In S. Amari and M. A. Arbib (Eds.), *Competition and cooperation in neural nets*, 430–441. New York: Springer-Verlag.

Uno, Y., Kawato, M., and Suzuki, R. (1989). Formation and control of optimal trajectory in human multijoint arm movement: Minimum torque-change model. *Biological Cybernetics, 61*, 89–101.

Uno, Y., Suzuki, R., and Kawato, M. (1989). Minimum muscle-tension-change model which reproduces human arm movement. *Proceedings of the 4th Symposium on Biological and Physiological Engineering*, 299–302, (in Japanese).

Uno, Y., and Suzuki, R. (1990). Quantitative relationship between internal model of motor system and movement accuracy, movement distance and movement time. *Proceedings of 1990 Annual Conference of Japan Neural Network Society*, 55 (in Japanese).

Wann, J., Nimmo-Smith, I., and Wing, A. M. (1988). Relation between velocity and curvature in movement: Equivalence and divergence between a power law and a minimum-jerk model. *Journal of Experimental Psychology: Human Perception and Performance, 14*, 622–637.

Werbos, P. J. (1988). Generalization of backpropagation with application to a recurrent gas market model. *Neural Networks, 1*, 339–356.

Wright, C. E., and Meyer, D. E. (1983). Conditions for a linear speed-accuracy trade-off in aimed movements. *Quarterly Journal of Experimental Psychology, 35A*, 279–296.

34 Strategies for Understanding Movement

Paolo Viviani

34.1 CONSTRAINTS AND FLEXIBILITY

One of the most fascinating aspects of biological movements, which sets them apart from others, is their apparent fuzziness. Basically, all movements are alike inasmuch as they are generated and controlled by physical principles that we understand fairly well. However, from the phenomenological point of view, biological and nonbiological movements are distinctly different. Whether they are simple or complex, nonbiological movements that are controlled by few identifiable agents appear to us as rigidly constrained and, therefore, predictable. All mechanical contraptions designed to serve a purpose, if they move at all, do so in a constrained and predictable way. Indeed, we want them to behave like this as a guarantee of their effectiveness. With a few exceptions, the price for effectiveness is dullness, as anyone who has watched a clock escapement for more than ten seconds can testify. Contrast this with a second category of nonbiological movements, those controlled by so many factors that the result seems to be free, unpredictable, and ever-changing: a leaf swirling in the wind or the rivulets in a mountain creek can be charming and graceful to us precisely because of their variability. But, of course, we do not expect them to accomplish anything.

Biological movements, and in particular those that we create, are so fascinating precisely because they seem to escape this dichotomy that is so deeply entrenched in our conception of physical motion. We can carry out the most demanding motor tasks requiring strength, or accuracy, or both, as the case may be. Yet our movements are never dull because they are never repetitive. Their accuracy is an intelligent one that concentrates on the overall result. The intermediate steps in the accomplishment of a motor goal, however, can be very variable indeed. For example, suppose we were to make a video recording of two pianists playing the same piece and then project the two images superimposed. The portions of frames containing the trunks and arms of the performers will appear quite confused, for no two pianists move in exactly the same way. Confusion, however, will diminish progressively as we get closer to the hands. Ultimately, the two images will overlap quite accurately at the fingertips, where it really matters for the performance. The robot pianists we are now able to build (one was demonstrated a few years ago at a technology fair in Japan) behave in a drastically different manner, because end point consistency requires consistency all the way back through the chain of moving segments. If robots were used in the above example, the two images would overlap everywhere.

This intrinsic and perspicuous quality of biological motions obscures somewhat a second, equally fascinating, aspect of these movements. We had to wait for the development of accurate techniques of measurement to become aware of the fact that our freedom to select equivalent ways of achieving a motor goal is far from unqualified. The situation bears some analogy with the production of language where many expressions can be used to express equivalent meanings, but each expression is constrained both syntactically and phonologically by the rules of the language. These constraints can be global, that is, pertaining to the temporal sequence of several utterances, or local, that is, concerning the modality with which each utterance is produced. The analogy should not be taken too literally because movements cannot be decomposed into units in the same unambiguous way that sentences can. However, we also see in movements the coexistence of both local and "syntactical" constraints which, within any acceptable solution to a specific motor goal, strongly reduce the variability of the geometric, temporal, and kinematical parameters of the motor act.

Many constraints are procedural and can be expressed as an *if-then* clause. This is the case in the instance of the empirical fact (known as the isochrony principle) that *if* the distance to be traveled by the relevant limb's end point increases, *then* the average velocity also increases (Viviani and McCollum 1983). Consequently, movement duration is kept far less variable than distance itself. The principle applies both locally, for individual strokes, and globally for sequences of strokes as complex as signatures. Sometimes the constraint applies to the selection of the trajectory. Thus, *if* I want to move from point A to point B, and *if* there is a mandatory via-point in C, *then* the tangent to the selected trajectory is specified almost uniquely by the position of A, B, and C. In other cases the constraint concerns the kinematics. It is well known, for example, that velocity in single-stroke movements has a stereotyped bell-shaped profile which scales very precisely with total stroke duration. In still other cases it is the covariation of trajectory and kinematics that is subjected to constraints. Thus, the so-called isogony principle states that curvature and tangential velocity in end-point trajectories covary in such a way as to reduce the variability of angular velocity (Viviani and Schneider 1991). Under certain circumstances, further reduction of freedom results from the phenomenon known as *homotetic scaling*: as one changes the overall tempo of a complex sequential action, the duration of the components scales proportionally, so that their ratios are kept invariant (Viviani and Terzuolo 1980). Finally, there is evidence that the temporal coordination and cooperation of motor components is subjected to certain compatibility rules which narrow down the number of possible combinations. For instance, in prehension movements the transport phase of arm and forearm invariably precedes the shaping of the fingers (see Jeannerod 1988).

Human movements, therefore, are characterized by a subtle interplay between seemingly contradictory aspects, freedom and constraint, neither of which can be ascribed to, or deduced from known physical principles. Aside from a few facts that can be accounted for in terms of dynamic laws and biomechanical properties of the limbs, most of the properties of human movements foreshadow the inner working of the underlying nervous control processes and, ultimately, should be explained within a comprehensive theory of these processes.

What strategies are available to make sense of the double nature of human movements? Is this double nature conceptually akin to that of language, as the previous metaphor might suggest? If so, are the constraints of this "motor language" isomorphic to—and derived from—a specific set of properties of the nervous hardware? Could they not be, instead, emerging properties, not related directly to the architecture of the motor system? I believe that, thanks to the flair of the organizers, the five papers presented in the session on Motor Control has provided a fairly representative coverage of the options that are available at the moment to answer these difficult questions. In the rest of the discussion I will review briefly these options, and I will attempt to highlight some of their strengths and weaknesses.

34.2   THE GLOBAL COST-MINIMIZATION APPROACH

The minimum torque-change model described by Kawato (chap. 33) is representative of a general approach to motor control theory based on the notion of optimality. As I have already noted, a motor goal can often be achieved by many different but equivalent movements. The idea behind this and other related models is that the nervous system eliminates the indeterminacy by always selecting the only solution that minimizes some appropriate cost function. Kawato's contention that the average square derivative of the joint torques is a more sensible cost function than other candidates described in the literature (such as energy or average square derivative of the acceleration) seems well founded inasmuch as this particular cost function takes into account directly the dynamic factors. Moreover, his model captures certain subtle features of real movements that may escape competing models. For the purpose of this discussion, however, I will neglect these differences, and concentrate instead on some general aspects of the optimality approach.

To begin with, the selection of the optimal solution is a global process which specifies at the same time both the geometry and the kinematics of the movement. Therefore, the approach predicts a specific covariation between curvature and tangential velocity, which can be compared with the experimental isogony principle mentioned above. Kawato has not verified this particular prediction of the model. By investigating the properties of a minimum-jerk model, however, Tamar Flash of the Weizmann Institute in Israel and I have demonstrated a satisfactory agreement on this point between data and theoretical predictions. Despite the use of a different cost function, it is very likely that Kawato's model fares just as well on this score.

The problem of movement timing has several aspects. All cost-minimization models share the property of being time scalable. Therefore, the total duration of the movement is a free parameter that must be adjusted on the basis of the data. By contrast, relative timing within the various parts of a movement (as measured, for instance, by the ratio of the duration of each part) is typically predicted by these models, and can be compared with the experimental observation. The test was performed by Flash and Hogan (1985) in the case of movements constrained by a mandatory via-point. Their minimum-jerk model predicted satisfactorily the experimental fact that the duration of each part is fairly independent of the length of the corresponding trajectory (relative isochrony, see above). Kawato has not addressed directly this aspect of timing control (but see Uno, Kawato, and Suzuki 1989). He did consider, however, a related issue, namely the relation between timing and accuracy known as Fitts's law. Given the fact that, for a fixed level of accuracy, Fitts's law implies a negatively accelerated relation between movement duration and extent, one could indirectly deduce that the minimization of the average torque rate also results in isochronous behavior.

An important feature of Kawato's chapter is the proposal to embody the principles of minimum-cost modeling into a neural network model. The attempt is based on the premise that priority should be given to explaining how we learn to reproduce a template model. Formal arguments are then advanced to assess the relative merits of three classes of solutions to the problem of how we learn under the supervision of a "distal teacher." It then is shown that each class corresponds to a functional architecture of the controlling network. Finally, it is argued that minimum-cost performance is an emerging property of one specific architecture among the three candidates. To the extent that the intermediate step in this progress (i.e., the formulation of a specific neural model) makes explicit reference to cerebellar structures, Kawato attempts to bridge the gap between the operational level, where the problems to be solved are formulated as abstract algorithmic requirements, and a descriptive level which is at least isomorphic to the actual brain machinery. The reference to the cerebellum is not very compelling, however. In fact, I do not believe that the argument advanced by Kawato would be weakened in any way if he had skipped this reference.

34.3 THE HARDWARE-TO-BEHAVIOR MAPPING

Requin and his coworkers (Requin, Riehle, and Seal, chap. 30) have provided evidence that the classical association of functional modules to anatomically identifiable areas of the motor cortex is somewhat unwarranted. Indeed, each area displays patterns of activity that are normally associated with different processing stages in the planning and execution of visually guided movements. Their main conclusion from these data is that "behavioral functions are implemented in widely distributed and flexibly interconnected neural networks of similarly organized modular units." The implications of this message depend on the general conception of the nervous system that one favors. Here I will

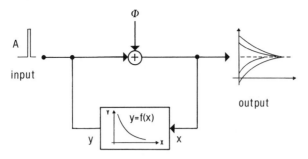

Figure 34.1 A hypothetical brain module. ϕ is a constant and $y = f(x)$ is a decreasing function. Under very general conditions, the response to a short input pulse converges after a transient to a value that depends only on f and ϕ, but not on the pulse amplitude A. The input-output relationship realized by this analog machine is differentiable with respect to its parameters.

only contrast the two main conceptions, which are sometimes referred to as the "analog machine metaphor" and the "computer metaphor." The following example dramatizes the differences between them.

Suppose that, with the help of suitable neurophysiological techniques, you have identified a module in the nervous system and you have come to the conclusion that the operation of the module is accurately described by the scheme depicted in figure 34.1. Everything in the scheme is fully specified. Thus, it should be possible to turn this implicit procedural description into a functionally meaningful description of the working of the module. In fact, it can be shown easily that if an input of amplitude A is fed into the module, after a transient phase the output converges to a value that depends only on the circuit parameter ϕ (for the sake of realism, the input amplitude can be thought of as the frequency of a spike train). In other words, the module always gives the same response, whatever the amplitude of the input. Of course, no "meaning" can be attached to this operation outside the broader context within which the module operates. Just how broad this context should be is a controversial and unsettled issue that need not concern us here. It is sufficient to note that a change in value of the parameter ϕ alters the numerical value of the output but not the nature of the operation performed by the module. According to the analog machine metaphor, all operations in the brain are accomplished by nervous structures that share the same basic property with our fictitious module: all the relevant variables within the module are differentiable with respect to its parameters (I'm making an abstraction that disregards the fact that certain nonlinear systems can give raise to chaotic behavior). The key consequence of this property is that a correspondence can be established between the topological structure of a given network and the logical structure of the operation implemented by the network. Thus, as Bernstein pointed out long ago (Bernstein 1967), to the extent that this operation maps into some characteristics of overt motor behavior, it may be possible to account for these characteristics in terms of the topology of the underlying hardware.

The computer metaphor—both in the original Neumanesque (serial) version, and in the more recent parallel embodiments—stands in sharp contrast with the preceding view. It assumes, in fact, that the nature of the operation being performed by a module depends not upon the topology of the network, but on the symbolic value assigned to certain state variables within a certain coding scheme (the program). A crucial distinction is introduced between these state variables and the variables which directly represent input quantities. Thus, changing the signal amplitudes somewhere in the network will have dramatically different consequences depending on whether input variables or state variables have been modified. Moreover, symbolic computing schemes of the parallel type are, in general, less clearly subdivided into identifiable functional units than their analog counterparts, and the same unit can play different roles at different moments. The consequence of adopting this view of the nervous system are momentous. In fact, as Jerry Fodor (1983) stressed in his well-known essay on the structure of the mind, the computer metaphor entails no less than the cognitive impenetrability of the central processor and, consequently, the impossibility of establishing any correspondence between overt behavior and the operations of certain nervous networks.

Let us try to place the results presented by Requin against the background provided by the distinction between analog and symbolic machines. Prima facie, it would seem that his conclusions square with the computer metaphor (in particular, the notion of hierarchical programming, which Requin retains as a useful heuristic concept, has no place whatsoever in an analog machine). If so, the chances of our to ever being able to trace back the structural properties of movements to those of the cortical networks are no greater that those of understanding what a computer program is doing by probing the voltages inside the processor unit. On the other hand, however, the pattern of results may also be compatible with the special type of analog machine adverted to by the connectionist school. As a price for this we must admit that no programming (of any kind) takes place in the areas investigated by Requin and his coworkers. In particular, the abstract plan for the movement—which indeed seems to require the flexibility of symbolic coding—must be set up elsewhere. Moreover, the specification of the program parameters resulting from sensorimotor integration should not be symbolic. Finally, it should be stressed that connectionist networks, albeit analog in nature, are notoriously opaque. Therefore, if in fact the somaesthetic, premotor and motor areas function in the connectionist mode, we should be reserved about the possibility of finding in those areas the justification for the observed regularities of the movements.

34.4   THE FUNCTIONAL APPROACH

As we have just seen, a conception of the nervous machinery can be entertained which at least leaves open the possibility to derive certain aspects of movement from the topology and functional properties of the wiring. It is precisely this possibility that provides the underpinning for the general epistemological project that cognitive scientists refer to as the "identity theory" (see Churchland 1988). Functionalism represents a somewhat less ambitious project. Functionalists do not consider that the quest for an isomorphism between behavior and the actual brain machinery is feasible. In fact they even doubt that such a quest is well founded in logic. Rather, it is assumed that overt behavior can be corresponded with (and explained by) a set of formal rules for manipulating functionally meaningful units. These units are defined post hoc from a purely operational point of view: they result from parsing mental or bodily behavior in a manner that satisfies as well as possible the conflicting requirements of parsimony and discrimination. The units do not correspond in any way to specific pieces of hardware. Thus, for instance, in most modern linguistic theories, speech acts are satisfactorily described as the result of principled transformations applied to linguistic primitives.

The functional approach is far less developed in the case of movement. No general consensus exists as to the rules for combining primitives, or, indeed, even as to how the relevant primitives should be defined. Rosenbaum's study of object manipulation (Rosenbaum, chap. 32) provides us with a fine example of the attempts being made to pursue the functional approach. The placing task that he analyzes can be carried out in two different ways (overhand and underhand grip) each of which may be construed as a possible unit of action. Following a line of argument that is characteristic of the functional approach, the experimental fact that unit selection is highly dependent on final posture is explained as a diachronic constraint on a potential sequence of such units. The apparent contradiction between freedom and constraint that I evoked above can be allied by segregating the former within the units, and ascribing the latter to between-units relationships. Within the context of the language metaphor entertained by Rosenbaum, this is reminiscent of the allophonic freedom that is permitted within phonetic boundaries. Since those aspects of the performance were not controlled in the experiments presented by Rosenbaum, it is likely that considerable variability was present in both trajectory and kinematics of the approach phase that preceded the bar grip, but, as long has these variations remained compatible with the chosen grip, they do not conflict with the rigid selection rules that are being applied. As in verbal communication, however, freedom can also be found in the choice and sequencing of the units. Thus, for example, it is well known that certain piano pieces can be played with different fingering techniques.

The hallmark of the functional approach is the countenancing of primitive, irreducible units. It is not necessary, however, for the units to coincide with identifiable segments of motion, as Rosenbaum suggests. Indeed, a large class of motor tasks are better analyzed by concentrating on rather abstract movement parameters. For instance, it could be argued that certain movements are adequately decomposed into a limited subset of specific muscle synergies (cf. Bernstein 1967). Similarly, as stressed in Wing's review (Wing, chap. 29), timing is often considered a primitive, irreducible variable of the motor plan. Also, time intervals provide in some cases the natural functional units for describing the movement. For example, it has been suggested that the essential characteristics of typing and piano playing movements are captured by the set of ratios of the intervals between keystrokes. The investigation by Ivry and Gopal of speech patterns (Ivry and Gopal, chap. 31) in cerebellar patients also focuses on timing as the basic control variable. The authors adopt the basic functional approach, quite independently from the fact that a specific nervous structure is held responsible for the regulating behavior under consideration. In fact, as Ivry and Gopal state explicitly, the study is part of a "research program aimed at identifying the elementary mental operations that underlie the performance of coordinated behavior." Within this framework, the very interesting hypothesis is put forward that computational modules can be shared across tasks. Indeed, shareability (as opposed to strict "vertical" modularity) is an essential precondition for these computations to enter into a combinatorial scheme and, therefore, to avoid the proliferation of ad hoc functional units. The import of the results vis-à-vis the stated hypothesis is controversial inasmuch as the expected connection between motor and perceptual effects of cerebellar lesions is not borne out by the experimental data. Cerebellar lesions are known to impair the production of accurately timed movements. However, while the same lesions also impair the ability to discriminate duration when the time interval is delimited explicitly, no impairment is observed in linguistic discrimination tasks where, in principle, only temporal parameters permit one to differentiate the items. This may suggest that when it comes to process language, special computational modules are brought to bear that do not coincide with those affected by the lesions.

The fact that the functional approach leads us to postulate units and rules that differ wildly across conditions, motor tasks and levels of description, does not necessarily detract from the interest of the approach. This diversity, however, may point to both a reason for concern and an intriguing possibility. Consider the movement by which we reach out for an object and grasp it with the hand. Consider, further, a complex behavioral context with respect to which it makes sense to consider such a gesture as a unit of motor behavior. In other words, let us assume that useful information about the organization of this complex behavior can be gathered by using a molar level of parsing of the behavior within which units as large as our grasping movement are functionally independent. The salient features of the entire motor behavior will then be expressed as regularities and constraints, both diachronic and synchronic, among the constituent units. Now, it is obvious that a grasping movement may, by itself, be considered as a (smaller) context. In this case it is perfectly legitimate to search for a possible parsing of this new whole into smaller units, such as transport phase, preshaping of the fingers, and grip phase. If the parsing is legitimate, we expect to be able to provide a functional description of the parsing again in terms of regularities and constraints which are now relative to the new, smaller units. In other words, the overall complex behavior may admit both a coarse and a fine parsing with the important qualification that orderly assembly of fine-grained units constitute coarse-grained ones. In fact this possibility is explicitly invoked by Rosenbaum to provide a rationale for his findings. This, however, places one very strong constraint on the nature of the rules that are assumed to be valid within each level: high-level rules must be deducible from low-level ones.

Such predicaments are commonplace in physics where, however, across-level compatibility is assured almost automatically by the unifying framework of mathematics. Thus, the empirical law of compressible gases $PV = RT$ emerges as soon as pressure P and temperature T (coarse-grained functional units) are broken up into kinetic molecular variables (fine-grained units) which are themselves described by the basic principles of statistical mechanics. The composition principles which permit us to build pressure and temperature from kinetic variables dictate automatically the form into which fine-grained statistical laws will be mapped at the phenomenological level.

Unfortunately, no unifying framework exists in motor control that is remotely comparable to mathematics, and across-level compatibility at this stage is mostly a matter of faith. I would like to stress, however, that the compatibility issue is not purely speculative. It arises, for instance, as soon as one attempts to apply the isochrony principle mentioned above to the analysis of complex drawing patterns (Viviani and Cenzato 1985). At any rate, it should be clear that this issue poses a conceptual challenge. Should it prove to be an impossible the challenge to meet, we would be left with a plethora of mutually incompatible levels of description, and the very foundations of the functional approach would be severely undermined.

NOTE

Preparation of this manuscript was partly supported by FNRS Research Grant #31.25265.88 (MUCOM ESPRIT Project).

REFERENCES

Bernstein, N. (1967). *The coordination and regulation of movements*. Oxford: Pergamon.

Churchland, P. M. (1988). *Matter and consciousness: A contemporary introduction to the philosophy of mind*. Cambridge, MA: MIT Press.

Flash, T. and Hogan, N. (1985). The coordination of arm movements: An experimentally confirmed mathematical model. *Journal of Neuroscience, 5*, 1688–1703.

Fodor, J. (1983). *The modularity of mind*. Cambridge, MA: MIT Press.

Jeannerod, M. (1988). *The neural and behavioral organization of goal-directed movements*. Oxford: Clarendon.

Uno, Y., Kawato, M., and Suzuki, R. (1989). Formation and control of optimal trajectory in human multijoint arm movement: Minimum torque-change model. *Biological Cybernetics, 61*, 89–101.

Viviani, P., and Terzuolo, C. (1980). Space-time invariance in learned motor skills. In E. G. Stelmach and J. Requin (Eds.), Tutorials in motor behavior, 525–533. Amsterdam: North-Holland.

Viviani, P., and McCollum, G. (1983). The relation between linear extent and velocity in drawing movements. *Neuroscience, 10*, 211–218.

Viviani, P., and Cenzato, M. (1985). Segmentation and coupling in complex movements. *Journal of Experimental Psychology: Human Perception and Performance, 11,* 828–845.

Viviani, P., and Schneider, R. (1991). A developmental study of the relation between geometry and kinematics in drawing movements. *Journal of Experimental Psychology: Human Perception and Performance, 17,* 198–218.

VII Symposium Discussant

35 A Word before Leaving

Donald E. Broadbent

35.1 INTRODUCTION

When I was first asked to contribute to this meeting, I counted on the organizers, and many of the participants, being friends of mine. I checked that they knew this to be the last Attention and Performance meeting before my retirement, and I assumed therefore that nobody would expect an old man to work very hard. After a time I began to have doubts about their friendliness, when I realized the scale of the task. I should have remembered that this group is also, without exception, made up of highly professional, creative, and energetic people. My final defense is to say that the task is impossible.

Yet something should be said as a conclusion. Five magnificent sections have gone before; but little has been said about their connections with each other. This is the time to relate each to the others, before the contributors return to the lab and I go off to my slippers, cat, and comfortable armchair. For me the first question, at the end of a life, has to be "Was it all worth while?" But for those who are carrying on there are then two much harder questions, "*Why* was this meeting a good thing, if it was?" and "What happens next?" The answers lie in the space between the sessions.

The arrangement of the meeting is itself an example of the input-processing-output structure that we all tend to assume.

We started with visual input, we then discussed selection of and attention to the input, next the time characteristics of decision, memory of the past, and only finally the way the person acts on the world. A perfect stages model, straight from the mind of Sternberg (1969) or indeed in less sophisticated form Broadbent (1958). As in the stages model, anything we learn in one stage may have no effect whatever on events in another stage; how far is that true of Attention and Performance, and does it matter?

I believe there is some truth in it, that it has not mattered so far, but that the time has come for another step. To argue for this, I shall go through the areas trying to strike a personal balance sheet. Too much general philosophy, however, is alien to the tradition of Attention and Performance. Before the grass-roots experimentalists all decide that nothing here concerns them, let me promise that I am going to introduce at least one fresh finding in each of the five areas. Perhaps that can be the bait that will lure you to consider the overall argument.

35.2 THE MORAL

Think back to the very first paper, by Van Kleeck and Kosslyn, because I want to use their framework. There have indeed been three historical stages of advance in attention and performance, of which the first was a rapid advance by the methods of traditional psychophysics and experimental psychology. (I shall be dissenting later about what has happened in the second and third stages.) Most of the enthusiasts for attention and performance still respect and carry on the tradition of the first stage, but the reason it was worthwhile is that it has changed the world; and unless one realizes that the world has changed, progress is going to stop.

We are, for example, now reaching a point where interdisciplinary collaboration has become essential if we are to go further. Computational modeling and neuroscience contributions have become essential allies. Yet even within a discipline and even within an area, it is now common for workers using one paradigm or set of concepts to avoid engagement with the data and ideas of other workers with a different paradigm. I remarked on this nearly a decade ago in the field of attention (Broadbent 1982), and the situation is now worse. In the field of chronometry, Townsend (1990) has expressed similar views. The problem of literature overload is shown quite clearly by the tutorial papers at this meeting. There is a greater tendency than in the past for each of them to take a highly personal stance and not to attempt to cover everything that has been published in the area.

To rectify this, as Van Kleeck and Kosslyn suggest, is going to involve deliberate thought about such things as the organization of the literature and of funding. That may not be part of the attention and performance tradition, but perhaps it should be.

35.3 ACHIEVEMENTS AND PROBLEMS OF THE PERIOD

The Motor Session

Now let us get concrete and return from the beginning of the meeting to the end. Motor performance has always been a neglected and deprived area of psychology. There are technical reasons for that; it is much harder to control what a person does than what stimulates them, and therefore harder to produce scientific laws of the type "A is followed by B." The last session, however, shows how these difficulties can be overcome and how the study of action can reveal the weaknesses of other areas. In these papers we can see clear evidence that the input-processing-output framework is insufficient.

Motor output depends on the intended final state (Rosenbaum), or on the predicted final outcome (Kawato); its neural substrate links together "sensory" and "motor" aspects (Requin). Preparation and anticipation are the core, not execution of an edict handed on by earlier processes in an open-chain fashion. The data and the concepts are hard, and our psychophysicists need not sniff at them; machines with feedforward components are as valid as open-chain ones are. Yet the same fundamental difference of orientation could be applied as much to the stages we cheerfully regard as "earlier" in processing. Vision, attention, decision, and memory certainly depend on purpose and on preparation. In the honorable tradition of experimental psychology, called by Van Kleeck and Kosslyn the first historical stage, processing only starts with the stimulus. In the real world, it is as likely to start with an intention or an unformulated internal disturbance that rouses a passive human being to start searching memory or searching the environment looking for a stimulus. I shall give examples where this point may have led us astray; for the moment, the students of motor behavior have at least given us an alternative structure.

Is there anything they can learn from other sessions? The success of the motor area has been based on analysis of single actions. Yet all the other topics have emphasized the importance of interrupting one activity by another, or of performing two at once; and it is a nontrivial problem in artificial intelligence to interrupt the execution of one plan and substitute another. Confining experiment to single actions therefore may not be enough. Allport and Driver are already studying the effects on motor processes of competing calls for action; and at the cognitive level, the interruption of a computer-based "adventure game" can produce quite large disruption of behavior (Gillie and Broadbent 1989). But the latter study is confined to symbolic behavior, not far removed from memory studies of retroactive and proactive inhibition; the extension of competition, interruption, and simultaneous performance to the subsymbolic level of motor processes may well lead to new insights.

A topic of interest both to motor performance and to memory is the role of action in producing learning. Funke and Müller (1988) studied the learning of a complex and dynamic system; some people in their study merely observed it, while others were able to take actual decisions affecting it. The effects of asking people to predict future events were also measured. Three kinds of dependent measures were used; the ability to predict the future, the ability to state the internal structure of the system, and the ability to control it successfully. Practice at prediction improved prediction, but not performance; both prediction and the experience of control were harmful, not helpful, to knowledge of the abstract structure. Yet performance was improved by the experience of control; action is in some ways essential to learning.

It is quite likely that this effect depends on the structure of the system being learned; Berry (1991) has found that mere observation of another person controlling a system may be sufficient to produce good learning, in a system with an unlagged link between action and effect. In that task, performance is well associated with verbal knowledge about the system (Berry and Broadbent 1988). When, however, the task employed the same system but with a lag between action and effect, Berry (1991) found that mere observation was less effective than action. The traditional view of memory as fed from the input is not enough; we must consider action as well.

The Memory Session

That leads to the strength of the memory session. Hintzman rightly points out that modern students of memory need to include productions, condition-action rules, in their models as well as static declarative representations, and that the learning rules used for the acquisition of productions are very similar to the rules devised by behaviorists of the supposedly primitive period. In the tasks of dynamic control that I have already mentioned, Marescaux, Luc, and Karnas (1985) have found that specific rather than general actions may be the basis for learning. People were tested after learning a control task of the type that gives dissociation between verbal behavior and performance. The later test of knowledge presented specific situations, some of which had been encountered by the particular subject while that person was being trained.

It was found that the experienced subjects could act more successfully in such situations than they could in randomly chosen situations—provided they had performed correctly on the previous occasion—and that the same action had then been correct. On a random sample of situations, without relation to personal experience, there was no evidence of learning. Dare one say, they succeeded when they had been "reinforced" for the required decision? Hintzman's emphasis on preserving the merits and insights of the past is fully justified, no matter how much one wishes to avoid older errors.

Let me also express sympathy with Hintzman's doubts about "ecological validity." I do so as an occupational psychologist rather than an academic. The mere use of a realistic setting does not mean that a study is valid; it may mean that some unmeasured accidental factor is contaminating behavior and making the results very dangerous to use in other practical applications. As an example, consider the effects of diazepam on driving efficiency. Laboratory tests (e.g., Brosan et al. 1986) show decrements in performance from that drug; yet it was at one time widely prescribed (Catalan and Gath 1984). Now, suppose one carries out an experiment in a more realistic situation, using a fast car and a measured task of cornering at speed by fit young men who have or have not taken diazepam. If you do this, it is quite possible that the performance might be unimpaired. The reason is that the pattern of laboratory findings is very similar to that of better-known inhibitory substances such as alcohol. Such effects are subject to complex interactions due to the level of motivation and stimulation in the situation (Broadbent 1971). Indeed, O'Hanlon (1984) has shown that impairments do appear in a real car, when one uses a long run at steady speed on a freeway and measures the wandering from side to side of the lane. In a real situation, it is much too dangerous to rely on a single "ecologically valid" experiment without a careful experimental analysis of the key factors in the situation.

Memory theorists are right therefore to preserve, or return to, the good things about the past. The speakers on memory are also right to distinguish different forms or types of memory: temporary and more lasting (Raaijmakers), declarative and nondeclarative (Squire), phonological input and phonological output (Howard). There is no single thing called memory, and the word is merely a convenient everyday label for a cluster of different functions. Both Howard and Squire link these differences to neuropsychology; the days of the empty organism are over.

Links to computing science, while present, are less evident in memory than they were in the motor section. That may explain the recent trend back to forms of input-output association rather than the more complex manipulations and operations found in machine systems. In the latter, there is debate and concern about the relative merits of symbolic and subsymbolic processes. There are computational advantages in systems that use condition-action rules, perhaps implemented in a distributed network mechanism. There are rather different advantages for systems that recombine or manipulate representations of the outside world into forms that they themselves have generated.

In the human case also, there is evidence against a straightforward path from input to output. Consider for instance a situation studied by Tattersall and Broadbent (1991). Their subjects received two simultaneous streams of visual material, with instructions to remember them both but to attach higher priority to one stream than to the other. After the material had arrived, they were told which stream to speak first. The material with higher priority, the "attended" stream, was recalled better; but this was much less true if that stream was the second to be recalled. The low-priority, "unattended" items were much less perturbed by some other recall.

This result has been found quite widely (e.g., FitzGerald, Tattersall, and Broadbent 1988). It looks very much as if the person creates a representation in the form that will be used for action, but is more likely to do so for attended than for unattended items. If then another action has to take place before the recall of the high-priority material, the representation of the latter is damaged; whereas the low-priority material, held in some form that is not ready for action, survives rather better. That interpretation is supported by a look at the effects of imposing articulatory suppression, the requirement to say some meaningless phrase continually during the task. Tattersall and Broadbent (1991) found that this extra task not only impaired memory but did so more for the high-priority material, and reduced the size of the priority/report-order interaction. That is what one would expect if an instruction to attend to an event caused that event to be coded immediately into internal speech, ready to issue into external speech. Losing the chance to do this would alter the size of the output-order effect.

Thus far, the results are complex but quite traditional; it has long been accepted that memory for visual events shows evidence for recoding into a phonological form. That is still consistent with an analysis in terms of a single chain of events from input to output. The first step is from vision into an internal but phonological form. The second step is onward from the internal to an external form. This is not a great change from a traditional S-R view, and there seems no need to suppose any symbolic, manipulable representation. To put it another way, recall can be viewed as the renewal of those processes occurring at input (Craik 1983).

The findings of FitzGerald and Broadbent (1985), however, raise a further problem. In that study, articulatory suppression had a larger effect on the attended material; but it made no difference to the effects of response order. There was a difference between their technique and that of Tattersall and Broadbent (1991); in the latter, the subjects spoke their recall, while in the former they wrote it. Recall by writing, in other words, does not disturb the part of the stored information that is held in internal speech. Yet people do still code attended material in an articulatory form, and then transform it again into a written form when it is needed.

What these experiments show is that some of the memory information is held in a form that is not an invariant part of the input-output chain. There appears to be a self-generated representation that can be detected by its indirect effects but does not appear overtly. Such a representation is, in the old-fashioned distinctions of forty years ago, a "symbol" rather than a "sign" (Yerkes 1943; Morris 1946). Because recall is not then a revival of the processes occurring at presentation, it needs more than a simple S-R chain to handle it. From that point of view the recent fashion for return to such open-chain theories is retrograde, although, as we shall see, models involving symbols are dangerously hard to distinguish by experiment. This is a good reason for pushing the open-chain theories as far as one can.

Chronometry

When we turn to the study of reaction latency, two immediate glories strike us. First, the concepts and assumptions are well described in public terms; one knows what each theory means, whether or not it is true. Second, experiments are done to test between alternative theories (Schweickert, Roberts, and Sternberg) rather than simply to confirm a single theory. That is the road to progress; confirming an existing theory advances us little, while disconfirming one theory without having an alternative leaves us totally agnostic. Would that other areas were as wise.

There are also some links with neuroscience, admittedly still tenuous compared with those of other areas, but still promising (Mulder). Perhaps however the greatest weakness is the lack of large-scale computational theory, without which it becomes difficult to test between particular theories about specific processes. As was mentioned in several papers, we know that speed trades off with accuracy, so that the decision process must involve a criterion that sets the stopping point. The usual assumption of theory is to leave this aside and to examine the distribution of latencies for evidence about the mechanism, keeping the criterion constant. Yet we know from the work of Rabbitt and Rodgers (1977) that criteria change dynamically during a session, errors being followed by abnormally slow responses. If dynamic changes of criterion are taking place, their effects have to be included in the predictions. It is hard from intuition to see what the final predictions will then be; on most theories, there will be a greater chance of false alarms as the numbers of processes increase, but perhaps a reduced chance of missed signals. Hence the criteria will move in a rather complex fashion.

If one builds a simple computational model, one can see what happens when the criteria are moved after each error in the way shown by Rabbitt's data (Broadbent 1987). With a parallel self-terminating search process, it turns out that such a model can give a linear increase of latency as the numbers of processes increase, with equal slope for positive and negative decisions. Thus, the total system will mimic the behavior of a serial exhaustive search. Although the point was not spelled out by Broadbent (1987), it is also true that latencies increase linearly with the level of "noise" assumed in each process. Thus, factors affecting the amount of noise will appear to have additive effects with each other even though they are clearly acting at the same stage. Such problems, arising from the structure of the total system, make it hard to derive clear predictions for the individual processes.

A related worry is provoked by two historical trends, very accurately summarized by Schweickert. One trend has been toward measurement of individual response times rather than the rate of continuous performance. I have doubts about this; response time ignores the preparation period and the recovery period. Those may be crucial for understanding the mechanism, and one cannot ignore them if one studies continuous performance as, for example, Kenneth Craik (1948) or Paul Fitts (Noble, Fitts, and Warren 1955; Alluisi, Muller, and Fitts 1957) did. The second trend has been away from measurement of information in the response, that is, probability, and rather toward a concentration on the set of stimulus alternatives that is searched. By returning to an analysis of reaction time in terms of number and kind of stimuli discriminated, rather than information transmitted, we tend to ignore criterion placements.

This latter trend is not peculiar to the chronometric area. It was notable in the discussions of memory that many contributors spoke of temporary or working memory as limited in "capacity"; that word was once a technical term, describing the quantity of Shannon-Weaver information that a system could discriminate. The one thing we are sure about in working memory is that it is not of constant capacity in that sense; it does not hold a fixed amount of information. If we use our magic seven items to recall digits, we can only discriminate ten million alternative sequences; but if we use them to recall letters, then that capacity goes up to a thousand times as many. (Of course, the size of the memory span is not strictly constant for different kinds of item, but does not vary enough to invalidate the argument.) What people mean is that working memory may be limited in number of items, or in the duration of an articulatory loop, or something of that sort.

The change in meaning of capacity seems to me a pity, although it is now so common as to be irreversible. It probably does not matter too much in the case of memory, simply because what matters in that field is indeed number of items and not the probability of each. However, in the case of chronometry it does matter because probability affects latency, and most likely it does so through criterion setting. Moreover, the lack of current interest in probability becomes most serious in the case of attention, as we shall see in a moment.

Attention

The good things in this session came in a variety of forms. First, there was the timely reminder by Allport that it is dangerous to appeal to attention as an explanatory concept, or even a single thing. We need definitions of each of the multiple processes involved when people cope with complex situations. He is not alone: it is worth recalling the words of another author who was putting forward a theory of the area in the language of information processing, without using the word "attention," and distinguishing quite different operations that are sometimes called by that name. After stating the approach, he turned to relate it to that of others, and said:

In the first place, the traditional language of consciousness and attention deals largely with the problems we have mentioned. . . . William James points out repeatedly the facts which are painfully restated in our different and unfamiliar terms. It is difficult to attend to two complicated tasks at once, though simple tasks may be made automatic. With practice they require little attention and fall almost out of consciousness. . . . Yet the traditional language has come off very badly in competition with other languages. The reason is undoubtedly that different people attach slightly different meanings to the words involved. Furthermore the words are often used with a frame of reference that causes great difficulties in practice. Consciousness is regarded as the experience of a subject who receives signals from the outer world but is himself a unity and the source of action. What then can we say of a man who turns out his electric fire while talking and cannot remember, on leaving the house, whether the fire is out or not? Was he conscious of turning out the fire? Did the action appear unconsciously? Or should we say it was conscious but at a low level of attention? Such alternatives seem to involve difficulties.

The author goes on at great length on the same point, urging the advantages of using everyday terms only as an indication of important problems, but adhering to a computational vocabulary to keep ideas clear; in similar vein he praises but ultimately rejects the language of stimulus-response psychology. This passage was written some time ago, as is revealed by language we would now call sexist; it was certainly not meant in a sexist fashion, as I can be sure because I wrote it (Broadbent 1958, 58–59). Unfortunately some readers absorbed the criticism of S-R language and ignored that of mentalism. Perhaps they thought it was merely a polite deference to behaviorist sensibilities; but it was not. The importance of breaking up "attention" into separate and functionally defined operations was as clear then as now; it is sad that it still needs to be urged.

If, however, one does distinguish between various kinds of bottleneck and selection system, then one can draw powerful conclusions; and the links with physiology are at last becoming clear and realistic. As was urged by Broadbent (1958), the original intake of information into the system is unselective (chap. 2), but is followed by various limited mechanisms (chap. 11). As was argued by Broadbent (1971), there are also a variety of optional strategies selecting in various ways (chap. 10; and also the distinction of the "what" and "where" systems made repeatedly throughout the meeting). The weak point of Broadbent (1958) was undoubtedly the use only of a pipeline or chain of processes leading from input to output; and here Duncan shows the shape of the future. The results of his group are more readily interpreted in terms of control and subordinate processes than of chains, and in this they are joined by a number of studies elsewhere. The German literature has for some years been considering human function in situations even more complex than that of driving, summarized in English by Funke (1988) and Dörner (1990). Quite often, success in such situations has been found to be unrelated to intelligence. Some tasks, however, do correlate (Putz-Osterloh and Lüer 1981), and this has been linked to the "transparency" of the system, the ease with which it can be represented cognitively. That concept may have aspects in common with the notion of "salience" found in the English-speaking literature. Thus, Berry and Broadbent (1988) interpret the differences between a lagged and unlagged control system, already mentioned, as due to the fact that key relationships are more obvious in the latter case. They link the findings to other methods of manipulating salience employed by earlier authors.

The position is not, however, completely cheerful. The key difficulty is the lack of models at the computational level, and this carries with it two problems that I have mentioned already. These problems are the neglect of preparation on the one hand and of probability on the other. In attention just as in motor performance, many of the key processes predate the arrival of the stimulus. In the early days of experiment on simultaneous streams of events, this may have been better realized than it is now. The reason was probably that it was necessary at that time to verify the existence of selection processes, to which the climate of the time was unfriendly. As Allport has said, it is not enough merely to show that spatial information helps a person to handle two streams of signals. Such a benefit might be due to better separation of the two tasks, and that was one of the possibilities considered by, for example, Broadbent (1958).

However, it was found that spatial separation helps some tasks and not others. If two streams of speech are arriving, and you only have to respond to one, spatial separation is certainly a help when you know in advance the voice that is important. If, however, you are only told which voice matters after the two messages have arrived, separation is much less helpful. So it is not the difficulty of making two overt responses, nor the packaging of the speech into two streams, that is helpful in itself. It is the selection of one stream to give rise to some internal event. There are even cases in which response to both of two streams of events is *hindered* by spatial separation, depending on the speed at which the events occur. Hence, Broadbent (1958) was able to exclude the alternative possibilities and show that selection was the most plausible explanation.

In the modern context these findings may well have been forgotten, but the point is still important. Preparation has its effects when the incoming event has *not* happened and adjusts the system into another mode. For example, McLeod and Posner (1984) asked people to say "high" when they heard the word "high." If they were also told to expect a pair of visual letters and to decide whether the letters were same or different, the speech response time showed no slowing at the moments when the visual stimuli were arriving, as compared with the time when they were merely expected. A less compatible reaction, of saying "low" when they heard a sound of 400 Hz., did slow down considerably as the letters appeared.

Yet the speech-speech task was much faster if the task was done alone, so that the subject knew that no visual stimuli would arrive. The results do not mean that the "privileged loop" is a separate input-output link wired permanently into the nervous system. Rather, it is a highly controlled process that is set up to operate in a slower fashion when other tasks are possible; the interference takes place in the preparation, not when the stimuli arrive.

This leads on to the second doubt about contemporary work on attention, the neglect of probability. It was manifest in the first days of the Attention and Performance meetings that simultaneous tasks are perfectly possible; people do talk and drive cars, sing while showering, sign letters while taking a phone call. Yet sometimes there are bad effects of task combination. The lesson of the 1950s and 1960s was that stimuli and responses do not necessarily interfere (apart from obvious peripheral and mechanical problems), but that there is difficulty in combining actions that transmit too much information in the technical sense. Doing two things at once is hard only if they are, at that time for that person, unlikely. In Ann Arbor it is especially appropriate for us to recall Paul Fitts, who showed in a number of experiments that people could emit complex motor sequences with only intermittent monitoring at another level, and that exactly the same stimuli and responses might or might not interfere depending upon the statistical structure of the task and the degree of experience that the person had with it (e.g., Bahrick, Noble, and Fitts 1954). Again, there is no clear way to explain such effects as due to problems of separating tasks or interference of goals, since those factors remain the same throughout the experiments.

The recent neglect of this old lesson is dangerous in three ways. First, if people imagine that "limited capacity" means that there should always be a problem about simultaneous response to two events, or that a "single channel" means serial processing, then they will believe those concepts to be invalidated by any experiments showing successful task combination or parallel processing. They are not.

Second, people may be surprised in the opposite way, by the extent of interference produced by apparently simple events. Pashler uses simple events, but he requires reaction to both, not merely to one. That really is necessary to transmit information; it misses the point to tell subjects to stop performing one task when the other needs action, and then to draw strong conclusions from the small amount of interference produced on the remaining task (Shallice, McLeod, and Lewis 1985). Pashler also uses unpredictable times of arrival to raise uncertainty; other investigators have produced uncertainty by varying the mapping between the input and the required output. In the results of McLeod and Posner (1984), such a mapping change might have increased confusion between one task and the other because the responses in one task became more compatible with stimuli in the other: but that cannot be the whole story. Broadbent and Gregory (1965) varied the S-R mapping purely within a tactile-manual task, and altered the degree of interference with memory for spoken letters. Pashler's results agree with many others in pointing to the existence of a major bottleneck in a process that we would now most naturally call the mapping of actions to conditions. That is why two actions are needed if one is looking for interference; it is a much less sensitive experiment to look at one reaction in the presence of stimuli that need no action.

The third danger in relapsing from information to stimuli is that it may divert effort away from devising concepts to handle these empirical data. Here, Rumelhart's brilliant Association lecture can give us a start. The problem is one of possible central representations for the input event. It was clear in the 1950s that the representation was likely to be distributed, because an efficient code would be one in which each part of the representation corresponded to many parts of the input and vice versa (Hamming codes); it would also be one in which increasingly specific representations are used for more and more probable events. The implausible feature of such a mechanism psychologically, however, was that it required an "optimum encoder," a mechanism that would change the representation to adjust to probability. Nevertheless, the experimental data suggested that (within limits) such adjustment does take place.

Rumelhart's examples illustrate how connectionist systems can adjust so as to create overlapping representations and produce interaction at the functional level that does not necessarily appear in the anatomy. Attention too therefore is in good shape, although it does need more development at the computational level.

The Visual Processing Session

In many ways, this session is a showpiece. For vision, Kosslyn's version of history is justified; after the mid-1970s, psychological research was truly joined by computational analysis to become a part of cognitive science. Equally, in the 1980s evidence from neuropsychology has been joined by improved knowledge of the physiology of vision, and by the newer techniques of scanning the brains of live and alert subjects. The widespread acceptance of the difference between "what" and "where" systems, and the separation of analyses of different primary features, have been cited by many speakers and carry echoes into other fields such as attention.

Let me give an example from a recent experiment of our own (Broadbent and Broadbent 1990). To appreciate the rationale for this experiment requires taking the following background into account: If people know in advance which of several events is to require reaction, then, as I noted earlier, there are advantages for performance. This is particularly true if the target event is marked out by some specific feature (e.g., spatial location) rather than merely by "what" it is, as in so-called filtering tasks. Nowadays a common method of exploring the phenomenon, due to Eriksen, is to present a visual letter for a choice reaction and also present distracting letters spatially separated from the target. Normally the nature of the distractors is important when they are near the target, but unimportant when they are more than about one degree of visual angle away from it. By the argument mentioned earlier, this is a selection effect, since it is helpful only when the location is known in advance and since separation is positively harmful if target identity rather than location is known.

Yet we do not know whether it is physical separation or visual angle that matters here. Because there are many separated projection areas for different visual features, and because these areas are normally arranged in a spatial map, the positions of corresponding points in different projection areas may be used to fuse different features into an integrated representation of an object. That would suggest, however, that it is angular location of the event in the visual field that matters, not true separation in space. Most experiments, however, have used tachistoscopes, or VDUs, at a constant viewing distance, thus confounding true physical separation with visual angle.

So what we did was to compare the effects of distractors at various true separations, seen at different distances to determine which of these factors really matters. We found that the true physical separation rather than the angular separation is important (Broadbent and Broadbent 1990). When the display is a long way off, one can ignore distractors whose separation is smaller than those that show a large effect if the display is seen from a short distance. The study is personally important as well; it will be our last experiment. It was finished immediately before Margaret ceased work, and I am left simply to write up the relics of thirty-two years of our intensive joint data collection.

There are, of course, many other examples of the interplay between attention and our growing progress in other disciplines. In this field the age of cognitive neuroscience has indeed arrived. The papers in the visual session, impressive though they are, form only a sampler of the extent of research in this domain. New information about the visual pathways, new psychological phenomena especially concerning movement and the combination of systems operating at different scales, and new computational techniques stimulated by the interests of roboticists are pouring into the literature. Those in other areas should admire and emulate.

35.4 A SUMMING UP

Yet, even in vision, what about preparation, purpose, and probability? And is Kosslyn's history true of attention and performance generally, or merely of vision? My own view is that it is not generally true, and my version of history differs slightly but importantly from that of Kosslyn. I would say that the mid-1970s did indeed mark a watershed in intellectual history; his first stage, the exploitation of experimental psychology, had shown its value by that time.

The second stage, however, was not simply a universal turning to cognitive science, in recognition or the new achievements it made possible. Rather, that epoch marked the appearance of a serious problem, to which psychologists reacted by different methods of coping. Only in the case of vision have the second and third stages followed the path described by Van Kleeck and Kosslyn.

The problem arose precisely from the intensive and successful pursuit of the methods of experimental psychology. Those methods seek to find causal relationships between factor A and factor B, and to make universally valid statements of those relationships. It had emerged by the 1970s that most psychological statements are true only if certain background conditions are specified. For example, reading experiments give different results depending on whether the person is using a grapheme-phoneme route or a semantic-articulatory route, attentional selection may be of different types, the laws of memory depend on the processing applied at the time of presentation, the effects of sleeplessness depend on the level of motivation, and so on. As Kosslyn said, there are still useful generalizations that can be made: but by the mid-1970s many of the areas of attention and performance were full of these qualifications and problems. It is because of this that Van Kleeck and Kosslyn are able to quote a crop of papers from that time questioning the possibility of progress; the doubts were quite widespread, and psychologists reacted in a number of different ways.

Some of these ways seem to be maladaptive. First there is the reaction of giving up the subject altogether; we can take it that nobody still here approves of that! A second reaction is to continue to describe oneself as a psychologist, but to develop increasingly the use of concepts derived from personal experience, such as consciousness and attention. My suspicion is that much of the sloppiness that Allport condemns has arisen since the mid-1970s; and Hintzman's strictures also apply to this kind of reaction. Then there is the more subtle reaction of denial, to go on doing experiments that search for "the" manner in which semantic memory is organized, or to assume that some module (say, language) *does* show invariant and regular behavior regardless of what may be happening elsewhere in the system. In the light of the evidence I would feel this is almost pathological; it can only be preserved by avoiding the literature produced by people who use different background conditions of experiment. The "spatial spotlight" effect, for example, may be different as a function of personality and of time of day (Broadbent, Broadbent, and Jones 1989), the degree of preference for reaction on the basis of "what?" rather than "where?" also depends on personality (Broadbent, Broadbent, and Jones 1986), and the precise form of the use of "where?" depends on anxiety (Broadbent and Broadbent 1988).

Much healthier was the appeal to other disciplines. David Marr demonstrated that this was possible and productive, and many have followed him. But he did so by a very careful and deliberate restriction of the problem space; he handled visual analysis up to the level of the "2.5-D sketch," not to the level of object identification. The next step would have introduced effects usually called expectancy, context, long-term experience, even values, and he rightly thought the time was not ripe. So the triumph of the visual sector is not only a matter of enlisting physiology and computing science. It is also a matter of simplifying the problem.

This is a traditional strategy of science; it is honorable, productive, and arrives at definite and communicable knowledge. It has been well repaid in vision, and I suspect it is about to show a similar flowering in the case of motor performance. In the case of attention, chronometry, and memory, the other sciences have been less help; but there too the investigators linked with this community have taken the path of simplification. That is why memory researchers are turning more and more to parts of their field that are less likely to show embarrassing individual differences, why chronometry leaves preparation and probability to one side, and why workers on attention still consider primarily those cases where people act "as if" they were open-chain systems. Within those constraints, they are doing well; and the current success is probably a result of the wisdom of the strategy. The limitations, however, are not ultimately acceptable. It cannot seriously be doubted that people act from internal causes rather than being stimulus-driven, that their actions have long-delayed consequences for which they are partially prepared, that their modes of attending, deciding, remembering, and acting are integrated. To abandon these areas as outside the realm of science is all very well as a temporary device, a tactic rather than a strategy, but in the long term it will not do.

35.5 A STRATEGY FOR THE FUTURE

Given these considerations, some conclusions are obvious. First, we need more interaction between the subareas of attention and performance; that will probably mean deliberate thought about journals, meetings, and possibly funding.

Second, we need computational theories of interaction between stages. As the number of theoretical entities increases in each area, it becomes increasingly hard to see the implications of combining them. Only computational systems can do this, and they will have the merit of stopping the laxness of definition noted by Allport and Hintzman.

Third, we shall probably need fresh kinds of data to supplement the tried and trusted technique of administering one stimulus, catching the response, and ignoring what happens before and after. My recommendation here is to study experimental interactions between people and exactly specified situations in which the environmental events are affected by the person as well as the reverse, and in which events at one time are affected by those at quite different times.

The fourth conclusion is that theory should not start with stimulation, but somewhere else; and this is where the difficulties begin. Data such as Duncan's suggest an analysis of levels rather than stages; such levels do not imply an anatomical hierarchy, but can perfectly well be discussed as a functional property of distributed codes. The key point, however, is the locus of control, the factor that decides whether event A will be followed by event B or event C.

There seem to me to be four possibilities for modeling this factor in current machine systems: invariant sequences of action, the firing of condition-action rules, temporary states that alter the rules and conditions, and manipulable symbols of the current goal. I suspect that all of these apply in the human case.

Two examples of possible misunderstanding are worth avoiding here. For my third option above (temporary states that modify rules), computational modelers sometimes use the term "working memory" to talk about a collection of contextual effects and information that may be very large. But this corresponds more to the functions that psychologists talk about as priming, or to the phenomena of drug and time-of-day effects. On the .other hand, the psychological usage of "working memory" is related to my fourth option (manipulation of goal symbols) and is functionally quite different. I would regard it as more useful to speak of "virtual memory" for the functions involved in the third option.

Another example is the term *central executive*. Some people seem to use it for the system that matches conditions to actions, which as we have seen may be distributed when multiple matches are taking place. Other people use it for a temporary memory of, say, reportable goals or intentions, which falls under my fourth option. One might also use it for the longer-lasting memory of permanent condition-action rules.

Sorting out these possibilities will be a major task, but a hopeful one. Some version of it will certainly be "What happens next," and the fact that we are now in sight of these fairly central topics of human existence is *why* this symposium was a good thing. These future activities will not of course be mine any longer; and I return to my personal question "Was it all worthwhile for me?" The answer, unhesitatingly, is "Yes."

REFERENCES

Alluisi, E. A., Muller, P. F., and Fitts, P. M. (1957). An information analysis of verbal and motor responses in a forced-pace serial task. *Journal of Experimental Psychology, 53,* 153–158.

Bahrick, H. P., Noble, M., and Fitts, P. M. (1954). Extra-task performance as a measure of learning a primary task. *Journal of Experimental Psychology, 48,* 298–302.

Berry, D. C. (1991). Learning to control complex systems: Observation versus participation. *Quarterly Journal of Experimental Psychology. 43A,* 881–906.

Berry, D., and Broadbent, D. E. (1988). Interactive tasks and the implicit-explicit distinction. *Quarterly Journal of Experimental Psychology, 36A,* 209–231.

Broadbent, D. E. (1958) *Perception and communication.* New York: Pergamon.

Broadbent, D. E. (1971). *Decision and stress.* London: Academic Press.

Broadbent, D. E. (1982) Task combination and selective intake of information. *Acta Psychologica, 50,* 253–290.

Broadbent, D. E. (1987) Simple models for experimentable situations. In P. E. Morris, (Ed.), *Modelling Cognition*, 169–1851. New York: Wiley.

Broadbent, D. E., and Broadbent, M. H. P. (1988). Anxiety and emotional bias: State and trait. *Cognition and Emotion, 2,* 165–183.

Broadbent, D. E., and Broadbent, M. H. P. (1990). Human attention: The exclusion of distracting information as a function of real and apparent separation of relevant and irrelevant events. *Proceedings of the Royal Society of London, B, 242,* 11–16.

Broadbent, D. E., and Gregory, M. H. P. (1965). On the interaction of S-R compatibility with other variables affecting reaction time. *British Journal of Psychology, 56,* 61–67.

Broadbent, D. E., Broadbent, M. H. P., and Jones, J. L. (1986). Performance correlates of self-reported cognitive failure and of obsessionality. *British Journal of Clinical Psychology, 25,* 285–299.

Broadbent, D. E., Broadbent, M. H. P., and Jones, J. L. (1989). Time of day as an instrument for the analysis of attention. *European Journal of Cognitive Psychology, 1,* 69–94.

Brosan, L., Broadbent, D. E., Nutt, D., and Broadbent, M. H. P. (1986). Performance effects of diazepam during and after prolonged administration. *Psychological Medicine, 16,* 561–581.

Catalan, J., and Gath, D. (1984). Benzodiazepines in general practice: Time for a decision. *British Medical Journal, 290,* 1374–1376.

Craik, F. I. M. (1983) On the transfer of information from temporary to permanent memory. *Philosophical Transactions of the Royal Society of London, B302,* 341–359.

Craik, K. J. W. (1948). Theory of the human element in control systems: II Man as an element in a control system. *British Journal of Psychology, 38,* 142–148.

Dörner, D. (1990). The logic of failure. *Philosophical Transactions of the Royal Society of London, B327,* 463–473.

FitzGerald, P., and Broadbent, D. E. (1985) Order of report and the structure of temporary memory. *Journal of Experimental Psychology: Learning, Memory, and Cognition, 11,* 217–228.

FitzGerald, P., Tattersall, A., and Broadbent, D. E. (1988). Separating central mechanisms by POCs: Evidence for an input-output buffer. *Quarterly Journal of Experimental Psychology, 40A,* 109–134.

Funke, J. (1988). Using simulation to study complex problem solving: A review of studies in the FRG. *Simulation & Games, 19,* 277–303.

Funke, J., and Müller, H. (1988). Eingreifen und Prognostizieren als Determinanten von System-identifikation und Systemsteuerung. *Sprache und Kognition, 7,* 176–186.

Gillie, T., and Broadbent, D. E. (1989). What makes interruptions disruptive? A study of length, similarity, and complexity. *Psychological Research, 50,* 243–250

McLeod, P., and Posner, M. I. (1984) Privileged loops from percept to act. In H. Bouma & E. G. Bouwhuis (Eds.), *Attention and Performance X,* 55–66. Hillsdale, NJ: Lawrence Erlbaum.

Marescaux, P.-J., Luc, F., and Karnas, G. (1989) Modes d'apprentissage sélectif et non-sélectif et connaissances acquises au contrôle d'un processus: évaluation d'un modèle simulé. *Cahiers de Psychologie Cognitive, 9,* 239–264.

Morris, C. (1946) *Signs, language, and behavior.* New York: Prentice-Hall.

Noble, M., Fitts, P. M., and Warren, C. E. (1955). The frequency response of skilled subjects in a tracking task. *Journal of Experimental Psychology, 49,* 249–256.

O'Hanlon, J. F. (1984) Driving performance under the influence of drugs: Rationale for, and application of, a new test. *British Journal of Clinical Pharmacology, 18,* 121S–129S.

Putz-Osterloh, W., and Lüer, G. (1981) Über die Vorhersagbarkeit komplexer Problemlöseleistungen durch Ergebnisse in einem Intelligenztest. *Zeitschrift für experimentelle und angewandte Psychologie, 28,* 309–334.

Rabbitt, P. M. A., and Rodgers, B. (1977) What does a man do after he makes an error? An analysis of response programming. *Quarterly Journal of Experimental Psychology, 29,* 727–743.

Shallice, T., McLeod, P., and Lewis, K. (1985) Isolating cognitive modules with the dual-task paradigm: Are speech perception and production separate processes? *Quarterly Journal of Experimental Psychology, 37A,* 507–532.

Sternberg, S. (1969) The discovery of processing stages: Extensions of Donders' method. In W. G. Koster (Ed.), *Attention and Performance II,* 276–315. Amsterdam: North-Holland.

Sutton, L., Teasdale, J. D., and Broadbent, D. E. (1988) Negative self-schema: The effects of induced depressed mood. *British Journal of Clinical Psychology, 27,* 188–190.

Tattersall, A. T., and Broadbent, D. E. (1991) Output buffer storage and the modality of recall. *Quarterly Journal of Experimental Psychology. 43A,* 1–18.

Townsend, J. T. (1990). Serial vs. parallel processing: Sometimes they look like Tweedledum and Tweedledee but they can (and should) be distinguished. *Psychological Science, 1,* 46–54.

Yerkes, R. M. (1943). *Chimpanzees: A laboratory colony.* New Haven: Yale University Press.

Reviewers

We are grateful to the following individuals for their generous and indispensable contributions in providing thorough reviews of the chapters in this volume:

Alan Allport
Don Bouwhuis
Claus Bundesen
Susan Chipman
Michael Coles
Max Coltheart
John Duncan
Martha Farah
Jennifer Freyd
Danny Gopher
Peter Gordon
Harold Hawkins
Herbert Heuer
Steve Hillyard
Doug Hintzman
David Howard
Glyn Humphreys
Dave Irwin
Richard Ivry
Ray Klein
Steve Kosslyn
Gordon Logan
Jay McClelland
Janet Metcalfe
Jeff Miller
Steve Monsell
Bert Mulder
Risto Näätänen
Ray Nickerson
Allen Osman

John Palmer
Harold Pashler
Karalyn Patterson
Michael Posner
Jeroen Raaijmakers
Roger Ratcliff
Keith Rayner
Jean Requin
Seth Roberts
Roddy Roediger
David Rosenbaum
Andries Sanders
Bepi Sartori
Roger Schwaneveldt
George Sperling
Saul Sternberg
Anne Treisman
Shimon Ullman
Paolo Viviani
Dirk Vorberg
Alan Wing
Ted Wright
Howard Zelaznick

Author Index

Names are listed in the form in which they appear in the references.

Ju, G., 45
Judd, D. B., 59, 60, 72
Julesz, B., 83, 122, 127, 129, 172
Junck, L., 782
Jung, J., 492
Juola, J. F., 489, 543, 616
Just, M. A., 49

Kaas, I. H., 765
Kahn, R., 362
Kahneman, D., 163, 164, 167, 170, 179, 184,
    185, 191, 192, 204, 248, 249, 300, 301,
    302, 318, 323, 331
Kalaska, J. F., 750
Kallos, T., 137
Kalmar, D., 260, 261
Kanade, T., 70
Kandel, E. R., 112
Kano, M., 825, 827, 840
Kantowitz, B. H., x, 536
Kanwisher, N. G., 283, 292
Kaplan, E., 463
Karis, D., 48
Karlin, L., 536
Karnas, G., 866
Karp, S. A., 331
Kartsounis, L. D., 159, 200
Kassell, N., 403
Katayama, M., 825, 835, 840
Kaufman, J., 268, 269, 270, 286, 292
Kawato, M., 705, 746, 817, 821–846, 854
Kay, B., 774
Kay, J., 440
Keane, M. M., 409, 410
Keele, S., 771, 773, 798, 799
Keele, S. W., 132, 184, 248, 249, 250, 592,
    724, 746, 756, 834
Kelley, K. L., 72
Kelly, M. H., 101, 103, 104
Kelly, W., 782
Kelso, J., 774
Kelso, J. A. S., 252, 714, 716, 717, 719, 722,
    738, 739, 825
Kelso, S., 803
Kenny, S., 704
Kent, J. T., 72
Kent, R., 774
Keppel, G., 361
Kertesz, A., 432, 446
Kestenbaum, R., 536
Keuss, P. J. G., 697
Kewley-Port, D., 776
Keyes, A. L., 234
Keysar, B., 185

Khoshbin, 773
Khurana, B., 171
Kidd, E., 362
Kim, J. K., 396, 407
Kimura, M., 113, 606
Kinchla, R. A., 280
King-Smith, P. E., 38
Kinsbourne, M., 159, 197, 199, 200
Kintsch, W., 354, 378, 489
Kirsner, K., 381
Kitano, M., 844
Klapp, S. T., 428, 726
Klatt, D., 776
Klima, E. S., 198
Kling, J., 779
Klinker, G. J., 70
Kluin, K., 782
Knezevic, S., 48
Knoll, R. L., 704, 714, 716, 722, 733, 746,
    756
Koch, C., 42, 46, 185, 196, 828
Koch, S., 375
Koenig, O., 45, 47
Koeppe, R., 782
Köhler, W., 361
Kohonen, T., 79
Kolers, P. A., 366, 408, 511
Kopelman, M. D., 403
Kornblum, S., ix, x, xii, 345, 536, 540, 541,
    572, 705, 712, 715, 716, 717, 718, 719,
    720, 721, 739, 746, 750, 834, 835, 836
Kornhuber, H. H., 540, 569
Kosslyn, S., 354
Kosslyn, S. M., 33, 37–52, 135, 169
Koster, W., ix
Kounios, J., 531, 532, 554, 622, 690, 691,
    697
Kozhenvnikov, V., 774
Kraft, L. G., 838
Kramer, A. F., 302, 581, 582
Krebs, M. J., 547
Krechevsky, I., 361
Krejci, J., 366
Krinov, E. L., 64, 65, 72
Kristofferson, A., 592
Kritchevsky, M., 398, 399, 400, 401
Krogh, A., 657
Kroll, J. F., 457
Kropfl, W., 122, 127, 129
Kuffler, S. W., 44
Kugler, P. N., 803
Kuhn, T. S., 382
Kulikowski, J. J., 38
Kulpe, O., 531

McClelland, J. L., 6, 43, 44, 45, 46, 135, 185, 319, 354, 372, 374, 375, 383, 497, 532, 533, 548, 551, 612, 616, 621, 625, 639, 648, 655–685, 692, 746, 747, 765, 828
McCollum, G., 852
McConkie, G. W., 122, 124, 129, 130, 131, 135, 166–167
McCorquodale, P. E., 375
McCracken, H. D., 717, 719
McDaniel, M. A., 364, 366, 512
McDermott, E. A., 428
MacDonald, C., 520
McDonald, J. E., 135
Mace, W., 730
McEvoy, C. L., 499, 500
McGaugh, J. L., 380
MacGregor, R. J., 46
Mack, A., 126, 136
MacKay, D. M., 139
MacKay, W. A., 749
MacKenzie, C. L., 712, 715, 717, 720, 721, 722, 726
MacKinnon, D. F., 403
Mackintosh, N. J., 605, 608
McKoon, G., 496, 497
McLachlan, D., 408, 409
McLaughlin, C., 724, 734
McLeod, P., 185, 247, 248, 260, 261, 323, 324, 724, 734, 872, 873
McLeod, P. D., 204
McLeod, S., 689
McMahon, T. A., 812
McMullen, P. A., 453
MacNeilage, P. F., 714, 733
McNeill, D., 380
MacQueen, G. M., 194
MacWhinney, B., 657
Maddox, I. J., 63
Madigan, S. A., 383
Maeda, M., 825, 828
Maeda, Y., 822
Maekawa, K., 843
Magliero, A., 572
Mahut, H., 393, 412
Maier, M. A., 749
Main, A. M., 266
Malamut, B., 369
Maljkovic, V., 43, 48
Maloney, L. T., 59–75
Mamelak, A. N., 348
Mandler, G., 371, 377, 381, 407, 409, 493
Mandler, J. M., 493
Mane, A., 312, 313, 316
Mangun, G. R., 219–239

Marcel, A. J., 196, 368
Marchak, F., 756
Mardia, K. V., 72
Marescaux, P.-J., 866
Maricq, A. V., 595
Marin, O. S. M., ix, 346
Markel, D., 782
Marley, A. A. J., 537
Marohn, K. M., 286
Marr, D., 33, 40, 41, 42, 43, 192, 205, 406, 821, 828
Marsh, R., 592
Marshall, J. C., 148, 200
Marshburn, E. A., 428, 726
Marteniuk, R. G., 726
Martin, R. C., 518, 519
Massaro, D. W., 646, 657, 663, 664, 665, 667, 672
Massey, J. T., 113
Massone, L., 827
Matelli, M., 191, 197
Matin, L., 137
Matsunami, K., 823
Matthews, P., 411
Mattingly, I., 799
Maunsell, J. H. R., 189
Mauritz, K. H., 756
Maussa-Ivaldi, F. A., 811
Mawafy, L., 101
Maximilian, V. A., 48
Mayer, M., 129
Mayes, A. R., 394, 399
Mead, C., 46
Meck, W. H., 595
Medin, D. L., 378
Medjbeur, S., 219
Meehl, C. G., 375
Mehta, Z., 453
Meijer, O. G., 756
Melara, R. D., 557
Melchner, M. J., 280, 281, 302
Melton, A. W., 370
Mensink, G. J., 362, 370, 382, 383, 472, 475, 478
Merchak, F., 804, 805, 806, 813, 814
Merikle, P. M., 267
Merisalo, A., 723
Mervis, C. B., 166, 378
Mesulam, M. M., 143, 148, 184
Metcalfe, J., 472
Metzler, J., 38, 39, 134
Meudell, P. R., 399, 400
Mewhort, D. J. K., 124, 125
Meyer, D., 773

Tulving, E., 354, 370, 381, 383, 394, 407, 408, 409, 410, 411, 489, 495, 499, 502, 511, 520, 522, 603, 608
Turnbull, J., 714, 717, 724, 728, 737, 738
Turock, D. L., 714, 716, 722, 733, 756
Turvey, M. T., 730, 803

Uhley, J. D., 51
Ullman, S., 42, 79–97, 164, 165, 166
Umiltà, C., 192, 301
Underwood, B. J., 361, 364, 370, 492
Ungerleider, L. G., 33, 44, 143, 160, 189, 219, 221, 239
Uno, Y., 705, 817, 822, 825, 826, 827, 828, 832, 835, 840, 844, 854
Upinder, S. B., 51

Vaglia, A., 453, 454
Vallar, G., 160, 193, 197, 198, 425, 426, 427, 444, 463
van Dellen, H. J., 570, 572, 581, 582
van der Ham, F., 612
van der Heijden, A. H. C., 124, 125, 185, 191, 200, 681
van der Meere, J. J., 581, 582
van der Molen, M. W., 551, 552
van der Valk, N. J. L., 736
Van Duren, L. L., 692
van Eerd, D. L., 712, 715, 717, 720, 721, 722
Van Essen, D. C., 189
Van Hoesen, G., 414
van Ingen Schenau, G. J., 812
Van Kleeck, M. H., 37–52
Van Sommers, P., 453
Van Voorhis, S., 220, 225
Van Zandt, T., 542
Varner, D. C., 75
Vaughan, H. G., Jr., 236
Vaughan, J., 148, 756, 803–818
Verfaillie, K., 101
Verplanck, W. S., 375
Vetterling, W. T., 642
Vickers, D., 538
Vickers, S., 538
Videen, T. O., 409
Vidyasagar, T. R., 172
Villa, G., 432
Vince, M., 246
Virzi, R. A., 185
Vitton, N., 749, 763
Viviani, P., 714, 736, 738, 851–859
Volkmann, F. C., 126
Volpe, B., 396
Volpe, B. T., 148, 194, 197

von Helmholtz, H., 59, 109, 122, 137, 368
von Helmholtz, H. L., 531
von Hofsten, C., 714, 730
von Holst, E., 122
von Kries, J., 61, 74
von Wright, J. M., 254, 267
Vorberg, D., 729, 731, 732, 733, 734, 736

Waddill, P. J., 366
Wade, D. T., 148
Wade, J., 48
Wadman, W. J., 704
Wagner, A. R., 374
Wald, A., 539
Walicke, P. A., 411
Walker, J. A., 148, 238
Wall, S., 543
Wallace, M. A., 192
Wallace, S. A., 704
Wallace, W. T., 490, 491, 493, 495, 496
Wallach, H., 126
Walsh, K. W., 324
Wandell, B. A., 61, 62, 64, 68, 69, 70, 73
Wang, G., 44, 45, 48, 169
Wann, J., 827
Wannier, T. M. J., 749
Warach, J., 189
Warren, C. E., 869
Warren, R. E., 498
Warrington, E. K., 47, 159, 164, 198, 199, 200, 399, 403, 407, 425, 452, 453
Waterse, G. A., 427
Watkins, M. J., 476, 489, 510
Watkins, O. C., 476
Watson, J. B., 365
Watt, R., 185
Watt, W. C., 100
Waugh, N. C., 353, 425, 510
Weber, A., 363
Weichselgartner, E., 266, 267
Weil, M., 313, 314, 315, 317, 318
Weintz, D. A., 616
Weir, L., 782
Weiskrantz, L., 394, 407, 411
Weismer, G., 774
Weiss, S. B., 48
Weisskopf, V. F., 70
Weldon, M. S., 366
Welford, A. T., 179, 180, 204, 246, 248, 250, 535, 536, 537, 555, 710, 712, 717, 718, 727
Werbos, P. J., 831
Wertz, R. T., 427
Wessinger, M., 231

Subject Index

Associative sets, intersection of, 494
Associative strength, measure of, 499
Asymptotic choice paradigm, 661
Asymptotic performance in identification tasks, 665
Ataxia, 783
Attention, ix, 149, 179, 183–206, 324, 864 870–873, 875. *See also* Neglect; Selection; Selective attention
  attended and unattended, 867
  benefits, 289–295
  computational theory, need for, 205
  control of, 299, 300, 319
  definition of none, 186, 187, 203, 206
  definitions of, 4, 86, 187, 203, 205, 206
  disorders of, 148, 149, 152, 157, 198, 208, 349
  divided, 276, 321, 323
  effort and, 302
  engagement and disengagement of, 195, 205
  facilitates local competition, 196
  as of feature detectors, 681
  filtering, 266, 274, 288
  focusing, 301
  as gain control, 220
  heterogeneity of, 189, 202–204, 206
  maintenance mechanism of, 145, 149, 153, 154, 160
  modulation of neuronal response, 193, 195, 196
  movement of, 148, 149, 155
  to multielement stimulus, 234
  network, 148
  orienting, 144, 148, 150, 153, 154, 159, 192, 193, 220
  peripheral, 314
  as prime, 681
  processes that require attention, 183, 188, 202–206
  resources, 259–260
  spatial, 220
  spatial orienting of, 192, 193
  spotlight of, 191
  strategies, 299, 313, 318
  switching, 238, 302, 345
  in visual recognition, 83
Attentional filtering, in selective-attention conditions, 288
Attention benefits, 289, 295
Attention disengagement, 148, 149, 152, 157
Attention engagement, 148, 149
Attention-management skills, 318

Attention-operating characteristics, 279, 280–282, 282–283, 290
Attention redirecting in space, 238
Attention systems, anterior and posterior, 345
Autoencoder, 10, 11
Automaticity, 246, 543
  capture of attention, 304
  classification, 236
  controlled processing and, 184, 188
  processing, 343

Balint's syndrome, 154, 158, 159
Basal ganglia, 606, 773
Binary-choice tasks, 627
Binary classification, 345
Biomechanics, 704
Boltzmann machine, 671
Bottleneck in processing, 247. *See also* Limited capacity
Brain imaging
  MEG, 48
  MRI, xiv, 228
  PET, 40, 48, 180
Brain-style computation, 3
Buffer model of STS, 468

Cancellation principle, 19
Candidate object in visual recognition, 88
Canonical view, 96
Capacity, 869, 872
  limitations (*see* Limited capacity)
Capacity sharing, 259–260
Cartesian product, 630, 648, 649–650
Cascade model, 532, 612, 621, 623, 640, 642, 643, 694
  additive factor effects and, 622, 624, 625, 644
  additivity and, 612–613
  evidence against, 638
  forbidden regions of the variance-change statistic and, 641
  neural network model and, 825, 828
  neural networks, stable equilibrium point in, 831
  and overadditivity, 625
  summation test and, 642, 649
  translation condition and, 615
  variance additivity and, 628, 639
Cascade neural networks
  model, 825, 828
  stable equilibrium point in, 831
Categorically organized knowledge, 462

Categorical perception, 775, 782, 793
    vs. continuous perception, 168
    in speech, 780
Categorical search, 543
Categorization, 115
Central executive, 188, 200–202, 204, 206,
    353
Central timing process, 773
Cerebal ischemia lesion, 416
Cerebellar disorders, 776
Cerebellar dysarthria, 790, 796
Cerebellar lesions, 792, 793, 798
Cerebellar patients, 782, 795
Cerebellar speech dysarthria, 783, 799
Cerebellar timing hypothesis, 790
Cerebellar timing system, 775, 782, 795
Cerebellum, 706, 772, 774, 841
Cerebral hemispheres, 260
Cerebral lesions, medial, 592
Cerebral localization of function, 586
Cerebrocerebellum, 841
Channel capacity theorem, 536
Choice RT task, 751
Chromatic adaptation, 73
Chronometry, 864, 868–869
Chunking, 324, 364
Cingulate cortex, 202
Codes, psychophysical approach to vision
    and, 38, 39
Coding in STS, 468
Coefficient of variation, 717
Cognitive development, 49
Cognitive impenetrability of the central
    process, computer metaphor, 856
Cognitive neuropsychologists, 525
Cognitive neuroscience, xii, 44, 183, 206,
    346, 349, 394, 763
Cognitive principles, interdependence, 665
Cognitive revolution, 359, 360, 382, 384,
    509
Cognitive science, 38, 509, 510
Cognitive skills, 408
Coincidence timing, 724, 734, 736–738
Collaboration, communication in science and,
    49
Color and color vision, 60, 61, 83
    color constancy, 34, 60, 172
    color signal, 61
    computational, 59
    grayworld assumption, 68
    intrinsic color, 59, 71
    Linear-Models Framework of, 60
    linear models of, 60
Components-levels theory of spacing, 481

Computational modeling, xii, 864, 869, 871,
    873
Computational theorizing, 45
Computed tomography (CT), 398
Computer game training, 319
Computer metaphor in learning, 361
Computer programs, as tools for formal
    analysis, 46
Computer simulation, 354, 355
Computer simulation models
    of learning, 381, 382
    of memory, 514, 515, 516
Concurrent memory load, 471
Concurrent process, 551, 555
Condition-action rules, 865, 866, 877
Conditioning, 367, 370, 374
Condition statistics, cascade model and, 638
Conjunction search, 149, 150
Connectionism, xiv, 354, 372, 374, 383, 697,
    706, 873
Connectionist models, 504
    additive factor effects and, 622
    the AP model and, 616
    of spatial attention, 681
Connectionist network, 3, 113
    inference and, 19, 21
    principle of inheritance and, 14, 17
Conscious experience, 168
Consciousness, 870, 875
    behavior and, 319
    learning and, 367
Consistency, within and between tasks, 454
Context
    effects on similarity, 80
    fluctuation, 474, 479
    memory and, 492
    as retrieval cue, 474
Continuity, discrete categories and, 116
Continuity criterion, of dynamic
    representations, 107
Continuity of time, 106
Continuous flow, 747, 765
Contrast, 83
Controlled processing, 343, 567. *See also*
    Attention
Coordinated movements, 729
Coordination, between head and eye
    movements, 738
Corpus callosum, 223
Corresponding features, in object
    recognition, 91
Cortical anatomy, 228
Crossed associates problem, 484
Crossover interaction, 619

Crystallized intelligence, 338
Cue combination model, for memory
    retrieval, 497
Cued locations, 234
Cued recall, with an extralist associate, 499
Cue overload principle in retrieval, 476
Cue set size, 499
Culture Fair Test, 330, 334
Current source density, 226
Cut-point, 552

Data structures, 38, 40, 43
Decision criterion (Beta), in signal detection,
    237
Declarative-episodic system, 520
Declarative knowledge, 354
Dentate gyrus, 400
Detection, 626–627
Detection thresholds, 39
Development, 348, 730, 737
    psychopathology and, 349
    of speech, 733
Diachronic and synchronic constraints, 858
Diazepam, 866
Dicoptic viewing, 269
Dimensional directionality, 105
Dimensions, of individual differences, 338
Dimension selection process, 605, 606, 608
Discrete, vs. continuous processing and
    transmission, 546, 585, 613, 692, 693,
    695
Discriminability
    differential, 286
    as a factor, 628
Disjunctive feature search, 149
Distributed codes, 873, 877
Distributed parallel network, 763
Distributed representation, sparse, 494
Divided attention, 276, 321, 323
Double dissociation, 521, 590
Double stimulation, 590
Double tasks, interference and, 697
Driving ability, 338
Driving skills, 327
d' sensitivity, 676
d' simulations, as a function of time, 676
2 1/2-D sketch, 40
Dual-task decrement, and g correlation, 327,
    333
Dual-task experiments, 307, 311, 425
Dual-task interference, 245–261
Dual-task performance, 303
Dual-task study, 331
Duration perception, 773, 782

Dynamics, of musculoskeletal system, 826
Dysarthria, 798

Ecologically valid analysis, of visual system,
    41
Ecological theories, of perception, 136
Ecological validity, 866
ECS (electroconvulsive shock), 404
ECT (electroconvulsive therapy), 404
Edge/bar detectors, 46. See also Line
    detectors
Edge detection, 43, 80
Electrical couplings, between neurons, 830
Electroconvulsive shock (ECS), 404
Electroconvulsive therapy (ECT), 404
Electromyogram (EMG), 570, 572, 578, 582–
    586, 704
Electrophysiological correlates, of RT, 540,
    547
Elementary operations, in motor control, 772
EMG (electromyogram), 570, 572, 578, 582–
    586, 704
Encoding
    priming, 354
    retrieval, 354, 512
    tasks, 365
    transfer of training and, 366, 367
Entorhinal cortex, 412, 417
Episodic memory, 354, 520
    semantic memory and, 394
Equal-probability mixture, 617
Equilibrium probability distributions, 661
Equilibrium trajectory, 844
Error rates, visual information processing
    and, 39
Event-related brain potentials, xiv, 180, 219,
    532, 567, 572
    NP80, polarity of, 230
    P_3 component, 572, 577, 579, 581
    polarity reversal, 222
    readiness potential, 569
Everyday (autobiographical) memory, 379
Evoked potentials, 553, 558
Evolution, 368
Execution-related neurons, 759
Executive control, 200–203
Executive supervisory functions, 324
Exocentric coding, 136
Experiment statistics, cascade model and,
    638–639
Expert, novice performance and, 326
Extinction, 596
Eye movements, ix, 33, 111, 166–167, 247.
    See also Saccades

Face-selective cells, 97
Failure of independence,
    interactive-activation model and, 673
Fast guess model, 538, 539, 545, 616
Feature detectors, 33
Feature differentiation, selective attention
    and, 288
Feature-integration theory, 185
Feedback error learning, 824, 836, 839, 841
Feedforward network, 9
Feedforward neural network model,
    mutilayer, 831
Figure ground, in game components, 314
Filtering, 874
    attentional, 288
Filter theory, 179
Fitts's law, 710, 718, 832
Fixed-interval schedule, 593, 608
Flanker displays, 573, 683
Flight training, 317
Forbidden region, in statistic space, 638
Force, 771
    of grip, 731
Force-time rescalability, symmetry and, 835
Foreperiod, in RT, 626
Forgetting, 354, 364, 396
Formant frequencies, 784
Forward, inverse modeling and, 836, 839
Forward-dynamics problem, 837
Forward-inverse sequential network, 829
Forward kinematics, 837
Forward model, of controlled object, 825,
    830
Free-recall task, 475
Frontal lobes, 396
    attentional, executive functions of and, 201
Functional architecture of brain, 183, 187–
    191, 206
    lesion data and, 47
Functional heterogeneity, of neural
    structures, 747
Functional visual field, 695, 696

Garner interference, 557
Gaze, 738, 739
g correlations, 324, 334
Gemination, 793
Generalization, 7, 18, 20, 27
Generation recognition, 502
Gestalt principles, 580
g factor, 339
GO–NOGO procedure, RT and LRP, 575–
    579
Graded activation function, 657

GRAIN model, 532
    principles of, 683
    of RT, 656
    Wickelgren's law and, 677
Grasping/reaching movement, 730
    hand aperture, 729
    hand transport, 730
    hierarchical representation, 729
Gstage model, 613, 620

Hamming distance, 24, 79
Handwriting, 709
Handwriting recognition, 100
Hardware-to-behavior mapping, in motor
    control, 854
Hick's law, 535
Hierarchical clustering, 20
Hierarchical models, 756
Hierarchical programming, of movements,
    856
Hippocampus, 355, 416
    CA1 region, 400, 416
    formation, 404, 406, 412, 417
    memory and, 520, 522
Homophone judgments, 428, 432, 445
Homotetic scaling, 852
Hull's learning theory, 373–376, 380, 381,
    383
Human-factors engineering, 180
Human performance, 344
Huntington's disease, 411
Hypothetical constructs, 513, 514, 515, 525

Iconic memory, 33
Identity theory, 857
Idiom, meaning of, 493
Illusory conjunctions, 165
Imagery, memory and, 363, 364
Imagery mnemonics, 362
Image segmentation, 147
Implicit memory, priming and, 407, 408
Impulse-variability model, 835
Independence constraint, on network
    architecture, 671
Independent-measures method, 590, 591,
    592, 593, 599
Individual differences, 181, 326, 339
Inference, connectionist network and, 14, 21
Information accrual, 537
Information measure (H), 535
Information processing
    approach, 524
    boxology, 765
    goals for a theory, 661

Information processing (cont.)
  paradigms, 661
  principles of, 656
  in a theory, 655
  in vision, 38
Input buffer, 442
Input variability, 668
Integration, of information, 748
Integrative visual buffer, 123
Intelligence, 323. *See also* IQ
Intensity, in RT, 626
Interaction contrast, 625, 628, 629, 634
Interactive-activation model, 532, 667
Interactive processing, 659
Interactivity, independence and, 667
Interference, forgetting and, 478
Interference theory, in learning, 370
Internal clock, 773
Invariant properties method, of shape-based
  object recognition, 90
Inverse, forward modeling and, 836, 839
Inverse-dynamics model, 837
Inverse-dynamics problem,
  agonist/antagonist tension setting, 823
Inverse-kinematics model, 837
Inverse-kinematics problem, system
  redundancy, excess degrees of freedom,
  and, 823
Inverse-reference model, 843
Inverse-statics model, 835
IQ, 332
IQ loss, *g* distribution and, 335
Isochrony principle, 852
Isomorphism between internal, external
  world and, 109, 110
Iso-voltage contours, 223

Kinematics, of musculoskeletal system, 826
Kinesiology, 704
Knowledge, of results (KR), 720, 734
Knowledge representation, 451
Knowledge systems, semantic, word form,
  structural, 522
Kolmogorow-Smirnov (K-S) test, 649–650
Korsakoff's syndrome, 398

Lags, effects of on repetition/delection
  performance, 281, 282
Language, 370, 383
Large-RT statistic, 637
Lateral cerebellar lesions, 592
Lateral geniculate nucleus, 230–231
Lateralized readiness potential, 532, 569,
570, 572, 575, 576, 578, 579, 581, 584–
585
Learning, xii, 3, 8, 353
  compatibility and transfer effects, 365
  control of skilled performance and, 323
  goal-directed, 839
  and memory, models of, 509
  memory systems and, 369
  relevant dimensions, 609
  which dimensions are relevant, 609
Left and right hemispheres, 168
Lesion experiments, 589, 608, 609
Lesion studies, electrophysiology and, 748
Letter matching, 132, 236
Levels of analysis, in information processing
  systems, 41
Levels of parsing, 858
Levels of processing, 365, 876
  framework of memory, 511, 512, 517
  memory and, 354
Levels of selection, 219
Lexical decision, 410, 457
Lexical priming, 496
Limited capacity, theories of, ix, 179, 185,
  187, 188, 195, 204, 205
Linear mapping, 95
Linear models, 62
Linear-Models Framework, 60–61, 70, 71,
  73, 75
Line detectors, 87. *See also* Edge/bar
  detectors
Lipreading, 429, 440, 441, 442, 446
List-length effect, 475, 500
List-search process, 502
List-strength effect, 476–478, 500
Location-based selection process, 238
Logarithmic transformation, 597, 598, 608
Logogen, 496
Long-term memory, 353
Long-term memory store, (LTS), 467
Long-term recency effect, 470, 471, 472
Long-term recognition network, 163, 166
Long-term store, 353

McCollough effects, 522
Magnitude estimation, 38
Main-effect difference statistic, 640
Maloney and Wandell algorithm, 68
Mammillary nuclei, 412
Manual tracking, 703
Masking, 124
Matching span, 430, 433, 437, 445
Means additivity, 618, 630, 647, 649

Measurement variability, 711
Mechanistic basis, of independence law, 672
Memory, xii, 353, 866–868
  coding of, 290
  consolidation in, 403
  declarative (explicit), 368, 407, 418
  matrix model of, 503
  modal model of, 510
  nondeclarative (implicit), 368, 407, 418, 484, 517
  primary, 353
  procedural, 522
  semantic-episodic, 483
  two-store model of, 467, 485, 510, 511, 513, 519
  units of, 482, 483
  visual, 166, 168
  working, 355, 370
Memory images, 472, 482
Memory matching, 268
Memory retrieval, 252
Memory scanning, 345
Memory span, 442
Memory structure, xii
Memory systems, 368
Mental abilities, 326, 338
Mental chronometry, ix, xii, 531, 567
Mental imagery, 48
Mental representations, 99, 108, 345
Mental rotation, 92, 134
Metabolic mapping, 589, 590
Metamemory, Korsakoff and, 399
Microfeatures, as network units, 6
Midline diencephalic lesions, 398
Minimum-jerk model, 825
Minimum motor-command-change trajectory, 825
Minimum muscle-tension-change model, 828
Minimum RT, as reflection of ideal processing, 717
Mixture, AP models and, 644–645
Mixture test, 617, 636, 637, 647
  AP model and, 635, 638, 644
  failures of, 620
  SI stage model and, 620, 647
  a stage model and, 619
  the summation test, cascade model and, 617, 618, 649
  summation test and, 635
  variance effects and, 618
Modality-specific cortex, 238
Modular conception, of brain, 765
Modularity, 771, 773, 798
Modules, 763, 764

cognitive, 116
networks of, 763
as stages, 568
Modules of visual processing, as stages, 40, 45
Monotonic, nonmonotonic time-accuracy curves and, 675
Moore-Penrose pseudoinverse matrix, 825, 840
Morse code, 27
Morton's independence law, 663
Motor. *See also* Movement
  command, 822, 827
  command space, 827
  cortex, 749
  delays, 720, 726, 737
  language, 853
  learning, supervised, 821, 836
  memory, 719
  output stage, 746
  performance, 864–865
  planning, 803, 820
  program, 252, 703, 704, 721, 746, 750, 756, 759, 760
  program buffer, 353
  skills, 522
  system variability, 706
Motor command, generation of, in voluntary movement, 822
Motor-command space, 827
Motor control, ix, xii, 756, 799, 857. *See also* Movement
  compatibility across levels, 859
  computational theory of, 821
  degrees of freedom, problem in, 704, 705, 756, 803, 809, 823
  direct and inverse modeling of, 838
  impedance control, 843
  problems of, 704
  trajectory formation, 821, 822
Motor-control problems, ill-posed and well-posed, 823, 840
Motor delays, 720, 726, 732
Motor language, 853
Motor learning
  supervised, 821, 836
  supervised with a distal teacher, 836
Motor memory, 719
Motor performance, 864–865
Motor programs, 252, 703, 704, 721, 746, 750, 756, 759, 760
Motor-program buffer, 353
Motor programming, 252
Motor programming stage, 746

Selection tests, 339
Selective attention, 183–206, 254, 265, 266, 267, 289, 292, 294, 295
  to objects, 199–200
Selective influence, 613, 616, 622, 646
Selective recall, 267
Selective task set, 200
Selective tracking paradigm, 171–172
Semantic memory, 252, 354, 371, 377, 483, 520, 522
  conceptual structure and, 378, 379
  episodic memory and, 394
  similarity and, 378
Semantic network, 13
Semantic pair recognition, 497
Semantic retrieval, 495
Sensitivity (d'), 237
Sensorimotor gradient, 751, 754, 763
Sensorimotor information, 137
Sensorimotor-type neurons, 752
Sensory/motor associations, 751
Sensory/motor function, of neurons, 749
Sensory store, 353
Sensory-type neurons, 752
Separately changeable measures, seriality of processes and, 593
Sequential-activation model, 495, 497
Sequential-intersection model, 497
Sequential processes, 551, 555
Serial, parallel systems and, 541
Seriality, parallel processing and, 747, 765
Serially arranged processes, 591, 592, 600, 604, 609
Serial-order problem, 704
Serial-position effect, 440, 502
Set size, as a factor, 627
Shadowing, 247, 261
Shape changes, in visual recognition, 80
Shape identification, 46
Shareability, 168
  of computational modules, 858
  of mental representations, 114, 115
Short-term memory, ix, 353, 425, 518, 519
Short-term visual repetition memory (STVRM), 269, 289, 292–296
Sigmoid activation function, 657
Signal detection experiments, 589, 591
Silhouette, with smooth bounding contours, 93
Similarity
  associative relationships and, 498
  learning and, 363
  of nontargets, 150–153
  in PDP networks, 7–9, 16, 22

in recognition, 80
RT slope and, 543
of targets in STM, 501
transfer of training and, 366
Simon effect, 249, 252
Simple reaction time, 234, 249
Simulation models, of visual processing, 43
Simultanagnosia, 199–200
Single-cell recordings, 706
SIstage model, 613, 633, 647
  AP model and, 635, 638, 644
  mixture test and, 620, 647
  summation test and, 614, 615, 650–651
  variance additivity and, 628
Skill acquisition and learning, 353, 724
Skilled and stereotyped behavior, 332
Skilled movement, 844
Skill learning, 407, 418
Skill specificity, 337
Sleep, 348
Small-RT statistic, 637
SOA. *See* Stimulus onset asynchrony
SOAR, 5
Somaesthetic cortex, 751
Spacing effect, in recall, 479, 481
Spasticity, 783
Spatial arrays, 267
Spatial coordinate systems. *See also* Attention
  reference frames, 192, 197, 198
  selection, 191–200
  working memory, 190
Spatial separation, 871, 874
Spatiotopic fusion and interaction, 122
Special-purpose processing systems, 325
Spectral reflectance, 59
Speech, 714, 715, 722
  disorders, 782, 799
  dysarthria, 782, 796
  perception, 774, 799
  production, 432, 706, 782, 796
  spectral analysis, 784
Speed-accuracy trade-off (SAT), 532, 586, 691, 696, 703, 705, 710, 718, 832
Spinocerebellum, 841
Spreading activation, 354
S-R alternatives, number of, 579
S-R compatibility. *See* Stimulus-response compatibility
Stage model, 532, 611–613
  additivity and, 645
  AP model and, 617, 619, 635–636
  cascade model and, 621, 625, 642
  mixture test and, 638
  summation test and, 629, 646, 648